P9-CFZ-127

# EUROPEAN CIVILIZATION SINCE THE MIDDLE AGES

*Medieval miniature showing teacher with students.*

# EUROPEAN CIVILIZATION SINCE THE MIDDLE AGES

Second Edition

EDWARD R. TANNENBAUM
New York University

John Wiley and Sons, Inc. New York . London . Sydney . Toronto

FRONT COVER:
Center of an industrial city planned by Claude Ledoux, 18th-century French architect to the court of Louis XVI.
Photo from The World Health Organization.

BACK COVER:
Model for an *arcology*, "Arc Cube," a self-contained city designed by Paolo Soleri utilizing a Euclidian (cube) form and other geometric shapes.
Photo, courtesy of The Whitney Museum of American Art.

FRONTISPIECE:
Miniature from a 14th-century *codice membranaceo.* (Milano, Biblioteca Braidense).
Photo from Madeline Grimaldi, G. Tomsich, Rome.



Library of Congress Catalogue Card Number: 74-125277

ISBN 0-471-84470-5

Printed in the United States of America

10 9 8 7 6 5 4 3 2 1

# PREFACE TO THE SECOND EDITION

THIS NEW EDITION of *European Civilization Since the Middle Ages* has been considerably revised and corrected. In recent years, Europe has been viewed more and more as the pioneer in modernization. This process has occured in different ways in different parts of the world, but the European experience retains its basic educational interest. Consequently, new material has been added to this book on the technological, economic, and organizational innovations of European civilization. The book also has been redivided into two equal parts: Part I, The Preindustrial age and Part II, The Industrial Age. The year 1848 now appears more crucial than the traditional year 1815 as the dividing point beyond which all aspects of European civilization moved irrevocably forward. Also the material on the period since 1945 has been expanded from one to two chapters. The purpose of this expanded coverage of the past 25 years is not merely to bring political events up to date but mainly to describe the dramatic social and cultural transformations in what is actually a postindustrial age. On the other hand, most of the other chapters have been shortened. Finally, a number of corrections have been made. Some of them are based on suggestions from readers, and others are the result of my effort to keep abreast of new information and new interpretations which concern a civilization that is unique in history and that is still, in many respects, the mother of us all.

EDWARD R. TANNENBAUM
*December, 1970*

# ACKNOWLEDGMENTS OF QUOTATIONS

Johan Huizinga's views on p. 46 are taken from his *The Waning of the Middle Ages* (London: Edward Arnold and Co., 1937), p. 18.

DeGaulle's comments on Napoleon on p. 358 are taken from his *France and Her Army* (London: Hutchinson, 1945), p. 60.

The quotation from Gilbert Murray on p. 539 is taken from "National Ideals: Conscious and Unconscious, "*International Journal of Ethics*, vol. 11 [1900], p. 21, cited in William L. Langer, *The Diplomacy of Imperialism*, New York: Alfred A. Knopf, 1956, p. 56.

Freud's letter of December 28, 1914, quoted on p. 639, is taken by permission from Ernest Jones, *The Life and Work of Sigmund Freud*, II: *Years of Maturity 1901–1919* (New York: Basic Books, 1955), 368–369.

The quotation from Nikolaus Pevsner on p. 647 is taken from *An Outline of European Architecture* (Harmondsworth, Eng.: Penguin Books, 1943), p. 265.

T. S. Eliot's opinion of Joyce, quoted on p. 647, is taken from W. Y. Tindall, in Alan Pryce Jones, *New Outline of Modern Knowledge* (New York: Simon and Schuster, 1956).

Jacques Prévert's *Late Rising* is quoted on p. 648 in the Selden Rodman translation, from *100 Modern Poems* (New York: The New American Library, 1951), p. 54.

The quotation from Dwight D. Eisenhower on p. 745 is taken by permission from his book *Crusade in Europe* (New York: Doubleday and Co., 1948) pp. 45–46.

General Spaatz's remarks on p. 746 are taken by permission from "Strategic Air Power against Germany," *Newsweek*, vol. 33, March 7, 1949, p. 28.

The quotation from General MacArthur on p. 752 is taken from U.S. Congress · Senate · Armed Services Committee · *Military situation in Far East . . . hearings on . . . the Relief of General Douglas MacArthur* (Washington, D.C.: U.S. Govt. Print. Off., 1951) Part I, pp. 57–58.

On p. 773, the quotation from Lord Crewe is taken from Sir Verney Lovett, *A History of the Indian Nationalist Movement* (London: John Murray, 1921), p. 89; the quotation from Lord Milverton is taken by permission from Harold Cooper, "Political Preparedness for Self-Government," *Annals of the American Academy of Political and Social Science*, vol. 306 (July, 1956), p. 71.

The excerpt from Norbert Wiener on p. 816 is taken by permission from his *The Human Use of Human Beings: Cybernetics and Society* (Boston: Houghton Mifflin Co., 1950), p. 71.

The observations of De Kooning and Dubuffet on p. 819 are taken by permission from *Daedalus*, vol. 89 (1960), pp. 11 and 95 respectively.

# CONTENTS

# LIST OF MAPS

**Maps by J. Donovan**

# A BIBLIOGRAPHICAL NOTE

## SUPPLEMENTARY READINGS AND BIBLIOGRAPHICAL AIDS.

Suggested readings for the student and the general reader appear at the end of each chapter. These books have been chosen to supplement the material presented in the text, except for a few specialized pioneer studies, which are do designated. Since many of the works listed are paperback editions, their publication dates often do not indicate when they were actually written or last revised. The paperback publication dates are nevertheless given (when available) for convenience in ordering.

There are many good collections of source materials and of varying views on specific problems. The staff of the Contemporary Civilization course at Columbia University has prepared three such works: *Introduction to Contemporary Civilization in the West* (New York: Columbia Univ. Press, 1960)—a two-volume general collection of sources; *Chapters in Western Civilization* (New York: Columbia Univ. Press, 1962)—a two-volume collection of long essays on major topics up to the twentieth century; and *Man in Contemporary Society* (New York: Columbia Univ. Press, 1964), a one-volume compilation of fifty short essays on problems of European civilization in the twentieth century—unlike those in the preceding works, these essays are written by philosophers, political scientists, anthropologists, literary critics, etc., rather than historians. The best one-volume collection of sources is *Great Problems in European Civilization* (New York: Prentice-Hall, 1965); edited by Kenneth M. Setton and Henry Winkler. Two new multivolume collections of sources in paperback are: *Sources in Western Civilization* (New York: The Free Press of Glencoe, beginning 1964), Herbert H. Rowen, general editor—Vols. 5–10 cover exactly the time span of this book; *Ideas and Institutions in Western Civilization* (New York: The Macmillan Co., beginning 1963), Norman F. Cantor, general editor—Vols. 3–5 cover the period 1300 to the present. The Heath paperback series, *Problems in European Civilization* (Boston: D.C. Heath and Co., beginning 1956), presents conflicting interpretations on important problems, from the nature of the Renaissance to the origins of the Second World War. Almost thirty booklets in this series have appeared; all are challenging and all have extensive bibliographies. Eugen Weber's *Paths to the Present: Aspects of European Thought from Romanticism to Existentialism* (New York: Dodd, Mead and Co., 1960), also in paperback, is an excellent selection of readings in intellectual and cultural history. Other collections of this type for specific periods are listed at the end of the pertinent chapters of the present work.

The standard bibliographical reference for all aspects of history is the American Historical Association's *Guide to Historical Literature* (New York: The Macmillan Co., 1961). It should be consulted for books on specific topics and for more specialized bibliographies. With this guide and with the book reviews since around 1960 in the *American Historical Review* and the *Journal of Modern History* the reader can keep abreast of all the important works in European and world history.

The American Historical Association also publishes an *Historical Pamphlet Series* for teachers. These pamphlets can be ordered from the Service Center for Teachers of History, 400 A Street, S.E., Washington 3, D.C. Almost sixty have appeared so far, with up-to-date bibliographies and summaries of recent research on a wide variety of topics.

### MULTIVOLUME HISTORIES.

For further background in European and world history the reader may consult the following multivolume series. *The Rise of Modern Europe* (New York: Harper and Row, beginning 1934), edited by William L. Langer and familiarly called the "Langer series," is, overall, still the best of its kind in English. Each volume is written by a single author and covers two or three decades. Each has a bibliographical essay that was up to date at the time of publication, but, unfortunately, most of these have not been revised. Except for the sixteenth century and the periods 1832–1852 and 1900–1939 the series is complete to 1945 and two new volumes on the twentieth century are forthcoming. The greatest merit of this series as an adjunct to the study of European civilization is its attention to economic, social, and cultural history, as well as political history. Most of the volumes have already been reprinted in paperback and are so listed in the suggested readings in this book.

The *New Cambridge Modern History* (Cambridge, Eng.: Cambridge Univ. Press, beginning 1957), is more up to date than the "Langer series," although it has certain drawbacks. Each volume covers roughly the same time span but is a collection of fifteen or more essays by different scholars. Like all cooperative ventures—especially international ones—these volumes lack a unifying point of view and are often uneven in quality. Many of the essays are unsurpassed; a few are wrongheaded. Finally, there are no bibliographies. Nevertheless, the entire series can be consulted with profit as a reference work on many specialized topics and particular areas.

An excellent French series on world history is the *Histoire Générale des Civilisations* (Paris: Presses Universitaires de France, 1953–1959), edited by Maurice Crouzet. Volume 3 covers the Middle Ages, Volume 4, the sixteenth and seventeenth centuries; and Volumes 5, 6, and 7, the eighteenth, nineteenth, and twentieth centuries respectively. Except for Volume 5, each is written by a single author. All the volumes stress civilization and culture more than politics and give more attention to the non-European world than the other series—an approach that sometimes leads to a rather summary treatment of Europe itself. Each volume has a selective bibliography and is revised periodically.

The outstanding world history series in German is the new, ten-volume *Propyläen Weltgeschichte* (Berlin: Propyläen Verlag, 1960–1965), edited by Golo Mann. Volumes 5 and 6 cover the Middle Ages and the Renaissance; Volumes 7–10, the end of the sixteenth century to the present. These volumes resemble those of the *New Cambridge Modern History* in consisting of chapters by different scholars of international repute, but the chapters cover longer time spans and are less specialized. Like the *Histoire Générale des Civilisations,* this series is designed to appeal to the general public, though its style is less lively and its viewpoint less uniform. A separate volume, *Summa Historica* (1965), contains the bibliographies for the ten volumes of the series. All in all, for those who read German, the *Propyläen Weltgeschichte* is probably the best series to use as an aid in teaching undergraduates. It is certainly the most expensive.

In French there are two excellent series that are more detailed than the *Histoire Générale. Peuples et Civilisations* began to appear in the late 1920s, but most of its volumes have been revised or replaced in the past two decades. Volumes 6 and 7 cover the eleventh through the fifteenth centuries; Volumes 8–20, the modern period. With few exceptions each is the work of a single scholar; all have fairly extensive bibliographies. The *Nouvelle Clio* series summarizes the latest research on major topics and has exhaustive bibliographies.

### GENERAL REFERENCE WORKS AND HISTORIES OF SPECIAL TOPICS.

The *Encyclopedia of World History* (Boston: Houghton Mifflin Co., edited by William L. Langer, is packed with information. In addition to a chronological narrative summary of all major events it has genealogical tables and lists of rulers.

*Westermanns Atlas zur Weltgeschichte* (Berlin: Georg Westermann Verlag, 1963) is the most up-to-date and detailed atlas for world history. William R. Shepherd's *Historical Atlas* (8th ed.; Pikesville, Md.: Colonial Offset Co., 1963) has been revised somewhat and is perfectly adequate, but it is more expensive and harder on the eyes than Westermann. The *Atlas of European History* (New York: Oxford Univ. Press, 1957), edited by Edward Whiting Fox, is a good inexpensive atlas for Europe alone —especially since it now exists in paperback.

The following histories of special topics are particularly useful (* indicates paperback edition): John Herman Randall, *The Making of the Modern Mind* (Boston: Houghton Mifflin Co., 1954); Jacob Bronowski and Bruce Mazlich, *The Western Intellectual Tradition: From Leonardo to Hegel* (New York: Harper and Row, 1960 —Torchbook*); Crane Brinton, *A History of Western Morals* (New York: Harcourt, Brace and World, 1959); William C. Dampier, *A History of Science and Its Relations with Philosophy and Religion* (4th ed.; Cambridge, Eng.: Cambridge Univ. Press, 1961); Morris Kline, *Mathematics in Western Culture* (New York: Oxford Univ. Press, n.d. *); Umberto Eco and G. B. Zorgoli, *A Pictorial History of Inventions from Plough to Polaris* (New York: The Macmillan Co. 1963); Abbot P. Usher, *A History of Mechanical Inventions* (New York: Oxford Univ. Press, n.d. *); Shepard B. Clough, *The Economic Development of Western Civilization* (New York: McGraw-Hill, 1959); *The Cambridge Economic History* (Cambridge, Eng.: Cambridge Univ. Press, 1942–1965, and continuing), of which six volumes have appeared so far; B. H. Slicher Van Bath, *The Agrarian History of Western Europe* A.D. *500–1850* (New York: St. Martin's Press, 1963); Charles Gide and Charles Rist, *A History of Economic Doctrines* (2nd ed.; Boston: D. C. Heath and Co., 1948); Marcel R. Reinhard, *Histoire de la Population Mondiale, de 1700 à 1948* (Paris: Domat-Montchrestien, 1961); for the most up-to-date demographic studies see the United Nations *Population Studies* (ST/ SOA/ Series A), which appear periodically; Peter N. Stearns, *European Society in Upheaval. Social History Since 1800* (New York: Macmillan, 1967*); Carl E. Landaver, *European Socialism: A History of Ideas and Movements from the Industrial Revolution to Hitler's Seizure of Power,* 2 vols. (Berkeley and Los Angeles: Univ. of California Press, 1959); Theodore Ropp, *War in the Modern World* (Durham, N.C.: Duke Univ. Press, 1959); John F. C. Fuller, *A Military History of the Western World* (3 vols., New York: Funk and Wagnalls Co., 1954–1956); Helen Gardner, *Art through the Ages* (4th ed.; Harcourt, Brace and World, 1959); E. H. Gombrich, *The Story of Art* (9th ed.; New York: Oxford Univ. Press, 1958); Nikolaus Pevsner, *An Outline of European Architecture* (Baltimore: Penguin Books, 1960, Pelican Books*); Paul Lang, *Music in Western Civilization* (New York: W. W. Norton and Co., 1941); *Columbia Dictionary of Modern European Literature* (New York: Columbia Univ. Press, 1963), H. E. Smith, ed.

E.R.T.

# GEOGRAPHY AND PEOPLES

Today the techniques, institutions, and values of European civilization can be found everywhere from Montreal to Buenos Aires, from Tokyo to Bombay, from Cairo to Capetown. Even the rabidly anti-Western Chinese have substituted Karl Marx for Confucius and steel tanks for paper dragons. It is also true that people who are not Europeans by birth or by descent have contributed much to the betterment of modern man. One has only to think of the Nobel prizes awarded to Japanese and Chinese scientists and, in the field of peace, to the black American Martin Luther King, Jr. and the black South African Albert John Luthuli. The fact remains that without the spread of European civilization throughout the world in recent centuries the achievements of these men might never have been made.

Although the scope of Euopean civilization is worldwide, this book will consider the rest of the world mainly in its relations with Europe. China, Japan, India, Southeast Asia, Africa, and the Near and Middle East each has its own history apart from that of Europe. Even the Americas are not merely "offshoots" of Europe. Their history has been strongly influenced by geography and climate and by the non-European peoples the European settlers found—or brought—there. World history cannot be understood through a knowledge of European history alone, but neither can it be understood without such knowledge. Hence this book will concentrate on the history of European civilization within Europe itself.

At first impression the physical map of Europe appears as a series of peninsulas jutting out in almost every direction. Even the British Isles seem almost like a peninsula. On a world map, Europe itself looks like a peninsular extension of the continent of Asia, with the Atlantic Ocean and the North Sea on one side and the Mediterranean Sea on the other. These impressions suggest a great deal about the historical development of Europe and its various subdivisions. Until about 1500 Europe borrowed important parts of its civilization from the Asian and African shores of the Mediterranean through its Balkan, Italian, and Iberian Peninsulas. After about 1500 Europe began to spread important parts of its civilization to the rest of the world from its peninsulas on the Atlantic.

Before 500 B.C. the civilized parts of Europe consisted only of Greece, and scattered Greek and Phoenician outposts along the southern coasts of Italy, France, and Spain. The main centers of civilization in the "West" were still in the ancient Near East: Mesopotamia, Egypt, Syria, Palestine, and Asia Minor. Beginning late in the fourth century B.C., Alexander the Great and his successors imposed the outward forms of Greek civilization on the educated city dwellers in most of the Near East. And by the time of Christ the Caesars of Rome conquered this area and imposed their own Latin language and civilization, which borrowed heavily from

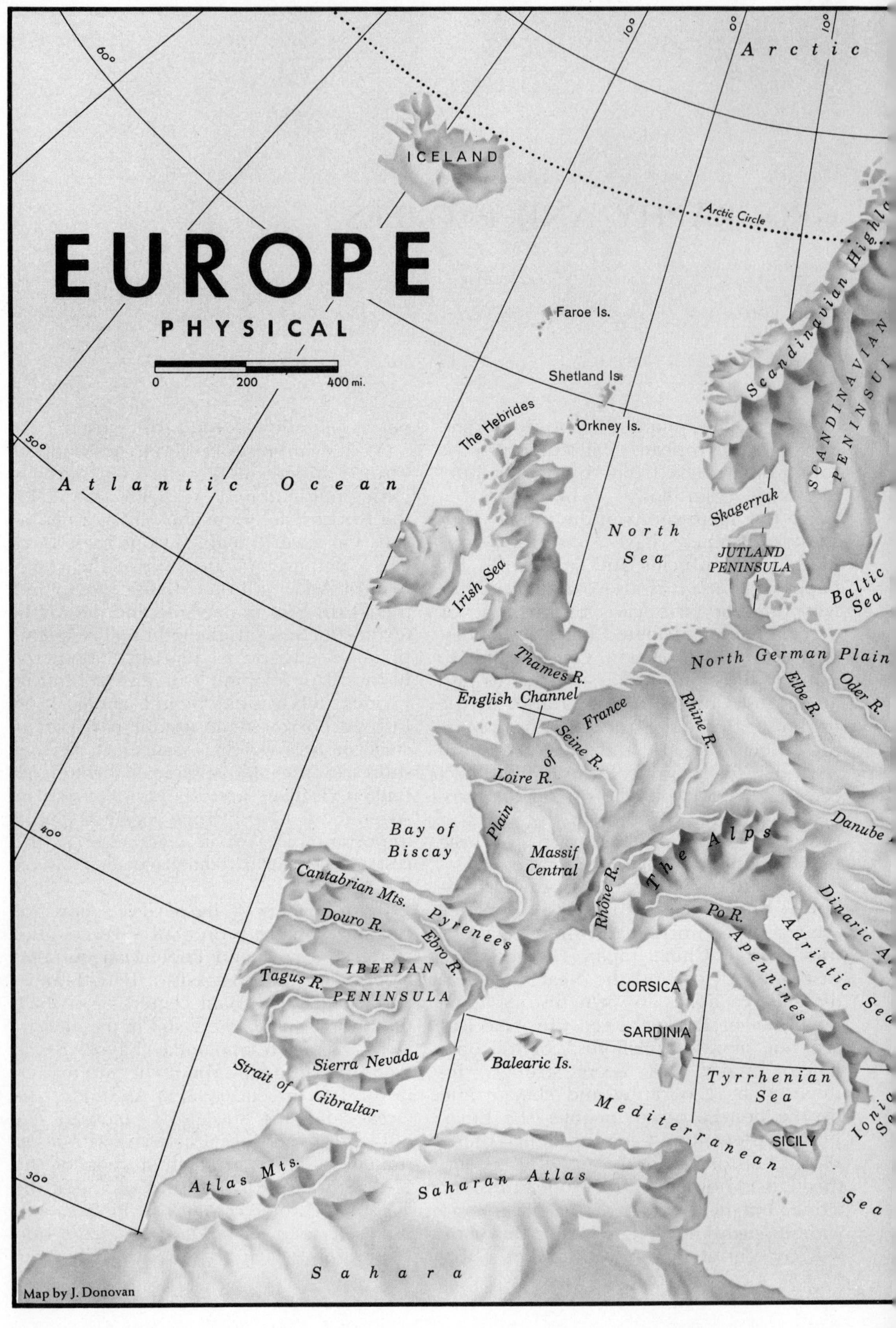

EUROPE
PHYSICAL
0
200
400 mi.
60°
50°
40°
30°
10°
0°
10°
Arctic
Arctic Circle
ICELAND
Faroe Is.
Shetland Is.
Orkney Is.
The Hebrides
Atlantic Ocean
North Sea
Skagerrak
JUTLAND PENINSULA
Scandinavian Highla
SCANDINAVIAN PENINSU
Baltic Sea
Irish Sea
Thames R.
English Channel
North German Plain
Elbe R.
Oder R.
Rhine R.
France
Seine R.
Plain of
Loire R.
Bay of Biscay
Massif Central
Danube
The Alps
Rhône R.
Cantabrian Mts.
Pyrenees
Douro R.
Ebro R.
IBERIAN PENINSULA
Tagus R.
Po R.
Apennines
Adriatic Sea
Dinaric A
CORSICA
SARDINIA
Balearic Is.
Sierra Nevada
Strait of Gibraltar
Tyrrhenian Sea
Mediterranean Sea
SICILY
Ionia Se
Atlas Mts.
Saharan Atlas
Sahara
Map by J. Donovan

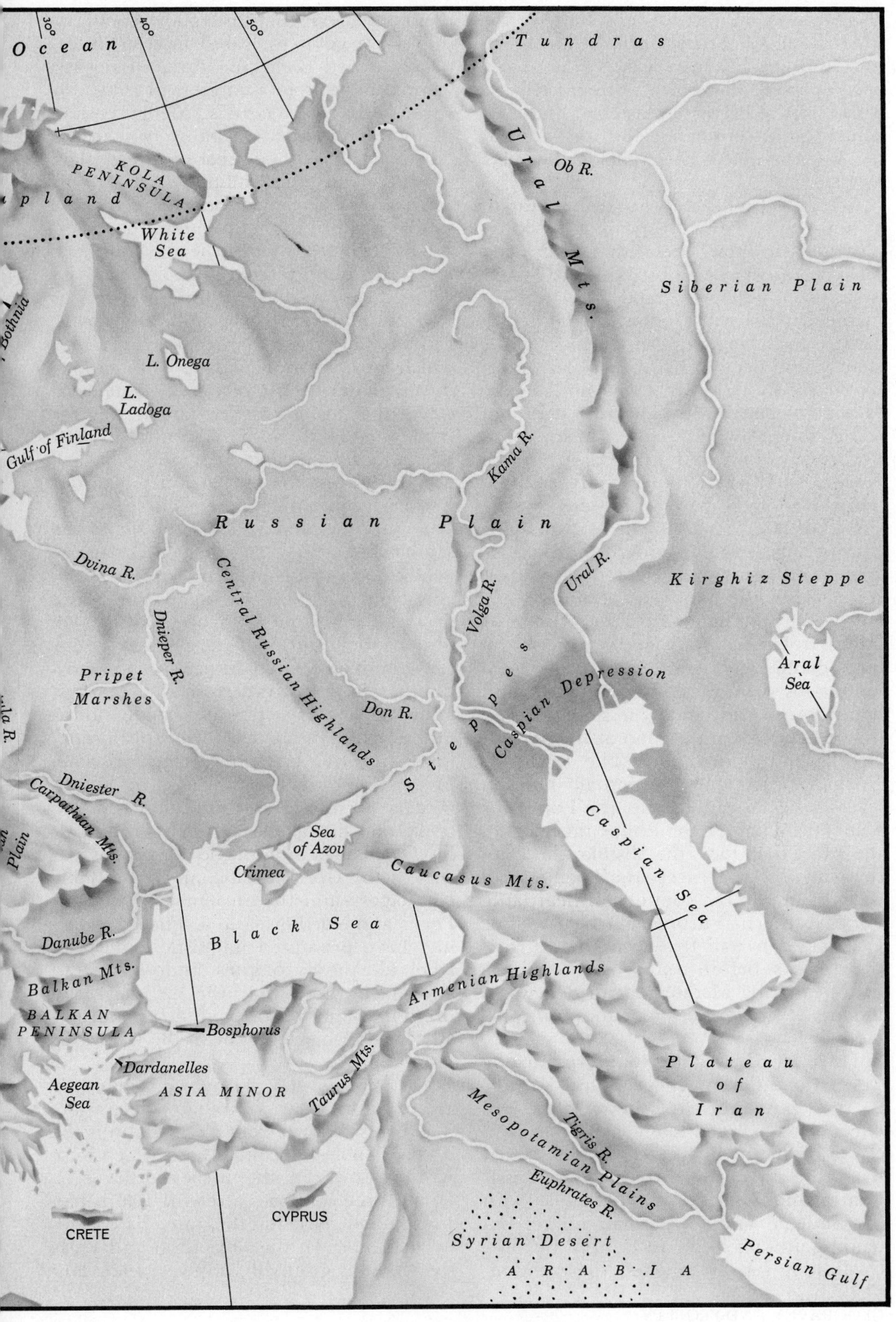

Ocean
30°
40°
50°
Tundras
KOLA PENINSULA
White Sea
Ural Mts.
Ob R.
Siberian Plain
Bothnia
L. Onega
L. Ladoga
Gulf of Finland
Kama R.
Russian Plain
Dvina R.
Central Russian Highlands
Dnieper R.
Volga R.
Ural R.
Kirghiz Steppe
Pripet Marshes
Aral Sea
Don R.
Steppes
Caspian Depression
Dniester R.
Carpathian Mts.
Plain
Sea of Azov
Crimea
Caucasus Mts.
Caspian Sea
Danube R.
Black Sea
Balkan Mts.
Armenian Highlands
BALKAN PENINSULA
Bosphorus
Dardanelles
Taurus Mts.
Plateau of Iran
Aegean Sea
ASIA MINOR
Mesopotamian Plains
Tigris R.
Euphrates R.
CYPRUS
CRETE
Syrian Desert
ARABIA
Persian Gulf

the Greeks, on the western half of the Mediterranean Basin. Until the fifth century A.D. the Roman Empire not only encompassed all of the ancient civilized world west of Persia but also had under its control all of continental Europe south of the Danube and west of the Rhine, plus England.

After the Roman Empire disintegrated, a new center of European life slowly emerged in those areas that had been most recently civilized by the Romans and then fallen into the hands of the Germanic barbarians: France, England, the Netherlands, and western Germany. The climate and geography of these lands differ markedly from what one finds in the Mediterranean Basin. The sun does not *always* shine on the Mediterranean coast, nor is it *always* cold and damp in the North. But there is much more rainfall, and the winters are often severe. In the early Middle Ages much of Northern Europe was covered by dense forests. As these were gradually cleared, a person could travel for hundreds of miles without seeing mountains or a large body of water. In Greece, Italy, and Spain, on the other hand, trees were sparse, the local mountains were usually in sight, and many towns had stood on slopes facing the open sea since the time of the ancient Greeks and Phoenicians. The towns of Northern Europe were eventually built on rivers—the Po, the Rhône, the Loire, the Seine, the Thames, the Rhine, the Scheldt, the Elbe, the Oder, the Vistula, the Danube—all of which, except the Thames, had their source in the continental heartland. For Northern Europeans the Atlantic Ocean was a wall to which they turned their backs before 1500. For Southern Europeans the Mediterranean Sea was a lifeline of communication and transportation.

Thus, Northern and Southern Europe were two different geographical worlds. As the physical map shows, they are effectively separated from each other by a chain of mountains extending eastward from the Pyrenees through the Massif Central and the Alps to the Balkans—with the Sudeten and Carpathian ranges extending upward into East Central Europe. Civilization hardly touched these mountainous regions before 1500. About all they were good for, until modern Europeans turned them into vacation resorts, were mining and summer grazing for sheep and goats. There is little flat land in the South but a vast expanse of it in the North and East. The great northern plain extends from the Atlantic Ocean clear across to Western Asia, and there is also a sizable plain in the middle Danube valley.

The peoples of Northern, Southern, Western, and Eastern Europe have developed historically in different ethnic as well as different geographical worlds. Ethnic comes from the Greek word *ethnos,* which means nation. This is not "nation" in the modern sense of a unified national state—the ancient Greek nation was far from *that.* Thus, to avoid confusion with the modern meaning of nation, we shall use the phrase "ethnic group" to distinguish a group of people who share the same customs and beliefs and speak the same language.

Most of the peoples of Europe speak languages of Latin, Germanic, or Slavic origin. It is beyond the scope of this book to trace the histories of these languages. A few examples should suffice to show how far they have evolved from their earliest known forms, as well as give some indication of when the peoples who speak them first appeared on the European scene, presumably from somewhere in Southwestern Asia. This presumption is based on certain similarities between all the Latin, Germanic, and Slavic languages—as well as the Greek, Celtic, and East Baltic languages—and the ancient languages of Persia and Northern India. These similarities have prompted linguistic experts to label all these tongues Indo-European and to imagine that the peoples who brought them to Europe and India orginally lived somewhere near the Caucasus Mountains.

The present-day Romance languages are of Latin—that is, Roman—derivation. The oldest known example of Latin is the Twelve Tables of Roman Law, which were written down in the fifth century B.C., about three centuries after the Latins had presumably settled in the immediate vicinity of Rome. In the next thousand years the Romans gradually imposed their language on most of the other peoples of Italy, France, Spain, Portugal, and parts of the Balkan Peninsula. By the fifth century A.D. the dialects of Latin spoken by these peoples already differed considerably from one another as well as from the language of the Twelve Tables. The collapse of Roman power, the invasions by other peoples, and the conditions of geographical and cultural isolation that prevailed thereafter, hastened the rate of transformation of these dialects. By 1500 they had coalesced into several distinct languages — Italian, French, Provençal, Catalan, Castilian (Spanish), Portuguese, Rumanian — each with its own local variants. Since then, each of these languages has evolved further into its present form.

The present-day languages of Germanic derivation are German itself, Netherlandish (Dutch and Flemish), Swedish, Norwegian, Danish, and English. There is no one form comparable to the Twelve Tables for Latin. The earliest written form of German was a Frankish oath dating from A.D. 842, almost five centuries after the Franks began to occupy western Germany. But other tongues of Germanic origin were also spoken at that time and had their own histories thereafter. One of these had been brought to England by Anglo-Saxon invaders in the fifth century A.D. Its earliest form is the epic poem *Beowulf*, which dates from the eighth century. Anyone who needs proof that the English language is of Germanic origin should look at this work. He should then compare it with Geoffrey Chaucer's *Canterbury Tales (c.* 1385*)*, which not only shows a marked evolution but also heavy borrowings from Latin and French. Even the language of William Shakespeare (1564 – 1616) has many forms and meanings that differ from the English of today.

Whereas the Romance languages predominate in Western and Southern Europe and the Germanic languages in Northern and West Central Europe, in East Central and Eastern Europe the languages are mainly of Slavic derivation. Today these are Russian, Ukrainian, Belorussian, Polish, Czech, Slovak, Slovenian, Serbo-Croatian, and Bulgarian. As in the case of the Germanic languages, no one original form is known, and there probably was none. The first surviving example of Russian is the *Ruskaia Pravda*, a law code dating from the eleventh century A.D., about two or three centuries after the East Slavic ancestors of the present-day Russians, Ukrainians, and Belorussians first emerged into the light of history. The West Slavs — Poles, Czechs, and Slovaks — have inhabited much of their present territory since the pre-Christian era, whereas the South Slavs — Slovenians, Croats, Serbs, and Bulgarians — moved into the Balkans in the sixth and seventh centuries A.D. From what little is known about the early forms of the languages of all these peoples it is clear that they too have evolved markedly.

East Central and Eastern Europe also include ethnic groups whose languages are not of Slavic origin. In the Balkans a modern form of Greek is still spoken in the land of its historic origin. A derivation of Latin is still spoken in Rumania, whose southern half used to be called Wallachia, from the word *Vlach*, which meant a Roman provincial in the Balkan Peninsula; there were Vlachs in Macedonia and Northern Greece until the end of the nineteenth century. Albanian is a local language of prehistoric origin. In the Eastern Baltic region Latvian and Lithuanian are Indo-European but not Slavic, while Estonian and Finnish are of Central Asiatic origin. Magyar, the language of Hungary, is also of Central Asiatic origin. Finally, between the eleventh and thirteenth centuries, German colonists settled in parts of Poland, Bohemia, Hungary, and the Eastern Baltic region and preserved their own language, especially in the towns, until they were evicted in the twentieth century.

In Western Europe there are several ethnic groups whose languages are of neither Latin nor Germanic origin. Like Albanian, the Basque language, spoken on both sides of the western Pyrenees, is a survival from prehistoric times. The Celtic peoples, who had occupied the British Isles, France, Switzerland, and much of Spain before the Latin and Germanic peoples moved in, survived on the northwestern fringes and in the mountain ranges of these countries. Even today Celtic languages are still spoken in north-

LANGUAGES OF EUROPE
NORWEGIAN
SCOTTISH GAELIC
North Sea
DANISH
IRISH (Gaelic)
ENGLISH
WELSH
LOW GERMAN
DUTCH
FLEMISH
HIGH GERMAN
Atlantic Ocean
BRETON
NORTHERN FRENCH (Langue d'Oui)
SLOVEN
RHAETO-ROMAN
Venetian
GALICIAN
SOUTHERN FRENCH (Langue d'Oc)
BASQUE
PROVENÇAL
Piedmontese
ITALIAN
Tuscan
Umbrian
PORTUGUESE
CASTILIAN
Aragonese
CATALAN
Sardinian
Andalusian
Mediterranean Sea
SICILIA
Map by J. Donovan

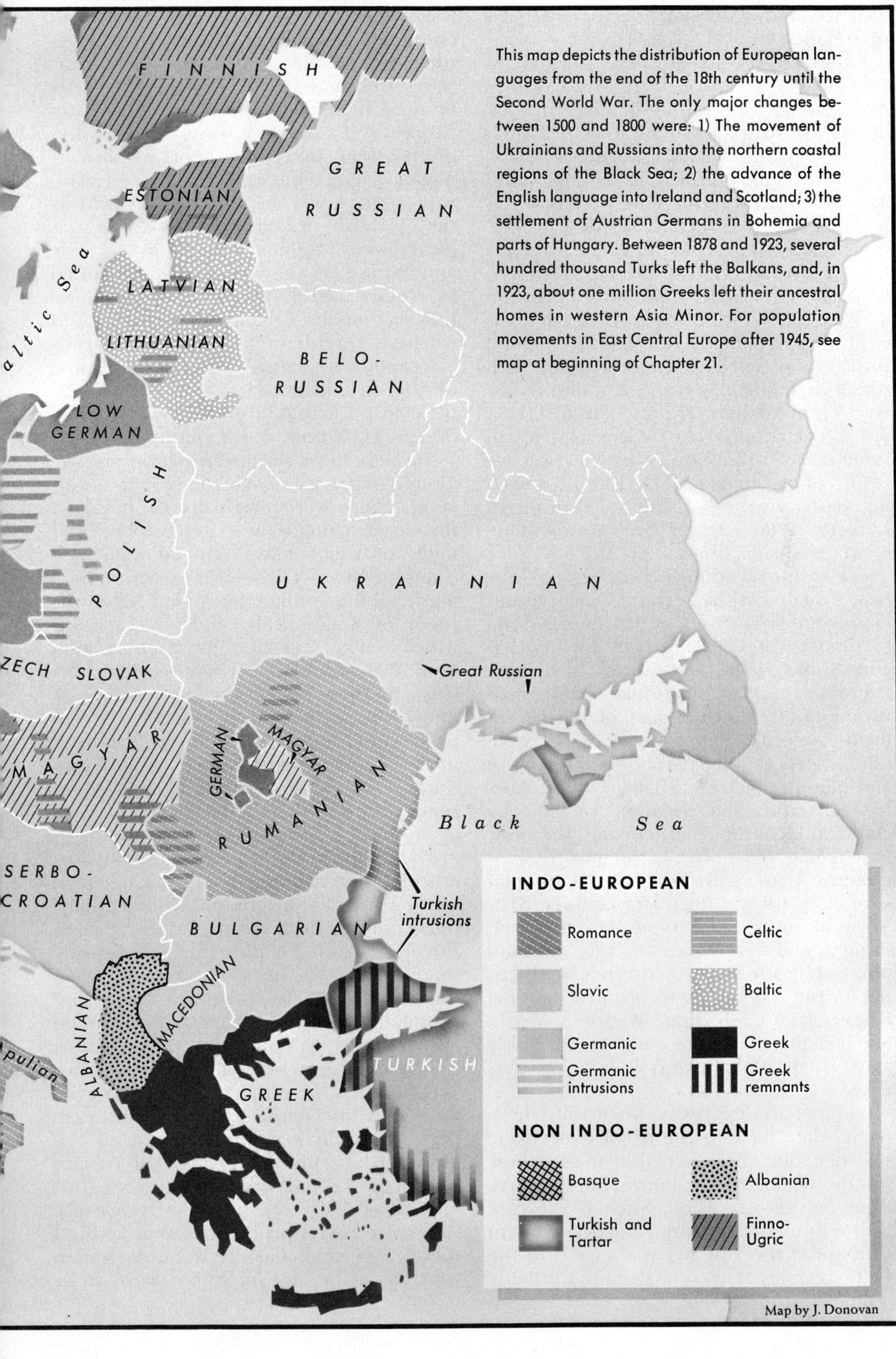

This map depicts the distribution of European languages from the end of the 18th century until the Second World War. The only major changes between 1500 and 1800 were: 1) The movement of Ukrainians and Russians into the northern coastal regions of the Black Sea; 2) the advance of the English language into Ireland and Scotland; 3) the settlement of Austrian Germans in Bohemia and parts of Hungary. Between 1878 and 1923, several hundred thousand Turks left the Balkans, and, in 1923, about one million Greeks left their ancestral homes in western Asia Minor. For population movements in East Central Europe after 1945, see map at beginning of Chapter 21.
FINNISH
ESTONIAN
GREAT RUSSIAN
altic Sea
LATVIAN
LITHUANIAN
BELO-RUSSIAN
LOW GERMAN
POLISH
UKRAINIAN
ZECH
SLOVAK
Great Russian
MAGYAR
GERMAN
MAGYAR
RUMANIAN
Black
Sea
SERBO-CROATIAN
Turkish intrusions
BULGARIAN
MACEDONIAN
ALBANIAN
pulian
GREEK
TURKISH
INDO-EUROPEAN
Romance
Celtic
Slavic
Baltic
Germanic
Greek
Germanic intrusions
Greek remnants
NON INDO-EUROPEAN
Basque
Albanian
Turkish and Tartar
Finno-Ugric
Map by J. Donovan

ern Scotland, Wales, Brittany, and parts of Ireland.

Language is only the most obvious aspect of a whole pattern of culture which distinguishes one ethnic group from another. Culture consists of ways of thinking, feeling, and behaving, which a person begins to acquire in his earliest childhood and which are reinforced by his contacts within a closed group throughout his life. A person's culture provides him with certain distinctive norms and patterns of behavior. It teaches him how to justify and rationalize specific forms of conduct; it also gives him a few broad, general principles of selectivity and ordering with which he tends to see and respond to the world around him. Even when an ethnic group has adopted a new language it can sometimes preserve other expressive forms of its culture. The English-speaking Irish are the best-known example in Europe today, but there were many others in earlier times.

The cultural differences among Europe's many ethnic groups have found expression at all levels. At the highest level of thought and art much of Europe has gone through the same series of distinctive styles, each with national and regional variations. In the first half of the seventeenth century there were noticeable differences in the baroque architecture and painting of Italy, Spain, France, Austria, Holland, and Sweden. During the eighteenth century mathematics, the most impersonal and universal form of human thought, had its British and continental schools. Until the twentieth century British philosophy was typically empirical, French philosophy rationalistic, German philosophy idealistic. A century ago serious music too began to acquire national characteristics, so that Wagner, Verdi, and Tchaikowsky were easily recognizable as German, Italian, and Russian respectively.

Some of the expressive forms of Christianity date back to the tribal and village societies out of which Europe's ethnic groups began to crystallize in the Dark Ages before A.D. 1000. Such is the case with a number of customs associated with Christmas: the yule log was sacred to the Celtic peoples of ancient Britain; mistletoe was venerated by both the Celtic and Germanic peoples of Northern Europe; the use of the fir tree for ceremonial purposes originated with Germanic peoples of pre-Christian times. Among the Latin peoples of Southern Europe the festivities of the week preceding Lent are also of pagan origin. One aspect of these Carnival festivities was the visit to this world by the spirits of the dead, whose role was played by young men wearing masks. The general license they enjoyed was justified by their useful function of bringing purification and driving away demons and witches. Torchlight and bonfire festivals associated with saints' days retained some of their primitive meanings of warding off the evil spirits that brought diseases to cattle and grain and of stimulating fertility.

Each modern European nation and region has its distinctive foods and beverages, which were originally products of the local climate and geography, and many of which have changed little in a thousand years. Olive oil is used for cooking in all the Mediterranean lands, but the foods of Spain, Italy, and Greece differ widely. The peoples in each region around the North Sea preserve their herrings in their own particular way. Even after Russia's peasants learned how to make vodka they also continued to drink mead, a fermented beverage made from water and the honey of wild bees. Beer remains the most popular alcholic beverage of all the Germanic peoples of Northern and Central Europe, again with dozens of different types. Grapes are grown as far north as the middle Rhine Valley, but wine has been *the* staple beverage of Europe's Latin peoples since prehistoric times, and it has always been used as an important item in religious ritual and hospitality. Even today many Frenchmen automatically welcome a guest or seal a business agreement with a glass of wine.

Differences in social relations and even in personality characteristics have been, in part, culturally conditioned. Not all Englishmen are phlegmatic, not all Italians are volatile, not all Russians are dour. But insofar as many are, it is partly because they were reared in cultures that favored these respective characteristics. A woman who has grown up in Rome *expects* to be pinched by passing men; a Dutch woman visiting Rome does not. When a Pole shrugs his shoulders he usually means "I don't know"; when a Frenchman makes the same gesture he usually means "That's life." Yet in both cases the context of the conversation may alter the meaning in a way that an outsider cannot fathom.

One's culture is a more intimate and meaningful part of one's life than one's civilization. Civilization consists of impersonal techniques, institutions, and values, and the economic framework within which these operate. Thus, the horse, the city, electricity, parliamentary government, monotheism, and monogamy are all elements of European civilization. Peoples all over the world have eventually adopted them. But even those of us whose ancestors came from Europe have developed distinctive cultures suitable to our new homelands. Meanwhile, in their old homelands, each European ethnic group has clung tenaciously to its own traditional culture. One of the most remarkable features of European civilization is the diversity of the peoples that have helped create it and yet maintain their cultural identity within it.

PART I

# THE PREINDUSTRIAL AGE

IN OUR MASS SOCIETY we must make a special effort to understand that, until little more than a century ago, the masses in Europe—and everywhere else—lived outside the mainstream of the civilization that dominated the world around them. From about the year 1000 until the middle of the nineteenth century, most Europeans never left their self-sustaining rural villages. (England was the only country where the transition from a mainly agricultural to a mainly urban-industrial population began before the nineteenth century.) These peasants knew practically nothing of the techniques, institutions, and values that gave European civilization its distinctive character. In many countries the very language of the upper classes was incomprehensible to the rural masses. They experienced even Christianity primarily through the familiar forms of their local folk cultures. Their geographical, social, and cultural isolation was reinforced by their almost complete lack of contact with the only mass medium of communication available before the late nineteenth century: the printed word. European civilization was the first to integrate its masses, but during most of its history it had little impact on their lives.

The integration of the masses is the most recent stage in the process of modernization. Today it is relatively easy for developing nations to borrow new knowledge and techniques from abroad and to produce leaders willing to force them on their tradition-bound countrymen. Originally, however, the accumulation of new knowledge and techniques and the rise of modernizing leaders developed slowly in Western Europe between the thirteenth and the eighteenth centuries. These first two stages in the process of modernization had to occur before the third stage, the economic and social transformation, could begin. Only after the middle of the nineteenth century did the predominantly rural and agricultural societies and economies of Western Europe and North America become predominantly urban and industrial. In the process their cultural patterns were also transformed, thus leading to the fourth stage: the integration of all individuals, social groups, and geographical regions into a national community. But cultural change always lags behind political, economic, and social change, especially when familiar values and ways of doing things are disrupted by major technological innovations.

About the year 1500 three major technological innovations—gunpowder, printing, and ocean-going sailing ships—began to alter the traditional European civilization of the Middle Ages. These innovations were exploited by men with a dynamic, restless, driving type of personality usually associated with the Renaissance. In addition to these generals, scholars, and explorers, a new type of monarch appeared. These new monarchs created strong central governments, which greatly increased the scope of warfare and commerce. But religion remained a very meaningful part of most people's culture and, when combined with the rebellions of overmighty aristocrats and princes, religious strife hampered the centralizing efforts of the monarchs. Nevertheless, by the eighteenth century, strong, secular-minded monarchies dominated most of Europe. By then the intellectual climate had become more scientific and cosmopolitan, and this new outlook was beginning to spread to the educated middle classes.

Between the mid-eighteenth and mid-nineteenth centuries the pace of modernization accelerated in Western Europe. The agricultural revolution gave more food with less labor and less land, while improvements in medicine reduced infant mortality and prolonged the life span. As a result, the world witnessed its first population explosion—first in the British Isles and then on the continent. The Industrial Revolution, which began with the harnessing of new mechanical inventions to the steam engine, helped to provide work for this expanding population while it also enriched the middle classes and increased the power of Europe's rulers. Even before the Industrial Revolution took hold in France, that country was partially transformed by Europe's first democratic revolution. Although, by 1815, Europe's counterrevolutionary monarchs had apparently succeeded in stamping out the more "subversive" political ideals of the French Revolution, its emphasis on modern, rational forms of government gradually reemerged during the next few decades. By the middle of the nineteenth century the railroad, the steamship, and the telegraph marked the true end of the preindustrial age. After that, modernizing leadership became a necessity—with or without political democracy—in order to deal with the economic and social transformation initiated by the revolution in transportation and communications.

CHAPTER I

# THE HERITAGE OF THE MIDDLE AGES

Around the year 1000 a new civilization emerged in Western Europe. The main features of this medieval civilization had been in the making for several hundred years, and it reached its peak in the thirteenth century. During the fourteenth and fifteenth centuries, seignorialism, feudalism, monastic culture, and the power of the church declined. Other medieval institutions and values—corporate social organization, regional and local attachment, privilege—persisted until the late eighteenth century. In representative government, municipal organization, law, and higher education, medieval traditions are still with us, usually (though not always) in forms more suitable to modern needs. Thus, historians now see a basic continuity in European civilization which in its medieval phase was predominantly agricultural, feudal, and church-oriented and which gradually became modern, that is, more secular, more urban, more politically centralized, and, finally, overwhelmingly industrial and scientific.

At the end of the tenth century this civilization showed little promise. Everything about it was a makeshift adjustment to conditions that had been getting worse and worse for hundreds of years. When the turbulent, uncouth Germanic rulers of Western Europe were not trying to repel new invaders they were fighting among themselves. Trade had ceased, the thriving cities of Roman times had disappeared, the population had dwindled, and the bulk of the people had become unfree peasants living at a subsistence level. The Roman Catholic Church preserved some elements of Roman law and administration and fostered the spread of Christianity. Otherwise the civilization of ancient Rome had disappeared, except in a few isolated monasteries where the monks copied ancient Latin texts, wrote naïve historical chronicles, and catalogued the small quantity of information and misinformation at their disposal.

## THE NEAR EAST AND EUROPE, *c.* A.D. 1000

In contrast to the main centers of civilization in the former territories of the ancient Roman Empire to the East and South, the Western remnant was just emerging from the Dark Ages. Indeed, the Latin-Germanic West struggled along in relative isolation from its more advanced neighbors until the middle of the twelfth century. Only then did contact with Muslim and Byzantine learning stimulate an intellectual revival in Western Europe. But in the tenth century Muslim civilization already held sway in Spain and Sicily, and Byzantine civilization was beginning to exert a decisive influence on the Slavic peoples of Eastern Europe through the Greek Orthodox Church. For these reasons we must cast a brief glance at the Byzantine and Muslim worlds before concentrating on the new civilization in the West.

### The Byzantine and Muslim Worlds

In the tenth century the Byzantine Empire, with its capital at Constantinople, controlled the Greek-speaking parts of the Balkan Peninsula, Asia Minor, and the islands of the Eastern Mediterranean. Although it continued to call itself the Eastern Roman Empire, it was culturally Greek and Near Eastern. (Historians later derived the descriptive label Byzantine from Byzantium, the original name of Constantinople.) The pomp and ceremony of the imperial court reflected the absolute power of the emperor. Even the patriarch, the head of the Greek Orthodox Church, was subordinate to him. Constantinople, a cosmopolitan city of a million people, was the commercial and manufacturing center of the Near East. Philosophy and letters flourished in its university, its theologians were unsurpassed in hair-splitting subtlety, and even Emperor Constantine VII Porphyrogenitus (912–959) was a serious student of art and history.

As well as affecting the Greeks themselves, who never forgot the power and splendor of their medieval empire, Byzantine civilization altered the lives of other peoples in Eastern Europe. In the late ninth century Cyril and Methodius, two monks from Salonika, converted the pagan Czechs in far-off Bohemia. They gave this people a modified Greek alphabet, religious texts written in the language of the country, a Slavic liturgy, and a Slavic church. The Magyar invasion of the Hungarian Plain in the tenth century separated the Slavs of Bohemia and Slovakia from those in the South and put them in the orbit of the Latin-Germanic West thereafter, along wtih the Poles and the Croats. But the Serbs, the Bulgarians, and the Russians were all converted to the Greek Orthodox rite by the end of the tenth century. All these southern and eastern Slavs used the language and liturgy invented by Cyril and Methodius and came under the ecclesiastical control and cultural influence of Constantinople. After the final split in 1054 between the Greek and Roman churches, these peoples developed independently of Western Europe.

Like Byzantine civilization, the civilization of the Muslim world reached its height between the ninth and eleventh centuries, which was the low point in the history of the Latin-Germanic West. It had originated around A.D. 630, when the teachings of Mohammed the Prophet had unified and invigorated the nomadic and semibarbaric tribes of Western Arabia. Mohammed conceived of God—Allah—as a person and at the same time as an all-powerful force. Allah demands "absolute submission of the heart"—Islam—to His Will. The Muslim—member of the faithful—who submits does not thereby resign himself to fatalistic inaction. On the contrary, he feels that he must express an uncompromising enthusiasm in order to secure his salvation in the next world. He may enjoy earthly goods as part of Allah's blessings, but he must shun superstition and miracles. The only true miracle is the gift of personal faith. In the name of this faith the Muslim must be prepared to fight unstintingly for Allah's cause and to practice the virtues of loyalty and generosity toward other men and, in contrast to traditional Arab custom, toward women.

Fired by this new faith the Arabs organized themselves into an irresistible fighting force and set out to conquer the world. Within twenty years they took over Syria, Egypt, Iraq (ancient Mesopotamia and Babylonia), and Persia. By the middle of the eighth century their empire extended to the Indus River and the plains of Central Asia in the East; in the West they controlled all of North Africa to the Atlantic Ocean.

Under the Abbasid dynasty (750–*c.* 1100) Muslim civilization made its most original and lasting achievements. In their capital at Bagdad the Abbasid rulers called themselves caliphs, the Prophet's representatives on earth. Unlike the popes in Rome, who were defining a comparable role for

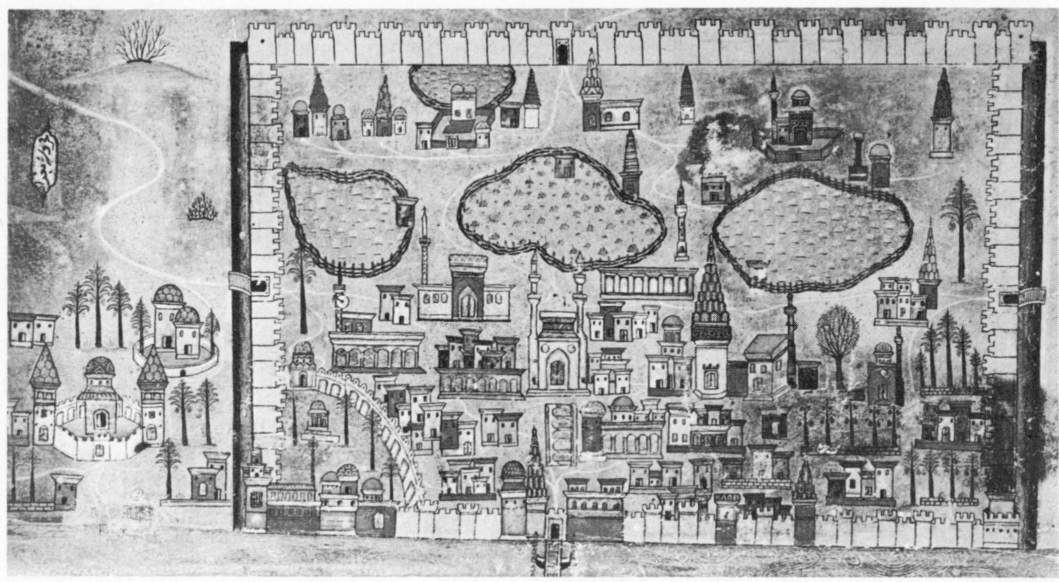

*Medieval Bagdad*

themselves, the caliphs were also able to make themselves supreme temporal rulers. They removed all distinctions between Arab and non-Arab Muslims and encouraged the Arabs to assimilate parts of the cultural heritage of the Near and Middle East. Thus, Arabic learning benefited from translations of literary and philosophical works not only from the Greek, but also from the Syriac, Persian, and Sanskrit. Arab scholars made original advances in science and mathematics and, borrowing some ideas from India, they invented algebra and the system of numerals, including zero, that the whole world uses today.

In Spain the Omayyad dynasty established a separate kingdom that lasted for almost three hundred years. Cordova, the capital, was a bustling city of half a million people. Its schools of medicine, philosophy, and mathematics made it the greatest intellectual center in Europe, outshining Constantinople itself. The poetry and music of Omayyad Spain rivaled those of the Abbasid caliphate in the Near East. Christians, Muslim converts, Jews, Arabs, and Berbers mingled freely in the most tolerant environment of the Middle Ages.

Between the end of the eleventh and the beginning of the thirteenth centuries Muslim Spain lost its northern territories to the Christian princes, while its southern territories were united with the Berber kingdom of Morocco. During this period Muslim Spain was a Moorish rather than an Arab state. Its intellectual and cultural activities continued unabated, and many ancient learned works were translated from Greek into Arabic. The outstanding contribution was made by Averroës (*c.*1126–1198), philosopher, physician, and commentator on Plato and Aristotle. Spanish Muslims also invented astronomical tables, which, along with Averroës' commentaries on Aristotle, were soon translated from Arabic into Latin. From Spain and Sicily (occupied by Berber Muslims called Saracens from the ninth to the eleventh centuries) these translations were to provide the basis for the revival of learning in Western Europe in the twelfth and thirteenth centuries.

## Foundations of the New Civilization in the West

In the year 1000, Latin Christendom rested on much more modest foundations than the civilizations of the Near East. There were no great cities, no commerce or industry, no strong central governments, no universities. Society was simple: there were those people who prayed, those who fought, and those who tilled the soil. Each of these three classes performed its function according to rules and customs prescribed by its own separate institution: the Church for the clergy, the feudal system for the warrior nobles, the seignorial system for the peasants. Yet these three institutions and their members also served each other. The peasants provided food and labor services to the feudal lords and the clergy; the feudal lords gave military protection; the clergy saved souls for the hereafter and gave meaning to a poor and often brutal existence in the here and now.

### The Teachings and Structure of the Christian Church

Until the Reformations of the sixteenth century the West had only one official Christian Church—the Roman Catholic Church. Its monotheism and emphasis on the Scriptures as the Word of God reflected the thought of its Jewish founders; its administrative organization and claim to universality were drawn from the Roman Empire. During the Middle Ages the Church developed these legacies from the ancient period in a unique way, though it should be noted that the Greek Orthodox Church, even after its eventual separation from the Church of Rome, retained the same basic teachings and structure.

Christ's teachings, as expounded by his disciples, were both moral and theological. His message of the dignity of the individual and the brotherhood of man, though phrased in a unique way, was less original than his promise of personal salvation through the gift of divine grace. The basis of this promise, and the core of Christian theology, is the doctrine of the Trinity. According to this doctrine, three distinct persons are united in one divine nature: the Father, the Son, and the Holy Ghost. A corollary doctrine is that a divine nature and a human nature are combined in the person of Christ. From this mystery Christian teaching developed is conception of the relation of man and God, and, indirectly, the idea that the Church is divine as well as human.

The Church teaches that communion with Christ is a form of union with divinity. Christ provided the means by which, after His departure from this world, future disciples might continue the union that His immediate disciples enjoyed with Him, though in a different way. These means were called sacraments, "outward signs instituted by Christ to give grace." This "grace" was a supernatural gift of God freely bestowed on man to prepare him for eternal life. Among the sacraments through which God bestowed the gift of grace were baptism, which made a person a Christian, and the Eucharist, which was a sacrificial repetition of Christ's last supper. The Eucharist—or Holy Communion—became the central act of Christian worship. To baptism and the Eucharist, the medieval Church added the sacraments of confirmation, penance, matrimony, extreme unction, and holy orders.

The structure of the Church was based on three separate doctrines. First, there was the doctrine that only an ordained priest could administer the sacraments. Hence, within the Church, the clergy was distinct from the laity. Second, according to the doctrine of Apostolic succession, those clergymen who came to be called bishops were the successors of the twelve Apostles, the immediate associates of Christ, who had been, as it were, the original clergy. The see (seat) of each bishop was a city, and a bishop's jurisdiction extended over an entire Roman diocese;* within each diocese, a number of parish churches were administered by priests, assisted by deacons. Third, according to the Petrine doctrine, the bishop of Rome, called *papa,* or pope, was Christ's deputy on earth, a role he inherited from Peter, whom Christ had designated as the founder of the Church and the first bishop of Rome. Until the eleventh century the popes had little real power outside the territory in central Italy known as the Papal States, and the bishops in the East never accepted the spiritual claims of the papacy. Nevertheless, the popes sponsored the conversion of the pagan peoples

*In Roman times a diocese was as large as a modern European country; in medieval times the Church created many new dioceses, subdivided the older ones, and grouped several dioceses under an archdiocese administered by an archbishop.

A Knight taking the oath of fealty

of Northern Europe, they corresponded with the bishops in the West as best they could, and they preserved some semblance of the universal language and administrative structure of ancient Rome.

In addition to the clergy that dealt directly with the laity—the secular clergy—there was the regular clergy, consisting of monks who retired from the world and lived according to a strict rule *(regula).* Until the late tenth century must continental monks followed the Benedictine rule and devoted their lives exclusively to prayer and contemplation. But Irish and English monks had already established traditions of scholarship, missionary work, and ecclesiastical reform. As we shall see presently, these kinds of monastic activity were to help bring medieval civilization to its greatest heights

### *Feudalism*

Like monasticism, feudalism developed as a response to the insecurity and uncertainty of the Dark Ages. It was a form of private government originally designed as a means of obtaining a reliable military force to dominate rebellious nobles and repel invaders, and of compensating those warriors who performed these services with the only form of wealth available in a backward agricultural economy—land. Thus, feudalism was a political system, a military system, and a system of land tenure.

Under feudalism political power rested in the hands of a landed nobility. Nominally these nobles were the *vassals* of some *lord* who gave them their land as a *fief.* In return, they served a given number of days in his army and at his court and fulfilled economic obligations called "relief" and "aid." The vassal became the lord's "man" and swore to perform these duties and fulfill these acts of *homage* (from the French word for man—*homme*). Their relationship was therefore both contractual and personal. It was sealed in a solemn ceremony in which the vassal knelt before his lord, placed his hands between his lord's hands, and took an oath of *fealty* to him. He promised to protect his lord from his enemies and never to serve anyone against him. Aside from homage and fealty, the feudal vassal was a free man; in many instances he was complete master of everyone in his fief.

The feudal system varied from place to place and adapted itself to changing conditions. Theoretically the hierarchy was a kind of pyramid, with a monarch at the top. The monarch had a few great vassals (dukes and counts) each of whom had a number of lesser vassals (barons and earls) each of whom had a group of knights—the lowest vassals in the hierarchy. In practice there were wide deviations from this theoretical model. Under the primitive conditions of the tenth century the local barons were usually the only effective rulers. After that there was a gradual concentration of power among the greater vassals. In the Norman kingdoms of England and southern Italy the king acquired some authority over the vassals of his vassals by the late eleventh century. In Germany the great dukes were virtually independent except under a few strong emperors. The king of France had some vassals—like the Duke of Normandy and the Count of Flanders—who were more powerful than he was and who were able to maintain law and order over more territory than he could. Conflicting and overlapping loyalties left plenty of room for private wars at all levels of the feudal hierarchy.

Despite the destructive and anarchical tendencies of many feudal nobles, the institution of the feudal monarchy itself had a strong moral basis. Sanctified by the Church and reinforced by personal oaths of fealty and homage from their vassals, the feudal monarchs became special personages in medieval society. Everyone acknowledged the Holy Roman Emperor in Germany as the temporal ruler of Latin Christendom, even though they did not pay much attention to his efforts to make this title a political reality. The kings of France and England also benefited from their moral ties with the Church and with their feudal vassals. Gone were the days when the Germanic kings of Western Europe could only count on the loyalty of their rough warrior "nobles" during a successful military campaign. The tribal chief had become an anointed sovereign.

### The Seignorial System

The third basic feature of medieval society by the tenth century was the seignorial (or manorial) system. It governed the relations between the agricultural workers and their masters, who by the twelfth century included almost every feudal vassal, bishop, and abbot (head of a large monastery). These landlords—*seigneurs*—held economic, political, and legal powers over their peasants, the great mass of whom were tightly bound to the master's will by ties that were socially degrading, as opposed to the voluntary agreements and contracts between members of the feudal hierarchy. A peasant's main obligation to his *seigneur* was to provide him with food and labor services. His social status was servile and his occupation menial. He lacked the rights and privileges of a free man—bearing arms, marrying whom he wished, being judged by his peers, moving to another locality—and was subject to corporal punishment. In France he was called a serf, and this term has been used loosely to denote unfree agricultural workers everywhere.

Many peasants had come to be bound in the chains of serfdom by no act of surrender, but by the eleventh century the procedure described in the following document from the monastery of Marmoutier was typical:

> " . . . William, the brother of Reginald, born of free parents . . . gave not only himself but all his descendants, so that they should forever serve the abbot and monks of this place in a servile condition."

William was then tied to the bell-rope and rang the bell three times to publicize his new "condition."

Seignorialism was a way of organizing the everyday lives of both the serfs and the free peasants. Usually they lived together in a village on the landlord's manor and went out into the surrounding fields during the day. Another arrangement predominated in uplands, forest areas, and poor soil regions. This was the hamlet system. Each hamlet consisted of a group of compact farms, usually cultivated by members of the same family, with each household living in a cottage in the middle of its own fields. Both the villages and the hamlets were small rural communities. They created close economic and cultural ties among the peasants and isolated them from the outside world. The *seigneur* of the land might be away much of the time—at the king's court, fighting other feudal vassals, or crusading against unbelievers. The peasants never went anywhere.

The peasants cultivated the land in various ways or engaged in animal husbandry or forest activities, according to the climate, soil, and topography of the area in which they lived. Until the late tenth century most of them tilled only half of their arable land in any one year, leaving the other half fallow in order to replenish its nutritive elements. This two-field system continued to prevail in much of Southern Europe, but in Northern Europe the peasants gradually switched to the three-field system. They planted one group of fields in the spring, another in the fall, and left only a third of their fields fallow at any given time. In general the fields of a village community were divided into strips, so that each peasant had some good and some poor ones. Most of the peasants did their sowing and harvesting cooperatively—on their own strips and on the master's domain, where they were required to work a certain number of days each week. Crop yields were so low that there was often just enough to feed the peasants and the master's household. Not until the eleventh century was the agriculture of the seignorial system able to produce a significant surplus for sale beyond the manor. In the ninth and tenth centuries Western Europe was barely able to support its small population at a subsistence level.

## THE HIGH MIDDLE AGES, ELEVENTH TO THIRTEENTH CENTURIES

In the eleventh century changing conditions helped Latin Christendom to move forward along new lines. The centuries-old peril of invasion was over: in the North, the aggressive pagan rulers of Norway, Sweden, and Denmark were tamed by Christianity; in the South, the Mediterranean was cleared of Saracen Pirates. The conversion of the Poles, Czechs, Hungarians (Magyars), and Croats to Roman Catholicism and their organization into feudal kingdoms established a vast protective buffer in Central Europe against future aggressors from the plains of Asia. At home, improvements in farming and the relative civil peace provided by the feudal system allowed more people to survive. Expanded agricultural production also increased the wealth of the feudal and clerical landlords, providing them with the means of purchasing imported luxuries, financing expeditions of foreign conquest, and supporting artistic and intellectual achievements.

But the new civilization in the West was not just the product of these preconditions, nor did it borrow anything of importance from other civilizations before the middle of the twelfth century. It was an original creation by men who used whatever physical, mental, and moral equipment they possessed in an effort to deal as best they could with the world as they found it. Some of these men organized new forms of trade and manufacturing. Others partially transformed brute force into legitimate political authority. The leaders of the Church gained a preponderant influence in politics, the arts, and learning. In all fields the movement of expansion that began around 1000 produced a unique and remarkably complex civilization that was to reach its peak around 1300.

### Economic Revival

Improvements in farming techniques and the clearing of more land for cultivation increased the food supply and, consequently, the population. A new type of harness with a rigid collar allowed a horse to deliver four times the tractive force it could in Roman times. This technological advance and the shift from the two-field to the three-field system were mainly responsible for the eleventh-century increase in food production. Other new farming techniques included the use of

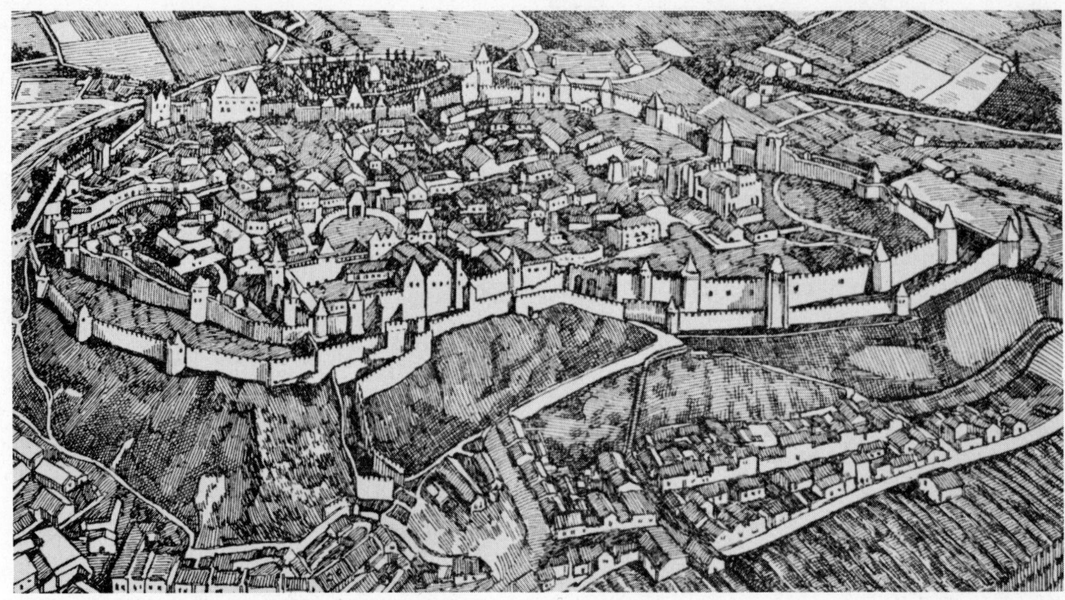

*Carcassonne, France in the thirteenth century*

windmills and draught animals in place of human muscle and the substitution of iron plows for wooden ones. The movement known as the Great Clearing involved the draining of marshes and the leveling of forests. Occurring first in France, the Low Countries, and England, it spread by the thirteenth century to East Central Europe in the lands conquered and colonized by the Germans.* Great abbots and feudal lords organized many of these reclamation and resettlement activities, but individual peasants also cleared small plots of land for new cultivation.

The appearance of agricultural surpluses stimulated a revival of trade. A few enterprising peasants were allowed to leave farming and specialize in simple forms of manufacture and commerce to meet the new demands of the rich. In Flanders, for example, they produced a fine woolen cloth. The craftsmen who made it could either sell it to the aristocracy of northern France and Germany or barter it with Norse merchants for furs, hawks, and honey. Then they could trade these products of the Scandinavian forests on the continent or in England, which had raw wool, tin, and silver to export. Wine was also much in demand in England after the Norman conquest. In the Burgundy and Bordeaux regions French producers supplied this demand and received English products in exchange.

Money soon replaced barter. The mines in Germany and elsewhere supplied the great feudal lords and kings with silver, which they minted into coins. These new currencies gained wide circulation; even humble craftsmen had to pay for their food. A lucrative market also developed from serving the small but increasing band of travelers—especially pilgrims—which sought food and lodgings. All this money usually found its way into the coffers of the landlords. The reappearance of a money economy also began to modify the relationship between masters and peasants. Slowly, payment for the use of land in services or in kind gave way to cash.

The growth of trade and a money economy brought a gradual renewal of urban life to Western Europe. Little is known about how the eleventh-century merchants originated. Some may have been agents of feudal or ecclesiastical lords who, while on a specific mission for their masters, began to do a little business on the side and eventually left their service to engage in full-time commercial activities. Others have been boatmen, teamsters,

*See p. 31.

and persons who made money serving travelers and then invested it in merchandise. Still others may have been runaway peasants or displaced persons. At first all were itinerants who conducted most of their business at rural fairs, but they needed a safe place to store their goods in off seasons, and they began, little by little to settle outside the walls of some castle, abbey, or episcopal see. These settlements were called *bourgs* in French, and the people who lived there came to be called *bourgeois*.

As these *bourgs* grew into towns of several hundred or a thousand inhabitants, their leaders banded together in *communes* to free themselves from the feudal and seignorial obligations they owed to the lord of the area. Since they had money, they were able to buy charters of immunity. The earlier town charters were granted at the end of the eleventh century in northern France. Soon thereafter other communes in Western Europe, especially in Italy and Flanders, gained "freedom of the city." The bourgeoisie became a new class outside of feudal society. Its main activity was commerce, and its members were legally free. The towns also became refuges for escaped peasants, who became free upon a year and a day's residence in them. Toward the end of the twelfth century these towns set an example for the peasants in the rural villages to ask the local lord to commute their obligations to money payments.

The rise of the free towns and the prosperity of the merchants were later to contribute to the dissolution of the feudal and seignorial systems. For the moment, however, they gave additional financial support to the expansionist activities of the dominant classes—the feudal nobility and the clergy.

### The Feudal Nobles

The feudal noble's most important function was to be a warrior. Indeed, until the eleventh century the knights fought foreign invaders and each other almost constantly. An armored knight on horseback was a formidable foe. In the eleventh century, adoption of the stirrup, improvements in the bridle, and better breeding methods increased the effectiveness of his mount. He could carry heavier weapons and wear heavier armor, and still move faster than a foot soldier. His metal helmet and long coat of mail (heavy leather meshed with iron) made him practically invulnerable to arrows or other missiles hurled from a distance and to the swords of knights on foot. Only another knight on horseback could fight with him on equal terms. Consequently, the main phase of any major battle became a cavalry charge. Balancing his weight on his stirrups, a knight could hold his shield in one hand and his lance in the other, charge an adversary head on at full gallop, and unseat him. Entangled in his coat of mail, a fallen knight was momentarily out of action.

The education of a knight was almost entirely aimed at this type of warfare. He underwent a rigorous training program of physical exercise, horsemanship, and weaponry. Even his leisure time was largely spent in hunting, jousting, and other pastimes that emphasized physical courage. He was also taught, however, to respect other noble warriors and never to attack an unarmed knight. These rules were to become part of a code of social behavior whose very name, chivalry, comes from the French word *chevalerie*, which means having to do with noble horsemen, *chevaliers*.

The emerging code of chivalry reflected a general effort to make warfare more "civilized." The Church persuaded most knights not to attack its personnel and property and to spare noncombatants. In addition, it tried to enforce the Peace and Truce of God, periods when armed combat was forbidden. The fact that the nobles were bound to most of their neighbors by oaths of homage and fealty also limited local conflicts. Indeed, the very goals of warfare changed; it became a path to glory and wealth rather than a brutal contest for survival. Instead of always killing one's enemy, one now tended to take him prisoner and hold him for ransom.

As feudal warfare became less destructive of life and property, both the population and the supply of food increased. The increase in population included a

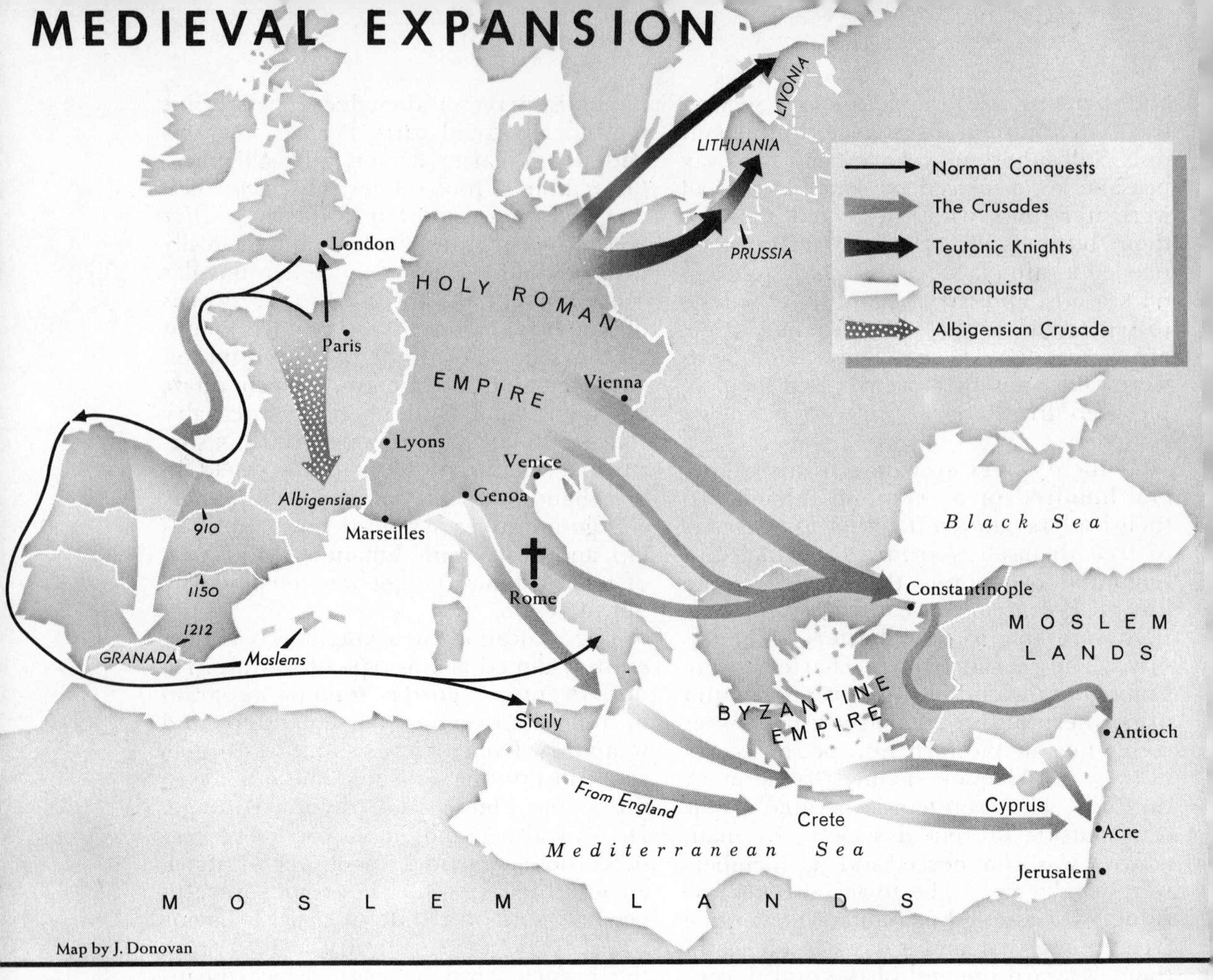


growing number of younger sons of the nobility who had nothing to do. With neither fiefs to manage nor wars to fight at home, these trained fighters sought adventure and fortune in distant lands.

### The Crusades

Beginning in the late eleventh century the knights of continental Western Europe began their campaigns of foreign expansion. During that period, at about the same time the Normans conquered England, southern Italy, and Sicily, the nobles of northern Spain launched a new type of military campaign, the crusade, against the Muslims who controlled most of the Iberian Peninsula. The Church sanctified the reconquest *(reconquista)* of that formerly Christian land and promised certain salvation to all knights who participated in it. The reconquest proceeded slowly, but by the mid-thirteenth century Moorish control had been eliminated everywhere except in the kingdom of Granada, on Spain's southern shore. By then the crusading knights of the Holy Roman Empire were conquering the pagan Slavs east of the Elbe and bringing the southern and eastern shores of the Baltic Sea under German, and hence Christian, control.

The most spectacular, but ultimately the least successful, crusades involved the reconquest of the Holy Land from the Muslims. The word crusade has lost its original meaning today. We now have "crusades" against everything from cancer to automobile accidents. In the Middle Ages a crusade *(croisade)* was a military campaign against unbelievers, in which the warriors bore the cross *(croix)* on all their equipment. The pope himself blessed the First Crusade in 1095 and promised redemption to the crusaders who delivered the tomb of Christ from the hands of the infidel. Knights from all over Latin Christendom responded to the pope's appeal. For the next two hundred years they took part in a series of campaigns, not only against the Muslim Arabs, but eventually against the Byzantine Empire as well. Between 1204 and 1261 they even set up a "Latin Empire" in Greece and Constantinople. They controlled some of the islands of the Eastern Mediterranean much longer, but lost their footholds in Syria and Palestine by the end of the thirteenth century. Nevertheless, the goal of a new crusade to recover the Holy Land haunted the nobles and the Church until early modern times.

The crusades permanently transformed feudal society and Western civilization in several ways, even though they did not succeed in keeping the Holy Land under Christian control: they reduced local warfare in Europe by siphoning off her surplus knights into foreign wars; they stimulated the revival of long-distance trade; and they altered the social behavior and taste of Europe's upper classes.

In the twelfth century large-scale trade between West and East became possible again for the first time since the "fall" of Rome. The Christian conquest of Spain, Sicily, and parts of the Near East ended Muslim control of the Mediterranean Sea and brought gold and other kinds of booty to the upper classes of Western Europe. Many returning crusaders had also acquired a taste for the more luxurious style of life of their Muslim enemies. Hence the merchant shippers who had transported them and the growing number of pilgrims to the Holy Land began filling their empty vessels with spices, alum, and luxury products on their return voyages to Barcelona, Genoa, Pisa, and Venice. They paid the Muslim merchants for these goods with gold and, despite the Church's opposition, with slaves and contraband arms. Then they sold the goods at high prices in the West. The crusaders provided the Italian merchants with trading stations in Syria and Palestine. Genoa and Venice also built regular navies which they used to conquer and retain their own coastal enclaves in other parts of the Near East long after the crusaders lost their holdings in the Holy Land. Once resumed, large-scale trade grew without interruption. By the end of the thirteenth century products imported by Italian merchants were being sold in France, the Low Countries, Germany, and England.

*Chivalry*

### *Chivalry*

The crusades also altered the social behavior of the feudal nobles. Historians disagree as to how much the change was due to contact with the Muslims and how much to the increasing influence of the Christian Church. In any case, the European warrior class became more civilized in the twelfth and thirteenth centuries. There were still cruel, selfish, and proud knights-errant—adventurers who often switched lords and who fought mainly for glory and booty. Rodrigo Diaz of Bibar, called *El Cid*, had been an outstanding example of this type in eleventh-century Spain. But by the mid-twelfth century *El Cid* was being transformed by literary legend into a dedicated and virtuous crusader. When not fighting the Muslims, knights-errant were supposed to right injustices and save damsels in distress. New crusading orders were founded in Spain (where they were partly modeled on Moorish societies for border defense), France, and Germany by men who took vows of chastity and devoted their entire lives to military campaigns in the name of Christianity. Finally, the great nobles and kings of Western Europe, such as Richard the Lion-Hearted in England and Saint Louis in France, spent part of their time crusading and set high standards of chivalrous behavior.

Chivalry was a system of ethical ideas which sprang from a variety of sources and were often inconsistent with one another. Feudal chivalry laid down the rules of behavior for the warrior nobles. It obligated them to be honorable toward their equals and generous toward their inferiors. This *noblesse oblige* did not prevent men of noble birth from beating peasant men and raping peasant women; generosity toward one's inferiors meant giving them money, not sparing their feelings. Only nobles were supposed to have feelings, and these had to be treated with elaborate forms of courtesy. The slightest affront could lead to a duel to the death and to bloody family feuds. Feudal chivalry comes to life in the *Chansons de Geste*, the long narrative poems that describe how various heroes hack their foes to pieces and intrigue against them at court.

The Church tried to divert the warrior nobles from such brutal activities. It developed the ideas of religious chivalry and the perfect Christian knight—like Sir Perceval (Parsifal) and Sir Galahad in search of the Holy Grail. The Christian knight took up the cross against the infidel, protected the Church in all situations, faithfully served his lawful prince, and cared for the weak and helpless. This kind of chivalry was too constraining for the rough and ready feudal warriors, but some of them accepted it, at least as an ideal.

A third kind of chivalry—the kind most people mean when they say it is dead today—concerned men's relations with noble women. In the Middle Ages it was called "courtly love." It originated in southern France in the late eleventh century. There professional entertainers called troubadours began writing songs glorifying great ladies and expressing the benefits a man of comparatively humble birth could derive from adoring them. In Southern France the troubadour placed his lady fair on a pedestal and worshipped her from a distance. In the North courtly love was more lustful. There the favorite literary model of the courtly lover was Sir Lancelot, who suffered disgrace and exile for the sake of an illicit love affair with his lord's wife, Queen Guenevere. But by the end of the Middle Ages (and well into modern times) the courtly lover was no longer expected to give up *everything* for love. His main function was simply to be around when his lady (whose husband was not supposed to treat her in a romantic way) wanted flattery and attention.

## The Universal Church and Medieval Culture

While the feudal nobles were conquering new lands and becoming more chivalrous, the Roman Catholic Church reached the peak of its influence, raising the spiritual and moral level of its own personnel and of the lay population in general. It asserted its complete independence from secular control, and it also sponsored a revival of international learning and art which produced the crowning achievements of medieval civilization.

### *The New Piety*

The eleventh and twelfth centuries were times of religious revival. Although Europeans had long been nominally Christian, many of them had not been much influenced by the teachings of the Church before the late tenth century. Only then did Christianity really begin to "get under their skins" and become a matter of personal conviction rather than of external forms and ceremonies. Religious revivals are always difficult to explain, and perhaps this one *was* related to the economic and military revivals. In any event, people began to worry more about behaving according to Christian standards and became more willing to follow the leadership of the Church. They did so not because they feared hell, but because they felt better when they conformed to the ideals of their society. By conforming they overcame their feeling of personal insignificance, and found meaning and direction in community life. The Church, in turn, reformed itself and used the great upsurge of popular piety to impose Christian ideals on all fields of endeavor.

The growing influence of Christian ideals on lay activities manifested itself in many ways. Kings and feudal lords gave large gifts to churches and monasteries, and, insofar as they supported the Peace and Truce of God, they protected noncombatants and limited feudal warfare. The other military manifestation of Christian ideals, the crusades, made war a foreign rather than a local affair. Even those crusaders who hoped for lands and booty were imbued with the popular piety of the age. As humans became more Christian, Christianity became more human. In the twelfth century both clergymen and laymen emphasized the human side of the Christian story—the infant Jesus, the Virgin Mary as a suffering mother and a merciful intercessor with the Divine Judge. Ordinary people built hundreds of churches dedicated to Our Lady (*Notre Dame*) with their bare hands as vivid and enduring testimonials of their faith.

Both the laity and the clergy were strongly influenced by the new monastic orders that were founded in the tenth and eleventh centuries. The two most important ones, the Cluniacs and the Cistercians, did not limit themselves to setting higher standards for monastic life. The Cistercians cleared wastelands and developed the most advanced agricultural and wool-growing techniques in Europe; Cluniacs became important public figures. Thousands of dedicated and talented men were attracted to these new orders. By the end of the eleventh century there were more monks and monasteries than ever before, and a few great abbots dominated the life of the age. The outstanding example was St. Bernard (1093–1153), abbot of the Cistercian monastery at Clairvaux, in Eastern France.

Bernard of Clairvaux, a mystic, became extremely active in public life. He wanted nothing better than to remain in his own monastery, which he made a model of piety and asceticism; yet he spent much of his time lecturing kings, advising popes, campaigning against subversive ideas, and preaching to crowds. Once he was even able to persuade the rulers of Europe to depose a pope he thought unworthy. He convinced the king of France and the emperor in Germany to launch the Second Crusade. His sermons and hymns to the Virgin appealed to the deepest yearnings of popular piety. He energetically opposed the heretical doctrines and rationalistic tendencies that began to appear in the twelfth century.* A word from him could save a lost cause or damn a successful one. For he was one of the great mystics of the Church, viewed by everyone as a saint in his own lifetime.

### *The Growth of Ecclesiastical Power*

While saints like Bernard of Clairvaux were guiding popes and kings and stimulating popular piety, able administrators and lawyers were strengthening the organization of the Church. This process began with Pope Gregory VII (1073–1085) and reached its high point under Pope Innocent III (1198–1216).

The first step was to free the Church from secular control. Even bishops and abbots had become part of the feudal system in the ninth and tenth centuries, and had had to provide armed forces to their lord, like any other vassal. The pope himself was often at the mercy of the local nobles in Rome and the emperor in Germany. Since all of these ecclesiastical offices brought prestige and large incomes to their incumbents, the feudal lords and monarchs sought to appoint their own relatives to them.

The man who did the most to end this scandalous situation was a Cluniac monk named Hildebrand. He helped to institute the College of Cardinals as the only agency that could elect a new pope. When he himself became Pope Gregory VII, he launched a campaign to eliminate the appointment of *any* high church official by laymen, a practice known as "lay investiture." He excommunicated the most powerful ruler in Europe, Emperor Henry IV, for resisting this campaign and absolved his subjects from allegiance to him.† Henry IV then donned the garb of a penitent and approached the pope at the castle of

*See p. 28.

†Excommunication meant almost certain damnation to the devout Christian, for it denied him communion with God through the sacraments of the Church. Gregory VII and his successors used it as an effective political weapon against secular monarchs who challenged the authority of the papacy.

Canossa, in northern Italy. After letting him stand in the snow for three days Gregory finally absolved him. Although the emperor temporarily regained his control over Germany, for two hundred years after Canossa few Western rulers dared to risk outright defiance of any pope. Hildebrand's successors assured the Church of the final say in all ecclestiastical matters and made the papacy the strongest political power in Latin Christendom.

In the twelfth century the age of great monastic leaders gave way to the age of great lawyers. The creation of an elaborate system of ecclesiastical justice was related to the growing rationalism of the age and to the parallel efforts of the secular rulers to improve their judicial systems. The law of the Church, canon law, was based on decrees of Church councils and papal decisions. In the mid-twelfth century the monk Gratian codified all this scattered material in his *Decretum*. Henceforth canon law was systematic, logical, and self-sustaining. It was applied throughout Latin Christendom in local courts staffed with trained lawyers. Appeals ran from them to the pope and his legal advisers. Having already taken its administrative affairs out of secular hands, the Church now became deeply involved in its own legal routine. The papal court (*curia*) in Rome became the hub of a vast administrative and judicial network that covered the whole Catholic world.

The papacy reached the zenith of its power and prestige under Innocent III. An energetic administrator, a master diplomat, and a skilled lawyer, Innocent almost succeeded in making the papacy the supreme political power in Europe. He declared that "Nothing in the world should escape the attention and control of the Sovereign Pontiff." Not only did he complete his predecessors' administrative and judicial reforms at the Fourth Lateran Council (1215), he also interfered in the secular affairs of Europe's leading rulers. He made and broke emperors and brought the king of England to heel by encouraging the king of France to invade his country.

Yet Innocent III, for all his political maneuvering, was sincerely concerned with religious matters. His Fourth Lateran Council clarified the dogma of Roman Catholicism and the rules of behavior that all good Catholics had to observe. The seven sacraments—baptism, confirmation, marriage, the Eucharist, penance, holy orders, and extreme unction—were decreed the channel to Divine Grace, with the Eucharist as the chief sacrament. The dogma of transubstantiation—namely, that the body of Christ was actually in the wafer eaten by the person receiving communion—was proclaimed. For Innocent III, Christendom was a single community, and everyone in it had to believe in the same things. To make certain that they did, he established the Inquisition to root out concealed heretics. This procedure became necessary after his suppression of a major heretical movement, the Albigensians, had driven its survivors underground.

### The Albigensian Crusade

The Albigensians were the most serious religious threat to the Church in the High Middle Ages. In the late twelfth century there were thousands in northern Italy and Spain, and they were especially numerous in southern France, where their settlement in the town of Albi gave them their name. They believed that everything material was evil, and their leaders renounced all worldly ties and lived ascetic lives. The dogma of the Albigensians was heretical in the extreme, since it made the God of the Old Testament a God of Evil, responsible for the death of Jesus, a God of Good. They had their own clergy and sacraments, and rejected all efforts of earlier popes to convert them. Innocent III finally summoned a crusade to suppress them. Actually, this "crusade" turned into a war of pillage and conquest by the northern French knights who carried it out. When some Catholic nobles in the south resisted this conquest along with the Albigensians, the ruthless northern "crusaders" cried: "Kill them all, God will know his own!"

The crushing of the Albigensian heresy did not solve the basic moral problem that had given rise to it: the growing worldliness of both clergy and laity. Consequently, Innocent III sanctioned the founding of the Dominican and Franciscan orders to combat this problem. Their founders, the Spaniard St. Dominic and the Italian St. Francis, had originally wanted to retire from the world, like earlier monks, but they soon found that their real mission was preaching to laymen. The Dominicans tended to concentrate on showing how the new rationalism of the age could be reconciled with the old faith on intellectual grounds. The Franciscans appealed more directly to the emotions. Unlike the regular monastic orders, the first Dominicans and Franciscans were mendicant friars, moving from town to town and begging for food and shelter. Thanks to their activities worldliness was checked, heresy was weakened, and the emotional and intellectual appeal of Christianity was strengthened in the first half of the thirteenth century.

Someone once said that, in religion, nothing fails like success. The monastic and mendicant orders, which had done so much to revive religious feeling and reform to the Church, ultimately developed vested interests in their own organizations and played a lesser role in the religious life of the community. By the end of the thirteenth century the old crusading orders, having lost their original function, became powerful landowners, like the Teutonic and Spanish orders, or wealthy bankers, like the Templars in France. The papacy became increasingly preoccupied with its temporal power, and its *curia* attracted men more interested in administration, law, and finance than in purely religious matters. This bureaucratization of the clergy was perhaps inevitable, given the problems it had to face in an increasingly complex world. But it made the Church less able to adapt itself to new crises.

### Learning

While still in its expansive and reforming stage, the medieval Church sponsored a great intellectual and artistic revival. This revival was stimulated by the economic and military expansion of the eleventh century. The increase in material well being allowed more churchmen to devote themselves to intellectual and literary pursuits than had been possible in the preceding Dark Ages. Also, the growth of towns and a money economy made it possible for scholars to leave their self-sufficient rural abbeys and move to the new cathedral schools that sprang up in the larger sees, especially in France. At the same time, military conquests brought the West into contact with the more advanced civilizations of the Muslim and Byzantine worlds, in Sicily and southern Italy, in Spain, and in the Near East.

Education began to improve. Until the middle of the eleventh century the "curriculum" of monastic and cathedral schools had consisted of the tools of learning, which were rather grandiosely called the seven liberal arts. First, there was the *trivium*—grammar, rhetoric, and logic—whose main purpose was to train the student to handle the Latin language. (In some ways it resembled the modern course in English composition.) Second, there was the *quadrivium*—arithmetic, music, geometry, and astronomy—whose main purpose was to have the student learn by rote the few texts available on these subjects. By the beginning of the twelfth century the teaching of grammar and rhetoric was improved by a more profound study of the Latin literary classics. Furthermore, these studies were now viewed simply as preparatory for the exploration of new fields, especially theology and its "servant," philosophy.

Other new fields opened up in the twelfth century. Contact with Muslim Spain spread mathematical knowledge to the French cathedral schools, where it enriched the study of music and made possible advances in architecture. The first medical schools appeared near the borders of the Muslim world, where they borrowed the ancient Greek prescriptions of Hippocrates from Muslim commentators: the school in Salerno had been founded in the tenth century, when the Saracens still controlled nearby Sicily; the school in Montpelier, in southern France, was founded in the twelfth century and borrowed its techniques from nearby Moorish Spain. Another new field was the law. The school that arose in Bologna, in north central Italy, became the main European center for the study of both Roman civil law and canon law.

The most remarkable advance in twelfth-century learning was rational speculation about theological problems, and its leading figure was Peter Abelard (*c.*1079 – 1142). This vain and impetuous young man set himself up as an independent teacher in Paris, after having learned all that its cathedral school could teach him. He became convinced that logic was a universal tool (as some people view higher mathematics today) which could solve old problems and reveal new knowledge. His most famous work – next to his love letters to Héloïse – is his *Sic et Non* (*Yes and No*). In it he tried to show that one could find arguments in the Bible and the writings of the early Christian theologians to prove or disprove any thesis. Sometimes the theses were deliberately shocking – for example, that sin is pleasing to God and the contrary, that God is a threefold entity and the contrary. This approach to knowledge came to be called *Scholasticism.* Abelard used it to try to make Christian doctrine more rational, not to contradict it. Nevertheless, St. Bernard condemned Abelard as a heretic and forced him to renounce the errors of his rationalism. But the future belonged to men who followed Abelard's Scholastic method, which was to dominate European thought until the beginning of modern times.

By the late twelfth century Western European scholars were asking all kinds of questions about the world for which there were no answers in the Latin writings available to them. The really advanced works in the sciences, medicine, and mathematics were in Greek or Arabic. Hence these scholars demanded translations of these works and got them in one way or another – from Spanish Jews, from Byzantine scribes, or by making them themselves. The man who seemed to have more answers than anyone else was Aristotle, and the study of the Latin translations of his works was to give a new dimension to medieval learning.

As the number of men interested in formal learning grew, some new institution was needed to coordinate their activities. Students wanted to get their money's worth from their teachers and from the innkeepers with whom they stayed. Professors had to be licensed and paid. Courses needed to be standardized and kept free from heretical ideas. Until the end of the twelfth century most students wandered from one cathedral or monastic school to another to listen to some famous lecturer or to study a particular subject. Most of the teachers in these schools had too many other duties to spend much time organizing a new educational system. There were no libraries, no deans, no registrars, and no dormitories. Indeed, there was no full-time faculty and no student body in any organized sense. But the Middle Ages was a time when every function had its own "body," or corporate organization: the feudal hierarchy, the secular clergy, the monastic and crusading orders, the communes, and the merchant and craft guilds. By the end of the twelfth century scholarship was recognized as a function, and students and teachers began organizing themselves into corporations called *universities.*

Pope Innocent III set the precedent for church control and protection of these new institutions. He himself had been a student at both Bologna and Paris, and he bestowed valuable privileges on the pioneer universities in those two cities. Later in the thirteenth century other universities appeared in Italy, France, England, and Spain. Teachers and students wore "uniforms" similar to those of the Dominican and Franciscan Orders and, as members of privileged corporations, enjoyed great freedom from the civil authorities, a privilege known as "benefit of clergy." In fact, all scholars were soon called clerics (clerks).

The university was one of the most important medieval contributions to modern civilization. Although new interests have added new subjects to the curriculum, the basic organizational features of the modern university stem from the Middle Ages. Students still attend regularly organized courses and prepare for examinations. Their achievements are still recognized by the granting of the same degrees – bachelor and master of arts, and doctor of philosophy, law, or medicine. Our system of tutorial residence halls and scholarships goes back to the founding of

*Classroom in a fourteenth century German university*

the Sorbonne College at Paris and Balliol College at Oxford in the mid-thirteenth century.

In the thirteenth century the universities took over the intellectual leadership of Western Europe. All the famous scholars of that age were university professors. University graduates, especially those with law degrees, filled most of the high offices in the Church and began to play an important role in the governments of the emerging secular states.

Although some universities resisted ecclesiastical control, the Church saw to it that no subversive doctrines were taught in the field of theology. The main problem here was to reconcile traditional dogma with the new knowledge acquired from the Greeks and Arabs—especially in the newly translated works of Aristotle. The crowning achievement of thirteenth-century learning was the resolution of this problem by the Italian scholar St. Thomas Aquinas (1225–1274), who was a professor at the University of Paris.

Aquinas epitomized medieval learning, which, in its highest form, was international, rational, all-encompassing, and fundamentally optimistic. He perfected the Scholastic method invented by Abelard and used it to reconcile reason and religion in his *Summa Theologica.* The approach of Scholasticism was to state a thesis and then prove it by listing citations from established authorities. Trying to answer all the questions of his time in this way, Aquinas used Aristotle as freely as he used the early Christian theologians (Church Fathers) as his source. He believed that everything made sense in the light of true reason and that the world was a harmonious whole. Until the beginning of modern times, most academic philosophers and theologians in Western Europe continued to seek knowledge by appealing to earlier authorities. Still, a few thirteenth-century scholars—notably the Englishman Robert Grosseteste (*c.*1170–1253)—were beginning to employ the experimental methods that were later to give rise to modern science.

### *The Arts*

Medieval art and literature also reached their high point in the twelfth and thirteenth centuries. The imposing but somber Romanesque style of architecture gave way to the loftier, lighter Gothic style.* Early thirteenth-century architects had much the same problem as the theologians. They, too, had to integrate the varied ideas of their predecessors into a consistent and harmonious pattern. Their success can still be seen in great Gothic cathedrals like Notre Dame de Paris and Notre Dame de Chartres. These cathedrals are triumphs of light and height, expressing the optimism and longing for the infinite of their age. They show the bare ribs of their structure as confidently as Aquinas showed the arguments with which he proved his theses.

But a Gothic cathedral was more than just a masterpiece of reason and planning. It summed up all the learning and beliefs of the Middle Ages in a way that ordinary people could understand. Only a few scholars could master the *Summa Theologica*; anyone could immediately recognize the meaning of the sculptured figures and the scenes in the stained-glass windows of a Gothic cathedral. Many of these illustrated ideas and allegories came from the popular literature and folklore of the day and from the miracle and mystery plays that were performed on the porches of churches. History, legend, the Christian story, the liberal arts, and the activities of daily life were all there. Learning was for the clerics, and imaginative literature was mainly for the nobility. Church art and architecture expressed the ideas and values of all classes.

Like the cowboy movies of our own day, new *Chansons de Geste* and stories about *El Cid* proliferated in the twelfth and thirteenth centuries. A new prose form, the romance, told tales of King Arthur's knights and courtly love. The *Roman de la Rose* was the most popular example of this type of romance from the thirteenth century to the end of the Middle Ages. Its first part is a thinly disguised allegory about courtship and seduction; its second part—written later in the thirteenth century by a different author—is more cynical about women and more voluptuous. The second half of the *Roman de la Rose* already reflects the decline of medieval idealism.

This decline was particularly evident in the *fabliaux*, short satirical stories written for worldly city dwellers. The heroes of these stories were clever tricksters, and their victims were stupid and naïve. In the *fabliaux* all women were lustful and all priests gluttons or lechers. The moral of these stories is: Enjoy youself as much as you can without getting caught. Although satire always exaggerates, the *fabliaux* showed that the leadership of the Church, despite temporary gains, was weakening in the face of a more secular outlook.

Yet the overriding influence of religion was still evident in the greatest poet of the Middle Ages, Dante Alighieri (1265–1321). Like St. Thomas Aquinas, he believed in the unity and meaningfulness of all human experience. His *Divine Comedy* has been called Aquinas put to verse; it was also a matchless commentary on human life. Its outline is well known: the classical poet Virgil leads Dante on a "tour" of Hell (The Inferno), Purgatory, and Paradise. Whether he was depicting the damned or the saved, Dante expressed the confident, optimistic, all-embracing spirit of the High Middle Ages.

### Economy and Society

By the thirteenth century the economic and social development of Western Europe reached a degree of stability and sophistication that was paralleled in the intellectual, cultural, religious, and political life of the age. We have already noted the effects of economic growth in the twelfth and thirteenth centuries. Agricultural expansion had made possible an in-

*See p. 67.

crease in population and the production of a food surplus, both of which had allowed more people to engage in commerce and manufacturing in the growing towns. The growth of towns, in turn, had made it possible for the bourgeoisie to become a free, independent social class and for run-away peasants to improve their status. Large-scale manufacture of woolen textiles had taken root in Flanders, and long-distance travel had been resumed by Italian merchants. In the thirteenth century the economic development of Central and Northeastern Europe compensated for a relative leveling off of agricultural expansion in the West and stimulated the continuing growth of large-scale commerce in Europe as a whole.

German colonization of the great plain east of the Elbe was a major event in European history. It began as a military conquest by dukes of the Holy Roman Empire in alliance with certain monastic orders. In some places the monks got there first and converted the Slavic chieftains, who then became vassals of the incoming German warriors. Within a few generations most of these Slavs were "Germanized" in language and culture, though a few pockets of Wends and Pomeranians* retained their Slavic language until the twentieth century. The Slavs became absorbed into the mass of German settlers, whom the new landlords attracted with promises of free land and lighter seignorial obligations than they had known in the West. In other places, notably in Prussia, the warriors got there first, killed off many of the pagan natives, and brought the monks in to convert the rest. German and Frisian settlers then moved into this sparsely populated land. Poland and Bohemia managed to survive as independent Slavic kingdoms, but the "finger" of territory between them, Silesia, became German: Twelve hundred new villages were founded there by German immigrants between 1200 and 1350. The other "finger" of Germanic expansion extended northeastward along the eastern shores of the Baltic, where the Teutonic crusading order ruled over the native Lithuanians, Letts, and Estonians. The German cities of Riga and Reval were founded here. Finally, groups of German peasants established themselves in isolated pockets in southern Poland, in the Hungarian Plain, and in Transylvania.

This German colonization was not limited to feudal warriors, monks, and peasants; it also brought in people with specialized economic skills. Miners exploited the metal deposits in the mountains of East Central Europe. Even more important were the businessmen. Towns arose where none had existed before. The new agricultural estates were able to supply large surpluses of grain on rich virgin land. Thus, the town merchants had an easily transportable product to sell elsewhere in Europe by way of the Baltic Sea. Another source of economic development was fishing; the best herring banks in Europe were in the Baltic Sea. Soon the merchants of northern Germany and its northeastern extension were supplying this easily preserved (with salt) fish to the Low Countries, France, and England. By the middle of the thirteenth century, the merchants in the Baltic towns had transformed their trading guilds into a political alliance, the Hanseatic League.

By modern standards the volume of medieval trade was small and its marketing techniques were primitive. The products of the local craft guilds were sold in shops, while local agricultural produce was sold in open markets on certain days in certain towns. The wholesale exchange of imported goods took place mainly in the great fair towns. In the twelfth and thirteenth centuries the busiest fair towns were in the Champagne area of northeastern France. There the products brought in by Italian merchants from the Near East were sold to jobbers who exchanged them for Flemish wool and for goods brought in from the North by merchants of the Hanseatic League. By the end of the thirteenth century the Champagne fairs declined in importance as Italian and Hanseatic shippers began transporting their merchandise along the Atlantic and North Sea coasts. Nevertheless, markets and fairs continued to be the main means of distributing retail goods well into modern times.

*See map p. 49.

Although nine-tenths of Europe's people remained in agriculture, their economic and social status changed. The peasants had begun to transform their seignorial obligations into money payments in the late twelfth century, and this process was accelerated thereafter. Although serfdom declined as an economic institution throughout Western Europe, the social cleavage between master and peasant did not disappear. Nor did most peasants become independent farmers. The fact that certain regions began to specialize in the production of meat, wool, wine, or cheese, partially altered the traditional village economy. Yet the village, like the town and the guild, continued as a closed corporation, preserving the precarious economic security and social cohesion of its members for the remainder of the Middle Ages.

The growth of the money economy also changed the position of the feudal nobility. At first these landowners had been glad to let their peasants substitute cash payments for obligations in kind and labor service; they needed money to buy newly available luxuries and to replace their wooden castles with stone fortresses. Then as prices rose in the twelfth and thirteenth centuries, the value of the peasants' fixed money payments declined. As a result, many impoverished barons and earls began to sell their feudal rights and their own services to more powerful lords. This development benefited certain princes and dukes whose fortified castles dominated important trade routes and market towns, and who drew large revenues from tolls and other duties on commerce. But the main beneficiaries of these economic changes were the feudal monarchs, who now began to tax the extensive territories under their nominal control and to force wealthy merchants to lend them large sums of money with which to strengthen their royal power.

## The Strengthening of the Medieval Monarchies

Between the middle of the twelfth century and the beginning of the fourteenth a fundamental change took place in the political organization of Western Europe —the rise of the secular state. Of prime importance in producing this change was the expansion of the money economy, along with the growing ease of contact among men and the germination of new ideas, which the revived study of Roman law helped to spread. Heretofore Latin Christendom had comprised kingdoms, principalities, feudal fiefs, and semi-independent towns. None of these was completely independent of external influence or completely supreme over everybody in its territory. Every ruler recognized the superior authority of the Church and granted immunities to various corporations and orders. The gradual development of centralized, independent, monarchial governments out of this hodgepodge had different aspects in different places.

The key feudal institution out of which the medieval monarchs fashioned their strong central government was the *curia regis*—the king's court. Originally it had been only a periodic assembly of the king's vassals for consultation and judicial proceedings on feudal matters. At the same time some kings began using the managers of their *private* affairs—chamberlains, overseers, keepers of the king's accounts, etc.—to administer the realm as a whole. Wherever strong centralized governments developed, they did so by building, on the foundations of the *curia regis* and the private household of the king, (1) a system of royal justice; (2) a royal bureaucracy; (3) a system of royal taxation in collaboration with some kind of representative assembly. Before a dynasty of kings could effectively use any of these three institutions it had to make its rule hereditary and gain real control over the territories under its nominal jurisdiction. In this crucial task the states of Western and Central Europe parted company.

At the end of the tenth century the Holy Roman Emperors had become the legal rulers over all of Central Europe from France to Poland and from Denmark to southern Italy, but they were never able to transform this vast area into a dynastic state that could be handed down from father to son intact. In Italy, both the papacy and the northern Italian cities challenged the imperial authority.

As a result, the emperors lost all real power in Italy after the mid-thirteenth century. Meanwhile their efforts to keep this power had weakened their position north of the Alps. There the secular princes and ecclesiastical rulers, by taking advantage of the emperor's frequent absences, consolidated their own political power. In 1356 they finally forced the reigning emperor to issue the Golden Bull, which made the Holy Roman Empire—with the new ending "of the German Nation"—into a loose confederation. The emperor was to be elected by seven electors—the King of Bohemia, the Dukes of Saxony and Brandenburg, the Count of the Palatinate, and the Archbishops of Cologne, Trier, and Mainz. There was to be a diet of three houses representing the electors, the secular princes, and the towns. For all practical purposes, succeeding emperors could not make any major move without the approval of this diet. The local rulers held effective authority, and the emperor became an elected figurehead.

In the kingdoms of East Central Europe—Bohemia, Hungary, and Poland—the reigning king was even weaker than the Holy Roman Emperor. The landowning nobility almost completely dominated the diets. In these East Central European kingdoms there were no great ecclesiastical princes and few large towns to compete with them. These eastern outposts of Latin Christendom were far from the main trade routes and less affected by the new ideas that were gradually transforming the West.

England, France, and the Iberian Peninsula all had hereditary dynasties by the twelfth century, but only England was a territorial unit. The King of France effectively controlled only his own royal domain around Paris. The rest of his kingdom was in the hands of powerful French and English vassals.* Thus, in the twelfth and thirteenth centuries one of the main tasks of the French kings was to extend the royal domain at the expense of these vassals. In the Iberian Peninsula, the kingdoms of Leon, Castile, Aragon, and Portugal had extended their royal domains by driving out the Moors, As we have seen, this *reconquista* was completed by the mid-thirteenth century, except for the Kingdom of Granada. It had temporarily united the feudal nobles around the kings, thus strengthening the royal authority, but once the Moorish danger was gone, the nobles and the communes turned against the kings. They used the *Cortes* (representative assemblies) in each kingdom to limit the monarch's power, and they opposed dynastic marriages that would have united the Iberian Peninsula under a strong ruler.

*Through marriage and inheritance the kings of England had acquired extensive territories in northern, western, and southwestern France. Their efforts to keep their dynastic holdings in France frequently distracted their attention from purely English affairs throughout the High and late Middle Ages.

*A king*

### England

Only in England and France did the dynastic kings make significant progress in creating a centralized territorial state. England had a head start. Ever since the Norman conquest the king had some control over the whole country. The Norman kings preserved the Anglo-Saxon system of local government by royal sheriffs and the Anglo-Saxon practice of reserving the most important criminal cases for the Crown.

On these foundations, the kings of the twelfth and thirteenth centuries strengthened their power by giving their subjects a uniform system of law administered by impartial judges. First they sent out circuit judges to settle difficulties in the local administration of justice. In the course of their work these judges began to build up a set of legal precedents that was soon to apply throughout the realm. It came to be called Common Law because it applied to all freeborn Englishmen. The growing use of juries, also promoted by the monarchy, gave the English people valuable training in self-government and increased the royal power by restricting the judicial authority of the feudal lords and by attracting the loyalty of the king's subjects to the Crown. By the end of the thirteenth century the courts of the feudal lords were all but eliminated and the jurisdiction of church courts restricted to purely spiritual matters, thus seriously limiting the immunity of the clergy from civil authority.

The Common Law courts were differentiated into (1) the Court of the King's Bench—concerned with criminal and Crown cases; (2) the Court of the Exchequer—dealing with royal finance; and (3) the Court of Common Pleas—handling all civil cases between private individuals. The *curia regis* became the supreme court of appeals from all other courts. At the new Inns of Court lawyers studied and transmitted the Common Law as a living force. It was one of the outstanding contributions of medieval England to the modern world.

The kings of England also had a head start over other European monarchs in their system of royal finance. The Norman conquerors had given the English monarchy a substantial revenue from royal estates and feudal dues. Additional income was later added from the sale of town charters, fees for royal justice, personal property taxes, and tariffs. Still, by the late thirteenth century the English kings constantly needed more income than their customary receipts provided. They borrowed money from Italian bankers, but even this was not enough. A modern government would simply tax its citizens to meet its financial needs. In the Middle Ages no ruler could simply tax anybody. Besides, in 1215 the nobles had forced the king to agree to abide by the law of the land in *Magna Carta.* Although this great charter was later to be viewed as a declaration of the legal rights of all Englishmen, it was a feudal document, designed to safeguard feudal privileges. No succeeding king openly dared infringe on such a basic legal right as freedom from arbitrary taxation.

In order to get their new taxes legally the English kings of the late thirteenth century began to appeal to their Parliaments. Initially, the word *parliament* was used the way "parley" is used today—to describe any occasion on which influential men talked (from *parler,* the French word for talk)* about important matters. By the mid-thirteenth century it connoted full meetings of the king's court (*curia regis*), which all the great lords attended. In this sense Parliament was still an administrative and judicial body rather than a representative assembly. The king intended to keep it that way—that is, a gathering that *he* called for his own purpose, whose delegates *he* chose, and which *he* could dismiss at will after it granted the taxes he demanded.

But Parliament became extremely popular with the wealthy classes. They saw it not only as a means of speeding up justice by appeals from the lower courts but also as a means of stating their grievances and forcing the king to enact their petitions into new laws. After 1295, not only the "lords temporal and spiritual," but the knights and burgesses (wealthy townspeople) attended its sessions, and the balance of power soon shifted from king to Parliament, as we shall see.

### France

The English situation was in direct contrast to the one in France. There the kings had a later start in strengthening royal authority but were ultimately to have far more control over their representative assembly than the kings of England.

Not until the late twelfth century had the French kings made their rule effective in the royal domain, and this was still only a small territory of a few thousand square miles around Paris. In the thirteenth century they began conquering the English holdings in Normandy and western France and bringing other provinces

*Norman French remained the language of government in England until the early fourteenth century, and of the law courts until the end of the fifteenth.

under their nominal authority. Even so, these provinces remained under the actual control of their dukes and counts until the end of the Middle Ages.

Since France was not a political unit like England, the French kings had to assert their royal authority in a different way from the English kings. They allowed each province to keep its local law and customs, while placing their own agents in positions where they could oversee the local governments. These agents, called *baillis* (bailiffs), were well-paid, well-trained men, chosen for their unflinching loyalty to the king. They kept the peace, collected large revenues for the king, and attached newly conquered provinces to the Crown. But unlike England, with its sheriffs and fairly loyal local nobles, France was united only by the king and his bureaucratic agents. The people of France therefore did not develop the training in self-government which the people of England received. The history of these two countries was to reflect these differences well into modern times.

The French monarchy also developed a system of royal justice. At first the king heard many appeals for justice himself, but as cases piled up he delegated more and more of his judicial authority to a section of his *curia regis*, which became known as the Parlement. Unlike the English Parliament, it remained exclusively judicial in character—the highest court of appeals in France. The judges in this Parlement were mostly university graduates trained in the Roman law. They worked out a jurisprudence favorable to the sovereignty of the king, one of the main concepts of Roman law. Their impartial judgments weakened the judicial power of the feudal lords and strengthened the king's position as the supreme guarantor of law and order throughout the realm.

As in England, the French monarchy initiated a system of royal taxation in collaboration with a representative assembly around 1300. But this assembly, called *Estates General*, did not have the prestige of the English Parliament, and the king never dared to collect a new tax solely on its authority. France was still a collection or provinces, each one having its own assembly. It was to these provincial assemblies that the king appealed through his royal agents. The great lords of France had not acquired the habit of working together at the *curia regis*, and the Estates General was not an outgrowth of this institution. Only the king's bureaucrats thought in terms of the kingdom as a whole. Nevertheless, the king sometimes got important backing from the Estates General when he needed it. Unlike the English Parliament, it was never to become a successful rallying point for opposition to the Crown.

### Secular Ascendancy

The secular monarchs of England and France gained strength at the expense of the Church as well as the feudal lords. Every increase in the king's power to judge, administer, and legislate meant a decrease in the power and privileges of the two formerly dominant classes in medieval society. Both the English and French kings limited the immunity of the clergy from civil authority and taxed its wealth. In so doing they clashed with what had been the most powerful monarchy in the twelfth and thirteenth centuries—the papacy.

The outcome of this clash reflected the declining influence and moral authority of the papacy as well as the growing strength of the secular monarchies. For some of the popes after Innocent III began to neglect spiritual leadership for secular matters. They tried to strengthen their administrative and fiscal structure; they fought wars with the Holy Roman Emperor; they used crusades for political purposes. And toward the end of the thirteenth century an unedifying struggle developed between rival Roman families for the papal throne itself.

Boniface VIII (1294–1303), the pope who finally won over his Roman rivals, soon felt the full humiliation of the triumph of the secular monarchies at the hands of Philip IV (1285–1314) of France. Like most popes of the thirteenth century, Boniface VIII had the canon lawyer's exalted opinion of papal authority. When Philip IV got the Estates General to tax the wealth of the Church, Boniface retaliated with the Bull *Unam*

A bishop

*Sanctam* (1302), in which he stated in its most extreme form the papal claim to superiority over secular rulers. What followed was one of the outstanding examples of tragic irony in European history. An agent of Philip IV went to Rome, broke into the pope's bedroom, took him prisoner, and tried to force his resignation. Boniface died shortly after this humiliating treatment. He had tried to extend the power of the papal monarchy at the very time when many men in England and France began to feel that the welfare of their kingdom was more important than the wishes of a secularized papacy. Two years after Boniface's death a French archbishop became pope and later took up residence at Avignon on the Rhône. During the next seventy years the Avignonese popes lost much of their predecessors' ability to guide and control Latin Christendom.

## THE LATE MIDDLE AGES, c. 1320-c. 1450

Medieval civilization reached its peak around 1300. Still predominantly agricultural, the economy of Western and Central Europe was able to feed a larger population than at any time in the past or for the next two hundred years. At the same time it could produce a surplus to support thriving towns and to exchange for imported goods. Thus, there was a working balance between town and countryside. A satisfactory—though precarious—balance also existed between central and local political powers, between Church and state, and among the different social groups. Each of these groups had its own corporate organization which gave its members a sense of belonging and a meaningful way of life. The clergy had the Church and various religious orders, the nobles their closed class, the merchants and craftmen their town and guild, the students their university, the peasants their village. Yet all these separate groups shared certain common religious beliefs and felt that they also belonged to a universal community called Christendom. The highest achievements of medieval art, thought, and literature—the great Gothic cathedrals, St. Thomas Aquinas's *Summa Theologica,* and Dante's *Divine Comedy* —were dedicated to these beliefs.

Then from the early fourteenth to the mid-fifteenth century the equilibrium of the High Middle Ages broke down in almost all fields. This was a period of material difficulties, political strife, and moral and spiritual crises.

### Material Difficulties

"Deliver us, O Lord, from war, famine, and plague!" This prayer became a regular part of rural church services everywhere toward the end of the Middle Ages. It reflected the main preoccupations of most people in the fourteenth and fifteenth centuries—staying alive and getting enough to eat.

#### *War*

Though in many ways a misnomer, the name Hundred Years' War serves to evoke the permanence of the major scourge of the late Middle Ages. This conflict began in 1338 over the English king's remaining territorial holdings in southwestern France, and ended only in 1453. It was a series of intermittent battles which lasted for more than a hundred years. When not fighting each other directly, the kings of England and France were often engaged in lesser wars with their immediate neighbors—the Welsh, the Scots, the counts of Flanders, the kings of Aragon. Added to these wars were the numerous revolts by feudal lords and princes taking advantage of the king's absence, the peasant uprisings and urban riots, and the individual acts of violence by soldiers of fortune, highwaymen, and pirates. No wonder people prayed for peace.

Throughout Latin Christendom, war was frequent if not constant. The Kingdom of Castile was torn by dynastic conflicts and civil wars in which the opposing sides sometimes allied themselves with the Moors, rather than completing their *reconquista* of the Iberian Peninsula. In the North, the kings of Norway, Sweden, and Denmark were in rivalry with each other, the English, and the Hanseatic League. The Teutonic Order continued its campaigns against the Slavs of northeastern Europe and tried to break the growing power of Poland. On the southeastern border of Latin Christendom the Ottoman Turks became a permanent menace after conquering the Orthodox principalities in the Balkans. In the Holy Roman Empire no power could curb the bellicose German knights, and Bohemia was ravaged by civil and religious wars for almost twenty years in the early fifteenth century.* The Italian Peninsula was entangled in the most complex and durable quarrels among its major city-states — Milan, Venice, Florence, Siena, and Pisa — and between the French and Aragonese princes who fought for control of Naples and Sicily.

War became an end in itself for a growing number of soldiers of fortune. It still preserved some of its feudal characteristics: letters of challenge, single combats, local truces, armies composed mainly of armored cavalry. But the temporary feudal levies of the traditional type could not be adapted to the permanence of war, and their hierarchial structure prevented the formation of flexible and homogeneous units. Hence the secular rulers began to resort to hiring companies of mercenaries — especially younger sons of impoverished noble families — for whom war became a regular profession.

The career of the Bascot (bastard) of Mauléon was typical of the fourteenth-century soldier of fortune. Having "won his spurs" in a tournament at Poitiers, the Bascot joined the "Great Company" of poor or illegitimate adventurers from all over Western Europe — an army which a French chronicler estimated at twelve thousand men. The "bands" from each region had their priests, their paymasters, their military police, their baggage trains, their valets and artisans, and their camp followers. These "bands" submitted to iron discipline, but although they worked together they retained their own identities. Fighting for the English, the Bascot and his companions pillaged castles, towns, and villages in the Rhône Valley, ransomed the pope at Avignon, and scoured the countryside of southern France. During a truce between the French and the English, the Bascot hired himself out to the King of Castile. He was soon joined in this adventure by the most famous soldier of fortune on the French side, Bertrand Du Guesclin. The resumption of Anglo-French hostilities recalled the two adventurers to their rival camps. But the Bascot fought above all for himself.

The development of regional "bands" into professional armies was paralleled by changes in the art of warfare. Although the heavily armored cavalry was still the main force of any army, it was now supplemented by an increasing number of infantry. Indeed, at the Battle of Crécy (1346) the infantry, which consisted almost entirely of commoners, broke the mounted knight's monopoly in winning battles. Here the English army defeated a French army twice its size by using archers armed with a new weapon: the longbow. These bows were over six feet long and could shoot arrows three times as far and with triple the impact of the older bows. Arrows, not lances, won the battle. During the fourteenth century gunpowder was also invented. It did not have an immediate effect on the art of warfare, but it did eventually make artillery an effective weapon in besieging fortified castles and towns.

Whether infantry or cavalry, the professional soldiers fought for wages, booty, and ransom. Only in rare cases, as when Joan of Arc inspired them against the English, did they fight out of patriotism. Add to the professional soldiers' quest for profits the secular rulers' appetite for ter-

*See p. 46.

ritorial gains, and we see why wars are easy to start and hard to stop, and why civilians suffered so much from their ravages in the fourteenth and fifteenth centuries.

### *The Black Death*

Man-made wars aggravated the insecurity of an existence constantly menaced by the blind blows of a virtually untamed nature. Too much or too little rain, a severe frost, or a plant disease could ruin a whole year's crops, thus creating widespread hunger and local famine. Sometimes speculators were able to buy up surplus food and ship it to an area hit by famine, but at such high prices that only the rich could buy it. The worst scourge of nature was epidemics of fatal diseases. Here, too, the men of the late Middle Ages were virtually helpless. Doctors were scarce and ignorant, and barbers, midwives, and astrologers often did more harm than good with their bleedings, their sealing out of fresh air, and their incantations and charms. The few attempts at public hygiene were virtually ineffective. In fifteenth-century Paris, for example, most people still disposed of their garbage and their excrement in the city's narrow streets or in the Seine River, despite a number of ordinances against this practice. One observer marveled that human beings who drank water from the river did not all die of incurable diseases.

The most widespread and devastating epidemic—or rather, series of epidemics—was the Black Death. It got its name from the hemorrhagic, blackening spots that appeared on the skin of its victims. This disease first appeared in Italy in 1347—allegedly brought there by a ship returning from the Near East—and it quickly spread all over Western Europe as far as England and Scandinavia. The rats that carried its germs had a field day in the filth of both the towns and the rural villages. The Black Death took three forms: bubonic, pulmonary, and intestinal. Whatever its form, its symptoms were horribly painful, and it was almost always fatal. It was also extremely contagious. The mortality rate ranged from one-eighth to one-third of the total population, depending on the region hit.

Although the worst wave was over by 1349, lesser epidemics recurred periodically. Poor public sanitation was not the only factor in their spread. Lack of private hygiene encouraged it, too—especially in the countryside, where people ate with their fingers out of a common bowl. Poor nutrition also weakened people's resistance. They ate too much salted fish and meat, starches, gravies, lard, and spices—too little fresh fruit and vegetables. But the main problem was that they often did not have enough of anything to eat, so that epidemics coincided with widespread hunger and famine.

### *Economic Regression*

War, famine, and especially the Black Death drastically reduced the size of Europe's population. Not only did millions of people die who would have had children, but many of those who survived showed little desire to reproduce in a plague-ridden, poverty-stricken world. Furthermore, people did not live as long as in the past. In England, the average life expectancy, estimated at 34 years in 1300, fell to 17 at the height of the plague and reached 32 years only in the first quarter of the fifteenth century.

This population decline prolonged a general economic regression that began in the early fourteenth century and lasted until the mid-fifteenth century. The intensity and duration of this regression varied from place to place. It ended sooner in Italy, took hold more slowly in England, and lasted longer and was probably most severe in war-torn France. The regression also had varying effects from one form of economic activity to another, and struck different social groups in different ways.

Yet the common factors of depression and the growing interdependence of Western Europe's regional economies led to a generalization of crises, while still allowing for local variations. The first cause of the decline from the relative prosperity of the thirteenth century was the growing imbalance between population and agricultural production. The signs and consequences of overpopulation (which means too many people in relation to the food supply) began to show up at the end of the thirteenth century in a halt to new land clearing, in the stagnation of agricultural technology, and in a slowing down in population growth. The Black Death removed the specter of overpopulation for at least three centuries, and readjustments of supply to demand temporarily improved the economic situation in certain countries. But these improvements were immediately compromised by chronic wars and especially by fluctuations in the value of money on a scale never before known.

Normally, prices decline during an economic depression. However, monetary instability altered this pattern after the mid-fourteenth century. Kings and princes periodically reduced the gold or silver content of their coins in order to have more gold and silver to pay for their wars and their growing governmental expenses. Each time such a devaluation occurred, prices rose, since it was impossible to keep the reduced value of any currency a secret for long. Then shrinking markets forced prices down somewhat. Between 1300 and 1500 the currency of Flanders lost 80 per cent of its intrinsic value, that of France 75 per cent, that of England 49 per cent. Yet the year-by-year decline was too small to stimulate a business revival. When prices did rise they did not do so at the same rate. The prices of manufactured goods, wine, meat, and wool rose much faster than the prices of grain, thus penalizing the majority of Europe's peasants.

During the economic regression of the fourteenth and fifteenth centuries an increasing percentage of people made their living by selling their goods and labor on the open market and were thus affected by monetary instability and price fluctuations. The Black Death caused a temporary shortage of labor everywhere. In the towns, guild masters were forced to grant higher wages to journeymen, whose proportion had increased as the masters made full guild membership ever more difficult. In the countryside, landowners gave their peasants various kinds of inducements to keep them producing grain, whose price was falling, instead of moving into other occupations. By the 1370s and 1380s, however, monetary devaluations destroyed the gains of both the urban and rural workers, who then began sporadic revolts, not only because they were poor, but also because they resented the social cleavage between them and the wealthy classes.

### Social Unrest

This social unrest was a protest against the increasing restrictions of the established powers in a time of shrinking economic opportunities. In the preceding period of economic expansion, peasants, businessmen, and crusading knights had been able to improve their status in new towns or in distant lands. Now these opportunities were gone, and people's status tended to become frozen. The merchants of Paris, led by Etienne Marcel, rebelled against the king's efforts to limit their political rights as leaders of the urban community. In the cities of Flanders and Italy the merchants led similar rebellions against their local princes. But the main unrest in the late fourteenth century came from the people with the lowest status.

In Flanders and Italy it was mostly the urban workers who expressed dissatisfaction; in England, France, and Germany the peasants played a larger role. The journeymen in the Italian and Flemish towns could no longer hope to gain the security and status of guild membership in the great textile guilds. They were becoming an urban proletariat, and they did not like this development at all. Along with the merchant guilds, which ran the town governments, the masters of the craft guilds were now a new privileged class whom the journeymen resented bitterly. When they tried to revolt, however, they were always suppressed. They had neither the equipment, the experience, nor the organization for sustained military action. The same was true of peasant revolts. In France a great peasant revolt —the *Jacquerie*—took place in the same year (1358) as Etienne Marcel's rebellion in Paris. Both were put down with trained military forces of the nobles and the king. In England the peasant's revolt of 1381, led by Wat Tyler, ravaged the countryside, destroyed records of seignorial dues, and killed landlords. In the end, however, it, too, was suppressed and its gains annulled. It was not peasant uprisings that destroyed seignorialiam; it was the growth of a money economy and the Black Death.

In the newly colonized lands east of the Elbe the seignorial system grew and benefited the feudal nobility, but in the rest of Western Europe the Black Death upset the labor market and hastened the system's decline. The noble landowners, already pinched for cash and now faced with a labor shortage, had to sell most of their remaining rights over their peasants. They also began renting some of their land to enterprising peasants or selling it outright to town merchants looking for safe investments during a business depression. On the land they kept, the nobles now had to hire workers for wages. Thus the countryside gradually changed. Instead of a few great manors farmed by serfs, the countryside now came to consist of smaller estates worked by day laborers and an increasing number of individual farms worked by free tenants.

The gradual disappearance of the seignorial system worked to the disadvantage of most nobles and even the rural estates owned by the Church. Not all nobles became impoverished, though. Some found other sources of income, such as spoils of war, pensions as retainers of kings and princes, and lucrative posts in secular and ecclesiastical government. But the main new form of wealth was capital, and it mainly enriched the merchants in the towns. Despite the long economic regression, these merchants were creating the foundations of early modern capitalism.

### Medieval Capitalism

Capitalism is a confusing word. Technically it means a system of economic organization in which the means of production are owned by the people who have invested their capital in them. By this definition, a small farmer who has bought his land and tools with his own money is a capitalist, whereas a banker who lends money to a government is not. Yet everybody knows that all bankers are capitalists, and that most small farmers are not. It would be simpler to say businessman instead of capitalist, but this would not be entirely accurate; only those businessmen who consistently invest important amounts of their income for further profit, instead of saving or spending it, are capitalists. What we are concerned with here is the accumulation of capital as stimulated by the investment of surplus income—which *is* capital when used in this way—for individual gain.

A capitalist, then, is a businessman who furnishes capital to other people to produce goods and perform services that create income, a share of which they return to him. Capital may take the form of land, tools, machines, raw materials, transportation and marketing facilities—or simply the money to acquire these. Even arms and munitions are capital when they are used, as they often were after 1450, for piracy, slave-raiding, or the conquest of trade routes and the wealth of foreign lands. Each time a businessman makes a profit he has more capital to invest. As more businessmen make more profits that they can invest, the total amount of capital in a given society increases. When there is enough to finance a significant proportion of a society's economic activities, we can speak of the rise of capitalism, which is simply large-scale business.

Businessmen had been accumulating capital in Western and Central Europe since the thirteenth century. Large-scale trade with the Orient and Northern Europe had begun to bring substantial profits to merchants in the cities of Italy and the Low Countries. The merchants reinvested these profits in trade and commerce, and, by the mid-fourteenth century, in manufacturing—especially woolen textiles—and loans to popes and princes. All these activities produced more profits for further investment, though there were losses, too—such are the risks of business. Another source of late medieval capital accumulation came from ground rents in growing cities; as the value of urban property increased, its owners received higher incomes, part of which they invested in other enterprises. By the mid-fifteenth century mining also became a profitable business and a source of investment capital.

In addition to accumulating capital, medieval businessmen developed new instruments of exchange and credit. Their need for hard money forced the cities of

*A money changer*

Italy and the states of Northern Europe to issue gold and silver coins with guaranteed fixed values—though these did not remain fixed, as we have seen. The Florentine *florin*, the Genoese and Venetian *ducat*, the English *sovereign*, and the French *livre* had approximately the same purchasing power—about $36 in 1450 at today's prices. Since the transfer of large sums of money over long distances was cumbersome and dangerous, businessmen devised the *bill of exchange* as a means of paying their debts. A bill of exchange was both an acknowledgment of receipt of goods and a promise to pay for them. In its simplest form it involved two people and might read as follows:

"I, Hans Olbrechts, have received goods from you, Giovanni Cipolla, at Bruges, October 1, 1353, to the value of 1,000 livres and I promise to pay you 1,100 ducats by July 1, 1354 in Venice."

Not only was this document a means of exchange, it was also a concealed loan. Cipolla was extending Olbrechts credit for nine months and charging him 10 per cent interest. By the late Middle Ages bills of exchange usually involved a third person—let us call him Jacques Lefevre—who owed money to the buyer of goods. A document in which Olbrechts directed Lefevre to pay Cipolla was known as a *draft*, an order to pay. If the third person expressed his willingness to comply with this order by writing the word "accepted" on the draft, it became an *acceptance*. In this form bills of exchange could be used as security to raise funds or they could be sold to banks, which charged a fee later known as a *discount*, for cash.

Other banking and commercial practices also aided the rise of businessmen in the late Middle Ages. In addition to lending money to ecclesiastical and secular princes, bankers extended credit to towns and to building and land speculators in return for perpetual "rents." When these "rents" became negotiable, as they did in Italy in the fifteenth century and in France in the early sixteenth century, they were in effect a new form of security for loans to those who held them. Businessmen pooled their resources for a specific undertaking—floating a large loan or financing a trading voyage—and divided the profits. Thus the temporary partnership was born. Commercial activities conducted over long distances required many letters, with two copies for one's files, in which the correspondent said what he had to say clearly and tersely, furnished local business news, and closed with the monetary exchange rates in his part of the world. Businessmen exchanged valuable information this way. They were also able to learn more about the state of their own finances after the invention of double-entry bookkeeping in fifteenth-century Italy allowed them to balance their credits and debits on two sides of the ledger.

A distinctive businessman's psychology grew out of this behavior and these practices. It was eminently rational, based on the calculation of profits and margins of risk. For the businessman the main purpose of money was to make more money. Hence he sought to safeguard his liquid funds. He extended credit mainly to move goods, with the expectation of being paid back in a short period of time. The Church condemned the lending of money at interest, but businessmen could profit without pangs of conscience from the concealed loans in bills of exchange, "rents," and other commercial and banking instruments. Kings might repudiate their debts, but businessmen dealt with each other on terms of mutual trust. They became masters at predicting and manipulating other people's behavior. Once they agreed on a transaction, however, they considered it "signed, sealed, and delivered."

The effects of these new business practices and attitudes were certainly limited by the long economic regression. Only the richest and most enterprising businessmen profited in the long run. And even they sometimes lost everything—as when the kings of England defaulted on their debts to the Bardi and Peruzzi banks in the 1340s. For the economic crises of the late Middle Ages were paralleled by a crisis in the political organization of Western Europe.

### Political Disequilibrium

In the fourteenth and fifteenth centuries Europe was in a state of political disequilibrium. Until then the secular monarchs had strengthened their power at the expense of the nobles and the Church, but they did not have the resources to support dynastic conflicts at home and frequent wars abroad. The kings of England and France also lost a good deal of public confidence and support by their excessive taxation and their increasingly arbitrary government.

Another change that had worked to the advantage of the secular monarchs at first but later worked against them was the decline of the feudal system. The old feudalism had begun to disappear in the thirteenth century, as kings and great lords gave money incomes instead of land fiefs to those who served them as vassals. By the fifteenth century this new feudalism of money gave way to a system that modern historians call "bastard feudalism." Now the vassal became a mere retainer, paid a regular fee for his services. The great princes, especially those related to the king, were able to buy retainers and build up virtually independent principalities. Thus the disappearance of the traditional feudal system gave way to the formation of princely and ducal parties that could challenge the centralizing policies of the kings. This development reached its peak in the fifteenth century in England and France, where public reaction against the excesses of monarchy was strongest.

In England the Duke of Lancaster usurped the crown from Richard II in 1399 and made himself King Henry IV. During the reign of his unbalanced grandson, Henry VI (1422–1461), the Houses of Lancaster and York began to dispute the English Crown in a series of dreary civil wars, called the Wars of the Roses, from 1455 to 1485. In the process the royal authority was badly weakened.

In France the royal dukes and princes who held *appanages* (semi-independent duchies and principalities only nominally attached to the kingdom) did not have the opportunity to dethrone the legal king. But neither could the king assert any real power in their realms. The Dukes of Burgundy, Bourbon, Berri, and Orléans copied the centralizing institutions of the French monarchy and acted like sovereign princes. In the fifteenth century the Duke of Burgundy was one of the most powerful dynastic rulers in Europe; he controlled the Low Countries and most of eastern France. Only in 1477 was King Louis XI finally able to defeat the current Duke of Burgundy, Charles the Bold, and reincorporate part of Charles's holdings in eastern France into his own kingdom.*

The medieval assemblies asserted themselves with varying degrees of success in different countries, but in England, France, and the Iberian Peninsula they helped to create a national basis for royal power. Except in the Holy Roman Empire, where the diet was a council of princes, these assemblies represented nations as they were conceived in the Middle Ages, that is, collections of legally defined classes called estates. Usually the "lords spiritual and temporal"—the high Church officials and the upper nobility—formed two separate estates, though in the English Parliament they sat together in the House of Lords. The participation of the wealthy townspeople was increasing slowly, but it continued to be constantly dependent on the king's need for money. In England these "burgesses" sat with knights in the House of Commons; in France they constituted the Third Estate; in Castile and Aragon they were represented by the towns, which were considered an estate—a kind of collective feudal person with the obligation of giving council to the king. In England the estates often argued with the king and did not always obey him, in Castile and Aragon the estates almost always argued with the king and often did not obey him; in France the estates bargained with royal agents but did not argue with the king—they obeyed the king.

Despite this disequilibrium the medieval assemblies helped to initiate the idea that the king and the nation were somehow related. They did not use the word sovereignty, but they behaved in a way that implied this concept as the thing they wanted to share with the king. As we shall see in Chapter III, the estates of continental Western Europe lost their influence as the kings began to consolidate their power after 1450. Only in England did the king and the national Parliament continue to share sovereignty into modern times.

*See map, p. 77.

### *The Papacy*

The papal monarchy also suffered a severe political crisis in the fourteenth and fifteenth centuries. During the seventy years in which the popes resided at Avignon—the so-called Babylonian Captivity—the secular monarchs became more determined than ever to control the Church in their own countries. For the papacy seemed to be losing its international character and becoming a French-dominated institution. In England especially, the royal government passed statutes limiting the influx of papal agents and forbidding judicial appeals to the popes in Avignon. Meanwhile, these popes tried to increase their revenue to support their own growing bureaucracy and the lavish palace they built for themselves on the banks of the Rhône. The kings, however, were trying to gain new revenue at the same time. Thus their competition with the papacy—now tarnished by its subservience to France and its grasping fiscal policy—for control of the upper clergy grew more acute.

The Babylonian Captivity was a minor scandal compared to what followed during the next half-century. In 1377 Pope Gregory XI moved back to Rome and died there a year later. The Romans had no intention of letting the next pope move back to Avignon, now that the papacy was once more within their grasp. They rioted and put heavy pressure on the College of Cardinals, now mostly French, to elect an Italian pope. Soon afterward, however, the cardinals declared this election void, returned to Avignon, and elected a French pope. There now seemed to be two popes. Half the countries of Catholic Europe supported one, half supported the other. This disastrous situation was known as the Great Schism. It was prolonged into the fifteenth century as rival groups of cardinals elected two new popes each time the old ones died.

The Great Schism brought to a head a movement for a representative assembly of the Church. Since the early fourteenth century political theorists like Marsiglio of Padua had been affirming the equality of all priests, attributing the supreme direction of the Church to a General Council, and declaring the pope's authority to be worth no more than that of any delegate. This attack on the whole hierarchical organization of the Church had, of course, been condemned by earlier popes. But during the Great Schism the conciliar movement gained ground among distressed Christians everywhere. The first attempt to end the Schism at the Council of Pisa (1409) only made matters worse. It elected a third pope, but the other two refused to resign. Finally, under strong pressures from the peoples and governments of Europe, a new Council met at Constance between 1414 and 1418. All three popes were deposed or forced to resign. Then a new pope was chosen and was generally recognized.

During the rest of the fifteenth century the new popes, now back in Rome, devoted themselves to restoring their supremacy over the General Council. They won the fight, but lost their political influence outside their own principality in central Italy. Now France as well as England began to move in the direction of a "national" church. The French king forced the reigning pontiff to sign the Pragmatic Sanction of Bourges (1438), which forbade the papacy to receive its traditional yearly income from France and granted the French church a large degree of autonomy. Preoccupied with their struggle with General Councils and their political power in Italy, the popes showed little interest in the reforms that sincere Christians were crying for in an age of spiritual and moral crisis.

### Moral and Spiritual Crises

One might think that the Great Schism, which had nothing to do with dogma, would not have caused much anxiety among ordinary people. Yet on top of all the other calamities that befell them it made them feel insecure and no longer sure of their moral and spiritual values. In an age of violence, early deaths, and growing contrasts between the rich and the poor, people longed for a better life and searched for new beliefs.

What is the truth? What are the world and man? The men of the fourteenth and fifteenth centuries asked these eternal questions with a special anxiety. Their quest for the answers mixed new ideas that became sources for modern thought with creative imagination and all the cold logic of traditional Scholasticism.

In the fourteenth century the Scholastic philosophers could no longer accept the sublime complacency of Saint Thomas Aquinas. John Duns Scotus rejected his reconciliation of faith and reason. He said the Scholastic reasoning could teach us the truth about the natural world, but that only an emotional revelation could lead us to God. Duns Scotus's emphasis on clear and distinct ideas got bogged down in theological obscurities, but it established a search for precise thinking which was later to lead to new kinds of knowledge. Another late Scholastic philosopher who rejected the Thomistic synthesis was William of Occam. He went even further by denying any reality to ideas. According to him, ideas were purely abstract and, as such, could be manipulated by logic in many different ways. Even more than Duns Scotus he heralded modern scientific thinking. But in his own time and to the end of the Middle Ages his new version of Scholastic reasoning proved sterile.

Other men turned to mysticism and new forms of piety in their search for spiritual certainty. They tried to enter into a union with God by intense contemplation, by practicing Christian living in a select community—like the Brethren of the Common Life in the Netherlands—or by renouncing the world and trying to imitate the life of Christ by oneself. Most people needed more dramatic forms of religious expression, like the veneration of relics, the cult of the Eucharist in the Corpus Christi festival, or various ways of exorcizing the Devil. One group, known as the Flagellants, went around beating themselves with whips. It was only a short step from some of these forms of mysticism and piety to open heresy.

#### *The Heresies*

The major heresies of the late Middle Ages were introduced by university professors. We have noted what might be called the "hardening of the arteries" of learning in connection with Scholasticism. Still, some of the same professors who

*Flagellants—15th century*

argued endlessly about abstract ideas also wanted to reform the Church and society. Both Marsiglio of Padua and William of Occam championed the conciliar movement. Indeed, Occam's logical subtlety made it possible for him to argue that the unity of the Church could be accommodated to a multiplicity of popes. Two other professors went much further and attacked the whole organization of the Church and its claims to hold the "keys to the kingdom" of heaven through its administration of the seven sacraments. These two men were John Wiclif (*c.* 1320–1384) at Oxford University and John Hus (1369?–1415) at the University of Prague. Both Wiclif and Hus put forth most of the ideas that were to appear again in the Protestant Reformation.

Beginning with the argument that the Church was being corrupted by wealth, Wiclif ended by attacking its whole administrative structure as being largely unauthorized by the Bible. According to him the priests had gone too far in setting themselves up as intermediaries between man and God through their control over the sacraments. He argued that ordinary men should commune with God through His Word, rather than through the priest's interpretation of it. Hence he translated the Bible from Latin into English, so that the wandering preachers could read it directly to the people. He wanted to abolish the practice of confession followed by penance, and he also began to cast doubt on the Catholic doctrine that the bread and wine in the sacrament of the Eucharist really were the Body and Blood of Christ. Wiclif also challenged the authority of the pope and said the kings should assume responsibility for the welfare of the Church in their own countries.

Wiclif was a university professor, not a leader of mass movements, but his ideas soon spread rapidly among the discontented English masses in the late fourteenth century. We have already mentioned the Peasants' Revolt of 1381. Wiclif's followers, called Lollards—literally, mumblers of prayers and psalms—also preached social revolution. If the Church had no right to property, they asked, did the barons and knights have any more right to it? Thus, the attack on the Church turned into an attack on the whole system of class and private property.

*When Adam delved and Eve span,*
*Who was then the gentleman?*

Naturally, the possessing classes joined the king in suppressing people who questioned the social and economic order in this way. Though the Lollard preachers were disposed of, Lollardy survived here and there among the masses. It was the first major expression of English nonconformism—a tradition that was to reappear in the late sixteenth century.

Meanwhile, Wiclif's ideas had been spread to Bohemia by Czech students returning from Oxford. John Hus took them one step further by preaching that the Bible alone was the ultimate rule of faith, that Christ, not the pope, was the true head of the Church, and that the sacraments of the Church were merely ceremonies, not miraculous doses of Divine Grace. For these heresies Hus was condemned at the Council of Constance and burned at the stake in 1415. But his doctrines lived on in Bohemia.

Just as Wiclif's ideas had become identified with social revolution in England. Hus's ideas became identified with anti-German national sentiment in Bohemia. The Kingdom of Bohemia was a part of the Holy Roman Empire of the German Nation. In the mid-fourteenth century Emperor Charles IV had sponsored a cultural awakening among the Czechs and founded the University of Prague. This cultural awakening soon faced two major deterrents: a corrupt and leaderless Church, and a steady influx of Germans into Bohemia and its great new university. After Hus was burned at the stake anti-German feeling spread when the current emperor tried to enforce the decrees of the Council of Constance against Hus's doctrines. The Hussites resented this interference in their national life. They organized themselves into an army and resisted the crusades launched against them by the pope between 1420 and 1433.

The Hussites were the only medieval revolutionaries to achieve any real success. In 1430 the papacy finally reached a compromise with their more moderate elements. Although the more radical Hussites, called Taborites, were suppressed, the moderates, called Utraquists, were accepted as true sons of the Church and given concessions unknown elsewhere in Christendom. They were to have their own national church and be given the cup of wine as well as the wafer in the Eucharist.

Latin Christendom remained nominally united at the end of the Middle Ages. All the same, it had suffered a series of devasting upheavals—upheavals that had expressed real anguish about the ability of the Church to save people's souls as well as a longing for a better life.

### *Literature and Art*

Anguish of existence and aspiration toward a better life—all the hesitations and contrasts that marked philosophical thought and the religious life—also expressed themselves in manners and in the arts. A debate began between emotion and reason, spontaneity and studied refinement, brutality and sensitivity. All sides asserted themselves without finding satisfactory answers.

People of the late Middle Ages showed striking contrasts in their behavior. The upper classes dressed in increasingly luxurious and fanciful clothes, yet still picked their noses, told lewd jokes, and mistreated their inferiors. The urban masses could be moved to tears and exaltation by an itinerant preacher and then howl with glee at seeing a condemned criminal hanged and quartered at a public execution. The most learned professors and the most worldly kings frequently consulted necromancers—people who claim to foretell the future by communicating with dead souls. As the historian Johan Huizinga put it:

"So violent and motely was life that it bore the mixed smell of blood and roses. The men of that time always oscillate between fear of hell and the most naïve joy, between cruelty and tenderness, between harsh asceticism and insane attachment to the delights of this world, between hatred and goodness, always running to extremes."

The literature of the late Middle Ages also varied in its modes of expression and its moral outlook. William Langland's *The Vision of Piers Plowman*, inspired by would-be reformers like Wiclif and the Lollards, criticizes every social class for its selfishness and worldliness and says that only by living according to the Gospel can the world be saved. On the other hand, Geoffrey Chaucer accepts life as he finds it, good-naturedly, but without hiding its weaknesses, in his *Canterbury Tales*. These penetrating portraits of a group of pilgrims give a better picture of late medieval society than any single work of literature. Elaborate poems about courtly love continued to be written, but with increasing cynicism about the chastity of women. At the same time, the bourgeois taste for satires of feudal society continued to nourish itself on the *fabliaux* and the adventures of Renart the Fox. François Villon's poems describe with gusto the life of the Paris underworld. Yet they also portray the fears and hopes of the poor and the outcast.

A common feature in most late medieval literature was a striving for realism and fullness of expression. There were plenty of sterile imitations of older classics, to be sure, but an age that produced a Chaucer and a Villon was still very much alive. These writers showed a remarkable perception of the realities of a turbulent and disoriented society, striving for something it could not find.

This striving for realistic detail was also evident in the painting of the late Middle Ages. An excellent example is the Flemish painter Jan van Eyck's *Madonna of the Chancellor Rolin*.* Here the three principal figures are very real people, though the Infant Jesus looks a bit old and wrinkled for his age. Every detail is carefully reproduced, from the embroidery on the robes to the tiles on the floor. This painting recalls the art of the miniaturist, which thrived in the late Middle Ages. Another artistic genre that stressed realistic detail was the Book of Hours—a sort of illustrated calendar of daily life in the country.

In contrast to this striving for minute realistic detail, there was also a tendency toward the pathetic and the macabre in late medieval art. This tendency reflected the emotional temper of the times. Its most widespread form was the woodcut of the Dance of Death (*Danse Macabre*), which shows Death as a skeleton leading a rich merchant or a bishop by the hand.

The architecture of the late Middle Ages was mainly an elaboration on the Gothic style. Here, too, the hypersensitivity and pathos of the time can be seen in all of its flamboyance. Indeed, this over-elaborate Gothic style is called "flamboyant." No surface was left undecorated —with cherubs, devils, gargoyles, or with flowers carved in stone. A late Gothic cathedral or secular building expresses the same anxiety and longing for a richer life that can be found in all the other arts.

*See p. 68.

In an age when everything was dramatized, perhaps the most typical and spontaneous art form was the religious play. In France its most popular "plot" was the Mystery of Our Lady; in Germany, the Passion of Christ. The actors were usually ordinary craftsmen or even peasants. Their performances of the miracles of the Christian story, amateurish as they were, brought the crowds into what seemed like living contact with these miracles.

Late medieval literature and art help to explain the responses of the people of the fourteenth and fifteenth centuries to the material difficulties that plagued them and the political and social upheavals of which they were both the instigators and the victims. Much of the unrest in Western and Central Europe in the fourteenth and fifteenth centuries expressed a desire to preserve or reform some aspect of medieval civilization. Etienne Marcel, Wat Tyler, John Hus, the advocates of Church councils, the journeymen of Florence and Flanders, and the Dukes of York, Lancaster, and Burgundy were all trying to resist the encroachments of the centralizing monarchs, the emerging capitalists, or an increasingly secular and fiscal-minded papal administration. They viewed these agencies as threats to their traditional rights and values. Much of late medieval culture also expressed a desperate feeling that something had gone wrong, and represented an exaggerated effort to reaffirm the old certainties as the only way of setting things right again.

Yet the fact that medieval civilization was changing irrevocably does not mean that it died, as Greco-Roman civilization died. The same Latin and Germanic peoples who had created it in the first place transformed it by themselves, with no intervening Dark Ages and with few major borrowings from other civilizations. Their contributions to the modern world show that continuity is as much a part of European history as change.

## THE ENDURING FEATURES OF MEDIEVAL CIVILIZATION

### Regional and Local Attachment

The Middle Ages bequeathed to modern European civilization a unique combination of cosmopolitanism, ethnic diversity, and provincialism. At the end of the fifteenth century Europeans had virtually no feelings about what their descendants came to call "race." The first explorers, merchants, and soldiers who came in contact with the natives of the Far East, Africa south of the Sahara, and the Western Hemisphere were to look upon these peoples as exotic, heathen, or barbarous, rather than as yellow-skinned, black-skinned, or red-skinned. Cultural and religious differences were what mattered. Between Russia and the Atlantic, between the Mediterranean and northern Scandinavia, there were many different physical types—from squat Ukrainians to angular Spaniards, from swarthy Sicilians to pale Danes. The overwhelming majority of Europeans rarely saw anyone who did not look like everyone else in their own rural villages. On the other hand, princes, merchants, scholars, and Church officials frequently had dealings with their counterparts from distant lands and were quite cosmopolitan in such cases. The important thing was not that one's skin was "white" but that one was a Christian and could communicate in some *lingua franca* —Latin for churchmen and scholars, some form of Italian, German or French for many merchants. Europe's ruling families intermarried with each other regardless of language, bone structure, or pigmentation.

Nevertheless, language and geography did divide Europeans into scores of different ethnic groups. Each of them was developing its own distinctive culture, but the multiplicity of dialects, the difficulties of transportation and communication, and the lack of strong central governments prevented any of them from being national in the modern sense. The Hundred Years' War encouraged the beginnings of national feeling in England and France; the reconquest of the Iberian Peninsula from the Moors stimulated a kind of cultural and religious self-awareness among the Latin peoples of Spain and Portugal; the Hussite Wars created an active national consciousness among the Czechs of Bohemia. But Europe was still a collection of ethnic groups ruled by princely dynasties rather than a system of nation-states. Each ethnic group had its own customs, style of dress, foods and beverages, and folklore. There was much borrowing among these groups. The English learned to drink wine from the French; the Italians learned to build ocean-going ships from the North Germans; the Spaniards learned more things than they cared to admit from the Moors and the Jews—from music, philosophy, and architecture to religious intolerance and the segregation of women. Yet each community clung to its identity and viewed all the others as foreign.

This kind of loyalty to one's native land remained provincial well into modern times. Until less than a hundred years ago a German referring to a *Landsmann*, an Italian referring to a *paisan*, or a Frenchman referring to a native of his *pays* meant someone from a particular province where the people felt themselves to be a cultural community because of their common traditions and their special dialect: Bavaria or Saxony for the German, Sicily or Venice for the Italian, Normandy or Provence for the Frenchman. Some small countries—*Länder*, *pays*—eventually became independent nation-states: Ireland, Norway, Portugal. Others were absorbed into larger unions: Scotland and Wales in Great Britain, Catalonia and Andalusia in Spain. But local loyalties have remained strong in these countries right down to the present. The Catalans in the sophisticated city of Barcelona still consider themselves superior to other Spaniards, who, of course, reciprocate the feeling. When Wales wins a football game from England, the victory calls for a "national" celebration in Cardiff.

### Corporate Social Organization

The corporate character of late medieval society persisted in the formal structure of the states of Europe until the nineteenth century. In most of them the subjects of

DIALECTS OF CENTRAL EUROPE
C. 1500
DANISH
SWEDISH
Baltic Sea
North Sea
Old Prussian
Pomeranian
West Frisian
East Frisian
Elbe R.
LOW GERMAN
Berlin
Weser R.
Low Franconian (Dutch)
(Flemish)
Wendish
Oder R.
German
POLISH
CENTRAL GERMAN
Rhine R.
NORTHERN FRENCH (Langue d'Oui)
Middle Franconian
Moselle Franconian
Rhenish Franconian
Prague
CZECH
UPPER
MORAVIAN
Strassburg
Alsatian
Swabian
Bavarian
Vienna
Alemannic
GERMAN
Zürich
Bern
Austrian
MAGYAR
SLOVENIAN
GERMAN
RHAETO ROMAN
VENETIAN
GERMAN
Venice
CROATIAN
ITALIAN
SERBIAN
PIEDMONTESE
PROVENÇAL
Map by J. Donovan

the king were divided into three estates: clergy, nobles, and commons. Some of the larger realms, like France and Germany, had regional as well as national assemblies consisting of the representatives of these estates. The stronger monarchs began dealing with some of their individual subjects on an informal basis in the early modern period. Yet legally the king's subjects had no political existence except as members of an estate, which was conceived as a collective body. This conception was closer to that of a present-day incorporated business concern than to that of a social or political class, though our habit of using present-day terms to describe past institutions has led many historians to call the medieval estates political classes.

Membership in each estate entailed special privileges and obligations, which were based on the original social role of each estate and some of which also survived well into modern times. Long after feudalism and seignorialism declined, the nobles alone retained the right to inherit titles and land, to be called sir or madam, to hunt in the forest, to carry a sword, and to demand certain forms of labor from their peasant tenants. The idea of feudal service as an honorable relationship between vassal and lord persisted in the idea of service to the crown. Until the early twentieth century many European noblemen still viewed the military and diplomatic service as the only honorable occupations for their class. In modern society the clergy continue to retain some privileges—like exemption from military service and the right to park cars in "no parking" zones. There were unworthy churchmen in both medieval and modern times. But most people still respect the clergy of all denominations because of their ideal of service to God and to the community. Although the members of the commons had no privileges, they occasionally had the right to vote on the taxes they were obliged to pay. In the eighteenth and nineteenth centuries they were to base their demands for a greater voice in government policy on this right and this obligation.

Each medieval estate had its own structure of corporate orders and ranks, each with its own *esprit de corps* and ethic. Within the clergy the ecclesiastical order consisted of the bishops and abbots; the lower ranks included the priests and the various orders of monks and friars; even the university students were considered clerics as well as members of their particular university corporation. The higher ranks of the nobility retained some of their feudal characteristics as an aristocracy—or ruling class—long after the lower ranks had become a service class. In fact, in England the knights—or gentry—sat with the burgesses in the House of Commons, rather than in the House of Lords. At the end of the Middle Ages the commons still consisted mainly of the rich merchants, manufacturers, and bankers, some of whom belonged to guilds and all of whom were burgesses of a chartered town. In the early modern period the commons gradually came to include more lawyers and other professional men who were neither nobles nor clerics. It continued to exclude the great mass of peasants, journeymen, and people who belonged to no fixed order: soldiers, sailors, actors, vagrants, Jews, Gypsies.

Although the term bourgeoisie is sometimes used as a synonym for the commons—or Third Estate—the social class it is meant to describe was never a corporate body.* Indeed, the very fact that it was not made some of its members eventually oppose all corporate bodies and the privileges that went with them. We have seen that the original burgesses—or bourgeois—were the wealthy merchants in the towns. But these merchants and the bankers, lawyers, and other educated commoners who later ranked as members of the bourgeoisie did not acquire the unity of outlook and the degree of organization necessary to make their class interests prevail before the late eighteenth century. Until then the "rise" of the bourgeoisie involved the creation of new forms of wealth and an increasing role in the de-

*A social class is an aggregate of individuals, often without specific inherent differentiating characteristics, who enter into and maintain relations with one another on a basis of equality, in contrast to other members of the community from whom they are distinguished by socially recognized standards of inferiority and superiority.

velopment of the techniques, institutions, and values that were to make European civilization modern.

In addition to local loyalty and corporate privilege, modern European civilization inherited from the Middle Ages a pattern of historical development in which the elites of power, wealth, education, and status brought about most of the major changes. What happened in the history of Europe, as in all history, was the result of three different kinds of causes. First, there were the voluntary actions of individuals and groups, each of which were often torn by uncertainties and inconsistencies, as well as pushed onward by reasoned decisions. Second, there were forces that were not the direct result of human intention: pestilence, famine, inflation, business depressions, population "explosions," and the destructiveness of certain major wars. Third, there were the individual and group actions governed by impulse, coercive authority, habit, and custom. On the whole it seems that the lower men stood in the hierachies of power, wealth, education, and status, the more their acts were of this third type. And, on the whole, acts of this type tended to foster continuity rather than long-range change. Not until the end of the eighteenth century did the lower orders begin to cause significant changes in the course of European history. And not until the late nineteenth century did the actions of the masses become a permanent factor in historical change.

Birth remained fundamental in distinguishing the status of a nobleman from that of a commoner, but wealth and education distinguished most bourgeois from the rest of the population. It was in this sense that the bourgeoisie was a "middle class." Although politics, diplomacy, and warfare remained almost exclusively under the control of the kings and nobles until the late eighteenth century, the middle class provided an increasing number of entrepreneurs, inventors, scholars, scientists, artists, and other kinds of innovators in both civilization and culture. The masses, especially the peasant masses, merely clung to their old ways. But the European peasant was also a part of the medieval heritage.

## The Peasants

It is difficult for an American today to understand what a European peasant was—in some places until only a generation ago. Centuries of serfdom and poverty had made him an ignorant, superstitious, servile brute. Long after he had gained his legal freedom he retained these characteristics. He frequently lived under the same roof with his barnyard animals in appalling filth and squalor. His diet, made up of rye bread, gruel, and cheese, was meager and monotonous. Village celebrations on saints' days or at marriages occasionally broke the monotony of his daily life; and, of course, he could always get drunk. Brute he was, and so was he viewed by everyone else. The very word *peasant* was a synonym for a rude and uncouth fellow in all European languages. He was a far cry from a present-day farmer, who often has a college education. The European peasant woman worked in the fields and was as uncouth and unkempt as her husband. She, too, was far different from the modern American farmer's wife, who gives herself a home permanent while the automatic washer is doing the laundry.

Yet the peasants were human beings, and they had their own folk cultures. These cultures included ways of dressing and cooking, rules for behavior, a whole system of beliefs, and popular arts and crafts. (The word *popular* is used here and throughout this book to mean "of the common people.") Superstitions and beliefs in witches and devils may have come down from prehistoric times, but they acquired the forms in which they persisted into modern times in the Middle Ages. Both the peasants and the urban masses had their oral literary traditions, which we call folklore. Some of their stories were later given a more refined treatment by professional writers. For example, Cinderella was a peasant girl in the folk version and the daughter of a nobleman in the later written version of her story.

Other folk stories were taken from the heroic sagas and fairy tales of the nobility. In the twelfth and thirteenth centuries these sagas and tales had expressed the feudal class's optimism and feeling of

*Peasants receiving their work assignments*

mastery over the world's problems. Long after this class ceased to believe these stories they filtered down to the lower classes, where, in a less sophisticated and courtly form, they provided images of the way the world should be. Popular fairy tales and sagas of princely heroes retained the naïve optimism of the earlier aristocratic stories well into the nineteenth century. The knight-in-shining-armor and the damsel-in-distress gave Europe's masses their notions of adventure, which had no place in their real lives; they never went anywhere, and spent all their time working or tending their numerous bawling infants. The well-born heroes and heroines also preserved the ideals of feudal society in the minds of the masses long after that society had disappeared.

Aside from its naïveté and its clinging to old traditions, folk culture differed from the cultures of the elites in having no written form. In an age when everyone can read and write we find it hard to understand the difference that literacy makes in the way people think. A person who can refer to a written text acquires a sense of sequence and precision which a person who has to rely on his memory alone lacks. In the late Middle Ages businessmen, as well as scholars and professional authors, learned to think logically through the discipline of writing down their thoughts and following rules of grammar and syntax. The daily use of arithmetic also helped to discipline their minds.

Thus, in the Middle Ages and well into modern times the ability to read and write clearly distinguished the middle and upper classes from the masses. By today's standards the most highly educated people of the Middle Ages were too much impressed with the authority of the written word. Nevertheless, they developed habits of analysis and precision which gave literate Europeans a distinct superiority over many of the world's peoples, as well as over the lower classes in their own society. It was they who made European civilization modern. The masses remained on the sidelines until the end of the eighteenth century in England and France, and until much later elsewhere in Europe.

## SUGGESTED READINGS


Trevor-Roper, Hugh, *The Rise of Christian Europe.* New York: Harcourt Brace and World, 1968.*
A brilliant and sweeping synthesis covering the period from the third to the end of the fifteenth centuries.

Dawson, Christopher, *The Making of Europe: An Introduction to the History of European Unity.* New York: Sheed and Ward, 1946.
A brilliant essay on the crosscurrents among Byzantine, Muslim, and Latin-Germanic civilizations in the early Middle Ages.

Hollister, C. Warren, *Medieval Europe: A Short History.* New York: John Wiley and Sons, 1964* and

Heer, Friedrich, *The Medieval World.* New York: Mentor, 1964.*
Two good up-to-date surveys.

Southern, Richard W., *Making of the Middle Ages.* New Haven, Conn.: Yale Univ. Press, 1953.*
Excellent social and cultural history of the eleventh and twelfth centuries, enlivened by well-chosen examples.

Diehl, Charles, *Byzantium, Greatness and Decline.* New Brunswick, N. J.: Rutgers Univ. Press, 1957.
The best short history in English.

Hitti, Philip K., *The Arabs: A Short History.* New York: St. Martin's Press, 1958*
An authoritative survey written in popular style.

Latourette, K. S., *History of Christianity.* New York: Harper and Row, 1953.
The authoritative work for all aspects of Christianity; Chapter 10–19 cover the Middle Ages.

Baldwin, Marshal W., *The Medieval Church.* Ithaca, N.Y.: Cornell Univ. Press, 1953.*
A first-rate summary of the organization and functioning of the Church.

Painter, S., *Medieval Society.* Ithaca, N.Y.: Cornell Univ. Press, 1951.*
This summary covers all social classes—especially good on the nobility.

Bloch, Marc, *Feudal Society.* Trans. L. A. Manyon. 2 vols. Chicago: Univ. of Chicago Press, 1961.*

The classic detailed treatment of the subject. A broadly conceived original interpretation.

Pirenne, Henri, *The Economic and Social History of Medieval Europe.* New York: Harcourt, Brace and World, 1956.*
Originally published three decades ago, this work is somewhat outdated, but still good on the origins of capitalism.

Cipolla, Carlo M., *Money, Prices and Civilization in the Mediterranean World, Fifth to Seventeenth Century.* Princeton, N.J.: Princeton Univ. Press, 1956.
Excellent introduction to the history of money and banking. Supercedes Pirenne as the best source, but is more difficult for beginners.

Pirenne, Henri, *Medieval Cities.* Garden City, N.Y.: Doubleday and Co., 1956.*
A pioneer work.

Mundy, John H. and Peter Riesenberg, *The Medieval Town.* Princeton, N.J.: D. Van Nostrand Co., 1958.*
A short synthesis based on recent scholarship.

Power, Eileen, *Medieval People.* New York: Barnes and Noble, 1963.*
Makes the six typical individuals it describes come alive.

Adams, Henry, *Mont Saint-Michel and Chartres.* Garden City, N.Y.: Doubleday and Co., 1959.*
A famous essay evoking the temper of medieval life.

Bolgar, R. R., *The Classical Heritage and Its Beneficiaries.* New York: Harper and Row, n.d. Torchbook.*
Stimulating presentation of broad ideas—covers thought and education in the Middle Ages and early Renaissance.

Haskins, Charles H., *The Rise of the Universities.* Ithaca, N.Y.: Cornell Univ. Press, 1963. Great Seal Books.*
Written in 1923 and still the best introduction to the subject.

Artz, Frederick B., *The Mind of the Middle Ages.* 2nd ed. New York: Alfred A. Knopf, 1958.
A good survey of medieval learning and cultural interests.

Clagett, Marshall et al, eds., *Twelfth-Century Europe and the Foundations of Modern Society.* Madison, Wisc.: University of Wisconsin Press, n.d.*
Especially good on medieval science.

Gilson, Etienne, *History of Christian Philosophy in the Middle Ages.* New York: Random House, 1955.
Authoritative and stimulating.

Jones, Charles W., *Medieval Literature in Translation.* New York: David McKay Co., 1950.
A fine selection.

Panofsky, Erwin, *Gothic Architecture and Scholasticism.* Cleveland: World Publishing Co., 1957. Meridian.*
Difficult but stimulating.

Perroy, Edward, *The Hundred Years' War.* New York: G. P. Putnam-Capricorn, 1967.*
A magnificent survey of major issues and problems in France and England in the late Middle Ages.

Huizinga, J., *The Waning of the Middle Ages: A Study of the Forms of Life, Thought and Art in France and the Netherlands in the Dawn of the Renaissance.* Garden City, N.Y.: Doubleday and Co. 1954.*
A classic interpretation.

*Paperback

CHAPTER II

# EUROPE BETWEEN MEDIEVAL AND MODERN TIMES: CULTURAL AND RELIGIOUS CHANGES

The transition of European civilization from medieval to modern form occurred at different times in different places. It began in the late fourteenth century in Italy and around 1500 in the rest of Latin Christendom; it was still going on in the early 1600s. Consequently, the whole period from the fifteenth to the seventeenth centuries was no longer strictly medieval nor yet decisively modern. This chapter and the two succeeding ones will emphasize the early modern aspects of European civilization, but the reader should constantly remind himself that most of the masses and some important elites resisted every change in their medieval way of life. He should also note that the Greek Orthodox Russian and Balkan lands were little affected by developments in Western and Central Europe before the late eighteenth century.

In this period of transition, educated men of all kinds began thinking and behaving in new ways and producing new works. We shall study these cultural and religious changes of the early modern period in this chapter, and political, economic, social, and military changes later. But we must remember that all these changes were often going on in the same place at the same time. We must also remember that men were moved as much by myths of golden ages, promised lands, and holy causes as by reason and self-interest.

The Renaissance and the Reformation, which ushered in the modern period of European history, began as attempts to change the current state of affairs by reviving an idealized version of the distant past. According to the men who made the Renaissance, medieval culture had strayed from the Greco-Roman ideal and become barbaric, benighted, and stultified. According to the men who made the Reformation, the medieval Church had corrupted the faith of the early Christians and set up a false doctrine of salvation through good works and the mediation of priests. To the men of the Renaissance and the Reformation the first centuries B.C. and A.D., respectively, seemed far superior to the fifteenth and sixteenth centuries. Both groups wanted to bring back the state of affairs of the earlier period and looked askance at the whole "Middle Age" between it and their own time.

## THE RENAISSANCE

Early modern history began when Europe's elites rejected the moral, intellectual, artistic, and political forms of the Middle Ages for new ones. These new forms expressed fundamental changes in the society that first created them—the Italian cities of the late Middle Ages. They then spread to those societies of Northern Europe that had undergone similar changes. Like medieval Christendom, modern Europe was to remain divided politically. But beginning in the early sixteenth century, educated Europeans north of the Alps acquired the basis for a new cultural and social unity through the forms of the Italian Renaissance.

Invented by Italian writers of the fifteenth century, the term Renaissance, or rebirth, is still used to describe the cultural innovations of early modern Europe. These writers thought they were fostering the rebirth of the culture of ancient Greece and Rome. To them the time when this culture had flourished had been a golden age, whereas the thousand-year "Middle Age" between the collapse of the Roman Empire and their own time had been a deathlike sleep, as it were. We know that this was not so. And we shall see that the greatest men of the Renaissance were not content merely to imitate the works of the ancient Greeks and Romans down to the smallest detail—the way some people today reproduce folk music or antique furniture. These men used the notion of a rebirth of classical culture as a myth to guide them in formulating new ways of thinking and acting, achieving new goals in politics and war, and creating a richer, fuller life for their own age.

**Background of the Italian Renaissance**

We cannot explain the "causes" of the Renaissance in Italy—especially the simultaneous appearance of so many great artists—but we can see how the Italian environment in which it took root was different from the rest of Europe in the late Middle Ages. The first important difference was the degree to which the "presence" of ancient Rome was still felt in its original homeland. Urban civilization and Roman law had survived in some form even during the dark ages of the tenth century and had begun to dominate the Italian scene much earlier than in the medieval North. By the thirteenth century Italy's feudal nobles lived in towns, so that the town, rather than the castle, set the tone of living for the upper classes; in the North the courts of the kings and the great dukes continued to set the tone until the end of the fifteenth century.

Medieval Italy had produced great theologians, like Anselm and Aquinas, and great religious reformers, like Francis of Assisi, but her most distinctive contribution to medieval civilization was the work of her lawyers. In the eleventh and twelfth centuries Irnerius and Gratian inaugurated the development of civil and canon law based on the Codes and Digest of Roman times. During the late Middle Ages, the study and practice of Roman law was far more influential in Italy than in Northern Europe.

The way Italy approached the study of law made it different from the North in several ways. The main emphasis of Italian learning was on practical, concrete problems of government and administration, rather than on metaphysical and theological problems. Italian universities taught grown men and linked grammar and rhetoric to the needs of the courtroom and the political polemic. Moreover, facilities for the education of lawyers were not restricted to university towns; they were widely diffused throughout the peninsula. Finally, the stress on law encouraged and was influenced by a secular bent in Italian intellectual life, a bent that was fortified by nonintellectual factors as well.

Medieval Italy also produced a class of merchants and bankers with international connections from England to the Near East. There were prosperous merchants in Northern Europe, to be sure, but they were more restricted politically and socially by the guilds, the great lords, and the kings than were their Italian counterparts. The Bardi and Peruzzi banking houses, which finally failed in the 1340s, had no equals anywhere until the end of the fifteenth century. The economic regression during the intervening period did not seriously alter the businessman's outlook of the Italian merchants and bankers—any more than it altered the aristocratic outlook of the Northern European nobility. There have been many instances in history of people clinging to class attitudes and status symbols in hard times.

The behavior, sentiments, and general world view of late medieval businessmen encouraged the cultural Renaissance in Italy and influenced the later development of the modern bourgeoisie, secularization, and urbanization in Northern Europe.

Finally, medieval Italy produced a type of political ruler, the despot, which was virtually unknown anywhere else in Europe. The rise of these *signori* (as the Italians called them) began in the early fourteenth century, when the popes were residing in Avignon and when the German emperors were no longer able to exercise their authority in northern Italy, even though this area was still nominally under their control. With no legitimate national ruler to interfere, the towns were free to fight among themselves, to harass their commercial rivals, and to increase their territory. They frequently hired a professional soldier of fortune (called a *condottiere*) to raise an army to do their fighting for them. Often this man, not satisfied with money and medals, seized political control of the city-state that had hired him. This procedure was made easier by the political and social dissensions within the city-state itself, which made one-man rule seem the only remedy. By the late fifteenth century Milan and the Papal States were under the sway of the most famous despots of the Renaissance, Ludovico Sforza (called *Il Moro*) and Cesare Borgia. Even in republican Florence, Cosimo and Lorenzo de' Medici were despots in all but name.

During this period of acute political strife and long economic regression, the peninsula was full of contrasts and political diversity. Within each town there were extremes of wealth and poverty. Italians expressed amazingly ambivalent attitudes toward religion and the clergy. Although Italy had more lawyers than any other single country, she also had almost as many saints and bishops as all the rest of Catholic Europe combined. Italians were sometimes brutally anticlerical and yet at other times exaggeratedly pious. A few fourteenth-century writers began to construct a myth of "Italy," but no ruler, Italian or foreign, succeeded in uniting the peninsula politically. It was not that some did not try. But Renaissance Italians identified themselves primarily with their own city-state and cooperated with another only to prevent the expansion of a third. In addition to this national disunity, there was a wide variety of political systems, ranging from the republics of Florence, Genoa, and Venice, through the despotism of Milan and the dynastic monarchies of Savoy and the Two Sicilies, to the clerico-feudal monarchy of the Papal States. The Renaissance began not as a cosmopolitan or even a national movement but as an ideological and cultural expression of local patriotism in republican Florence.

## The Early Renaissance. Florence, 1340–1440

Evidence of a Renaissance in Italy during the fourteenth century was confined to a few individuals and isolated monuments. In literature and the arts it was the age of the *dolce stil novo*—the fresh style of the vernacular writings of Dante, Petrarch, and Boccaccio, and gay new musical forms like the madrigal—of the "liberating" influence of northern Gothic on the Byzantine and Romanesque styles that had dominated Italian art and architecture for centuries. The real beginning of the Renaissance occurred with Petrarch's re-establishment of moral philosophy as a secular study and with his insistence on the value of literature—especially classical Latin literature—as a means of self-improvement and improvement in society. Petrarch's enthusiasm for classical antiquity was then propagated by Boccaccio, made the basis for a new educational program, and taken over for political purposes by Coluccio Salutati, the patriotic chancellor of Florence from 1375 to 1406.

### *The Secularization of Wisdom: Petrarch and Boccaccio.*

Francesco Petrarca (1304–1374), better known as Petrarch, was thus the originator of Italian humanism. Humanism (*studia humanitatis*) meant the study of the pagan classics, rhetoric, poetry, and history in conjunction with moral philosophy. Petrarch's bequests to his successors were his passionate identification of study with life and his insistence that new interests could be stimulated and satisfied through a sympathetic concern with antiquity. Yet his own personaity and career illustrated the lack of logic and consistency we must expect in most people, as well as the fusion of the old and the new, which was typical of the whole late-medieval-early-modern period.

Petrarch was born in the Tuscan town of Arezzo and grew up in Avignon, to which his exiled father, a Florentine merchant, had migrated. He moved about a great deal in Italy and France during his lifetime, withdrawing periodically from his active life to a rustic retreat near Avignon. Petrarch, who as a young man studied law and theology, became a clergyman in order to have a steady income from a benefice, but he then turned his back on lawyers and Scholastic theologians. His fondest ambition was to gain fame as a writer. He wrote heroic epics and learned treatises in pure classical Latin and lyrical love sonnets in the Tuscan vernacular to his mistress Laura.

Petrarch's greatest contribution to the later development of the humanist outlook in public affairs was his discovery (1345) of some hitherto unknown letters of Cicero to his friend Atticus. These letters reveal Cicero as an active Roman citizen trying to save the Republic from the despotism of Julius Caesar and from civil war; the relevance of this example in Florence was soon to become all too clear. Despite his admiration for Cicero, however, Petrarch disapproved of him for not having detached himself from "so much worthless strife." In his *Secretum* (1342–1343), a soul-searching, imaginary dialogue with St. Augustine, Petrarch himself had accepted the Christian doctrine of withdrawal from worldly affairs. Throughout his life he felt misgivings about his vanity and the worldly activities that he tried to transplant from Roman times to his own day.

Nevertheless, it was Petrarch's worldly side that influenced the growth of humanism, and it was his contemporary Giovanni Boccaccio (1313–1375) who helped to spread this influence. Boccaccio's best-known work, the *Decameron*, was not particularly important in the development of the new humanist spirit. This series of short stories was in the same tradition as the French *fabliaux* and Chaucer's *Canterbury Tales*. Indeed, for sheer bawdiness, it does not always equal them. It was Boccaccio's *Genealogy of the Gods*, written in Latin, that diffused the basic knowledge necessary for understanding ancient poetry, which was full of allusions to classical mythology. In manuscript copies and in many printed editions beginning in the late fifteenth century this source book helped to make Petrarch's enthusiasm for Latin literature as a guide to life popular among the Florentines.

The reasons for the early popularity of the humanist outlook in Florence were the distinctive economic, social, and political features of that Tuscan republic. A number of Florentines had grown rich through a combination of banking and the manufacture and processing of woolen cloth, while the bulk of the population had been reduced to the level of insecure wage earners. The fourteenth-century businessmen (called *grassi*, which means fat ones and was a synonym for rich in those days) were still suspicious of the nobles (*grandi*), from whom they had recently taken political power, and apprehensive of the underprivileged townsfolk (*populo minuto*), whose resentment sometimes led to open rebellion—as in the case of the textile workers (*Ciompi*) in 1378. All the same, they frequently had to appeal to "the people" for support in their efforts to keep rival factions among themselves from controlling the municipal government. Their extremely active interest in local politics also sharpened their awareness of the contrast between the teachings of the Church and the realities of daily life—Petrarch's dilemma of withdrawal or commitment. They knew that it was not easy for a rich man to get into heaven.

### *Politics and Education*

The most serious threat to the Republic of Florence came from the outside in the late fourteenth and early fifteenth centuries. For two generations the despots of Milan tried to extend their control over all northern and central Italy. The leadership of Florence in Tuscany, her access to the sea, and sometimes even her independence seemed to be in the balance. A new and original cultural development arose out of the combination of these dangers and the popularization of Petrarch's program for the active perusal of classical studies for their moral guidance, their practical importance, and their inspiration in literature and the arts. The man who first used this program for political—today we would say ideological—purposes was Coluccio Salutati. In his office of chancellor, an administrative rather than a political post, he wrote letters and polemics in defense of Florentine liberty and on the duties of the patriotic citizen. One of his main arguments was that Florence had inherited the liberty of republican Rome. Since his city had been founded before the time of the ancient Roman Caesars, it had all the virtue necessary to resist the Caesarian ambitions of the current Milanese despot. Salutati also used the argument of cultural nationalism when he claimed that the homeland of Dante, Petrarch, and Boccaccio represented the truest and finest aspects of the Italian tradition. This kind of propaganda had a strong appeal to the civic pride of the Florentines and was an effective weapon in their relations with other states.

Salutati and his friends did not merely use humanistic studies for propaganda purposes in diplomacy and war; they derived a whole new secular outlook from ancient literature and philosophy. While Petrarch had reproached Cicero for his involvement in politics, Salutati praised him precisely because he had been such an active citizen. The dynamic political atmosphere of early fifteenth-century Florence and a growing interest in antiquity prompted other humanists to uncover unknown Latin works and to study Greek texts brought in by Byzantine scholars. Many Florentines scorned the humanists' efforts to imitate the style of classical Latin in their own Latin and vernacular writings. But their tendency to stress accommodation to the here-below, as opposed to the next world, was in tune with the spirit of the age. One humanist, quoting Cicero, said, "the whole glory of man lies in activity." Another, paraphrasing Aristotle, said, "the possession of external goods affords an opportunity for the exercise of virtue." By the mid-fifteenth century the ascetic monk no longer had a monopoly on virtue. The professional soldier, the civil servant, the poet, and the family man could be virtuous, too. Their outlooks were now respectable.

As humanist scholars formulated new moral values, humanist teachers made these the basis of a new kind of education. In Florence, in Mantua, and in other parts of Italy young men from well-to-do families went to newly founded boarding schools featuring a curriculum of classical studies and physical exercises. The active life replaced the religious ideal of earlier education. As Vittorino da Feltre, the head of a very famous fifteenth-century boarding school, said:

"Not everyone is called to be a lawyer, a

physician, a philosopher, to live in the public eye, nor has everyone outstanding gifts of natural capacity, but all of us are created for the life of social duty, all are responsible for the personal influence which goes forth from us."

Thus the goal of the new education was to mold active citizens and balanced personalities through the humanities. Poets, orators, historians, and essayists were to be studied for use in action and for discourse on all subjects. The power of expression, especially an elegant literary style, was declared essential to the educated layman in all fields. The preparatory schools of the Western world were to cling to this educational program until well into the twentieth century. It was the most influential and lasting creation of the Italian Renaissance.

### *Art*

The secularization of wisdom, politics, and education also found expression in Florentine art during the early fifteenth century. Many people had long pictured the world privately as it was portrayed in the detailed realism of late Gothic painters. But beginning with Masaccio (1401–*c.*1428), this realism was expressed in a new manner, which set the style not only for Italian Renaissance painting but for all European art until the late nineteenth century. Masaccio mastered the technical problems of perspective, of light and shadow, and of giving the appearance of roundness and depth to his figures and scenes. Unlike the Fleming Van Eyck, who was already painting in oils, he sacrificed minute, photographic details for the dramatic realism of his central figures, and highlighted the intensely human emotions of his subjects.* He replaced the late Gothic concern for decoration with a "classical" conception of unity in composition. Thus Masaccio shared the basic goal of Florentine art and architecture in the early fifteenth century: to achieve a uniformity of total effect. No matter how rich their content or how full their detail and color, the artistic creations of the Renaissance seem fundamentally simple and homogenous, particularly when compared with those of the late Middle Ages.

*See p. 69.

Just as Masaccio was the father of the new style of painting, two other Florentines, Donatello (*c.* 1386–1466) and Filippo Brunelleschi (1377–1446), were the fathers of Renaissance sculpture and architecture respectively. Donatello's religious subjects were no longer merely a part of the wall decoration of a church. He made them stand foursquare in a niche and endowed them with physical realism and earthly beauty.† His equestrian statue of Gattemalata became a landmark in the history of art. The subject is a completely secular *condottiere*, and the style is thoroughly classical; Gattemalata looks like a Roman general. Donatello began the practice of measuring human figures so as to produce the ideally proportioned figure in sculpture. Brunelleschi made the measuring of ancient ruins the acknowledged method of producing a combination of the most perfect forms and harmonious proportions in architecture.

Like the humanist scholars, early Renaissance architects regarded the cultural remains of ancient Rome as visible evidence of the virtues that had made her great. They too hoped to recapture some of the grandeur of classical times by copying its style. But the truly talented architects of the Renaissance were not mere imitators. While Brunelleschi's buildings combined many antique, Early Christian, medieval, and Byzantine elements, they had a striking originality of their own. In a sense, Brunelleschi crowned Florence with a new physical appearance just as he crowned her cathedral with its superb dome.*

## The High Renaissance in Italy

By the middle of the fifteenth century the Renaissance was spreading from Florence and a few other centers to the rest of Italy. Although ruled by princes, most of the Italian city-states found little difficulty in adapting to their own needs the Florentine secularization of virtue and wisdom,

†See p. 71.
*See p. 71.

*Portrait of Pope Leo X, by Raphael*

the justification of accumulating wealth, and the use of the arts and letters for political purposes. In administration and diplomacy the humanist chancellor and the humanist ambassador-in-residence became permanent fixtures of the Italian scene. The Florentine republic had used history and rhetoric in attacking its enemies and in getting favorable peace treaties. Almost in self-defense, other states hired clerks, diplomats, and orators who could serve them with the same classical allusions and stylistic flourishes. Florentine styles in building and the decorative arts were also taken over elsewhere and blended with local elements. These changes occurred first in the small princely courts, whose rulers were anxious to bolster their power and prestige. But it was in Rome that the Renaissance reached its peak under the greatest Italian princes of them all—Popes Julius II and Leo X.

### Papal Patronage

Even in Rome princely patronage of the humanities and of the new style in building and painting was partly a prop for weak government. The popes channeled the productions of most writers and artists—with a few outstanding exceptions—into propaganda pieces. Pope Julius II (1503–1513) devoted the bulk of his time to consolidating his power as an Italian prince and as the head of an international church. Personally leading a number of military expeditions against the rebellious nobles of the Papal States, he brought the whole of that territory under his control. The ceremony and pomp with which he celebrated his victories imitated the triumphal processions of the Roman emperors. Julius II also engaged in wars with Venice and Florence and (in defiance of the king of France) called the Fifth Lateran Council in 1512 to assert the supremacy of the papacy. In all these endeavors he used the services of humanist diplomats and scholars for monarchical ends, just as Florence had done to save its republic. From the papal chancery diplomatic messages poured forth to all Europe in the humanist script, which, in its printed form, was henceforth called "Roman."

Julius II not only wanted to be the greatest prince in Christendom, he also wanted to improve what we would call today his public image, for he was well aware of how he scandalized the faithful with his military exploits, his unscrupulous political maneuvering, and his neglect of his spiritual functions. He even sought to perpetuate a favorable image of himself for posterity by having Michelangelo build him an enormous tomb surrounded by forty huge marble figures. The original plan was not carried through, but some of Michelangelo's most powerful statues—Moses, the two Slaves in the Louvre, and the Victor and four unfinished Captives in Florence—were created to glorify a pope who one pious humanist said would never get into Heaven.

Julius II and Leo X were also determined to make papal Rome the cultural capital of the Christian world. They could spend more money on culture than the princes, despots, bankers, and merchants of Italy, and they succeeded in luring the outstanding artists of the High Renaissance into their service. Raphael covered the walls of their private apartments with murals, and Michelangelo spent four years on his back painting the ceiling of their private chapel. Their most gigantic public gesture was the building of the biggest, most impressive church in the world over the grave of St. Peter. Bramante's design was austere, monumental, and crowned with a mighty hemisphere of a dome; though later modified, it brought the grand manner of High Renaissance church architecture to a climax. Despite the great wealth of the papacy, however, Leo X had to seek the new sources of income in order to insure the completion of St. Peter's. His issuance of a special indulgence for this purpose was to spark the Lutheran revolt against the papacy itself.

### *The New Individuality of the Artist*

Just as Julius II and Leo X had other things to do besides patronizing the arts, the artists themselves created works that transcended the interests of these worldly popes and of the despots and bankers of northern Italy. They transformed the harmony and symmetry of earlier Florentine art into a more heroic and idealistic style. When dealing with religious subjects, they created a sublime vision of God become man—as in Raphael's late Madonnas, Leonardo da Vinci's "Last Supper," and Michelangelo's frescoes on the ceiling of the Sistine Chapel. Their secular subjects, on the other hand, expressed a spiritual ideal of refined humanity, as in Leonardo's "Mona Lisa" and Raphael's "School of Athens," or a conquering heroism, as in Michelangelo's giant statue of David, nude like an ancient warrior. They changed their idiom to suit the subject matter.

The Renaissance artist differed from earlier artists in emerging from the anonymity of the medieval craft guild; and his "public" also differed from what it had formerly been. In the Middle Ages there had been no clear distinction between art for the elite and art for the masses. There had been a courtly literature and courtly love songs, but painting, sculpture, and architecture, which were mainly in the churches, had been accessible to all members of the community. Even the works of Masaccio, Brunelleschi, and Donatello still had some appeal for most Florentines. But by the end of the fifteenth century and thereafter, important works of art were commissioned by and catered to the tastes of a highbrow elite that understood their classical allusions and symbolism. Just as the literary humanists tried to create a kind of cultural monopoly for themselves, so the princes, popes, educated bankers, and courtiers set themselves up as exclusive connoisseurs—a new concept—of the arts. They gave free reign to the genius—another new concept—and versatility of the individual artist, who, in turn, produced works of increasing grandeur and subtlety. Raphael's Madonnas* seem easy enough to understand today, but they were not created for the masses of the early sixteenth century. The elite for whom they were painted saw in them a deeper metaphysical meaning than the obvious representation of a mother and child, surrounded by "cute" little angels.

By the beginning of the sixteenth century the versatility of the artist came to be considered the ideal for all educated men to cultivate. The humanist credo now was: I am a man, and nothing human can be strange to me. He believed in the fullest expression of all aspects of the mind, the heart, the body, and the spirit. None of these could be rejected, for they were all human. Ideally, the Renaissance man should try everything and participate fully in everything he tried. The two unpardonable faults were bad taste and a narrow mind. Everything was permitted, as long as one carried it through with style and grace, whether one was composing a poem or a diplomatic dispatch, discussing philosophy, or poisoning an enemy. Such an outlook was obviously restricted to a small elite with enough money, talent, and leisure to pursue life to the fullest. It was turned into a formula in the most popular "how to" book of the sixteenth century, Baldassare di Castiglione's *The Courtier*. Castiglione transformed the public-spirited citizen, which the earlier humanistic educational program had tried to produce, into the gentleman, trained to use his mind and body with charm and elegance, and encouraged to pursue every ambition and noble passion befitting human nature.

### *Scholarship*

The Renaissance was not all high living and artistic virtuosity; it also opened up whole new fields of scholarship, which were soon developed in Northern Europe as well as Italy. The humanists made available—in Latin and eventually in vernacular translations—the entire body of ancient Greek learning for later use by professional scientists and philosophers. Artists and engineers made discoveries in optics, perspective, archaeology, and building construction, which were also taken over by professional scientists after the middle of the sixteenth century. Lorenzo Valla (d. 1457) founded the disciplines of classical philology and textual criticism by proving that the Donation of Constantine was a forgery. Valla showed that the Latin style and some of the references in this document—in which the Emperor Constantine had allegedly given the Papal States to the bishop of Rome—could only have been written several centuries after Constantine's death. Valla's "Notes on the New Testament" in its original Greek version was to have an enormous effect on Biblical studies and on the development of vernacular literature. For only after they had absorbed the achievements of humanism in style, vocabulary, grammar, and subject matter were the vernacular languages able to replace Latin in every area of expression.

Another field of scholarship to emerge from the Renaissance was the modern writing of history. Medieval historians had accepted the divine ordination of a universal empire—heir of Rome—and stereotyped legends about the origins of nations, noble families, and cities. Most of them had not clearly distinguished one period from another and therefore had little sense of development through time—which is the main point of history. Here, too, early fifteenth-century Florentines launched a new approach. Leonardo Bruni made the writing of history a means of defending Florentine liberty, but he purged it of mythical and religious influences, gave it a new narrative form, showed a new seriousness in the treatment of his sources, and, most important of all, sliced time up in a way that clearly marked off one part of the past from another. Historians in other Italian states soon followed Bruni's example in concentrating on specific geographical areas and limited periods of time. Finally, in the

*See p. 72.

mid-sixteenth century, Francesco Guicciardini wrote his *History of Italy* for the years 1492–1532 which, along with some earlier regional studies, became a model for historical writing on contemporary political developments all over Western Europe.

### Machiavelli

The Italian Renaissance did not produce a philosopher who measured up to Plato or Aristotle, but it did produce one man who equaled the ancient Greeks as a political theorist. Niccolò Machiavelli (1469–1527) served Florence as a diplomat in the last days of the republic. When the Medici took over permanently in 1512, he was forced into exile. Soon thereafter he wrote *The Prince* and the *Discourses on the First Ten Books of Titus Livy* (the Roman historian). In the former he said that only a prince who was completely ruthless could rule successfully; in the latter he praised the civic virtues of the ancient Greeks and Romans as the basis of a free, self-governing community. Ever since these two works appeared, scholars have argued about what Machiavelli really meant. In the context of Italy in his own time he seemed to be saying that his countrymen had lost their earlier civic virtues and thus required a strong government from above—to keep order among themselves and to protect them from French and Spanish invaders.* For Machiavelli this situation was tragic, but he faced it squarely and described it as he saw it.

Although *The Prince* was mainly concerned with the troubles of Italy in the early 1500s, it has greater significance as the foundation of modern political theory. Having detached politics from religion and moral philosophy, Machiavelli tried to describe its "effective reality," rather than its ideal form. This "effective reality" was an unholy and unscrupulous struggle for power over the lives of men through control of the state. For the actors in this struggle politics was an art; for the student of behavior, politics was a science. Both actor and student must remember that private life is different from public life and that the rules of the one have no relevance for the other. Politics is politics and must be conceived and practiced according to its own rules, aims, and motives, which are eternally the same. By defining politics in this way Machiavelli was not telling the princes of Europe much that they did not already know from their own experience. His real originality was in insisting that the only way to understand their behavior was to study it from the point of view of a scientist.

### Persistence of Medieval Ideas

Despite their scientific and rational approach to certain questions, many men of the Renaissance clung to medieval beliefs about miracles, magic, witchcraft, and the necessity for preparing for the next world, to which God or the stars would call them at some fixed time. According to them, statues of the saints and the Holy Virgin perspired in order to foretell momentous events, and witches could put the body of the Devil into the bodies of their victims in the form of a mysterious powder—just as the body of Christ was absorbed during the Catholic Mass in the form of a wafer. God "emanated a mysterious fluid" which, through the intermediary of the stars, affected the lives of all living things. By studying the relationship of heavenly bodies to parts of the human body an astrologer could tell a doctor how to treat a patient. For example, the best time to bleed a person whose bile was acting up was when the moon was under the signs of Leo and Saggitarius. Even Popes Julius II and Leo X retained the services of astrologers. Finally, no matter how much the men of the Renaissance admired pagan antiquity, most of them never abandoned their belief in a divine Providence, and some of them still yearned to escape from a purely secular world. The replacement of God by Reason and Science was still in the future.

Their belief in a "revival" also placed the men of the Renaissance closer to the Middle Ages than to modern times. They still assumed that human nature was always the same, that history repeated itself in cycles, and that when civilizations became "corrupt" they were "revived" by the virtuous efforts of reforming leaders and a reversion to the true principles of their

*See p. 114.

golden age. The Renaissance showed little belief in *progress*, the most characteristic idea of modern times. This idea seems to be closely linked to economic growth and scientific and technological advances, none of which was outstanding until the mid-sixteenth century.

### The Renaissance in Northern Europe

The High Renaissance had transformed the neoclassical styles and attitudes of republican Florence into a grand manner more suitable to popes and princes, but it underwent further transformations after the 1520s. Something of the Florentine identification of culture and political liberty was transplanted to the aristocratic Republic of Venice, where it survived until the beginning of the seventeenth century. Elsewhere in Italy, republics succumbed to despots and foreign domination. The Sack of Rome by the troops of Emperor Charles V in 1527 dealt a severe blow to the prestige of the papacy and dramatized its political weakness. At about the same time (though through no demonstrable causal relationship) Italian artists began to overstrain the forms of the High Renaissance in order to achieve a more personal and emotional effect. Perhaps they were trying to make art triumph over life and prevent it from fading into soulless beauty. In any case, beginning with the later work of Michelangelo, they developed a style called Mannerism, which copied the "manner" of the High Renaissance but left the artist freer to express his subjective feelings. This Mannerist style was especially adaptable to the taste of Northern European princes in the sixteenth century.

#### *Northern Europe in the Fifteenth Century*

The outward forms of Northern European civilization remained medieval throughout the fifteenth century, but the way people lived was changing. In politics, "bastard feudalism" was fighting a losing battle against the territorial monarchies. The rise of the independent businessman was threatening the economic monopolies of the guilds. Burghers and gentry were acquiring an increased political and social influence in many places. There were technological innovations in printing, mining, warfare, navigation, and cartography, though their economic and cultural effects were still modest. Meanwhile, economic insecurity and spiritual uncertainty caused some people to seek salvation through lay piety and mysticism, and others to take on a morbid preoccupation with witches, the Devil, and Death.

Learning, literature, and the fine arts elaborated on traditional forms. Scholasticism still dominated the universities, poets developed an exaggerated rhetorical style, and late Gothic art and architecture became increasingly ornate. Stress on realistic detail appeared in the *Canterbury Tales*, the second half of the *Roman de la Rose*, the paintings of Jan Van Eyck, and minor artistic genres. But despite the realism of the arts, Northern Europe was still imprisoned in the cultural forms of the past, just as it was physically imprisoned by the advancing Turks in the East and the Atlantic Ocean in the West. The Renaissance, along with the Reformation and the economic effects of new geographical explorations, helped it to break out of this prison.

In the North, as in late medieval Italy, there was a marked conflict between what men did and what they were told. There, too, priests and friars were mocked in popular literature. There, too, the curriculum of traditional education became progressively irrelevant to the practical needs of the day. In England and France new schools sprang up to instruct the sons of the gentry and burghers in law and classical letters, so that they might better provide their resurgent monarchs with newer, more advanced techniques of administration and diplomacy. The courtiers and noble landowners showed a renewed interest in the knightly norms for behavior of ancient Troy and the world of King Arthur's Round Table: Sir Thomas Malory's *Morte d'Arthur* was very popular in England; Duke Philip the Good of Burgundy took a personal hand in preparing the *Stories of Troy;* Courts of Love in France continued to judge delicate questions of chivalrous behavior. But the courtiers and nobles were ready for a worldlier model of the gentleman, and some Northern scholars were becoming interested in the Latin classics and the critical study of the Bible—the Englishman John Colet, the Frenchman Jacques Lefèvre d'Etaples, the Dutchman Desiderius Erasmus.

### *The Renaissance Moves North*

By the beginning of the sixteenth century Italian innovations had finally begun to acquire forms that were intelligible to the North, where society was still mainly princely and aristocratic. Italy (Ludovico Ariosto's *Orlando Furioso*) and Spain (Garci Rodriguez di Montalvo's *Amadis de Gaula*) supplied the rest of Europe with refurbished daydreams in epic poems depicting medieval chivalry, knightly exploits, and feudal loyalty. Renaissance models for behavior in the real world came from more prosaic sources. Castiglione's *The Courtier* and other works like it taught the squires and courtiers of England and France a reasoned code of service, a taste for expensive leisure, and the rewards of an active life. The professional diplomat and the professional general fitted the requirements of the Northern kings in the more serious business of power politics. In education, the humanist program gradually took over. Morality was based on Cicero as well as Scripture, and the schoolmaster emerged as a purely secular figure.

In the arts and letters Italian ideas were transmitted by Italian scholars and artists in the North, Northern visitors to Italy, and the circulation of books and works of arts. It was especially through the woodcuts and engravings of the German artist Albrecht Dürer (1471–1528) that the whole Northern world learned to appreciate the Italian art of the High Renaissance. After Dürer, however, German art came increasingly into the service of the Lutheran Revolt, and it was in France that the Renaissance flourished in all the graphic arts. In the field of scholarship, the principal Italian influence was on Biblical studies. Classical Latin, written in the humanist script, became the standard form in diplomatic documents in England; ironically, the first evidence of this change is the signed renunciation of the authority of Rome by the English Church in 1534. Italian humanists had served the dynasties of Western and Central Europe during the fifteenth century, and many Northern clerks and diplomats frequented the Roman *curia* and other Italian courts. These exchanges left their mark on Northern letters.

The meeting of Northern scholarship and the Italian humanistic Renaissance gave a new direction to European culture for the next two hundred years. "Classical" forms and themes survived in the fine arts, literature (even after the vernacular languages replaced Latin) and drama. Rabelais, Shakespeare, Rembrandt, and Bach owed much to the achievements of the Renaissance. The upper classes of Italy, France, England, the Netherlands, and Germany acquired a new social unity through a common education in the humanities and a common code for gentlemanly behavior. An international community of scholars continued to thrive in these countries and to communicate freely with one another in humanist Latin. The Protestant and Catholic Reformations, the open challenge of secular values to religious values, and the wars of the sixteenth and seventeenth centuries tend to obscure this social and cultural unity. Yet the Renaissance had a unique and unifying effect. Henceforth, it distinguished those parts of Europe that had gone through it from those that had not. This was also true of the Reformations, as we shall see.

### *Christian Humanism: Erasmus*

Before the Protestant reformers broke completely with the papacy, a number of outstanding writers and statesmen tried to save the Church by bringing the new learning into its service. These included Cardinal Ximenes de Cisneros of Spain, Ulrich von Hutten of Germany, and Sir Thomas More of England.

The most famous and influential of the Christian Humanists was Desiderius Erasmus (1469?–1536), born in Rotterdam, but a true European in every sense of the word. Although his parents were poor and obscure, he managed to get the best education available in Northern Europe at the time. At the age of thirty, he was still studying Greek at the University of Paris, having already become a priest, served as

PICTURE GROUP A

# *Medieval and Renaissance Art and Architecture*

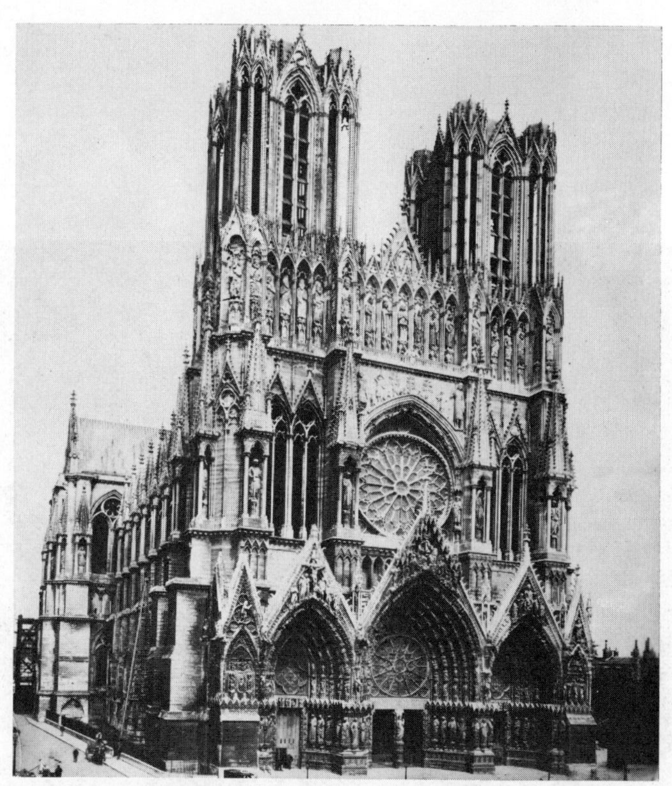

Left:
GOTHIC ARCHITECTURE:
*Rheims Cathedral*

Art Reference Bureau

Below:
ROMANESQUE ARCHITECTURE:
*The Cathedral of Worms*

Marburg/Art Reference Bureau

JAN VAN EYCK: *The Madonna of the Chancellor Rolin*
Musée Nationale du Louvre, Paris

Above:

ALBRECHT DÜRER: *The Four Horsemen of the Apocalypse*

National Gallery of Art, Washington, D.C., Rosenwald Collection

Left:

MASACCIO: *Expulsion of Adam and Eve*

Brancacci Chapel, Church of the Carmine, Florence

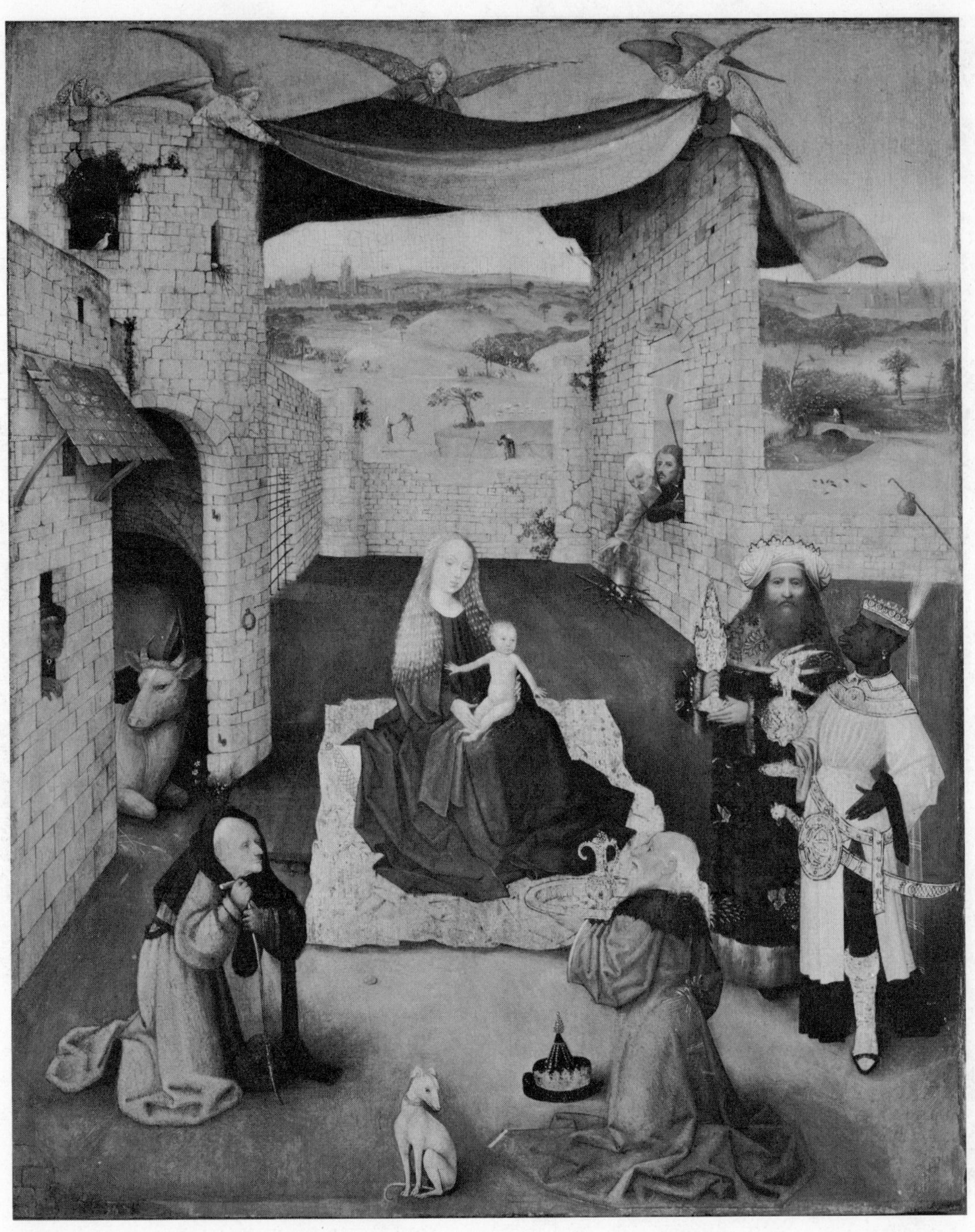

HIERONYMUS BOSCH: *The Adoration of the Magi*

The Metropolitan Museum of Art, Kennedy Fund, 1912

MICHELANGELO BUONARROTI: *David*

Alinari

DONATELLO: *Saint George*

FILIPPO BRUNELLESCHI: *Dome of Florence Cathedral*

RAPHAEL: *Sistine Madonna*
The Dresden Museum

ROME: *Municipal Center (Campidoglio)* Alinari

TITIAN: *Paul III*
The Naples Museum

FRANCOIS CLOUET: *Francis I, King of France*

Alinari

*Erasmus and his secretary*

secretary to the Bishop of Cambrai, earned a degree in theology, and mastered the Latin classics.

Erasmus combined all aspects of the Christian Humanists: their criticism, their scholarship, their educating mission, and their search for a new Christian ethic. He wrote his *Manual of the Christian Knight* (1503) to teach the layman—whom he said the priests left uninstructed—how to practice true Christian piety. In this work he developed a new "philosophy of Christ" by combining the classical virtues with an inward feeling for the spirit of the Gospel. Erasmus told his readers that they could not be saved by routine—and often superstitious—observances of the letter of the Scriptures and the performance of external "ceremonies" such as fasting, going on pilgrimages, praying to the saints, and buying indulgences. His *Praise of Folly* (1511) and his *Colloquies* (1522) poked fun at all kinds of foolish and hypocritical behavior, though their main targets were the institution of monasticism, the ignorance and abuses of the higher clergy, and outward conformity as a substitute for the true Christian spirit. These two works, like his *Adages* (1508), were also important contributions to Latin literature. The *Adages* is a collection of quotations from classical authors with elucidations and sophisticated comments on them and on the contemporary scene. It became a standard reference work for writers and scholars and went through sixty editions in Erasmus's own lifetime. His own scholarly contributions included a new Latin translation of the New Testament influenced by Valla's textual criticism, a critical edition of its Greek original, and critical editions of the writings of the early Church Fathers. Erasmus believed that these purified texts would help to purify Christian life. But his efforts were unable to stop the Protestant Revolt.

## THE REFORMATIONS

### The Church around 1500

Just as by 1500 the medieval forms of culture, society, and politics were losing their relevance to the way men were thinking and behaving, so were those of the Christian Church. The sheer inertia of this enormous and complex organization and the drag of its powerful vested interests seemed to have made it incapable of adapting itself to new needs. The minority of educated and wealthy laymen (and even some high churchmen) were developing worldly tastes and interests that were increasingly unrelated to the Church's teachings. The extension of the money and market economy of the towns to agriculture had broken down the personal ties between landlord and tenant and upset the economic and social "harmony" that the Church had seemed to sanctify as an expression of divine justice. Although the peasants of Western Europe generally benefited from rising prices, which made their fixed rents easier to pay, they and the town wage earners were mentally unprepared for the insecurity their new independence entailed. Moreover, they were haunted by fear of death and pestilence. When they turned to the Church for guidance they became more resentful of familiar clerical abuses than they had been in the past. In an age of spiritual uncertainty, epidemics, and the threat of the advancing Turks in the East, they saw the chief symbol of Christendom, the papacy, steeped in worldly politics and even accepting money from the Sultan.

While the papal monarchy had finally won out in its constitutional struggle with the Church councils, the Church itself was losing much of its power to secular monarchs. England had limited the financial, judicial, and administrative independence of the Church as early as the fourteenth century. By the 1520s Cardinal Wolsey, Archbishop of York, created a centralized dictatorship over the English Church, which made it almost self-sustaining even before Henry VIII finally broke with Rome in 1534. In Spain, Ferdinand and Isabella set up a kind of national church —with its own Inquisition—which gave them effective control over ecclesiastical appointments, taxation, and jurisdiction by the early 1500s. Francis I of France gained many of the same powers for his country through the Concordat of Bologna, which he negotiated with Pope Leo X in 1516.

The papacy's power was most extensive—and most bitterly resented—in the Holy Roman Empire, including such Swiss and Rhineland cities as Zürich, Basel, Geneva, and Strasbourg, where no secular ruler was strong enough to stand up to the pope. Insofar as the emperors were involved, they tended to take a share of ecclesiastical taxes and allow the rest to flow on to Rome. The same was true of some German princes and archbishops. Albert of Hohenzollern's relations with Leo X are a case in point. This younger son of the Elector of Brandenburg wanted to bribe the pope into letting him occupy two archbishoprics and a bishopric; both the bribe and the holding of more than one church office were common abuses at the time. Albert borrowed the money from the Fugger bank to pay the pope, whom he also persuaded to allow him to "sell" papal indulgences in these episcopal sees. Leo X got about half the "contributions," which he wished to use for the completion of St. Peter's; Albert and the Fuggers pocketed the other half. It was no accident that the Reformation began in Germany, where the Church hierarchy was richer, more independent, and more worldly than anywhere else in Europe.

In earlier times, the Church had been able to reform itself, put down heresies, and resist the secular princes while maintaining its doctrine intact; but in the first half of the sixteenth century it faced a fundamental and widely supported religious controversy—a controversy that ended the unity of Western Christendom. This unity was replaced by uniformity within state and local churches, for the Protestant Reformation was not a movement toward religious liberty. It replaced the authority of the popes with the authority of the Bible, as interpreted by the local church. Like the Renaissance, its energizing myth involved an ideal in the past that had to be restored.

Where lay rulers favored a break with Rome, the Protestant Reformation triumphed; it rarely survived where the civil authorities decided to suppress it.

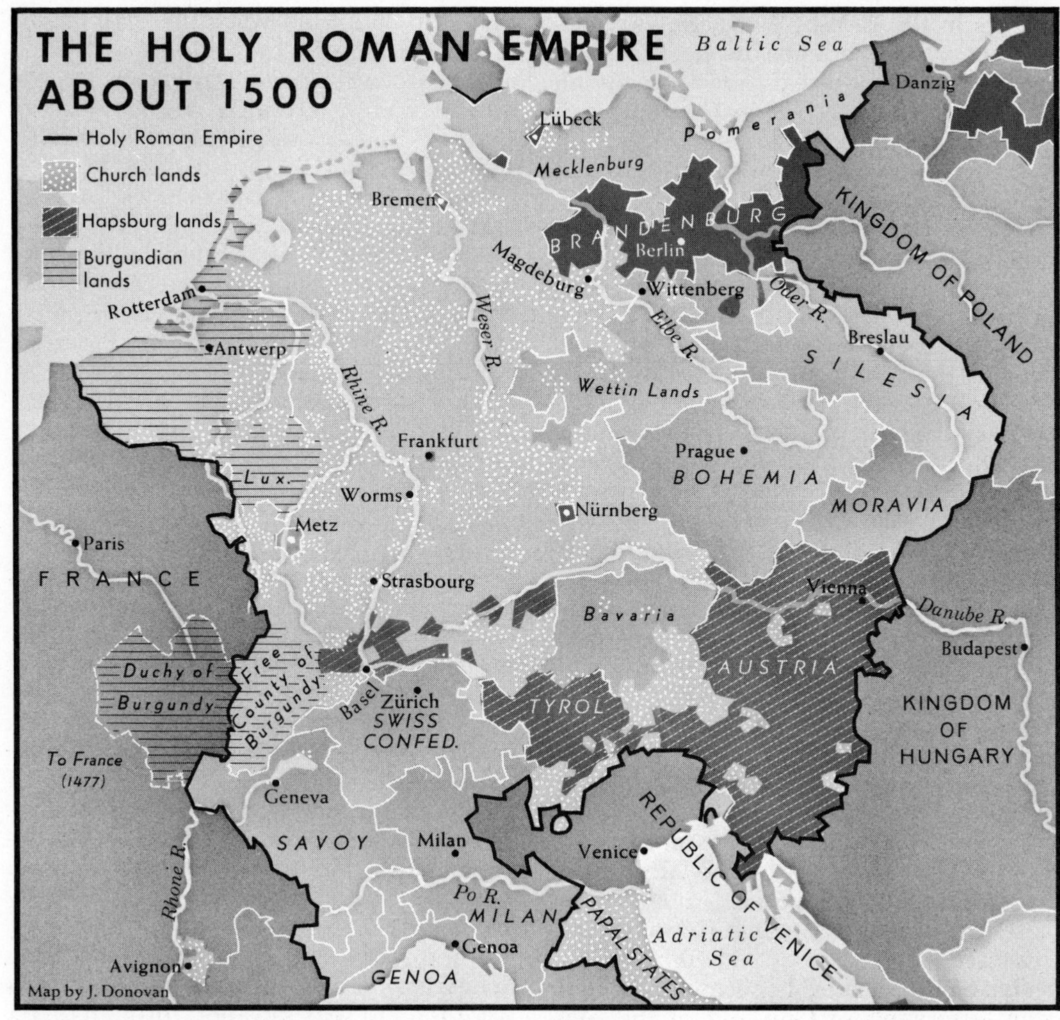


Nevertheless, it began as a movement of the spirit with a new religious message. Its preachers attracted followers in most places even before the princes and civil magistrates had made their decision, though the religious and lay leaders tended to support each other.

The main leaders of the Protestant Reformation wanted to *restore* the *true* Church, not to break it up. Martin Luther rejected the doctrines of the theologians and the popes as well as the power of the clergy to help men gain salvation. In their place he put the authority of the New Testament. He wanted all Christians to seek salvation the way he had found it —by faith in Christ's sacrifice as told in the Bible. Calvin too restored the authority of the Bible, with added emphasis on the Old Testament as God's Law of how Christians should live.

### Luther and the German Reformation

Just as the Italian Renaissance had begun as a search for a new truth through arts and letters, the German Reformation began as a search for a new truth through religious faith. Many German princes were to use the Reformation to strengthen their authority, just as many Italian princes had done with the Renaissance. Even so, Lutheranism, unlike humanism, did not initially express the interests of an elite of wealth, power, education, or status. As in the case of Italy, the explanation for what happened in Germany lies largely in the special environment in which it took root. But in Germany this environment favored a religious rather than a cultural break with the current state of affairs.

The situation in Germany was unique in several ways at the beginning of the sixteenth century. Except for the cities of the south, particularly in Bavaria, Germany had been less affected by economic change than Italy and other advanced areas of Western Europe. Most of Germany did not yet feel the secularization of existence and the fading of the Christian ascetic ideals of the Middle Ages. This was one reason that criticism of the worldliness of the papacy and German ecclesiastics was especially strong. On the one hand, the division of Germany into many weak territorial states had made it virtually impossible for any secular ruler to mitigate the abuses of the Church, as the kings of Spain, France, and England had done. Only Bavaria had any degree of autonomy from papal control and, significantly, Bavaria was to remain Catholic. On the other hand, monks and priests who lived up to the ideals they proclaimed still exercised an enormous authority among the pious Germans who criticized these abuses. Their authority reflected the medieval conception of their role as servants of God and of the community as a whole. Since Germans from all sections of society resented the unique hold the papacy had on their weak and divided land, they were thus especially receptive to the message of a reformer like Luther, who was both a monk and a priest.

Luther rejected the Christian Humanists' optimism about man's ability to be taught how to lead the good life and thereby gain salvation. According to Luther, man was born a sinner. Nothing he *did* could restore him to the justness and righteousness that God had given Adam and Eve when he created them in his own image. Adam and Eve had lost this perfection—symbolized by their expulsion from Paradise—by breaking God's Law. The taint of their original sin was passed on to all their descendants and proved that man could not resist the temptations of the Devil by his own efforts, no matter how hard he tried. But God, in His infinite mercy, promised to save him in spite of his wickedness. He did this by showing Himself in Jesus Christ. The life, teachings, and final sacrifice of Christ, as told in the Bible, were God's promise of salvation. Only by believing in this promise with utter humility and resignation could man be born anew—that is, in a state of grace—and end in Paradise. Nothing else would save him.

This was the basis of Luther's message. He discovered it gradually while he was a monk and teacher in the early 1500s. At first he did not see that it contradicted the teaching of the Church, but only some of its practices. Eventually, however, he said: "What differentiates me from previous reformers is that they attacked the life whereas I attack the doctrine." Luther broke with the Church not only over the sale of indulgences; other pious Catholics were equally as indignant about this. He rebelled because he felt that the Church's teaching obscured the biblical picture of man's plight and the way to salvation. Unitl he found the way himself he was obsessed with the imminence of his own damnation, and he derived no security from the intercession of the saints and the Virgin, from acts of penance, or from Scholastic theology. Other tortured souls were soon to seek salvation through direct contact with God and His Word, but Luther is the outstanding example of a man whose own quest for salvation made him the leader of a new evangelical movement.

### The Man Luther

Martin Luther was born in the Thuringian town of Eisleben in 1483. A year later his parents moved to nearby Mansfeld, where his father, a former peasant, became a successful operator of smelting furnaces and mining shafts; his mother came from a burgher family. The Luthers regarded their son's intellectual gifts with gruff pride and provided him with an excellent education and expensive books. Their harsh methods of child training and the somber and superstitious atmosphere of their home were normal for the

Germany of the time. Neither could Luther's experiences at school be blamed for his ultimate revolt against the Church. He was reared in an atmosphere of Catholic piety and given the traditional medieval tools of learning. To please his parents, he enrolled in the law school at the University of Erfurt in 1505, though he would have preferred to devote himself to religion. A few months later, he suddenly decided to enter the local monastery of the Augustinian order of Hermits. According to tradition, he made this decision when thrown to the ground by a flash of lightning. He himself said later: "Not freely or desirously did I become a monk . . . but walled around with the terror and agony of sudden death, I vowed a constrained and necessary vow."

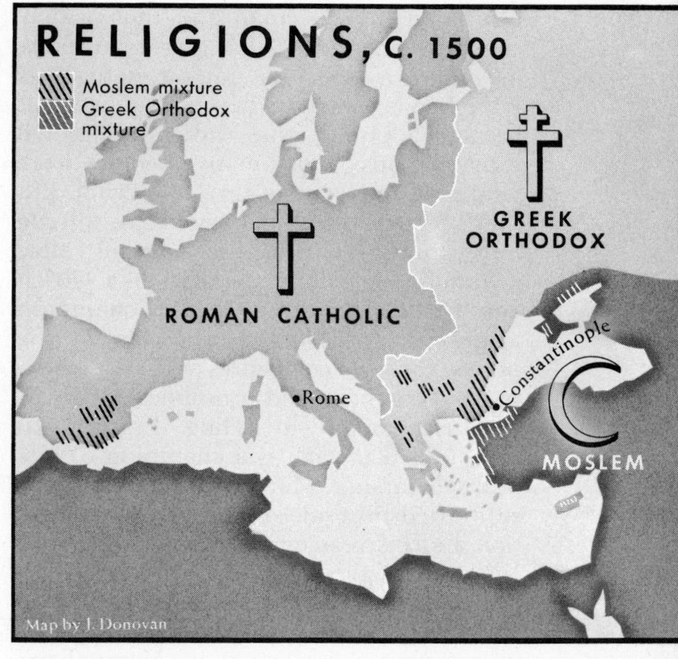


Between 1507 and 1517 Martin Luther tried desperately to convince himself that he could cleanse himself of sin through fastings, scourgings, and prayer beyond the rule of his monastic order. The kindly vicar of the order, Johannes von Staupitz, tried to divert this high-strung, conscience-stricken young monk from his torments. He gave him administrative duties, encouraged him to preach in the local pulpit, and, in 1511, had him appointed Professor of Bible at the new University of Wittenberg. While preparing his lectures there Luther finally found his answer in one of St. Paul's letters to the Romans: Man could become righteous (just) only by confessing his innate sinfulness, throwing himself on God's mercy, and accepting His grace. Here was the essence of Luther's doctrine of justification by faith alone. Luther did not immediately see how it conflicted with the Catholic doctrine. He simply hoped to emphasize it by giving the Bible a larger place in Christian education, just as the Christian Humanists were doing. It took personal contact with the indulgence controversy and the later attacks of his enemies to make Luther realize the full implications of his personal religious discovery.

The fact that Luther was a priest brought him into direct contact with the indulgence controversy. Elector Frederick of Saxony had forbidden the sale of Pope Leo X's indulgences in his own territories, but some of his subjects in Wittenberg were securing them in nearby towns across the frontier. Luther was outraged by the way his parishioners had been misled into believing they had bought pardons for their dead relatives in purgatory and preferential treatment for their own future sins. The monk who hawked these indulgences had allegedly said: "As soon as the coin in the coffer rings, the soul from purgatory springs." This crass, sixteenth-century version of the "hard sell" affronted Luther's hypersensitive awareness of the awful cost of true redemption. Determined to bring the moral home, he wrote out ninety-five theses, along with a covering letter to Archbishop Albert, and posted them on the door of the Wittenberg castle church on All Saints' Day, 1517. Most of these propositions were not revolutionary. The main controversial ones said that the pope had no jurisdiction over purgatory and that he could not transfer the "surplus" of good works accumulated by past saints to the "credit" of present sinners through his indulgences. According to Luther, "the true treasure of the Church is the holy gospel of the glory and grace of God."

Luther had written his ninety-five theses in Latin for disputation with other theologians, but within two weeks they were translated into German and then widely circulated in print. What might normally have been a "squabble among monks," as Pope Leo X called it when he first heard it, became a public issue with international repercussions. Too many people were aware of the controversy to permit Luther's ecclesiastical superiors to muzzle him through ordinary administrative channels. German nationalists like Ulrich von Hutten saw Luther as a champion against the grasping fiscal policy of the popes. Luther's colleagues at the University of Wittenberg and a number of Christian Humanists, including Erasmus at first, rallied to him as a champion of biblical scholarship. Many ordinary Germans supported his criticism of current corruption and his reassertion of ancient truths. In addition, Elector Frederick was protecting him, and both Emperor Maximilian and the pope needed Frederick's support in securing the election of Maximilian's grandson Charles to the imperial crown. Meanwhile, Luther took an increasingly revolutionary position in public debate. By 1520 he had denied the divine origin of the papacy and praised John Hus, whom the Council of Constance had condemned as a heretic just over a hundred years earlier. Pope Leo X finally issued the bull *Exsurge Domine*, proclaiming that, if Luther did not take back everything he had said, he too, would be condemned as a heretic.

Between the time this bull was issued in June 1520 and the time it reached him in October 1520, Luther appealed directly to the public in a series of printed tracts and pamphlets. His *Address to the Christian Nobility of the German Nation* called on the secular princes to reform the Church themselves, since the popes and councils had failed to do so. Here was an invitation to take over church property and found state churches. *The Babylonian Captivity*, addressed to the clergy and the learned world, argued that the Roman Church had "captured" the sacraments of the true church and had falsely claimed that its priests had the sole power to make them "work." Luther abandoned all but three of the sacraments—baptism, penance, and the Eucharist, which he called the Lord's Supper—and altered their meaning. Priests, whom Luther called ministers, should still preach the Gospel and administer the sacraments, but they had no miraculous powers.

In December 1520, Luther publicly burned the works of canon law and the papal bull, thus completing his defiance of Rome. Death at the stake seemed the only possible outcome. But Elector Frederick, though he never broke with the Church himself, insisted that Luther be given a fair hearing before being condemned. He suggested to the newly elected emperor, Charles V, that this hearing should take place at the imperial diet, which was to meet in the town of Worms in April, 1521. The emperor promised to give Luther a twenty-day safe conduct from Wittenberg to Worms and back. Papal legates tried unsuccessfully to avoid the publicity of an open hearing, for Luther had many sympathizers, even in Worms itself. Their worst fears did not anticipate the dramatic effect of Luther's stand in the face of the emperor and the impressive assembly of ecclesiastical and secular princes. In his simple monk's garb, Luther told his august audience:

> Unless I am convicted by Scripture and plain reason—I do not accept the authority of popes and councils, for they have contradicted each other—my conscience is captive to the Word of God. I cannot and will not recant anything, for to go against my conscience is neither right nor safe. God help me. *Amen.*"

Charles V told Luther to go home while his safe conduct was still in effect. Then he issued the Edict of Worms, placing Luther under the ban of Empire.

Outlawed by both pope and emperor, Luther retired temporarily from public life. Actually, he had been "kidnapped" with the connivance of Elector Frederick, who hid him in his castle of the Wartburg. In this place of exile Luther set about translating the New Testament from Erasmus's critical edition of the Greek original into German. Since man could only be saved through God's Word, he should be able to read it in his native language. Luther's German Bible was a literary master-

*Luther preaching his revolutionary doctrines*

piece as well as an inspired spiritual guide; he later also wrote great hymns. Yet Luther soon found that being a reformer entailed more than preaching a new doctrine. He also had to build a new church.

Luther became disturbed at the way other people were using his doctrine for their own ends. In Wittenberg his earliest supporter, Carlstadt, preached an extreme lay puritanism, denouncing all pictures, images, and music in the church service and all distinctions between ministers and laymen. Luther decided that he had to come out of hiding and set matters straight in Wittenberg. Thus, he and his associates began a series of visitations there and elsewhere which led to a standardized liturgy and catechism and an organized clergy—with married ministers and no monks or nuns—wherever Lutheranism was eventually adopted. A group of poor German knights wanted to make war on the Catholic bishops and increase their power in the Empire at ecclesiastical expense. Luther refused to sanction the use of the sword on priests, and the rebels were defeated. Then, in 1524–25, the peasants of southwestern Germany tried to use his name in a mass uprising against their feudal lords. Luther was horrified by what he called these "murdering, thieving hordes of peasants," and he urged the civil authorities to destroy them. More and more, he found himself supporting the princes in temporal matters and reserving "Christian Liberty" for the spirit.

### Lutheranism Established

By the late 1520s Lutheranism thus acquired its two most distinctive features: a religion of the inner life and a church under direct princely control. Unlike Calvin,* who wanted religion to be a dynamic element in society, Luther emphasized the

*See pp. 86-88.

private side of religion and the desirability of obedience to princely authority in public affairs. Luther abandoned his early efforts to convert individual Germans by the mid-1520s, and he repudiated those popular preachers and movements that tried to give his message a social or economic interpretation. During the next twenty years Lutheranism became the religion of the small, economically backward territorial states of northern Germany through the decision of the princes, not through mass conversions.

The German princes were already becoming divided between the Catholic and Lutheran positions by the late 1520s. Because he was under the ban of Empire, Luther could not attend any of the diets at which they clashed. His colleague, Philip Melanchthon, was his spokesman on these occasions, at which the evangelical princes pressed their right to institute Luther's innovations and "secularize" church property in their territories. At the Diet of Speyer in 1529, the Catholic majority forbade them to do any more of this sort of thing. The evangelical princes replied with a *Protestation* from which they later acquired the name Protestant and which solidified them as a political force.

The division became permanent a year later at the Diet of Augsburg. Emperor Charles had been fighting wars outside of Germany ever since he had issued the Edict of Worms. Now he was present in person and hopeful that the combination of the Turkish danger and an appeal to the loyalty of the Lutheran princes to the Empire would bring about a reconciliation. He asked all parties—including some Rhineland and Swiss reformers who denied the presence of Christ in the Lord's Supper—to prepare statements of faith for discussion. The result was three separate Confessions: Catholic, Lutheran, and Swiss-Rhineland Reformed.* Melanchthon and his associates stood by their Augsburg Confession, which became the lasting basis for a separate Lutheran Church. Though there was talk of restoring religious unity for the next twenty-five years, the schism was complete. The issue was now a political one and in the hands of two rival leagues of princes.

*See p. 86.

### The Spread of Lutheranism to 1555

Charles V refused to consider the possibility of a permanent religious division in the German-speaking parts of the Holy Roman Empire. Both his Catholicism and his position as emperor made such a possibility inadmissible. The Empire's claim to being Holy and Roman had meaning only in a Catholic world. The word catholic *means* universal. In this sense, even the early Protestants regarded Western Christendom as an indivisible unit, and they wanted to convert everyone in it to their conception of Christianity. Despite Luther's denunciations of the use of force, the Lutheran princes formed the Schmalkaldic League and were ready to fight the emperor himself, if he should try to make them abjure their faith and give up the church property they had seized.

The Lutheran princes refrained from open warfare until 1547, partly out of deference to Luther, who died in 1546, but mainly because Charles V was too busy fighting the Turks to force the issue in Germany before then. In 1532 he declared an imperial peace on religious matters, until a general church council should be called. This arrangement merely postponed the final break. It soon became clear that, if a council were to be called at all, it would be under papal auspices and hostile to all Protestant views. Meanwhile, the temporary legality of Protestanism during the imperial peace encouraged its expansion. Virtually all the princes in north Germany and a few in the south had become Lutherans by 1545, when the pope finally called a general council to meet at Trent. The Protestant refusal to attend finally required the emperor to take action.

The issue in the wars between the emperor and the Lutheran princes was mainly political, and it was settled in a political way. In 1547 the emperor defeated the forces of the Schmalkaldic League, but war broke out again a few years later. The Lutheran princes were fighting for their liberties against the emperor. They even went so far as to buy military support from Catholic France in return for the transfer of the imperial archbishoprics of Metz, Toul, and Verdun to the French crown. Their victory, plus the intransigence of the Council of Trent,* destroyed Charles's hopes for a Catholic empire through the reunification of the churches. A broken man, he handed over his title as emperor to his brother Ferdinand, who in September 1555 had to agree to the Peace of Augsburg.

This settlement formally recognized the right of each German prince to choose the Lutheran or Catholic faith as his own and to impose it on all his subjects. The principle involved was *cuius regio, eius religio* —the religion of the realm must be that of its ruler. Dissenters would not be tolerated and had to move to a state where their faith was the official one. Calvinism and other sects continued to gain followers, but they had no legal status. Germany was now about equally divided between Lutherans and Catholics, and the Reformation there was over.

By 1555, however, Lutheranism had spread to other parts of Northern and Central Europe. In Poland, Bohemia, and Hungary it was able to exist as the faith of a minority owing to the loose political structure of these kingdoms. But in the Baltic lands outside of the Empire the rulers declared it the state religion. The territories of the Teutonic Order—Estonia, Livonia (Latvia), and East Prussia—all adopted the principle of *cuius regio, eius religio* and remained Lutheran after they were annexed by Sweden and Brandenburg. The combined kingdoms of Denmark-Norway and Sweden-Finland set up national Lutheran churches in 1536. In most cases, the majority of the Catholic bishops and priests remained at their posts as Lutherans and taught the people the new catechism. In the Scandinavian countries the churches were somewhat freer from princely control than those in Germany, in spite of the fact that the Scandinavian Reformation had occurred as an act of state and the king was the ultimate ecclesiastical authority.

### The Reformation in England

Nowhere was the Reformation more exclusively an act of state than in England. While a few Cambridge and Oxford theologians flirted with Lutheranism in the 1520s, almost all Englishmen, from King Henry VIII on down, adhered to Catholic orthodoxy. In fact, Henry wrote a book denouncing Luther, for which a grateful pope gave him the title of Defender of the Faith. Many ordinary people disliked paying tithes and being ruled by arrogant ecclesiastics like Cardinal Wolsey, and the gentry coveted the wealth of the Church, which owned almost a third of the land in England. Still, these feelings alone would not have led to a break with Rome if the king had not been thwarted in getting the pope to let him divorce Catherine of Aragon. Until this happened, it had not occurred to Henry that he could not have his way. When he found that he was wrong, he severed all ties with the "foreign potentate" in the Vatican. After Henry made himself supreme head of the English Church in 1534, it was he who decided what his subjects should believe and how they should practice their religion. It should also be noted that foreign-policy considerations often determined these decisions for Henry and his successors during the next hundred and fifty years.

Without the divorce issue there would probably have been no Reformation in England. Henry's motives for wishing to divorce Catherine were clouded, but his determination to do so was inflexible. He needed a male heir, which his middle-aged wife could no longer give him, and he was in love with Anne Boleyn. Yet the reason he gave for wanting the divorce was that Catherine was the widow of his brother and that, according to the biblical law, he was living in sin with her. Henry was not being hypocritical. A supreme egotist, he really believed that right was always on his side. In 1527, when he "realized" that his present marriage was "sinful," he confidently expected the pope to accede to his righteous demand for its dissolution. Unfortunately for him, Catherine had another relative, her nephew Charles V, who refused to see her mistreated in this way and who was in a position to prevent the pope from doing so. For the next five years Henry tried to force papal compliance by numerous

*See pp. 93–94.

threats and appeals. Then, in 1532, he allowed himself to be convinced by his able adviser, Thomas Cromwell, that the divorce did not need the sanction of the pope and that Parliament could settle the matter.

Between 1532 and 1534 Parliament, guided by Cromwell passed a series of acts that created the independent Church of England. The Act in Restraint of Appeals (1533) destroyed the pope's most powerful weapon in interfering in English affairs by prohibiting appeals to any court outside the realm. The new Archbishop of Canterbury, Thomas Cranmer, forthwith used his power as the highest ecclesiastical judge in the land to declare Henry's first marriage void and to marry him publicly to the pregnant Anne Boleyn. In 1534 Parliament then transferred all other papal powers—granting dispensations, appointment of bishops, right to tax—to the Crown. The Act of Supremacy declared the king to be the head of the Church of England, and another act made it a treasonable offense not to regard him as such. Henry was now able to claim that by virtue of his kingship he was also God's vicar in a sovereign national state.*

Henry had no intention of using his supremacy to alter the doctrine and worship of the English Church. His main innovation was the dissolution of the monasteries. The monasteries were rich, the Crown needed money, and the gentry wanted land. So, between 1535 and 1540, the wealth of the monasteries was expropriated, and the monastic orders dissolved, with pensions for the dispossessed abbots and monks. Surely this policy was a break with the ecclesiastical past, but it did not affect religious worship and practice. The only change here was the introduction of an English translation of the Bible into the churches. Otherwise, the English Church was still as Catholic as Rome itself when Henry died.

The first moves toward Protestantism took place during the brief reign of Henry's adolescent son (by his third wife), Edward VI (1547–1553). Clergymen could now marry and were to be considered simply ministers of the Word. Archbishop Cranmer produced his book of Common Prayer (1549–1552) and revised the doctrine and ceremonies of the English Church along the lines of the continental Reformed Churches in his Forty-Two Articles (1553). England was legally a Protestant country now, but the old forms of worship—especially Holy Communion—continued to be used in many places. Time was needed to educate the people in the new faith, but Edward VI was a sick boy, and when he died, time ran out. He was succeeded on the throne by Mary, Henry's daughter by Catherine of Aragon. And Mary, a devout Catholic, was determined to stamp out Protestanism and restore the supremacy of the pope in the English Church.

Mary Tudor's reign (1553–1558) was a short-run disaster for Protestantism and a long-run disaster for Catholicism in England. Her father had executed a few recalcitrant Catholics, including Thomas More, but Mary had almost three hundred Protestants burned at the stake, thus earning for herself the name "Bloody Mary." While her brief restoration of the Roman rite temporarily wiped out all Protestant innovations, it created a permanent hatred in the English people for Catholicism as a cruel and persecuting religion. Foreign affairs also turned the nation back to Protestantism when she died. For Spain was emerging as England's number one enemy, and Mary's husband, Philip II of Spain since 1556, kept trying to interfere in English affairs.

Since Mary had no children, the crown passed to Elizabeth I, Henry's daughter by Anne Boleyn. Whatever Elizabeth's private religious convictions may have been, she could only rule England as a Protestant. Not only was she an illegitimate child in Catholic eyes, but the bulk of the nation had had enough of Catholicism. The nation had also had enough of persecution, so Elizabeth did not launch a Catholic witch-hunt. She restored the Act of Supremacy and the Book of Common Prayer, which again became uniform for

*For the political significance of this claim, see p. 102.

the whole country. Although Englishmen could interpret church doctrine in several ways, they all had to follow the same liturgy. The Thirty-Nine Articles (1563) became the prescribed faith, but they were deliberately vague, so as to satisfy as many people as possible. Unfortunately for Elizabeth and her successors, this settlement did not end the religious controversy. In addition to a sizable minority of English Catholics, the Irish, who were ruled by the English Crown, resisted the forced imposition of the Anglican Church on them and clung to their Catholicism. Before the end of Elizabeth's reign the English Puritans began to challenge Anglicanism, too. The Puritans were outstanding examples of the newer, more radical forms of Protestantism which spread rapidly after 1555.

*Queen Elizabeth I*

### New Forms of Protestantism

Whereas the English Reformation resembled the Lutheran Reformation after 1530 in being an act of state, the reform of the Church in the cities of the Rhineland and Switzerland differed from it for several reasons. On the fringes of the Empire, these cities were virtually independent of outside control and could interfere in local ecclesiastical affairs to a degree unknown elsewhere. Zürich, Basel, and Strasbourg were centers of humanism, and, unlike Luther, their reformers carried something of the humanist spirit over into their new doctrines. These cities, along with Geneva, were also compact enough for all prominent citizens to know each other by name. This fact made the notion of a Christian commonwealth especially attractive to them. Luther had reformed the Church by stressing the Word and the sacraments, while leaving civil matters to the princes. The Swiss and Rhineland reformers added a third feature, "the discipline of Christ." Martin Bucer in Strasbourg, Johannes Oecolampadius in Basel, and John Calvin in Geneva wanted evangelical pastors and godly magistrates to work together in creating God's kingdom on earth. Ulrich Zwingli in Zürich took a more extreme position in stressing the duty of the civil authorities to control the religious and moral life of the community.

#### *Zwingli*

Zwingli was born in 1484 into a family of Alpine shepherds in eastern Switzerland. Through the good offices of an uncle who was an influential priest he was able, despite his humble background, to acquire an advanced humanist education in the Universities of Vienna and Basel. He apparently never felt the kind of self-questioning that tormented the young Luther, nor did he see any incompatibility between his studies of the pagan classics and his duties as a priest, which he began in 1506. During the next thirteen years he continued to study Greek in order to understand the Scriptures better while at the same time making a reputation for himself as an effective preacher. For a time he looked on Erasmus as his intellectual master and devoured the Dutch humanist's critical edition of the Greek New Testament, but he gradually outgrew his enthusiasm for Erasmus as he subordinated literature to religion. For all his humanist learning, Zwingli was a man of the people and was determined to bring the Gospel directly to them in their own earthy language.

From the moment he was appointed as a priest in Zürich in 1519 Zwingli exalted the conception of a Christian community living according to God's Word. In that same year the plague killed some of his close relatives and parishioners, while his own survival strengthened his Christ-centered faith. Within the next few years he repudiated the authority of the church hierachy and denounced the indulgences, the monastic orders, the invocation of saints, the doctrine of purgatory, and fasting during Lent and other Catholic ceremonials. He had the backing of the magistrates and the majority of the priests in the Zürich canton at a public disputation—in German so that all could understand—over his doctrine in 1523. By the end of that year the community formally renounced the jurisdiction of the bishop of Constance and the pope. Soon thereafter it abolished all images and music from the churches and adopted the Zwinglian interpretation of the Mass as a remembrance of Christ's sacrifice, not a reenactment of the sacrifice itself.

Like Luther, Zwingli had to build a new church, but unlike Luther—and the Catholics—he made no clear distinction between civil and ecclesiastical authority. In the mid-1520s the godly magistrates of Zürich set up a court to regulate marriage and passed statutes for the general overseeing of public morals. For Zwingli the church was the community of God's elect. All those who adhered to the Reformed faith in Zürich belonged to it, while dissenters had to be driven out. The sacraments of baptism and the Lord's Supper were to be viewed as signs of belonging to the commonwealth of God. Since the Bible was the final authority for community life as well as for faith, only those offices named in the New Testament should be allowed in the church.

Zwingli differed from Luther in being very active in local politics. He had to deal more directly with Anabaptist* dissenters in his midst than the Wittenberg reformer. Zwingli was also intensely patriotic, and he carried on an active campaign against the hiring of Swiss mercenary soldiers to fight and die for the king of France and the pope. Zwingli's protests antagonized the Catholic cantons, which were already hostile on religious grounds. In order to spread his message and to protect Zürich from its enemies Zwingli sought military alliances with the Reformed cantons and several southern German cities in the late 1520s. But these alliances were short-lived. In October 1531 the Catholic cantons, assured of aid from the pope, sent their armies against Zürich. Zwingli himself served as chaplain to his troops and died in battle.

*See p. 89.

After Zwingli's death, the Reform in Zürich took a more moderate path under the leadership of Henry Bullinger. Although Zürich was now isolated politically from the other Swiss cantons, Bullinger corresponded with the reformers in Basel, Berne, and Geneva and made modifications in Zwingli's doctrine in an effort to produce a common confession for all the Swiss Reformed Churches. Bullinger's doctrines, along with those of Martin Bucer of Strasbourg, also influenced the development of Protestantism in England. In 1566, most Swiss Reformed Churches, including Geneva, accepted Bullinger's second Helvetic Confession. Bullinger's moderation made possible the transition of Reformed Protestantism from Zwingli to Calvin.

### Calvin

Jean Cauvin, known in English as John Calvin, was born in the northern French town of Noyon in 1509. His father, a local lawyer and civil administrator, had high ambitions for his son and sent him to the best schools: Paris for theology and Orléans for law. Until his mid-twenties Calvin thought of himself primarily as a man of letters, and although he later became a dedicated preacher and an authoritarian church leader, he retained his scholarly interests throughout his life. His first book was the *Commentary on Seneca's Treatise on Clemency* (1532), a typical product of Erasmian humanism. Soon thereafter, however, he experienced a sudden conversion, which transformed him into a seeker of knowledge of God. The Bible became his chief literary study and his guide and authority in knowing God and His Law. In Paris he became associated with dangerous friends, humanist reformers who publicly denounced the French king's persecution of men who criticized the Catholic Church. Calvin fled from France in 1534 and lived for a while in Basel and Italy before taking up residence in Geneva in 1536. It was during this period that he published the first edition of his most important work, the *Institutes of the Christian Religion.*

The *Institutes*, which was to be enlarged and perfected in later editions in both Latin and French, was a massive synthesis of Calvin's doctrines. It was the clearest and most authoritative statement of Protestant theology to come out of the Reformation, and it was to have appeal in more places than any other. Here was a convincing and logical—rather than emotional, as in Luther's case—demonstration of how man should live in close communion with his Creator. Calvin showed people that the experience of living according to high ideals made a mockery of materialistic pleasure-seeking. The main goal of the true Christian was to know God. As Creator He is known both through the outward universe and Holy Scripture; as Redeemer He is known through Scripture alone.

While Luther was primarily concerned with *how* man was saved, Calvin wanted to know what man was saved *for.* Calvin's famous doctrine of predestination has sometimes been misunderstood. God did indeed decree that some men would have eternal life and that others would suffer eternal damnation. Yet He was a merciful Savior as well as a stern Father. Those men whom He had selected for salvation could not see into His mind, but they could learn, through His Word, to know the meaning of Christ's sacrifice as overcoming the malignity of sin. Once they acquired this knowledge, they had to have faith in God's mercy and justice and stop worrying about their fate. If they felt their communion with God in their hearts, dedicated their behavior to His glorification, and partook regularly of the Lord's Supper—in which Calvin, unlike Zwingli, saw the true spiritual presence of Christ's sacrifice—they were justified in believing themselves to be among the elect. Thus, far from making people anxious and pessimistic about their salvation, Calvin's doctrine of predestination gave them confidence and hope.

The damned are those people who lack faith, whose behavior does not show a desire to glorify God, and who neglect the Lord's Supper. Alienation from God was Calvin's hell, which he and later Calvinist ministers vividly portrayed in terms of fire and brimstone. The purpose of their sermons was to remind those who felt saved that damnation too was an aspect of divine Providence. In a seemingly illogical, but very human, way Calvin and his followers were both for and against sin. They were for it as a lesson to themselves and against it as an affront to God. Sinners in their midst made the abstract conflict between good and evil more immediate and personal. Without them, knowledge of God's Will would have been less dramatic. On the other hand, the task of discovering and rooting out sinners from the community served the conscious end of doing God's Will and the unconscious end of justifying the austere lives of the elect. From a psychological rather than religious point of view the temptation to sin—that is, to indulge in nongodly forms of personal gratification—is both titillating and threatening. By discovering and punishing others who succumb to the temptation, one savors the forbidden act vicariously and then punishes oneself vicariously. Such an arrangement is more reassuring and more comfortable than wearing a hair shirt or beating oneself.

Since Calvin differed from Luther in wanting to make religion a dynamic social force, he was particularly concerned with the nature of a community of the elect. The fact that this community turned out to be the French-speaking Swiss city of Geneva seemed fortuitous, but to Calvin it was a manifestation of God's Will. Several years prior to his arrival there in 1536, Geneva's leading citizens had revolted against their Catholic bishop and their temporal overlord, the Duke of Savoy, and introduced the Reformation by throwing the images of the saints down the wells. But the municipal council was divided over religious matters, and a large section of the ordinary inhabitants were still Catholics at heart. The fiery Protestant evangelist William Farel could not make his views prevail. When Calvin happened to be passing through the city, Farel used all his persuasive powers to convince the young French scholar that God would condemn him to hell and damnation if he did not heed His call to build His church in Geneva. Calvin heeded the call and stayed.

Unlike Zwingli, Calvin did not gain the full backing of the civil magistrates immediately. His program called for a church that would regulate the religious and moral life of the community—including the right of excommunication—through pastors, teachers, elders, and deacons. The municipal council refused to give the church so much power and forced Calvin to leave the city. He spent the years 1538–41 in Bucer's Strasbourg, until unrest and lack of discipline in Geneva finally prompted the civil magistrates to call him back. Athough they did not accept all of his clerical program at once, they became captive to his religious message and eventually let him have his way in placing the church on a par with the state and giving it the power of excommunication. Another reason for Calvin's ultimate mastery in Geneva was the changing composition of the city's population. Calvin's preaching won over the majority of its thirteen thousand inhabitants. Those who remained Catholics were excommunicated and forced to leave, but they were more than replaced by six thousand Protestant refugees (most of them French), before Calvin's death in 1564. These people became his staunchest supporters in overcoming the hesitations of the civil magistrates.

By 1555 Calvin had completely made over Geneva into his version of the ideal Christian community. He had succeeded in dividing all legislative, judicial, and administrative functions between the municipal council and a church consistory of pastors, teachers, elders, and deacons. This division of civil and ecclesiastical functions was more realistic and more effective than Zwingli's attempt to place all power in the hands of godly magistrates. Calvin was a stern taskmaster. In addition to the regularly constituted authorities, he insisted that each citizen was his brother's keeper and should spy on his neighbor. Twice a year a commission of pastors and elders inspected every house in town to see that there were no superstitious pictures on the walls and that all residents were diligently attending the five weekly sermons and receiving the Lord's Supper regularly. The council passed edict after edict forbidding such ungodly things as card-playing, dice, light songs, and dancing. It even regulated the way people dressed, thus initiating the simple Puritan style that was to appear wherever Calvinism took root for over a century. The Bible served as the guide for everything, including the names with which infants were to be baptized. There were fines and punishments for all kinds of offenses, and the worst offense of all was open heresy. Calvin saw to it that the Spanish scholar Michael Servetus (1511–1553) was executed for publicly denying the doctrine of the Trinity in a Geneva congregation. The community of the elect had to deal mercilessly with such a crime. That was God's Will.

### *Anabaptists*

Once the Protestant reformers had rejected the exclusive authority of the Catholic Church to interpret God's Will, they opened the way for schisms among themselves. Luther, Zwingli, and Calvin had different ideas about the meaning of the Lord's Supper, the use of art and music as material aids to religious feeling, and the relationship between church and state. Yet all three men—and, of course, the Anglicans—agreed that every individual in a given community should belong to the same church and should fulfill his obligations to the state. They had wanted to restore the true church of early Christian times, but they did not go all the way. For during the first three centuries A.D. the Christian communities of the Roman Empire had been self-conscious minorities of people who had accepted adult baptism as a sign of their conversion and who had refused to serve the state as soldiers and

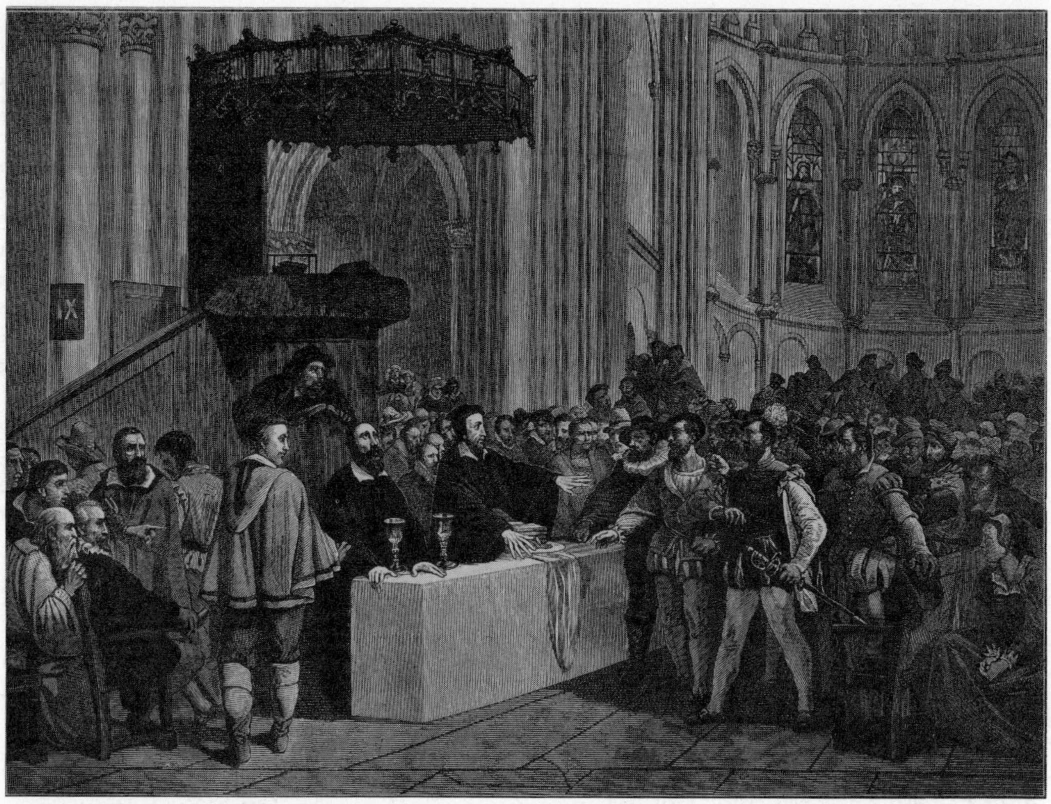

*Calvin's Geneva*

magistrates. Groups of men and women tried to restore this ideal in Switzerland in the 1520s and in Germany and the Netherlands during the following decades. Their enemies called then Anabaptists.

The Anabaptists, who lived in various parts of Europe, differed among themselves in many ways. Most of them were pacifists, but some were revolutionaries, like the group that took over and held the west German town of Münster by force in 1534–35. Some even abolished private property and practiced polygamy, which they justified from the Old Testament. But most of the Anabaptists shared the same three basic principles: (1) the church is a voluntary association; (2) church and state should be separate; (3) religious liberty should prevail. This program threatened all the existing churches, both Protestant and Catholic, for they all insisted that the church and the state had the same boundaries and that there was no room for dissenters within these boundaries.

The Catholics and all the other Protestants were as merciless with these radicals as the pagan Romans had been with their spiritual ancestors. Only their methods of execution were different. Instead of throwing their victims to the lions, the Catholics burned them and the Protestants drowned them. Zwingli and Calvin were especially disturbed by the heresy of rebaptism—hence the name *ana*-baptist—though the Anabapists denied that this was what they were doing, since infant baptism had no meaning for them. Luther viewed the Anabaptists' refusal to serve as soldiers and magistrates as a threat to the very existence of the state and hence seditious to it. The Catholic and Protestant authorities had executed tens of thousands of Anabaptists by the mid-sixteenth century in Northwestern and Central Europe. Those who managed to escape this blood bath fled to the loosely organized kingdoms of East Central Europe—especially Bohemia and Poland—where they survived as the Brethren,

Hutterites, and Mennonites. The Mennonites were to filter back into Germany, and eventually to North America, in the more tolerant eighteenth century.

### *Spread of Calvinism*

In the sixteenth century both Catholics and Protestants insisted on religious conformity for a whole community, but the Calvinists went farthest in trying to restore the interpenetration and identification of the church and the world. Actually, this ideal had been realized most fully in the period 450–1050 A.D., when there had been close cooperation between the secular monarchs and the church, and when the monastic orders—a kind of medieval elect—had been the keystone of this equilibrium. In Geneva the elect tried to impose its austere way of life on everybody else, thus eliminating any distinctions between the church and the world. Strong rulers protected the state churches, and state churches supported strong rulers, but ultimate sovereignty rested with the secular rulers.* Attempts to create the Kingdom of God on earth could not last in an emerging society of secular states.

This trend did not stop Calvinism from spreading to many parts of Northwestern and Central Europe in the mid-sixteenth century. Calvin had created a doctrine, a catechism, and a program of church discipline with great potential appeal. He also founded an academy in Geneva in 1559 for the instruction and training of ministers. Hundreds of Protestant leaders from other countries flocked to Geneva to study at Calvin's academy and then bring his teachings back to their native lands. They modified these teachings to suit local conditions, without abandoning their essence. Thus, in the western German state of the Palatinate, the Elector insisted on strong governmental control of doctrines and discipline. This modification of the Genevan model was later adopted by some Calvinists in England and Scotland. The English Calvinists under Elizabeth were to become particularly concerned about "purifying"—hence, the name Puritans—the Anglican Church of "popish" elements in the ritual, such as elaborate vestments, instrumental music, and incense. In 1560 John Knox, who had studied in Geneva, persuaded the Scottish parliament to accept a confession drawn up in the spirit of Calvin and to organize a state church, which was called Presbyterian. Elsewhere the Calvinists became a persecuted minority and emphasized the right to revolt against governments that interfered with the establishment of God's kingdom on earth. This was especially so in France, where Calvinists were known as Huguenots, and in the Netherlands, as well as in England. Refugees from these three countries also spread Calvinism to Germany, Poland, Bohemia, and Hungary. In most places the main enemy of the Calvinists was not the secularized state but the Counter-Reformation.

*See chapter III on the new monarchies.

## The Catholic Reformation

The Catholic Reformation was both a movement for reform *within* the Church and a campaign against Protestantism. The campaign against Protestantism, called the *Counter-Reformation*, involved the efforts of the Jesuits, the Inquisition, and the Hapsburg rulers of Spain and Austria to win Protestants and Catholic backsliders back to the Roman faith. These efforts achieved their main results after 1560 and will be discussed later. But they were sparked by a resurgence of religious feeling among Catholics and by the reforming work of the Council of Trent. These two developments emanated primarily from Spain and Italy in the first half of the sixteenth century.

### *The Spiritual Revival: "Methodical Prayer"*

Many Catholics revived their spiritual lives through the practice of "methodical prayer," sometimes pushed to the point of mysticism. This type of spiritual "exercise" had been invented by the medieval mystics and had been perfected by the Brethren of the Common Life. In the early 1500s it became popular in various parts of Europe, especially Spain. For at least an hour each day a person "exercised" his soul by means of prescribed forms of prayer and meditation designed to blot out the world around him and put him in personal communication with God.

This practice tended to make people's daily behavior conform to official doctrine and to remove doubts, hesitations, backsliding, and a separation of faith from life. It became an integral part of the lives of the clergy by the second half of the sixteenth century and was taken up by pious laymen as well. "Methodical prayer" was of major importance in reviving religious feeling among Catholics in the Reformation period.

A number of saintly men and women (e.g., St. Teresa of Avila) devised various forms of "methodical prayer," the best known being that of St. Ignatius Loyola (1491–1556). The *Spiritual Exercises* of this ex-soldier were to become the heart of the most influential religious order of modern times: the Jesuits. Loyola came from a knightly Basque family and until his thirtieth year led the life of a Spanish soldier and courtier. In 1521 he received a grave leg wound in the defense of Pamplona against the French. During his long and painful convalescence he devoted himself to reading about the lives of Christ and the saints. He renounced his former habits and dedicated himself to a religious career. When he was well enough to move about, he visited the shrine of Monserrat, confessed his sins, and distributed his worldy goods to the poor. Then he moved to Manresa, where he lived for eight months as a beggar and a self-punishing penitent. In Manresa, Loyola underwent a series of religious experiences and illuminations which formed the basis for his future career and were incorporated into his *Spiritual Exercises.*

This little book was a manual for disciplining the soul. The goal of its program of prayers and meditations was to provoke intense feelings of love and hate and to make people so hypersensitive to religious words and symbols that these would henceforth elicit a flood of images and emotions and lead the will irresistibly toward pious acts. All the senses were to come into play, so that it would be impossible to imagine hell without trembling with horror and revulsion or to think of Christ without one's body quivering with tenderness and one's heart melting with love. These "exercises" required many hours of concentration and reflection on one's own sins and on steeling oneself as a soldier of Christ. Here was a Christian discipline that made religion intensely emotional and personal. Only a minority of Catholics practiced it, but this minority helped revive the Catholic faith in the sixteenth century.

### New Religious Orders

Several new religious orders were founded at this time in Italy with the purpose of reviving the pastoral and charitable calling of St. Francis of Assissi. Their numbers and their zeal showed that Catholicism was far from dead in the homeland of the Renaissance. The inspiration for their development came from a kind of guild called the Oratory of Divine Love, which was founded by a group of pious men in Rome in 1513. These men earnestly felt that the soul should be consumed with a wholly disinterested love of God, and that one must devote oneself wholeheartedly to the needs of one's fellow man. Since the late fifteenth century Italy had been racked by wars, plagues, famine, and a new scourge, syphilis. The new religious orders devoted themselves not only to preaching but also to helping the victims of these calamities, especially by founding hospitals.

The members of these Italian orders were called clerks regular. Like monks, they were well-organized, well-educated, conditioned to obedience, and detached from the temptations of a worldly life. Unlike monks, however, they had no local ties and no requirements for group participation in liturgical and community observances. They were priests living according to a rule (hence regular) but they subordinated their own concerns to furthering the welfare of other people. Many of the ecclesiastics who helped reform the papacy and the Church in the mid-sixteenth century also came from their ranks. Actually, though, the most important order of clerks regular for both the reform within the Church and the campaign against Protestantism was not Italian, but international. It was Loyola's Society of Jesus.

Once Loyola had dedicated his life to religion, his first idea had been to go to the Holy Land as a simple friar and con-

*St. Ignatius Loyola, founder of the Society of Jesus*

vert the Muslims. He went there in 1523 but he was soon forced to leave. When he returned to Spain he broadened his goal to teaching others the way to God as he had discovered it himself at Manresa. In order to become a teacher, he had to acquire an education himself. Hence, from 1524 until 1535 he went to school, starting in a Latin class with little boys of eleven in Barcelona and finishing in theology at the University of Paris. In Paris he formed a group of six disciples among his fellow students, and in 1534 they bound themselves to poverty and chastity and set out to work for God—if possible, in the Holy Land, if not, then in the service of the pope. After they completed their studies they tried unsuccessfully to reach Palestine. Then they gathered in Rome, where, in 1537, Loyola experienced a revelation in which he claimed that God had "set him along with his Son." Thus, when he and his companions decided to form a religious order, they named it the Society of Jesus—popularly known thereafter as the Jesuits. In 1540 the pope gave them a charter. A year later Loyola was elected general of the order, and his six companions took their solemn vows.

Loyola directed the activities of his order from Rome until his death in 1556. Its original aims, aside from the sanctification of its own members, were the defense of the faith and the promotion of spiritual health through the usual priestly activities of preaching and administering the sacraments. In addition, the Jesuits set themselves the special task of instructing boys in the truths of Christianity. The rule of the Jesuits differed from that of the monastic orders: it freed them from common recitation of the church liturgy, severe bodily mortifications, and fasts. Their lives were active, not contemplative. The novitiate of a Jesuit was longer and more rigorous than that in other orders, and he received an advanced education in the humanities, philosophy, and theology. He was required to respond to commands "like a corpse that one can turn in any direction." At the same time, he had to be capable of giving an up-to-date and intelligent presentation of the faith he preached to Catholic and infidel alike. There were three grades of membership. Out of about 1,000 members in 1556, only forty-three had reached the top grade, which entitled them to take a special vow directly to the pope and be sent on foreign missions. By that time the activities of the Jesuits included not only missionary work in heathen lands (mainly Asia—especially through St. Francis Xavier—and Africa) and education, but also engagement in the fight against Protestantism in Europe.

The Jesuits were the spearhead of the Counter-Reformation in their teaching and their pastoral activities. They decided that the only way to save Catholicism in the Holy Roman Empire was to train a new generation of priests and laymen in a more positive and confident kind of faith, and they founded colleges there for this purpose. Later on, rich laymen, including some Protestants, sent their sons to Jesuit colleges in other countries, not only because of their high academic standards, but also because of their instruction in athletics and in the modern social graces. The Jesuits also developed a talent for handling confessions; they convinced the sinner that he had not really sinned at all unless he had fully intended to do so. This talent, plus their other merits, ingratiated the Jesuits with the rulers of Bavaria, Austria, and Poland, with whose help they were to stamp out Protestantism in these lands by 1590. St. Peter Canisius, working out of Cologne, was largely responsible for stemming the tide of Lutheranism and reviving Catholicism in the Lower Rhineland areas of Germany and the Netherlands. The Jesuits championed a personal and emotional religion, combining the rigors of "methodical prayer" with a vivid and dramatic style of church art, including lifelike wax statues, painted angels that seemed to fly down from the ceiling, and sumptuous church buildings. Finally, the Jesuits played an important role in reaffirming official Catholic theology at the Council of Trent.

### *Council of Trent*

The first pope willing to summon a general church council was Paul III (1534–1549). He was still a Renaissance pope in his political and diplomatic style, but he was determined to reform the Church from within. As a first step, he renovated the College of Cardinals by appointing men dedicated to reform, though there were still some very worldly cardinals left. In 1536 he issued a summons for a General Council, though for various reasons—mainly the wars between Charles V and the king of France—it did not meet until 1545. Meanwhile, Pope Paul III appointed a committee of cardinals and other prelates to advise him on what reforms were needed. The opening statement of the committee's report said that the Christian Church was in ruins and that the evil was especially active in the Roman curia itself. The report censured the preceding popes for their hypocrisy and selfishness and for their sale of offices and dispensations for profit. Many of the report's recommendations for the reform of abuses were adopted at the council, which finally met at Trent, in northeastern Italy, in three separate sessions: December 1545–September 1549, May 1551–April 1552, and January 1562–December 1563. Only a small proportion of the eligible members of the Catholic hierarchy attended the meetings, yet its work completed the reform within the Roman Catholic Church and became the basis for modern Catholicism down to the present.

On doctrine the Council of Trent proposed only to make clear the official Catholic position on specific points disputed by the Protestant reformers. Its references were to wrong doctrines, not to individual reformers. The Council reaffirmed the official Catholic view: man's nature is tainted by original sin, but not irredeemably compromised; God offers His grace to everyone. The core of Catholicism is not original sin, but redemption through Christ. Each man can earn this free gift of grace through love of God, which he demonstrates through faith and good works. Each man chooses to accept it or reject it of his own free will. The Church alone is his guide in interpreting Christ's teachings, which include the Holy Scriptures and the writings of the Church Fathers. It alone administers the seven sacraments, clarified at Trent, which are the visible signs of God's grace. All Catholics are compelled to accept this doctrine on pain of excommunication. Despite the efforts of the Jesuits, however, the Council of Trent did not declare the pope to be infallible. The doctrine of papal infallibility did not become official until 1870.

The main reforms of the Council of Trent consisted in eliminating abuses within the clergy. To raise the educational level of the parish priests the council required every diocese to have a seminary to train them. It strengthened the authority of the bishops, forbade them to hold more than one benefice, and required them to reside in their dioceses. It also placed severe restrictions on the wandering friars, many of whom had loose morals and taught superstitious notions to the uneducated masses. When it adjourned the council handed the following tasks over to the Holy See, which completed them in the next six years: (1) publication of an *Index* of books forbidden to read, (2) compilation of a catechism for the use of parish priests, (3) revision of the breviary, (4) revision of the missal.

The next two popes, particularly Pius V (1566 – 1572), completed the reform within the Church and then took up the work of the Counter-Reformation in earnest. The "Holy Office" of the General Roman Inquisition, founded in 1542, tried an increasing number of suspected heretics, including a few men connected with the Oratory of Divine Love. Spain's territorial conquests in Italy* also helped Jesuit influence to repress Italian thought. Outside of Italy, Spain introduced its own Inquisition into most of its far-flung possessions. In 1559 the Spanish Inquisition condemned some of the writings of Erasmus and certain manuals of "methodical prayer," and publicly burned a group of suspected heretics at the stake. It was soon to become the chief nonmilitary instrument of Philip II's anti-Protestant crusade.

## POSTSCRIPT: PRINTING

Printing from movable type, which was first introduced in Europe in the middle of the fifteenth century, initiated cultural changes that made it possible for Europeans to become modern before any other peoples of the world. It did this by influencing not only what they thought but also how they thought and felt. Print emphasized the visual over the other senses. The repetitive, lineal patterns of the printed page conditioned people to view all kinds of problems in ways that could be expressed in such patterns. As with movable type, the breaking up and rearranging of actions, functions, and roles could be applied wherever desired. Scientists in the late Middle Ages had already discovered the principle of translating nonvisual matters of motion and energy into visual terms. Printing applied this principle to writing and language, thus making it possible to codify and transmit every kind of learning. By doing so, printing initiated a technological breakthrough whereby experience could be processed through "linear thinking," which emphasized quantification and repeatibility.

Thus the change that began to set literate Europeans apart from all the other civilized peoples of the world was not the

*See p. 114.

content of Renaissance art and thought but rather their new modes of thought and imagination. Beginning in the Renaissance, Europeans were moving in the direction of visualized measurement and quantification of life. There was much resistance to this change, especially among artists and men of letters, who continually lamented its effects in numbing the other senses, relegating religious and aesthetic experiences to the realm of the "irrational," and divorcing science from art. Nevertheless, this kind of specialization by dissociation was the basis of the power and efficiency of European civilization. Printing made possible a technology tending to process experience by homogenizing it. With this technology European society was eventually able to control natural forces and organize human effort in ways undreamed of elsewhere.

The new effects of printing on European thought and feeling took hold slowly at first. From the mid-fifteenth to the mid-seventeenth centuries one of the principal tasks of print was to serve as a mass medium for an earlier culture; just as TV today retransmits old movies, so in the sixteenth century the great body of printed matter was of medieval origin. There is an exact parallel between the popularity of medieval romances of chivalry in early printed books and the popularity of "Westerns" in recent TV programming. Next to these medieval romances most people read illustrated books of hours, almanacs, the Bible, and prayer books. Students and teachers at the universities, a smaller minority than now, benefited from printed editions of classical texts and the major treatises of the traditional scholastic arsenal.

Nevertheless, the new modes of thought and feeling conditioned by printing affected many of the developments of the early modern period, as suggested by the following quotations from Marshall McLuhan's *The Gutenberg Galaxy.*

"Renaissance Italy became a kind of Hollywood collection of sets of antiquity, and the new visual antiquarianism of the Renaissance provided an avenue to power for men of any class." (p. 119) During the Reformations ". . . The homogeneity of the printed page seemed to inspire a subliminal faith in the validity of the printed Bible as bypassing the traditional oral authority of the Church. . . . It was as if print, uniform and repeatable commodity that it was, had the power of creating a new hypnotic superstition of the book as independent of and uncontaminated by human agency." (p. 145) "The Machiavellian mind and the merchant mind are at one in their simple faith in the power of segmental division to rule all—in the dichotomy of power and morals and of money and morals." (p. 174) (Marshall McLuhan, *The Gutenberg Galaxy*, Univ. of Toronto Press, 1962. paperback edition, 1966.)

: : :

Like the Renaissance, the Reformations made a permanent difference between those countries that experienced them and those that did not. In Eastern Europe the Orthodox populations of Russia and Turkey were untouched by the Protestant Reformation, though the Jesuits were to make a few Catholic converts among those in Lithuania.† After having inspired the Catholic Reformation, Italy and Spain succumbed to the Inquisition and the austerity of Philip II. The Reformation that began in 1517 with Luther's Ninety-Five Theses was over in 1560 only in Northern Germany, the Scandinavian countries, and the Baltic states. Great Britain, France, and the Netherlands were to be torn by religious strife for almost another hundred years; the Calvinists were still on the march, and here their influence was to have a profound effect. In southern Germany and Bohemia the Jesuits and the Hapsburgs were to restore Catholicism between 1618 and 1648 during the bloodiest religious war in European history.

Nevertheless, the intensity and extension of religious concern between 1517 and 1648 did not bring a corresponding decrease in the flow of energy and activity in a secular direction. Neither Calvinist nor Jesuit zeal could destroy the cultural innovations of the Renaissance, for these innovations expressed the changing ways in which Europe's educated elites lived

†See p. 109.

and thought. From double-entry bookkeeping and Machiavellian politics to education and the arts, the secularization of European civilization was an irreversible development. Although the leaders of the Renaissance and the Reformations were still medieval in some ways, and their original energizing myths had been reactionary rather than progressive, yet their willingness to change and the dynamism they exhibited in both secular and religious matters were definitely modern.

## SUGGESTED READINGS


Ferguson, Wallace K., *The Renaissance in Historical Thought.* New York: Harper and Row, n.d. Torchbook.*

Excellent summary of varying interpretations over five centuries.

Helton, Tinsley, ed., *The Renaissance: A Reconsideration of the Theories of the Age.* Madison, Wis.: Univ. of Wisconsin Press, 1961.*

Based on a scholarly symposium. Brings Ferguson's account up to date.

Burckhardt, Jacob, *The Civilization of the Renaissance in Italy.* 2 vols. New York: Harper and Row, 1958. Torchbook.*

Written over a century ago, this famous classic retains its fascination. But most scholars no longer accept Burckhardt's view.

Baron, Hans, *The Crisis of the Early Renaissance: Civic Humanism and Republican Liberty in an Age of Classicism and Tyranny.* 2 vols. Princeton, N.J.: Princeton Univ. Press, n.d.*

A pioneer work of the newer scholarship. For a short general treatment incorporating Baron's views, see:

Hay, Denys, *The Italian Renaissance in Its Historical Background.* New York: Cambridge Univ. Press, 1961.*

Bishop, Morris, *Petrarch and His World.* Bloomington, Ind.: Indiana Univ. Press, 1964.

A judicious and graceful study of "the first modern man" and his world.

Brucker, Gene, *Renaissance Florence.* New York: Wiley, 1969.

Cassirer, Ernst, Paul O. Kristeller, and John H. Randall, eds. *The Renaissance Philosophy of Man.* Chicago: Univ. of Chicago Press, 1955.*

Selections from six representative thinkers of the Renaissance, with critical introductions.

Kristeller, Paul O., *Renaissance Thought.* New York: Harper and Row, 1961. Torchbook.*

Scholarly essays by one of the great modern authorities on humanism.

Berenson, Bernard, *Italian Painters of the Renaissance.* Rev. ed. Greenwich, Conn.: New York Graphic Society, 1957. Meridian.*

The classic presentation.

Gombrich, E. H., *The Story of Art.* 9th ed. New York: Oxford Univ. Press, 1958.

The brief section on the Renaissance is excellent.

Pevsner, Nikolaus, *An Outline of European Architecture.* Baltimore: Penguin Books, 1960. Pelican.*

Excellent on the Renaissance.

Chabod, Federico, *Machiavelli and the Renaissance.* Trans. Davis Moore. Cambridge, Mass.: Harvard Univ. Press, 1958.

A stimulating interpretation.

Elton, Geoffrey R., *Reformation Europe, 1517–1559.* New York: Harper-Row, 1966.*
A fine, up-to-date interpretation.

Dickens, Arthur G., *Reformation and Society in Sixteenth Century Europe.* New York: Harcourt Brace and World, n.d.*

Harbison, E. Harris, *The Christian Scholar in the Age of the Reformation.* New York: Charles Scribner's Sons, 1956.*
A fine study of Christian Humanism.

Phillips, Margaret M., *Erasmus and the Northern Renaissance.* New York: Collier, n.d.*
A good popular account.

Bainton, Roland H., *Here I Stand: A Life of Martin Luther.* Nashville, Tenn.: Abingdon Press, 1959. Apex Books.*
The authoritative biography—sympathetic and thorough. Stresses religious aspects of the Reformation.

Barraclough, Geoffrey, *The Origins of Modern Germany.* New York: G. P. Putnam's Sons, 1967*
Excellent introduction to the medieval setting of the Lutheran Reformation.

Holborn, Hajo, *A History of Modern Germany: The Reformation.* Vol. I. New York: Alfred A. Knopf, 1959.
An authoritative work—stresses political aspects of the Reformation.

Rilliet, Jean, *Zwingli: The Third Man of the Reformation.* Trans. H. Knight. Philadelphia: The Westminster Press, 1964.
Sympathetic and scholarly.

McNeill, John T., *The History and Character of Calvinism.* New York: Oxford Univ. Press, 1954.
The standard work.

Hughes, Philip, *A Popular History of the Reformation.* Garden City, N.Y.: Doubleday and Co., 1957.*
By an eminent Catholic scholar. Especially good on the Catholic Reformation.

Bainton, Roland H., *The Age of the Reformation.* Princeton, N.J.: D. Van Nostrand, 1956.
An Anvil original.*
A comprehensive selection of the writings of the great reformers.

McLuhan, Marshall, *The Gutenberg Galaxy.* Toronto: University of Toronto Press, 1962.*

*Paperback

CHAPTER III

# EUROPE BETWEEN MEDIEVAL AND MODERN TIMES: POLITICAL CONSOLIDATION AND OVERSEAS EXPANSION

Although the leaders of the Renaissance and Reformation proposed new ideas of what the world should be like, they concerned themselves mainly with forms of thought, art, and faith. With few exceptions, such as Salutati, More, Calvin, and Loyola, they left the practical development of new institutions and new techniques of organization to kings, generals, businessmen, explorers, and lawyers. These men reorganized the political, diplomatic, military, and economic life of Western and Central Europe and began the exploration, exploitation, and colonization of other parts of the world. Their activities, in turn, produced new ways of gaining wealth and power. Nations and social groups that adopted these ways forged ahead of those that did not.

These changes took place over such a long period of time that people were often unaware of what was happening. Although its origins date as far back as 1300, the modern state did not reach full development anywhere until around 1700; and the first phase of modern capitalism and European expansion overseas lasted approximately two hundred years—from 1450 to 1650. Furthermore, setbacks to and reactions against the dominant trends were many, and parts of Europe were completely untouched by them. Nevertheless, between the discovery of America in 1492 and the permanent division of Europe into independent sovereign states by 1560, there occurred a number of dramatic events which clearly showed that European civilization was changing.

## THE BEGINNINGS OF THE MODERN EUROPEAN STATE

The Renaissance and the Reformation paved the way for the development of the modern state in several respects. They made it possible for Europe's monarchs to free themselves completely from the dominance of the medieval Church and to base their authority on purely secular principles. The Renaissance secularized politics and introduced the professional administrator, the professional general, and the professional diplomat. In most places where the Reformation occurred it eventually led to the subordination of national churches to national states. At first, some reformers—both Protestant and Catholic—wanted their church to have an independent existence, but such an arrangement was impossible in the face of the revived religious passions of the sixteenth century. On the one hand, political opponents of the crown used religion to challenge its authority. This challenge was to become most serious in France and the Netherlands in the latter third of the sixteenth century. On the other hand, the crown used religion to bolster its political power and to stimulate patriotism. The so-called wars of religion increasingly involved constitutional issues at home and power politics in the international arena.

Both the form of the state and relations between states changed in the sixteenth century. In general, the larger, stronger states triumphed over the smaller, weaker ones, and national monarchs consolidated their power at home by restricting the "liberties" of nobles, towns, and representative assemblies. The larger states—especially France, Austria, and Spain—were still held together mainly by dynastic ties, with peripheral and recently acquired provinces retaining their own cultures and laws. Independent middle-sized states began to disappear. This tendency was especially evident in Italy, where only Venice survived as a power after 1560. Elsewhere, Wales, Burgundy, Granada, and Novgorod-the-Great were absorbed by England, France, Castile, and Russia respectively. Neither the "bastard feudalism" of the late fifteenth century nor Charles V's "universal monarchy" worked. The modern state acknowledged no sovereignty other than its own and began to compete with other sovereign states for power. Dynastic and religious motives still obscured the interests of the state as such, but these interests increasingly influenced foreign policy, even to the point of bringing about temporary alliances with religious enemies and traditional dynastic rivals—as when England allied herself with France against Charles V.

### The New Monarchies

In its ideal form the modern state is an integrated society, at once a community and a power. It is a community insofar as it has the unconditional agreement of its members to cooperate, a high degree of division of labor, and a belief in a common good—more or less broadly and clearly defined. It is a power insofar as it possesses a monopoly over the legitimate use of force and can exercise its authority directly on all individuals within its borders. No European state had achieved this ideal by 1560. But France, England, and Spain were moving toward it and setting an example for others.

Since the thirteenth century the kings of France, England, and the Iberian Peninsula had been strengthening the powers and the public image of the medieval monarchy. They developed their royal councils from private advisory bodies into public ministries, extended the authority and number of royal officials and royal law courts, and used their representative assemblies to gain additional revenue and public support for their policies. At the same time, political theorists began to identify the king with the state and to say that the rights and powers of the crown endured, whatever happened to the individual who wore the crown. Thus, the king never died. He had two bodies, one physical and personal, one metaphysical and immortal. When his physical body died, his incarnation of the undying principle of monarchy passed on to his heir. This theory explains the meaning of the phrase: "The king is dead, long live the king!" In France, for example, the mystical body of the dead king was treated as if it were still alive until the coronation of the new king, which might occur many weeks—or even months—later. During the intervening period the high dignitaries of the realm continued to act out the ceremonies due a reigning sovereign in front of the king's regally decorated coffin.

Every state has some kind of constitution. Whether written down or merely implied in the traditions, customs, and institutions of the society concerned, it defines the relationships between the rulers and the ruled. In other words, the constitution of a state *is* its form of government. In the late fifteenth century the kings of France, England, and Spain consciously tried to change the constitutions of their realms in order to increase their powers. Their efforts to do this earned them the label New Monarchs. They gave new functions to medieval traditions, customs, and institutions, and they created new agencies of strong, central government. Their progress was aided by a widespread desire among their subjects for a strong leader. The king thus acquired the aura of a hero. By 1560 the transition from the medieval to the modern form of monarchy was well under way. But there was strong resistance to this change in most places, and the constitutional issue was not easily settled.

### France

The kings of France were in many ways the most successful of the New Monarchs. At the end of the fifteenth century France was the largest, most populous (twelve million people), and most advanced state in Christendom. After more than a hundred years of devastating wars her kings had managed to expel the English and to secure their own authority with a royal army and the right to levy taxes without summoning the Estates General, which was not to meet between 1484 and 1560. Though still a conglomeration of semifeudal provinces and special interest groups, France had begun to acquire a feeling of being a national community.

The first of the New Monarchs, Louis XI (1461–1483), reasserted the authority of the Crown over what had previously been semi-independent principalities and reduced the importance of the princely and ducal parties. We have already seen that he annexed the Duchy of Burgundy in 1477. In the 1480s the territories of the extinct house of Anjou also reverted to the French Crown; they included the strategic county of Bar, on the eastern frontier, and Provence, with its port of Marseilles, which opened Mediterranean commerce to France. Using the considerable revenues and powers at his disposal, Louis XI expanded the royal army and strengthened the machinery of the central government. His successors Charles VIII (1483–1498), Louis XII (1498–1515), Francis I (1515–1547), and Henry II (1547–1559) consolidated these gains and put France on the path toward a strong, centralized monarchy. Almost constant wars kept the nobility—which still comprised the officer corps of the army—busy, and prevented it from causing disorders at home.

Francis I brought the New Monarchy to the peak of its power. In 1516 he gained a large degree of control over the Catholic Church in France through the Concordat of Bologna. Like his predecessors, he swelled the ranks of the royal officials with non-nobles, especially lawyers, and divided their functions in an increasingly complex bureaucracy and judicial system. In this way he increased the directness of his control over individual subjects at the expense of local officials and local courts. The lawyers, in turn, bolstered the royal authority with a body of juristic opinion based on various legal traditions, but particularly on the absolutist principles of Roman law. They said that the king derived his power directly from God and that he could make his own laws without regard for tradition, custom, or the historic "liberties" of any interest group. The king's pleasure was the law of the land.

Like the other French kings of the first half of the sixteenth century, Francis I was an ambitious, capable, and popular ruler. Combining Castiglione's refined courtier with Machiavelli's opportunistic prince, he personified the ideal Renaissance monarch. He won the gratitude of the growing merchant class by not overtaxing it and by maintaining order. Although some of his officials tried to upset existing constitutional forms in order to augment their own power, Francis himself was careful to show respect for the privileges of various provinces, towns, and social classes. While retaining their loyalty in this way he gained an increasing proportion of his revenue from the sale of offices and the one-tenth of the Church's income to which he was entitled. Francis patronized the arts and built a sumptuous Renaissance court at Fontainebleau, about forty miles southwest of Paris. This new court, created in the image of a powerful monarchy, attracted a new class of royal servants, to whom Francis sold, or gave, offices, honors, privileges, and noble titles. He consolidated his own power by keeping the different privileged groups in constant rivalry and making them all dependent on him.

Still, the apparent power of the French king had its practical limits. He usually made his will prevail when he intervened personally in some affair. Yet he could not intervene everywhere nor all the time, given the small number of officials—one for every 1,250 inhabitants in the early sixteenth century compared with one for ever seventy inhabitants in the 1930s—and the slowness of transportation and communication in what was for that era an immense country. Local authorities preserved a good deal of initiative in the provinces, which still maintained their political and cultural diversity. Medieval traditions of local loyalty, privilege, and corporate social organization died hard. Hence royal institutions outside their framework were still viewed as temporary expedients to meet the needs of diverse and constantly changing situations. A man or a group of men who should have had specialized functions had, in reality, a collection of ill-defined and variable powers and rights over a complex of seignorial, urban, and ecclesiastical jurisdictions. Finally, the power of the king was limited by the very officials he created. Once they had bought their offices, they held them as property rights and could not be legally deprived of them. With this kind of security they began to act like a new privileged class. They enriched themselves at the expense of the royal treasury, which was already being depleted by continual wars, and furthered their own interests, which were not always those of the king.

#### *England*

When Henry Tudor became King Henry VII (1485–1509), the first of England's New Monarchs, the country had come a long way from the glorious days of Henry V (1413–1422). The nobles and common soldiers had rallied behind that royal hero and had helped him to conquer more than half of France. But after his untimely death the English, by 1453, lost all of France except the port of Calais. Then, from 1455 to 1485, the great families of York and Lancaster fought each other for the crown in the Wars of the Roses. The noble claimants slaughtered one another to such an extent that in effect they reduced their power as a class and England's rank among the European states. Indeed, when Pope Alexander VI drew up the first diplomatic ranking of the Christian powers in 1493, he placed England below Portugal. Although the majority of England's four million people was not directly involved in these feudal wars, the last of their kind there, it longed for an end to the prevailing anarchy. Thus the English welcomed the end of the Wars of the Roses and the accession of Henry VII to the throne. The new king promised peace and stability and established the Tudor dynasty, which was to rule for over a century. He dealt with the remaining rebellious nobles by prohibiting them from maintaining private armies and by setting up the Court of the Star Chamber to punish them.* By staying out of foreign wars and by developing an efficient, if arbitrary, royal financial system, he increased his revenues and at his death left a surplus in the treasury.

One of the most original political moves of Henry VII and the later Tudors was to seek the support of the lesser gentry and the middle classes. Henry VII created a new peerage from their ranks, which greatly outnumbered the decimated older nobility. His son, Henry VIII (1509–1547), enabled these new peers to enrich themselves with the lands of the dissolved monasteries. Some of the impoverished backwoods gentry remained henchmen of the great lords. In general, though, they served as the king's unpaid justices of the peace, as the local administrators of all decrees of the central government, and as its tax collectors. The merchants did not challenge the political power of the gentry and the Crown as long as they were permitted to make more money in commerce and through the capitalistic organization of household manufacturing.† Under Henry VIII middle-class lawyers like Thomas Cromwell and Thomas More rose to the highest ranks in the royal government.

Like Francis I, Henry VIII had all the attributes of a Renaissance monarch. He

*See p. 103

†See pp. 136–138.

*The House of Lords with Henry VIII on the throne*

prided himself on his versatility. When young, he was not only slim and somewhat frivolous, but also an accomplished athlete, musician, and sailor. Even when he became old and fat and ruthless he continued to live life to the fullest. The majority of his subjects idolized him as a person, even when they resented his policies.

With the great nobles largely subdued and the gentry and middle classes in tow, Henry was able to go further than any other monarch of his day in asserting the complete sovereignty of the state. Nevertheless, he had to share this sovereignty with Parliament, which during the Tudor period lost its medieval cast and became the king's equal partner. Only Parliament could change the law of the land and grant new taxes. Yet, in practice, Henry — and Elizabeth I later on — managed to get Parliament to do his bidding. As we have noted, he forced Parliament to pass the Act of Supremacy, which gave the English monarchy the biggest single addition to its powers since the time of William the Conqueror.

In England, as in France, old agencies were transformed, and, when this was not possible, new ones were created for the real work to be done—with varying degrees of success. Parliament was the outstanding example of an old institution acquiring new functions. Other examples included the offices of the king's household. Thomas Cromwell made his office of king's secretary into an all-powerful ministry by 1534. He also tried unsuccessfully to centralize the government's machinery for collecting taxes. Like France, England failed to solve the problem of securing revenue adequate for the needs of a modern state, and the treasuries of both countries were empty by the end of the 1550s.

England had a more uniform and more centralized judicial system than any of the New Monarchies. Her Common Law was the same for all social classes and all parts of the realm. To England's existing system of national courts, Chancellors Wolsey and More added the Court of Chancery to act on the growing body of administrative law. In addition, the Court of the Star Chamber, originally established to suppress disorder and to punish men too powerful and influential for the ordinary courts to handle, soon began taking private disputes out of the hands of the Court of Common Pleas by introducing imaginary riots into bills of complaint. As the king's ministers could pass arbitrary judgments in the Court of the Star Chamber, this court became a major instrument for strengthening royal power.

### Spain

In the late Middle Ages, Spain developed in a different setting from that of England and France. The story of her political and religious unification and the strengthening of her central government involves dynastic marriages and intrigue, mass expulsions and conversions of Muslims and Jews, monarchs playing off the cities against the nobles and the nobles against the cities, and the use of the Church and its institutions for political ends. The New Monarchs who launched these policies were King Ferdinand of Aragon (1479–1516) and Queen Isabella of Castile (1474–1504).

In the late fifteenth century the Iberian Peninsula was still divided into a number of political, ethnic, and religious units. The largest kingdom, that of Leon and Castile had over six million inhabitants. In the west, the Kingdom of Portugal had less than two million; in the east the Kingdom of Aragon had less than one million, excluding the inhabitants of Sardinia and Sicily; in the south the Kingdom of Granada had about half a million; and in the north, the Kingdom of Navarre had less than one hundred thousand inhabitants. The population of Granada was almost exclusively Muslim, and there were several hundred thousand Muslims in Castile and Aragon. There were also about a quarter of a million Jews, mainly in Castile but also in Aragon. The majority of people in Castile spoke Castilian Spanish; in southern Aragon the Valencian dialect of Spanish was spoken, but in northern Aragon, whose capital was Barcelona, the language was Catalan. The Muslims spoke Arabic, the Jews spoke Spanish. Basque was spoken in parts of Navarre and northern Castile, and Portugal had her own language.

The marriage of Ferdinand and Isabella in 1469 was the first step in transforming all the Iberian Peninsula except Portugal into a politically united and exclusively Catholic state. At first the "union" of Aragon and Castile was purely dynastic. Each state retained its own Córtes, political institutions, laws, courts, armed forces, taxation, and coinage. Castilians and Aragonese continued to consider themselves separate nations and to be suspicious of each other. It was Castile that colonized the New World, conquered Granada (1492), and annexed Navarre (1515). Aragon was to retain many of its rights and privileges until the middle of the sixteenth century, but it was never able to break the tie with Castile completely. Meanwhile, Ferdinand and Isabella's strengthening of the central government in Castile created the basis for Spanish power.

As in England and France, the New Monarchs in Spain set themselves the task

of taking power away from the nobles and concentrating it in the royal government. In the past, the Castilian nobles had been able to gain Crown lands from weak kings, to engage in feudal wars, and, in general, to challenge the royal authority. Ferdinand and Isabella ended this situation in 1480 by summoning the Córtes of Toledo (the capital of Castile until Philip II transferred it to Madrid in 1560). In order to avoid new taxes, the Córtes, dominated by representatives of the cities, authorized the monarchs to get the revenue they requested by taking back former Crown lands from the nobles. It also banned the building of new fortified castles and the waging of private war; Ferdinand and Isabella even demolished many existing castles. They gradually removed the great nobles from important political offices, replacing them with university-trained jurists of humble birth, and forcing them to live at the royal court. At the same time they allowed them to retain their privileges, including exemption from taxation, and even granted them new honorific titles. Finally, the Crown took over the administration and revenues of the semi-independent military orders from the nobility, though financial pressure was to force it to mortgage and sell the estates of these orders after 1529.

Ferdinand and Isabella gained the support of the Córtes and the cities in adapting another medieval institution to the needs of a modern state. This was the *Hermandad* (Brotherhood), a municipal militia. They used it in their war against Granada (1482–1492), thus augmenting the strength of the royal army, and then transformed it into an instrument for maintaining civil order in the countryside. The new *Hermandad* received extraordinary powers to prosecute and punish crimes not yet under the jurisdiction of the ordinary courts: robbery, arson, and, especially, rebellion against the royal authority. It succeeded in suppressing crime and disorder, keeping the local nobility in line, and making the royal authority strong and universally respected. By 1498 its task was completed, and many of its activities were transferred to other agencies. Meanwhile the cities, having served their purpose in supporting the Crown against the nobles, were in turn brought more directly under royal control. From 1480 on, a *corregidor* (corrector) appointed by the Crown sat on every municipal council in Castile. These *corregidores* were the eyes and ears of the monarch and they acted as his administrative agents throughout the realm. The Córtes too gradually declined in importance in Castile, though not yet in Aragon, as Ferdinand and Isabella extended their own power. Under their successors the monarchy was to establish its exclusive right to make and enforce laws.

When Isabella died in 1504 the future union of Castile and Aragon was assured because the Córtes of both states had taken an oath of allegiance to Joanna, the daughter of Ferdinand and Isabella. Joanna's husband, Philip, was the son of Maximilian of Austria and Mary of Burgundy. The heir of this couple would therefore inherit not only Castile, with her growing overseas possessions, and Aragon, with her Italian possessions, but also the domains of the Austrian Hapsburgs and of the House of Burgundy, which consisted mainly of the Netherlands and the Franche-Comté. This heir was to be the future Emperor Charles V. Before Charles became the king of Spain in 1516, however, Ferdinand carried on a campaign of intrigue to retain control of Cas-

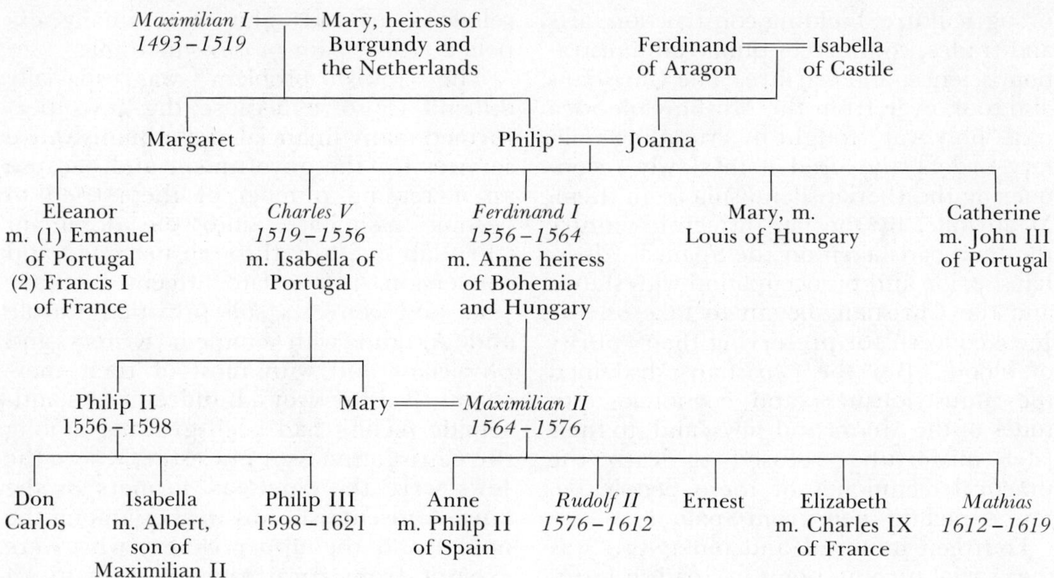


*The House of Hapsburg in the sixteenth century. Names and dates of Holy Roman Emperors are given in italics.*

tile. He was still the king of Aragon, to be succeeded by Joanna upon his death, and he tried to deprive Joanna and Philip of their rights in Castile. Two accidents helped him in this endeavor. Philip died in 1506, and Joanna went mad. Joanna's insanity allowed Ferdinand to rule Castile in her name until his death in 1516. Then the aged Cardinal Ximénes de Cisneros served as regent until Charles arrived a year later.

Although Charles V was the king of Spain—where he was called Charles I—for almost forty years, he showed little concern for that country and was viewed as a foreigner there. He had been raised in the Netherlands, he spoke no Spanish, and many of his court officials were Burgundians. His main interest in Spain was the revenue and troops it could provide for him for his wars elsewhere in Europe. In 1520 the popular and radical elements (*Comuneros*) in the Castilian towns rebelled against Charles' rule. Only when this revolt threatened the estates of the nobles did they finally help the king repress it. By late 1521 the power of the monarchy was restored in Castile and was not seriously threatened again under the Hapsburgs. Charles allowed the towns to keep some of their autonomy, but he reestablished the powers of the *corregidores.* He continued the practice of excluding the great nobles from the government, of giving them new honors and titles, and of exempting them from taxation—though not from the jurisdiction of the Inquisition. It was the common people who bore the main tax burden. But, as we shall see shortly, they were given the "psychological compensation" of the Inquisition. As for the Aragonese and Catalans, Charles allowed them to retain their traditional privileges in return for helping him run their territories in Italy, including those he added.*

Ferdinand, Isabella, and Charles created the modern Spanish state, but in order to make it into a nation they had to do something about the Jews and the Moors. For almost eight hundred years Christians, Jews, and Muslims had lived together without developing a sense of community. In spite of their separation, Spain's three religious groups had influenced one another's language, behavior, and thought patterns. Hundreds of Castilian (and Portuguese) words were borrowed from Arabic, especially for activities in which the Muslims were superi-

*See p. 114.

or: agriculture, building construction, arts and trades, commerce, public administration, science, and warfare. The Christians also took over from the Muslims the idea of a "holy war" fought by crusading military orders and used it in slowly reconquering the Iberian Peninsula from them. Meanwhile, by the late fifteenth century the Jews had taken on the Spanish Christians' pride and preoccupation with status, and the Christians began to take on the Jews' concern for preserving their "purity of blood." But the Christians disdained the industriousness and economic aptitudes of the Moors and Jews, and, to their later misfortune, refused to learn the practical techniques of these people before expelling them from Spain.

Fourteen hundred and ninety-two was the crucial turning point in Spanish history. In that year Columbus discovered the New World, the last Muslim kingdom in the Iberian Peninsula fell, and the Jews were expelled from Spain. At the time, the conquest of the Kingdom of Granada seemed more significant than the other two dramatic events. Ferdinand and Isabella granted liberal terms to the conquered Moors, allowing them to retain their religion, laws, language, and customs. For the next ten years attempts to convert the Muslims by persuasion proceeded slowly. Isabella finally sent Cardinal Ximénes de Cisneros to speed up the process, but the mass conversions he instituted goaded the Moors into open rebellion. Then, in 1502, all Muslims over fourteen who did not accept baptism were forced to leave Granada.

Thousands of Moriscos (Muslim converts to Christianity) intermarried with "Old Christians" and added their "blood" and their temperament to the Spanish nation. Nevertheless, despite the later policy of resettling the Moriscos in other parts of the country, and despite increasingly stringent laws forbidding the use of the Arabic language and Moorish customs, most of the Moriscos remained unassimilated. They revolted again in 1571, and the Spaniards feared that they would ally themselves with the Turks and the Muslim rulers of North Africa in an attempt to take over the country. Thus they seemed dangerous on political as well as religious grounds and were finally expelled from Spain *en masse* in 1609.

The "Jewish problem" was especially difficult to solve because the Jews performed many financial and administrative services for the government and because an increasing number of them tried to become assimilated into the dominant Christian majority through marriage and conversion. In the late fifteenth century Jews and converts still provided Castile and Aragon with eminent writers and physicians and with most of their merchants. But for over a hundred years antisemitic feeling had been growing among the Christian masses in Castile, where the Jews were the chief tax farmers of the king. Antisemitism was weaker among the nobles and the upper clergy, who were exempt from royal taxes and many of whom used the Jews to handle their own financial affairs, but on the other hand, the Church resisted the royal authority because much of its administration was in Jewish hands. Consequently, a major reason for the persecution of Jewish converts beginning in 1480 and the final expulsion of all Jews in 1492 was to rally the Church and the common people to the Crown. The Christian masses would no longer tolerate the preeminent position of the Jews now that Castile had conquered Granada and was becoming a powerful and efficient state. Along with most of the monastic orders and the priests, they wanted to be rid of the Jews, even though there was no one to replace them in the essential tasks they had performed in the community for centuries.

Thus, in 1492 between one hundred and fifty and two hundred thousand Jews were forced to leave what they considered their homeland. They preserved the Spanish language and their feeling of superiority as a group wherever they went. The majority moved to the Ottoman Empire; others to Italy and Portugal. When Portugal was annexed to Spain in 1580 a few of the Jews there went to southwestern France, the rest to the Netherlands, whence some came to North America in the seventeenth century. But the "Jewish problem" persisted with regard to the thousands of Jewish converts who remained in Spain. It was to deal

*The Inquisition*

with them that Ferdinand and Isabella had already established the Inquisition in 1480.

From its original function of investigating the Christian orthodoxy of converted Jews the Inquisition became the most effective institution the Spanish monarchy had for strengthening its own political power. Popular hatred for the converts undoubtedly prompted Ferdinand and Isabella to set up such an agency. The pope's desire for Ferdinand's aid in Italian diplomatic affairs probably influenced him to allow the royal Castilian government to operate the Inquisition independently of the Church's authority. In any case, the Crown appointed the inquisitors, gave them their instructions, paid their salaries, and commanded that confiscations made by them should be paid into the royal treasury. Within a few decades the Inquisition was introduced into Aragon, Sicily, Sardinia, and the American colonies. Ruled by a royal council, it was the only institution with jurisdiction in all the territories of the monarchy. Under the guise of protecting the purity of the Catholic faith in Spain the Inquisition created a reign of terror against all potential opponents of the royal authority.

The Spanish Inquisition became notorious for its devious methods of inquiry and for the extreme forms of conformity it stimulated. Heresy was the crime it was supposed to deal with, but its main victims were people accused of being relapsed Jews. It built its case against a suspect on the word of informers and gossips whom he was not allowed to confront. Once arrested, he was usually doomed to months or years of imprisonment before being tried. The best way to avoid suspicion was to proclaim one's hatred for Jews and turn informer. Since "New Christians" were the likeliest suspects, many of them became more viciously antisemitic than the resentful masses of "Old Christians." Some converted rabbis became bishops and even inquisitors, although a few eminent converts, like the philosopher Luis Vives, were humane and enlightened. The Inquisition stifled freedom of thought and expression by making Catholicism a totalitarian, state religion—which it had not been before in Spain and which it never was anywhere else. Not to think and not to know became protections against the sadism and plundering instincts of the Inquisition. Many people even refused to learn to read for fear of being contaminated by subversive ideas.

In the sixteenth century Spain was able to compete successfully for power and empire, partly owing to the strengthening of her royal government and to her excellent soldiers, but mainly to the fortunate accident of the wealth that poured in from the New World after the 1540s. The price she paid for her political, religious, and ethnic unity was the loss of the most dynamic people in her economy: the Jews and the Moors and, after 1609, the Moriscos. Thirteen per cent of the population consisted of *hidalgos* (gentry), who paid no taxes, performed no work of any kind, and lived like a closed caste. They were very honorable but very useless. Many of the ablest men and women took refuge in the Church. By the seventeenth century the Church came to own one-half of the national wealth but did little to improve the country's material and social well being. Spain was the strongest, most unified Christian state in sixteenth-century Europe. Still, the forced fanaticism of the Inquisition did not forge deep social ties among her people, and she wasted her wealth and manpower in a glorious but fruitless crusade against Protestant Europe. She produced Cervantes, Lope de Vega, El Greco, Velásquez, and a world empire that was to last for three hundred years. But she failed to keep up with the new scientific, economic, and technological developments in the more progressive countries of Western Europe.

### Central Europe

While the New Monarchs in the West were transforming their medieval kingdoms into centralized states, the monarchies of Central Europe retained their decentralized, medieval character. No states comparable to France, England, and Spain developed in Central Europe in the sixteenth century. On the one hand, there were two medieval elective monarchies: the Holy Roman Empire and the Kingdom of Poland. On the other hand, there were many dynastic territories, church lands, and imperial cities. The most important dynasty, the Hapsburgs, controlled its ancestral holdings in Austria, a few enclaves in south Germany, and, after 1526, Bohemia, which was part of the Empire, and Hungary, which was not. In addition, there were several middle-sized dynastic territories including Bavaria, Saxony, Brandenburg, Brunswick, Hesse, Württemberg, and the Palatinate. Both the elective monarchies and the dynastic territories had their medieval parliaments—usually called diets in Central Europe. The landowning nobility held sway in the territorial diets; the electors and princes dominated the Diet of the Holy Roman Empire. Insofar as the concept of sovereignty was recognized, it was considered to be shared by the diet and the monarch.

The Holy Roman Empire of the German Nation was none of the things its name implied by the middle of the sixteenth century. Emperor Charles V tried to restore its meaning as the secular center of a united Christendom and to lead it against its external enemy, the Muslim Turks, and its internal enemy, the Lutheran heretics. But to the Germans he was a French-speaking Burgundian, whose main interests lay with his *dynastic* empire outside of Germany. The Lutheran revolt expressed a kind of German nationalism, but Charles's attempt to make Catholicism prevail encouraged the very particularism he wanted to overcome. Rome—that is, the papacy—saw Charles V as a threat to its territorial security because of his control of Naples and Milan and to its spiritual supremacy because of his efforts to mediate the differences between Protestants and Catholics in Germany. Although Germany and Rome were willing to support his crusade against the Turks in his role as Holy Roman Emperor, they felt little sympathy for his wars against the French in his role as the dynastic head of a "universal monarchy" with its main source of strength in Spain. By the early 1550s Charles lost the support of the Catholic as well as the Protestant princes in Germany. After the Peace of Augsburg (1555) the imperial Diet became a congress of diplomats representing virtually sovereign states. The Empire had ceased to be Holy, Roman, German, or a Nation.

Charles V viewed himself as a "universal monarch" because marriage alliances and inheritance had given him control over half of Europe. Yet he ruled his dynastic holdings like a family patrimony. Because he had sworn to maintain the laws and customs of each area, he never attempted to impose a centralized imperial administration on them. He governed most of his far-flung possessions through members of his own family; only in his Italian domains did he appoint nonroyal viceroys. His governors-general in the Netherlands were first his aunt, Margaret of Austria, and then his sister, Mary of Hungary. By the late 1540s his son, Prince Philip, was already running Spain in his name. Charles gave over his rights in the ancestral Austrian lands to his brother Ferdinand in 1521–1522, and Ferdinand was elected king of Bohemia and Hungary in 1526. When Charles abdicated in 1556, Ferdinand "inherited" the Holy Roman Empire. The rest of the Hapsburg holdings went to Philip. Charles had failed to make Germany the center of his "universal monarchy" along medieval lines.

The future of the German-speaking lands lay with the dynastic territories. There the princes reorganized their finances, developed new fiscal agencies out of their private councils, and could often muster enough income for their needs from other sources than their tax-granting diets. They also relied increasingly on civil lawyers in building up some form of central administration. In the Austrian crown lands Maximilian I (1493–1519) had begun this development by setting up a council of government and a central treasury, with separate departments for receipt, audit, and expenditure. He also tried to enforce the collective responsibility of permanent commissions and the separation of functions. These principles, along with the increasing use of Roman law, were continued by his successors in Austria and adopted by other German princes.

Meanwhile, the Austrian Hapsburgs were creating the basis for a new, multinational dynastic state in Central Europe. When Ferdinand became King of Hungary and Bohemia he replaced the royal executive offices of these kingdoms with those of Austria. Even so, the Hungarian and Bohemian diets still had to vote on any laws or taxes presented to them by their Hapsburg sovereign before these became effective. There was no royal army, no uniform system of law or administration, and no national community. There were Croats, Slovenes, and Serbs in Austria and Hungary and Germans in the Silesian part of Bohemia. The bulk of the Hungarian kingdom was to be under Turkish rule between 1526 and 1699, but Ferdinand had strengthened the monarchial power in Austria, Bohemia, and the sliver of Hungary that was left to him. The dynastic union of these three lands was to last for almost four hundred years.

The Kingdom of Poland followed the path of political decentralization in the sixteenth century, though not as far as the Holy Roman Empire. The Jagellon dynasty had succeeded in monopolizing the elective crown since the fourteenth century, but after Sigismund II died without issue in 1572, the nobles elected whomever they pleased, thus weakening the royal power. Although the Jagellons had created an embryonic system of royal justice and administration in earlier times, the monarchy was already growing weaker at the beginning of the sixteenth century. The Polish *szlachta* (diet) forced each succeeding king to give up some of his power in return for its support in his foreign wars. Dominated by the landowning nobles, the *szlachta* became a bulwark of aristocratic privilege, rather than a national parliament. When the Grand Principality of Lithuania was integrated into the Kingdom of Poland in 1569 (it had been held by the Jagellons since 1380 but only in a dynastic union), its nobles received the legal and economic privileges of the Polish *szlachta.* This expanded Kingdom of Poland was larger than any other Christian state. Most of the inhabitants of its Lithuanian half were Belorussian and Ukrainian peasants. They hated their "Polonized" nobles and the Jews* who acted as their overseers and who, along with German settlers in the Polish towns, performed what little commercial services there were. Some of the peasants were forced to join the Uniate Church, which kept the Orthodox rite but accepted the authority of the pope; the rest clung to

*The bulk of Europe's Jews outside of Spain had been expelled from Germany in the fourteenth century and had migrated to Lithuania and Poland. There they lived in ghettos, spoke the Yiddish dialect of German, and constituted the largest concentration of Jews in the world until the twentieth century.

*Tsar Ivan IV ("The Terrible")*

the Orthodox Church and hated the dominant Polish Catholics. Politically weak, and divided by religious and ethnic antagonisms, the Kingdom of Poland nonetheless remained a sovereign state and a military power of sorts until the eighteenth century.

### Russia

Poland was the eastern limit of Latin Christendom; beyond it lay the Grand Duchy of Moscow and a number of other Russian principalities, all of which had been cut off from Europe by their Tartar masters since the mid-thirteenth century. Before that time a kind of medieval monarchy had developed in southern and central Russia. Missionaries from Constantinople had converted the people of this area to Greek Orthodox Christianity, and the church they established there gave Russian culture a strongly religious and Byzantine character. Then in 1227–1240 one of Genghis Khan's generals conquered most of the lands inhabited by the Great Russians. In order to escape the "Tartar yoke" the Russian princes in what are now Belorussia and the Ukraine had placed themselves under the rule of Lithuania, and their subjects henceforth developed along different lines from the Russians under Tartar rule. The Tartar Khans maintained their sovereignty over the Great Russian princes and granted them their authority over their local subjects for over two hundred years. Until the late fifteenth century their forces continued to carry out punitive raids against any Russian territory that did not pay its heavy tribute or whose prince broke his oath of fealty to the Khan. During this time all contact with Constantinople and the West ceased.

The Tartar period was the Russian Dark Ages. The masses lived almost exclusively by farming, but whatever surplus they produced was taken from them by their princes, who acted as the Khan's collection agents. Only their religion and language gave them any sense of identity as a group. The princes and nobles aped their Tartar overlords in administering cruel forms of punishment, in segregating their women in harem-like seclusion, and in showing contempt for their inferiors. Despite their Orthodox faith, the Russian territories that had been under Tartar rule continued to seem "Asiatic" and backward long after this rule disappeared. Muscovite Russia did not experience the Renaissance, the Reformation, the rise of capitalism, or the new developments in science and technology in Western and Central Europe.

After they freed themselves from the Tartars at the end of the fifteenth century the Moscow princes absorbed the neighboring principalities, including the vast northern city-state called Novgorod-the-Great, and established themselves as the sole rulers over the Great Russian people in the sixteenth century. The most important ruler in this period was the brilliant maniac Ivan IV (1533–1584), often called "The Terrible."

Ivan's main achievements were his weakening of the power of the hereditary nobility, his conquest of Tartar territory in the Southeast, and his adoption of the title Tsar of All the Russias. Tsar (Czar—from Caesar) was the Russian name for the Eastern Roman (Byzantine) Emperor in Constantinople, which the Russians called Tsargrad. Soon after the last Byzantine tsar had been overthrown by the Turks (1453), his niece had married Ivan IV's grandfather. Ivan could thus claim the right to this title through his grandmother. The Russian branch of the Orthodox Church also supported his claim by inventing a theory that Moscow was the "Third Rome." Ivan, in turn, strengthened the authority of the Russian Church, and his successor managed to give its head the title of Patriarch in 1589, thus making him the equal of the Patriarch in Constantinople. From a purely constitutional view, Russia was now a centralized monarchy with a loyal state church. Nevertheless, her backwardness in all other respects marked her off from the states of Western Europe.

Ivan IV increased his power through sheer cruelty and police state methods, but he failed to create any feeling of community among the Russian people. He set up a new governing agency called the *oprichnina*—which combined some of the qualities of the Spanish Inquisition, the English Court of the Star Chamber, and the French royal administration—to assert the tsar's authority and put down all treason to the state. The power of the *oprichnina* was not accepted as legitimate by the Russians, and it did not survive Ivan's reign. Ivan also tried to destroy the hereditary land-owning class and create a new nobility, whose titles and privileges were contingent on service to the tsar. In order to keep these service nobles loyal to him he had to grant them large tracts of land, some of which were confiscated from the hereditary nobility.

It was Ivan's treatment of the hereditary nobles that earned him the name, The Terrible. First he accused them of treason, then he seized their land and had them murdered. Those hereditary nobles who survived were completely alienated from the monarchy, and most of the rest of the population was ready to resist its authority at the end of the sixteenth century.

Whereas Englishmen, Frenchmen, and Spaniards were beginning to think of the state as a national community, the Russians saw it only as the tsar's personal patrimony. When Ivan's son died in 1598 without any heir, there was no one to be loyal to. For the next fifteen years Russia went through a period of civil war and foreign occupation. This Time of Troubles almost brought the ruin of the Russian state before the power of the monarchy was finally restored.

Tsarist power rested on a different socioeconomic base from the contemporary national monarchies in the West. Russia was an underdeveloped country: her main forms of wealth were land and a labor force to work the land; her agricultural techniques were primitive and produced little for great human effort. Ivan's service nobles, who spent most of their time fighting his wars, found it difficult to keep their peasant tenants on their estates. In most instances, these peasants were already in debt and were supposed to remain where they were until their debts were discharged, which often meant indefinitely. Nevertheless, many of them fled to the south and east in order to escape both their debts and their heavy taxes to the tsar's government. Partly to satisfy the demands of the service nobility for a reliable labor force, and partly to keep the peasants where he could tax them, Ivan IV passed a series of laws binding the peasants to the soil for life. Thus, serfdom, which had disappeared in England, France, and Spain, became a new and permanent institution in Russia in the late sixteenth century. The power of the tsar came increasingly to rest on the political and military support of a landed nobility whose power, in turn, rested on the economic exploitation of their serfs. This system impeded the development of a wealthy and educated middle class, which provided the kings of England and France with new sources of income and loyal servants of the Crown.

### The Ottoman Empire

The Orthodox Christians of the Balkan Peninsula had been even more strongly influenced by Byzantine civilization than had the Russians and were then cut off from the West for an even longer time by an Asiatic conquerer. For over four hundred years they were to remain subject peoples of the Ottoman Turks. Each ethnic group had its faith and folk culture, both of which allowed it to endure as a homogeneous peasant mass, separate from the Muslims. But all lacked native intellectual and political leaders, and knew nothing of the new learning or the scientific and artistic developments that were transforming Western Europe. The history of Southeastern Europe is part of the history of the Ottoman Empire.

Having displaced most of the Greek population in Asia Minor the Ottoman Turks invaded southeastern Europe in the late fourteenth century. Then Sultan Mohammed II (1451–1481) captured Constantinople and completed the conquest of the Balkans south of Belgrade. Turkish ferocity and military prowess were awe-inspiring, but the task of the conquerors was made easy by the dissatisfaction of the Bulgarian, Serb, and Greek peasants with their own feudal overlords. These were mainly native nobles, with some Venetians in the coastal areas of the Adriatic and Aegean Seas. Already facing a rebellious peasantry when the Turks arrived, the native leaders disappeared as a class with the Turkish conquest. The peasant masses accepted Ottoman rule, which they found to be more efficient and no more oppressive fiscally than that of their former masters. Furthermore, the Ottomans allowed the Orthodox population to keep its faith under the leadership of the Patriarch of Constantinople.

By the mid-sixteenth century the Ottoman Empire included the whole section of the world that Western Europeans called the Near East. To his holdings in Asia Minor and the Balkans, Selim I (1512–1520) added Syria, western Arabia, and Armenia. Suleiman the Magnificent (1520–1566) extended his European frontier into Hungary, Transylvania, and what is now northeastern Rumania and the southwestern part of the Ukraine, as well as conquering Iraq in Asia and all of North Africa up to Morocco. The Ottoman Turks were considered non-Europeans because of their Muslim faith rather than their Asiatic connections. Yet almost half of their fifty million subjects lived in Europe, and the majority of these were Christians.*

After the death of Suleiman in 1556 the first signs of a long-term decline appeared. One of its main causes was the problem of succession. Each sultan had many sons by different mothers (who were often Christian slaves), and when he died there was usually a struggle for the throne. The son who finally got it could eliminate his rivals only by having them all strangled. In the seventeenth century the sultans began to designate children as their successors, but this practice led to long regencies in which the mother ruled. The sultans sank increasingly into debauchery. Murad III (1574–1595) became a father one hundred and two times. Ibrahim I (1640–1648) turned into a sex maniac and had to be strangled for the good of the realm. Surrounded and dominated by the women of the seraglio (harem), the sultans lost contact with the affairs of government, and many of them ceased to lead their soldiers in wars. Thus, despite its wealth and strength in the sixteenth century, the Ottoman Empire did not develop the self-sustaining institutions of a modern European state. The Ottoman state was the sultan, his advisors, and his administrators. When the sultan was weak, the empire was weak.

The other long-term weakness of the Ottoman Empire was its cultural, intellectual, and technological stagnation. Despite some notable achievements in poetry and architecture, many fields of Ottoman culture never freed themselves from the traditional forms of the past. In the sixteenth century the Ottomans borrowed European muskets, cannon, and ships, and they continued to import European technicians

*The inhabitants of Hungary were mainly Roman Catholics or Protestants, though some Orthodox Serbs had fled there to escape Turkish rule in the fifteenth century. Most of the Albanians, the Serbs of Bosnia, and a few Bulgarians became converted to Islam. Over a million Muslim Turks and Tartars were eventually settled in the Balkans by the Ottoman government, and several hundred thousand Gypsies came there uninvited. There were also almost one hundred thousand Jewish refugees, who were invited, from Spain. All the Greeks and Rumanians and the majority of the Serbs and Bulgarians remained Orthodox Christians.

of all sorts thereafter. But they never developed their own technicians, and most of them viewed science as the work of the devil right down to the twentieth century.

By the nineteenth century the Ottoman Empire was to be called the "Sick Man of Europe," and its subject nationalities were to find its rule intolerable. In the sixteenth century, however, it was a vigorous world state, larger than any since ancient Rome. It waged war and made alliances with the greatest powers of the time and was to remain a major participant in European international relations long after it began to decline internally.

## DIPLOMACY AND WAR, 1494–1560

Modern international relations are conducted by sovereign states. Even under the most favorable conditions the relations between the states are those of an unintegrated society, in which cooperation is limited and conditional, and in which the allegiance of the members is directed toward distinct groups—in this case the nation-state—rather than the whole they constitute. Each state is a community and a power; there is no world community ruled by a central power. The states may set up international institutions, but these have no direct authority over individuals. Each state reserves this kind of authority for itself and claims a monopoly over the right to use diplomacy and war in order to promote its interests against those of other states. Thus, the world in which international relations take place is at best a society and at worst a battlefield.

### The Italian Wars

At the end of the fifteenth century the

relations between the emerging states of Europe began to move toward the modern pattern. The dynastic wars of the fourteenth and fifteenth centuries had been struggles between royal monarchs for control over each other's territorial possessions: Plantagenets and Capetians in France, the Houses of Aragon and Anjou in Sicily, and France and Burgundy in eastern France. In 1494 a series of wars between France and Spain for control over parts of Italy launched a new phase in international relations by involving states of unprecedented size and power in a struggle for control over territories outside their boundaries. The pretexts of dynastic claims to these territories were medieval; the techniques of war and diplomacy used to conquer them were modern.

Between 1494 and 1559 Italy served as the main battleground of Europe. Except for Sicily, which was part of the kingdom of Aragon, the Italian states had already approximated the modern type of international relations among themselves by the late fifteenth century. Each one used hired armies and professional diplomats in safeguarding its own interests and in trying to prevent any of the others from becoming too strong. But their rivalries and their search for allies outside the peninsula soon made them the prey of French and Spanish aggression.

The ability of France and Spain to engage in warfare for control of Italy was a consequence of their internal revival under the New Monarchs. In 1494 Charles VIII of France decided to seize the crown of Naples, whose king had just died, Ferdinand of Aragon had as good a dynastic claim to Naples as Charles through his family connections with the House of Anjou. During the next sixty-five years the kings of France and Spain fought intermittently for control of Naples and Milan, which they also both claimed, with their own professional armies and in shifting alliances with the other Italian states. The French won their most notable victory at Marignano in 1515 and suffered their worst defeat at the Battle of Pavia in 1525. At Pavia, Francis I was captured, taken to Spain and held for ransom, and forced to give up all his claims in Italy. Then, in true Renaissance fashion, he repudiated his treaty engagements as soon as he was freed. Not until 1559, when both sides had exhausted their financial resources, did the French permanently abandon Naples and Milan to the Spaniards in the treaty of Cateau-Cambrésis.

### Extension of the Struggle

Beginning in the 1520s the Italian wars became part of a larger struggle between the kings of France and Emperor Charles V. Here the issue seemed to be Charles's attempt to create a universal monarchy versus France's determination to counter this threat to her national existence. In a truly Machiavellian way, Francis I supported Charles's rebellious subjects in Spain (the *Comuneros* in 1520–1521) and Germany (the Schmalkaldic League in 1546–1547), put pressure on the pope to turn against Charles, and scandalized Europe by seeking help from the infidel Turks against the secular leader of Christendom. England formed temporary alliances with Charles V against France, but she gradually developed the policy of maintaining the balance of power against any state that threatened to dominate the continent. Thus she did not hesitate to join her traditional enemy, France, when Charles seemed to be getting too strong. Charles also put pressure on the pope when the pope supported the French (though the emperor was not directly responsible for the Sack of Rome by his mercenary soldiers in 1527), encouraged some of the great princes of France to rebel against their king, and used the treasures of the New World and the soldiers of Spain to fight the French and their Protestant allies in Germany.

In addition to the French and the German Protestant princes, Charles V had to deal with the advancing Turks on a third major "front." A year after his victory over the French in Italy at Pavia he faced the disastrous consequences of the Battle of Mohács (1526) in Hungary, for three years after their defeat of that unfortunate kingdom the Turks were besieging Vienna. But the Turks as well as Charles had too many irons in the fire—they were still digesting Syria and Egypt, pushing westward in the Mediterranean, and contemplating a war with Persia—and time, distance, and new Hapsburg armies under King Ferdinand forced them to withdraw from Vienna. Still, the Turks occupied two-thirds of Hungary (until 1699) and continued to harass the Hapsburgs, both in southeastern Europe and in the western Mediterranean.

By the end of the 1550s the pattern of European international relations for the next century and a half had begun to take shape. Over sixty years of war and diplomacy had produced a stalemate among the major powers and ended the threat of a universal monarchy with the Holy Roman Empire and the Mediterranean as axes. Charles V had been unable to subdue France, and the Turks had been "contained." In the West the principal protagonists were henceforth to be France and the Hapsburgs—now divided into a Spanish and an Austrian branch—with England trying to maintain a balance of power between them. Russia, Poland, and the Ottoman Empire were to suffer their ups and downs but they were to remain the dominant powers in Eastern Europe until the eighteenth century. In 1560, then, Europe was well on its way to becoming a society of independent sovereign states competing and allying with each other for power. What these states still lacked was adequate financial resources for permanent standing armies and continuous large-scale wars.

### Changes in Diplomatic and Military Techniques

The emerging system of international relations required new methods of action. Between 1492 and 1560 frequent wars were followed by periods of peace that served as truces for preparing other wars, or, more accurately, as opportunities for continuing warfare by nonmilitary means. In response to these new conditions diplomacy underwent a revolution. As the speed with which armies could be mobilized and alliances could change quickened, each state, especially the weaker ones, had to keep in closer touch with the intentions of the others. Previously, special embassies of high dignitaries had visited foreign courts on specific matters of business and then returned home. It now became necessary to have permanent embassies at all the important foreign courts. The first resident ambassadors and their staffs were essentially spies and troublemakers and were viewed as such by the local authorities. They collected information from paid informers, held secret meetings with potential traitors, and tried to bribe influential persons close to the government. Only gradually did diplomacy become respectable and bring immunity and prestige to the office of resident ambassador.

Renaissance diplomacy was war on another level. Its habitual "arms" were the lie and the ruse. The diplomat had to be able to create the impression of wanting to do one thing and then do something else. He developed a number of classic "gambits" into a new kind of performing art. In order to mollify an ally about a conference to which it had not been invited, the ambassador assured it that his own sovereign had met with the rival power only in the interest of peace and had made no commitments. To rekindle the zeal of a lukewarm ally, the ambassador suggested that his sovereign might prefer another ally and was at that very moment coming to terms with it. To impress a recalcitrant minister, an embassy feigned a wish to break off negotiations and began packing its bags. Yet, for all their cunning, Renaissance diplomats were sometimes obtuse and irrational. They confused eloquence with common sense and believed that dramatic personal intervention "at the summit" could take the place of prolonged expert negotiation. For example, the famous meeting of Henry VIII and Francis I on the Field of the Cloth of Gold near Calais in 1520 merely complemented the work of the professional diplomats and resulted in no new decisions. Belief in the possibility of a crusade and in the effectiveness of a general church council symbolized the coexistence of a medieval outlook with modern methods.

The art of war also underwent considerable changes in the transitional period between medieval and modern times. A good example of a major army at the end

A Landsknecht

of the fifteenth century was the one with which Charles VIII of France invaded Italy in 1494. Its units were already combining troops armed with shooting weapons which prepared attacks by weakening and demoralizing the enemy from a distance, armored shock troops bristling with pointed hand weapons for plowing into enemy lines or stopping for enemy attack, and lightly armed troops for reconnaisance, probing tactics, and pursuit. The cavalry troops and their horses were heavily armored and fought with long lances. They were covered from the rear by archers. The infantry—outnumbering the calvalry for the first time—was a huge mass of men. Half of them were armed with long pikes, others with axes for hand-to-hand combat, and about one-tenth with harquebuses, a kind of small hand cannon fired from a portable forked stand. (A mixture of saltpeter, sulphur, and wood charcoal had been invented in the fourteenth century, but the use of this gunpowder to discharge a metal ball from a cylindrical chamber did not become common until the late fifteenth century.) There were also men armed with crossbows, on foot and on horseback. The artillery consisted of one hundred and forty muzzle-loading bronze cannon.

The army of Charles VIII was an army of mercenaries. Warfare had become a profession requiring individual and group training in which men were drilled like machines. Each country specialized in a particular type of combat. The heavy cavalry consisted of French nobles, paid by the king, to whom they still felt a feudal loyalty. It was an elite corps of irresistible shock value, the main force of the army. The bulk of the heavy infantry was composed of pikemen—mainly Swiss, but also some German *Landsknechte*—who were the sons of artisans and well-to-do peasants and who equipped themselves at their own expense. There were also armored harquebusiers grouped into regiments; these included some nobles, for the stigma of fighting on foot was beginning to disappear. Their colonel was a military entrepeneur with a recruiting patent from the king. The heavy infantry was a solid mass without initiative. The light infantry was made up of Frenchmen from Picardy and Gascony, brave, flexible, and full of initiative, but less solid than the Swiss and the *Landsknechte*.

The standardization of combat tactics in Italy allowed Gonsalvo de Cordova to revolutionize the Spanish army in 1503 by creating the division as a self-sufficient unit consisting of twelve thousand infantry, sixteen hundred heavy cavalry, sixteen hundred light cavalry, and forty-four cannon. He increased the armor of his pikemen and armed more of his other infantry with harquebuses. Thereafter most European armies placed increasing emphasis on heavy shock troops and on fast, lightly armed infantry and cavalry. Gonsalvo de Cordova also equipped almost half of his infantrymen with knives and short swords, so that they could dodge between the Swiss and German pikemen and stab them in the stomach. He made it easier to switch from marching formation to battle formation by breaking his battalions into companies which, with a right-flank turn, could quickly present a solid, three-deep line against the enemy. Finally, he imbued his troops with a sense of discipline and pride that was unmatched in any other Christian infantry.

The wars between Francis I and Charles V brought further advances in military technology and tactics. Artillery was simplified and standardized. Improvements in the mining and forging of iron ore made it possible to manufacture cannon with this metal instead of bronze; cast iron was used by the middle of the sixteenth century. Mortars were improved with springs to break their recoil. In turn, improvements in artillery necessitated improvements in fortifications. Walls thick enough to repel cannon balls were eventually replaced by stone screens with forward bastions from which the attackers could be hit in the flank. By the second half of the sixteenth century quick victories were no longer possible against a well-defended fortress. This fact changed the whole character of military campaigns and, consequently, their financial and diplomatic background.

Improvements were also made in hand arms. Originally the harquebus was so heavy that it had to be fired from a support, to which it was attached by a fixed hook. After 1520 the Spaniards made it with a bent stock and a longer butt, so that it could be fired from the shoulder. The original matchlock mechanism that ignited the gunpowder was replaced by a wheel-lock and finally a flint. A few further changes in the second half of the sixteenth century transformed the harquebus into the musket, which remained the chief infantry firearm for the next three hundred years. The Germans invented a smaller, lighter version of the harquebus, the pistol, which could be fired with one hand and which soon became standard equipment for the light cavalry.

The composition and spirit of armies were far different in 1560 from what they had been in 1494. Improvements in armor allowed the chivalrous knights on horseback to have their final fling at glory

*A harquebusier*

in the first half of the sixteenth century. They retained their tactical effectiveness, but their supply was limited. Since common foot soldiers could be equipped more cheaply and recruited in apparently limitless numbers from Switzerland and Germany, the infantry increasingly outnumbered the cavalry. But the Swiss were expensive, the *Landsknechte* drank too much, and both had the unfortunate habits of pillaging, plundering, and changing sides for higher pay. Though all armies had to continue to employ some mercenaries, the major rulers began to recruit native troops and try to instill into them a sense of national loyalty and patriotism.

In the second half of the sixteenth century military strategy was increasingly determined by recruitment, finance, transport, the relationship between fortification and siegecraft, and the composition of armies. Only large states with extensive resources could carry on sustained wars. Even France and Spain had to quit in 1559. After that, armies became smaller and had less elaborate materiel. France was handicapped economically as well as politically by civil strife, but all the Western European states suffered from the first crisis of modern capitalism.* The fragmentation of Western Europe into nations, factions, and clans also diminished the resources of each. Warfare was a battle of wits for the generals and of nerve for the common soldiers. Both war and diplomacy were taking on their modern forms and becoming increasingly linked with each other in a Machiavellian world of sovereign states.

## THE BEGINNINGS OF EUROPEAN EXPANSION OVERSEAS

The Renaissance, the Reformation, the foundations of the modern state, and new techniques of war and diplomacy were all momentous developments in the history of Europe. But other civilizations have also experienced cultural and religious revivals, created complex and durable political institutions, made notable contributions to the arts of diplomacy and war, and then stagnated, fallen apart, or been conquered by barbarian invaders. Early modern European civilization might well have faltered on a new plateau and then declined like the others if it had not broken out of its geographical and economic confines in the late fifteenth century.

On the eve of the great "discoveries" Latin Christendom was merely one of dozens of civilizations and cultures—each a "world" unto itself—on a vast planet whose true dimensions nobody knew. There were roughly three hundred million human beings—one-tenth of the present world population—living in virtually every land area inhabited today. Some of these territories were heavily populated, others sparsely settled; but all were "known" by someone. Arab navigators made regular voyages across the Indian Ocean; Chinese junks utilized the coastal waters of the Far East and reached Africa; Polynesians moved about from one island to another in the South Pacific. Thus, the Europeans were not the first people to "discover" these seaways.

Outside of their own "world," Western and Central Europeans had first-hand knowledge of only the Turks and the Moors. No European had been known to have explored Africa, Southeast Asia, Australasia, or the Western Hemisphere. Scandinavian adventurers had visited parts of North America around the year 1,000, but their findings were not known in the fifteenth century. Marco Polo's account of his experiences in North China in the thirteenth century was known, but it was little help regarding the geography of the Far East, and it misled Europeans into believing that a Great Khan friendly to Christianity still ruled in "Cathay" two centuries later. By then most learned Europeans accepted the theory of Claudius Ptolemy, an Alexandrian Greek of the second century A.D., that the Earth was a sphere. Although they knew that the Far East lay somewhere to the west, they found it difficult to give a visual form to such an apparent paradox. The first crude globe was constructed by the German astronomer Martin Behaim only in 1492, and in the late fifteenth century Genoese navigational charts showed only the Mediterranean coast, the Atlantic shores from Morocco to England, and the Canary, Azores, and Madeira Islands, which had been "rediscovered" in the early 1400s. Beyond them some map makers placed a large mythical island called "Antilia."

Religion, politics, and the lure of adventure prompted Europeans to probe the unknown, but their main motive was economic. Like their Roman ancestors in the third century A.D., they were running out of precious metals with which to pay for the goods they imported from India and the Far East. By the fifteenth century the spices and herbs of Southeast Asia, which Europeans referred to vaguely as "the Indies," had become essential for the preservation of food and in pharmaceutical products. Their cost had always been high. Italian merchants had long monopolized their distribution from the ports of the Eastern Mediterranean, where they had bought them from Egyptian and Syrian merchants, who had bought them from Asiatic caravan masters and Arab sea captains, who had transported them thousands of miles over land and water. Each intermediary who handled these goods took exorbitant profits, and the

*See pp. 140–141.

*The transfer of spices from the overland route to the sea route*

Egyptian government added further charges for the use of its ports. The Europeans had nothing that Asia wanted in return except silver and gold. Thus, they had to find new sources of precious metals and a cheaper trade route to the Far East, if they were to continue to import its products.

In the late fifteenth century Europeans began to change the course of history by taking to the open sea. The Portuguese were the first to discover the all-water route around the southern tip of Africa to "the Indies," and they succeeded in controlling it for almost a hundred year. On the way they found not only gold, but also a new source of wealth, slaves, in West Africa. This find was to have unanticipated consequences in connection with the discovery and colonization of the New World, which was itself an unforeseen result of the efforts of other nations to find an alternate sea route to "the Indies" and new supplies of precious metals. The silver of far-off Peru was to stimulate a price revolution in Europe; the discovery of exotic alien civilizations was to alter European thought patterns; the struggle for wealth and empire was to bring about the dominance of the Atlantic powers in world affairs.

## Early Explorations

Europe's triumph lay in her ships and their voyages, which linked together the uncharted ocean routes of the world for the first time. Since the end of the thirteenth century Italian merchant galleys had been plying the coastal waters of the Atlantic as far as the North Sea, and their navigators had gained much experience in seamanship. Northern and southern shipbuilders learned new methods of construction from each other. In the fifteenth century the Portuguese adopted the sternpost rudder from the North. It was a great improvement over the older lateral rudder, which had been little more than a wide oar held in the water from the stern of the ship by several men. The fixed stern-post rudder could be steered by one man from the interior, and it allowed the ship to tack and to sail to windward. Perhaps the greatest "breakthrough" in fifteenth-century navigation was the elimination of oarsmen and the entire dependence on sails for ocean voyages. The caravel, which was soon to carry Vasco da Gama and Columbus half way around the world, had broad rectangular sails to catch the wind from the back and slender triangular sails for tacking. This combination allowed ships to use both the east and west trade winds.

Finding the right wind at the right time was relatively easy; knowing where one was on the open seas was more difficult. The lodestone compass indicated the approximate direction of the North Pole by day or night. A fifteenth-century invention, the astrolabe, allowed a navigator to calculate the angle of the line of his vision to the North Star and thus deduce his approximate latitude. The biggest problem was finding one's longitude. Fifteenth-century navigators knew that there was an hour's difference between two places fifteen degrees apart, but they had no practical means of calculating the difference in time between their present position and their point of departure. They had glasses filled with sand, which they kept turning over every twenty-four hours in order to keep their time of origin. Until the invention of the chronometer in the eighteenth century, calculations based on sand clocks or on the position of the moon and the stars produced errors of up to ten degrees, or six hundred miles.

The world's oceans posed as many problems to their first explorers as outer space to the astronauts of our own time. Fear of going through a layer of cosmic dust at the limit of the Earth's atmosphere in the 1950s was paralleled by fear of crossing the equator five hundred years earlier. At that time the equator was believed to be a zone of boiling waters with magnetic rocks that pulled ships to the bottom of the sea and with fantastic marine monsters that attacked men and ships. These terrors declined with experience. But real dangers remained, such as storms, tidal waves at the Cape of Good Hope, and the risk of famine on crossings of uncertain duration in sailing ships whose captains lost their longitude. Nourishment was poor at best, consisting mainly of dried meat, dried fish, dried beans, and moldy bread full of worms. When the wine ran out, the men had only stale, brackish water to drink. The heat of the tropics made them break out in pimples and helped worms to breed in their clothes. Diseases such as scurvy, smallpox, and typhus took a heavy toll. Rarely did a week pass without one or two burials at sea. Yet a peculiar restlessness drove the explorers ever onward in the face of all these hardships.

The Portuguese were the first Europeans since the ancient Greeks to organize expeditions for exploration as an end in itself. Prince Henry (1394–1460), called The Navigator, was the leading figure in this endeavor. After participating in the capture of the Moroccan seaport of Ceuta, immediately across the Strait of Gibraltar, in 1415, he became intensely interested in Africa, its peoples, its trade routes, and its resources. Since the eighth century Western Europeans had created fantastic legends about what lay beyond the solid mass of Muslim territory in North Africa and the Near East. These medieval legends told of immense gold stores and of a Christian king called Prester John. Prince Henry wanted to find them both. He also had some of the anti-Muslim crusading spirit of the Iberian Peninsula and hoped to find a way of attacking Morocco from the rear. Prince Henry was never king, and he used private funds to set up a school of navigation at the southwestern tip of Portugal. There he assembled an international group of seamen and astronomers to carry on explorations down the west coast of Africa. His explorers reached Cape Verde in 1445 and the Guinea coast—where they found their first gold and slaves—by the time of his death.

Prince Henry probably did not begin to think about finding a sea route to India until his later years, but under Kings John II (1481–1495) and Manuel I (1495–1521) Asia became the principal concern of the Portuguese government. Bartolomeu Dias rounded the southern tip of

Africa in 1488 and ventured a short way up its east coast. Vasco da Gama made the first successful voyage by a European across the Indian Ocean and arrived on the west coast of India in 1498. He brought a few samples of spices and other oriental luxuries back to Lisbon. Now that the way was known, a real trading expedition was needed. In 1500 King Manuel fitted out a fleet of thirteen ships under the command of Pedro Alvares Cabral. Seeking the South Atlantic trade winds that would carry him eastward, Cabral inadvertently reached the coast of Brazil and claimed it for Portugal, though it was not settled by Europeans until much later. Then, having found his west winds, he sailed eastward past the Cape of Good Hope into the Indian Ocean and finally arrived in India. He brought back a larger cargo of spices than Gama, though still not enough to pay for the ships he had lost in storms and in encounters with hostile Arab merchants.

While the Portuguese explorers were still probing their way southward down the coast of Africa, a Genoese sea captain whom we call Christopher Columbus asked King John II to sponsor him on a voyage to the west. Every schoolchild knows that King John turned him down and that it was Queen Isabella of Castile who finally subsidized Columbus's four westward voyages in search of "the Indies" between 1492 and 1502. Columbus mistook Cuba for Cathay—home of the Great Khan—and Haiti for Japan. Until his death in 1506 he continued to insist that he had discovered the *true* (East) Indies and that somewhere down the coast of South America, which he believed was part of the Malay Peninsula, there was a strait leading into the Indian Ocean.

Columbus claimed the lands he *had* discovered for Spain, and the Portuguese were determined to keep the Spaniards from claiming any new lands in Africa. The two powers signed the Treaty of Tordesillas in 1494, giving Portugal title to all territories east of a line through the mid-Atlantic and giving Spain everything west of it. It was later discovered that Brazil lay to the east of this line and hence "belonged" to Portugal. The Spaniards established colonies in Haiti, Cuba, Jamaica, and Puerto Rico between 1493 and 1512, and Vasco Nuñez de Balboa became the first of the great *conquistadores* of the American mainland. In 1513 Balboa discovered the Pacific Ocean on the western side of the Isthmus of Panama. His discovery showed the Spaniards how narrow a strip of land separated the Atlantic from the Pacific and encouraged them to seek an all-water route to the East Indies somewhere through the bothersome land-mass that barred their way.

The conquest of Central America was in a sense an incident in the race between the Portuguese and the Spaniards to find the sea route to the Far East. Portuguese explorers from India established footholds in Malacca, thereby gaining control of the Malay Straits, in 1511, the Moluccas Islands in 1513, and Macao on the South China coast in 1517. Two years later Hernando Cortés conquered Mexico, and Ferdinand Magellan sailed westward from Spain. Magellan finally found the southern tip of South America, crossed the Pacific, landed in the Philippines and claimed them for Spain. Since the Philippines were only five hundred miles north of the Moluccas, a new line of demarcation was needed to determine whether they really belonged to Spain or Portugal. In 1529 the Portuguese took advantage of Emperor Charles V's financial difficulties and gave him three hundred and fifty thousand ducats in return for his acceptance of the seventeenth-degree longitude as this line. Although the Philippines were legally in the Portuguese zone, the Spaniards remained and fought the Portuguese off. But the Spaniards had lost the race for control of the shortest all-water route from Europe to the Far East.

While Portugal consolidated her hold on the sea route to India and Spain began colonizing Central and South America, the monarchs of England and France sent out explorers to find the Northwest Passage to the Far East. Sailing from England, John Cabot (Giovanni Caboto) sighted Nova Scotia as early as 1496. His son, Sebastian, found the entrance to Hudson's Bay in 1509 but had to turn back because of the cold. Under King Henry VIII no further English expeditions were sponsored. Then, in the late 1570s, Mar-

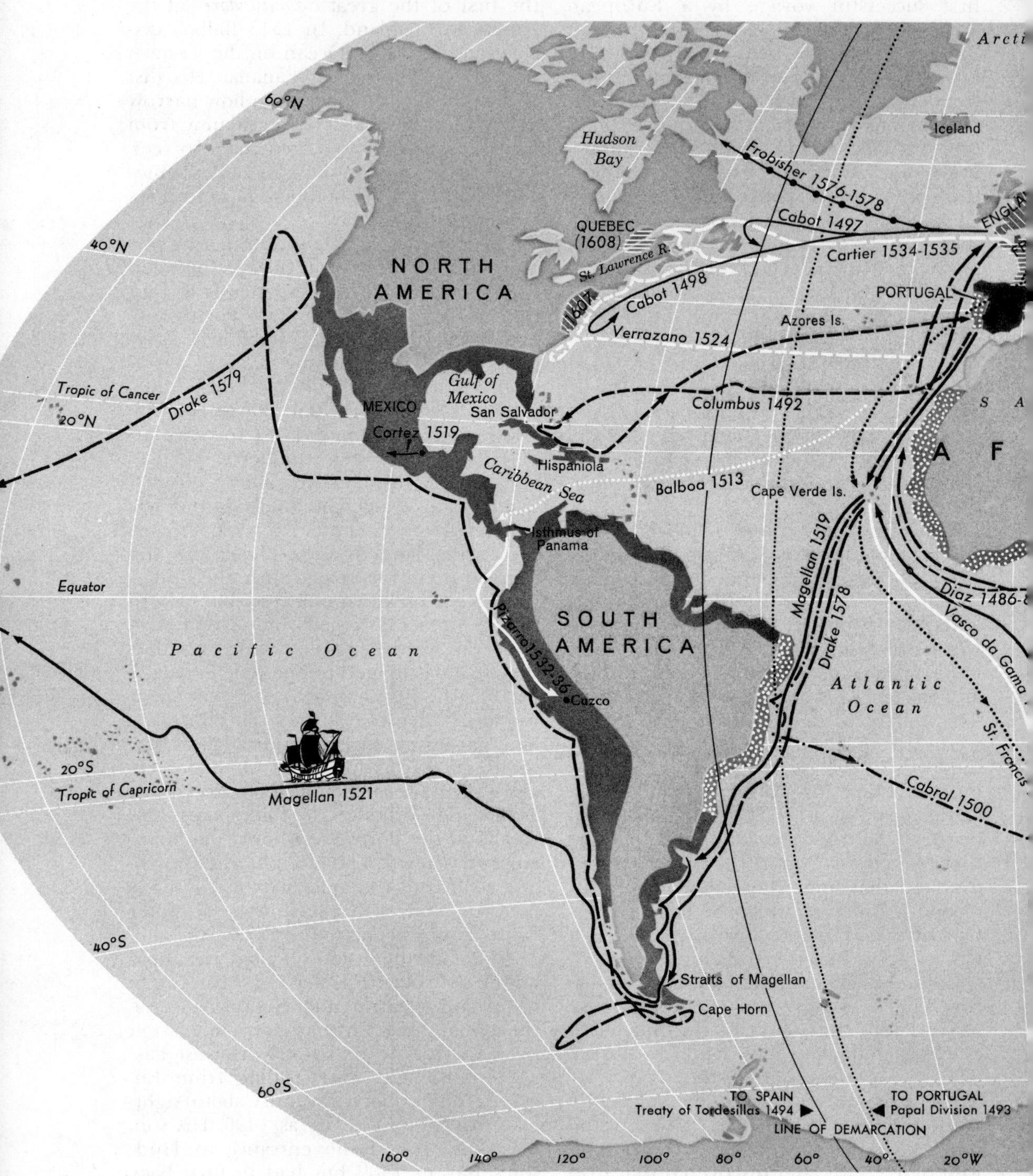

Arcti
60°N
Iceland
Hudson Bay
Frobisher 1576-1578
QUEBEC (1608)
Cabot 1497
ENGLA
40°N
NORTH AMERICA
St. Lawrence R.
Cartier 1534-1535
Cabot 1498
PORTUGAL
Azores Is.
Verrazano 1524
Tropic of Cancer
Drake 1579
Gulf of Mexico
Columbus 1492
MEXICO
San Salvador
20°N
Cortez 1519
Hispaniola
A F
Caribbean Sea
Balboa 1513
Cape Verde Is.
Isthmus of Panama
Magellan 1519
Equator
Drake 1578
Diaz 1486-
SOUTH AMERICA
Pizarro 1532-36
Vasco da Gama
Pacific Ocean
Atlantic Ocean
Cuzco
St. Francis
20°S
Tropic of Capricorn
Magellan 1521
Cabral 1500
40°S
Straits of Magellan
Cape Horn
60°S
TO SPAIN
Treaty of Tordesillas 1494
TO PORTUGAL
Papal Division 1493
LINE OF DEMARCATION
160°
140°
120°
100°
80°
60°
40°
20°W

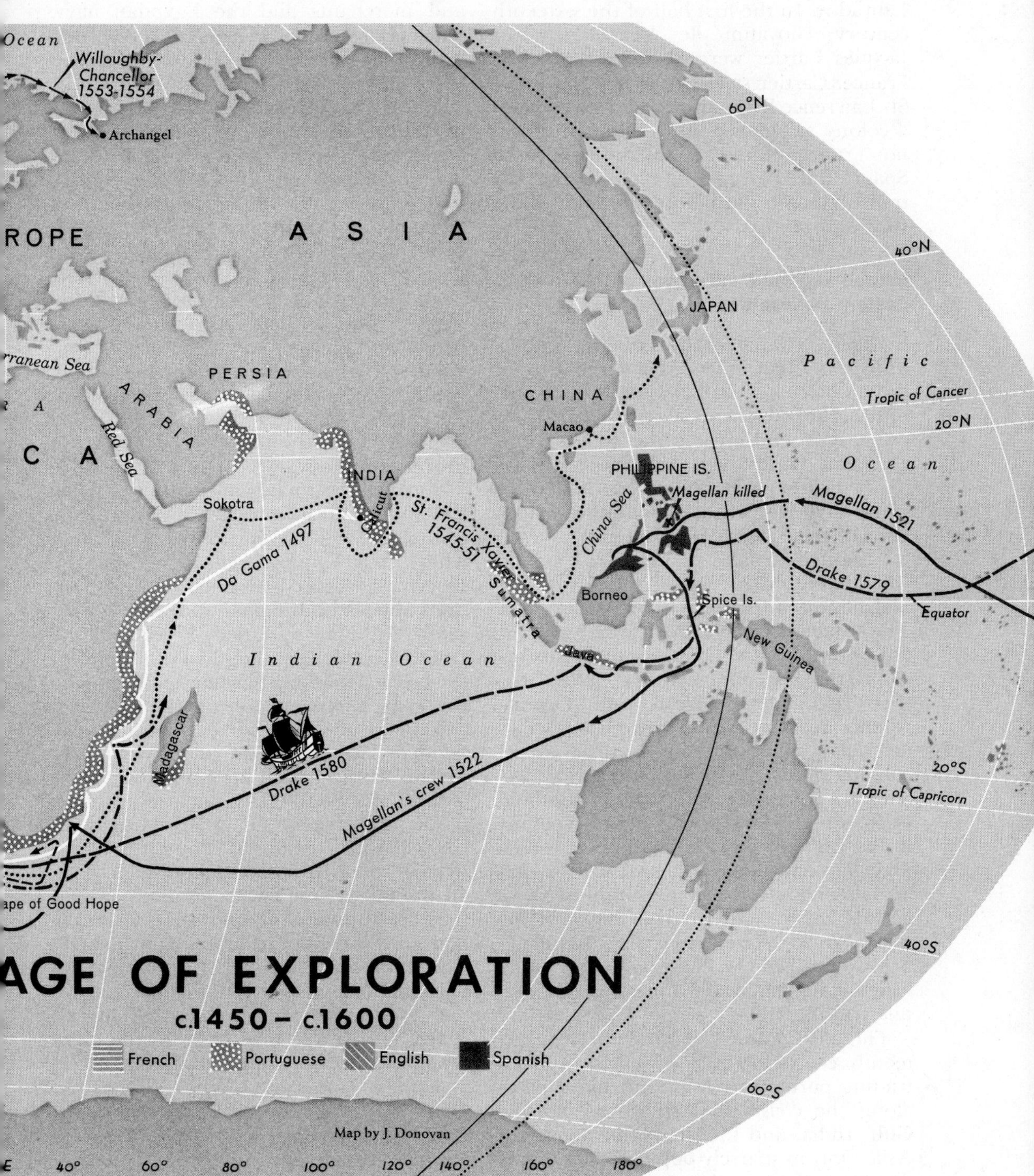

Ocean
Willoughby-Chancellor 1553-1554
Archangel
ROPE
ASIA
rranean Sea
PERSIA
ARABIA
Red Sea
CA
INDIA
Sokotra
Calicut
Da Gama 1497
St. Francis Xavier 1545-51
CHINA
Macao
JAPAN
PHILIPPINE IS.
Magellan killed
Magellan 1521
China Sea
Borneo
Spice Is.
Drake 1579
Sumatra
Java
New Guinea
Indian Ocean
Madagascar
Drake 1580
Magellan's crew 1522
Pacific Ocean
60°N
40°N
Tropic of Cancer
20°N
Equator
20°S
Tropic of Capricorn
40°S
60°S
ape of Good Hope
AGE OF EXPLORATION
c.1450 – c.1600
French
Portuguese
English
Spanish
Map by J. Donovan
E
40°
60°
80°
100°
120°
140°
160°
180°

tin Frobisher again took up the search for a northern sea route to Cathay beyond Labrador. In the first half of the sixteenth century Giovanni de Verrazano and Jacques Cartier were also searching, for France. Cartier sailed quite a way up the St. Lawrence River and even tried to plant a colony at Quebec. But neither England nor France offered serious competition to Spain and Portugal in colonization or transoceanic trade before the end of the sixteenth century.

### Europe and the Civilizations of the Eastern Hemisphere

By the second half of the sixteenth century Europeans had explored a large part of the globe. They had mastered its ocean routes, linked these together for their own profit, and created the first tenuous economic bonds between different parts of the world. Still, they were unable to make any real inroads against the civilizations of the Eastern Hemisphere.

Although Spain wanted to spread Christianity to the rest of the world, she had almost no success in Africa or Asia. The Spaniards' age-old hatred of the Moors led them to try to conquer Morocco in the sixteenth century. They also tried to conquer Algeria and Tunisia, whence Barbary pirates preyed on Mediterranean shipping. But, aside from occupying Tunis and Oran for a few decades, they gained no permanent foothold in North Africa. The only Spanish colony in the Far East was the Philippines, which Magellan had discovered in 1521. Spain's actual conquest and colonization of these islands began in 1565 from bases in the New World. Thereafter the Spaniards slowly occupied the Philippines and established a regular trade route between Manila and Acapulco.

The Portuguese "empire" in the sixteenth century was a series of isolated trading ports, fortresses, and naval bases along the coasts of Africa, the Persian Gulf, India, and the islands of Southeast Asia. Only in sparsely populated areas like Angola and Mozambique (and Brazil) did small Portuguese settlements eventually take root in the hinterland. Trade with "the Indies" was Portugal's central concern. In order to gain and keep this trade, Portugal had to fight local Muslim rulers and merchants and the Egyptian navy. Since her resources were small, she needed the profits of trade to wage war. Between 1509 and 1515 Alfonso de Albuquerque ruled as the governor of the Portuguese in India and created the beginnings of a maritime empire, with Goa as its "capital." Albuquerque advanced Portuguese trade and increased his country's holdings from Malaya to the Persian Gulf, but he could not prevent interlopers and smugglers from engaging in private trade. The royal government's share of the Asian trade did little more than pay the expenses of war and government overseas and contribute to the embellishment of Lisbon. By the late sixteenth century the King of Portugal's "empire" in the Indies had somehow turned into an all-but-bankrupt grocery business.

Portugal was unable to extend her political and cultural influence beyond a few coastal enclaves on the continent of Asia, where great empires went their own way. Her missionaries converted several hundred thousand Indians, and a few thousand Portuguese settled in the coastal cities of India. But the Muslim Empire of the Great Mughals continued to dominate the sixty million people in the northern two-thirds of that country, and an independent Hindu empire ruled over thirty million in the south. In China the Ming dynasty (1368–1644), though declining in power, was able to eliminate virtually all contacts with foreigners. The Emperor in Peking ruled his sixty million subjects as an absolute despot and continued to claim that his Middle Kingdom was the center of a world of tributary states. Inordinately proud of their ancient civilization, the Chinese looked down upon all foreigners—especially Europeans—as barbarians. A few Portuguese merchants in the guise of ambassadors bearing tribute carried on a limited trade at Canton. Otherwise China was to remain closed to Europeans until the nineteenth century.

Japan was the one Asian land that experienced a certain amount of European influence in the sixteenth century; this happened for several reasons. The country was weakened by political rivalries and civil wars. In theory, the "divinely descended emperor" (*Mikado*) was the head of a centralized state whose chief military and civil leader was called the *shōgun*. Actually the feudal lords (*daimyō*) supported by their knightly retainers (*samurai*) exercised complete authority in their own domains, constantly made war on one another, and disregarded the central government. Although the national religion was Shintōism, which involved the worship of deified natural forces, Buddhism had penetrated Japan from China with great success, and the wealthy Buddhist monasteries were political rivals of the *daimyō* and the *shōgun*. Moreover, some outsider was needed to carry on Japan's trade with China, which Chinese merchants had abandoned.

In this situation the Portuguese came in 1542 with their silks from China, their harquebuses, and their missionaries. The Jesuits, led by St. Francis Xavier, were especially skillful in explaining Christianity in terms their audience could understand. By 1577, one hundred thousand Japanese had accepted the new faith. The *daimyō* did so partly to get the luxuries of China and the new weapons of Europe, partly to weaken the political influence of the Buddhists, partly out of sincere conviction. But at the beginning of the seventeenth century a strong new *shōgun* reversed the trend by restoring the power of the central government, exterminating the Christians, and closing Japan to foreigners.

Thus, all the civilizations of Asia and Africa rejected the feeble efforts of Europeans to conquer them and convert them to Christianity. The Orient remained a mystery to the Portuguese and Spaniards long after their first contacts with it. Their ignorance of its basic geography seems astounding today. A missionary in Goa wrote in 1551 that China, or at least the Mongol Empire, which had long since disappeared, bordered on Germany. A generation later the Jesuits in Goa did not know of the existence of the Himalayas. Until the end of the sixteenth century European map makers extended China into the middle of the Pacific Ocean, and still had no idea that it was Marco Polo's Cathay. Such ignorance, and the distance from Europe, nourished illusions about the power of Asia for a long time.

### Spain's New World Empire

The Spaniards concentrated on the New World. The fact that they did so may have helped to save Asia; for, in the Western Hemisphere, they destroyed three civilizations and many cultures, and transformed the lives of the native peoples.

The first stage of Spanish colonization was restricted to the Caribbean. In 1497 Columbus's brother Bartolemé built the town of Santo Domingo on the island of Hispaniola (Haiti); it was the capital of the Spanish Indies for over half a century, and is now the capital of the Dominican Republic. In the early 1500s the Spaniards established farming and mining settlements in the other islands of the Greater Antilles. The native Tainos and Caribs declined in numbers as a result of forced labor and European diseases like smallpox and measles. The *encomienda* system divided the Indians of the Caribbean area among the Spanish settlers and, in 1512, the first European colonial code (Laws of Burgos) defined their status. They were free men, not slaves; they were required to work; and they were to be converted to Christianity by peaceful means. The *encomenderos*—their Spanish masters—were to protect them, give them religious instruction, and treat them humanely. Administration of the colonies was directed from Spain through local governors and judicial courts (*audiencias*). After 1520 these beginnings in native policy and colonial administration were to be applied throughout the mainland of America from Mexico to Peru.

The Spanish *conquistadores* were a unique breed of men. Most of them came from the rough highlands of northern and western Spain. They were used to hot summers, cold winters, and modest food, and to fighting the Moors and the French. Whatever their social background—Cortés was a nobleman, Pizarro was a peasant's son—they thought of themselves as *hidalgos*, too proud for any occupation except war. Their psychological makeup combined a wolfish greed for gold, land, and slaves, a passionate desire to destroy heathens and win souls for Christ, and a longing to surpass the deeds of the great heroes of antiquity. Their banners carried the following words in Latin: "Comrades, let us follow the Cross, and if we have faith, in truth we shall conquer with this symbol." The *conquistadores* often showed contempt for the wealth they thought they were looking for. When they acquired it, many of them, including Cortés, squandered it in organizing further conquests. They were grave, stiff, steadfast, and brutal, yet always burning with a consuming passion for "Gold, Gospel, and Glory."

On the eve of the Spanish conquest there were, perhaps, 80 million Indians in the Americas, most of them south of the Rio Grande. Recent studies estimate the population of Mexico alone at 25 million. This figure includes the Aztec Empire, with its capital at Tenochtitlán (Mexico City) in central Mexico, and the declining Maya civilization, in southeastern Mexico and Guatemala. The most extensive and most populous Indian state was the Inca Empire of Peru, which stretched two thousand miles from present-day Colombia to northern Chile. Brazil and Paraguay were sparsely settled by the Tupi-Guarani Indians, whose culture was more advanced than that of the tribes in the remaining regions of South America, These tribes, like those of North America, were too primitive to be assimilated and were either wiped out or displaced by the Europeans who eventually colonized the Western Hemisphere.

The Indians whom the Spaniards conquered most quickly and assimilated most easily into a mixed civilization dominated by Europeans were precisely the most advanced – those of Mexico and Peru. These peoples were used to large-scale political organization and submission to a central authority. They had also developed mental habits and expressive forms that were close to those of Europe. Their scientific and artistic achievements were all the more remarkable in view of their limited technology. None of them employed the wheel, and only the Incas had beasts of burden, the rather ineffectual llama. Yet they built great stone temples and pyramids, drained lakes, supplied large cities with food and water, made notable achievements in astronomy and mathematics (the Mayan calendar was more accurate than that of Europe), produced remarkable works of sculpture and painting, and developed systems of hieroglyphic writing. But the Aztecs and the Incas were aristocracies of conquerors ruling over masses of downtrodden subjects. When the Spaniards arrived, some tributaries of the Aztecs were ready to revolt, and the Inca princes were engaged in civil war.

Despite physical hardships and almost incredible mountain marches, Hernando Cortés conquered the Aztecs (1519–1522) and Francisco Pizarro and Diego de Almargo conquered the Incas (1532–1536) with a few hundred men. Their small number of harquebuses and horses frightened the natives; but their main advantages were their over-riding confidence in their invincibility, their superior military discipline, and their ability to find collaborators among their potential victims. Cortés, for example, made use of an Aztec woman who became known as Doña Marina. Not only did she serve him as an interpreter and a diplomatic agent, but she secured the alliance of the inhabitants of Tlaxcala, which furnished him with thousands of soldiers and porters. Pizarro and Almargo played off the rival claimants to the Inca throne and then killed them, leaving the Inca armies without leadership. The *conquistadores* seized all the treasure they could lay their hands on, took many lives, and tried to destroy the native civilizations of Mexico and Peru. Cortés tore down the temples and houses of Tenochtitlán and founded a new capital, Mexico City, on its ruins. Pizarro chose to abandon the Inca capital of Cuzco and to establish Spanish power at Lima, which was closer to the sea.

The *conquistadores* divided the conquered lands into vast feudal *encomiendas* and paid only nominal allegiance to the King of Spain. They substituted themselves for the native aristocracy and exercised seignorial rights over the Indians. Ignoring the Spanish government's policy of assimilation, they maintained themselves as a superior race and tried consciously to give the natives a feeling of

*Aztec emissaries before their conquerors*

inferiority. In Mexico there were more mixed marriages than in South America, but the growing number of half-breeds (*mestizos*) were treated as second-class Spaniards by the dominant whites. The *encomenderos* faced a perennial shortage of labor. Consequently, they overworked their own Indians and reduced conquered tribes to virtual slavery. These conditions were hardly favorable to missionary activity, which progressed in spite of them.

The Spanish government tried to weaken the *encomienda* system and to limit the exploitation of the Indians, but its anti-feudal and pro-Indian policies were no longer enforced by the 1570s. Thereafter the government of the colonies became increasingly decentralized. Partly owing to the financial burdens of his wars in Europe, Philip II tended to transfer the costs of colonization to local officials, abandoning some of his authority to them as compensation. The rapid decline of the Indian population and the decline in the real value of money tribute caused by mounting inflation made agriculture based on the *encomienda* system less and less profitable. The Spanish settlers then turned to the more lucrative economic activities of mining and ranching. Both types of enterprise were carried on by private capitalists, and the government in Madrid had to be content with its royal fifth from the silver mines and with other forms of taxation.

By the end of the sixteenth century a new type of seignorial estate, the *hacienda*, developed in Mexico. The *hacienda* was an extensive self-sufficient community, with its own grain fields, grazing lands, and domestic industry. Its master was a true feudal lord. He maintained order, administered justice, and had absolute control over his native serfs—contemptuously called *peons.** Their foreheads bore the brand of their owner's name: "Marques del Valle," "Doña Ysabel de Villaneva." Most of the rural Indians remained an inferior race in the eyes of the Spaniards, including many of the priests, who despised and segregated them. Even the friars lost their original missionary zeal, and their abbots began to behave like *hacienda* lords. Meanwhile, by 1600, the Indian population was literally decimated, having plummeted from 25 to 2.5 million. This demographic catastrophe was due mainly to massive epidemics of European diseases against which the Indians had no immunity. In northern Mexico, cattle far outnumbered people by the beginning of the seventeenth century.

Charles I and Philip II tried to develop a consistent and enlightened colonial policy, and their achievement in governing the New World was an impressive one. They provided courts staffed by salaried professional judges, they issued decrees protecting the Indians from outright slavery, and they supported the humanitarian efforts of the Roman Catholic Church, though Philip also introduced the Inquisition into the New World in 1569. Spain showed the other Atlantic nations the economic value of colonies for the power of the modern state, and she created the model of a new government policy—mercantilism*—that would best promote this value. But, like much sixteenth-century legislation in Europe, the legislation of the Spanish Crown was imperfectly enforced in the colonies.

Yet, despite its abuses and shortcomings, the Spanish colonial empire succeeded in spreading European power and influence to a large part of the Western Hemisphere. The majority of the Indians became at least nominal Christians, and those in the towns adopted the language and culture of Spain. A slow but steady immigration from the mother country and a large number of *mestizos* assured the permanence of Hispanic civilization in the New World. Universities and printing presses were established in Mexico City and Lima in the mid-sixteenth century. The subjugation of the natives and the destruction of their leaders, their institutions, and much of their culture removed the possibility of organized rebellion against European rule. The colonists gradually developed their own way of life, and it was they, not the Indians, who were ultimately to break their political ties with Spain.

*People who walked, as opposed to *caballeros,* who rode on horseback.

*See p. 139.

### The Impact of Overseas Expansion on Europe

The discovery and exploitation of new lands and seaways eventually affected all of Europe. During most of the sixteenth century Mediterranean commerce remained more important than that of the Atlantic and Indian Oceans. Barcelona, Marseilles, Genoa, and Venice continued to send the products of Southern Europe to the North and to trade with the Near East despite the Barbary pirates, the often hostile Turks, and the Portuguese water route to the East Indies. But by the end of the century the prosperity of the Mediterranean world was over. Not only Italy, but Germany, too, declined economically as Atlantic ports replaced the Rhineland and southern German cities as commercial and banking centers. Even remote Russia was inadvertently "discovered" in the 1550s by English explorers searching for the Northwest Passage. Tsar Ivan IV welcomed them and allowed them to establish regular trade with his country through the Muscovy Company.

By the second half of the sixteenth century Frenchmen and Englishmen as well as Italians, Spaniards, and Portuguese were becoming aware of the exotic civilizations and cultures outside of Europe. In that age of nascent nationalism and religious strife, a few educated individuals began to question some of the inherited assumptions of European civilization. The Frenchman Michel de Montaigne (1553–1592) became convinced that everything human was relative and that all beliefs were merely a matter of custom. His skepticism was not typical of his time, to be sure, yet it stemmed at least in part from new knowledge of the non-European world. Much of this knowledge took the forms of legends about El Dorado, the "noble savage," and inscrutable orientals. Even so, it made some Europeans broaden their mental horizons, and it spurred Roman Catholic missionaries to undertake anthropological studies of far-away cultures in order to find ways of communicating Christianity to their people in terms they could understand.

While the Atlantic powers drew on cosmopolitan scientific and navigational skills, they organized and financed exploratory and trading expeditions in an intensely national way. European concepts of trade and diplomacy changed radically as new ambitions and new rivalries developed over colonies, transoceanic trade, and the amassing of hoards of precious metals. Hapsburg Spain was receiving huge quantities of silver from the New World—sixty million pounds from Potosí alone—in the late sixteenth and early seventeenth centuries. The reserves of the other countries seemed inadequate in comparison, and the scramble for bullion became a major goal of the diplomatic machinations of that period. Not only did the English and the French dispute the wealth of the New World with the Spaniards, they subsidized privateers like Francis Drake, John Hawkins, and Jean Fleury to seize Spanish silver on the high seas.

The wealth of the New World allowed Spain to live beyond her resources and helped the economic development of other Atlantic states more than her own. Spain could not supply her colonists with all the goods and labor they needed. The rigidity of the Castilian economy made it impossible for industry and agriculture to respond to the stimulus of a demand that was increasing—both in quantity and as a result of rising prices. In fact, Spain used much of her newly acquired metals to buy foreign goods and services for domestic consumption, and to finance her abortive attempts to dominate Western Europe by force of arms. Moreover, who can say how many men of courage and ability went to the colonies to seek their fortunes, and thus were lost to Spain?

The diffusion of American bullion stimulated the growth of capital and the spirit of enterprise among merchants, bankers, and manufacturers in Northwestern Europe to an even greater extent than the opportunities for smuggling goods and African slaves into the labor-hungry Spanish colonies. The social effects of the "Price Revolution" will be discussed in the next chapter. Here we need only mention the part the new bullion played in financing technical improvements in manufacturing, in enlarging units of production, and in expanding markets.

: : :

By the second half of the sixteenth century a dynamic minority of Western Europeans was creating some strikingly new ways of gaining power and wealth. These kings, generals, lawyers, and explorers did not reject medieval values and institutions as self-consciously as did the leaders of the Renaissance and the Reformation. They adapted some of these values and institutions to new purposes, but they also did things that had been unthinkable in the Middle Ages. Medieval monarchs could not have relied primarily on middle-class lawyers to run their countries or used resident ambassadors to keep in touch with foreign courts. Medieval generals had not even considered bombarding infantry troops with gunshot. No one in the Middle Ages had dreamt of sailing westward in order to arrive in the East. In Europe itself England, France, and Spain were becoming strong centralized states. But the most portentous event of the period covered in this chapter—and this is why 1492 is the one date everybody knows—was the "discovery" of the New World. There Spain gained more wealth and power than any European state since ancient Rome.

## SUGGESTED READINGS

Elton, Geoffrey R., *England under the Tudors*, Vol. IV of *The History of England*, ed. Charles Oman. New York: Barnes and Noble, 1955.
Autoritative survey.

——— *The Tudor Revolution in Government.* New York: Cambridge Univ. Press, n.d.*
Specialized study of the formation of the New Monarchy in England.

Castro, Américo, *The Structure of Spanish History.* Princeton, N.J.: Princeton Univ. Press, 1954.
This controversial interpretation stresses the importance of Jewish and Muslim influences in early modern Spain.

Elliott, John H., *Imperial Spain, 1469–1716.* New York: St. Martin's Press, 1964.
A learned and readable work—the best source on Spain's new monarchs.

Lynch, John, *Spain under the Habsburgs*, Vol. I (to 1598). Oxford: Blackwell, 1964.
Another excellent scholarly work.

Brandi, K., *The Emperor Charles V.* Trans. C. V. Wedgwood. London: Cape, 1960.
Excellent biography.

Pollard, Albert F., *Henry VIII.* London and New York: Longmans, Green and Co., 1954.
Best scholarly biography.

Holborn, H., *A History of Modern Germany: The Reformation.* Vol. I
See comment in readings for Chapter I.

Stavrianos, Leften S., *The Balkans since 1453.* New York: Holt, Rinehart and Winston, 1958.
Useful on the Ottoman Empire at its height.

Potter, G. R., ed., *The Renaissance*, Vol. I of *The New Cambridge Modern History.* Cambridge, Eng.: Cambridge Univ. Press, 1961.
See J. R. Hale's fine chapter on the art of warfare.

Nef, John U., *War and Human Progress.* Cambridge, Mass.: Harvard Univ. Press, 1950.
Reissued as *Western Civilization Since the Renaissance.* New York: Harper and Row, 1963. Torchbook.*
Even though this thoughtful and learned work is not always convincing in its effort to disprove any positive correlation between war and technological advances, the chapters on early modern economic and military development are excellent.

Mattingly, Garrett, *Renaissance Diplomacy.* Baltimore: Penguin Books, 1964.*
Lively and definitive.

Nowell, C. E., *The Great Discoveries and the First Colonial Empires.* Ithaca, N.Y.: Cornell Univ. Press, 1954.*
A good introduction.

Parry, J. H., *The Establishment of European Hegemony: Trade and Expansion in the Renaissance.* New York: Harper-Row, 1966.*
An excellent broad survey.

——— *The Age of Reconnaissance.* New York: New American Library of World Literature, 1963.*

Full of interesting information on the techniques of European expansion.

Cipolla, Carlo M., *Guns, Sails, and Empires: Technological Innovation and the Early Phase of European Expansion.* New York: Funk and Wagnalls, 1967.*

An interesting scholarly account.

Morison, Samuel Eliot, *Admiral of the Ocean Sea.* 2 vols. Boston: Little, Brown and Co., 1942.

The standard life of Columbus—stresses his voyages.

Díaz del Castillo, Bernal, *The Conquest of New Spain.* Trans. J. M. Cohen. Baltimore: Penguin Books, 1963.*

A classic, first-hand account by a common soldier.

Haring, C. H., *The Spanish Empire in America.* New York: Harcourt, Brace and World, 1963.*

Stresses institutional development.

*Paperback

CHAPTER IV

# EARLY MODERN EUROPE IN AN AGE OF CRISIS, 1560–1648

New conditions create new kinds of crises. By 1560 European civilization had achieved a degree of dynamism unknown anywhere until then. An important minority of Europeans was acquiring an organizing energy and a capacity for constructive change that could legitimately be called modern. Europe had more people, more money, and more overseas contacts than ever before. But Europe had to adapt herself to all these new conditions. Could she feed her growing population, adjust her economy to new price levels, and consolidate her tenuous overseas contacts?

In addition to impersonal ingredients like rising prices, population increase, and the growth of sea power, the crisis of the early modern period involved a whole range of human choices between opposing jurisdictions, loyalties, and outlooks. Overmighty subjects opposed their centralizing monarchs and were often supported by religious opponents of the established church. Such combined opposition threatened the civil order and security of France and the Netherlands in the second half of the sixteenth century and of Germany and England in the first half of the seventeenth century. Conflicts between Catholics and Protestants set a painfully high price on weakness or errors of judgment in the struggle for secular power between dynasty and region and between competing dynasties in the new European power game. For the opposition between rival religious groups left less room for accommodation than conflicting secular loyalties. Meanwhile, the struggle to reconcile religious yearnings with the new secularism found cultural expression in the baroque style.

Spain played a preponderant role in European affairs between 1560 and 1648, but she was to be the least successful of the major states in adjusting to the new material conditions of the age. Having overreached herself in every field of endeavor, she eventually went into a proud decline. Although she did not experience the kind of domestic strife she so cunningly encouraged in the Netherlands, France, and England, these countries took the leadership of the modern world away from her in the seventeenth century. Philip II's crusade against them stimulated their contending parties to work out political and religious compromises in the interest of temporary national unity. The Hapsburg Crusade was also a struggle for power on land and sea, and here too the

Dutch, the English, and the French soon outdistanced the Spaniards. No country became truly modern economically until the Industrial Revolution, but England, Holland, and France left Spain far behind in economic growth based on commercial capitalism.

## ECONOMIC EXPANSION AND ITS CONSEQUENCES

Having seen the intense activity of the sixteenth century in the arts, religion, politics, war, diplomacy, and geographical exploration, we turn now to the economic expansion of that exuberant age. This expansion was well under way before the importation of precious metals from America transformed a steady rise in prices into a "revolutionary" inflation. In the Mediterranean area and Germany the economic surge was over by 1600; in northwestern Europe it lasted until 1650. Prices had begun to rise in the late fifteenth century as a result of population growth, the monetary devaluations and soaring budgets of governments, and the extension of world trade and domestic commerce. Labor and capital were plentiful, and new techniques of organization and exchange put them to more effective use than ever before.

Yet the economic expansion of early modern times produced its own crises. Trade and commerce played a dynamic role in allowing specialization and better use of available resources by the mid-seventeenth century, but the material gain barely sufficed to support the accompanying increase in population. There was a limit to what new techniques of organization and exchange could accomplish in a pre-industrial civilization. Instead of raising the overall level of living they created a few more rich people and a great many more poor people. The resulting strains in the social order were intensified by the disintegration of the medieval corporate ethic and its gradual replacement by an ethic based on individual initiative.

### Early Modern Capitalism, 1450–1650

Early modern capitalism developed in a cyclical pattern. There were overlapping periods of expansion and regression. In one region the economy prospered, while elsewhere it declined. Sometimes capital accumulated from commerce in goods; sometimes it was lost in loans to governments or through speculation on the value of money, securities, and land. It should be noted—especially in our age of extreme specialization—that big businessmen often engaged in several kinds of activity at once. Still, certain basic trends and periods are discernible for Western and Central Europe between the late fifteenth and the late seventeenth centuries.

#### *Commerce and Banking*

The period roughly between the 1450s and the 1530s has been called the period of the Fuggers, not only because of the great wealth of this family, but also because its business activities were typical of the age. Hans Fugger had come to the southern German city of Augsburg in 1380 and had founded the family fortune from profits in the large-scale manufacture of cloth. His son Jacob, and his grandsons, Ulrich, George, and Jacob (later called The Rich), continued in the cloth trade and extended their activities into banking, mining, and foreign commerce. In addition to lending huge sums of money to the Austrian Hapsburgs and the Elector of Saxony, Jacob the Rich (1459–1523) also invested considerable capital in mining enterprises in Bohemia and Saxony and furnished most of the silver of his time. The House of Fugger had important branches in Venice, Lisbon, and London, and in Antwerp, which was the main center of commerce in Europe until it was sacked by the Spaniards in 1576.* It was there, rather than at Lisbon, that the bulk of Portugal's imports from the Indies was marketed.

Taking high profit margins on merchandise was the most characteristic capitalist operation in the century of the Fuggers, but in the second half of the sixteenth century many businessmen became more active in dealings in money and interest-bearing loans than in trade. The main stimulus to this new activity was the need

*See p. 144.

of the Spanish government to transfer vast amounts of silver from America to various places in Europe in payment for merchandise and troops. Having expelled their own Jewish businessmen, and disdaining such transactions themselves, the Spaniards had to turn to foreigners. The activities of Genoese bankers in handling Spain's finances were typical.

The Genoese financiers signed contracts (*asientos*) in which they agreed to pay the Spanish government's obligations elsewhere in Europe in return for silver to be collected later. In effect, they were extending credit to the kings of Spain. Regular fleets made the run from Barcelona to Genoa, where the bankers traded their cargoes of silver against bills of exchange obtained in other Italian cities. These bills of exchange might be payable in gold in Antwerp to Spanish armies fighting the rebellious Dutch or to merchants who had sold manufactured goods for shipment to the Spanish colonies overseas. The Genoese not only put their own money to work in these transactions, they also solicited investment funds all over Europe. Profit margins were less than 5 per cent, but the large amounts involved made the enterprises worthwhile. Unfortunately, the kings of Spain frequently defaulted on their debts (1557, 1575, 1607, 1627, and 1647).

These repeated government bankruptcies shook the foundations of capitalism at a time when the influx of gold and silver from America allowed Europe to live beyond its means and to invest beyond its savings. Spain's wars wasted rather than accumulated capital. The Genoese credit manipulators and speculators recovered part of their losses at the expense of their clients and by effecting compromises with the bankrupt governments; less sophisticated investors were ruined.

Other businessmen throughout Italy had compensated for the loss of Asian trade to the Portuguese by concentrating on banking in the sixteenth century. Some of them had also turned to the manufacture of silks and luxury goods for export to Northern Europe, where everything from the homeland of the Renaissance was in great demand. Others profited from the still active commerce within the Mediterranean Basin. Like everyone else Italian businessmen suffered from the financial crisis at the end of the sixteenth century, but they were unable to benefit from the subsequent recovery based on a revival in transoceanic trade. It was the Atlantic merchants, particularly the Dutch, who gained the ascendancy in the seventeenth century.

The period from the 1590s to about 1650 was a new golden age of overseas trade with large profit margins. At the beginning of the sixteenth century the Portuguese had brought the first merchandise from India and Southeast Asia to Europe by sea and stimulated the beginning of modern capitalism. By the middle of the century, however, they had allowed the trade to languish. After Portugal was annexed to Spain in 1580, the Dutch, who were rebelling against Spanish rule, decided to take over the Portuguese maritime "empire." In the early 1600s they captured almost all of Portugal's holdings in the East Indies and extended their control over those islands. They also took Ceylon and the Portuguese base at the Cape of Good Hope by the middle of the seventeenth century. Their new transport ships were bigger and faster than any in the world, and they carried unprecedented amounts of goods. When the spice trade fell off, the Dutch introduced coffee, tea, and cocoa into Europe.

The Dutch tried to maintain a monopoly over all trade with the Far East by forming the East India Company in 1602, even though a group of English businessmen had already organized their own East India Company two years earlier. Both organizations prospered, and their prosperity stimulated the Dutch and English economies. These companies introduced a new form of business organization, the joint-stock company. It was a permanent partnership of shareholders who received periodic profits on their investments. During the course of the seventeenth century other such companies were organized not only for colonial trade but also for domestic banking and mining. The main advantage of the joint-stock company was that it could mobilize large amounts of capital for long periods of time. Shares of owner-

*An armed merchant ship on the route to the Indies*

ship were eventually offered on stock exchanges, thus creating a new business occupation, stockbroking. Indeed, by the late seventeenth century the Amsterdam Stock Exchange was to become the scene of speculation and financial manipulation that boosted the price of stocks out of all relation to their value as investments. Then Dutch capitalism, like earlier Italian capitalism, was to have difficulty in finding new investment opportunities and to turn primarily to banking.

Thus, the history of early modern capitalism is the history of a number of regional capitalisms held together by instruments of credit, ties of commerce, and exchanges of precious metals. Each of these regional capitalisms went through cycles of concentration on trade, speculation, and government loans. Investment opportunities in agriculture and manufacturing were limited by backward organizational structures and poor technology. Early modern capitalism was primarily commercial capitalism, with banking and trade providing the main accumulations of capital.

### Economic Growth

Economic growth means an increase in the amount of goods and services per capita of population. It requires the presence of capital, and it requires instruments for creating credit, for making investments, and for combining the savings of many persons. We have seen how Europe developed these instruments, and how the influx of precious metals from the New World filled Europe's need for more money. These two factors helped to stimulate commercial expansion, but economic growth also depends upon improvements in the utilization of natural resources and labor.

Between 1450 and 1650 population growth was far more significant than technological progress in fostering such improvements. During those two centuries the population of Europe west of Russia doubled. This increase was especially important in an age when production depended primarily on human power. The only other sources of energy were wood, a few water wheels and windmills, and domestic animals—which were scarce and scrawny because most available land was farmed rather than left for grazing. In part, the population expansion was made possible by the cultivation of lands abandoned during the century of population depletion following the Black Death. As more food was produced, more people could live in cities and work in manufacturing and commerce. In the sixteenth century at least twenty European cities had over fifty thousand inhabitants; Venice, Naples, and London had over 100,000; Paris had 300,000; and Istanbul had 700,000. Thus, there were increases in the total work force, in the division of labor, and in the number of consumers. All of these increases stimulated economic growth.

Unfortunately, this economic growth could not keep pace with the increase in population. Soon there was little good land left to bring under new cultivation. Agricultural techniques remained backward and crop yields low, so that by the seventeenth century Europe was beginning to have difficulty feeding itself. Furthermore, as more human beings competed on the labor market, real wages declined. This decline limited the amount of goods the poor could buy. It was partially offset by the growing number of middle-class people with money to spend, to be sure. Still, the main hindrance to economic growth was technological backwardness.

The only permanent way to increase the amount of goods and services for a whole society is to improve productivity—to raise output in relation to input. Between 1450 and 1650 Europeans made only modest advances in this direction. Their major achievement was increased reliance on water transportation.

It takes only 1/35 as much power to move a given weight over water as it does over land. The nations on the Atlantic coast benefited most from this fact. England could import forest products and furs from Russia via the White Sea, which her explorers had inadvertently discovered in their search for the Northwest Passage. The Dutch could import grain from Prussia and Poland via the Baltic. Cannon, textiles, ships' riggings, and other manufactured goods could be brought from England, the Low Countries, and France to Cadiz and then shipped on to Spanish colonists in the New World. Spices, silks, dyestuffs, cotton, coffee, tea, cocoa, tobacco, and sugar could be shipped from Asia and America to Europe. Although the masses of Europeans continued to consume only local products, the opening up of the world's sea routes provided a notable increase in the amount of goods available to those people who could afford them.

Productivity in manufacturing improved more than in agriculture, but was still inadequate. Since the Middle Ages the guilds had tried to monopolize the production of consumer goods, especially textiles, and had resisted technological innovations. Machinery was introduced primarily in the newer "industries": printing, mining, metallurgy, and armaments. Even then it was manipulated mainly by human power, and it brought only a modest increase in productivity. The big leap forward was not to come until the late eighteenth century, when a new kind of power, steam, was harnessed to machines.

The most notable advance in sixteenth-century manufacturing was organizational rather than technological. It has been called the *domestic system*, or cottage industry, from the fact that the work was done in rural homes rather than in urban shops. The guilds retained their local markets in the growing cities, but their restrictive regulations prevented them from meeting the general demand for textiles. Hence enterprising merchants organized the manufacture of cloth in the

Early printing

countryside. A new type of businessman had come into being, the entrepreneur. He supplied individual villagers with raw materials, tools, and models. One group of workers specialized in spinning the yarn. After the entrepreneur collected the yarn and paid these workers he gave it to others who wove or knitted it into cloth. In the late sixteenth century he was able to provide his knitting workers with a new machine, the stocking frame, with which they could make many times more stitches per day than they had formerly done by hand. The entrepreneur finally took the cloth to still other workers who dyed and finished it.

While most of this work was done by individuals in their own homes, it was organized on a capitalist basis. The entrepreneur controlled the means of production, paid the workers, and undertook to find markets for their products. The word *entrepreneur* means someone who undertakes an enterprise. In some cases he solicited capital investments from other people and paid a commission to still other people to sell his merchandise. He was essentially an organizer, a promoter. The entrepreneurial spirit, which was soon to spread to other kinds of economic activity, was the most important stimulus of all to the rise of early modern capitalism.

### Social Consequences

Economic expansion and rising prices upset Europe's traditional social structure. They lessened the distinctions between rich bourgeois and nobles, increased the separation between these two classes and the poor masses, and divided all three into subgroups.

In the late Middle Ages the bourgeoisie had been a relatively stable class of merchants, guild masters, and professional men (mainly lawyers and doctors). All these people had lived comfortably in towns and had treated each other as social equals. By the sixteenth century, however, some rich merchants were already buying country estates and town houses from impoverished nobles, patronizing the arts, and trying to make Renaissance ladies and gentlemen out of their children. An increasing number of the highest government officials came from the families of merchants and lawyers. The more prosperous guild masters maintained a middle-class income and were sometimes able to send their sons into the liberal professions or government service. Yet they felt a certain rancor toward the more successful merchants, who were now upper-middle class. Meanwhile, the masters of the lesser guilds became indistinguishable from the ordinary shopkeepers, who were already lower-middle class.

The transition from the medieval corporate structure to the modern class structure reflected individual ambitions as well as growing differences in income. Although the hereditary noble order was still distinguishable by its special privileges, the richest businessmen copied its style of life as best they could. The rulers of England and France carefully regulated the granting of titles of nobility to their highest officials, but the petty princes of Italy and Germany had virtually no way of stopping people from calling themselves barons and counts. Half of the men of Spain called themselves *hidalgoes*, and all Spanish women demanded to be treated as ladies. The daughters of English shopkeepers dreamed of marrying dashing knights; the sons of French royal officials began to carry swords. Anyone who could afford the price could dress and live like a noble lady or gentleman. But many real nobles could no longer afford the price, for prices more than tripled between 1500 and 1600.

#### *The Price Revolution*

This Price Revolution was the first manifestation of the now familiar phenomenon of inflation. In the sixteenth century almost no one understood that it was caused by a decline in the value of money in relation to the value of goods. The flood of gold and silver from America "inflated" the amount of money in circulation. Since the amount of goods did not increase nearly as fast, prices rose.

The Price Revolution was aggravated by speculation on the value of money itself. Speculators came to a country with foreign money inferior in gold or silver content to the money of that country. They offered to buy this dear money at a higher price than its legal value but paid for it with cheap foreign money. The speculators hoarded the dear money in the hope of using it at a later date, when it would be worth more. In the meantime, more and more cheap money circulated, causing prices to rise still higher. In his famous law, Sir Thomas Gresham (1519? –1579) described the process whereby cheap money drives dear money out of circulation.

While Gresham was one of the few people who partially understood the causes of inflation, everyone whose income did not rise as fast as prices felt its effects. Those nobles whose income came from fixed rents on small estates were ruined. Thousands of *hobereaux* in France, *Rittern* in Germany, and squires in England sold their lands to pay their debts and became a restless pool of recruits for all sides in the civil and religious wars in these countries. In Spain, those *hidalgos* whom war did not absorb sometimes stooped to thievery and even begging.

But not all the nobles in Europe were adversely affected by inflation. Some big landowners—both old and "new" nobles—in France were able to buy out peasants who paid fixed rents on small hereditary holdings and to regroup them on larger, more efficient holdings. For peasants too went into debt when there were bad harvests, when their land was devastated by war, or when their landlords "rediscovered" long-forgotten obligations. In their new arrangement with their tenants the enterprising landowners furnished them with oxen for plowing and took half of their crop, instead of a fixed money rent. The gentry of northern England engaged in large-scale sheep raising and sold the wool to merchant entrepreneurs in the textile industry. As a means of increasing their own grazing lands they began to "enclose" the common lands of their villagers. The gentry then bought out the more marginal peasants, adding their lands to these "enclosures" and forcing them out of agriculture entirely. In Russia, Poland, Prussia, and Bohemia, the nobles practically reduced their peasants to slavery in order to have a cheap work force to produce crops for export.

Class differentiations and class antagonisms increased in the cities as well as the countryside. The rich got richer, and the poor got poorer. Journeymen became lifetime day laborers with virtually no hope of achieving the security of guild membership. To make matters worse, their real wages failed to rise as fast as prices. They organized secret "unions" and tried to rebel against their employers, but the businessmen, backed by the princes, maintained the upper hand. An increasing number of poor people became beggars, bandits, and highwaymen. Minor Italian princes often welcomed their neighbors' outlaws in order to make use of them themselves. Spain had its *picaros*, France had its *gueux*, England had its "vagrants." These people divided their time between begging and stealing and, sometimes, prostitution. They had their haunts and their Thieves' Market in each major city. In 1601, England passed its first Poor Law, which required the parishes to help their paupers. But there, as elsewhere, the urban poor became a segregated, closed class with its own loyalties and a growing hatred of the rich.

### Mercantilism

Despite this social impoverishment, economic expansion and population growth strengthened the emerging national states. Bankers supplied their rulers with bigger loans; corps of royal officials collected increasing amounts of taxes for them; the precious metals of America replenished their reserves of hard cash. The increase in population provided them with more taxpayers, more soldiers, and more producers of goods and services that could be sold abroad and bring additional wealth to the nation's economy.

The territorial rulers tried to make the most of the material and human resources at their disposal through a policy called *mercantilism*, which was an early form of economic nationalism. In the sixteenth century Spain was the strongest state in Europe, and Spain had the largest supply of precious metals. The mercantilist theorists of the time thus equated national power with large reserves of bullion. According to them, those states that lacked bullion had to acquire it by selling goods and services to foreigners, and (unofficially, of course) by subsidizing freebooters to seize Spanish shipments of gold and silver on the high seas. The Dutch concentrated on selling services: commerce, shipping, and banking. England and France gave more emphasis to the export of manufactured goods.

Mercantilism—or the mercantile system—required government supervision of all these kinds of economic activity in the interest of state power. The government tried to regulate standards of workmanship in order to preserve the reputation of its country's exports. It encouraged investment in trading companies by giving them monopolies in various parts of the world. It undertook—not too successful-

A royal tax collector

ly—to protect native producers by preventing the smuggling in of cheaper, or better, foreign products. With even less success than in its efforts to eliminate smuggling it tried to keep all of its subjects busy doing productive work. Finally, again following the example of Spain, the English, Dutch, and French governments sought to acquire colonies as cheap sources of raw materials and as protected markets for manufactured goods. (See Chapters V and VI.)

### The Crisis of Scarcity

The economic crisis of early modern times was a crisis of scarcity. Certainly the necessities—not to mention the luxuries—of life had always been scarce. But by the late sixteenth century they became more *expensive* than they had ever been before. The Price Revolution was not just the result of new supplies of precious metals; it also reflected a growing disparity between the number of people and the amount of goods available to them. Despite the increase in capital and labor and the development of new techniques of organization and exchange, most Europeans saw no improvement in their level of living. Economic expansion benefited the merchants and bankers and those noblemen who made a business of agriculture, and it increased the number of activities that kings could undertake. Yet these people also found themselves competing more intensely than ever for land, raw materials, markets, colonies, and, above all, money. Here, too, the more competitors there were, the scarcer the things they competed for became.

## RELIGION AND THE EMERGING STATES OF WESTERN EUROPE TO 1588

Economic and political competition among states was still a long way from its modern form in the latter part of the sixteenth century. Dynastic marriages counted far more than nationalism in the policies of Europe's monarchs, and even in the Dutch and English wars against Spain the Catholic-Protestant split was at least as important as national feeling. The most acute struggles between Protestantism and Catholicism occurred in those countries of Western Europe where Calvinism had gained the most followers. In France and in the Netherlands some Calvinist extremists called their Catholic rulers "tyrants" and challenged the principle of monarchy itself. More often, however, the rebels of one country appealed to the monarch of another for help. Several civil wars thus turned into one international war. In its various phases, however, this war between Protestantism and Catholicism in Northwestern Europe became increasingly involved in the struggle for control of the world's sea routes.

Within each state the civil strife was to follow the same general pattern for almost a century: political opposition to centralized monarchy by certain privileged groups, supported by religious opposition to the established church. Regional and religious loyalties clashed with loyalty to the dynasty in England, Scotland, France, the Netherlands, and even Spain itself, where the Catalans were to revolt against their king in 1640. Except in England, where the Catholic minority opposed Queen Elizabeth I and the Anglican Church, Catholicism generally supported the territorial rulers, and Calvinism was widely used by sections of the nobility and the wealthy middle class in their struggles against "tyranny." The French Calvinists, or Huguenots, were always a minority, as were the English Calvinists, or Puritans. Yet the Puritans were to overthrow the Stuart dynasty and the established church temporarily in the mid-seventeenth century, as we shall see in the next chapter. Only the Scottish Calvinists, or Presbyterians, became a majority and established a state church in the late sixteenth century. Calvinism became the official religion in the Dutch half of the Netherlands in the early seventeenth century, but other religious groups were to be tolerated thereafter: Catholics, Portuguese and Spanish Jews, Arminians—Calvinists who rejected the doctrine of predestination—and many other sects. Between 1618 and 1648 the theretofore quiescent Holy Roman Empire was to experience the longest and most devastating civil war of all. Although the main opponents of the Hapsburg emperor were territorial princes themselves, they resembled the opponents of the monarchs of Western Europe in their desire to preserve their "liberties" and in their opposition to Catholicism.

We shall discuss the Thirty Years' War and its consequences for Germany later in this chapter; here we shall begin with the religious, civil, and international conflicts between 1560 and 1588. At that time everybody still believed that everybody else should belong to the same church. The monarchs of England, France, and the Netherlands were intolerant of religious minorities, who, in turn, conspired to replace them with rulers of their own faith. And ever ready to intervene in all three countries was Philip II of Spain.

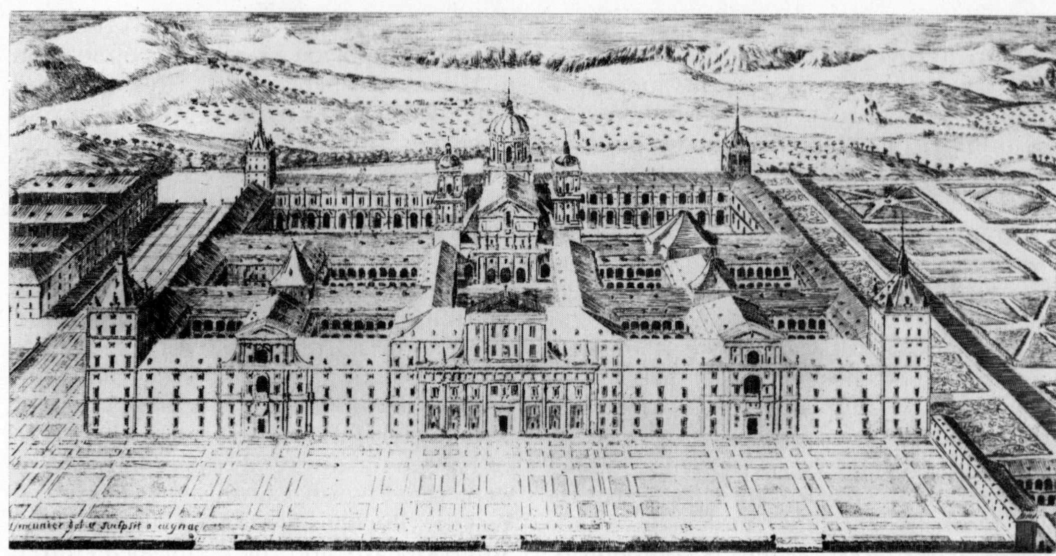

The Escorial

## Philip II

Philip II (1556–1598) was the most powerful man of his time. The wealth of Mexico and Peru more than compensated him for the imperial crown, which now belonged to the Austrian branch of the Hapsburgs. Philip had Spain, the Netherlands, Franche-Comté, over half of Italy, and a vast empire overseas. From his new capital in Madrid he kept his personal representatives in Brussels, Naples, Milan, Mexico City, Lima, and Manila under constant surveillance. He had the largest army, navy, and bureaucracy in Christendom, and he made himself the chief clerk of his global empire. Thus, in addition to being the most powerful man in the world he was the busiest.

The bureaucrat-king also wanted to be a monk-king. Brought up by priests and women, Philip became immersed in piety and made himself the champion of the Catholic Church as the only true church and as the indispensable support of monarchy and morality. Although he had some affairs in his youth, he was a faithful husband and a devoted father and lived simply, even austerely. The bureaucrat-king preferred office memoranda and behind-the-scenes intrigue to the glitter and crowds of court life; the monk-king even tried to regulate the dress and morals of his subjects. For example, he banned the saraband, which was apparently a rather sensuous dance before it later achieved its artistic dignity. During the last thirty years of his reign Philip gradually gave up the few simple things he loved: flowers, paintings, country excursions, and the company of his family. He spent most of his waking hours poring over state papers in his cubicle in the Escorial, the monumental palace-monastery he had constructed twenty-seven miles northwest of Madrid.

Rarely has a man's "home" expressed his temperament and aspirations as dramatically as the Escorial. This powerful and forbidding quadrangle of gray granite buildings was an architectural expression of Philip's bureaucratic and monkish sides. It also symbolized his conception of Spain as a monolithic Catholic state and his determination to make the ascetic spirit of the Counter-Reformation prevail throughout Christendom.

Aside from the abortive revolt of the Moriscos in 1569–1571, Spain gave Philip little trouble. The nation continued to develop along the paths already described. Its economy did not decline until after Philip's death. Philip was simply unable to mobilize all the economic resources at his disposal, and the government was often short of funds. But he had the best soldiers, sailors, and diplomats in the world and he mobilized *them* with great skill.

In a sense Philip's main problem was distance. He had to maintain contact with his far-flung agents, assure the transport of goods and men, and supervise innumerable transfers of money and bills of exchange. His navy spent most of its time trying to protect trans-Atlantic shipments of precious metals from English and Dutch marauders. The temporary withdrawal of France from international affairs* allowed Philip's fastest couriers to ride directly from Madrid to Brussels —a distance of 900 miles—in three weeks. His soldiers had to take a more circuitous route from Italy through the mountain passes of Switzerland and up the Rhine. Even in the Mediterranean Sea, which seems so small today, the Barcelona-Genoa run of 400 miles took ten days. Philip compounded the problem of distance with his habit of delaying decisions for months and sometimes years. In the end, however, he overcommitted his resources in a futile attempt to conquer England and France.

Until he launched his famous crusade against these countries Philip was fairly successful in keeping his empire together and enhancing its power. He consolidated his hold on the Kingdom of Naples and the Duchy of Milan and exerted considerable influence in Tuscany. Along with Venice, he participated in the great naval victory over Spain's long-standing enemy, the Turks, at Lepanto in 1571. His half-brother, Don Juan of Austria, commanded the victorious fleet and brought new glory to the Hapsburgs. Turkish pirates no longer molested Spanish shipping in the western Mediterranean, though Spain was unable to maintain her footholds on the North African coast. In 1580 Philip asserted his dynastic claim, through his mother, to the crown of Portugal. Philip then annexed Portugal and her overseas possessions, which were to remain under Spanish rule until 1640. He seemed to be at the peak of his power. Yet ever since 1566 he had been trying to subdue his rebellious subjects in the Netherlands.

*See p. 147.

### The Netherlands Revolt

The Netherlands were the bane of Philip's existence. Not only were many of the rebels heretics, thus threatening the Catholic unity of his empire, but they threatened its political unity as well. Philip drew two-fifths of his total revenue from these seventeen provinces, yet had to spend considerably more money than this trying to maintain military control over them. In the past the Dukes of Burgundy and Charles V had allowed the Netherlands to go about their own business and manage their local affairs. They felt no sense of national unity. The northern provinces spoke Dutch, the middle provinces Flemish, the southern provinces the Walloon dialect of French. Their constitution was medieval, with a reigning sovereign, an estates general, and the usual local "liberties." Philip wanted to change all that. To him, the Netherlands were Spanish and should submit to royal authority and Catholic orthodoxy. The fact that many Walloons, Flemings, and Dutch had become Calvinists and achieved religious solidarity by adopting the Belgic Confession in 1566 made them doubly determined to resist such pressure.

Their resistance turned into the first revolution for national independence in modern history. The Dutch Declaration of Independence in 1581 was the forerunner of the document signed by the American colonies almost two hundred years later. Revolt began in the Netherlands in 1566, when two hundred nobles of the various provinces, both Protestants and moderate Catholics, petitioned Philip not to introduce Spanish conceptions of government. Their prime motive was to preserve their "liberties." When Philip's representatives refused their petition, the nobles were unable to control the mob violence that broke out spontaneously in the major cities. The rank-and-file of the rioters were disgruntled journeymen expressing their social and economic grievances by pillaging churches and destroying all the symbols of "popery" they could find. They were bitterly anti-Catholic and anti-Spanish. Philip made no distinction between the moderate nobles and the fanatical masses. In 1567 he sent the

Duke of Alva with an army of 20,000 Spaniards to crush the revolt and punish its leaders. Alva's "Council of Blood" executed thousands of people, confiscated the estates of the rebel nobles, and levied new taxes to cover the expenses of his operations. These measures united the "natives" of all classes in their opposition to "foreign" rule.

Both sides practiced terrorism and economic warfare. The Dutch Calvinists took the initiative at first. William of Orange, a prince of the Empire, used his title as *Stadholder* (regent) of the Province of Holland to issue patents to sea captains who preyed on Spanish shipping and raided Spanish-held ports. By 1573 these "Water Beggars" had freed many cities in the northern provinces from Spanish control. William, called the Silent, regretted their brutality in killing priests and destroying churches, but he had no control over them. There were insubordination and undisciplined violence on the Spanish side, too. In late 1576 the garrison at Antwerp mutinied—because the men had not been paid—and sacked the city. This "Spanish Fury" gave the final blow to the prosperity of what had been, until the revolution began, the financial and commercial center of the Western world.

A few days after the sack of Antwerp representatives of all the provinces signed the Pacification of Ghent, by which they united to drive out the Spaniards. They wanted to form a loose federation, without regard for ethnic and religious differences, keeping their ancient "liberties" and still recognizing the nominal sovereignty of Philip. But neither Philip nor William the Silent would accept such an arrangement.

Within five years the Netherlands became permanently split in two. Philip's brilliant new commander, Alexander Farnese, Duke of Parma, subdued the Walloon provinces. By promising that their old liberties would be restored Parma was able to unite them in the Federation of Arras (1579). The Dutch provinces thereupon formed the Union of Utrecht and proclaimed their independence from Spain two years later. The great northern Flemish cities, including Antwerp and Ghent, also joined the Union of Utrecht. William of Orange and Parma each tried to reconquer the whole of the Netherlands, but the division nevertheless remained permanent. Parma was eventually to bring the Flemish cities back into the Spanish Netherlands, thus forming the territory that was to become modern Belgium. Meanwhile, the seven Dutch provinces, called the United Provinces, became the first state in modern history to dissociate the idea of the nation from that of loyalty to a dynastic monarch.

In 1584 the Dutch suffered two serious setbacks, the assassination of William of Orange and the loss of Antwerp to Parma's forces. At that point Queen Elizabeth I came to their aid. Her fear of Spanish intervention in England from across the Channel finally overcame her dislike for helping rebels against a legitimate sovereign.

### England and Scotland

Elizabeth's open aid to the Dutch was soon to transform the civil war in the Netherlands into an international war between England and Spain. These two countries and, as we shall shortly see, the two extremist parties in France, had already been engaged in undeclared warfare for some time. At present, however, we shall concentrate on the domestic situation in the British Isles, which is complicated enough in itself.

The key figure in Scotland was Mary Stuart. After her father, James V, died in 1542, her mother, Mary of Lorraine, acted as regent and had her raised as a French princess. At sixteen she was married to the dauphin of France, who became King Francis II 1559, and died less than two years later. The appealing nineteen-year-old widow was now ex-queen of France but she was still the Queen of Scotland, and in 1561 she went "home" to sit on the throne of her father. The majority of her Scottish subjects had just accepted John Knox's brand of Calvinism, and they viewed her as an enemy—another example of religious loyalty versus loyalty to the crown. In order to keep her crown Mary needed outside help, from France or even England. No help came. In 1565 her subjects rebelled when she married Henry Stuart, Lord Darnley, her cousin and also a Catholic. Immediately after Darnley was killed two years later, Mary married his alleged assassin, James Hepburn, Earl of Bothwell, thus casting considerable suspicion on herself as having been privy to her husband's murder. (She had in fact stopped loving him soon after their marriage.) That was all John Knox needed. He insisted that Mary be desposed and that her infant son by Darnley be crowned King James VI. Within a year Mary lost Scotland and her third husband and fled to England. There Queen Elizabeth kept her unwanted "guest" under house arrest for almost twenty years.

During Mary's long imprisonment Philip's commanders in the Netherlands were periodically distracted by pressures from continental Catholics to liberate her. This distraction weakened their efforts to crush the Dutch rebels, while fear of Spanish intervention worsened Philip's relations with England. Mary Stuart was not only the deposed Queen of Scotland; she was also a descendant of Henry VII and hence had a claim to the English crown. Many English Catholics viewed her as their true queen, and all they thought they needed to depose Elizabeth was military help from across the Channel. When Don Juan of Austria was governor of the Netherlands (1576–1578) he longed to use his army for just his purpose. He intended to make himself King Juan by making the thrice-widowed Mary his wife. In this way he could restore Catholicism in England—and perhaps even in Scotland—make that country a Spanish satellite, and remove a potential hindrance to crushing the Dutch revolt.

Philip was much too cautious to sanction an overt attack against his rival Elizabeth. He preferred behind-the-scenes intrigue with the English Catholics. This approach was less expensive and less dangerous than war. Besides, Philip felt that any support he might give to Mary Stuart would benefit her French relatives, not Spain. Elizabeth was also a cautious and skillful intriguer; she had more need to be than Philip.

### *Queen Elizabeth I*

When Elizabeth came to the throne the English nation was weak and demoralized. Her sister, Mary Tudor, had been almost as unpopular a queen in England* as Mary Stuart was in Scotland a decade later. Mary Tudor had opened the country to Spanish and Catholic influence, forced many Protestants into exile, and lost Calais, England's last foothold on the continent, to France. The English people longed for unity and peace. Elizabeth was able to avoid foreign entanglements simply by never getting married, though that solution could last only as long as she lived. Unity at home was harder to achieve, for the Catholic and Protestant factions hated each other. Any concession Elizabeth made to one of them was bound to antagonize the other. She decided that the only way to rule successfully was to play down the religious issue and to cultivate the patriotic loyalty of the people to herself as the embodiment of the nation.

Elizabeth combined the Renaissance versatility of her father with all the feminine wiles she could think of. She had to, as a woman doing a man's job. She wooed her subjects with innumerable public appearances, making herself as beautiful and beguiling as possible. They in turn idolized her as their Good Queen Bess, their Gloriana, their Faerie Queen. In foreign affairs Elizabeth avoided war and played off one suitor against another in the diplomatic game of "Who will be the King of England?" At home she followed her father's practice of relying on commoners and the new gentry as the main support of royal power. She also patronized the humanist scholars, the arts, and the theater.† Many Englishmen resented her religious policy, but were very grateful for low taxes and domestic and foreign peace.

Religion was the issue on which Elizabeth showed the greatest degree of shrewdness and flexibility. Here, too, her personal preference was that of her fa-

*See p. 84.

†See p. 162.

ther—an independent state church that retained most of the Catholic ritual and dogma. She compromised with the returning Protestant exiles on dogma by allowing Parliament to pass the Thirty-Nine Articles in 1562, but she resisted every effort of the growing number of Puritans in Parliament to alter the organization or ritual of the Church of England along radical Calvinist lines. Puritans and Catholics might think as they wished in private, but they all had to attend the services of the established church. Ths policy, despite the fines for nonattenders, was bearable enough to prevent civil disobedience. Except for an abortive uprising by some Catholic nobles in northern England, and sporadic armed resistance in Ireland, Elizabeth managed to make her will prevail throughout her realm. Papal attacks on the legitimacy of her rule and secret plots by Catholic zealots against her life forced her to become more positively Protestant. They also strengthened her popularity, even among the Puritans.

But Elizabeth was more interested in sea power than in Protestantism. We have already seen how Frobisher, Hawkins, and Drake carried on extensive overseas explorations during her reign. Although Elizabeth also secretly subsidized English "sea dogs" who preyed on Spanish shipping, her main concern was with her regular navy. Her predecessors had already established the tradition of spending a larger proportion of their revenue on ships of war than other European monarchs, and the growing enmity with Spain made control of the sea increasingly important. In the 1570s and 1580s the queen gave Sir John Hawkins a free hand in building up a fleet of ships that were faster and more adaptable to the wind than any others in the world. When Philip II finally attacked England in 1588, control of the sea was as important to him as striking a blow at Protestantism. Before discussing that event, however, we must turn to one other participant in the international events leading up to it, France.

#### Religious Wars in France

Whereas Elizabeth was able to preserve royal power, maintain civil peace, and strengthen England's naval power, in France the whole achievement of the New Monarchs was threatened by a constitutional and religious struggle that lasted for almost thirty years. Despite official persecution, the number of Huguenots had grown steadily in many provincial cities in the 1550s. Then, almost half of the nobility also adopted Calvinism in the 1560s and 1570s. These nobles refused to be persecuted like ordinary artisans because of their faith. They intended to resist and, if necessary, to revolt. The weakness of the Valois monarchy encouraged their determination to do both. After Henry II died in 1559, his widow, Catherine de' Medici, tried to rule France in the name of her sons, Francis II, who died in 1560, Charles IX, who died in 1574, and Henry III, who died in 1589. But neither Catherine nor her weak sons could command the kind of loyalty that Elizabeth had in England.

Three religious factions fought each other for political power in France. Catherine and the moderate Catholic nobles sometimes joined forces with the ultra-Catholic House of Lorraine and Guise against the Huguenots in the name of religious unity, but the effort of the Guises to take over control of the state prevented such alliances from lasting very long. It also caused some of the leading moderate Catholics—most notably Gaspard, Admiral de Coligny, and his two brothers—to change their religion and become leaders of the Huguenots. The Huguenot faction had two other powerful leaders in Prince Louis of Condé and King Henry of Navarre, who were princes of the blood in the Bourbon line. Although the religious wars were not originally a struggle against the Valois kings, in the end of Bourbons were to claim their right to the crown through their descent from Louis IX, and the Guises were to claim it through their descent from Charlemagne.

The importance of dynastic marriages in the late sixteenth century was especially evident in France. In 1571 Catherine de' Medici tried to reconcile the Catholics and the Huguenots by marrying her daughter Margaret to Henry of Navarre. She also proposed the marriage of her son Francis, the Duke of Alençon, later Duke of Anjou, to Queen Elizabeth of England, hoping thereby for an English alliance against Spain. This proposal failed, but Francis' brother Henry fared better. William the Silent proclaimed him "Defender of the liberty of the Low Countries" in an effort to get a French alliance; Poland elected him her king; and he was finally to become King Henry III of France, the last Valois ruler of that country. Meanwhile, the current king, Charles IX, was betrothed to another Elizabeth, daughter of Emperor Maximilian II, who, again for dynastic reasons, gave his daughter Anne in marriage to his Hapsburg cousin Philip II. Philip had become a widower after the death of his third wife, Elizabeth of Valois, another daughter of Catherine de' Medici, and was later to claim the French throne on the basis of his former marriage to her.

Until the final victory of Henry, King of Navarre, in the 1590s, the civil and religious wars kept France in a state of near anarchy. There was no continuous battlefront behind which civilians could go about their business in safety. At any moment a town or whole province on one "side" might revolt and start a local war of its own. France's impoverished but still bellicose nobles served all the contending factions in no less than nine successive wars. At first they claimed to be trying to free the king from the pernicious influence of their rivals, but many of them were actually rebelling against the centralizing tendencies of the monarchy itself. While the nobles rebelled in the name of their lost feudal "liberties," Calvinist political theorists justified rebellion in the name of religious liberty. They put forth the idea that government was based on a contract between the sovereign and his subjects and that the King of France had violated this contract by persecuting the Huguenots. Such was the message of François Hotman's *Franco-Gallia* and the anonymous tract, *Vindicix Contra Tyrannos.*

Unable to maintain order at home, the French government lost influence in international affairs. Indeed, some of its subjects were willing to call in foreign help, thus involving their own civil war in the international struggle of the 1560s and 1570s. The Huguenots offered to give Calais back to England if Elizabeth would send them aid. The Guises risked making France a Spanish dependency in return for money from Philip II to help them gain the French throne. While France was at peace with England and Scotland, the Guises plotted with English and Scottish Catholics to make Mary Stuart, their niece, the queen of those two countries. While France was at peace with Spain, the Huguenots offered to help the Dutch Calvinists in their struggle against Philip II. The existence of France as a sovereign nation-state was threatened by this conflict between national, dynastic, and religious loyalties.

Terrorism and counterterrorism mounted as the wars in France continued with no end in sight. Rival families and neighbors slit one another's throats. Roving bands of soldiers—including the German and Swiss mercenaries used by both sides—devastated the countryside and committed atrocities against civilians. The worst was the Massacre of Saint Bartholomew, on the night of August 25, 1572, when several thousand Huguenots were dragged from their beds and slaughtered. Catherine de' Medici, prompted by the Guises, had ordered this action as a means of eliminating the Huguenot leaders who had assembled in Paris for the marriage of her daughter to King Henry of Navarre. Then the Parisian masses, unleashed by their fanatical priests, went on a rampage of cruelty toward everyone suspected of being a heretic. Similar massacres occurred in a number of provincial towns during the next few months. Henry of Navarre escaped with his life by temporarily becoming a Catholic, but thereafter the Huguenot masses also got out of hand in their passion for revenge. Whole towns in southwestern France rose up against their royal governors, tortured priests, and pillaged the treasures of the Church.

Under King Henry III (1574–1589) the French monarchy became increasingly weaker. Trying to play off the Guises against the Huguenots, he lost his independence in the process. Although he was not without intelligence and personal courage, his penchant for pretty young men tarnished the already fading dignity of the Crown and divided the court into factions around his favorites.

Yet there were Frenchmen who wanted to restore the authority of the monarchy and play down religion as an excuse for everlasting war. They called themselves *politiques*, that is, people for whom political considerations were more important than anything else. The political philosopher Jean Bodin said that every society must have a monarch strong enough to force everybody to obey the law of the land. He was thus the first advocate of the modern idea of the sovereign state and royal absolutism. Henry of Navarre was also a *politique*, as we shall soon see. But both King Henry III and Duke Henry of Guise still barred his way to the throne in the late 1580s. Since Philip II was to become involved in the outcome of the dynastic struggle among the three Henry's we must return to his activities.

## THE HAPSBURG CRUSADE AND ITS AFTERMATH

Philip II was a reluctant crusader. He did not openly declare war on England until 1588 or on France until 1589. His main concern was to keep his dynastic empire intact. He also wanted to keep it completely Catholic, but he was not willing to force Catholicism on "heretics" elsewhere unless they threatened his own possessions. For almost three decades he had been giving surreptitious support to the English and Scottish Catholics and to the Guises in France. Still, if there had been no revolt in the Netherlands, there would probably have been no Hapsburg Crusade. It was mainly to keep his sovereignty there that Philip finally agreed with his more avid advisers that he had better control England, Scotland, and France, as well.

The pope, the Jesuits, and the Guises had been plotting a Catholic restoration under Mary Stuart in England and Scotland for twenty years. English fears of such a plot had prompted Elizabeth to aid the Dutch rebels in 1584 and to sign Mary Stuart's death warrant three years later. Mary's execution gave Philip a good excuse for an invasion and removed the danger that it would put a pro-French queen on the English and Scottish thrones. Philip also concluded that it would be cheaper to assemble a gigantic invasion force than to continue indefinitely to pay the cost of protecting Spanish galleons from English and Dutch "sea dogs." The other Catholic plotters on the continent prayed for his success but gave him no financial support. Thus their "Enterprise of England" became a purely Spanish undertaking.

### The Armada

The plan of this crusade was that a fleet assembled in Spain would sail to the Netherlands and escort Parma's army across the Dover Straits to the English coast. After many delays, the Invincible Armada, commanded by the Duke of Medina Sidonia, arrived at the western end of the English Channel on July 31, 1588, on its way to Parma's army. It was the most formidable concentration of naval power the world had ever seen: 130 ships weighing 58,000 tons; 30,000 men; and 2,400 pieces of artillery. The English fleet, smaller in tonnage but faster and more maneuverable, was waiting for it at Plymouth. It was commanded by Lord Howard of Effingham, with Drake, Hawkins, and Frobisher playing leading roles in the battles that followed. Medina Sidonia's task was to sail directly eastward through the Channel to the Flemish port of Dunkirk —a distance of about 200 miles. The English task was to destroy his fleet before he got there.

In the ten days between the Armada's appearance off the coast of Plymouth and its passage through the Dover Straits it fought four separate battles with the English fleet, battles that ushered in a new era in naval warfare. Each side had to change its prearranged tactics, and each made mistakes and suffered heavy losses. The main reason for the Spanish failure was that Parma's invasion barges, blockaded by a Dutch fleet, could not get out of Dunkirk harbor when the Armada arrived as near to it as its deep-draught ships would allow. The livelier English ships dealt a major blow to the Armada in the narrow Dover Straits. Had Parma's barges been ready, the Armada might still have

*The English fleet battles the Spanish Armada*

accomplished its task. As matters stood, however, the pursuing English forced it to keep moving northward. Medina Sidonia took it around the northern coast of the British Isles and back to Spain—defeated.

Like many historical events, the defeat of the Spanish Armada gave rise to legends not supported by the facts. The Armada was not a broken remnant after its last encounter with the English, nor were all the English ships small and all the Spanish ships large. Part of the Armada was wrecked in storms off Scotland and Ireland, but two-thirds of the fighting ships and half of the total fleet that had originally left Spain managed to get back eventually. The losses in the northern waters were due as much to faulty construction as to the great "Protestant wind" that supposedly drove the ships off their course. It was natural for the English to adopt the legend of the "Protestant wind" as material proof that God was on their side. Even the Spaniards accepted it, preferring to believe that God had let them be defeated *this* time for their past sins without releasing them from fighting for His cause another time.

There was not to be another time. By magnifying the real defeat of the Armada the legends made its effect decisive. England had been saved from invasion, and Spain had been humiliated. Europe's Protestants were confirmed in their belief that God Himself was a Protestant. The Catholics outside of Philip's empire felt a certain relief in learning that Spain was not, after all, God's chosen champion. Spain was to remain at war with France until 1598, England until 1604, and the United Provinces until 1609, and her preponderance on the continent was to last for more than a generation. But after 1588 the emerging national states of northwestern Europe felt increasingly free to develop in their own way without conforming to any externally imposed creed.

### England after 1588

The defeat of the Armada was a dramatic high point in the most expansive period in English history. We call it the Elizabethan Age although it lasted from 1575 to 1625. It is difficult to explain why a nation exhibits a particularly high level of striving and achievement at any given time. Whatever the explanation, in England this level was reached early enough to save the country from invasion and then sustained for a generation by this success. During the period in question the expansive spirit of England's businessmen developed the country's industries and resources at such a pace that their achievements have sometimes been called a first "industrial revolution." In government this was a period of increased efficiency of administration and of growing claims by the House of Commons for a share of power. It was England's golden age of drama and music.* It was also an age in which English influence penetrated into the surviving pockets of Celtic culture in Wales, Cornwall, and Ireland. Especially important for the future, it was an age of geographical expansion and the beginning of overseas colonization.

Elizabeth I was able to maintain the essentially aristocratic structure of society despite the vitality of England's ambitious commoners and gentry. Faction and rivalry kept life at court intense and vigorous; newly rich landowners were often unscrupulous in enclosing the peasants' common lands; the officers of the new joint-stock companies filled their own pockets at the investor's expense. Even enterprising apprentices—like the heroes of the American writer Horatio Alger—could aspire to wealth and success. Once rich, people dressed ostentatiously and talked extravagantly ("I hunger and thirst to serve thee"), but Elizabeth was able to keep these upstarts within bounds by the doctrine of "degree, priority, and place." She supported the new gentry as strengthened by her father and managed to avoid watering down the value of aristocracy by not creating too many new peers.

Bolstered by the victory over the Armada, Queen Elizabeth was able to maintain national unity until her death. Englishmen became prouder than ever of being English. Their patriotism expressed itself in popular songs, in parliamentary speeches, and in the theater. We can see it in Shakespeare's plays. The following excerpt from *Richard II* is typical:

*This earth of majesty, this seat of Mars,*
*This other Eden, demi-paradise . . .*
*This blessed plot, this earth, this realm, this England.*

Both Catholics and Puritans rallied to Elizabeth as the embodiment of national glory. When she died in 1603, it was even possible for the same monarch to assume the crowns of both England and Scotland with each nation keeping its established church.

Yet when James (Stuart) VI of Scotland became James I of England (1603–1625), the seeds of disunity that Elizabeth had kept dormant began to germinate. In the seventeenth century England could not avoid the kind of religious and civil strife that was already rampant on the continent. Elizabeth's successors were unable to share sovereignty with Parliament the way she did. The English were ultimately to discover, along with everyone else, that sovereign power cannot be shared by two determined claimants. The Stuarts lacked Elizabeth's popularity and her ability to keep the loyalty of her opponents. James I's persecution of the Catholics prompted a group of them to try to blow up the Houses in Parliament in the famous Gunpowder Plot of 1605. He then succeeded in antagonizing both the Puritans and the House of Commons during the rest of his reign.

The Stuarts were also unable to preserve Elizabeth's royal power. In the last decade of her reign the authority of the Crown was already relying heavily on favoritism and bribery. These were considered normal in a situation where courtiers and government officials received only nominal salaries. But with Elizabeth's restraining influence and the foreign danger gone, the system got out of control. James I—for all his bigotry—was a weak ruler. He did not know when to say "No."

### France after 1588

In France the defeat of the Armada strengthened Henry III's determination to resist the Guises and to restore sover-

*See pp. 162, 165.

eignty to the Crown. Just before the Armada had arrived off the coast of England, Duke Henry of Guise had seized the royal palace in Paris, and King Henry III had fled. After the Armada had been defeated, Henry III summoned the Estates General at Blois. Since it would not support him against the ultra-Catholic league, he had the Duke of Guise murdered (December, 1588). At the news of this event, the league launched an open revolt against the king himself. He fled to the Huguenot camp and sought the protection of Henry of Navarre. There he was murdered (July, 1589) by a fanatical monk. On his deathbed, however, he had confirmed Henry of Navarre as his successor. Thus, the remaining Henry—now King Henry IV (1589-1610)—embodied the undying principle of kingship.

But Henry IV was a Protestant, and the ultra-Catholics joined Philip II of Spain in an all-out effort to depose him. France now became the main battleground of the Hapsburg Crusade. Philip viewed Henry IV as the strongest ally of the English and the Dutch, with whom he was still at war. He proposed to dismember France, transferring her border provinces to neighboring Catholic states. Then he wanted to marry his daughter to the young Guise heir, who would become king of what was left. With all of continental Western Europe up to the Dutch border on his side, Philip might have been able to crush the Dutch and launch another attack against England. Spanish and Guise armies effectively prevented Henry IV from taking Paris, and, until he could do this, his cause was in jeopardy.

As in England, it was patriotism that foiled Philip's plan in France. Except for the Catholic extremists, most Frenchmen did not want to risk making their country a satellite of Spain. The problem was how to make Henry IV acceptable to the Catholic majority without alienating the Protestant minority, of which he was the nominal leader. The solution was provided by the *politiques* of both sides: Henry would guarantee religious liberty to the Huguenots and then adopt the faith of the majority of Frenchmen himself. Having done these two things, Henry was able to break the power of the ultra-Catholic league and to march triumphantly into Paris in 1594. As long as he could keep his power as the monarch in a united nation, Paris seemed "well worth a Mass." The rallying of the French people to their own Catholic king was in some ways a more decisive blow to the Hapsburg Crusade than the defeat of the Armada.

The Hapsburg Crusade and the religious wars in France ended in 1598 when Philip II signed the Treaty of Vervins, in which he renounced all claims on French territory. He died a few weeks later, a broken man. Henry IV then opened a new era in French and European history by recognizing the legal existence of two religions in the same state. This he did with the *Edict of Nantes.* Protestantism was excluded from all episcopal cities and from any place within twenty miles of Paris, but the Huguenots were to have access to all public offices and the same civil rights as Catholic Frenchmen. In addition, they obtained some fortified towns in southwestern France and were recognized, to a certain extent, as an armed political party. Later rulers were to limit the rights of the Huguenots, but the Edict of Nantes was of momentous significance in introducing the principle of toleration to the European world.

During the next generation, France's rulers occupied themselves with the tasks of reconstruction of home and of restoring French influence in international affairs. The country's economy had suffered badly from decades of political anarchy and military devastation. Henry IV's able assistant, the Duke of Sully, restored France's communications system, making rivers more navigable and rebuilding bridges and roads. Sully also encouraged agricultural prosperity by lowering taxes, facilitating the marketing of grain and dairy products, and draining marshes. Old industries were revived and new ones—especially the manufacture of silk—were established with the help of the government. During the reign of Louis XIII (1610–1643) France's role as a European power was strengthened, first by Louis' mother, Marie de' Medici, and then by his able minister, Cardinal Richelieu.* The Hu-

*See p. 170.

guenots and the nobles still caused trouble from time to time, but Henry IV, like Elizabeth of England, had made the monarchy a popular symbol of national unity. Having already experienced their religious and civil wars, the French people were more firmly committed to the Crown after the death of their beloved sovereign than the English after the death of theirs.

### The Dutch Netherlands after 1588

Spain's interference in the French religious wars prevented her from reconquering the Dutch half of the Netherlands. No sooner had the defeat of the Armada released the Duke of Parma from the "Enterprise of England" than he found himself obliged to use much of his army against Henry of Navarre in France. Sporadic and inconclusive fighting continued between the Spanish and Dutch forces until a Twelve Years' Truce was arranged in 1609. This settlement virtually established the independence of the seven Dutch provinces, which we shall call the Dutch Republic hereafter; its legal name was the Republic of the United Provinces. When the truce expired, the Spaniards resumed hostilities. But the Dutch had grown rich and powerful at sea and were able to defend themselves until Spain finally gave up all claim to their territory in 1648.

The growth of Dutch economic and naval power was a direct result of the Hapsburg Crusade. After the Duke of Parma recaptured Antwerp in 1585, the Dutch rendered it useless by closing the mouth of the Scheldt River. The Spanish Netherlands were eventually to recover some of their former prosperity, but the permanent Dutch blockade of the Scheldt allowed Amsterdam to replace Antwerp as the "economic capital" of Western Europe. Meanwhile Philip II's attempt to keep Dutch shippers out of Spanish and Portuguese ports prompted the Dutch to take over the East Indies trade themselves. We have already noted how they captured parts of the Portuguese "empire" at the turn of the seventeenth century. As the century progressed, the Dutch built up both their merchant and naval fleets and began trading and colonizing in the Western hemisphere as well. By 1614, Holland alone had more sailors than England, Scotland, France, and Spain combined.

At home the Dutch began an interesting experiment in modern government. The Union of Utrecht in 1579 had been a military alliance, not a political federation. Nevertheless, the Estates General of these seven provinces had begun meeting regularly at the Hague, in Holland, after 1593. Its members were wealthy bourgeois, called High Mightinesses (*Hooge Moogende*). In the early seventeenth century this elite of merchants and bankers vied with the landed aristocracy for political power. At first the nobles gained some support from the lower classes, who felt exploited by the bourgeois oligarchy and whose Calvinism was a much stricter brand. A religious controversy thus complicated the political issue for a while, but as in England and France, it was settled in the name of national unity. The legal government of the Dutch Republic remained its Estates General. Not part of it, but often equally powerful, was the House of Orange-Nassau, descended from William the Silent. Throughout the seventeenth century this family had a virtual monopoly on the elective office of *Stadholder*. In theory there were seven *Stadholders*, one for each province; in practice, one member of the family was usually elected to all seven offices. The *Stadholder*, although the executive, had little power in time of peace; in time of war, however, he had effective authority as the military leader.

Philip II's attempt to conquer England, France, and the Dutch Republic stimulated these countries to resist and strengthened their patriotism. They settled their religious differences, at least temporarily, and introduced the novel idea that everyone need not be of the same faith. The Dutch Republic became the most tolerant state in Europe. The English and the French were to persecute their religious minorities again in the name of political unity, but no foreign power was ever able to make them forget that they were Englishmen and Frenchmen first, Catholics

and Protestants second. In addition, the English and the Dutch successfully challenged Spain's control of the seas and became colonizing powers themselves.

### THE THIRTY YEARS' WAR, 1618-1648

Germany was unable to resist Hapsburg imperialism and emerge as a strong independent state, as had England, France, and the Dutch Republic. The Holy Roman Empire of the German Nation had no effective central government and no national or religious unity. Its German-speaking peoples were divided into several distinct "nations," each with its own dialect and folk culture: Brandenburgers, Prussians, Pomeranians, Hessians, Swabians, Saxons, Bavarians, Austrians, Alsatians, and others.* Furthermore, the hundreds of principalities, duchies, counties, ecclesiastical lands, imperial cities, and knights' fiefs into which this "state" was splintered did not correspond to its ethnic divisions. When the Austrian Hapsburgs tried to reimpose Catholicism and imperial authority on Germany in the first half of the seventeenth century, that country became Europe's main battleground. Like the low-pressure center of a cyclone, it sucked in

*See map, p. 49.

storms—in the form of invading armies—from all directions.

### The Four Aspects of the War

The Thirty Years' War began as a struggle between the estates and the monarchy in the territories of the Hapsburg dynasty, but it soon became a German civil war, a conflict between Catholicism and Protestantism, and an international power struggle. These four aspects of the war did not coincide exactly with its four conventional chronological divisions: the Bohemian and Rhineland Period (1618-1625), the Danish Period (1625-1629), the Swedish Period (1630-1635), and the Swedish-French Period (1635-1648). Nevertheless, the issue between the Bohemian and Austrian estates and the Hapsburg dynasty was settled in the first period, the German civil war and the religious conflict were largely over by the end of the third period, and the international power struggle reached its climax in the fourth period.

#### *The Estates versus the Monarchy*

After the death of Ferdinand I in 1564 the Austrian Hapsburg dynasty had become weak; indeed, it seemed unable to keep even its personal domains united and free from Protestantism. Its religious policy had fluctuated between tolerance of Protestants and Counter-Reformation militancy, and by the early 1600s many of the nobles in the Austrian, Bohemian, and Hungarian territorial estates were non-Catholics. In 1619, however, Ferdinand II became the single heir to all the family holdings and to the imperial Crown. He intended to subdue the estates. Educated by Jesuits, he was also determined to lead a new Catholic crusade and to use Hapsburg power to transform the Holy Roman Empire into a centralized state with himself as its real as well as its nominal ruler.

#### *The German Civil War*

The religious and political situation in the Empire had not remained as it had been fixed at the Peace of Augsburg in 1555.* By the 1580s Lutheran princes had taken over ("secularized") additional ecclesiastical lands upon the death of the current archbishop, bishop, or abbot; and the rulers of the Rhineland and Bavarian Palatinate had officially adopted Calvinism. After the 1580s the Counter-Reformation, led by the Jesuits, began to reconvert parts of southern and western Germany to Catholicism. These early successes of the Counter-Reformation encouraged the Austrian Hapsburgs to reassert their political claims in the Empire, as well as to begin thinking of a new Catholic crusade. The Peace of Augsburg had put the Imperial Chamber (supreme court) under the control of an equal number of Catholic and Protestant representatives. But toward the end of the sixteenth century the Imperial Chamber lost its effectiveness by the withdrawal of the Protestant princes, and the existence of the Diet itself was imperiled. As early as 1598 the Emperor was issuing judgments affecting the political situation in the Empire from his own Aulic Council in Vienna, to which most of the imperial administrative functions had gravitated since its creation at the beginning of the century.

*See p. 83.

#### *The Religious Conflict*

Not content with peaceful proselytizing, both the Catholics and Protestants in Germany formed military leagues in the early 1600s. Led by Maximilian of Bavaria and backed by the Hapsburgs, the Catholic league was the stronger of the two. The Lutherans and Calvinists lacked unity, but they could, on occasion, call in outside aid. In 1610 war was narrowly averted by the assassination of Henry IV of France, who had promised to help the German Protestants prevent the Hapsburgs from taking over a small principality in the lower Rhineland. Although this particular issue was settled peacefully, the cyclonic character of the Empire was becoming increasingly apparent to outsiders.

#### *The International Power Struggle*

The majority of the German princes who had chosen Protestantism had done so in order to use it as a protective shield of traditional local life against a centralizing Catholic monarchy. In this respect they resembled the nobility of the Hapsburg dynastic lands and the Huguenot noblemen of France. Only in England and Scandinavia had Protestantism been connected from the beginning with the trend toward a strong national state. Protestantism had started as a movement of the noble estates in the Netherlands, but the rise of the Dutch burghers to commercial preeminence in Europe made Protestantism there an agent in the birth of a nation. In the first half of the seventeenth century the resumption of the Dutch revolt against Spain contributed to the survival of German Protestantism and the territorial sovereignty of the German princes by diverting some Spanish armies from the wars between the Austrian Hapsburgs and the Protestant princes. Swedish and French intervention was far more crucial in helping to put the territorial churches of Protestant Germany more firmly under the control of the secular rulers than anywhere else in Europe.

This final outcome was certainly not the original aim of any of the powers that transformed the German civil war into an international conflict. Spain, France, and Sweden sent their armies into Germany to further their own imperialist aims. Almost every power in Europe was to fight somebody at some time or other between 1618 and 1648—and Spain and France were to continue fighting until 1659. These struggles were all directly or indirectly related to the efforts of the Austrian Hapsburgs to destroy Protestantism in the Holy Roman Empire and to transform that "cyclonic center" into the dominant military and political power in Europe.

#### Austrian and Spanish Imperialism. Bohemia and the Rhineland, 1618–1629

We have already noted that the Austrian Hapsburgs had been consistently elected to the Bohemian Crown since 1526. We have also noted that Lutherans, Calvinists, and Anabaptists (called Brethren) had set up churches in Bohemia. The Hapsburgs had granted these Protestants a degree of toleration and had respected most of Bohemia's "liberties." Then, in 1617, they launched an anti-Protestant campaign. Like their Dutch predecessors, the Bohemian Calvinist nobles revolted. A year later they threw two Hapsburg governors out of the window of the royal palace in Prague. The governors landed in a pile of manure, so they were not physically hurt. But their "defenestration" could not go unpunished, especially since its perpetrators had the further impudence to elect a Protestant king in 1619. This revolution in Prague marks the beginning of the Thirty Years' War.

The elevation of Elector Frederick of the Palatinate to the Bohemian Crown was a slap in the face to the new Hapsburg emperor, Ferdinand II, who considered himself Bohemia's rightful king. Ferdinand was determined to depose Frederick and destroy Protestantism in his rebellious Bohemian lands. He enlisted the military assistance of Maximilian of Bavaria, a staunch Catholic, by promising him Frederick's title of Elector of the Empire. Together the forces of Ferdinand and Maximilian crushed Frederick's army at the Battle of White Mountain (1620), a short distance west of Prague. As a result of this defeat, Bohemia lost her "liberties," and tens of thousands of Bohemian Calvinists and Brethren became the first modern "displaced persons" in Western Europe, where the word *bohemian* soon came to mean a rootless individual. Ferdinand confiscated the lands of the Protestant nobles and redistributed them among German-speaking Catholics. Frederick fled to Holland, and Bohemia was reduced to the status of a mere province of Ferdinand's dynastic empire. The conquest of Bohemia also strengthened the monarchial authority in the Austrian lands, ending the power of the provincial estates and forcing many Protestant noblemen into exile.

Meanwhile, the defeated Frederick became the focal point of several European issues. First, the Emperor's arbitrary decision to transfer his electoral title to Maximilian of Bavaria aroused the other German princes to defend their "liberties." Second, Frederick's efforts to gain English and Dutch support in recovering the Rhineland Palatinate threatened to block Spain's supply route to her possessions in the Netherlands and brought Spanish troops into the war. Third, the conquest of the Palatinate by Ferdinand's Spanish and Bavarian allies brought other Protestant princes to Frederick's aid against the new Catholic crusade.

With Bohemia and the lower Rhineland firmly under Hapsburg control, Ferdinand set out to subdue the rest of Germany. He was aided in this endeavor by the outstanding *condottiere* of the age, Albert of Wallenstein, a member of the Bohemian Catholic gentry. Together with his Bavarian allies, Wallenstein defeated the combined forces of the Protestant princes in a series of brilliant military campaigns. (The King of Denmark also tried to stop the Catholic crusade and almost lost his kingdom in the process.) In 1629, Ferdinand's Edict of Restitution forced the Protestant princes to give up all lands that had been secularized since 1552. Ferdinand's arbitrary action was not only a triumph for the Counter-Reformation, it was the high point in his attempt to bring the Holy Roman Empire under his direct personal rule.

Beginning in 1621 Ferdinand II had been aided and abetted by his Spanish cousin, Philip IV (1621–1665)—or, rather, by Philip's chief minister, the Count-Duke Olivares. Thus, the danger of Hapsburg imperialism and the new Catholic crusade came from both Madrid and Vienna. While Ferdinand was crushing Bohemia, Olivares resumed Spain's war against the Dutch, the Twelve Years' Truce having expired in 1621. Olivares wanted the war to continue in Germany so that he could occupy strategic points on the overland route from Italy to the Netherlands. This Spanish imperialism threatened France with encirclement. In order to break Dutch control of the North Sea, the Spanish navy needed German port facilities on its coast. Wallenstein obliged by conquering both the North Sea and Baltic coasts of Germany. But instead of collaborating with Olivares, he began building his own navy there. This imperialism threatened Sweden's effort to build her own empire in the Baltic.

The main diplomatic opponent of the Count-Duke Olivares was the Cardinal-Duke Richelieu, first minister of France from 1625 to 1642. Richelieu was not in a position to do battle with both the Spanish and Austrian Hapsburgs at first. At home he had to deal with political conspiracies and a major Huguenot rebellion; in foreign affairs he had to stop England from helping the Huguenots and to stir up the Swiss and Italian states that bordered on Spain's lifeline to the Rhineland. Richelieu reduced the status of the Huguenots from that of an armed political party to that of a tolerated sect. He silenced his opponents at court and strengthened the power of the royal bureaucracy at the expense of the nobles.* Finally in 1630 he persuaded the King of Sweden, Gustavus Adolphus (1611–1632), to fight for France by giving him a large sum of money. Thus the Catholic Richelieu, persecutor of the French Protestants, fought the Catholic Olivares by allying himself with the Swedish and German Protestants who were fighting the Catholic Ferdinand II.

### Swedish Imperialism, 1630–1635

Whereas Richelieu thought of Gustavus Adolphus as merely a tool, the Swedish king had his own imperialist ambitions. He had modernized his country's government, sponsored commerce and industry, and invited Dutch and French experts to help him transform his peaceful subjects into disciplined soldiers. Having built up a first-class army, he had conquered Carelia and Ingria from Russia, thus connecting Finland and Estonia, both of which Sweden already controlled. In a war with Poland he had conquered Livonia (present-day Latvia) and extended Swedish influence in Courland (present-day Lithuania). A few footholds on the North German coast would almost have made the Baltic a Swedish sea.

Religion was still a major issue in Germany when Sweden entered the war on the side of the Protestants. The Edict of Restitution had destroyed the Lutherans' gains of three-quarters of a century and denied the Calvinists all legal standing. What was needed was a William the Silent or a Henry of Navarre to stem the tide of the Counter-Reformation. Unfortunately for Germany, no such national champion

* As every reader of Alexandre Dumas knows, Richelieu destroyed the nobles' fortified castles and even tried to prohibit dueling.

*A Swedish attack on Prague toward the end of the Thirty Year's War*

appeared. Gustavus Adolphus, although a good Lutheran whose small Swedish army landed in Germany singing hymns, was a foreigner, and his most likely allies, the Electors of Brandenburg and Saxony, hesitated to accept his military leadership. They only did so after an imperial army sacked the city of Magdeburg and massacred most of its inhabitants in May 1631 in an attempt to enforce the Edict of Restitution there.

For the next year and a half Gustavus Adolphus seemed on the point of forming a great Protestant Swedish empire in Northern Europe. He was a brilliant general, and his artillery and infantry were lighter and more mobile than those of most of his opponents. In 1631 he won his first major victory in Saxony, in the heart of Germany. From there he marched triumphantly westward to the Rhine and then southward into Bavaria. Even after he was killed in battle in November, 1632, his minister, Axel Oxenstierna, kept the Swedish alliance with the German Protestants going and pursued the goal of empire with the skill of a Richelieu or an Olivares.

The meteoric career of Gustavus Adolphus threatened the whole Hapsburg cause and forced Emperor Ferdinand, much against his will, to give Wallenstein uncontrolled command over a new army. Just as the Swedish king had shown that he was no mere hireling of the French, so Wallenstein tried to create an independent position for himself in the Holy Roman Empire. He had already been given the titles and lands of the Dukes of Friedland and Mecklenburg. Drawing on his own domains he was able to recruit and supply a larger army than any German prince. By 1633 he was even carrying on his own diplomatic negotiations with the Swedes, the Saxons, and the French. His goal was to "liberate" the Emperor from Spanish influence and compel him to make peace with the Protestants.

Clearly Wallenstein was not the answer to Ferdinand's needs. Thus, in February, 1634, the Emperor formally deposed him from his command. A week later this Bohemian soldier of fortune was murdered by an English soldier of fortune on his own staff. Intrigue and politics had not only removed the Hapsburg's strongest military commander, they had also negated the religious character of the Thirty Years' War.

In 1635 the Peace of Prague seemed to mark the end of the civil and religious war in Germany. Some Lutheran princes, especially the Elector of Saxony, were just as fearful as the Catholics of Swedish imperialism. Consequently they settled their differences with the Emperor in order to make common cause against the Swedes. The Calvinists, who could bring no military aid to this cause, were disregarded in the Peace of Prague. Yet by virtually annulling the Edict of Restitution the Emperor allowed the Lutheran and Catholic princes to recover all the lands they had held at the outset of the war. The Peace of Prague also increased the monarchical powers of the Emperor by providing for the dissolution of the armed forces of the princes and the maintenance of one imperial army. Confidence in the Emperor had not died, and patriotic sentiment made it possible to hope that internal disorders could be ended by the expulsion of the foreigners.

Unfortunately, this new unity was not sufficient to expel the foreigners. The Peace of Prague had deprived Sweden and France of their territorial gains, and they were determined to continue fighting. Furthermore, Spain had already prepared for a full-scale attack on France. Neither religion nor the German constitution was the issue any longer. Although Emperor Ferdinand III (1637–1657) continued to engage the French and the Swedes and those few German princes who later joined them, he wished for nothing more than an end to the interminable fighting.

### The International Power Struggle

The last phase of the Thirty Years' War was a modern power struggle in both its military and its diplomatic aspects. After 1635 the days of the *condottieri* were over. The armies of France, Spain, and Sweden were national armies fighting for imperialist goals. By 1638 the fact that all the German princes were temporarily allied with the Emperor removed the last vestiges of restraint on these plundering armies, which brought greater devastation than ever to Germany. Even dynastic ties lost their former importance as the Austrian Hapsburgs began to fear their Spanish cousins as much as their declared enemies. Spain wanted to consolidate, within the Empire, a belt of Spanish territory from Switzerland to the Netherlands. Sweden still hoped to make the Baltic a Swedish lake. The Dutch fought not only for their political independence but also to keep Antwerp landlocked and thus preserve their commercial supremacy.

But France was the main imperialist aggressor. In order to "make Europe safe for France" Richelieu and his successors gave military support to everybody who fought the Austrian or Spanish Hapsburgs. They sent armies into Germany to help the Swedes; they openly aided Portugal and Catalonia when these territories rebelled against Spain in 1640; they threatened the Hapsburg domains in Hungary by intriguing with the Protestant Prince of Transylvania; and they cooperated with the Dutch in attacking the Spanish Netherlands. In 1643, a year after Richelieu's death, the French won a great victory over the Spaniards at Rocroi. Thereafter France began to replace Spain as the strongest power in Europe. The outcome of the war between these two countries, which continued to 1659, will be discussed in the next chapter. Here we are concerned with showing how the French reduced Germany to impotence for the next century and a half.

After 1635 the war in Germany had degenerated into an interminable and devasting conflict of all against all. German and foreign armies ravaged the country without achieving any decisive victories. The soldiers were poorly and irregularly paid, many became deserters, and new recruits constantly had to be lured into the ranks, often by force. Armies had to be allowed to requisition food and lodgings from the civilian population. They pillaged, raped, tortured, burned, and spread terror wherever they went. Sometimes famine drove victorious troops out of territories they had just invaded. In such cases they destroyed everything they could not take with them: houses, vines, grain fields, livestock. Some towns became almost deserted, and many peasants temporarily fled to the forests where they were reduced to eating grass, bark, and wild fruit. During the winter the mercenary soldiers dispersed if their commander could not furnish them with good quarters.

Those who were quartered in towns were as harsh with the inhabitants as troops in the field were with the peasants. In addition, there were the inevitable camp followers—hordes of women (and children) who lived off the countryside and spread disorder and disease wherever they went.

Gone were the days of brilliant victories like those of Gustavus Adolphus and Wallenstein. Few generals could pursue an opposing army until it was completely disorganized and destroyed, and most battles were long sieges. By the mid-1640s Ferdinand III and Maximilian of Bavaria could no longer hold out against the French and the Swedes. They had begun peace negotiations with the French and the Swedes in the Westphalian towns of Osnabrück and Münster in 1643, but they continued fighting in the hope of gaining better terms. The final peace settlement was not signed until 1648.

### *The Peace of Westphalia*

French and Swedish imperialism triumphed in the Peace of Westphalia. Sweden gained several enclaves on the northern German coast as well as control over the mouths of the Oder, Elbe, and Weser rivers. Her Baltic empire was thus temporarily secured. France strengthened her eastern frontier by formally annexing parts of Lorraine and gaining the right to govern and garrison several imperial cities in Alsace. She was not to remove the Spanish threat completely until 1659, but she had triumphed over the Austrian Hapsburgs and replaced them as the dominant outside power in the affairs of the Holy Roman Empire.

The Peace of Westphalia ended the religious wars in the Empire and permanently divided it into an approximately equal number of Protestant and Catholic states.

The Hapsburg restoration of Catholicism in Bohemia and Austria was left intact. Otherwise, all the gains of the Counter-Reformation since 1624 were wiped out. Several of the larger Protestant states acquired considerable territory at the expense of former bishoprics and archbishoprics. The principle of *cuius regio, eius religio* was followed; thus there were to be no tolerated minorities within any Catholic, Lutheran, or Calvinist state, although dissenters could move to a neighboring state if they so chose. There were some three hundred states within the Empire, so a dissenter did not have to move very far.

The Peace of Westphalia also confirmed the political disintegration of the Holy Roman Empire into a hodgepodge of small sovereign states. This development had been well under way for some time. The treaties merely made it legal. Two states, the Swiss Confederation and the Dutch Republic, severed all ties with the Empire and gained complete independence. Except for Bohemia and some French-speaking territories west of the Rhine, the Empire was now completely German. Yet never was it more disunited. In the name of religion and their medieval "liberties" the German princes had successfully resisted the centralizing efforts of Emperor Ferdinand II. Each prince was now completely sovereign and had the right to conduct his own foreign as well as domestic affairs. France and Sweden made themselves the guarantors of this new "constitution," which was the negation of everything a constitution was supposed to be. For, henceforth, the Empire's "government"—its electors, its diet, its supreme court—had no real power.

This political disintegration paralleled Germany's economic decline. The loss of lives and property during the Thirty Years' War, though more devastating than in France and the Netherlands a half-century earlier, aggravated rather than initiated this decline. France and the Netherlands, and England after 1650, recovered from the ravages of their religious wars partly because they were in a geographical position to benefit from the revival of transoceanic trade and partly because they had strong central governments. In land-locked Germany, economic regression had already set in by 1600, and it became steadily worse during and after the Thirty Years' War. In the seventeenth century her town-centered economies could not expand at the same rate as the emerging national economies of England, France, and the Dutch Republic; no single German state had resources or markets comparable to these. The entrepreneurial spirit was not lacking among German businessmen, but they had no strong governments to back them.

The Thirty Years' War and the Peace of Westphalia also set a new course for international relations. Diplomacy came into its own with first-rate ministers like Richelieu, Olivares, and Oxenstierna. Hundreds of diplomats participated in the negotiations at Osnabrück and Münster. They represented almost every state, large and small, in Central and Western Europe. Out of their deliberations there emerged two basic notions: (1) that individual sovereign states were the central forces of political life; (2) that relations between sovereign states were subject to mutually accepted rules. International relations were thus frankly secularized; but the fact that religion ceased to be an excuse for imperialist crusades did not lessen the frequency of wars among sovereign states.

The Dutch political theorist Hugo Grotius (1583–1645) had formalized the idea that relations between states were governed by natural rather than divine laws in his *Law of War and Peace.** For almost one hundred and fifty years after the Peace of Westphalia the European states were to pay at least some attention to the principles of international law. Even so, all that diplomacy could (and can) do was to introduce an element of rational calculation into the relations among these states.

## EARLY MODERN LITERATURE AND ART

Europe's creative artists became hypersensitive to the crises of the early modern period. In the late sixteenth century many

*He also invented the idea of freedom of the seas, but England contested it.

of their works reflected the fractionalization of Europe along national lines. Italy and Germany had experienced the earliest national cultural awakenings and then seen these stifled by war, political disunity, religious bigotry, and economic regression. The rising nations along the Atlantic seaboard escaped this fate. But they did not escape the growing tensions of the age, and by the early seventeenth century their artists, writers, and composers—like those in Italy and Germany—expressed their anxieties in the baroque style.

### The Development of National High Cultures

In the sixteenth century Western Europeans created distinct national forms in literature and the arts within the general framework of Renaissance society and culture. Literary and artistic currents crossed political frontiers as never before, just as the Price Revolution broke through all economic barriers. Worldly ladies and gentlemen exhibited the same forms of social behavior almost everywhere. Like fashions in clothes, the fashions, techniques, and themes of literature and the arts knew no frontiers. At the same time, however, each national culture gave them its own peculiar stamp. Creative writing increasingly reflected national peculiarities; indeed, this "nationalization" of literature was a kind of secular parallel to the "nationalization" of religion fostered by the Reformation.

France produced two outstanding writers whose works provided models for the heroic and reasonable sides of early modern Europeans. François Rabelais (*c.* 1490–1553) in his *Gargantua and Pantagruel* had pictured man as a giant who could do anything. Writing in the exuberant age of King Francis I, Rabelais was not overwhelmed by the emerging conflict between religious and secular values. Whereas Rabelais reflected the exuberance of the Renaissance, Michel de Montaigne (1533–1592) expressed in his *Essays* the skepticism of a moderate and tolerant philosopher in the period of the religious wars. In that era of slaughter in the name of dogma, Montaigne asked "What do I know?" (*Que Sais-je?*) "After all," he said, "it is setting a high value on our opinions to roast people alive on account of them." Montaigne devoted his life to studying human nature at first hand, with himself as his main subject. His *Essays* taught the lesson he had learned from his own experiences: Be skeptical and reasonable and avoid living dangerously.

Besides expressing two fundamental aspects of the modern French temperament, Rabelais and Montaigne, though still remarkably cosmopolitan in their outlook, were the founders of their country's national literary language. France's high culture was to reach its full development only when Cardinal Richelieu gradually subdued her conflicting religious and political factions. For, in addition to strengthening the national state, Richelieu founded the French Academy in 1635 and endowed it with the power to discipline the vocabulary and grammar of the national language. Later we shall see how Louis XIV (1643–1715) tried to regiment the high culture of his time for the glorification of his reign. On the other hand, Spain and England experienced their cultural golden ages almost a century earlier without any regimentation from royal governments or academies.

Like Rabelais and Montaigne, Miguel de Cervantes Saavedra (1547–1616) and William Shakespeare (1564–1616) created literary prototypes of modern, secular man in a distinctly national cultural setting. Whether idealistic and heroic or skeptical and down to earth, their conceptions of character were broader and richer than the medieval contrast between good and bad men and the contemplative versus the active life. Many Spaniards claim that Cervantes' novel *Don Quixote* expresses the true Spanish character—half visionary hero (Don Quixote), half practical-minded skeptic (the faithful servant Sancho Panza). Others see it mainly as a satire on outmoded knightly values. Like Shakespeare, however, Cervantes partially transcended his own time and country and created a vision of man with universal appeal. Shakespeare's significance for the theater will be discussed presently. Suffice it to say here that he too contrasts the heroic and self-indulgent sides of man. One has only to think of Henry V and Falstaff.

Nowhere was the emergence of secular national cultures more fully expressed than on the stage. As in art and music the theater borrowed many of its conventions and techniques from post-Renaissance Italy. For example, in each country the theater adapted the stock characters and situations of the *commedia dell'arte** to its own national setting. But unlike art and music, the early modern theater was a truly popular artistic form, shared by urban people of all social classes. Hence the playwrights and the actors had to give them something they all could understand and enjoy. This common denominator was man—with all his passions and prejudices, nobility and meanness, elegance and coarseness—man trying to sleep with someone else's wife, man defending his honor, man making a fool of himself. Still, the audiences in each country wanted these actions to be related to their own national values and expressed in the language and gestures of their own culture.

The most popular writer of the early modern theater in Spain was Felix Lope de Vega (1562–1635). His plays are often cited as examples of the baroque style, but we shall concentrate on their peculiarly Spanish characteristics. As we have seen, the Spaniards took themselves and their world mission very seriously. Thus Lope de Vega glorified Spain's religious zeal, the valor of her soldiers, the honor of her noblemen, and the beauty of her women. He expressed vividly the Spanish sense of tragedy, which sees men and women as victims of their uncontrolled passions and constantly threatened by violent death and the avenging hand of God. In some of his best plays Lope de Vega also dramatizes the struggles of the Spanish peasantry against injustice, though his main purpose was to entertain. His two thousand plays deal with every subject, but he excelled in cloak-and-dagger plots where the action often turned on the "point of honor"—preventing an unauthorized suitor from "compromising" the heroine. Here the characters are not developed; only their actions are important.

Shakespeare was as English as Lope de Vega was Spanish, but his appeal is more universal because of the range and depth of his characters. Macbeth, Hamlet, Lear, and Falstaff brought a new dimension to the modern theater. Not since the ancient Greeks had man as an individual been so fully explored and displayed on the stage. Yet Shakespeare, like Lope de Vega, had to give his audiences what they wanted in order to butter his bread. And Elizabethan audiences loved violence, bawdy dialogue, and glorifications of their past. Hence, along with soul-searching monologues, Shakespeare gave them Gloucester having his eyes gouged out, Mercutio and Juliet's nurse joking about sex, and a rewritten history in which the English always beat the French during the Hundred Years' War. Like Lope de Vega, he appealed to the patriotism of all social classes.

While Shakespeare stressed the glory of England's past, Ben Jonson (1573?–1637) exposed the seamier side of London life at the turn of the seventeenth century. We have seen how corruption and bribery increased at that time. Lust for money was rampant, and all sorts of quacks and confidence men were ready to fleece greedy fools and even each other. Ben Jonson satirized all of these foibles in *Volpone* and *The Alchemist.* Volpone (The Fox) is a lascivious miser who tricks a series of legacy hunters into filling his pockets and his bed so that he will remember them in his will. Sir Epicure Mammon claims to be able to transform all kinds of metal into gold. In *Eastward Ho*, which Jonson wrote with two collaborators, even the motives of overseas exploration are shown as mean and selfish. Sir Walter Raleigh has become a worthless adventurer called Sir Petronel Flash.

The rootless lower classes in Spain were immortalized in the picaresque novel. As we know, an increasing number of people

*The Italian *commedia dell'arte* came into existence in the late sixteenth century. It consisted of a group of strolling players who improvised their dialogue and gestures on a simple standardized "set." They wore masks, and the characters they portrayed were all fixed social and regional types: the Spanish captain, the vicious old dotard (Pantaloon) from Venice, the buffoon (Polichinelle) from Apulia, the blundering servant (Harlequin) from Bergamo. Eventually the popular theater in each Western European country had its stock characters and situations. This tradition has survived in farce, burlesque, and vaudeville—and in slapstick and "situation comedy" on television.

became beggars, bandits, and highwaymen by the beginning of the seventeenth century. Unlike Ben Jonson's moneygrubbers, these *picaros* were really poor. The novels in which their adventures are described make them lovable in their efforts to outwit the authorities and pathetic in their quest for food and shelter. Beneath the surface, however, the picaresque novels express a radical pessimism and a contempt for official law and order, whose moral standards are shown to be no better than those of the bandit heroes in these novels. Poverty and lawlessness were as much a part of the Spanish scene as nobles dedicated to honor and saints dedicated to God.

Printing had a decisive influence on both the national and the international trends in literature and learning. Most educated Europeans read more than one language, and most writers knew and imitated the literary products of other countries. There was an extensive international book trade, not only in literary translations but also in reference works. Dictionaries, encyclopedias, histories, and collections of texts made all the accumulated knowledge of the past available to a growing audience. Printed books were the first mass medium of communication, and, like the more recent mass media, they disseminated misinformation and propaganda as well as fact and art. On the other hand, they also set uniform standards for a few great literary languages, which gradually replaced both Latin and the multiplicity of local dialects. All Englishmen learned to read the language of the King James Bible, all Frenchmen that of Montaigne, and most Spaniards that of Cervantes. Verse survived in the Bible, the theater, and folklore, but in most printed literature prose gained over poetry and sense gained over sound. Although Latin was still the international language of learning in 1648, it was soon to be challenged by French.*

## The Baroque

By the seventeenth century national expressions of Renaissance exuberance gave way to a more intense and agitated style that reflected and aggravated the crises of that troubled age. The baroque style conveys feelings of strain and tension, of conflicts between opposing forces, and of great human effort to contain all these strains, tensions, and conflicts in some kind of dynamic equilibrium. It uses words, sounds, colors, and shapes in overelaborate and often distorted ways. It is art because it has form, but the form always seems dangerously close to dissolving into some inner or cosmic chaos. It points up the fact that the crises of the seventeenth century were not merely clashes between armies, governments, religious and political factions, and social classes. Seventeenth-century man felt a psychological rupture within himself and a fear of losing contact with the eternal and the universal—in other words, with God. That was why baroque painters and sculptors made their religious figures appear so intensely human, why baroque composers invented complicated effects to give vital import to the impersonal cosmos, why baroque writers overdramatized the emotional conflicts of their characters.

### Architecture and Sculpture

In architecture and sculpture the baroque originated as a style of church art in Italy and spread throughout most of Europe as an expression of both religious and secular feelings. The Jesuits built the first baroque church in Rome in the late sixteenth century. Within a few generations that city was dominated by churches in this style. Gian Lorenzo Bernini (1598–1680) created the great colonnaded plaza of St. Peter's and introduced baroque sculpture and architecture to France in religious and secular forms. The Jesuits built baroque churches in all the Hapsburg lands from Austria to Spanish America. By the late seventeenth century the baroque had also become the dominant style for palaces, theaters, and heroic statues of Europe's kings.

Even a casual tourist can tell something about the way people think and feel from the cities they build. The great cities of continental Europe have changed considerably since the seventeenth century, but many of them still bear the baroque

*See pp. 196–197.

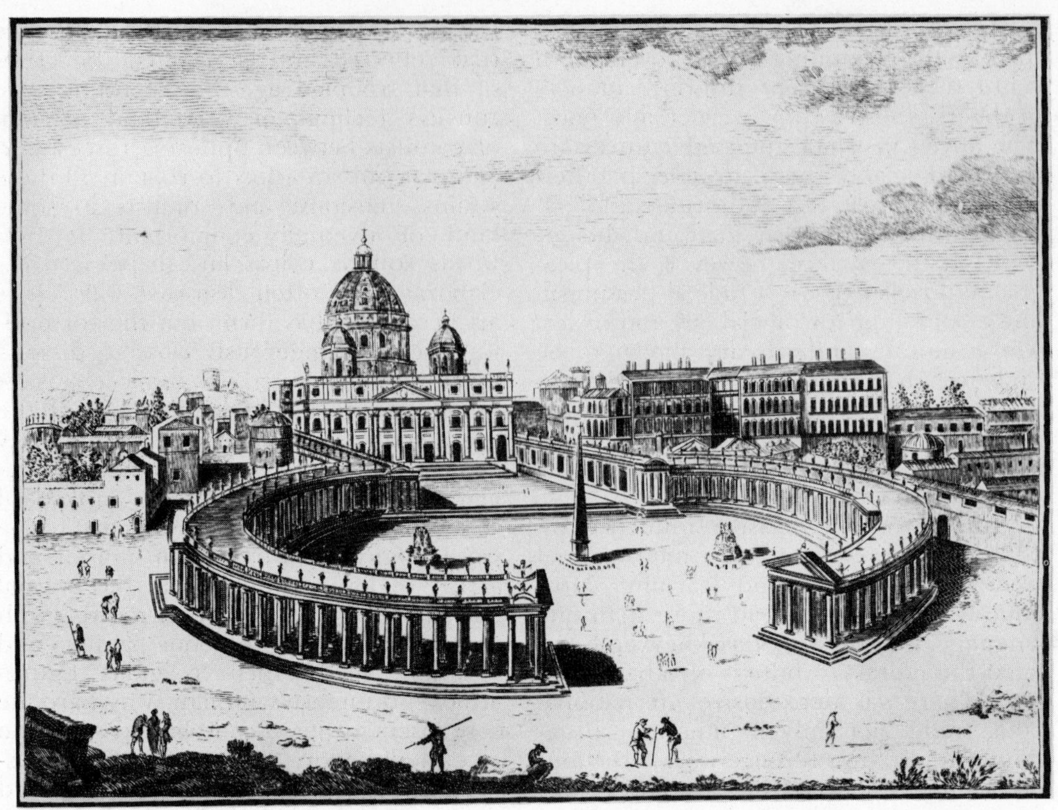

*Bernini's colonnaded plaza, St. Peter's*

stamp. Their architecture and sculpture were meant to express conflict, tension, and a sense of power, and so they do in the public places of Europe's major cities. There are statues everywhere, almost always suggesting agitated movement. There are baroque churches, palaces, and theaters, with richly ornamented façades, broad sweeping staircases, and ceilings covered with painted angels and cherubs that seem to be flying down from the sky. Solid stone comes to life on a monumental scale. Everything is busy. The very columns that support some of the roofs seem to move. One senses immediately a striving for power and grandeur, an effort to reproduce everything the human mind can know or imagine, and an anxiety over having missed some unknown or unimagined mystery.

### Painting

It is more difficult to classify the painting of the early modern period than the architecture and sculpture. The mature works of El Greco (1548?–1614) and Peter Paul Rubens (1577–1640) are clearly baroque and strongly suggestive of the Counter-Reformation spirit, though both painters studied with Titian and Tintoretto, who nourished the controlled grandeur of the High Renaissance in Venice in the late sixteenth century. Indeed, El Greco has been described as Venice fanaticized by the Spanish Inquisition. Rembrandt van Rijn (1606–1669) had nothing to do with either Venice or the Counter-Reformation, yet this Dutch master was the most baroque of all painters; and, whereas the baroque style is supposed to be especially expressive of the Spanish outlook, a Renaissance clarity is still apparent in the works of Rodríguez de Silva y Velásquez (1599–1660) and Bartolomé Esteban Murillo (1617–1682). As a final example, the outstanding French painter of the seventeenth century, Nicholas Poussin (1594–1665), who spent the major part of his life in Rome, home of the baroque, gave most of his paintings an ordered and classical feeling.

Although the three outstanding baroque painters differed in what they had to say and how they said it, they had certain stylistic traits in common: the extensive use of tonal gradation rather than clear colors, a tendency to eliminate distinct outlines and to merge objects into the surrounding background, the contrast of light and shadow, and the piling up of large quantities of pigment on the canvas. El Greco evolved a unique style, with austere, elongated bodies symbolizing souls reaching for heaven. Rubens is best known for his plump Flemish women ("riots of unimpeded flesh"), his suffering Christs, and his scenes depicting the majesty of royal power and the splendor of the court ritual. Rembrandt pushed the characteristics of baroque painting to extremes. He inserted movement into solid forms with an almost miraculous use of light and shadow. The faces of his subjects express not only their personalities but their very souls, with all their contradictory longings and inner power.

### Opera and Music

The fullest expressions of the baroque style were those that combined several forms and levels of sensation in a dynamic equilibrium. Such was the case in baroque churches or palaces, where the exterior was sculptured, gilded, and colonnaded; where the interior was both divided and held together by majestic staircases and vast corridors; where the ceilings and the walls seemed to be letting in the world outside and at the same time assuring the viewer that the figures and scenes represented were human creations. Perhaps the supreme example of the baroque in this sense was opera.

To many Americans today opera is an artificial and unconvincing art form. The plots are silly, and the sets are clichés. Until recently the performers did not look even remotely like the characters they portrayed, and the words they sang were in a foreign language. In view of their inability to act this was probably just as well. Besides, who sings when he is fighting a duel, making love, or dying?

Yet opera was originally conceived as a living representation of the full range of human passions through all the combined effects of the theater and music. Claudio Monteverdi (1567–1643) was the first composer to give this form the baroque spirit of unity and power, of deep emotion and stately ritual. Among the best of his many works are *Orfeo* (1607) and *The Coronation of Poppea* (1642). By the late seventeenth century opera became the rage in France as well as in Italy. Though less receptive to baroque forms than the continent, England produced one of the most moving and dramatic operas of the century, Purcell's *Dido and Aeneas* (1689).

Music is the most personal and the most cosmic of all the arts, and, perhaps as a result, it reached its highest baroque expression in Italy and Germany. Shorn of earthly power and strong institutions, Italians and Germans seemed especially receptive to the power of music to transport the listener outside the world around him, to make him feel the unnameable mysteries of the cosmos in his inner being. Seventeenth-century Italian composers created almost all the forms of modern music: the solo song with instrumental accompaniment, the opera, the oratorio, the cantata, the sonata, the concerto, and the orchestral suite. The best-known of these composers were Arcangelo Corelli (1653–1713), Alessandro Scarlatti (1659–1725), and Antonio Vivaldi (1675–1743). In Germany the more somber and spiritual side of the baroque flourished in the church music of Dietrich Buxtehude (1637–1707), and Johann Sebastian Bach (1685–1750) and George Frederick Handel (1685–1759) brought baroque music to a climax in all its forms.

### Poetry and Drama

In literature and drama the baroque expressed itself more as a special type of heroic character than as a formal style. An extreme example is the character of Satan in John Milton's *Paradise Lost* (1667):

*. . . aspiring*
*To set himself in Glory above his Peers,*
*He trusted to have equalled the most High,*
*If he oppos'd; and with ambitious aim*
*Against the Throne and Monarchy of God,*

*Rais'd impious War in Heav'n and Battel proud,*
*With vain attempt.*

The legendary figure of Don Juan was a more typical model of the seventeenth-century hero than Satan. He appeared in plays by Tirso de Molina (1571–1648) and Molière (1622–1673) not only as a seducer of other men's wives, but as a man who assumed many guises in an everlasting search for personal fulfillment. In Molière's play Don Juan ends up in the same place as the fallen arch-angel, and for the same sin: pride. Another type of baroque hero was the noble warrior, as in Corneille's play *Le Cid* (1637). And real-life d'Artagnans fought for France's rebellious princes against Richelieu the way similar heroes sought glory in literature and drama. The heroes and heroines of the seventeenth-century stage sacrificed everything—love, honor, status, loyalty to family and prince, and even life itself—for personal glory. They were thus in dramatic conflict with themselves as well as with their antagonists in their striving to satisfy their pride through a sense of power, which was what glory meant in the baroque age.

We can even see evidence of the theatrical side of the baroque in the lives of Europe's elites in the seventeenth century. Whether their passion for the theater reflected their inner needs or whether they merely imitated the kinds of behavior they saw there, they seemed to think of themselves as living on a stage, and they calculated their actions to produce a desired effect. Only a few tried to equal the exploits of Don Juan and other heroes in real life, but many indulged in masquerades of various kinds. With a mask and an elaborate costume one could disguise one's true self and play any role one wished. One writer sees the wig as the most revealing symbol of the baroque tendency to push things to extremes and to cultivate the theatrical exaggeration of reality. By the mid-seventeenth century European noblemen wore wigs of long flowing curls whenever they appeared in public. Ladies' fashions became increasingly elaborate and often bordered on disguise. Wealthy people also tried to create a theatrical decor in their homes. They filled these with exotic bric-à-brac, rugs from Turkey and China, scenic tapestries, full-length mirrors, and *trompee-l'oeils*—which were make-believe windows painted stereoscopically to deceive the spectator. The extraordinary, the intense, and the striking dominated the daily life as well as the arts of the baroque age.

: : :

By 1648 the main trends of early modern European history had clearly emerged. The shift from religious to secular values was well under way in politics, the arts, and thought. Capitalism and the entrepreneurial spirit had fostered a major economic expansion, and Europe's population had doubled in two centuries. Overseas explorations had begun to give some people a new outlook toward the physical world, an outlook that was also influenced by new scientific theories, as we shall see in the next chapter. But none of these trends had triumphed completely in 1648. The first wave of Europe's economic expansion ended without providing the means to feed a growing population. Although religion ceased to be a factor in international politics, it remained a critical issue in the internal affairs of England and France. Through the baroque style many sensitive individuals everywhere strove anxiously to reconcile their religious yearnings with the new secularism. In the next chapter we shall see how this conflict was also expressed in new forms of Catholicism and Calvinism. The struggle to adjust to new material conditions and new modes of thought made Europe's elites more dynamic and more restless than ever.

The one trend that had pretty well established itself in Western Europe by 1648 was the development of national high cultures in the emerging national states. Elizabeth I, Philip II, William the Silent, Henry IV, and Gustavus Adolphus had laid the groundwork of national unity and strong central government in their respective countries. England and Spain had already experienced their literary and artistic golden ages, and France was about to enter hers. Sweden was a full-fledged

Western European nation with her own literature and her great university at Upsala. The Dutch Republic transformed its low-German dialect into a national literary language, produced a group of brilliant painters, and became a center of learning.

On the other hand, religious preoccupations, foreign aggression, and economic stagnation stunted the development of a national state and a national high culture in Italy and Germany. Although Italian styles in art and music continued to have an international influence in the seventeenth century, the last great work in Italian literature was Torquato Tasso's *Jerusalem Delivered* (1575). The Counter-Reformation and Spanish domination effectively silenced the national literary spirit outside of Venice. Germany's cultural decline began in all fields except music in the second half of the sixteenth century. The painters Albrecht Dürer, Hans Holbein, and Lucas Cranach were all dead by then. After the death of the poet Hans Sachs in 1576 German national literature languished for almost two centuries. Germany's universities attracted fewer students than in Luther's time and fell into an interminable rut of theological controversies. By 1600 even educated Germans had become increasingly provincial and superstitious. Then the Thirty Years' War tore the German nation to pieces and made it a cultural wasteland.

After 1648 Spain followed Italy and Germany on the path of decline. Henceforth, it was Northwestern Europe that was to set the pattern for modern times.

## SUGGESTED READINGS


Clough, Shepard B., *The Economic Development of Western Civilization.*
Chapters 8, 9, and 10 of this book cover the early modern period.

Parry, J. H., *The Age of Reconnaissance.**
See comments in readings for Chapter III.

Nef, John U., *Industry and Government in France and England, 1540–1640.* Ithaca, N. Y.: Cornell Univ. Press, 1957.
Detailed and authoritative.

Ogg, David, *Europe in the Seventeenth Century.* 8th ed. New York: The Macmillan Co., n.d. Collier Book.*
An older survey—still very useful.

Clark, G. N., *The Seventeenth Century.* 2d. ed. New York: Oxford Univ. Press, 1947.*
An interpretive survey.

Elliott, John H., *Europe Divided, 1559–1598.* New York: Harper-Row, 1969. Torchbook.*

——— *Imperial Spain 1469–1716.*
See comments in readings for Chapter III.

Lynch, John, *Spain under the Habsburgs*, Vol. II (1598–1700). Oxford: Blackwell, 1969.
Authoritative treatment of Spain and the New World.

Geyl, Pieter, *The Revolt of the Netherlands.* New York: Barnes and Noble, 1958.
A detailed history.

Neale, John E., *Queen Elizabeth I.* Garden City, N. Y.: Doubleday and Co., 1957. Anchor.*
The standard biography.

Rowse, Alfred L., *The Expansion of Elizabethan England.* New York: St. Martin's Press, 1955.

——— *The England of Elizabeth: The Structure of Society.* New York: The Macmillan Co., 1951.
Lively and detailed.

Elton, Geoffrey R., *England under the Tudors.*
See comments in readings for Chapter III.

Bindoff, S. T., *Tudor England.* New York: Penguin, n.d.*
Based on recent scholarly research.

Mattingly, Garrett, *The Armada.* Boston: Houghton Mifflin Co., 1959.*
Superlative history of Western Europe as it was affected by the events of 1588. Beautifully written.

Harbison, E. Harris, *The Age of Reformation.**
See comments in readings for Chapter II.
This book is also good on the religious wars in France and the Netherlands.

Notestein, Wallace, *The English People on the Eve of Colonization, 1603–1630.* New York: Harper and Row, 1962. Torchbook.*
Excellent survey of institutions and social life.

Bridenbaugh, Carl, *Vexed and Troubled Englishmen.* New York: Oxford Univ. Press, 1968.
Describes the early English colonists and why they came to North America.

Geyl, Pieter, *The Netherlands in the 17th Century, 1609–1648.* Vol. I of 2 vols. Rev. ed. New York: Barnes and Noble, 1961.
A detailed history.

Holborn, Hajo, *A History of Modern Germany.*
The section on the Thirty Years' War incorporates the latest scholarship.

Nef, John U., *War and Human Progress.**
See comments in readings for Chapter III.

Roberts, Michael, *The Military Revolution, 1560–1660.* Belfast: Boyd, 1956.
Especially useful on the Thirty Years' War.

Wedgwood, Cicely, *The Thirty Years' War.* Garden City, N. Y.: Doubleday and Co., 1961. Anchor.*
A well-written conventional history.

Friedrich, Carl J., *The Age of the Baroque, 1610–1660.* New York: Harper and Row, 1962. Torchbook.*
Excellent volume in the Rise of Modern Europe series.

*Paperback

CHAPTER V

# EMERGENCE OF THE MODERN STATE AND MODERN SCIENCE, *C.* 1648–1715

In 1648 Western Europe had failed to resolve its early modern crises. Both France and England were in the midst of civil war. In England the constitutional issue was complicated by religious and social conflicts and by the Scottish and Irish questions. In France some powerful opponents of the royal authority were willing to ally themselves with their country's archenemy, Spain. Economic crisis plagued even the most advanced countries; production was inadequate to feed a growing population and to provide governments with sufficient revenues for their frequent wars. Governments were beginning to observe some rules in their relations with each other, but they still confused dynastic considerations with national interests, and the military spirit of the "nobility of the sword" encouraged them to go to war on the slightest pretext. The lure of empire in Europe and overseas also remained a danger to any temporary peace settlement. Still, the most upsetting aspect of the seventeenth-century crisis was the impact of the scientific revolution on the thought and feeling of Western Europe's educated elites.

Between 1648 and 1715 Western European leaders made significant strides in resolving some of their crises. They established the unquestioned sovereignty of the state and created techniques of government that have endured down to the present, and in science and philosophy they constructed a basic outlook that was to sustain their descendants for two hundred years. The dominant figures of the age were King Louis XIV, René Descartes, and Sir Isaac Newton. These men imposed the principles of Authority, Reason, and Order on the world around them.

## FRANCE IN THE AGE OF LOUIS XIV

No man struggled longer and more resolutely against the seventeenth-century crisis than King Louis XIV of France. He tried to eliminate all opposition to the absolute authority of the state and to make everyone in his personal government absolutely loyal to him. He also tried to make all of his twenty million subjects subordinate their own interests to those of the state: Protestants had to adopt the state religion or leave the country; merchants and manufacturers had to provide the state with increased revenues. Even artists and writers had to glorify the state in the person of its sovereign.

Louis XIV made disorder give way to

order and substituted authority for liberty. The traditional label for his political system is *absolutism.* But no seventeenth-century ruler could have absolute control over every aspect of his subjects' lives, given the limited resources and the slow means of transportation and communication of that age. Only in the twentieth century have totalitarian dictators achieved the kind of power that the word absolutism suggests. Louis XIV was not a dictator; he was a sovereign who ruled by divine right. Everyone in France accepted his claim that his authority came from God. (No twentieth-century dictator has ever claimed that.) Hence the best label for his political system is *authoritarianism.*

### The Legacy of Louis XIV's Predecessors

The centralizing policies of the royal government had been frequently challenged during the half-century preceding Louis XIV's assumption of personal power in 1661. Henry IV had made the new Bourbon dynasty popular by restoring peace and prosperity, and by promising "a chicken in every pot." He had subdued the great princely and ducal parties, guaranteed the privileges of the Huguenots, and refrained from levying new taxes. But soon after his assassination in 1610 it became clear that many Frenchmen still opposed the royal authority and were determined to resist its encroachments on their interests. The Huguenots, the princes of the blood, and the great nobles rebelled against Richelieu's efforts to limit their pretensions to independence. Peasants and urban workers attacked royal revenue agents in protest against the new taxes—especially the one on salt—that Richelieu had got King Louis XIII to levy for his wars. Since the Bourbons did not call the Estates General after 1614, they had no trouble from that quarter, but the Parlements (royal law courts) tried to take over its role as an independent legislative body. From 1648 to 1653, along with the princes of the blood, they launched a series of rebellions, called collectively the Fronde.

In 1648 Louis XIV was only ten years old. His mother, who acted as regent, entrusted the reins of government to her first minister and secret husband, Cardinal Mazarin.* This was the political situation when the hereditary judges in the Parlement of Paris persuaded the disgruntled citizens of that city to set up barricades and to riot against the royal authority. These magistrates posed as champions against arbitrary taxation, but their real goal was to preserve their own entrenched positions and those of other officials who held their posts as property rights—rights they unconvincingly called constitutional liberties. Thus they failed to enlist strong popular support in the country as a whole. No sooner did the royal military forces put down their insurrection than a second one was started by the Prince of Condé and the boy-king's uncle, the Duke of Orléans. These "overmighty subjects" claimed the ancient right of vassals to switch their allegiance to another lord, in this case the King of Spain. Mazarin was unable to suppress the disorder and violence of these civil wars for several years. In the end, however, most Frenchmen recognized the essentially selfish ambitions of the insurgents and were willing to accept an authoritarian government that would maintain order and tranquility in the kingdom. The Fronde had convinced them that they needed a strong ruler.

When Mazarin died in 1661 he left Louis XIV not only a loyal populace but also the leadership of the first power in Europe. The wily cardinal was at his best as a diplomat. He realized Richelieu's dream of making France safe from the Austrian Hapsburgs by negotiating the Peace of Westphalia (1648). His final diplomatic triumph was the Peace of the Pyrenees (1659), which concluded France's long war with Spain and marked the end of Hapsburg leadership in Europe. To seal the peace settlement, the King of Spain sent his daughter Maria Theresa to France to become the bride of the young Louis XIV. Her marriage contract renounced her claim to the Spanish throne,

*Mazarin (Giulio Mazarini) was born in Italy and became a naturalized Frenchman in 1639. He got his cardinal's hat from Louis XIII, but he was not a priest, so his probable marriage to Louis' widow was not as shocking as it might seem, though it was certainly not recognized by the Church.

but other clauses in the contract nullified her renunciation and were to give her husband an excuse to claim the whole Spanish inheritance later on.*

Mazarin also left Louis XIV the makings of an authoritarian government. Richelieu and Louis XIII had strengthened the royal bureaucracy by transferring important functions from people and institutions that held them on a hereditary basis to people who could be appointed and dismissed at will. Under Richelieu and Louis XIII the royal secretaries had begun to emerge as heads of ministries and of special policy-making councils. Louis XIII had initiated the use of the *lettre de cachet*, a letter bearing the royal seal, to notify personally a disobedient subject or official of his arrest, imprisonment, or exile. In this way he asserted his authority as the legal source of justice. Richelieu had created the new office of *intendant*, a traveling official who made the king's authority felt throughout the realm. These king's men undermined the power of the traditional town authorities and of the great nobles who traditionally governed the provinces. All these makings of an authoritarian government had been put to a severe test during the Fronde. It was Mazarin who saved them and passed them on to the new king.

### Louis XIV and His Personal Government

Louis XIV had an exalted conception of his role as king. To him, a king was God's lieutenant on earth, the provider of all law and justice, and a conquering hero. Though no genius, Louis was a man of more than average ability, and he was better educated than most kings. Mazarin had initiated him into the ways of statecraft, and, along with the queen mother, had made him believe that he could be a great ruler if he would only apply himself to the task. This Louis did with great seriousness and long hours of work. He resolved to be his own first minister, so that only he would understand the totality of affairs and thus be indispensable.

Partly out of vanity and partly in order to live up to the exalted role of king, Louis made himself a dazzling and awe-inspiring public figure. From the time His Majesty arose in the morning until the time he retired at night his every action demanded a ceremony with elaborate rules of protocol. Princes of the blood vied with each other for the honor of helping him put on his shirt. His meals were artistic productions of many courses. A typical evening's entertainment "at home" might include a troupe of ballet dancers, a masked ball, and an extravagant display of fireworks. Everyone around His Majesty bowed, curtsied, and catered to his every wish. His courtiers compared him to the Sun, and his emblem said that no one was his equal. Louis XIV made a cult of majesty.

Louis also made himself the source of law and justice. He silenced the Parlements—which had claimed equal power in these matters during the Fronde—by ordering them to confirm his power to tax and to register his edicts immediately and without change. In addition, he began the practice of issuing royal law codes to apply to all Frenchmen, a practice that was to be completed in the Napoleonic Code in the early 1800s.* Crimes against His Majesty were crimes against the state, which Louis ferreted out through use of *intendants* and police spies. On the slightest suspicion anyone accused of the crime of lese majesty—an affront to His Majesty—found himself in the Bastille. Like the *lettre de cachet*, this converted fortress on the east side of Paris became a symbol of political oppression and the absence of civil rights.

Obviously the king could not keep in touch with every minor official in his greatly expanded bureaucracy but he wanted at least the major ones to view themselves as his devoted personal servants. Even his highest ministers had to convey notes to his lady friends and to look after his bastard children by the royal mistresses. As Louis said in his memoirs, "His good graces were regarded as the sole source of all possessions; one thought of raising oneself only to the extent that one might approach his person or rise in his esteem." Louis sought to utilize the old sentiment of vassalage to bind

*See p. 186.

*See Chapter IX.

his officials to their sovereign through a personal tie. In this way, no less than in the exercise of personal power, he concentrated the state in himself and, in doing so, prepared Frenchmen to advance eventually to the concept of the impersonal modern state.

More and more, it was one's service to the sovereign, the embodiment of the state, that determined one's social rank. In the highest offices of the realm Louis gradually replaced hereditary nobles—nobility of the sword—with men of bourgeois origin. He felt that these bourgeois would be more devoted servants than the nobles since their new social status depended entirely on his will. But he also wanted to bring the struggle between the two classes to an equilibrium that would assure his personal power and maintain order, unity, and hierarchy in the government and the state. In order to do this, Louis conferred hereditary titles of nobility on his highest bourgeois officials, making them a nobility of the robe—so called for the robes worn by French magistrates.

Still, Louis also had to mollify the nobles of the sword, who despised the "vile bourgeois" nobles of the robe and who resented the social leveling the king seemed to be bringing about. He continued to appoint them as governors and to reserve most of the higher ranks of the army and the Church for them and their sons; his wars provided them employment and opportunities for achieving glory and enhancing their prestige. At the same time, the king insured their servility with pensions, dowries, and ecclesiastical benefices. His most spectacular means of domesticating the nobility of the sword was to keep its higher members busy at court. No longer were they to be allowed to raise the standard of rebellion in the provinces. The princes of the blood and the great nobles now had to spend most of their free time participating in an unending series of courtly ceremonies and festivals. They fawned over the Sun King like lesser gods over Jupiter. In order to create a proper setting for this imitation of the life of the immortals Louis XIV built the palace of Versailles ten miles outside of Paris.

Versailles* not only served as a gilded cage for all who counted among the French nobility, it also became a symbol of Louis XIV's power in France and in all of Europe. It was a world in itself, with scores of bedrooms, vast reception halls, extensive formal gardens, a chapel, a theater, and government offices. Only the richest king in Europe could have built such a palace; it cost 100 million dollars. Its classical exterior awed the viewer with a feeling of ordered power. Its baroque interior seemed to breathe extravagance and pleasure on a grand scale. Louis XIV became the model absolute monarch. Long after his death the kings and princes of Europe constructed smaller versions of Versailles and tried to emulate his cult of majesty.

## Louis XIV's Instruments of Power

In addition to building up the royal bureaucracy and surrounding himself with devoted ministers and officials, Louis XIV developed his country's military and economic resources to strengthen the state at home and in its relations with the outside world. We shall discuss Louis XIV's wars presently; but it is essential to note here the importance of the needs of war in strengthening the state. The organization and maintenance of a large standing army and a regular navy added to the functions of the bureaucracy and prompted the government to foster economic growth so that it would have more wealth to tax. Here too, Louis XIV provided models for the other rulers of Europe.

### *Armed Forces*

The trend toward standing armies, which had been developing in Europe for a century, reached fulfillment in France after 1661. Louis XIV was acutely aware of his need for an overwhelming military force to prevent the kinds of rebellions he had experienced as a child. He wanted to be sure that, henceforth, all armed persons in France fought exclusively for him. There were to be no more bands of mercenaries, loyal only to their captains. All

*See p. 204.

*A military drill*

soldiers were now paid, fed, clothed, and equipped by the king's commissioners and commanded by officers who took their orders from the king's minister of war, a new function in the royal bureaucracy.

Louis established a clear chain of command in the military ranks and made all soldiers submit to a strict discipline. He made himself the supreme commander, both to nurture his image as a military hero and to let his generals know who their real boss was. Along with the generals, the colonels and captains were still mostly noblemen who had bought their commissions and who were used to making their own decisions. Louis therefore created the ranks of lieutenant and lieutenant-colonel to keep an eye on them. The colonels now recruited their troops under government supervision and had to make periodic reports on their condition. From reveille to taps the common soldiers followed a regular program of drill worked out by General Martinet, whose name still stands for a military disciplinarian.

The standing army was Louis XIV's most successful and most widely imitated creation. At full strength its 400,000 men constituted the largest and best-disciplined military force in Europe. Other countries were soon to copy its techniques and even its terminology.

In building up his new instruments of military power Louis made use of the most talented men of the age. Michel Le Tellier (1603–1685) and his son Michel Le Tellier, Marquis de Louvois (1641–1691) brought infantry, cavalry, and artillery units under a unified command, established schools for cadets, and organized a new branch of the army, the corps of engineers. Sébastien Le Prestre, Seigneur de Vauban (1633–1707) used the engineers to construct an imposing system of fortifications along France's frontiers. Permanent garrisons could now defend the country more effectively from attack and menace its neighbors from these installations. Finally, Jean-Baptiste Colbert (1619–1683) built the foremost navy of the day.

### Economic Controls

Colbert was the prime example of the bourgeois minister on whom Louis XIV relied so heavily. The son of a textile merchant, Colbert had worked his way up in the royal service under Mazarin. He served Louis XIV in many capacities and instituted reforms in many fields. As minister of commerce and finance he worked tirelessly to increase the national wealth as a means of bolstering the political and military power of the state. His economic reforms came to be known under the name of Colbertism, but Colbert himself was the first to admit that "the great Cardinal Richelieu" had proposed many of the innovations he carried through. Furthermore, both England and the Dutch Republic were following a similar policy, and it was to be imitated by the states of Central and Eastern Europe in the eighteenth century.

Colbertism was merely the most famous example of the mercantilist policies that many states used to combat the seventeenth-century economic crisis. As we have seen, the original goal of mercantilism was to have a country export more than it imported as the best means of maintaining reserves of gold and silver to pay for the king's wars. Colbert went several steps further. According to him: "The trading companies are the weapons of the king and the industries of France his reserves." Thus, Colbert sponsored trading companies to compete with the Dutch and the English in the East Indies, the Levant (Near East), Africa, and America so that French money would not be paid to foreigners for the products of these areas. He also encouraged the king to found colonies in North America to serve as cheap sources of raw materials and as markets for French manufactured goods. Like the English and the Dutch, Colbert tried to regulate all unavoidable commerce with other Europeans. He did this through protective tariffs against competing manufactured goods and prohibitions against the exportation of foodstuffs—the latter measure was to keep the masses quiet by holding down the price of bread.

Colbert's most advanced innovations were his efforts to promote economic growth at home. He was not very successful in doing this for agriculture, whose productivity did not increase much anywhere in seventeenth-century Europe. But he achieved considerable success in increasing France's production, if not productivity, of manufactured goods in the guilds, in domestic industry, and in new workshops that supplied the royal army and navy. He encouraged new business enterprises by lowering the interest rate for investment capital, granting tax exemptions and out-and-out money subsidies, restricting imports, and keeping wages down.

Colbert viewed the workers as an industrial army whose mission was to assure the power and greatness of the state, and the government backed the employers in maintaining strict discipline and high standards of workmanship. The workers' interests were sacrified to the needs of economic growth; they served long apprenticeships, received only subsistence wages, and had to work long hours with few holidays. Colbert even launched the very modern policy of trying to increase the size of the labor force by granting tax exemptions to heads of large families. He also persuaded foreign workers to come to France and introduce new crafts there.

Yet even the great Colbert could not solve all of France's financial and fiscal problems, particularly in the face of the severe and prolonged depression the country experienced after 1650. French manufactured goods brought in considerable profits from abroad and new sources of taxable income at home. The government collected more taxes than ever before, but it still could not tax the wealth of the privileged classes, especially the landed nobility. This weakness in the nation's tax structure was to plague French governments throughout the eighteenth century. As a result of Colbert's efforts Louis XIV had more wealth at his disposal than his predecessors had ever dreamed of. But Louis was soon to waste much of his economic power in costly wars, and his successors were to go increasingly into debt.

### Religion and the Arts in the Service of the State

Like most seventeenth-century rulers Louis XIV was more successful in enforcing religious uniformity on all his subjects than in controlling their economic activities. His ideal was: One faith, one law, one king (*"Une foi, une loi, un roi"*). When he assumed personal power there were still about one million Huguenots in France, and they had come to accept the royal authority as unquestioningly as the Catholics. But authoritarian regimes tend to be suspicious of minority groups, however loyal they may insist they are. Thus, Louis put increasing pressure on the Huguenots to convert to the official religion of the state. First he sent Catholic missionaries into their midst; then he deprived them of their remaining legal privileges. When these measures proved to be too slow, he began quartering troops in Huguenot homes. Finally, in 1685, he revoked the Edict of Nantes, making the "so-called Reformed religion" illegal in France. Tens of thousands of Huguenots emigrated to England, Holland, Germany, and America. Not all of those who remained in France gave up their Calvinist faith, but they had to suffer all the penalties of a persecuted minority.

With the Revocation of the Edict of Nantes the ideal of one faith, one law, and one king became a reality. The French Church accepted the spiritual authority of the pope in Rome, but the king controlled its administration and used it to bolster his political authority. Its priests fostered loyalty to the king and obedience to all the constituted authorities of the realm. Even the workers in the government-sponsored workshops were forced to attend Mass regularly and to listen at mealtime to priestly harangues about duty and obedience.

While the Church disciplined people's private thoughts and feelings, the government tried to regiment the arts and letters—and science, as we shall see later in this chapter—for the glory of the state. It controlled the printing and sale of all books and periodicals; it censored all theatrical productions. There was to be no public criticism of the king or his policies, even in the most innocuous comedy. Still, royal supervision had its positive as well as its negative side, since the king became the main patron of all the creative arts.

In addition to giving France's artists and writers individual commissions and subsidies, the king made them dependent on him through his control of the French Academy and his founding of academies of architecture and music. Charles Le Brun (1616–1690), who glorified the king in his own paintings, taught other artists to do so in his post as director of Louis' new Academy of Painting and Sculpture. Thus the king extended his control to all the arts.

Not since ancient Rome had a European ruler gone as far as Louis XIV in using artistic display for his own glorification. He had his military victories celebrated in triumphal arches, in heroic statues of himself in public squares, and, of course, in paintings and tapestries in his palaces. Like the great nobles at Versailles, the members of the French Academy came to view themselves as lesser gods in the service of the Sun King; eventually they even came to be called the "forty immortals." France's greatest playwright, Jean Racine (1639–1699), once said: "All the words of the language, all the syllables seem precious to us because we regard them as so many tools with which to serve the glory of our Illustrious Patron."

### Classicism and the Spread of French Cultural Influence

Not only did Louis XIV use his artists and writers to glorify him as the personification of the state, he also wanted them to impose a sense of order and unity on the world. They obliged him by developing a new aesthetic style, classicism. Partly owing to their own notable achievements and partly to the prestige of France during the late seventeenth century, this style spread French cultural influence to many parts of Europe.

The Jesuits continued to use baroque painting, sculpture, architecture, and even the theater "for the greater glory of God," but they also helped to form the classical spirit in their educational institutions. As we have seen, in the seventeenth century most of the elite groups in Catholic countries sent their sons to Jesuit schools. There they learned rules of etiquette as a form of self-discipline and as a means of making themselves agreeable to other people. The Jesuits taught them to

*Classical architecture—the Louvre*

control their emotions by exerting their will power and to appreciate the value of abstract ideas through their God-given ability to reason. By stressing discipline, order, and a sense of proportion and appropriateness in thought and behavior, and by affirming the power of the human will, this type of education contributed to the classical spirit in the arts.

The essence of classicism is that reason controls artistic expression. It justifies the rules of each art form and keeps the imagination from going astray. Reason is permanent and universal, the same at all times and in all places. It dictates the canons of good taste and gives the arts their moral functions of purifying the emotions and of setting standards of what is beautiful and what is appropriate. It prescribes the rules of verisimilitude in portraying nature and human behavior. In each case this portrayal must avoid imperfection and confusion. The artist or writer must not mix serious and frivolous elements, he must not make his characters behave in ways unsuitable to their social status, he must avoid the crude, the bizarre, or the strange. A play must not present events that last for more than one day or that occur in more than one place. A painting must have a central focus with everything else around it arranged to form a complete and self-contained whole. Inspired by reason and a desire for order, classicism is an aesthetic of unity.

Like the Italians of the Renaissance, the French classicists looked to ancient Greece and Rome for inspiration. Greek mythology and Roman history provided settings and characters for the tragedies of Jean Racine and Pierre Corneille (1606–1684) and for the allegorical paintings of Nicholas Poussin (1594–1665).* The ancients were admired for the order, unity, and simplicity of their creative works. Unlike that of the Greeks, however, French aesthetic restraint was not an overcompensation for turbulent passions and a disordered political life. For France's artistic and social elites classicism was not merely an artistic style, it was also a style of life.

In life, as in the arts, the Age of Louis XIV strove for perfection. Corneille's tragedies show men how they could be and how they are when they have the courage to be men. Jean Baptiste Molière (1622–1673) ridiculed all kinds of extravagance and immoderation in personal behavior in his own society; his comedies immortalized the snob, the miser, the religious zealot, and the woman-hater. But just as too many rules eventually began to stifle artistic creation, they also took much of the warmth and spontaneity out of human relations in polite society. According to the classical outlook nothing natural was perfect until it had been tamed by human reason and the human will. Just as shrubs had to be pruned and shaped into geometrical forms, even an idle flirtation had to be cultivated and contrived with an eye to perfection. Everything, from the clothes one wore to the food one ate, had to be a perfect work of art.

By the beginning of the eighteenth century classicism had not completely succeeded in resolving the crisis in thought and feeling. Baroque tendencies persisted in both art and behavior. Italian opera—that "insult to human reason"—conquered all of Europe from Vienna to London. People began to weep un-

*See p. 207.

ashamedly, on the stage and in private. Some writers began challenging Louis XIV's authoritarian conception of government as well as classicism in the arts. For Louis was making serious errors of judgment in foreign policy and becoming more despotic at home. His insatiable quest for glory and power ultimately weakened the magnificent façade of order and well being that his ministers had created.

Nevertheless, classicism and absolutism retained their appeal as ways of imposing order on the world. They continued to be imitated in France and in most of Europe long after the Age of Louis XIV. France's elites had created what seemed to be a new kind of civilization. It was artificial, it lacked warmth and spontaneity, and it stifled freedom of thought and expression. Yet it had an elegance and a predictability that endeared it to most European aristocrats throughout the eighteenth century.

## CONSTITUTIONAL CRISIS IN ENGLAND

By the time England finally went through her civil and religious wars, English society had become integrated enough to prevent the state from falling apart as it had in Germany and as it almost had in France under similar circumstances. Between the 1640s and 1680s the English beheaded one king and deposed another, submitted to a dictatorship of generals and Puritan "Saints," and made basic transformations in their constitution, all without ceasing to be a community and a power. Unlike France and Germany, England had tamed her princes and great nobles militarily in the sixteenth century. Henry VIII and Elizabeth I had favored the gentry and university-trained laymen, utilizing them as loyal servants of the Crown. England was also freer from the influence of the clergy than most European countries. The abolition of the monasteries by Henry VIII and the redistribution of their lands to the gentry had given members of this class the incentive to engage in capitalist agriculture and sheepraising. The Renaissance had glorified the active life in France as well as in England, but French aristocrats were active primarily in warfare. English aristocrats had acquired more of the acquisitive outlook of capitalism than their counterparts across the Channel. Hence, they began to raise the question of the best form of government when the Stuart kings who ruled after the death of Elizabeth mismanaged the country's foreign affairs and threatened to bolster their absolutism by restoring clerical influence at home.

The burning question was: Who embodied the supreme authority of the state, the Stuart kings or Parliament? The struggle over this constitutional question raged intermittently from the time James I (1603–1625) came to the throne until the time James II was deposed in 1688. In the 1640's and 1650's it was complicated by religious and social conflicts within the parliamentary faction and by the ascendancy of a strong military leader, Oliver Cromwell. Although the religious issue also complicated the final stage of the constitutional conflict in 1688, the basic question was whether England should be ruled by an absolute monarch or by a Parliament representing the aristocracy.

This aristocracy still consisted primarily of the landowning nobility and gentry, but it had long since abandoned its feudal opposition to a strong centralized state. By the 1640's, it promoted the first modern example of a strong state ruled by a corporate elite, rather than by an absolute monarch or a federation of aristocrats. Indeed, during the Civil War the English aristocracy—also for the first time—gave a large number of commoners a role in public affairs, if only temporarily.

Through intermarriage and cooperation in business the landowning gentry and the city merchants had developed a common interest in translating their wealth, which now exceeded that of some great nobles, into political power. Yet the gentry and the great nobles shared a common education in Latin grammar schools, where they acquired the rhetoric and ideals of the aristocratic Roman Republic. Their representatives in Parliament were clever politicians and debaters who knew how to appeal to public opinion, how to use their university learning to discover legal arguments for their demands, and how to develop an effective committee system in the House of Commons for organizing their attacks on Stuart policies.

The Stuarts were unable to make royal absolutism triumph in England the way the Bourbons did in France, but they certainly tried. They tried to develop their Privy Council into a strong executive agency composed of ministers and high officials personally devoted to the king. They tried to monopolize the power to make laws. They tried to use the highest royal courts to condemn opponents of their policies and to imprison these people without due process of law. They tried to impose taxes without consulting Parliament. They tried to maintain a standing army to enforce the royal will.

Those parliamentary politicians who opposed royal absolutism thought of themselves as traditionalists rather than revolutionaries on the constitutional issue. To them, it was the Stuarts who were trying to change the basic law of the land, the Common Law, which was intended, above all and from the earliest times, to protect both private property and the rights of the individual. They insisted that the king was bound by this law. Hence they viewed the Stuarts' efforts to monopolize the various organs and functions of government as illegal.

### Background of the Civil War

Under the first two Stuarts, both relatively weak kings, Parliament became too strong to handle. James I and Charles I (1625–1649) lacked Elizabeth's touch and they no longer personified the national ideal the way she had, yet they constantly rebuked the Commons for meddling in affairs of state. For example, when the Commons criticized James I for trying to marry Prince Charles to a Spanish princess, the king contemptuously ordered the ushers to "bring stools for these ambassadors." That was hardly the way to get the new self-styled elite of the nation to grant the king money.

And the Stuarts always needed money. They needed it to build up their military instruments of power, to maintain themselves in a more lavish style than their private incomes allowed, and to pay for their royal bureaucracy. "The king's servants" numbered about eighteen hundred persons. Had they been more competent, they might have become a bulwark of absolutism; instead, they made the government of the Stuarts cumbersome, inefficient, and increasingly expensive.

Every time the Stuarts asked Parliament for more money, it demanded that they give up some of their authority. Finally, Charles I dissolved Parliament in 1629 and governed without calling it again for eleven years. He tried to raise money for a peacetime navy in 1634 by extending a traditional levy called "ship-money" from seaboard towns to the whole country. A rural squire named John Hampden made a test case of his right to refuse to pay this tax. Since the royal judges were in the king's pay, Hampden lost his case in court. Even so, he had helped focus public opposition to royal absolutism on a specific grievance.

The Stuarts' religious policies also aroused increasing opposition both inside and outside of Parliament. James I and Charles I took their job as head of the Anglican Church seriously. They wanted to keep its elaborate ritual and episcopal organization intact. After the failure of the Gunpowder Plot in 1605* Catholic opposition subsided. Also, bishops were restored to the Scottish Church, which otherwise remained Presbyterian. The main opponents of the Stuarts were now the Puritans. Although a handful of them fled to Holland and thence to Massachusetts, the majority wanted to take over the Church of England and "purify" it of its "popish" ritual and organization. They provided the most dynamic leadership in Parliament against the king. The printed sermons of their preachers were the "best sellers" of the day. A surprising number of these preachers were in Anglican pulpits; hence, from the royal point of view, they were real subversives, boring from within. Under Charles I, Archbishop Laud, the primate of the Church of En-

*See p. 150.

gland, set up a system of spies against them and removed the more radical ones from their benefices. This underhanded example of royal absolutism made all Puritans cry "tyranny and oppression!" For, unlike the Huguenots in France after the 1630s, the English Calvinists retained their hatred of all hierarchies and institutions that tried to limit their individual liberty as God's children.

Charles I might have weathered the attacks of the English Puritans and avoided a civil war if he had not also got himself into serious trouble by trying to impose Anglicanism on Scotland. Charles was the king of Scotland and Ireland as well as England and he was determined to assert his absolutism wherever he ruled. But Scotland had its own state church, its own Parliament, and the ability to raise a regular army. Thus, when Charles ordered the Anglican liturgy to be read in Edinburgh, the Scots formed a national league to resist any changes in their religion and openly prepared for war. In trouble in Scotland and financially distressed in England, Charles *had* to call a new session of Parliament.

Between 1640 and 1642 the struggle between king and Parliament came to a climax. Charles had agreed to pay both the Scottish and English armies with the proceedings of a new tax to be granted by Parliament. Then, in 1641, a major rebellion broke out in Ireland because the Irish feared that Protestant England would use their Catholic religion as an excuse for seizing their lands. Charles needed a new army to crush the rebellion in Ireland, where thirty thousand Protestants were massacred in Ulster. But, despite its anger over this Catholic atrocity, Parliament refused to grant Charles his tax or to trust him with a new army until he redressed all its grievances. It had already impeached Charles's chief advisers, Archbishop Laud and the Earl of Strafford; now Charles ordered the impeachment of five of his leading opponents in the Commons. By the summer of 1642 the breach was irreparable. Parliament appointed a committee of public safety in London, and the king raised the royal standard at Nottingham.

### Civil War, Commonwealth, and Protectorate, 1642–1660

At first neither side wished to get rid of the other completely, but six years of intermittent fighting transformed the English Civil War into a real revolution. The Cavaliers, led by the great Anglican and Catholic lords and the conservative Anglican gentry, fought for the king. The Anglican clergy and most of the peasants were also royalists. The supporters of Parliament, whom the royalists contemptuously called Roundheads because they did not wear wigs, included the majority of the urban middle classes and the Puritan and Presbyterian gentry. As the war dragged on this apparent division along social and religious lines became blurred. Soon members of the same family were fighting on opposite sides. The parliamentary side eventually became divided within itself, with the more radical Puritans demanding a republic and religious freedom, and the Presbyterians still hoping to preserve the monarchy and a state church for the whole of the British Isles. In the end the Puritan army dictated the most revolutionary changes that any European country had yet experienced.

Compared with the civil and religious wars in Germany and France, the war in England was fought in a fairly gentlemanly manner. No cities were destroyed; no civilians were massacred. The Cavaliers had the initial military advantage with their superior cavalry. But the Roundheads learned to ride, and their great military leader, Oliver Cromwell (1599–1658) created a New Model Army that eventually proved unbeatable. In addition to its superior organization and discipline, the New Model Army had the advantage of believing that it was fighting for God. Charles bought the military services of some Irish Catholics and in the last year of the war he got the Scots to come over to his side. Cromwell then defeated the Scots as well as the Cavaliers.

No sooner was the war over than the Puritan army and Parliament were at each other's throats. The Parliament that had been elected in 1640 is called the Long Parliament because, technically, it re-

*The House of Commons—as shown on the Second Seal of Commonwealth (1651)*

mained in session until 1660. In late 1648 its Presbyterian majority was still negotiating with the king and the Scots. It wanted to preserve the monarchy and a moderately Calvinist state church for England, Scotland, and Ireland. The Puritan army would have none of this. One of its officers, Colonel Pride, forcibly "purged" the ninety-six Presbyterian members from Parliament. Since its Anglican and Catholic members had joined the royalist side in 1642, only a "Rump" of Puritans remained.

In 1649 the Puritans consummated their revolution. The "Rump Parliament" tried and executed the king and abolished the monarchy and the House of Lords. Charles I's brave behavior at the execution block was to give the royalists a rallying point later on. But for the next decade the Puritans ruled. They made England a Commonwealth, retaining the legislative power for Parliament and giving the executive power to a Council of State. Ultimate sanction for the Commonwealth rested with the army and its leader Cromwell.

Although Cromwell was satisfied with this arrangement, the more radical elements in his army were not. As early as 1647 a group of extreme democrats, the Levelers, had circulated their pamphlets among the common soldiers, who discussed them around their campfires. Not only did the soldiers demand to be paid, they also argued with their officers for a government in which everybody would have a say. As country squires, Cromwell and his generals opposed this kind of political and social leveling: thus, it did not win out. But since it continued to cause trouble, Cromwell was able to prolong his military rule for eight years.

The irony of the Puritan Revolution was that it had fought the king in the name of constitutionalism and the rule of law only to succumb first to rule by a small faction and then to a personal dictatorship—a pattern that was to repeat itself in the French and Russian Revolutions later on. Cromwell was a reluctant dictator, but dictator he was. Not only did he have to crush the Levelers, he also had to subdue the Scots and the Irish by armed force, and by 1652 he was also fighting the Dutch. Thus the army was never demobilized. It became the main political force in England. In 1653 Cromwell dissolved the "Rump Parliament" and made himself "Lord Protector of the Commonwealth of England, Scotland, and Ireland." But Cromwell's regime was unable to gain any backing from the great aristocrats, many of whom had fought for Charles I in the hope of bringing him around to their view of government. This was one basic weakness of the regime. Another was that the Lord Protector had no traditional claim of legitimacy.

If Oliver Cromwell had been a hereditary monarch, he might have done for England what Louis XIV did for France. He was a stronger leader than any of the Stuarts and a more astute statesman than Louis XIV. Under Cromwell England's international position improved considerably. He built up the navy to protect the country's overseas trade and passed the Navigation Acts to help the British merchant marine break the Dutch monopoly over the importation of goods into England. In addition to implementing these mercantilist policies successfully, Cromwell also won wars against the Dutch and the Spaniards. At home, the Instrument of Government by which he ruled was the first modern constitution based upon the division and balance of governmental authority and the first to recognize freedom of religion—as long as there was no pope and no bishops! Still, the people of the seventeenth century were not ready to accept a ruler whose authority was not sanctioned by tradition. And there was no tradition for a Cromwell in English history, unless one went all the way back to Julius Caesar, who had once conquered England but who was certainly not *English.*

Like Louis XIV, Cromwell believed that his power came from God, used religion in the service of the state, and tried to impose a new style of life on his countrymen. But unlike Catholicism and classicism in France, Puritanism as a faith and a code of behavior was alien to the English nation. Cromwell himself was not as bigoted as the major generals and "Saints" who tried to force English life and art into a Puritan strait-jacket. He loved good living and was fairly tolerant of other Protestants as long as they did not challenge his political authority. He would even have liked his regime to rest on popular support as expressed in free elections. Since the majority of Englishmen had come to hate him, this was not possible. Cromwell ruled reluctantly as a military dictator, with a hand-picked Parliament to give his authority some semblance of legality; but with no popular or traditional base his regime quickly crumbled after he died in 1658.

The story of the end of the Protectorate and the return of the Stuarts can be told briefly. Cromwell's son Richard ruled for a few months and was overthrown by a military conspiracy (1659). The generals then began quarreling among themselves. One of them, George Monk, ended the impending anarchy by leading his army from Scotland to London and taking control. General Monk threw in his lot with the civilians, who viewed a return to the monarchy as the only solution. A new Parliament was elected, and it invited the son of the beheaded Charles to return from exile. In May 1660 the new king returned to London as Charles II. The crowds cheered him, but he knew that it was freedom from Puritan "tyranny" rather than his own popularity that made them cheer.

### The Restoration and the Glorious Revolution, 1660–1689

In many ways the period of the second two Stuarts seemed like a repeat performance of the first. The monarchy and the House of Lords were restored, and a new House of Commons took office. Even the names of the performers were the same: Charles II (1660–1685) and James II (1685–1688). The "plot" was also the same: royal absolutism versus parliamentary supremacy and the rule of law. Nevertheless, the two major sides were chastened by their recent defeats and tried to avoid going to extremes. The struggle between them became almost exclusively *political.* Moreover, foreign help played a larger role after 1660 than it had before.

Charles II wanted to live and let live.

Having no desire to return to exile, he did not openly do anything that might force his opponents to remove him from the throne. He replaced the strait-laced moral regime of the Puritans with a permissive and fun-loving one; the London theaters, which the Puritans had closed, became famous for their racy and licentious tone.

The new king also sincerely desired to establish religious toleration. But he had to share power with Parliament, and the overwhelmingly Anglican Cavalier Parliament (1661–1679) insisted on religious conformity to the Church of England. It passed a series of acts discriminating against both Roman Catholics and Protestant Nonconformists—also called Dissenters. The Test Act of 1673 compelled all public servants to take the sacrament of the Church of England, and the Papists' Disabling Act of 1678 excluded Roman Catholics from Parliament.

Although Charles II was unable to oppose Parliament on the religious issue, he did find two ways of increasing his power at its expense. The first was to imitate as far as possible the form of government established by Louis XIV in France. Charles' admiration for Louis led him to conclude an alliance with him, and Louis gave Charles regular subsidies. These subsidies were bribes to keep England out of France's war with the Dutch.* Many English merchants wanted England to go to war against France, a commercial rival, but Charles managed to keep his bargain with Louis and at the same time strengthen his power against his Parliaments.

Charles' second technique of dealing with his Parliaments was to manipulate some of their members, a practice that led to the development of political parties. With favors and bribes he bought the support of a considerable number of Anglican Cavalier members, who came to be known as Tories (literally, Irish robbers). The opposition party, called Whigs (literally, Scottish cattle thieves), included many sons of Roundheads. Neither group was a real party yet; both lacked formal organization, discipline, and a consistent platform. The Tories tended to represent the interests of the conservative country gentry, whereas the Whigs tended to represent the modern capitalist landlords and the wealthy middle classes in the towns. In the eighteenth century the two parties were gradually to acquire more cohesion. But under Charles II, and until 1715, about one hundred members of Parliament—mostly Tories—were paid agents of the king.

*See p. 185.

Disagreeing on most issues, the Whigs and Tories both opposed Catholicism and royal absolutism. Charles II had kept his Catholic sympathies to himself and had increased his personal power by devious means; his brother James II was less circumspect. James tried to create a standing army as an instrument of the royal will. He also disregarded the Test Act by appointing Catholics to high public offices and due process of law in suppressing his opponents. Still, an anti-papist, anti-French succession seemed assured by the fact that James's daughter Mary was safely Protestant and married to William of Orange, *Stadholder* of the Dutch Republic, and grandson of Charles I. Then in 1688 his second wife gave birth to a son, whom James said would be raised as a Catholic. (The lullaby *Rockabye Baby* was originally a Whig political ballad directed against this heir.)

The danger of a Catholic monarchy with absolutist pretensions and pro-French leanings temporarily united the Whigs and Tories, and together they made the "Glorious Revolution." They invited William of Orange to come to England with an army and make James II abandon his pro-Catholic policies. James might have retained his throne if he had submitted to this pressure, but when his own army melted away he fled to France.* The revolution was thus a bloodless one. In 1689 a new Parliament imposed substantial limitations on the rights and powers of the English monarchy. These limitations were then incorporated into the Bill of Rights.

The Bill of Rights reaffirmed and ex-

*The French kings supported James II, his son James, and his grandson Bonnie Prince Charlie in later efforts to restore the Stuarts. The Jacobite (Jacob means James) movement remained active until the mid-eighteenth century, but the Stuarts were a lost cause.

tended the rights of Englishmen as set forth in Magna Carta and gave a permanent constitutional form to all the restraints that Parliament had tried to put on the Stuart kings. Its most important provisons were: (1) making or suspending any law without the consent of Parliament is illegal, (2) levying taxes without the consent of Parliament is illegal, (3) maintaining a standing army without the consent of Parliament is illegal, (4) elections of members of Parliament must be free, (5) there must be freedom of debate in Parliament, (6) Parliament should meet frequently, (7) Englishmen have the right to petition the sovereign, (8) Englishmen have the right to keep arms, (9) Englishmen have the right to trial by a jury, (10) excessive bail should never be demanded. The Habeas Corpus Act of 1679 was also reaffirmed. According to this act, judges were obliged to issue a writ of *habeas corpus* ("you may have the body") to a prisoner's lawyer, who could then demand that the jailor free his client if he could not show cause for his imprisonment. William of Orange, now William III, and his wife, Mary, took an oath to preserve these rights and restraints when they accepted Parliament's offer of the vacant throne.

In England things are not usually done in a nice tidy way, with everything in one statute. The Toleration Act (1689) granted Protestant Nonconformists the right of free public worship, while still barring them from public office. The Act of Settlement (1701) provided for the peaceful succession of the English crown to the nearest relative of the Stuarts who was willing to rule as an Anglican.* It also said that no king could involve England in a foreign war without the consent of Parliament, and it secured the independence of the judiciary by making judges removable only by an act of Parliament. Finally, in 1707, England and Scotland were united under the name of Great Britain.

*Queen Anne, Mary s sister, reigned from 1702 to 1714 and died childless. Since her brother James was a Catholic, her only acceptable Protestant successor was a German prince who was a great-grandson of James I. Thus Elector George of Hanover became King George I of England, Scotland, and Ireland in 1714, adopted the Anglican faith, and established the Hanoverian dynasty.

### Significance of the English Revolution

The English Revolution made permanent changes in the British political system, but it did not result in democracy. No more people were allowed to vote, as the Levelers of the 1640s had wished. There was no change in the class structure; Whigs and Tories represented two different outlooks among the wealthy classes, not two different classes. The English Revolution put the state in the hands of the wealthy classes and made it subservient to the law. Even so, the state itself grew stronger than ever.

Satisfied with their control over the state through Parliament, England's wealthy classes were willing to place more money at its disposal than any continental monarch— even Louis XIV—could muster. Not only did they pay more taxes, they also allowed the government to establish a national debt. They set up the Bank of England (1694) to lend money to the government and issue the national currency. The investors who supported this new institution made it possible for England to defeat France and become a world power, as we shall see in the next section.

In addition to strengthening the financial power of the state, the war against France also helped to extend further the ascendancy of Parliament over the monarchy. William III was no Whig, but he made concessions to his opponents in Parliament in order to keep England in the war on the side of his homeland, the Dutch Republic. The war, in turn, required expenditures that made William and his successor Anne increasingly dependent on Parliament for money. By 1713 Parliament virtually controlled the royal finances and granted the monarch only enough money outright to pay for his household expenses. This grant, called the civil list, was more than just pin money, but it was not enough to run a state.

At first glance it would seem that Great Britain was developing along different lines from the rest of Western Europe at the beginning of the eighteenth century; a closer look shows that it was not so different after all. From the mid-fifteenth to the mid-seventeenth century England's relative aloofness from continental affairs had certainly had its effects on English institutions and on the English national character. So had the country's seafaring tradition. But by 1715 Great Britain had become a major world power, closely involved with the other powers. Although the British government did not persecute its religious minorities the way Louis XIV did, it made a clear distinction between conformists and nonconformists in religion and denied certain political rights to the latter. In other respects, however, the British political system did differ from any on the continent. It was a constitutional monarchy in which the king still possessed discretionary powers, especially to defend the state in a crisis; in which Parliament had the supreme power to make laws; and in which the judiciary was independent of both the executive and the legislature. For later history the independence of the judiciary was the greatest safeguard of the liberty of the individual.

Great Britain had become a modern state; but still, despite all these obvious differences, so had France. In both countries the independence of the medieval estates was gone. In both countries the central government monopolized the military, political, and legal instruments of power. The British solution to the seventeenth-century constitutional crisis was to prove more lasting than the French. It was eventually to provide a model of government, complete with political parties and parliamentary committees, for free men wherever the British settled and in much of Western Europe as well. Later we shall see the importance of John Locke in translating this model into a political theory with widespread appeal.

## THE DEVELOPMENT OF THE EUROPEAN STATE SYSTEM

We have seen how the needs of war helped to strengthen the power and authority of the state in England and France; in Chapter VII we shall see a similar pattern in Austria, Russia, and Prussia. The wars of the late seventeenth and early eighteenth centuries involved all five of these countries and others as well. Indeed, these wars embraced the whole of Europe from Russia to Spain and began to affect certain European colonies overseas. They were not very destructive and not very passionate. Power, rather than religion or revenge, was the principal motive of Europe's rulers in going to war. They wanted to take over one another's men and property, not to destroy them. When the wars began (1667) France was the only state with enough power and authority at home to threaten the independence of other states. When the wars ended (1714 in the West and 1721 in the East) there were four others. During the course of the wars these countries had not only acquired the characteristics of the bureaucratically organized modern state, they had also worked out a system of in ternational relations.

### The Wars of Louis XIV

Like the English, most seventeenth-century Europeans retained their traditional belief that the only legitimate basis for political authority was dynastic. The cry, "The king is dead, long live the king!" still meant that kingship passed from the dead king to his nearest living heir in an unbroken succession, even if this heir was a foreigner. A ruler without a dynastic claim for his authority, like Cromwell, did not last very long. On the other hand, a royal personage with a proper dynastic claim to some other ruler's territory had a fighting chance of making his claim prevail.

Since most of the royal families of Western and Central Europe were related to each other, a birth or a death in any family made new dynastic combinations possible. The Hapsburgs had been particularly lucky in building up dynastic empires in the past. In the late seventeenth century the King of Spain, Charles II (1665–1700), was still the sovereign of a dozen territories in Northwestern Europe and Italy and the ruler of a world empire. Emperor Leopold I (1658–1705), Archduke of Austria and King of Bohemia and Hungary, was a Hapsburg too, and he was married to Charles II's sister. Louis XIV, the Bourbon King of France, also had Hapsburg blood in his veins and was married to Charles II's other sister. Both Leopold and Louis thus had dynastic claims

Louis XIV at war

to the Spanish inheritance as soon as Charles II should die. Everybody assumed that this sickly and dimwitted king would never have children, and they were right. But Charles took a long time dying.

Louis XIV's family claims to Spanish territories were a major factor in European international relations throughout his reign, but, as the personification of the French state, Louis tried to identify his own interests with those of France. Today we speak of the "national interest"; in Louis' time and throughout the eighteenth century this was called "reasons of state." It meant preserving and extending the political, military, and economic power of the state by all possible means. For "reasons of state" Louis XIV gave large sums of money to Charles II of England to keep him from allying himself with the Dutch and supported James II's claim to the English throne to stir up trouble against William III. For "reasons of state" Louis XIV fought the Dutch to enlarge French commerce at their expense. For "reasons of state" he tried to annex the Spanish Netherlands and German territories on the west side of the Rhine to strengthen his military frontier. Between 1701 and 1713 he fought the War of the Spanish Succession against a Grand Alliance including England, Holland, Austria, and a number of lesser states. But, for "reasons of state," he had become willing to make peace as early as 1709. Costly military defeats, crop failures, and excessive taxation were weakening France to a dangerous degree. Hence Louis XIV had to give up his dream of acquiring the Spanish dynastic empire for himself.

In the late seventeenth century "reasons of state" came to determine how wars were fought as well as why they were fought. As bureaucrats took the place of nobles of the sword in making government policy they introduced an element of caution and economy into the conduct of their countries' wars. The function of bureaucrats was—and still is—to serve the state. They were suspicious of soldiers who wanted to risk the whole army in a single battle. Troops were becoming too valuable to be wasted in this way. Thus land warfare became an affair of maneuvers and sieges, and naval warfare mainly a matter of blockades and raids on commercial shipping. This was the way Louis XIV's first three wars were fought: the War of Devolution (1667–1668) against the Spanish Netherlands, the Dutch War

(1672–1678), and the War of the League of Augsburg (1688–1697). This third war involved a French invasion of the Rhineland, a trade war against the English and the Dutch, and minor skirmishes with the English in North America. (Simultaneously, Austria, Venice, Russia, and Poland were fighting the Ottoman Empire in Eastern Europe.)

### *The War of the Spanish Succession*

Cautious bureaucrats did not always have their way when the stakes were really high, and in the War of the Spanish Succession (1701–1713) the stakes were the highest anyone could imagine. A world empire was "up for grabs." Just before he died, Charles II of Spain had willed this empire to Louis XIV's grandson, who became Philip V. Although Emperor Leopold prepared for war, the English and the Dutch were willing to accept this arrangement as long as the French and Spanish crowns remained separated. But Louis pushed his luck too far. He insisted that French merchants receive preferential treatment in all Spanish markets at the expense of their English and Dutch rivals. In addition, he expelled the Dutch garrisions along the southern border of the Spanish Netherlands, which they had gained the right to control at the end of an earlier war. The response in London and The Hague was the emergence of war parties. By 1701 all the rulers of Western and Central Europe were ready to go to war, while their bureaucrats and ministers shook their heads.

The War of the Spanish Succession showed that the states of Europe could not annihilate one another by military means. Armies were larger and better disciplined than ever before. In battle each side consisted of a five-deep line of smartly uniformed infantrymen with their new trigger-firing muskets and bayonets. When one soldier fell, another filled his place in line. The days of armored cavalry charges and mobile sharpshooters were over, and decisive battles were rare. Brilliant generals like the Duke of Marlborough, fighting for England, and Prince Eugene of Savoy, fighting for Austria, won spectacular victories in Italy, Germany, and the Spanish Netherlands, but they could not break through Vauban's system of border fortifications to the heart of France. The French held their own at home and in Spain, but they could not conquer the rest of Europe.

Thus, the champions of "reasons of state"—the bureaucrats—turned out to be right after all, and the war ended with a compromise peace settlement. The new Tory ministers in England paved the way for peace by removing Marlborough from his military command and deserting their Dutch and Austrian allies. Without English support these countries had to stop fighting, and the diplomats of all the belligerent states signed the Treaties of Utrecht and Rastadt (1713–14).

These treaties divided the lands of the Spanish Hapsburgs as follows: Louis XIV's grandson, Philip V, retained Spain, the Spanish overseas empire, and part of Italy; the Austrian Hapsburgs received the Spanish Netherlands and part of Italy; Britain gained Gibraltar and the slave-trading concession in Spain's American colonies. In North America England also took over Nova Scotia and Newfoundland from France. The Dutch regained the right to garrison the border fortifications in the now Austrian Netherlands. Finally, the French agreed that France and Spain would remain permanently separated.

### The Emergence of the Balance of Power

The War of the Spanish Succession had shown that, opposed by a combination of other powers, no single power could dominate Europe. The Treaties of Utrecht and Rastadt sought to preserve this "balance of power" as the permanent basis of European international relations. That was why the Austrians and the Dutch were given control over France's northern neighbor, the former Spanish Netherlands, and why her southern neighbor, Spain, was separated from the French Crown, even though both countries were now ruled by Bourbons. Having helped to "contain" France in this way on the continent, Great Britain could now dominate the Western Mediterranean and the Atlantic approaches to Europe with her navy and her new stronghold at Gibraltar.

By 1715, then, Western Europe had

brought some semblance of order to the seventeenth-century crisis in international relations. No longer could religious and civil rebellions be used by foreign powers for imperialist ends. Louis XIV gave up his support of the Stuart Pretenders against the new Hanoverian dynasty in England. Fixed political frontiers now replaced dynastic rights as the limits of state power. Control of the sea also became increasingly important as a means of preserving the balance of power—and here Great Britain emerged supreme.

The balance of power could not insure permanent peace, but it did create a system in which each state could defend its independence against foreign aggression. In 1715 the three great powers—France, England, and Austria—kept one another's imperialist ambitions in check by cooperating with the lesser states. The Dutch Republic had lost its commercial supremacy and lacked the resources and fighting spirit to compete with the new great powers. Its wealthy burghers settled down into a comfortable complacency with the assurance that, if one of the great powers attacked them, the others would intervene to preserve the balance of power. In Central and Eastern Europe other older powers (Sweden, Poland, and Turkey) were also declining, and new ones (Prussia and Russia) were rising. We shall deal with them in Chapter VII. The point to remember here is that Europe as a whole had developed a complex pattern of international relations which allowed culturally diverse states to develop independently and to form alliances for mutual protection against any state that threatened to upset the balance of power.

## THE SCIENTIFIC REVOLUTION

Modern science, like the modern state, was a product of the seventeenth-century search for new sources of authority and order. Just as power acquired a new basis, so did knowledge. In each case the change created a conflict between the champions of the old and the champions of the new; in each case the latter won out. Even more than the modern state, modern science gave European civilization a directive force unique in the history of the world.

What is knowledge? Men have argued for centuries about how we acquire it, but they have usually agreed that it is a correspondence between ideas and "reality." Whatever this reality may be, we want our ideas about it to be true, and we want to be able to express these true ideas in some kind of language. Whatever the words or symbols of this language may be, we want to be able to say: "This is so." Hence, to know something is to be able to make a true statement about it.

What is reality and what is the source of true statements about it? These were the crucial questions in the seventeenth century. They were crucial because the old sources of knowledge seemed inadequate to some men and because old statements about reality were being openly challenged. We have already seen such challenges in the changing artistic styles and the religious controversies of the early modern period. Let us turn now to the challenges posed by the new science and the new philosophy of the seventeenth century.

### From Natural Philosophy to Natural Science

Although much of European civilization from the eleventh to the seventeenth century was an original creation, educated Europeans had borrowed heavily from the civilization of the ancient Mediterranean world in thought and letters; we have seen the importance of Aristotle in medieval philosophy and of Cicero and other Roman writers in Renaissance humanism. Greek achievements in science and mathematics began to be known through Latin translations in the thirteenth century and in authentic Greek texts during the Renaissance. By the mid-sixteenth century the whole body of Greek scientific knowledge was readily available in printed books.

In medieval and early modern times thoughtful men were more the slaves of the Greek (that is, Aristotelian) explanation of the physical universe than if they had invented it themselves. Beginning in the fourteenth century they faced perceptible difficulties in some areas, especially where patches of ancient science were still undiscovered. Yet even when they performed experiments and pushed back the frontiers of thought they were still playing on the margin of the Aristotelian system; and when anything needed explaining they would not derive their theories from their own observations. Instead, until the mid-sixteenth century, they continued to draw on the explanations of ancient philosophy. To be sure, some late medieval scholars began to question Aristotle's theory of motion, and they and a number of early modern scholars prepared the way for the scientific revolution. But it was nevertheless a revolution—a true break with the past which gave a new dimension to European civilization.

In the late medieval and early modern periods there was no clear distinction between science and philosophy. Philosophy seeks knowledge through speculation and logic; science seeks it through experimentally controlled theories. The Greeks had produced Archimedes and other scientists, yet only in the seventeenth century did the experimental *method* of Archimedes gradually replace that of Aristotle as an accepted source of knowledge about the natural world. Until this happened, the study of nature was more philosophical than scientific.

The picture of nature offered by Aristotelian philosophy, supplemented by Christian theology, held sway for so long not only because of its traditional authority but also because it was so satisfyingly complete. Everything fitted into some neat category. Furthermore, everything had a purpose. Hence the supporters of the traditional picture of the world—especially the churches and the universities—used all their authority to condemn the men who made the scientific revolution.

In the year 1543 two books made the first major attacks on traditional natural philosophy on the two separate levels of fact and theory. In his *On the Fabric of the Human Body* the Belgian Andreas Vesalius (1514–1564) showed how new facts could be learned about human anatomy by dissection and experiment, while retaining the theory of the Greek authority on the subject, Galen. In his *On the Revolution of Heavenly Bodies* the Pole Nicholas Copernicus (1473–1543) accepted the observations of the Greek astronomer Ptolemy but substituted a new *interpretation.* Although these two books were to have momentous consequences for the scientific revolution, neither Vesalius nor Copernicus had bridged the medieval gap between the realm of speculative thought and the bewildering complexity of the natural world. Natural science did not completely replace natural philosophy until fact and theory were brought together.

### Copernicus

The outstanding example of the transition from medieval to modern thinking about the natural world was Copernicus. He rejected Ptolemy's mathematical theory of the universe, while retaining the predominantly Aristotelian descriptive and physical cosmology, whose objective was to understand the heavenly universe and relate it to the rest of man's knowledge. Ptolemy's *geostatic* theory made the mean center of the Sun's supposed orbit around the Earth the focal point of the universe. Copernicus made the mean center of the Earth's orbit around a Sun "at rest" the new focal point, and his theory is therefore called *heliostatic.* It was truly revolutionary to say that the Earth moved. But according to Copernicus the orbits of the planets were still perfect circles, and the categories of motion and matter on Earth were still fundamentally different from those in the rest of the universe. Furthermore, Copernicus' heliostatic theory used eccentric circles—circles having different centers—to confirm what could be seen with the naked eye just as Ptolemy's geostatic theory did.

As a pioneer of modern science Copernicus is more significant for having invented a mathematical planetary system than for having postulated a moving Earth and a stationary Sun. Ptolemy's theory was so arranged as to deal with each planet separately and individually. There was no single mathematical connection among these several models, only a general similarity in the mathematical methods used for each. Copernicus was the first to devise a mathematical link that welded the whole into a *system.* Now the way was opened for a new type of think-

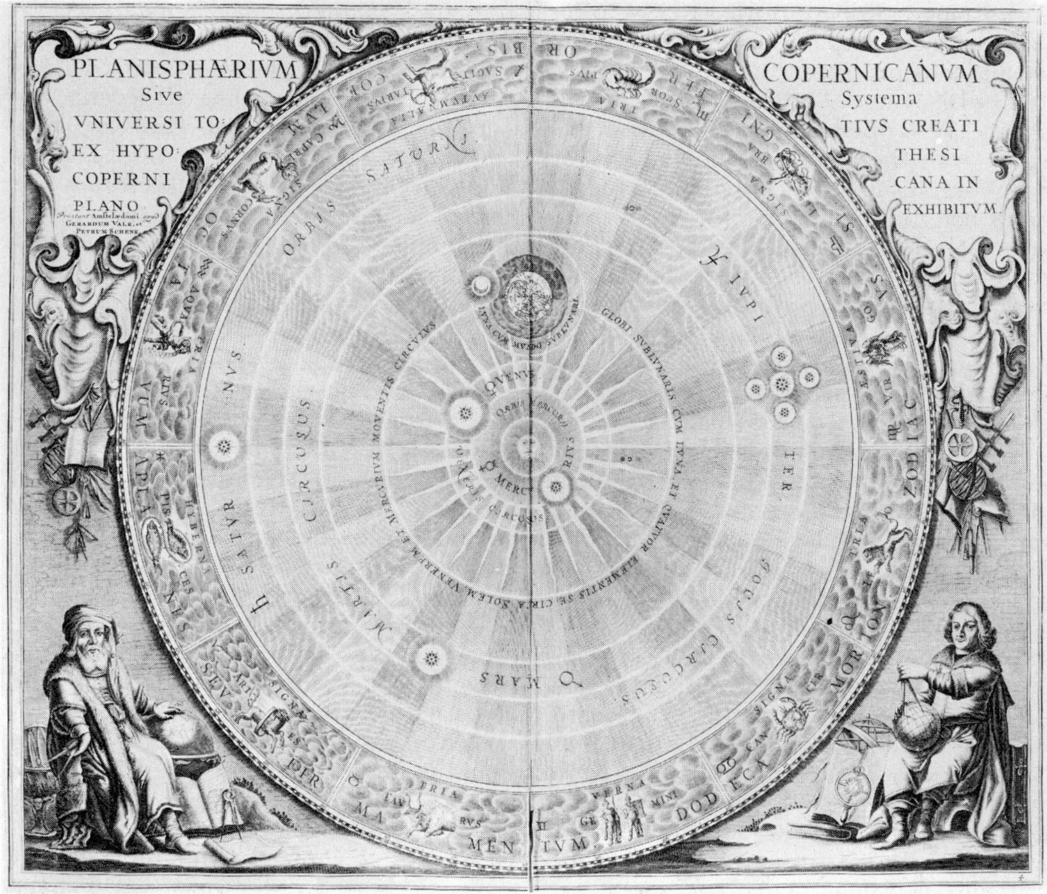


*Copernicus' planetary system*

ing, which was to explain the movement of bodies in the heavens *and* on Earth in terms of mathematically explainable natural laws. In mathematics the value of most symbols is a *function* of something else. It now remained for the notion of functionality to triumph in the laws of the natural world.

### *The Accumulation of New Knowledge*

Many practical factors helped to bring about a scientific attitude in the sixteenth and seventeenth centuries. Travel and exploration broadened men's knowledge of the world and made them more receptive to new ideas. The habit of quantitative thinking that introduced rational accounting into business also affected the way scientists began to think about nature. Through long-continued contact, experimentation and observation were taken over into science from art and architecture, from mining, from map making, and from skilled handicrafts in general. The solution of practical technological problems became increasingly urgent as the new economic, military, and navigational needs of an expanding society emerged. Indeed, a major concern of many seventeenth-century scientists was to find an accurate way to compute longitude at sea. The solution to this problem did not come until the eighteenth century, when modern time computing and other new techniques were applied to it.

The revolution in astronomy, physics, and mathematics is our central concern, but we must note that it did not occur in a vacuum. There was a tremendous expansion of the intellectual and physical horizons in other fields as well. William Harvey (1578–1657) discovered the circulation of the blood; Robert Boyle (1627–1691) made pioneer experiments in chemistry and gaseous pressures; Marcello Malpighi (1628–1694) and Anthony Leeuwenhoek (1632–1723) opened up new fields of research with their microscopic analyses of living organisms. Some of their achievements had an immediate influence; others had to be developed further before their full import became clear. Nevertheless, the sheer mass of new information and the bold challenges to traditional views in so many fields acted as an exciting stimulus for a radical reevaluation of man's attitudes toward nature and society.

We must also note several important points about the way seventeenth century advances in science were made. First, they were international: Galileo Galilei (1564–1642) was an Italian, Johannes Kepler (1571–1630) was a German, René Descartes (1596–1650) was a Frenchman, and Sir Isaac Newton (1642–1727) was an Englishman. Second, new technical aids—like the telescope—and new mathematical tools—trigonometry, logarithms, analytical geometry, infinitesimal calculus—were very important. Third, the development of new theories and the accumulation of new facts led to far more profound readjustments between theory and fact than the original innovators could foresee. Fourth, the greatest early modern scientists were less interested in achieving practical results than in finding a fixed and necessary order of nature formulated with quantitative precision and elaborated with the techniques of mathematics. The first modern physicists and astronomers were as eager as earlier natural philosophers to find the divine plan of the world. What made them revolutionary was their insistence on controlling their new theories with observations and experiments.

### Galileo and Kepler

Galileo was the first modern scientist to support mathematical theories about the physical world with an experimental base. He directed the mind toward problems that were amenable to measurement and calculation. According to him, shape, size, quantity, and motion were the primary qualities that the scientist should seek to examine, rather than common-sense phenomena and the ordinary appearances of bodies, with which all his predecessors had primarily dealt. Many of Galileo's famous experiments—like dropping objects from the Tower of Pisa—are now known to have been "thought experiments" only. We should therefore avoid imputing his intellectual achievements too definitely to the experimental method itself.

Although Galileo's most significant advances were in the field of physics, he also destroyed classical astronomy with his telescopic observations; we shall examine the latter work first. Borrowing the techniques of a Dutch lens maker, Galileo constructed his own telescope in 1609 and turned it toward the heavens. Men had been gazing at the stars for thousands of years, but no one had ever seen what Galileo saw. He saw four of the satellites of Jupiter and regarded them as a visible model of the whole solar system. By observing that Venus had phases like the Moon, he deduced that this planet revolved around the Sun. Galileo also saw that the Moon had mountains and the Sun had spots.

Galileo's observations vindicated Copernicus against Ptolemy, and they dealt a crushing blow to Aristotle. For Galileo could *demonstrate* to anyone who would look through his telescope that the universe was a physical structure containing two types of physical bodies, stars and planets. Contrary to Aristotle, the heavens were not perfect, invariable, and essentially different from earthly things. The Earth was a planet. It was composed of the same kind of physical matter as Venus, Mars, Mercury, and Jupiter, and, contrary to Ptolemy, all these planets revolved around the Sun.

Some university professors refused to look through Galileo's telescope; all astrologers went on talking about the supposed influences of the stars on human behavior; and in 1633 the Roman Inquisition compelled Galileo to "abjure, curse, and detest" the Copernican doctrine as a heresy. Someone thought he heard Galileo mumble the words "and yet it *does* move" under his breath just after he had "abjured, cursed, and detested" this idea in a loud voice. The mumbling was a legend, but Galileo's real convictions were clear. Aristotle's natural philosophy was inconsistent with the new physical astronomy. The new natural philosophy, which Galileo helped to found, had to view the universe in terms of laws of motion.

Galileo's greatest achievement was in the mathematical analysis of motion. We cannot describe all the physical and mental experiments and mathematical calculations he went through to discover the principle of inertia. Suffice it to say that here too he completed the refutation of Aristotle, whose theory of motion had already been under attack for two hundred years. According to Aristotle, the "purpose" of a moving body was to seek a resting place, and it required a continuously acting force to remain in motion. To Galileo, a body in motion along a straight line would not only go on moving indefinitely without any continuously acting force, it would also require some other force to stop it.

From this single discovery Galileo was able to build up a whole theory of mechanics. Herein lies the magnitude of his achievement. It showed a rapid evolution in thought requiring clarity of definition, a systematic elaboration of mathematical expression, the re-thinking of the nature of motion, and an ingenious recognition of functions that made quantitative calculations possible.

Galileo never compared the motion of a projectile with that of a planet; it was his contemporary Kepler who first described the laws of planetary motion. The two men referred favorably to each other's work and corresponded regularly for many years, but they followed independent paths in their studies. The synthesis of their two distinct points of view was not to come until a generation after both had died.

These two founders of modern science were utterly different kinds of men. Despite his mathematical ingenuity and his interest in astronomy, Galileo was "down to earth" both temperamentally and in his main scientific concerns. He became a conscious propagandist for the new natural philosophy and wrote many of his books in Italian so that even nonexperts could read them. His *Dialogues on the Two Chief Systems of the World*, published in 1632, was a truly popular book. Kepler was the prototype of the Central European mathematical genius—retiring, eccentric, and incapable of communicating his thoughts in ordinary language. He was "up in the clouds" both temperamentally and in his main scientific concerns. His books, which were written in abstruse Latin and permeated with number-mysticism, show the kind of man he was. The two that best show his mysticism are the *Cosmographic Mystery* (1597) and *The Harmonies of the World* (1619).

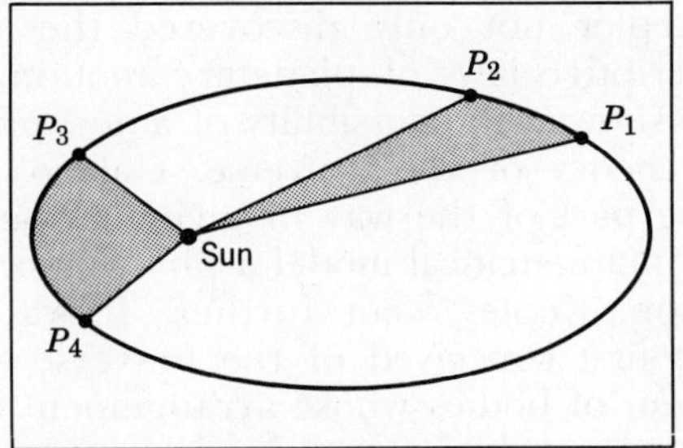

*Kepler's First Two Laws of planetary motion*

Yet part of Kepler's genius lay in his ability to overcome his superstitions about the mystical meanings of numbers and perfect geometrical forms in the interest of quantitative accuracy. In his search for the true orbits of the five known planets of his day he would have liked them to have been perfect circles and to have corresponded to the five regular solids. But this fantastic scheme did not fit the set of *quantitative* observations he had fortunately acquired from his patron and friend, the Danish astronomer Tycho Brahe (1546–1601). As a true scientist, therefore, Kepler revised his theory to fit the best set of facts available to him. The result was that he discovered the first two laws of planetary motion: (1) The planets move on elliptical, not circular, orbits with the Sun at one focus; (2) the line joining the Sun and a planet sweeps out equal areas in equal times. With the aid of the improved trigonometry of his day and the invention of logarithms by the Englishman John Napier (1550–1617), Kepler discovered his third law of planetary motion; namely, that the squares of the period of the orbit are proportional to the cubes of their mean distances from the Sun.

Kepler not only discovered the new descriptive laws of planetary motion, he also showed the possibility of a new physical theory of the universe. Galileo had gone part of the way in giving Copernicus' mathematical model a physical explanation. Kepler went further. It was he who first conceived of the universe as a system of bodies whose arrangement and motions could be explained by universal generalizations demonstrable from qualitative observations and checked by accurate quantitative measurements. This was the true significance of the scientific revolution.

Neither Galileo nor Kepler saw that the same mechanical laws might apply on Earth and in the heavens; Descartes suggested that a Universal Mathematics was needed to describe the universal laws of motion; but not until Newton combined mathematics with new experiments was the synthesis of Galileo's earthly mechanics and Kepler's celestial mechanics fully achieved.

### Descartes and Newton

René Descartes came closer than anyone else to making himself the Aristotle of the new science and the new philosophy. Like Aristotle, he was a philosopher first. Like Aristotle, he established an apparently foolproof method of acquiring knowledge, as we shall presently learn. Unlike Aristotle, however, Descartes made significant contributions to the science of physics, and was one of the world's great mathematicians.

Seventeenth-century physical scientists, as we have seen, were striving toward an explanation of the behavior of matter in motion. Descartes not only provided such an explanation, he also thought it explained everything in the natural world. He provided the explanation by *defining* matter and motion in such a way as to include everything else—except God and the human soul. According to Descartes' definition, matter is that which occupies space. In other words, it is extension. All other qualities of matter—weight, color, texture, etc.—can be reduced to combinations of its extensive or spatial qualities. Motion is the displacement of matter. That was all there was to it! Descartes said: "Give me motion and extension, and I will construct a world."

The world Descartes constructed is purely mechanical. Bodies in motion continue to move in a straight line unless they are acted upon in some way. When bodies like the planets move in circular orbits (Descartes did not accept Kepler's elliptical orbits) there must be some kind of centripetal force that makes them do so. Whether circular or straight, motion is the result of the impact of material bodies on each other. There is no such thing as empty space, and there are no intangible "forces" like gravity. The world consists entirely of particles of matter hitting one another in fixed mechanical patterns. The forms of matter vary in size from tiny "corpuscles" to the largest planets. We can see the movement of the planets and visible objects on Earth, but even a chair or a table is nothing more than a combination of particles of matter whose motion maintains them in the forms familiar to our senses.

Descartes made a famous philosophical assumption—the autonomy of the human mind—that hampered his work as a scientist. When he was in his early twenties he experienced a psychological crisis. He wanted to know reality as it really was, and he began to doubt all the traditional sources of such knowledge. So he threw them all out one night: Scholastic reasoning, in which he was well trained, holy scripture, the senses—everything. There was only one thing that he could not throw out—the fact of his doubting. Here was the basic certainty: "I think, therefore I exist." (*Cogito, ergo sum*). From this indubitable starting point he could advance afresh with full confidence in the knowledge his thinking would reveal. As we have observed, Descartes came to explain all natural phenomena, including the human body, as matter in motion. Yet he continued to view the human mind as something different, a kind of ghost, or soul, in the machine. This notion was inconsistent with his own mechanistic view of nature. It also led him to overrate the ability of the mind to reproduce models whose properties, motion and extension, were exact replicas of those of the real world and hence explained it.

Descartes was too optimistic in hoping that the mind could duplicate the mechanics of the universe in the abstract symbols of a universal mathematics. The idea had great appeal, though, and it made him the most influential thinker of the seventeenth and early eighteenth centuries. Nonetheless, Descartes and his followers made some serious mistakes about the physical world with their purely mental constructions. For example, Descartes was mistaken in denying the possibility of a vacuum, as another French scientist, Blaise Pascal (1623–1662), was to show. He was also mistaken in thinking that when a moving body hit a stationary body it bounced off in another direction without losing any of its momentum. He believed this not because of any experiments he conducted or any mathematical demonstration he made; he did not know of the infinitesimal calculus with which the German mathematician-philosopher Gottfried Wilhelm von Leibniz (1646–1716) was to prove this notion to be false. He deduced it from the principle of the conservation of motion. In fact, Descartes' fullest description of the natural world, *The Principles of Philosophy* (1664), is almost completely nonmathematical.

Even though Descartes did not always practice what he preached, he was a great mathematician, and he had a profound influence on modern science as well as on philosophy. His principal contribution was his method of abstract model-building. Today's scientists no longer view their models as ultimate explanations, but they have fully vindicated their use as the best way to make some sense out of what happens in the infinite and infinitesimal "worlds" we cannot see.

Descartes also invented an important mathematical tool, analytical geometry. Since he believed that the more abstract a concept was the truer it was, he decided to improve the traditional geometry of his day. He eliminated the "accidental" visual aspects of geometrical figures by expressing lines and curves in numerical symbols and their relations in equations. In addition, he introduced the idea of movement, which was lacking in Greek geometry. He determined the position of a point on a graph by its distance from the sides of the graph and thus invented the plotting of a curve. In doing so, Descartes coordinated the geometrical idea of representation with the algebraic idea of two variables in an equation having an indefinite number of simultaneous values. In this way he strengthened the seventeenth-century scientists' habit of viewing everything as a *function* of everything else.

By the late seventeenth century a number of thinkers had advanced man's knowledge of astronomy, physics, and mathematics considerably, and the time was ripe for someone to bring all this knowledge together into a grand synthesis. Things do not always happen when the time is ripe for them, but Isaac Newton "happened" at just the right time. Although he did not see all problems in ways unimagined by his contemporaries, he exercised greater ability and mathematical skill in solving them. He established the developing physical sciences at a new level, a level at which they remained until the nineteenth century was well advanced.

Newton brought those branches of physical science that were studied in the seventeenth century to a peak of achievement. He made optics a branch of physics by demonstrating that the theory of light and the theory of matter complemented each other. He gave the principles of dynamics their explicit form and formulated general laws of motion from which Galileo's principle of inertia and Kepler's three laws of planetary motion all followed as necessary consequences. For example, he showed that the Moon's motion, given its distance from the Earth, conformed to the same law as that of freely falling bodies at the Earth's surface. In this and other ways he advanced the idea of a universal gravitational force acting between all particles of matter with an intensity inversely proportional to the squares of their mutual distances. The gravitational force emanating from the Sun is sufficient to keep the planets in their orbits, while such a force emanating from a planet keeps its satellites in their orbits.

Like most great scientists, Newton had to invent new techniques for solving problems that the old ones could not handle.

The most pressing problem of this type was the mathematical analysis of continuous changes. Now that practically everything was conceived as being in motion, the old kinds of measurements no longer worked. So, in order to carry through his mathematical deductions, Newton invented infinitesimal, or *fluxionary*, calculus,* which was analogous to partial differentiation and partial integration. With this tool he was able to calculate the infinitesimal decrease in the force of gravity at increasing distances from the earth.

In mathematics, as in astronomy and physics, Newton was drawing on work done by his predecessors. The calculus was a remarkable invention, but its crude components had already been sketched by Newton's time. What Newton did was to realize Descartes' ideal of a universal mathematics that would bring all the familiar physical phenomena of the Earth and the heavens into a unified system. He made the various laws and theories of this system derivable from a few physical principles taken as axioms and verifiable by experiments conducted on the surface of a minor planet.

Newton shared Descartes' conception of nature as a mechanistic order. He tied this order together with the principle of gravity, but he was unable to explain the *cause* of gravity. His most famous book was *The Mathematical Principles of Natural Philosophy* (*Philosophiae Naturalis Principia Mathematica*), first published in 1678 and amended in a second edition in 1713. In this book —usually referred to simply as the *Principia*—he developed a theory that accounted for all matter in motion "as if" it were regulated by gravity. This explanation "worked" better than Descartes' notion of impact. Still, Newton's world was a dull affair, soundless, scentless, colorless. It consisted merely of particles of matter hurrying endlessly and meaninglessly, but in an ordered way capable of being expressed in mathematical formulas. The disciples of Descartes and Newton believed in the same new philosophy. Their main quarrel concerned the proper method of the new science.

*Leibniz developed a similar calculus with a superior notation independently in Germany a few years later. The charges and countercharges of plagiarism between the two men illustrated a new type of problem in scientific research and had the unfortunate result of cutting England off from continental discoveries in pure and applied mathematics until the early nineteenth century.

### The Scientific Method

Newton's *Principia* influenced the development of modern science for the next two centuries. It established a mechanistic system of the universe that remained valid within the limits of the "world" Newton knew even after the discovery of the subatomic "world" and the "worlds" outside our own galaxy two hundred years later. It defined mass and the laws of motion and gave to science the formal concepts of space and time. It virtually created theoretical physics as a mathematical science in a form that lasted until the end of the nineteenth century. Finally, it illustrated a new method of obtaining knowledge about the natural world—a method still in use.

In the seventeenth century the method of the physical sciences, excluding chemistry, tended to be abstract and mathematical; that of the biological sciences tended to be concrete and descriptive. Indeed, classification and description were to remain the chief activities of anatomy, botany, physiology, and zoology until the latter half of the nineteenth century. Despite this variety, the question of the proper method of science became a major issue in the seventeenth century.

As we have noted, the intellectual elite of that time was looking for a new source of certainty. Some believed that this lay in observation and experiment; others believed that it lay in general ideas. The former approach is called *empirical*, the latter *rationalistic* or *analytical*. The advocates of both approaches agreed that the scientist should doubt everything initially. Beyond that they differed radically about what he had to do to achieve certainty.

From a purely logical point of view the difference between the empirical and rationalistic approaches to knowledge is a difference between inductive and deductive reasoning. Inductive reasoning begins with observations of individual things or events. It sorts these out into classes or species and then seeks, by experiment, to discover relations between particular things or events in each class or species—assuming that controls can be set up to eliminate variables not under study. For example, the botanist observes a large number of individual red objects. He then classifies them all as roses. After performing experiments on them he is able to make generalizations that serve to predict and control the way they reproduce themselves, the effect of varying amounts of water and sunshine on their growth, the possibilities of cross-breeding, etc. This is pure empiricism.

The first modern prophet of pure empiricism was the philosopher Francis Bacon (1561–1626), who also served as Lord Chancellor of England under James I. Like Descartes, Bacon "rang the bell and called the wits together" in the assault on traditional ideas, prejudices, and preconceptions. In his *New Organon*—which was to replace Aristotle's collection of logical treatises of the same name—Bacon insisted on the organizing and recording of experiments as the only sure method of acquiring new knowledge. Unlike Descartes, Bacon performed no experiments himself, but his manifesto inspired a number of seventeenth-century British scientists to do so. By the mid-eighteenth century French scientists were also to favor the empirical approach and to glorify Bacon out of proportion to his actual importance. For, by harping on the virtues of inductive reasoning, Bacon missed the point that the new physics and the new astronomy were inconceivable without mathematics, which is the most abstract form of deductive reasoning.

Deductive reasoning starts with what are called first principles—the most general and supposedly self-evident truths—and works down through a series of statements at increasingly less general levels until it reaches a particular case. Thus, it starts with a first principle like "All men are mortal," combines this with a classifying statement "Aristotle is a man," and concludes with the particular case "therefore, Aristotle is mortal." With this kind of reasoning Descartes deduced the whole order of the universe from the first principles "matter is that which occupies space" and "motion is the displacement of matter."

In his *Discourse on Method* (1635) Descartes gave the classic presentation of the rationalist, or analytical, method, which is sometimes called the *Cartesian* method. First, one must be sure that one's basic ideas are clear, distinct, and true. Second, one must break down a complex issue into its simplest separate components; this is the process of analysis. Third, one must build up an ordered arrangement of these components into a logical whole; this is the process of synthesis. Fourth, one must be meticulously complete in detecting all the relevant items that belong in the final synthesis. Descartes and his many admirers believed that, with this method, reason could explain everything there was to know.

Thus, empiricism gives priority to knowledge gained through the senses, while rationalism begins with abstract ideas. In practice, however, Galileo, Newton, and even Descartes—when he was being a scientist rather than a philosopher—combined both approaches.

Even the most self-conscious empiricist does not begin from ignorance. He knows that roses are roses and he usually has a great deal of prior knowledge about their behavior. Consequently, he does not ask questions about them at random. He sets up an experiment in order to bring forth a single, unambiguous response to a specific question he has thought out in advance.

The only way the scientist can design such questions is through the use of mental constructs and generalizations that are derived from the specific reality but that are abstract rather than real. For example, in Newtonian mechanics the law of gravitation had to be taken as descriptively correct, although gravity was not explainable in terms of matter and motion. In other words, gravity is a mental construct, and the law of gravitation is a generalization. Both are derived from the description of matter and motion, which seventeenth-century scientists took to be the basic realities. Even so, these realities are not the *cause* of gravity.

Descartes challenged the validity of purely descriptive constructs and generalizations derived from sense perceptions. According to him, they did not *explain* anything. Only the "clear and certain ideas" of the mind could tell us *why* bodies were attracted to each other and *why* the planets stayed in their orbits. But Newton and Galileo were right in denying the possibility of touching any cause more fundamental than a construct or generalization derived from the description of some specific phenomenon. This was the great methodological discovery of the scientific revolution. Once this discovery was made, the distinction between description and explanation began to lose its significance in science.

Newton fused the empirical and analytical methods in his own work and established this combination as the model for scientific investigation in all fields. His method operated as follows. First, by inductive reasoning, he discovered the fundamental principles embodied in phenomena. For example, by observing that a number of apples fell to the ground he could have reasoned that all apples fall to the ground. Second, he generalized these principles by abstracting them from any real objects – in this case apples – and then expressed them mathematically. In this form the principles would apply in all cases of falling objects. Finally, he showed the physical validity of these mathematical generalizations by appealing to observation and experiment. (What do you mean, all objects don't fall? Look!)

Until the mid-eighteenth century Western European thinkers were divided between the followers of Descartes and the followers of Newton. Although Descartes offered a deeper kind of certainty, Newton's appeal to experiment was contagious and was finally to win out. Let us remember, however, that both the Cartesians and the Newtonians agreed on two fundamental methodological assumptions: (1) that reason is infallible when rightly used; (2) that things always happen in the same way under the same conditions. This second assumption is called the principle of *determinism.* Along with "right reason" it was to remain unchallenged in European science for two hundred years.

## The Organization and Spread of Scientific Knowledge

So far we have discussed science as a new philosophy of nature, a new body of knowledge, and a new method; in none of these respects did science have any immediate effect on the thinking of the masses of Europeans. But between about 1665 and 1720 science as an *activity* became a part of European life. The churches gradually dropped their objections to it, and some universities began to offer courses in the new mathematics and the new natural philosophy, though not in the experimental sciences. Furthermore, the practical usefulness of scientific activity became apparent to government officials, and national governments founded or chartered the first permanent scientific societies, the two most important being The Royal Society of London for the Promotion of Natural Knowledge, chartered in 1662, and the French Académie Royale des Sciences, founded four years later. What both institutions provided for scientists was honor and fame and a place to discuss their work. In return, the government officials who sponsored them expected practical inventions that would help the nation economically and give it an advantage over competing nations. Occasionally a government sponsored some group project, but the private researches of the academicians were more important than their cooperative undertakings. National partisanship also hampered the growth of international cooperation among scientists. Yet the disinterested pursuit of scientific knowledge was firmly established in all "schools" in all countries. Beneath the academic and national rivalries a new community of thought and activity became a part of European civilization.

The members of the scientific community kept up with one another's activities mainly by private correspondence and the frequent exchange of their respective publications; but another new institution, the scholarly journal, gave them at least a superficial picture of the total scientific activity in Europe. The *Philosophical Trans-*

Louis XIV visiting the French Académie Royale des Sciences

*actions* of the Royal Society printed original research papers, which were also translated into Latin for specialists on the continent. The *Journal des Savants*, published in Paris, surveyed the whole field of learning, published book reviews, and reported the meetings of scientific societies. In the 1680s Pierre Bayle, of whom we shall learn more shortly, launched the first semipopular journal, *News of the Republic of Letters* (*Nouvelles de la République des Lettres*), which followed the broad pattern of the *Journal des Savants.* Its very name, and the fact that it was published in Holland, symbolized the international character of the scholarly community.

## CHANGING PATTERNS OF THOUGHT

The scientific revolution did not resolve the European crisis in thought and feeling. Classicism and Cartesian rationalism tried to restore a sense of proportion and order to the "ordinary" world, but neither could cope with the infinite and infinitesimal worlds newly revealed by experimental science. As a result, some thought that science should usurp the place of philosophy, supersede religion, and supply the answers to all the longings of the human heart. Others reasserted the primacy of faith and feeling. A few became skeptical about all forms of truth. Already divided into different religions and competing states Europe became a whirlpool of new ideas toward the close of the seventeenth century.

## Science and Philosophy: New Visions of the World

Descartes and Newton, and, as we shall see presently, Leibniz too, combined the role of scientist with that of philosopher. Thus, the new philosophy—the vision of a mechanistic universe—naturally sprang from the new science. During the course of the eighteenth century, however, philosopher and scientist became separated. Philosophy came to deal with the mind of man, the nature of his thought, and the ends of his action. Science came to disregard the idea of purpose; it sought causal laws that would explain the world of matter. But until 1715 it was the scientists themselves who gave educated Europeans their new philosophical visions of the world; and these visions were to dominate eighteenth-century thought.

The vision of an orderly, rational universe governed by immutable laws was not new; what was new was Newton's idea of God Himself as the master mathematician-architect Who had created this universe and Who kept it going on its mechanical way. This idea was based on a philosophical argument: Everything has a cause, and since the causes also have causes, there must be a first cause. Put "first cause" in caiptal letters and you have God. Newton's God, a kind of eternal engineer, was an affront to pious Christians. There was nothing *personal* about Him. He was only a "Lord of things." Moreover, Newton's cosmology neglected the possibility of change. For he could not believe that anything so reasonable and orderly as the planetary system or the bodily structures of living things could ever have been different from what they were.

With Newton science seemed well on its way to dominating both philosophy and religion; he was able to transfer his optimism about the possibilities of scientific method to a philosophical vision. But Newton himself viewed science as a detached intellectual pursuit, not a cure-all for the problems of his time, and he shied away from the religious and social implications of the scientific revolution. It was his archrival, Leibniz, who tried to change the course of civilization.

Leibniz was the last European thinker to master the whole of knowledge; he was a great humanitarian, a dreamer, a universal genius. He believed that God had made the best of all possible worlds and that it was up to man to consummate the possibilities of harmony and unity in this world.

> "In God there is *Power*, which is the source of all, also *Knowledge*, whose content is the variety of ideas, and finally *Will*, which makes changes or produces products according to the principle of the best."

With Power, Knowledge, and Will, Leibniz believed that man could complete God's work.

Even Leibniz's scientific and mathematical discoveries pointed toward a vision of a harmonious and unified world. For example, his discovery of the infinitesimal calculus seemed to show the transition from the noncontinuous to the continuous in the physical world. The apparently instantaneous impact of two bodies hitting each other was really a succession of infinitesimal movements involving a slowing down, a reciprocal deformation of the bodies, a stop, a re-establishment of their original form, and a resumption of their movements. If the whole physical world was harmony and unity, Leibniz asked, why should Germany be disunited? Why should the states of Europe not lay down their arms and live in perpetual peace? Why should the Protestant and Catholic Churches not establish a new harmonious relationship? Why should there not be a universal language as clear and logical as the language of algebra?

Throughout his life Leibniz worked to realize his vision. He traveled all over Europe trying to bring about a reconciliation among the churches. He proposed a

European confederation, which would give each state a zone to conquer in some other part of the world in order to avoid rivalries in Europe. In his search for a universal rational language he anticipated many of the recently discovered principles of mathematical logic. He conceived of all substance as consisting of particles of energy called *monads* to show the ordered dynamism of the physical world. In his own varied career he gave the world an example of a seemingly inexhaustible dynamic force that never ceased to replenish its stock of facts, ideas, feelings, and human interests.

This extraordinary man epitomized all the strivings of Europe's sensitive elites. In his concern with power and in his combination of the rationalistic and empirical approaches to knowledge he was most representative of his age; and his striving for perfection made him one of the true founders of the philosophy of the Enlightenment.*

Leibniz's idea of science as the key to progress was first "popularized" by Bernard le Bouvier de Fontenelle (1657–1757). As the permanent secretary of the Académie des Sciences Fontenelle kept abreast of the latest scientific developments and wrote many popular books. His theme was progress with a capital P. Today's men of genius, he maintained, have revealed gravitation to us; tomorrow, other secrets will be brought to light, so that we shall eventually know everything about the mighty machine that is the universe; and all this knowledge will give us the power to add comfort and convenience to our daily lives and even to make us better morally. Fontenelle explained the mechanistic universe with such lucidity that any interested amateur could understand it. He also asserted that "true physics will be exalted to the point of becoming a kind of theology."

### Science and Religion: Deists and Doubters

Fontenelle was right; the physical sciences did become the basis of a new natural theology called Deism. The Deist conception of God closely paralleled that of Newton: God created the world-machine and then conveniently stepped out of the picture, leaving man to order his life with his own natural reason. It was useless to pray to such a God. No longer need His wrath be feared. Nor was there any use in sacraments, rites, fasting, or going to a church, chapel, or synagogue. The Bible was a book like any other book; there was nothing supernatural about it. Still, there *was* a God, and since He established the laws of nature as well as nature itself, these laws had to be obeyed.

The new natural theology reflected the growing secular and rationalistic spirit of the late seventeenth century. Many prominent men were Deists at heart, and some of the more openly radical ones became Freethinkers. They believed that the logical power of their own reason was enough to order their lives in the direction of true happiness, that man was the master of his own fate as he was of the universe. Still, even these radicals felt a moral obligation to society and a desire to adhere to the ethical norms prescribed by reason. In the early eighteenth century a number of them banded together into the first Masonic lodges.* With its rites and its oaths Freemasonry was the most famous example of a new type of secular religious movement in modern Europe.

The Deists, Freethinkers, and Freemasons hedged on some of the implications of a rationalistic, mechanistic conception of the universe; it was Baruch Spinoza (1632–1677) who pursued these implications to the bitter end. His radicalism was far ahead of his time. In his *Tractatus Theologico-Politicus* (1670) Spinoza blandly declared that a clean sweep would have to be made of all traditional beliefs, all organized religions, and all illogical political systems. Only then could there be a fresh start based on Cartesian rationalism. Obviously people thought Spinoza was the archsubversive of the age. His moral message completely escaped them; his skepticism about the established political order seemed anarchical; his religious mysticism was rank heresy. The Jewish colony in Amsterdam ostracized him, and the Catholics and Protestants called him an atheist.

*See Chapter VIII.

*See pp. 291–292.

But Spinoza was not an atheist; he was a pantheist. He started with God and into that rational God he reintegrated man. Pantheism is the belief that God is everywhere. He is the unique substance constituted by an infinite number of attributes of which each expresses something of His eternal and infinite essence. God is thought, God is extension. And man, body and soul, is a mode of this pervasive Being. Man's desire to identify himself with God thus becomes the fundamental element in the moral life. Man becomes free when he is able to direct and control his bodily appetites through the power of reason and to subordinate them to the love of God.

Attacked from all sides, Spinoza had at least one admirer, the French writer Pierre Bayle (1647–1706), who also lived in the tolerant atmosphere of Holland. Bayle was definitely a man of his time, for he expressed the growing *skepticism* of the educated classes in words that everyone could understand. He started with the assumption that certainty could be affirmed of nothing, that nothing could be known beyond all doubt. Then he rather inconsistently set out to show, beyond all doubt, that there was no common ground between religion and philosophy. This was so, according to Bayle, because there is an element of mystery in every religion, and mystery is incompatible with reason. It is one thing to believe, it is quite another thing to employ one's reason. There can be no picking and choosing in order to find a middle course. Bayle lumped all "religionaries" together: Catholics and Calvinists, Jews and Muslims, and Deists too. He also attacked the "Rationalists" in the opposite camp. "A man stakes his all on reason only to find that he has been leaning on a broken reed. For Reason cannot hold out against feelings." Bayle resisted complete skepticism, though. His determination to fight against error was stronger than his doubts about accepted truth.

Bayle's *Historical and Critical Dictionary* (1697) became the skeptic's bible. It cast doubt on most of the widely accepted principles of morality and religion. Nowhere was the challenge to traditional authority more boldly stated. Bayle, a Huguenot refugee living in Rotterdam, attacked Louis XIV at the height of his power, attacked the divine basis of this power, attacked the authority of the state and the way this authority was used to persecute nonconformists.

A strange mixture of toleration and persecution pervaded the European scene in the period 1648–1715. Increasing contact with the world beyond Europe made some men more open-minded. So did the growing secularism, rationalism, and scientific discoveries of that age. Some educated people became unorthodox and even skeptical in private while paying lipservice in public to the established orthodoxies in religion, politics, and thought. In Holland especially and in England after 1689 this kind of private doubt was one of the factors that encouraged religious toleration. On the other hand, Louis XIV revoked the Edict of Nantes in 1685, and pious zealots continued to burn witches in Germany, in Denmark, and in Massachusetts.

Yet even these examples of persecution showed a kind of improvement. Louis XIV persecuted the Huguenots for "reasons of state," not out of bigotry. The bigots who conducted witch-hunts were uneducated; the educated elites no longer believed in witches. By the end of the seventeenth century they were moving away from the idea of religion as a dogma to be imposed on everyone by force. Some "enlightened" people began to see religion primarily as a guide to personal morality and as a bulwark of social stability. For others, however, the official religions were becoming too "comfortable" and needed reforming.

### Faith and Feeling

Many educated men felt that an inner experience of God was more important than any ritual. But, in contrast to the optimistic Deists and Pantheists, they were pessimistic. They believed that man is basically bad, a slave to his passions and appetites. Without God's gift of grace he is utterly doomed. Yet he cannot enter into the necessary mystical communion with

PICTURE GROUP B

# *Seventeenth-Century Art and Architecture*

REMBRANDT VAN RIJN: *The Jewish Bride*

Rijksmuseum Amsterdam

**PETER PAUL RUBENS:** *The Triumphal Entry of Henry IV into Paris*

The Metropolitan Museum of Art, Rogers Fund, 1942

**GIOVANNI LORENZO BERNINI:** *Fountains in the Piazza Navona, Rome*

Italian Cultural Institute

DIEGO RODRIGUEZ DE SILVA Y VELASQUEZ: *Philip IV of Spain*

Copyright The Frick Collection, New York

JOHANNES VERMEER: *Young Woman with a Water Jug*

The Metropolitan Museum of Art, Gift of Henry G. Marquand, 1889

CLASSICAL ARCHITECTURE: *Versailles*

Musée Nationale du Louvre, Paris

BAROQUE AND CLASSICAL ARCHITECTURE: *St. Paul's Cathedral, London, by Sir Christopher Wren*

British Travel Association photo

Right:
FRANZ HALS: *Portrait of Descartes*
Musée Nationale du Louvre, Paris

Below:
LOUIS LE NAIN: *Peasant Meal*
Musée Nationale du Louvre, Paris

NICHOLAS POUSSIN: *The Blind Orion Searching for the Rising Sun*

The Metropolitan Museum of Art, Fletcher Fund, 1924

CHARLES LE BRUN: *A section of the Hall of Mirrors at Versailles*

Alinari Photo

God unless he renounces all personal pride and worldly vanities. This pessimistic view of man and religion has cropped up many times in history. Perhaps it asserted itself so strongly in the seventeenth century because pride and worldly vanities were so rampant in that baroque age. It permeated many sects, but we shall examine only two of them: the French Jansenists and the English Puritans.

Taking its name from the teachings of the Flemish scholar and bishop Cornelius Jansen (1585–1638), Jansenism spread to France in the 1640s and troubled sincere Catholics there throughout the reign of Louis XIV. Its headquarters (until Louis destroyed it in 1713) was the convent of Port Royal, on the western edge of Paris. The pious scholars who settled there were seeking the quiet and seclusion they felt they needed in order to discover God. Their denial of man's freedom to choose or reject God's grace and their doctrine that Christ had died for a small elite smacked of predestination and were therefore heretical. Their radically ascetic attitude particularly irritated the Jesuits, who, as we have seen, were becoming increasingly worldly and rationalistic. The Jansenists might have been quietly crushed if they had not had as their champion one of the foremost thinkers of the time, Blaise Pascal (1623–1662). Pascal's *Letters to a Provincial Friend* (1656–57) attacked the moral laxity of the Jesuits and defended the Jansenist way of life. These *Letters* were widely read and they caused many French Catholics to doubt the effectiveness of routine piety in bringing salvation.

The example of Pascal shows that the most rational and penetrating minds are not immune to the appeal of irrational views. This eminent scientist, mathematician, philosopher, and prose stylist was truly a baroque thinker. On the one hand, he could invent a calculating machine and discover the principles of barometric pressure; on the other, he could totter on the brink of despair until he finally felt a mystical contact with an intensely personal God. This sense of mystery gave Pascal and the Jansenists an exalted quality that troubled and exasperated their more rational contemporaries. They could be unjust—as when Pascal accused Descartes of being a Deist. But they could be disarmingly human, too.

The English Puritans also burned with the "inner light" of revealed religion, though they were less docile than the Jansenists. We have already seen how they waged war on their rightful king, how they finally beheaded him, and how they tried to impose their strait-laced morals on English life under Cromwell's rule. Their perseverance in carving a commonwealth out of the wilderness in America is known to every schoolchild. So is their bigotry and intolerance. The very word Puritan has come to mean a narrow-minded conception of morality, a hostility to pleasure, and a self-righteous assurance of doing God's will on earth.

Like the Jansenists, the English Puritans produced a great writer with a lofty moral message, John Milton (1608–1674). Just as Pascal championed reason and free inquiry in the case of Galileo, so Milton fought passionately for freedom of speech in England. And the author of the awe-inspiring *Paradise Lost* could also be warmly human in his lyrical poems and in his private life.

Another attack on the rationalistic, mechanistic vision of man and the world was made in the name of feeling. This attack was not to achieve its full force before the mid-eighteenth century, * but it began in the late seventeenth century. We have already noted the rehabilitation of feeling in art, in the theater, and in opera. The English philosopher John Locke (1632–1704) made sensation the primary reality of the mind and uneasiness the prime mover of the soul.

"The uneasiness a man finds in himself upon the absence of any thing, whose present enjoyment carries the idea of delight with it, is what we call desire; which is greater or less, as that uneasiness is more or less vehement. Where, by the by, it may be of some use to remark, that the chief, if not the only spur to human industry and action is uneasiness.†"

*See pp. 309–313.

†John Locke, *Essay Concerning Human Understanding*, 1690, Book II, Chapter 20. This is the first major book to postulate the senses as the source of knowledge.

*Psychological* truths alone were certain, according to Locke. Hence he tried to see how the mind turns seemingly random sensations into ideas, how it combines these ideas, and how the memory retains them. We must recognize the limitations of our understanding and accept them; there are no "innate ideas," as Descartes believed; the mind is a blank page, a *tabula rasa*, until the senses "feed" it material to work into coherent thoughts.

Locke saw some of the moral consequences of this daring theory, though not all of them. For example, he tried to remain a religious man in spite of his basically materialist outlook. But he did see the importance of child training and education in molding the kind of free and uninhibited individual who could think for himself. His ideas on these matters were far too revolutionary for his time. Not until our own era were they really put into practice. It is virtually impossible for an American student today to understand how revolutionary it was to suggest to European parents in 1690, or even in 1910, that they refrain from spanking their children, that they put as little restraint as possible on them, and that they try to justify the lessons they made them learn.

With Locke individual liberty became the first good. We shall now see how he translated this moral principle into a theory of society.

### Man and Society

Freedom versus authority, natural law versus divine law—these were the issues in the great debate over what was the best form of society. The theoretical arguments on these issues reflected the real political crises of the seventeenth century, the clash between science and religion, and the overriding interest in Nature. Economic and social considerations entered into these arguments, as we saw in the case of the English Levelers. Nevertheless, the main focus was on the state as a political body. What was the true basis of its power? What had society been like before the state had come into existence?

#### Bossuet

The outstanding champion of authority and divine law as the true bases of the state's power was Bishop Bossuet (1627–1704), theologian, historian, and tutor to Louis XIV's heir-apparent. He gave the *authoritarian* outlook its classic form. God's law is the supreme authority. Since He established the Church, we must obey its authority too. As for government, Bossuet said that its primary example was parental authority. Just as there is only one head of a family, so there can be only one head of the state. Bossuet also advanced other arguments for the authority of the monarchy. It was the most general, the oldest, and the most natural form of government. Then Bossuet brought God in again. God created men to be obedient subjects and kings to rule them. A king thus ruled by *divine right*. He was answerable to God, but his subjects had to submit to him without question. If he abused them, they could only pray that he might have a change of heart. For he ruled his subjects in accordance with God's inscrutable will.

The living example of Bossuet's doctrine was, of course, Louis XIV. Together the doctrine and the example became a tradition that continued to appeal to the authoritarian temperament of many Europeans right down to the present.

#### Hobbes

In England, Thomas Hobbes (1588–1679) published his *Leviathan* (1651). Like Bossuet, he favored the doctrine that the ruling prince should have absolute power, but Hobbes based this doctrine on natural law as discovered through reason. For Hobbes, the state was a gigantic artificial man, a monstrous machine that governed men by treating them as instruments, as tools. (The name Leviathan is taken from the monster described in the Book of Job.) There was no operating example of Hobbes' Leviathan in the seventeenth century. But the link between his doctrine and the *totalitarian* regimes of our own time seems almost as clear as the link between Bossuet's doctrine and the authoritarian regime of Louis XIV.

We cannot dismiss Hobbes' doctrine simply because we do not *like* it. We have to imagine what life would be like in a country where all public services have ceased to function, where armed bands loot and rape at will, where there are no law courts, no policemen, and no regular supplies of food and water, before we can understand what real anarchy means. Hobbes had only a mild taste of it during the English Civil War. But it was this experience that made him look for a political system to restore order and security to his country.

Furthermore, Hobbes was a born pessimist. He had a very poor opinion of his fellow men. If left to themselves, they would tear each other to pieces, as they seemed to be doing in the wars of his day and as he presumed they did in the original "state of nature." By "state of nature" Hobbes meant the time before men became reasonable enough to create the political state in order to secure peace and safeguard their lives and property from one another's predatory instincts. In the anarchy of the "state of nature" men were free, but their freedom was constantly threatened by the war of all against all. They therefore decided to give up their freedom in exchange for safety.

Since men gave up their natural freedom for life and security, it was only natural that they should make the guardian of their lives and security—the state—as strong as possible. According to Hobbes, sovereign power was indivisible, inalienable, and unlimited. Because men could never agree among themselves about what was right or wrong, they had to leave such decisions to the state, Its authority, wrote Hobbes "is to trump in card-playing, save that in the matter of government, when nothing else is turned up, clubs are trumps." Any form of violence was justified to maintain civil order. To insist that a subject possessed inalienable rights would be to destroy all authority. Furthermore, to admit that there could be a possible conflict between the authority of the executive, legislative, and judicial functions of government would be to undermine the whole basis of the state. For Hobbes, then, power was its own justification.

### Locke

Not so for Locke. He maintained that the powers of government were limited, that the sole basis of its authority was the "tacit consent" of the people, that it had to operate within the framework of a rule of law, that the different branches of government should act as checks and balances against each other, and that an unjust and unlawful sovereign might be lawfully resisted. This theory of government formed the basis for the *liberal* political tradition from Locke's time onward.

Like Hobbes, Locke based his political doctrine on natural law as discovered by reason. He, too, conjured up a picture of an imaginary "state of nature" as the starting point for showing the source of state power. And though Locke, like most liberals, was basically optimistic about his fellow men, his "state of nature" was as anarchic as that of Hobbes. The law of nature tells men that "no one ought to harm another in his life, health, liberty, or possessions." But in the "state of nature" there are no effective means of enforcing this law; hence the need to set up a government. In contrast to Hobbes, however, Locke believed that when men set up a government they did not forfeit their natural rights of life, liberty and property.

Natural rights! This was a new concept in the history of mankind. How do we discover them? The same way we discover natural law: through reason. Yet Hobbes and Bossuet found no such "rights" through reason, and they certainly cannot be discovered scientifically. It is pleasant to think that Locke's "natural rights" —called the "inalienable rights" of life, liberty, and the pursuit of happiness in the American Declaration of Independence —are real. Nevertheless, Locke the empiricist was resorting to Cartesian "innate ideas" on this point.

Locke said that the duty of a government was to protect and guarantee the rights of its citizens. This was why they had set it up in the first place. The natural law applies to sovereigns as much as to individuals in a "state of nature." If a sovereign infringes on it, he can be overthrown. For government by rule of law is the essence of political liberty.

But Locke was no democrat. He wanted only property owners to have a voice in the affairs of government, which was exactly what happened as a result of the Revolution of 1688. His "natural rights" were *civil* rights. *Political* rights—the right to vote and to hold office—he reserved for the wealthy. Locke's liberalism lay instead in his desire to limit the power of the state. He believed that in setting up a government men agreed to surrender only so much of their natural liberty as they thought necessary for the assurance of an ordered society.

For all their differences, Bossuet, Hobbes, and Locke agreed that the state was necessary to any society and that in order to serve the public good it must be strong. The Fronde in France and the English Civil War had shown the danger of anarchy when the authority of the central government broke down. To be sure, the eighteenth century saw the weakening of the French state and the championing of the rights of the nobility and the Parlements, but the trend toward a strong, centralized state was a permanent one, in practice and in theory.

: : :

The intellectual, spiritual, and moral crises were not completely resolved by the beginning of the eighteenth century. Newton's synthesis imposed Reason and Order on the physical world and was to last for almost two hundred years. Soon many thinkers were to try to impose Newtonian Reason and Order on man and society as well. But European man and European society refused to be tamed in this way. Within each man, faith and feeling continued to be in conflict with Reason. Within each community, conflicting classes and interest groups struggled against an Order that seemed to favor one and discriminate against another. These psychological and social conflicts were to acquire an increasing intensity and to spill over into politics more and more in the next two centuries.

In 1715, however, the intellectual, moral, and spiritual crises were pretty well restricted to the realm of thought. Furthermore, only a small intellectual elite was involved—except for a few radical religious sects. The masses of Europeans still accepted the Authority of traditional beliefs and institutions without question. Organized revolt was practically impossible in the face of the strong modern state and the established churches. Despite undercurrents of restlessness and protest, Western European society "worked" better than at any time since the thirteenth century. The long transition between medieval and modern civilization was over.

Western Europeans had established what seemed to be an ordered and reasonable way of life. The modern state had apparently solved the problem of civil and religious disorder. It had also tackled the problem of the "creation of plenty" with some success through its mercantilist policies. In both France and England the central government monopolized political power. In international relations a balance of power was achieved among the sovereign states, a balance that seemed to protect even the weaker states from complete annihilation. Descartes had enthroned Reason without dethroning God; Newton had given a convincing picture of an ordered and harmonious Nature; and the classical style had imposed a sense of order on the arts. Western Europe was now ready to assert its supremacy over other parts of the world.

## SUGGESTED READINGS

Nussbaum, Frederick L., *The Triumph of Science and Reason, 1660–1685. New York: Harper and Row, 1962. Torchbook.**

Excellent volume in the Rise of Modern Europe series.

*Wolf, John B., The Emergence of the Great Powers, 1685–1715*. New York: Harper and Row, 1962. Torchbook.*

Another excellent volume in the same series.

Friedrich, Carl J. and Charles Blitzer, *The Age of Power.* Ithaca, N. Y.: Cornell Univ. Press, 1957.*
A shorter survey covering the same period as the preceding work. Also excellent.

Ogg, David, *Europe in the Seventeenth Century.**
See comments in readings for Chapter III.

Clark, George N., *The Seventeenth Century.**
See comments in readings for Chapter III.

Aston, Trevor, *Crisis in Europe 1560–1660.* New York: Doubleday-Anchor, n.d.*
Discusses issues arising from the recent debate over the "seventeenth-century crisis."

Goubert, Pierre, *Louis XIV and Twenty Million Frenchmen.* New York: Pantheon, 1970
Shows the interrelationship between the people and the power of their ruler, using a new, demographic approach to history.

Wolf, John B., *Louis XIV.* New York: W. W. Norton, 1968.*
Excellent, up-to-date biography of Louis as "soldier administrator."

Lewis, W. H., *The Splendid Century: Life in the France of Louis XIV.* Garden City, N. Y.: Doubleday and Co., 1957.*
Lively and rich in detail.

Stone, Lawrence, *The Crisis of the Aristocracy, 1558–1641.* New York: Oxford University Press, 1966.*
A pioneering new interpretation of the role of the aristocracy in the development of early modern England.

Hill, Christopher, *Reformation to Industrial Revolution, 1530–1780,* Vol. I of *The Making of English Society.* New York: Pantheon, 1969.
A sophistocated essay in social history, Especially interesting on the English Civil War.

Davies, Godfrey, *The Early Stuarts, 1603–1660,* Vol. IX of *The Oxford History of England.* 2nd ed. New York: Oxford Univ. Press, 1959.
A good political study.

Clark, George N., *The Later Stuarts, 1660–1714,* Vol. X of *The Oxford History of England.* 2nd ed. New York: Oxford Univ. Press, 1955.
Another good political study in the same series.

Wedgwood, Cicely V., *The King's War.* New York: The Macmillan Co., 1959.
One of the best books by this prolific author. Stresses military events of the English Civil War.

Firth, Charles H., *Oliver Cromwell and the Rule of the Puritans in England.* New York: Oxford Univ. Press, 1953.
Best scholarly biography.

Hall, A. R., *The Scientific Revolution, 1500–1800: The Formation of the Modern Scientific Attitude.* 2nd ed. Boston: Beacon Press, 1956.*
The best introduction to the subject.

Butterfield, Herbert, *Origins of Modern Science, 1300–1800.* Rev. ed. New York: The Macmillan Co., 1961. Collier Books.*
This brilliant survey stresses the difficulties in placing science on a firm foundation.

Clagett, Marshall, ed., *Critical Problems in the History of Science.* Madison, Wis.: Univ. of Wisconsin Press, 1959.

Dampier, William C., *A History of Science and Its Relations with Philosophy and Religion.*

See note on readings at beginning of book.

Santillana, Giorgio de, *The Crime of Galileo.* Chicago: Univ. of Chicago Press, 1955.

Brilliant, controversial study of Galileo's life and trial.

Hazard, Paul, *The European Mind, 1680–1715.* Cleveland: World Publishing Co., 1963. Meridian.*

An all-encompassing intellectual history of this exciting period. The best work of its kind.

*Paperback

CHAPTER VI

# WESTERN EUROPE'S WORLD SUPREMACY, c. 1713–1774

After 1715 western european influence made itself felt more and more in other parts of the world. Overseas the Anglo-French struggle for wealth and empire led to the exploitation of the Caribbean islands with African slaves, the growth of the North American colonies, and the subjugation of India. The rising powers of Central and Eastern Europe also felt the influence of the more advanced countries. As Austria, Prussia, and Russia became part of the European state system, their rulers adapted the military and bureaucratic institutions of the West to their own needs. Their aristocracies also copied its social and cultural models, especially from France. But aside from this Westernized upper crust, Eastern European society, with its mass of serfs and its insignificant bourgeoisie, remained backward.

Despite the economic and social differences between Eastern and Western Europe, until 1789 the political systems of most of the major states resembled each other, at least in form, to a greater extent than in any earlier or later century. Under these systems—called collectively the Old Regime—the monarch was sovereign, but the hereditary aristocracy retained its social and cultural dominance. Indeed, as long as land remained the major form of wealth, sections of the nobility were able to use their influence on the royal governments to reassert their political influence in many places.

The Old Regime was not the same in all countries; there were important differences among the major states. At one extreme were Russia and Prussia, where the only limits on the authority of the monarch were imposed by the efficiency of the bureaucracy and the strength of the army. At the other extreme was Great Britain, where the old institution of Parliament and the emerging institutions of the cabinet and the political parties acted as fundamental checks on the power of the king. France, Spain, and the Austrian Monarchy occupied an intermediate position between the two extremes. The theoretically absolute rulers of these states had to struggle to overcome the stubborn opposition of privileged groups and institutions in their efforts to create an efficient administrative machine. After about 1750, a number of these rulers tried to accomplish this task through the new approach of "enlightened despotism."

Yet even in those countries where centralized monarchy was strongest and most "enlightened," government and administration were still carried on largely by amateurs with the help of intermediate agencies between the individual and the state. These agencies, all of which were medieval in origin, included guilds, chartered towns, universities, legal corporations, village communes in Eastern Europe, the French Parlements, and, in England, the local justices of the peace. In principle these agencies accepted the authority of the monarch; in practice they could and sometimes did oppose him.

Western Europe forged ahead of the rest of the world because of its rational principles of organization and its scientific and technical advances. Let us always remember, though, that most Western Europeans continued to resist new ideas and new ways of doing things as long as the old ones seemed to work. This was especially so with regard to the political systems of France and Great Britain. We should also remember that under the Old Regime the common people benefited little from economic and technical advances. They still did all the work, paid the bulk of the taxes, and did most of the fighting. Though legally free, they remained at the mercy of the tax-collector, the overseer, the recruiting sergeant, and the master-at-arms, all of whom stood between the mass of the organized and the elite of organizers. The power and affluence of Western Europe benefited a "happy few" of less than 5 per cent of the total population – a growing minority, but still a minority.

## THE PERFECTION OF TECHNIQUES

By the late eighteenth century Western Europe had perfected its techniques about as far as possible before the "breakthrough" of the Industrial Revolution. Most of these advances were the work of craftsmen and entrepreneurs rather than scientists. But these nonscientists were indirectly influenced by the new experimental and rational outlook, and they used their new knowledge to increase their country's power and their countrymen's well being. They invented new comforts and conveniences to make the daily lives of the "happy few" more pleasant. They built more and better ships to bring them the products of far-away places and to give them control of the seas. They produced and equipped better armies with which to conquer new lands. They perfected their methods for financing economic enterprises and exploiting the labor of other people. In fact, they began to put the rest of the world to work for them.

*Military exercises*

### Military and Naval Advances

Superior military and naval power gave Western Europeans their main advantage over other peoples. As we know so well today, new weapons require new tactics and new methods of disposition; in the eighteenth century the problem was how to make the best use of the new trigger-firing musket* and the smooth-bore cannon. We have seen how new firearms revolutionized warfare in the sixteenth century and how large standing armies came into being toward the end of the

*The trigger-firing musket, invented in the late seventeenth century, could be loaded and fired more quickly than the older muskets. In 1740 the substitution of an iron ramrod for a wooden one made loading the powder and the shot into the muzzle even faster. With the introduction of the cartridge in 1744, a soldier could fire three shots a minute.

seventeenth century. By 1715, these armies consisted primarily of unwieldy lines of infantrymen backed by immobile cannon of varying quality and size. (Although the cavalry survived, it served mainly in making breaches in the enemy line.)

The trigger-firing musket's potential for rapid and concentrated firepower was still limited in 1715 by the way the soldiers were arranged in battle formation. It took over an hour for a column of marching infantrymen to break ranks and reassemble for combat. In that time the enemy could simply march off if he chose not to fight. There was no room for maneuvering the battle lines once they were formed, and no possibility of pursuing and destroying the enemy army. Each soldier still stood in a fixed position five or six feet from his comrades on either side, as in the days when they had had to ignite the powder of their muskets with burning wicks. Behind them stood similar rigid lines of infantrymen five or six feet deep, as in the days when the army with the most replacements won the battle. The soldiers in the front line were more concerned with pulling the trigger at the same time as their comrades than with killing the enemy. Meanwhile, the potential firepower of the soldiers standing behind them was wasted.

During the course of the eighteenth century these difficulties were overcome by new types of organization and tactics. The Prussian and French armies developed the familiar right-flank, left-flank, and oblique turns to facilitate a quick change from a marching column to a battle line. The maneuvers seem childishly simple today, but they made it possible to force an enemy army to do battle at any time. The Prussians also began to use a three-deep line, with the front line on its knees, the second line crouching, and the third line standing straight. This arrangement increased the firepower of the line threefold. The Austrians and the French gradually came to allow their infantrymen to fire at will after the first salvo. They also began to use individual sharpshooters to prepare a bayonet charge, to protect their flanks, and to disrupt the enemy line. In these ways the true destructive potentialities of the trigger-firing musket were finally utilized.

The most striking improvement of the period was in artillery. A French artillery officer named Jean-Baptiste Vaquette de Gribeauval (1715 – 1789) made all parts of any type of cannon interchangeable, so that repairs would be possible near the battlefield. In order to make his lighter cannon more mobile (the heavier ones he reserved for sieges), he improved the harness with which the horses pulled them. They could now be drawn into battle at a trot over rough terrain. Finally, he improved the accuracy and range of his cannon with sights and elevating mechanisms. Thus, through specialization and improved techniques, the smooth-bore cannon became a deadly weapon in the service of a more mobile and better organized infantry.

By the late eighteenth century the destructive power of navies had also improved. Although it was not to be fully utilized until the Napoleonic wars, it developed during the wars of the mid-eighteenth century and gave Western Europeans complete mastery of the sea in most parts of the world. By the 1770s mathematicians and specialized engineers brought the construction of sailing vessels and the practice of navigation close to their technological ceilings.

A naval ship-of-the-line was the largest and most complicated machine produced by eighteenth-century European ingenuity and craftsmanship; it was 190 feet long and required two thousand oak trees for its construction. By the 1760s ships-of-the-line had three decks, ninety to one hundred and twenty cannon, and nine hundred to twelve hundred men; frigates—which were used for reconnaisance and raids on enemy shipping—carried twenty to forty cannon; even the corvettes—used mainly to carry orders—were armed with twelve small cannon and could play an auxiliary role in combat. Both merchant and naval vessels had cleaner lines and more sails than ever before, and sailors also learned to trim their sails in such a way as to allow them to sail almost directly into the wind. Moreover, the invention of the chronometer in the 1770s finally solved the old problem of finding one's longitude. With a chronometer—a precision clock whose spring, escapement, and pendulum compensate for changes in latitude and temperature—and a record of the distance one has traveled from one's home port, one can calculate one's longitude almost anywhere on the open sea with reasonable accuracy.

The increased size and firepower of naval vessels made battles at sea resemble land battles, with two solid opposing lines firing away at each other. The ships-of-the-line did the bulk of the fighting. The line was sacred; each vessel had to stay in formation, even when it was sinking, rather than let the enemy breach the line. Maneuverability was extremely limited, and an iron discipline had to prevail in the face of continuous enemy broadsides. Battles of this type were costly without being decisive, for at a certain point the whole line of the "defeated" side would withdraw rather than risk annihilation. Not until the 1790s did the British find new tactics to outflank an enemy line and really destroy it. Thus more and better ships made naval warfare costlier; but in peacetime they also made possible a great increase in commerce.

### Personnel and Discipline

Discipline, as important as new tactics in giving Western Europeans their military and naval superiority, was perfected by eighteenth-century armies from the innovations of Louis XIV. The officers, who were almost exclusively noblemen or gentry in all countries, had already become a professional caste. They had their own code of behavior and a sense of dedication to the service of their sovereign; and there was no more room for adventurers or upstarts. The enlisted men were also expected to regard the army as a long-term career. They learned to obey orders automatically during interminable hours on the drill field: "By the right flank, *march*! By the left flank, *march*!" The purpose of these familiar commands was to condition a company of infantrymen to maintain its ranks on the battlefield. Fear of their officers and feeling of solidarity with their comrades also kept the soldiers in line under fire. The penalties for disobedience or cowardice were severe. Flogging was the commonest form of corporal punishment. And then there was running the gauntlet, which was used in the British navy as well as in most armies. In this case, each of the culprit's own comrades beat him as he dragged himself past them.

Recruiting methods also became more rational in the eighteenth century. Though all soldiers in the ranks were (and still are) called *enlisted men*, many of them "enlisted" very much against their will. There was no official conscription of all able-bodied youths—this would have taken too many economically useful men away from their plows and workbenches—but woe to the drifters and misfits when a recruiting sergeant appeared in the local tavern or public square! He could use virtually any means to force his victim to "sign up." Sometimes he simply hit him over the head and carried him off to camp; sometimes he softened him up with liquor; and occasionally he even had a female assistant to "convince" an unsuspecting loafer of the advantages of army life. In his own calculating way the recruiting sergeant kept the army at full strength without interfering with efficient functioning of his country's economy. After he had done his work, the drill sergeant took over.

The personnel and disciplinary methods of the British and French navies resembled those of the army in many ways. One important difference was that the officer ranks were more open to men from the middle classes. Once in the navy, however, these men acquired the same sense of dedication and the same code of behavior as army officers. As in the army, the enlisted men came from the lowest classes. But good sailors were harder to find than good soldiers, so their recruitment was more ruthless and more highly organized. Although some common criminals were taken from the jails, press gangs preferred to comb the waterfront taverns for real sailors, who were easily spotted by their distinctive walk and habits. In wartime the navy raided its country's own merchant ships for able sailors. Soldiers could run away if they found army life intolerable; sailors at sea had no place to run to, and mutiny meant disaster for the whole ship. Hence the master-at-arms maintained an even sterner discipline than the drill sergeant.

#### Economic Advances

Rational principles of organization had been applied to business since the late Middle Ages. We have seen how they made possible a major commercial expansion between 1450 and 1650; in the eighteenth century, they stimulated a more spectacular upsurge in world trade and led to the beginnings of an industrial revolution as well.

After 1715 there was a large increase in the total amount of money and credit available for economic growth. New silver mines were put into operation in Mexico, and gold was discovered in the Portuguese colony of Brazil. These new supplies of precious metals were not risked in long-distance transactions; instead, businessmen made use of letters of credit and bills of exchange on an expanded scale. The most striking expansion was in the use of paper money. The Bank of England and the Bank of Amsterdam received large stocks of precious metals for safekeeping in their vault and issued bank notes that were promises to pay a given amount of gold or silver to the bearer on demand. Experience showed that all the bearers of these notes did not demand such payment at the same time. Consequently, the banks issued more paper money than their reserves of precious metals could cover. This paper currency added greatly to the total amount of money available for business transactions and new investments.

Stocks and bonds provided the major capital for all kinds of enterprises. We have seen how joint-stock companies organized Europe's trade with other parts of the world in the early seventeenth century. From then on the number and variety of joint-stock companies increased markedly. By 1715 there were 140 in England alone. Stock exchanges facilitated the sale of stocks to the public in Amsterdam, in London, and in Paris after 1724. We have also seen how the British government borrowed money from the Bank of England. Other governments also began to borrow money in this way and to issue bonds in return, not only to banks but also to private individuals. In England these bonds could be bought and sold through brokers; thus they were negotiable securities. In France government bonds were less fluid, a factor that had dire consequences in the first great speculative boom in modern times.

##### *The "Bubbles"*

Nothing could have been more rational than the scheme of the Scottish banker John Law for financing a French company for trade on the Mississippi with paper money issued by a bank that held two-thirds of its capital in French government bonds. In 1718, Law's bank became a royal enterprise, and the trading company extended its activities from the Mississippi Valley to Canada, the West Indies, the Guinea Coast of Africa, and the Far East. Possibilities for profit in such a company seemed enormous, and they were carefully exaggerated by official publicity and inside "tips." As a result, large-scale buying forced the value of the company's stock up from 500 to 18,000 livres a share. When the company announced a 40 per cent dividend at the end of 1719, those people who had bought their stocks at the current market price could get only 1 per cent. The speculators panicked and started a wave of selling. Loss of confidence soon spread to Law's bank as well, and the mass of the speculators presented their paper money for payment in gold. The bank had to close its doors, for the bulk of its assets were not in gold, but in nonnegotiable government bonds.

Law's venture, called the "Mississippi Bubble," had mixed consequences. It eased the national debt, since the government did not have to honor the bonds held by Law's defunct bank. It also stimulated French trade in the Upper Mississippi Valley, but it strengthened Frenchmen's already widespread suspicion of paper money and large, centralized banks. This reaction was unfortunate, for it retarded France's commercial and industrial growth. Furthermore, Frenchmen's distrust of the financial stability and even honesty of the government, along with the inequitable and inefficient system of taxation, discouraged the growth of a national debt of the British type.

The English "South Sea Bubble" burst a year after the "Mississippi Bubble" in France. The operations that produced this "Bubble" began soon after the Treaty of Utrecht (1713) gave the government-sponsored South Sea Company the slave-trading concession (*asiento*) and other trading rights in Spain's American colonies. As in France, the national bank took over some of the state's obligations and issued paper money on them to finance the South Sea Company. Speculators bid the price of the company's stock way up in anticipation of easy profits. In the fever of speculation, other joint-stock companies were founded for the wildest purposes —to develop a perpetual-motion machine, to distill fresh water from the ocean, to insure female chastity. When the South Sea Company collapsed in 1720, so did these others.

In England the results were not as disastrous as in France. Speculators lost their money, to be sure, but the Bank of England did not close its doors, and the government did not repudiate its debt. Furthermore, Parliament passed the "Bubble Act" requiring any new joint-stock company to obtain a government charter. Within a few years, Englishmen forgot their mistrust of these institutions, and new ones were formed for insurance against losses at sea, fire, theft, and other hazards. The most famous of these companies was Lloyd's of London. Along with commercial and financial companies, these new insurance companies provided outlets for capital and opportunities for investment.

### Manufacturing and Agriculture

Reason and order were also applied to agriculture and manufacturing. Although the domestic (cottage) system predominated in the manufacture of most kinds of consumers' goods throughout the eighteenth century, the factory began to make its appearance in England and to a lesser extent in France after 1750. This development was encouraged by the invention of machines driven by water, wind, and, ultimately, steam power. Manufacturers also learned that they could have a more efficient division of labor when all the workers were under one roof. Some of the new factories began to produce cotton cloth to compete with the calicos, ginghams, and chintzes imported from India, and "china" to compete with the imported original. Others refined sugar, roasted coffee, and made paper out of wood pulp. But the greatest improvement in the organization of the labor force was the plantation system in the colonies, which we shall discuss presently.

The first important break in traditional methods of farming occurred in the eighteenth century. Again it was on the one-crop plantations of the New World that the greatest gains in productivity were made; but in England gentleman-farmers like Jethro Tull and Lord (Turnip) Townsend were applying rational principles of organization to Old World agriculture. By careful experimentation Tull finally discovered the now-obvious method of dropping seeds into rows of holes instead of the traditional method of simply throwing them on the surface of the ground —which delighted the birds but lessened the crop yield. Townsend discovered the now equally obvious fact that crop rotation preserved the nutritive elements in a given plot of land better than letting it lie fallow periodically. Furthermore, the turnips and clover that he rotated with wheat provided forage for livestock. Another Englishman, Robert Bakewell, introduced the idea of selective animal breeding. The result was better meat and heavier cattle, sheep, and hogs to feed an ever-growing urban population of well-to-do citizens.

### *Living Conditions*

During this period life for the rural masses remained as unpleasant as ever; but, for a growing number of city dwellers—and, of course, the landowners—living conditions improved markedly. Urban planning, which had been rediscovered in the seventeenth century, now provided great city squares, public gardens, and paved embankments along the Thames and the Seine for promenades. People with modest incomes could afford cheap imported products like tea, coffee, cocoa, sugar, tobacco, and, in the latter part of the century, cotton clothes, which had been a luxury for the rich at first.

Skilled craftsmen gave the rich many new pleasures to enjoy. Theatrical and operatic performances became more polished and sophisticated than ever before. There were new musical instruments—like the pianoforte—and there were more comfortable chairs, adapted to the contours of the seated body, to listen to them in. The chefs of the great French nobles invented such delectable dishes that eating became a subtle art almost on a par with flirting. Even the farmers catered to the good-living demands of the upper classes by creating *pâté de foie gras*, rich cheeses, and vintage wines.

Although eighteenth-century standards of health and hygiene were considerably improved from those of earlier times, they seem very low today. Rich people might take mineral baths at spas to cure their ailments, but at home they bathed themselves one day a week and used perfume on the other six. They were not concerned about dirt and germs (or indeed about any preventive medicine); they simply wanted to smell good. On the other hand, some medical advances were being made. Doctors began diagnosing illnesses by taking the patient's pulse and temperature. Surgeons began to get special training at newly founded surgical schools and learned to perform delicate operations with great technical proficiency.*

## Growth of a Global Economy

With their new techniques, wealth, and amenities Western Europeans brought their material civilization about as far as it could go in pre-industrial times. Commercial capitalism came out of its seventeenth-century economic crisis by putting the rest of the world to work for it. Merchant-entrepreneurs marketed unfinished goods produced by masses of slaves and serfs in America, Africa, and Asia. They built factories to turn hemp into rope, tobacco into snuff, and beaver pelts into hats. All these products sold in an ever expanding market in Western Europe and the colonies. Wherever there were people with money to spend, the merchant-entrepreneurs were ready to show them a need for some new product. And the largest markets of all—the first mass markets—were the standing armies and navies of the great powers.

### *Factors in Economic Growth: Trade and Slaves*

Economic growth is conditioned by four major factors: (1) increased capital-output ratio (productivity)—that is, a larger output for a given amount of capital input, achieved through greater organizational or technological efficiency; (2) increased supply of savings; (3) increased demand for investment; (4) population expansion.

The four factors in eighteenth-century economic growth were obviously interdependent. Population growth in Western Europe increased the number of both producers and consumers. But if there had not also been an unlimited supply of slaves in Africa, then less sugar, coffee, and tobacco would have been produced, and hence there would have been less

*Well into the eighteenth century surgeons were merely glorified barbers; and barbers themselves continued to pull teeth, sew up skin cuts, and set broken limbs. The name "barber" (from *barbe*, the French word for beard) indicated only their *primary* occupation; even poor men viewed shaving as a "surgical" operation and had a barber do it. The eighteenth century was not a "do-it-yourself" age.

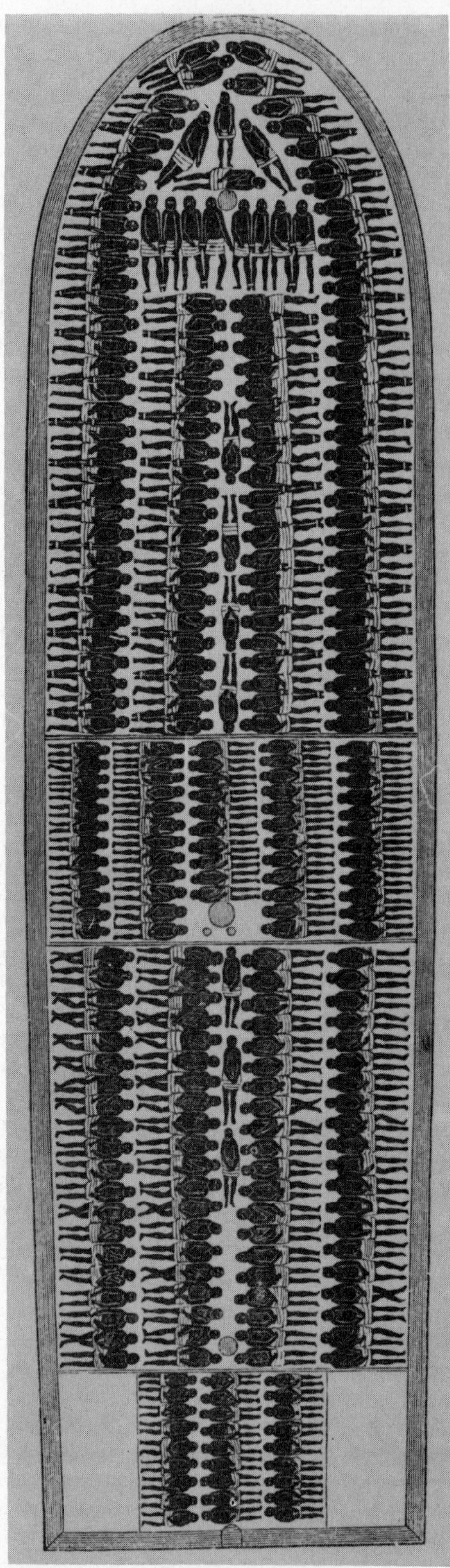

*Loading plan of a slave deck*

trade between Western Europe and America. Or, if there had not been a growing supply of savings in Western Europe, then there would not have been enough capital to finance new foreign trade. The increase in trade made more people rich; in turn, they bought more goods, thus fostering further increases in trade, which then created new demands for investment. Trade expansion and slavery were what made England and France richer than any other countries in history. Today, the main stimulus to growth is an increase in the capital-output ratio resulting from mechanization in industry and agriculture. In the eighteenth century this variable was of minor importance.

The growth in world trade and shipping in the eighteenth century was truly spectacular. British and French trade increased fivefold. The Dutch, whose trade and shipping had formerly been greater than those of England and France combined, fell into third place after 1715. By 1763 British ships alone were carrying about one-third of all the goods entering and leaving the ports of Europe. The Americas accounted for the largest growth in trade and bulk shipping, but there were also substantial increases in Western European commerce with Eastern Europe and Southeast Asia. Deprived of the spice trade by the Dutch, the British East India Company began importing tea from China, coffee from southern Arabia, and cotton textiles from India. More and more, the Dutch turned to financing and insuring the trade of others, especially the British. For they could not compete with the British and the French in the manufacture of goods for export.

Foreign trade stimulated industrial growth in both Britain and France. Except in the Far East, both paid for their new imports with finished or semifinished products. French manufactured goods equaled those of the British in total value but were of different kinds. The French exported mainly fine furniture, tapestries, porcelains, clocks, and fancy clothing accessories. Their main market for these products was in Europe itself, though some rich colonists bought them too. The British exported cheap textiles and hardware. Most striking however, was the growth of British re-export trade in colonial goods. In 1724, for example, more than four million pounds of tobacco came into Liverpool and more than three million were re-exported. The Atlantic ports of Britain and France experienced a rapid growth of population, and their ship owners, sugar-refiners, and brokers in tobacco, cotton, cheese, sugar, and rum made huge profits on goods produced by others.

Never in history have slaves been used to produce so much wealth as in Europe's American colonies in the eighteenth century. In ancient Rome, in Asia, and in the Muslim world slaves were used mainly as servants rather than as producers of marketable commodities. In eighteenth-century America, from Virginia to Brazil, most field workers literally worked to death producing crops to enrich the plantation owners and the merchants who marketed their products all over Europe.

The slave trade itself also produced wealth, for slaves were a marketable "commodity" of great value. Enterprising British and French sea-captains herded the unfortunate Africans into the holds of their ships like cattle, battened down the hatches, and transported their "cargo" to the West Indies to be sold on the auction block. They shipped the sugar the slaves produced to England, France, or Massachusetts, where it was made into rum. Then they took some of the rum back to Africa to corrupt the natives and buy more slaves. This three-way trade enriched the auctioneers, the plantation owners, the slave traders, the distillers, the merchants, and the rum runners. Here was the seamier side of Europe's economic supremacy in the eighteenth century.

### Mercantilism in the Eighteenth Century

Historians disagree on the extent to which government policies stimulated economic growth in the eighteenth century. Some say that mercantilist efforts to control foreign trade were rendered ineffective by widespread smuggling and privateering. Some say that wars wasted resources and capital. But most historians agree that in peacetime the standing armies and navies maintained by the major powers constituted a new and important market for goods and services.

The French army and the British navy were good examples. In 1740 the former had 160,000 men, the latter close to 100,000. Every man had to clothed, fed, housed, and provided with arms. The government furnished everything—down to each British sailor's daily allotment of rum and each French soldier's daily ration of red wine. Compared to today's military forces, those of the eighteenth century were small, and their needs modest. Nevertheless, the servicemen of that period were the first mass consumers in modern history. The manufacture of 250,000 uniforms, for example, provided work for countless ordinary people and profits for a significant number of private merchants and investors. The governments themselves subsidized the manufacturers of ships, cannon, and muskets. All the money earned from equipping and servicing the military forces acted as a further source of demand for other people's goods and services, both at home and abroad.

As foreign trade brought growing prosperity, the governments of the eighteenth century tried to strengthen their control over it for the good of the state. This control meant subsidizing the home export industries, supporting a national merchant marine, and limiting imports to those that were essential, that did not compete with native products, and that could be paid for with exportable goods rather than cash.

These mercantilist policies achieved their greatest success in Great Britain for several reasons. The British government was more responsive to commercial interests than any other except the Dutch, who, because of their military and political weakness, became increasingly dependent on British sea power and British commercial interests. The British navy had undisputed control of the sea during much of the eighteenth century. Also, Great Britain was able to force most merchants selling goods to her and her colonies to transport them in British ships. Oliver Cromwell had passed the first Navigation Act to this effect in 1651 in order to break the Dutch monopoly on world shipping at that time. Eighteenth-century British governments not only reinforced the earlier Navigation Acts but also saw to it that Britain had a large enough merchant marine to handle all of her shipping needs. (It should be noted that the French government had to rely partially on ships operated by the Dutch and by the British colonists in North America for her West Indies trade.)

Despite the successes of her mercantilist policies, Great Britain had to pay cash for some imports. The Chinese would accept nothing else for their tea, the Indians little else for their cotton. Britain also had an unfavorable balance of trade with the Baltic countries. Before the invention of a practical means of smelting British ore with coal, Britain had to import smelted Swedish ore because of her own declining supply of wood. She also had very little tar, pitch, or hemp for making rope. Her growing navy and merchant marine needed these naval stores, and their greatest single source was the Baltic.

The need for hard cash to pay for some imports explains Great Britain's greed for bullion and her determination to exploit her colonies in North America and the West Indies. For purposes of imports these colonies were considered part of Britain; for purposes of exports they were not.

### *The Colonial Empires*

As we saw in Chaper III, the first Europeans came to the New World in search of treasure and an all-water route to the Orient. In the sixteenth century the Spaniards claimed and partially occupied all of the Americas from California and Florida south, except for Brazil. Then other Europeans arrived. In the seventeenth century Swedes and Dutchmen established small colonies in Delaware, New Jersey, and eastern New York, and Danes took over the Virgin Islands in the Caribbean. But from the mid-seventeenth century on, the British and the French became the sole contenders for control of most of North America and the West Indies. The original English settlers in New England (Puritans), Maryland (Catholics), and Pennsylvania (Quakers) had come to America to escape religious discrimination at home, and some French Huguenots had settled in the English coastal colonies after the Revocation of the Edict of Nantes (1685). Nevertheless, the majority of Englishmen and Frenchmen who migrated to the New World came for economic reasons.

By 1715 the French and British empires in North America were pretty well established. From their original settlement in Quebec (1608) the French had extended their holdings from the mouth of the St. Lawrence to the mouth of the Mississippi. In the Treaty of Utrecht (1713) they had lost Newfoundland, Nova Scotia, and the Hudson Bay Territory to the British. Otherwise they controlled all of eastern Canada, the Great Lakes region, and the Ohio, Mississippi, and Missouri Valleys. The main French settlement was in the St. Lawrence Valley, where there were about 20,000 French settlers in 1715 and about 65,000 by 1763, an increase mainly through natural reproduction rather than further immigration. Otherwise the French empire in North America was a vast, sparsely populated forestland. There were about 400,000 Indians, a handful of Jesuit missionaries who tried to convert and "civilize" them, and a few thousand fur trappers who intermarried with them.

The British colonies along the Atlantic seaboard resembled the French in their separation into distinct groups and their autonomous spirit, but they had a larger population and a higher level of production and commerce, and they were overwhelmingly Protestant. Their population had increased from 255,000 in 1700 to 1,640,000 in 1763, mainly through immigration by Scottish Presbyterians from Ulster, Germans from the Rhineland, and black Africans. In the South—Maryland, Virginia, the Carolinas, Georgia (founded in 1732)—plantation farming of rice, tobacco, and indigo predominated. The plantation owners controlled local affairs and became an untitled landed aristocracy. In New England—New Hampshire, Massachusetts, Maine, Rhode Island, and Connecticut—the bulk of the people were small farmers, though fishing and shipping became increasingly important. In the Middle Atlantic colonies—New York, New Jersey, Pennsylvania, Delaware—agriculture was diversified and commerce thrived in cities like Philadelphia and New York. Unlike the French Catholics, the English Protestants made few efforts to convert the Indians. They merely pushed them off the land and annihilated those who fought back. As we shall see, the colonists' relations with the Indians became complicated by wars between England and France.

According to mercantilist theory, the main function of the colonies was to bolster the economy of the mother country. Most of the British and French colonies had been founded and originally controlled by trading companies licensed in London or Paris. In the eighteenth century the colonists themselves managed most of their local affairs, while the royal governors saw to it that they obeyed the laws of the home government, especially in matters of foreign trade. But as the British colonists in North America began to pursue their own economic interest, friction arose. In 1732 Parliament prohibited the importation of hats from the colonies and restricted their manufacture. A year later, under pressure from British planters in the Antilles, it passed the Molasses Act. This Act placed prohibitive duties on the sugar and molasses the colonists were importing from the French Antilles, where prices were 40 per cent cheaper than in the British islands. In 1750 the British government forbade the manufacture of iron products in New Jersey. It said: "If America should take it into its head to manufacture so much as a nail, England will make it feel the full weight of her power."

In the eighteenth century the British and French islands in the West Indies were the ideal type of colony. They furnished goods completely lacking in the mother country and they produced almost nothing that the mother country produced. We have already noted how they bought their manufactured goods in England and France and their slaves from English and French entrepreneurs operating along the coast of West Africa. The population of the Antilles, which by 1763 was 90 per cent black, equaled that of the whole of British and French North America. A few rich European planters lorded it over the mass of the slaves and lived in fantastic luxury. Indeed, their wealth and commercial importance made the home governments cater to them more than to the North American colonists; the Molasses Act certainly proved this.

Despite the efforts of the colonial powers to regulate trade and manufacturing in the colonies, smuggling was rampant. In peacetime, illegal traffic was probably greater than legal trade between the British and French colonies in North America and the West Indies. The profits from smuggling usually benefited the colonists more than the mother country. But the British government valued its merchants' illegal trade with the Spanish colonies enough to go to war against Spain in 1739 when that country "deputized" private "coast guards" to capture their ships and cargoes.

Smuggling was not the only factor that limited the effectiveness of mercantilism. A glance at the map shows how France's North American possessions encircled the British colonies; thus the French had the geographical advantage over the British settlers in the fur trade. They also had a better system of forts and communications in the hinterland, giving Montreal and New Orleans more furs than Albany and New York. When the British settlers tried to establish themselves in the Ohio Valley, the French built a fort at Vincennes (1732) to stop them from advancing further. The governments in London and Paris tried to ignore these colonial wars until the 1740s, but ultimately the French and British colonists themselves forced them to go to war to foster these American (rather than European) interests. When they finally did go to war against each other, they were to find that their colonists were developing their own "national" interests, both economically and politically.

By the mid-eighteenth century the New World was beginning to live up to its name. The most typically colonial areas—the West Indies and Brazil—were to remain under European rule for at least another century. But everywhere the European settlers ceased to think of themselves merely as producers of raw materials for the mother country and consumers

Plantation scene

of her manufactured goods. They were still "white" and they still spoke English, French, Spanish, or Portuguese, but they were becoming increasingly different from their countrymen back home. Indeed, they no longer thought of England, France, Spain, or Portugal as "home." Many of them had lived in America all their lives.

The geography and economy of the New World, plus intimate contact with Indians and black slaves, transformed the European settlers. From Virginia to Brazil slavery gave plantation owners a racist outlook unknown in Europe; and fur trappers in Canada, western Pennsylvania, and Virginia had little in common with the peasants of France or northern Ireland. The nations of America were acquiring their distinct cultural characteristics even before the wars of the second half of the century aided the independence movement among the European colonists. Both the English and Spanish-speaking colonists began to call themselves "Americans," the Portuguese-speaking colonists "Brazilians," the French-speaking settlers in Quebec "Canadians."

The growing cultural differences between the colonists and their compatriots "back home" did not alter the fact that the New World was part of a global economy operating primarily for the benefit of Western Europe. We shall see later how trade between Europe and America continued to grow and how European capital began to pour in even after some of the colonies became independent. Meanwhile, the British, French, and Dutch intensified their competition for the trade of the Far East, and the British and the French began to clash in their commercial dealings with India. Directly or indirectly, the rest of the world was working increasingly for Europe and enriching its middle and upper classes.

## SOCIAL AND POLITICAL CONSEQUENCES OF INCREASED WEALTH AND THE GLOBAL ECONOMY

The expansion of trade, the growing importance of colonial empires, and the enrichment of the middle and upper classes all had important effects on the social and political life of Western Europe. In England, France, the Dutch Republic, Sweden, Denmark, and even Spain, the modern bureaucratic state had entrenched itself. No longer could private groups successfully challenge its monopoly over political and military power. What they could and did do was to insist that the state respect their property and privileges. Thus began the struggle between private and public interests. In the eighteenth century it involved only people of wealth and position, but their number was growing, and they became increasingly self-conscious about preserving and extending what was *theirs*. In England they worked fairly well together in keeping the state on their side; in France they were in conflict with one another as well as with the state.

### Property and Privilege

Before the eighteenth century property had meant immovable wealth (land) and titles, neither of which could be legally separated from their rightful owners. A bishop received his title and the income from the land that went with it for as long as he lived, but he could not sell the title or the land to somebody else. Both belonged to the Church in perpetuity (*mortmain*). A hereditary nobleman could never sell his title; he might mortgage or lease out his land, but usually he could not sell it outright without a special legal dispensation, for feudal laws of entail still survived in many parts of Western Europe. A king could sell judgeships, army commissions, and administrative posts, but even these tended to become lifetime property rights for the men who held them.

In the eighteenth century, however, a new situation arose: never before had there been as much private property, and never had it been so consciously exalted as a value in itself. Governments protected it; insurance companies insured it; Locke called it an inalienable natural right. As trade and commerce grew, more and more private property took the form of movable wealth, such as ships, warehouses, stocks and bonds, and just plain money in the bank. Traditionally this kind of property had never been considered quite respectable, and in many places the law did not always give it full protection. To take an extreme example, as late as 1745 a court in the French city of Angoulême dismissed the suit of a group of banks against their debtors, because it was still illegal to lend money at interest there. But by and large bourgeois property owners were winning their fight to make movable wealth as sacrosanct as the older types of property rights.

Many wealthy bourgeois wanted to have the best of both worlds. They wanted complete freedom to dispose of their movable wealth and they wanted the kinds of privileges that went with immovable wealth. Since the sixteenth century rich commoners had tried to move up the social ladder by purchasing land and titles. As this practice grew through the increase in movable wealth in the eighteenth century, the hereditary nobles tried to become more exclusive, especially in France. The main status symbols now had to do with privilege: the privilege of being presented at court, of being called "sir" or "madam," of going to the opera, of wearing a wig, of not paying taxes (in France), of having one's own coach-and-four, and most especially, the privilege of not working. No matter how rich a new noble was, his property seemed somehow incomplete unless he could consider himself a member of the privileged classes.

Legalized privilege can be very alluring. American society has never had it with regard to class, though many of its white members have known the satisfaction of having certain public facilities reserved exclusively for them. In Europe class privilege had been supported by law since feudal times, and the older privileged orders clung to it as an inalienable right in the eighteenth century. Not only did the hereditary nobles continue to hold most of the high offices in the state, the army, and the Church, but they also still owned many of the large rural estates and still set the standards of taste and manners. They thought they were the best people, the real aristocrats, because they had been "born that way." No wonder so many wealthy people who had not been "born that way" tried to acquire similar privileges.

Only the top level of the western European bourgeoisie could aspire to aristocratic privileges in the eighteenth century, and outside of England most people at this level were not "in trade." The richest

Dutch burghers were now *rentiers* living in idleness on interest (*rentes*) from government bonds and bank accounts. The most prosperous members of the French bourgeoisie were bankers and the tax farmers, who received 7½ per cent of all the taxes they collected for the royal treasury. In the 1750s the total income of the 600 tax farmers and assistant tax farmers exceeded 600 million livres. All doors were open to millionaire bankers and tax farmers, and they "lived nobly." But it was less easy in France than in England for a rich merchant or a manufacturer to buy a large rural estate and end his days as a country gentleman. As early as 1726 Daniel Defoe described the English situation as follows:

"In short trade in England makes gentlemen, . . . for the tradesman's children, or at least their grand children come to be as good gentlemen, statesmen, Parliament men, privy counsellors, judges, bishops, and noblemen as those of the highest birth and the most ancient families." (*The Complete English Tradesman* [1726], pp. 376–7.)

While some wealthier members of the bourgeoisie entered the ranks of the aristocracy, some hereditary noblemen began to lose their aversion for making money. In both England and France a number of them farmed their estates with a keen commercial sense. They also invested their savings in distilleries, sugar refineries, and banking, while many bourgeois invested theirs in land. The resulting marriage between property and privilege was therefore not a one-sided affair, although much hostility remained between the nobles and the upper bourgeoisie, especially in France. But as the wealth of both classes increased, they both intensified their efforts to preserve the social order that had made this increase possible. In order to do so effectively they sought to control the instruments of public power.

## Society and Politics in England

The eighteenth-century British political system allowed the wealthiest landowners and the wealthiest businessmen to dominate the country in their own interest. The system was corrupt, it neglected the lower classes, but it got things done. As in no other European country, the "best people" ruled in Great Britain; Britain had a government of the aristocracy, by the aristocracy, and for the aristocracy.

The core of the eighteenth-century British aristocracy was the one hundred and forty peers of the realm. Whether dukes, viscounts, or earls, they alone were addressed as "Lord" and had the privilege of sitting in the upper house of Parliament along with the bishops, or "Lords Spiritual." Nevertheless, great accumulations of land allowed others besides peers to enter the ranks of the aristocracy. Despite the formal separation between Lords and Commons, the members of the lower house were mainly landowners, and many were related to those in the Lords and owed their seats to the money and influence of some peer.

The eighteenth-century aristocracy was mainly a Whig aristocracy. Its members stood for limited monarchy and the supremacy of Parliament, for the Bill of Rights and the Protestant succession, for hostility to France, for the promotion of commerce and the security of property, whether movable or immovable. The Tories had supported the Stuarts and gone down in defeat. George I of Hanover, not the exiled "James III," had succeeded Queen Anne in 1714. Tories continued to sit in Parliament and to vie with the Whig aristocrats in local politics; but their alleged sympathies for the Stuart Pretenders made them partially suspect, and they failed to produce national political leaders. From 1714 until 1760 the Whigs ran the government and the country in their own interests.

### *The Form of Politics*

Whig supremacy insured the interests of the wealthy classes, and it was epitomized by the political leadership of Sir Robert Walpole. As First Lord of the Treasury he controlled the British government for over twenty years (1721–1742). Walpole was perfectly suited to his role, combining as he did the country gentleman's experience in ruling men, the expensive tastes and overbearing manners of a great aristocrat, and the temperament of a first-rate businessman. Under his rule men of

*Walpole (standing) being addressed by the speaker of the House of Commons*

wealth invested increasing amounts of money in trade, land, and domestic building. They also lent money freely to the government, *their* government, at low interest, allowing it to accumulate a national debt unparalleled anywhere in the world.* They felt that their money was in safe hands with Walpole as First Lord of the Treasury, and with a Parliament that they controlled guaranteeing the debt and auditing the public accounts. With so much cheap money available in the form of loans Walpole was able to foster commerce by abolishing import duties, formerly an important source of revenue. He also helped his Whig allies in Parliament gain more land and high government offices by an adroit use of Crown influence.

Under Walpole's rule British politics took on the form it was to retain until 1832.* Legally the king alone held executive authority. In practice, however, his government could not function without a majority in Parliament; thus the king had to choose his ministers from the relatively small number of men who could muster

*The British national debt had been £1,000,000 in 1688. It rose to £80,000,000 by the mid-eighteenth century, yet the interest rate on government securities fell to 5 per cent in 1717, 4 per cent in 1727, and 3 per cent in 1749.

*See Chapter XI.

such a majority. Out of this situation arose the three main features of British politics: the cabinet, the party system, and rigged local elections.

In typically British fashion, modern cabinet government developed without anybody defining its responsibilities; and although the ministers sometimes forced the King's hand, they never claimed the right to do so. Walpole has been called the first true prime minister, but he held no such title. As First Lord of the Treasury his preeminence in the cabinet rested on his direction of national finances and his control of the great volume of patronage. Future First Lords, however, could not claim the same preeminence. Between 1757 and 1761, for example, Secretary of State William Pitt the elder was the real leader of the cabinet* in which the Duke of Newcastle was the First Lord of the Treasury. The premiership was not to take on its full modern form until leadership of a political party gave an independent source of power and a special standing in the cabinet to one person. In the first years of his reign George III (1760–1820) reasserted the authority of the Crown over its ministers and curbed the power of the Whig aristocrats who had been running the country for almost fifty years. He did this by building up in Parliament a party of the "King's friends" with Tory aid and by the now usual means of bribery and patronage. In the Tory cabinets of the 1760s and 1770s George III held the upper hand.

Corruption, the influence of the Crown, and the lack of issues among the wealthy classes hampered the development of disciplined political parties. Only the Jacobite issue really divided the Whigs and the Tories before the mid-eighteenth century. Besides, these two parties included only a third of the members of the House of Commons. A third always voted for the government, and another third had no party affiliation at all. Those Whigs whom Walpole had excluded from office frequently stood against their nominal leader not because they disagreed with his policies, but in order to gain a share of power. Nevertheless, after 1780, the nuclei of a conservative (Tory) and a liberal (Whig) party were there.

The fact that both parties represented only the rich can be clearly seen in the way their members were elected. Each borough in England and Wales returned two members to the House of Commons. In the more populous urban boroughs the leading landowner had to gain the necessary votes for himself or his "man" by promises of patronage to the more influential citizens. In rural boroughs from which many people had moved to the cities he could intimidate the handful of forty-shilling freeholders who were qualified to vote. The fact that the voting was open, by a show of hands, made opposition dangerous. Besides, many freeholders still retained a medieval kind of loyalty to the local lord and looked on him as their protector. Successful control of the representation of a borough meant greater influence in Parliament and increased local authority. The struggle for such control was an integral part of the process by which the "best people" survived in eighteenth century English society.

### *Forces of Stability*

Through its control of the government the English aristocracy maintained social stability. By the mid-eighteenth century the great landowners were displacing the country gentry in local politics and putting them in a position of dependency for favors and patronage, and friction again arose between the great landowners and the small farmers with the renewal of the enclosure movement. Nevertheless, an alliance between landed and business wealth forestalled all opposition from below. For the rich, private property was sacred; and any threat to it was viewed as a threat to the social order itself.

All Englishmen were proud of their constitutional liberties, but the ruling class imposed legal restraints on these liberties in the name of social order and the protection of private property. Since Parliament made the law, an Englishman's liberty consisted in doing only what Parliament considered respectable, and since the execution of the law was in the hands of local authorities, he had to observe it as they interpreted it. Public agitation was

*See pp. 241–244.

# PARLIAMENTARY REPRESENTATION IN GREAT BRITAIN AT THE END OF THE 18TH CENTURY

County boundaries

Boroughs and Scottish Burghs •

Towns not represented ○

0 20 40 60 mi.

Map by J. Donovan

ORKNEY IS.
CAITHNESS
SUTHERLAND
CROMARTY
ROSS
NAIRN
ELGIN
BANFF
ABERDEEN
INVERNESS
KINCARDINE
FORFAR
PERTH
ARGYLE
CLACKMANNAN
KINROSS
FIFE
DUMBARTON
STIRLING
LINLITHGOW
HADDINGTON
BUTE
RENFREW
LANARK
EDINBURGH
PEEBLES
BERWICK
DUR.
SELKIRK
ROXBURGH
AYR
DUMFRIES
KIRKCUDBRIGHT
WIGTOWN
NORTHUMBERLAND
CUMBERLAND
DURHAM
WESTMORE-LAND
YORK
LANCASHIRE
LINCOLN
FLINT
ANGLESEY
CARNARVON
DENBIGH
CHESHIRE
DERBY
NOTTINGHAM
MERIONETH
MONTGOMERY
SALOP
STAFFORD
LEICESTER
RUTLAND
NORFOLK
CAMBRIDGE
HUNTINGDON
NORTHAMPTON
WARWICK
WORCESTER
RADNOR
CARDIGAN
SUFFOLK
BEDFORD
HEREFORD
PEMBROKE
CARMARTHEN
BRECON
BUCKINGHAM
HERTFORD
ESSEX
OXFORD
GLOUCESTER
MONMOUTH
MIDDLESEX
London
GLAMORGAN
BERKS
SURREY
KENT
WILTS
HANTS
SOMERSET
SUSSEX
DEVON
DORSET
CORNWALL

rare in the eighteenth century, but the frequency of sporadic rioting* made upper-class Englismen view the common people as potential enemies. Consequently, they imposed severe penalties on any threats to property or the social order. By the 1750s over three hundred and fifty offenses were punishable by death, but fortunately for the criminals, though not for their victims, there was no regular police force. As a result, lawlessness actually increased. Englishmen were willing to accept this situation as the price for their extraordinary freedom from government regulation, for they viewed the police and all agents of a strong central government as instruments of despotism.

The law was not the only instrument fostering social stability; religion helped too. The Church of England, like all state churches, was extremely conservative. It supported an ordered social hierarchy and taught children to obey their masters and be diffident toward their betters. Protestant Nonconformists were less committed than Anglicans to the established order, for it excluded them from its highest offices. But this group was not powerless. It included many of Britain's most enterprising merchants and manufacturers. These people could vote, and they joined the great landowners and Anglican businessmen in the Whig party. The wealthier Nonconformists had abandoned their seventeenth-century revolutionary tendencies and accepted their inferior political status as long as their property and social position were safe. The English Catholics were treated as resident aliens, and the Irish Catholics had no rights at all. Yet by the mid-eighteenth century even they ceased to agitate for changes in the established order.

Social stability was further fostered by the fact that really talented individuals could better themselves. The son of a small Nonconformist freeholder joined the Established Church and ended his days as Archbishop Secker. Philip Hardwicke, the son of a country attorney, became Lord Chancellor and an earl. The outstanding example of a commoner rising to the heights of power and status was William Pitt (1708–1778). Unlike Walpole, Pitt had not been born into a solidly established, centuries-old, landed family exercising traditional authority and political power. Nevertheless, his outstanding leadership in the wars against France in America and India was to earn him the title of First Earl of Chatham.

*The most savage riots of the eighteenth century occurred in 1780, when London was at the mercy of an angry and destructive mob for several days. These Gordon Riots were directed mainly against Catholics, but they also expressed the deep discontent of the urban lower classes in the face of the nation's disastrous defeats in the American Revolution.

The successful functioning of eighteenth-century English government depended upon the wish of a sufficient number of influential and dedicated men to make it work. Local justices of the peace, often unpaid members of the gentry, executed the law as best they could. They were honest though not very efficient, especially in the assessment and collection of taxes. But for the political reasons already mentioned, the central government did not try to interfere with the local authorities. At the national level politics and patronage often subordinated the public good to private interests. Yet the upper ranks of the civil service included many impoverished young gentlemen who, although political appointees, brought traditional standards of honesty and upright conduct to their new profession. The lower ranks as well were devoted and fairly efficient. Furthermore, those young gentlemen who could not get into the civil service carried these same standards into the legal profession and the business world.

### Society and Politics in France

France did not adapt herself nearly as well as Great Britain to the economic and social changes of the eighteenth century. Private interests and the public good rarely coincided. On the one hand there was the royal government, dedicated to the public good, but lacking a Louis XIV to make it work as it was organized to work. On the other hand, there were the privileged orders, unable to control the royal government but determined to prevent it from doing anything that threatened their rights and status. If some of them had worked together, they might have been able to enforce a policy of their own. But they were as jealous of one another as they were of the Crown. If the royal government had been stronger it might have made the institutional changes necessary to meet the new conditions of French society. But the entrenched traditions of divine-right monarchy, the weakness of Louis XIV's successors, and the resistance of the privileged orders forbade such a solution.

It is difficult to say how much more effective the French royal government might have been if it had had stronger leadership, yet the political system itself had certain weaknesses that even Louis XIV had not been able to overcome. He had given France the most highly centralized bureaucracy in Europe. In the eighteenth century the royal *intendants* presided over the thirty administrative units – *généralités* – into which the country was divided. Still, other administrative units overlapped the *généralités:* the ecclesiastical dioceses, the jurisdictions of the Parlements, the 39 military *gouvernements* – not to mention the many semi-independent areas that had been annexed to France over the centuries. Although royal edicts applied throughout the kingdom, many provinces and even counties had their own traditional legal systems. All this administrative confusion would have weakened the effectiveness of even the strongest and most unified central government.

### *Louis XV*

As it was, the government of eighteenth century France was weak and divided at its center, the royal court. Louis XV reigned from 1715 to 1774. Since he was only five years old when his reign began, a Regency ruled in his name at first. The princes of the blood came into their own again, and court intrigue became a permanent habit for the rest of the century. One faction worked against the other and prevented the Regent and his ministers from doing anything positive. From 1726 to 1743 a strong minister, Cardinal Fleury (1653 – 1743), tried to rule France the way Walpole was ruling England. When Fleury was prime minister in all but name, the rivalries of factions did not dominate French policy,* but after he died the real trouble began; the king decided to run the state himself. He played off one minister or court faction against another, intrigued against his own ministers, and let himself be swayed by his "chief mistress," Madame de Pompadour. During the late 1740s and throughout the 1750s this daughter of a clerk, promoted to the rank of marquise, was the prevailing influence at the royal court. Bankers, politicians, generals, and artists flocked to her boudoir. For the back stairs from there to the royal chambers were the surest route to the king's favor.

Louis XV was a handsome, charming, intelligent, well-intentioned man, but a weak king. Brought up amid court intrigue, he became bored with the duties of kingship at an early age. He alleviated his boredom with women and hunting. On the days when he did not hunt, the court bulletin said "the king is not doing anything today." His fatal incapacity for making decisions paralyzed the machinery of the state. Yet he clung to the divine-right prerogatives he had inherited from his great-grandfather, Louis XIV. His ministers got him into fruitless wars that bankrupted the royal treasury; his court nobles and his mistresses loaded themselves with favors and privileges. In the later years of his reign it became increasingly difficult for him or anyone else to carry out a consistent government policy. The public good was in danger of being drowned in a sea of selfish interests. Still, Louis XV and Madame de Pompadour believed that the flood would not come as long as they lived.

### *Class Divisions*

France's political system had ended the political and religious disorders of the early modern period, but it could not adapt itself to the changing conditions of the eighteenth century. By then France's middle and upper classes viewed the sanctity of property second only to the

*See p. 238.

sanctity of the king. Theoretically absolute, the French government was less able than the British government to tap the private wealth of its subjects for public purposes, especially wars. As a result it faced chronic financial distress, despite the tremendous increase in private wealth. It gained considerable income from the sale of offices that made their holders nobles of the robe. But nobles, whether old or new, linked their offices to family patrimony and to constitutional resistance to the Crown in defense of property. Unlike those in Great Britain, France's men of property and privilege did not feel that the national government was *their* government. They had no institution comparable to the British Parliament through which they could directly control public policy. All they could do was to defend their private interests against government encroachment. The hereditary nobles refused to pay taxes; the wealthy commoners were reluctant to lend money to a government that did not represent them; and, as we shall see shortly, the Parlements reasserted their right to block royal efforts to raise new forms of revenue.

There was also less harmony of interest among the privileged classes in France than in England. The country gentry shared the great nobles' hostility to the royal officials who had taken away their local political powers, but they also resented the ability of the great nobles at court to get the lion's share of patronage and honors. The nobility of the robe was split between the *intendants*, who supported royal absolutism, and the magistrates in the Parlements, who opposed it. Moreover, in the first half of the eighteenth century the high-ranking members of the nobility of the sword tried to reassert their role as France's true aristocracy. They brought fresh talent and vigor into their ranks by "taking in" new recruits from the nobility of the robe, but they despised the wealthy bourgeoisie, and during the 1750s they closed their ranks to its members. From then on the nobles virtually monopolized all the highest offices in the Church, the state, and the army. Some of France's wealthiest bankers and financiers had managed to gain exemption from taxation, like the hereditary nobles. They too looked down on other bourgeois who were trying to climb the social ladder, but they knew that they were second-class aristocrats at best.

The middle classes had as little in common politically as the privileged ones. Some of the bigger merchants and shipowners wanted the government to restrict the privileges and tax exemptions of the aristocracy; others wanted it to allow them to buy noble titles and rural estates for themselves. Independent manufacturers wanted to eliminate the guilds, which Colbert had strengthened; the guild masters wanted to keep their privileged monopolies. A growing number of second-string government officials, lawyers, and other professional men also swelled the ranks of the bourgeoisie, But, though more clearly defined than in England, the bourgeoisie in France was not a homogeneous class united in political interest.

The French monarchy was unable to unify the changing society. Everybody seemed to think that somebody else was getting more than his share of wealth and privileges and wanted the state to rectify the situation in their favor. Some ministers tried to foster commerce and trade, but there was no alliance between business and landed wealth as in England. The peasants, who constituted 80 per cent of the population, bore the brunt of the tax burden and resented the state as well as the landlords. As long as the privileged orders refused to be taxed, there was little the government could do except get its revenue where it could. When it tried to institute tax reforms in the mid-eighteenth century it found itself thwarted by the one institution that had a legal claim to check its actions, the Parlements.

### The Parlements

As we have seen, the Parlements insisted that they were the repositories and rightful defenders of the fundamental laws of the kingdom. Louis XIV had restricted their powers, but they had recovered them during the Regency that followed his death. Each time a strong minister

tried to institute a tax on landed property the Parlement of Paris declared it illegal and the provincial Parlements followed suit. In each case they were backed by all the privileged orders. The magistrates of the Parlements also gained some support from the unprivileged masses by pronouncing high-sounding phrases like "the king's subjects are free men, not slaves."

The Parlements were the closest thing to an organized political opposition in eighteenth-century France. But even though they could rally temporary support on specific issues, they really represented no one except themselves. In other words, the robed magistrates were just another privileged order defending their property rights in their land and in their offices. The royal government periodically tried to exile the magistrates, but they always managed to come back and find some new issue on which to attack it.

One such issue was the Jesuits. The exaggerated fear and hatred felt for this Order everywhere in Protestant Europe was equaled in many parts of the Catholic world by the middle of the eighteenth century.* Louis XV and the majority of the French bishops wished to preserve the

*The Jesuits were expelled from Portugal in 1759 and from Spain and Naples in 1767. In 1773, under pressure from the kings of France, Naples, and Spain, Pope Clement XIV abolished the Society of Jesus throughout Catholic Europe. It was not revived until 1814 during the general reaction against the French Revolution and Napoleon.

Eighteenth-century French aristocracy

Order's existence, but most of the Parlements had long viewed it as a subversive alien organization. The magistrates considered themselves good Catholics, so their opposition to the Jesuits was on political rather than on religious grounds. In 1762 the Parlement of Paris finally ordered the abolition of the Society of Jesus on the ground that its doctrine were "perverse, destructive of all principles of religion, and even of honesty, injurious to Christian morality, pernicious to civil society, seditious, hostile to the rights of the nation and the power of the king." This independent legal action constituted the Parlement's oldest claim to represent the true interests of the nation. The fact that the king could do nothing about it showed how weak he really was.

### Persistent Weaknesses

Although the abolition of the Jesuits was not meant to be a direct attack on the Catholic Church in France, it had broad implications for the established social and political order. The critical and scientific spirit of the eighteenth century was turning many enlightened people away from religion. Their antireligious feeling was an implicit threat to a monarchy founded on divine right, and their resentment against the Church as a privileged estate could lead to changes in the structure of French society. In Great Britain, where these changes were already occurring, even the Nonconformists did not resent the Established Church as much as Catholic Frenchmen resented their own Church for standing in the way of these changes.

By not changing with the times the political and social order in France fostered deep-seated resentment among wealthy but unprivileged Frenchmen. The Revolution was still a generation away in 1763, and the old order defended itself well. A stronger government might have kept the aristocracy more "open," thus strengthening the social basis for its authority. This was England's way of accommodating itself to the changes brought about by the enrichment of its middle classes. But the weakness of the French monarchy only encouraged the privileged few to become more exclusive than ever and to make their own bid for political power. Barred from both power and privilege the wealthy bourgeoisie was eventually to see that it could only improve its status by open rebellion.

## THE QUEST FOR WEALTH AND EMPIRE

While social and economic changes were transforming domestic life in Great Britain and France, each state continued to foster its commercial interests overseas. The government of France was less responsive to the social and political demands of its businessmen than the government of Great Britain, but both governments pursued mercantilist policies to strengthen their national economies. Although they tried to avoid using their armies and navies in open warfare to defend purely economic interests, this was not always possible. For the British and the French had their dependents and allies in Europe, Asia, and America, and these people always seemed to be getting into trouble. Thus the Anglo-French struggle for wealth and empire inevitably led to war.

The wars of the mid-eighteenth century were fought in many parts of the world, but they were not the kind of world wars the twentieth century was to know. First of all, the big and little powers of Central and Eastern Europe were involved only tangentially in the conflict overseas. Moreover, eighteenth-century international relations were conducted by professional diplomats and professional soldiers, with a minimum of effect on civilians. This chapter will discuss the British and French struggle for world supremacy and its effect on the European balance of power; the next chapter will complete the picture of the European state system in the eighteenth century by examining the internal developments of the other powers and their relations with one another.

### England, France, and Europe, 1713–1748

Both England and France were tired of war in 1713. They had fought each other almost without interruption since 1689 and they were determined to avoid another war for as long as possible. The fact that they were to resume hostilities in the early 1740s and to continue fighting off and on until 1815 has given the name "Second Hundred Years' War" to the whole period 1689–1815. But England and France remained at peace for almost thirty years in the first half of the eighteenth century, and between 1716 and 1733 they were actually allies. This unusual alliance expressed each country's desire to stop other countries from fighting in Europe now that *they* had stopped fighting there. England got practically all she wanted at the Treaty of Utrecht, and France needed peace in order to rebuild her economy and her diplomatic position on the continent. Neither country wanted to see the precarious balance of power upset or to be dragged into wars started by the Russians, the Spaniards, or the Austrians.

Although the Anglo-French *rapprochement* did not stop other European powers from fighting among themselves, it did limit the extent of the fighting until about 1740. The main areas of conflict, besides the Baltic, were Poland and the Western Mediterranean. The War of the Polish Succession (1733–1735) involved France, primarily because Stanislas Lesczynski, the king whom the Austrians and Russians deposed, was Louis XV's father-in-law. Even in this instance Great Britain and France were able to localize the conflict. France did not succeed in keeping Stanislas on the Polish throne, but she got Austria to give him the Duchy of Lorraine and the County of Bar, which were to go to France on his death (1766).

### *Spain and Italy*

Meanwhile, the newly established Bourbon dynasty in Spain set out to recover its lost possessions and influence in Italy. Philip V (1700–1746) and his French advisers cut down the excessive formalities and delays of Spanish administration, improved the tax system, and built up the navy. Even so, Spain remained impoverished, burdened by a reactionary nobility and clergy, and hampered by inadequate resources. Philip's second wife, Elizabeth Farnese, the niece of the Duke of Parma, was a woman of strong character and narrow outlook. She dominated her husband and with the aid of Abbé Giulio Alberoni, an Italian adventurer and master at diplomatic intrigue, forced Spain into a series of wars to secure Italian thrones for her two sons.

In 1713 some Italian states had exchanged one foreign master for another. The Austrian Hapsburgs had taken Milan and Naples from Spain, thus gaining a preponderant influence in the peninsula. Flanking the Duchy of Milan were the two decaying commercial republics of Venice and Genoa. In the northwest the rising state of Piedmont-Savoy became the Kingdom of Sardinia after its acquisition of that Mediterranean island in 1720; though one of the most conservative and badly governed of the Italian states, Piedmont-Savoy was already showing a capacity for territorial expansion which none of the others could equal. Further down the peninsula were the small duchies of Parma and Piacenza, the Grand Duchy of Tuscany, the Papal States, and the Austrian dominanted territories of Naples and Sicily—henceforth called the Kingdom of the Two Siciles. Venice still produced notable painters, Rome remained the capital of the Catholic world, Naples was the schoolmaster of European musicians, and Tuscany and Naples were later to contribute to the economic and intellectual advances of the century. But defenseless Italy remained the natural victim of ambitious foreign dynasties.

In the 1730s and 1740s the Spanish Bourbons and Austrian Hapsburgs exchanged several Italian territories through minor wars and diplomatic agreements. In 1735 Spain received the Two Sicilies, which came under the rule of Elizabeth Farnese's eldest son, Don Carlos. The descendants of this Spanish Bourbon were to rule the southern half of Italy for the next century and a quarter. In exchange for the Two Sicilies Austria received the Grand Duchy of Tuscany, which was given to Francis of Lorraine, the husband of the Hapsburg heiress, Maria Theresa,* in compensation for his own duchy, which went to Stanislas Lesczynski and eventually to France. Hapsburg rule in Tuscany was to last almost as long as Bourbon rule in the Two Sicilies. Austria also took Parma and Piacenza in 1735, but in 1748 these two duchies came under Bourbon rule when they went to Don Filipo, Elizabeth Farnese's younger son.

Great Britain and France resisted most of the efforts of Elizabeth Farnese and Alberoni to draw them into Italian affairs. They cared little who ruled what territories in Italy as long as competition for these territories did not involve *them.* Nevertheless, by the end of the 1730s many Englishmen began to notice that the principal losers in 1713, Spain and France, had recovered much lost ground in Europe, and France again was making her diplomatic influence felt everywhere on the continent, just as if there had been no Treaty of Utrecht. While Walpole prided himself on promoting commerce and keeping England out of Europe's wars, Fleury was quietly rebuilding France's status as a world power.

### Renewal of Anglo-French Rivalry

Fleury wanted to harass England's position in North America and the West Indies, *not* to become involved in a general war. Walpole did not want war either. But both ministers failed to prevent groups with special interests from making their countries fight. English business interests won out over the public good in 1739, when England went to war with Spain to protect the South Sea Company's trade with the Spanish West Indies. Walpole commented, "They are ringing the bells now, they will soon be wringing their hands." In France, Fleury's failure was more serious. There, in 1740, a court faction of the nobility of the sword won out over the public good when France went to war with Austria for no apparent reason other than territorial aggrandizement and because the leader of the French war party, Marshal Belle-Isle, wanted France to take advantage of the change in the Hapsburg succession to eliminate her ancient rival. Thus Fleury's efforts to cultivate Austria's friendship and to reserve France's military forces for an eventual duel with England were negated.

The story of the War of the Austrian Succession (1740–1748) will be told in

*See p. 257, footnote.

Chapter VII; here we are concerned with France's reasons for getting entangled in it. Emperor Charles VI (1711–1740) had persuaded most of the states of Western and Central Europe to sign the Pragmatic Sanction, a document guaranteeing the territorial integrity of the Hapsburg domains after his death. Louis XV had signed the Pragmatic Sanction, and France was in no danger when the King of Prussia, who had also signed it, invaded Austria in 1740. But the French war party had no sympathy for Fleury's policies. The cautious Cardinal was almost 90 years old and no match for the dashing young officers who supported Belle-Isle. As we have seen, the French aristocrats were less involved in commercial enterprises than their English counterparts. War on land was their profession, and the House of Austria was France's traditional enemy.

England restricted her involvement in the War of the Austrian Succession to giving financial subsidies to Austria and to fighting one battle in 1742; the bulk of France's army got bogged down in a long, fruitless war which, in the end, benefited only Prussia—which annexed the Hapsburg province of Silesia—and intensified anti-French feeling in England and Austria. In the process, France lost several opportunities to gain the upper hand over England in America and India.

*Slave auction*

## The Struggle for Supremacy in America

Until the mid-1750s Great Britain, France, and Spain tried to avoid a showdown for control of North America and the West Indies. The war between Great Britain and Spain, The War of Jenkins' Ear,* lasted from 1739 to 1748. Although it resulted in no transfer of territory, it made Great Britain give up her long attempt to force the Spaniards to allow direct trade with their colonies. After 1750 the Spanish government managed to maintain its monopoly and to strengthen its trade system. Illegal trade between the British West Indies and Spanish America continued, but the French steadily enlarged their share of the legal trade at the expense of the British. They did this by the traditional method of consigning goods for Spanish America through Spanish merchants at Cadiz. At the same time the French increased their commercial competition in the West Indies and their strategic pressure in North America. Until the 1750s, however, the British and French governments restricted their military activities in the New World to naval blockades and allowed the local authorities to organize most of the land operations.

Between 1744 and 1748 the war between Great Britain and France in the West Indies expressed the bitter rivalry between these two countries' sugar colonies rather than the desire of the home

*We have already noted the conflict between English smugglers and Spanish "coast guards" that caused this war. One Englishman, a Captain Jenkins, had his ear cut off by the Spaniards. He made a dramatic appearance in Parliament, where he produced his severed ear from a handkerchief. The war party prevailed as a result of this spectacle. Hence, England's war with Spain was called the War of Jenkins' Ear.

governments to acquire new territories or new trade routes. The French islands —larger in area and with their soil less exhausted—were increasing their competition with the British inlands in the production of cheap sugar and in trade with Europe and British North America. As we have seen, the British planters had practically forced the home government to pass the Molasses Act in order to reduce this competition; but the Act was difficult to enforce, and the British planters urged the home government to take more direct action. From 1744 to 1748, the British navy tried to cut off the trade of the French West Indies by starving them of provisions and slaves and by preventing them from selling their sugar. Because it was in a temporary state of disrepair, it could not force the issue. Besides, the British colonists in North America continued to trade with the French islands during the war, buying their sugar and selling them grain and timber. Under these conditions the war with the French ended inconclusively in 1748.

The end was also inconclusive in the Anglo-French war in North America. After having lost Newfoundland and Nova Scotia (Acadia) in 1713, the French built the fortress of Louisbourg at the mouth of the St. Lawrence in order to dominate access to the river and to their vast empire in the hinterland. During the American phase (King George's War) of the War of the Austrian Succession, British colonists from New England captured Louisbourg with naval support from the mother country. The British colonists also clashed with the French in the territory between the Great Lakes and the Ohio Valley and in the Cherokee country west of Carolina and Georgia. All these conflicts ended inconclusively when the governments in London and Paris signed the Treaty of Aix-la-Chapelle in 1748. Louisbourg was restored to France, and the French retained their precarious hold on the Ohio and Mississippi Valleys. But peace settlement of Aix-la-Chapelle was only a truce.

### *The French and Indian War*

In their long-term struggle for the territory west of the Appalachians both the French and the British colonial authorities tried to find Indian allies. After all, this *was* Indian country, and until the 1740s it had virtually no British settlers, and only a small French settlement in southern Illinois. The Iroquois, organized into a Confederation of Six Nations, controlled most of the territory from western New York to the Ohio Valley and collected most of the furs and pelts from the tribes further west. Both French and British traders tried to persuade the local Indians to sell these goods to them in exchange for rum, hardware, and cheap textiles. Despite this interference with their trade the Iroquois refused to get involved in the Anglo-French conflict of the 1740s. Their neutrality, plus the fact that a Neutrality Party also controlled the New York colonial Assembly, limited the military conflicts between the British and French colonists during King George's War (1744–1748).

It was while their home governments were technically at peace (1748–1756) that the colonists intensified their struggle for control of North America. In 1749 a group of Virginians organized the Ohio Company to develop the land west of the Appalachians. Its purpose was settlement as well as trade. Since both the French and the Indians claimed the territory the Ohio Company wanted to develop, they began to work together to resist British penetration. In the early 1750s the French Governor-General, Marquis Duquesne, built a series of forts from Niagara to the site of present-day Pittsburg. With these forts and their Indian allies, the French hoped to stop the westward migration from Virginia. Meanwhile, at the mouth of the St. Lawrence, the British government expelled several thousand French settlers from Nova Scotia and resettled that territory with an almost equal number of Britishers. Thus by the early 1750s the British and French colonists not only wanted to control North America for commercial purposes; they also wanted to occupy it themselves.

As long as their home governments remained at peace, no showdown was possible. Each side had its weaknesses. The French had more Indian allies than the British, but they themselves were fewer in numbers; the British colonists were disunited. In 1754, when Benjamin Franklin proposed a plan of union to a colonial convention assembled in Albany, the other colonists refused to fight for the Virginians and their Ohio Company. The British government then decided to send a small expeditionary force under General Braddock to aid the Virginians against the French and the Indians. In the summer of 1755 the combined forces of Braddock and the Virginians suffered complete defeat a few miles from Fort Duquesne. This successful attempt at limited warfare convinced the French to strengthen their system of forts in the Great Lakes and Ohio regions. By the end of 1755 they and their Indian allies were pushing the British back beyond the mountains to their seaboard bases. In the face of this kind of setback the British government finally decided that it had to drive the French out of North America. At this point the struggle for North America merged with a new general war between Great Britain and France in Europe.

### *The European Phase*

In 1755 it was clear that Great Britain and France had increasingly subordinated their European interests to their commercial and colonial rivalries. Still, the King of England was also the Elector of Hanover, and this North German state was vulnerable to attack by Prussia and France, the allies of the War of Austrian Succession. The British would have preferred to have Austria do the fighting against Prussia and France and reserve the bulk of their own forces for the struggle overseas. But Austria was now concerned primarily with Central European affairs, and France could not count any longer on her ally Prussia to do her fighting on the continent. Austria and Prussia were mainly interested in their own struggle for supremacy in Germany, and they wanted to use Great Britain and France as much as these powers wanted to use them.

A new system of alliances came into being as a result of the rise of new powers in Central and Eastern Europe and the preoccupation of the British and the French with their overseas interests. The rise of Prussia meant that Great Britain had an alternative to Austria as an ally against France, and that Austria's enemy was no longer France but Prussia. The rise of Russia meant that her diplomacy could upset the balance of existing alliances. We shall discuss the diplomatic maneuvering that led to the new alliance system in Chapter VII. Here all we need to know is that it came to a head when Great Britain signed a subsidy treaty with Russia in 1755. Since Russia was already allied with Austria, Prussia, fearing encirclement, also signed a subsidy treaty with Great Britain (January, 1756). France was furious at this apparent Prussian betrayal and formed an alliance with her traditional enemy, Austria. This last action was what made people speak of a Diplomatic Revolution.

The ease with which Great Britain and France could exchange allies in Central and Eastern Europe showed how completely independent their colonial interests were from those of the continent. At first it seemed that Great Britain had gained most from the Diplomatic Revolution; she now had two allies, while France had gained only one. Russia, however, did not keep her bargain with Great Britain. Fearing that Prussia was now too strong, she remained loyal to Austria. So when Prussia again dragged Europe into war in 1756, as she had in 1740, she had most of the continental countries against her. We shall see the outcome of the Seven Years' War in Chapter VII. What is important here is that France devoted more effort to it than Great Britain did and thus lost the struggle overseas.

The man who made possible Great Britain's victory in the Seven years' War (1756–1763) was William Pitt, the First Earl of Chatham and the real leader of the British government between 1757 and 1761. Pitt said that England would win an empire on the plains of Germany. She would do this by giving Prussia large sums of money to keep fighting France and her allies on the continent. Pitt's policy worked. The war in Germany prevented the French from looking after their navy and their colonies. Whereas they were able to send a total of only a few hundred men to reinforce their garrisons in Canada, the British were to increase their naval strength and eventually to send 60,000 reinforcements to America.

### *The British Victory in North America*

When Pitt took office in 1757 the British position in the New World was precarious. French commercial competition in the West Indies was growing, and French strategic pressure in North America had become more and more menacing since General Braddock's futile attack on Fort Duquesne two years earlier. With their commanding line of forts from Louisbourg to New Orleans, the French could direct their Indian allies to raid British settlements from Nova Scotia to Georgia. There were to be some large-scale naval battles in the Caribbean, and by 1763 the British were to take Martinique, Guadeloupe, and all the other French islands there except Haiti. But in Pitt's mind the major purpose of the French and Indian War, the American phase of the Seven Years' War, was to safeguard British North America by seizing Canada.

Within a year, Pitt's leadership reduced the French advantage. Pitt sent enough military and naval forces to North America to allow the British to capture Louisbourg in the summer of 1758. A few months later they destroyed French ascendancy in the Ohio Valley by taking the site of Fort Duquesne, now abandoned by the French; it was later named Pittsburg. They also threatened French communications between the St. Lawrence and the Great Lakes by capturing Fort Frontenac on Lake Ontario. Most ominous for the French was the ability of the British to prevent naval reinforcements and supply ships from reaching Canada. The Governor-General, the Marquis of Montcalm, not only had to rely increasingly on his own meager military forces, but he also began to lose the allegiance of his Indian allies, since he had no more European goods to trade with them.

In 1759 the British began their all-out assault on the St. Lawrence Valley from their newly won bases. The crucial campaign was General James Wolfe's attack on Quebec. Starting from the mouth of the St. Lawrence, Wolfe moved his amphibious force slowly upstream toward the capital of New France. It was a hazardous operation in every respect: hostile Indian fighters attacked the British whenever they moved too close to the shore; in midstream the waters of the St. Lawrence were treacherous and required expert seamanship. Wolfe also faced frequent opposition from his junior officers, who questioned his judgment and resented his stern aloof manner. When the expedition finally reached Quebec, it had to scale the high cliffs on which the citadel stood. Montcalm was now isolated, and his food supplies were running low. At last he sent his troops out of the fortress to do battle with the British on the famous Plains of Abraham. Quebec surrendered five days later (September 18, 1759), after both Wolfe and Montcalm had lost their lives.

With the capture of Quebec the British had almost achieved their goal of driving the French out of the St. Lawrence Valley. Almost, but not quite, for they were still dangerously exposed to counter-attack from the remaining French forces in Montreal. The final victory depended on whether French or British reinforcements reached the valley the following spring. Unfortunately for the French, their naval power was shattered in November 1759, when it was assembled to invade England. In April 1760 the British navy dispersed a relief convoy from Bordeaux, and a month later it was British, rather than French, ships that sailed up the St. Lawrence to Quebec. With these reinforcements the British consolidated their hold on the entire lower St. Lawrence. Montreal finally surrendered in September.

Thus by the end of 1760 the British had won the struggle for North America. They had done so through the organizing genius of Pitt, the superiority of their navy, and the professional competence of their regular generals, who eventually learned the techniques of forest warfare. The American colonists had provided abundant supplies and some invaluable auxiliary troops, but the full force of Great Britain's army and navy had been required to destroy France's entrenched position in the New World.

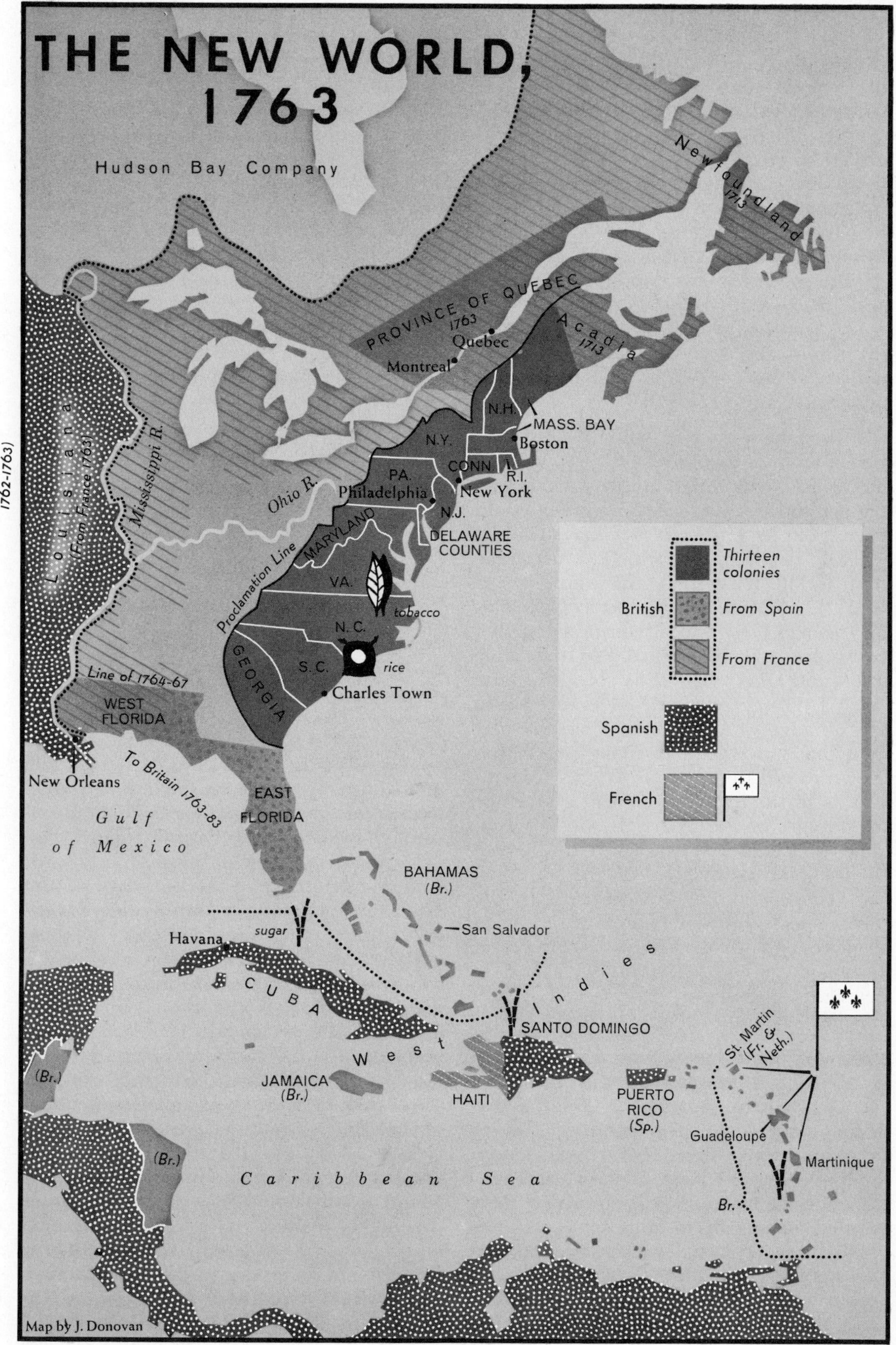
THE NEW WORLD, 1763
Hudson Bay Company
Newfoundland 1713
PROVINCE OF QUEBEC 1763
Quebec
Montreal
Acadia 1713
N.H.
MASS. BAY
Boston
N.Y.
CONN
R.I.
PA.
Philadelphia
New York
N.J.
DELAWARE COUNTIES
MARYLAND
VA.
tobacco
N. C.
S.C.
rice
GEORGIA
Charles Town
Ohio R.
Mississippi R.
Proclamation Line
Louisiana (From France 1763)
Line of 1764-67
WEST FLORIDA
New Orleans
To Britain 1763-83
EAST FLORIDA
Gulf of Mexico
Thirteen colonies
British
From Spain
From France
Spanish
French
BAHAMAS (Br.)
San Salvador
sugar
Havana
CUBA
West Indies
SANTO DOMINGO
JAMAICA (Br.)
HAITI
PUERTO RICO (Sp.)
St. Martin (Fr. & Neth.)
Guadeloupe
Martinique
Br.
(Br.)
(Br.)
Caribbean Sea
Map by J. Donovan

1762-1763)

### *The Aftermath*

The Anglo-French conflict lasted almost three more years, and its outcome for North America depended upon other factors besides British conquests there. Pitt wanted to continue the war until France would agree to terms that insured British supremacy. Louis XV's foreign minister, the Duke of Choiseul (1719–1785), countered with a threat to draw Spain into the conflict unless Pitt agreed to more moderate terms. Choiseul's maneuver was so clever and so typical of eighteenth-century diplomacy, that it is worth citing his motives as he later described them in a memorandum to Louis XV:

> "I then proposed to your Majesty two games to play together: one to keep up negotiation with England in such a way that if it did not succeed this time it would serve from its simplicity as a base for the general negotiations which must take place if Pitt fell before the influence of Bute. [Lord Bute did in fact replace Pitt in October, 1761 and advocate a conciliatory policy toward France.] At the same time—and this was the second game which I thought essential—I entered into an exchange of views with Spain, so devised that if we were to make peace that Crown would find it to its interest to support us in the negotiation, and guarantee the stability of the treaty. If, on the contrary, we failed in this, my plan was that Spain should be drawn into the war, and that France would be able to profit by the events which this new complication might produce, and repair her losses. Finally, if the event proved unfortunate, I had in view that the losses of Spain would lighten those which France might suffer."

Spain did in fact go to war with England in 1761, but this action did not save French North America. Only Great Britain's desire to stop fighting and to gain some concessions for Prussia, whom she had abandoned in Germany, persuaded her to let the French keep any of their colonial possessions at all.

The three colonial powers signed the Treaty of Paris in 1763. France was given back her West Indian islands, and Great Britain kept Canada and all of North America west to the Mississippi. Many Englishmen would have preferred to have kept the former, which were richer, and relinquish the latter, but strategic considerations won out over economic ones. The British understood that they had to eliminate the French threat to the expansion of their mainland colonies. They also eliminated the Spanish threat by forcing Spain to give up Florida and compensating her with all former French holdings west of the Mississippi, called the Louisiana Territory.

Not only the French, but the Indians, too, lost out in the British conquest of North America. Within a few months after the treaty of Paris was signed, Pontiac, the chief of the Ottawas, organized an uprising against the British-held former French posts between the Great Lakes and the Ohio Valley. The Algonquins, some of the Iroquois, and some of the tribes of the lower Mississippi also participated in what the British called the Conspiracy of Pontiac. The British eventually crushed this uprising and began to allow their colonists to move into Indian territory. In 1768 treaties with the Creeks, Cherokees, and Iroquois extinguished Indian rights in large areas. On the eve of the American Revolution the American Indians were being driven out of Tennessee and Kentucky by agents (including Daniel Boone) of land companies from Pennsylvania, Virginia, and North Carolina.

In 1774 the British empire in North America included all territory east of the Mississippi. Although the British practically eliminated Indian resistance to their colonists' westward expansion, they made two mistakes that were to incite the colonists to revolt against them. First, they increased the colonists' taxes and continued to put mercantilist restrictions on their trade and manufacturing. Second, they tried to limit their expansion north of the Ohio by extending the boundary of Quebec Province to that river. The Quebec Act (1774) had an ironic effect. It found a satisfactory way of incorporating the 65,000 French settlers into the British empire, while antagonizing the British colonists in whose interests the mother country had defeated the French and Indians.

In 1776 the revolt of the colonists was to negate most of Great Britain's gains against the French and the Indians of North America. The British were to find that the permanent foundations of their world empire lay in an entirely different setting.

## The Struggle for India

The British Empire in India was undoubtedly the most important single example in modern times of European supremacy overseas. Founded in the mid-eighteenth century, it remained Great Britain's prime possession until 1947. Moreover, its founding set a pattern for later European expansion at the expense of other old but declining civilizations in Asia and North Africa, an expansion that required new techniques and new types of men. Since India was so different from any area that the English and the French had dealt with before, we must look at it as it was before they tried to take it over.

### *The Setting*

At the end of the fifteenth century the majority of India's 90 million inhabitants were Hindus. The northern two-thirds of the country was divided into numerous principalities most of which were ruled by Muslim chieftains and their armies; the southern third formed an independent Hindu empire. The traditional Hindu way of life prevailed almost everywhere, even under the Muslim rulers. Each Hindu was born into a specific caste, which he could never leave and which was separated from the other castes by all sorts of barriers. The caste system allowed the Hindus to live side by side with people of other civilizations; it saved their own civilization under Muslim conquerors and the British later on. Any conqueror who did not respect Hindu customs and rituals risked a general uprising.

In the early sixteenth century a new Muslim dynasty, the Great Mughals, installed itself in India and reached the peak of power and brilliance under Akbar (1556–1605). Akbar conquered almost all of the northern two-thirds of India. He tried to rule his empire on the basis of tolerance and understanding with the Hindus, an efficient fiscal system based on fairly mild property taxes, and a well-trained public administration approaching that of a modern state. Later in his reign he even tried to unite his subjects of different religions through a new monotheistic faith. Yet this grandiose scheme came to naught, and after Akbar's death the empire of the Great Mughals went into a long decline.

The Mughal dynasty in India declined for the same reason as the Ottoman dynasty in Turkey*—it got soft at the top and oppressive at the bottom. Harem life debauched the Mughal ruling class, and Akbar's administrative institutions deteriorated in the hands of corrupt and inefficient officials. Emperor Aurangzeb (1659–1707) conquered most of the Hindu territories in the south, divided them into two provinces, and appointed a *Nizam* (Viceroy) to rule them in his name. But Aurangzeb could not control his subordinates, and he enraged the hitherto docile Hindus with fanatical religious persecution throughout his empire. He also increased the Hindus' taxes so much that the majority of the peasants lived dangerously close to the subsistence level. Hindu revolts threatened the unity of the Mughal Empire even before Aurangzeb died. Soon after his death revolts by most of the *nawabs* (provincial governors) accelerated its collapse, for the nawabs became virtually independent in their own provinces, giving only nominal allegiance to the puppet emperors who succeeded Aurangzeb at Delhi.

By the mid-eighteenth century the Mughal Empire had completely disintegrated. A group of rebellious Hindus, the Marathas, had conquered the whole central third of India and set up a new Hindu empire there. Mysore to the south and the Rajput States to the north also became independent Hindu principalities under their own rajahs. An aggressive Persian ruler had conquered the northwestern provinces of the Mughal Empire and stolen the Emperor's bejeweled Peacock Throne from his palace in Delhi. (If he could have dismantled the Taj Mahal, he would have taken that too.) Soon thereafter these provinces became the nucleus

*See pp. 112–113.

of an Afghan Empire. In the south the Nizam controlled only the state of Hyderabad; in the north the Mughal empire was restricted to a state of comparable size around Delhi. Along most of the eastern coast Muslim nawabs ruled as independent princes; the two main states there were Carnatic in the south and Bengal in the north.

This vast, politically disunited subcontinent was the India in which British and French adventurers sought to extend their power beginning in the 1740s. Until then the European trading companies had remained aloof from India's internal politics. The Portuguese had lost all their trading settlements except Goa and two other tiny enclaves. In the seventeenth century the English and French companies had acquired footholds at Pondicherry (French) and Madras (English) in Carnatic and at Chandernagore (French) and Calcutta (English) in Bengal. The English also worked out of Bombay on the west coast. In all instances European trade was at the mercy of the local princes. Yet this trade had increased enormously during the eighteenth century, and with little open conflict among the Europeans. Then, soon after war broke out between England and France in 1744, the East India Companies of these countries became involved in a life and death struggle for power in eastern India. The two principal leaders in this struggle were the Marquis Joseph François Dupleix (1697–1763), and Robert Clive (1725–1774).

### Dupleix and Clive

Dupleix was the first of the new imperialists in India. Though born a nobleman, he became a renegade to his class and an adventurer. As governor-general of the French East India Company (1741–1754) he began his intervention in Indian political affairs for commercial reasons and for private gain. Only gradually did he begin to dream of a French empire in India, but when he did, his fertile imagination and boundless ambition showed him the way. First he tried to get his own candidates recognized as Nizam and as nawab of Carnatic. His purpose was to make these puppet rulers grant him part of the revenues of their states. He did this because his company's resources were inadequate for his purposes, and he asked for no money from the government in Paris. Since France could spare him only a few thousand recruits and a handful of officers, Dupleix supplemented his military forces with European-trained Indian troops called *sepoys*. With these techniques he extended his control over southeastern India.

Dupleix's fatal mistake was his underestimation of the power and the resolute opposition of the English. If he had had only the Indian princes to contend with, he might have consolidated his rule in southeastern India. But the English opposed him there in the early 1750s even though they were officially at peace with France. The French government did not give Dupleix the money or military resources to compete with the larger English army and navy, and it forced him to return to France in 1754, where he died in poverty and disgrace nine years later. The English, not the French, were to build an empire in India, and England's first empire-builder was also an adventurer, very much like Dupleix.

Robert Clive was a soldier and an officer in the British East India Company. Dazzled by Dupleix's successes, he tried to follow his example. He won several native rulers away from the French with bigger and better promises, threats, and intrigues. And he got more military and naval support from his home government than did Dupleix.

Clive founded the British Empire in India by taking over the rich and populous state of Bengal. The nawab of that territory was bitterly anti-British, and in 1756 he sent a large army against the English settlement in Calcutta. Many of the Europeans escaped before the attack, but the nawab captured 146 of them and packed them all into a prison cell called "The Black Hole." Only 23 of them survived until the next morning, the rest having died from suffocation. Outraged by this atrocity Clive resolved to capture Calcutta. After he had succeeded in doing this, he decided to dethrone the nawab. At the Battle of Plassey (1757) Clive's forces won an easy military victory over the nawab and replaced him with a puppet. Henceforth, the British were the real rulers of all Bengal.

The Battle of Plassey was of supreme importance for the growth of British power in India. It was the first major European victory over an oriental potentate on his own soil. Not only did it establish British supremacy in northeastern India, it virtually settled the outcome of the struggle with the French. For it was from his secure base in Bengal that Clive launched his first attack on the French holdings along the southeast coast. Naval support from England and the inflexibility of the new French commander at Pondicherry also helped insure the British victory there in 1761. So did an Afghan raid in the northwest, which temporarily weakened the Marathas and gave Clive time to consolidate his power in Bengal.

After 1761 the French position in India rapidly declined. According to the terms of the Treaty of Paris (1763) Pondicherry and the other French trading posts were restored; they could still carry on trade, but could have no military forces. A few years later the French government dissolved the Company founded by Colbert and took over its moribund trading posts. In India, as in North America, the British had won a decisive victory in their struggle for world supremacy.

### *Early British Rule*

It took a while before the British learned how to administer their budding empire in India. As governor of Madras and then of Bengal, Clive tried to reduce corruption in the East India Company while at the same time enriching himself. In 1767 he returned to England as a "nabob"—a nickname for Englishmen who became wealthy in India—and became a member of Parliament. But the problem of governing Britain's possessions in India remained a difficult one as long as the East India Company had the final authority in all dealings with the nominally independent native rulers it controlled.

In 1772 the Company made Warren Hastings (1732–1818) virtual dictator of Bengal, a role he played effectively and ruthlessly for the next dozen years. Back in London, however, Englishmen were outraged by parliamentary reports on the corruption in the East India Company and its exploitation of the natives. (Clive himself was impeached, though never convicted.) The British government decided that Britain's possessions in India should have a centralized administration over which it should have some control. To this end it passed the Regulating Act of 1773. Hastings now became governor-general of Bengal, with other governors under him. In his dual role as head of the East India Company and Britain's top official in India he used high-handed means to enhance the British position and to reap profits for his company. He made the natives hate British rule, despite his reforms in taxation and coinage. At the same time he waged wars against several independent potentates and brought more territories in eastern India under British control.

Although Warren Hastings laid the real foundations of Britain's rule in India, the British government wanted more control over what went on there. In 1784 it passed the India Act in order to achieve this goal. The East India Company was still allowed to exploit India economically and to have a voice in choosing Britain's top-ranking officials there. But the Crown was to appoint the governor-general and supervise civil and military administration through a Board of Control. This clumsy "double government system" was to last for almost three-fourths of a century.* Hastings himself was impeached for his "crimes" in India. He was ultimately acquitted, but his impeachment, along with Clive's, showed that the British government had found a new imperial role for itself in India immediately following the great European wars of the mid-eighteenth century.

## Diplomatic Consequences

Although we have neglected the wars of the mid-eighteenth century in Central and Eastern Europe because both Great Britain and France subordinated them to their overseas interests, these wars had important consequences for the international position of the two Western powers. As we have seen, they had tried to use

*See Chapter XV.

the two main German powers—Prussia and Austria—to keep part of each other's forces deadlocked on the continent. The French had got more involved there than the British, but in 1763 both had to make concessions to each other in the interests of their Central European allies. Great Britain allowed France to keep her West Indian islands in order to get more favorable peace terms for Prussia. France agreed to restore the territory of Great Britain's lesser German allies—Hanover, Hesse, and Brunswick—in order to salvage some of Austria's influence in Central Europe (Prussia agreed to vote for the Hapsburg archduke as the next Holy Roman Emperor). In effect, the powers of Central and Eastern Europe had emerged as the masters of their won affairs by 1763. During the next generation neither France nor Great Britain had much influence on what happened in that part of the world.

This temporary decline in British and French influence on the continent had its repercussions on the continuing struggle between the two Western powers for world supremacy. Great Britain may have won Canada and India in Germany during the Seven Years' War, but she was to lose the Thirteen Colonies not only at Yorktown, but also in Europe, for she had no friends left there after 1763. France was unable to do anything about the spectacular Russian conquests in Eastern Europe in the 1770s and 1780s. But by purchasing Corsica from Genoa in 1768 she prevented Great Britain from acquiring a strategic position near her southern coast. And she was to get her real revenge by helping the American colonists detach themselves forever from the British Empire.

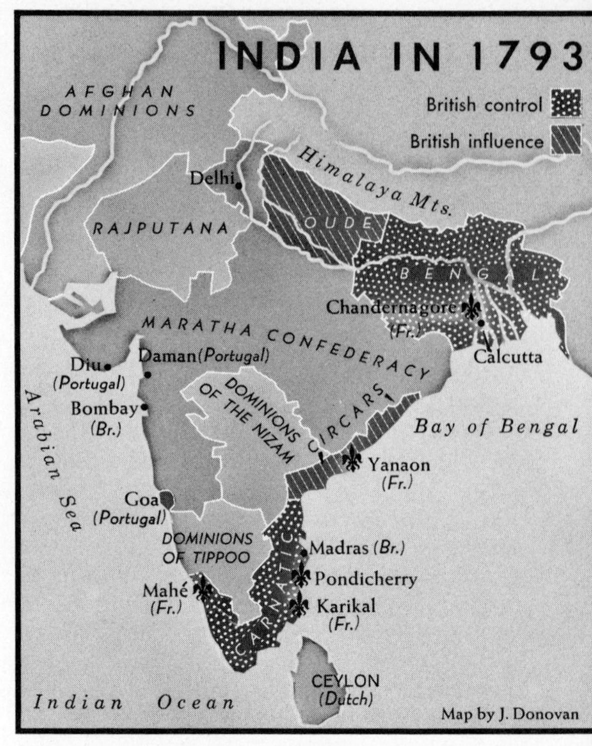


: : :

Great Britain and France remained supreme in wealth, in technical and scientific development, and in social and political organization, despite the rise of great military powers in Central and Eastern Europe. The defeats of the Seven Years' War had shaken the prestige of the French monarchy, but its collapse was still a generation away. France's foreign trade increased at a higher rate than ever before, and as we shall see in Chapter VIII, French science led the world in the second half of the eighteenth century. The English political system was the envy of European liberals everywhere. It seemed to reconcile individual liberty with strong government and to insure social harmony among all the classes that really counted. The British had more capital and made more productive use of it than anyone else, and British inventors were already launching the Industrial Revolution.

In their struggle for wealth and empire the British and the French had an enormous superiority over non-Europeans in the eighteenth century. This superiority consisted not only in materiel and in military tactics, but also in discipline and training, which seemed to make the European a type apart, cool-headed, energetic, tenacious, and brave—though also quite ruthless. In India, where the bravest fighters were subject to disastrous panics because of lack of discipline, one native potentate said to an English general, "What soldiers you have! Their line is like a brick wall. And when one falls another fills the breach. That's the kind of troops I would like to command!" This superiority earned the Europeans not only victories and subjects, but also allies and friends. It was one of the principal means of their penetration in all parts of the world and their march toward control of most of the world.

## SUGGESTED READINGS


Anderson, Matthew S., *The Eighteenth Century, 1718–1783.* New York: Oxford University Press, 1964.*
A very good survey in comparative history.

Roberts, Penfield, *The Quest for Security, 1715–1740.* New York: Harper and Row, 1963. Torchbook.*
Another volume in the Rise of Modern Europe series.

Dorn, Walter L., *Competition for Empire, 1740–1763.* New York: Harper and Row, 1963. Torchbook.*
One of the most original volumes in the Rise of Modern Europe series. Contradicts Nef's thesis concerning war and progress.

Clough, Shepard B., *The Economic Development of Western Civilization.* Chapters IX-XI.
See note on readings after table of contents.

Laslett, Peter, *The World We Have Lost.* New York: Scribner, n. d.*
Good on demographic, economic, and social patterns of pre-industrial England.

Ashton, Thomas S., *An Economic History of England: The Eighteenth Century.* New York: Barnes and Noble, 1955.
This scholarly study is especially useful on agricultural, manufacturing, and commercial techniques.

Goodwin, A., ed., *The European Nobility in the Eighteenth Century: Studies of the Nobilities of the Major European States in the Pre-Reform Era.* New York: Harper-Row, 1966.* Torchbook.
Excellent comparative study.

Plumb, J. H., *England in the Eighteenth Century.* Baltimore: Penguin Books, 1950. Pelican.*
Excellent survey.

Plumb, J. H., *Chatham.* London: Collins, 1953.
An authoritative biography of the elder Pitt.

Ford, Franklin L., *Robe and Sword: The Regrouping of the French Aristocracy after Louis XIV.* New York: Harper Row, 1965.* Torchbook.
Scholarly study of the social and political resurgence of the French aristocracy in the period 1715–1750.

Mitford, Nancy, *Madame de Pompadour.* New York: Random House, 1954.
Popular biography—lively descriptions of court life under Louis XV.

Barber, Elinor, *The Bourgeoisie in Eighteenth-Century France.* Princeton, N.J.: Princeton Univ. Press, 1955.*
A sociological study showing the complexity and the contradictory attitudes of this "class."

Wright, L. B., *The Atlantic Frontier: Colonial American Civilization, 1607–1763.* Vol. III of the New American Nation Series, ed. Richard B. Morris and Henry S. Commager. Ithaca, N.Y.: Cornell Univ. Press, 1963.*
An authoritative survey.

Pares, Richard, *War and Trade in the West Indies, 1739–1763.* Oxford, Eng.: The Clarendon Press, 1936.
The standard scholarly work.

Priestly, Herbert I., *France Overseas through the Old Regime: A Study of European Expansion.* New York: Appleton-Century-Crofts, 1939.
A good survey.

Graham, Gerald S., *Empire of the North Atlantic: The Maritime Struggle for North America.* 2d. ed. Toronto: Univ. of Toronto Press, 1958.
The best summary.

Wilbur, Marguerite, *The East India Company and the British Empire in the Far East.* New York: R. R. Smith, 1945.
Covers political as well as economic development of the British empire in India.

*Paperback

CHAPTER VII

# CENTRAL AND EASTERN EUROPE IN THE EIGHTEENTH CENTURY

Success in war brought Austria, Prussia, and Russia into the European state system as major powers. All three adapted the most advanced military and administrative techniques of the West to their own needs, and, at one time or another, both France and Great Britain gave financial subsidies to Prussia and Austria. These three new powers more than made up for their economic and social backwardness with strong leadership. The most effective European rulers after 1713 were not Louis XV and XVI or the first three Georges; they were Peter I and Catherine II of Russia, Frederick William I and Frederick II of Prussia, and Maria Theresa of Austria.

Whereas Great Britain and France achieved their most important military successes overseas, Austria, Prussia, and Russia gained theirs at the expense of their weaker neighbors in Europe itself. The map on page 253 shows the political boundaries of Central and Eastern Europe in 1660 and 1795—*before* and *after* the developments described in this chapter. The most striking feature of the *after* is the complete disappearance of Poland, whose territories had been gobbled up by all three of her stronger neighbors. In addition, Sweden had lost her holdings in the Eastern Baltic to Russia, and Turkey had lost considerable territory to both Russia and Austria. There is still no state called Germany; but the fact that Prussia and Austria already control half of what still seems to be the Holy Roman Empire suggests that one of these two powers is soon going to take over the rest of it. The story of how Prussia finally did so in the 1860s will be told in Chapter XII.

The rise of new powers in Central and Eastern Europe in the 1740s changed the course of European history. For well over a hundred years thereafter, Austria, Prussia, Russia, Great Britain, and France constituted the "Big Five" in international relations. In the early twentieth century Austria ceased to be a power, but during the two World Wars Germany, having been unified under Prussian leadership, came close to dominating the entire European continent. And after World War II Russia, having been revitalized by Communism, gained a preponderant influence in East Central Europe and the Balkans. Since the origins of German and Russian power lay in the eighteenth century, we shall henceforth give as much attention to Central and Eastern Europe as to the West.

## CONTRASTS BETWEEN EAST AND WEST

The appearance of the so-called "Iron Curtain" in the late 1940s obscured the earlier meaning of the terms Central and Eastern Europe. For it ran straight through the heart of an area whose people had participated in the same civilization as their western neighbors since the Middle Ages—one has only to remember Hus, Luther, Dürer, Copernicus, Kepler, and Leibniz. This area, traditionally called Central Europe, comprised the Holy Roman Empire plus the western parts of Hungary and Poland. Its eastern and southeastern boundaries were roughly the dividing line between Latin and Orthodox Christendom; its northern, western, and southern boundaries were where people stopped speaking German. Today, West Germany, Switzerland, and Austria are west of the "Iron Curtain"; East Germany, Poland, Czechoslovakia, and Hungary are east of it. But, traditionally, Eastern Europe meant only the territories of the Russian and Ottoman empires as shown on the map of 1795.

Before going any further, therefore, we must try to understand what Central European meant in the eighteenth century—and continued to mean well into the twentieth. First, it meant people who spoke German, Czech, Magyar (Hungarian), and Polish. Second, Central Europe had inherited a number of common institutions and practices from medieval Catholic Christendom: the Holy Roman Empire, the feudal liberties of the landed aristocracy in Poland and Hungary, the rule of law, and the use of the German or Latin language for official purposes. Third, the great cities of Central Europe acquired their baroque façade and their unique tempo of life in the mid-eighteenth century. Until the 1930s Vienna, Prague, Budapest, Dresden, and Warsaw resembled one another more than any of them resembled London, Paris, or Moscow.

Yet, for all its historical uniqueness and the cultural ties of its educated classes with the West, Central Europe was divided in certain important respects by a line similar to the "Iron Curtain" after 1948. This line had no check points or border guards, and it did not represent the conscious effort of any state to isolate itself from its neighbors. It most resembled the kind of line that separates a rich district from a poor one in a large modern city. Even though it is invisible, one knows when one has crossed it by the way the people on the other side live and work and by their relations with one another and with the authorities.

Socially West Central Europe tended to resemble France and East Central Europe tended to resemble Russia in the eighteenth century. East of the invisible line the mass of peasants had sunk into a kind of serfdom in which they had to do forced labor for their lords on large estates. West of the line most peasants owed little or no forced labor and tilled small plots of land as tenants, sharecroppers, or, in some cases, as independent proprietors. Class barriers were more rigid in the East than in the West. There were the nobles at the top, the serfs at the bottom, and not much in the middle. The bourgeoisie, which was growing in size and influence in the West, became increasingly insignificant the further east one went.

The social backwardness of East Central and Eastern Europe reflected the economic and political backwardness of these areas. Some of the big landowners exchanged their agricultural and forest products for the luxury goods and services of Western Europe. Because the productivity of their unfree peasants was low, there was little economic growth at home. Cities like Vienna, Budapest, Warsaw, and Moscow were mainly administrative capitals rather than commerical centers. There were some merchants, to be sure, but they lacked the dynamism and the rational techniques of organization shown by their more numerous counterparts in the West. Prussia and Austria began to build up professional bureaucracies, but there were few bourgeois lawyers, magistrates, or statesmen to challenge the political authority of the big landowners in the East.

Although landowning aristocracies remained dominant in almost all of eighteenth-century Europe, there were important differences between those in the East and those in the West. The aris-

tocrats of England and Sweden leased most of their lands to tenant farmers over whom they had relatively little economic control, whereas Polish and Hungarian squires still personally supervised the running of their estates. Even the landlords' local political power in England was not as absolute and unchallengeable as in Hungary and Poland. French noblemen retained their hold on conservative and constitutionalist judicial courts and provincial estates, both of which limited the extension of state power. Such institutions lost their importance in Prussia in the early eighteenth century and had never really existed in Russia. The service nobilities created by the sovereigns of Russia and Prussia had little in common with either the classes that produced Walpole and Choiseul or the increasingly functionless aristocracies of Spain and Italy.

During most of the eighteenth century the states of western Germany—like Scandinavia, Switzerland, Italy, Spain, and Portugal—were the backwaters of Western Europe. Their ruling families provided marriage partners for European royalty everywhere; their writers, composers, and scholars produced many notable works. They stagnated politically, but at least they were ruled by kings and aristocrats who spoke their own language. In East Central and Eastern Europe the opposite situation prevailed, and political frontiers had little to do with national cultures.

## THE AUSTRIAN MONARCHY

The Austrian Monarchy comprised the dynastic lands of the Hapsburgs in Central Europe. We have seen how Maximilian I laid the administrative foundations of this "state" in the mid-sixteenth century* and how Ferdinand II tried to extend its power in Germany during the Thirty Years' War.† We also know that it included three main parts: the Crown lands of Austria, the Kingdom of Bohemia, and the Kingdom of Hungary—most of which was occupied by the Ottoman Turks between 1526 and 1699. The eldest son of the reigning Archduke of Austria, King of Bohemia, and King of Hungary usually inherited all three titles from his father. This fact above all held the Austrian Monarchy together. But this assemblage of dynastic holdings did not become a state in the true sense until the mid-eighteenth century. And before it did, it almost disintegrated.

*See p. 109.
†See pp. 155–158.

## The Austrian Monarchy and the Holy Roman Empire

In his role as Holy Roman Emperor (a title all the reigning Hapsburgs held almost without interruption from 1438 to 1806), the head of the Austrian Monarchy controlled the formal institutions of the Empire and the lands within it—but only in principle. In practice the princes and free cities of the Empire had their own independent governments, and the head of the Monarchy had no control over them.

The formal institutions of the Empire were the Diet, the Imperial Chamber, and the Aulic Council. After 1663 the Diet met permanently at Regensburg in Bavaria. Although its nine Electors (Hanover became the ninth Electorate in 1692) chose each new Emperor, the "perpetual diet" was a completely ineffectual legislature—"a bladeless knife without a handle." After 1689 the Imperial Chamber met permanently in Wetzlar, which, like Regensburg, was outside the hereditary Hapsburg lands and hence outside the Emperor's control. Since the Aulic Council—the administrative "supreme court" of the Empire—met in Vienna, the Emperor had some control over it, but even this institution had no real political power. Its main function was to settle disputes among the princes and knights of the Empire over matters of protocol. Still, it gave the Hapsburg monarch in Vienna a degree of prestige that no other European ruler had. He remained *the* Emperor.

At the end of the seventeenth century only a few institutions were common to all three basic units of the Austrian Monarchy itself. These included the Court Chamber dealing with financial administration, the Secret Council competent in foreign affairs, and the Court War Council. Ferdinand I had extended the authority of these purely Austrian agencies to Bohemia and Hungary in the sixteenth century, and his successors had developed them further. In practice, however, a separate chancellery in Prague administered Bohemia, and the Hungarian diet safeguarded the autonomy of the Magyar landowners on their own seignorial estates. The Austrian Monarchy remained a fairly workable dynastic state by seventeenth-century standards, but it lacked a common army, common taxes and economic policies, and a unifying legal structure.

## The Complexity of the Hapsburg Lands

Nowhere did legal frontiers correspond less with ethnic communities than in the Austrian Monarchy. There were Czechs, Germans, and some Poles in the Kingdom of Bohemia. There were Magyars, Slovaks, and Croats in the sliver of Hungary held by the Hapsburgs until the 1690s. The rest of Hungary, which was reconquered from the Ottoman Turks at that time, included Rumanians, Ruthenians (Ukrainians), Germans, and Serbs. Finally, the Austrian Crown lands included Croats and Slovenes in their southeastern provinces. Nevertheless, in each of the Monarchy's major subdivisions one or two national groups held a dominating position: Austrian Germans and Croats in the ancestral Hapsburg lands, Austrian Germans and Czechs in Bohemia, and Magyars in Hungary. It was they alone, rather than the ethnic minorities below them, who tried to maintain their independent historic political traditions in the face of Hapsburg efforts at centralization.

The man responsible for the military successes that transformed this loosely consolidated, multinational dynastic state into a great power was, appropriately enough, a non-Austrian: Prince Eugene of Savoy (1666–1736), an international aristocrat of French origin. He won spectacular victories over Austria's traditional enemies, France and the Ottoman Empire, an achievement all the more remarkable since these two states were again allied in the last two decades of the seventeenth century.* In the Treaty of Karlowitz (1699) the Turks permanently abandoned almost all of the vast medieval Kingdom of Hungary, which Emperor Leopold I (1658–1705) proceeded to incorporate into his hereditary lands. In the Treaty of Rastadt (1714) the Austrian Monarchy received Spain's Italian possessions and

*It will be recalled that Francis I had allied his country with the Turks against the Hapsburgs during the sixteenth century. See p. 114.

*Turkish cavalry in the late seventeenth century*

the Spanish Netherlands, both of which Louis XIV had fought for long and hard. Prince Eugene not only added considerable territory to the Austrian Monarchy, he also reformed the supply, equipment, training, and command of its standing army. He had made "Austria" a great military empire of twenty million people. Freed permanently from the Ottoman Turkish threat, it could now concentrate on consolidating its power in Central Europe.

But Austria had difficulty controlling its new Hungarian holdings. Soon after Prince Eugene took them from the Turks, a rebellion broke out against Hapsburg rule. Led by Prince Francis Rákóczy of Transylvania, a semi-independent principality in eastern Hungary, this revolt lasted from 1703 until 1711. It expressed the proud, stubborn resentment of the Magyar landlords against Hapsburg inroads on their traditional liberties. Under Turkish rule the Magyar landlords had had the same kind of political and religious independence as the German princes in the Holy Roman Empire. Now the Vienna government was denying them the right to be Protestants and to maintain their own armed forces. In addition, it had disregarded their diet in assuming the Hungarian crown and had given Austrian Germans large tracts of land in order to weaken Magyar control in the countryside.

Since the Magyar nobles and their retainers constituted almost 10 per cent of the population of Hungary, their revolt under Rákóczy may be considered an early form of modern nationalism. It was finally crushed in 1711. Rákóczy took refuge in Turkey, and the other rebels accepted Hapsburg rule after the Vienna government promised to respect the constitution that Emperor Leopold had granted them in 1689. Throughout the eighteenth century Hungary retained its own system of administration, dominated by the gentry and based on their county assemblies. In spite of the efforts of the government in Vienna, this class gained exemption from all taxation (1731) and strengthened its powers over its serfs. The Magyar nobles retained their independent and nationalistic spirit and were to challenge Austrian authority several times again in the eighteenth and nineteenth centuries.

After the crushing of the Hungarian revolt the Austrian Monarchy still faced the problem of how to keep its many dynastic lands under one ruler. The problem took on a particular urgency when it became clear that Emperor Charles VI (1711–1740) would have no male heir. In order to make certain that his daughter, Maria Theresa, would inherit all the Hapsburg lands Charles VI first issued the Pragmatic Sanction in 1713. Gradually, the diets of the Hapsburg lands signed this document; so did most of the rulers of Europe. It remained to be seen, however, whether all the signers would keep their word and respect the territorial integrity of the Austrian Monarchy.

Meanwhile Charles VI did little to strengthen the political power of the state whose unity the Pragmatic Sanction was supposed to preserve. Prince Eugene's improvements in the standing army survived, but they could not be consolidated without increased revenue. Charles VI tried to enrich the state by expanding its international trade. To this end he founded an East India Company at Ostend in his new Netherlands possessions (Belgium), but he had to abandon it a few years later in order to get the competing Atlantic powers, especially Great Britain, to sign the Pragmatic Sanction. He then developed the Adriatic port of Trieste, which was in the original Austrian Crown lands. During Charles' reign the Bohemian and Austrian lands lost most of their local nationalism, but Hungary retained hers, despite Charles' efforts to weaken it by mixing Germans and Serbs with the local population. Finally, Austria's wars against Spain, Turkey, and France left the treasury empty without producing any territorial gains. Charles VI died a mortified man in October 1740.

### Consolidation

Before the 23-year old Maria Theresa (1740–1780) had collected all the crowns she was supposed to inherit, the War of the Austrian Succession began. We shall discuss the details of this war later. Here we are interested in its effects on the consolidation of the Austrian state.

The first effect was to reinforce the special position of Hungary in the Austrian Monarchy. Within a year foreign armies overran all of the Hapsburg lands except Hungary and the eastern provinces of Austria. Maria Theresa's only hope was that, as Queen of Hungary, she could persuade the diet of that country to provide her with an army to recover what she had lost. The young queen made a dignified speech to the assembly of Hungarian aristocrats, declaring that she entrusted the fate of herself, her crown, and her newly born son Joseph to their valor and their loyalty. Stirred by feudal chivalry the assembled magnates could not resist the appeal of their distressed sovereign. They cheered when she showed them her baby and swore to defend her with their lives and their blood.

The Hungarian diet's gesture of support greatly strengthened Maria Theresa's international position. Other parts of her realm rallied to her cause, and Great Britain came to her aid as a means of distracting France's armies on the continent. By the end of the war (1748) the young Hapsburg heiress had recovered all her father's lands except the Bohemian province of Silesia, which Prussia kept.

After having retrieved most of the territories guaranteed by the Pragmatic Sanction Maria Theresa and her advisers set about strengthening the Austrian state. The war had taught them the need for a centralized administration to collect taxes and superintend the army and the police. The Belgian and Italian provinces, which were ruled by viceroys, and Hungary, with its separate administrative and legal systems, were largely left alone; most of Maria Theresa's reforms only applied to Austria and Bohemia. The administration of these lands was combined in a single chancellery in Vienna, where a central bureaucracy assessed and collected taxes without consulting the local diets and estates. The former feudal nobles also lost their control over the administration of justice. For the first time in their history the Austrian and Bohemian lands were given a unified judicial system, with judges trained in Roman law. Finally, Maria Theresa raised the technical efficiency of the army by founding a military academy, establishing regular camps, introducing maneuvers, and improving the living conditions of the officers and men.

Slowly and in a rather haphazard fashion Austria acquired a bureaucracy and a professional standing army staffed by aristocratic officers from all over the realm. Along with the Hapsburg dynasty itself, these institutions held the Austrian state together under Maria Theresa and afterward. She retained the loyalty of the leading Hungarian aristocrats by inviting them to live at her court, showering them with honors, and entrusting them with important diplomatic and military posts. Though administratively separate, Hungary remained loyal to the House of Hapsburg as long as her landowning gentry were given a free hand with their serfs and exemption from taxation. Elsewhere in the realm professional bureaucrats strengthened the authority of the central government in Vienna and gradually acquired an *esprit de corps* of their own. The officers in the Austrian army also acquired an organizational and psychological unity that was remarkable in view of their different national origins.

The Roman Catholic Church also served as a unifying force in the Austrian Monarchy. Over 80 per cent of the people in the realm belonged to it, and the Hapsburgs were notoriously devoted to its interests. The Jesuits had long since rooted out Protestantism in the Austrian Crown lands and in the eighteenth century were finishing the job in Bohemia.

Maria Theresa herself set an example of piety and family devotion for all her subjects. This plump, blond, rosy-cheeked matriarch was an eighteenth-century Queen Victoria. With her numerous children and her devoted husband, she seemed to personify Mother Austria. She set a high standard of respectability at her court and took a sober interest in religious and political affairs. She also did more than any ruler of her time to protect the serfs in her domains (except Hungary) from the arbitrary exactions of their landlords. But without her shrewd advisers she could never have created a strong central government for the realm.

While the territorial princes and nobles opposed Hapsburg centralization, the high court nobility favored it. After all, they had the privilege of serving the most exalted dynasty in Europe.* Moreover, all the highest offices of the state, the Church, and the army went to them. Whether they were Italian, Czech, Hungarian, Croatian, or Polish, they learned to speak German and became devoted to the Crown.

### Unity without a National Culture

In 1740 a German superstructure was still a possible basis for a political community in the Austrian Monarchy. Like most of Austria, about half of the Kingdom of Bohemia was German-speaking; the Bohemian province of Silesia had a large German majority, with a Polish minority in its rural areas; and hundreds of thou-

*Maria Theresa is sometimes referred to as an empress, but it was her husband, Francis I of Lorraine, who was Holy Roman Emperor from 1745 to 1765. Thus their son, who became Emperor Joseph II (1765–1790) did not have a Hapsburg father. Technically, the imperial house was now called Hapsburg-Lorraine.

*The Palace of Schönbrunn*

sands of Germans had also been settled in Hungary, Transylvania, and Croatia. Then the loss of Silesia in 1740 and the acquisition of Polish, Ruthenian, and Rumanian territory beginning in the 1770s† weakened the German superstructure. Henceforth, the Germans constituted no more than 25 per cent of the total population.

Thus, the Austrian Monarchy was not a German community. It was a dynastic state held together by loyalty to the Hapsburgs, Roman Catholicism, the armed forces, the bureaucracy, and the court aristocracy. The fact that it successfully survived as a power in the wars of the mid-eighteenth century also strengthened it. Although the Hapsburgs were German, the language of administration was German, and everybody who counted throughout the realm spoke German—and often French, too, whatever his native language may have been, the non-German-speaking masses had no sense of political or cultural identification with their masters. As we have seen, the majority were unfree peasants. Their community was their own village or province; their culture was the local folk culture.

†See pp. 277–278.

Unlike Paris and London, Vienna did not produce a *national* high culture to be shared by all educated people outside the capital. Viennese culture was at once local and cosmopolitan. Half the repertoire at Vienna's great new theater consisted of Italian opera, the other half of broad popular farces in the Viennese dialect. Maria Theresa had her new Schönbrunn palace built according to a French plan, with Spanish and Italian embellishments. The members of the high court aristocracy had their sumptuous town houses constructed as close as possible to the fount of honor. Equally splendid, equally numerous, and equally late baroque were the churches built by the Jesuits. Artists, architects, musicians, and fashion designers from all of Western and Central Europe gave the Hapsburg court a unique style. The music of Mozart epitomized the aristocratic, cosmopolitan high culture of eighteenth-century Vienna.

Despite the dominant position of the court and the aristocracy, upper-middle-class bureaucrats began to make their influence felt. By 1776 a candidate for office in an Austrian provincial bureau had to have studied public finance at the university. Just below the top levels of administration, these educated civil servants were beginning to introduce the rational principles of organization of the West into Hapsburg government and to form the nucleus of an intellectually and politically conscious elite that was to have great significance for future developments.

By the late eighteenth century, then, the Austrian Monarchy had many sources of strength. Except for the Hungarians, its national minorities posed no threat to its political unity. As long as most of them remained encased in their local folk cultures the German-speaking elite was able to impose its will everywhere. The dynasty, the high aristocracy, the Church, the army, and the bureaucracy gave the state a unified superstructure and the ability to survive until the early twentieth century as one of Europe's five great powers.

## THE GROWTH OF PRUSSIA

At the beginning of the eighteenth century Prussia resembled the Austrian Monarchy in several ways. It was essentially a collection of diverse lands held together by obedience to a ruling dynasty—the House of Hohenzollern. It had a rigid social and economic structure dominated by large landowners and sustained by the inefficient labor of unfree peasants. The part of it that was inside the Holy Roman Empire had suffered the debilitating effects of the Thirty Years' War. The part of it that was outside the Empire (East Prussia) had only been freed from the overlordship of Poland in 1660—just as the bulk of Hungary was reconquered from Turkey in 1699.

There were also several important differences between Prussia and Austria in 1713. Prussia was much smaller in size and population, predominantly Protestant, and almost completely German in language and culture. But the most important difference was that the Hohenzollerns had gone considerably further than the Hapsburgs in transforming their dynastic lands into a modern state. The "Great Elector," Frederick William (1640–1688), laid the foundations upon which his grandson, King Frederick William I (1713–1740), was to transform Brandendurg-Prussia into a budding European power, which King Frederick II (1740–1786) was then to transform into a great one.

### Brandenburg-Prussia to 1713

The Hohenzollern dynastic inheritance comprised several territories scattered over northern Germany. Its nucleus was the margravate of Brandenburg, centered at Berlin and straddling the Elbe and Oder Rivers, which since the early fifteenth century had been an Electorate of the Holy Roman Empire. In the seventeenth century the Brandenburg branch of the Hohenzollern family began acquiring other lands. In 1614 it inherited the Rhineland Duchy of Cleves, and the counties of Mark and Ravensburg, also in western Germany. In 1618 it inherited the Duchy of Prussia (east Prussia), a fief of Poland on the southeast Baltic coast. At the Peace of Westphalia (1648) it added Farther Pomerania and the Archbishopric of Magdeburg to Brandenburg itself.

In the seventeenth century these three separate blocks of territory offered little prospect of developing into a strong unified state. The small western enclaves hardly counted, and Brandenburg and ducal Prussia were poor agrarian lands, sparsely populated and open to invasion from all sides. Each province had its own laws and customs and its own diet. The estates of these diets were dominated by the lesser nobility and the town corporations, which had become independent of their feudal superiors when money payments replaced older types of obligations at the end of the Middle Ages.

#### *The Great Elector*

The first Hohenzollern who tried to establish an effective central government over all these lands was the Great Elector. Seeing his territories weakened by the Thirty Years' War, he decided that the only way to maintain the interests of the dynasty was to have a standing army that could serve him in his scattered provinces without interference from their estates. These estates saw no necessity for such an army, especially if they had to pay for it, and they had no wish to get involved in

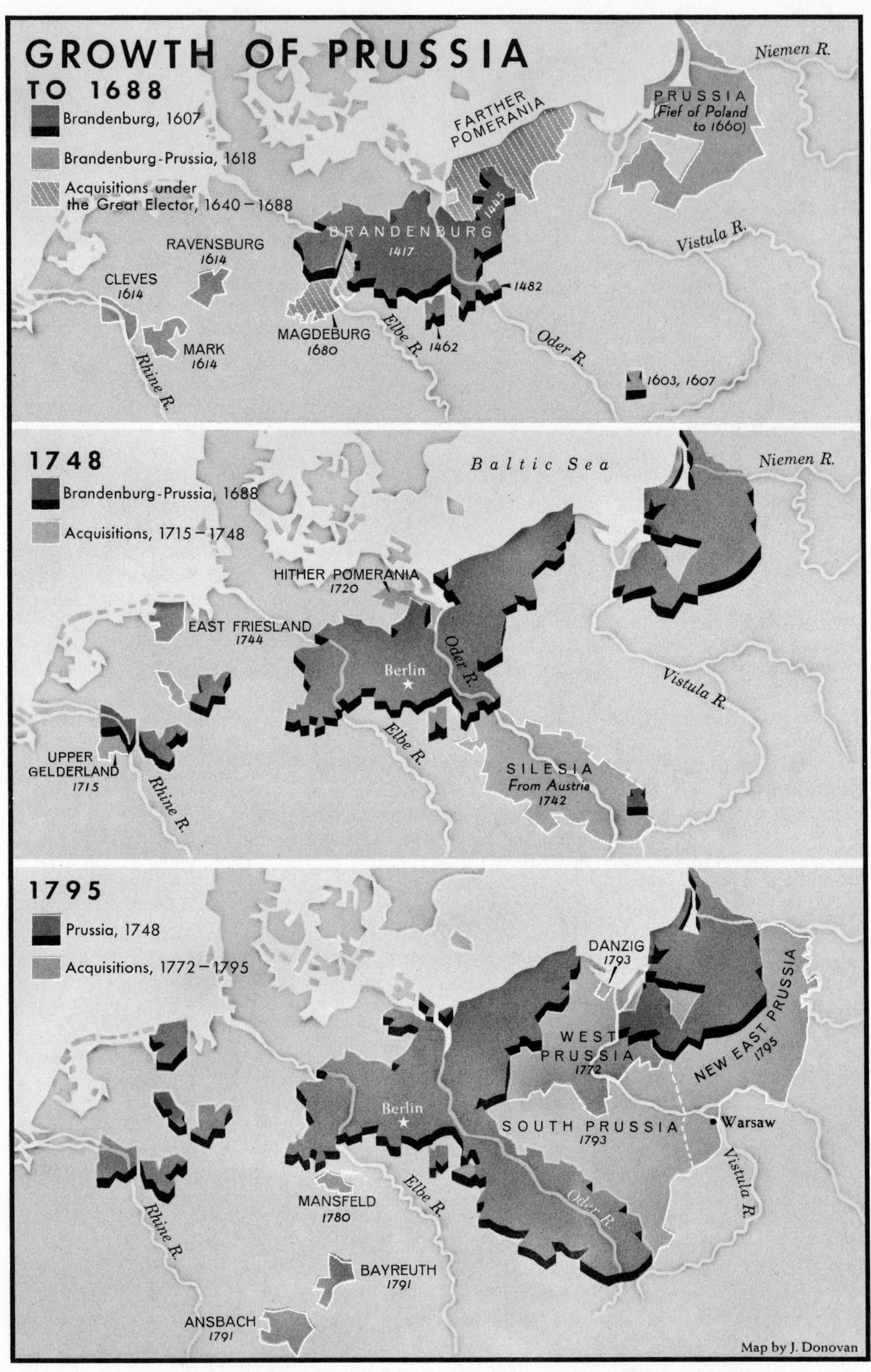
GROWTH OF PRUSSIA
TO 1688
Brandenburg, 1607
Brandenburg-Prussia, 1618
Acquisitions under the Great Elector, 1640–1688
FARTHER POMERANIA
PRUSSIA (Fief of Poland to 1660)
Niemen R.
BRANDENBURG
1417
1445
1482
1462
Vistula R.
RAVENSBURG 1614
CLEVES 1614
MARK 1614
MAGDEBURG 1680
Elbe R.
Oder R.
Rhine R.
1603, 1607
1748
Brandenburg-Prussia, 1688
Acquisitions, 1715–1748
Baltic Sea
Niemen R.
HITHER POMERANIA 1720
EAST FRIESLAND 1744
Berlin
Oder R.
Vistula R.
Elbe R.
UPPER GELDERLAND 1715
Rhine R.
SILESIA From Austria 1742
1795
Prussia, 1748
Acquisitions, 1772–1795
DANZIG 1793
WEST PRUSSIA 1772
NEW EAST PRUSSIA 1795
Berlin
SOUTH PRUSSIA 1793
Warsaw
Vistula R.
MANSFELD 1780
Elbe R.
Oder R.
Rhine R.
BAYREUTH 1791
ANSBACH 1791
Map by J. Donovan

the international disputes of the seventeenth century. But the Great Elector got his way. First he organized a new tax-collecting and police agency to manage his own extensive farm lands and increase his personal revenue. With this additional income he created a small standing army which was not organized by province, and which he used to browbeat the recalcitrant provincial diets into voting for a permanent tax, thus weakening their traditonal hold over him. Then he enlarged his army and sold its services to various foreign powers, thereby adding to his income and making himself more independent of the provincial estates.

Nevertheless, the Great Elector made significant concessions to the aristocracy. Like Louis XIV, he reduced its political influence over the central government, but, unlike Louis, he cemented a working alliance with its members, who were called *Junkers* in Prussia. The Great Elector confirmed the Junkers' absolute authority over their serfs and their political preponderance over the towns, a concession that tended to limit economic growth. He also encouraged the Junkers to serve the state, especially as army officers. Hence, unlike most other European monarchies, the Old Regime of the Hohenzollerns rested on the cooperation of the sovereign and the aristocracy, not on their mutual antagonism.

In the process of building up his army the Great Elector created the beginnings of a bureaucratic central government for all the Hohenzollern holdings. He did this by gradually extending estates to non-Crown lands and by building up a war commissariat to serve the needs of the army. In the countryside his private tax collectors and bailiffs gradually began to displace the older officials of the provincial diets. In the towns his commissaries watched over everything in the government interest, cooperated with the garrison commander, and tried to improve the local economy so that it would produce more revenue for the Crown. The Great Elector made no effort to coordinate the activities of his nascent bureaucracy, and competing jurisdictions survived until the beginning of the nineteenth century. Still, he made an important start in giving his bureaucrats a sense of loyalty to Brandenburg-Prussia as a state including all the Hohenzollern lands.

Getting people to adopt new loyalties was an extraordinary achievement anywhere in the seventeenth century, but especially in the backward and fragmented Hohenzollern lands. At that time loyalties to traditional groups—town, guild, province, estate—came first. The Great Elector began to alter this pattern by moving his civilian and military officials from place to place and by making them responsible to the central government wherever they went. A Pomeranian tax collector in East Prussia or the Rhineland thus lost his local allegiance and began to think of himself as a servant of an organization bigger than any town or province. Brandenburg-Prussia was the first state where the modern "organization man" appeared. Under the Great Elector's successors the type reached its most extreme form in the officers of the standing army, as we shall soon see.

The Great Elector also introduced the policy of mercantilism into the Hohenzollern lands. His private income, even when supplemented by foreign subsidies, was not large enough to support his army. In order to increase his revenue, he tried to develop his country economically, especially in manufacturing. His standing army provided a ready market for manufactured goods; but he had no ready supply of capital and skilled labor. Thus, in backward Brandenburg-Prussia, the government took the entrepreneurial initiative. The Great Elector lured foreign craftsmen and businessmen to his lands with all sorts of inducements, from moving expenses to tax exemptions. When Louis XIV revoked the Edict of Nantes, the Great Elector "imported" 20,000 French Huguenots. Their superior organizing techniques helped him to initiate and finance new industries, which his bureaucrats then supervised in many ways. Thus, the Hohenzollern state exercised a greater degree of control over its economy than those Western states where private capitalism was more advanced.

Elector Frederick III (1688–1713) did not equal his father's achievements in strengthening the Hohenzollern state, but he gave it a new formal status among the European powers. Just as the Great Elector had sold the services of his army to the King of Poland in return for the recognition of his sovereignty over ducal Prussia in 1660, so his son sold them to the Hapsburg Emperor for the title of King in Prussia in 1701. At first Elector Frederick III could not call himself King Frederick I *inside* the Holy Roman Empire,* but by the time he died, he was doing just that. Henceforth, the Kingdom of Prussia meant all the Hohenzollern lands, both inside and outside the Empire. But it still had only a million and a half people in 1713, when Frederick William I became king.

Frederick William I inherited a medium-sized German state, better organized, but no more populous and less advanced economically than Saxony, Bavaria, or Hanover. All these states maintained standing armies at home and resident ambassadors abroad. They too entered into alliances and wars with the great powers. The Elector of Saxony was also the King of Poland from 1697 to 1763; the Elector of Hanover was also the King of England after 1714; and from 1742 to 1745 the Elector of Bavaria was also the Holy Roman Emperor. In the early eighteenth century, then, the Elector of Brandenburg, who was also the King of Prussia, did not seem any stronger or any more important than these other German majesties. It was Frederick William I and his son Frederick II who made Prussia the main competitor of Austria for domination over all of Germany.

### Prussia's Rise to Power

Together Frederick William I and Frederick II did many things for Prussia which Louis XIV had done for France. The father strengthened the army and the political and economic power of the state; the son made himself a conquering hero. Like Louis XIV, Frederick William I brought the techniques of absolutism to their peak. Like Louis XIV, Frederick II exhausted his country in foreign wars, but he was luckier in these wars than Louis XIV had been in his. By the 1770s Frederick II had doubled Prussia's size and almost tripled its population. Thus, these two Prussian kings transformed their backward, scattered lands into a great power in little more than half a century. In doing so they created the most successful authoritarian society in Europe.

### *Frederick William I*

Frederick William I has been called the "garrison king" because he ruled the Prussian state the way a hard-drinking, cigar-smoking colonel ran an out-of-the-way garrison. He did not bother with the social graces expected of eighteenth-century sovereigns. His language and manners were coarse, he showed no gallantry to the ladies, and he preferred his slightly seedy uniform to the trappings of royalty. When the King of France wanted somebody to do something, he conveyed his message through a minister, who phrased it with all the polite forms appropriate to the rank of the person who was to receive it. Frederick William simply said: "Do this, that's an order!" He expected everyone in his realm to obey him without question. And he showed no respect for the traditional rights of institutions or individuals. His own son, the future Frederick II, ran away from home to escape his bullying. Frederick William himself worked long and hard for the good of the organization—the state. Why shouldn't everybody else?

The army was Frederick William's true love, and he made all his subjects serve it in one way or another. First, he required the younger sons of every noble family to take commissions in it. Second, he established a recruiting system for enlisted men by dividing the whole country into "cantons" of 5,000 households. Each canton had to provide replacements for a particular regiment stationed in or near the district. In addition, almost a thousand professional recruiting officers brought in conscripts from outside Prussia through the tactics described in Chapter VI. Third, Frederick William fostered production and internal colonization to meet the heavy

*The only king allowed within the Holy Roman Empire was the King of Bohemia, and since he was the same person as the Hapsburg Emperor, there was no possibility of conflict between two rival monarchs.

Frederick William I of Prussia reviewing his Potsdam guards

cost of his constantly expanding army—an army he loved so much that he never risked it in a war.

Within the army the garrison king had a special affection for the guards regiment of his palace at Potsdam, just outside Berlin. His only extravagance was buying tall men for this regiment. Even a six-footer (the minimum height) was worth from seven hundred to a thousand thalers at a time whan a common soldier earned only two-and-a-half thalers a month and a lieutenant only twelve. And Frederick William willingly paid much more for real giants.

Under Frederick William I the officer class of the Prussian army acquired a strong corporate spirit. At first many nobles opposed their forced militarization, but the king overcame their opposition by establishing a corps of cadets for the education of the Junkers, by making military service a criterion of social distinction, and by setting a personal example of devotion to the army and the state. Unlike France, where only a small minority of the 50,000 adult nobles habitually served as officers, in less populous Prussia nearly all the noble families had at least one son in the army. The Prussian officers' code stressed service, duty, and sacrifice as the supreme human virtues. An officer was promoted on the basis of merit; he could not buy his rank with money or family influence. His fellow officers saw to it that he obeyed the code and never shirked his duties. In a society where being an army officer came to be essential to a nobleman's dignity and status, one had no choice but to conform.

Frederick William I also strengthened the corporate spirit of the bureaucrats. They too came to look upon themselves as a closed group dedicated to the service of the state, and, as in Austria, those who came from the middle and upper-middle classes acquired special prestige in the social hierarchy. But in militaristic Prussia the bourgeois bureaucrats stood in awe of the aristocratic officer class and were never to develop any political or intellectual independence. Both Frederick William I and Frederick II showed little respect for their intelligence and limited their responsibilities to a minimum. The Prussian "organization man," whether army officer or civil servant, was supposed to carry out orders, not to take the initiative himself.

The Prussian bureaucracy became more centralized under Frederick William I. He combined the administration of the royal domains with the war commissariat into a General (Finance and Domains) Directory in Berlin. In the provinces, too, the bureaucrats of both groups now worked together in one service. The General Directory administered the whole kingdom, managed its finances with military needs as a primary concern, and supervised trade and industry in the interests of general economic prosperity. It had to find ever-increasing revenues to pay for itself and for the growing army.

Yet centralization did not eliminate conflicting jurisdictions. Each of the four ministers in Frederick William's General Directory was responsible for a whole complex of affairs in an assigned area and for a particular type of affairs in all areas. There was similar confusion of purpose all the way down the line. The king made the real decisions, and his bureaucrats had to decide who was to carry out his orders. Frederick II later complicated matters further by creating additional ministries alongside the existing ones. The system worked only when the king himself was energetic and efficient. Not until the early nineteenth century was the Prussian bureaucracy to become the kind of self-sustaining, smoothly functioning machine of which it has been the prototype ever since.

Frederick William I used his bureaucracy to enforce his mercantilist policies. Like his grandfather, he tried to foster new business enterprises in order to avoid buying manufactured products abroad. He also forbade the importation of foreign grains and the exportation of raw wool. But Prussia's native industries were still in their infancy and were hampered by the traditionalism and inefficiency of the guild system. Frederick William I therefore brought the guilds under strict state control. Private enterprise increased, though always under bureaucratic supervision, and the working man was controlled in a more impersonal way by the state than he had ever been in the old guilds. Like the Great Elector, Frederick William I encouraged immigration from abroad in order to strengthen his manpower resources. During his reign hundreds of thousands of soldiers, craftsmen, and peasants came to Prussia from other countries and settled there permanently.

When Frederick William I died in 1740 he had accomplished the first of Germany's modern "miracles." He had raised the population of Prussia from one-and-a-half to almost two-and-a-half millions; Berlin itself had 100,000. Frederick William had also created a centralized bureaucracy and increased the government's revenue to about seven million thalers a year—with a surplus of nearly eight million thalers packed away in casks in the cellars of the royal palace. He had transformed the bulk of the nobility into a dedicated military caste, brought the workers under state supervision, and forced the peasants to provide recruits for his army and pay about 40 per cent of their income in state taxes. He had installed habits of discipline and obedience into his subjects and made the state an armed camp. Finally, with the small population and still backward economy at his disposal, he had built up the fourth largest and best trained army in Europe. This was the army with which his son defied the great powers during the wars of the mid-eighteenth century.

### Frederick The Great

Frederick II differed from his father in every way except in his sense of duty to something greater than himself combined with a love of power. He was short and thin, with a sharp nose and cynical lips, a lover of the arts and philosophy, and a writer of talent—in French. His father feared that he would turn into a "little marquis," a foppish dilettante with no courage and no seriousness of purpose. How wrong he was! Frederick became one of the most impressive kings of modern times. He ran his country with as much dedication as his father and earned the title "the Great" as a result of his military and political achievements. We shall discuss his wars presently and touch on his role as an enlightened despot in the next chapter. Here we shall deal only with the way he used his domestic resources and foreign conquests to strengthen the power of the Prussian state.

Frederick continued his father's system of authoritarian government, but with more self-confidence, and a greater ability for sustained effort. He knew he was brilliant and he believed that anything he set his hand to, as well as his mind, would turn out better than if left to some subordinate. With grim humor he bore his immense burden of inspecting his kingdom each summer and his army each autumn. He insisted on reading and commenting on every dispatch from his ambassadors, every letter from his nobles, and every important petition and state document. Like all autocrats, however, he had to rely on the written reports of officials who preferred to tell him what he wanted to hear rather than unpleasant truths. He introduced new functional ministries for mining and forestry and a new tax-farming system directed by a staff of French officials. He even had one group of officials spy on another and report back to him. In short, Frederick tried to run the state almost by himself. He set a model of kingship that only a superman could follow successfully.

Frederick the Great's wars weakened Prussia economically, but this effect was only temporary. In the long run, the conquest of Silesia in the early 1740s more than paid for itself, adding almost two million people and rich natural resources to the national economy. Frederick did little to improve the lot of Prussia's peasants, but he forced them to grow—and eat—new crops like the potato and the sugar beet. In the early 1770s there would have been a danger of famine without the potato. In the end this humble tuber was more effective than all of Frederick's elaborate measures for controlling the grain trade. Frederick encouraged the domestic system of manufacturing under private entrepreneurs and started Berlin on the path toward industrialization in the production of silk and woollen textiles. As under his father, nearly two-thirds of the state revenue went to the support of the army. But under Frederick the improved national economy was able to sustain a peacetime army of almost 200,000 men, nearly 4 per cent of the population.

The one area of Prussian life in which Frederick made a pioneer effort was the administration of justice. His father had taken no interest in the legal rights of his subjects. Frederick II did. In 1746, with the help of the Prussian chief justice, Samuel von Cocceji, he set out to establish a single centralized judicial system, to weed out incompetent lawyers and judges, and to codify the law for the whole realm. Although the legal code was not completed until 1795, the first two goals were achieved within five years. The government continued to interfere in the administration of justice on matters affecting the "public interest." Still, the civil and criminal courts became independent, at least in theory. The ordinary citizen now had greatly increased security in his civil rights, especially with regard to property. Frederick's judicial reforms thus laid a firm basis for capitalistic development under private entrepreneurs. They also completed the process of consolidating the power of the state.

Prussia was the most secular state in all eighteenth-century Europe. Though a pious man himself, Frederick William I had sought to bring together as good citizens both the Lutheran majority and the Calvinist minority, which included his own family. He refused to allow the ministers of any religion to interfere in lay matters, thus breaking with the tradition of state churches in the small Lutheran states of Germany. Frederick the Great's conquests in Silesia and Poland* added almost two million Catholics to the king-

*See pp. 277–278.

dom, who, together with those in the small Rhenish provinces, constituted over a third of the total population. Frederick himself was a Deist, and he tolerated even Jews and Jesuits whose services might raise the economic and educational level of his realm.

Under the Old Regime no state was a true national community, but Prussia remained more divided socially and culturally than France or even Spain. As in these countries, social barriers remained rigid, and people of different classes were taxed and rewarded in unequal ways. In Prussia, however, the Junkers served the state as an exclusive millitary caste and prevented the king from abolishing the forced labor of their unfree peasants. Prussia's business and professional classes lacked initiative and did little to further the intellectual life of the country. The leading lights at Frederick the Great's court and at the Berlin Academy were mostly foreigners. Neither religion nor a native high culture gave Prussia a community spirit; the power of the state alone provided its unifying superstructure.

## THE EMERGENCE OF RUSSIA

The rise of Prussia was the most spectacular success story of the century. By sheer will Frederick William I created a disciplined, hard-working society of loyal subjects and a first-class army. By sheer audacity Frederick the Great comquered the rich province of Silesia. These two kings used the rational principles of organization of the West to convert a backward section of East Central Europe into a powerful modern state. We shall now see how two Russian rulers, Peter the Great and Catherine the Great, tried to transform their backward country into a great power along Western lines.

### Muscovite Russia in the Seventeenth Century

What was the situation in Russia when Peter the Great (1682–1725) tried to "westernize" her and make her a European power? In Chapter III we noted that the reign of Ivan IV (1547–1584) was followed by a virtual collapse of the Muscovite state. This "Time of Troubles" was marked by mass uprisings and Swedish and Polish invasions, as well as civil war among rival claimants to the throne of the tsars. Finally, in 1613, the Poles were driven out, and the *zemsky sobor*—an assembly that briefly played the role of medieval Western parliaments—placed a new dynasty, the *Romanovs*, on the throne. During the remainder of the seventeenth century the Romanov tsars consolidated their authority. (Like the Hohenzollerns and the Hapsburgs, their dynasty was to last until the early twentieth century.) These early Romanovs emerged as modern autocrats, despite their indolence and personal incapacity. They were able to do so mainly because they faced little organized opposition.

Muscovite Russia was not a political community. Unlike the English Parliament, the *zemsky sobor* never developed into an independent body capable of organizing community resistance to the will of the monarch. The classes that it represented harbored irreconcilable grievances against one another: the tax-paying merchants versus the tax-exempt nobility, the great merchant families of Moscow versus inferior commercial groups, the big landlords versus the provincial gentry. Ivan IV had done his work well in destroying most of the wealth and power of the hereditary nobles (*boyars*) and in creating a new service nobility loyal to the tsar. These service nobles (*dvoriane*) had no need for a representative assembly. They wielded administrative, military, judicial, and police power in the whole country and became the absolute masters over the peasants on their estates. They accepted the role of humble servants of the tsar, who, in turn, allowed them to extend and consolidate their control over the mass of the population. At court Tsar Alexis (1645–1676) imported all sorts of Western luxuries: gilded coaches, brass bands, German toys and clothes for his children. Some of his ministers began to think about modernizing the army and fostering trade, but no concerted effort toward "westernization" was made until Peter the Great.

Life in Muscovite Russia in the seventeenth century was a mixture of Byzantine and Tartar forms grafted onto old Rus-

*Russian noble dress in the seventeenth century*

sian customs. At court the tsar and his noblemen all wore long beards and dressed in long flowing robes with wide sleeves. Their women were kept veiled and housed in seclusion, like the wives of the Tartar princes. Among the noblemen superstition and rigorous adherence to protocol and rank were the prevalent basis for behavior. The small group of merchants and craftsmen in the towns remained as custom-bound and unenterprising as the rest of the population. In the 1660s the patriarch of the Russian Church tried to reform the liturgy and ritual, which had deviated from the Byzantine rite in centuries of isolation from Constantinople. But his efforts antagonized the masses, who felt that any change in the old ways—for example, making the sign of the cross with three fingers instead of two—was a sacrilege. In fact, a significant minority broke away from the official church, and thus weakened it.

Meanwhile Russia remained backward and poor. Part of the poverty of the peasant masses resulted from the low productivity of their agriculture; the harvest usually returned only two or three times the amount of seed sown. Russian peasants lived at a near-subsistence level constantly threatened by famines, which, as we have seen, were beginning to disappear in the West. Their monotonous fare was rye bread and cabbage, supplemented on special occasions by a little meat and salted fish. The usual drinks were mead (a fermented honey wine), kvas (a kind of warm beer), and, by the eighteenth century, vodka (a distilled spirit made from potatoes). The consumption of alcoholic beverages was directly related to the people's misery, and the Russian masses were to hold the record in Europe well into the twentieth century.

Impoverished by their own backwardness Russia's peasants became increasingly brutish and servile in their relations with the noble landowners. More and more of them sank to the level of serfs as they could not meet their obligations, which consisted either of rent in labor (*barshchina*) or rent in goods (*obrok*). By the beginning of the seventeenth century the *barshchina* took as much as half of the peasants' labor time. The *obrok* was eventually superseded, at the landlords' demand, by rent in money, which placed an even greater burden on the peasants. On top of this they had to pay taxes to the tsar's government. By the mid-seventeenth century an increasing number voluntarily became serfs—in effect, the private property of their masters—because serfs did not have to pay taxes.

The discontented masses did not always accept their lot without protest, especially those in Russia's southern and southwestern borderlands. Groups of fighting frontiersmen known as Cossacks tried to lead an independent existence in the vast plains of the Ukraine from the Dnieper to the Volga River. Led by Bogdan Khmelnitsky, those in the west rebelled against the nominal sovereignty of Poland and switched their allegiance to the Russian tsar in 1653. After Khmelnitsky's death Russia and Poland fought for control of the Ukraine, and in 1667 Russia annexed the territory east of the Dnieper River from Smolensk through Kiev and almost to the Black Sea Coast. It took a long time thereafter for the Moscow government to subdue the Dnieper Cossacks. Further east a Don Cossack named Stenka Razin led a revolt that assumed the proportion of a national uprising in 1670. Peasants began killing their landlords as far north as Moscow itself. The government put down these revolts and executed Razin, but he became a legendary hero among the Russian masses, and similar revolts were to be repeated in later centuries.

### Peter the Great

Such was the Russia that Peter the Great tried to organize into a European power. Like his ancestor Ivan IV, he was determined to make himself a supreme autocrat and to engage in foreign conquests. But whereas Ivan had fought against the weak and backward Tartars in the East and Southeast, Peter had to defeat the powerful and modern army of the Swedes in his effort to gain a short water route to Europe and Baltic bases for a navy. As some historians have said, he wanted a Window on the West. In order to succeed in this endeavor, he had to modernize his own army. This was the first motive for his so-called policy of westernization. The second motive was to create an efficient, loyal bureaucracy that would make his political power absolute. What Peter wanted from the West was the *techniques* that would give him a strong army and a strong government.

Peter himself was an impressive person. He was well over six feet tall and physically attractive, despite a slight nervous twitch. His energy was enormous, and his mind inquisitive. In many respects, however, he was the opposite of his older contemporary Louis XIV of France. He wore simple clothes, beat his courtiers with a club, and used foul language, and his other habits were also crude. To Western Europeans Peter seemed like an Asiatic potentate who had discovered technology and who tried to force his superstitious and benighted subjects to become engineers and mechanics overnight. Even as a boy Peter was fascinated by anything having to do with mechanics and construction. Shortly after becoming tsar he made a tour of Western Europe, where he was especially captivated by the shipbuilding techniques of the Dutch and the English. Peter then decided that Russia must strengthen her navy.

Peter's determination to make Russia a sea power involved him in a major war with Sweden. In 1696 he had already captured the Black Sea town of Azov from the Turks; in 1700, he attacked Sweden's East Baltic territories. Unfortunately, this first attack was a disaster, despite the fact that it was launched in alliance with Denmark and Poland.* His army was destroyed at the Battle of Narva in 1700 by the Swedish king, Charles XII. Luckily for Peter, however, Charles XII turned his attention against Poland instead of following up his victory over the Russians. During the next few years, Peter was able to remodel his army and build up his navy with the help of technicians and generals imported from Western Europe.

*See p. 273.

As we shall see, the war with Sweden dragged on until 1721, when Russia finally emerged victorious. She received all of the Swedish lands on the Baltic Sea from southern Finland to Poland, all inhabited by non-Russians. Spectacular celebrations attended by representatives from many European countries marked the final achievement of the long-sought and hard-earned victory. Peter had already begun the construction of a new capital called St. Petersburg, near the Baltic coast, his new Window on the West, and changed his title from "Tsar of all the Russias" to "Emperor of all the Russias."

Like most of Peter's celebrated reforms, the new town and the change of title were direct or indirect outgrowths of military needs. Because Peter's wars consumed tremendous amounts of money, he instituted tax reforms to increase the government's income. In order to levy and collect taxes more efficiently he took a census, which, by lumping peasants and serfs together, in effect degraded the peasants to serfdom. Peter also had to improve and enlarge his bureaucracy to carry out his tax reforms and to make educational reforms that would provide a supply of trained administrators. One reform led to another with no long-range planning; most of them were hastily improvised under wartime pressures. The only governing principle behind Peter's reforms was his conviction that every one of his subjects, from the highest noble to the lowest serf, should pay taxes and serve the state in some capacity.

Peter's determination that no one should escape state service weighed most heavily on the lower classes. Unattached free men were conscripted into the army, assigned to the estate of some landlord, or put into forced labor in state-owned forests and mines. By a new recruiting system, one youth for every seventy-five peasant households had to serve in the army for life. The census of 1718 created more male serfs and made them all liable for the new poll (head) tax. State peasants—those who worked the lands owned by the Crown—were technically free. As their very name indicates, they were in the service of the state, but their lives differed little from those of the serfs.

The middle and upper classes also felt Peter's harsh demands for state service. City people already constituted a separate legal class. Peter organized the craftsmen into associations and guilds and encouraged the wealthier merchants to found new industries. He even allowed these merchants to use serf labor—a practice the nobles resented and succeeded in abolishing after Peter's death. But he forced them to pay heavier taxes than ever and to submit to close government supervision. Even the nobles were all required to enlist in the service of the state for life. Peter abolished the titles and privileges of what remained of the old hereditary nobility. He tried to establish the principle that everyone, noble or commoner, should earn his rank by working up to it in some agency of the state.

In 1722 Peter set up a "Table of the Grades in All Ranks of Military, Civil, and Court Service." There were fourteen ranks altogether, and membership in the nobility came automatically to anyone who succeeded in rising into the top eight ranks. The very highest classifications conferred hereditary nobility on their holders, and the old service nobles retained their special privileges as long as they fulfilled their obligations to the state. Hating these obligations, they tried to evade them whenever possible. Nevertheless, Peter's Table of Ranks was his most lasting reform. It created an official class that kept the masses in check and served the state until the twentieth century.

Peter reorganized the state administration with names borrowed from the West (his government departments were called "colleges" and were supervised by a "Senate") and he tried to give his various provinces a uniform administration. These reforms did not work well, mainly because Russia lacked the trained and conscientious officials necessary to run a modern state. It takes years to create an efficient bureaucracy, and Peter died before the schools he founded for the purpose could produce the needed administrators. Indeed, of his schools, only his military and naval academies survived him, plus an Academy of Science. During the rest of the eighteenth century Russia's noblemen gradually evaded their obligations to the

*A contemporary caricature of one aspect of Peter's forced westernization*

state, and there were no middle-class lawyers, as in Western Europe, to take their place as administrators. Hence Russia remained badly governed.

The Church did not escape Peter's attention, either. In earlier centuries the Russian Orthodox Church had supported the tsar's government and grown rich. It had also dominated the intellectual and artistic life of the country, so that Russia had no national secular culture, like the countries of Western Europe. The level of religious art and thought never reached that of the Roman Catholic Church in the West, and the Russian Church sponsored few schools, hospitals, or charitable organizations. Millions of people still observed the formal ritual, but it had lost much of its spiritual force. Peter felt that whatever influence the Church still had over the masses should be placed directly in the service of the state. He abolished the office of patriarch and put a layman in charge of the newly created Holy Synod for Church Affairs. There was opposition to this plan, but it lasted until the twentieth century.

In his later years, Peter placed a new emphasis on Western cultural models, at least for his court nobles. His first step was to issue a translation of a German handbook on gentlemanly behavior (1717). Gentlemen would henceforth not pick their noses or clean their teeth with a knife, they would spit to one side and not in the midst of a group, they would doff their hats to acquaintances at three paces distance. Peter forced the noblemen to shave off their beards and to don wigs and Western-style clothing, and he even succeeded in forcing the noble ladies out of their accustomed seclusion and onto the dance floor.

For all his reforms, to what extent did Peter the Great really change Russia? His emphasis on Western culture was new, but it affected only a thin upper crust of Russian society and even there remained a parody of the real thing. Only gradually during the eighteenth century did the court and the higher nobles adopt the behavior and thought patterns of the West. The new names that Peter gave things simply reflected new forms for old relationships; Russia's class structure, political institutions, and economic practices remained basically unchanged. Still, like Frederick William I of Prussia, Peter did succeed in giving his realm a militaristic stamp. And, like Frederick the Great, he made his country a great power.

### Catherine the Great

Catherine II (1762 – 1796), a German princess, came to power in the last of the palace revolutions that had become the standard pattern of succession to the throne since the death of Peter the Great. Except during the reign of Peter's daughter Elizabeth (1741 – 1762), the succession had been frequently upset by the noblemen in the palace guards. Partly as a result, the emperors and empresses of this period had neglected the needs of the people in favor of the nobility, especially those in the palace guards. They needed the guards' support against rival claimants to the throne and in order to get it they had considerably reduced the nobles' obligations for state service. Then Peter III, Catherine's husband, dramatically released them from these obligations altogether.

Peter III's gesture should have ensured the nobles' loyalty to him, but he antagonized those in the guards regiments by forcing them to wear Prussian uniforms and by threatening to use them in his own private war against Denmark.* Catherine, who was determined to rule alone, took quick advantage of their discontent. She won their backing and with it overthrew the emperor. After deposing her husband and recognizing her as empress, her zealous backers killed the unfortunate Peter III. As in so many other cases (Queen Elizabeth I and Mary Stuart, Emperor Ferdinand II and Wallenstein) the monarch disowned the assassins who had eliminated a major threat to her authority. But, since Catherine had no legal claim to the throne and was utterly dependent on the nobility, their triumph seemed to be complete.

Why, then, did eighteenth-century Russia not develop into an aristocratic state like England or Hungary instead of the bureaucratic autocracy it remained? One reason was the change in the composition of the guards' regiments; the nobles, "emancipated" by Peter III, were now willing to serve only as officers, and it became necessary to recruit the rank and file from the lower strata of society. Furthermore, the Russian nobles did not have the class-consciousness of Western European aristocrats. They had become more genuinely "cultured" since Peter the Great's time, but they lacked the feudal traditions of their English and Hungarian counterparts, and in the eighteenth century they had no parliament or diet through which to express their class interests. The Russian nobility also still felt the need of a strong central government to repress frequent outbreaks of peasant discontent. As a result, it was impossible to transform Russia's basic power structure. The only real possibility was the traditional one of replacing the autocrat. Moreover, during the course of her reign Catherine restored the ancient bond between the sovereignty of the monarch and the power of the landlords over their serfs. The greatest mass uprising in Russia's history made this restoration possible.

*Peter III was also the Duke of Holstein and he wanted to add the neighboring Danish territory of Schleswig to it.

This revolt began in 1773 among the Cossacks of the Ural region and was led by Emilian Pugachev, who claimed to be the supposedly dead Peter III. Within a year it turned into a fierce peasant uprising against the landlords. Pugachev moved up the Volga and was enthroned at Kazan. In 1774 his forces threatened an advance on Moscow itself. Only the imperial army was able to stamp out this rebellion. Pugachev himself was finally captured and publicly quartered in Moscow's Red Square in 1775. A byproduct of his defeat was the permanent subordination of all the Cossacks to the central government.

Catherine and the nobles had had a real scare. Both parties agreed that the nobles should be given absolute authority in the provinces in order to suppress future peasant revolts before they got out of hand. Catherine did not create an efficient professional bureaucracy at the national level. But she did succeed in maintaining her own power over all her subjects by frankly recognizing the position of the nobility as a specially privileged ruling class at the local level in her Charter to the Nobility of 1785. This Charter also implicitly recognized the peasants' status as chattel slaves with no legal rights against their landlords. Catherine gave the nobles everything they wanted, including freedom from obligations to the state, complete control of local government, and the right to buy and sell serfs, thus separating serfs from their families and detaching them from the land.

Catherine was an intelligent and forceful woman. She corresponded with the most brilliant writers of Western Europe, had many lovers, and tried to create an image of herself as an enlightened despot.* Her armies added hundreds of thousands of square miles and several million non-Russian people to the Russian Empire.† Yet, aside from further enslaving the Russian masses, she changed Russia even less than Peter the Great had done.

*See p. 319.
†See pp. 277–278.

#### Russia's Backwardness

Perhaps the best way to see what Russia was like in the eighteenth century is to compare it with Western Europe. First, Russia lacked the rational principles of organization in government and economic behavior which had been given to Western Europe by three groups of people: (1) capitalist businessmen, generals, engineers, and administrators; (2) bourgeois lawyers; and (3) political philosophers. Peter the Great tried to copy the organizing principles of the first group, and Catherine the Great paid lip service to the ideas of the third. Both rulers failed. They failed because these principles and ideas, and the techniques necessary for implementing them, were not native to Russia. Russia had not experienced the great forward-moving developments of Western Europe: the Renaissance, the rise of capitalism, the Reformation, and the development of modern science. Nor did any of its people develop the spirit of individualism and free inquiry—much less the rational principles of organization—that these movements stimulated.

These principles cannot be imposed on a poor, backward people by a mere government decree. Some dynamic minority—some aristocracy in the true sense of the word—must set the example and give the other people an incentive to follow it. In Russia there was no such dynamic minority, and even if there had been, it could not have budged the enslaved masses. For what incentive could make slaves work harder and more efficiently?

In Russia there were two basic groups of people, the nobility and the peasants, living in two different worlds. Aside from a few high churchmen, who had no influence in public life, the nobles were the only educated Russians, the only candidates for the dynamic minority. But they were amateurs in everything they did—except in military affairs, where they managed to keep Russia's army on a par with those of the rest of Europe. They owned much of the land, but took little interest in increasing its productivity. They held all the important government posts, but they did not run the country efficiently. With isolated exceptions, there was little creativity in thought, the arts, science, or technology. In these fields the Russian upper classes simply borrowed from the West as dilettantes. They could not and would not reorganize Russian life in a rational way and they would not abandon their artibrary and often brutal control over their serfs. Instead, they devoted their energies and imagination to outdoing their aristocratic Western European teachers in extravagant and irresponsible living. They spoke French (the international language of the cosmopolitan eighteenth-century aristocracy); they built lavish palaces in St. Petersburg; they had as little to do as possible with their estates and the miserable wretches whose forced labor provided them with their income. The rural masses, on the other hand, lived in abject poverty and ignorance and preserved their ancient folk cultures as best they could.

For all the Western European trimmings of its empress and its noblemen, Russia still resembled an Asiatic despotism. A small minority was rich and powerful; the masses were poor and ignorant. By the end of the eighteenth century England, France, and Spain were *national* states—though still not national communities—of free peoples. Russia was a multinational empire with over half its population enslaved.

### THE WARS IN NORTHERN AND CENTRAL EUROPE TO 1763

War brought more changes in the history of eighteenth-century Europe than any other activity or policy. At the beginning of the century it had prevented France from upsetting the balance of power in the Netherlands, the Rhineland, and Spain and had recovered Hungary from the Turks. Later on it substituted Spanish for Austrian influence in southern Italy and made Lorraine a French province. War endowed Great Britain with a great colonial empire and almost unlimited opportunities for further expansion. Large standing armies and navies created the first mass market for goods and services; and the need to create powerful fighting forces in backward economies forced the rulers of Prussia and Russia to

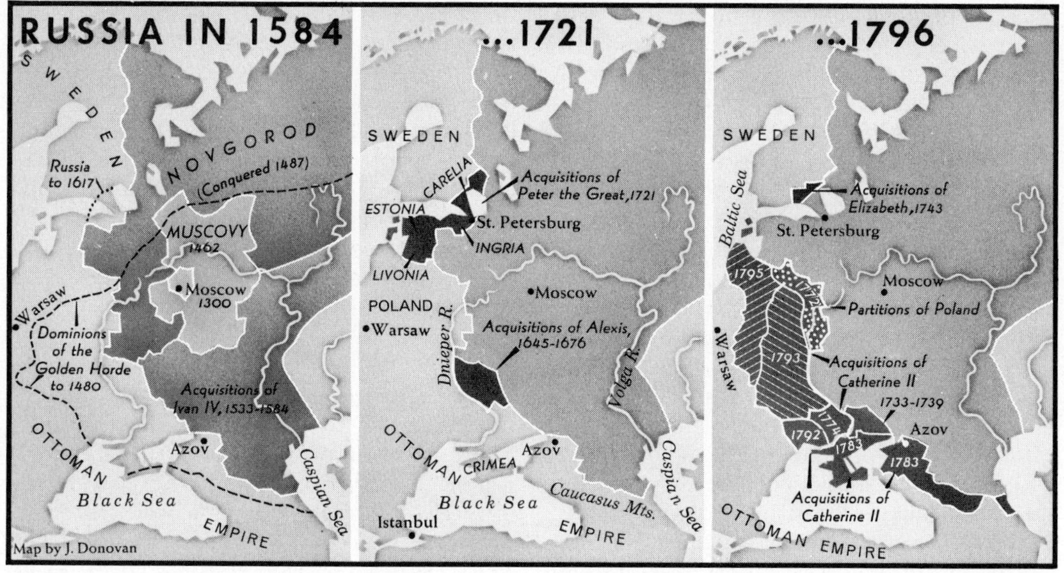


impose an unprecedented degree of militarization on their subjects.

For Europe as a whole the growing power of Russia, Prussia, and Austria was even more important than the duel between Great Britain and France for overseas empire. The Great Northern War (1700–1721) gave Russia the status of a great power and seriously reduced the influence of Sweden in the Baltic. The War of the Austrian Succession (1740–1748), the diplomatic revolution, and the Seven Years' War (1756–1763) made Prussia a major competitor of Austria for control of Germany and further enhanced Russia's international position. All three powers took part in the partitions of Poland (1772, 1793, 1795), which wiped that ancient kingdom completely off the map. Finally, Russia's conquest of large tracts of Turkish territory (1774, 1792) made her a Black Sea power and accelerated the Ottoman Empire's decline.

### The Great Northern War

When Charles XII (1697–1718) came to the Swedish throne, at the age of 15, Russia, under Peter the Great, was challenging Sweden's supremacy in the Baltic region. Meanwhile, Augustus II, Elector of Saxony and King of Poland, wanted to reconquer Livonia; the King of Denmark, Scania. These three rulers formed a secret alliance against Charles XII and launched the Great Northern War in 1700. Within a few months Charles forced the Danes to make peace and also defeated the Russians at Narva. During the next seven years he drove Augustus II out of Poland, overran Saxony and Silesia, and set himself up briefly as the master of Central and Eastern Europe.

But Charles XII's brilliant exploits could not be sustained. His home base, Sweden proper, had only a million-and-a-half people and meager resources. The rest of his possessions—Finland, Carelia, Ingria, Livonia, and Nearer Pomerania—were poor and unreliable. His hold on Poland through a puppet king was precarious, and he had no real allies. Louis XIV, who wanted Charles to attack Austria, was in no position to help him against his main enemy, Russia. Charles got as far as he did because of his superior generalship and army, but his battles cost him tens of thousands of casualties, and he eventually ran out of trained replacements.

The decisive turning point came in 1709 at the Battle of Poltava, in the plains of southwestern Russia. Peter the Great lured the Swedes far into the Russian interior, exhausted them, and risked a pitched battle only when he had "six Russians to play off against one Swede, with time, space, and hunger, for allies." By the spring of 1709 the Swedish invasion force had been reduced from 44,000 to 18,000 men. Peter had transported the last year's grain harvest to the fortress of Poltava, and Charles knew that he had to seize it to keep his troops from dying of hunger. For almost two months he besieged the fortress. Finally, on July 8, 70,000 Russian troops surrounded the decimated Swedish forces, killing thousands of them and driving the scattered remnants of Charles' once invincible army out of the country. Charles himself was wounded and barely escaped with his life. The Battle of Poltava completely reversed the political situation in Northern and Eastern Europe. Russia replaced Sweden as the dominant power there from then on, not only in the Baltic but in Poland as well.

Charles XII made valiant but futile efforts to revenge himself against Peter the Great but by 1713 he was without allies and when he was killed in battle in 1718, the war was lost. The final settlement of the Great Northern War was written into the Treaty of Nystadt in 1721. Sweden lost all of Gustavus Adolphus's conquests in Germany, and she permanently ceded all her possessions from Finland to Courland to Peter the Great. Henceforth, Sweden (plus Finland) and Denmark plus Norway) were secondary powers of approximately equal strength. Although Russia interfered in the affairs of both countries periodically, the new equilibrium in Scandinavia and the Baltic remained unchanged for the remainder of the century.

## The Contest for Germany

Unlike the duel between Sweden and Russia in the Baltic region, the struggle between Prussia and Austria in Central Europe did not end in the clear-cut supremacy of the rising power over its older rival. In the War of the Austrian Succession Austria fought a combination of continental powers almost alone except for British help; in the Seven Years' War Prussia fought a combination of continental powers almost alone except for British help. The only major German territory that changed hands during these two wars was the Austrian province of Silesia, on the Oder River between Saxony and Poland. Prussia's acquisition of this rich and populous province made her a great power. Still, the Austrian Monarchy retained the rest of its ancestral holdings, and the struggle for supremacy in Germany was far from over at the end of these two wars.

### *The War of the Austrian Succession*

Although Frederick II of Prussia "started" the War of the Austrian Succession in 1740, a number of other rulers quickly joined him in trying to despoil Maria Theresa of territories whose integrity they had agreed to respect in the Pragmatic Sanction. Two months after Frederick's quick conquest of Silesia in April 1741, France signed an alliance with Prussia, which Bavaria and Saxony quickly joined. Spain too entered the conflict in the hope of conquering some Hapsburg possessions in Italy.

The War of the Austrian Succession was a typical example of eighteenth-century international relations. Like the war of the Spanish Succession forty years earlier, it involved dynastic claims, "reasons of state," sheer aggression, and the maintenance of the balance of power. As always, Great Britain aided the enemies of France, though in the 1740s this meant mainly Austria. But as each belligerent pursued its own goals the alliance against Austria gradually disintegrated. In the Treaty of Aix-la-Chapelle (1748), however, Maria Theresa recovered all her possessions except Silesia and some small Italian territories. Yet, like all eighteenth-century peace treaties, the Treaty of Aix-la-Chapelle did not settle the future of Central Europe any more than it laid to rest the conflict between Great Britain and France.

### *The Diplomatic Revolution*

Between the Treaty of Aix-la-Chapelle and the outbreak of the Seven Years' War a diplomatic revolution took shape; it was instigated by Prince Wenceslas Anton von Kaunitz (1711–1794), Maria Theresa's state chancellor, who had been planning a

reversal of the traditional alliance system as early as 1749. He wanted to bring France and Russia into a grand alliance that would leave Prussia isolated. But Kaunitz did not get his French alliance until the other three powers played into his hands.

Great Britain took the first step by signing a convention with Russia in September 1755. In return for a subsidy, Empress Elizabeth promised to attack Frederick II from the rear in case he should join France in an attack on Hanover (the English king's homeland). Frederick now faced the threat of a combined onslaught on him by Great Britain, Austria, and Russia. In January 1756 he escaped from this threat by signing his own convention with the English. This convention, by making Prussia, rather than Russia, the guarantor of Hanover, was supposed to exclude Germany from the Anglo-French war that had already broken out in North America.

The Anglo-Prussian convention at last persuaded the French that Kaunitz was right, that Austria and France should forget their ancient rivalry and work together against their now common enemies. The French reaction to this convention was somewhat irrational, because the neutralization of Germany, by forcing France to concentrate her energies on the colonial struggle with Great Britain, would have served her real interests. Although still unwilling to contemplate offensive action against Prussia, the French wished to punish Frederick for his scarcely concealed contempt for them. Hence, they signed a defensive alliance with Austria in May 1756. To seal the bargain, Maria Theresa gave her daughter Marie Antoinette in marriage to the heir-apparent to the French throne, the future Louis XVI. Kaunitz thought of everything. His diplomatic revolution was completed when Russia, also resentful of Frederick's *rapprochement* with Great Britian, finally joined the Franco-Austrian alliance at the end of the year.

### *The Seven Years' War*

Frederick the Great's fortunes rose and fell several times during the Seven Years' War (1756–1763). In November 1757 he won his greatest victory at Rossbach over Franco-Austrian forces twice the size of his own. Nevertheless, in the years 1758–1761 Prussia's military position steadily worsened. Frederick's salvation came in early 1762 as a result of the most unforeseen development of the war, the defection of Russia. Empress Elizabeth, in some ways a more inveterate enemy even than Maria Theresa, died on January 5. Peter III, her unstable successor, was a fanatical admirer of Frederick and he ordered an immediate armistice. With Russia out of the war and the British victory over the French almost complete, Maria Theresa could no longer hope to recover Silesia.

The Central European phase of the Seven Years's War ended in February 1763 with the signing of the Treaty of Hubertusburg. As in the Treaty of Aix-la-Chapelle fifteen years earlier, the magic phrase was *status quo ante bellum.* The relative positions of Prussia and Austria in Germany had not really changed since 1742. But a great deal else had changed. Great Britain and France had reversed their alliances with the German powers. The Treaty of Paris, which ended the Anglo-French phase of the Seven Years' War, gave Great Britain complete mastery in North America and India. And British concessions to defeated France in the West Indies gave Prussia more favorable terms than she could have expected on the basis of her own performance.

Ironically, the real victor of the Seven Years' War was Russia; in 1763 she was a stronger force than ever in European international relations. When Peter III's wife Catherine became empress she withdrew from the war entirely. For the moment she concentrated on consolidating her power at home; then she was ready to embark on her own program of expansion of Eastern Europe. Neither Prussia nor Austria had really won the Seven Years' War. Whereas they had to be satisfied with the *status quo ante bellum* in Germany until almost the end of the century, Russia took the lead in partitioning the vast territories of Poland and the Ottoman Empire.

## THE WARS IN EASTERN EUROPE AFTER 1763

At the beginning of the eighteenth century all of Eastern Europe was under the rule of Russia, Poland, and Turkey. In the past these three states had fought each other periodically without altering the basic equilibrium among them. All this changed with the emergence of Russia as a great power. After 1763 both Poland and Turkey lost considerable territory to her. Prussia and Austria shared in the partitions of Poland, which were to cause trouble among the three new powers until 1815. Austrian rivalry with Russia for control of Turkey's Balkan provinces opened the Near Eastern Question, which was to threaten the peace of Europe until 1914.

### The Dismemberment of Poland

Eighteenth-century Poland simply could not defend herself against her more powerful neighbors. Neither her elected king nor her diet had any real political authority.* The nobles jealously guarded their medieval liberties, by which they ruled their own bailiwicks without interference from the central government, and formed confederations for the purpose of waging war against the king. Since the 1660s any member of the diet could stop any positive action by casting a negative vote—a *liberum veto.* A state so constituted was the antithesis of a power. It could not maintain a large standing army, a bureaucracy, national law courts, or a national taxation system.

Indeed, there was little that was national about it. The Catholic Polish half of its population of eleven million was concentrated in the west. In the east lived the Orthodox Russian third of the population. The remaining sixth comprised Lutheran Germans, Lithuanians (divided among Catholics, Orthodox, and Lutherans), and Jews. Poland's cities were few and far between, and their bourgeois inhabitants were mainly Jews and Germans. About 72 per cent of the popula-

*See p. 109.

tion consisted of serfs dominated by 20–30,000 families of small nobles who in turn served as retainers for about twenty great landed families. This backward, caste-ridden, multinational hodge-podge was a landlord state *par excellence*.

Like their Hungarian counterparts, however, the Polish nobles developed a kind of national patriotism in the eighteenth century. In 1764 the Czartoryski family tried to initiate reforms that would strengthen their country in the face of the aggressive great powers. They succeeded in getting their relative, Stanislas Poniatowski, an ex-lover of Catherine II, elected king. With his cooperation they sought to bolster the royal power and abolish the *liberum veto*. Catherine felt duped; she rewarded all of her ex-lovers well, but she thought that a man who had been given a whole kingdom should have been more loyal to her interests. Seeking a pretext for establishing Russian influence in Poland, she decided to become the protectress of the Orthodox minority there. She sent an army into the kingdom and forced King Stanislas to grant his Orthodox subjects equal rights with Catholics. The infuriated Polish nobles formed the Confederation of Bar (1768) and fought Stanislas and the Russians for four years.

Since France supported the nobles, the Polish Question became an international issue. France had viewed Poland, Sweden, and Turkey as her traditional allies against the Hapsburgs and she wanted to preserve her influence in Eastern Europe against any new threat to the balance of power. Hence, she persuaded the Turks to declare war on Russia. With a Turkish War on her hands Catherine could not concentrate all her forces against Poland. Meanwhile, her victories against the Turks so alarmed the Austrians that they seriously considered declaring war on Russia. Frederick the Great feared that he too would be dragged into the conflict. Thus he took the diplomatic initiative and organized the First Partition of Poland in 1772.

This land grab illustrated perfectly the cynicism and hypocrisy of eighteenth-century rulers. "In the name of the Holy Trinity . . . and out of fear of the total disintegration of the Polish state" Maria Theresa annexed the privince of Galicia, with its two-and-one-half million inhabitants. She cried, but she considered Galicia just "compensation" for the loss of Silesia. Frederick took most of West Prussia with over half a million inhabitants, thereby filling in the gap between East Prussia and the main part of his kingdom. He did not cry; he felt that he was entitled to do what everyone else was doing. Catherine had to be content with a slice of eastern Lithuania, with 1,700,000 inhabitants.

### Catherine's Conquests in the South

Since Catherine's preoccupation with the Turks kept her from getting more of Poland in 1772, we must see what they were about in the eighteenth century. As we observed earlier, the Ottoman Empire had gone into a long internal decline after the death of Suleiman the Magnificent. Yet the Turks had continued to play an important role in international affairs and had shown a major burst of power when they besieged Vienna in 1683. Then they lost all of Hungary to the Hapsburgs in 1699 in the Treaty of Karlowitz. In the late 1730s Austria and Russia had both attacked the Ottoman Empire, but this time the Turks held their own. They were able to do so for two reasons. First, they had outside allies—France in the first half of the eighteenth century and Austria after 1768. Second, their influential Greek subjects tried to breathe some new life into the decrepit empire. Under Turkish rule the Greeks virtually monopolized the country's trade, held high administrative positions in its central government, and even ruled some of its provinces.* Knowing that conquest by foreigners would make them lose their advantageous position they did all they could to bolster Ottoman power. But they could not halt the military advance of Russia in the 1770s; they were manipulators, not soldiers.

Despite brilliant Russian victories, the domestic difficulties that led to the Pu-

*Phanariot Greeks (so called because they came from the Phanariot district of Constantinople) ruled Moldavia and Wallachia as *hospadors* and made the Greek language official in those Rumanian-speaking provinces.

gachev revolt forced Catherine to accept a compromise peace in 1774. According to the Treaty of Kuchuk Kainardji, Russia acquired the whole northern shore of the Black Sea and detached the Crimea from Turkish control. In the Danube Valley, however, she had to give up her conquests and allow Austria to annex the Ukranian-speaking province of Bukovina. The bulk of the Ottoman Empire still stood, but its territorial integrity was threatened by a provision in the treaty vaguely authorizing Russia to protect the Orthodox churches within its borders.

This provision of the Treaty of Kuchuk Kainardji thus opened a new era in European politics. Russia was to use it again and again as an excuse to interfere in Turkish affairs, taking another slice of territory each time. Although Austria had taken her share of Turkish land, she was soon to join France and Great Britain in defending the Ottoman Empire against Russian aggression. This happened after Catherine's second war against the Turks, 1787–1792.

Catherine was a determined imperialist. She had a "Greek Project" for partitioning all of Turkey's possessions in Europe. The area of present-day Rumania and Bessarabia was to become a Russian protectorate, while Greece, Macedonia, and Thrace were to be made into a restored Byzantine Empire with Catherine's second grandson (born in 1779 and significantly named Constantine) as its ruler in Constantinople. In the 1780s Austria made an alliance with Russia in return for "compensation" in Serbia and then deserted her new ally. The "Greek Project" came to naught when Russia again had to make a compromise peace with Turkey in 1792. Worried by Prussian activity in Poland, Catherine signed the Treaty of Jassy. This treaty confirmed all of Russia's conquests along the Black Sea, including the Crimea (annexed in 1783). Catherine pushed her country's border westward to the Dniester River, but she returned Moldavia and Bessarabia to Turkey.

#### Poland's Subsequent Partitions

Having accomplished this much in the south, Catherine again turned toward the west, that is, to Poland. There she was faced with a concerted effort of the Polish patriots to reform their kingdom. Led by Poniatowski they had put through a new constitution (in 1791), which made the monarchy hereditary, conferred the executive power on the king and a council of state, gave the legislative power to a diet of two chambers, and abolished the *liberum veto.* Preoccupied with the French Revolution Prussia and Austria accepted this change,* but Russia once again threw her armies into Poland. Prussia then followed her example, and in 1793 these two powers made the Second Partition of Poland. Russia took most of Lithuania and most of the Western Ukraine—three million people altogether. Prussia took Danzig and Thorn and the rest of western Poland—over one million people altogether. The new Polish constitution was annulled, and what was left of the Kingdom of Poland became virtually a Russian protectorate.

The Polish patriots made one last desperate stand before their country was wiped completely off the map. In 1794 Thaddeus Kosciuszko (1746–1817) led a national uprising against superior Russian and Prussian forces. But the uprising was crushed within a year, Kosciuszko was captured, and Warsaw was occupied. In 1795 the three "interested" powers brought about the Third Partition of Poland. Russia took what was left of Lithuania and the Ukraine—one million inhabitants. Prussia took what was left of northern Poland, including Warsaw—one million inhabitants. Austria took what was left of southwestern Poland, including Cracow—one million inhabitants.

All three of the "interested" powers had been "compensated." The Partitions of Poland had transformed contempt for the rights of states and peoples into a system.

⁝ ⁝ ⁝

The extent of Russia's backwardness was dramatized by the effect of her newly conquered territories on her internal development. As we have noted, the further east one went in Europe, the more back-

*See Chapter IX.

ward society became. The bulk of the territories annexed by Prussia and Austria in the eighteenth century were to the east, and hence more backward than the original realms; the bulk of territories that Russia annexed were to the west, and usually more advanced than the original realm. All three of the new great powers became multinational empires as a result of their eighteenth-century annexations, but the Russian Empire had the most trouble in assimilating its conquered minorities. Its Baltic provinces were almost entirely non-Russian; except for the immediate vicinity of the new capital at St. Petersburg they were inhabited by Estonians, Latvians, Lithuanians, and Germans. The Russian government generally allowed the German landlords to rule the Baltic area as they had done for centuries, at the same time using their superior military and administrative abilities for national purposes. It had greater difficulty absorbing the millions of Belorussians, Ukrainians, Lithuanians, Poles, and Jews it had taken from the old Kingdom of Poland. These troublesome minorities—especially the Poles and Jews*—were to make Russian governments increasingly intolerant and reactionary.

At the end of the eighteenth century Prussia and Austria also became reactionary in many respects. Austria had created the beginnings of a modern bureaucracy and judical system, but noble princes in Hungary and Galicia still ruled the local populations like semifeudal seignors. Prussia was the most tightly organized of the three eastern powers, but she had bitten off more than she could chew in Poland and was becoming complacent at home. The social structures of Russia, Austria, and Prussia remained rigid, and serfdom still prevailed. In foreign affairs the three eastern powers were also to become bulwarks of reaction for the next hundred years.

Despite their backwardness and their reactionary outlook, Austria, Prussia, and Russia were catching up with Great Britain and France in political and military organization and in their techniques of foreign policy. In the next chapter we shall see how some of their elites also tried to catch up culturally and socially. By the late eighteenth century Berlin, Vienna, and St. Petersburg had taken their places among the great capitals of Europe. Prussia and Austria had gone further than Russia in creating an efficient system of government. The only Russian institution that was up to Western standards was the army—the first product of Peter the Great's reforms. With this army Catherine the Great added more territory and people to her realm than any other ruler on the European continent. Declining British and French interest in Central and Eastern Europe after 1763 also opened the way for a new balance of power there.

*By 1795 the bulk of Europe's Jews lived in the Russian Empire.

By the late eighteenth century the modern European state system was fully developed. There were five great powers, each with a strong central government, a sizable military establishment, and a sophisticated diplomacy. The declining states on the periphery of Western Europe—Spain, Portugal, the Dutch Republic, Denmark, Sweden—managed to carry on an independent existence. But the days of the weaker states in Central and Eastern Europe were numbered. Poland disappeared completely from the map by 1795, and the Turks had been pushed back into the Balkans. The smaller states of Germany and Italy were already the playthings of the great powers, for power alone decided the relations between states in eighteenth-century Europe. Yet this political jungle was still a garden culturally, as we shall now see.

## SUGGESTED READINGS


Anderson, Matthew S., *The Eighteenth Century, 1718–1783.*
See comments in readings for Chapter VI.

Goodwin, A., ed., *The European Nobility in the Eighteenth Century: Studies of the Nobilities of the Major European States in the Pre-Reform Era.*
See comments in readings for Chapter VI.

Gooch, George P., *Maria Theresa and Other Studies.*
London and New York: Longmans, Green, 1951.
See especially the suggestive appraisal of Maria Theresa.

Carsten, Francis L., *The Origins of Prussia.* New York: Oxford Univ. Press, 1954.
Early history to the Great Elector.

Schevill, Ferdinand, *The Great Elector.* Chicago: Univ. of Chicago Press, 1947.
Good biography.

Ergang, Robert R., *The Potsdam Führer: Frederick William I, Father of Prussian Militarism.* New York: Columbia Univ. Press, 1941.
The only biography in English.

Gooch, G. P., *Frederick the Great: The Ruler, the Writer, the Man.* Hamden, Conn.: Shoe String Press, 1947.
Presents Frederick in a favorable light—draws heavily on his own words.

Lindsay, J. O., ed., *The Old Regime, 1713–1763.*
Vol. VII of *The New Cambridge Modern History.* Cambridge, Eng.: Cambridge Univ. Press, 1957.
The chapter by David B. Horn on the diplomatic revolution is outstanding.

Halecki, Oscar, *Borderlands of Western Civilization: A History of East-Central Europe.* New York: Ronald Press Co., 1952.
A general survey, See especially the sections on Poland and Hungary in the eighteenth century.

Sumner, B. H., *Peter the Great and the Emergence of Russia.* New York: The Macmillan Co., 1962. Collier Books.*
The best study in English.

Blum, Jerome, *Lord and Peasant in Russia from the Ninth to the Nineteenth Century.*
New York: Atheneum Publishers, 1962.*
See the sections on the seventeenth and eighteenth centuries.

Soloveytchik, George, *Potemkin: A Picture of Catherine's Russia.* London: T. Butterworths, 1938.
Delivers what the title promises.

Clarkson, Jesse, *A History of Russia.* New York: Random House, 1961.
An excellent textbook, very helpful for this chapter.

CHAPTER VII

# THE AGE OF ENLIGHTENMENT

In the eighteenth century many educated Europeans began thinking of themselves as the most civilized people the world had ever known. In the preceding two centuries Europeans had conquered America and learned much from the older civilizations of the East: now, they believed that they surpassed even the ancient Greeks and Romans in artistic and intellectual creativeness. Never before had war been so tame, manners so polite. Never before had so many people lived so comfortably and enjoyed so much leisure.

The more civilized these educated Europeans thought they were, the more concerned they became with what was still uncivilized in their society. This concern was the guiding force of the intellectual movement known as the Enlightenment. Its leaders believed that the "light" of the scientific method—which they called Reason—would make ignorant beliefs and smug intolerance disappear and help informed and unselfish minds find the best ways for improving man's lot. The Enlightenment could not completely accomplish these goals, but it did give the intellectual climate and social policies of the second half of the eighteenth century a new direction. It also fostered values that are still relevant to the Western world today: reason, toleration, humanitarianism, social usefulness, and a liberalism that believed in allowing each individual to realize his greatest possible potential.

Although the Enlightenment gave eighteenth-century civilization its distinctive tone, it did not eliminate the underlying conflicts and insecurity bequeathed to it by the preceding century. After the 1760s its rationalism and qualified optimism were to be challenged in literature, in the arts, and even in science, as well as in moral philosophy. There were also to be nationalistic reactions against its cosmopolitan character and against French culture in particular. The Enlightenment drew its followers from the aristocracy, the bourgeoisie, and even some of the clergy without diminishing the tensions between these classes. Finally, by the 1770s, Reason itself was to be used to justify two contradictory political ideals: enlightened despotism and representative government.

## THE ENLIGHTENMENT AND ITS SPREAD

The Enlightenment was above all a search for new, secular ideas about the nature of man and his place in society.

Each great age in Western Civilization has illuminated some facet of man's complex nature which earlier ages left in shadow. The philosophical image of man apprehending virtue through the use of reason and following its demands originated among the ancient Greeks; Christianity had added the religious image of man controlling his sinful impulses and redeeming his evil nature through transfigured love. The Renaissance introduced power and will to the political image of man controlling his social environment and using his energy to create the state and the national ideal alongside the religious one.

In the eighteenth century new psychological, social, and political images of man overshadowed the religious ideal, but the most original and enduring contribution of that age was a rational justification of man's interest in property, things, and money. This novel use of reason gave rise to the idea of *economic man.* Its creators postulated natural laws that transformed the individual good into the common good. In the nineteenth century other economic and social theorists were to use the idea of economic man to sharpen the basic political conflicts between economic classes. But in the eighteenth century the idea of economic man already reflected an increase in wealth, the growth of world trade, and the social and political aspirations of the propertied classes.

### The Philosophes

Although the writers who spread the ideas of the Enlightenment called themselves *philosophes,* a number of important *philosophes* were neither French nor professional philosophers. The Enlightenment was centered in France, but it was shaped by men of many nations. Even the two most typical French *philosophes*—Voltaire and Diderot—were not philosophers in the way that the Scotsman David Hume and the German Immanuel Kant were. They were philosophizing publicists whose main purpose was to convince the general reader to adopt their way of thinking.

The *philosophes* flouished between the 1730s and the 1780s, but their outlook had it origins in the late seventeenth century. By then the Cartesian method of logical analysis, shorn of Descrates' "innate ideas," had become pretty well accepted. Locke's *Essay Concerning Human Understanding* furnished a new theory of knowledge with the senses as the *source* of ideas, and Newton had shown what the combination of Cartesian rationalism and Lockean empiricism could achieve. His laws of motion and his orderly "clock universe" became the basis of eighteenth-century dicussions of religion and ethics as well as science. Pierre Bayle joined Locke and Newton as one of the early idols of the Enlightenment because of his fearless insistence that every belief must be doubted until justified by history and logic. From Bayle, the *philosophes* learned how to focus the empirical-analytical attack on tradition.

### *Diderot and the Encyclopedia*

Denis Diderot (1713–1784) might be called the *philosophe's philosophe.* He epitomized the modern intellectual not only in his modest origin (his father was a prosperous craftsman), but also in his lively curiosity and in his sophisticated knowledge in so many fields. Diderot was best known in his own time for his great work on the French *Encyclopedia,* his interest in science and technology, and his reputation as a freethinker; his best works on drama and art criticism, his novels, and his philosophical writings were not published until after his death. This was the case with *Rameau's Nephew,* Diderot's most original literary creation. In this imaginary dialogue between the author and a depraved youth Diderot pilloried all the chief enemies of the *philosophes* and attacked the abuses of a social organization that forced talented but needy men to cater to the whims of haughty and often unworthy patrons.* Diderot went even further and asked if the disintegrating society of late eighteenth-century France could ever be reformed effectively unless some way were found to curb the inherent baseness of human nature itself.

So many of the *philosophes* wrote articles for the *Encyclopedia,* their most influential

*It should be noted, however, that Diderot wrote *Rameu's Nephew* before his fame prompted Catherine II of Russia to provide for his last years by purchasing his library and giving him a disguised pension for guarding the books as her "librarian."

propaganda medium, that the term Encyclopedists became almost synonymous with *philosophes.* In his article under the heading *Encyclopedia* Diderot summarized the program of all the contributors. Their aim, he said,

" . . . is to assemble the knowledge scattered over the face of the earth; to explain its general plan to the men with whom we live, and to transmit it to those who will come after us, so that the labors of past centuries may not be useless to future times; so that our descendants, by becoming better informed, may in consequence be happier and more virtuous; and so that we may not die without having deserved well of the human race."

According to Diderot's co-editor, the mathematician Jean le Rond d'Alembert (1717–1783): "The truth is simple and can always be made accessible to everyone." D'Alembert contributed articles on mathematics, and in his famous introduction he committed the other contributors to the empirical-analytical theory of knowledge, which the *philosophes* called Reason.

Since many of the *philosophes* challenged the existing authorities they had to find ways of getting around the censors. In the *Encyclopedia* Diderot cleverly used footnotes and cross references for this purpose, and also managed to include his beliefs in what appeared to be mere grammatical definitions; for example, he concluded his brief definition of *Anarchy* with the sentence: "We can assert that every government tends toward despotism or *anarchy.*" The reader could hardly miss the warning. Other writers put their indictment of European political institutions, irrational religious beliefs, and barbarous customs into the mouths of exotic foreigners. Charles de Secondat, the Baron de La Brède et de Montesquieu (1689–1755) did this n his *Persian Letters* (1721), which has been called the first book of the *philosophe* movement. Voltaire sometimes wove his criticisms into apparently innocuous novels.

### Voltaire

Francois Marie Arouet, better known as Voltaire (1694–1778), is the most famous

Portrait of Diderot

example of the new type of writer in the eighteenth century. He had established a reputation as a poet and playwright in his native Paris while in his thirties. Then he visited England. On his return to France in 1734 he became a publicist for Locke's psychology, Newtonian science, and what he took to be English religious and political freedom. He also wrote novels, moral essays, and a *Philosophical Dictionary* summarizing the whole outlook of the *Encyclopedia.* His *Century of Louis XIV* became a model for a new cultural approach to the study of history—an approach that stressed how people lived and expressed themselves, as well as kings and battles. In all his writings Voltaire sought to maintain a high literary standard while at the same time expressing what he had to say as clearly as possible. Here was the modern professional writer, in his full glory: clever, testy, vain, independent, and, above all, civilized.

Voltaire wrote for all educated people, not just kings (though he spent three years at the court of Frederick the Great) and aristocrats (though he had many friends among them). Of bourgeois origin himself, Voltaire firmly believed that the ruling classes had no monopoly over intelligence and creativeness. Indeed, he often ridiculed the stupidity of princes, judges, and priests. He called upon a new enlightened elite to eliminate such uncivilized features of eighteenth-century society as intolerance, superstition, and legalized cruelty. Voltaire was no democract, though. According to him, the mass of ordinary people had to be kept in line by the traditional forces of order.

### Ideas of the Philosophes

The way in which the *philosophes* used their combination of analysis, empiricism, and skepticism gave the Enlightenment its unique character as a cultural movement. It limited the kinds of questions they asked to those that could be answered by an appeal to reason and experience. "True nature" was comprehensible to "right reason." Everything else was "supernatural" or "unnatural," and hence not worth talking about—except to be exposed as a fraud. The rationalism of the so-called Age of Reason assumed that, though the world was imperfect, men could improve it by making certain choices; many evils could be eliminated, many institutions could be reformed, many superstitions could be argued out of existence. All these possiblities were "within reason."

#### *Initial Assumptions*

Their specific brand of reason gave the *philosophes* two basic standards of value: *humanity* and *social utility*. As the English poet Alexander Pope said:

The bliss of man (could pride that blessing find)
Is not to act or think beyond mankind.

Man is the measure of all things. He seeks his personal happiness here and now, not in some supernatural hereafter. Whatever helps him to achieve this happiness is good; whatever hinders him from doing so is bad. But "man" means society as well as individuals.

The *philosophes* had a very strong social consciousness and they frankly admitted that some socially useful things conflicted with others. Was an act that immensely benefited a few people preferable to one that slightly improved the lot of a huge majority? Each *philosophe* had his own moral arithmetic for measuring the goodness of any act or idea for society. They all agreed, however, that social utility was the basic standard.

One final assumption of the *philosophes* needs to be stressed. In addition to "right reason," "true nature," humanity, and social utility, they all believed in *change*. The world was obviously different from what it had been fifty, a hundred, or a thousand years earlier. Whether it was *better* or not was a more complicated matter.

The *philosophes'* celebrated belief in progress was limited by their underlying pessimism about man and history. Whatever improvements they hoped to make in society, most of them accepted human nature—with its passions as well as its reason—as something one could not change. It was simply there, like any other fact of nature. The triumphs of the human mind in astronomy showed what human nature was capable of as it was. Reason could perhaps direct the *education* of future generations and so achieve a comparable degree of progress in other fields. But no man could be educated beyond his natural capacity.

Nor did most *philosophes* believe that the history of mankind proved the inevitability of progress. The Italian Giambattista Vico (1668–1774) said that history moved in cycles. According to this view each civilization repeated the same life pattern of birth, growth, old age, and death—the same development from barbarism, to primitive organization, to higher organization. Other *philosophes* said that history moved in an aimless way dictated largely by chance—as in Voltaire's repetition of Pascal's quip that the whole history of the world might have been different if Cleopatra's nose had been a fraction of an inch shorter. Hardly any of the *philosophes* believed in inevitable decline, but those who preached an unqualified doctrine of the perfectibility of man and civilization were exceptional. Indeed the crowning work of eighteenth-century historical writing, Edward Gibbon's *Decline and Fall of the Roman Empire* (1776–1787), tried to show how Christianity had undermined the confidence and sapped the strength of the most impressive civilization within the ken of Western man.

### Human Understanding

The majority of the *philosophes* accepted Locke's view that all knowledge comes from the five senses, but they went even further than Locke in trying to explain how sensation bridges the gap between external objects and events on the one hand, and ideas in the mind on the other. The senses give us our first simple ideas of qualities like cold, hot, bitter, sweet, extension, shape, movement. Some of these are subjective, but our ideas of extension, shape, solidity, movement, and number represent things as they are. The mind compares, unites, and transposes these simple objective ideas to form more complex ideas of cause and effect, morality, politics, etc. Each sensation increases the mind's powers of imagination, memory, judgment, will, and logical reasoning. Thus, the most complex ideas are nothing more than transformed sensations of the real world. Our passions sometimes prevent us from adapting our actions to the world and to other people as they really are. Nevertheless, when we use our natural tools of comprehension, we can be sure of understanding an external reality that is essentially orderly and predictable.

Not all eighteenth-century thinkers accepted the infallibility of empirical knowledge. The Scottish philosopher David Hume (1711–1776) denied it in his *Treatise on Human Nature* (1740). According to Hume, all the inferences derived from experience—even the apparently incontestable idea of cause and effect—are merely the result of habit or custom. A man living in England grows accustomed to the idea that lowering the temperature of water to 32° is the cause of its freezing. But he has no way of knowing that this was always the case in the past or that it will always be so in the future. Besides, everybody's experience is limited by his environment. A king of Siam could never have believed that there was a country where water became solid enough to support the weight of an elephant. Hume's writings disturbed but did not convince the *philosophes*. Yet they were extremely important in showing where a rigorous skepticism could lead. They have, in fact, led to twentieth-century notions of relativity and probability.

### Religion

Religion was a much touchier question than human understanding for the *philosophes*. Not only did critical inquiries about religion risk sanctions from the established authorities, they might also undermine even the most rational moral order, if pushed too far. For almost all the *philosophes* believed that religion could still lend stability to society and direction to individual lives. Their task, as they saw it, was to simplify religion, scrape it clean of encrusting superstitions, and bring it into accord with nature and reason.

Reason led different men of the Enlightenment to several views about God. Deism remained a comfortable resting place for those who did not wish to push their inquiries too relentlessly. But Diderot, Franklin, and many others eventually abandoned Deism after deciding that they did not know enough about God to conceive of him even as the expert clockmaker, "Author of the Universe." They took the position that we could not know whether God exists or not—a position that was later to be called agnosticism. Only a few French *philosophes* adopted the view of uncompromising atheism: "there is no God." Agnosticism is simply a skeptical attitude about God; atheism is a new kind of militant faith. As such, it did not suit the temper of an age that was critical of all dogmas.

The *philosophes* were more interested in religion as an historical and social phenomenon than in theology. They speculated about why and how men had invented gods in the first place. Some said that the first gods were deified natural objects (fetishes) or forces (the stars, the wind, the rain); some said they were human heroes apotheosized through myths: some said they were expressions of unconscious fears and brutal panic—sometimes invented by rulers to control their ignorant subjects. Some said that tales of the gods were allegories of vices and virtues. These speculations about mythology reflected the eighteenth-century curiosity concerning man's nature and customs. They were also related to theories of progress and the "demystification" of Christianity itself.

In our age of perpetual crisis it may seem strange that the eighteenth-century *philosophes* should have condemned organized Christianity as the main obstacle to the advance of civilization. The *philosophes* were luckier than they knew in having no worse enemies than priests and censors, who were far more lax than the thought-controllers in today's dictatorial countries. To them however, the intolerance of the established churches was the greatest evil of their time. They particularly decried the continued discrimination against Catholics in Great Britain and Ireland and the persecution of Protestants in France.

Voltaire launched the battle cry, *écrasez l'infâme* ("crush the infamous thing"), in his effort to clear the memory of Jean Calas, a Protestant put to death on the charge—based on mere rumor—of murdering his son to prevent his conversion to Catholicism. If people still wanted to believe in the "superstitions" of organized Christianity, that was their business. But Voltaire insisted that the churches should be divested of all influence in public life: education, censorship, politics, and the regulation of public morals. Thus Voltaire became the champion of *toleration* and *anticlericalism* as essential policies in a civilized society. Both the friends and the enemies of the Enlightenment have viewed Voltaire in this guise as its main symbol ever since.

### Ethics

The *philosophes*' approach to ethics was best expressed in the subtitle of Hume's *Treatise on Human Nature*: "An attempt to introduce the experimental method of reasoning into moral subjects." We have already noted the Hume was a more original and advanced thinker than the average *philosophe*. Nonetheless, his approach to ethics expressed the typical view of the Enlightenment. If religious principles were, in Hume's words, "sick men's dreams," then "healthy" men had to take the responsibility for ameliorating the evils of this world in the light of other moral standards.

In rejecting theology the *philosophes* did not repudiate the need to define good and evil. Some said that there was a "natural morality" based on the "laws of nature." Others, as we have seen, based their ethical judgments on the standard of social utility. In either case "the experimental method of reasoning" showed that men had a mutual need for each other and that this need imposed certain reciprocal obligations on them. The ideal good man was sympathetic toward mankind, intolerant only of superstition and fraud, and receptive to new ideas even if these threatened him personally. He respected life, freedom, and property. He might indulge his passion for pleasure, but he refused to let it overpower his reason. Although no *philosophe* quite lived up to this ideal, it marshaled humanism, utilitarianism, and rationalism behind generous moral demands.

### Law and Government

The liberalism of the *philosophes* rested on their belief that society should promote the happiness of its individual members under the rule of law. Most *philosophes* tended to be less interested in the formal structure of a government than in setting its moral and social goals. They looked for the laws of human society sometimes in history, sometimes in the aspirations to justice they observed all around them. But most of them still believed that certain basic rules of justice applied in all societies. The main point was to discover these rules somehow and to substitute them for irrational custom and arbitrary control.

The most influential appeal for the reform of criminal law in accordance with reason was written by the humanitarian Italian jurist, Cesare Bonesana, Marchese di Beccaria (1735–1794). In his *On Crimes and Punishments* (1764) he expounded the revolutionary idea that society should concentrate on preventing crime, not just on punishing it. Good police work, by increasing the likelihood of arrest, would do more than severe punishments to deter crime. Beccaria deplored the senselessness of making hundreds of petty crimes punishable by death, as most countries still did in the eighteenth century. He used reason to show that keeping the death penalty for crimes of petty theft, for example, only encouraged sneak thieves to go on murdering witnesses, since this

*Public hanging at Tyburn, eighteenth century*

helped their chances of escape. Torture, too, was irrational, for it only tested the coarseness or sensitivity of a suspect's nerve fiber, not his truthfulness. Few books of the Enlightenment had as prompt and powerful an effect on the conditions of European life as Beccaria's *On Crimes and Punishments.*

Montesquieu's *Spirit of the Laws* (1748) was the most ambitious investigation of the organization of society as a whole to use the approach of the *philosophes.* Despite frequent appeals to "natural relations" and common sense Montesquieu did not prospose to discover a universal set of laws for all societies. Instead, he tried to show how differing social customs, historical traditions, and geographical environments gave a different *spirit* to the laws of each society. Thus, the vast empires of the ancient Mediterranean world and of Asia tended to be despotisms supported by the spirit of fear. Small city-states—like Athens, Venice, and Geneva—were usually republics supported by the spirit of virtue—that is, civic virtue, an active participation in community affairs and, when necessary for the public welfare, a certain self-effacement. Finally, large Western European states, especially England and France, tended to be free monarchies supported by the spirit of honor—that is, by their noblemen's consciousness of the privileges and obligations of rank, which is often called *noblesse oblige.* Montesquieu obviously favored what he called free monarchy, but he insisted that the specific laws of any type of state should provide the maximum liberty and humaneness possible within its constitutional limits.

Although Montesquieu was a liberal in his insistence on personal liberty and the rule of law, he was a conservative in defending the French aristocracy against encroachments by the royal administration. As a member of the nobility of the robe he included the Parlements and other intermediate bodies—clergy, guilds, towns—as moderating influences on the Crown. Insofar as his ideal for France was what he took to be the balance among King, Lords, and Commons in England, he was a Lockean liberal. But in the second half of the eighteenth century the conservatism of the Parlements and the resurgence of the "feudal" nobility led most French *philosophes* to feel that the nobles of the sword and of the robe were holding back social progress in order to preserve their own selfish interests.

Few major *philosophes* openly took the side of the absolute monarchs against the reactionary intermediate bodies. Even Voltaire did so only in connection with specific issues, and not because he was an advocate of despotism. To the *philosophes* the existing monarchies were the best available agencies for reforming society. They could do this, however, only by reforming themselves as well.*

### Economic Theory

While on political matters most *philosophes* put their faith in properly enlightened kings rather than in noblemen, an important group of them stressed freedom from government interference on *economic* matters. They criticized the mercantilist policies of eighteenth-century governments as being contrary to the laws of nature. Indeed, the French opponents of mercantilism called themselves *physiocrats*,† that is, advocates of physiocracy, or the government of nature. They wanted to make political economy into a science, just as Montesquieu had tried to transform the study of society into a science, sociology. They insisted on Montesquieu's conception of man's liberty without his reservations for different types of society. According to the physiocrats, economic phenomena constituted an order of facts that obeyed certain laws derived from the nature of things. The natural situation was for each individual to pursue his own economic interest. The natural role of governments was to let him do this with as little interference as possible: *laissez faire, laissez passer* (let it be done, let it get on).

The physiocrats tried to prove that their position benefited the community as well as the individual. According to them, the mercantilists were mistaken in seeing money as the true measure of wealth; they should learn that the real wealth of nations came from products that could be consumed without diminishing the capital that created them. These products were obviously agricultural, and this capital was obviously land. Industry merely transformed the raw materials of agriculture, including animal husbandry and forestry; commerce merely exchanged them. Land was the main producer of a nation's wealth. The government should therefore encourage and favor the landowning classes by safeguarding their private property and removing all feudal and communal restrictions on it. Then the landowners would be able to produce more goods, thus enriching the community and providing more revenue for the state.

This economic philosophy with its emphasis on free enterprise (*laissez faire*) and private property was to become the gospel of bourgeois capitalism for the next 150 years. But the French physiocrats spoke for the landowning class, which was still largely noble in eighteenth-century France and England. According to them, this was the most essential class in any society. Next came the farmers who worked the land. Last came the "sterile class"—including all the merchants, manufacturers, and professional men—which produced nothing new.* The true founder of economic liberalism from the bourgeois capitalist point of view was the Scottish moral philosopher Adam Smith (1723–1790).

Like the physiocrats, Adam Smith tried to prove that free enterprise and private property benefited the community as well

*See pp. 317–321 on enlightened despotism.

†The most important physiocrats were François Quesnay (1964–1774), Mercier de la Rivière (1720–1797), and Louis XVI's sometime finance minister (see p. 320) Anne Robert Jacques Turgot (1727–1781). Pierre-Samuel Dupont de Nemours (1739–1817)—whose son later established what was to become the world's largest chemical corporation in the United States—invented the name physiocracy. Turgot invented the phrase, *laissez faire, laissez passer.*

*Contrast this classification with that of the Abbé Siéyès' *What Is the Third Estate?*, which gives the middle-class view of the most useful classes in society.

*Illustration of a pin factory from Diderot's* Encyclopedia

as the individual, as the title of his classic work indicates: *An Inquiry into the Nature and Causes of the Wealth of Nations* (1776). Unlike the Physiocrats, however, Smith argued that the person who transformed raw materials into manufactured goods did increase their value, and hence the total wealth of the community. Furthermore, the more people concentrated on those aspects of production in which they were best suited, the more goods they would be able to produce. Writing before new machines and new sources of energy had shown their real potential, Smith demonstrated how national prosperity could be increased by organizational improvements. He took as his example a pin factory, as described in Diderot's article on pinmaking in the *Encyclopeida*. By dividing the manufacture of pins into several specialized operations, the owners of his factory became able to get their workers to produce ten times as many pins per day as the same number of workers could produce if each one performed all the operations himself.

Smith used the idea of division of labor as the key to the wealth of nations to justify a revolutionary new policy: *free trade*. According to him, reason dictates that whole nations, as well as individual men, should concentrate their labor on the forms of production for which they are best suited. It is foolish to buy inferior goods at high prices in one's own country when comparable goods of better quality can be bought more cheaply abroad and paid for by exporting goods that can be produced most efficiently at home. Each region and each nation of the world should use its comparative advantages of climate, materials, and skills. These comparative advantages, along with its freewheeling capitalists, were the true wealth of nations—not hard cash, as the mercantilists argued, or land alone, as the physiocrats argued. Even so, free trade should not apply in cases where it would aid potential enemies. Nor did Smith believe that division of labor required a nation to abandon its own production of the minimum needs of war.

Although a staunch moralist, Smith refused to see the implications of unfettered free enterprise for the working man. He justified the morality of his economic philosophy with the familiar values of the *philosophes:* reason, individual liberty, natural law, social usefulness. His economic man was both rational and acquisitive. If allowed complete freedom to pursue his self-interest he would know how to make the most out of his capital and his skill. A whole society of such free economic men would produce more wealth than any other kind of society. The natural laws of supply and demand would eliminate the inefficient producers, thus giving the consumers the best products at the lowest prices. As the nation's wealth increased, some of it would eventually filter down to the workers themselves. As a political economist Smith was content that he had described the best, that is, natural, functioning of a nation's economy. As a moralist he felt impelled to add an "invisible hand" that made this system a just one. Later British political economists in the Adam Smith tradition were to drop the "invisible hand."

The writings of the *philosophes* showed theoretical defects, but they had a significantly beneficial effect on the society of their day. Men like Adam Smith, Diderot, Voltaire, and Beccaria did indeed change ordinary men's ways of thinking. They hastened the eventual. triumph of empiricism and the scientific spirit. They also fostered a humanitarian movement such as the world had never known, a movement that began the progressive elimination of systems of organized cruelty. If they did not make all men reasonable and civilized, they at least made many men feel that they ought to be so.

### The Social and Cultural Setting

The desire for improvement and "enlightenment" made educated Europeans modern, although it may seem a strange label for those who wore the powdered wig and danced the minuet. If so, it is because we see these two symbols as representing the whole culture of the age. Actually, they expressed only the outward style of life of the dominant social class, the French and Frenchified aristocracy. Furthermore, economic changes increased the influence of the urban middle classes in the West, and by the 1770s the simpler tastes of these classes began to affect even the aristocracy itself. Under Louis XVI, for example, noblemen began to carry simple bourgeois canes instead of swords. French culture was imitated by Central and Eastern European aristocrats until almost the end of the century. But in France itself this culture was challenged from England, from the German cities, and from the non-European world.

Thus, we must not be deceived about people's thoughts and feelings by their dress and manners nor judge an age by these standards. Many of the same aristocrats who danced the minuet also developed a passion for science. Although most men in powdered wigs and knee breeches continued to defend the Old Regime, others, like George Washington and the Marquis de Lafayette, were to lead revolutions. Much of the social and cultural life of the eighteenth-century upper classes had a make-believe quality about it; Queen Marie Antoinette, for example, dressed up like a simple milkmaid and carried a pail around a thatched cottage she had had constructed in the park of the Versailles palace. Having noted this let us now turn to the realities of the age.

In the eighteenth century the Old Regime defended itself from criticism as best it could. The alliance between throne and altar fostered obedience to established authority through the law courts, the police, education, sermons, and censorship. But this absolutism was often inefficient and sometimes easygoing. Prussia, for example, was known for its toleration long before Frederick the Great said: "My subjects may think and say what they like, as long as they do what I like." In France, censorship was relatively lax, and an author could sometimes evade its control by using a pseudonym and giving a foreign city as the place of publication for his work.

European culture acquired a broader social base in the eighteenth century. No longer did it cater exclusively to closed groups like the clergy, the king's courtiers, and the higher nobility. The growth of the urban middle classes provided an educated public with new cultural demands. Some members of the upper bourgeoisie wanted nothing better than to follow the artistic and literary tastes of the aristocracy. But the bulk of the commercial and professional people developed distinctive tastes of their own—tastes that fostered the triumph of new public forms of expression such as the novel, the symphony, and the newspaper.

People seeking higher status also broadened the base of eighteenth-century culture. Despite the prevalence of class distinctions everywhere, talented men and attractive women could move out of the lower social ranks as individuals. We have already seen how fortunes were to be made in the slave trade and the colonies. Though they never became as rich as nabobs, writers like Voltaire, Samuel Johnson, and Benjamin Franklin made a comfortable living from their journalistic and literary works and ended their lives as honored guests of high society. Madame

Du Barry, the illegitimate daughter of a seamstress, became Louis XIV's last mistress and a sponsor of the arts. While courtesans needed royal or noble patronage to become "ladies," writers and composers tried to improve their social status by freeing themselves from such patronage. Kings and nobles treated them as servants; the new public began to treat them as "artists." For artistic and intellectual culture became *fashionable* as never before.

To be sure, the bulk of the European population remained socially and culturally isolated. Free or unfree, peasants were still peasants. Their inability to read barred them from the literary and intellectual culture of the age; they knew only their traditional folk cultures. Even in the towns and cities the lower classes were mostly illiterate and socially segregated. Eighteenth-century culture was restricted to the middle and upper ranks of urban society—perhaps 3 or 4 per cent of the total population in England and France, and considerably less as one moved eastward.

In our own age of universal literacy and mass culture this cultivated minority seems very small. But in comparison to earlier times it was a momentous gain. And if we consider numbers rather than percentages it is even more impressive. In the late eighteenth century Paris and London had 600,000 and 750,000 inhabitants respectively. The cultivated minority included about 10 per cent of the city population. These 60,000 Parisians and 75,000 Londoners constituted a larger public than had ever existed.

The new public interest in cultural matters created a market for popularizations of available knowledge about them. Richard Steele's *Tatler* and Joseph Addison's *Spectator* were the first weekly newspapers to bridge the gap between the scholar and the more or less educated general reader, between the fastidious aristocrat and the matter-of-fact bourgeois. Their pseudoscientific articles, literary journalism, and moral essays stimulated their subscribers to read real books. As comparatively wide sections of society acquired a taste for serious literature, books as well as periodicals adapted their style and tone to the new reading public. Their language became less precious and less ornate, their ideas became simplified and more closely related to contemporary life. The novel developed into an intensely personal description of human behavior of all kinds, and by the 1770s even the theater turned to exposés and satire. Finally, Diderot's *Encyclopedia* was the most successful and enduring medium of high-level popularization in all fields.

Public interest in literature, science, and social philosophy fostered other new media for diffusing new ideas. Aristocratic ladies organized cultural and intellectual evenings in the *salons* of their town houses. There noted writers conversed with the ladies and gentlemen of high society eager to learn the latest ideas—along with the latest gossip, of course. More important than the salon was the *café*, or coffee house. In this typically urban, middle-class institution men gathered periodically to talk and to read the many journals and newspapers to which it subscribed. Meanwhile, the lending library made it possible for people to read more books than they could afford to buy. The number of learned academies increased rapidly; in France alone, fourteen provincial academies were founded in the first half of the eighteenth century. Even more characteristic of the educated amateurs' longing for "enlightenment" were the private clubs that were formed to discuss current books and articles and reports on their members' own research. These clubs included nobles and bourgeois, professional men and priests—another sign of the broader social base of culture.

Freemasonry, another important medium for spreading the ideas of the Enlightenment, got its start in England in the early eighteenth century. At that time a group of educated Englishmen took over the guilds of mason-builders which had survived from medieval times. They preserved many of the symbols and secret rites of these guilds but replaced the old professional masonry with a "philosophical" masonry. By 1725, lodges of Freemasons appeared in France and spread all over the continent by midcentury. Everywhere their members dedicated themselves to renovating the moral and social order with the ideas of liberty and brotherhood. They were Deists who worshiped the Great Builder of the Universe. Despite repeated condemnations by the papacy, the movement continued to attract followers from all social classes in Catholic as well as Protestant countries. Practically anybody who was anybody was a Freemason: Benjamin Franklin, Voltaire, the Prince of Bourbon-Condé, King Frederick II of Prussia, Emperor Francis I of Hapsburg-Lorraine. Enlightened despots joined these secret organizations both to keep them under surveillance and to assure themselves of their support.

In addition to producing new media for the diffusion of new ideas, the cultural tone of the century stimulated many people to try their own hand at new activities and experiences. Everybody has heard about Benjamin Franklin's experiments with electricity. Frederick the Great wrote poems and plays in French, George III was an amateur botanist, Voltaire dabbled in mathematics, the Abbé Nollet gave a regular course in experimental physics for 600 interested amateurs in the auditorium of the Royal Garden in Paris. Few monarchs of any age have had as many lovers as Catherine the Great, and few aristocrats have glorified their eroticism with as much energy, shamelessness, and persistence as the Marquis de Sade. Yet in perhaps no other century were personalities like Casanova and Fanny Hill so widely tolerated and even lionized.

The eighteenth century was above all an age of curiosity. Many people who professed an interest in science still viewed it as a kind of magic. The same audience that watched the Abbé Nollet's demonstrations also flocked to watch the Italian charlatan who called himself Alexander de Cagliostro evoke the spirits of the dead. People also filled the auditoriums of Paris and Vienna to see the German doctor Franz Mesmer demonstrate his theory of animal magnetism. So effective was his ability to put volunteers from the audience into a hypnotic trance that it gave birth to the word "mesmerize." Curiosity about strange, far-away places was stimulated in 1771 by accounts of the real discoveries of Captain Louis Antoine de Bougainville in the South Pacific and of Captain James Cook in Australia and New Zealand. But much of the travel literature of the day catered to the popular idealization of primitive lands, especially America, as havens for the poor, the persecuted, and the maladjusted. People wanted to hear about "noble savages," not cannibals. Still, whatever curiosity cultivated Europeans showed about the overcivilized Chinese or the unspoiled Iroquois, they believed that their civilization, though nourished by the others, had surpassed them all.

## EIGHTEENTH-CENTURY SCIENCE

The faith of the educated public in science reached its first great peak in the eighteenth century. Here is the way D'Alembert put it in his *Elements of Philosophy* (1759):

"Natural science from day to day accumulates new riches. . . . The true system of the world has been recognized. . . . The discovery and application of a new method of philosophizing, the kind of enthusiasm which accompanies discoveries, a certain exaltation of ideas which the spectacle of the universe produces in us; all these causes have brought about a lively fermentation of minds."

But this "lively fermentation of minds" produced two contrasting views about the purpose of science among philosophers and among some scientists themselves. On the one hand, there was a continuing effort to follow Descartes or Newton in perfecting mathematical theories of the physical world. On the other hand, there was a concerted movement to follow Bacon in observing and experimenting with those aspects of nature that could be grasped by the senses.

### Mathematics and Its Critics

Eighteenth-century mathematicians developed procedures for defining the fundamental concepts of astronomy and mechanics more neatly and exactly and for explaining new facts revealed by observation. Newton and Leibniz had left the calculus very imperfect; their successors made it into an instrument for measuring infinitesimal variations of all kinds under any conditions. With this improved calculus the Frenchman Count Louis de Lagrange (1736–1813) in his *Analytical Mechanics* (1788) deduced all the equations of motion from the principle of least action: when any change occurs in nature, the amount of action—or work—necessary for this change is the least possible. The value of the calculus for astronomy was confirmed by another Frenchman Claude Clairaut (1713–1765). With it he predicted the exact day (March 13, 1759) on which Halley's Comet, last seen in 1682, would reappear at the closest point in its orbit to the Sun. Clairaut thus showed that comets as well as planets were subject to the principle of universal gravitation.

The *Celestial Mechanics* (1799) of Pierre-Simon, Marquis de Laplace (1749–1827) was the crowning achievement of the eigh-eighteenth-century French mathematicians. It completed Newton's work by molding the whole of mechanics and astronomy into a beautifully complete and harmonious series of equations. Improvements in the telescope had greatly increased the size of the visible universe and corrected Newton's doubts about the eternal stability of the solar system. Newton had thought that God had to intervene every so often to keep all the planets in their orbits. Laplace made this hypothesis unnecessary by extending in time the laws that Newton had traced in space. With its almost arrogant self-confidence, with its delight in the essential logic and simplicity of the structure of the universe, Laplace's *Celestial Mechanics* sums up one side of eighteenth-century science.

No comparable opus sums up the other side, but the controversy between the mathematical and experimental approaches is vividly expressed in two short works by Diderot. In his *Thoughts on the Interpretation of Nature* (1754) Diderot rejects the claim of mathematics to be the true language of science. Not only does it idealize, he held, it falsifies by depriving bodies of the perceptible qualities in which alone they have any real existence. Mathematics is not only arrogant, it is inhuman. The true route to a science of nature moves toward a threefold object: Existence, Qualities, Use. In *D'Alembert's Dream* (1769) Diderot has his friend, himself a geometer, say that the kind of scientist best qualified to point out this route is a doctor, the universal doctor who sees physical nature across the perspective of human nature.

Diderot did not believe that nature was merely an unstructured aggregate of elements. He tried to explain the development of animal and human life as a continuous process in which the qualities of the different species penetrated one another to some degree. Man with his many different organs attained unity in diversity. Even a swarm of bees, "all clinging to one another by the feet," is "a being, an individual, an animal of sorts." And the solidarity of the universe resembled the organic community that the social insects knew.

### Biology and Natural History

Diderot's organic conception of nature had little influence in an age in which biology—the very name was not yet in use—was still struggling to distinguish itself from natural history. Since the sixteenth century naturalists had studied and catalogued thousands of examples of flora and fauna. Then, in the late seventeenth century, natural history showed signs of becoming a science by adopting the skills of the human anatomist and physiologist, the chemist, and the physicist. The observations of Leeuwenhoeck and Malpighi with the microscope seemed especially promising. But neither the techniques nor the ideas of other disciplines provided an adequate theory or even workable hypotheses to guide scientific research into the life processes. Hence, eighteenth-century naturalists devoted their main efforts to the systematic classification of everything in the natural world.

The greatest eighteenth-century achievement along this line was that of the Swedish naturalist Carl Linnaeus (1707–1778), who developed systems of classification for the animal, vegetable, and mineral kingdoms. The tenth edition (1758) of his *System of Nature* is still the standard work of reference, especially for plants. Linnaeus classified all living things according to differences in kind (genus) and differences

*Lavoisier in his laboratory*

in variety (species). Although his standards of differentiation were arbitrary, his new terminology had the great merit of simplicity. Henceforth, all plants would have only two names—one for their genus and one for their species—instead of a string of descriptive adjectives, as in the past. Late in his life, Linnaeus began to lose faith in his belief in the immutability of species, but this notion remained his chief legacy to biology.

In the eighteenth century evolutionary ideas were applied to the formation of the earth's crust, rather than to its living creatures. The French naturalist Georges Cuvier (1769–1832) founded the science of paleontology. He accounted for fossils of extinct species by saying that successive catastrophes—of which the Biblical Flood was the most recent—had swept the earth of old species, and that successive creations had people it with new ones. Cuvier's compatriot Georges-Louis Leclerc, Count de Buffon (1707–1788), developed a more sophisticated theory of the evolution of the earth. He pushed its origin back 74,000 years (instead of the 6,000 of the theologians) and divided its history into seven geological epochs. In the epochs before our own, animals had been larger and perhaps even man had been a giant, and according to Buffon, many current species were degenerated forms of earlier ones. For example, he thought the donkey to be a horse that had degenerated under the influence of climate and nourishment. Buffon abandoned the notion of the immutability of species; but only in the next century did evolution become the concept that explained the origin of specific differences.

### Chemistry

The greatest advances in eighteenth-century science were made in chemistry. Chemists passed from the description of appearances to the discovery and qualitative analysis of simple elements. Through innumerable experiments they built up their knowledge of the different forms of inorganic matter—minerals, acids, alkalies, gases. These experiments showed that the substances themselves were the really active participants in their own transformation. But chemists had no way of measuring the exact gain or loss of weight due to the participation of a gaseous element in a reaction. The French chemist Antoine Laurent Lavoisier (1743–1794) solved this problem in the latter part of the century by inventing a precise balance scale.

Lavoisier's achievements constituted a real revolution in chemistry. Like Newton, he gave his science a universal principle, the *conservation of matter*. In his *Elements of Chemistry* (1789) he said:

> "We may lay it down as an incontestable axiom that, in all the operations of art and nature, nothing is created; an equal quantity of matter exists both before and after the experiment; the quality and quantity of the elements remain precisely the same; and nothing takes place beyond changes and modifications in the combination of these elements."

The balance scale showed this. Chemistry now became a *quantitative* science. Lavoisier also provided this science with a new vocabulary. He and two of his colleagues established simple symbols and names for all the known substances and chemical processes.

From all these scientific developments it became evident that the method of Newton *was* more fruitful than the method of Bacon. Those sciences that still relied purely on data provided by the senses made little progress. On the other hand, the combination of theory, hypothesis, and factual reporting was to produce a revolution in biology in the nineteenth century, just as it had in mechanics and astronomy in the seventeenth and in chemistry at the end of the eighteenth.

Nevertheless, Lavoisier's material algebra would have disappointed Diderot had he lived to see it. He and other philosophers were already beginning to express concern over the shroud of obscurity that mathematically oriented scientific geniuses drew between nature and sensitive nonscientists. In the eighteenth century this concern did not affect the majority of the educated public, which continued to view science as a producer of marvels, a "glorious entertainment." Yet it did indicate a potential rift between the humanistic outlook and the outlook of professional scientists more concerned with perfecting their own theories than with the human consequences.

## ARTISTIC CULTURE

As in science and moral philosophy, the eighteenth-century conflict between the abstractions of the Enlightenment and the flesh-and-blood realities of human existence found expression in literature and the arts. There the issues were classicism versus the cult of sensibility, cosmopolitan versus native forms, universal versus individual and personal values, and—though this is an oversimplification—reason versus emotion. Part of the conflict reflected changing taste and class cleavages. But the main characteristic of eighteenth-century literature and art was a restless search for purely secular expressive forms.

Art does not merely reflect the spirit of the civilization in which it appears. It has a life of its own, which is molded by individual geniuses and limited by specific techniques. Moreover, the greatest art expresses universal human feelings, not just those of a particular time and place. Nevertheless, the dominant artistic *styles* in any age are determined to a large extent by the aesthetic conventions of that age. People learn these conventions partly by their education within a given culture and partly by a growing familiarity with the works of influential innovators.

### Neoclassicism

During the eighteenth century the dominant style in most traditional art forms was some kind of classicism. According to classical standards, the function of art is to refine taste and—especially through poetry and drama—to illustrate moral precepts. It is to do these things by stressing the general, universal, and unchanging aspects of nature and man. Modern classicism had originated in the age of Louis XIV as a way of imposing a sense of order and unity on the world through the control of reason. This intention explains in part the continuing appeal of classicism, or more properly neoclassicism, in various new forms through the eighteenth century.

In contrast to the anxiety and tension of the baroque style, neoclassicism expressed the controlled optimism about man and civilization which dominated the thought of the Enlightenment. By the middle of the century it was drawing its models directly from the ancient Greeks, whose conception of beauty was especially congenial to enlightened Europeans because it reinforced their belief that everything was governed by natural laws. The fact that neoclassicism reached its peak in the last third of the century also seems directly related to the efforts of many rulers of that time to use the ideas of the Enlightenment to bolster the order and unity the Old Regime was supposed to provide. Indeed French art, architecture, poetry, and drama remained strictly neoclassical throughout the Revolutionary and Napoleonic period. It was the opponents of the new order of that period, not its champions, who first turned to romanticism.

#### *Architecture*

In all art forms, the neoclassical ideal was to follow the rules of "good taste." English and French architects of the early eighteenth century found these rules in the textbook of the Renaissance architect Andrea Palladio (1508–1580). Their adaptations of "Palladian" ideas of regularity, symmetry, and restraint in external ornamentation were especially well suited to the town houses of the great aristocrats.* To Americans the most familiar example of eighteenth-century neoclassicism in architecture is the Georgian, or "colonial," house of red brick with a white portico.

The rediscovery of ancient Greek and Roman buildings in the 1740s brought a new wave of neoclassicism in public architecture, the Greek revival style. It expressed perfectly the outlook of the champions of Reason. The most impressive example is the group of buildings surrounding the Place de la Concorde (originally named after Louis XV). The church of the Madeleine, which can be seen from this square, is a direct copy of a Greek temple. Other late eighteenth-century examples of neoclassical public architecture include the Paris stock exchange, the Brandenburg Gate in Berlin, and the Winter Palace in St. Petersburg.

### Painting

European painting in the first half of the eighteenth century is more difficult to classify than the architecture. By then Italy had become the museum and school of Europe, and Venice was its playground. Countless painters filled huge canvases with grand but lifeless scenes of that city's waterways. The few good artists that Italy still produced were admired mainly for their success in imitating their Renaissance ancestors. In France the Flemish-born Antoine Watteau (1684–1721) painted dreamlike parks where gallant ladies and gentlemen dressed in sparkling silk cavorted in a world divorced from all hardship and triviality. François Boucher (1703–1770) depicted, under the guise of classical mythology, the more erotic side of court life at Versailles. In England the upper classes also preferred idealized portrayals of elegant society. For this reason they refused to take seriously the most original English artist of the period, William Hogarth (1697–1764). He learned his technique in the school of classicism and reason and he wrote a book, *The Analysis of Beauty*, in which he showed his belief in teachable rules of taste. But most of his paintings and engravings laid bare the weaknesses, the follies, and the misery of English life in his own time. His famous picture-series, "The Rake's Progress" and "The Harlot's Progress" appealed more to the middle-class public than to the aristocratic connoisseurs.

Although French painting did not adopt a vigorous neoclassical style until Louis David in the 1780s, neoclassicism dominated English painting during the entire second half of the century. The elegant society of the period at last found its ideal painter in Sir Joshua Reynolds (1723–1792). He portrayed the wealth and beauty of his aristocratic patrons not in the libertine manner of Boucher but in the minutely correct, carefully posed style of a Velazquez. Like all classically inspired painters, Reynolds believed that the only hope for an artist lay in the careful study and imitation of the Renaissance masters—the draughtsmanship of Raphael, the coloring of Titian. As the head of the Royal Academy of Art, founded in 1768, Reynolds tried to make his neoclassical standards permanent. And so they remained for over a century in academic art.

### Interior Decoration

The most characteristic eighteenth-century style in interior decoration is known as *rococo*. It originated in France around 1700 and dominated much of Europe during the period of Louis XV. Watteau's paintings helped to mold it, but the rococo style was mainly restricted to the interior walls and furnishings of royal and aristocratic dwellings. Here it abandoned cherubs and ornate columns for floral and curved designs on flat surfaces whose very essence lay in their unreality. These designs, called *arabesques*, had a playful, transitory, dreamlike quality that permitted the most fanciful union of varied elements. In fact, an outstanding feature of the rococo style was its use of new materials for ornamentation: porcelain, stucco,

*See pp. 301–307 for examples' of eighteenth-century art and architecture.

seashells, and artificial rockwork. *Rocaille*, the French word for this, was transformed into the mildly contemptuous rococo by its critics.

In France the rococo style expressed with decent restraint the best side of the aristocracy—its grace, its gaiety, its gentleness; in Germany and Italy, however, it was grafted onto late baroque and used to decorate something grand but dead. Even in France rococo decorative artists soon ran out of new ideas. Some of them turned to Chinese art for inspiration. Just as the first translation of Confucius had given Montesquieu, Voltaire, and other *philosophes* an image of Chinese life governed by rational and enlightened thought, the large-scale importation of Chinese porcelains stimulated European efforts to imitate them. In the aristocratic and cosmopolitan eighteenth century porcelain became the typical material of rococo art, from Sévres to Dresden.

As in architecture and painting, neoclassical influences appeared in interior furnishings after 1760. In England the cult of the exotic—comparable to the French cult of *chinoiseries* (things Chinese)—had prompted Horace Walpole to decorate his neo-Gothic country house at Strawberry Hill with Moorish screens and Persian rugs. Even the early pattern-books of Thomas Chippendale and other cabinet makers showed the stylistic confusion of the 1750s. Then Sheraton and the brothers Adam began to design interiors and furniture with an extremely fine sense of proportion. In France, too, the style known as Louis XVI developed a classic simplicity and symmetry.

### Music

Because of its transcendant character music is less easy to label as baroque, rococo, or classical than the visual arts. In addition to this limitation, we should also remember that the style we usually associate with the eighteenth century—the classicism of Franz Joseph Haydn (1732–1809) and Wolfgang Amadeus Mozart (1756–1791)—took hold only after the 1750s. Until then the baroque music of Johann Sebastian Bach (1685–1757) and George Frederick Handel (1685–1759) and the rococo music of François Couperin (1668–1733) and Domenico Scarlatti (1685–1757) dominated the scene. Changes in musical style have an inner development of their own. When one style becomes "used up," composers seek to express themselves in a new one—as is true of all kinds of artistic and literary creation. Nevertheless, in music there was a direct connection between the shifts from baroque to rococo to classicism and the audiences for whom works in these styles were composed.

As in art and architecture, the shift from the baroque to the rococo style in music reflected the change from the church to the aristocratic salon as a cultural center. But the salon, like the church, soon faced the competition of another cultural center, the public concert hall. The first concert societies were formed in the 1750s. Soon thereafter their bourgeois patrons hired large halls where musicians played for payment to ever-growing audiences. Although Haydn and Mozart continued to write "occasional" pieces commissioned by a nobleman for a single performance, in composing symphonies for an anonymous concert public they tried to create "immortal" works in a self-consciously classical style.

Mozart epitomized the artistic scope and universal appeal of this classical style. In his opera *Don Giovanni* he expressed the full range of human feeling. In his chamber works Mozart experimented with every possible combination of instruments. Within the strict classical limits of form and tonality he gave his last three symphonies a degree of breadth and profundity seldom exceeded by later composers. His music appealed not only to the cosmopolitan aristocrats of his native Vienna, it was equally well received in Paris, London, and Prague.

Like the Greek revival in architecture, the style of the Viennese classicists prevailed into the early decades of the nineteenth century. In addition to Haydn and Mozart, these composers included Ludwig van Beethoven (1770–1827) and even Franz Schubert (1797–1828) to some extent. It may seem paradoxical that architecture and music—the most concrete and abstract of the arts—should have retained their classical mold during the upheavals

*Mozart with his sister and father (by Johann N. de la Croce.*

of the Napoleonic era. Yet despite these upheavals, the spirit of the Enlightenment lived on. Its ideas of man's common nature and of the human capacity for moral progress were most vividly expressed in Haydn's *Creation* and *The Seasons* and in the "Hymn to Joy" in Beethoven's *Ninth Symphony.*

**Sensibility and the Novel**

The cult of sensibility had appeared in the late seventeenth century, but it acquired a new intensity and new forms in the mid-eighteenth century. According to the new aesthetic theory of this cult, the writer or artist should concern himself with the individual, intimate, and fluctuating aspects of his subject. In the novel especially, the new heroes and heroines were no longer universal types but intensely individual characters. The reader could thus take a personal interest in their triumphs and sufferings.

In England the popularity of the novel came from stories depicting credible characters living in a familiar atmosphere. Samuel Richardson's *Pamela, Or Virtue Rewarded* (1740) was the first and most enduring model of the modern female success story. The heroine, an irresistible but virtuous governess, withstands the wiles of seduction and induces her presumptuous employer to marry her. Henry Fielding's *Tom Jones* (1748) takes its hero, a foundling, through all sorts of lusty adventures and has him end up with a country estate and the lovely Sophia, who corrects his natural tendencies to vice. Here, however, the moral of "virtue rewarded" is only a polite pretense; indeed, Fielding is consciously making fun of *Pamela.* The main interest in *Tom Jones* is its realistic—and sometimes spicy—portrayals of contemporary human behavior.

The sensibility of continental readers was more attracted by sentimental stories about suffering heroes, particularly as expressed in semiautobiographical "confessions." Through his hero Des Grieux in *Manon Lescaut* (1733) the Abbé Prevost d'Exiles described in fictional form an episode in his own youth, in which his passion for a woman of easy virtue had almost destroyed them both. The most famous example of the subjective fictional confession was the *Sorrows of Young Werther* (1774) by Johann Wolfgang von Goethe (1749–1832). Here the young lover's hopeless passion leads him to suicide. Goethe was soon to turn to more robust forms of literature and drama and to become Germany's greatest writer.* Meanwhile, young Werther had many imitators

*See p. 300 and Chapter XI.

and evoked a cult of sensibility that spread far beyond Germany. Few of Werther's imitators actually went so far as to die for love, but their pose of tearful despair added another dimension to the eighteenth-century search for individual self-expression.

### An Age of Satire

By Voltaire's time the novel of social satire had already gained a wide audience. Daniel Defoe's *Robinson Crusoe* (1720) emphasized the bourgeois virtues of industry, endurance, inventiveness, and common sense, which overcome all difficulties in an environment free from the restraining forces of traditional society. Jonathan Swift's *Gulliver's Travels* (1726) attacked the stupidity and pettiness of contemporary social and political behavior by having his hero encounter them in fantastic races like the Yahoos, who are incapable of reasoning, and the Lilliputians, who are physical as well as mental dwarfs. Similarly Voltaire's *Candide* (1759) describes the ultimate disillusionment of a good-natured, well-meaning hero in a cruel world. Like Gulliver, Candide travels to many strange places and undergoes all sorts of misadventures in order to find out how cruel the world really is. His main foils, however, are Europeans like Dr. Pangloss, who personified the kind of self-deluding optimism that bars the way to even modest reforms.

In the late eighteenth century the theater also produced a number of realistic comedies that mocked and criticized the current social scene in a variety of ways. In England Richard Sheridan's *The Rivals* (1775) and *The School For Scandal* (1777) satirized the snobbery (Mrs. Malaprop) and extravagance (Lady Teazle) of the "status seekers" of that time. In Germany, Gotthold Efraim Lessing's comedy *Minna von Barnhelm* (1767) gave a poignant portrayal of a poor soldier's hopeless love for a young noble woman. Far more realistic and more pointedly critical of the existing social system were two plays of the Frenchman Pierre Beaumarchais: *The Barber of Seville* (1775) and *The Marriage of Figaro* (1784). In each of them the lowly barber Figaro sympathetically portrays the personal hopes and disappointments of many commoners in the audience. He spends so much of his time criticizing and outwitting the aristocracy that Napoleon Bonaparte later called these two plays "the Revolution already in action."

### The German Cultural Revival

In Germany a cultural revolution was already under way before the French made their political revolution. In fact, it began as a reaction against the cosmopolitan, French-inspired culture of the Old Regime. The writers who revived German literature—after nearly two centuries of virtual stagnation—shared many of the attitudes of the Enlightenment: humanitarianism, hostility to established authority, religious toleration, and scientific curiosity. But they dissociated themselves from the French *philosophes*, whom they dismissed as flippant, insincere, and superficial, and they condemned the prevailing French influence on upper-class German culture. They wanted to give German culture a new orientation and to shape the German language into a superior medium of expression.

The first phase of the German cultural revival—the *Sturm and Drang* (Storm and Stress) period—could be termed a frustrated German Revolution. It took the form of a literary rather than a political protest against the Frenchified German aristocracy. Lessing's *Minna von Barnhelm* was the first important play to hint at this protest. Goethe's novel *The Sorrows of Young Werther* was more outspoken in expressing the protest of many spirited young Germans against the disunited, apathetic, and caste-ridden society in which its hero foundered. For *Werther* was more than a superbly written love story. It also told of the frustrations of an ambitious young commoner in the face of the aristocratic prejudices that prevented him from achieving social and professional acceptance.

By the 1780s the *Sturm and Drang* had spent itself, and the German cultural revival took a more positive direction. Goethe and Lessing tried to create new standards for German literature and drama. Unlike England and France, di-

*The late eighteenth-century theater*

vided Germany had no one great intellectual metropolis, and most of the German princes showed little interest in German culture. The one major exception was Duke Karl August, who made his tiny ducal capital at Weimar a haven for men of letters. Goethe, now famous, became the duke's minister of state and lived most of his life in Weimar. The dramatist Friedrich Schiller (1759–1805) also spent his remaining years in Weimar after 1787. Schiller had made his contribution to the *Sturm and Drang* in his first play, *The Robbers*, which tells the story of a young nobleman who is driven by injustice to become an outlaw but is ultimately reconciled to law and order. At Weimar Schiller gave the German stage its greatest classical dramas: *Don Carlos, Wallenstein, The Maid of Orleans, Maria Stuart, William Tell.*

Another pilgrim to Weimar, Johann Gottfried Herder (1744–1803), gave the German cultural revival its philosophical manifesto in his *Ideas on the Philosophy of the History of Mankind* (1784). In it he contended that all true culture must arise from the native masses, the *Volk,* not from the cosmopolitan upper classes. Herder thought French ways more frivolous and shallow than German ways. If he had known anything about French peasants Herder might have seen how different their ways were from those of the French upper classes. But he assumed that each *Volk*, whether French or German, had its own national character—*Volksgeist*—which it should develop in its own way. No national culture was better than another; they were simply different. Nor did Herder put his argument for cultural diversity into political terms. The German people had long been excluded from the affairs of their separate states and they thought little about the political rivalries of their princes with other European rulers. Nevertheless, cultural nationalism was soon to give rise to political nationalism, first in Germany, and then in the other "emerging nations" of Europe.

As Herder, Schiller, and Goethe grew older they seemed to return to the general spirit of the European Enlighten-

PICTURE GROUP C

# *Eighteenth-Century Art and Architecture*

ABOVE:
NEOCLASSICAL ARCHITECTURE:
*Chiswick House, Middlesex*
Historical Pictures Service, Chicago

RIGHT:
LATE BAROQUE INTERIOR:
*Staircase in Pommersfelden Castle*
Marburg/Art Reference Bureau

NEOCLASSICAL ARCHITECTURE: *The Royal Crescent Bath, England*
Mansell Collection

RIGHT:
SEVRES PORCELAIN VASE: *designed by Duplessis with painted panels by Francis Aloncle*
Copyright The Frick Collection, New York

ROCOCO INTERIOR DECORATION: *San Souci Palace, Potsdam, Germany*
New York Public Library

JEAN ANTOINE WATTEAU;
*Musical Conversation*
The Metropolitan Museum of Art,
Bequest of Lillian S. Timken, 1959

THOMAS GAINSBOROUGH: *The Mall in St. James's Park*


LEFT
FRANÇOIS BOUCHER: *Summer*

WILLIAM HOGARTH: "The Orgy at the Rose Tavern" from *The Rake's Progress*
Historical Pictures Service, Chicago

JEAN-ANTOINE HOUDON: *Rousseau*
Musee' Nationale du Louvre, Paris

JOSHUA REYNOLDS: *Mrs. Richard Brinsley Sheridan (?)*
The Metropolitan Museum of Art, Bequest of Mary Stillman Harkness, 1950

JACQUES LOUIS DAVID: *The Oath of the Horatii*
Musee' Nationale du Louvre, Paris

ment. But they were more concerned with championing artistic culture and intellectual freedom than with reforming society. This approach is understandable partly as a reaction against the extremes of the French Revolution and partly as a reflection of the lack of social intercourse among the educated middle classes in the cities of divided Germany. Weimer was no substitute for Paris or London, and it did not long remain even the provincial cultural center it had been in the 1780s and 1790s. After the deaths of Schiller and Herder, Goethe alone remained the voice of the Enlightenment in Weimar, and despite his early role in the German cultural revival Goethe was essentially a classicist in literature and an advocate of peaceful enlightened absolutism in politics.

## RESISTANCE AND COUNTERACTION

The main challenges to the civilization of the eighteenth century did not come from its writers and artists. Like politics, economic activity, and social structure, the artistic culture of the Old Regime clung to traditional forms and conventions. Despite temporary excursions into rococo, *chinoiseries*, cultural nationalism, and even the tearful realm of sensibility, it nearly always returned to some variation of classicism. The strongest reactions against the dominant rationalism and materialism of the age stressed the primacy of the heart, the spirit, and personal fulfillment. They included religious revivals in England and Germany, Rousseau's pleas for new departures in politics and education, and Kant's effort to establish a new basis for knowledge and morality.

### Religion

The age of Voltaire also produced John Wesley (1703–1791), the founder of Methodism, whose work serves to remind us that many "revivalist" religious movements had their origins in the eighteenth century. While still preparing for the Anglican ministry at Oxford, Wesley began his campaign to revive religious "enthusiasm" (meaning "filled with God") in the world. His fellow students derisively called him and his associates "Methodists" because of the strict rules of conduct and systematic study they introduced into their religion. In the face of the formalism and coldness of the Anglican Church and the unbelieving Deists, Wesley preached the simple message of salvation through Jesus. During his long life he traveled some 250,000 miles and preached almost 40,000 revivalist sermons in barns and in the open air. Wesley stirred hundreds of thousands of townsmen, farmers, and miners to repent and have faith. Though he remained an Anglican minister himself, he lived to see the founding of the Wesleyan Methodist Church in England and the Methodist Episcopal Church in the United States. Other offshoots of Wesleyanism appeared soon afterward.

The religious sects that grew out of Wesley's teachings appealed especially to the lowly and the miserable, for, in addition to emphasizing direct communion between God and man, they sponsored humanitarian activities of all kinds to alleviate the poverty and suffering among the poor and humble people to whom they preached. They also encouraged movements for prison reform, penal codes, public hospitals, and poorhouses, and for the abolition of slavery.

With Wesleyanism, other revivalist sects represented a widespread movement to make Christianity more personal and to break down the formalism of the state churches in the eighteenth century. The Pietists, who flourished in the Lutheran sections of Germany, resembled the Methodists in many ways. They too worked within the established church at first, emphasizing meditation, Bible reading, and good works that gave meaning to one's Christian faith. They too stressed personal religious feeling over doctrine and had a strict code of personal behavior. The eighteenth-century English Baptists believed that people should not be baptized until they were old enough to recognize their sins, confess them, and accept Christ's message; many of the revivalist sects in America today are offshoots of the early Baptists. By the eighteenth century the Quakers, or Society of Friends, no longer "quaked" when the divine truth came to them. But they still believed that an "inner light" would guide them to it without the aid of priests, sacraments, or rituals.*

Aside from the persistence of Jansenism in France there were no revivalist movements in the Roman Catholic Church comparable to those in the Anglican and Lutheran Churches. The Roman Catholic Church survived attacks from all sides as best it could. "Enlightened" kings continued to defend it in principle and to exploit it for their own purposes. Meanwhile, its creed and its ritual retained their hold on millions of ordinary Catholics who were untouched by the antireligious propaganda of the *philosophes.*

*In the late eighteenth century there were also nonreligious cults that offered their followers supernatural sources of comfort and wisdom. One was founded by the Swede Emmanuel Swedenborg (1688–1772), who claimed to have direct contact with the spiritual world. Another was the Rosicrucians, who claimed to be able to unlock the secrets of nature with special powers superior to reason.

## Rousseau

Jean-Jacques Rousseau (1712–1778) was the great rebel against eighteenth-century civilization, especially as he saw it in France. He thought it artificial, its manners too elaborate, its taste too sophisticated, its people of refinement too hypocritical and frivolous, its religion too formal, and its unbelief too glib. For Rousseau all this went against nature, by which, in his later writings, he meant man's nature. Going "back to nature" did not mean "going around on all fours," as Voltaire charged. Rousseau pleaded for a civilization that would allow the strong emotional side of man's nature to develop in a harmonious way. His main complaint against the *philosophes* and the aristocratic culture of his time was that they neglected man's emotions.

More than anything else in the world Rousseau longed to be free to be himself. Rousseau was born in Geneva and imbued with the puritanical outlook of that Swiss city. He lived mostly in France, though he spent a year in Venice as secretary to the French embassy, a post of considerable prestige. Yet even after he became famous, Rousseau always felt awkward in the company of his social superiors. As he approached the age of forty he decided that emotional freedom was impossible in the civilization of his day. He began his personal "reform" by giving up the outward symbols of civilized living. In his *Confessions* he says: "I gave up gold lace and white stockings, took to wearing a round wig, and put aside my sword." Henceforth Rousseau devoted his writings to describing the possible ways of reforming civilization so that other men could also be free to be themselves.

Rousseau passionately believed that man was born free and inclined toward moral good. Man was not responsible for the emotional ingredients of his nature. It was up to society to help him realize his full capacity for self-determination—through good laws and institutions and through the right kind of education and religion.

This "philosophy of the heart" was a major challenge to the whole civilization of the Enlightenment. In his most popular work, the novel *The New Héloïse* (1761), Rousseau showed how man's innate sense of moral values could triumph over his baser emotions. In *Emile* (1762) Rousseau proposed a system of education which would preserve a child's native goodness, innocence, and natural sincerity into adulthood. Emile's tutor does this by carefully sheltering his pupil from all the artificial aspects of eighteenth-century civilization and allowing him to develop his natural personality and aptitudes with as little constraint as possible.* When Emile is twenty, a Savoyard Vicar gives him a "Profession of Faith" in a personal God and a religious conscience as a guide to moral behavior. In religion, as in everything else, Rous-

*Johann Pestalozzi (1746–1827), a Swiss educator and humanitarian, tried to adapt Rousseau's educational program to the practical requirements of the classroom. In his experimental school he taught geography, drawing, carpentry, and other practical subjects, and he reacted against the traditional method of teaching by a combination of endless drill and bodily punishment. But most European schools retained both the classical curriculum and traditional classroom methods. Not until the twentieth century did American and finally European educators begin to follow the ideal of Rousseau and Pestalozzi—namely, that children should be treated as children, not miniature adults.

seau rejected the cold rationalism of the *philosophes* and made feeling, properly guided by one's inner conscience, the key to human happiness.

Rousseau's idea that governments had no authority apart from the individuals over whom it was exercised was truly revolutionary in the eighteenth century. In his *Social Contract* (1762) he states explicitly that *the people is sovereign* and that *government is its agent.* "The depositories of executive power are not the masters of the people, but its officers. . . . the people may establish or remove them as it pleases." Like Locke, Rousseau said that people in a "state of nature" formed a government through a mutual agreement, a social contract. But unlike Locke, Rousseau did not grant even a limited degree of sovereignty to a government thus formed. According to Locke the governed accept the sovereignty of their government as long as it protects their civil rights. According to Rousseau, "each person gives himself to *all*, but not to any *individual*." Rousseau calls the will of this "all" the "general will."

*A scene from Rousseau's Emile*

He tried to use his idea of the general will to reconcile his concern for individual liberty with his recognition of the need for organized government. In the *Social Contract* he defines liberty as obedience to a law that we prescribe to ourselves by our own individual wills. Then he argues that the general will is an expression of the better side of each individual will. It is "a pure act of understanding that, in the silence of the passions, reasons about what a man can demand of other men and what they can rightfully demand of him." In other words, there is a moral law which each person discovers within himself and which is the same for everybody in a given community. A government that expresses the general will has the right to force its citizens to obey this law, since people form governments in the first place—that is, in an anarchic "state of nature"—in order to guarantee their individual liberty. Those who violate the general will not only jeopardize the liberty of others but also harm the better side of themselves. Rousseau says that they must therefore be "forced to be free."

Rousseau based his idea of the general will on another revolutionary idea, the people as a community of individuals. He thus challenged the traditional and legal conceptions of society as consisting of corporate groups—classes, orders, estates, guilds, towns—each with its own privileges and interests. This kind of society, Rousseau thought, was a perversion of what the people had wanted when they had made the social contract among themselves. They had done this because as a community of individuals they had agreed unanimously on the need for a government to express their general will. Minorities are bound to question specific policies of such a government, but when the majority makes these policies it expresses the general will of the community. As long as the minorities consider themselves a part of the community they must accept the ruling of the majority. Otherwise, the community falls apart, and its members lose the possibility of realizing their individual potential for self-determination.

Another revolutionary idea of Rousseau's was that all men are equal. On this point too Rousseau blamed civilization as it had evolved to his time for destroying the natural equality of men. For as society had become more civilized it had created forms of wealth and power with which some men exploited others. Rousseau did not believe that everyone should necessarily have the same degree of wealth and power. He simply wanted the law to limit each person's share to the point where it could not suppress the liberty, self-respect, and self-determination of another individual. "It is precisely because the force of things always tends to destroy equality that the force of legislation should always tend to maintain it." Thus, the law should force men to be equal as well as free.

Later critics of Rousseau have charged him with favoring the tyranny of the masses, but Rousseau himself did not believe that a government based on the sovereignty of the people—that is, a democracy—could be achieved in a large state. It could only work in a small city-state like Geneva, and only then if all the citizens participated in it directly. In fact, when Rousseau later suggested reforms for the constitution of Poland, he recommended the preservation of the elective monarchy, the privileges of the nobles, and even serfdom until the serfs had been taught responsibility.

We must try to understand Rousseau in his own time and on his own terms. In the eighteenth century dominant minorities imposed their will on powerless majorities everywhere. To Rousseau this arrangement was morally wrong. He believed that he had found the true moral basis of society, law, and government in man's natural equality and capacity for goodness. We may consider this belief naïve. But is it any more naïve than Adam Smith's belief that the sum of individual acts of economic self-interest naturally produces the greatest public good—or Montesquieu's belief that men of privilege naturally feel more obligations toward their fellow men than ordinary people—or Locke's belief, incorporated into the American Declaration of Independence, that all men are born with certain natural rights? In a way all the *philosophes* were naïve in thinking that there was a sure way of knowing how society could best be organized. Rousseau differed from them mainly in seeking this knowledge through the heart rather than through reason.

### Kant

Just as Rousseau's "philosophy of the heart"—with its emphasis on feeling and individual fulfillment—was to find its fullest expression in nineteenth-century romanticism, Kant's doctrine that the ultimate reality lies in the world of ideas and the spirit rather than in sense experience launched a second major nineteenth-century movement, *idealism.*

In his *Critique of Pure Reason* (1781) the German philosopher Immanuel Kant (1724–1804) went through a series of mental "experiments" concerning the "facts" of human reason—that is, the kinds of propositions with which reason operates. Then he found the laws that tied these facts together. Finally he discovered the principle on which these laws depended. Most philosophers in the past had started with objects in the natural world and asked how they "came into" the mind. Kant started with the mind and asked how it knew objects in the world outside itself. He granted that these objects were real but he denied that the mind could know them as they truly were. It knows them only as *forms* (phenomena), not as things in themselves.

According to Kant we experience the world in terms of certain basic assumptions that already exist in our minds: space, time, cause, quantity, quality, means, relations, etc. These assumptions, or categories, exist *a priori*—that is, prior to our experience—and they transcend (go beyond) what is given by experience. It is these *a priori*, transcendental categories alone that dictate the forms by which we know the objects of the natural world. The principle upon which these categories, which Kant thought comparable to Newton's laws, depend is the existence of the mind as a living reality, prior to and transcending the senses.

Kant wanted his investigation of the problem of morality to be as "scientific" as his study of the problem of knowledge. Hence, following Newton's method, he analyzed all existing moral conceptions in order to find the one principle on which they all depended. He found this principle to be "good will," the will to do one's duty toward one's fellow man. This principle turned out to be an innate part of human nature, much as Rousseau had seen it. Man's natural feelings impelled him toward good will, but reason had to guide his judgment. And reason told him that whatever the circumstances, a true act of good will had to follow a rule that he would not hesitate to see become a universal law. "Do unto others as you would have them do unto you." Kant called this moral law the "categorical imperative."

Like his categories of pure reason, Kant's "categorical imperative" is an absolute idea, independent of all individual examples and circumstances. Human reason can grasp it quite apart from, and even in contradiction to, what seems socially useful or emotionally desirable. Under certain circumstances the assassination of a tyrant may seem like a useful service to society. But no one in his right mind would want the rule "assassinate all tyrants" to become a universal law. A lonely man in a strange city may find emotional satisfaction in making love to an equally lonely woman and then leave her broken-hearted. Here, too, the "categorical imperative" tells him that such an act is morally wrong. In fact, a corollary maxim tells him to act "so as to treat humanity, whether in thine own person or in that of another, always as an end, never simply as a means." Kant based his view of morality on his stern demand that man take full personal responsibility for respecting the dignity and rights of other men.

The importance of Kant lies not only in his reevaluation of the philosophy of the Enlightenment but also in his role in the German cultural revival. Just as the empiricism of Bacon and Locke had become characteristically British and the rationalism of Descartes had become characteristically French, so the idealism of Kant became characteristically German. Each national culture provides its own way of viewing the world, which philosophy reflects and molds even more emphatically than literature and the arts. Goethe, Schiller, and Herder gave educated Germans a national literary culture before the German nation came into existence. Kant gave them a theory of knowledge based on ideas that transcend what is given by experience. The idea of the nation was not a part of Kant's philosophy. But German philosophers in the Kantian tradition were soon to give not only the idea of the nation but also ideas like the state, class, and even the historical process a transcendental character that made German culture unique in the nineteenth century.

Kant shared the growing demand of the late eighteenth century for a higher morality and a greater autonomy for the individual personality. In 1784 he proclaimed that "Enlightenment is man's release from his inability to make use of his understanding without direction from another." Like Rousseau and Diderot, he challenged the mechanistic assumptions of Newtonian physical science as arrogant and inhuman. All three attacked conformity to the external customs of the civilization of their time as inimical to man's personal and cultural expression. This idea of a divorce between culture and civilization was to reappear in early nineteenth-century romanticism and periodically thereafter. Meanwhile, this idea became associated with the new stress on individuality, a higher morality, and the validity of emotion. Together they openly challenged the political as well as the artistic and intellectual assumptions of the eighteenth century.

## THE ENLIGHTENMENT AND POLITICS, 1763–1789

In the last third of the eighteenth century the political reorientation of European civilization took the form of a democratic revolution—the demand for governments representative of and responsible to the people. Although most of its advocates still limited "the people" to taxpayers, their goal represented an early version of modern political democracy. The advocates of this goal usually faced the opposition of an aristocracy that was trying to reassert or extend its own privileges and powers. Caught between these two contending forces, many of Europe's monarchs sought to preserve their authority by reforming society from above—a policy known as enlightened despotism.

All three groups used the ideas of the Enlightenment to justify their behavior. But although these ideas were "in the air," they did not *cause* the American Revolution or the subsequent democratic revolutions in Europe, including the French Revolution itself.

### The American Revolution

Revolutionary wars have a way of simplifying issues. One must be either for the revolution or against it, a patriot or a traitor. All other issues that formerly divided the insurgents must be temporarily submerged in the struggle against the common enemy. When this enemy begins to be viewed as a foreign power the struggle molds the previously divided insurgents into a national community. If the insurgents have certain common traditions, this community coheres after its victory over the enemy, especially if the majority of the "traitors" has permanently left the scene. The revolt of the thirteen American colonies against British rule was the first successful example of this pattern of events. As such it had an immediate impact on Europe and became a model for later revolutions in Latin America.

Since we are primarily concerned with the impact of the American Revolution on Europe, a few comparisons between America and the Old World are necessary. Some historians contend that the Thirteen Colonies were a unique frontier society having practically nothing in common with Europe. This view seems too extreme. Certainly the British colonists had never known hereditary feudal nobles, state churches,* and oppressive kings the way their European cousins had in the past. But these conservative forces were already waning in Western Europe. Even before the French Revolution of 1789, Dutch, Belgian, Swiss, Irish, and English democrats were demanding more representative and responsible government in their respective countries. They faced stronger opposition from kings, aristocrats, and established churches than the American colonists, but they shared similar aspirations.

In the decade leading up to 1776 the Thirteen American Colonies *were* different from Europe, but they had a king, and they had an untitled aristocracy, although its influence was weaker than in Europe. They also had traditions of liberty and equality, whose influence was stronger than in Europe. The oldest colonies had been founded with a large degree of independence from Great Britain. By the eighteenth century, each colony had a royal governor, but it also had its own assembly elected by a wider suffrage than any in Europe—80 per cent of adult white males in Massachusetts, just over half in New Jersey, a little under half in Virginia. These assemblies exercised a considerable degree of self-rule. In addition to sharing these traditions of political equality and political liberty, the white population enjoyed all the civil liberties of Englishmen.† The distribution of wealth in colonial America was far more equal than in the Old World, but the rich and the poor were far enough apart to cause trouble.

Despite their internal differences, most Americans disapproved of Great Britain's efforts to strengthen her control over the Thirteen Colonies in the decade before the Revolution. These measures-increased taxes and limitations on westward expansion (Quebec Act, 1774)-were largely products of the French and Indian War.

The Stamp Act of 1765 united almost all the colonists against Britain for the

*The Anglican Church was established in New York and in the South, the Quakers tried to dominate Pennsylvania, and the Congregationalists (Calvinists) still had a strong influence in New England in the eighteenth century. But there was no alliance between throne and altar and no legal discrimination against dissenters in most colonies. In fact, a larger proportion of Americans belonged to no church at all than in any European country.

†Though half of all the white immigrants into the colonies south of New England arrived as indentured servants, their indentures expired after a few years and they soon merged with the free population.

*A society of patriotic American ladies signing a pledge to drink no more tea until the liberation*

first time. They viewed this act, which placed a tax on newspapers, playing cards, and all legal documents (wills, contracts, licences, etc.) as an "unconstitutional" innovation. They raised the question of taxation without representation, despite the fact that the British Parliament had passed the Stamp Act to produce revenue for the military defense of the colonies. While rich merchants retaliated by boycotting British goods, mobs of poor people rioted, intimidated the king's officials, and destroyed property. But when Parliament repealed the Stamp Act in 1766, the momentary unity of the colonists disappeared.

Then new efforts to make the colonies serve British interests provoked mounting resistance. New import duties in the late 1760s caused further rioting, and when the British decided to station a military force in Boston, radical patriots called Sons of Liberty stoned the soldiers. In one incident the soldiers fired on the crowd, killing five people; the citizens were especially enraged when the commanding officer was acquitted at his trial. In 1773 a group of citizens disguised as Indians dumped a whole shipload of tea into Boston harbor. They did this in protest against the Tea Act, which deprived American shippers and retailers of the profits of the tea trade by giving the British East India Company a monopoly over it. In 1774, to punish Massachusetts for the "Boston Tea Party," Parliament passed the "Intolerable Acts." These acts closed the port of Boston, forbade town meetings, and compelled the province of Massachusetts to provide food and lodging for British soldiers sent there to enforce these disciplinary measures.

In September 1774 the American Colonies moved from isolated acts of protest to organized revolution. A Continental Congress representing all the colonies except Georgia met in Philadelphia. At first the purpose of the delegates was to recover their "just rights and liberties" and to restore "union and harmony between Great Britain and the colonies." But the Tory-dominated British Parliament refused to back down. The incident that brought the conflict past the point of compromise was open fighting between the people of Massachusetts and the king's troops at Lexington and Concord in April 1775. Violence spread, and local militias were formed to maintain law and order. In May 1775 a second Continental Congress organized these militias into a "Continental Army" under the command of General George Washington. The demand for complete separation from Great Britain increased when the British government placed the insurgent colonists outside the protection of the British Crown in December 1775.

Thomas Paine's widely circulated pamphlet, *Common Sense* (January 1776), helped to spread the argument for independence among the general public. Paine, a former British exciseman and new arrival in America, gave the classic democratic argument against the "remains of aristocratical tyranny in the House of Lords" and the "remains of Monarchical tyranny in the person of the King." Even General Washington called Paine's argument for independence in the name of democracy "sound doctrine and unanswerable reasons."

The formal Declaration of Independence on July 4, 1776 was based on practical considerations as well as ideals. If the British Crown refused to maintain law and order in the colonies, the colonists would have to form their own government to do so. If financial aid was to be sought from France, the French would have to be convinced that it was for the purpose of breaking up the British Empire and undoing the British victory of 1763. Thus, a little over a year after the Battle of Lexington, the Continental Congress announced the arrival of the United States of America as an independent state "among the powers of the earth."

America won its independence from Great Britain after five years of hard fighting and with considerable outside help. At first the Continental Army made little headway against the superior British forces, even though the French had been giving money and supplies to the insurgents since the start of the rebellion. Then in 1778 the French formed a military alliance with them. This alliance was crucial not only because of the French soldiers and naval forces it brought to America but also because of its diplomatic effect on Great Britain. It reopened the world struggle for colonial supremacy with France and with Spain and Holland, who joined France in her war against the British. Other European states created a League of Armed Neutrality in 1780 to resist British searches of their ships bound for America.

Britain now paid the price for having antagonized practically every power on the continent in 1763. Furthermore, she was divided at home. Some Whigs were ready to recognize American independence so that they could blame the king's friends for ruining the empire—and thereby turn them out of office. Ireland also was restive and required British troops to maintain order. For all these reasons Great Britain made a separate peace with the United States after Cornwallis's defeat at Yorktown in October 1781.

Whereas the final *military* victory of the American colonists owed much to outside factors, the emergence of the United States as the modern world's first democracy was a purely American achievement. We must not forget that a prominent minority of the colonists opposed a complete break with Great Britain. These loyalists came from all classes, but a high proportion of them identified themselves with the values of the British governing class. By the end of the war over 60,000 loyalists out of a total population of 2,500,000 (including 500,000 slaves) had permanently emigrated to Canada. This loyalist emigration was extremely important in removing a potential conservative force from American society. Those untitled aristocrats who became patriots accepted the principle of equality during the war and incorporated it into the Constitution in 1787.

In a sense, the Constitution of the United States reaffirmed the traditions of liberty and equality of colonial times, but it was truly revolutionary in explicitly stating that all public power came from the people. The people had exercised their sovereignty in framing the Constitution, in giving themselves alone the power to change it, and in agreeing to live under the restraints imposed by it. Their elected legislators could pass other laws, but they could not change the organization of public power—the law of the land. It was this example of liberty, equality, and rule of law that immediately captured the imagination of so many Europeans, including the French.

Books, newspapers, magazines, clubs, and the Freemasons brought the American dream to the European consciousness; so did soldiers returning from the war. Almost 20,000 Hessian mercenaries returned to Germany and told their neighbors what they had seen in America; thousands of British and French enlisted men did the same thing in their respective countries. Prominent young aristocrats had served as officers in Washington's army and become inspired with democratic ideas: the Pole Thaddeus Kosciuszko, the Prussian Count Neithardt von Gneisenau, and, most famous of all, the Marquis de Lafayette. This impressionable young Frenchman, who had come to America primarily for military action, became closely associated with Washington and tried to emulate him. His experience in the American Revolution gave him his idealistic love of liberty and made him try to spread his liberal political sentiments after his return to France.

The young American Republic also had its own spokesmen in Europe, of whom Benjamin Franklin was the most famous and most successful. Parisian society lionized this genial *philosophe* from the New World when he was America's minister to France from 1776 until 1785. Thomas Jefferson followed Franklin in this post. Though he could not duplicate Franklin's personal triumph, he published many articles on America in French and encouraged others to do so. In fact, shortly before going home in the summer of 1789 Jefferson was to help Lafayette with a draft of a French Declaration of the Rights of Man. John Adams played a similar role in publicizing American ideals in Holland, where he arrived in 1780.

Through all these channels of communication the American Revolution had a great impact on Europe. It gave a new content and new dimensions to the political ideas of the Enlightenment: liberty, equality, humanity, and the rule of law. It substituted America for England as the model for those seeking a better world. It brought constitutional conventions and declarations of rights into the realm of the possible. Whether seen in a factual way or fantastically idealized, America made European society seem more unjust than ever to many middle- and lower-class people and to aristocrats like Lafayette, who wished them well.

## Enlightened Despotism and the Aristocratic Resurgence

Most European aristocrats were poles apart from Lafayette. Far from wishing the democrats well, they tried to crush them wherever they could. In the 1780s they succeeded in doing so in Great Britain, Ireland, Holland, Belgium (Austrian Netherlands), and Switzerland. Elsewhere they concentrated their attacks on strengthening their own powers and privileges at the expense of enlightened despots.

### *Great Britain*

In Great Britain the three-way struggle between democrats, aristocrats, and the king ended in a stalemate between the latter two in the 1780s. The struggle began in the 1760s when Parliament, the stronghold of the Whig aristocracy, was challenged by the democrats and the king at once. George III (1760–1820), though no enlightened despot, reasserted his political influence by appointing his personal favorites, especially Lord North, as his chief ministers, thus breaking the monopoly that the Whig aristocracy had held over the government since 1713.

Democratic criticism of the Whig-dominated Parliament was first inspired by the quixotic John Wilkes, who, as a newspaper editor and member of the House of Commons, campaigned for greater political and civil liberty and an end to "corruption." By the beginning of the American Revolution other men were demanding that the House of Commons be made more representative of and responsive to the existing electorate. Indeed, in 1780, some extremists even proposed that a General Association elected by all the people replace the aristocratically controlled Parliament. This kind of agitation was fed by growing dissatisfaction with the government's handling of the American Revolution; but some Whigs used that issue as a means of shifting popular discontent from Parliament to the Crown. Moreover, the ugly violence of the Gordon Riots* dampened the democratic ardor of men like Wilkes. For eighteen years after 1784 both the king and the aristocracy accepted a series of Whig governments under William Pitt the Younger. Both had their reservations about him, but under his leadership they closed ranks against the democratic revolution that threatened them at home and in all of Western Europe after 1789.

### *Austria, Russia, Prussia*

Whereas in Great Britain the political stalemate between the king and the aristocracy precluded any basic changes, enlightened despotism had made notable gains in France, Sweden, and the Austrian Monarchy† in the decades preceding the American Revolution. The monarchs of these countries put through administrative reforms and reduced the powers of the aristocracy. Maria Theresa worked persistently to alleviate the burdens of serfdom; Louis XV's ministers initiated important reforms in tax assessment and judicial organization; in Sweden, King Gustav III (1771–1792) ended half a century of aristocractic domination and restored the royal authority. He then abolished torture, improved the poor laws, and proclaimed religious toleration and freedom of the press.

These were the kinds of things enlightened despots did. Many of their reforms were based on the practical need to increase revenues and manpower resources for their wars. Others, however, reflected a desire to justify monarchical rule in the cold light of reason and social usefulness. The example of the Austrian Monarchy is especially instructive for the period after 1776 because its ruler, Joseph II (1765–1790) tried harder than any other eighteenth-century ruler to make enlightened despotism work.

Joseph II's outlook and policies earned him the title "the revolutionary Emperor." Though he regarded the *philosophes* as presumptuous intellectuals, Joseph was the very type of enlightened ruler to whom they looked to put through the reforms they wanted. He had no respect for the organized nobility and the established church; on the contrary, he regarded them as impediments to his humanitarian efforts to help his various peoples by direct government action. Joseph's anticlerical policies included the suppression of most monastic houses, the legalizing of civil marriage, transferring to the state the Church's responsibility for poor relief and care of the sick, and the legal toleration of Protestants and Jews. He also encouraged anti-Catholic propaganda in the press and on the stage. The Emperor reduced the privileges of the nobility by subjecting those of its members convicted of crimes to the same humiliating penalties as everybody else, by making noblemen pay the same kind of tax as other landowners, by giving free rein to commoners in his civil service, and by allowing Jews to become officers in his army.

Most revolutionary of all Joseph's policies was his "abolition" of legal serfdom. As we have seen, the peasants in most of the Hapsburg lands lived under some form of hereditary subjection. Joseph gave them the legal freedom to leave the

*See footnote, p. 232.

†There were also enlightened despots in Spain, Portugal, Naples, Tuscany, and Denmark.

estates of their landlords, to marry without permission, and take up new trades. But those peasants who remained as agricultural workers on the estates owed the same obedience and labor service as before. Joseph's ultimate aim was to convert the peasants of his realm into independent property owners and taxpayers, like those in France and western Germany, but, since he also wanted the noble landlords to draw substantial taxable incomes from their peasant labor, he was never able to achieve this aim. The main effects of his legal abolition of serfdom were thus to increase the peasants' hostility to the nobles and the nobles' hostility to him.

Joseph II's "revolution from above" failed for several reasons. He could not have both a nation of peasant proprietors and a taxpaying nobility whose main income was still derived from forced labor. Furthermore, his whole program expressed no public demand by groups of interested parties with formulated ideas and habits of working together, as in the more advanced countries of the West. The state represented only itself. There was no large merchant class. Enlightened commoners worked in the state bureaucracy, but even here there were enough noble officials to sabotage imperial orders. Finally, Joseph aroused national resentment among the Czechs and Magyars by disregarding their traditional diets and by making German the only language for official business.

Under Leopold II (1790–1792) the aristocratically controlled provincial diets forced the repeal of most of Joseph's reforms. Though Leopold had been an enlightened despot when he was the Grand Duke of Tuscany, he had to yield on all fronts to the aristocratic resurgence once he became Emperor. He managed to maintain the peasants' legal freedom, but those peasants who stayed on the land—as most of them did in the pre-industrial era—remained subject to forced labor and corporal punishment.

The legally constituted privileged orders triumphed in Russia as they did in the Austria of Leopold II. Catherine the Great's Charter to the Nobility* insured their ascendancy in 1785. In an enormous agrarian empire resting on serf labor and military force, this charter guaranteed the privileges of those persons without whom the monarchy could not control its subjects. Joseph II had tried to weaken his nobility and free the serfs of his empire; Catherine II completed the development of the Russian nobility into a legally privileged and irresponsible aristocracy better able to dominate the Russian serfs. Joseph II was a true enlightened despot; Catherine's reputation for enlightenment rested mainly on the carefully cultivated image that she conveyed to her *philosophe* friends in the West.

In Prussia enlightened despotism was not the pure sham that it was in Russia, but there too the monarchy had to make concessions to a resurgent aristocracy. Frederick the Great's law code, which we have already mentioned, was completed after his death and promulgated as the Prussian General Code of 1791. It began with a statement of natural rights in the spirit of the Enlightenment. But it gave *more* rights to the existing privileged classes—the landed nobility and the high civil servants—than to the rest of the population. These two classes were so close in their values and attitudes that one historian has recently called them together an "aristobureaucracy."

Thus, in Austria, Russia, and Prussia, enlightened despotism gave way to a new understanding between the monarchy and the privileged aristocratic "estates." This new arrangement was to survive the French Revolution, and, in general, to last until the beginning of the twentieth century in most of Eastern Europe.

### France

In France the pattern of development was quite different. There the monarchy antagonized both the commoners and the privileged estates. Both groups opposed the despotism of Louis XVI until the summer of 1788 when the First and Second Estates—the clergy and the nobility—openly defied him. But in France this "aristocratic revolt" led directly to a revolt by the Third Estate—the commoners—against the other two. The last part of this story will be told in the next chapter.

*See p. 271.

*Fragonard's "The Swing"*

Here we shall concentrate on the failure of enlightened despotism and the aristocratic resurgence up to 1788.

The failure of enlightened despotism in France was partly a failure of "public relations." Louis XVI and his ministers shrouded their most justifiable policies in administrative secrecy and showed the most objectionable features of their despotism to the public. When Louis XVI came to the throne in 1774 he wanted to be a good king. Although no dullard, he had neither the glamor nor the shrewdness of a Frederick II, a Catherine II, or a Joseph II, and he lacked the will to carry through a consistent policy of reform. Moreover, he did not know how to gain support from any section of society for the individual reforms his ministers proposed.

The most pressing need was to find new sources of revenue in the face of a mounting public debt, which French aid to the American Revolution had greatly increased. Yet not until 1787 did any finance minister try to convince the public that the crisis was real and that France's traditional fiscal system was unjust. All the public knew about the king's government was that it was arbitrary, devious, and extravagant. The "Diamond Necklace" scandal in 1783 damaged the monarchy's public image considerably, involving as it did a cardinal enamored of the queen and a piece of jewelry for which the king had to pay one million livres in order to save his wife's reputation.

But poor "public relations" was only one side of the story. The other side involved the resistance of the Parlements, the nobles, and the church hierarchy to all government efforts to infringe on their "constitutional liberties." Louis XVI's first acts as king were to restore the Parlements, which Louis XV had abolished, and to appoint the reformer Turgot as his chief minister. Within two years the Parlement of Paris wrecked Turgot's program to equalize the tax burden and to reduce the privileges of the nobility. It objected particularly to the conversion of the *corvée royale*, the week's labor service of peasants on the royal highways, into a money tax to be paid by landowners of all classes. Although the *corvée royale* was only fifty years old, the Parlement of Paris equated it with the very essence of France's constitution, the prerogatives of birth, and divine justice. Later ministers met similar resistance in the name of "constitutional liberties" whenever they tried to tax the nobility or the clergy.

In the 1780s the French aristocracy intensified its effort to increase its privileges and powers—an effort it had launched during the minority of Louis XV. Not all nobles were hereditary, and some bourgeois mixed socially with the nobles, especially in Paris. On the whole, however, the aristocracy became increasingly self-segregating and class conscious. The Parlements restricted their membership to men born into the nobility of the robe. In the 1780s, all of France's 135 bishops were noblemen. Almost all the royal ministers and all the royal intendants were of noble birth. Finally, in 1781, the aristocracy forced the passage of an army ordinance requiring all future officer candidates to show proof of four generations of noble descent. In the crises of 1787–1788 the aristocrats resisted the royal government in the Parlements, the Church, the government service, and in the newly convened assemblies of notables.* Thus, enlightened despotism failed, and the aristocratic resurgence reached its peak on the eve of the French Revolution.

Enlightened despotism failed everywhere. Its reforms were always incomplete, for it could not eliminate overlapping jurisdictions, traditional privileges, and the sanctity of the crown. The combination of an aristocratic resurgence and a democratic movement—both using claims of constitutional liberties and natural rights—ruined any chance of its ever working.

: : :

The *philosophes* were reformers, not revolutionaries. By the 1770s most of them wanted to eliminate oppression, but none of them openly advocated the overthrow of any existing government. Indeed, Voltaire sometimes took the side of despotism when it tried to make some specific reform opposed by the Parlements and the aristocracy. Diderot and Rousseau were not deceived by enlightened despotism. Yet even they preached the need of using available political means, which generally meant monarchy. Only the British colonies in North America actually revolted before 1789, and the Declaration of Independence was more influenced by Locke than by the French *philosophes*. Only after the American Revolution had taken place did the possibility of a direct challenge to existing political institutions occur to democratic-minded Europeans. By then the political and social strife between the ambitious middle classes and the resurgent aristocracy was more important than the ideas of the *philosophes*, most of whom were dead anyway.

In the early 1790s the cosmopolitan character of the French aristocracy was to damn that class in the eyes of nationalistic commoners almost as much as its political and social pretensions. The death of Antoine Caritat, Marquis de Condorcet (1743–1794) was to symbolize the triumph of nationalist feeling over the cosmopolitan spirit of the *philosophes*, of whom Condorcet was the last. His most famous work expressed an ardent belief in the unlimited progress of mankind. He allegedly took poison in 1794 in order to escape the guillotine, to which he had been condemned by the nationalistic revolutionary government of that time. For the French Revolution was not only the first great democratic revolution in Europe, it also gave birth to the first fully developed form of modern nationalism.

*See Chapter IX

## SUGGESTED READINGS


Smith, Preserved, *The Enlightenment, 1687–1776.* Vol. II of *The Origins of Modern Culture.* Collier Books.*

First published over three decades ago, this work is still very useful for all aspects of eighteenth-century cultural history except science.

Hazard, P., *European Thought in the Eighteenth Century: From Montesquieu to Lessing.* New Haven: Yale Univ. Press, 1954.

A very good survey.

Cassirer, Ernst, *The Philosophy of the Enlightenment.* Boston: Beacon Press, 1955.*

A thoughtful analysis.

Cobban, Alfred, *In Search of Humanity: The Role of the Enlightenment in Modern History.* New York: George Braziller, 1964.

One of the best reevaluations of the significance of the Enlightenment.

Havens, George R., *The Age of Ideas: From Reaction to Revolution in Eighteenth Century France.* New York: Holt, Rinehart and Winston, 1955.*

A very readable and accurate survey; particularly good on Diderot.

Gay, Peter, *Party of Humanity: Essays on the French Enlightenment.* New York: Alfred A. Knopf, 1963.

Argues that the *philosophes* were level-headed reformers rather than utopian dreamers.

——— *The Enlighenment. An Interpretation,* 2 vols. New York: Random-Vintage, 1968–69.*

Presents a fresh view of the Enlightenment in all its complexity and contradictions.

Manuel, Frank E., *The Eighteenth Century Confronts the Gods.* New York: Athenenm, 1965.*

Stresses the *philosophes'* interest in mythology and its retrograde influence on human progress.

Brinton, Crane, ed., *The Portable Age of Reason Reader.* New York: Viking, 1956.

A good selection of the writings of the Enlightenment.

Hall, A. Rupert, *The Scientific Revolution, 1500–1800: The Formation of the Modern Scientific Attitude.**

See especially the section on the revolution in chemistry in the late eighteenth century.

Green, Frederick C., *Jean-Jacques Rousseau: A Critical Study of His Life and Writings.* New York: Cambridge Univ. Press, 1955.

Scholarly and authoritative.

Blanchard, William H., *Rousseau and the Spirit of Revolt.* Ann Arbor: University of Michigan Press, 1968.

Relates Rousseau's efforts to fuse liberty and law to his inner personal conflicts.

Kimball, Sidney F., *The Creation of the Rococo.* Philadelphia: Philadelphia Museum of Art, 1943.

Detailed description of the development of this "typically" eighteenth-century style—by an art historian.

Gombrich, Ernest H., *The Story of Art.*

Good section on neoclassicism.

Hauser, Arnold, *The Social History of Art.* 4 vols.; New York: Random House, 1960. Vintage.* The first five chapters of Volume III give a provocative though not always convincing interpretation of the relationship between artistic and social trends in the eighteenth century.

Bruford, W. H., *Germany in the Eighteenth Century: The Social Background of the Literary Revival.* New York: Cambridge Univ. Press, n.d.*
Excellent analysis of the relationship between social and cultural trends.

Palmer, Robert R., *The Age of the Democratic Revolution.* Vol. I. Princeton, N.J.: Princeton Univ. Press, 1959.
An impressive attempt to relate democratic movements in all countries from the American colonies to Russia. Challenging comparative history for the advanced reader.

Pares, Richard, *George III and the Politicians.* 2nd ed. New York: Oxford Univ. Press, 1964.*
A thoughtful essay.

Rossiter, Clinton L., *Seedtime of the Republic: The Origin of the American Tradition of Political Liberty.* New York: Harcourt, Brace and World, 1953.

Stimulating analysis of intellectual currents in the colonies on the eve of the Revolution.

Alden, John Richard, *The American Revolution, 1775–1783.* Vol. IV of The New American Nation Series. New York: Harper and Row, 1951. Torchbook.*
The best general survey.

Gottschalk, Louis R., *Lafayette between the American and the French Revolutions (1783–1789).* Chicago: Univ. of Chicago Press, 1950.
Part of a massive, day-by-day account of the life of Lafayette by the acknowledged authority on the subject. This volume stresses Lafayette's role in spreading the ideals of the American Revolution in France.

Gershoy, Leo, *From Despotism to Revolution, 1763–1789.* New York: Harper and Row, 1963. Torchbook.*
Another excellent volume in the Rise of Modern Europe series.
The best general account of Enlightened Despotism.

Padover, Saul K., *The Revolutionary Emperor: Josepth the Second, 1741–1790.* New York: R. O. Ballou, 1934.
A good original biography.

CHAPTER IX

# THE ERA OF THE FRENCH REVOLUTION AND NAPOLEON, 1789–1815

After 1750 the acceleration of economic and social change in the more advanced parts of Western Europe brought into question the whole system of estates, orders, and other traditionally organized groups. Population growth, the increased circulation of money, and the intensification of foreign trade made prices rise, opened new markets, and multiplied profits. These were quantitative rather than qualitative changes. Nonetheless, their cumulative effect made Western European society significantly different by 1789 from what it had been in 1715. The middle classes had grown considerably in size and wealth. They viewed the power of the privileged orders with mixed feelings, depending on the degree to which they could aspire to share in it. But in the 1770s and 1780s a growing number of them began to express open resentment toward new efforts by the aristocracy to protect its traditional privileges. In response to this "aristocratic resurgence," a minority of educated commoners launched the first "democratic revolution" in modern history.

Thus the *evolutionary* developments of 1715–1789 helped produce the *revolutionary* developments of 1789–1815. Although this second period has a unity of its own, it belongs more to the eighteenth century than to the nineteenth. The French Revolution and Napoleon transformed much of Europe in accordance with the new ideas of the eighteenth century, not those of the nineteenth—although the latter found isolated (and usually abortive) expression during the period. And the people who finally overthrew Napoleon did so with the hope of restoring as much as they could of the Old Regime.

## THE COMING OF THE REVOLUTION IN FRANCE

Although the revolution in France was a phase of a wider upheaval in the Western world, it was nevertheless the most important manifestation of the upheaval, both in its magnitude and in its influence on other countries. France was the most populous nation in Europe (one European out of seven was a Frenchman in 1789), and her wealth was second only to that of Great Britain. Yet in France royal "absolutism" was feebler and more irresolute than anywhere else, and the revolutionary forces were more dynamic and powerful. Provoked by the aristocratic resurgence, which prevailed almost everywhere, the bourgeoisie, the peasants, and the urban masses in France formed alliances that would have been impossible elsewhere. Beginning in 1789 these three forces, led by the most radical middle-class elements, destroyed the Old Regime more thoroughly than in any other country. They also drove the dispossessed aristocracy and clergy irrevocably into the royalist camp which, beginning in 1792, was to provoke an international counterrevolution against the revolution in France and in almost every other country where it manifested itself.

### Causes of the Revolution

We can look back now and see the causes of the revolution in France. But, until a unique combination of circumstances prompted the king to call the Estates General for the first time in one hundred and seventy-five years, hardly anyone expected to see the Old Regime overthrown by force. Many people knew that something was wrong. There was an economic crisis aggravated by population pressure; the aristocratic resurgence exasperated sections of the bourgeoisie and the peasantry; enlightened political ideas were raising constitutional issues, and enlightened despotism was not working very well. Many Frenchmen were losing confidence in the justice and reasonableness of the existing government and its laws. As their old loyalties faded they felt their obligations as impositions and their forced respect for their superiors as a form of humiliation. Existing sources of prestige and hitherto-accepted forms of income and wealth seemed undeserved. Frenchmen lost their sense of community. In this situation the former bonds between social classes were broken by jealousy and frustration. Thus the first cause of the French Revolution was widespread dissatisfaction with the existing order.

But no revolution can succeed without able leaders, and, in 1789, the most dynamic and effective leadership was on the side of change; this was the second cause of the French Revolution. Neither the king nor his ministers could control the events they set into motion. They appealed to public opinion and then lost the leadership of this opinion to the revolutionaries in the Estates General, in the streets, and in the press.

The third cause of the French Revolution was the weakness of the government of the Old Regime itself. In the second half of the eighteenth century the machinery of the royal government was gradually falling apart. Neither the king's ministers nor the *intendants* who ran much of provincial France could stay this process under the ineffective leadership of Louis XV and Louis XVI. Only a determined monarch could have abolished France's overlapping administrative jurisdictions, reformed the tax system, and eliminated the obsolete medieval survivals in the law. The courts too needed a thorough overhaul to make them serve the needs of all the king's subjects. At the end of his reign Louis XV had cancelled the privileges of the Parlement of Paris when the judges of that court thwarted Turgot's program for fiscal reform. But one of the first moves taken by Louis XVI was to restore its full authority. Like so many high officials, the judges bought or inherited their posts, which they continued to regard as a means of private enrichment rather than as a public trust. Under the Old Regime France lacked the dedicated amateurs who ran the civil service and local affairs in England and, unlike Prussia and Austria, she had not yet begun to use trained professional bureaucrats.

Like the machinery of the royal government, the social and economic structure of the Old Regime was crumbling. The First and Second Estates—that is, the higher clergy and the nobility—no longer performed many of the functions that had formerly justified their wealth and privileges. These ecclesiastical and social elites might have been able to retain their ascendancy over the Third Estate—the bourgeoisie—had they not hopelessly antagonized the rising elite of wealth and talent in this estate. The eighteenth-century French bourgeoisie consisted of the well-to-do commercial and professional classes. Although these people had diverse inter-

*This French caricature shows an aristocrat cursing the Revolution and a democrat expressing her contentment over the Declaration of the Rights of Man, a copy of which she holds in her hand*

ests and aspirations, they all came to hate the snobbery and privileges of the first two estates, especially their exemption from taxation. They also resented the success of the resurgent aristocracy in acquiring a virtual monopoly over the better posts in the government, the Church, and the army.

Although members of the bourgeois elite were to lead the Revolution, they received indispensable backing from the urban and rural masses. Ordinarily, the lower classes had little in common with the bourgeoisie, and during the course of the Revolution the interests of these two heterogeneous groups were to clash repeatedly. What brought them together in 1789 was their common hostility to the Old Regime in a time of economic crisis.

This economic crisis resulted partly from rising prices and partly from a population "inflation." In 1789 France had twenty-six million people, an increase of almost 40 per cent in two generations. This increase was caused by the fact that civil peace and improved means of transporting food to areas of famine allowed greater numbers of people to survive, particularly among the poor. Still, many of the poor could not find enough work, and even those who could saw their wages lagging behind rising prices, which were driven up by new supplies of gold and silver from Brazil and Mexico. By 1789 there was much unemployment, among both the town workers and the peasants who earned part of their living in domestic manufacturing.

Population growth and rising prices also aggravated the problem of hunger in the face of a severe bread shortage. Bread was the principal food for the lower classes, and the grain harvest of 1788 had been disastrously bad. Because of the shortage, the price of bread was higher than at any time in the preceding hundred years. Hordes of landless workers flocked to the cities or roamed the countryside in search of work and food. These "brigands" frightened the small peasant proprietors and urban craftsmen as well as the rich, as we shall see presently.

Millions of peasants were bitter about France's outmoded and unjust system of land tenure. Most of them held small, scattered bits of land which they had come to think of as their property. It was and it was not—and this was the main source of their resentment against the existing order. Only recently have historians figured out the approximate distribution of landed property among—though not within—the various classes in 1789: 10 per cent for the clergy, who constituted less than 1 per cent of the population; almost 25 per cent for the nobility, less than 2 per cent of the population; over 20 per cent for the bourgeoisie, about 5 per cent of the population; a little more than 40 per cent for the peasants, almost 80 per cent of the population. Even these figures would have given cause for complaint, and at the time most peasants believed that the clergy and the nobility alone owned over half the land.

What was worse, the privileged orders were reasserting their seignorial claims on those small parcels of land the peasants considered their own. Since the twelfth and thirteenth centuries many peasant tenants had acquired hereditary rights to the land for which they still paid fixed quitrents. In early modern times inflation had reduced the value of these rents to a pittance. Then, in the eighteenth century, in the face of a new rise in prices, the nobles began trying to find ways to increase these payments in order to boost their revenues. This "feudal reaction," which corresponded to the aristocratic resurgence in political matters, brought the discontent of the small peasant landowners to fever pitch, especially since they also resented the heavy taxes of the government and the compulsory tithes of the Church during the economic depression.

In 1789 the grievances of the small landowners combined with those of the urban craftsmen, who were very different from factory workers. Those who were "in business for themselves" resented the guilds for their restrictive regulations, the government for its heavy taxes, and the privileged estates for their tax exemptions. Those who did piecework or who were paid in wages blamed the merchant-entrepreneurs for the decline in their real income, but the government made a better target. The mass of small producers and nonpropertied classes of the towns and the countryside did not wear *culottes* (knee-breeches), like the bourgeoisie and the nobility. Indeed, in the revolutionary fervor of 1789–1794 they were to glory in their status as *sans-culottes.* But they carefully distinguished themselves as "the people" from the mob of jobless "brigands."

The hopes and grievances of all sections of French society coalesced when the king promised to summon the Estates General for May 1789. He made this move only after all his other efforts to gain new taxes to stave off the mounting financial crisis failed. Heavy expenditures during the American Revolution had worsened the chronic financial difficulties of the government, and by 1787 it was on the verge of bankruptcy. In that year Louis XVI tried to persuade the nobles, the Church, and the Parlements to grant him new taxes; when they refused, he stripped the Parlements of most of their powers. This reversion to "despotism" also antagonized the leaders of bourgeois opinion, who at first sided with the privileged orders in their demands for constitutional government, taxation by consent, and civil liberties. It was this combined opposition that forced Louis XVI not only to convene the Estates General but also to have the delegates elected by nearly universal manhood suffrage, to give the Third Estate twice as many delegates as the First and Second, and to request Petitions of Grievances (*cahiers de doléances*) from it. Sizable portions of these Petitions dealt with local problems, like the noblemen's restrictions on poaching, or the destruction of the woods to supply fuel for iron smelters. But other portions expressed the bourgeois program of reform: equality of taxation for all classes, the sanctity of private property, unlimited access to the highest offices of the realm, freedom from arbitrary arrest and imprisonment, freedom of the press.

### The Revolt of the Third Estate

All Louis XVI had wanted was new taxes, but within less than two months of its opening session the Estates General was to transform itself into a National Assembly ready to make a revolution. It was the leaders of the Third Estate, backed by a few liberal noblemen and churchmen, who were to bring about this transformation. The key issue was whether the delegates would vote together by head or separately by estate. Only a vote by head could have given the Third Estate—with its representation doubled plus a small number of allies in the other two—a majority. The king knew this and used all kinds of pressure to make the three estates meet separately.

At the formal opening session on May 5 at Versailles the delegates of the Third Estate were too loyal to defy the king openly when he commanded each estate to verify its own credentials and to organize itself as a separate body. Hence for six weeks they engaged in parliamentary maneuvering, refusing to verify their credentials as a separate estate and urging members of the other two estates to join them. A number of parish priests heeded this call, but the bishops and the great majority of nobles ignored it.

The deputies of the Third Estate included the most active, persistent, articulate, and politically conscious commoners in France. Though elected by nearly universal manhood suffrage,* they were essentially bourgeois. Over half of the 648 deptuies were lawyers, 166 of whom were in private practice; 278 deputies—most of whom had legal training—held some kind of government office; 85 deputies were merchants or business men; 67 lived by the income or management of their property (usually land); and 31 were doctors or other professional men. There was not a single peasant or workingman in the entire delegation. This situation was not peculiar to the period—even today there are few such people in the democratically elected legislatures of the Western world. Indeed, in 1789, the smaller agricultural tenants and laborers, the hordes of domestic servants, and many wage-earning artisans willingly accepted the preeminence of the nobility or the bourgeoisie. What is significant is the fact that the delegates themselves came from those sections of the bourgeoisie whose ambitions were most thwarted by the existing order and who were best able to state their case against it.

Ironically, the first outstanding champion of the Third Estate was a liberal clergyman, the Abbé Siéyès. In his widely read pamphlet, *What Is The Third Estate?*, he said that it alone was the nation and that the privileged orders were useless. "What a society," Siéyès exclaimed, "in which work is said to *derogate*, where it is honorable to consume, but humiliating to produce, where the laborious occupations are called vile, as if anything were vile except vice, or as if the classes that work were the most vicious! ' Siéyès' pamphlet, which had first appeared in February 1789, demanded full political rights for the Third Estate. "The Third Estate alone, they [the privileged orders] say, cannot constitute the *Estates General.* Well! So much the better! it will form a *National Assembly.*"

In June the deputies in the Third Estate transformed Siéyès's demands into the first acts of the Revolution. On the 17th, they solemnly proclaimed themselves the National Assembly, the only true representative of the French people. They even claimed the right to withdraw their "authorization" of existing taxes, should the king and the privileged orders prove obdurate. The king replied to these revolutionary claims to power on the 20th by closing down the hall at Versailles in which the deputies met. Undaunted, they moved into a large indoor tennis court nearby and took an oath "never to separate. . . . until the Constitution of the kingdom was established and affirmed on a sound basis." The Tennis Court Oath

*The voting was indirect. Nearly all adult males—almost ten million of them—voted for representatives to 40,000 local assemblies. These representatives then voted for electors in about 200 district assemblies. It was these electors who finally elected the 648 deputies to the Third Estate. The 300-odd deputies of each of the first two estates were also elected through district assemblies, though only by the two or three hundred thousand adult males who belonged to these two orders.

*David's "The Oath of Tennis Court"*

was one of the great dramatic gestures in modern history. All but one of the deputies defied the king by asserting that they were the National Assembly in this playroom of the court aristocracy or anywhere else they might meet.

By late Jine, then, the Third Estate was asserting itself in a way that no one had dreamed was possible a few weeks earlier. Men who had never seen each other before had forged a bond of unity and found their spokesmen. These included not only the liberal clergyman Siéyès, but also the liberal nobleman Honoré Gabriel, Count de Mirabeau, who rose to prominence by reasserting the sovereignty of the National Assembly when the king again tried to force the three estates to meet separately on June 23. Mirabeau told the king's emissary: "Go tell those who sent you that we are here by the will of the people, and that we will leave our seats only at the point of bayonets."

These words showed that the representatives of the people were now hostile to the aristocracy and the royal government itself. On June 27, Louis XVI seemed to give in when he ordered the absent members of the first two estates to join the majority. But he was merely stalling for time while he moved his army regiments to Versailles and Paris. It seemed as if bayonets were going to be used after all. And the aristocrats were probably plotting their own revenge; or so it seemed. These fears aroused the masses of Frenchmen into action in July. Henceforth the Revolution became a truly popular movement.

## REVOLUTIONARY FRANCE

The mass uprising of the summer of 1789 infected the army, disarmed the government, and disabled the nobles in the ultimate strongholds of their landed estates. It finally enabled the bourgeois elite to triumph over the aristocracy; it made it possible for the National Assembly to remain in existence, and forced it in some ways to go beyond what its boldest leaders had originally intended. This body, which began calling itself the Constituent Assembly, did not disband until September 1791. But commencing in the summer of 1789 the more radical leaders of the bourgeoisie decided to destroy not only the aristocracy but all the existing institutions that thwarted their aspirations.

Thus was France propelled into a series of revolutionary experiences unprecedented in the history of the world. During the next six years the country went through three constitutions, rebellions by the extreme Right and the extreme Left, a totalitarian dictatorship, and an international war in which modern ideological issues played a crucial role. The French Revolution not only overthrew the Old Regime and brought class antagonisms into the open; it also forged a nation. Millions of Frenchmen suddenly began to think of the revolutionary government as their government. They differed as to how it should be constituted and what its policies should be, but they agreed in their desire to defend it against its enemies at home and abroad.

Through all these upheavals, however, the new, modern order based on the "principles of 1789" remained. These principles created a constitutional monarchy in the name of the sovereignty of the people. They abolished all forms of privilege and gave every citizen individual liberty and equality of rights. They rid the institution of private property of feudal entail and began to replace laws based on status with laws based on contractual agreements. They did away with the guilds, internal tariff barriers, and other hindrances to the freedom to hire labor, the freedom to produce, and the freedom to buy and sell. They expropriated the wealth of the Church and refashioned this institution into an agency directly dependent upon the state. Finally, they gave France rational administrative and judicial systems that have lasted until our own time.

### The Revolt of the Masses

In early July, 1789, the beginning of the alliance between the revolutionary bourgeoisie and "the people" was marked by the formation of a bourgeois militia (National Guard)—including journeymen but excluding unemployed drifters—and the installation of a revolutionary government at the Hôtel de Ville (City Hall). For all their fears of the urban masses, the bourgeois spokesmen for the Third Estate feared a royal or aristocratic reaction more. Hence under their leadership, and with the help of the dissident troops in the city, the people of Paris vented their accumulated rage on the Bastille.

The storming of the Bastille was a unique event in the magnitude of its impact on the political situation. Tens of thousands of Parisians took part in it, and one hundred and fifty of the attackers were killed or wounded. The victorious crowd slaughtered the handful of defending troops, impaling their heads on pikes. Almost everyone interpreted the intoxicating news that the Bastille had fallen as a major defeat for "depotism." The victors not only freed the seven political prisoners in the fortress-prison, they also tore it down stone by stone. At Versailles the news frightened the king so much that he sent away his troops.

The news of the fall of the Bastille and of aristocrats fleeing across the frontier also unleased the mass upheaval in the countryside. In the last weeks of July the peasants became convinced that the "aristos" were inciting the "brigands" to attack them. As the Great Fear mounted in intensity, the peasants, armed against nonexistent brigands, turned their weapons against the hated *seigneurs* and their bailiffs. They stormed the châteaux and government offices where the records of their "feudal" obligations were kept and burned them. Neither the police nor the government officials did anything to stop them, and the law courts were suspended. This anarchy in the countryside forced the Constituent Assembly (as the National Assembly called itself by September) to go beyond its goal of political reform to more radical changes in France's social structure.

Already on August 4–5 the deputies at Versailles had abolished the vestiges of feudalism and on August 27 they recognized the civil equality of all Frenchmen in the Declaration of the Rights of Man and the Citizen. The noblemen renounced their remaining seigneurial rights; the clergy renounced its tithes. Henceforth, all land could be bought and sold outright by anyone, and every Frenchman was to be subject to the same rates of taxation and to have equal access to all public

*The storming of the Bastille*

offices. The main accent of the Declaration of the Rights of Man and the Citizen was on liberty, "the power to do anything that does not injure others." The first Article declared that "men are born and remain free and equal in rights." Article Two defined man's natural rights as "liberty, property, security, and resistance to oppression." According to Article Three, sovereignty belongs to the nation, not to the king. The Declaration went on to say that only the law could limit the exercise of men's rights, and that the law was the expression of the general will. "All citizens have the right to take part personally or by their representatives in its formation. It must be the same for all, whether it protects or punishes." The law protected all citizens against arbitrary arrest and imprisonment and punished no one for his opinions or free expression of them in the press.

The king did not approve of the August 4 decrees and the Declaration of Rights, but the people won because they were organized. Never had any Europeans expressed such a burst of civic spirit as the French in 1789. Bourgeois patriots met in clubs to discuss reforms. watch over local affairs, and prod the authorities. There were many such political clubs, the most energetic being the Jacobins, of whom we shall learn presently. The *sans-culottes* in the towns did the same things in their popular assemblies, which controlled the new communes. People from many sections of society joined the local branches of the National Guard and began organizing them into regional federations. Finally, the press kept the citizens alert.

The revolt of the masses continued when, on October 5, a crowd of women, accompanied by the National Guard, marched to Versailles and brought the royal family back to Paris the next day. As in July, a bread shortage precipitated the uprising. The women wanted the king to give them bread *and* to come to Paris, where they could keep an eye on him.

Whether or not Marie Antoinette told her husband "let them eat cake," she was certainly against everything the Revolution stood for and opposed to leaving Versailles. The Marquis de Lafayette, who had fought with George Washington and who now headed the National Guard, tried to pacify both sides by appearing on the balcony with the queen, kissing her hand, and assuring the crowd that she and her husband would gladly go back to Paris. They were not glad, but they went, accompanied by wagonloads of bread from the royal bakeshop.

The victory of the Parisian masses seemed completed when the Assembly followed the king into the capital. Thereafter the king was their prisoner, and the Assembly was constantly subjected to the intimidations of the more aggressive political factions in Paris. For the next two years the Assembly governed France like a sovereign while framing a constitution that the king could no longer reject. But the constitution itself reflected the aspirations of the bourgeois leadership more than those of the masses.

## BUILDING THE NEW ORDER, 1789–1791

Despite all these pressures, the bourgeois patriots framed the kind of constitution they wanted. Its main features were a weak executive and decentralization. The Constitution of 1791 has been called a triumph of the bourgeoisie. Its emphasis on individual liberty, limited monarchy, and weak government bears out this description, and so, to some extent, does its electoral procedure. All citizens were to have civil rights. But only male citizens over twenty-five who paid direct taxes equal to the income of three days' work were to have the right to vote for electors in local assemblies. These *active* citizens included almost two-thirds of France's adult males; the rest were *passive.* There were higher property and income qualifications for electors and for deputies, which only members of the bourgeoisie could meet.

In addition to its main work of framing a constitution, which was to endure for less than a year, the Constituent Assembly issued a number of longer-lasting decrees in line with the principle of equal rights set forth in August 1789. In the spring of 1790, it abolished all outward signs of social privilege; henceforth noblemen were forbidden to use their former titles or to display their coats of arms, and every Frenchman was to be addressed simply as Citizen so-and-so. All Frenchmen could now enter any form of employment. Social classes remained fairly closed, but there were no longer any legal distinctions among them. Money and talent replaced privilege and birth as the main criteria of social status.

The administrative and judicial reforms of the National (Constituent) Assembly had less profound effects on people's daily lives than its social decrees, but they were actually more radical and longer lasting. In 1789 the map of France was a complicated and illogical mosaic of provinces, bailiwicks, civil and ecclesiastical dioceses, conflicting local administrations and degrees of self-government, military districts, and unequal judicial divisions. The Assembly abolished all of these and reorganized the nation into 83 departments (counties) of approximately equal size. The new judicial divisions were provided with a uniform system of courts. All judges were to be paid by the state and (at first) elected the local citizens. Juries were also introduced into the criminal courts. France had to wait until the time of Napoleon for its civil code, but the Assembly inaugurated a standard judicial procedure and a uniform penal code based on the new enlightened ideas of Beccaria.

Unlike the social and administrative revolutions, the economic reforms of the National (Constituent) Assembly did not make radical changes in the structure of the existing order. Nonetheless they altered this order profoundly. In accordance with the Enlightenment principle of *laissez faire,* the Assembly abolished the monopolies and privileges of all existing economic organizations. These included chambers of commerce, manufacturers' associations, trading companies, and craft guilds. Now both businessmen and workers were forbidden to organize. In February 1791, the Le Chapelier Law finally abolished the guilds while retaining the old ordinances against strikes and unions. The new legal equality of enterprise obviously favored the employers over the workers, but it was perfectly consistent with the doctrine of economic liberalism. The assembly also abolished all internal tariffs and duties and other indirect taxes on consumers' goods. Complete freedom of trade in France itself was a major innovation with many ramifications. It helped the development of banks, financial societies, and credit. The Assembly also facilitated economic activities by instituting a uniform system of weights and measures—the metric system. The suppression of indirect taxes on consumers' goods temporarily increased the purchasing power of the poorer classes; but it deprived the government of much-needed revenue.

The Constituent Assembly temporarily solved the government's desperate need for revenue by nationalizing the lands of the Church and selling them to the public. In November 1789 the government sold bonds, called assignats, with which people could buy plots of land. As people paid for national property with these assignats they were supposed to be burned on their return to the state, and the money received for them was to be used to pay off the huge deficit inherited from the Old Regime. But the government was soon forced to make new issues for other purposes. It had to reimburse the former holders of suppressed offices and pay the salaries of the clergy, and there were all the regular expenses of running the government. Since the new direct taxes were not yet coming in, the state used new issues of assignats to meet its financial obligations. Soon the assignats became a kind of legal tender for all monetary transactions though partly as a result of lack of public confidence and partly because of their sheer weight of numbers, they had declined one-third in value by early 1792.

The policy of selling Church lands was more successful in solving the immediate financial crisis than in redistributing these lands among the poorer peasants. The government tried to favor these peasants by requiring only a small down payment, but when the lands went on sale in May 1790 the majority of the landless day laborers simply did not have even that much money. Furthermore, since the sales were by public auction, the larger lots could not conveniently be broken up for the benefit of small buyers. Thus, the people who profited from the sales were mainly peasants who already owned land, some nobles, and, most especially, the bourgeoisie. The principal gains of the peasants from the French Revolution were the elimination of all outside claims on their lands and, by 1793, the abolition of all compensation to their former landlords for the right not to pay them quitrents any more.

Meanwhile, the Assembly's reform of the Church itself divided the French people more seriously than any of its other reforms. The Civil Constitution of the Clergy suppressed the monastic orders, made the priests and bishops servants of the state and required them to take a loyalty oath to the revolutionary regime. In April 1791 Pope Pius VI formally condemned the Civil Constitution and the Revolution itself. About half of the French clergy obeyed the pope in refusing to take the loyalty oath, and Louis XVI, who bitterly repented approving the Civil Constitution, took a "non-juring" priest as his private chaplain. This split between the "juring (those who took the oath) and "non-juring" clergy spread all through France.

Within a year after the National (Constituent) Assembly disbanded, the political system it had created disappeared. Whereas the American colonists had learned to run their local affairs before they obtained their own national government, the French people had to acquire this kind of experience on the spur of the moment. Indeed, the very structure of the French system handicapped it from the start. The militant leadership at the local level was usually more radical than the national government, and political decentralization widened the gap between the two. Moreover, the executive—that is, the king—and new Legislative Assembly refused to cooperate most of the time. France had no George Washington to reconcile opposing factions and symbolize national unity. She had,

*Camille Desmoulins calling the people to arms in the garden of the Palais Royal (by Honoré Daumier)*

instead, Louis XVI, whose heart was with the forces of counterrevolution.

This system also failed because of continuing opposition from the radical Right and the radical Left. The radical Right tried to persuade the monarchs of Central Europe to invade France, crush the Revolution, and restore the king and the Church to their former status. The radical Left wanted to depose Louis XVI and eliminate the distinction between active and passive citizens. In April 1792 France did, indeed, go to war against Austria.* The king supported the war hoping that the revolutionary government would lose. The bourgeois leaders of the new order launched it hoping that it would rally the "passive citizens" to the defense of the nation. Instead, the people of Paris made a "second revolution" on August 10, 1792.

*See p. 346.

## THE REVOLUTION FIGHTS FOR ITS LIFE, 1792–1794

The insurrection of the Paris Commune on August 10, 1792 was the first example in modern history of a successful revolution led by the masses. The insurgents seized the royal palace and tried to arrest the king and queen. While the attackers were slaughtering their Swiss Guards, the royal couple fled next door to the meeting hall of the Legislative Assembly. It too had to bow before the conquerors of August 10. After deposing the king and letting the Commune imprison him, it voted itself out of existence. But first it announced the election, by universal suffrage, of a new Constituent Assembly, to be called the Convention.

This Convention immediately abolished the monarchy and decreed that its own acts would be dated from the Year I of the Republic (September 22, 1792). In December, the Convention tried Louis XVI for treason, and on January 21 the king was guillotined in the great square built by Louis XV and renamed the Place de la Révolution. Louis XVI's execution dealt a decisive blow to monarchical feeling in France. It also bound the counterrevolutionaries irrevocably to the European war against the regicides and made it impossible for the latter to obtain a compromise peace.

Although the main purpose of the Convention was to frame a new constitution, it also had to consolidate the Revolution, maintain a government, and wage a war against the rest of Europe. In each of these tasks the Convention faced formidable obstacles. And, to make matters worse, its deputies were deeply divided among themselves. The Girondists favored economic freedom and a federal republic; they sat on the Right. The deputies of the Left supported the policies of the Parisian Jacobins. Both factions were thoroughly middle class and property-minded. but the Left insisted on the necessity of economic controls and strong central government, at least for the duration of the war. Then the events of 1793 strengthened the forces of the counterrevolutionary Right and the radical Left outside the Convention and divided its two main factions into moderate and radical wings.

At first, all the Girondists accepted the Republic and devoted their main efforts toward driving the enemy out of France and spreading the benefits of the Revolution to her neighbors. These policies, plus the execution of the king, brought other European powers into the war on the side of Austria and Prussia (First Coalition) in February 1793. Under the crushing weight of their forces the French army caved in, and its commander, General Dumouriez, went over to the enemy in early April. The new threat of foreign invasion again roused the revolutionary groups that had appeared spontaneously in August and September of 1793. Led by the pro-Jacobin Commune of Paris they demanded the ouster of the Girondists from the Convention. Despite their parliamentary immunity, twenty-nine Girondist deputies were arrested on June 2, 1793. The rest fled to the provinces. Although many of them continued to think of themselves as "patriots," others joined the forces of counterrevolution.

The Revolution was indeed fighting for its very life by the summer of 1793. Its armies were being driven back on almost all fronts, and counterrevolutionary uprisings were spreading in the provinces. Incited by non-juring priests and agents of the émigrés, the peasants of the Vendée had already begun their open rebellion in March. (They rebelled especially against the army draft, as we shall see shortly.) The Girondists rose up in June in Normandy, the Gironde, Lyons, and Provence. By July, more than two-thirds of the country was in open rebellion against the Convention. Coupled with the foreign menace this mounting counterrevolutionary violence at home called for extreme measures, if the Revolution were to survive at all.

### The Committee of Public Safety and the Terror: Robespierre

For a year, beginning in July 1793, France lived under a Jacobin dictatorship. The Convention framed a far more democratic constitution than the one it superseded but was never able to put it into effect. Instead, it delegated extraordinary powers to the Committee of Public Safety and the Committee of General Security and declared that the provisional government of the Republic was to be "revolutionary until the peace." While the Committee of Public Safety tried to control every aspect of French life from Paris as well as instituting the terror there, the Jacobins in the provinces carried out their own reign of terror against suspected slackers and traitors.

There is no doubt that the Committee of Public Safety's military mobilization saved France from invasion. In February

1793, the Convention had already decreed a levy of 300,000 troops (which had provoked the revolt in the Vendée). Then, in August, the Committee decreed a levy-in-mass. This decree made all bachelors from 18 to 25 subject to call into the army and declared that the entire population—both sexes and all ages—was liable to service of one kind or another. Conscripts and volunteers were merged with the old army of professionals into a mammoth force of over a million men. Most of the raw recruits received their "training" on the battlefield from the example of the professionals, and their patriotic fervor partially made up for their inexperience.

The levy-in-mass was doubly revolutionary in that it included the nation's material resources as well as its manpower. It was harder to mobilize the economy than to draft young men, but still, munitions factories, textile plants, and workshops were soon supplying the new mass army with its basic needs. In late September the Committee of Public Safety made provision for nationwide controls over prices and wages in the Law of the Maximum. This law was designed to promote equality of sacrifice at home, as at the front. No one was supposed to get rich from the war, and no one was supposed to go hungry. The Committee of Public Safety and the local authorities were to force the peasants, the manufacturers, and the merchants to sell their products at specified ceiling prices. Although the system of controls was never fully worked out, and the Maximum was frequently violated, it did prevent a catastrophic fall of the assignat and insured the provisioning of the armies.

In September 1793, again under pressure from the Paris radicals, the Convention organized the Terror. This new technique of coercion promised death to Frenchmen who evaded the controls of the levy-in-mass. Its main purpose, however, was to punish traitors and prevent further counterrevolutionary uprisings. In order to make the Terror effective, the Committee of Public Safety drafted a Law of Suspects, which the Convention passed on September 17. According to this law anyone suspected of any kind of unpatriotic behavior—or even thoughts—was to be arrested. During the next ten months over 300,000 Frenchmen were imprisoned. Of these, 16,594 were executed as a result of trials, and over 20,000 were shot without trial or died of disease or other causes while awaiting trial in prison. Anyone was eligible; no one was safe. That was what the Terror meant.

Without the help of organized local patriots the Committee of Public Safety and the Committee of General Security could never have enforced the Terror. In theory, agents and representatives of the national government supervised the activities of the revolutionary surveillance committees and Jacobin clubs in the provinces. In practice, these popular organizations often acted on their own. They hounded their fellow citizens into patriotic conformity by forcing them to carry "certificates of civism." These "certificates" were required identity cards and had to be renewed frequently. In addition, the local patriotic organizations compiled their own lists of suspects. They often tried and executed their victims without consulting the Revolutionary Tribunal in Paris. As a result, a number of innocent people died with a larger number of guilty ones.

The Terror served its main purposes of quelling treason and mobilizing the patriotic energies of the nation for the war effort, an achievement all the more remarkable in view of its makeshift character, for, even at the top, the revolutionary dictatorship was far from being "monolithic." The Committee of Public Safety included men with a variety of talents and political views. Nominally the "twelve who ruled" were all Jacobins, but there were cliques within cliques among them. Most powerful among them was Maximilian Robespierre (1758–1794).

Although Robespierre continued to share power with his own clique, his personality and his views largely determined the nature of the Terror. He came from the lower ranks of the professional bourgeoisie, a social stratum that was naturally hostile to the nobility but almost equally opposed to the wealthy bourgeoisie, which stood so much higher in the social hierarchy. With the help of scholar-

The Terror: arrest of a suspect

ships he was able to go to the best school in Paris. There he studied classical literature, the philosophy of the Enlightenment, and Rousseau, whose powerful influence colored his political and social ideals and his emotional sensitivity and lent severity to his tone of expression. In 1781, at twenty-three, Robespierre returned to his home town of Arras, where he earned a modest living as a lawyer and moved in middle-class social circles.

From this environment, as well as from Rousseau, Robespierre acquired the values of honesty, hard work, dignified morals, and decent appearances. Robespierre was a staunch patriot and a champion of political democracy conceived as universal male suffrage and equality of civil rights. During the Terror he showed exceptional political shrewdness. Yet, though often ruthless in his means, he remained dedicated to the defense of the Revolution and the nation. Indeed, he earned the nickname The Incorruptible.

Robespierre helped to organize the Terror in response to a unique set of conditions. In 1793 France was gripped by a hysteria induced by fear of foreign invasion, fear of counterrevolution, and fear of the *sans-culottes'* demands for social as well as political democracy. For many people the Revolution meant no government, no taxes, and no quarter for the rich. The Committee of Public Safety thus faced the task of running a revolutionary government without the sanction of traditional legitimacy, which engenders the habit of obedience. Under such conditions Robespierre and his colleagues had to set up an emergency dictatorship. He reconciled his democratic principles with this dictatorship by calling it the "despotism of liberty"; as Rousseau had suggested, he was "forcing men to be free" and destroying the "enemies of the people." But "the people" were becoming divided among themselves.

### The Sans-Culottes versus the Jacobin Dictatorship

Almost all the revolutionary agencies that had sprung up in 1789 continued to grow. Only the more conservative clubs and newspapers disappeared with the fall of the Girondists (June 2, 1793), and by that time the Jacobin clubs had almost half a million members throughout France. As we have already noted, they played an increasingly active role in local affairs, aside from dominating the national government. This mass minority of activists saw to it that most of the government's emergency decrees were carried out and helped to stimulate the civic spirit and patriotism of the more passive major-

A Parisian sans-culotte with his pike and the cockade in his hat

ity. Just below this group was a larger mass minority of activists, those underprivileged townspeople who believed that they had made the Revolution and that now anything was possible.

It must be remembered that, large as this group of activists was, it was also a minority of its class, even in Paris itself. This class included shopkeepers, craftsmen, wage earners, domestic servants, café waiters and proprietors, barbers, and even some small merchants and manufacturers. Many of these people had no desire to compete with their social betters and hated the social disorganization brought about by the Revolution. In fact, many were executed as counterrevolutionaries under the Terror.

The true *sans-culottes* were fanatical on the subject of equality. To them true democracy meant their direct participation in the political life of their local neighborhoods, and by sheer numbers they dominated the popular assemblies that controlled the municipal communes in 1793–94. They also refused to accept a subordinate position in social relations. As one contemporary observer put it: "Citizens of poor outward appearance and who in former times would not have dared to show themselves in those places reserved for more elegant company, were going for walks along with the rich, and holding their heads high." They made a virtue of their long trousers, their familiar form of address (the equivalent of calling everyone by his first name), and their emancipation from the tutelage of the former privileged orders. Their hostility to the clergy made some of them openly favor the "dechristianization" of French life and the development of their own civic "religion," complete with trees of liberty, patriotic festivals, and popular songs.

Although the combination of an unprecedented release of human energy at the base and dynamic leadership at the top saved the Revolution and the nation, the Committee of Public Safety and the *sans-culottes* were working at cross purposes by early 1794. The *sans-culottes'* conception of direct democracy was anarchic and unworkable; the Jacobin dictatorship worked, but was despotic. Furthermore, the *sans-culottes* held economic and social views incompatible with those of the bourgeois economic liberals, including most of the Jacobins. To the *sans-culottes* the ideal society was one of small independent producers, each owning a field, store, or workshop large enough to maintain his own family. They wanted to redistribute the land on the big estates among the poor and to curb the monopolies and profits of the large traders, not just during the emergency but permanently. To the bourgeoisie of all levels, property was sacred, and profits should be determined solely by what the market would bear.

In April 1793 Robespierre himself had expressed his belief in the ideal of a society of small independent producers, but once he came to power he saw that he could not yield to the *sans-culottes* without

*Robespierre being brought to the guillotine. The bandage covers his broken jaw, which some say was the result of an attempted suicide*

terrifying the property-owning bourgeoisie, which formed the main base of his government. Thus, he made just enough concessions to the *sans-culottes* to attach them to the revolutionary regime. The most extreme of these concessions were the Ventôse* decrees, at the end of February, 1794, which proposed the confiscation of the property of the "enemies of the Revolution" and its redistribution among "indigent patriots." But despite their seemingly "socialistic" character, the Ventôse decrees made little impression on the *sans-culottes*. Their interests were basically opposed to those of the Jacobins, and the alliance between the two groups stood only until the worst threats of foreign invasion and counterrevolution had passed. Meanwhile, the Terror provided the *sans-culottes* with the severed heads and gushing blood of thousands of their betters. The terrorist exaltation of the *sans-culottes* led them to idealize the guillotine as the "popular ax," the "scythe of equality," which would both rid France of her enemies and increase the supply of bread.

The open break between the *sans-culottes* and the Jacobin dictatorship came in the spring of 1794. At that time Robespierre arrested and executed the leading *sans-culotte* demagogue, Jacques Hébert, and a number of his "enraged" lieutenants (the *enragés*). Thereafter the *sanculottes* began to lose faith in the Jacobin-dominated Committee of Public Safety. In the end, Robespierre was deserted by both the *sans-culottes* and his fellow Jacobins who wore knee-breeches, just as he did.

*A new calendar replaced the old Christian calendar in the fall of 1793. It started with the Year I of the Republic (September 22, 1792) and gave new names to the months. These names corresponded to the weather and the seasons: Ventôse (month of the wind), Thermidor (the hot month), Brumaire (the foggy month), etc. The revolutionary calendar remained in effect until Napoleon became emperor in 1804 (the Year XII).

### The Thermidorean Reaction

The reaction began on the 9th Thermidor (July 27, 1794), Robespierre and several of his colleagues were arrested, and the Committee of Public Safety was overthrown. Their downfall resulted from a political plot within the Convention and the two government committees. It was the first major event of the Revolution in which the *sans-culottes* did not play a major role. After trying to defend his position in the Convention, Robespierre submitted to arrest. He hoped that the Commune of Paris would rise up on another one of its "days" in his defense, but he had stripped it of many of its powers and disillusioned most of its supporters. Less than a day after his arrest The Incorruptible himself was executed by the guillotine to which he had sent so many other victims.

The goal of the conspirators of the 9th Thermidor had been to get rid of Robespierre, not to end the Terror. Yet most people yearned for the end to this nightmare. Besides, it now seemed unnecessary in view of France's military successes in the spring of 1794. The nation was no longer in grave danger, and, indeed, the armies of the Republic were advancing into enemy territory on several fronts.* Thus the Jacobin leaders who overthrew Robespierre fell out of favor themselves. The survivors of the Girondist faction came back to the Convention in December 1794, and the majority of the deputies abolished most of the emergency measures of the Committee of Public Safety.

The Thermidorean Reaction brought a more conservative political regime and reprisals against the Jacobins. In the last year of its existence (July 1794–October 1795) the Convention reaffirmed the liberal and individualist ideals of the first phase of the Revolution. The new constitution it drafted resembled that of 1791 in giving the right to vote only to those Frenchmen who paid direct taxes, but it differed from its predecessor in maintaining the Republic and in placing much more executive power in the hands of five "directors" than the king had had under the first constitution. Meanwhile, middle- and upper-class youths attacked the Jacobin supporters in the streets, and the power of the Jacobins was ruined by crippling restrictions on all organized political activity. After the initial wave of revenge, the new regime, called the Directory, settled down to four years of uninspired rule.

*See p. 346.

## THE PERIOD OF CONSOLIDATION, 1795–1814

Many historians claim that the French Revolution ended with the Thermidorean Reaction and the rise of the Directory in 1795. Napoleon Bonaparte himself said that it ended when he became dictator (under the title of First Consul) in November 1799. According to him, his accession to power ended the period of innovation and civil strife and initiated a period of consolidation and internal stability. Nevertheless, the Directory too had tried to maintain a middle course between Left-wing radicalism and counterrevolution; it was its failure to do so that allowed this famous general to take over the job. Whenever the Revolution was *over*, it had not entirely *failed*. Until 1814, and to some extent even afterward, the bourgeois elite managed to safeguard the "principles of 1789"—with the important exceptions of political democracy and representative government—as well as unrestricted capitalist enterprise.

### The Directory and the Rise of Napoleon Bonaparte

The character of the Directory (October 1795–November 1799) can be briefly summarized. Politically it was controlled by 20,000 electors, who chose the two chambers of the legislative assembly (the Council of 500 and the Council of Ancients, an upper chamber of 250 members) and all the important provincial officials. The chambers chose the five Directors, who constituted the executive and gave the whole regime its name. Socially the Directory catered to the bourgeoisie at the expense of the other classes. Economically it failed to provide reasonably priced food for the masses or to solve its chronic fiscal problems. Official corruption and private profiteering aggravated domestic unrest and hampered the war effort.

Yet certain stabilizing forces soon came into being. Not only the bourgeoisie but also millions of other Frenchmen longed for political and economic stability. This longing was a force in itself. The army also acted increasingly as a force for maintaining order at home. Since the summer of 1793, troops had been used to put down counterrevolutionary uprisings in the provinces. Then, in April 1795, for the first time since the Revolution began, they were brought to Paris itself, where they crushed bread riots by the *sans-culottes.* In October 1795 royalist mobs protested against the way the Convention tried to pack the new legislative assembly with its own members. Having already accustomed itself to using the army for political purposes, the Convention, in one of its last acts, called on a twenty-six-year-old general named Napoleon Bonaparte to put down the royalist mobs. The "whiff of grapeshot" with which he did this made the Directory dependent on military protection from the outset, and in the next four years it relied more and more on this kind of protection. It was only a question of time before the army would decide the fate of the government itself.

Napoleon Bonaparte (1769–1821) was the most famous example in modern times of a military hero who seized power from a weak liberal regime and ruled successfully as an enlightened despot. The fact that he was born in Corsica in 1769 helped him to realize his ambition for power and glory. This Italian-speaking island had just been annexed to France. Therefore, as the son of one of its noblemen, young Napoleon found it possible to gain admission to a French military school and to become a lieutenant in the king's army. The the Revolution gave him his chance to rise rapidly in rank, since many of the senior royalist officers deserted. He was a brigadier-general in 1795 when he dispersed the royalist mob in Paris and, a year later, he received command of an army in Italy. From then on he piled one military victory on top of another. He ruled the Italian territories he conquered like a sovereign prince and made the government of the Directory dependent on him for funds and booty. Finally, the weakness of the Directory gave him his chance to seize power.

Napoleon used his extraordinary personal qualities to his best advantage. Although short and dark, he was solidly built and not unattractive. He did not have the fancy manners of a true aristocrat, nor was he "nice" by bourgeois standards. He lost his temper and could be grossly insulting. There was always something of the schemer about him, yet he was completely fearless in the face of personal danger. Behind his flashing eyes one could almost see the brilliant mind and vivid imagination constantly at work. Always alert, his brain tirelessly seized on new facts and ideas, which his memory filed away for later reference at a moment's notice. He could concentrate for hours and fall asleep at will. Despite his changing moods, he was able to captivate and dazzle anyone who had any inclination to follow him. His soldiers adored him, and many eminent civilians could not help but admire his rapid decisions and his quick grasp of complex problems. With a sure intuition, Napoleon singled out the aspects of the Revolution that were closest to the heart of the nation and the ones that would best serve his own power. But he never relied on his intuition alone. Through extensive reading as a young officer he had thoroughly absorbed the cultural outlook of the eighteenth century. Reason was his surest guide. He once declared that "every operation must be carried out according to a system, because nothing succeeds by chance." He also had a completely "classical" conception of a unitary state, all of a piece, and constructed according to a simple and symmetrical pattern.

But it was Bonaparte the general, not Napoleon the intellectual, who seized power in 1799. In the autumn of that year, several leaders of the Directory were looking for a general to quell unrest at home. Bonaparte then left his forces in Egypt and returned to Paris to join a group of conspirators, including one of the Directors, who were plotting the overthrow of the existing government. On the 18th Brumaire in the Year VIII (November 9, 1799), his soldiers, with bayonets drawn, expelled the members of the two legislative councils from their meeting halls. The victorious conspirators then replaced the Directory with a new regime, called the Consulate. A rump assembly met and appointed three provisional Consuls, with Bonaparte as First Consul, to govern France.

Three weeks later Frenchmen had a new constitution, which told them: "Citizens, the Revolution is firmly rooted in the principles that began it; it is finished." Bonaparte the "stabilizer" had taken it over.

### The Reforms of Napoleon

Napoleon consolidated his personal power by rallying the nation behind him in three ways. He invented the plebiscite—a popular referendum based on universal suffrage—to approve his dictatorship in 1799 and 1802 and his crowning himself Emperor of the French in 1804. He gave his regime a broad social base by preserving the doctrine of "careers open to talent" while at the same time reconciling some of the *émigrés* with new offices and new titles. In 1801 he ended the ten-year split in the Church by signing a mutually acceptable Concordat with the pope. This Concordat was to last for more than one hundred years. It restored some of the pope's powers over the French bishops, but the Church's property was not restored, and the state was to remain purely secular, paying the salaries of the priests and of Protestant ministers and Jewish rabbis. By temporarily disarming the counterrevolution the Concordat was Napoleon's most successful tool for promoting conciliation and stability in France.

With these goals achieved, Napoleon began to renovate the nation's institutions; his guiding principles in this endeavor were: equality, authority, efficiency. He gave France the most highly centralized modern bureaucracy in the world, with the Council of State at the top and thousands of well-paid professional administrators. He maintained the local administrative units created in 1790 but introduced a new representative of the central government—the *prefect*—as the final authority in each department. Napoleon's economic and financial reforms consolidated the gains of the Revolution and completed the emancipation of bourgeois capitalism from the restraints and inefficiency of the Old Regime. He established a corps of national tax collectors and created the Bank of France on the model of the Bank of England. In 1804, the Bank of France issued a new, stable currency, the franc, which was to retain its gold value of twenty cents for more than one hundred years. Napoleon also created a centralized system of secondary and higher education for training his new elite of talent.

Napoleon's most famous and most enlightened reform was his codification of the laws. The Constituent Assembly had already given France a new penal code and a code of criminal procedure; Napoleon's legal experts added the Civil Code, a Code of Civil Procedure, and a Commercial Code. Promulgated in March 1804, these codes made France legally and judicially uniform. They consecrated the great gains of the Revolution: individual liberty, free enterprise, freedom of conscience, the secular state, and the legal equality of all citizens. At the same time they preserved some aspects of the Old Regime. Working men were still forbidden to organize unions, and their word was not acceptable in court against that of their employer. The head of a family retained extensive powers over his minor children and his wife's property.

For most people the Napoleonic Code meant the Civil Code, which was widely adopted outside of France, as we shall see presently. Not since the Roman Emperor Justinian had anyone defined all the possible legal relations involving private individuals and their property in such a rational and comprehensive way. There was a statute for everything. Nothing was left to custom or chance. The Civil Code incorporated the whole modern conception of private property from John Locke through the French Revolution. In making contracts rather than status the basis of civil society it marked the permanent triumph of the bourgeoisie. Most bourgeois Frenchmen were even willing to give up their political liberties in return for this blessing.

Napoleon remained a dictatorial ruler until his downfall. His secret political police arrested and deported all known opponents of his regime; books, plays, and the press were strictly censored. Yet Napoleon was a modernizing leader, as his reforms demonstrated. It was his military ambitions, not his domestic policies, that brought about his final downfall. But before turning to the Napoleonic wars, we must first examine the spread of revolution outside of France.

## THE FRENCH REVOLUTION AND THE WORLD

What happened in France was not an isolated phenomenon. As we have already noted, there was widespread political unrest on both sides of the Atlantic during the last third of the eighteenth century. In fact, some historians now speak of a revolution in the Western world, beginning around 1770, reaching its climax between 1789 and 1815, and reappearing in many places until 1849. France and the United States played a preponderant role in this upheaval, but it also included all of Western and Central Europe and Latin America, and it even touched Poland and parts of the Balkan Peninsula. The main issues in Western and Central Europe were liberty and equality versus despotism and privilege. In the remaining areas affected, national independence was the primary issue, though it did not necessarily exclude the others.

The revolt against privilege and inequality had begun outside of France before 1789 and it preceded any French military occupation in a number of places thereafter. In the Dutch and Austrian Netherlands and in parts of Switzerland democratic revolts—albeit unsuccessful ones—had occurred before the summer of 1789. There had also been unrest in the British Isles. Like the American revolutionaries, the English and Irish radicals of the 1780s were generally hostile to the aristocratic British Parliament, and although the authorities managed to sidetrack all movements for basic political changes, radical groups reappeared in England in the 1790s. There was also a mutiny in the British navy in 1797 and a violent insurrection in Ireland in 1798. Between 1790 and 1796 there were revolutionary incidents, clubs, and plots in Germany, Italy, Austria, Hungary, and Poland, in which French influence was remote and indirect. The same may be said of the revolutions in Spain's New World colonies between 1810 and 1814.

On the other hand, revolutions followed the arrival of the French armies in many places. In Belgium, Holland, Switzerland, and Italy the French did little more than give assistance to local "patriots," but in the Rhineland in 1794 and in Malta and Egypt in 1798 they brought in a complete, prefabricated revolution. French military occupation did not, however, automatically bring revolution in its wake. In Spain, which the French occupied from 1808 to 1814, the main changes were made by the counterrevolutionary opposition.

Whatever the revolution's origins, however, its opponents blamed the French and fought a long and bloody series of wars against them. These wars involved the traditional struggle for empire and the balance of power as much as the extermination of the revolution. Yet the slogans of counterrevolution as much as anything else bound France's enemies together. They hated Napoleon for his military conquests; they also hated him as a "Jacobin."

### Revolution: A Contagious Disease

The first news of the Revolution in France received a favorable response throughout Europe. Kant, Goethe, and many other educated commoners saw it as a great step forward for the cause of humanity and read smuggled French pamphlets and newspapers avidly. Meanwhile, Paris and Versailles soon thronged with sympathetic tourists and "pilgrims of liberty" like the Prussian scholar Karl Wilhelm von Humboldt, the English poet William Wordsworth, and Thomas Paine from the new American Republic. Even some liberal nobles and churchmen admired the Third Estate's initial challenge to royal despot-

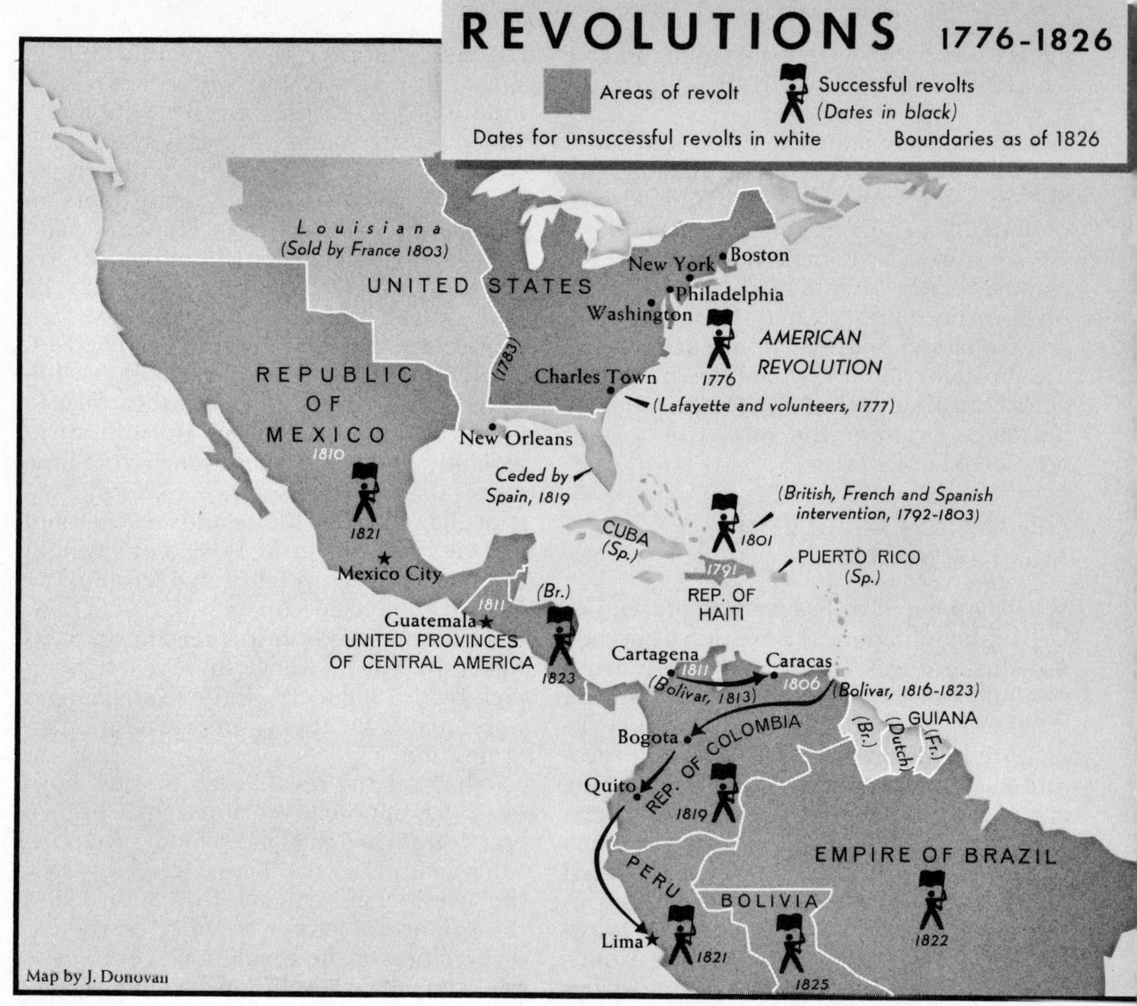


ism in June of 1789. On the other hand, many statesmen saw the events of 1789 as a confirmation of France's weakness.

But once the Revolution became contagious, responses to it divided sharply between those foreigners who wanted their countries to "catch" it and those who literally wanted to avoid it "like the plague." Part of Belgium had already risen up against Austrian rule in early 1789. In the summer the Revolution spread to other provinces of the Austrian Netherlands and to the Archbishopric of Liège. To the north, the Dutch patriots opposed the *Stadholder.* And along France's eastern borders local patriots began agitating for radical reforms in Rhineland Germany, in Italy, in Switzerland, and in Savoy. In the opposite camp, Europe's crowned heads became worried by the constraints put on Louis XVI in October, and the suppression of feudal rights and privileges and the nationalization of Church properties in France turned foreign nobles and churchmen against the Revolution. Each new reform in France exhilarated its friends and irritated its enemies abroad. Still, the armed conflict between revolutionary France and the rest of Europe did not come until the leaders of the Revolution provoked it with the principles on which they claimed to base their foreign policy: the sovereignty of the people and the liberty of all peoples to determine their own nationality.

The right of national self-determination had grave international consequences. In Alsace, for example, it threatened the seignorial rights of a number of German princes. If the people of Alsace consid-

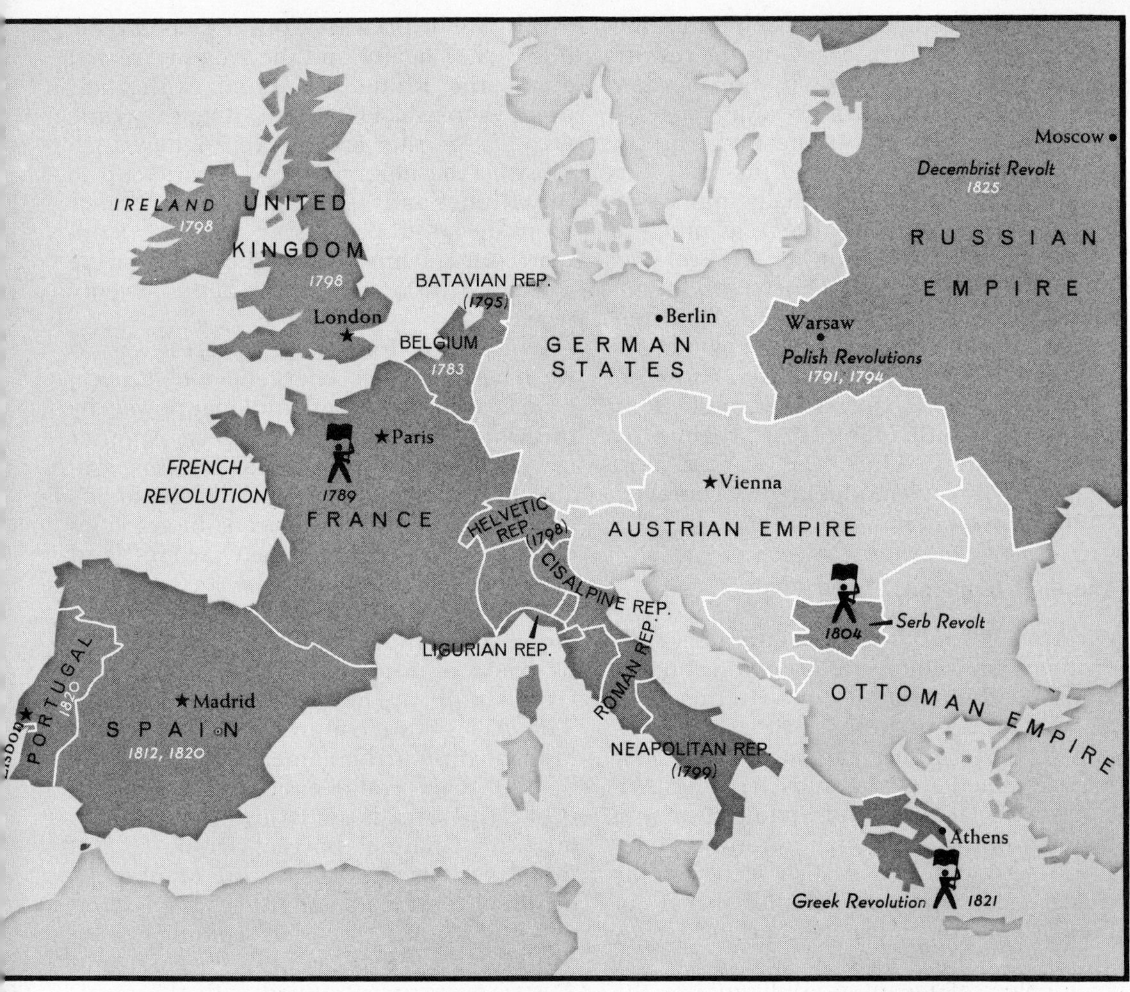


ered themselves French, they would have no reason to compensate these princes for the abolition of their rights. In October 1790 one deputy to the Constituent Assembly put it this way:

"Today . . . now that the sovereignty of the people has finally been established . . . what does it matter to the people of Alsace, or of France, that in despotic times certain agreements brought the two peoples together? The Alsatian people have united themselves to the French because they wish to do so. The rights of nations are not subject to regulation by the treaties of princes."

This declaration was an open challenge to traditional international law. In July 1791 the assembly finally voted in favor of the right of other peoples—Belgians, Savoyards, Swiss, Avignonese*—to union with France. This vote spread fear among all the monarchs of Europe.

Another group of Frenchmen, the *émigrés*, also helped to bring on the war between revolutionary France and counterrevolutionary Europe. These *émigrés* carried lurid tales of atrocities, sacrileges, and outrages against the royal family to all the foreign courts that gave them asylum. The Hapsburg court at Vienna was especially eager to intervene, since Marie Antoinette was the Emperor's sister. And, as we have seen, the French king himself secretly favored foreign intervention.

At first the monarchs of Europe hesitat-

*At the request of the inhabitants, the Assembly annexed the papal enclave of Avignon to France in September 1791 without consulting its sovereign, the pope.

ed to launch an armed invasion and limited themselves to threats against the revolutionary government, but it soon became clear that no compromise was possible between the Revolution and Old Europe. Although the *émigrés* helped to make this so, the rulers of Europe finally intervened to protect their rule at home as much as to crush the Revolution in France. For displaced Belgian and Dutch revolutionary patriots clamored for war so that they might return in victory to their own countries. Swiss, Savoyards, Italians, and Germans also hoped that a war might help them to establish democratic regimes in their countries. Thus, the wars against France took on an ideological character from the start.

### The First Coalition, 1792–1795

On April 20, 1792, the revolutionary government of France declared war on the Hapsburg Emperor. It did so in the name of "the righteous defense of a free people" against "unjust aggression." In July Prussia joined Austria, and Great Britain, along with Holland and Spain, became a member of the First Coalition in February 1793. Although the British were mainly concerned with the age-old threat of French control of the Netherlands, they quickly gave their participation in the war an ideological meaning. William Pitt the Younger (1759–1806), their prime minister almost continuously from 1783 to 1806, had at first hoped to check the French threat to the Netherlands by negotiation. But when the French refused to bow to his will and declared war on Great Britain, Pitt said: "It is a question of life and death for civilization . . . for the safety of Europe and for civil society. We must reconcile ourselves to a long war, a war without mercy, until we have destroyed this plague."

Until the spring of 1794 neither side gained a decisive advantage. During the six months following September 1792, when the French stopped the Prussians at Valmy, they took the offensive and occupied Belgium, Savoy, and parts of the Rhineland, but between March and December 1793 the forces of the augmented First Coalition pushed the French back within their prewar frontiers. Then the tide turned again, and the Allies retreated across the Rhine. Beginning with their great victory at Fleurus, in Belgium (June 26, 1794), the French reconquered almost all the neighboring territories up to the Rhine and the Alps, which France soon declared to be her "natural frontiers" and from which the Allies were unable to dislodge her for almost twenty years.

One reason for France's success was, as we have seen, the energetic mobilization of national resources and manpower by the Committee of Public Safety. Another reason was the weakness of the First Coalition itself. In contrast to the Republic's levy-in-mass, the European monarchies continued to recruit their armies and mobilize their resources in the old way. Pitt used his country's traditional technique of commercial warfare, but his blockade of France did not prevent her from supplying her own material needs. The Allies also continued to play their familiar diplomatic game. In the summer of 1793 they could easily have marched on Paris. Instead, the British preferred to take the Channel port of Dunkirk, and the Austrians the fortress of Maubeuge, on the French side of the Belgian frontier, as pawns for the coming peace conference. Furthermore, Prussia and Austria were preoccupied with the partitions of Poland from the beginning of 1793 to the end of 1795.* These partitions kept Russia out of the war against France altogether, and they diverted Prussia's best troops to occupation duty in the newly annexed Polish provinces. By the spring of 1795 Prussia was so uncertain about Austrian designs on these provinces that she signed a separate peace with France. Thus, the preoccupation of the three eastern powers with Poland, whose own revolution also "invited" aggression, may well have saved the French Revolution.

In the spring and summer of 1795 the defection of Prussia, followed by Holland and Spain, broke up the First Coalition and left France with a tier of occupied territories from the North Sea to the Mediterranean. The Convention voted to annex Belgium, Savoy, and Nice. It post-

*See p. 278.

poned a decision on the German territories on the left bank of the Rhine, since the Austrians were still fighting there, but the French trusted that their armies would be aided by German and Italian patriots, whose delegates flocked to Paris. After all, the Dutch patriots had aleady returned to their country with the French army. There they set up France's first satellite state, the Batavian Republic, in May 1795.

### The "Sister Republics"

By 1795 territorial conquest and plunder were becoming more important to the French then the "liberation" of peoples. Furthermore, the people in the occupied territories discovered that their "liberation" came at a high price. The French helped them to get rid of their princes and prelates and to set up democratic regimes. But the French also requisitioned everything in sight for their war needs. Even after they suppressed their "evacuation agencies" the "evacuation" continued—it took everything from food, horses, and precious metals to works of art and the locks on the doors. In two years Belgium experienced three invasions; the third, which installed the French definitively, almost ruined her.

Under the Directory the French continued their combined policy of the "liberation" of peoples and territorial conquest in Italy and Switzerland, where, with the aid of French armies, "sister republics" were set up by local patriots. Although these patriots had been actively campaigning against the Old Regime in their own countries before the French arrived, the other powers continued to view the French Republic as the source of the revolutionary disease. The English philosopher-statesman Edmund Burke had already diagnosed the nature of this disease in 1790 in his *Reflections on the Revolution in France*. In the late 1790s he called on the "civilized world" to destroy the "Directory of regicides."

The Batavian Republic became the model of the other five "sister republics." In 1797 Napoleon himself set up the Cisalpine Republic and the Ligurian Republic (Genoa) after driving the Austrians out of Northern Italy and "compensating" them, in the Treaty of Campo Formio (October 17, 1797), with Venice and Venice's territories along the eastern Adriatic. Other French generals helped local Italian patriots to seize the territories of the Papal States and the Kingdom of the Two Sicilies, which they replaced respectively with the Roman Republic in February 1798 and the Parthenopean Republic in January 1799. The revolution in the Neapolitan part of the Kingdom of the Two Sicilies was more spontaneous than elsewhere, and its bourgeois patriots were joined by some enlightened nobles. In fact, during its brief existence, the new Parthenopean Republic also experienced a popular peasant revolt, similar to the one in France in 1790, against its moderate leaders. But elsewhere in Italy, as in Holland and Switzerland, where the French helped to set up the Helvetic Republic in April 1798, the revolutionary patriots were almost exclusively urban and middle class.

### The Second Coalition, 1798–1802

The revolutionary hopes of the Dutch, Swiss, and Italian patriots were thwarted by both French imperialism and English resistance. These patriots became increasingly distressed by the ironic contradiction between French promises of national independence and the burdensome realities of French interventions and requisitions, which, in turn, were made necessary by the continuing war against England. In 1798, under cover of an invasion threat to the British Isles, Napoleon persuaded the Directory to allow him to strike at India by way of Egypt, then a semi-independent vassal of Turkey. He conquered the Mediterranean island of Malta in May and then proceeded to occupy the delta of the Nile. But in August, in the Battle of the Nile, his fleet was destroyed by Horatio Nelson, who henceforth became the enduring symbol of England's salvation through her supremacy at sea. While Napoleon remained a prisoner of his conquest in Egypt, England persuaded Austria, Russia, and several lesser states to join the Second Coalition in December 1798. Together the three major Allies planned to drive the French out of the Netherlands, the Rhineland, Switzerland, and Italy.

The wars of the Second Coalition were predominantly imperialistic in character. Although Nelson restored the Neapolitan king to his throne, the elimination of the French threat to the British Empire was the main English goal. France's main aim was to break up the Coalition and to extend French influence even further. In the summer of 1799 French armies defeated the Anglo-Russian armies in Switzerland and Holland, and, in August, Napoleon deserted his troops in Egypt and returned to Paris. While plotting to overthrow the Directory he also found time for diplomatic intrigue with the unbalanced Emperor Paul (1796–1801) of Russia. In October Paul took his country out of the Coalition, partly because he felt that the English were not cooperating with his armies, partly because he suddenly became an admirer of Napoleon's military genius, but also because Napoleon encouraged his imperialistic ambitions in the Balkans and Malta. A month later Napoleon declared that the revolution in France itself was "finished" when he made himself First Consul.

In early 1800 Napoleon began to extend French influence into western Germany as well as Italy. Austria was the main enemy of this endeavor, and by the end of the year his armies had thoroughly eliminated her from both places. In February 1801 Austria signed the Treaty of Luneville, in which she not only had to confirm France's preponderance in Italy but also to accept a large-scale reorganization of German territory.

The terms of this treaty practically finished the Holy Roman Empire. Its Hapsburg Emperor could do nothing to stop the German princes from courting the First Consul for new territories east of the Rhine in compensation for those they had lost to France or to Italian dukes who had formerly been Austrian protegés. By 1803 most of the ecclesiastical territories and imperial cities had also been "reassigned" by the covetous German princes. Their recommendations were adopted by the imperial diet as the famous *Reichsdeputationshauptschluss* ("final decision" of the imperial "deputation"—consisting of leading electors and princes). In 1804, when Napoleon crowned himself Emperor of the French, he decided that there was not room in Europe for two imperial dynasties. Two years later he was to abolish the Holy Roman Empire of the German Nation for all time.

Meanwhile, in March 1802, England had also made peace with France in the Treaty of Amiens. The terms of this treaty were far more favorable to France than to England. They left France in virtual control of all of Western Europe from the North Sea to the Mediterranean; even Spain was now her ally. But the peace of 1802 was only a truce. Napoleon not only continued to represent the hated Revolution in England's eyes, he also threatened her world empire with the resources of half of Europe behind him. Besides, Austria, Prussia, and Russia would not tolerate his disruption of the balance of power indefinitely. Hence the international ideological war and the traditional power struggle would have to go on together.

### Napoleon's Imperialism, 1802–1812

History is full of "might-have-beens." In 1802, if Napoleon had been satisfied with what he already had, he might have united Western Europe and thus prevented the rise of German nationalism, the First World War, the Russian Revolution, which occurred during that war, and all the succeeding upheavals. Yet as long as that elusive yet overwhelmingly real thing called power is concentrated in sovereign states, the men who wield it are tempted to use it against real or imagined rivals. And when a Napoleon is one of these men, the "might-have-beens" lose their plausibility.

After 1802 Napoleon's ambitions increased with each addition to his already immense power and prestige. He provoked a theatrical series of wars in which the stakes were "double-or-nothing." In the process his military subordinates became increasingly engaged in a competition organized and judged by the emperor, with glory and riches as the prize. In the end his military machine seemed to exist only to serve the dictator, his grasp-

*Napoleon I inspecting his troops*

ing and quarrelsome relatives, and the self-seeking "battlefield nobility" around him.

#### *Britain's Supremacy at Sea*

In the early 1800s Napoleon's only serious failure was the frustration of his colonial ambitions. The Treaty of Amiens had returned Egypt to Turkey, but Napoleon tried to reassert French influence in the Near East soon thereafter. He even dreamt of conquering Persia and India. All these schemes came to naught because of the superiority of British sea power, and in the New World he lost the most important colonies he already had. The slaves of Haiti had driven the French out and set up an independent state in the mid-1790s. Napoleon sent a large military force there to restore French control, but though some of the rebel leaders were executed, Napoleon finally abandoned the island in 1803. The loss of Haiti plus the impending new war with Great Britain then prompted him to sell the vast Louisiana Territory* to the United States rather than risk having it fall into British hands.

Some historians doubt Napoleon's intention of ever invading England, but he certainly convinced everybody at the time that that was what he was planning to do between 1803 and 1805. First he extended his power in Western Europe by annexing Piedmont outright, tightening his hold on the satellite Helvetic Republic, and making deals with various German princes. In the face of these actions the British refused to give up Malta, which they had agreed to do in the Treaty of Amiens. Napoleon then used this refusal as a pretext for reopening the war with Great Britain in May 1803. He massed troops in the Channel ports from which they would presumably row across. But Napoleon wanted to avoid a naval battle,

*Louisiana had been transferred to Spain in 1763, but Spain had returned it to France in 1800. At first Napoleon had hoped to make it the granary for France's West Indian sugar islands. He finally sold it to the United States for the reasons mentioned.

and the troops sat there for a year-and-a-half, until the British fleet could be diverted into other waters and the main naval forces of France and Spain could cover their invasion. This strategy failed on October 21, 1805, when the naval battle Napoleon had tried to avoid took place off Cape Trafalgar, near the entrance to the Mediterranean.

The Battle of Trafalgar assured British control of the seas for over a century. In the Battle of the Nile (1798) Admiral Nelson had already broken with eighteenth-century naval routine as decisively as General Bonaparte had broken with routine on land. At Trafalgar, Nelson repeated his new technique of concentrating on part of the enemy line by breaking it in the center or by putting two ships on one where the enemy had no room to maneuver. As a result, he destroyed or captured twenty-two of the thirty-three French and Spanish ships-of-the-line.

Meanwhile, the British had formed the Third Coalition with Austria, Russia, and Sweden in the summer of 1805. To meet this challenge on land Napoleon was already moving his troops from the Channel ports into Central Europe before the Battle of Trafalgar.

### *The Defeat of Austria*

On December 2, 1805, at Austerlitz (about one hundred miles north of Vienna), Napoleon won one of his greatest victories by defeating the combined Austrian and Russian armies. The Russians retreated, and Austria signed a separate peace with France (December 26). Not only did she give up her remaining territories in Germany and the former Venetian Republic, but eight months later (August 6, 1806) she had to accept the final dissolution of the Holy Roman Empire. During this time, Napoleon annexed parts of Italy to the French Empire and reorganized the rest of it into two satellite kingdoms. (Republics were "out" now!) Between those parts of Germany he annexed in the west and Prussia and Austria in the east, Napoleon established the Confederation of the Rhine. Almost all the German princes joined this confederation as French puppets and were to remain so until 1813.

### *The Defeat of Prussia and Russia*

In 1806 and 1807 Napoleon also defeated Prussia and Russia. Prussia went to war against France for the first time in eleven years because Napoleon's domination of the rest of Germany now threatened her on her own borders. But the heirs of Frederick the Great were no match for Napoleon's military machine. The French defeated them in the Battles of Jena and Auerstädt on October 14, 1806. Then, on June 14, 1807, the French defeated the Russians in the Battle of Friedland.

These campaigns showed the French military system at its peak. Napoleon's forces were usually superior in numbers at the decisive point. When they were not, as at Auerstädt, the tactics of one French general enabled him to defeat a Prussian army twice the size of his own. And in each campaign the French were able to live off the country, hundreds of miles from home.

In July 1807 Napoleon sealed his victories over Prussia and Russia in the Treaties of Tilsit. Prussia had to give up half of its territory either to France and her German dependencies or to the Duchy of Warsaw, which Napoleon set up as a new satellite state in Eastern Europe. In addition, Prussia had to reduce her standing army to 42,000 men, pay a large indemnity, and support 150,000 French occupation troops until this indemnity was paid. Russia lost no territory, but she had to recognize the Duchy of Warsaw and join France in an alliance against England. Thus, after Tilsit Napoleon controlled all of Europe from the Spanish to the Russian borders. Only England continued to fight him.

### *The Conquest of Spain*

The Iberian Peninsula was the only part of Europe where England could still threaten Napoleon's control of the continent. Hence, in 1808, he invaded Spain, overthrew the Spanish Bourbons, and made his brother Joseph that country's new king. The British then landed in Portugal, and the Spanish people began the first, and most important, national resistance to the French. For the next six years the Peninsular War went on intermittently. It was fought by hundreds of thousands of Spanish partisans, as well as the regular British and French armies and a makeshift army organized by a handful of liberal Spanish patriots. This war was the bloodiest and most ruthless of all the wars of the Napoleonic period—the Spanish artist Francisco de Goya y Lucientes portrayed its horrors vividly in a series of drawings called *The Disasters of War.* Whatever else Napoleon did thereafter in the rest of Europe, he had to keep a considerable part of his armed forces in Spain.

Nevertheless, Napoleon was at the peak of his power and prestige in 1810–1811. He had beaten Austria for the fourth time in 1809 and forced her into a direct alliance with France. Every continental country except Turkey and Portugal was now either an ally or a satellite. Furthermore, in 1810 Emperor Napoleon had married the young Hapsburg archduchess Marie Louise—a member of the "best family" in Europe—after divorcing Josephine for not having provided him with an heir. England had not yet been brought to her knees, but Napoleon had already made his plan to bring down the British government. He would do this through a financial crisis caused by the exclusion of British exports from the whole continent, which he nominally controlled in one way or another.

**The Continental System**

The Napoleonic empire with its west German and Italian dependencies corresponded almost exactly to today's Common Market.* The organization of its economy around the interests of France was one purpose of what Napoleon called his Continental System; its other purpose was to destroy the export trade of Great Britain. For the latter, Napoleon had to make his allies, as well as his satellites, boycott British exports.

The Continental System failed to destroy Great Britain economically mainly because her sea power gave her other sources of supply and other overseas markets. By 1807 the British had captured the Dutch colonies in the East Indies, South Africa, and South America and the remaining French colonies in Africa and the Caribbean. They thus tightened their monopoly over the re-export trade in sugar, tea, coffee, and tobacco. Napoleon's boycott considerably restricted the entry of these products, as well as British manufactured goods, into the continental market, though smuggling got some colonial wares through to eager European buyers. The American Embargo and Nonintercourse Acts of 1807 and 1809 also severely cut British trade with the United States. But Napoleon's occupation of Spain opened Latin America to British merchants; British exports there rose from £300,000 in 1805 to £6,300,000 in 1809. And despite the Continental System, British cotton exports more than doubled in the same four-year period.

Aside from leaks in the continental boycott, British sea power and the Industrial Revolution foiled Napoleon's mercantilist policies against Great Britain. As we have seen, the British navy and merchant marine opened up new markets and new sources of supply overseas. Then the Industrial Revolution increased British national income so much that the government was able to borrow twice as much money in 1812 as in 1809. Thus it did not go bankrupt, even though the carrying charges on its debt took half of its revenue. Indeed, British subsidies were to save Austria, Russia, and Prussia from impoverishment, and British arms were to help equip their new armies for the final campaigns against the French in 1813 and 1814.

The Continental System also failed to unite Europe economically. At first Napoleon was able to stir up feelings against the British monopoly over foreign trade. For in their blockade—the counterpart of the Continental System—the British insisted that all non-British ships trading with the continent pass through British ports and operate only under British licenses. The British blockade too was designed to destroy the enemy's commerce, credit, and government revenues, but the Continental System did not equalize the sacrifice among all its members. Relief from British competition did stimulate new industries in Western Europe. Never-

*See map, Chapter XXI.

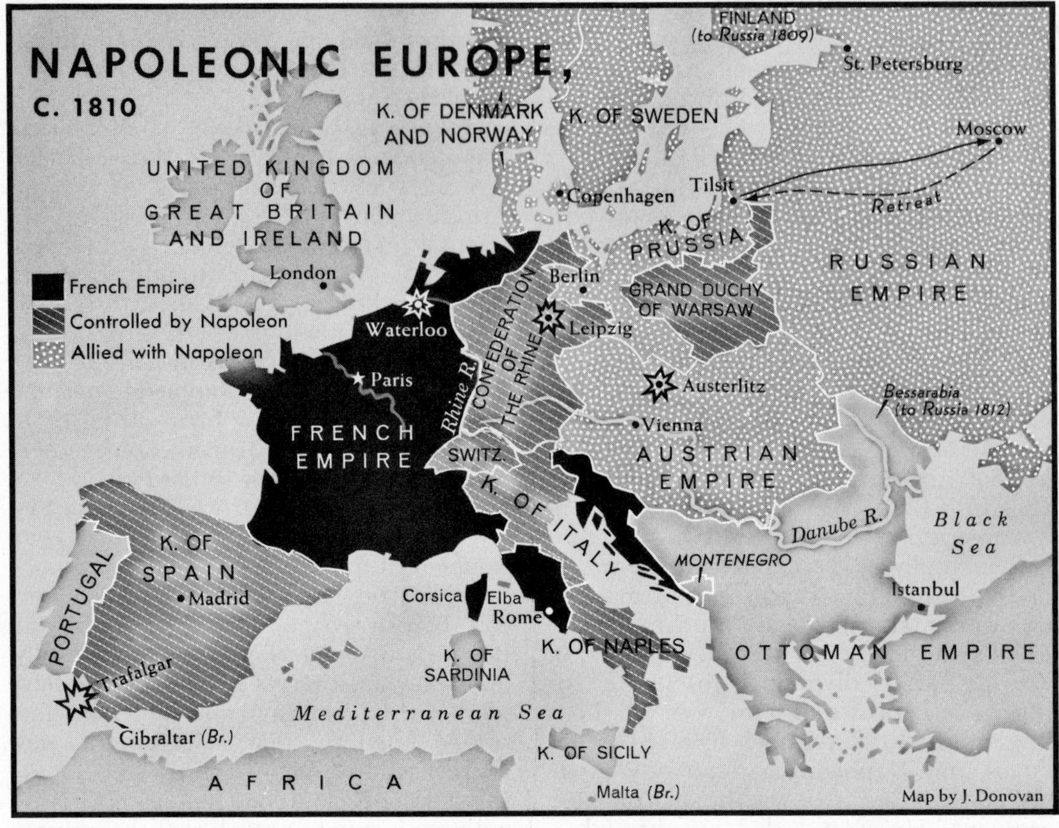


theless, the exchange of these goods within the continental market was hampered by British control of coastal traffic. Although new roads were built over the Alps, a purely continental economy was impossible to maintain before the age of railroads. Another obstacle was tariffs. Unlike the Common Market today, Napoleonic Europe was not a free-trade area. Napoleon retained French tariffs on imports, even from those territories he had annexed politically. At the same time, he prevented his satellites from placing tariffs on French goods. His policy was "France First," and within Europe the Continental System was partly a struggle of French manufacturers to take over markets from the British.

This aspect of the System caused widespread antagonism to the Napoleonic regime. It was to be one of the reasons why the Eastern European powers eventually renounced their alliances with Napoleon. French policy also served to alienate the "natural," that is, democratic, allies of France in other countries, and thereby played into the hands of the counterrevolutionaries. Even some of Napoleon's most loyal satellites in Western and Central Europe began to resent his economic discrimination against them. Before they were finally "liberated," however, they had been partially transformed by his political and social policies.

### The Spread of Modern Institutions

Under Napoleon all of Europe from Spain to Poland got a taste of what it was like to live in a modern society. Since his political reorganization of the continent did not survive his military defeat, only its general outlines need to be noted. By 1810 the French Empire itself included Belgium and Holland, the left bank of the Rhine, the German coast as far as the western Baltic, and the Italian coast as far as Rome. All these territories were organized into departments and governed by prefects who reported directly to Paris.

Beyond them lay various kinds of dependent states. All except Switzerland were now monarchies. Napoleon installed members of his own family in the satellite states of Naples, Spain, Holland, and Westphalia, a synthetic kingdom in west Germany, made up principally of Hanoverian and Prussian territories. In the Confederation of the Rhine and the Duchy of Warsaw Napoleon dictated policy to nominally sovereign German kings and princes.

But everywhere Napoleon initiated the same plan of reform. As he had already done in France, he wanted to integrate the gains of the Revolution into a new kind of enlightened despotism. Anything that smacked of feudal or clerical privilege was abolished, and all citizens were now legally free, irrespective of their religion or former servile status. No corporate or territorial organization was to stand between them and the authority of their highly centralized governments.

Those territories that had been under French control the longest were the most affected by the new forms of political and social life. Only in Belgium and the Rhineland did the seignorial regime disappear completely and without compensation. East of the Rhine Napoleon had to compromise with the landlord class at the expense of the would-be peasant proprietors. In the Duchy of Warsaw the Polish nobles retained all the land, whereas the serfs received only nominal freedom, and the Jews, who were initially given civil rights, were then denied them in 1809. The principle of "careers open to talent" was also less rigorously enforced in the more recently acquired French dependencies. Yet even there the nobility lost its legal privileges in taxation, office holding, and military command.

More than any single instrument, the Napoleonic Civil Code permanently transformed the social institutions of every territory where it was applied. It brought the "principles of 1789"—the equality of persons, forms of property, and inheritances; religious toleration; the secular state; and divorce—to Belgium, Holland, Rhineland Germany, and Italy (where Catholicism managed to eliminate divorce). In 1810 the Code was promulgated in Warsaw. Napoleon even tried to apply it in Spain, despite the fact that his religious program was largely responsible for keeping the Spanish people in a state of chronic rebellion. Although the Civil Code was revoked in 1814 in Spain and Italy, it strongly influenced the new national law codes of these two countries in the late nineteenth century. By then it had also been adopted in modified form in Rumania, Egypt, Haiti, Quebec, Louisiana, and half a dozen Latin American countries.

Even more than under the Directory, France's conquered and dependent territories had to pay for the blessings of the Revolution with their money and their blood. Napoleon made them defray the cost of the French armies of occupation in order to keep taxes low in France. He also forced them to supply more and more soldiers for his later campaigns. By 1812, Germans, Dutch, Belgians, Italians, Poles, and even some Spaniards were to constitute together almost two-thirds of the army with which he invaded Russia. Hence, Napoleonic Europe was finally to welcome the end of French control, even though it was to retain many of the reforms this control had brought.

## THE OVERTHROW OF NAPOLEON'S EMPIRE

Napoleon's disastrous defeat in Russia marked the crucial turning point in his fortunes. After that his enemies were ultimately able to combine and concentrate superior military power against him. The rise of anti-French feelings helped, and so did British money and arms and the reorganization of the Prussia and Austrian armies. Yet the great powers, even in their alliance for victory, did not neglect their own imperialistic aims.

### The Big Four: Domestic Developments

So far we have focused attention on Napoleonic Europe, but there was a non-Napoleonic Europe as well. France never succeeded in destroying the four other great powers. Great Britain completely escaped invasion and plundering; Russia survived Napoleon's effort to conquer her and drove him out in less than six months. Even defeated Austria and truncated Prussia maintained lives of their own after 1806. By and large, all four countries escaped the Revolution.

Of the four great powers Austria changed the least. Two years before Emperor Francis II (1792–1835) lost the Holy Roman Empire, he consolidated his Danubian possessions into an Austrian Empire, of which he became Emperor Francis I. In 1809 Prince Clemens von Metternich, a dispossessed Rhineland nobleman, became his foreign minister and successfully guided Austrian foreign policy for almost forty years. The emperor and the aristocracy accepted certain changes in the organization of the army, changes that strengthened the war effort in its final stages. But the Old Regime survived the Napoleonic period intact.

Great Britain also escaped political and social revolution. To be sure, she was experiencing her own Industrial Revolution, but it brought no institutional changes before 1815. Meanwhile, foreign radicalism made Britain's leaders cling more tenaciously than ever to their eighteenth-century institutions. In his *Reflections on the Revolution in France* Burke had warned his countrymen against making changes not shaped by their traditions and their national history. The one political reform of the revolutionary and Napoleonic period strengthened rather than weakened the traditional British system. In 1801, as a reaction against the Irish insurrection three years earlier, Pitt persuaded Parliament to enact the legislative union of Great Britain and Ireland under the name of the *United Kingdom.* This Act of Union abolished the Irish Parliament in Dublin. Thereafter the Irish had to send representatives directly to the British Parliament in London, where they would be an ineffective minority.

Prussia changed the most between 1806 and 1813. No great European power had ever suffered such humiliating treatment as she had at Tilsit; yet displaced German patriots viewed Prussia as their main hope for overthrowing French domination and took refuge there. The four men who rebuilt the Prussian army and strengthened the Prussian state were all non-Prussians: Count Neithardt von Gneisenau (1760–1831), General Gerhard von Scharnhorst (1775–1813), Baron Heinrich von Stein (1757–1831), and Prince Karl August von Hardenberg (1750–1822). Their reforms were indirectly influenced by the Revolution, especially their efforts to create civil equality, careers open to talent, and a sense of participation in the national community. But they initiated these reforms in the name of enlightened despotism in order to prevent the Revolution from spreading to Prussia and to defeat it at its source.

Scharnhorst and Gneisenau concerned themselves mainly with the army. In order to circumvent the restriction on the size of Prussia's standing army they set up a system that later developed into what we call universal military training. All young men were to serve for a short term in the regular army and then become part of the reserves. In its final form (1818) the new conscription law was in some ways more democratic than that of revolutionary France, especially in eliminating the possibility of buying substitutes. It was to become standard everywhere on the continent in the late nineteenth century.

Stein and Hardenberg tried to make Prussia into a real political community. They modernized the state administration by eliminating overlapping jurisdictions. They gave the middle classes a greater voice in municipal affairs and opened the lower officer ranks of the army to them. Stein's "abolition" of serfdom gave legal status and freedom of movement to the mass of the population, but many peasants remained dependent on their landlords as hired laborers. The position of the Junkers became stronger than ever, for they gained a third of the land of every peasant who wanted to convert the other two-thirds of his tenture into private property. In laying the foundation for a modern state and a modern economy through their legal reforms, Stein and Hardenberg actually strengthened the power of the king and the aristocracy. They had hoped for something more, and in this sense their reforms were a failure.

Russia escaped both the Revolution and effective reform at home. Tsar Alexander I (1801–1825) tried to return to a kind of enlightened despotism in the first decade of his reign. Influenced by his Swiss tutor, the "Jacobin" La Harpe, he even dreamt of giving Russia a constitution. He appointed a committee of liberal young noblemen to draw up such a constitution and to modernize Russia's administrative and judicial structure. Then after the defeat at Friedland, Alexander's affections, turned away from these young friends to Michael Speransky, a talented administrator of non-noble origin. Speransky prepared an elaborate project for the social and administrative reconstruction of the empire. This project included a deliberative body called the State Duma, a Council of Ministers, a uniform law code, and financial reforms. Though modeled on Napoleonic France in many ways, Speransky's proposals maintained class privilege and serfdom. Alexander I even launched a program to "assimilate" the several million Jews in Belorussia and the Western Ukraine. The bulk of Europe's Jews lived in this area, called The Pale, and were indeed a separate cultural group. Alexander proposed "to weaken their fanaticism" by uprooting them from their autonomous communities and traditional occupations and turning them into "good Russian peasants." The Napoleonic invasion ended this program, as well as Speransky's reforms. After 1812 Russia became the most reactionary country in Europe.

### The War of 1812

Napoleon invaded Russia in June 1812 with a Grand Army of almost 700,000 men. His main reason was that the tsar had withdrawn from the Continental System and resumed commercial relations with England. As in the past, he planned a short war and a quick peace settlement.

But everything went wrong in the Russian campaign. Napoleon's formerly invincible military machine could not function in the vast plains of Russia, hundreds of miles from his Central European base of supplies, Since the Russians destroyed all the local food stocks as they retreated, Napoleon's men and horses often went hungry. Yet he could not force the Russian army into a pitched battle until Borodino, less than a hundred miles from Moscow; though he won the battle there, the Russian army was able to withdraw in good order. Less than three months after the start of his campaign Napoleon entered Moscow. Now, he thought, surely the tsar would surrender. But Alexander stayed in St. Petersburg, and most of the inhabitants of Moscow had been evacuated. Almost immediately the deserted city went up in flames. Napoleon occupied a ruin.

After five weeks of indecision the baffled French emperor decided to retreat—an undertaking that very quickly turned into a rout. Armed Russian peasants butchered the stragglers, and tens of thousands of Napoleon's soldiers died of starvation. By November a heavy frost also began to take its toll. Discipline broke down, and Napoleon's international army dissolved into a horde of individual fugitives. In December only 50,000 of the original Grand Army crossed the border into the Duchy of Warsaw; 400,000 had died of battle wounds, starvation, and exposure; another 100,000 had been taken prisoner; the rest were simply "missing." Napoleon had rushed ahead to Paris to raise another army, but his catastrophic defeat in Russia had also turned Prussia and Austria against him.

### Nationalism and Power Politics

In 1813 the European powers finally united in a concentrated effort to destroy Napoleon's empire. Traditionally these wars are called the Wars of Liberation, with the assumption that native nationalism played a major role in driving the French out. Actually the rulers of Russia, Austria, Prussia, and England utterly abhorred the revolutionary principle of national self-determination. So did lesser powers like Sweden, which annexed Norway from Denmark in January 1814, and Bourbon Spain, which tried to suppress revolts in its Latin American colonies even while its king was in exile. In 1813–1814 they all used the anti-French feelings of their subjects to bolster their own war efforts, even though their primary goals were to restore the balance of power and gain additional territories for themselves. We must therefore examine the nature of this new phenomenon of nationalism.

It was indeed new in the late eighteenth

century. Tribal exclusiveness and local patriotism had existed since ancient times, and we have seen outbreaks of anti-foreign feeling in the dynastic and religious wars of the fifteenth and sixteenth centuries.* Modern nationalism is rooted in such feelings, but it expresses much more self-conscious and explicit attitudes of loyalty and pride toward one's own nation as well. These attitudes first appeared in the late eighteenth century, when patriotism came to mean devotion to the nation, and not simply to the dynasty. The first goal of the patriots was that all members of their nationality—or at least all the taxpayers—be united in one nation, independent and indivisible.

Most Europeans had to be made aware of themselves as nationalities before they began thinking about unity and independence. Somebody had to *tell* them that they were Germans, Dutch, Belgians, Swiss, or Italians; nobody was *born* with a knowledge of his native tongue and his nation's customs and prejudices, and with an inherent national character. In each case the first step was for a self-conscious minority of patriots to convince their countrymen that their common way of life, their common historical traditions, and, wherever possible, their common language made them a distinct national community. Only then could they be made to fight for unity and independence.

The Napoleonic wars stimulated this kind of nationalism against the French, but in most places, particularly in Germany, the self-conscious patriots did not really get their point across to the masses. We have already noted the German national cultural revival in the 1760s and Herder's pronouncements concerning the *Volksgeist*.* After the French conquered Germany another German philosopher, Johann Gottlieb Fichte (1762–1814), took up Herder's idea of the *Volksgeist* and gave it a strongly political tone. In 1808 Fichte delivered a series of *Addresses to the German Nation* in French-occupied Berlin. He argued that the German nation was not only unique but also nobler than the others. It must be liberated at all costs from foreign, and especially French, influence. Later generations of Germans were to regard Fichte as a national hero for his *Addresses*, but they had few hearers when he gave them. In fact, the French garrison commander considered them too academic even to bother suppressing them. Elsewhere in Germany other professors were collecting examples of German folk tales with which they hoped to stimulate national feeling. Ernst Moritz Arndt wrote patriotic poems, and Ludwig Jahn organized the Tugendbund, a "league of virtue and manliness," in which patriotic students went on hikes and did calisthenics in order to develop their "innate Germanness."

None of these philosophical, philological, literary, or athletic activities had much effect on the German people as a whole. By 1813 Prussian civilians and soldiers heeded their king's appeal "to my people" to drive out the French—a response that the democratization of the Prussian army helped to make possible. But the rest of Germany was not directly involved, and the voices of the patriots who wanted German unity were quickly silenced.

Insofar as patriotism helped to defeat Napoleon it was usually the more spontaneous, traditional kind. The Spanish patriots had little control over the peasant partisans who tied down a considerable part of Napoleon's forces during almost five years of guerrilla warfare. These *guerrillas*—little wars—were not fought by regular soldiers but by fanatical civilians driven by an elemental hatred for the invader.* Napoleon met the same kind of spontaneous, nonideological, mass resistance in Russia. Only in England did the more modern, self-conscious kind of nationism play a major role in the struggle

*See p. 37 on the French in the Hundred Years War, p. 46 on the Czechs in the Hussite wars, pp. 82–83 on the Germans in the Lutheran Revolt, p. 149 on the English at the time of the Armada.

*See p. 300.

*"Like avenging vultures [they] followed the French columns at a distance, to murder such of the soldiers as, fatigued or wounded, remained behind. . . . The women . . . threw themselves with horrible shrieks upon the wounded, and disputed who should kill them by the most cruel tortues; they stabbed their eyes with knives and scissors, and seemed to exult . . . at the sight of their blood." (M. de Rocca, *Mémoires sur la guerre des Français en Espagne*, Paris, 1814, pp. 145, 191.)

*Goya's "The Third of May, 1808"—French soldiers executing Spanish guerrilla fighters*

against him. It was aptly expressed in the following verse from "Rule Britannia":

*The nations not so blest as thee*
*Must in their turn to tyrants fall*
*While thou do flourish great and free*
*The dread and envy of them all.*

Although the combined military power of the Allies was more important than nationalism in defeating Napoleon, nationalism was to become an increasingly dominant force in the nineteenth century. Nor was it restricted to Western and Central Europe. Nationalist revolts that were to be consummated after 1815 had already begun in Latin America and the Balkans during the Napoleonic period. There too the great powers tried to use native nationalism for their own imperialist ends.

In South America the British began supporting native nationalist revolts against Spanish rule as early as 1806. They gave aid to the three great patriots who led these revolts: Francisco de Miranda (1756–1816), José de San Martin (1778–1850), and Simón Bolivar (1783–1830). The British had always wanted trading rights in South America, and the fight for independence in the region of the Rió de la Plata, around Buenos Aires, was promoted by the British in their attempt to gain territory there as well. They had to abandon this project after Napoleon occupied Spain in 1808, for they then became allies of the exiled Spanish Bourbons. As we shall see in Chapter XI, however, the British were again, after 1820, to prefer a free South America to one controlled by Spain.

The Russians followed a similar policy in the Balkans. Between 1804 and 1813 the Serb patriot George Petrovich (Kara George) (1766–1817) led a major revolt against Turkish rule. The rebels only sought control of their own garrison in Belgrade at first, but when Russia went to war against Turkey in 1806–1812, she encouraged the Serbs to seek complete independence. Russia's war against Turkey was one of many examples of how the powers continued to pursue their own imperialist aims even while Napoleon was the number-one menace. Thus, in the interim between Tilsit and the invasion of June 1812, Russia used her temporary understanding with Napoleon to annex the province of Bessarabia before concluding peace with Turkey in March 1812. Russia also made war on Sweden during this period and annexed Finland from her. Then Russia deserted the Serb nationalists, whom the Turks soon suppressed. But later in the nineteenth century she was to resume her policy of encouraging nationalist revolts against the Ottoman Empire in order to spread her own influence in the Balkans.

### The Final Victory

Let us return now to the defeat of Napoleon. In 1813 he had finally managed to make the four great powers concentrate their main efforts against him. Not only did their combined armies at last outnumber his everywhere, but now the bulk of his own soldiers were raw, teen-age recruits. Also, middle age and overwork began to make the emperor lose some of his sure touch. General Charles de Gaulle, who 150 years later was accused of harboring Napoleonic ambitions, had this to say about Napoleon in that period:

"Still undismayed, and still resolved to tempt Providence once more, he suddenly found himself without soldiers or weapons, and saw, towering above him and ready to break, the swollen wave of ill will, of cowardice and treachery which was to engulf his genius."

One by one Napoleon's former allies and dependent rulers turned against him. Finally, in mid-October, they defeated him in the Battle of Leipzig, which the Germans called the Battle of the Nations.

After this decisive defeat, Napoleon's empire quickly fell apart. The Duke of Wellington drove the French out of Spain, and most of the remaining satellite territories joined the anti-French alliance. The Allies made mistakes and quarreled among themselves, but they did not make the supreme mistake of giving Napoleon a winter to recuperate. They crossed the Rhine at the end of 1813 and made their victorious entry into Paris on March 31, 1814. Napoleon was then exiled to the island of Elba, off the west coast of Italy. His return to the throne and his defeat at Waterloo the next year were little more than a theatrical epilogue; Napoleon and his empire were finished. The Allies had already restored the Bourbon pretender to the throne of his fathers and his dead brother. Louis XVIII indicated the tone of the whole post-Napoleonic period when an aide brought him the joyous news. "Sire! You are the King of France!" The new sovereign coldly replied, "And when have I been anything else?"

### The Peace Settlements, 1814–1815

The peace settlements of 1814–1815 marked the complete triumph of the balance of power in international affairs. For "reasons of state" the aspirations of mere peoples were simply shelved. Power alone counted. The international ideological war had long ceased to be an overriding consideration, and it ended with France's military defeat. In fact, now that France was safely Bourbon again, she was quickly accepted into the club of the four other great powers. Lesser powers, dispossessed sovereign princes, and nationalist pressure groups had no influence on the peace settlements; the Big Five reorganized Europe and the colonial world to suit themselves.

In the first Treaty of Paris (May 30, 1814) the Allies were lenient with France. They let her retain her 1792 boundaries in Europe and some remnants of her former colonial empire. In their desire to strengthen the new Bourbon regime, they abandoned all claims for indemnities or reparations. They had already signed a Quadruple Alliance to enforce the peace settlement with France and had agreed to deal with other questions at an international congress in Vienna.

*The Congress of Vienna*

Before consenting to a general conference, both Russia and Great Britain "settled" many of their own imperialist claims themselves. Russia retained Bessarabia, Finland, and some recent conquests in the Caucasus. Great Britain confirmed her domination in the Mediterranean by keeping Malta and the Ionian Islands, off the northwest coast of Greece. She also insisted on her right to control all the other sea lanes of the world. To assure this control she kept the former Dutch colonies of Ceylon and the Cape of Good Hope and the former French island of Mauritius in the Indian Ocean, as well as three French islands in the West Indies. With these lands, Canada, Australasia, and additional conquests in India, Great Britain remained the only important colonial power for the next seventy years. The others were mere remnants.

The Congress of Vienna (September 1814–June 1815) decided the fate of Europe. The fact that this brilliant international conference met in the Hapsburg capital seemed to symbolize its counterrevolutionary character. So did the delegates themselves, with their silk knee breeches, their ancient titles, and their elaborate attention to protocol. But behind the scenes the chief negotiators of the Big Five—Metternich for Austria, Hardenberg for Prussia, Castlereagh for Great Britain, Talleyrand for France, and Alexander I himself for Russia—showed little desire to restore the state of affairs before 1789. On the contrary, they wanted to settle the differences that had long divided them in order to prevent future wars. France was to be "contained" within her prewar borders, of course, but she was to remain an equal partner in maintaining the new balance of power. Each of the other four powers sought to strengthen its place in this equilibrium with little consideration for ancient frontiers or the "legitimate" claims of formerly sovereign princes.

There was little argument over the settlement in Western Europe. Everyone agreed that there should be a barrier of strong states along France's northern and eastern frontiers. Thus, a new Kingdom of the Netherlands was formed, combining the former Dutch Republic and Belgium (former Austrian Netherlands), and Prussia was given almost all of the German left bank of the Rhine. The Kingdom of Sardinia got back Piedmont and, eventually, Savoy and was also given the

old Republic of Genoa. In compensation for Belgium, Austria got the remainder of northern Italy—to be called the Lombard-Venetian Kingdom. The old ruling families were eventually restored in central and southern Italy as well as in Spain and Portugal. Switzerland was restored as an independent confederation—the only republic in Europe.

It was far more difficult to reestablish the balance of power in Central and Eastern Europe to everyone's satisfaction. Only the territory of the Duchy of Warsaw was included in the new state, later called "Congress Poland," with Alexander I as its "constitutional" king. Some Poles remained in Prussia and Austria, but Russian influence now extended two hundred and fifty miles farther west than it had after the third partition of Poland in 1795. Prussia did not get as much of her demands as Russia did—only two-thirds of Saxony. The rest of Saxony and the Napoleonic kingdoms of Bavaria, Württemberg, and Hanover were kept virtually intact. They formed a part of the loose German Confederation of thirty-nine states, whose borders corresponded pretty much to those of the Holy Roman Empire. But the Holy Roman Empire itself was not restored, and all the other formerly sovereign princes were left with nothing but their empty titles and their memories.

Meanwhile, the settlement with France was momentarily threatened in the spring of 1815. In March Napoleon escaped from Elba, returned to Paris, and raised a new army. For a Hundred Days he was once more the emperor, but on June 18 the combined English and Prussian armies defeated him for the last time at the Battle of Waterloo, in Belgium. After that Napoleon was exiled to the island of St. Helena, in the South Atlantic. In the second Treaty of Paris France was restricted to her 1790 frontiers and required to pay an indemnity of 700,000,000 francs.

The Hundred Days had renewed the dread of revolution and aggressive war among the victors, but the basic peace settlement remained unchanged. Great

Britain, Austria, Prussia, and Russia renewed their Quadruple Alliance and agreed to settle future disputes at international congresses like the one at Vienna. Alexander I, now grown quite mystical, wanted the powers to promise, by signing the Holy Alliance, to uphold the Christian principles of charity and peace as well. Though the statesmen did not take Alexander's Alliance seriously, the repressed nationalists, liberals, and democrats saw it as a reactionary conspiracy against liberty and progress.

It was the necessities of the balance of power, not the Holy Alliance, that prevented Europe's peoples from achieving sovereignty and national self-determination. The peace settlements of 1814–1815 had the great merit of doing what they were designed to do. They did indeed maintain the new balance of power for a good part of the nineteenth century. No series of wars of comparable magnitude has ever been followed by such a long period of international peace as those that ended in 1815.

. . .

The Congress of Vienna had restored outward peace and order, but it could not restore the civilization of the prerevolutionary age. Radical changes swept the whole Western world between 1789 and 1815. To be sure, many achievements of the past endured. The Newtonian view of the physical world was to persist for almost another century. Sovereign states simply became stronger and more imperialistic than ever. Economic development proceeded at about the same pace as before; only in England did industrialization change it radically before 1815. Nevertheless, many basic features of European civilization were never to be the same again.

The traditional class structure lost its legal basis in most of Western and Central Europe. Although social classes were to remain an important part of European life long after 1815, never thereafter were noblemen to have the kinds of power and privilege they had enjoyed in the past. The middle classes had come into their own, and the masses had begun to assert themselves.

War changed too. In order to defend their Revolution against foreign attack the French put a million men into the field of battle. In order to defeat them, other states finally mobilized mass armies themselves. The age of gentlemanly wars fought by mercenaries was over. Once the masses became involved, wars acquired an increasingly nationalistic flavor.

The needs of war and the ascendancy of the bourgeoisie also made government more efficient and more rational. Here too the French initiated the change, and other nations followed suit. They developed modern civil administrations run by talented commoners. Many countries also adopted the Napoleonic legal code, with its emphasis on logical consistency, equality before the law, and the sanctity of property.

The great upheavals of this period also stimulated a new outlook in all the arts. Writers, composers, and painters sought to build something new on the ruins of the old order of things. This was the main purpose of romanticism, which we shall examine in Chapter XI.

Finally, the ideals of political democracy and national independence became part of the European consciousness. By 1815 democratic government survived unscathed only in the new American Republic; but the French had given this ideal to their fellow Europeans, and it was to reassert itself in France and elsewhere within a few decades. The French and the Americans gave the ideal of national independence to the people in Latin America as well as in Europe, and although it too was thwarted in most places in 1815, it was to reappear shortly thereafter.

The most permanent legacy of the era of the French Revolution and Napoleon was its radicalism. A radical is someone who cherishes values incompatible with those embodied in existing institutions. He is so deeply estranged from these institutions that he refuses to compromise with them in any way. The radical of the Left insists on the destruction of the old order and the creation of a new one. The radical of the Right insists on the destruction of the new order and the recreation of the old one. Each type of radical had appeared from time to time before 1789.

But in that fateful year the conflict between them began an epidemic of revolutions and counterrevolutions which still plagues many parts of the world today.

## SUGGESTED READINGS


Lefebvre, Georges, *The Coming of the French Revolution.* Trans. Robert R. Palmer. New York: Random House, 1961*
Excellent analysis of the immediate causes of the Revolution.

Gershoy, Leo, *The Era of the French Revolution: Ten Years That Shook The World.* Princeton, N. J.: D. Van Nostrand, 1957. An Anvil original.*
Excellent brief survey incorporating newer interpretations.

Lefebvre, Georges, *The French Revolution.* 2 vols. New York: Columbia Univ. Press, 1964.
The most balanced and thorough account of the Revolution, placed in a world context.

Lefebvre, Georges, *Napoleon*, 2 vols., New York: Columbia Univ. Press, 1969.
The great French historian's account of the Napoleonic Period.

Brinton, Crane, *A Decade of Revolution.* New York: Harper and Row, 1963. Torchbook.*
A very good older account in the Rise of Modern Europe series.

Stewart, John Hall, *A Documentary Survey of the French Revolution.* New York: The Macmillan Co., 1951.
The best collection of sources.

Rudé, George, *The Crowd in the French Revolution.* New York: Oxford Univ. Press, 1965.*
Reflects recent emphasis on the role of the *sans-culottes.*

Soboul, Albert, *The Parisian Sans-Culottes and the French Revolution, 1793–4.* Oxford, Eng.: Oxford Univ. Press, 1964.
A masterly, detailed study of the subject.

Williams, Gwyn A., *Artisans and Sans-Culottes.* New York: W. W. Norton, 1969.*
Excellent short social history of popular movements in England and France at the end of the eighteenth century.

Hampson, Norman, *A Social History of the French Revolution.* Toronto: Univ. of Toronto Press, 1967.*
Stimulating and novel.

Palmer, Robert R., *Twelve Who Ruled: The Committee of Public Safety during the Terror.* New York: Atheneum, n.d.*
A brilliant study of the Committee of Public Safety.

Thompson, James M., *Robespierre and the French Revolution.* New York: The Macmillan Co., 1953.*
A good, balanced study.

Palmer, Robert R., *The Age of the Democratic Revolution.* Vol. II. Princeton, N.J.: Princeton Univ. Press, 1964.
Carries the theme of the French Revolution as part of an Atlantic Revolution through the 1790s—more diffuse than the first volume.

Herold, Christopher, *The Age of Napoleon.* New York: Harper and Row, 1963.
Readable and accurate.

Brunn, Geoffrey, *Europe and the French Imperium, 1799–1814.* New York: Harper and Row, 1963. Torchbook.*

A good survey of the Napoleonic period—in the Rise of Modern Europe series.

Markham, Felix, *Napoleon and the Awakening of Europe.* New York: Collier, 1965.*
An admirably compact and up-to-date biography.

Geyl, Pieter, *Napoleon, For and Against.* New Haven: Yale Univ. Press, n.d.
Compares conflicting interpretations.

Tarlé, Eugene, *Napoleon in Russia.* New York: International Publishers, 1942.
Exciting description of the War of 1812 and the Russian resistance, by a leading Soviet historian.

Shanahan, Willian Oswald, *Prussian Military Reforms,* 1786–1813. New York: Columbia Univ. Press, 1945.
A specialized study of reforms that were to have a lasting influence in Germany.

Webster, Charles K., *The Congress of Vienna,* 1814–1815, 2nd ed. London: Oxford Univ. Press, 1934.
Detailed and authoritative.

CHAPTER X

# THE INDUSTRIAL REVOLUTION (TO 1850)

The Industrial Revolution lacked the drama and the glory of the French Revolution. There were a few working-class demonstrations against the new machines, and the appearance of the steam locomotive aroused considerable public reaction at first. But no Bastilles were stormed, no kings lost their heads, and no Lafayette, Robespierre, or Napoleon gave events the stamp of his personal leadership.

Yet, in its undramatic and inglorious way the Industrial Revolution was to transform modern civilization more than all the other revolutions we have studied thus far. For industrialization became a continuous process of change at an ever accelerating pace. It is still going on—with no end in sight.

The Industrial Revolution got under way in Great Britain at the same time as the political and social revolution in France, that is, in the 1780s and 1790s. It was then that the steam engine rapidly took hold in textile manufacturing and made possible heavy concentrations of factory production in Lancashire and Yorkshire. It was then that the double process of puddling and rolling made cheap wrought iron available as the major structural material of the new industrial economy. The first stage of the Industrial Revolution was completed by 1850, when new chemical processes, machine tools, and railroads were firmly established. By then it had also taken root in Belgium, France, and Germany, as well as in Great Britain.

This revolution in technology transformed the economic, political, social, and cultural life of the countries affected, though these transformations were more gradual than those brought about by the French Revolution. Even in 1850 agriculture and domestic service were still the most important occupations in Great Britain, and most of the labor force was still engaged in industries of the older craft type—building trades, tailoring, shoemaking—and in unskilled work of all sorts. The old order was even stronger in Belgium, France, and Germany. Nevertheless, by 1850 a new kind of civilization was clearly emerging. In three generations Western man had increased his nonagricultural productive capacity more than he had in ten thousand years. Industrialists and their allies in trade and finance had gained a preponderant influence over domestic government policy in much of Western Europe. The mill town and the urban slum had created a new kind of proletariat, rootless, anonymous, and—in contrast to the apparently boundless optimism of its employers—hopeless.

In this chapter we shall see that the

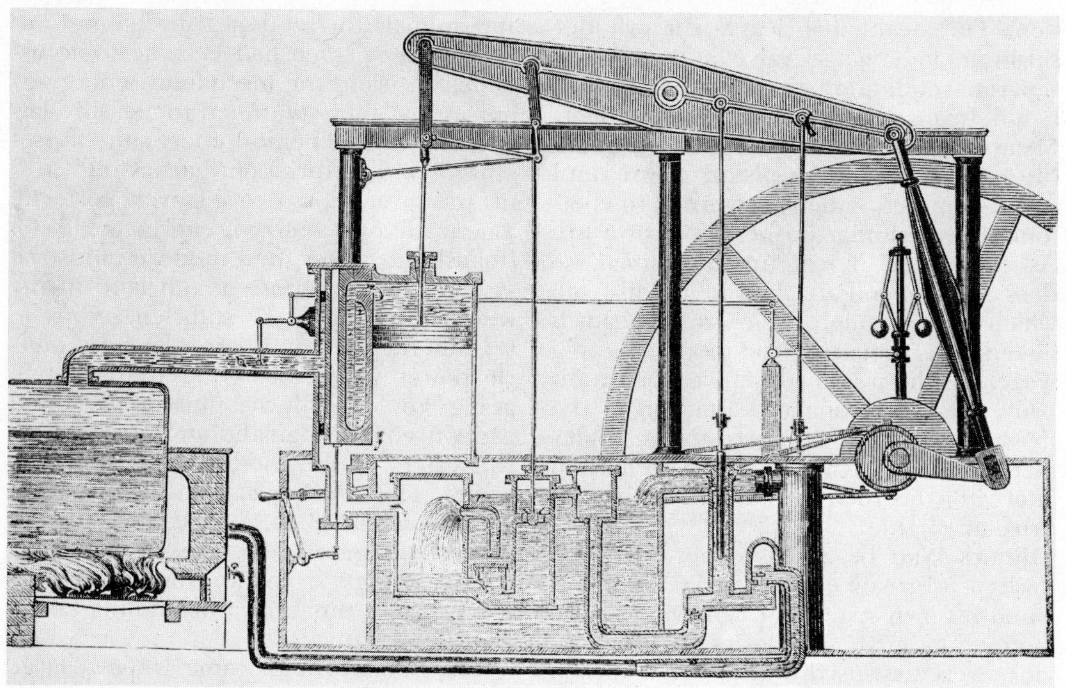

*Watt's low-pressure steam engine, an early version*

Industrial Revolution was first of all a technological revolution. After that we shall examine the economic, social, and political factors that made it appear first in Great Britain: expanding markets, abundant natural resources, growing accumulations of capital, a strong, centralized government catering to private capitalists, a highly developed entrepreneurial spirit, urbanization, and an organizable pool of cheap labor. We shall then see how the Industrial Revolution spread to the European continent. Next we shall consider the social and cultural effects of urbanization and the factory system on the new working class wherever it appeared. Finally, we shall note the first ideological reactions to the Industrial Revolution: economic liberalism and utopian socialism.

## THE REVOLUTION IN TECHNOLOGY

The most revolutionary aspect of the Industrial Revolution was the way it changed the production and transportation of goods. It substituted machines driven by steam power for hand tools and muscle power. In the new forms of production many workers became tenders of machines rather than fashioners of things. Those workers who extracted the raw materials—especially coal and iron—probably used more muscle power than ever, and so did those who laid the railroad tracks and shoveled coal into blast furnaces and boiler engines. But these boiler engines, blast furnaces, and railroad tracks *then* served to produce and transport goods in ways that the skills and strength of mere human beings and draught animals could never match.

### New Sources of Power and Energy

It all started with steam and coal.

A steam engine is a device that transforms heat energy into mechanical energy. It does this in several stages. First, the heat energy of coal is released as the coal is burned in a firebox, and the heat transforms water in the boiler of the engine into steam. This steam then enters a cylinder through a valve arrangement, and its pressure exerts force upon the piston which is translated into piston motion. The steam then leaves the cylinder through an exhaust valve and enters a separate condenser, where it is cooled into liquid form and returned to the boiler. Meanwhile, the vacuum thus created in the cylinder pulls the piston down until steam admitted under pressure at the bottom of the cylinder pushes the piston up. As the piston moves up and down, so does a piston rod attached to it. This rod, which runs through the cylinder head, is linked by a connecting rod to a crank on a wheel. As the piston rod moves longitudinally, the connecting rod attached to the flywheel translates the force to the rotary motion of the flywheel. The mechanical energy of this rotary wheel can be used to drive an engine.

James Watt began his experiments on this type of steam engine in 1763 and patented his own system for achieving rotary motion* in 1781. Ten years later his engines were first used to drive machines in textile mills. By 1800 Great Britain had perhaps five hundred such engines, totaling less than 10,000 horsepower. Half a century later, her steam capacity was up to about 1,300,000 horsepower and was being used in the metallurgical industry, ships, and railroads as well. Earlier inventors had prepared the way for Watt's achievement (Newcomen patented the first steam engine in 1705), and later ones adapted it to new uses. The same is true for most inventions. Our purpose here is not to single out James Watt as a greater inventor than the others. It is to see his steam engine as *the* device that harnessed a new form of energy to the productive process.

Until the late eighteenth century man had been more or less limited to the energy of living organisms. There were some windmills and watermills, and all sailing ships were wind machines in a sense. But 80–85 per cent of the total energy came from plants, animals, and men—who used plants for food and fuel and animals for food and mechanical energy. Indeed, men had become so accustomed to using the mechanical energy of horses that they continued to measure later forms of mechanical energy in "horsepower" and to speak of "harnessing" it to functions no horse could ever perform. The traditional kinds of energy could not furnish the power for a modern industrial system. There is not enough land in the whole world to grow sufficient crops to feed all the men and animals whose muscle power would be required to keep it going. For not only are muscles weak and easily tired, but men and animals are poor converters of the food energy they consume. The mechanical energy a horse supplies is only 3 to 5 per cent of the energy of the green fodder used to feed it. As for energy from non-fossil fuels, the chief supply, timber, was dwindling fast in Western Europe.

The breakthrough came when a large number of inanimate converters, steam engines, turned a new source of energy, coal, into motion. Coal had been used commercially as fuel in England since the late sixteenth century, but its use was limited by the cost of producing and transporting it. By the early eighteenth century mines had to be dug deeper in the ground and were constantly being flooded. The first primitive steam engines were used to pump the water out. When later steam engines were perfected and used on barges and railroads, it became possible to produce more coal and to transport it at a much faster rate. More coal in turn meant more machine power. Thus, new sources of power and energy started the Industrial Revolution and kept it going at an ever accelerating rate of growth.

### The Textile Industry

The first application of the new sources of power and energy came in textile manufacturing, especially the manufacture of cotton cloth. Textile manufacturing was certainly not new. Woolen fabrics had been the principal manufactured staple in international trade for almost a thousand years. They had enriched Flanders and Italy in the Middle Ages and England

*Because patent rights prevented him from using the aforementioned system he devised the "sun and planet" system for transmitting power from the piston to a beam and then to a shaft. He put geared teeth on the shaft; these teeth engaged a small geared wheel; and this wheel then transmitted its power to a larger wheel.

since the sixteenth century. By the late eighteenth century the manufacture of cloth (mainly woolens and worsteds) employed more British workers and capital and yielded products of more value than any other form of production except agriculture. But it was still done mainly at home by frequently indifferent workers on hand-driven machines.

During the course of the eighteenth century new inventions intermittently speeded up the processes of spinning and weaving. John Kay's flying shuttle (1733) made it possible for one weaver to do the work of two. The spinners of yarn could not keep up with the increased demand until James Hargreaves invented his spinning jenny (a multiple spinning wheel) in 1765 and Richard Arkwright perfected his water frame, a true mechanical departure since it was driven by water power, four years later. Then in 1779 Samuel Crompton combined features of the jenny and the water frame in a machine called the mule. Now the weavers could not keep up with the flood of cheap yarn. This bottleneck was not completely broken until the perfection of the machine loom driven by steam power. Edmund Cartwright invented a primitive version in 1787, but the power loom did not really take hold until the 1820s.

All these inventions except the flying shuttle found their first effective application in the cotton rather than the wool industry. The vegetable cotton fiber lent itself to mechanization far better than wool, and both the supply of the raw material and the demand for the finished product responded more easily to changes in price in the younger industry. As we saw in Chapter VI, it had been cheaper to import cotton cloth from India than to produce it in Great Britain until the late eighteenth century; but from 1760 to 1840 the price of British yarn fell to one-twentieth of what it had been. The invention of the cotton gin by the American Eli Whitney in 1793 facilitated rapid development in production. In 1787 Britain consumed 22 million pounds of raw cotton; by 1849 the figure was 630 million. Cotton had displaced wool as Britain's chief manufacture.

As a result of this spectacular growth, the cotton industry became the heart of the Industrial Revolution in Great Britain. By the mid-1840s it employed over half a million people, 340,000 of them tending power-driven machines in factories rather than working at home. Furthermore, its expansion created new demands for the products of other industries. In this way it turned what might otherwise have been an isolated phenomenon into a new system of production.

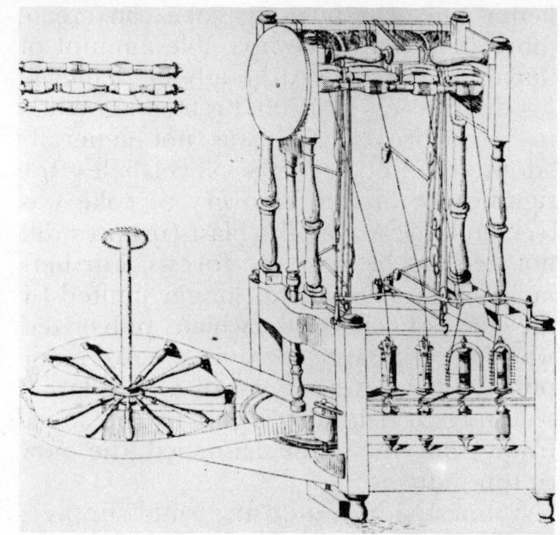

*Arkwright's water frame*

### Heavy Industry and Transportation

By the late eighteenth century the iron industry was able to meet new demands by transforming itself with the use of coal as a new source of energy. Traditionally, iron ore had been smelted and refined with charcoal, and the iron works had had to be near the source of wood. But, as we have seen, Britain's wood supply was rapidly dwindling, not only because it was burned as fuel but also because so much of it was used in shipbuilding. Hence, Britain had to rely more and more on imports of iron from Sweden and Russia.

An ironmaster named Abraham Darby eliminated the bottleneck when he found a way of blast-firing his ore with coke —the carbon residue of coal after its volatile elements had been driven off. By discovering how to produce coke Darby not only found a new source of energy but a better one, for burning coke can create more heat than a comparable amount of burning charcoal. Although he achieved his first success in 1709, his technique had to be improved and was not generally adopted until the 1760's. Nevertheless the significance of the discovery of coke was tremendous. At last the blast-furnaces did not need to be near the forests. Furthermore, their size was no longer limited by the use of charcoal, which pulverized when used in large quantities. Coke made possible the development of a new, large-scale pig iron industry, just as the water frame and the mule launched the new cotton industry.

Before the iron industry could supply a satisfactory structural material for machines another technological advance had to be made. For pig iron is hard and brittle and will not stand up under pounding or the stress of rapid movement. Another iron master, Henry Cort, found the way to make wrought or malleable iron in 1784 with his double process of puddling and rolling. Puddling is the process by which most of the carbon and other impurities are removed from pig iron through a combination of heat, oxidation, and frequent stirring in a small reverberatory furnace. Rolling is the process of shaping the heated metal by passing and repassing it between a set of rolls. In this way it can be shaped into plates, bars, rails, wheels, or any other form desired.

Cort's discoveries opened the way to a modern metallurgical industry. From the end of the eighteenth century on, cheap iron became available as the major structural material of the new industrial economy. Other transformed metals were later to replace iron, as we shall see, but the first stage of the Industrial Revolution was an iron age. Its great blast furnaces altered the British countryside in an even more spectacular way than the new textile mills. Here is a late eighteenth-century description of the famous Carron iron works in lower Scotland:

"Four giant furnaces forty-five feet high devour enormous masses of coal and minerals day and night. . . . Each furnace is kept going by four huge air pumps. . . . The draft, compressed in iron cylinders and forced toward the flames through a narrow pipe, produces such a sharp hiss and such a violent commotion, that a man who had not been warned about it in advance would have difficulty controlling his terror. . . . Such a concentration of air is indispensable to maintain at the highest heat a forty-five foot pile of coal and minerals: this draft of air is so swift and so active that it shoots up brilliant flames six feet above the chimneys."

Two further developments in heavy industry—chemicals and machine tools—completed the first stage of the Industrial Revolution. In the new chemical industry the key innovations were the lead-chamber process of producing sulfuric acid, developed by the British in 1746, and the Leblanc technique of making soda from salt, developed by the French in the 1780s and put into commercial use in France and Great Britain in the early nineteenth century. Both sulfuric acid and soda replaced earlier, more expensive agents in the process of bleaching textiles. The other new development in heavy industry was the manufacture of machine tools, which carried the revolution in handicraft one stage further by using machines to make machines. One of many innovators in shaping metals according to plan was John Wilkinson, whose boring machine helped to make James Watt's steam engine a success.

A brief final word is necessary on the application of iron and steam to rail and water transportation. In our age of diesel locomotives and trucks, atomic-powered ships, and jet planes, it is easy to forget that the steam locomotive and the steamship were the world's chief forms of transportation until the 1940s. Hence, we cannot close this section without mentioning the familiar achievements of Robert Fulton in perfecting the first successful steamboat in 1807 and of George Stephenson in completing the adaptation of the steam engine to the railroad in 1814. The first general railway for transporting passengers as well as goods was opened between Liverpool and Manchester in 1830. Within the next twenty years, Great Britain built 6,500 miles of track linking every major industrial and population center.

The construction of railway networks promoted and substantially completed the first stage of the Industrial Revolution in Great Britain by 1850 and in other Western European countries soon thereafter. This cheap new form of transport reduced the costs of manufacture and expanded in even greater proportion the demand for finished goods. In addition, it increased the demand for the products of the coal, iron, and machine-tool industries, thus provoking numerous technological advances and promoting a general shift of capital into heavy industry. The railroad opened up new markets and new sources of raw materials. It also had far-reaching social effects, especially in redistributing the population.

## ECONOMIC GROWTH AND THE INDUSTRIAL REVOLUTION IN GREAT BRITAIN

We must now ask ourselves *why* the Industrial Revolution took place first in Great Britain and *how* her people found the resources, capital, enterprise, skills, and labor to carry it through; for it was more than a series of technological advances. The first requisite of economic growth is a particular kind of society. Some of its people must have a strong sense of economic values and considerable powers of economic calculation. They must be willing to adopt new techniques and to perceive the alternative results of using resources, capital, and labor in new ways. By the mid-eighteenth century British society had more of these features than any other in the world.

### Expanding Markets

Not only was Great Britain the world's leading trading nation, but she also had thriving handicraft industries, especially in woolen textiles. Both at home and overseas the demand for British manufactured goods was so great that existing techniques of production could not keep up with it. The necessity to increase output did not *cause* the technological breakthrough, but it made the manufacturers especially willing to exploit the inventions and discoveries that appeared: the jenny, the water frame, and the mule, the factory to house them, the steam engine to power them, and the use of coal as energy for the steam engine. In the end all these innovations helped the new cotton industry most, although they were conceived for wool.

Since the sixteenth century Great Britain had become the world's main producer and exporter of woolen cloth. England had the largest flocks of long-haired sheep in the world, and, in the seventeenth century, she prohibited further export of wool in order to prevent its manufacture by competitors on the continent. Most of her woolen cloth was produced by rural "cottage" labor organized by independent entrepreneurs—a system that did not limit output and prevent innovation as the guilds did on the continent. These advantages, plus the fact that labor was cheaper in the countryside than in the towns, helped to increase the supply of cheap British woolens. Finally, in the eighteenth century, the demand for these woolens also increased, at home and overseas.

The home market for all goods expanded in the eighteenth century for several reasons. First of all, though the majority of Britishers were poor, they had more money to spend than people on the continent; wages for similar occupations were twice as high in England as in France and higher yet than in the countries further east. Second, the rapidity of urbanization* also stimulated the home market. Furthermore, in England, many rural people in the handicraft industries acquired urban buying habits. Finally, British retail traders were more energetic and enterprising than those on the continent; they sold where and when they wished and competed freely on the basis of price, advertising, and credit.

Britain's sales abroad had grown spectacularly; including re-exports, they increased almost fourfold between 1660

*By the middle of the eighteenth century 25 per cent of the population of England and Wales lived in towns of 5,000 or more, as compared with 10 per cent in France and even less in Germany and Eastern Europe.

and 1760, and grew at an even faster rate after that. Moreover, the desires of Britain's customers overseas further aggravated the crisis of production. They wanted the same woolens, hardware, and other cheap, standardized goods for which there was a growing demand at home. Without a technological breakthrough, Britain's domestic system of manufacturing could not have kept up with the total demand.

#### Capital, Resources, and the Role of Government

By the eighteenth century the British economy was already being transformed by changes in men's attitudes to enterprise, particularly the enlargement of their concept of capital. Capital is the surplus from economic activity which is invested in further growth. Traditionally, it was viewed as a purely physical thing: land, buildings, a store of gold or commodities. From the seventeenth century onward, however, stocks and bonds also provided capital for all kinds of enterprises. The collapse of the "South Sea Bubble" in 1720 (see p. 220) strained the connection between tangible and intangible forms of wealth to the point of disaster. Nevertheless, businessmen were learning from experience to adapt themselves to new economic horizons.

An eighteenth-century British entrepreneur could set forth on a career of manufacturing with a relatively small capital investment. He could borrow his working capital from the suppliers of his raw materials and the purchasers of his finished products. They were happy to give him six months or a year to pay, as long as the interest rate* was attractive and his credit was good. In textile manufacturing his fixed capital was modest because the early machines were of rudimentary construction, not much more costly than the hand-operated devices they replaced; and there was soon an active market in used equipment. If the entrepreneur could not afford to buy his power and plant, he could usually lease them from owners of industrial property.

In heavy industry and transportation, where the capital requirements generally surpassed the means of a single entrepreneur, partnerships and joint-stock companies were the rule. Although the anonymous, limited liability corporation was still a long way off, these early British firms were already more open to outside investors than the family businesses of other countries. Moreover, some firms in the iron industry were able to secure long leases on mineral-bearing land at very low rates—until the proprietors became aware of its true value. Once started, an industrial firm could grow by reinvesting its profits. These were very large because of the low cost and high productivity of the early machines. Still, some investment capital had to come from other parts of the economy for heavy industry, and especially for the costly initial outlays of railroad construction.

Here the supply of savings was important, particularly the accumulated wealth of Britain's landowners, professional classes, and merchants. British agriculture, already more profitable than any other, was assured a good market in the rapidly growing urban population. The enclosure movement that had begun in the sixteenth century was greatly accelerated in the eighteenth century, and, like improved techniques, raised productivity. Many big landowners, both nobles and commoners, operated their agricultural estates on a capitalist basis and were ready to invest their savings in other sections of the economy. So were Britain's merchants. Indeed, profits from overseas trade and domestic commerce constituted the largest supply of savings available for investment in new industries. Lawyers, doctors, and government officials had also gained increased income and savings from Britain's pre-industrial economic growth.

Great Britain's advanced banking and

*The interest rate on government bonds had fallen to 3 per cent by 1749 (see footnote on p. 229). Hence the higher rates for short-term business loans were much sought after. Businessmen also raised investment capital by mortgaging their factory buildings to some neighboring landowner, widow, or prosperous lawyer. Mortgages at 5 per cent remained attractive securities for such people until the coming of the limited liability corporation in the 1850s and 1860s (see Chapter XIII).

credit institutions facilitated the transfer of savings from other parts of the economy into industry. By the 1790s around four hundred private provincial banks made the savings of their investors available to businessmen either in the form of credit or by discounting their bills of exchange. The center of the money market was the few square blocks in London known as the City. There discount houses and banks bought up the bills of exchange of provincial trade and industry. At the top of the system stood the Bank of England, which rediscounted the bills for the banks, thus providing them with a steady supply of liquid funds. In these ways money was able to flow rapidly and efficiently to the areas of highest return, which, by the late eighteenth century, meant new industries.

In addition to her economic and financial advantages Great Britain had easy access to natural resources and raw materials. As we shall see later, there were important deposits of iron and coal in Northwestern Europe, but these were less easily accessible and less concentrated than those in Great Britain, and many were not discovered until the nineteenth century. The coal and iron basins in Great Britain were especially rich and particularly close to each other, a fact that reduced the cost of transportation. She was also particularly well endowed with raw materials for her non-wool textile industries. By the time her cotton industry really got under way, her main source of raw cotton, the southern United States, was no longer a British possession. But during the Napoleonic wars the British navy controlled the Atlantic, and the British merchant marine alone was able to import American cotton. Long after 1815 the cotton-producing areas of the young American Republic remained dependent on the British market and catered to its needs.

The British government itself aided economic growth in several ways. At home it had eliminated all regional tariff barriers, thereby providing a larger domestic market than any other country before France removed her internal tariffs during the Revolution. Since the mid-seventeenth century the British government had also licensed private monopolies and trusts to build and operate turnpikes, canals, and docks. These utilities not only facilitated trade, but also produced profits that added to the stock of available investment capital. Once the process of industrialization was under way, the government helped to increase the mobility of labor too, as we shall see presently.

No government was as responsive to the desires of its mercantile classes and as alert to the commercial implications of war as that of Great Britain. Unlike most of its continental rivals, this island kingdom did not fight frequent wars for European territory. Instead, it built up a trading empire overseas, which cost less and paid better in the long run. The British government also encouraged foreign trade by supporting a large, aggressive merchant marine and the banks and joint-stock companies that sustained it. When war did become necessary, the British navy championed British commercial interests against all comers.

### Skill and Enterprise

It is not easy to explain the remarkable concentration of technical skill represented by the eighteenth-century parade of British inventors. Some historians stress the freedom of British invention from guild restrictions and the open recruitment of mechanical and engineering talent. Indeed, some children of good families acquired technical skills by being apprenticed out to weavers and joiners. The early inventors came from all sections of society: John Kay was the son of a substantial farmer; Edmund Cartwright, the son of a gentleman, was a graduate of Oxford; James Watt was the son of an unsuccessful merchant and very poor himself; John Roebuck, the discoverer of the lead-chamber process for sulfuric acid and one of the founders of the Carron iron works, had studied chemistry and medicine at the Universities of Edinburgh and Leyden.

Other historians emphasize the influence of the rational-empirical outlook of the scientific revolution in aiding the inventors of the eighteenth century. This kind of influence is difficult to prove, though highly probable. But Great Britain was not the only country to undergo this revolution, and indeed in the late eighteenth century France, not Great Britain, was the main center of practical scientific activity. There were French inventors too. We have already mentioned Nicholas Leblanc's soda ash process, and René-Antoine Ferchault de Réamur, the inventor of the thermometer, also pointed the way for turning wrought iron into steel. Technical advances were made in other countries as well; German chemists invented new industrial dyes, and by the early nineteenth century American inventors were to lead the field in creating new machine tools. Moreover, in Great Britain as elsewhere, some inventors had scientific training and some did not.

What was unique in Great Britain was, W. S. Jevons has said, a "union of certain happy mental qualities with material resources of an altogether peculiar character." There the scientific outlook and the concentration of technical skill coincided with a shortage of a traditional form of energy (timber), the presence of large supplies of coal, and a very active group of entrepreneurs created by a prolonged growth of mercantile activities.

The spirit of enterprise *was* stronger in Great Britain than anywhere else in the eighteenth and early nineteenth centuries. Everybody noticed it. Napoleon's quip about "a nation of shopkeepers" was made with contempt, but it recognized a fact. All Englishmen were certainly not shopkeepers, and after 1800 many nobles and professional men looked down increasingly on people "in trade." The English, however, were generally less prejudiced against manual work and moneymaking than other Europeans.

British entrepreneurs were versatile as well as enterprising. They shifted their money and energy wherever the rewards were the greatest. An outstanding example was James Watt's partner, Matthew Boulton (1728–1809). Boulton, the son of a silver stamper and piecer in Birmingham, entered his father's business at an early age and began expanding it. In 1760 he married Anne Robinson of Lichfield; her dowry gave him additional capital, which he used to found the Soho Works in 1762. Water power was used to produce silver buttons and buckles in this factory, but as it grew, Boulton began looking for a more abundant source of power. James Watt was already being subsidized by John Roebuck, but when Roebuck went bankrupt in 1772 (there were business failures as well as successes), Boulton bought up his share in Watt's first patent. He took Watt on as a partner, and his energy and encouragement kept the inventor going until he achieved the hoped-for results.

Not only did Boulton use Watt's engines in his own factory, he also helped to promote their use elsewhere and to get the patent extended for twenty-four years through an act of Parliament. Boulton devoted all his own capital and all he could raise from other sources for the promotion of the steam engine. He brought himself to the verge of bankruptcy before the engine became a commercial success. Not until 1790 did he begin to make a profit.

Manufacturing buttons and promoting the steam engine were not Boulton's only activities. He also minted coins at Soho on several presses he set up in 1788 and worked with steam, a process he patented in 1790. After making large quantities of coins for the East India Company and several foreign governments, he undertook the production of a new copper coinage for Great Britain in 1797, in his sixty-ninth year! He then helped to organize the exploitation of copper mines in Cornwall and became involved in engine building there. In 1805 he supplied machinery for a new government mint that coined a large part of Britain's money for the next three-quarters of a century. With all his business ventures Boulton still found time to be an active member of the Royal Society and of the Lunar Society, an outstanding eighteenth-century organization of amateur and professional scientists.

### Labor

At the beginning of the Industrial Revolution people were abundant but factory labor was scarce. How could this have been so? In our rootless, urban civilization we think little of moving to another place for a better job. But in the late eighteenth century most Britishers were still rooted in a traditional agricultural civilization and hesitated to break away from their familiar surroundings. Population pressure in the countryside created a "push," but there had to be a "pull" too. Workers had to be recruited, just like soldiers and sailors.

As we already know, population growth had been stimulated in Western and Central Europe after the mid-eighteenth century.* Improvements in agriculture and increasing imports of corn to feed livestock produced more and better food. The potato, another import from America, saved Prussia from famine in the 1770s and allowed the population of poverty-ridden Ireland to increase as fast as that of prosperous England. By the 1840s the potato had been incorporated into the daily diet of the common people in much of Europe, including Russia. The fact that one could grow two to four times as much food in potatoes as in wheat or other grains on the same amount of land made possible earlier marriages and larger families than in the past. The main resistance to the potato was in the Iberian, Italian, and Balkan Peninsulas, and these were the areas of the smallest increase in population from 1750 to 1850.

*Women and children in the coal mines (from the Report of the Royal Commission, 1842)*

Between 1700 and 1800 the population of England and Wales grew from 5 1/2 to 9 million; by 1850 this last figure was nearly doubled. Historians differ widely over the explanation of the population explosion in the British countryside in the second half of the eighteenth century, when the new labor supply was first being organized. Some attribute it primarily to the declining death rate brought about by fewer epidemics and more food; others stress the rising birth rate, caused by earlier marriages. Lack of sufficient evidence allows the advocates of each argument to criticize the other without offering a final answer.

One point is clear: Britain could not have absorbed her rapidly growing population into her existing economic structure. After the mid-eighteenth century there were already more people in the British countryside than there was land or work for them. The situation was worse in Ireland. A large number of British citizens began emigrating to North America, but most of the rural masses continued to eke out a living in their rural slums until the prospects of jobs in the new factories and mines lured them away. News of these prospects was spread by the press and the town crier and by ordinary word of mouth. And just as recruiting agents signed up people to go to America as indentured servants, they also recruited them for the owners of the factories and mines at home.

Yet in the eighteenth century there were many impediments to the movement of labor from one place to another. Travel on foot was not always safe; if a man took to the road he might be picked up by a press-gang or kidnapped and sent to the plantations. Even in London, in 1756,

*See pp. 221–223.

James Watt was afraid to go into the street at night. The English Poor Laws were a more serious obstacle than the dangers of city streets and country roads. Although the law of 1601 required each parish to provide workhouses for its paupers, the law of 1662 permitted the local authorities to refuse to take in outsiders. One was an outsider until he had been settled in a new parish for a full year. If he lost his job before the year was up, he could be forced to move back to his own parish. This fact made him think twice before leaving his native village to seek work far away. In addition, many parishes gave supplementary relief whose rates varied inversely with the wage earner's normal earnings, thus destroying the incentive of the worker to demand, or the employer to offer, higher wages. This practice aggravated overpopulation in the agricultural villages and reduced the pressure on the laborers to move.

It was also difficult at first to move from one occupation to another. As in earlier times, most crafts bound their apprentices for six or seven years and enforced severe penalties on those who left their employer before the end of the period. Boulton and Watt made their engine erectors agree to serve for three or five years. Also, employers often failed to engage a man from another district because they were unable to offer work to other members of his family. To solve this problem some iron masters set up textile works near their furnaces in order to provide employment for the women and children.

The individual craft workers themselves often refused to move into new kinds of factory work. A male weaver would not think of stooping to the less skilled task of spinning, which was traditionally women's work. It was equally unthinkable for his wife and children to leave their home for a nearby factory. Fear of the unknown, resentment against supervision, and an aversion to the relentless demands of the machine all combined to make people view the factories as monstrous workhouses, or, as William Blake called them, "dark satanic mills."

With all these impediments, where did the new factory workers come from? At first they were the squatters of the countryside and the paupers of the towns—that is, the surplus population that agriculture and the traditional crafts could not absorb. Until the late eighteenth century the population of the countryside increased faster than that of the towns. But as the number of cotton mills in the towns grew, landless rural people flocked to them in order not to starve, and once there, they continued to have many children and thus augment the natural increase in population growth, and urbanization. Each was necessary for the continuation of the other.

The government helped too. In 1795 it passed a new law establishing freedom of movement for labor by withdrawing the right of local authorities to send poor people from other parishes back whence they came. Now the adults could move to the factory and mining communities and go on relief *there* when they were out of work. Moreover, their abandoned children could be sent to other factories as "apprentices." Since the early textile machines were easy to operate, and since the men shunned them at first, the majority of the workers in the new cotton mills were women and children.

As British workers moved gradually into the factories, poor Irish immigrants took their places in the fields, on the docks, and, after the 1820s, along the railroads. Some of these Irishmen saved a few pounds and then declared themselves penniless and got the Poor Law authorities to give them free passage home. Many, however, remained in Britain, where, as in the United States a few decades later, they did the dirty work of the Industrial Revolution: the digging, hauling, and loading. Eventually some of them worked in the mills in Scotland. Others replaced the English hand-loom weavers, who began to desert their dying occupation once the power loom reduced their earnings to a pittance.

By the 1830s Great Britain had gradually obtained a body of mobile, wage-paid workers in one way or another. Except for Irish immigration, there was no mass exodus from the countryside to the industrial towns. Nevertheless, a series of short waves of local migrations resulted in a long "wave" movement from the south and east to the Midlands and the north. Men and women who had previously divided their activities between agriculture and weaving or mining gradually came to work full time at the loom or the coal face, often without having to move their households. Parents insisted less and less on imposing their own occupations on their sons and daughters. As a result, factory employment also expanded by drawing in more children. In all these ways the "push" of population pressure and the "pull" of new job opportunities created a market for a new "commodity"—labor. Finally, the towns themselves, despite inadequate housing and abominable sanitation facilities, produced their own increase in population, which had no place to go except to the mills.

The Industrial Revolution in Great Britain made it possible for economic growth to keep ahead of population growth for the first time in history. Previously war, pestilence, and famine had always limited the size of the population to the available economic output. The British managed to break out of this trap by means of a fortunate combination of expanding markets and the resources, capital, enterprise, skills, and labor to satisfy the needs of these markets. We shall see shortly how the workers in the new factories and mines were exploited in order to make possible the "leap forward" in productivity and total output. But in the long run the Industrial Revolution laid the foundation for a spectacular rise in the level of living for all classes.

Already by the beginning of the nineteenth century the changes in the British economy were something new in human experience. Since the 1770's the output of the cotton industry multiplied tenfold; that of the iron industry fourfold. The steam engine was already helping to reduce costs in other industries, and large amounts of private capital were being spent in the construction of a canal system. The population of manufacturing cities like Manchester and Glasgow trebled. Most important, by 1800 the total national output of Great Britain was growing at a rate of 2 per cent a year and at a yearly rate of 1 per cent per capita, despite a rapidly growing population.

## THE INDUSTRIAL REVOLUTION ON THE CONTINENT

Once Britain had made the technological breakthrough, other European nations could learn from her. Yet even the most advanced ones moved slowly at first. For one thing, the Napoleonic wars disrupted contact between Great Britain and the continent until 1815; by then British technology was already a generation ahead. But there were more deep-seated hindrances within the continental countries themselves.

The flow of goods was restricted in countries like France and Germany. They were larger and less densely populated than Great Britain, and thus transport costs were higher and markets were fragmented. Political fragmentation and frequent customs barriers aggravated the fragmentation of markets. Until 1790 even France had its internal tariffs, while Germany, and to a lesser extent Belgium and Italy, remained a patchwork of kingdoms, principalities, bishoprics, and free cities, each with its own laws, courts, coinage, and tariffs.

Continental entrepreneurs were generally less enterprising and less versatile then those in pre-industrial Britain. In manufacturing they traditionally catered to orders from the wealthy few at home and were not geared to produce cheap, standardized goods for foreign markets. Except for Holland, whose financial activities were virtually ruined during the Revolutionary and Napoleonic period, the continent possessed less advanced banking and credit institutions than Great Britain. Most continental businessmen had a strong prejudice against taking outside capital entailing unwanted advice into family firms. Furthermore, most nobles and many would-be gentlemen looked down on all kinds of business activity. They preferred to put their savings into land, honorific titles, and privileged offices, until these were abolished by France at home and in her satellite states.

Traditionally, a government that wanted to build up its country's manufactures often took the initiative in organizing and financing these itself. All these factors limited the enterprise and versatility of the private entrepreneurs.

Nonetheless, in the late eighteenth century people in the more advanced continental countries began to think about industrialization. Government leaders recognized its political and military importance in maintaining their nation's status as a great power. Manufacturers soon saw that machine-made British goods would annihilate the less efficient industries of the world, as they were already undermining handicraft cotton production in India.

Neither the Napoleonic wars nor Britain's efforts to keep her industrial secrets could prevent British technicians from bringing their know-how to the continent. Some were entrepreneurs already and helped build new industries and railroads in Belgium, France, and Germany. Others were skilled workers who trained the first generation of industrial workers in these countries. By 1825 there were at least 2,000 skilled British workers on the continent. Thereafter some workers in Belgium and northern France became entrepreneurs and educated other workers from areas further east and south. In these ways, along with the founding of its own technical schools, the continent soon won its technological independence from Great Britain.

### Belgium

Belgium was the first continental country to overcome the handicaps to rapid industrialization.* It was an area of efficient agriculture and had a long tradition of textile manufacturing and metallurgy. Belgium's small size made transport relatively easy, and, above all, she had rich deposits of coal. The invasions of the early 1790s had badly disrupted her economy, but annexation to France provided enterprising manufacturing centers like Verviers with a large market, despite Napoleon's efforts to limit Belgian "imports." The increased pressure on the Belgian system of handicraft production brought the same consequences as similar pressure in Britain. But the Belgians did not have to invent new techniques themselves.

An emigrant English artisan named William Cockerill set Belgium on the path of rapid technological advance. In 1799 two wool entrepreneurs of Verviers engaged him to build carding and spinning machines and mechanical looms. Cockerill soon got other contracts, and within a few years he and his three sons were building equipment for the entire textile industry in Belgium and shipping their products all over Western Europe. The Cockerill family then branched out into steam engines, coal, iron, railway rolling stock, steamboats, and armaments. By the 1830s the Cockerill enterprises were one of the largest integrated complexes in Europe.

Belgium's precocious alliance between finance and production speeded the process of industrialization. Bank support helped the expansion of the Cockerill enterprises and paved the way for a spectacular boom in heavy industry and mining. The Société Générale (1822) and the Banque de Belgique (1835), both of Brussels, were the first joint-stock investment banks in Europe. Nourished by injections of French capital their investments helped Belgian coal output rise from 2,300,000 tons in 1831 to 5,660,000, a record figure on the continent, in 1847. The Belgian iron industry, which had barely learned to smelt with coke in the 1820s, turned out 2,484,000 tons of pig iron in 1847. By 1850 Belgium had a steam engine capacity of 51,000 horsepower in industry. Finally, thanks to her small size, Belgium entered the railway age ahead of France and Germany, and her strategic location made her government-built trunk lines the nexus of Western Europe.

Significantly, Belgium's textile industries did not develop nearly as fast as her heavy industry and railroads. After 1815 her domestic market was again restricted by separation from France, and her European market was again open to British

*It will be recalled that Belgium consisted of the former Austrian Netherlands and the Bishopric of Liège. These territories were annexed to France in 1793. In 1814 they were joined to Holland, and they finally won their independence in 1830.

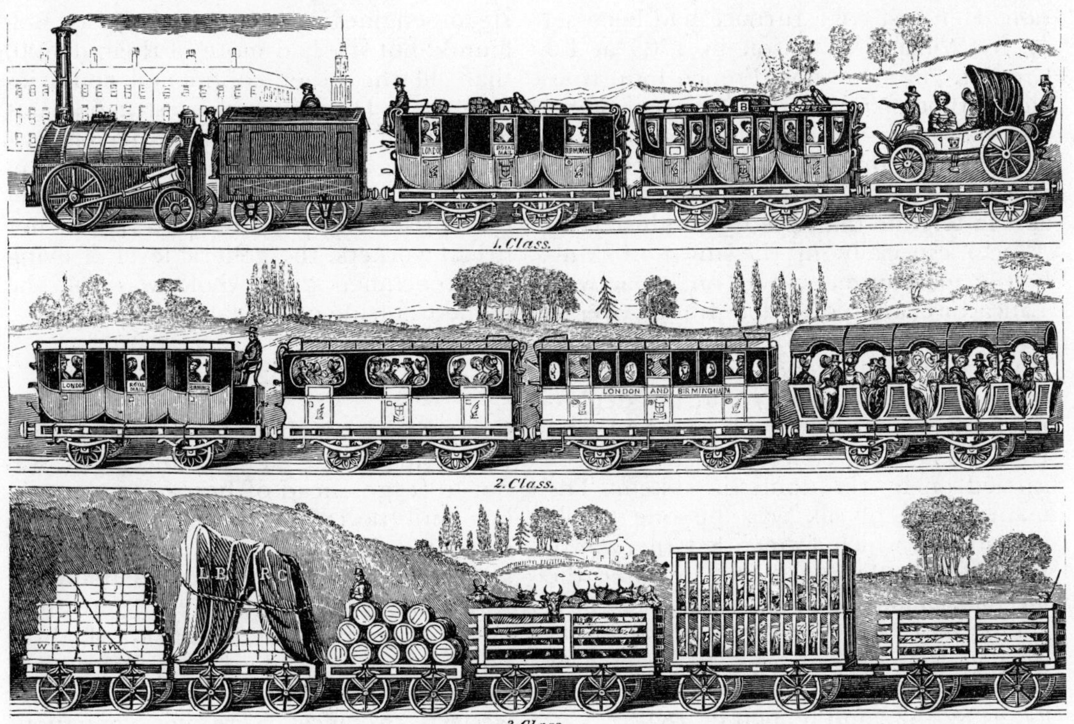


*The London and Birmingham Railway carriages: first, second, and third class*

competition. Belgium became increasingly a land of coal and iron, much of which she exported to France and Germany.

### France

France industrialized at a much slower rate than Great Britain and Belgium. Her economy was handicapped by high transportation and fuel costs; in 1850 she imported two-fifths of her coal requirements. Furthermore, much of France's limited supply of coal was inconveniently located far from the iron ore and was unsuitable for coking. These facts delayed the development of heavy industry. French railway construction was held up until the early 1840s while the legislature debated what routes the principal lines should follow and how much financial support the state should give. The failure to attract sufficient capital also held back industrial growth. There were no joint-stock companies other than public utilities, and the private banks did not invest in manufactures on the same scale as those in Great Britain and Belgium. The government discouraged the spirit of enterprise among manufacturers by maintaining high tariffs that protected them from foreign competition. Finally, France's slow rates of population growth* and urbanization in the nineteenth century did not give French industry the same stimulus of a rapidly growing home market and an expanding supply of factory workers which other great manufacturing states enjoyed.

Despite these basic handicaps, France began her slow process of industrializa-

*In France the 1820s was the last decade to show a large excess of births over deaths. The slowly declining birth rate thereafter was partly the result of manpower losses, estimated at three-quarters of a million, during the Napoleonic wars and partly the result of conscious efforts at birth control by peasant landowners who did not want to divide their petty holdings among two or more children. In 1846–1851 a severe depression, complicated by a cholera epidemic in 1849, inaugurated almost a century of virtual stagnation, during which the birth rate barely kept ahead of the death rate.

tion. Her first coke furnace had been set up by William Wilkinson in 1785 at Le Creusot, but as in most French industries old methods continued to be used along with new ones—even in 1850 over half of France's pig iron was still smelted with charcoal. Cotton manufacture advanced at a faster rate than the iron industry. In Alsace, especially in the town of Mulhouse, mechanization was on a par with Lancashire, and power looms took over in both areas in the 1820s. But the other main centers of French cotton manufacture, notably Normandy and the department of the Nord, were less progressive. Until 1850 the woollen industry was still carried on by the domestic system. The manufacture of silk was the one textile industry in which France led the world. Joseph-Marie Jacquard had invented the mechanical loom for silk weaving in 1801, and France began raising her own silkworms after 1815. Lyons, the center of silk manufacturing, had 42,000 Jacquard looms by 1832 and 60,000 by 1847.

Industrial expansion before 1850 affected only certain parts of France: the Paris Basin, the northeast, the eastern provinces, and isolated communities like Lyons and Le Creusot. Even in these areas most enterprises employed fewer workers and used smaller steam engines than comparable enterprises in Great Britain and Belgium. They could not compete on the world market and they survived at home mainly because of protective tariffs. French industry was more diversified than any in the world, with its triving chemical, glass, ceramic, and paper manufactures. Yet these too adopted new techniques slowly and were usually carried on in small establishments. Not until the major railroad trunk lines were completed in the 1850s did France become a unified national market. Not until the business depression of the late 'fifties and the lower tariffs of the early 'sixties were the more efficient entrepreneurs compelled to lower their prices and the more backward elements of French industry seriously threatened with extinction.

Still, it would be wrong to underestimate the extent of the French advance. By 1850 France remained far and away the richest country on the continent. Her steam engines were not as big as Belgium's, but she had more of them (6,800) than all the other continental countries combined. Her railroad construction was well under way, and some of her big private banks were beginning to invest in other public utilities and manufacturing enterprises. Despite the poverty of her urban workers, the general level of living of Frenchmen as a whole was still the highest outside of England.

### Germany

Germany, a much poorer country than France in the late eighteenth century, was not to forge ahead of her western neighbor until the 1870s. The Napoleonic wars disrupted her economy, and the peace settlement of 1815 still left her politically fragmented, although there were now only thirty-nine states instead of three hundred. Prussia alone had almost half the territory and population, but her western provinces were not contiguous with the rest of the state, and internal as well as external tariff barriers continued to hamper trade all over Germany in 1815.

The Prussia that took the lead in fostering economic growth at home and in the rest of Germany after 1815 was no longer the Prussia of Frederick the Great. *That* Prussia had suffered a shattering defeat at Jena in 1807. We saw how this defeat stimulated a series of political and social reforms designed to revive and modernize the Prussian state. Some of the national drive toward revival and expansion rubbed off on Prussia's businessmen and made them more aggressive than those in other parts of Germany and in France after 1815. From then on the leaders of both the state and of industry worked hard to build up Prussia's wealth and to extend her power in Germany.

The most significant contribution of Prussia's leadership was in tariff reform. In 1818 the Prussian government eliminated all internal customs and tolls. This free trade area was extended to most of the south German states in 1834 through the *Zollverein* (Customs Union). Almost all the remaining German states in the north and west west to join the *Zollverein* by the 1850s.

The Crystal Palace

Next to the *Zollverein*, the most important stimulus to German economic growth was the railroad. By the end of the 1850s the unification of the German market was to be completed by a system of trunk lines connecting most major economic centers. Already in 1850 Germany had 3,840 miles of track in operation, while France had only 1,738 miles.

Industrial growth progressed more slowly in Germany than in Great Britain, Belgium, and France, but the foundations were laid by the middle of the nineteenth century. The output of her major coal fields—the Ruhr, the Saar, and Upper Silesia—rose from one million tons in the 1820s to six million tons in 1850. Improved machines, some of them driven by steam, were introduced in the 1830s and 1840s. Most of the steam engines drove either pumps in the mines or spinning machines and power looms in the textile factories of Prussia and Saxony. By 1850 almost one-third of the non-agricultural working population was employed in factories. Even so, the textile industry was still dispersed and technologically backward, and the Ruhr did not have its first coke-blast furnace until 1849.

By and large, German industry used cheap rural labor and concentrated on finishing rather than rough work. The forges and workshops of the Ruhr and the Rhineland worked imported British and Belgian iron into hardware, cutlery, and machines. Merchant-entrepreneurs bought cheap English yarn and put it out to rural weavers who worked for even less than the Irish in Lancashire. Meanwhile, German industry accumulated capital, trained a cadre of skilled workers, and exploited newly discovered coal deposits to meet the growing demand.

On the continent only Belgium, France, Germany, and to a lesser extent Switzerland had begun their process of industrialization before 1850; but the other continental countries were not all equally backward. Their progress toward a modern economy ranks as follows: (1) the Bohemian and Moravian provinces of the Austrian Empire and Piedmont in northern Italy, (2) Holland, Scandinavia, the rest of the Hapsburg domains west of Hungary, and the other states of northern Italy; (3) Eastern Europe, southern Italy, and the Iberian Peninsula. With some notable exceptions, especially Ireland, the areas closest to the homeland of the Industrial Revolution were the most advanced, and those furthest away were the most backward.

In 1851 Great Britain celebrated her industrial triumphs at the Crystal Palace Exposition in London. The building itself was a triumph of advanced construction with iron and glass. Inside, seventeen thousand exhibitors proudly displayed samples of their technological achievements to hundreds of thousands of visitors to this first World's Fair. The Crystal Palace Exposition showed that Great Britain was far ahead of everybody else. This little island, with less than two-thirds the population of France, produced two-thirds of the world's coal and more than half of its iron and cotton cloth. It was literally "the workshop of the world."

Yet Britain and especially the continent still had a long way to go on the path to industrialization. Outside of agriculture most of the British labor force worked in nonmechanized occupations. Domestic service alone accounted for over a million workers, and in London accounted for one out of three adults. The average British mill still employed less than two hundred people, the average continental mill less than fifty. By 1851 about half the people in England and Wales lived in towns or cities; in France and Germany the proportion was about a quarter. Industrialization and urbanization strengthened rather than weakened the crafts that catered to the daily needs of busy urban dwellers: baking, butchering, cobbling, saddlery, tailoring, and especially housing construction.* The domestic system of textile production declined in Britain, but it grew on the continent until the 1840s as the availability of cheap semifinished manufactures, often imported from Britain, provided new employment for rural labor.

By 1850 Northwestern Europe had experienced a rapid expansion of a new mode of production in a context of overall economic growth. The general prosperity helped to preserve many non-industrial crafts. Nevertheless, a real revolution was taking place, and it had important material and social effects.

## MATERIAL AND SOCIAL EFFECTS OF INDUSTRIALIZATION

Although the new mode of production did not yet affect the majority of people in the most advanced countries by 1850, it was already changing the lives of a growing minority. We shall have to distinguish the material and social effects of industrialization on the new proletariat from those of concurrent and in part independent developments like urbanization and population growth. What would the effects of the "population explosion" and overcrowded cities have been *without* an increase in machine manufactures that could be exchanged for food? We shall also see that the growth of the industrial proletariat was soon to be matched by a proliferation of service and professional people, white-collar workers, civil servants, and engineers. The middle class became larger and much more heterogeneous, and the nobility and the peasants did not disappear. Industrialization made European society more complex and added new class antagonisms to existing ones.

Morally the Industrial Revolution was neutral. Degraded working and living conditions went far back into history, and neither the possession of capital nor the extensive use of machines were needed to make men callous and brutal. Some men had been that way from time out of mind. On the other hand, the human agents who promoted industrialization had no more far-sighted visions for the betterment of humanity than the human agents who caused the increase in the population. Only the public authorities, learning by experience with the new conditions of industrialization and rapid urbanization, could take action to alleviate the squalor and insecurity that these conditions imposed on masses of helpless workers. Such action came slowly.

### Working Conditions

The factory system created a new type of industrial proletariat. There had been some landless workers with nothing to sell but their labor since the late Middle Ages, but these journeymen had worked on the fringes of the traditional craft guilds. There had also been a few large workshops, such as those that turned out armaments or refined sugar, in which traditional unmechanized labor operated under supervision. The Industrial Revolution not only greatly increased the size of the pro-

*There was also a host of water-carriers, chimney-sweeps, street-lamplighters, ragpickers, and other menial workers in the cities. Some skilled French craftsmen called *compagnons* revived the corporate spirit of the medieval guilds and made their *Tour de France* before settling down in one place.

letariat, it also concentrated it in larger work units. In the new mills and factories power-driven machines produced goods formerly fashioned by hand. And the term "hand" came to mean an interchangeable operative who simply tended the machines.

At first the handicraft workers hated the machines. Would they not do away with work, create unemployment, and reduce wages? The weavers and finishers of wool cloth reacted especially violently. In both England and France they sent petitions to the government, marched in protest demonstrations, and sometimes went so far as to smash the machines. The most notorious machine-wreckers were the "Luddites" (named after their legendary leader Ned Ludd), who spread terror in the English Midlands in 1811–1812. It took an army as large as the one Wellington was leading in Spain to put them down. As time went on, the workers saw that machines did not eliminate the need for labor, and the wrecking rampages finally ceased. But each technological innovation thereafter met with the same initial hostility.

It is difficult today to imagine the adjustment the factory required of its new workers. In pre-industrial shops and home workrooms craftsmen had worked just as hard, but at their own pace. Now the relentless click-clack of the machine set the pace. Boulton managed to discipline his workers to operate with such a degree of regularity that the slightest dissonance in the noise of the hammers and bellows indicated a stoppage or an accident. Furthermore, everybody now had to begin work on time. Today we expect everyone and everything to be on time, but in the early years of the Industrial Revolution the inexorable demands of the clock seemed inhuman. When the Duke of Bridgewater reproached his factory workers for being late in returning from the midday break, they excused themselves by saying that they had failed to hear the stroke of one; the Duke immediately had the clock altered so that henceforth it struck thirteen. The workers were taught not to be late or absent by having their wages docked severely for each offense. They also had to learn not to leave their posts without permission and not to gossip on the job. This new type of worker was supervised and disciplined by the foreman, a new offshoot of an older breed, the drill sergeant.

The worst evils of the early factory system were not the pace of the machines and the harsh discipline of the foremen. Most workers eventually got used to these demands. Nor were low wages, long hours, or the exploitation of women and children anything new. The worst evils were unsafe and unsanitary working conditions and a complete lack of any kind of security against unemployment, injury, illness, or old age.

Several variables must be taken into account in any discussion of wages. In the war years 1793 to 1815 the cost of living rose faster than wages in England. Thereafter, however, prices fell and wages continued to rise. The 1831 the cost of living was 11 per cent higher than in 1790, while urban wages were 43 per cent higher. On the other hand, the wages of agricultural workers fell in the overpopulated countryside, as did the income of the hand-loom weavers and other craftsmen who were fighting a losing battle against machine production. Moreover, women were paid half the wages of male adults in industry or mining, and children employed as factory "apprentices" were paid only a quarter of a man's wages. The pauper children of the parishes received only their food and lodging.

The mass employment of young children as "apprentices" in the early cotton mills was partly the result of technological change and partly of the fact that, as one contemporary said, it was "nearly impossible to convert persons past the age of puberty, whether drawn from rural or from handicraft occupations, into useful factory hands."

In 1796 a Manchester doctor named Percival made the following observations:

"1. It is clear that children and other persons employed in the big cotton mills are particularly exposed to contagious fevers and that . . . these diseases . . . spread rapidly . . . to their families . . . and to the whole neighborhood.

"2. The big factories generally have a pernicious influence on the health of those who work there, even when there is no epidemic, because of the narrowly confining life they impose, because of the debilitating effect of their overheated and unpure air, and because of the lack of physical exercise . . . .

"3. Night work and long working days . . . not only tend to . . . destroy the vital energy of the rising generation, but too often encourage the laziness, extravagance, and vice of the parents who, contrary to the rule of nature, live by the exploitation of their children."

Only gradually, and in the face of vigorous resistance, did the British government try to alleviate the appalling working conditions of the early factory system. Its regulatory laws of 1802 and 1816 had no effect because they were not enforced. The first effectively applied law was the Factory Act of 1833. It forbade the employment of children under nine years, restricted the labor of those between nine and thirteen to 48 hours a week or 9 in a single day, and those from thirteen to eighteen years to 69 hours a week or 12 in a day. Children under thirteen years were to have 2 hours of schooling a day. A system of paid inspectors was set up to enforce these and other provisions. In 1844 another law tried to reduce the numerous accidents that women and children suffered in the factories. It required the shielding of dangerous moving parts of the machines and said that women and children should not be allowed to clean them until the machines were stopped. Similar laws were soon adopted in France and Germany. Like many laws, these early factory acts tell us more about the conditions they were supposed to remedy than they do about their own effectiveness.

The worst thing that could happen to a member of the new industrial proletariat was to be unemployed. Those who were too sick, too maimed, or too old to work at all became charity cases, unless they were lucky enough to have a family that was willing to keep them. Those who were able-bodied but could not find employment were put into a workhouse. In England this was a worse fate after 1834 than it had been before, for, in an effort to cut down the charity rolls, the new Poor Law of that year set up even more sinister workhouses in the industrial north than the earlier ones in the rural south. Charity was only for the unemployable now. The Poor Law of 1834 made this clear by abolishing the supplementary relief that had previously been doled out to people with abnormally low wages.

### Living Conditions

The well being of labor during the first stage of the Industrial Revolution depended on several variables. First was the changing ratio of productivity to population growth. When the former kept ahead of the latter, the workers' level of living rose along with everyone else's. But in many instances the outcome of the race was unfavorable to labor. Such was the case of those workers whom the machine left behind or ignored: the hand-loom weavers, the sewing girls, and the journeymen tailors in the "sweat shops" of London and Paris. Such was the case of agricultural laborers in the overcrowded countryside. Such was also the case of unorganized casual labor in the mill towns, especially the Irish immigrants. On the other hand, the skilled male workers in the factories and mines definitely benefited from rising wages—which usually kept ahead of rising prices—when they worked.

This last qualification indicates a second variable, unemployment. Like periodic downswings in the business cycle, fluctuations in special kinds of demand put people out of work. This happened all over Western Europe in 1815 with the cessation of wartime production needs. It also happened at the end of each railroad construction boom.

A third variable was the especially heavy investment of capital in industry, transport, and trade in the transition to an industrial economy. The choice in wartime was guns or butter, in peacetime it was factories and railroads or butter. When the choice was made against butter, that is, consumers' goods in general, the workers' level of living usually went down.

The wage earners lost most in housing. Urban slums were nothing new. But the simultaneous growth of cities and indus-

*"Coketown," 1850*

try multiplied them at an astronomical rate, despite all the belated efforts of civic-minded municipalities to alleviate the squalor and overcrowding. In the newer mill and mining towns, houses were built back-to-back along narrow alleys, or around courtyards closed in on all four sides and entered by a tunnel. Most of these tenements had no running water and had to rely upon water carriers, selling by the pail. There were no fountains in picturesque town squares. In fact, there were no squares or other open spaces at all. Inside the houses, lack of ventilation intensified the stench of garbage and excrement. Here is a description of a working class tenement in Stockton:

"Shepherd's Buildings comprise two rows of houses with a street seven yards wide between them. Each row consists of two lines of houses back-to-back . . . There is one outside toilet for each row . . . Each house contains two rooms, a common room, and a bedroom above it; each room is three yards square. In a typical house there are nine people belonging to the same family, and the mother about to give birth to a tenth. There are 44 houses in the two rows and 22 cellars all the same size."

Those people who could not afford, or find, a room lived in the cellars and courtyards. In 1850, 15,000 people lived in cellars in Manchester; in Liverpool 39,000 people lived in 7,800 cellars and 86,000 in 2,400 courtyards. A few years later 3,000 of the 3,600 cellars in the working-class district of Lille, France "housed" over 15,000 people within their damp, leaky walls.

In contrast to these squalid living conditions the housing "developments" built by a few far-sighted factory owners seemed like paradise. They were usually near a country factory or mine, rather than in the mill towns and great cities. In England Edmund Ashworth built his cottages with two rooms upstairs and two downstairs, with an oven and a good kitchen grate, and a small garden in the back. In France the Dollfus and Koechlin factories built a model community outside of Mulhouse, with tree-lined streets. Here the workers were encouraged to save money and buy the houses. More commonly, the factory owners remained the landlords, thus reinforcing the state of dependency and inferiority which their workers seemed to accept without hesitation. The majority of workers in Britain and on the continent lived neither in model developments nor in cellars, but in the kind of slum described in Stockton, and their health and home life suffered for it.

Living conditions in the urban slums were not necessarily worse than in the rural slums from which most of their inhabitants came, but they had more harmful social effects. Again, we must distinguish between the effects of industrialization and the effects of urbanization and population growth. Life in a cellar in Manchester was undoubtedly preferable to death on the roadside in overpopulated Ireland. Still, the fact that father, mother, and children spent most of their waking hours in a factory broke down family life, and the lack of community and church life in the cheaply-built urban slums made matters worse. Children received practically no moral or religious instruction, and those who did not work played in the streets with no supervision. They also lacked the warm contacts with older relatives that country children had. There was no grandmother to tell them folk tales, and they usually did not see their father even on Sunday, for he was often drinking up the remainder of the wages he had received the night before. The mother, or sometimes an older sister, bore the whole burden of keeping the family together. Rural folklore created the old woman who lived in a shoe and had so many children she didn't know what to do. In Stockton or Glasgow her plight was a great deal more visible to well-meaning reformers.

Many urban people ate better food and lived longer than their country cousins, but they were often less healthy. Lack of sleep and exercise stunted their growth; foul air and indoor work gave them a sickly pallor and bad lungs. Worst of all, overcrowding and hopelessly inadequate sanitation facilities exposed them constantly to contagious diseases.

The cholera epidemic of 1831–1832 struck rural as well as urban areas, but it took a heavy toll in mining towns like Newcastle, where housing conditions and sanitation were particularly bad. It also struck the older cities with better municipal facilities, causing 1,400 deaths in Berlin, 6,700 in London, and 18,600 in Paris. The poor people of Paris accused the authorities of poisoning them in order to reduce their swelling numbers.

The number of people in Western Europe's cities was indeed swelling. Between 1801 and 1851 Manchester grew from 95,000 to 401,000 inhabitants; Birmingham from 71,000 to 232,000; Glasgow from 77,000 to 329,000; London from 980,000 to 2,363,000; Paris from 600,000 to 1,053,000.

In great metropolitan centers like London and Paris, the middle and upper classes lumped all poor people together into one "dangerous class." They made virtually no distinction among honest working people, paupers, and delinquents. But there were differences. The delinquents—mainly thieves and prostitutes—lived in an underworld of their own, with "traditions" dating back to the late Middle Ages. They had their own jargon, their own "hangouts," and their own group loyalties. There were simply more of them now that the cities had grown so tremendously in population; there were 100,000 pickpockets in London in the 1830s, including children like those in Dickens' *Oliver Twist.* The honest working people usually worked in "sweat shops" or as casual laborers in hauling, loading, and construction, for there were few big textile mills and little heavy industry in London or Paris before 1850. These people were poorly paid and constantly threatened with unemployment and eviction from their tenements. Some workers became paupers, and some paupers became delinquents. But few delinquents became paupers or workers, both of whom the police and the relief officials could handle. The delinquents were dangerous because they flouted the laws of respectable society and protected each other from its enforcement agents. In time, however, many workers adopted the jargon of the underworld and its hostility to the police. Their forced segregation in the slums, their stunted growth and sickly appearance, and their dirty clothes and uncouth speech all made them seem like social outcasts too, and hence "dangerous."

### Class Conflicts

Industrialization, urbanization, and population growth seemed to divide the most advanced countries into two hostile "nations." On the one side were the "haves," from the rich noblemen and bankers to the small independent farmers and shopkeepers. On the other side were the "have nots," the "other nation" of landless workers completely dependent on their uncertain wages for survival. The concentration of this growing proletariat in cities and mill towns made it more visible to the "haves" and reinforced the workers' own sense of deprivation and injustice. But before examining some of their early efforts to improve their lot through mass action, let us take a closer look at Western European society in the first half of the nineteenth century. For as we have noted, technological, economic, and social changes were actually making this society more complex, not simpler.

Even the working class, "the other nation," was divided into several sub-nations. The economic, educational, and temperamental gulf between skilled and unskilled workers in industry made the former a kind of lower-class elite. Even the non-mechanized artisans in the urban "sweat shops" considered themselves superior to the unskilled factory workers and the people who worked on the docks, the railroads, and as casual laborers in construction. The village laborers became increasingly distinct in outlook from the town laborers. They were also less easy to organize, being either content to defer to their betters or cowed by the authorities. By the 1830s in England and somewhat later on the continent the rural hand-loom weavers were the most miserable. These tragic victims of the rise of the machine had little in common with the new industrial proletariat.

At the other end of the social scale, the nobles held their own fairly well in the face of economic and social changes. As in the eighteenth century, the English nobility was less exclusive than the French. But in both England and France many nobles had large incomes from urban as well as rural property. In England the higher offices in the state church remained a source of wealth for the nobility and gentry. In all countries these classes still held high public offices, especially in the army and diplomatic corps. We shall discuss their resistance to the social and political strivings of the wealthy members of the middle class in Chapter XI. Here we need only note that, before 1850, the highest social class retained much of its role as a ruling class—that is, an aristocracy—in many parts of Europe.

In the long run, however, industrialization benefited the middle class the most, making it wealthier, larger, and more heterogeneous. It provided vastly expanded opportunities for enrichment in industry, banking and commerce, as well as advancement in government service, the professions, and letters. There was a great difference in income, origin, and education between multimillionaire bankers and modest shopkeepers or government clerks. Yet people from these two extremes and everyone else in between all considered themselves middle class. As the famous sociologist W. I. Thomas once said: "When situations are defined as real, their consequences are real." The nineteenth-century middle class defined itself as being different from the working class, and its upper ranks defined themselves as potentially equal to the aristocracy. These definitions created a middle-class state of mind, which expressed itself in a particular style of life, modest for the lower ranks, lavish for those at the top, yet distinct from that of the nobility or the proletariat.

Although the middle class was larger, more varied, and more "open" at both ends than ever before, the bulk of the workers had no means of entering its ranks. There were no *legal* obstacles to such a move, but it did require a minimum amount of savings, clean hands, and suitable clothes. Thus, "the other nation" remained segregated, and its members tried to fight for their class interests by two means: mass demonstrations and trade unions.

The famous "Peterloo Massacre" in 1819 was the prototype of the modern

*The "dangerous class"—a London slum (by Gustave Doré)*

working-class demonstration and its repression. In August of that year 80,000 workers attended a mass meeting in St. Peter's Field in Manchester. Their purpose was to demand government reforms for the alleviation of their poverty, which was especially acute during the depression that followed the Battle of Waterloo in 1815. At first there was no violence, just speech making and verbal protests. Then the local authorities sent in mounted troops to arrest the leaders and disperse the crowd. The troops soon panicked and fired indiscriminately on the seething mass of demonstrators surrounding them. Within minutes St. Peter's Field was cleared, except for the four hundred killed and wounded demonstrators, one quarter of whom were women. With tragic irony, sensitive Englishmen called this "victory" of law and order over "the other nation" in St. Peter's Field "Peterloo," the shameful epilogue of the victory over the French at Waterloo.

Despite their ineffectiveness, mass demonstrations of the "Peterloo" type reappeared in later crises, especially on the continent. In 1831 the silk workers of Lyons actually took control of the city. They claimed that they were not making a political revolution and they did no damage to public or private property: "We are fighting for bread and work." Nevertheless the government in Paris feared the worst, having just come to power through a political revolution a year earlier itself.*

*See pp. 403–404.

It sent an army to Lyons to quell the revolt. Yet the thousand dead and wounded workers at Lyons failed to discourage later, more violent proletarian uprisings in France and Germany during the Revolutions of 1848.

The other means of defending working-class interests, trade unions, had hardly any more success than mass demonstrations before 1850. In England the first unions and "friendly societies" appeared at the end of the eighteenth century. Then, in 1800, the government passed a law forbidding their existence, not in the name of the authority of the state, but because they constituted a threat to private employers. In 1824 the right of workers to organize was restored, and between 1831 and 1834 a number of large national unions appeared in the various British trades. There was even an effort to unite them in the Grand National Consolidated Trade Union. Under the leadership of the industrialist-reformer Robert Owen, this organization wanted "not to obtain some paltry rise or prevent some paltry reduction in wages, but to establish for the productive classes a complete dominion over the fruits of their own industry." We shall discuss this form of utopian socialism further shortly. Here all we need to note is that the G.N.C.T.U. quickly collapsed under the weight of divided leadership, lack of cooperation of other unions, and pressure from employers. Not until the 1850s did an effective and realistic trade-union movement get under way among the skilled workers. The unskilled remained unorganized until almost the end of the century.

The trade-union movement did not even begin outside of Great Britain before 1850. In France the Le Chapelier Law of 1791 still kept the workers in a state of legal and actual inferiority and denied them any means of organizing for their own defense. Some French workers, beginning with the miners, had founded friendly societies, which gave them nominal assistance in cases of sickness and accidents, and to which they and their employers both contributed. But even these were closely supervised by the government in the 1830s and 1840s. Not until 1864 was the right to organize and to strike to be made legal in France, and not until 1881 in Germany.

Thus, in the first half of the nineteenth century the European proletariat was an underprivileged and virtually segregated class. Only a minority of skilled workers, mainly in England, managed to better their material lot. Most employers showed little interest in the welfare of their workers, and neither governments nor unions could make them do so.

The concentration of a growing number of workers in urban centers heightened the concern of sensitive writers and reformers with the social and material effects of industrialization. While they began proposing collectivist solutions of various kinds the champions of laissez faire argued that nothing should (or could) be done. Thus began a great ideological debate that persisted almost to our own time.

## IDEOLOGICAL RESPONSES TO THE INDUSTRIAL REVOLUTION

The way to recognize an ideology is to look for a word standing for a value, with an "ism" tacked onto some form of it. Thus: nation – nationalism; social justice – socialism; capital – capitalism; liberty – liberalism; authority – authoritarianism; equality – equalitarianism. This rule of thumb does not always work: Baptism is not an ideology; vegetarianism is. An ideology is a program of action for the purpose of achieving some basic value. The two basic values brought into open conflict by the Industrial Revolution were individual liberty and social justice. We shall now examine the programs of action proposed by the early champions of these conflicting values. In Chapter XI we shall discuss the other "isms" of the first half of the nineteenth century.

### Economic Liberalism

The father of economic liberalism, Adam Smith, wrote before the Industrial Revolution; his successors, Thomas Robert Malthus (1766 – 1834) and David Ricardo (1772 – 1823) adopted his ideas* to the

*See pp. 288 – 290.

new economic and social problems caused by industrialization and population growth. Like Smith, they viewed economic liberty, or free enterprise, as the greatest value, and, like him, they advocated laissez faire as the best way to achieve it. Malthus and Ricardo also justified this program of action, that is, government inaction, by an appeal to "natural laws."

### Malthus

In his *Essay on Population* (1798, revised in 1803) Malthus introduced his "natural law"—that living creatures multiply faster than the food supply. He pointed out that population had a tendency to increase in a geometrical progression (2:4:8:16:32), whereas agricultural production could increase at most in an arithmetical progression (2:4:6:8:10). And the ways in which the rate of population growth might be checked were either ineffective or bad. The desire to maintain or improve their status by having fewer mouths to feed prompted some men to use "moral restraint" in sexual relations with their wives, but Malthus had no faith in its effect on population statistics. As an Anglican clergyman Malthus also considered contraception immoral. To avoid impregnating their wives, men sometimes frequented prostitutes; this was bad because it encouraged vice. The "positive checks" on population enumerated by Malthus were also bad because they shortened the duration of human life: unwholesome occupations, severe labor and exposure to the seasons, extreme poverty, bad nursing of children—and, of course, war, pestilence, and famine. By saying that nothing more "positive" than these abominations could check the population explosion Malthus was in effect formulating a law of increasing misery.

### Ricardo

Along with Malthus, Ricardo helped to give the study of economics, or "political economy" as it was called in their day, its reputation as the "dismal science." Malthus had implicitly said that the state should not try to help the working classes—except to promote schemes of education that would encourage "moral restraint" in marriage—and that they should not be allowed to organize in their own defense. Ricardo said this explicitly in his *Principles of Political Economy and Taxation* (1817) and justified it with his "iron law of wages." According to this law, when the market price of labor is high enough to give the workers a decent level of living, they have more children, thus increasing the labor supply and bringing an inevitable fall in wages. Even when the market price of labor rises, owing to a temporary shortage of labor or an increase in capital investment, the cost of living rises faster. Like the law of supply and demand, the "iron law of wages" is a "natural law," according to Ricardo.

The great liberal economists were not as rigid or as uncompromising as this brief summary of their theories indicates. Nevertheless, in the first half of the nineteenth century there was widespread objection to all government interference and all government expenditure. This objection was founded not only on laissez-faire theory, but also on the belief that government interference was likely to be selfish and incompetent and governeent expenditure likely to be corrupt. Such had certainly been the experience of the eighteenth century, and the belief that it would always be so died hard.

Ricardo and thc later economists of the Manchester School, notably Richard Cobden and John Bright, argued that, despite inevitable hardship among the less able members of society, private individuals were better qualified than the state to run the economy. Ricardo especially opposed the Poor Laws, which he said only encouraged the poor to marry young and to have more children. Society had enough "parasites" to cope with already. The only way for the workers to escape misery was to practice thrift and birth control. "Self help" was the social message of economic liberalism. The economists of the Manchester School vigorously opposed the Factory Acts of 1833 and 1844 as infringements on the rights of free enterprise. They also advocated the abolition of all restrictions on foreign trade.

Although they abandoned Adam Smith's idea of an "invisible hand," the Manchester liberals remained basically optimistic about the benefits of free enterprise to the community as a whole. They rightly saw that the individual entrepreneurs were the main creators of new wealth. The saw, again rightly for their own time, that money spent on higher wages or social welfare would have to be diverted from new capital investments that, in the long run, would increase production *and* raise living standards. These spokesmen for the new capitalist elite were no more indifferent to the plight of the masses than earlier aristocratic or ecclesiastical elites had been. "The poor are always with us" was an old old saying. The economic liberals simply refused to let their concern for the poor stand in the way of what they considered true economic progress.

### Collectivism: Robert Owen and the French Utopian Socialists

Socialism as a movement appeared first in Great Britain and France as a protest against the poor living and working conditions of the early nineteenth century. As we have seen, urbanization and population growth were as much to blame as industrialization for these conditions. But the socialists concentrated their attacks on the industrial capitalists themselves. They were viewed as the real culprits because they concerned themselves exclusively with the *production* of goods. To the socialists the main concern of society should have been the just *distribution* of these goods.

The opponents of economic liberalism argued that only some form of collective action could benefit the community as a whole. They decried the evils produced by unrestrained competition among individuals. Yet they refused to view society as divided into irreconcilable conflicting classes, as Karl Marx and his disciples were to do later;* they hoped to achieve their goal of social justice through *cooperation.* Whether it involved the working class alone or the whole society, cooperation would lead to a new harmony among all social groups.

Robert Owen (1771–1858), the founder of the idea of social harmony based on cooperation, was a Manchester manufacturer. This fact is significant because it shows that not all "industrialists" were morally neutral. Most were, but Owen was not alone in trying to better the lot of his own workers and of the working class as a whole. Around 1800 Owen moved to New Lanark, where his well-kept mills and community institutions soon became showplaces. He argued that social environment determined individual character, and he tried to persuade the British ruling classes to plan productive relief for the poor and to seek for a better social order. Failing to win their support, Owen devoted his energies to building model communities in which drastic changes could take place without outside interference. The most famous example, New Harmony, Indiana, collapsed in 1828. After that Owen returned to England and made a concerted appeal to the "laboring class." He convinced a small group of disciples that "working men sustained the whole superstructure of society" without fully sharing in its benefits. The Owenites then tried to organize cooperatives in production and in retail stores which would help the workers get a fuller share of the benefits of industrial society. Owen's cooperative movement survived on a small scale. But in the 1830s he failed to turn the Grand National Consolidated Trade Union into an effective working-class movement, as we have already seen.

In France, Claude Henri de Rouvroy, Count de Saint-Simon (1760–1825) was the earliest and the most influential of the so-called utopian socialists. His mercurial personality and the revolutionary times in which he lived made him change his ideas periodically. During the Terror this descendant of one of the most aristocratic families in France renounced his titles and became a paragon of republican virtue. He made and lost a fortune in real estate speculation and shared the libertine cynicism of the Directory era. During the Empire period he sent crackpot projects to Napoleon, challenged the scientific geniuses of the age to spiritual combat, and became ever poorer. In 1813 he went insane, but he recovered a year later. Under Louis XVIII, Saint-Simon became a propagandist for the supremacy of the

*See pp. 502–506.

*Robert Owen's model factory at New Lanark*

bourgeois industrialists and bankers, but these people soon dropped him, and in a fit of despair he tried to commit suicide in 1823. Then in the last two years of his life, he surrounded himself with a group of disciples who were to perpetuate, and partially transform, his message.

Despite its inconsistencies, Saint-Simon's message contained one overriding idea: technology and science in the service not of profit making but of all mankind. Saint-Simon was the first thinker to foresee industrialization as the key to a higher level of living for all classes. His ideology was "socialist" chiefly in the sense that it prescribed some collective social enterprises in the form of vast engineering projects run by technical experts. Whereas most socialists were mainly concerned with the equitable distribution of available goods, Saint-Simon said that boundless production would create surpluses. He argued that technological innovation would place a higher value on the skills of the workers by relieving them of routine drudgery. Private property would be maintained, but it would be governed by laws dictating the total utilization of resources rather than being subject only to the selfish will of its owners. The economy would still operate under the profit system, but it would be responsive to the demands of an expansive society dedicated to the public welfare.

Many of the material and administrative aspects of Saint-Simon's ideal industrial society are now being realized in Western Europe and North America, but his social and religious views remain as utopian as they were in his own time. Saint-Simon wanted society to be reorganized around three functional classes, based on the three "psychophysiological" types of mankind: motor, rational, emotive. In Saint-Simon's utopia men would engage in motor activity either as administrators or workers, in pure research as scientists, and as moralizers and inspirers, appealing to human emotions through preaching and the arts. Each "capacity" would labor in its respective branch, and there would be no misfits or class confiicts. Perfect harmony would prevail, the power of the state would disappear, and men would devote themselves to exploiting nature rather than to exercising dominion over one another. Since Saint-Simon felt that traditional Christianity was in contradiction with "the system of the sciences and modern industry," he wanted to replace it with a "New Christianity." The supreme religious duties of the "New Christianity" would be brotherly love and the fulfillment of all human capacities in society.

Saint-Simon's chief rival, Charles Fourier (1772–1837), offered a quite different solution to the problems of industrial society. It was frankly escapist. Whereas Saint-Simon's industrialized super-society was to encompass all of Europe, Fourier wanted mankind to be organized into agricultural "phalansteries" of 1,700 and 1,800 persons each. Like the other utopian socialists, Fourier condemned the civilization of his day as ruthless, cruel, and incapable of allowing men and women to express their natural capacities for love and meaningful labor. Only the "phalanstery" could provide the degrees of harmony and variety that would give its members true happiness through free love and work freely chosen in accordance with their natural capacities. No such "phalansteries" appeared in France; the best-known examples of Fourier's scheme were those of the Brook Farm "movement," in far-off Massachusetts in the 1840s. Fourier has much to say to our own age about the relationship between love and work and the ideal of total fulfillment. But withdrawal into small harmonious agrarian communities was not the answer to the problems of industrial society in Fourier's time or in ours.

Louis Blanc (1811–1882), another early French socialist, thought he had a more practical answer: state socialism. Although he too condemned the society and government of his time for their injustices toward the working class, he had no faith in Saint-Simonian elites or Fourierist "phalansteries." The workers themselves had to gain control of the government through a political revolution that would establish universal suffrage and transform the traditional state into a "social republic." This "social republic" would then reform the economic structure by acting as the "poor men's banker." It would distribute credit and create the capital equipment for production. It would also float a loan for the establishment of national workshops which would bring into being workers' production associations. The resultant elimination of private capitalists conformed more to the standard notion of state socialism than the schemes of Saint-Simon and Fourier. Still, Blanc's scheme was utopian in making the workers' production associations alone the basis of social harmony and efficient production.

. . .

The Industrial Revolution transformed European civilization more than all the political revolutions we have studied thus far. Coal, steam, and new kinds of machines gave man the means for increasing his productivity faster in three generations than he had in the preceding ten thousand years. The new industrial technology made it possible for economic growth to keep ahead of population growth for the first time in history. It also revolutionized the conditions of work in ways that seemed almost inhuman at first and, along with urbanization, it created new social and moral problems in the mushrooming industrial slums.

Even though the majority of Europeans were not yet directly affected by industrialization before 1850, a number of sensitive thinkers concerned themselves with the problems of those who were. The early champions of individual liberty and social justice held opposing views on how to solve economic and social problems. But most of them agreed on one thing: the traditional state was not the answer. According to the economic liberals, the main function of the state was to protect private property; the "natural laws" of economics would do the rest. According to the utopian socialists, the state was an outmoded "superstructure," a remnant of the Old Regime, with no legitimate function in the brave new world of the future.

Why did most thinkers concerned with the problems of the Industrial Revolution lack confidence in the state? We shall find the answer in the next chapter. There we shall see that after 1815 the state was controlled by people who were concerned with preserving the political status quo, not with solving new economic and social problems. Except for some rudimentary labor legislation in Great Britain, the states of Europe hardly acknowledged the existence of these problems before the Revolutions of 1848.

## SUGGESTED READINGS


Ashton, Thomas S., *The Industrial Revolution, 1760–1830.* New York: Oxford University Press, n.d.*

*The Cambridge Economic History of Europe*, Vol. VI, *The Industrial Revolutions and After.* Cambridge, Eng.: Cambridge University Press, 1965.
See especially Chapter I, "The Growth of National Incomes" (W. A. Cole and Phyllis Dean) and Chapter V, "Technological Change and Development in Western Europe, 1750–1914," by David S. Landes. An expanded version of this chapter is now available as a book, *Prometheus Unbound.* Cambridge, Eng.: Cambridge University Press, 1968.*

Cipolla, Carlo, *Economic History of World Population.* Baltimore: Penguin Books, 1962. Pelican.*
Includes a stimulating short treatment of industrialization.

Chambers, Jonathan D., *The Workshop of the World: British Economic History from 1820 to 1880.* London: (Oxford) Home University Library, 1961.
Excellent brief survey incorporating new interpretations.

Thompson, Edward P. *The Making of the English Working Class.* New York: Vintage, 1965.*
Excellent social history.

Kitson-Clark, George S. R., *The Making of Victorian England.* New York: Atheneum, 1966.*
A fine, balanced account that counteracts, in part, the "bleeding heart" version of early working-class life.

Young, George Malcom, *Victorian England: Portrait of an Age.* 2nd ed. New York: Oxford Univ. Press. 1953.*
An impressionistic survey—excellent for the reader already familiar with the basic facts.

Hobsbawm, Eric J., *Industry and Empire: the Making of Modern English Society.* Vol. II. *1750 to the Present Day.* New York: Pantheon, 1969.
A remarkable, up-do-date survey by a prominent social historian.

Briggs, Asa, *The Age of Improvement.* London: Longmans, Green and Co., 1959.
Excellent social and cultural history of nineteenth-century England.

Henderson, W. O., *The Industrial Revolution in Europe: Germany, France, Russia, 1800–1914.* Chicago: Quadrangle Books, 1961.
The best survey available, though not altogether satisfactory.

Plamenatz, John, ed., *Readings from Liberal Writers, English and French.* New York: Barnes and Noble, n.d.*
Valuable on the ideas of the Manchester liberals.

Manuel, Frank E., *The Prophets of Paris.* New York: Harper-Row, 1964. Torchbook.*
See especially on Saint-Simon and Fourier.

**CHAPTER XI**

# PAST VERSUS FUTURE: REACTION AND THE "ISMS," 1815–1848

In the first half of the nineteenth century Europe became a conglomeration of social and national groups, each trying to find itself and competing with the others in an age that was between the traditional civilization of yesterday and the industrial civilization of tomorrow. There were the contrasting rural societies of East and West and the capitalist societies that varied from city to city and from nation to nation; an upper class whose world was the salon in town and the castle in the country and a proletariat that lived and died in the new urban slums. The social group that came closest to finding itself and winning out over the others was the bourgeoisie. Yet its struggle for representative government and free enterprise was partially thwarted by political reaction from above and fear of proletarian uprisings from below. In such an atmosphere, people who wanted constitutional rights and the vote for all taxpayers were considered radicals, while those who sought national independence or the emancipation of labor were treated as subversives and outlaws.

Each competing group developed its own ideology—or "ism". Indeed, the whole nineteenth century and the first half of the twentieth have been called the "age of ideology." We shall see later how the ideologies of democracy, nationalism, socialism, fascism, and communism were ultimately to represent mass movements. But in the first half of the nineteenth century, like-minded people of all kinds were already identifying themselves with ideological labels. For the first time there were philosophical "isms" and "isms" in the arts. In politics the façade of reaction and restoration settled nothing; in fact, its champions also felt the need to resort to an ideology in order to defend it. The chief opponents of this reactionary ideology were liberalism and nationalism. Meanwhile, another kind of nineteenth-century "ism," radicalism, began to protest against all constraints, both of the old and of the emerging new orders.

Liberalism and nationalism threatened the status quo in individual countries, although they threatened the European state system itself less before 1848 than they were to do later. Both liberals and nationalists supported each other across state boundaries, partly because they were fighting a common foe (the reactionary monarchies), partly because the late eighteenth-century ideals of brotherhood and the Rights of Man retained much of their appeal, but mainly because neither liberalism nor nationalism was as yet exclusively identified with the state (as was to happen later in the nineteenth century and especially in the twentieth century). Even so, all the major powers except Great Britain did their utmost—including military intervention in other countries—to maintain existing political systems everywhere against liberal and nationalist revolts. For they viewed such revolts as threats to international peace as well as the domestic status quo.

A passionate search for something more, something better, gave the period 1815–1848 its distinctive style. Romanticism originated as a movement to make the arts, as well as thought, a new instrument for finding the truth in a revolutionary age. Poets, composers, and painters were particularly torn by a conflict in which their intelligence, deprived of sure answers rooted in an orderly cosmos, refused to cooperate with their emotions. While they tried to resolve this conflict through the arts, other sensitive Europeans sought new meaning for their lives through identification with other creative "forces:" "the People," "the Church," "History," "the Nation." Some joined secret societies; others merely assumed outlandish poses in their personal behavior. A few artists, and the rebellious bourgeois youths who tried to imitate them, set a precedent for "bohemian" behavior that has reappeared many times since the 1820s. Broadly speaking, then, the romantic style combined rebellion against existing constraints with a mighty effort to create a new and better world.

## RESTORATION AND REACTION, 1815–1830

In 1815 the old ruling classes were in the saddle everywhere. Those in Great Britain and East Central and Eastern Europe had never really been out of it; those that had been unseated by the French Revolution and Napoleon were restored in Spain, Italy, Germany, the Low Countries, and France itself. Only France, Sweden, and a few southern German states had any kind of written constitution, and their monarchs clung to their royal prerogatives as tenaciously as any others. States that were stronger than ever enforced rational legal codes and protected property rights. But their ruling classes refused to share the saddle of power and privilege with any other section of the population.

The dominant outlook of those in the saddle was one of reaction against the French and Industrial Revolutions. By appealing to tradition and order the ideology of reaction sought to quell the new forces these revolutions had unleashed. Its spokesmen looked to the past for solutions to present problems. They believed that only the monarchy, the aristocracy, and the church working together could keep the world they had tried to restore from going to pieces again. Some of them even hoped to revive the medieval guilds as the proper form of organization for an industrial society. All of them rejected the eighteenth-century ideas of natural law and the rights of man. In their view, these ideas had led directly to the Revolution of 1789 and all its catastrophic consequences.

### Domestic Conflicts

Edmund Burke had once said: "Kings will be tyrants from policy when subjects are rebels from principle." This was the conservative view. But according to the liberal view, subjects would be rebels from policy when governments were repressive from principle.

These two opposing views explain much of the domestic conflict in the countries of Europe after 1815. Well-meaning conservative rulers felt forced to resort to repressive measures that made their opponents call them reactionary. Well-meaning liberals felt forced to resort to secret conspiracies and armed uprisings that made the conservatives call them revolutionary and take repressive measures against them. In such an emotionally charged situation, it does not matter who "starts" a particular cycle of incidents. Each side is so inherently hostile to the other that it feels forced to go to extremes in order to achieve its goals. Then the professional extremists come in, on both sides. The reactionaries claim that *any* concessions involving change will destroy the status quo and lead to anarchy; the revolutionaries argue that *any* compromise with the status quo is a betrayal of the utopia—democratic, nationalist, or socialist—toward which all true believers must strive.

### France

The pattern of reaction varied in different parts of Europe between 1815 and 1830. In France, King Louis XVIII (1814–1824) was a good example of the well-meaning conservative pushed toward a policy of reaction by extremists of both the Right and the Left. Louis—old, fat, and tired of traveling—wanted to settle down on the throne of his ancestors and enjoy his declining years. In an effort to reconcile the nation to the restored monarchy, he had granted it a Charter in June 1814. This Charter safeguarded individual rights and gave the new regime a constitutional and parliamentary form, with a Chamber of Deputies elected by about 90,000 voters and a Chamber of Peers consisting of hereditary members. Louis was still a Bourbon, however, and he insisted on his own hereditary rights. Most Frenchmen did not bother about this inconsistency; they were glad to have peace and prosperity. But the minority of Right-wing extremists, called the Ultras, thought Louis was not royalist enough. They disapproved of the Charter and wanted to restore the Old Regime in all its aspects.

The reactionary ideology of the Ultras was best expressed in the writings of a poor but talented Savoyard nobleman, Joseph de Maistre (1753–1821). According to De Maistre, Louis XVIII had not been restored to the throne of his ancestors, he had simply taken over the throne of Bonaparte, which was tainted with the evils of the French Revolution; De Maistre wanted a "real" restoration to the "real" throne. He wished to restore the divine right of kings and to give back to the Church a degree of power and influence it had not enjoyed since the Middle Ages. De Maistre wanted to undo everything the Revolution had achieved—from the confiscation of ecclesiastical and aristocratic lands to the abolition of the guilds. Here was reaction in its purest form.

Meanwhile, a minority on the Left wanted the Chamber of Deputies, not the king's ministers, to rule; the Left-wing extremists preferred an outright republic. In February 1820 an obscure fanatic assassinated the Duke of Berri, presumed to be the last of the Bourbon line.* This act provoked a temporary anti-Leftist reaction and helped the Ultras persuade Louis to appoint a new minister, the Count of Villèle, who was sympathetic to their cause.

When Louis XVIII died in 1824 his hope of reconciling the nation to Bourbon rule was far from being achieved; his successor, Charles X, assured its ultimate failure. Charles was an uncompromising reactionary who tried to revive every form and practice of the Old Regime. First he had himself crowned and anointed in an elaborate ceremony at Reims. Then he gave the former *émigré* nobles a sizable indemnity for the estates they had lost during the Revolution. Dedicated to the prerevolutionary alliance between throne and altar he increased the power of the Church, especially in education, and made sacrilege a crime punishable by death. Villlèle, who remained his chief minister until 1828, enforced strict censorship of the press and imprisoned the open critics of the regime. All these policies merely increased the opposition. A more conciliatory policy might have preserved the regime, but Charles X made the fatal mistake of alienating almost everybody except the Ultras. Even the conservative Chamber of Deputies turned against him in 1830. When Charles tried to rule without it in July, the conflict between the king and the nation turned into a revolution.*

*Since Louis XVIII was childless, he would be succeeded by his brother, the Count of Artois (b. 1757), who would become Charles X (1824–1830). The Duke of Berri, Artois' son, was the only Bourbon young enough to produce a male heir. Actually, his wife did produce a son eight months after his death. This son, the Count of Chambord, lived until 1883 but never became king.

*See pp. 403–404.

### Great Britain

In Great Britain, as in France, the government increased the severity of its repressive policies in the face of threats to the existing order, but there were important differences between the two countries in the period 1815–1830. First of all, the powers of the British king were clearly limited by the country's unwritten constitution. George IV had ruled as regent since 1811, when his father, George III, had been declared legally insane; he was king from 1820 to 1830. Both his debauched personal behavior and his reactionary political views made him extremely unpopular. When he died in 1830, even the arch-conservative *Times* said: "There never was an individual less regretted by his fellow-creatures than this deceased King." The British monarchy became really popular only in time of Queen Victoria (1837–1901), but it had the great advantage of being taken for granted as an institution, whatever the character of any individual ruler. Moreover, it lacked power, and hence nobody, not even the Left-wing extremists, demanded its overthrow.

The Tory regime in Great Britain also differed from the government of France in its eventual willingness to move toward moderate reforms, although it was particularly repressive between 1815 and 1820. This was a time of economic and social unrest springing from the depression following the end of the Napoleonic Wars. The Left-wing extremists demanded parliamentary reform as the country's only salvation, and, whenever they resorted to violence, the government took extreme measures against them. In 1817 it passed the Coercion Acts, which, among other things, suspended *habeas corpus* for the first time in English history. Then in August 1819 it perpetrated the Peterloo Massacre. Further repressive actions lost the Tories much of their support, but in February 1820 the Cato Street Conspiracy helped them regain the allegiance of the middle-class moderates. This plot by twenty extremists to assassinate the entire cabinet with a bomb, occupy the Bank of England, and set up a revolutionary government was discovered, and the arrest of the conspirators marked the end of extremism, of both the Left and the Right, in Great Britain. Returning prosperity after 1820 also helped.

The relative calm of the 1820's allowed the Tory governments to follow a less repressive policy. Their leaders included reactionary Tories like the Duke of Wellington, the Victor of Waterloo, and liberal Tories like Robert Peel,* an Oxford-trained, independent-minded son of a self-made factory owner. These governments rescinded earlier measures preventing political agitation and labor organization. They even sponsored the removal of the long-standing discriminatory acts against non-Anglicans: in 1828 Parliament repealed the Test Act against Protestant Nonconformists; a year later it passed the Catholic Emancipation Bill.

These moderate reforms did not satisfy the English liberals or the Irish nationalists. Although the former were soon to gain some of their demands, the latter were to remain a chronic problem for all British governments well into the twentieth century. The Tory government had passed the Catholic Emancipation Act only in the face of threatened disorder and violence in Ireland, and it took away with one hand much of what it had given with the other. It disenfranchised the mass of small Irish freeholders, thus reducing the electorate in Ireland to only 26,000, as compared to 200,000 before 1829. The government also suppressed the nationalistic Catholic Association in Ireland, thus taking away political liberty while granting religious equality. Anglo-Irish relations were thereby poisoned for another half-century.

### Germany and Italy: Metternich's Role

The situation in Central Europe differed from that in Great Britain and France. Here no strong national state held undisputed sway. Austria itself remained the multinational empire it had been in the eighteenth century, with new acquisitions in northern Italy.† In addition, Hapsburg

*Peel gave Great Britain its first reliable machinery for keeping public order by creating the metropolitan police of London—called "Bobbies" after their founder.

†See map, p. 360.

princelings ruled in serveral central Italian states, and Austria had the preponderant influence in the German Confederation. Before the 1830s even Prussia did not seriously challenge this arrangement. And Metternich, its chief architect, dedicated his life to preserving it.

Metternich was not a reactionary extremist by temperament or design. He was a cosmopolitan, eighteenth-century aristocrat serving the interests of the most illustrious dynasty in Europe, the Austrian Hapsburgs. At the Congress of Vienna he had served these interests by doing his best to reconstruct Europe as it had been before 1789. On the international scene this meant the Concert of Europe; on the domestic scene it meant benevolent despotism. Metternich's desire to preserve this traditional system after 1815 made him a true conservative, and he might have remained one if everyone had simply taken the system for granted. But the nationalists and liberals who challenged the status quo in Germany and Italy forced him to adopt increasingly repressive measures against them. For their nationalism threatened the historic international balance of power and civic order within each state, while their liberalism threatened the principle of absolute monarchy.

Sir Thomas Lawrence's "Metternich"

The subversive organizations in the German states were mainly associations of university students, called *Burschenschaften.* They had originated as patriotic societies during the Wars of Liberation against Napoleon. After 1815 they tried to perpetuate the spirit of these wars and combine it with a strong religious feeling and an enthusiasm for German unity. The students at each university came from many German "provinces"; and they hoped to extend their own feeling of academic solidarity to one of solidarity in the nation as a whole. On October 18, 1817, three hundred *Burschenschaften* held a great "national" festival at Wartburg, the place where Luther had translated the Bible into German three hundred years earlier. In addition to singing patriotic songs and listening to speeches, they publicly burned a number of reactionary symbols: books condemning the patriotic spirit of the Wars of Liberation, a Hessian wig, a corporal's baton, a Prussian guardsman's corset. These youthful acts of bravdo seemed ominous enough to the authorities. Then, seven months later, an adult fanatic killed a police spy who had heckled a patriotic speaker at another public meeting.

Metternich decided to crush the "revolutionary" movement in the German universities. In July 1819 he called a meeting of eight German monarchs at Carlsbad. There he persuaded them to adopt a series of measures abolishing the *Burschenschaften,* outlawing all political activities by students, and imposing strict censorship over what professors said in the classroom or in print. These Carlsbad Decrees effectively stunted the spontaneous growth of liberalism and nationalism in Germany as a whole. In the 1820s the university movement went underground and reorganized itself into secret clubs.

The 1820s were the golden age of revolutionary secret societies throughout Europe. There were the Philomathians of Poland (modeled on the *Burschenschaften),* the Russian Union of Salvation, the Spanish liberal organizations, and a host of others. Italy had more than any other country, and the most famous one there,

*Student's Wartburg Festival (1817)*

the Carbonari (Charcoal-burners), had affiliates in Spain and France as well. The Carbonari attracted army officers, small proprietors, and a few outright adventurers. They derived some of their ritual, initiation ceremonies, secret signs, and passwords from the Freemasons, but they were far more radical than the Freemansons in their desire to overthrow "tyranny" and foreign rule. The Carbonari favored heroic insurrections as the answer to all existing evils. Since they risked their lives if they failed, they felt compelled to work under conditions of secrecy and mystery. Stendahl's novel *The Charterhouse of Parma* and Puccini's opera *Tosca* both deal with men of this kind.

The Carbonari were the classic example of the extremists who forced Metternich to adopt increasingly repressive measures everywhere. They made him suspect practically every native Italian except the pope of being a potential subversive; for Napoleon's conquest and reorganization of the peninsula had shown the Italians the advantages of enlightened laws and administration and had awakened their desire to free themselves from foreign rule. After 1815 the restoration of the Old Regime under Austrian domination made revolution against existing governments seem the only way to achieve these goals.

Metternich's suspicions of Italians were confirmed in 1820–1821 when, first in Naples, then in Piedmont, revolutions broke out against the local reactionary monarchs. The revolutionaries, led by the Carbonari, had forced each to grant the kind of constitution that Napoleon had given to Spain in 1812. The situation had gone too far for measures like the Carlsbad Decrees; only direct military intervention could reverse it. Metternich therefore sent the Austrian army into Naples and Piedmont and crushed the revolts.

Ironically, Metternich had less influence in Austria itself than in the rest of Central Europe. In the years immediately after 1815 he had presented plans for the reorganization of the Hapsburg Monarchy along somewhat decentralized lines. He wanted to maintain a balance of forces within that multinational state comparable to the balance of power he tried to preserve in the relations among states. But the timorous and narrow-minded Emperor Francis I (1806–1835) refused to accept any change. Francis' "system" consisted merely of police control and the suppression of all forms of political expression in the provinces and in the capital itself. His ideal was to make the Viennese carefree, frivolous, and immune to any kind of civic-mindedness with the waltz, the opera, and the secret police. Metternich had hoped to maintain order at home in other ways. Yet he gave in to the emperor in order to keep his office as foreign minister, which he held until 1848.

### *Prussia*

The other major power in Central Europe, Prussia, was not as reactionary as Austria, but the fact that she became as conservative as she did was a great disappointment to all German liberals. As we saw in Chapter IX, they had begun to look to her for leadership after 1807, when reforming ministers like Stein and Hardenberg abolished serfdom, emancipated the Jews, reformed the disciplinary code of the army and opened its officer corps to talented commoners, and broadened the powers of local government. King Frederick William III (1797–1840) had even promised to give his subjects a constitution in 1815. He broke his promise, however, and he frustrated other attempts to rebuild Prussia's greatness on liberal foundations by resuming authoritarian rule and enforcing Metternich's Carlsbad Decrees.

Thus the country that had seemed to be in the vanguard of German liberalism reverted to a settled conservative order. The old reforming spirit was gone. Nevertheless, the ruling classes had a greater sense of duty and responsibility than any other in Europe except in England. This was especially true of the newer bureaucrats, who fostered efficient administration, education, and tariff reforms.*

The man who came closest to expressing the new Prussian conservatism was Georg Wilhelm Friedrich Hegel (1770–1831), a distinguished professor of philosophy at the University of Berlin. His grandiose philosophical system† influenced many aspects of German and European thought until the late nineteenth century. Here we can only touch on one aspect of it: the reinforcement of the idea of a strong, conservative state.

Unlike the traditionalist De Maistre, Hegel saw the state as the highest synthesis to date of the dialectic between opposing forces in history. He then used Prussia as the outstanding example of a state, although the principle that the individual could find true freedom only within the state applied to others besides Prussia. For Hegel true freedom meant complete identification with the world spirit, or absolute reason, whose final embodiment was the state. These were novel conceptions of freedom, reason, and the state, and in philosophical terms they were too abstruse to have much influence on public life. But Hegel made his point more simply in his *Philosophy of Right* (1821), where he said that since the French Revolution the peoples of Europe had become deaf to the voice of freedom and had swung from mob tyranny to princely despotism. Hegel gave the servants of the Prussian state an ideology based on reason and history, but Hegelianism could be turned against the existing order by people like Karl Marx, who were later to argue that it did not embody the forces of history and reason in their final form.

### Russia

Russia followed the pattern of Austria rather than of Prussia. Alexander I (1801–1825) became increasingly reactionary in the last decade of his rule. Gone were all his plans for a constitution and political reforms, at least for Russia. He did allow some degree of self-government to the two most sharply defined national groups under his rule, the Finns and the Poles. Like the Irish, however, the Polish patriots were not to be satisfied with anything less than complete national independence.

*See p. 378 on the *Zollverein*.

†See p. 415.

Meanwhile, in Russia itself, a handful of frustrated liberals worked for their goals through secret societies. The name of the most important of these, the Union of Salvation, expressed the utopian outlook of the liberal noblemen who dominated it. Their situation was truly pathetic. Not only did they have no way of influencing government policy, but the tsar's government knew everything they did through the police spies it "planted" in their midst.

Alexander's death, in December 1825, sparked the only attempt at a liberal revolution in Russia in the whole nineteenth century. The secret societies chose this time because of the confusion over which of the deceased tsar's brothers should succeed him on the throne. The elder brother, Constantine, had renounced his right to it in 1822, but the younger brother, Nicholas, did not know this. Hence, an absurd situation arose in which Nicholas proclaimed Constantine tsar in St. Petersburg, while Constantine, who was in Warsaw, proclaimed Nicholas. It took almost three weeks to get matters straight. (It was winter, and Warsaw is over seven hundred miles from St. Petersburg.) The conspirators had the idea that Constantine was the more liberal, and when Nicholas finally ascended the throne, the secret societies and a section of the army staged a revolt in St. Petersburg, with the battle cry, "Constantine and a Constitution." It is said that the more ignorant soldiers thought that "Constitution" was Constantine's wife. Whether this is true or not, it shows how little there was in common between the liberal nobles and the rest of the population. In any case, the revolt lacked adequate preparations and a clear plan, and Nicholas crushed it with great severity.

The memory of the Decembrist Revolt colored Nicholas' notion of benevolent despotism throughout his reign (1825–1855). Although the new tsar sincerely wanted to carry out needed reforms from above, unfortunately for him, and for Russia, this was an impossible task within the existing framework of the country's political and social system. Most of Russia's noblemen were unwilling and unable to be efficient administrators, and the new professional bureaucracy that Nicholas tried to create was handicapped by irresponsibility at the top and red-tape and corruption at the bottom. (Gogol's story *The Overcoat* dramatizes the futility and cynicism of Nicholas' bureaucrats.) Nicholas therefore relied increasingly on censorship, control of studies, and the secret police to repress all unofficial aspirations for change of any kind. He continued to consider himself a benevolent despot. But his despotism far outweighed his benevolence, and he was viewed everywhere as the most reactionary ruler in Europe.

### International Relations: Revolts of the 1820's

The Congress System provided a means of peaceful change through periodic consultations among the great powers. It sought to find a middle way to give Europe as a whole some degree of order and unity, a way between the Napoleonic method of conquest from above and the eighteenth-century method of shifting alliances based on purely selfish state interests. The idea behind the Congress System was that of a Concert of Europe—a group of independent "players" working together in a common endeavor. Unfortunately, the "conductor" of this concert, Metternich, rewrote the "score" for the almost exclusively conservative purpose of preventing change of any kind. In this way he drove one of the principal players, Great Britain, to quit.

In 1815 the four major powers that had defeated Napoleon were in complete agreement on one matter: their determination to prevent further French efforts to impose order and unity on Europe by military conquest. They renewed the Quadruple Alliance (November 20) for this purpose and, at the urging of Lord Castlereagh, they also agreed to hold periodic congresses to discuss common international problems and interests.

This was as far as the British were willing to go; the leaders of Russia and Austria had more grandiose ideas. Alexander I and, to a lesser extent, Metternich, viewed themselves as the delegates of divine Providence with the mission of protecting "Religion, Peace, and Justice." They persuaded Prussia to join them in signing the Holy Alliance (September 26), in which they pledged themselves to uphold this policy of reactionary paternalism.

As the members of the Holy Alliance sought to extend their mission beyond the borders of their own states, the difference in principle between them and the British began to cause serious friction and to undermine the effective functioning of the Congress System in international affairs. In September 1818 the first postwar congress met at Aix-la-Chapelle (Aachen). There the four powers brought their occupation of French territory to an end and allowed Bourbon France to join them in the newly formed Quintuple Alliance. Tsar Alexander I then presented a memorandum to the conference suggesting that the member states guarantee all legitimate regimes everywhere. Lord Castlereagh refused to commit Great Britain to such a pledge, and the question was dropped. It came up again in less than two years in connection with revolts in Spain and Italy. By then, Metternich as well as Alexander wanted to generalize the principle of intervention to preserve the status quo in other countries. Again the British said no, and Castlereagh refused to attend the congresses at Troppau and Laibach in late 1820 and early 1821. Meanwhile, Austrian armies crushed the revolts in Naples and Piedmont. The last congress attended by all the Big Five took place at Verona in October 1822. Here Great Britain was unable to prevent Austria, Russia, and Prussia from authorizing France to send troops into Spain, and the new British foreign minister, George Canning, gave notice that his country would not attend any more meetings of this kind.

The revolts of the 1820s took place in the most economically and culturally backward parts of Europe and the Atlantic world: Spain, Portugal, Latin America, Naples, Piedmont, the Ottoman Empire (Greek Revolt), and Russia (Decembrist Revolt). All except Piedmont had bigoted or incompetent monarchs, corupt and inefficient administrations, censorship and church control of what little education there was, and a degree of mass illiteracy and poverty unmatched in Northwestern Europe. Only a handful of people in each of these places had any understanding of abstract concepts like constitution or national self-determination. In Spain the revolt against the existing regime was sparked by the army, in Italy by the Carbonari, in Greece by merchants and writers, in Russia by liberal noblemen. But almost everywhere the masses were so deeply immersed in their own ignorance and squalor that they would not have believed in a better future even if the revolutionary leaders had been able to communicate such an idea to them.

With the important exceptions of Latin America and Greece, all the revolts of the 1820s were crushed by one or more of the great powers, and even these exceptions were made possible mainly by the action, or inaction, of these powers. No longer "in concert," the Big Five still managed to avoid wars among themselves. It was the weaker states, especially Spain and Turkey, that felt the direct effect of military operations and suffered the territorial losses.

### Spain

Spain experienced two revolutions in the early 1820s, one at home and one in her Latin American colonies. There was a direct relationship between the two, for it was the army, expanded by King Ferdinand VII to put down rebellion in Latin America, which led the revolt against him at home in January 1820. Demoralized by their low pay and poor working conditions the soldiers refused to be sent overseas to fight what they considered to be his battles there. Their refusal assured the independence of Spain's former colonies and encouraged liberal civilians to riot in the large cities of Spain itself. The insurgents forced the king to reinstate the Constitution of 1812, and they controlled Spain for almost three years. Then 100,000 French troops crossed the border and restored Ferdinand and his reactionary regime to power. The masses of the Spanish people viewed the liberals as heretics and subversives and had no understanding of their goals of a constitution and representative government. They cheered the restoration of king and Church, the only "institutions" they did understand.

The members of the Holy Alliance

would also have liked to restore Ferdinand's New World possessions to him, but in this case they were thwarted by Great Britain and the young republic of the United States. Although his country was not to become a power until the end of the century, James Monroe issued the first famous "Doctrine" to be associated with an American president's name, in his annual message to Congress in December 1823. The substance of the Monroe Doctrine was a warning to all European states that any threat on their part to the independence of any country in the Western Hemisphere would be treated as a danger to the peace and safety of the United States. This warning was aimed at Great Britain as well as the members of the Holy Alliance, but the British turned it to their own advantage. Not only did they alone have the naval power to protect the New World from invasion, they also had good reason to keep the South American republics independent. For British trade with them had increased tremendously since their liberation from Spain, and the British were beginning to invest large sums of money in them. In addition to securing her own economic interests in South America, Great Britain was able to convert her "hands off" policy there into a diplomatic victory over Russia and Austria, which compensated for her diplomatic defeat at Verona.

### *Turkey*

The revolt that involved the great powers most directly in 1820s was the Greek struggle for independence from the Ottoman Empire. The Turks had had to cede the northern shores of the black Sea to Russia in the preceding decades, but their vast empire still stretched from Algeria to the Persian Gulf and from the mouth of the Danube to the upper Nile. Western Europeans called this whole area the Near East. They considered it all—including the Balkan Peninsula, which was a part of Europe and predominantly Christian—as "beyond the pale of civilization." But in the early 1820s they suddenly remembered that, in Shelley's words, they were all Greeks in the sense that Greece had been the cradle of their civilization. This view aroused much public sympathy in the West for the modern Greeks when they rose up against their Turkish overlords and slaughtered every Turkish soldier and official in sight, and when the Turks fought back with equal savagery.

Despite this popular sympathy for the Greek Revolution, the governments of the major powers viewed the strife with mixed feelings. On the one hand, it was a revolt against legitimate authority and a threat to the territorial status quo; on the other hand, any intervention by one of them might upset the balance of power in the Near East and force the others to intervene. For these reasons, all the powers refrained from entering the conflict until 1825.

The Greek Revolution was the first successful nationalist revolution in European history.* It was inspired by a group of propagandists and scholars who successfully aroused the pride of their compatriots in their national heritage. Not only the Greek merchant class, but sailors, peasants, and even brigands from the mountains risked their lives to throw off the Turkish yoke. Their determination and their heroism—as well as their brutality—set an example for other nationalists aspiring to independence in Europe and the Near East for over a hundred years. Each time a national group tried to break away from the Ottoman Empire, the powers were faced with a diplomatic crisis and the temptation to intervene in order to protect their own interests or to prevent the intervention of others.

Beginning in 1826 the Greek Revolution became an international conflict that

*In Chapter IX we saw how, in 1804, the Serbs first rebelled against Turkish rule with Russian support, which was withdrawn in 1812. By 1815 Kara George had fled, and the Turks had ruthlessly supressed the remnants of the rebellion. Then another rebel leader, Miloch Obrenovitch, began to force concessions from the sultan through a combination of guerrilla warfare and diplomatic bargaining. The Greek revolution and the intervention of the powers obliged the sultan to make further concessions to the Serbs between 1826 and 1830. Miloch Obrenovitch was proclaimed hereditary prince of an autonomous and strictly Christian Serbia. The Turks took a fixed yearly tribute and occupied key fortresses in the principality. But the Serbian rebellion lacked the cultural and ideological basis for a truly nationalist revolution.

benefited the Russians more than anyone else. Russia temporarily detached herself from the Holy Alliance and joined Great Britain in trying to force the Turkish sultan to give self-rule to the Greeks. When he refused, Russia, Great Britain, and France formed an alliance in June 1827 aimed at achieving complete independence for Greece. The combined navies of these three countries defeated the Egyptian fleet that sailed into the Aegean Sea in the service of the Turks. After this victory, first the British and then the French withdrew their forces, but the Russians carried on open warfare against the Turks until the latter sued for peace in the summer of 1829. The fate of the Greeks was settled separately in London in February 1830, when Great Britain, France, and Russia formally guaranteed the independence of the new Greek nation. In September 1829, in the Treaty of Adrianople, the Russians had already forced the Turks to give up their control over the mouth of the Danube and to vacate the Danubian principalities (later to be called Rumania), which they then took over as a virtual protectorate. Henceforth Russia was to try to use every nationalist uprising in Turkey's Balkan provinces as an excuse for extending her own power in that area.

## THE TRIUMPHS AND FRUSTRATIONS OF LIBERALISM IN THE 1830S

Beginning in July 1830 a series of revolutions swept France, Belgium, Poland, and parts of Italy and Germany. Liberalism was the main force behind most of the revolutions on the continent and the parliamentary reform in Great Britain.* Its goals were constitutional rule, broadening the franchise, and civil rights, which was what *liberty* meant above all else. In the 1830s liberalism triumphed almost exactly in proportion to the degree of industrialization in each country. (As we saw in Chapter X, the most industrialized countries in descending order were Great Britain, Belgium, France, and parts of Germany.) Many other factors explain the triumphs and frustrations of liberalism later on, but this correlation with industrialization was paramount in the 1830s.

*The unsuccessful Polish revolt had primarily nationalist goals and will be described later.

### The Revolutions of 1830 and Their Aftermath

#### *France*

The July Revolution in France was a largely spontaneous uprising of the people of Paris against Charles X. As we have seen, this stubborn Bourbon had finally decided to abolish all vestiges of constitutional rule by issuing the July Ordinances, which dissolved the new Chamber before it met, altered the electoral system, deprived the wealthy bourgeoisie of the right to vote, and stripped the press of any semblance of liberty. Not only was Charles stubborn, he was also naïve; he expected no disorders and he did not try to reinforce the small garrison in the capital. During the "three glorious days" (July 27–29) that followed the announcement of the July Ordinances, students and workers threw up barricades in the narrow streets and drove the royal troops out of the city. Their leaders wanted to set up a republic with Lafayette, now 74, as its president. The "hero of two worlds" had revived the defunct National Guard and had ensconced himself in the City Hall, which the republican forces had captured, as the Jacobins had done in August 1792. But Lafayette felt that most Frenchmen did not really want a republic and he deferred to the candidate of the conservative liberals, the Duke of Orleans.

When the excitement died down, the Orleanists confiscated the revolution. These bankers and politically ambitious newspaper editors wanted a reformed monarchy, not a radical—that is, democratic—republic. The Duke of Orleans suited their needs perfectly. He was descended from a younger brother of Louis XIV, and hence could establish a new hereditary dynasty. At the same time he was a wealthy, thrifty man, a model of bourgeois virtues, willing to play the role of constitutional monarch. On July 30 his backers covered Paris with posters calling for the transfer of the crown to him. The next day he went to the City Hall amid glowering crowds of workers, students,

*Louis Philippe, King of the French*

and shopkeepers, who could see that their revolution was being taken away from them. At the City Hall Lafayette played his last balcony scene by embracing the Duke and telling the crowd: "Here is the best of republics!" Charles X fled to England, and ten days later the two chambers of Parliament proclaimed Orleans king as Louis Philippe, "King of the French by the Grace of God and the will of the Nation."

The constitution of the July Monarchy was more liberal than the Charter of 1814, but it was certainly not democratic. It widened the electorate from 90,000 to 200,000, abolished censorship, guaranteed civil rights, and eliminated the influence of the Ultra noblemen and the Church. Still, it was ambiguous about the key factor of representative government: the responsibility of the king's ministers to an elected Parliament. Under the July Monarchy French politicians began to gain valuable experience in parliamentary behavior, and there was even the beginning of a kind of two-party system: Right-Center and Left-Center. But these two factions represented a narrow segment of the population.

Indeed, the regime itself represented only those elites that rallied to Louis Philippe. The elite of wealth was solidly behind him, and, though many noblemen remained loyal to Charles X and retired from public life, others participated in the new king's government. The members of the French Academy and many university professors became thoroughly Orleanist too. On the other hand, many of France's leading intellectuals and creative artists were soon to find the regime stifling. The mass of the population, which was still rural, remained indifferent to politics. From the beginning, however, the regime faced an actively disloyal opposition from the supporters of Charles X (who now called themselves Legitimists), from the republicans, and from the surviving Bonapartists. By the 1840s the growing working class began to look to socialism for leadership.

The narrow social base of the July Monarchy made it difficult to find the *juste milieu*, or golden mean, its leaders were looking for. They wanted to hold a balance between liberty and order, between parliamentary and authoritarian rule, but the disorders incited by the opposition made the government limit freedom or organization and expression. At the same time, Louis Philippe's determination to govern and not merely reign weakened the power of Parliment. In fact, less than a year after the July Revolution the prime minister of the new regime told the Chamber of Deputies: "The trouble with this country is that there are too many people . . . who imagine that there has been a revolution in France." No wonder the people who had made it felt cheated!

### Belgium

The July Revolution in France had immediate repercussions beyond her borders. The most successful revolution occurred in Belgium, the country where the existing government was most out of touch with society as it had developed there by 1830.

The Belgian revolution expressed both liberal opposition to the rule of the Dutch king and nationalist desires for independence. Both the Walloon and Flemish Catholics in the Kingdom of the Netherlands had resented their forced union with the Dutch since it had been imposed on them in 1815. Now they began to think of themselves as an oppressed minority, like the Irish or the Poles. But they outnumbered the Dutch two to one, and their economic life was becoming more dynamic than that of their northern overlords. Thus, the old Catholic nobility joined the younger middle-class liberals in an insurrection in Brussels. Having cleared Belgium of Dutch troops, they proclaimed her independence in October 1830.

Strictly a native affair, the Belgian Revolution still owed part of its success to foreign intervention; for the Dutch did not give up easily and they reoccupied much of Belgium in 1831. The French disappointed the other revolutionaries in Europe, but they came to the aid of the Belgians, and the British also intervened by blockading the coast of Holland. Meanwhile, the British and French governments had called a conference of the powers in order to prevent Austria, Prussia, and Russia from trying to intervene against the Belgians. In January 1831 the five powers recognized Belgium's independence and her perpetual neutrality.

The new Belgian regime was the most liberal one on the continent of Europe. It chose as its king a particularly agreeable and attractive German princeling, Leopold of Saxe-Coburg-Gotha. Leopold adhered more faithfully to his oath to honor the constitution than Louis Philippe, and the Belgian constitution was more liberal than that of the July Monarchy. It recognized the sovereignty of the people more clearly, it guaranteed a larger range of civil rights, and it created a legislature of which both houses were elected though the proportion of eligible voters – 46,000 out of over 4 million – was almost as small as the 200,000 of 31 million in France. And in the true laissez-faire spirit, Belgium did even less than Great Britain and France for her industrial workers.

### The Era of Reform in Great Britain

After 1830 the British government adapted itself with the most success to rapidly changing conditions, and it did so within the traditional parliamentary system. Despite changes in the electoral law, the aristocracy still held the reins of power, but it was traditionally more open and more flexible than the ruling classes on the continent. By accepting, and even initiating, moderate reforms it satisfied some of the new purposes of the industrial and commercial classes. In addition, though it did little for the growing number of industrial workers, it managed to keep radical agitation from leading to open revolution.

The first noteworthy reform was a change in the system of representation in the House of Commons. On the eve of the Reform Bill of 1832, not more than a third of the members were freely chosen. The existing system of apportioning constituencies had reflected gross inequalities when it had been last revised over a hundred years earlier, and the subsequent growth and migration of population had exaggerated these inequalities. New industrial cities like Manchester had the same representation as depopulated rural boroughs. Some of these boroughs had less than fifty inhabitants, and the few residents who could vote were controlled by bribery and the influence of the local landlord; these were the "rotten boroughs." Then there were the "pocket boroughs," in which the patron had the absolute right of returning candidates, and the "close boroughs," in which self-perpetuating municipal boards controlled elections.

The Whig leaders who undertook to redistribute parliamentary seats and to extend the franchise were just as aristocratic as the Tories and just as hostile to the (then) radical doctrine of democracy. They too believed that the growing mass of the working class was unfit to take any responsible or intelligent part in politics. The Whigs differed from the Tories only in a more realistic readiness to forestall violent mass pressure by granting moderate reforms that would "afford sure ground of resistance to further innovation." Only in this way could the rest of the nation be reconciled with the governing aristocracy. Besides, the death of King George IV in June 1830 made new elections mandatory, the Whigs needed a good campaign issue, and public interest in parliamentary reform was stimulated by the July Revolution in Paris. For all these reasons they decided to launch the great Reform Bill.

From 1830 until 1832 the new Whig ministry of Earl Grey struggled to get "The Bill" enacted. Only when Grey forced King William IV (1830–1837) to threaten to create enough new peers to give the Whigs a majority in the House of Lords did the Lords bow to the wishes of the Commons and of public opinion. As in the case of the Catholic Emancipation Act, the conservative forces yielded rather than risk further violence and civil strife; for there had been serious riots in 1831, and a mob had held control of Bristol for two days.

Actually, the Reform Bill of 1832 was much less democratic than its title or the stormy events that preceded it suggest. The main change it made was to redistribute the strength of the constituencies. It eliminated the "rotten" and "pocket" boroughs and gave their seats to the new industrial, port, and mining towns. It also shifted the representation of the counties in a way that strengthened the smaller landowners against the big landlords. These changes did not destroy the preponderance of the great landowners; well over sixty members of the House of Commons were still directly dependent on them. But the industrial and commercial classes were given a large enough share of parliamentary power to enable them to assert their interests. Furthermore, the Reform Bill protected both the landed and industrial interests against the dangers of democracy by other provisions. It increased the old electorate of half a million, which was already larger than that in any European country, by 50 per cent in England and Wales, but it preserved the property qualifications in the boroughs, where a voter had to be the owner or tenant of a property worth at least £10 annual rent. This provision effectively kept almost all the working classes out of the electorate. The lack of provision for a secret ballot meant that the old electoral methods of bribery, influence, and intimidation remained as effective as ever.

Still, the Reform Bill enhanced the prestige and powers of the Commons in relation to the Lords and brought to the lower house men who broadly represented all the well-to-do classes in the country. It also made resistance to further changes – such as the labor legislation described in Chapter X and the abolition of slavery in the colonies in 1833 – more difficult when the mass of opinion demanded them.

The Municipal Reform Act of 1835 did as much to make local government more representative as the Reform Bill of 1832 had done for the national government. It replaced the self-electing oligarchical boards in the boroughs with new borough councils elected by all householders who paid the tax that supported the workhouses. This electorate was narrower than the national one, but it was wide enough to include most of the wealthier merchants and manufacturers in the large towns. As time went on, the borough councils were to expand municipal services in health, sanitation, and education.

Between 1834 and 1846 most British cabinets were led by two men dedicated to moderate reforms: Lord Melbourne was a conservative Liberal; Sir Robert Peel called himself a liberal Conservative. The terms Liberal and Conservative began to replace Whig and Tory in this period, but party alignments continued to shift, especially on the issue of free trade.* This characteristically British ability to change labels and attitudes to meet new needs helped to spare Great Britain the revolutionary upheavals on the continent, though it could not prevent radical agitation. The Reform Bill of 1832 had itself been a complicated compromise framed to meet a pressing need. Peel had opposed it without hope, and Melbourne had assisted it without enthusiasm. Yet whatever their views on specific issues were, the prime ministers of the era of reform helped Great Britain move toward a

*See pp. 419–420 on the repeal of the Corn Laws.

greater degree of representative government and individual freedom. In this sense they were all liberals.

### The Ideology of Liberalism: Mill and Tocqueville

The liberal ideology and the kind of people that expounded it varied from country to country according to what had already been achieved. Before 1848 both liberals and liberalism were still considered subversive in Central and Eastern Europe. Consequently, the "best people" there continued to shun it. The governments of Great Britain, France, and Belgium had at least formally accepted constitutional rule, representative assemblies, and civil rights. Many of the "best people" there wanted to call a halt at that point. These liberals of the 1820s became the conservatives of the 1830s and 1840s. British and French liberals of those decades wanted something more, something better. The two whom we shall now consider never reached the top of the ruling elite, but they were both internationally known authors and quite "respectable" in their own right.

John Stuart Mill (1806–1873) was one of the most remarkable Englishmen of the whole nineteenth century. Extremely precocious intellectually, he had begun to study Greek and mathematics at the age of three. As a young man he became an official at India House (the home office of the East India Company), a position that gave him a comfortable income and ample time for writing. His *System of Logic* (1843), *Principles of Political Economy* (1848), and *On Liberty* (1859) were epoch-making works in their respective fields. Here we shall concern ourselves only with the way Mill and others used his ideas as guides to action.

In his youth Mill had belonged to the movement known as Utilitarianism, founded by Jeremy Benthan (1748–1832) and propagated by Mill's own father, James Mill. The Utilitarians accepted the predominance of the educated middle classes as their starting point and called for reforms that would promote "the greatest happiness of the greatest number." They believed that this goal could best be achieved by the strict avoidance of government interference in private affairs; the function of the state was to promote gradual political reform and a long-range program of secular education. Though numerically a small group, the Utilitarians—who were also called Philosophical Radicals—had considerable influence in getting Parliament to repeal the combination Acts against labor organizations in 1824 and to grant religious minorities greater freedom in 1828–1829.

By the late 1840s Mill modified his views on laissez faire. The widespread misery of the new industrial proletariat made Mill and some other liberals propose government efforts to regulate the distribution, though not the production, of goods in order to spread them to a greater number. Mill also changed his views on other matters. At first he was against factory legislation, then for it; at first he was for extending the franchise, later he opposed it. Still, he was always fearful of the power of the state—so fearful, in fact, that he sought to check its influence in education.

Mill also remained true to the basic value of liberalism—liberty. He defined it in the first sentence of his *On Liberty:* "civil, or social liberty: the nature and limits of the power which can be legitimately exercised by society over the individual." Mill believed that free men should be allowed to arrange their lives as they saw fit. But, in order to be free, a man had to be educated and financially independent. The situation of the poor and the ignorant could be improved with public and private help. Until it was, however, the tyranny of the masses was to be feared as much as the tyranny of kings and churches.

Mill's closest counterpart on the continent was the French writer Alexis de Tocqueville (1805–1859). He too was well-educated and financially independent, though unlike Mill he was a titled aristocrat. For nine years he served as a member of the Left-Center faction in the Chamber of Deputies under Louis Philippe. Like Mill, who admired his writing and helped introduce them to an English speaking audience, Tocqueville stressed liberty as the highest value, but he was less optimistic than Mill about its eventual triumph in his own country. His two main works—*Democracy in America* (1835) and *The Old Regime and the French Revolution* (1856)—show how democracy as well as despotism could stifle liberty.

According to Tocqueville, the United States had managed to achieve democracy without abandoning liberty because certain of its features were unique. Its vast size and its natural wealth created prosperity, which in turn, inspired respect for private property among its citizens. In addition to its vastness, the absence of bellicose neighbors allowed the United States to enjoy a decentralized government. Other important institutional features included service on juries and local self-rule in town meetings, which made Americans "feel that they have duties which they are bound to discharge toward society and that they take part in its government." Above all, Tocqueville saw the spirit of the American people as the greatest guarantee of liberty—their respect for the law, their habit of voluntary association, their religious devotion, and their patriotism.

Since America was unique, Tocqueville looked more to post-1832 Great Britain as a model for France. There the traditional ruling classes had managed to create a liberal society without risking the dangers of majority rule, that is, political democracy. Unfortunately, France followed neither the American nor the English pattern. For, according to Tocqueville, neither the Old Regime nor the Revolution had provided the institutions and habits that would prevent democracy from degenerating into tyranny, as it had under Napoleon I and as it was soon to do again under Napoleon III.

Tocqueville's ideal liberal society was one based on social and political inequality—that is, aristocracy. By this Tocqueville did not mean hereditary nobility; his political and social elite would be open to all men of substance and talent. The rest of the people would have no direct voice in governing the state, but the state would guarantee their basic liberties as private individuaals and would exercise as little constraint over them as possible. For, like all liberals since Locke, Tocqueville believed that "each man, being presumed to have received from nature the necessary lights to guide his actions, brings with him into this world an equal and imprescriptible right to live independent of his equals in everything that concerns only himself and to determine his own destiny as he sees fit."

Tocqueville was more "aristocratic" than Mill in both his temperament and his ideas. Still, he expressed the essence of nineteenth-century liberalism, namely, that individuals should have complete freedom in their private affairs, including economic freedom, freedom of conscience, and all the usual civil liberties, that they should obey the law in their public affairs; that with proper conditioning through education and example the majority might someday acquire the sense of duty and responsibility which would entitle them to the political rights of the privileged few. Both Mill and Tocqueville opposed the democrats, who wanted *these* rights for everybody immediately. Not until the last decades of the nineteenth century was democracy to become an integral part of the liberal ideology.

## NATIONALISM

In the 1830s and 1840s nationalism and liberalism remained closely associated with each other in many places. Both ideologies opposed the political settlement of 1815; both proposed paths of action for the achievement of "self-rule"—of the individual for liberalism, of a whole nationality for nationalism. One reason so many nationalists tended to be liberals was that they and almost everyone else still associated nationalism and liberalism with the revolutionary "patriots" of the 1790s. They especially remembered how nationalistic the French revolutionaries had been, and they thought they saw a logical connection between nationalism and popular sovereignty. Another reason was that, after 1830, Great Britain, France, and Belgium served as models for the achievement of both individual and national "self-rule" together. Here the logical connection seemed to be between political progress and economic and cultural growth.

But there were already important exceptions to all these associations by the 1830s. In economically and culturally backward Ireland and Poland many nationalists were less concerned with representative government then with preserving native traditions and the Catholic religion (so much so that the Irish and the Poles remained the most intensely Catholic peoples in Europe well into the twentieth century). Yet more nationalists were liberals in these two countries than in Germany, which was economically and culturally more advanced. In Germany liberalism, inspired by the French Revolution, ran counter to the conservative nationalist ideology inspired by Fichte and Hegel. Finally, the great powers continued to have a crucial influence on the frustration or realization of nationalist goals, wherever they chose to interfere.

### The Awakening of Nationalities

There were two kinds of nationalism. The first kind was restricted to nationalities that had not yet achieved their political independence; the second kind was that of independent nations seeking to increase their power and prestige. Before 1848 only the French and the English were much affected by the latter kind. Most of the other peoples of Europe were just beginning to discover that they were distinct nationalities and that they ought to be independent nations. We shall concentrate on their kind of nationalism here.

The nineteenth-century French writer Philippe Buchez defined nationality as meaning "not only the nation, but also something by virtue of which a nation continues to exist even when it has lost its autonomy." What was this "something" more? Liberal nationalists emphasized community of purpose and free institutions; conservative nationalists emphasized power. But all nationalists agreed that a nationality was a group of people with common cultural traditions and a shared historical experience.

It is understandable, then, that the national awakening occurred earliest among the so-called historic peoples, that is, peoples who had known some degree of self-rule or independent cultural development in the recent past. In the main, these were the Poles, the Magyars, the Germans, the Italians, and the Irish.* Yet among these peoples only a small educated minority attached any special importance to the historical and cultural heritage that made them distinct nationalities.

Even this self-conscious minority of nationalists differed over the goals they wished to achieve: sovereignty, independence, unification. In Italy most nationalist writers wanted those Italian-speaking territories under Austrian rule to become independent and to be joined with the already independent Italian states in some kind of union. But these writers differed markedly on the question of sovereignty. Some wanted a federal monarchy in which the pope would be sovereign; others wanted a centralized republic in which the people would be sovereign. Independence from the foreign rule seemed clear enough in the case of the Irish and Poles. In Hungary, however, some Magyar nationalists wanted sovereignty but not independence from the Hapsburg Monarchy; others wanted both. The problem of unification was especially difficult in Germany. Should a united Germany include the German-speaking Austrians? Should it include the Poles in Prussia and the Czechs in Bohemia, who had always been a part of the Holy Roman Empire and who were in the German Confederation?

In Eastern Europe most nationalities were still at the "emerging" stage in the early nineteenth century. They had no history as far as anyone knew. And their upper classes still tended to speak German or French, to look to Vienna or Paris for their cultural models, and to have practically nothing in common with the peasant masses. Peasant culture remained folk culture, and most languages spoken by the peasants had no written form. Thus, before 1848, the nationalists in Eastern Europe devoted most of their

*Until the Act of Union of 1801 (see Chapter IX, p. 354) the Irish had had their own Parliament in Dublin. Moreover, the Catholic Emancipation Act of 1829 gave some religious liberty to the Catholic majority in Ireland, but it further limited Irish poltical liberty. Irish Catholics still had to support financially the Church of Ireland, which was Anglican, not Catholic.

efforts to reviving and organizing their historic cultures. Only in this way could they awaken a feeling of nationality in the small educated minority.

Like German nationalism, from which it borrowed heavily, nationalism in Eastern Europe was mainly cultural at first. Like Herder, the Grimm brothers, and Ernst Moritz Arndt, a handful of East European scholars collected folk tales and ballads. They also composed dictionaries and grammars, often for the first time. In 1830 the Croat philologist Ljudevit Gaj published his *Short Outline of Croat-Slovene Orthography*, a work that paved the way for the development of the modern unified Serbo-Croatian language. Creative writers wrote pioneer literary works in their mother tongues. In his *Book of the Polish Nation* (1832) the great Polish poet Adam Mickiewicz developed a new concept of his country's Messianic role among nations, the great martyr in the cause of human freedom. Historians also played a major role in stimulating the national consciousness of their compatriots by giving them a new pride in their common past. The most famous example was the *History of the Czech People* (1836–1838) by Francis Palácky.

The situation in Hungary showed how the awakening of nationalities was already creating animosities between different subject peoples in the Austrian Empire. Hungary had never fully become a nation in the Western sense. Although her institutions were very old and the Magyar nobles had periodically sought self-rule from the Austrian Hapsburgs, but these Magyar nobles had failed to assimilate their own Magyar peasant subjects or reconcile them to their own rule. In the 1830s and 1840s the simultaneous growth of cultural nationalism among Hungary's subject peoples and the Magyars themselves created new tensions between them. Only five million out of the eleven million people in Hungary spoke Magyar. Yet, in 1843–1844 the Magyars forced the Vienna government to make their language compulsory in official business and public instruction. (Formerly the official languages had been Latin and German.) The educated Croats, who were developing their own natural language, bitterly resisted the new law, which was itself a prelude to demands for Magyar political independence in 1848.

### The Frustrations of Nationalism

Nationalism made little headway before 1848. Except for Greece and Belgium, both of which gained their independence with foreign help, no nationalities achieved the coveted goals of independence, sovereignty, and unification. Their failure was due to three factors: the continuing resistance of the great powers, the ineffectiveness of the nationalist movements themselves, and the persistence of particularism, especially in the economically and culturally backward countries.

#### *Poland*

In their abortive revolution of 1830–1831, which had been inspired by the July Revolution in France, the Polish nationalists suffered the most from the resistance of the great powers to further changes in the status quo. A secret society led by university students succeeded in expelling the Russian garrison from Poland in November 1830. Then the rebels set up a provisional government consisting mainly of Polish noblemen. Whereas these noblemen wanted to bargain with the tsar for reforms, the more radical nationalists wanted to declare him deposed. The tsar took advantage of this split and sent a Russian army back into Poland in February 1831. Now the only hope was western intervention. Unfortunately for the rebels, both the British and the French governments refused to help them, and the tsar's army was able to crush the Polish Revolution by the autumn of 1831. The Russians then took severe repressive measures. They closed the University of Warsaw, they took away the few political rights granted in the Constitution of Congress Poland, they subjected the country to military government, and they greatly curtailed cultural and religious activities. Nearly 10,000 Poles fled to Western Europe, especially to France, where they continued to hope in vain that some government would allow the formation of a Polish legion. Private citizens in Paris and London set up societies called "Friends of Poland." But their governments resolutely

Polish revolutionary forces, 1831

refused to help the Polish independence movement in any way.

### Germany and Italy

Particularism was a major obstacle to the spread of nationalist feeling, especially in Germany and Italy. In these two areas, which Metternich wanted to remain mere "geographical expressions," most people still felt a primary loyalty to their local region and their local ruler. The idea of "Italy" meant nothing to a Sicilian peasant or a Piedmontese artisan. And most Bavarians and Württembergers preferred staying as they were to being swallowed up in a "Germany" dominated by Austria or Prussia. They viewed these countries as foreign, despite the fact that their people all spoke some form of German. Insofar as they did believe in a united Germany they wanted it to be imperial and federal, as it had been under the Holy Roman Empire in early modern times.

In our age of universal literacy, mass communication, and speedy tranpsortation we assume that any manifestations of regional particularism we see are just for the tourists—that the quaintly dressed "natives" concern themselves with affairs outside the village and have clothes like ours to put on later. Actually, industrialization, and its attendant urban mass culture, spread slowly and even left many regions of France and the British Isles untouched. Moreover, as one went eastward and southward in Europe, the number of people who could read decreased to insignificance. Although there were certainly nationalists in countries where factories, railroads, and newspapers were still novelties, the masses of "natives" in these countries were simply too ignorant to understand what these nationalists were talking about.

### Mazzini

Even in the more economically and culturally advanced countries, the nationalists were ill prepared and ill organized for the practical achievement of their goals. An outstanding example is the Young Italy Movement, founded in 1831 by Giuseppe Mazzini (1805–1872). This famous Genoan spent his entire adult life as a revolutionary journalist and agitator. After the collapse of the Carbonari revolts of the 1820s and the 1830–1831 risings in Modena and Parma he fled to France and launched his new movement in Marseilles. By 1833, Young Italy had attracted 60,000 supporters, with local branches in all the main Italian cities. Mazzini hoped to convince his disciples that national unification was a religious duty and that continual insurrections made people conscious of their power and of how to use it in executing God's purpose. Yet Young Italy's first major revolutionary attempt (1833) failed because of poor organization and lack of effective preparation.

Undaunted, Mazzini founded a still more ambitious society called Young Europe, with branches in Poland, Germany, and Switzerland. Mazzini was first of all an Italian patriot, but he wanted the youth of all nations to fight for liberty, equality, and the brotherhood of man. "Every people has its special mission, which will cooperate toward the general mission of Humanity. That mission is its nationality. Nationality is sacred." Like Young Italy, Young Europe was to work for national independence and unity in each country under a republic and for a kind of European federation of nations. This republicanism and internationalism soon alienated some members of Young Europe and also caused the authorities to disband the movement in 1836. Mazzini then went into exile in England, where he continued to preach his message of the sacredness of nationality, the virtues of republicanism, and the brotherhood of man.

Many other nationalist leaders in the 1830s and 1840s were utopian intellectuals like Mazzini, and most of their followers were also university students; still, not all European nationalists shared Mazzini's democratic, and therefore radical, goals. Magyar aristocrats in Budapest and exiled Polish aristocrats in Paris advocated a much more conservative brand of nationalism. In Germany many nationalist intellectuals emphasized the folk aspects of nationality, in the tradition of Herder, and the need for a powerful Prussia, in the tradition of Hegel, as the agent of unification. There was really no more *logical* connection between the *Volksgeist* and the *Zollverein* than between Mazzini's republicanism and internationalism. This lack of logic escaped the notice of most people, who did not understand what the intellectuals were driving at anyway. But, along with secret societies and impractical insurrections, it expressed perfectly the romantic style of the age.

Even though the nationalists were frustrated in their political goals before 1848, they had given the *idea* of nationality widespread currency. In the second half of the nineteenth century the leaders of the most economically and culturally advanced parts of Germany and Italy were to exploit this idea in unifying these two countries. It also played a major role in the cultural revival among the intellectuals in Eastern Europe, which was to lead to national independence for many peoples of that area. The idea of nationality had such great influence because it gained attention at a time when old beliefs and old institutions had been profoundly shaken by the French Revolution and the beginning of industrialization. Ever since, it has continued to offer something more, something better, to all peoples trying to find themselves in a period of rapid change.

## ROMANTICISM

Like the other ideologies of the early nineteenth century, romanticism expressed a longing for something new, something better, in a disoriented age. The romantics differed considerably in the kinds of change they wanted, but most of them shared a common temperament. They were primarily concerned with expressing new forms of feeling and thought. And they all expressed their desire for change in a new style in literature, painting, music, criticism, and philosophy.

### Romanticism as a Temperament

In each major period we have studied so far, what united creative artists and thinkers was the dominant problem they were trying to solve. In the Renaissance the problem had been to find new forms to express the new secularization of life, and the men of that period turned first to the forms of ancient Greece and Rome to replace those of the Middle Ages. In the Baroque Age the Protestant and Catholic Reformations had reasserted the importance of religion, so that the problem was to reconcile a secular outlook with still very strong religious feelings. Beginning in the late seventeenth century classicism attempted to resolve a new crisis of thought and feeling, by making reason impose rules of order and unity on all forms of creative art. Yet the imperfections and confusion that classicism was supposed to avoid became all too clear in real life by the late eighteenth century, and Rousseau's *The New Heloïse* and Goethe's *Werther* gave a preview of the romantics' rejection of the existing conditions of life at that time.* Then the French Revolution, the Napoleonic Wars, and the Industrial Revolution brought all traditional beliefs and institutions into question. The youth of the early nineteenth century felt that it had to build something new or perish. This urge was the essence of the romantic temperament.

This temperament is more than a mere combination of human traits: sentimentality, irrationalism, indolence, individualism, utopian aspirations, love of nature, hatred of injustice, or preoccupation with the exotic and the mysterious. These traits exist in every age. They happened to be especially suited to the revolutionary period that began in the late eighteenth century and that virtually destroyed the old framework of fundamental beliefs about the meaning of life. Faced with the collapse of this cosmos many creative artists felt impelled to discover the meaning of life in their own individual souls. Their search for truth through the arts turned out to be endless, since every new discovery was brought into question by a still subtler suspicion. Their outlook was one of a generation that no longer believed in the old absolute truths and could no longer believe in any truths without thinking of their relativity and their historical limitations.

The German dramatist Schiller once called the romantics "exiles pining for a homeland." During the Napoleonic period the poet François-René Chateaubriand (1768–1848), a literal as well as a figurative exile, exemplified this type in France. At the same time, many German writers sought their "homeland" in an idealized vision of the Middle Ages, which they peopled with valiant knights, gracious ladies, pious monks, and happy peasants. Ludwig Achim von Arnim's and Clemens Brentano's *Des Knaben Wunderhorn* (1805–1808), with its devotion to the lyrical spontaneity of the folk-song, is the prime example. The romantics remembered past time as if it were a previous existence and preferred it to the present, which they feared because they saw it as a period of struggle and flux.

*See pp. 298 and 310.

### *German Romanticism*

In Germany the rejection of eighteenth-century civilization took the form of subjective idealism, an intensely personal and ultimately frustrating search for the absolute. As we saw in Chapter VIII, the German cultural awakening began in the 1770s with the short-lived *Sturm und Drang* movement in literature and drama. By the 1790s Goethe and Schiller had accepted "classical" laws and forms, for which ancient Greece served as a model. They believed that the task of all artistic and philosophical effort was to lay bare these forms and laws and to make them effective in a higher perfection of the individual. Meanwhile, Kant had made both reason and external objects subject to universal laws. In the early nineteenth century German romantic poets, critics, and philosophers rejected this separation of spirit and reality in the world and proclaimed that understanding depended upon the inseparable emotional and rational sides of man, best exemplified in his aesthetic sense.

Any discussion of the German literary movement must begin with the towering figure of Goethe. His literary activity spanned half a century, from *Werther* in 1774 to the second part of his drama *Faust* in 1831. Though his last words were "more light," Goethe never shared the *philosophes'* concern with social conflicts and sufferings. The miracle of his genius lay in the interplay of his artistic imagination with the passionate search for the perfection of his personality. In *Faust* he tried to show that human self-perfection was achieved not through society or the state but through the individual.

*Faust* tells the story of man who gets everything that Werther wanted and

*Faust, Act One (a lithograph by Eugène Delacroix)*

much more. When the play opens, God and Mephistopheles wager that the latter cannot satisfy the eternal longing of man. The test case then becomes Faust, a distinguished middle-aged scholar. Mephistopheles appears before him and promises him youth, knowledge, and power. Faust wagers that none of these things will give him ultimate satisfaction and agrees to let Mephistopheles take his soul if they do. At first he uses his regained youth to seduce and ruin a young girl, Margaret, and her family. Margaret's death ends Part I. In Part II, Faust moves on to bigger things. With his devil-given knowledge and power he becomes the right-hand man of the medieval German Emperor. He saves the Empire's finances by coining counterfeit money and its political unity by defeating a military rebellion. He even proves able to raise Helen and Paris, the beautiful lovers of Greek legend, from the dead. Toward the end of Part II Faust becomes a ruler in his own right and creates a land of plenty for his subjects. He has done everything that a man could ever dream of doing, both good and bad.

But what of Faust's pact with the Devil? In the original bargain Faust had agreed to his ultimate damnation only if Mephistopheles could force him to cease striving for new triumphs and to "hail the moment flying: 'Ah, still delay—thou art so fair!'" When Faust finally utters these words, he dies, but he is saved rather than damned; for the "moment" he wanted to stay was a vision of a liberated mankind on a liberated earth. He had "beat the Devil" not by his accomplishments but by his striving toward the unattainable.

Goethe's message was "the triumph of the purely human." Faust symbolized modern European man, with his incessant striving and his endless longing for the moment that would stay. Goethe himself was a Faustian man—without Faust's monumental sins—striving poetically toward universal knowledge, beauty, and liberation. For Goethe the object of man's striving was the truth he could never fully know. "Man was not born to solve the problems of the universe but rather to seek to lay bare the heart of the problem and then confine himself within the limits of what is amenable to understanding."

Although Goethe himself was not a romantic, his personality and work became the greatest single inspiration for the German romantics, who admired the poetic genius as the highest personification of man's power. They concluded that individuality ought to be left free to follow its own inner law and mode of life. Only in this way could the poet gain the empathy with and the awareness of participation in the eternal becoming that was the life of the universe. The German romantics did not produce any literary genius comparable to Goethe or Schiller, but they represented a vast range of talent and achievement: Friedrich Schlegel (1772–1839) the critic, August William Schlegel (1767–1845) and Ludwig Tieck (1773–1853) the translators of Shakespeare, Heinrich von Kleist (1777–1811) the short-story writer, and Friedrich Hölderin (1770–1843) the poet.

In the early nineteenth century it was characteristic of the German intellectual movement to advance by alternating between aesthetic vision and philosophical contemplation. Kant had already demonstrated how the ideas of the mind determine our understanding of reality; Hegel carried Kant's philosophical idealism much further. He wrote of the "mind mourning over the loss of its world," then "rising above it," and finally "creating out of its [the mind's] own pure self, its [the world's] true nature. Hegel's dictum that "whatever is not rational is not real" meant that the only reality was the World Spirit and that the only way to approach knowledge of this reality was through reason. Hegel's "objective" idealism explained the world as the necessary development of the Absolute or divine spirit. Through a continuous dialectic of self-assertion, self-opposition, and restored unity, the Absolute unfolds in the world in order to realize its potentialities (we have already noted Hegel's view of the state as the final synthesis of this process on the political level). At the same time, man, through his rational consciousness, becomes aware of the ordered movement of the absolute spirit as the supreme law of the universe. He puts himself, so to speak, in tune with the dialectic.

In the 1820s and 1830s Hegel's absolute idealism gained the greatest following in Germany, but Friedrich Wilhelm Schelling (1775–1854) was closer to the romantic temperament with his *Naturphilosophie* (philosophy of nature). For Schelling nature, not spirit, was the true reality, and it was understandable through aesthetic intuition rather than reason. Schelling and his followers conceived of nature as an organism and sought a single unifying principle for all natural phenomena. In the end Schelling thought he found this principle in an irrational striving for radical change and freedom.

### English Romanticism

Many English romantics also turned to nature in their search for truth and beauty in a disoriented world. This was particularly true of the poets William Wordsworth (1770–1850) and Percy Bysshe Shelley (1792–1822) and the painters Joseph Turner (1775–1851) and John Constable (1776–1837). Wordsworth sought his inspiration in the Lake District of England and later set down the emotions he had felt there in such poens as his *Ode: Intimations of Immortality from Recollections of Early Childhood,* which begins:

*There was a time when meadow, grove,*
*and stream,*
*The earth, and every common sight,*
*To me did seem*
*Apparell'd in celestial light,*
*The glory and the freshness of a dream.*

Shelley expressed the desire of many English romantics for art itself to be more "natural" in his *To a Skylark:*

*Hail to thee, blithe spirit!*
*Bird thou never wert—*
*That from heaven or near it*
*Pourest thy full heart*
*In profuse strains of unpremeditated art.*

Turner and Constable, who pioneered in painting seascapes and landscapes directly from nature, also believed that they could see their true emotions reflected only in nature, and that the vision they put on canvas in a free and personal form was the only vision of truth.

Yet the English romantic poets were seeking more than mere personal fulfillment in nature. Samuel Taylor Coleridge (1772–1834) already seemed to sense the drabness of early industrial society for the urban proletariat.

*Work without hope draws nectar in a sieve,*
*And Hope without an object cannot live.*

Shelley too gave way to this kind of despair in his later poems, but not before rebelling against everything legitimate and conventional in the society of his day. George Gordon, Lord Byron (1788–1824), exhibited in his own life and in his poem *Don Juan* another side of the romantic temperament: the restless and aimless hero. Through Byron the romantic's feeling of isolation developed into a resentful cult of solitude, the loss of faith in the old ideals into anarchic individualism, the boredom with conventional civilization into a flirtation with life and death. (Byron himself died on his way to fight in the Greek Revolution.)

The Byronic hero captured the imagination of many sensitive Europeans in the 1820s and 1830s. Like the baroque Don Juan,* Byron's Don Juan is a proud aris-

*See p. 166.

tocrat, but he does not suffer his tragic fate at the hands of a cosmic force (God) beyond his control; his failure and tragedy are caused by man-made institutions and standards. Still, because he is an aristocrat, he is too proud to challenge the existing order of society. So he hurls himself and all who come in contact with him to destruction. The Byronic hero appears in two outstanding examples of Russian literature: Alexander Pushkin's *Eugene Onegin* (1826) and Michael Lermontov's *A Hero of Our Time* (1840). In French literature the poet in Alfred de Vigny's play *Chatterton* (1835) undergoes the agony of a spirit deserted and victimized by God and the world. But in real life the French poets of the 1830s affected a more plebeian kind of anti-conventionalism than Byron. They abandoned the aristocratic dandyism of the 1820s for bohemianism, which meant defying the existing order of society, and entailed living in garrets, not washing, letting one's hair grow long, and having no visible means of support.

### Romanticism as an Ideology

Like the other ideologies that first appeared in the early nineteenth century, romanticism tried to substitute new beliefs for those that the revolutionary age had destroyed. Its main beliefs were that truth could best be discovered through intuition and that aesthetic truth was the highest kind of truth. The English poet John Keats (1795–1821) had given poetry its new function and meaning in the last lines of his *Ode on a Grecian Urn:*

> *Beauty is truth, truth beauty,—that is all*
> *Ye know on earth, and all ye need to know.*

Like the other romantics, Keats believed in a transcendental, world-pervading spirit as the source of poetic inspiration and identified it with the spontaneous creative power of language.

The German literary critic Friedrich Schlegel spelled out the way the poet attained artistic truth and how the reader understood it. According to Schlegel, we cannot understand any work of art by subjecting it to logical rules like those of classicism. "It is the beginning of all poetry to abolish the law and method of the rationally proceeding reason and to plunge us once more into the ravishing confusion of fantasy, the original chaos of human nature." In other words, the source of poetry, and of all art, is in the mysteries of our unconscious life. In itself, this idea is not especially controversial or distinctly romantic. What *is* controversial and distinctly romantic is the idea that the highest truth is the truth of an aesthetic vision spontaneously brought to light from some world-pervading spirit that lurks in our unconscious.

It was but a short step from this version of the romantic ideology to the dogma of Art for Art's sake. The French writer Théophile Gautier (1811–1872) first pronounced this dogma in the preface to his novel *Mademoiselle de Maupin* (1835). His later poems mark a turning point in the history of romanticism—the point at which the poetic self rejected the excess of private and subjective outpourings and avenged itself on a hostile world by setting up an autonomous world of poetry. Since their world existed completely for its own sake, Gautier and his fellow bohemians felt no need to bring "bourgeois" standards of behavior into it. Even so, it had its own artistic laws, and in calling for absolute obedience to them Gautier reintroduced the classical virtue of form to romanticism.

The dogma of Art for Art's sake was the ultimate expression of the main source and theme of romanticism: the estrangement of the imagination and of the nobler passions of the mind from "reality." We have seen that the estrangement of the mind itself from the real world was the source and theme of the principal philosophy of the romantic period—Hegelianism—which, in turn, forecast the "absolute art" of the late romantic poets. Both were supreme attempts to bring the unique character of the individual into harmony with some form of rational "reality."

### The Romantic Style

One generalization that can be made about the romantic style is that it emphasizes the subjective and emotional possibilities of each artistic medium and neglects its formal and structural aspects. The romantic writer, painter, or composer tries to cut short the road of communication to his audience by eliminating what he believes to be unnecessary formal conventions. Not unlike an electrical short circuit, this technique gives romantic works of art a kind of "high tension." We have already noted examples of this directness of subjective communication in the sentimental novels of Rousseau and the early Goethe (to which should be added the historical novels of Sir Walter Scott, 1771–1832), the poems of Wordsworth and Shelley, and the paintings of Constable and Turner. It reached its climax in France around 1830 in the paintings of Eugène Delacroix (1798–1863), the verse plays and novels of Victor Hugo (1802–1885) and the music of Hector Berlioz (1803–1869).

### French Romanticism

Each of these Frenchmen consciously rebelled in his own way against the formal conventions of his particular art. Hugo expressed the meaning of their revolt in his preface to *Cromwell* (1827). He said that the new style should be based on nature, truth, and inspiration; that it should stress violent contrasts, local color, and the characteristic rather than the beautiful; and that, above all, it should be dramatic. Hugo then created a public sensation with the first performance of his play *Hernani* (1830). A riot broke out over the following exchange: "*Est-il minuit?*" ("Is it midnight?")—"*Minuit bientôt.*" ("Midnight soon.") This sounded too commonplace, too direct, too listless, to theatergoers accustomed to more allegorical and allusive verse in a tragedy. One critic (Stendhal) thought the answer should have been:

"*. . . l'heure*
*atteindra bientôt sa dernière demeure.*" ("the hour [that is, the day] will soon attain its final resting place.")

Hugo not only made verse more flexible and commonplace, he also destroyed the unities of time and place. By taking these liberties in public before the habit-ridden Parisian audience, Hugo was declaring a revolution in all the arts.

Delacroix, who was in the audience, soon grew to hate the label romantic, but he nonetheless incarnated romanticism in his paintings. In his *Death of Sardanapalus* (1828)* Delacroix avoids the heaviness of modeling and color, the formal symmetry, and the central focus of classical painting. Instead, he tries to achieve a sketchiness that evokes the violence and contrasts of the death of a debauched Assyrian king of ancient legend.

Although Berlioz (who was also present at the premiere of *Hernani*) supported Hugo on the unities, he failed to see why Hugo attacked the rigid, four-square line and the stopping of sense with rhyme. Yet Berlioz himself broke with the rigidity and squareness of classical music in his melody and rhythm. In fact, Berlioz was *the* creator of romantic music.

The dissonance, clashing rhythms, and complicated tonal qualities of his *Fantastic Symphony* created almost as much of a sensation in 1830 as the revolutionary innovations of *Hernani*. The *Fantastic Symphony* expressed the aesthetic principle of all Berlioz's subsequent compositions: the development in sounds of certain unnamable elements that life and music hold in common. In this work Berlioz organized each musical moment around a single subject, at once musical and dramatic. He called his unifying device an *idée fixe* and carried it through in each of the five movements of this work. Berlioz made this (then) strange music more acceptable to his audience by putting a "story" in the program. This, too was an important romantic innovation, though for Berlioz himself the music always came first.

The romantic style lasted the longest, and is most familiar today, in music. Beginning with the Frenchman Berlioz it quickly became international. Its all-pervading subjectivism took new forms in the symphonic poens of the Hungarian Franz Liszt (1811–1880), and the character pieces for piano of the Pole Frederick Chopin (1810–1849) and the German Robert Schumann (1810–1856). Its attempt to combine music and drama in an all-inclusive representation of life reached its most exhaustive (and exhausting) form

*See p. 487.

in the operas of the German Richard Wagner (1813–1883).*

In painting and the novel the romantic style began to change after 1830. Delacroix looked for surroundings more real, more probable than those of ancient legend for the tempetuous scenes he wanted to paint. He found them on a journey to Morocco in 1831. Thereafter he painted lion hunts in the desert, and battles with sheiks and slaves, and with women being raped—all in a way that made them appear to be happening in his own time. In *The Hunchback of Notre Dame* (1831) Hugo anticipated the new preoccupation with "the people" in the social novels of the 1840s and his own *Les Misérables* (1862). The style of the earlier novel is completely romantic, with its setting of a Gothic cathedral, its calculated melodrama, its macabre images, and its heroic climaxes. Yet its hero is a deformed bell-ringer and its heroine a gypsy dancer. All the reader's sympathy goes to Quasimodo and Esmeralda, as againt the corrupt archdeacon who symbolizes the injustice of misplaced power.

The romantics of the first half of the nineteenth century did not withdraw entirely into self-pity and a dream-world of nature or legend. Many of them fought for greater freedom in life as well as in art. Nor were their creative works as untamed as their ideological pronouncements would suggest; they broke the traditional rules in order to develop new artistic forms. Their emotions fought an endless battle with their intelligence in both their behavior and their works. But both were inspired by reason as well as fire.

## THE GATHERING TIDAL WAVE OF THE 1840s

In the 1840s all the forces described in this chapter and in Chapter X came into open conflict with each other. As newly awakening social and national groups made demands for recognition, the ruling elites became increasingly defensive. In Central Europe the liberals and nationalists were still striving for goals that had already been achieved in Great Britain and France. At the same time, the governments of these two countries had to cope with more radical and democratic demands. Between 1840 and 1846 uncontrolled economic growth led to overpopulation and to overproduction in industry. Meanwhile, crop failures in 1846 drastically reduced the purchasing power of rural people. A year later a financial crisis halted the new capital investments needed to restore economic prosperity. By the end of 1847 masses of miserable peasants and unemployed workers were demanding sweeping social reforms. Their demands were to come flooding through the breach that the political revolutions of 1848 opened in the old structure.

Democracy emerged as the most important ideology in Great Britain and France in the 1840s. In Great Britain the limited franchise, the lack of a secret ballot, and the preservation of boroughs that could be bought or influenced kept the government safe from radical pressure. In France the limited franchise and the system of buying off opposition deputies with lucrative government posts accomplished a similar purpose. Disenfranchised middle-class people began demanding universal suffrage and a drastic overhaul of the electoral system as the only means of removing abuses of this kind in both countries. It was clear to all that the wealthy minority was able to use its rights to vote and hold public office to promote and protect its own interests. Hence, even the working classes came to believe that democratic political reforms were the first and necessary step toward economic and social reforms.

### The 1840s in Great Britain

The Chartist movement in England launched the most radical challenge to the British constitution in the country's history. Against the liberal doctrine of the sovereignty of Parliament, it raised the democratic principle of the sovereignty of the people. The movement arose out of popular discontent with the Reform Bill of 1832, out of economic and social unrest in the industrial Midlands, and out of the failures of early experiments in trade unionism. All these forces fused together in 1838 in support of the "People's Charter,"

*See p. 500.

*Bread riot at the entrance to the House of Commons, 1815*

a six-point program calling for universal male suffrage, equal electoral districts, removal of the property qualification for members of Parliament, payment of members of Parliament, secret ballot, and annual general elections. The last of these demands was the most radical of all—a House of Commons subject to annual elections would have been an instrument of direct democracy, thus transforming the whole character of the parliamentary system.

Chartism quickly became a nationwide movement. In London it was supported by the respectable and self-educated artisans. In Birmingham and Leeds fiery orators like the Irishman Bronterre O'Brien aroused the enthusiasm of hungry factory workers by hawking the Charter as a panacea for all social ills. The climax came in the summer of 1839, when the movement presented Parliament with a petition signed by nearly a million and a quarter people urging the enactment of the Charter. When Parliament rejected the petition, the leaders of the movement split on what to do next. The moderates urged further campaigns of peaceful agitation and popular education; the extremists provoked riots, local strikes, and even mass insurrections. A second petition was presented and rejected in 1842, and yet another in 1848. The Chartist movement was the first effective and spontaneous working-class organization in England or any other country. It drew the attention of all classes to the urgency of social reforms, and, despite its failure, it gave an eventual impetus to further reforms. (All the demands of the Charter except annual elections were to be granted piecemeal in the late nineteenth century.)

Meanwhile, the major issue in Great Britain in the 1840s was no longer the Charter but Free Trade, and the main conflict was between the conservative agricultural interests and the liberal manufacturing and commercial interests. The prosperity of Britain's growing cotton industry depended directly on foreign trade, which was hindered by the Corn Laws, enacted in 1815 to protect homegrown grain and keep its price high. In Parliament the Tories argued as eloquently for the retention of the Corn Laws as the Whigs for their repeal. Outside of

Parliament the repeal of the Corn Laws and Free Trade in general aroused popular agitation on a scale comparable to the Charter. In 1843 the Anti-Corn Law League held twenty-four mass meetings in London, and its weekly newspaper reached a circulation of over 20,000. As its activities spread to the countryside, the farmers retaliated with organized violence.

The real crisis began in 1845, when a devastating disease ruined the potato crop in Ireland. Since potatoes rather than grain were the staple diet there, acute famine resulted.* The Anti-Corn Law League demanded the immediate repeal of all laws that kept out imported food when families were starving. Both political parties were confused over the free-trade issue, and Sir Robert Peel brought about the final split in the old Tory Party by abandoning protectionism for free trade. His budgets of the early 1840s had already abolished almost all duties on the import of raw materials. In 1846 he got Parliament to abolish completely the duty on corn and fixed only a nominal duty on all other grains. Backed by widespread popular support the manufacturing and commercial interests had won a great victory.

This victory was won through reforms and compromise rather than revolution. Unlike the French Legitimists in 1830, the English Tories did not simply retire from politics in disgust. They shared power with the Liberals and were soon to find ways of attracting working-class support.† Cheap food and cheap raw materials did not solve Britain's social ills, nor did they make her government more democratic. But along with continuing industrial growth, they brought reviving trade and greater prosperity, developments that killed the Chartist movement and helped make working-class agitation less violent. In these ways Great Britain avoided the revolutionary upheavals that were to sweep the continent in 1848.

*Ireland has never recovered from this disaster. A steady flood of immigrants left the country, especially for the United States. The island's population, which had been over 8 million in 1844, declined to less than 4 million within the next century.

†See p. 440.

### The 1840s in France

The Orleanist regime in France did not duplicate Britain's achievement. By the 1840s France had settled into political stability and a business boom, but stability and prosperity did not conceal the corruption in high places, the narrowness and rigidity of the ruling elite, and the frustrated aspirations of the middle and lower classes in a society on the threshold of industrialization.

Louis Philippe's chief minister, François Guizot (1787–1874), tried to enforce a middle-of-the-road policy and the idea of government by all the elites. (Guizot himself was a prominent historian.) To those Frenchmen who wanted to share the political privileges of the elites he said: "Get rich." Guizot was not being facetious; he lacked both the will and the wit for that. He really believed that if people could not better themselves, the fault lay not in an unjust society but in their own limitations. His main goal was to keep political power in the hands of those elites whose leisure, wealth, and intelligence gave them the capacity to seek for and discover the divine law of truth and justice through reason. This self-righteous conservative was both unpopular and blandly indifferent to popularity. Guizot remained in power from 1840 to 1848 because he perfectly embodied the king's desire to make the cabinet responsible to the Crown and not to the Chamber of Deputies.* His talent as a parliamentary tactician also helped him to win the support of opposition deputies.

The opponents of the Orleanist regime were divided on what they wanted. In general, the disenfranchised middle classes wanted a broadening of the suffrage and the prevention of deputies from holding salaried posts in the government—a practice that created a "conflict of interest" between the two roles. These were milder demands than those of the Chartists in Great Britain, but Guizot always managed to prevent the passage of such measures in Parliament. A small group of radicals wanted to abolish the

*The Constitution of 1830 was ambiguous on this point; see p. 404.

regime entirely and replace it with a democratic republic. There were also the socialist followers of Louis Blanc† who wanted not only a republic but a *social* republic. A number of prominent writers also became hostile to the regime for one reason or another. The poet Alphonse de Lamartine expressed a widespread contempt for its lack of glamor—especially Guizot's "safe-and-sane" foreign policy—when he said: "France is bored." Meanwhile, the romantic novelists Victor Hugo, George Sand, and Eugène Sue developed a cult of the common man and played with doctrines of democracy and socialism. And Jules Michelet made "the people" the collective hero of all his books on the history of France.

These Parisian writers and intellectuals gave the ideological movements of the 1840s a romantic rhetorical style, a style that also appealed to the foreign liberals and nationalists who made Paris their haven. There they talked and wrote about all the brave new worlds that they would like to build in their homelands in Central Europe. There the poet Heinrich Heine, the *enfant terrible* of German romanticism, satirized political conditions in Germany in his *Germany—A Winter Fairy Tale* (1844). These European intellectuals laid the ideological groundwork for the coming revolution, but it might not have come when it did without the severe economic crisis of 1846–1847.

This crisis began in agriculture in 1846, when bad weather brought crop failures in many parts of Western and Central Europe. Although not as severe as the potato famine in Ireland, these crop failures caused scattered outbreaks of peasant violence from southern Italy to the Austrian part of Poland. Then came the financial and industrial crises of 1847. The problem was that, except in Great Britain, Europe's credit and banking facilities could not keep up with the needs of industrial expansion and the railroad-building boom of the 1840s. Since in 1847 all available credits had to be used to import food, "capital hunger" in industry and railroad building caused widespread unemployment. The handicraft workers in the Central European countryside also suffered as the depression made it difficult for them to sell their wares.

†See p. 391.

Thus, a whole complex of forces led to the Revolution of 1848. There was the liberal and nationalist impatience with the old order in Germany, Austria, and Italy and the varied opposition to the Orleanist regime in France. There was the changing economic and social structure in all these countries. Finally, there was the economic depression of 1846–1847.

. . .
. . .

The ramparts of the restored Old Regime of 1815 faced a mounting tidal wave by 1848. The civilization of yesterday was being openly challenged by the civilization of tomorrow. Various "isms" helped emerging social and national groups to find themselves, while the hardships of industrialization brought them into sharp conflict with each other. Of the advanced countries, only Great Britain and Belgium were to escape the revolution that swept across the continent to the borders of benighted Russia.

## Suggested Readings

Nicolson, Harold G., *Congress of Vienna: A Study in Allied Unity, 1815–1822.* New York: Viking Press, 1961.*
Entertainingly written history of international relations.

Kissinger, Henry A., *A World Restored: Metternich, Castlereagh, and the Problems of Peace, 1812–1822.* New York: Grosset and Dunlap, 1964.*
A probing analysis by a political scientist.

Droz, Jacques, *Europe Between Revolutions, 1815–1848.* New York: Harper-Row, 1969. Torchbook*
The best and most up-to-date survey.

Artz, Frederick B., *France under the Bourbon Restoration, 1814–1830.* New York: Russell and Russell, 1963.
A reprint of a good older account.

Beik, Paul, *Louis Philippe and the July Monarchy.* Princeton, N. J.: D. Van Nostrand, 1965. An Anvil original.*
An excellent up-to-date account.

Thomson, David, *England in the Nineteenth Century.* Baltimore: Penguin Books, 1950.*
A fine survey—well written and stimulating.
See also George Kitson-Clark's *The Making of Victorian England,* cited in readings for Chapter X.

Gash, Norman, *Politics in the Age of Peel: A Study in the Technique of Parliamentary Representation, 1830–1850.* New York: Longmans, Green and Co., 1953.
Valuable scholarly examination of the functioning of Parliament and English society.

Shafer, Boyd C., *Nationalism: Myth and Reality.* New York: Harcourt, Brace and World, 1955.
A thoughtful essay on all aspects of European nationalsim, though lacking in sepcific details.

Plamenatz, J., *The Revolutionary Movement in France, 1815–1871.* London: Longmans, Green and Co., 1952.
A scholarly study.

Halévy, Elie, *The Growth of Philosophic Radicalism.* Boston: Beacon Press, 1955.*
Splendid analysis of the doctrines of radical reform in England.

Ruggiero, Guido de, *The History of European Liberalism.* Boston: Beacon Press, 1959.*
The standard account—originally published in 1927 but still serviceable.

Mill, John Stuart, *Autobiography.* New York: Bobbs-Merrill Co., 1958.*
One of the great classics of European civilization.

Tocqueville, Alexis de, *The Recollections of Alexis de Tocqueville.* Cleveland: World Publishing Co., 1959. Meridian.*
Somewhat disjointed, but indispensable for Tocqueville's views.

Talmon, Jacob L., *Romanticism and Revolt, 1815–1848,* New York: Harcourt Brace & World, 1967.*
Interpretative intellectual and social history.

Barzun, Jacques, *Berlioz and His Century: An Introduction to the Age of Romanticism.* Cleveland: World Publishing Co., 1956. Meridian.*
Excellent life-and-times biography—sympathetic and stimulating.

Hugo, H. E., ed., *The Romantic Reader.* New York: Viking Press, 1957.
A good selection of the writings of the romantic period.

Graña, Cesar, *Modernity and its Discontents*: French *Society and French Men of Letters in the Nineteenth Century.* New York: Harper-Row, 1967.Torchbook.*
Excellent analysis of the beginning of the alienation of modern writers.

See also the sections on early nineteenth-century arts and thought in the following works listed at the beginning of the book:

Bronowski, Jacob and Mazlish, Bruce, *The Western Intellectual Tradition*; Gardner, Helen, *Art through the Ages*; Lang, Paul, *Music in Western Civilization.*

Part II

# THE INDUSTRIAL AGE

POLITICAL, ECONOMIC, AND SOCIAL CHANGES were resisted by the aristocratic and monarchical forces until the middle of the century, but they were to triumph in Central as well as Western Europe thereafter. In the latter half of the century both nationalism and liberalism altered their own earlier outlooks when they were confronted with revolutionary socialism, which grew apace with industrial capitalism. The social composition of the conservative forces varied considerably between Western and Eastern Europe. In Great Britain the Tories, who supposedly represented landed wealth, tried to "buy" working-class support by extending the francise and encouraging moderate labor reforms, while the Liberals continued to back a government that fostered laissez faire. In Russia, the landowners and the government wanted to repress both the workers and the bourgeois liberals who asked for laissez faire, thus driving both groups into a position of radical opposition. Furthermore, since Russia's industrialization did not really gain impetus until the 1890s, "capitalists" and workers were a small proportion of the population and were too weak to change the Old Regime before the twentieth century.

After 1815 the victorious Allies and a chastened France had tried to replace the eighteenth-century balance of power with a Concert of Europe, in which present and future relations would be planned by the "Big Five." But Prussia, Austria, and Russia worked with a different set of principles from Great Britain and France. Besides, the insurgent nationalism in Germany and Italy—and among the subject peoples in the Hapsburg Monarchy, the Ottoman Empire, and Russia later in the century—was too self-centered and threatened the status quo too much to be controlled or planned by all the powers in agreement. Concert slipped back into balance in the 1850s and 1860s, and balance, in turn, was replaced by the precarious equilibrium of the Bismarckian era, with its insurances and reinsurances. Beginning in the 1890s imperialist rivalries overseas put additional strains on this equilibrium. In the decade preceding 1914 precarious equilibrium was to degenerate into an obvious disequilibrium of rival alliance systems and an armaments race, which led to the cataclysm of the First World War.

European civilization became increasingly scientific and industrial in the late nineteenth century; everybody and everything eventually had to bow before it. Art and religion fought what became increasingly a rear-guard action against it. The railroad and the city uprooted millions of people from their traditional folk cultures, which public education and the popular press began to replace with a new, mass culture. Indeed, everything became organized on a mass scale: states, businesses, armies, and navies. And Europeans used their scientific, economic, political, and military power to extend their undisputed dominion over a large part of the globe. The British Empire alone covered a fourth of it by 1905.

Like the period 1789–1815, the period 1905–1919 was transitional. On the one hand, the nineteenth-century power structure persisted until the last months of the First World War in all the major countries except Russia. On the other hand, the social and political tensions that led to the wartime and immediate postwar revolutions in Central and Eastern Europe originated in the prewar decades. Thus, the collapse of the European system during the First World War is really the end of the story of the nineteenth century. The twentieth-century revolution in science, philosophy, and the arts began around 1905 but attained its full impact only after 1919.

Never before the twentieth century had war led to so many domestic political upheavals. Between 1919 and 1939 only Great Britain, France, and the smaller countries of Northwestern Europe survived as parliamentary democracies. All the parliamentary regimes established in Central and Eastern Europe at the end of the First World War gave way to some form of dictatorship in the next two decades. In fact, Italian democracy, which had been "in the making" before that war, was the first victim of its aftermath (the brief Provisional Government in Russia in 1917 had been the first victim of the war itself) and succumbed to fascism in 1922. During the Second World War the German fascists imposed their New Order on the bulk of the continent. Their defeat in turn led to the imposition of Communist regimes on the countries of Eastern Europe by the Soviet Union and the restoration of parliamentary democracy in Western Europe—including Italy and a large part of Germany—under the aegis of the United States.

The economic history of Europe since 1919 has been closely linked to its international and domestic politics. In the first decade after each world war the economies of Europe floundered or prospered as a direct result of events on the other side of the Atlantic. Just as the Great Crash of 1929 in the United States precipitated the worst depression that modern Europe had known and aided the rise of the Nazis, so the Marshall Plan, beginning in 1948, helped the nations of Western Europe to remove the threat of Communist subversion and to reach new heights of production through their own efforts. These nations have lost their former economic predominance in the world as a whole. They have nonetheless managed to provide a higher standard of material well being for their own citizens than in the days when the French financed the Suez Canal and Russian railroads, the Germans dominated the market in Southeastern Europe, and the British navy and merchant marine ruled the waves.

War, politics, and economic growth have also transformed European society. They have hastened the breakdown of the traditional class structure and have given the urban masses new levels of aspiration. The depression of the early 1930s intensified the hostility between the middle and lower classes, both of which became attracted to mass political movements that promised to alleviate their social and economic frustrations. Outside the Soviet Union the pre-1914 elites continued to fight a rearguard action against the revolt of the masses until the Second World War. Since then these elites have been completely destroyed in the new Communist regimes of Eastern Europe and are being increasingly displaced by a new group of experts and managers in the democratic regimes of the West. Even east of the so-called Iron Curtain, this group seems to be establishing itself as a "new class," open to but distinct from the real "toilers." And everywhere from democratic Britain to Communist Russia the masses have forced their governments to give them health, education, and welfare services on an unprecedented scale.

Unfortunately, the economic and social gains of the past half-century have had little effect in reconciling culture and civilization. Indeed, the rift between them has apparently widened more than ever, not only in the higher forms of artistic culture but also in the new mass culture that has overwhelmed traditional ways of thinking, feeling, and behaving. The rift has been exposed in avant-garde literature and art in such movements as Expressionism, Existentialism, and the cult of the absurd. Even in that most synthetic form of mass culture, the movies, Charlie Chaplin portrayed the pathos of a man with a handcart mind struggling to adapt himself to an automated world. Some writers and artists have consistently remained prophets of gloom and doom regarding the future of European culture. Others have turned periodically to Communism, socialism, nationalism, or fascism for its salvation. But, just as no historian has yet been able to give cultural meaning to the scientific-technological civilization of the twentieth century, neither has any creative artist or philosopher. Since the First World War philosophers have challenged all traditional values and beliefs, one school going so far as to deny meaning to all philosophical questions except those dealing with the language of science. Meanwhile, artists, literary writers, and composers have come forth with a bewildering variety of new styles, each claiming to be the true expression of contemporary reality.

CHAPTER XII

# REVOLUTION AND CONSOLIDATION 1848–1871

The Revolution of 1848 marked the end of an era. Ever since the late eighteenth century, liberal patriots had tried to overthrow the old order in one country after another, but the old order had always recovered its power. In 1848 the same thing happened simultaneously in several countries, and it finally became clear that the goals of individual liberty and national independence could not be permanently established by revolution from below.

The Revolution of 1848 did not turn out the way its instigators had hoped it would, but it had many unanticipated consequences. All the countries that experienced it (and some that did not—like the United States and Russia) underwent a profound transformation during the next two decades. In politics, ideological rigidity and impassioned oratory gave way to hard-headed realism. Seemingly irreconcilable conservative aristocrats and liberal bourgeois began to work together in many places. This period also saw the end of serfdom in Central and Eastern Europe and of slavery in the United States. As a result, the landlord class that serfdom and slavery had supported declined, and underemployed rural wokers in Europe were able to seek better economic opportunities in the cities or on new farm lands in the plains of North America and Siberia. This large-scale movement of peoples was also facilitated by improvements in transportation; for in the 1850s and 1860s European civilization passed from the age of the stage coach and the sailing ship to the age of the railroad and the steamship. All these changes in turn contributed to the consolidation of nation-sates and the emergence of a new balance of power.

The key to all these transformations was industrialization. It made Europe's rulers see that political power had to be based on material and technological progress, rather than on the preservation of a reactionary ideal. It also forced them to promote the interests of the bourgeois capitalists who built the railroads, the banks, and the armaments that made the state strong. Nor could Europe's rulers any longer ignore the aspirations of the uprooted masses that industrialization produced. In the 1850s and 1860s the governments of the most advanced industrial countries already began to seek the allegiance of the masses by fostering some of the goals of nationalism and democracy from above.

## THE REVOLUTION OF 1848

In many respects the Revolution of 1848 recapitulated in Central Europe what the Revolution of 1789 had done in France, and it anticipated what the Revolution of 1905 was to do in Russia. In each case there was a significant minority of educated middle-class people dedicated to the principle of representative government and to the ideal of the nation as a political community including all social classes. The time lag in Central and Eastern Europe reflected the lag in the economic and cultural conditions that produced this significant minority. Not until the 1840s did Germany, Italy, and Austria reach the general economic and cultural level of France in the 1790s; and not until the end of the nineteenth century was Russia to reach it. This fact helps to explain why Russia had no revolution in 1848. A major reason Great Britain and Belgium also escaped revolution in 1848 was that, by then, they had already achieved a degree of representative government and national cohesiveness which satisfied their educated middle-class minorities. This was not the case in France, and that country went through the whole cycle of events of 1789–1799 once again in 1848–1852.

Like all historical parallels, these are not exact. France was not as *industrially* developed in the 1790s as parts of Central Europe in 1848, which in turn were less industrialized than parts of Russia in 1905. By 1905 Russia had passed the degree of industrialization of France in 1848 and was approaching its general cultural and economic level. As a result, socialism as a movement of *industrial* workers played practically no role in France in the 1790s or in Central Europe in 1848, a fleeting role in France in 1848, and a considerable role in Russia in 1905. The composition of the educated middle-class minorities that made all these revolutions was also somewhat different. There were more lawyers and even noblemen in the revolution of 1789, more professors in 1848 and in 1905. Only in Germany and Italy were these people concerned with territorial unification in 1848. The immediate circumstances that gave rise to and determined the outcome of each revolution also varied in 1789, 1848, and 1905 and from place to place in 1848.

Nevertheless, the similarities remain between the revolutions of 1789, 1848, and 1905. All were led by middle-class intellectuals; all were supported by a nascent proletariat in the cities. And all removed any remaining seignorial obligations of the peasants, thus making the rural masses at least nominal members of a national community. Finally, all these revolutions established the forms of constitutional rule and representative assemblies.

Twentieth-century Russia is mentioned at this point because it was to take over the ideological rigidity that the West finally abandoned after 1848. This ideological rigidity had first appeared in France in 1789; its chief characteristic was its search for a final solution to all the problems of society. Between 1815 and 1848 it had reappeared in such diverse forms as English Chartism, French utopian socialism, and the radical nationalism of Mazzini. After its disastrous defeat in the West, it was to wander eastward and ultimately to win dominance in Russia after 1917 and in China after 1949. Of all the unanticipated consequences of the Revolution of 1848, this was the most remote but the most significant for the world today.

### The Outbreak of the Revolution and Its Initial Successes

In early 1848 revolution broke out almost simultaneously in Paris and in all the major cities of Italy, Germany, and Austria. Everywhere the revolutionaries seemed to demand similar changes and to proclaim similar slogans. Monarchs cringed, constitutions were promulgated, and the map of Central Europe seemed about to be altered beyond recognition. Yet despite the simultaneity and apparent similarity of the revolutions, they originated in dissimilar situations, took different forms, and produced conflicting results.

We must therefore keep the differences as well as the similarities in mind as we follow the complicated pattern of events.

In Italy we must distinguish between the revolution in Austrian-held Lombardy and Venetia and the events in the independent states: Piedmont in the north, the Duchies and the Papal States in the center, the Kingdom of the Two Sicilies in the south. In Germany we must distinguish between the movement for national unification and the revolutions in the individual states, especially Prussia. In the Austrian Empire we most distinguish between the revolution in Vienna as an Austrian affair and the revolutions in Hungary, Bohemia, and Lombardy-Venetia—all of which were anti-Austrian.

### Paris

The February Revolution in Paris began with a banquet and ended on the barricades. Denied the right to hold public political meetings, opposition leaders had been denouncing the government and drinking toasts to reform at private banquets for several months. The government's patience finally broke when a huge banquet was scheduled for February 22, with a hundred opposition deputies on the invited list and with a popular demonstration to accompany them through the streets of Paris. Guizot banned both the banquet and the demonstration. Though most of the deputies stayed at home, the organizers of the demonstration went ahead with their plan, and students and workers began clashing with the police on the 22nd. When the king called out the National Guard, the privates, who felt no attachment to a regime under which they could not vote, refused to move. On the next day Louis Philippe reluctantly decided to dismiss Guizot and to promise electoral reforms. These concessions came too late. Republican firebrands were helping the workers to throw up barricades at the main intersections of Paris' narrow streets. Meanwhile, a crowd gathered outside of the Ministry of Foreign Affairs, shots were exchanged, and twenty civilians and one soldier were killed. This encounter roused the rest of the city to revolt by the morning of the 24th. With the revolutionaries surging toward the royal palace, Louis Philippe quietly slipped away in a cab. Like the July Revolution of 1830, the February Revolution of 1848 had deposed a king in three days.

The republican leaders brushed aside any discussion of retaining the monarchy under Louis Philippe's grandson. On February 25, in response to the demands of the crowd that invaded the Chamber of Deputies, they declared France a republic and proclaimed the principle of universal manhood suffrage. They also set up a provisional government—including the poet-historian Lamartine and the radical deputy Ledru-Rollin—to rule the nation until its citizens had a chance to elect a constituent assembly in April. In addition, a Government Commission for Workmen was formed under the leadership of Louis Blanc. This commission persuaded the provisional government to take emergency measures for the thousands of jobless workers who had flocked to Paris. But despite the revolutionary pressure from below and a worsening economic crisis, the republic was unopposed.

### Italy

By early March the news of the events in Paris stimulated the revolutionary process that was already under way in Italy. This process had begun in 1847, when Grand Duke Leopold of Tuscany and the newly elected Pope Pius IX (1846–1878) granted a number of civil rights and seemed to be making their bids for the moral leadership of Italy. Alarmed by these threats to his "system," Metternich sent Austrian troops into the Papal States. This step aroused liberals all over Italy and helped fan anti-Austrian sentiment. In Piedmont, King Charles Albert (1831–1849) introduced liberal provisions for local government and a looser censorship. These minor concessions were insufficient to satisfy the Piedmontese liberals or to outbid Leopold and Pius IX, not to mention Mazzini, for leadership of the independence movement against Austria.

For Italy's national resurgence, called the *Risorgimento*, was in full swing. In late 1847 a new newspaper, significantly entitled *Il Risorgimento*, argued for further political changes in Piedmont as the first step toward Italian unification. One of the editors of this newspaper was Count Camillo Benso di Cavour (1810–1861), the man who was later to succeed in uniting Italy after all others had failed.

In early 1848 the Italian revolutionary movement was achieving its greatest successes. It triumphed first in the Kingdom of the Two Sicilies, where hunger and Bourbon misrule prompted an insurrection in Palermo (Sicily) on January 12 and forced King Ferdinand II (1830–1859) to promulgate a liberal constitution on February 10 in Naples. Leopold of Tuscany followed suit on February 17, as did Charles Albert of Piedmont on March 4 and the pope on March 14. Then Lombardy and Venetia rebelled against Austrian rule. The people of Milan threw up barricades in the streets and in five days (March 18–22) of heroic fighting drove the Austrian forces to the eastern borders of Lombardy; the people of Venice also expelled the Austrians and proclaimed a Venetian Republic on March 22. On that same day, Charles Albert of Piedmont declared war on Austria. Within the next few weeks volunteers from all over Italy formed to help the Lombards and Venetians, and Charles Albert triumphantly entered Milan.

### Vienna

In March 1848 the Austrian Empire itself seemed on the point of disintegration. The news from Paris aggravated the financial and industrial crisis that had begun there, as elsewhere, in 1847. While members of the emperor's court intrigued against Metternich, a radical named Louis Kossuth (1802–1894) made a daring speech in the Hungarian diet, demanding a liberal constitution and self-rule for his country. Then, on March 13, a Viennese mob of middle-class radicals and students clashed with the police and invaded the palace grounds. Metternich resigned and left the country. By March 15, Vienna, like Paris, had its barricades. On that day the emperor promised a constitution and granted freedom of the press. Within three weeks he also accepted the virtual independence of Hungary and promised to call a constituent assembly for Bohemia. Independence movements also broke out in Croatia, Galicia, and Transylvania, as well as in Lombardy and Venetia. In mid-May the emperor and his family fled from radical Vienna to Innsbruck. The climax of the revolution in the Hapsburg Monarchy came in June, when a Pan-Slav Congress met at Prague under the presidency of Francis Palácky. This congress proclaimed the solidarity of the Slavic peoples, especially the Czechs, against the Germans.

### *Germany*

The revolutions in Paris and Vienna sparked the revolutionary movement in Germany. As in the Austrian Empire, this movement was both national and liberal, but its national goal was unification, not disintegration. Furthermore, in various parts of Germany there were peasant revolts and riots by craftsmen threatened with extinction by the beginnings of industrialization.

The middle-class movement based on liberalism and nationalism proceeded in two stages, with the consolidation of liberal gains coming first. Between March 1 and March 12 all the rulers in western Germany refashioned their ministries along liberal lines and made profuse promises of further reforms. In the northern German cities of Hamburg, Bremen, and Lübeck, peaceful revolutions turned oligarchic regimes into democratic republics. Middle-class leaders in the Prussian Rhineland and Westphalia demanded representative institutions, seized control of the municipalities, and formed National Guards. These sweeping changes were effected rapidly and without bloodshed. On March 31 a "preliminary parliament" in the Rhineland city of Frankfurt ordered the holding of elections throughout Germany by direct manhood suffrage. Hopes ran high for the National Assembly that these elections would produce.

But Berlin, not Frankfurt, was the third major revolutionary center in 1848, along with Paris and Vienna. For Berlin was the capital of the largest and most economically advanced state in Germany, Prussia; it was also the most industrialized city on the continent. Unemployed workers had begun to demonstrate in early March for emergency relief, but they lacked the guidance of socialist theorists, as in Paris. Then the crisis on the Berlin stock exchange was aggravated by the revolutions elsewhere. On March 18 the news from Vienna prompted a mass demonstration in front of the royal palace, where shots were fired. Soon thereafter barricades went up, and a general insurrection began against the royal garrison. Extremely agitated, King Frederick William IV (1840–1861) issued a proclamation "to my beloved Berliners" promising that the hated troops would be withdrawn if the barricades were removed.

The insurgents exulted in their victory. They forced the king and the queen to salute the men who had died on the barricades and to grant concrete political concessions. Frederick William was swept off his feet by events. Although he was incapable of accepting a liberal program sincerely, he was also incapable of fighting it manfully. He promised full civil rights and a constitutional government responsible to a Parliament elected by universal suffrage.

The capitulations of the Prussian king and the Austrian emperor were the high points in the German revolution. The kings of Bavaria, Hanover, and Saxony had to follow their lead in promising reforms. Meanwhile, more radical groups began to threaten the already reformed regimes in western Germany. Thus, when the Frankfurt National Assembly met on May 18, a new Germany seemed to be in the making.

After its initial successes the many-sided Revolution of 1848 followed divergent paths in each country. Liberals and democrats jostled each other and the conservatives, and the socialists briefly entered the fray in Paris and Rhineland Germany. As this happened, nationalism emerged as the only unifying force. And it too lost out everywhere, except in France.

### The Course of the Revolution in France to 1851

On Easter Sunday (April 23), 1848, 84 per cent of all the male adults in France went to the polls to elect their representatives. The results of this election showed that rural France wanted the republic to be much more conservative than Paris did. Even in Paris the radical and socialist candidates ran well behind the moderate republicans. Of 900 deputies in the new Constituent Assembly, moderates who were at least nominally republican numbered about five hundred, avowed monarchists three hundred, radical republicans and socialists only eighty. This Assembly immediately reorganized the provisional executive committee to reflect its own moderate republican majority. The socialists, angry at losing all share in power, attempted a second revolution by organizing an attack on the Assembly on May 15. They failed miserably, and their leaders were arrested.

This incident helped turn the moderates against any kind of social or economic reform—even emergency work-relief. The national workshops established at the end of February were not the producers' cooperatives envisioned by Louis Blanc;* they were public works projects for the unemployed. Their cost was bitterly resented by most middle-class and peasant taxpayers, especially since the persistent economic and financial crisis precluded any possibility of reforming the tax structure.

After May 15 the government itself began to view the national workshops as hotbeds of socialist agitation as well as an unjustified financial burden. Over 100,000 unemployed provincial workers had swelled the ranks of the national workshops by June. There was simply not enough work in all Paris for a labor force of this size. The Ministry of Public Works put some men to work digging holes in the Champ de Mars and others filling them up again. They got forty cents a day, while the idle workers got thirty-five cents. A radical deputy wanted to nationalize the private railroad-building projects in order to provide additional jobs. That scheme smacked of socialism too. Finally, the government forced all the idle workers to choose between going back to the provinces or joining the army; on June 21 it abolished the national workshops altogether. In response to this action, the mass of Parisian workers again raised the barricades and revolted against the government.

For four days (June 22–26) the workers and the government fought a bloody civil war. The workers's battle cry was "Bread or Lead!" But in addition to "bread" they wanted to replace the existing bourgeois government with a true "social republic." The "have-nots" were turning against the "haves" in open class warfare. Bourgeois deputies, fearing for their property, gave emergency powers to General Cavaignac. He waited until the workers had entrenched themselves in strong positions and then blasted them with artillery shells, rather than mere lead bullets. In this way over a thousand workers lost their lives on the barricades. Several thousand more were either killed or deported in the settling of accounts that followed this cruel repression of industrial Europe's first "revolt of the masses."

Comparative calm followed the catastrophic "June Days." General Cavaignac shut down the radical newspapers and maintained law and order. Meanwhile, the Constituent Assembly went about its business of drafting a constitution. This constitution, which went into effect in November 1848, was more democratic than any other in Europe. It provided for a single legislative assembly chosen for three years and a president for four, both to be elected by universal manhood suffrage. Still, no mention was made of "the right to work" or other socialist proposals. The Second Republic was politically democratic, but socially and economically it adhered to the principle of laissez faire. It supposedly achieved an ideal arrangement between an executive and a legislature that would be too busy competing with each other to threaten liberty or property.

*See p. 391.

This presidential system was completely new in Europe. Only in the republics of the New World was the chief executive —combining the offices of head of state and prime minister—elected by the people and responsible to the people. In Europe, the head of state was traditionally a prince, a king, or an emperor, and it did not take the French long to revert to this tradition. In fact, it took them exactly four years—from the time Louis Napoleon was elected the first president of the republic in December 1848 until he made himself Napoleon III, Emperor of the French, in December 1852.

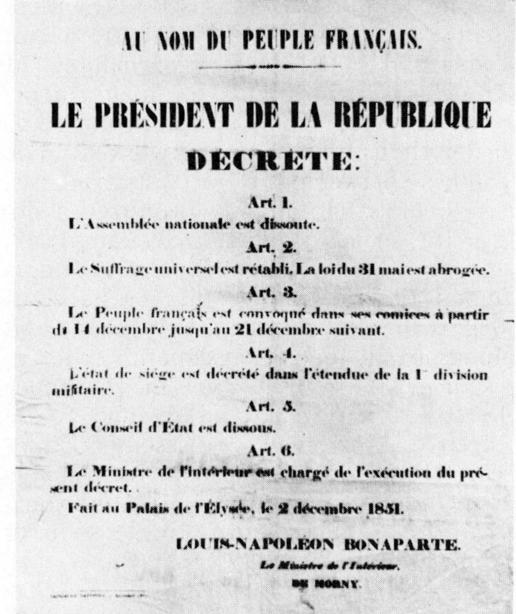
AU NOM DU PEUPLE FRANÇAIS.

LE PRÉSIDENT DE LA RÉPUBLIQUE

DÉCRÈTE:

Art. 1.

L'Assemblée nationale est dissoute.

Art. 2.

Le Suffrage universel est rétabli. La loi du 31 mai est abrogée.

Art. 3.

Le Peuple français est convoqué dans ses comices à partir du 14 décembre jusqu'au 21 décembre suivant.

Art. 4.

L'état de siège est décrété dans l'étendue de la 1[re] division militaire.

Art. 5.

Le Conseil d'État est dissous.

Art. 6.

Le Ministre de l'intérieur est chargé de l'exécution du présent décret.

Fait au Palais de l'Élysée, le 2 décembre 1851.

LOUIS-NAPOLÉON BONAPARTE.

*Le Ministre de l'Intérieur,*

DE MORNY.

*Proclamation of the coup d'état*

Louis Napoleon (1808–1873) was a nephew of the first Emperor of the French. He had grown up in exile, mainly in Germany and England. In 1840 he tried to invade France by crossing the Channel with fifty men and, according to legend, a tamed eagle. This farcical exploit earned him only ignominy and a sentence of life imprisonment. But Louis Napoleon escaped from prison in 1846 and went back to England. He returned to France after the February Revolution, accompanied by a motley group of supporters and a blonde English actress named Miss Howard. (She was more helpful than the tamed eagle—she had money.) Some politicians supported his candidacy in the first presidential election in France because they thought that his name would draw votes and that they could then manipulate him for their own purposes. No one anticipated the Bonapartist landslide that this election produced. Louis Napoleon polled 5,500,000 votes; his nearest rivals were Cavaignac, with 1,500,000 votes, and Ledru-Rollin, with 370,000 votes.

The French people, who were still predominantly rural, also showed their desire for a monarch in the election of the Legislative Assembly five months later. The moderate republicans were almost wiped out. Although the radicals won almost 200 seats, the real victors were the Legitimist and Orleanist monarchists, with 400 seats.

Until late 1851 Louis Napoleon collaborated with this conservative, monarchist, and Catholic majority. In foreign affairs he sent an occupation force to Rome to protect the Pope from Italian revolutionaries.* At home he supported the Falloux Law of 1850, which allowed Catholic secondary schools to operate freely alongside the state schools, and which increased Church supervision of all primary schools. But Louis Napoleon catered to the traditional conservatives and clericals out of sheer opportunism. He himself was relatively indifferent to religion, and espoused many of the ideas of Saint-Simon regarding economic growth and social reform. Above all, Louis Napoleon wanted to be emperor.

Louis Napoleon transformed himself from a prince-president into an emperor in two stages. In December 1851 he used the army to overthrow the constitution of the Second Republic by a *coup d'état.* In its place he created a regime that provided for a ten-year presidential term and a sharp cut in the legislature's power. Like his uncle before him, he then appealed to the nation to ratify the new regime in a plebiscite. A year later he made himself emperor and arranged another plebiscite. This time his majority was 97 per cent.

Why did the February Revolution end in an authoritarian monarchy? Admitted-

*See p. 438.

ly some intimidation was used in the plebiscites, but the name of Bonaparte meant order and national glory to millions of French peasants and to many army officers. Louis Napoleon also promised to better the condition of the workers. The conflicts between the socialists, radicals, and liberals had already produced a desire for strong leadership by late 1848, and thereafter Louis Napoleon undermined the support of these groups, as well as the conservatives, by posing as all things to all men. Consequently, the resistance to his *coup d'état* in December 1851 was too weak and divided to be effective. As we shall see presently, Napoleon III used nationalism conservatively to include social reform in an authoritarian order. Other countries were soon to adopt a similar arrangement.

### The Course of the Revolution in Germany

Unlike the revolution in France, the revolution in Germany did not take place within an already existing national framework. The delegates who met at Frankfurt represented the people of separate sovereign states. They had no army, no law courts, no bureaucracy, no police force, and no revenue. All they had was an idea of a united German empire, and they did not even agree on what territories this empire should include or on who should be its monarch. There were really only two choices: the Emperor of Austria or the King of Prussia. As long as these two sovereigns were busy trying to recover their authority at home, the delegates at Frankfurt could make their plans somewhat independently. But neither the Prussian king nor the Austrian emperor intended to see his state swallowed up in a new Germany, and, in the end, it was the political and military power of thse two historic states, not the delegates at Frankfurt, that determined the outcome of the German revolution.

This was particularly so regarding Prussia. By the time the National Assembly at Frankfurt had constituted its new German empire (on paper), Prussia had liquidated her own revolution and was the only real power within its borders. Hence, we must examine the outcome of the revolution in Prussia first, in order to understand the outcome of the German revolution as a whole.

#### *The Prussian Constitution*

As we saw earlier, Frederick William IV had promised all sorts of reforms in a moment of weakness. The newly elected Prussian Constituent Assembly met in late May, and at first the liberals and radicals predominated. They in turn were driven by further popular agitation to destroy the still intact institutions of the Old Regime and to build a new democratic state. In July, however, the conservatives—the Junker landlords, the Lutheran clergy, the royal court, and the army—began reorganizing their forces. As in France, the peasants were generally opposed to radicals in the capital, though there were some peasant revolts against the remnants of servile obligations, especially east of the Elbe. By September, the king recovered his nerve and used the army to suppress working-class agitation in Berlin. Two months later, he appointed a conservative ministry under Count Brandenburg and transferred the Assembly to the provinces. On December 5 he dissolved the Assembly altogether and promulgated his own constitution.

Thus, the revolution in Prussia was over by the end of 1848. Frederick William's constitution granted equality before the law, universal suffrage, and two legislative chambers which the king could dissolve at will. The other German monarchies followed Prussia's lead in granting constitutional concessions while opposing democracy and popular sovereignty. When the radical democrats rose up in Saxony, the Palatinate, and Baden in the spring of 1849, it was the Prussian army that crushed them. Then, in May 1849, Frederick William nullified the concessions to liberal ideas in his constitution by restoring the old restricted franchise.

By January 1850 the Prussian Constitution was published in its final form. (It lasted until 1918.) It abolished the last vestiges of serfdom in East Prussia and appeared to guarantee the rights of all

*A member of the Frankfurt Assembly tries to stop fighting between the Prussian army and radicals, September 1848*

individuals. Nevertheless, the king reserved the right to nominate and dismiss ministers independently of Parliament. The upper chamber became simply a house of lords, and the lower chamber was elected by a three-class system of voting. The big taxpayers elected one third of its deputies, the middle range of taxpayers one third, and the small taxpayers the remaining third. Hence, despite universal suffrage, the Prussian Parliament (like the British Parliament before the Reform of 1867*) was dominated by the country's noble and wealthy elites.

It was this constitution, not the one proclaimed at Frankfurt in early 1849, that was soon to dominate the political life of Germany. At the time, however, hope for another kind of Germany was running high.

*See p. 440.

### The Frankfurt Assembly

The Frankfurt National Assembly embodied this hope, but, aside from its lack of real power, it was divided within itself. The Left wing wanted social and political democracy under a king; there were even a few republicans. The Right wing represented the interests of the individual states, especially Prussia and Austria. The Center, which comprised the majority of the delegates, wanted a liberal, self-governing, federally unified Germany. It differed over details, but it made the constitution that was the noblest expression of nineteenth-century German liberalism.

Unfortunately, these liberal constitution makers confused ideas with reality. Many of them were professors and lawyers, conscientious, earnest, rigid of purpose, but completely lacking in political experience.

They were idealists in both the ordinary sense and in the philosophical sense. They believed that they could conjure up ideas of "Germany" that included or excluded Austria, Bohemia, and Prussian Poland, and that each of these ideas was real. They believed that by willing themselves sovereign they were sovereign. Their most tragic illusion was their confusion of a paper constitution with the way power was actually constituted.

In reality, sovereign power remained with the individual German states, and whenever the delegates at Frankfurt needed power they had to turn to them. Thus, in the summer of 1848, when they decided that the Danish provinces of Schleswig and Holstein should become a part of the new Germany, they had to ask Prussia to send troops to the disputed area.* In September 1848 radical riots broke out in Frankfurt. Again, the Assembly had to call in troops from Prussia, and other states as well. Thereafter, it met under Prussian protection.

The final disillusionment came in the spring of 1849. By then the Frankfurt Assembly had at last completed its constitution. It guaranteed all the basic civil rights, set forth a common law for all Germany, and created a federal empire to be ruled by a legislative assembly and a limited monarchy. There had been long debates over what territories this empire should include. The Left wing had wanted it to include Austria and Bohemia, which were already part of the German Confederation. This was the "Greater Germany" idea. The liberals thought it wiser to leave Austrian territory out because of its large non-German population. This was the "Lesser Germany" idea. The "Greater Germany" idea, which would include Austria and Bohemia but not Hungary, meant the break-up of the Hapsburg Monarchy. Since the Austrian emperor had just put this state precariously together again,† the advocates of "Greater Germany" were forced to see the unreality of their idea. The "Lesser Germany" idea also proved to be unreal, for King Frederick William IV of Prussia refused to become its sovereign. (In private, he spoke with contempt of a "pig's crown" that did not come by the grace of God but by the grace of "master bakers and butchers.") After that, most of the delegates simply went home. Their "realities" had all been unmasked as illusions.

*Prussia, however, quickly concluded an armistice in August 1848, and the Frankfurt Assembly had to acquiesce. By the time the great powers settled the Schleswig-Holstein question in 1852, there was no Frankfurt Assembly and no "Germany."

†See pp. 437–438.

#### Reaction

Between the summer of 1849 and the autumn of 1850 Prussia and Austria each tried to reassert its influence in Germany. Frederick William wanted a federation of the lesser German monarchies under his leadership, and he was perfectly willing to accept a crown from his fellow princes. Austria, fully recovered by 1850, threatened war if this federation should come into being. Frederick William was not willing to risk war, so, with the help of Russian diplomatic intervention (the tsar also frowned on the idea of a united Germany), Austria was able to make him drop his plan in a conference held at Olmütz, and the German Confederation of 1815 was restored soon thereafter. Under this system Prussia and Austria were once again to defend jointly a conservative, traditional Germany against revolution. Even so, the restoration of this system did not prevent many Prussians from viewing their "humiliation" at Olmütz as a shameful defeat.

The real defeat, however, was that of the several simultaneous revolutions of the German people themselves. As in France in 1789, the success of the middle-class constitutional revolution was made possible by peasant revolts and working-class riots, especially riots by craftsmen threatened by industrial capitalism. But unlike what happened in France in 1789, these German "*sans-culottes*" quickly repudiated the liberal revolutionaries without being able to organize a more radical revolution of their own (as did the Commune of August 10, 1792). Furthermore, without a threat of foreign aggression, there was nothing to hold the diverse German revolutionaries together after their joint defeat of the Old Regime at home. In this situation the German constitutionalists clung to their middle-class preference for liberty over social justice, for the rights of property over the needs of men. Unlike the Jacobins of 1793, they refused concessions to the disgruntled masses as a matter of expediency. Meanwhile, before their eyes, the political conservatives and economic traditionalists formed a coalition that was to destroy them.

In industry this conservative coalition championed the handicraftsman over the mill owner; in the countryside it agreed to the surrender of "feudal" judicial and police privileges, the commutation of servile dues, and the establishment of rural credit institutions. In these ways the conservatives brought about a realignment of popular forces that made possible the restoration of the old order. Many middle-class advocates of a united Germany under a liberal or democratic constitution were forced to emigrate; others decided to leave of their own free will, especially for the United States. When the time for a readjustment to changing social conditions came around once again, Central Europe was to embrace the machine age under the auspices of a policy of blood and iron.

## The Course of Revolution in the Austrian Empire

As in France and Germany, the conservative forces in Austria began to recover their strength by the end of 1848. This recovery meant disaster for the liberals, democrats, and nationalists throughout the empire. It also defeated the movement for Italian unification by reintegrating Lombardy and Venetia into the empire.

As we have seen, Emperor Ferdinand and his family had fled Vienna in May, 1848. The city remained in radical hands until the end of October, but the army remained loyal to the dynasty. Under General Windischgrätz, part of its forces suppressed the Czech revolutionary movement by ruthlessly bombarding Prague on June 17. Then, on July 24, General Radetsky defeated the Piedmontese-Italian army at Custozza and reestablished Austrian control over Lombardy. Although Venetia still remained in republican hands and although Piedmont was to reopen the war briefly in March 1849, the Hapsburg dynasty could now concentrate on restoring its authority in Vienna itself, and in Hungary. It did this in two ways: it played off the subject peoples against one another, especially the Croats and the Rumanians in Transylvania against the Magyars and the Czechs against the Austrian Germans; it called a Constituent Assembly to win over the liberals and isolate the radicals.

### *The Constituent Assembly*

This Constituent Assembly, the only full imperial Parliament in the history of the Austrian Empire, met in Vienna from late July until October, 1848 and in Kremsier until March, 1849. It represented a double compromise: the liberals accepted the empire and the dynasty; the dynasty, for the moment, accepted liberalism. In addition, the Czech nationalists accepted the dynasty out of fear of German nationalism, for the Vienna radicals wanted Austria and Bohemia to join the "Greater Germany" being proposed at Frankfurt. The liberal Austrians feared the disruption of the empire by Viennese radicalism or its capture by the Slavs. They also feared the vague social aspirations of the Viennese workers. Hence they and the Czechs supported the work of the Constituent Assembly.

The democratic constitution drawn up by this assembly, like the one drawn up at Frankfurt, was never to go into effect; its only lasting reform was the emancipation of the peasants. In most of the Hapsburg Monarchy the peasants had to perform compulsory labor for their landlords in return for the use of the land. This labor-rent—*robot*—was abolished on September 7, 1848. Thereafter the landowners had no further interest in keeping a large peasant population tied to the soil, and peasants with very small holdings sold out and moved to the cities. The class struggle between the landed nobility and the peasants thus ceased. In the countryside the great estates benefited by the increased efficiency of paid laborers, and the compensation given by the government for the elimination of *robot* provided the big landlords with capital for other enterprises: mills, breweries, hotels, coal mines. On the other hand, the lesser gentry were soon ruined, especially in Hungary.

For the moment, however, the Magyar gentry were busy trying to gain their independence from Austria. They and the Viennese radicals were the only real threats to the dynasty and the empire in the fall of 1848.

### *The Magyars*

The Hapsburgs resorted to their centuries-old policy of "divide and rule" by pitting the Croats against the Magyars. When the Croats declared their autonomy from Hungary in June, Emperor Ferdinand, who was also King of Hungary, opposed them, but by September he needed a new army to defeat the Magyar rebels themselves. He therefore allowed the Croat leader, Baron Jellachich, to form such an army and to invade Hungary. Things went badly for the dynasty in early October. The Magyars pushed Jellachich's army back to the gates of Vienna, and inside the city the radicals led a new uprising against Ferdinand's move to suppress the Magyar revolt with Croatian troops. For, like the German radicals, the Austrian radicals opposed the nationalist aims of "mere Slavs," be they Poles, Czechs, or Croats.

However, the dynasty soon won out. On October 31, Windischgrätz and Jellachich bombarded Vienna into submission, and a few days later they ruthlessly executed the radical leaders. Thereafter, the causes of liberalism, democracy, and nationalism were doomed in the Austrian Empire. On December 2, Emperor Ferdinand abdicated in favor of his nephew Francis Joseph (1848–1916). This move was inspired by Radetsky and engineered by the new government strong man, Prince Felix Schwarzenberg, who reasoned that the new emperor would not be bound by his predecessor's promises to the Magyars, the Croats, and even the Austrian liberals. Francis Joseph did not disappoint them. In March 1849 he disavowed the constitution proclaimed by the Kremsier Assembly and restored absolutism everywhere in the empire, including Hungary.

But Hungary still had to be reconquered. Goaded into resistance by the return to Hapsburg absolutism, the Magyar gentry proclaimed their country a republic, with Kossuth as its president. Austrian military power alone could not defeat the rebels, so, in June 1849, Francis Joseph finally accepted the offer of Tsar Nicholas of Russia to send an army of 100,000 men into Hungary from the east, while a new Austrian army attacked again from the west. At the same time, the Magyars faced revolutionary movements among the Serbs in the south and the Rumanians in Transylvania. They could not hold out for long against such odds. By August 1849 the last Magyar resistance collapsed, and Kossuth joined the many exiles of the revolutions of 1848.

### The Course of the Revolution in Italy

Meanwhile, the revolutionary movement in Italy went its separate way to military defeat. In the south King Ferdinand had destroyed the revolution in Naples in May 1848 and altered the spirit of his "irrevocable" constitution. A year later he overran Sicily and restored his power there. Pope Pius IX had also disregarded his promise to rule as a constitutional monarch. This action prompted a revolution in Rome, which forced the pope to take refuge in Neapolitan territory in November. For the first three months of 1849, Rome was a republic. Mazzini, for the first and last time in his life, held political power as its virtual dictator.

In Rome it was the French, rather than the Austrians, who intervened. They met with considerable resistance from improvised forces led by Giuseppe Garibaldi (1807–1882), a veteran of several earlier revolutions in Italy and South America. Only in July did the French finally crush Garibaldi's forces and restore Rome to the pope, along with a permanent French garrison to protect him.

Elsewhere in Italy the Austrians did more than their share in suppressing the revolutionary movement. In March 1849 they defeated Charles Albert of Piedmont a second time at the battle of Novara. After this defeat, Charles Albert abdicated in favor of his son Victor Emmanuel II (1849–1878). Piedmont retained her constitution, but henceforth it was clear that she could not drive the Austrians out of

Italy without foreign help. In May 1849 the Austrians occupied the Duchies in north central Italy and restored Grand Duke Leopold to his throne. Finally, in August, they overthrew the Venetian republic, which had lasted since March 1848. With the French in Rome and the Austrians in Lombardy, Venetia, Tuscany, and Modena, Italy became occupied territory more than ever.

### Significance of 1848

The Revolution of 1848 was an explosion of liberal nationalism—along with democratic and socialist sputterings—which missed its mark. It failed partly because of divisions among the revolutionary forces and partly because of the political ineptitude of its leaders. But it failed mainly because the conservatives were able to use the armies of the great powers to annihilate it. The Prussian army put down uprisings all over Germany. The Austrian army destroyed the revolutionary movements everywhere within the empire except Hungary. There the Russian army finished the job. In France too, Cavaignac and Louis Napoleon used the army to suppress all opposition. Finally, the Austrian and French armies restored the old order in Italy.

The attitude of the peasants was crucial, for they constituted the majority of the population and the bulk of the soldiers everywhere. In France they opposed the revolution from the beginning; in the Austrian Empire they lost interest in it after the abolition of the *robot.* Even in Germany and Italy, where some of them had at first hoped to improve their economic situation, most of the peasants remained obedient to the traditional authorities.

Still, despite its failures, the Revolution of 1848 changed the course of European history. By ending the vestiges of serfdom in Central Europe, it paved the way for industrial capitalism there as well as in the West. Nor were the goals of liberalism and nationalism permanently lost. In the 1850s and 1860s professional politicians were to succeed where the poets and professors of 1848 had failed. They were to unify Italy and Germany and make France more liberal; for the Revolution of 1848 showed that conservatives had nothing to fear from universal suffrage and that they could use popular nationalism for their own ends.

## NATIONAL CONSOLIDATION AND MATERIAL PROGRESS IN WESTERN EUROPE AND NORTH AMERICA

In Great Britain and France the nation-state was already the supreme authority, and the ties between government and governed were being strengthened through new methods of administration and social organization and through the promotion of material progress. Along with Great Britain the smaller constitutional monarchies of Northwestern Europe slowly gave their citizens a greater feeling of participation in national life through representative institutions. The Second Empire in France provided an alternative model for the modern nation-state. This model was to be widely adopted later in Latin America and, ironically, in the new nation-state that came into being with the Second Empire's defeat—namely, imperial Germany.

National consolidation and economic growth were not confined to Europe alone. In the 1860s the United States and Canada also acquired the structural framework of an emerging industrial civilization. Even remote Japan began to build railroads, telegraph lines, and steamship companies and to set up a strong central government inspired by European models.* These developments had important consequences for the history of Europe. The United States and Japan were soon to join the ranks of the great European powers; the Canadian method of national consolidation was ultimately to be extended to the bulk of the British Empire.

### Mid-Victorian Britain

From 1846 to 1867 the aristocracy and the wealthy businessmen of Great Britain shared power under what is sometimes

*See Chapter xv.

called the Victorian Compromise. During this period, Britain's ruling elites were more intersted in money-making and world power than in domestic reform. They ran the country and the Empire for the good of the nation, but they maintained the gulf between the masses and themselves. Although the aristocrats had a tradition of paternalsim toward the rural masses, they joined the businessmen in trying to avoid helping the "dangerous" urban classes during this period. Only in 1867 did the maverick Conservative leader Benjamin Disraeli (1804–1881) conceive the idea of an alliance between the aristocracy and the working classes against the bourgeoisie. Only in 1868 did a new kind of Liberal leader, William Ewart Gladstone (1809–1898), try to narrow the gulf between the ruling elites and the rest of the nation. Meanwhile, the Liberal party dominated British life during much of the 1850s and 1860s under its aristocratic leader Lord Palmerston (1784–1865). Its ideology remained that of laissez faire: every man (who matters) knows what is best for himself and can develop his talents and interests best with the least possible interference from the state.

Under the Victorian Compromise British political life remained the preserve of a privileged elite. This elite included the members of both houses of Parliament, as well as the Church of England, the high-ranking civilian and military officials, and, of course, the Crown. In the 1850s Queen Victoria insisted on playing an active role in foreign policy. She was even able to force Palmerston's dismissal in December 1851, when he arbitrarily approved Louis Napoleon's *coup d'état* in France. The Crown lost some of its popularity and influence when the queen withdrew from public life in 1861 after the death of her beloved husband, Prince Albert. Although the force of public opinion became more powerful and active, and party cohesion in Parliament continued to grow, these two developments remained disjointed from each other until the Reform Bill of 1867 brought them together.

This Second Reform Bill doubled the British electorate. By lowering the tax and rental qualifications it extended the vote from 1,000,000 to 2,000,000 male adults (a third of the total), including many skilled urban workers. Ironically, a Conservative government headed by Disraeli finally pushed this ill through Parliament, only to be ousted in the first election held under the new franchise. But henceforth both the Conservatives and the Liberals tried to strike their roots among the new mass of voters.

Gladstone inaugurated a new era in British political life in his first ministry (1868–1874). His reforms were designed to strengthen the cohesion between the state and society, just as the extension of the franchise tied the political parties closer to the people. The Forster Education Act of 1870 established a national system of primary education to meet the needs of an industrial age; a year later the legal status of the emerging craft unions was confirmed (the first of these, the Amalgamated Society of Engineers, had been founded in 1851); in 1872 the ballot was at last made secret; and the Judicature Act of 1873 made the law courts more responsive to modern needs. Other reforms effected liberal changes in the army, the civil service, and the universities. All these reforms were aimed at reducing privilege and at giving all men of talent an equal opportunity to pursue careers in Britain's great public institutions.

### The Second Empire in France

Despite the opportunism of his methods, Louis Napoleon seems to have had three long-term goals: to give France a modern industrial economy of the kind he had seen in England, which would raise the material level of living of her urban and rural masses; to use this industrial base to restore French political influence in Europe and the world; and to realize these first two goals through an imperial dictatorship supported by universal suffrage.

From the beginning Napoleon III tried to make his centralized despotism seem legitimate in three ways. He used universal male suffrage in his plebiscites and in the elections to the Legislative Body; in this way he gave the masses a feeling of participation in the nation's political life, while reserving the real power for himself. He also maintained the shadow of parliamentary government in the form of packed assemblies. The government prefects did their best to influence the elections for the Legislative Body, while he himself appointed the members of the Senate for life. Actually, the Legislative Body had little real power, since cabinet ministers were responsible only to the emperor, and the main duty of the Senate was to see that legislation did not conflict with the constitution. The third way in which Napoleon III tried to gain mass approval for his centralized despotism was to give France policies that he thought would be both popular and beneficial to the nation.

In the 1860s, the government of the Second Empire gradually became more liberal. Parliament regained its power to question cabinet ministers; freedom of the press was restored; a political opposition was allowed to develop inside and outside of Parliament; the cabinets of the late 1860s even included some ex-republicans and ex-Orleanists. In May 1870 Napoleon III set forth a new constitution that gave Parliament the right to initiate legislation, as well as to amend bills proposed by the government. Over 7,000,000 Frenchmen voted "*oui*" to this constitution in Napoleon III's last plebiscite.

There are several possible explanations for the liberalization of the Empire in the 1860s. One is that Napoleon III's mistakes in foreign policy forced him to grant concessions at home. Another is that he sincerely wanted to reconcile the conflicting traditions inherited from France's past and adapt them to the needs of an industrial society. Still another explanation is that Napoleon III was a mere opportunist trying to stay in power by whatever means he judged convenient. Each of these explanations has some validity. But, despite the political concessions and personal favors proffered them, many prominent Frenchmen never accepted Napoleon III's upstart regime. Consequently, he was less successful than Disraeli and Bismarck in combining aristocracy with democracy. France had a livelier democratic tradition than Great Britain or Germany, but in these countries the elites did not question the legitimacy of the regime.

Plebiscites install dictators, not dynasties. One of the main weaknesses of the Second Empire was its lack of legitimacy, notwithstanding the emperor's efforts to give it all the trappings of a traditional monarchy. Unlike his uncle, who had been able to marry a Hapsburg archduchess, Napoleon III had to settle for a Spanish countess, Eugénie de Montijo. She was beautiful, but she was not *royal.* Their court at the Tuileries, though more luxurious and showy than that of Vienna, St. Petersburg, Berlin, or London, was largely shunned by the old aristocracy. Empress Eugénie set the fashions for France and all of Europe, and every major ruler except the Tsar Nicholas I called the emperor "my dear brother." Yet the monarchs of Europe and the elites in France never forgot that Napoleon III was a usurper.

Despite the handicap of its illegitimacy the Second Empire was not only popular with the French masses, it also brought them notable economic and social advantages. Napoleon III was really miscast. Because he *was* a Bonaparte, he had to play the role of the "man on horseback." But, unlike his uncle, he had no talent for military affairs. He was not even a particularly shrewd diplomat, as we shall soon see. More than anything else he wanted to be known as the chief engineer of economic and social progress. In this role he resembled a Saint-Simon, more than a Napoleon I – "on horseback."

### Economic Expansion

With Napoleon III's active encouragement, France began the most rapid economic expansion in her history. In 1852 the imperial government met the need for banking institutions that would make long-term investments in new productive enterprises by granting charters to two joint-stock deposit banks:* the *Crédit Mobilier* and the *Crédit Foncier.* The *Crédit Mobilier* financed railways, shipping companies, and new mining and metallurgical enterprises. The *Crédit Foncier* put its funds into mortgages on land, especially in Paris, though it was less active in the other role it was supposed to play, namely, making long-term loans for the im-

*See Chapter XIII.

*The modernization of Paris: a new boulevard*

provement of agricultural production. In the 1860s two larger and more permanent deposit banks, the *Crédit Lyonnais* and the *Société Générale*, received their charters. Napoleon III also sanctioned the formation of limited liability corporations in 1867. One of these completed the construction of the Suez Canal two years later.

In addition to encouraging private enterprise, Napoleon III fostered vast public works projects. One of his prefects, Baron Haussmann, made Paris the most modern capital in Europe, with wide boulevards,* gas lighting, a vast network of underground sewers, and spacious railroad stations. These and other projects stimulated the economy as a whole and gave the masses the feeling that the government was doing something for them. They had the added advantage of not being built at the expense of the taxpayers; they were financed by government-backed corporations in which people were glad to invest their money.

Indeed, the Second Empire was a speculator's paradise. People made fortunes on the stock exchange (though many small investors lost their savings when the *Crédit Mobilier* collapsed in 1867). In imitation of the lavish imperial court, bourgeois ladies, *demi-mondaines* ("half-ladies"), and businessmen dressed and lived ostentatiously. More than ever before, money was king.

Napoleon III also tried to pose as the champion of the new industrial workers, even to the point of calling himself a socialist. His only concrete reform on the workers' behalf was his legalization of the right to strike in 1864. But he promised them their just share in the general economic progress, and the building boom during much of his reign did alleviate the problem of unemployment.

In his catering to the workers, as in everything else, Napoleon III was part

*There was a political as well as an economic and an aesthetic motive for building these boulevards. In the past, Parisian revolutionaries had been able to barricade themselves in narrow streets, inaccessible to attacking cavalry troops. The boulevards ended this danger.

opportunist and part dreamer. He sincerely wanted to reconcile liberty and authority, to promote the welfare of the nation, and to rule with the support of the masses. All these goals were part of the Bonapartist dream. Above all, however, *this* Bonaparte wanted to stay in power and to pass on the imperial crown to his son. He tried to achieve this goal by being all things to all men, but by the late 1860s, in failing health and exercising poor judgment, he lost his political touch. As we shall see in the next section, he was soon to blunder into a disastrous war with Prussia, a war that ended his power as well as his dreams.

Although the Second Empire helped France through a rapid process of industrialization with a minimum of hardship, it had unfortunate political consequences. It deepened the fear of a strong ruler among French republicans and liberals, and it reinforced the general French suspicion of all governments. By 1870 the Second Empire came closer to being a liberal parliamentary regime than either the Bourbon or Orleanist monarchies had been, and it certainly had the backing of the majority of the population. If it had lasted, the emperor's new liberal supporters might have been able to convert him into behaving like a British monarch, subordinate to Parliament's wishes. But the fact that it went down in the wake of a military defeat seemed to show its major weakness as the character of Napoleon III himself. When a ruler of doubtful legitimacy loses a war, everything about him comes up for criticism. People remember his dictatorial side more than his economic and social accomplishments. This was to happen in France in the 1870s, when the Third Republic was shaped in an atmosphere of violent revulsion against everything the Second Empire stood for.

Yet with all its shortcomings the Second Empire set the pattern of the modern national state as a community and a power. This pattern developed on the continent under the guidance of strong rulers, rather than idealistic intellectuals. These rulers also learned to get popular support for their policies. What Napoleon III did in France, Cavour and Bismarck were to do in Italy and Germany. They too were to emphasize material progress over political freedom; they too were to consolidate national unity and state power through wars—at Napoleon III's expense.

### Canada

In contrast to that of Germany, Italy, and the United States, the consolidation of the Canadian nation took place without serious warfare. Yet it required the solution of two delicate sets of relationships: between the English- and French-speaking inhabitants of Canada itself, and between the Canadians and the British Crown.

In the early nineteenth century British North America consisted of a number of provinces unconnected with one another. In Lower Canada (Quebec) French civil law, the French language, and the French Catholic Church were protected by the British Crown. Upper Canada (Ontario) was settled by the descendants of the United Empire Loyalists who had fled from the United States during the American Revolution. Thereafter, a continuous stream of working-class immigrants from Great Britain flowed to both Lower and Upper Canada. The Maritime Provinces, Newfoundland, and Labrador were governed separately from London, and the Hudson Bay Company controlled the vast area from Lake Winnipeg to the Rockies.

In addition to territorial disunity, friction developed between the French majority and the growing British minority in Lower Canada and between the original United Empire Loyalists and the newer British immigrants in Upper Canada. In 1837 both provinces rebelled against the London government. The rebellion was put down with almost no bloodshed, but it prompted the reforming Whigs in England to find a new colonial policy.

In 1838 the Whig government appointed Lord Durham Governor-General of all British North America, and he published his recommendations a year later. His Report has ever since been regarded as the charter of British Commonwealth development. It recommended the reunion of Upper and Lower Canada as the nucleus for a future federation of all the British territories in North America. It also recommended making the executive authorities of the provinces directly responsible to their legislative assemblies instead of to the London government, which was to control only external affairs. Most of Lord Durham's Report was quickly accepted. In 1840 Lower and Upper Canada were united, and the British army was withdrawn. Henceforth, the Canadians moved slowly but steadily from discontent and disunity to self-government and national cohesion.

Canada acquired the political framework of responsible self-government in 1867. In that year the Canadians themselves drafted their own federal constitution, which the British Parliament passed as the British North America Act. This Act established the Dominion of Canada with its own Parliament and its own cabinet. After 1867 the Dominion was to move slowly forward from independence in internal affairs to independence in such external matters as diplomacy, tariffs, and decisions on war and peace.

The development of national cohesion also proceeded slowly. French- and English-speaking Canadians learned to work together, if not to like each other. The Dominion took over the territories of the Hudson's Bay Company in 1869 and from them created the provinces of Manitoba in 1870 and British Columbia in 1871. The Canadian Pacific Railway, the vital link between the western and eastern provinces encountered many obstacles; not until 1885 did the first train run from Montreal to the Pacific Coast. As in the United States, the railroad made possible the development of the prairies, and the provinces of Saskatchewan and Alberta were added to the Dominion in 1905.* And, like the United States, Canada eventually became a highly industrialized country.

The Canadian approach to national consolidation and responsible government was ultimately adopted in other parts of the British Empire. Australia acquired Dominion status in 1901, New Zealand in 1907, and the Union of South Africa in 1910. A half-century later, it was finally extended to non-European peoples in Great Britain's former colonies in Asia and Africa.

*Eventually, all the other territories of British North America became provinces of Canada. Newfoundland was the last to join, in 1949.

### United States

In the history of the United States the Civil War (1861–1865) is the great pivotal event. It destroyed slavery, it assured the triumph of industrialization and finance capitalism, it preserved the Union, and it stabilized—if it did not indeed create—the modern American nation. The alignment of forces was different from that in the wars of unification in Germany and Italy. In the United States the ideals of nationalism and democracy were fused, and the force that resisted national consolidation was sectionalism within the existing federal union.

By 1860 the United States had vastly expanded its original territory and experienced rapid economic and population growth. In 1790 the original seaboard states had a population of 4 million people; in 1860 the country stretched to the Pacific Ocean and had 31 million. In the 1840s American nationalism had become extremely vocal in the struggle to acquire the Pacific Northwest from Great Britain, and especially in the war against Mexico, as a result of which the United States annexed Texas, New Mexico, and California. The United States began building its railroad and telegraph networks, and the Northeastern states entered the first stage of industrialization.

Yet by 1860 the emerging American nation as falling to pieces. The South had developed a sense of sectionalism not unlike the nationalism felt by many peoples in Europe. This section of the country was controlled by a minority of white planters, and its economy depended on slave labor. For several decades Southern leaders had wondered if they could maintain their way of life in the Union their ancestors had helped to create. The situation came to a head in 1860 with the election of a Republican president, Abraham Lincoln (1809–1865). Although Lincoln himself belonged to the moderate wing of the new party, the more extreme Republicans favored policies that catered almost exclusively to Northern interests: free Western lands for small farmers, a higher tariff, transcontinental railroad building, a central bank of issue in place of state banks, and, above all, the abolition of slavery. Hence in early 1861 the Southern leaders solemnly withdrew their states from the Union and organized them into a new independent nation, the Confederate States of America, reaching from Virginia to Texas. President Lincoln ordered the armed forces to defend the territory of the United States, and the Civil War, or War for Southern Independence, began.

The war itself falls outside the scope of this book. Suffice it to say that it was fought with the same new military techniques as the wars in Europe and that it lasted far longer and was far bloodier than any European war between 1815 and 1914. Here we are concerned with its effect on the national consolidation of the United States. Although the immediate question was whether the Union could win, the more fundamental question was whether victory could restore an American nation.

Throughout the fighting, President Lincoln tried to make the preservation of the Union the grand object and to infuse the ideology of American nationalism with a broadly democratic philosophy. He waited until he was convinced that "slavery must die that the nation might live" before issuing the Emancipation Proclamation* on January 1, 1863. Lincoln based his defense of the Union not upon the exaltation of the American state, but upon the universal cause of democracy. In his Gettysburg Address he did not use the word "American;" he spoke of the Civil War as a test of whether *any* nation "conceived in liberty and dedicated to the proposition that all men are created equal" could long endure.

Lincoln did not live to see the restoration of the Union based on voluntary loyalty. His assassination soon after the Northern victory allowed the Republican extremists to take their vengeance on the South in the period of Reconstruction. Twelve years after Lincoln's death the spirit of American nationalism seemed weaker than at the beginning of the war. Military victory had restored political unity, but the restoration of the bonds of national cohesion required a longer social process, a kind of folk reconstruction. Only gradually did the white Southerners develop an emotional longing for reconciliation with the North. This longing expressed itself in many ways, such as the poem of Francis Miles Finch honoring both "The Blue and the Gray" in 1867; the funeral of General Grant, at which former Southern generals served as pallbearers in 1885; and the rush of Southern volunteers to serve under the flag of the Union during the Spanish-American War in 1898. On the other hand, Americans of African descent gained little from the restoration of political unity. Although legally free, the majority of them remained poor and segregated in the South. The true emancipation of America's black citizens made little headway for almost another hundred years; it is still going on.

Meanwhile, the United States moved forward to become a great industrial power. In 1869 the first railroad to span the American continent was completed. As in Western Europe, finance capitalism and large corporations triumphed after 1870. Factories and mines boomed; cities grew; a mass market for goods was created. And, as in the France of Napoleon III, newly rich businessmen built pretentious mansions and set the tone for bourgeois capitalist society in its most flamboyant age.

*This proclamation did not interfere with slavery in the loyal slave states of Delaware, Maryland, Kentucky, and Missouri. Not until December 1865 did the Thirteenth Amendment abolish slavery throughout the restored Union.

## NATION-BUILDING IN CENTRAL EUROPE AND THE EMERGENCE OF A NEW BALANCE OF POWER

Between the mid-1850s and 1870 the map of Central Europe was radically changed. War and diplomacy succeeded in doing what revolution had failed to do; they created two new national states, Germany and Italy, and profoundly altered the structure of Austria. In the process, the character of war and diplomacy changed considerably too. By 1870 a new and much more precarious balance of power had replaced the one that had lasted from

1815 to 1854. The turning point was the Crimean War.

### New Trends in War and Diplomacy. The Crimean War

The Crimean War (1854–1856), the first major war since 1815, involved Russia on one side and Turkey, Great Britain, and France on the other. Russia had fought Turkey many times before, but this was the first time in the nineteenth century that Great Britain and France tried to stop her. Although the dispute began as a test of prestige between France and Russia over control of the Holy Sanctuaries in Palestine, the main issues were Russian attempts to control the Turkish government and British fears of Russian expansion in the eastern Mediterranean. Finally, in 1854, Great Britain and France decided to join the Turks in their war against Russia in order to preserve the balance of power in the Near East.

Despite blunders on both sides, the Russians experienced a humiliating defeat on their own soil in the Crimean War. The Treaty of Paris (1856) made them give up their influence in Wallachia and Moldavia (which were united into the new principality of Rumania in 1862) and their control of the mouths of the Danube and forbade them to have a navy in the Black Sea. Even more serious was Russia's loss of international prestige. From the time of Catherine the Great, Russia had expanded steadily westward, and by 1815 she had become the strongest and most feared power on the continent. Then the reactionary regime of Nicholas I had isolated itself from the new technological developments in the West. It paid the price in the Crimean Peninsula. There, Great Britain and France had landed and supplied over 150,000 men, thanks to their new steamships. As a result, the Colossus of the East suffered its most disastrous defeat in over one hundred and fifty years.

The Crimean War had shown that Russia was no longer interested in preserving the balance of power she had helped to establish in 1815; it also made the other powers change their attitude toward the existing distribution of forces on the continent. As one historian has written: "There remained in 1857 no great political force irretrievably committed to the preservation of things as they stood."* Russia was now willing to consider agreements with other revisionist powers that might promise to support her Black Sea claims if she would not interfere with their designs elsewhere. The existing balance of power was also jeopardized by Great Britain's growing tendency to withdraw from continental troubles.

A new fluidity and a new "realism" marked the relations among the powers after the Crimean War. In the period before 1854, alliances and diplomatic alignments had been generally defensive. They had been concluded to protect the partners from the threat of such things as revolution or an attempt by another power or group of powers to extend its influence in such a way as to disrupt the existing balance. After 1856, alliances and diplomatic "understandings" were generally concluded for an aggressive purpose. Sometimes they tried to secure the collaboration of the partners for a projected war against a third party; sometimes they tried to facilitate the designs of one of the partners by assuring him of the benevolent neutrality of the other.

In the 1850s and 1860s the most successful exponents of the new techniques of power politics were Cavour in Italy and Bismarck in Germany. They used the currents of economic change to the greatest advantage, and they exploited the new fluidity and "realism" in diplomacy to the fullest. Both men were hard-headed statesmen, not idealistic nationalists; their primary goal was always to increase the power and prestige of the monarchs they served. In pursuing this goal they added two new powers to the European state system.

### Cavour and the Unification of Italy

In the 1850s the task of building a united Italy fell to the Kingdom of Piedmont (Sardinia) and its prime minister, Cavour. The prophets of republicanism had driv-

*R. C. Binkley, *Realism and Nationalism 1852–1871*, New York, 1935, p. 179.

en the prophets of a united Italy under the pope into extreme reaction after 1849. Henceforth, all the partisans of unification were anticlericals. They continued to conspire, but Cavour would have nothing to do with them—at least publicly. He was ready to champion the idea of unity only when public opinion was ready for it and only if it did not compromise the interests of Piedmont or the monarchy. Meanwhile, he needed Mazzini in the opposition in order to frighten the conservatives at home and abroad into aiding his own more orthodox brand of revolution.

For Cavour the *Risorgimento* was not simply a revolt against foreign oppression, but an internal revolution designed to introduce economic, political, and civil liberty. He wanted to bring this revolution to Piedmont first. Only in this way would she become unquestionably and for the first time the leading state of the Italian Peninsula. Then Cavour could convince the rest of Europe that Italians, under Piedmontese leadership, were able to govern themselves without Austrian tutelage.

In background and temperament Cavour was quite different from Mazzini, whose role in the making of Italy he usurped during his eight years as prime minister (1852–1859, 1860–1861). Cavour too had edited a newspaper and traveled widely in England, France and Switzerland, but he had concentrated on learning advanced western methods in agriculture, industry, and parliamentary government. By 1850 he had made a fortune out of applying modern scientific methods and mechanization to the farming of his family estates; he had also become a director of the Bank of Turin and the Turin-Genoa railway. He was a rationalist in religion and a liberal conservative in politics. His belief in the separation of Church and state made him especially hateful to Pope Pius IX. Mazzini combined prophecy with conspiracy; Cavour combined skepticism with shrewd political and diplomatic maneuvering.

Cavour always claimed that his liberal ends justified his often illiberal means at home. He sincerely believed that "free institutions tend to make people richer."

Liberalism *paid*. But economic and social modernization under liberalism also had to be *paid for*. Cavour had to overcome considerable unpopularity for the taxes he levied to help build more railroads and a modern army and navy. He also had to contend with the opposition of the reactionary Piedmontese nobles and bishops. In order to achieve his goals in the face of these obstacles he set the tradition of taking action first and then asking Parliament for retrospective consent. He preferred to manipulate Parliament rather than abolish it, and to disarm opposition peacefully wherever possible. Yet he did not hesitate to bribe and suppress opposition newspapers, and he freely used the civil service to secure the election of government candidates to Parliament—another Italian political tradition about which we will learn more later. As one of his colleagues put it, Cavour was a cross between Robert Peel and Machiavelli.

### Cavour and Napoleon III

Cavour was even more unscrupulous in pursuing his goal of bringing all of northern Italy under Piedmontese control. The first step was the conquest of neighboring Lombardy from Austria. In order to manage this without the approval or knowledge of his cabinet, Cavour goaded the Austrian government into breaking off diplomatic relations with Piedmont and then hurried Napoleon III into war against Austria for Italy's benefit. In July 1858 he met the French emperor secretly at the resort town of Plombières, where he persuaded him to allow Victor Emmanuel to revive the old Napoleonic kingdom of northern Italy down as far as Bologna. He also promised to help the present Napoleon carve out a separate kingdom in central Italy for a member of his own family. In January 1859 a formal treaty confirmed the transfer of the Piedmontese territories of Nice and Savoy to France in compensation for French intervention in Italy.

The French kept their part of the bargain, up to a point. In June 1859 Napoleon III and his armies drove the Austrians out of most of Lombardy. Then, without consulting the Piedmontese, he suddenly concluded an armistice with Emperor Francis Joseph and temporarily abandoned his claim on Nice and Savoy. He had discovered that Cavour had surreptitiously sent agents to prepare the annexations of the Duchies of central Italy to Piedmont. This action violated the agreement at Plombières that these Duchies were to form a separate kingdom under Napoleon's cousin. The French withdrawal from the war had so compromised Cavour that he resigned temporarily as prime minister, even though the French had already won most of Lombardy for Piedmont. But Cavour returned to power in early 1860 and again offered Nice and Savoy to Napoleon if he would allow the annexation of Central Italy, now in open revolt, to Piedmont. Both Napoleon and Cavour quickly "arranged" plebiscites for their respective annexations. In the year ending with the spring of 1860, the Kingdom of Sardinia had more than doubled its size; and it now included almost half the population of Italy.

### Cavour and Garibaldi

Cavour still had no plans for unifying *all* of Italy. He hoped to consolidate his position in the north. Meanwhile, he would try to appear moderate and conservative, so that France might help him to win Venetia and, perhaps, finally withdraw her garrison from Rome. He had no designs on the Kingdom of the Two Sicilies and, in 1860, he continued to cultivate that state as an ally and an equal partner. The southern half of Italy belonged to the Bourbons, and Cavour had no desire to see another revolutionary insurrection against them.

But Cavour had not counted on Garibaldi. This famous revolutionary soldier had been leading guerrilla uprisings in Italy since the 1820s. Except in 1849* he had always failed not only because he had inadequate troops but also because he had very little popular support. In 1860 the situation was different, and Garibaldi at last played his great role in the unification of Italy.

In May 1860 Garibaldi and his Thousand Redshirts landed in Sicily. From their base in the Piedmontese city of Gen-

*See p. 438.

*Garibaldi with his troops fighting in the streets of Palermo (Sicily)*

oa they had originally hoped to land at nearby Nice (Garibaldi's home town) and prevent its transfer to France. Cavour managed to divert the expedition to Sicily, where he thought it would do less damage, but a widespread peasant's revolt was disrupting the Bourbon administration there and it helped to terrify a large army into surrender. Some Bourbon soldiers even joined the Redshirts. In less than two weeks Garibaldi set up a provisional government at Palermo. By late August he had crossed the Straits of Messina and was marching toward Naples, where many people were eagerly awaiting the great revolutionary liberator.

Cavour had to change his tactics quickly. First, he hoped to foment a more conservative insurrection in Naples as a means of forestalling Garibaldi. While still pretending to treat with the Bourbons, he had his agents bribe the more important generals and ministers. When Garibaldi arrived at Naples first, Cavour had to find a way to prevent him from moving northward against Rome and Venetia. Cavour engineered popular uprisings in the Papal States as a pretext for invading them in order to "save them from the revolution." He annexed most papal territory except the area around Rome and sent the Piedmontese army southward to head off Garibaldi. Despite his hostility toward Cavour, Garibaldi remained loyal to King Victor Emmanuel. Hence he allowed the Kingdom of Piedmont to annex all of southern Italy and retired temporarily from public life.

Almost before people could see what was happening, Cavour had in fact unified all of Italy except Venetia and Rome. He then held the usual rigged plebiscites to give his achievement popular sanction. The first Parliament of the Kingdom of Italy met in Turin in 1861. A new power of twenty million people had come into existence. It was more materialistic and less religious than Mazzini had wished it to be, and, like Garibaldi, though for different reasons, he was bitterly disillusioned. Other Italian nationalists were more grateful, but the mass of the population, especially the peasants in the south, were more interested in land and economic security than in "Italy."

Cavour did not live to see the annexation of Venice and Rome to the Kingdom of Italy. He died in June 1861 at the age of 52, but his successors followed his policy of exploiting European wars (these were initiated by Prussia in her effort to gain control over the bulk of Germany) to acquire new territories in Italy. Prussia's war against Austria in 1866 gave Italy Venetia; her war against France in 1870 gave Italy Rome.

## Bismarck and the Unification of Germany

In Prussia, as in Piedmont, the political climate of the 1850s remained obstinately conservative and provincial and held out little hope for German unification. Like Piedmont, Prussia also experienced rapid economic development in this period. The railway network was developed and completed; coal production rose; the urban population increased in the industrial areas of the Ruhr and Silesia. And even more than in Piedmont, the liberals in Prussia sacrificed their lofty principles to the needs of *Realpolitik.*

The word *Realpolitik* (political realism) first came into the thinking of Prussian liberals in 1853 through an anonymous pamphlet called "Foundations of Political Realism." According to this pamphlet, "To be sovereign means to exercise power, and only he who possesses power can exercise it. This direct connection between power and sovereignty is the fundamental truth and the key to the whole of history." The pamphlet went on to advocate a strong united German national state as the ultimate embodiment of this kind of power. This conception of political realism produced the National Liberalism of the 1860s and enthusiastic support for the forcible unification of Germany under Prussian leadership.

Prince Otto von Bismarck (1815–1898) was to dominate Prussian and German politics and European diplomacy for almost thirty years. We shall examine his career from 1870 to 1890 in later chapters; here we are concerned with his predominant role in the Prussian constitutional conflict and the German national struggle between 1862 and 1870. He expressed his views on both in his first speech as Prussia's Minister-President in September 1862:

> "Germany is not looking at Prussia's liberalism, but at her power. . . . Prussia must preserve her power for the favorable moment, which has already several times been passed. Prussia's frontiers are not suited to a healthy national life. The great questions of our time will not be decided by speeches and majority decisions—that was the mistake of 1848–49—but by Blood and Iron."

The meaning of *Realpolitik* could not have been put more clearly.

What kind of man was this, the most successful exponent of *Realpolitik* in the nineteenth century? Bismarck came to power at the age of 47, after having served as Prussion ambassador to the Diet of the German Confederation (1851–1859), to the court of the Russian tsar (1859–1862), and to France (1862). He was a man of great physical vigor and penetrating intelligence, and despite his gruff exterior he could exercise real charm when he chose to do so. In his youth he had seemed like just another bigoted Prussian Junker, devoted to his estates and contemptuous of the landless middle classes of the cities. He never lost this outlook completely. But once in power, he did not hesitate to override the interests of the reactionary aristocrats when they interfered with his wider aims. The same was true of his Protestant religious beliefs. They were strong, but he did not allow them to influence the morality of his public conduct. Like Machiavelli (and Cavour), Bismarck believed that private and public life were two distinct worlds, with different standards of behavior. Yet he was not a mere free-wheeling opportunist. Throughout his life Bismarck remained a loyal servant of the Prussian monarchy. Everything he did—every act of political intrigue and diplomatic duplicity—was calculated to increase its power and prestige.

From the beginning, Bismarck exploited his successes in war and diplomacy to reinforce the power of the monarchy in the face of liberal demands for parliamentary rule at home.

The Prussian constitutional crisis had begun in 1860, when the liberals opposed the army reforms put forth by the new war minister, General Albrecht von Roon. He wanted to increase the term of military service for enlisted men to three years and to incorporate the officers of the middle-class Reserve Army into the professional officer corps. The liberals hoped to block these reforms by refusing to vote appropriations for them in the Prussian Parliament. If they could win this test, they then hoped to assert the authority of Parliament over all other functions of government as well. This constitutional crisis reached its height when Bismarck became minister-president in September 1862. A few months later he told Parliament that he would get the money without its consent, taking advantage of a provision of the constitution which said that taxes once voted continued to be levied until actually repealed by Parliament. For the next four years he governed Prussia in defiance of Parliament and in violation of the constitution. Meanwhile, he weakened his parliamentary opposition by winning over some liberals to the feeling that Prussian leadership alone could achieve German national unity. As in Great Britain, the success of government policy depended on such a liberal-aristocratic compromise.

### *Bismarck's Contest with Austria*

By early 1866 Bismarck's minimum goal was to break up the German Confederation, in which Austria had always claimed to be the paramount power, and to set up a Prussian-controlled north German federation. The southern German states would then be left "floating" between it and a predominantly non-German Austrian Empire; Bismarck would deal with them later, as soon as a suitable opportunity arose.

All through the 1860s Bismarck pursued his program by combining appeals to German nationalism with brilliant diplomatic and military victories for Prussia. First he induced Austria to join him in a brief and successful war against Denmark for the provinces of Schleswig and Holstein. All German nationalists resented the attachment of these two territories to the Danish Crown. A convenient excuse for seizing them had occurred in 1863, when a new Danish king tried to eliminate their special privileges and virtually to annex Schleswig. Bismarck wanted a war that would involve Austria in a joint occupation of the two provinces, an arrangement that would leave ample room for a quarrel with her later. He also wanted to try out his new army and to raise Prussia's prestige among the German nationalists. Hence, in February 1864, he sent a Prussian-Austrian army against Denmark and won a quick and inexpensive victory. Prussia occupied Schleswig, and Austria occupied Holstein, but the two powers were uneasy partners, and Bismarck was already setting the diplomatic stage for his war against Austria.

Bismarck managed to prevent France, Great Britain, and Russia from interfering in this second war as successfully as he had in the first. Although Palmerston blustered, the British remained neutral. Bismarck had won the friendship of Russia in 1863 by backing her during a Polish insurrection; thereafter, he could continue to count on her benevolent neutrality toward his ambitions in Germany. As for Napoleon III, Bismarck simply gambled that he would be unable to decide which side to support and would thus remain inactive. The French emperor, hoping somehow to gain something—perhaps Italian friendship—persuaded Austria to cede Venetia to Italy through him in return for his neutrality. This cloudy scheme played right into Bismarck's hands, for the Prussian chancellor wanted Italy as an ally. He signed an alliance with her, and it was his forthcoming military victory, not Napoleon III's cheap diplomacy, that gave her Venetia.

The Austro-Prussian War settled the struggle for supremacy in Germany. In reality this was a civil war in which, as in the American Civil War, the key issue was states' rights. A majority of the territorial sovereigns in the German Confederation sided with Austria, for in their eyes an increase in the power of Prussia was synonymous with a reorganization of Germany along centralized lines. Unlike the American Civil War, however, the Austro-Prussian War was short and relatively bloodless. It began in June 1866, and within three weeks Prussia defeated Austria and her German allies. The decisive battle took place at Sadowa (Königgrätz), in Bohemia, on July 3. Bismarck did not want to destroy Austria, nor did he want

the war to spread, so he ended it quickly and offered Austria fairly generous terms. Aside from Venetia she lost no territory, but she was henceforth excluded from German affairs. Prussia now became the dominant power in Germany. She annexed Hanover, Hesse-Cassel, Schleswig-Holstein, and the free city of Frankfurt. Bismarck then forced all the other states in the northern two-thirds of Germany to join his projected North German Confederation and brought the southern German states into alliances that placed their armies under Prussian command in the event of a foreign war.

### The North German Confederation

Bismarck not only settled the pattern of German unification, he also ended the constitutional struggle in Prussia. Many liberals who were unwilling to oppose the victor of Sadowa joined the majority of the Prussian Parliament in adopting a bill of indemnity legalizing all Bismarck's violations of the constitution over the past four years. In this way they sacrificed their liberal ideals for something even more precious—a German national state.

In 1867 this state, the North German Confederation, received its constitution, which was adapted, with little change, to the needs of the German Empire four years later. It was federal in structure. The member states retained their monarchs and administrations and were represented in a federal council called the Bundesrat. Here Prussia predominated. This predominance remained conservative because the differential voting system* in Prussia's lower house favored the wealthy classes and kept Prussian politics conservative. The second federal assembly, the Reichstag, represented people, not states, and it was "elected by universal and direct election with secret voting." This was indeed a democratic innovation. But, at first, the Reichstag had less power than the Bundesrat, and most important, the federal chancellor—Bismarck, of course—and his ministers were not responsible to either assembly. The constitution simply said he was "responsible," but not to whom; in practice he and his successors were to be responsible to the monarch alone. Thus, Bismarck and his ministers headed a central government and administration that was to become increasingly stronger than both the federal Parliament and the local administrations of the states. From the very beginning the armed forces of all the member states were under its control, and Bismarck already exerted considerable influence in most of the southern states.

Bismarck now set the stage for his third and last war, this time with France. He wanted to use this war to incorporate the southern German states into the North German Confederation and thereby complete the unification of Germany under Prussia. His plan was to goad France into declaring war. In such an event the southern German states would be obliged (according to their alliance) to place their armies under Prussian command, and their subjects would be moved by a wave of national enthusiasm. Their subsequent inclusion in a new German Empire would then be easy.

### *The Franco-Prussian War*

In 1870 Bismarck's foreign policy triumphed over Napoleon III's. After the successes of the French emperor in the Crimean War and the war against Austria in 1859, he was no longer able to bolster the prestige of France and his own popularity with cheap military and diplomatic victories. During the 1860's his support of the pope in Rome alienated the Italians, while the failure of his Mexican adventure* weakened his position at home. As the showdown with Bismarck approached, Napoleon III, who was in poor health, left the direction of foreign policy increasingly to second-rate subordinates.

The diplomatic background of the Franco-Prussian war is too complex to examine in detail. All the major powers were concerned, but, in the end, France fought alone, and Prussia was joined by all of Germany. Bismarck succeeded in isolating France diplomatically by persuading the other powers that Napoleon III, not he, had imperialist designs. This was easy to do, since the French emperor did indeed have such designs, though he still thought he could satisfy them through old-fashioned diplomatic bargaining. Since many Frenchmen viewed Sadowa as an implicit defeat for their country, Napoleon III wanted some form of "compensation" on the left bank of the Rhine or in Belgium. Bismarck asked him to put these proposals in writing and then published them in 1870. In this way he turned the other powers against France. Then, at the last moment, he found a suitable pretext for war in, of all places, Spain.

The question of the succession to the Spanish throne was the immediate cause of the Franco-Prussian War. For over twenty years Queen Isabella II had scandalized her subjects with her flagrant love affairs and oppressed them with her reactionary rule. In 1868, her corrupt despotism broke down under the weight of its own inefficiency and under the attack of two military politicians. Isabella fled to France, and the two generals tried to set up a liberal constitutional monarchy. This

*See pp. 434–435.

*In 1863 Napoleon III tried to create a new overseas empire in Mexico by using the French army to install his own puppet emperor, the Hapsburg Archduke Maximilian. But after the end of the American Civil War, the United States government demanded the withdrawal of French troops, claiming that their presence in the Western Hemisphere violated the Monroe Doctrine. In 1866, Napoleon III unceremoniously abandoned Maximilian, who was quickly executed by Mexico's national hero, President Benito Juarez.

was an almost hopeless task, given Spain's economic and social backwardness and lack of a parliamentary tradition. Still, the country wanted a new monarch, and the search dragged on into the summer of 1870. Finally, at Bismarck's instigation, the Spanish crown was offered to a Catholic cousin of the Hohenzollern king of Prussia. France was horrified at the thought of a Hohenzollern on her southern border. On July 6 her foreign minister announced that unless the Hohenzollern candidate was withdrawn, France would treat the matter as a cause for war. The Prussian king did not want war, and he persuaded his cousin to withdraw. Bismarck was furious. *He* wanted war. Injured French pride and a fortuitious telegram gave it to him.

On July 13, 1870, Bismarck's agent sent him a telegram from Ems, a resort where King William was staying. It told how the French Ambassador, Count Vincent Benedetti, had pressed the Prussian king to promise never to let his cousin's candidature for the Spanish throne come up again. It also told how the king had said he could not make such a promise and how he had walked away. Bismarck edited the telegram to make it seem to say that Benedetti had discourteously pressed an unreasonable demand on William, and had been rebuffed with equal discourtesy. Then he made sure that his revised version was published. In both Paris and Berlin the Ems telegram, as it was called, was viewed as a national insult. With public passions thus aroused, both Bismarck and Napoleon III were ready to fight. Bismarck had succeeded brilliantly in making the French declare war, which they did on July 19.

Prussia and her German allies quickly defeated France.* On September 2, Napoleon III surrendered at the front, and two days later a Paris mob overthrew the Second Empire. The French nevertheless kept fighting the Germans for almost six more months. (We shall discuss the political changes in France in Chapter XIV.) On January 18, 1871, ten days before Paris capitulated, William I was proclaimed German Emperor† in the Hall of Mirrors at Versailles. This was France's greatest humiliation and Bismarck's greatest triumph.

Once on the winning side, the four south German states decided to stay there. Consequently Bismarck had little difficulty in persuading them to join the North German Confederation, now renamed the German Empire. Bismarck also annexed the provinces of Alsace and Lorraine, thus removing any future French threat on the Rhine. Apart from this fatal (as we shall see later) error, Bismarck had limited the territory of the new German Empire to what Prussia could conveniently digest.

The German Empire that Bismarck created clearly showed that he was a Prussian monarchist, not a German nationalist. A true German nationalist would have wanted to incorporate all the millions of Germans in Austria and Eastern Europe into one state, an idea Bismarck never dreamt of. He had made the Prussian monarchy the strongest power in Europe; that was as far as he wanted to go. He had no wish to unleash the nationalist passions in the Hapsburg Monarchy. Indeed, he was henceforth to seek to preserve that state as a bulwark of order in the rest of Central and Eastern Europe. Bismarck's unification of Germany by *Realpolitik* had created a new state dominated by Prussia. The German nation as a community and a power was thus able to come into being.

### Austria and the Compromise of 1867

Bismarck's military victories had crucial consequences for France, Italy, and Austria. In France they brought the collapse

*See pp. 456–457.

†King William I did not want to accept the title of "Emperor of Germany" because of its associations with what the German liberals had wanted in 1849. Bismarck therefore got the senior of the other German ruling houses, King Ludwig II of Bavaria, to invite the Prussian king to accept the alternative title "German Emperor" in their name. Bismarck did this by suggesting that a Bavarian king might someday be elected emperor and by giving Ludwig a large annual subsidy for building more fancy castles (one of the extravagances that soon earned him the title "Crazy Ludwig.") In this inelegant fashion the German Empire was founded.

of the Second Empire, the loss of Alsace-Lorraine, and the establishment of the Third Republic. Italy annexed Venetia after Sadowa and occupied Rome (September 20, 1870) after the French removed their garrison there during the Franco-Prussian War. Two weeks later Rome became the Italian capital, and the papacy's temporal power was ended. But Austria suffered the most crucial consequences of all.

In the Compromise of 1867 the Austrian Empire was transformed into a new hybrid state called Austria-Hungary. The Magyars had finally gained their independence in the wake of Sadowa. They still accepted Emperor Francis Joseph as their king and they agreed to cooperate with the Austrian government in matters of foreign affairs, defense, and finance. But Hungary was now governed by her own laws and free from any control by Austria over her internal affairs.

Unfortunately, the Compromise of 1867 did almost nothing for the peoples of Hungary and Austria who did not happen to be Magyars or Germans—and they were the majority. Only a federal structure could have held all these Czechs, Slovaks, Croats, Serbs, Rumanians, Poles, and Italians together permanently. The Austrian Germans had had enough difficulty trying to hold the empire together alone; now they divided the effort with the Magyars. The nationalities problem was to plague Austria-Hungary until her final collapse a half-century later.

The Compromise of 1867 was an ingenious effort to evade the principles of national unification and independence that triumphed in Germany and Italy. In their place it substituted the partition of territory and the division of political power between the German and Magyar ruling minorities. Cavour and Bismarck had created states that were designed to become nations; the state created by Hapsburg ingenuity was designed to do the opposite. Both efforts succeeded.

### The New Balance of Power and the Changing Nature of Warfare

After 1870 the European state system was much simpler than it had been in the past. There were now six major powers—Great Britain, Germany, France, Russia, Austria-Hungary, Italy—plus the smaller states of Western Europe. The new nation-states of Germany and Italy had swallowed up all the formerly independent kingdoms and principalities in Central Europe. Even the papacy lost the temporal power it had held for a thousand years. In Eastern Europe Serbia and Rumania had achieved self-rule within the Ottoman Empire, but, legally, the Turks were still sovereign everywhere in the Balkans except in Greece. Never before (or since) had the map of Europe been so uncluttered.

Yet never before had the existing situation been more open to change. Great Britain retained her industrial and commercial supremacy and remained the number-one power in the world for another generation. But while she tried to maintain her "splendid isolation" from the continent, Germany was to strengthen her position there considerably. In the 1870s Bismarck was to try to bring two of the weakened powers, Russia and Austria-Hungary, into a new diplomatic alignment against the third weakened power, France. Russia was soon to strike out on her own in the Balkans and to support new nationalist revolts against Turkish rule there, which were to endanger the precarious control of Austria-Hungary over her own subject nationalities and to make her increasingly the junior partner of the German Empire. Finally, France and Italy were to seek to strengthen their places in the existing system by adhering to new and unforeseen alliances: France with Russia, Italy with Austria-Hungary and Germany.

Power alone counted in the new age of *Realpolitik*, and the power of each state now had to be based on an advanced degree of industrialization and military technology. The wars of the 1850s and 1860s were the first to be fought with the new weapons and techniques of the Industrial Revolution. Strategically, the most important of the new inventions were the railroad, the steamship, and the telegraph, which made it possible to mobilize, supply, and command large masses of fighting men. Tactically, the breech-loading

*The Franco-Prussian War (1870)*

rifle enabled the infantry to delivery more fire at longer ranges. It outmoded the Napoleonic artillery tactic of smashing the enemy's tight formations beyond musket range, and it ended the old superiority of a lancer on horseback to a single man on foot with a blunderbuss. In the Crimean War, the range and accuracy of the rifle helped to develop an early version of trench warfare. Rows of rifle pits, each holding one man and covered in front by sandbags, were connected by trenches. Parts of these trenches gave shelter to continuous ranks of riflemen.

In the Franco-Prussian War the decisive factor was not the mere existence of railways, but the uses to which the Prussian General Staff put them. It made the timetable of mobilization, concentration, and the first moves of an offensive the center of its planning. France's railways were just as good as Germany's, but the French did not use them as efficiently. Their field armies had a larger number of professional soldiers than those of Prussia; perhaps this was why they neglected plans for the efficient mobilization of reservists. A French reservist was supposed to go to his regimental depot to be equipped and then catch up with his unit. One such French reservist reported in Strasbourg, was sent to Marseilles and then to Africa for his equipment, and finally joined his unit back in Strasbourg.

Moreover, the Prussian War Academy was creating a new breed of officers trained in the systematic application of general principles. Just as Roon reformed the organization of the Prussian army, so Helmut von Moltke tried to make it function with "scientific" precision. His generals and staff officers no longer depended on the old rules of thumb that had previously put the commanders of all European armies on a common level. French officers fought with great physical courage, but they could not adapt themselves as quickly to new situations as the Prussians, who were taught to have a coordinated plan for every eventuality.

In August 1870, having encircled Marshal Bazaine's army at Metz, Moltke assumed that the rest of the French army would retreat westward over the Moselle. He therefore allowed the German Third Army to move toward Paris, supposedly in pursuit of the main enemy force. But Napoleon, fearing the psychological effect of a strategic withdrawal, ordered Marshal MacMahon to push northeastward of the advancing Germans in an attempt to relieve Metz. The German Third Army now wheeled north on to the flank of MacMahon's army, which had already been headed off by part of the German forces moving on past the isolated French position at Metz. Trapped against the Belgian border, near Sedan, MacMahon's army was compelled to surrender on September 2, with 82,000 men. This was merely the most famous example of the flexibility of Prussian military thinking. The Prussian educational revolution changed the character of modern warfare as much as railways, steamships, and rifles.

Prussia's military successes were soon to make the other powers adopt another feature of the Prussian system: universal military training. As we have seen, Prussia had improvised an early version of this after her defeat at Jena in 1807. The idea was to train all able-bodied youths for a limited period—usually one to three years—and then put them on active reserve. In this way the peacetime army would have only a few hundred thousand men at any one time, but could be quickly expanded, with the efficient use of railways, when war came. In 1870 the combined German field armies were almost double those of the French, though the two countries were approximately equal in population and industrial production. Thereafter, France and all the major continental powers were to build up the same proportion of reserves to population as Germany through universal military training.

## RUSSIA

Russia's defeat in the Crimean War showed what could happen to a great power that did not keep up with advances in military technology and organization. It prompted the government and the ruling class to reexamine the country's economic and social structure, which had been "frozen" under the reactionary rule of Nicholas I. Clearly no state could hope to rank as a great power without becoming industrialized, and the growth of industry also demanded an abundant supply of free labor, thus requiring the abolition of serfdom.

But a traditional society and culture cannot simply "put on" the trappings of industrial power, like another new style of clothes. In a literal sense, *these* "clothes" transform the wearer. Russia's rulers wanted factories, railroads, a modern army and navy, a mobile labor force, and an efficient administrative and judicial system—in other words, the structural frame work of industrial civilization. At the same time, they wanted to maintain the old social and cultural barriers between the nobility and the peasants. They especially did not want a disorderly urban proletariat or aggressive capitalists.

In the long run this reluctance to accept the social and cultural consequences of industrialization was to cause the complete collapse of the Old Regime in Russia. Nevertheless, the more perceptive landowners were questioning the value of compulsory labor even before the process of industrialization began in earnest. Partly out of "liberal" conviction, but mainly out of economic interest, it was they themselves who encouraged the new tsar, Alexander II (1855–1881), to abolish serfdom.

### The Abolition of Serfdom

Several considerations prompted the nobles to seek an alternative to serfdom. In general, the serf-owning nobles were not prospering. By the mid-nineteenth century, two-thirds of their serfs were mortgaged for a total sum equal to half the market value of all the serfs they owned. Also, as in other underdeveloped countries, the rural population of Russia grew faster than the amount of available work. Thus the nobles were still responsible for their underemployed serfs but got no economic benefit from them. Large landowners in the black-soil provinces of the Ukraine wanted to grow wheat for export to Western Europe with wage laborers whom they could hire and fire. They were willing to contemplate emancipation as long as the serfs were not given land. In the older central provinces the land was less suited to modern commercial agriculture; there the nobles derived their main revenue from the nonagricultural activities of their serfs: mining, forestry, household manufacturing. They favored emancipation, but with compensation for the loss of compulsory labor.

*Russian peasants*

A final consideration was the continuing restlessness of the serfs themselves, which kept alive memories of the Pugachev Revolt.* Both the landowners and the tsar feared another such revolt after Russia's defeat in the Crimean War. Speaking of the need to emancipate the serfs, Alexander II said: "Better that this reform should be effected from above than from below."

The new tsar had a humanitarian concern for the lot of the serfs, but he was not a liberal in the Western sense. Carefully educated in the duties of an absolute ruler, Alexander II had no intention of giving Russia a constitutional regime. At the end of the Crimean War he canceled the restrictions on university teaching and on foreign travel. But his main concern was not to promote individual liberty; it was to make the Russian state more efficient. Since this could not be done within the framework of the old order, he resolutely set about the task of finding a solution for the crippling burden of serfdom. Like the nobles, the tsar viewed any change in the old order with distaste. Still, it had to be done.

*See p. 270.

After four years of preparation the terms of the emancipation of privately owned serfs were finally published in March 1861. The juridical authority of the noble over the persons of his peasants was terminated, without compensation to the former owner. The peasants gained neither complete individual freedom nor legal equality with their former masters; instead, they became members of a legally recognized group, the village commune, which controlled their freedom of movement. Nor did they immediately become the proprietors of the land to which they were now entitled—about half of the total arable land in Russia. They had to pay for it first—again as members of the commune, rather than as individuals. Since the peasants had no money, the government devised a plan by which they could "redeem" their share of the land in annual payments spread over forty-nine years. The state, in turn, undertook to compensate the landlords for this land. Meanwhile, it technically belonged to its former owners, who were now entitled to rent for its use.

The emancipation of the privately owned agricultural serfs was soon extended to other categories of peasants. The "courtyard people" (household serfs), like the American slaves, were freed without land. Most of those who did not stay on as servants in their old homes migrated to the cities. Another category of serfs, the so-called state peasants,* were also granted the lands they already cultivated, with somewhat smaller redemption obligations.

The abolition of serfdom intensified class antagonisms and irrevocably upset the old order in Russia. The peasants resented their redemption payments to the state, and they now became bitter economic enemies of the landlords. They wanted high wages and low land rentals and prices, while the noble landlords wanted the reverse. Their status and power had rested on the ownership of land and serfs, and despite the compensation they received, they declined as a class. Already in debt, most of the landlords were unable to run their estates successfully on a commercial basis, and their power over the peasants was taken over by bureaucratic officials. As the power of the landlord class declined, so did that of the regime that rested upon it. On the other hand, the grant of freedom released a dynamic force in Russian life, even though the economic conditions of the peasants worsened in the short run.

### Other Reforms

Other reforms were also needed to achieve the goal of increased governmental efficiency. The existing bureaucracy was simply not equipped to deal with the peasants now that they were no longer under the control of the nobles. Consequently, participation in the country's complex public life had to be extended to other sections of Russian society. National consolidation, not liberalism, was the motive of the reforms in local government, the judiciary, and the army.

In 1864 the Russian government created new local councils, called zemstvos. These organizations were given the task of supervising public education, public health, and other social services, as well as promoting the local economy. Their members were elected by three separate classes: the private landowners, the peasant communes, and the townspeople. The nobles still dominated the zemstvos, but they now had to work side by side with other classes. This new situation represented the "All-Class Principle" that was supposed to weld the nation together. But the peasants and the lower classes in the towns resented the zemstvos because of the additional tax they had to pay to support them. At the same time, the zemstvos never had enough funds to carry through the kinds of improvements their often well-meaning leaders—both liberal landowners and professional people—proposed. And when these zemstvo leaders began discussing liberal political reforms on the national level, their activities were quickly curtailed.

A second reform of 1864 incorporating the "All-Class Principle" concerned the judicial system. The government made the judges permanent and independent and simplified the court procedure; henceforth all subjects were to be equal before the law, irrespective of class. Yet the equality of subjects before the law was not intended to establish a distinction between the law and the will of the tsar. It was rather to reduce the erstwhile highly privileged nobility to the level of subjects governed by a bureaucracy responsible to him alone. Like the emancipation of the serfs, the judicial reform contributed to the mounting isolation of the autocracy, which was finally to lead to its overthrow.

The reform of the army was the only one carried through in the spirit of its planners, namely, to create an "all-class," well-trained army capable of contending with the military forces of the West. In 1874 Russia replaced forced recruitment for twenty-five years with the Prussian system of universal military training. On their twenty-first birthday all Russian males now became liable to a six-year period of service, followed by nine more in the reserve. Aside from exemptions for men with dependents, the only privileges accorded were based on education. University students had to serve only six

*In 1858 eleven million "souls" (males of all ages registered for poll-tax purposes) were privately-owned serfs, while thirteen million were state peasants. These state peasants worked on land owned and administered by the state, whose officials acted like landlords in dealing with the peasants.

months, high-school graduates two years, and elementary-school graduates four years. In 1875 a further reform made literacy one of the objectives of military training, thus providing an important substitute for an adequate system of primary instruction in Russia.

Democratic as the obligation for military service now was, the mass of soldiers still lacked the feeling that the government they served was their government. For both in the army and in society as a whole, peasants were still treated as second-class citizens, despite their legal equality. Besides, by the time of the army reform, the tsarist regime had reverted to a reactionary outlook.

### Reaction

The switch to reaction was partly conditioned by the Polish Revolution of 1863. A year earlier Alexander had tried to win the support of the Poles by substantially restoring their pre-1830 rights. This concession placated the moderates but incited the extreme nationalists to fight for complete independence. Without an army they could only wage a guerrilla struggle and hope for outside help. But the British, Austrian, and French governments restricted themselves to diplomatic protests, which provoked a wave of patriotic support among the Russian people for *their* government. This support strengthened the government's position and reduced the need for further liberal concessions. Meanwhile, the Russians crushed the Polish revolt by 1864, and the very name of Poland was obliterated. The old Congress Kingdom was now administered as a Russian province, and the Russian language became obligatory in all public business. (A Warsaw housewife could ask for meat from her butcher in Polish, but he had to answer her in Russian.) And, to drive deeper the wedge between the Polish classes, the peasants were given especially favorable land allotments when they were emancipated from their landlords.

In April 1866 the first attempt by radical terrorists to assassinate Alexander II confirmed him in his new reactionary outlook. This reaction, which lasted with a few short pauses until 1905, brought much evil to Russia. It disturbed the peaceful development of the country under the new reforms, and it drove not only the radicals, but the liberals as well, "underground." The reaction could cripple and distort the reforms of the new order, but it could not bring back the old. The emancipation and the decline of the landowning nobility were irreversible.

By 1870 Russia was still far behind the major states of Western and Central Europe in economic progress and national consolidation. Her railroad and telegraph networks were beginning to take shape, but she lacked the capital for large-scale industrialization. The peasants benefited from the emancipation and from the judicial and army reforms, but, though legally a part of the nation, they were not a part of it in practice. Some Russian peasants moved to the cities, some to Siberia, and some to North America. The majority remained where they were, land-hungry and alienated from the rest of the nation. Even among the educated elites, many writers and members of the gentry wanted constitutional government. Thus, Russians from all classes lacked a feeling of identification with the Russian state, while the subject nationalities were not really assimilated, only repressed.

: : :

The great nation-builders of the nineteenth century—Napoleon III, Cavour, Bismarck—seemed ready to sacrifice the individual in the name of the state and national power. Only Lincoln demanded that government of the people, by the people, and for the people be preserved at any cost. Yet, as we shall see in Chapter XIV, democracy was to advance in Europe as well as in North America after 1870. By that time the strong nation-state had been achieved in almost all the economically advanced countries, and its power and its ties with the people increased as industrialization broke down the self-sufficiency of rural society. The liberals generally opposed these developments; they still thought that the well-to-do and the well-educated could take care of themselves, But no modern state could ignore the needs of the masses after 1870.

## SUGGESTED READINGS

Bruun, Geoffrey T., *Revolution and Reaction*, 1848–1852. Princeton, N. J.: D. Van Nostrand, 1958. An Anvil original.*
A well-written, up-to-date survey.

Duveau, Georges, *1848: The Making of a Revolution.* New York: Vintage, 1968.*
An impressionistic and exciting social history of the rising in Paris, stressing the mechanics of revolution.

Fejto, Francois, ed., *The Opening of an Era: 1848 an Historical Symposium.* New York: H. Fertig, 1968.
Presents the views of various scholars on the significance of the revolutions.

Hamerow, Theodore S., *Restoration, Revolution, Reaction: Economics and Politics in Germany 1815 –1871.* Princeton, N. J.: Princeton Univ. Press, n.d*

Binkley, Robert C., *Realism and Nationalism*, 1852–1871. New York: Harper and Row, 1960. Torchbook.*
Another volume in the Rise of Modern Europe series. Especially useful on the changing character of international relations following the Crimean War.

Morazé, Charles, *The Triumph of the Middle Classes.* New York: Doubleday-Anchor, 1968.*
Describes the way in which the European bourgeoisie used its economic and social skills to conquer Europe and the world.

Briggs, Asa, *Victorian People: A Reassessment of People and Themes, 1851–67.* New York: Harper and Row, 1963. Colophon.*
Excellent social history.

Thompson, James M., *Louis Napoleon and the Second Empire.* New York: Noonday Press, 1955.
The best of a number of unsatisfactory biographies of this somewhat enigmatic emperor.

Williams, Roger, *Gaslight and Shadow.* New York: The Macmillan Co., 1957. Called *The World of Napoleon III, 1851 –1870* in the paperback edition. Collier Books.*
Amusing and revealing vignettes of various aspects of the Second Empire.

Whyte, Arthur J., *The Evolution of Modern Italy,* New York: Norton, 1967*
Focuses mainly on the Risorgimento and its aftermath.

Martin, George, *The Red Shirt and the Cross of Savoy: The Story of Italy's Risorgimento (1748–1871).* New York: Dodd, Mead & Company, 1969.
An up-to-date narrative.

Mack-Smith, Denis, *Cavour and Garibaldi, A Study in Political Conflict.* Cambridge, Eng.: Cambridge Univ. Press, 1954.
A brilliant and detailed account of how Italy was unified.

Pflanze, Otto, *Bismarck and the Development of Germany, the Period of Unification, 1815–1871.* Princeton, N.J.: Princeton Univ. Press, 1963.
A scholarly, comprehensive account.

Craig, Gordon A., *Politics of the Prussian Army: 1640–1945.* New York: Oxford Univ. Press, n.d.*
See the section on the issue of militarism in the 1860s.

Medlicott, W. N., *Bismarck and Modern Germany.* New York: Harper-Row, 1966.*

A readable, up-to-date account.

Blum, Jerome, *Lord and Peasant in Russia from the Ninth to the Nineteenth Century.* New York: Atheneum, n.d.*
Excellent on the effects of emancipation on the serfs. See also the pertinent sections of Jesse Clarkson's textbook referred to at the end of Chapter VII.

Mosse, Werner E., *Alexander II and the Modernization of Russia.* New York: The Macmillan Co., n.d.*
Discusses the reforms of the "Tsar-Liberator."

CHAPTER XIII

# THE TRANSFORMATION OF EUROPEAN LIFE, 1850–1905

In the second half of the nineteenth century, more people lived longer than ever before and pursued new kinds of occupations far from the homes where their parents and grandparents had lived and died. They were uprooted physically by the railroad and the steamship and culturally by the city. Indeed, Darwin described man as a creature that even in a more natural environment had evolved from earlier forms of life.

Optimism about man's future based on scientific and technological progress became the dominant response to Europe's changing civilization. To be sure, clergymen with empty churches, like impoverished noblemen and underemployed peasants, had little to be optimistic about. Religious leaders lamented the growing preoccupation with material things and the spreading belief that science could explain away the mysteries of man and the universe. Many writers and artists despaired over a civilization in which money was king and beauty and truth seemed to be at a discount. And Marx, who produced the most influential new ideology of the age, condemned the prevailing political, social, and cultural order as a mere "superstructure" masking the exploitation of the proletariat by the bourgeoisie.

The bourgeoisie that Marx condemned was at the peak of its power and self-confidence in the second half of the nineteenth century. The twentieth century was to show that other nations, other races, and other classes could make just as good use of science and technology; until then the European bourgeoisie considered them its exclusive possessions, and its style of life set the tone of the age.

All these changes in European life were primarily the result of industrialization and its spread. New discoveries in physics and chemistry were improving the efficiency of the steam engine and introducing the electric age. Man was even creating new forms of matter—steel, dyes, and explosives—and in the 1890s Germany and the United States began to outstrip Great Britain in steel production. Europeans employed in both the newer and the older industries found themselves increasingly dependent on large, impersonal markets, for the railroad and the steamship that uprooted men also carried goods over an ever larger area. As national markets merged into one huge world market, the price of wheat in Winnipeg and Odessa threatened the very livelihood of the French farmer. Not only did international trade and investment continue to alter life in the advanced countries, they also began to bring the means of economic change—railroad equipment, engines, mining gear, machinery—to backward ones.

By 1870 the supply of goods and services was increasing faster than the demand for them, and the competition for markets forced businessmen to adopt larger and more efficient forms of organization. Industrial capitalism gave way to finance capitalism. In the process, industry came increasingly under the control of men who were primarily concerned with selling, accounting, and similar money affairs, while the actual production of goods and services was managed by a new class of salaried professional people. Businessmen also began to form monopolistic combinations in order to reduce the number of producers and to keep the bulk of the available market for themselves. The concentration and specialization so typical of twentieth-century business activity were already beginning to challenge free competition.

## THE SPREAD OF INDUSTRIALIZATION

The first stage of the Industrial Revolution was concerned primarily with production; the second stage was launched by innovations in transportation, communication, and finance. In 1850, when this second stage began, Great Britain was still far ahead of the rest of the world. During the next two decades, however, other countries in both Europe and North America acquired the structural framework of industrial civilization: railroads, telegraph networks, corporations, and new kinds of banking facilities to finance further growth. As we saw in Chapter XII, industrialization was indispensable to national consolidation during the 1850s and 1860s, not only in Great Britain and France, but also in Germany, Italy, the United States, Canada, and even still-backward Russia.

### Applications of Science to Technology

Although science and technology became more closely related than they had been in the past, they still remained independent types of activity. The one is mainly concerned with theory, with *why* things happen; the other is exclusively concerned with practice, with *how* things happen. Science is the rational correlated knowledge of natural phenomena, with mathematics as its logic and with experiment and observation as its means of verification. Technology is the creation and perfection of techniques of production, construction, and transportation, with empiricism as both its logic and its means of verification.

Whereas traditional trial-and-error methods were still used well into the twentieth century in many industries, isolated amateurs used science increasingly as an aid in their inventions. One has only to recall Alexander Graham Bell's telephone in 1876, Gottlieb Daimler's internal combustion engine in 1886 and automobile in 1887, Gugliemo Marconi's wireless telegraphy (the basis for radio broadcasting) in 1895. These inventions were no longer the result of accident or trial-and-error probing. Bell, Daimler, and Marconi knew what they were looking for, and they consciously applied the new theories of physics to their own experiments. Though not creative scientists themselves, these men introduced scientific methods into practical research.

In addition to becoming increasingly specialized, science itself became a more organized and professional activity in the late nineteenth century. By and large, it was each specialist's business to keep up with his field in all parts of the world and to learn the languages in which the growing number of new books and journals were published. Methods of research also became more highly organized and purposeful, especially in the universities and technical schools of Germany. There the scientific amateur changed imperceptibly into the professor, and laboratory training and instruction in research became standard features in scientific teaching. The new, efficient Germany of Bismarck took the lead in organizing teams of researchers to work on a given project in order to attain a specific result. Other countries were to adopt this method later, and it has reached an astonishing degree of bureaucratization today, with specialized institutes, pilot projects, and phases of research distributed over a whole nation. As the philosopher-mathematician Alfred North Whitehead once said: "The greatest invention of the nineteenth century was the invention of the method of invention."

### *Energy Conversion*

Energy was the most important new concept to be defined beginning in the mid-nineteenth century. Hitherto almost all physical scientists had accepted Newton's theory of nature as matter in motion and Lavoisier's theory of the conservation of mass. Heat had been conceived as an impalpable fluid, and magnetism, electricity, and light had all been imagined as "flowing" through some elastic medium of transmission. The new concept of energy helped to explain the behavior of these phenomena far more satisfactorily than the older material theories. Although the full equivalence of matter and energy was not to be understood until Einstein, physical scientists learned that the former could be converted into the latter in the second half of the nineteenth century. This discovery not only had momentous theoretical implications, it also unlocked new sources of power for industry and transportation.

The discovery that heat could be converted into work, and vice versa, led to the formulation of the laws of thermodynamics by Hermann von Helmholtz (1821–1894) and other German scientists around 1850. These laws state that in all ordinary physical processes energy is conserved in one form or another, that there is a theoretical limit to the efficiency of a heat engine, and that the more a given amount of heat energy is transformed the less of it is available for doing useful work. Further research helped make steam engines more efficient by reducing the loss of energy in the form of heat and ultimately proved the superiority of the internal combustion engine. In addition, the liquification of gases by compression made possible the development of refrigeration, achieved by releasing the liquified gases, which then absorbed heat.

### *Electrical and Chemical Industries*

Electricity, the most important new source of energy developed in the nineteenth century, had been considered essentially useless until two Britishers, Michael Faraday (1791 –1867) and James Clark Maxwell (1831 –1879), discovered the relationships between electricity and magnetism and showed how to achieve a continuous electric current with the use of a dynamo. This rotating machine could be used as a generator to convert a mechanical energy input from machines driven by steam and later water-power into electrical energy output, or as a motor to convert electrical input into mechanical output. As a result, electric lighting, electric streetcars, and electrically driven motors of all kinds came into general use in the 1890s. So did the telephone.

New discoveries in chemistry also helped to create new industries. While the laws of the conservation and dissipation of energy were being formulated, chemists like Justus von Liebig (1803–1873) began to view organic matter itself as subject to the laws of mechanical energy. In the 1860's, both organic and inorganic chemists finally accepted the molecule, not the atom, as the least free particle. They began using the law of atomic weights of the Italian physicist Amadeo Avogadro di Quaregna (1776–1856) and creating new syntheses of organic and inorganic elements. Within a short time a whole new industry of artificial dyes and a whole new industry of explosives came into existence. Heretofore explosives had been simple mixtures of inorganic combustible materials. Now a much greater explosive force could be obtained with combinations of organic materials and azotic acid. The Swede Alfred Nobel (1833–1896) made a fortune manufacturing dynamite (and left a good part of it for a yearly prize to the man who did the most to promote peace).

Along with the new electrical and chemical industries the shift from iron to steel

*A 100-ton steam hammer, constructed in 1876, used in forging steel*

characterized the second stage of the Industrial Revolution. In 1857 Sir Henry Bessemer developed an ingenious closed converter that transformed iron ore into steel by adding carbon to it with hot air blasts from burning coke. The Bessemer process, by eliminating the use of fuel in earlier stages, reduced the cost of producing steel to about one-seventh its former level. Bessemer steel was uneven in quality, a difficulty that an alternative method soon overcame. William Siemens, a British subject of German origin, and the Martin brothers, French metallurgists, developed the open hearth process in the 1860s. The Siemens-Martin process used a large, shallow pan in which the molten metal was processed slowly and remained under precise control at all times. But neither the Bessemer converter nor the open-hearth process worked well on iron ore containing phosphorus, as most ore in continental Europe did. In 1879 the Englishman Sidney Gilchrist Thomas and his cousin Percy Gilchrist developed the Thomas-Gilchrist process for removing the phosphorus by lining a Bessemer converter or an open hearth with a basic substance that would combine chemically with it. All these new procedures helped steel to replace iron as the main structural material in industry and transportation. It was lighter, harder, and more malleable as well as cheaper and longer lasting.

### The New Financial Structure

Until the mid-nineteenth century the principal functions of banks had been commercial. Banks facilitated business transactions by discounting (cashing) all sorts of paper promises to buy, sell, or deliver goods and thus extended short-term credit to merchants and manufacturers. Private banks as well as the central banks of issue (Bank of England, Bank of France) issued banknotes of their own, which were promises to pay hard cash to the bearer. In this way they put more money into circulation. Before 1850 banks contributed less to the financing of new business enterprises than to the extension of the operations of existing ones, and long-term bank loans still went almost exclusively to governments. Thus, as we saw in Chapter X, the early factories and mines had been largely self-financing.

The House of Rothschild is the most famous example of private commercial banking. Mayer Amschel Rothschild, who founded the family fortune in the Frankfurt ghetto in the late eighteenth century, began with money-changing, discounting, and the selling of goods. Then he managed to persuade the Elector of Hesse to let him handle his large investments in real estate and British government bonds. With this capital at his disposal Mayer Amschel made his first foreign loan, to the Kingdom of Denmark, in 1804. By the end of the Napoleonic period his sons had set up independent but closely connected banks in four major capitals of Europe: Nathan in London, James in Paris, Solomon in Vienna, and Karl in Naples. The fifth son, Amschel, remained in Frankfurt.

All five sons continued their commercial banking operations and government loans on an ever increasing scale, and the wealth of the Rothschilds became legendary. The French branch had almost complete control over the sale of government bonds and the importation of tea under Louis Philippe; the Austrian branch invested heavily in railroad building; the English branch lent the Disraeli government twenty million dollars to purchase almost half of the shares in the French-owned Suez Canal Corporation in 1875. Each branch sent information to the others and was ready to provide additional capital when needed. Nevertheless, aside from financing the building of some railroads, the Rothschilds remained essentially private commercial bankers. And it should be remembered that they were unique among traditional bankers in the scope of their operations.

The financial crisis of 1847 had shown that Europe's credit facilities were inadequate for an industrial economy. The traditional banking system facilitated business sales by discounting short-term notes, but the building of railroad networks, steamship lines, and telegraph systems required long-term credits on a scale beyond its capacity. Consequently, the completion of these projects was held up until the appearance of two new types of financial institution: the joint-stock deposit bank and the limited liability corporation.

The joint-stock deposit bank had several advantages over the older type of private bank. First of all, by selling its stocks to the public, it acquired a larger fixed capital. Second, it acquired a larger working capital by accepting deposits from the public in the form of checking accounts. It used the bulk of this working capital to extend credit to business enterprises. At the same time, the checks drawn on its customers' deposits eventually became as acceptable as paper currency in business transactions. These checks thus increased the amount of money in circulation. This new system of finance capitalism worked better than the self-financing methods of the older industrial capitalism in supplying money and credit to an expanding economy.

The second new financial institution was the limited liability corporation. Like most banks, most business organizations had previously been controlled by a few big stockholders, and these stockholders had been legally responsible for all their company's debts. The limited liability corporation was a much larger and more impersonal organization as its French name, *société anonyme*, indicates. It attracted far more investment capital, particularly from small investors, because a stockholder could not lose more than the par value of his stock. Also, limited liability corporations had to publish balance sheets and other information about their operations so that the stockholders knew how their money was being used. Even banks and credit institutions began to invest in these new corporations. They were ultimately to gain controlling interests in some of them, as we shall see presently.

In the 1850s and 1860s limited liability corporations mushroomed in Great Britain, Belgium, and parts of Germany. The French restricted them to railroads and banks until 1867. Thereafter business enterprises of all kinds could incorporate on a limited liability basis in France. But the French people remained wary of investing their money in private businesses over which they had no control. They preferred government bonds and government-sponsored public works enterprises, like the modernization of Paris.

### Transportation and Communication

The completion of modern transportation and communication networks accelerated capitalist economic development in the 1850s and 1860s. Between 1850 and 1870 the railroad mileage* of Great Britain

*By 1910 the total railway mileage in Great Britain was 23,400; in France 30,000, in Germany 37,500, in Italy 10,000, in Russia 47,000, in Canada 37,000, in the United States 240,000.

*The opening of the Suez Canal, November 17, 1869 (from a watercolor by Edouard Riou)*

rose from 6,000 to 14,400 that of France from 1,800 to 10,400, that of Germany from 3,600 to 12,000, and that of Italy from 300 to 3,600. The electric telegraph and the steamship also came into large-scale use during this period. On the national level, however, the railroad had the most immediate economic effects. It absorbed more new capital and created more new jobs than any other type of enterprise; it opened up new markets and new sources of raw materials; it promoted the growth of new towns. No other part of the new economic framework had as great an impact on European and North American life as a whole. The railroad caused the gradual disappearance of old ways of living and thinking. Social groups that had formerly lived in isolation began to participate haltingly in the activities of the national community. The class system remained, in passenger trains as in social relations. Even so, there was something inherently democratic about riding on the same train as one's social betters, even though one sat in a different compartment. The nationalizing and democratizing consequences of the railroad also reinforced the constitutional trend toward equality of classes and representative government, and the increasing cohesion between the state and society.

In 1872 the novelist Jules Verne's Phileas Fogg made a trip around the world in eighty days. He performed this unprecedented feat by using the latest improvements in transportation and communication. Starting from London, he crossed the Channel by steamship and arrived in Paris by train. Verne had his hero travel from Paris to the Mediterranean by balloon, but Phileas Fogg could have gone by train, for the main railroad lines of France, Spain, and Italy were nearing completion in the early 1870s. He took a steamship from the Western Mediterranean through the Suez Canal (opened in 1869), the Red Sea, and the Indian Ocean. Then he crossed most of India by train, where the main trunk lines were already under construction. After sundry adventures in Southeast Asia, Phileas Fogg crossed the Pacific by sailing ship, the United States by the first transcontinental railroad in history (completed in the same year as the Suez Canal), and the Atlantic by steamship. On the first phase of his trip he had used the services of the new Cook's Travel Agency, and at various times he was able to make reservations by the newly laid transoceanic cables.

Within a few years after Phileas Fogg's journey, bulky cargoes were being transported over thousands of miles by railroad and steamship, and orders for goods and services were being expedited by telegraph and cable. By the early 1900s the Trans-Siberian railroad linked Moscow with the Pacific, and the other railroads of the world had replaced their iron rails with steel ones. Improvements in marine engines brought about the complete triumph of the steamship over the fastest clippers. After 1880 Western Europe was able to import wheat from North America and Russia at a lower price than that of home-grown wheat. She could also export steel rails and heavy machinery to any part of the world.

### A Worldwide Economy

Technological advances in power and metallurgy, the spread of modern transportation and communication networks, and a remarkable system of international capital investments and money transactions made possible a phenomenal growth in world trade. Between 1875 and 1905 the volume of this trade almost trebled. Great Britain continued to play a leading role in international economic affairs, but, in contrast to the first half of the century, she was no longer supreme. By the beginning of the twentieth century almost all of Western and Central Europe had become the workshop and banker of the rest of the world.

Improvements in transportation and the industrialization of other countries besides Great Britain altered the character of world trade as well as its volume. Long before 1850 Great Britain had become dependent on the agricultural products of the tropics and sub-tropics and had paid for her imports with exports of cotton and wool textiles. She had also exported coal, metals, and machinery to Europe and the United States, but by the 1880s Germany and the United States were producing these items for themselves, and Germany was beginning to compete with Great Britain in exporting them. As Germany, France, the United States, and other nations put up tariffs to protect their own textile industries, Britain's foreign market for textiles became limited primarily to India and China. Even there local mills began to appear at the turn of the century. More and more the character of world trade involved a division of labor between those nations engaged in heavy manufacturing and those producing food and raw materials.

### *"Invisible" Exports*

Ironically, the British, and to a lesser extent the French, helped the less advanced countries develop into potential competitors. After 1850* the British invested heavily in the building of North and South American railroads; the French built railroads in Italy, Spain, and Austria-Hungary; and the French indemnity after the Franco-Prussian War helped to complete the construction of the German railroad system. In the last third of the century British, French, Belgian, and German capital and technicians were also helping Eastern Europe and Latin America to develop railroads, telegraph lines, mining, and light manufacturing.

Although the large-scale exportation of capital eventually stimulated competition from newly industrialized countries, it benefited the exporting countries in several ways. New, and hence risky, Latin-American railroads, South African gold mines, and Malayan rubber plantations would pay much higher interest rates than established enterprises at home. Hence, the Europeans who increased

*We have already seen (Chapter X) how British capital and technicians aided the first stage of industrialization in Belgium and France before 1850; one trace of the British engineers in North America is the Chicago and Northwestern Railroad, which to this day runs its trains on the left track instead of the right.

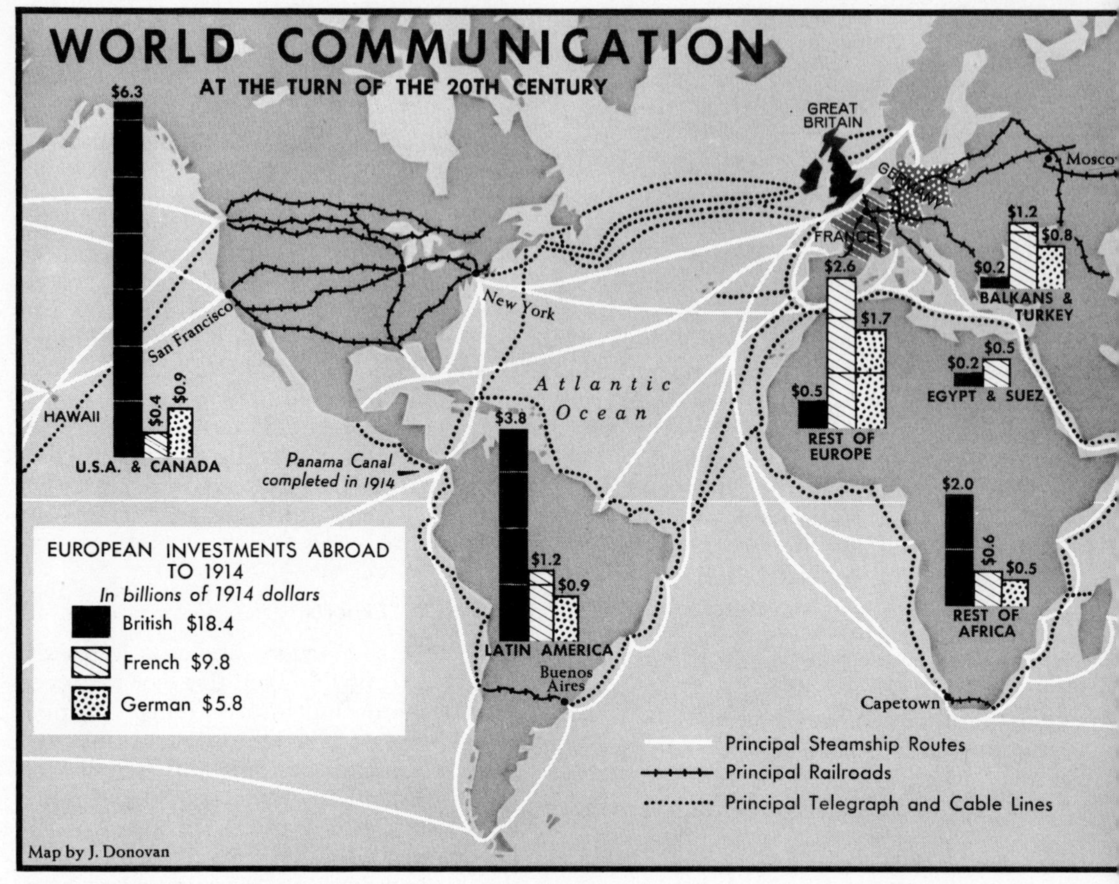


their income from overseas investments bought more goods and services at home, thus stimulating economic growth there. At the same time, the overseas countries in which their capital was invested could buy more industrial products from Europe. Finally, the income from foreign investments allowed the European countries to import more "visible" goods than they exported.

Capital was not the only "invisible" export. The advanced countries of Europe also earned income from banking services, insurance, and shipping. Great Britain alone increased her shipping earnings from eighteen million to nearly seventy million pounds a year between 1850 and 1905, despite increasing competition from Germany, Norway, and other countries that were building their own merchant marines. For example, Great Britain earned Argentine pesos for carrying Argentine hides to Germany, German marks for insuring the shipment, and Italian lire for transferring the pesos to the bank account of an Italian merchant who wanted to buy Argentine beef.

### *The Gold Standard*

These monetary transactions were facilitated by the fact that from the 1870s to the First World War the currencies of all major countries were on the gold standard; that is, they were convertible into gold at a fixed value. This ready interchangeability encouraged the development of a world market, but it also had effects on prices of goods and services in Europe. The discovery of gold in California* and Australia lowered the price of gold and thus of money, and hence stimulated the economic boom and the rise in

*Captain Sutter made his strike, which led to the gold rush of 1849, at the time of the February Revolution in Paris.

prices of goods and services of the 1850s and 1860s. This boom was followed by a depression that lasted, with a few partial upswings, from 1873 to 1895. After that, new supplies of gold found in South Africa and Alaska helped a new boom.

### World Prices

Although gold was a factor in determining prices, market conditions were a much greater one. The rising tide of goods that flowed in the wake of overseas capital investment and the services that eased their movement created a world market governed by world prices. Transportation in bulk became so inexpensive that the lowest price anywhere for a particular commodity became the price at which producers everywhere had to sell. This fact tended to squeeze out the less efficient producers and to make each area of the world specialize in the kind of economic activity in which its prices were competitive—just as Adam Smith and the Manchester School had said they should.

From 1873 to 1895 prices in the industrial countries fell because the demand for their goods and services did not keep up with the supply. This change first became evident in the completed railroad systems of Europe, then in industry, and finally in agriculture, where large-scale imports of grain and meat from Russia, North America, and Australia forced down the prices of Eurpoean agricultural products. The only answer to this threat that Europe's farmers could think of was high tariffs, and by the 1890s most continental governments tried to alleviate the domestic agricultural depression in this way. The new captains of industry met the problem of falling prices in other ways. They reduced their costs of production through mechanization and larger plants; they sought new markets overseas; they formed monopolistic organizations with which they drove their competitors out of business in cut-throat fashion.

Hence, just as the first stage of the Industrial Revolution had been partially stimulated by the need to supply growing markets, the second stage was partially stimulated by another kind of necessity: falling prices. These falling prices threatened the economic security of manufacturers and farmers who could not meet them. In the long run, however, they stimulated economic growth by forcing producers to increase their efficiency. Furthermore, the industrialization of new countries created new wealth and thus helped the growth of world trade. Every country had to buy some goods and services abroad, and improvements in transportation made these available in an ever rising volume. The result of all these developments was a truly worldwide economy.

### Big Business

The multimillionaire business tycoon was a typical product of the second stage of the Industrial Revolution. Samuel Cunard built and operated a vast steamship line between Great Britain and the Western Hemisphere. Charles Ritz founded a chain of hotels in France and other European countries. In Europe and North America there were department store tycoons, railroad tycoons, steel tycoons (Andrew Carnegie), oil tycoons (John D. Rockefeller), and even newspaper tycoons (Gordon Bennett, William Randolph Hearst). Whether they furnished goods or services, these men controlled enterprises whose scale of operations was bigger and more highly organized than anything dreamed of before 1850.

Just as the first stage of the Industrial Revolution had been the age of the steam engine, the second stage was an age of electricity, and the outstanding business tycoons in this field were the Siemens brothers in Germany. These ten brothers, born on a farm in Hanover between 1816 and 1836, headed the most prodigious complex of industries in Germany by the end of the century. Ernest, the eldest, had joined the artillery corps at eighteen, and during his sixteen years in the army acquired a passion for electricity. He learned the process of electrotypy and, as director of the Berlin arsenal, he developed an electrical charge for underwater mines and organized the construction of Prussia's electric telegraph system. In 1850 he resigned from the army and set up his own telegraph equipment business. Ernest and his nine brothers constructed telegraph lines in the rest of northern Germany and in Russia, and, along with other firms, in South America and South Africa. Siemens Brothers, as the firm came to be called, built the first electric streetcars in Berlin in the 1880s. Brother William, as we have seen, perfected a new process for making steel, and was ultimately made a baron in England; another brother founded glass factories in Saxony and Bohemia. By 1900 Siemens Brothers controlled gas works, steel mills, telephone and telegraph manufacturing as well as many branches of the electrical industry.

In order to increase their profits, especially in a period of falling prices, some business tycoons attempted to monopolize the market in one way or another. The first way was the cartel, in which several autonomous firms combined by agreement, usually for a limited time. An outstanding example was the Rhenish-Westphalian Coal Syndicate that grew up among the coal producers of the Ruhr Valley. Its avowed objectives were (1) to end price competition; (2) to establish profitable prices; (3) to regulate production; (4) to minimize fluctuations in output. The second type of business combination was the trust, or holding company, in which a separate financial concern controlled the voting shares of several operating joint-stock companies, an arrangement extensively employed in the United States until the anti-trust laws of the early 1900s. The third type of business combination was the direct merger and amalgamation of the assets of several previously independent firms. This type was the closest to a pure monopoly. A good example was the Coats cotton sewing thread industry in Great Britain. In 1896 J. & P. Coats merged with four of its rivals to form a virtual monopoly within the domestic market, and it expanded its foreign activities until it dominated the whole world market. Coats was able to prevent rivals from undercutting on prices by refusing to sell to dealers who sold other brands at lower prices. By fixing its own prices for a product whose sales volume was insensitive to price changes, Coats regularly earned annual profits of 20 per cent and more!

Large-scale business stimulated the growth of large-scale banking to supply it with long-term credits, and the banks in turn became increasingly allied with large-scale business. It was more profitable to deal in the securities of larger and better-known enterprises than in those of small business. Hence small business lost out in the competition for investment capital as well as in the competition for markets. Many business tycoons managed to retain their independence from the big investment banks, but the general trend was toward an ever closer alliance between industry and finance.

### Germany

In no other country was the alliance between banking and industry closer than in Germany. The Imperial Bank (*Reichsbank*) chartered in 1875, performed functions similar to those of the Bank of England and the Bank of France, but it was soon regulating the country's banking activities more strictly than these older national banks. Owing to Germany's backward financial organization in the third quarter of the nineteenth century, the joint-stock deposit banks had done a far more miscellaneous business than that of a typical contemporary bank in England, and from the beginning they had developed the closest possible association with the country's industrial development. After 1875 the most powerful business banks were the *Deutsche*, *Dresdner*, *Diskontogesellschaft*, and *Darmstädter*. The credits they issued to industrial concerns became longer and longer until they amounted almost to partnerships, with industrialists and bankers sitting on each others' boards of directors. These banks also fostered the cartel movement, which was more extensive in Germany than anywhere else, in order to shield from competition those industrial concerns in which they had financial interests.

The fact that the industrialization of Germany took place mainly during the second stage of the Industrial Revolution gave her certain advantages over Great Britain, France, and Belgium. It gave her a more modern financial structure, a strong lead in the new electrical and chemical industries, and the ability to begin large-scale steel production with the latest equipment. It also gave her a far larger world market than had been available to the other three countries when they had begun to industrialize in earnest. The lack of a liberal economic tradition plus the precedent of the *Zollverein** allowed Bismarck to gain a ten-year lead in using a policy of moderate tariff protection to reserve the home market for native producers.†

But the rapid pace of German industrialization had unfortunate political and social consequences. The political history of the German Empire will be discussed later; however, we should note here that the dependence of German Big Business on state regulation helped to prevent it from developing a strong political organization of its own. The double achievement of national union and economic growth under Bismarck made it difficult for liberals to oppose his authoritarian methods. And if the propertied middle class was not granted a share in the government, what could the working class expect to obtain in answer to its political demands? The rapid pace of German industrialization enabled the cities to absorb nearly 30 million new citizens between 1849 and 1910—almost the entire increase in the total population from 35,128,000 to 64,926,000. Nevertheless, half a century was too short a time in which to integrate such a mass of uprooted people into a fast-changing national society and culture. By the early twentieth century imperial Germany had not evolved a sense of national purpose other than the further extension of her growing economic and military power.

## SOCIAL AND CULTURAL CONSEQUENCES OF INDUSTRIALIZATION

Industrialization, urbanization, and population growth interacted with one another in the second half of the nineteenth century to produce ever accelerating social and cultural changes. Between 1800 and 1900, the proportion of people of European origin in the world increased from one-fifth to one-third. Some of these people moved from their rural birthplaces to newly opened farmlands overseas; the majority moved to the growing cities of Europe. These unprecedented migrations were made possible by cheap rail and steamship transportation. Meanwhile, division of labor in the economy reflected itself in a more complex social structure than European civilization had ever known. Among the middle and lower middle classes, there was a vast increase in the number and kinds of professional people. Of the older professions, only the army officers and the clergy remained relatively static; the rest burgeoned. Moreover, the structure of the new industrial civilization required new cadres: managers, engineers, technicians, civil servants, judges. Nonprofessional occupations also became more demanding; even semiskilled factory workers had to be able to read and write. The growth in the urban population provided an increased demand for all sorts of services, both old and new.

### Education and Specialization

Concentration, specialization, and continuing economic growth provided a host of new occupations in the service industries. By the end of the nineteenth century there were hundreds of white-collar employees in the offices of industrial firms like the Siemens Electrical Company in Berlin, in transport organizations like the Great Western Railway in London, and in department stores like the Bon Marché in Paris. New forms of industry, transportation, and communication also required engineers and technicians, traveling salesmen, railroad conductors. As governments furnished increasing services to growing populations, the number of civil servants—from bureau heads to postmen—swelled too.

These service occupations formed a part of the economy that was neither agricultural nor industrial; economists call it the third, or "tertiary," sector. Included in

*See p. 378.

†Bismarck's tariff was instituted in 1879. Comparable tariffs in France, Russia, and the United States came only around 1890, and Great Britain was to cling doggedly to free trade until 1931.

it was also a growing number of specialized professional people. The largest group, and the one that trained all the others, was the teachers.

While the number of teachers and students increased in the secondary schools and universities, education at these levels changed slowly in the nineteenth century. Secondary schools continued to use the classical liberal arts program based on Latin and Greek, although now supplemented by courses in mathematics and science. Universities added new schools in the sciences, medicine, surgery, and pharmacy to the traditional ones of law, theology, and philosophy. Except in Germany, technical high schools and colleges were insufficient to meet the growing needs of an industrial civilization.

Secondary and higher education were still restricted to the bourgeois and aristocratic elites; the real revolution in nineteenth-century education came at the elementary school level. Earlier, the few schoolmasters there were had had little formal training and often had to hold a second job in order to make a living. Teaching had consisted of rudimentary instruction in reading, writing, arithmetic, and religious and moral homilies, given with the aid of the proverbial hickory stick. "Children can never receive enough blows," said a typical eighteenth-century German schoolmaster.

The hickory stick lasted throughout most of the nineteenth century, but the quantity and quality of instruction improved with state-supported elementary schools and normal schools for the training of teachers. Prussia led the world in these developments, though her normal schools remained under the control of the churches; as early as 1864 Prussia had 36,500 elementary-school teachers for around three million pupils. In 1833 the French government had passed a law regulating the hours of instruction and the curriculum of all elementary schools, establishing a normal school in each of the country's eighty-three departments, and requiring each community to pay its teachers a regular salary. The normal school spread to all advanced countries in the second half of the nineteenth century and made teaching a specialized and autonomous profession. With the coming of compulsory primary education in the 1870s and 1880s* the number of teachers and pupils skyrocketed in all the advanced countries.

Meanwhile, the older professions of medicine and law became more specialized and were entered by more men. Medicine particularly exemplified the scientific outlook of the age. Surgeons ceased to be glorified barbers and now received the same degree of training as other doctors. Pharmacy too became scientific. There were few factory-made drugs before the end of the nineteenth century (a German chemist named Bayer invented aspirin only in the 1890s), and the pharmacist had to be able to fill complicated prescriptions by doctors versed in the new discoveries in chemistry. Folk remedies and elixirs held their own, especially in rural areas, but more and more people recognized medicine as a truly scientific profession.

The law remained the most popular single field of study, but it now trained men for many specialized activities. Big Business brought an enormous increase in civil litigation, especially in torts and contracts. In the past, judges with little or no legal training had bought their posts or been appointed to them. By the late nineteenth century they had to pass an even more rigorous examination than the lawyers of the bar before they could preside in most countries. Perhaps the largest new field for men with legal training was the civil service. Already well established in France and Prussia, the professionalized civil service finally began in Great Britain in 1870 and in 1883 in the United States—each with examinations, a seniority system, and an *esprit de corps* of its own.

### Population Growth

The professional people were only a small part of the population in the advanced countries; we must now turn to the population of the world as a whole. The accompanying table shows the increases in different parts of the world between 1650 and 1967. In the present discussion we

*See p. 440 for Britain, p. 512 for France.

are concerned with the increases between 1800 and 1900. During that period the population of Europe (and Asiatic Russia—of whose 22 million people in 1900 at least a third were Europeans) increased by almost 120 per cent, compared to a 44 per cent increase in Asia and a 41 per cent increase in Africa. In 1900 nine-tenths of the population of North America and Oceania and at least one-third of the population of Central and South America were of European origin. The total percentage of "Europeans" in the world was therefore about one-third, and the total number a little over five hundred million.

In every major area except China (for which no reliable figures are available before 1900) the nineteenth-century increase in population outside of Europe can be traced to European influence of one sort or another. In Asia—especially British India—and Africa European methods of maintaining civil peace, of economic enterprise, and of hygiene and sanitation brought a decrease in the death rate. In most of the Western Hemisphere and Oceania the major increase came from immigrants from Europe and from the birth of second- and third-generation European settlers.

Population growth is the direct function of three variables: the fertility rate, the

**ESTIMATES OF WORLD POPULATION BY REGIONS, 1650–1967[1]**

Estimated Population, in millions

| Series of Estimates and Date | World Total | Africa | North America | Latin America | Asia (exc. USSR) | Europe and Asiatic USSR | Oceania | Area of European Settlement[2] |
|---|---|---|---|---|---|---|---|---|
| Willcox's estimates[3] | | | | | | | | |
| 1650 | 470 | 100 | 1 | 7 | 257 | 103 | 2 | 113 |
| 1750 | 694 | 100 | 1 | 10 | 437 | 144 | 2 | 157 |
| 1800 | 919 | 100 | 6 | 23 | 595 | 193 | 2 | 224 |
| 1850 | 1091 | 100 | 26 | 33 | 656 | 274 | 2 | 335 |
| 1900 | 1571 | 141 | 81 | 63 | 857 | 423 | 6 | 573 |
| Carr-Saunders' estimates[4] | | | | | | | | |
| 1650 | 545 | 100 | 1 | 12 | 327 | 103 | 2 | 118 |
| 1750 | 728 | 95 | 1 | 11 | 475 | 144 | 2 | 158 |
| 1800 | 906 | 90 | 6 | 19 | 597 | 192 | 2 | 219 |
| 1850 | 1171 | 95 | 26 | 33 | 741 | 274 | 2 | 335 |
| 1900 | 1608 | 120 | 81 | 63 | 915 | 423 | 6 | 573 |
| United Nations' estimates | | | | | | | | |
| 1920 | 1834 | 136 | 115 | 92 | 997 | 485 | 9 | 701 |
| 1930 | 2008 | 155 | 134 | 110 | 1069 | 530 | 10 | 784 |
| 1940 | 2216 | 177 | 144 | 132 | 1173 | 579 | 11 | 886 |
| 1950 | 2406 | 199 | 166 | 162 | 1272 | 594 | 13 | 935 |
| 1967[5] | 3420 | 328[6] | 220 | 259 | 1907 | 678 | 18 | 1175 |

[1]United Nations, *The Determinants and Consequences of Population Trends* (1954).
[2]North America, Latin America, Europe and the USSR, and Oceania (Australia-New Zealand).
[3]Walter F. Willcox, *Studies in American Demography* (1940).
[4]Alexander Carr-Saunders, *World Population, Past Growth and Present Trends* (1936).
[5]United Nations, *Population and Vital Statistics Report, January 1969.*
[6]This figure is based on new census data indicating that United Nations estimates for 1920–1950 were too low.

death rate, and migration. Each of these variables in turn is influenced by a variety of factors. The fertility rate, which is the average number of babies born to women of child-bearing age, is influenced primarily by nutrition and hygiene. Migration is influenced primarily by the desire to better one's economic condition. Lesser factors also have their influence too: the fertility rate in a particular community goes down when a large proportion of its men are away for long periods of time, in wars, for example; wars can also influence the death rate; some people migrate to other countries to escape religious or political persecution.

The phenomenal growth in the population of Europe in the nineteenth century was due primarily to an ever-decreasing death rate. This fact is all the more significant when one considers that the fertility rate fell steadily in all the industrialized countries and that, between 1835 and 1914, 60 million Europeans migrated overseas. Malthus was wrong. The death rate went down, the total population grew, and the food supply increased faster than the total population, resulting in better health and a better level of living. As more people advanced beyond the level of bare subsistence they limited the size of their families in order to maintain their higher level of living. This pattern appeared earliest in France, and by the 1880s the fertility rate was falling as fast in Great Britain, Germany, and Italy as in France. But since more people lived on into the middle and older age groups, the total population in all European countries except France and Ireland continued to rise well into the twentieth century.

In view of today's population explosion in the rest of the world, Europe's experience in the nineteenth century is most instructive. It shows that the rate of population growth is fastest during the early stages of industrialization, when better hygiene, more food, and more jobs allow more people to live longer. It also shows that, as more and more people achieve a level of living that can only be maintained by limiting the number of children they have to support, sooner or later they find ways to have fewer children. Neither the French nor the bourgeoisie as a whole had a monopoly over thrift and birth control. Even skilled industrial workers and farmers eventually acquired these habits when public law and the professionalization of work required them to keep their children in school instead of sending them out to work at the age of ten. In one important respect, however, Europe had an advantage over Asia, Africa, and Latin America today. She could send part of her surplus population overseas.

### Overseas Migration

Between 1835 and 1914 the principal areas of emigration were Europe (60 million) and Asia (no figures available); the principal areas of immigration were the United States (32 million), Latin America (8 million), Siberia (7 million), Canada (4 million), Australia-New Zealand (2½ million), and Africa (1 million to South Africa and ½ million to Algeria and Tunisia).

In most cases the immigrants were landless people from overcrowded rural communities seeking cheap land in underpopulated areas. There were some major exceptions, though. The Irish tended to work as domestic servants and unskilled nonagricultural labor in the United States; some Chinese set up small businesses in Southeast Asia and in the Western Hemisphere; Eastern European Jews often specialized in petty merchandising and the clothing trades in the United States; East Indians worked in the mines of South Africa and on the plantations of British Guiana in South America. But the majority of these people were also proletarians in the true sense, without land and with no economic security. Only a minority of the overseas emigrants left Europe because of political or religious persecution; even many of the Jews from "The Pale" of Russia fled poverty as much as pogroms.

Like the migrations within Great Britain in the first stage of industrialization, the vast exodus from Europe after 1850 was caused by the "push" of lack of economic opportunities at home, the "pull" of economic opportunities elsewhere, and relative freedom of movement. After 1850,

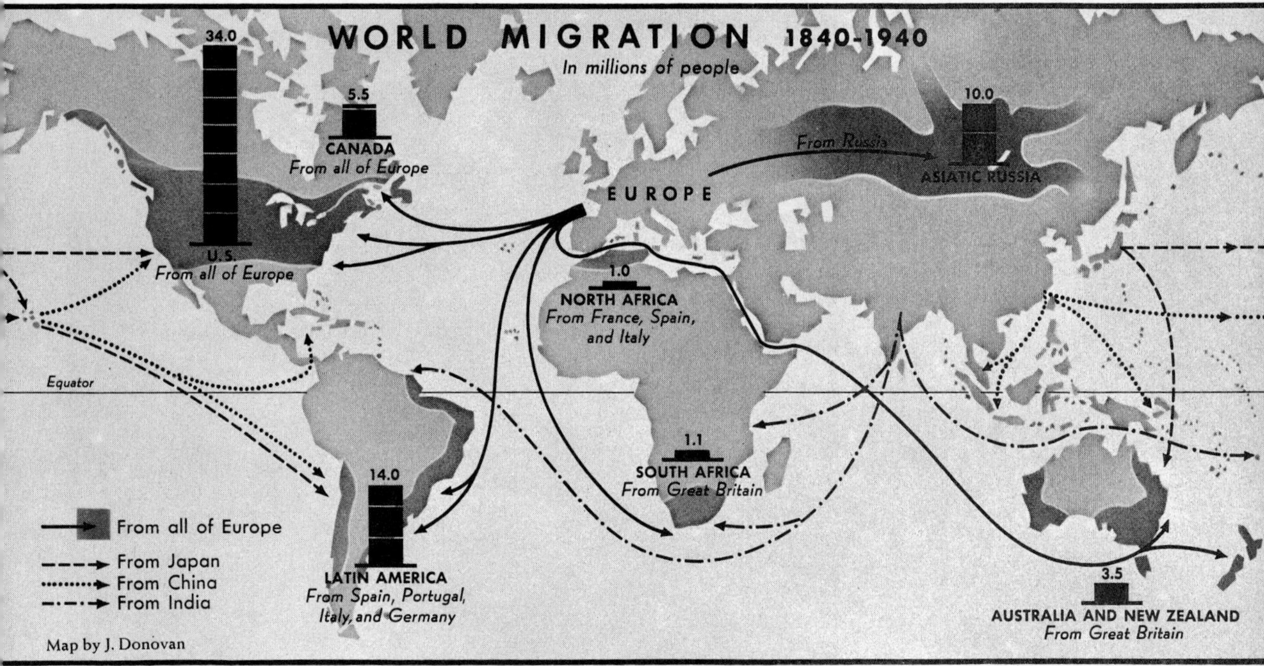


however, the "pull" of opportunities elsewhere and freedom of movement increased considerably. Much of Western North American was a vast wilderness of prairie land, and the American and Canadian governments actively encouraged its settlement as well as the immigration of cheap casual labor of all kinds. Once the abolition of serfdom in Central and Eastern Europe allowed peasants to leave the land, the new railroads brought them to the ports of the Atlantic and the Mediterranean and to Siberia. And the holds of new steamships provided all emigrants with cheap, though extremely uncomfortable, passage to America.

The accompanying graph shows the numbers and the countries of origin of the Europeans who emigrated overseas. The largest numbers left from the areas of the greatest underemployment: landless Irishmen and Scots, hand-loom weavers from the countryside of England and Germany, and, after 1880, southern Italians, Russians, Poles, Slovaks, Ruthenians, and Jews from the countryside and nonindustrial towns as well. Spain, Protugal, and Sweden also disgorged several million emigrants by 1914. France was the only large country that did not experience a significant emigration. The reason was simple: the economic "push" was weak. France had more good land per capita and a lower rate of population growth than any major European country.

The bulk of the emigrants from the British Isles went to English-speaking countries; the overwhelming majority of Spanish emigrants went to the Spanish-speaking republics of Latin America; most Portuguese went to Brazil. These people became quickly assimilated and lost their Old World ways. On the other hand, immigrants from Germany, Italy, Austria-Hungary, and the Russian Empire often formed sub-communities of their own, especially within the larger cities of the United States. These sub-communities, kept alive by fresh waves of immigrants, had their own newspapers, their own social and religious organizations, and sometimes even their own schools.

In the long run, however, the Europeans tended to adopt the dominant culture of their new homelands and yet, in certain places, to give this culture something of their own. By 1914 one-fourth of the population of New York City was Jewish,

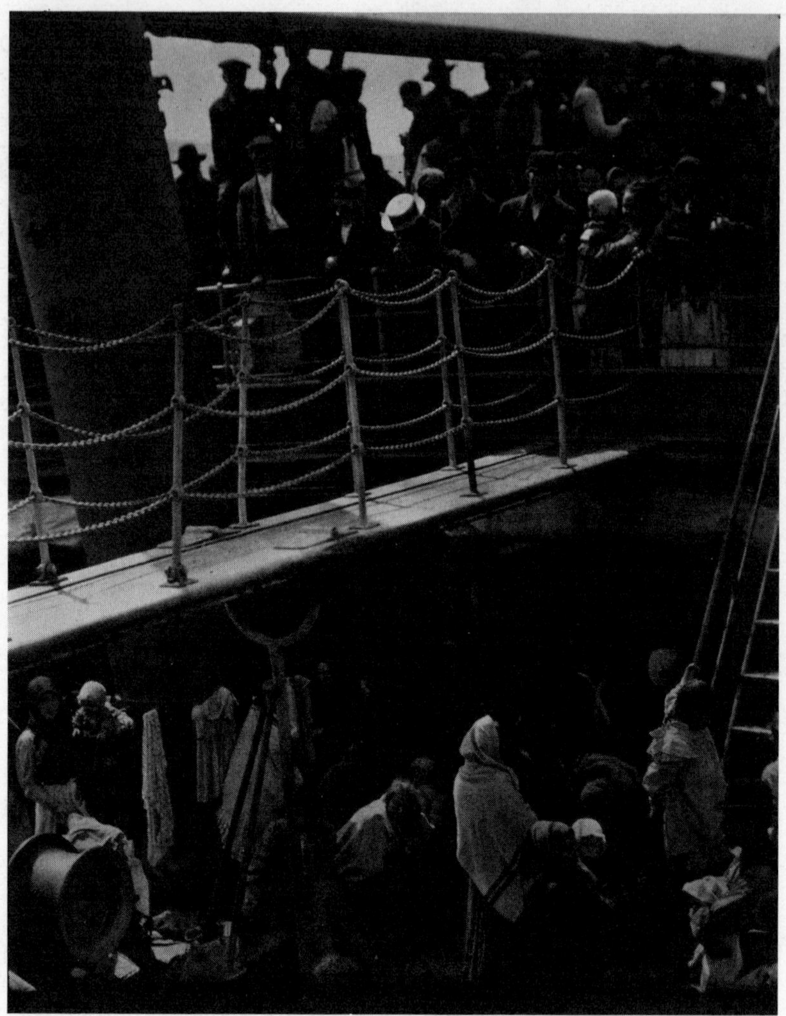

*Alfred Stieglitz's "The Steerage" (1907).*

one-fourth of Boston Irish, one-fourth of Milwaukee German, and one-sixth of Chicago Polish. These large European minorities gave each of these American cities a distinctive style of work, play, and politics.

### Urbanization

Of the net increase in European population, only one out of every seven went overseas; the other six moved to the towns and cities of Europe itself. It was much easier for underemployed rural people to move to the capital or the new mill towns of their own country than to some promised land abroad. The cities could provide them with jobs and food, they thought, and the railroad gave them a quick and cheap way to get there. The unprecedented exodus from the countryside to the city made the population and the civilization of Europe predominantly urban by the beginning of the twentieth century.

This process of urbanization occurred most rapidly in Western and Central Europe, but it left no major country untouched. In 1815 less than 2 per cent of all Europeans had lived in cities of over 100,000 inhabitants; in 1910 the figure was over 15 per cent. By then six urban agglomerations had more than a million people, fifty-five more than 250,000, one

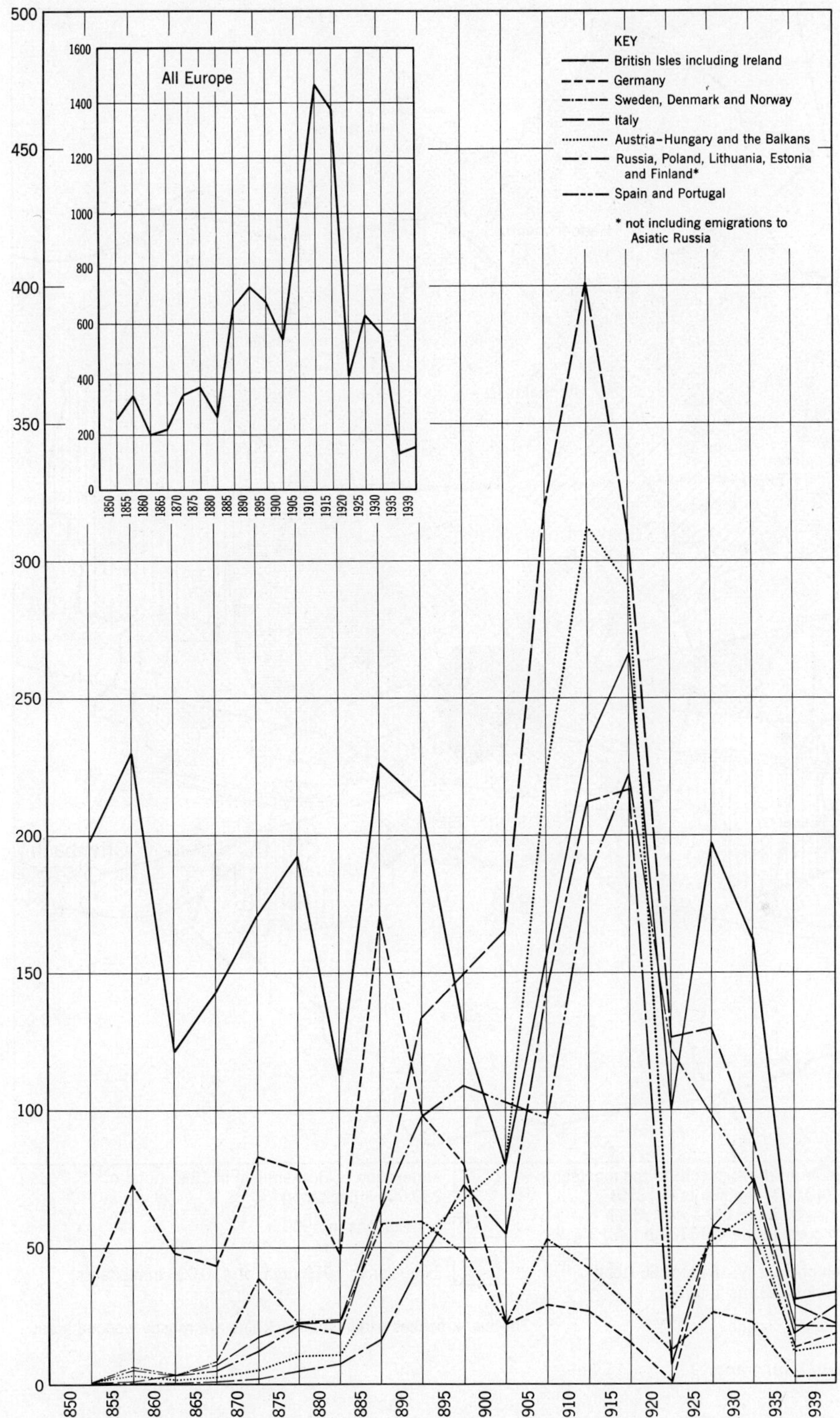


*Average annual overseas emigration from Europe, 1846–1939 (thousands)*

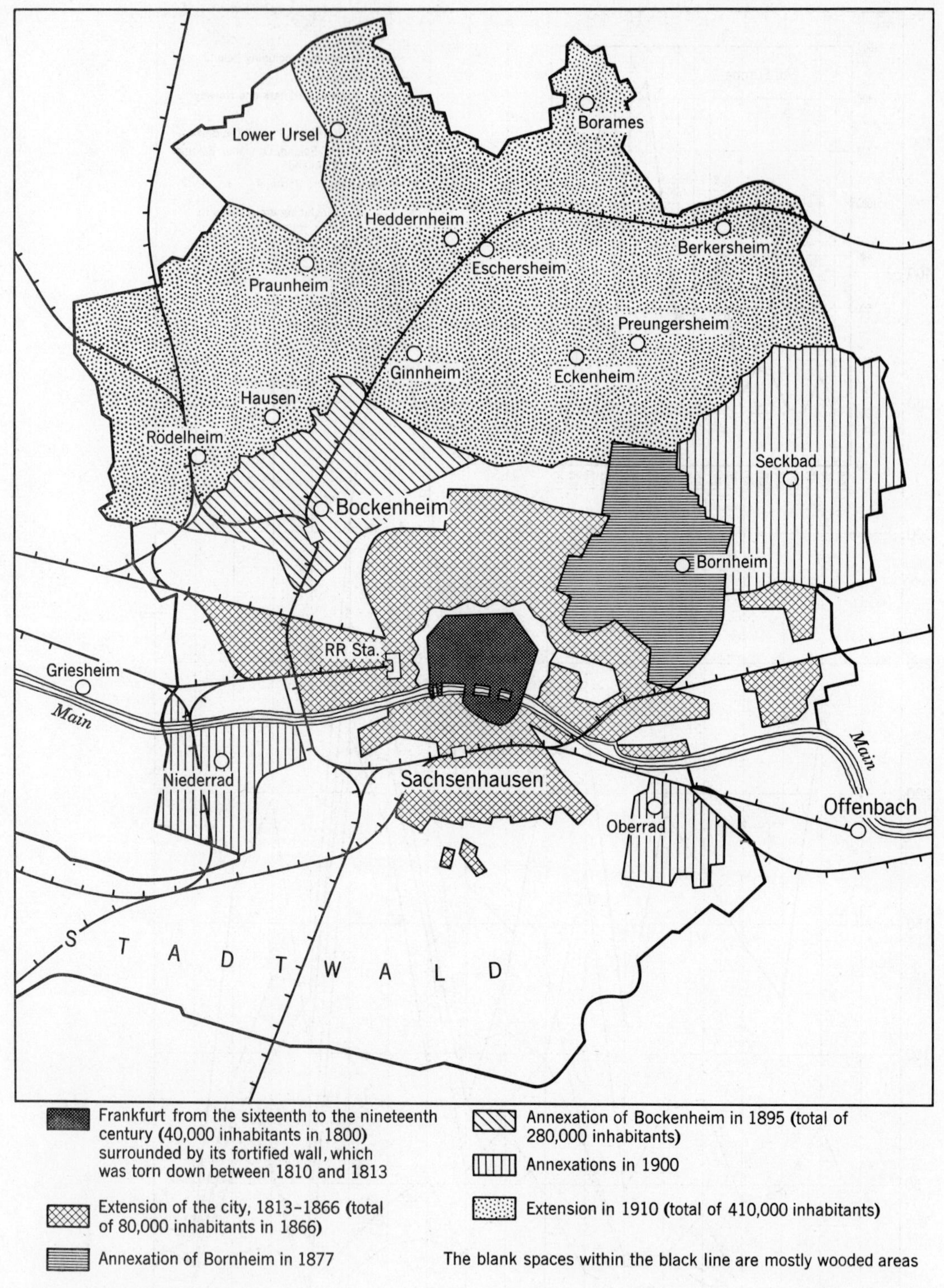


*Frankfurt-am-Main, Germany*

hundred and eighty more than 100,000. The growth of the great capitals was especially striking. By 1880 London had 4 million Englishmen out of a total of 30 million; Paris had almost 3 million Frenchmen out of a total of 37 million. Within a century St. Petersburg and Moscow had increased their populations by 300%, London by 340%, Paris by 345%, Vienna by 490%, Berlin by 872%. There were more Londoners than Belgians.

The tremendous growth in population transformed the physical character of Europe's cities. Until the middle of the nineteenth century many of them were still surrounded by a wall and gates of entry. Since there was no more room within these walls, new factories and new working-class slums sprang up outside them, along the new railroad lines, in nearby rural villages, or along the river that usually wound through the city. Little by little the municipal governments annexed these built-up areas and tore down the city walls. The inner zone of the large city became increasingly the exclusive domain of the middle and upper classes, with its town houses, apartment buildings, public gardens, theaters, offices, restaurants, and department stores. Property in this area was too valuable for low-income housing, so many of the old city tenements were torn down, and the poor people who had always lived in them moved out to new slums in the industrial suburbs.

This physical segregation reinforced the cultural differences between the various classes of city dwellers. Before 1850 rich people and poor people had milled about the public squares in the center of Europe's great cities, and had often lived on the lower and upper floors of the same building. They did not *know* each other, but at least they *saw* each other once in a while. At the end of the nineteenth century the factory workers rarely ventured out of their own neighborhoods, and when a few middle- and upper-class people "went slumming" to a working-class cabaret, they thought of themselves as tourists in a foreign country. Indeed, in London, Paris, Vienna, and Berlin the neighborhoods of the different social groups were so distinct that each had its own accent and its own brand of slang, which was often incomprehensible to outsiders.

The impersonality and segregation of city life was especially hard on the millions of uprooted newcomers. In 1895 only 37 per cent of the inhabitants of Munich had been born there, only 50 per cent in the French city of Saint-Etienne. The figures were typical of hundreds of Europe's cities. Former farm laborers lived brutish lives in the new industrial slums, although they were hardly harsher than their lives in the country. But there was one great difference; the new city dwellers, unlike the immigrants abroad, lacked "colonies" of people from their old cultural environment to make the transition easier. This was especially hard on the new white-collar employees. They came into daily contact with the bourgeoisie through their employment and had to acquire a modicum of refinement in their speech and dress and yet they had to keep their social distance. When they went home from work, they found no circle of friendly neighbors in the impersonal apartment houses in which they lived. Nobody seemed to care what happened to anybody. If a person was hit by a street car, the police removed the body and the sanitation department cleaned up the mess.

Eventually many uprooted newcomers acquired a certain pride in being Parisians, Londoners, or Berliners, but it was impossible to sing the praises of Lille, Sheffield, or Düsseldorf. In these and hundreds of other overgrown mill towns life was much drabber than in the great cities – with their neighborhood vaudeville houses, street entertainers, circuses, and political demonstrations. In the typical mill town the factories, the railroad depot, and the slums occupied the central district, while the rich business and professional men built their mansions in the rural suburbs, away from the smoke and noise. The rich traveled to the capital or to the new seaside resorts for relaxation and diversion; the lower classes never went anywhere.

By the 1890s falling prices and a growing supply of cheap manufactured goods helped to raise the material level of living of the urban workers, but these people were culturally poorer than their country cousins. The peasant village rooted its members in the traditions of a self-sustaining community. Young children in the village were brought up chiefly by their grandparents, while the parents spent most of the day in the fields. This close association between the most malleable and the most inflexible generations was a major source of cultural continuity in many traditional peasant societies. But the grandparents usually did not accompany their adult offspring to the city, where lower-class children ran loose in the streets and often rebelled against parents who had little to teach them and who were unsure of their own relation to the city. Thus, as they grew up, slum dwellers lost contact with the surviving rural folk cultures, and except in a few great cities, they did not begin to identify themselves with the newer forms of urban culture until well after 1905.

### Changes in Rural Europe

The lives of people who stayed on the land were also affected by industrialization, urbanization, and population growth. By the end of the nineteenth century, many farmers in Northwestern Europe had adapted themselves to specialization, intensive farming, and a market economy. Denmark experienced a genuine revolution in its agricultural methods, concentrating particularly on dairy products for export; Holland specialized in cheeses, butter, and flowers; French winegrowers secured their world market by planting new wines after the old ones had been killed by phylloxera in the 1880s. The small independent proprietor survived in modest circumstances from Sweden to northern Italy and from the Atlantic to the Elbe. In contrast, the majority of the peasants of Spain, southern Italy, and Eastern Europe had no way of raising their miserable level of existence. They continued to grow more wheat and rye, weave more baskets, and have more babies than anybody wanted. There had never been just one rural class in Europe, but by 1905 the contrast between a prosperous dairy farmer in Denmark and a poverty-ridden agricultural laborer in Bulgaria was enormous.

This contrast was cultural as well as economic. True folk culture expresses the beliefs, longings, and traditions of people engaged in meaningful kinds of work. Sailors, craftsmen, and peasants each had their own lore and their own way of looking at the world. These forms began to break down in the face of the technological and organizational forms of industrial civilization. Farmers in Nowthwestern Europe had harvest ceremonies involving the symbolic use of bundles of grain cut with a scythe, but these ceremonies lost their meaning as the scythe was replaced by modern tools. Even in Southern and Eastern Europe, peasant folk culture was being altered by store-bought clothes, the railroad, and the decline in the influence of religion.

By 1905 the majority of Englishmen, Germans, and Belgians lived in cities and towns, as did over a third of all Frenchmen. The growing number of white-collar employees was already identifying itself with the popular culture of the urban bourgeoisie, which was to become a truly mass culture by the mid-twentieth century. Both white-collar employees and uprooted proletarians were seeking integration into the dominant society and culture of their newly industrialized countries. This fact, along with the extension of the franchise, universal military training, compulsory primary education, and the concentration of masses of people in urban areas, was to have decisive political effects; both the socialists and the nationalists were to seek their support here.

Urbanization, industrialization, and population growth also began to break down the traditional cultural and social patterns of rural life. As farmers grew rich, they did not necessarily become middle-class, but their political interests began to clash with those of the rural proletariat. The old folk culture was dying away, but it had not yet been replaced, and rural people were to be even slower than city blue-collar workers in accepting the bourgeois culture.

## THE LIFE SCIENCES: THEIR IMPACT ON SOCIETY AND THOUGHT

The general public became increasingly aware of the new wonders of science, technology, and medicine in the second half of the nineteenth century. In 1851 the Crystal Palace Exposition in London had attracted hundreds of thousands of visitors. Thereafter other great cities held international expositions that were attended by millions. Not only the exhibits themselves but the structures around them were triumphs of man's mastery over nature. The most spectacular example was the Eiffel Tower, built for the great Paris Exposition of 1889. A thousand feet high, this awe-inspiring structure showed the seemingly limitless possibilities of steel in building construction. With the invention of photography and the electrically driven rotary press, millions of people who did not visit international expositions could see pictures of them and read about them in the newspapers. Both city-dwellers and farmers felt the benefits of new discoveries in surgery and preventive medicine. But the most epoch-making new scientific discovery of the nineteenth century, Darwin's theory of evolution, caused some consternation among the general public and the churches.

### Microbiology and Medicine

Medicine also benefited enormously from new scientific discoveries. The most notable, the germ theory of disease, was first put forth by the Frenchman Louis Pasteur (1822–1895). In his studies of fermentation and putrefaction Pasteur began to ask himself if the microorganisms that produced them might not attack living tissues as well. Before, everyone had assumed that putrefaction took place spontaneously in dead organic matter. In 1859 Pasteur demonstrated that nothing could putrefy unless living agents were introduced into it. He did this with experiments in which putrefiable materials were kept wholesome in heat-sterilized vessels protected from contamination by airborne dust. Then, drawing on his discovery that some kinds of bacteria caused fermentation, he showed how other kinds of bacteria—carried by dust—caused putrefaction. Finally, he evolved the theory that still other kinds of bacteria caused disease in living tissues. Meanwhile, the German Robert Koch (1843–1910) worked from Pasteur's new theories to develop what were until recently the standard techniques of bacteriology and to discover the tuberculosis bacillus (1882). Pasteur himself soon gave practical application to his theory by successfully combating a silkworm disease caused by bacteria. Later he discovered means of inoculating cows against tuberculosis and human beings against rabies. Medicine could now not only cure, it could also prevent disease.

In Britain, the surgeon Joseph Lister (1827–1913) was disturbed in his early medical experience by the infection that inescapably accompanied surgery and began to think that the suppuration of tissues and the putrefaction of dead matter had similar causes. He adopted Pasteur's theories and found a powerful agent in organic chemistry to hinder infection. In his own practice, he eliminated microorganisms from every possible source of infection by spraying carbolic acid on instruments, the patient, the operators' hands, the dressings, and even the air itself. He introduced his new method of antiseptic surgery at Glasgow in 1865, and thereafter surgery acquired a scope and security hitherto inconceivable.

### Evolution: Darwinism

Charles Darwin (1809–1882) did not originate the idea of evolution; he marshaled the evidence for it, explained how it worked, and developed it into a theory of all forms of life. Over fifty years before the appearance of Darwin's *Origin of Species* in 1859, the French naturalist Jean-Baptiste Lamarck (1744–1829) had emphasized the dynamic aspect of nature, but he had overstrained credulity by claiming that living organisms were able to pass on acquired characteristics to their posterity. In 1830 the British geologist Charles Lyell (1797–1875) had already assigned the Earth an age of 100,000,000 years and described some of the changes in its long physical development. But he still followed Cuvier, the father of palaeontology, who had ascribed the disappearance of extinct species to successive catastrophes.* Darwin spent twenty years collecting specimens of different species

*See p. 294.

A DARWINIAN IDEA.
SUGGESTED BY THE CATTLE SHOW.
THE OLD SORT.
THE MODERN IMPROVEMENT.
WHAT IT MUST COME TO.


*Punch cartoon, December 23, 1865*

of plants and animals in many parts of the world and observing the variations within each species. Finally, in 1859, he explained both the differences among species and the variations within a species as adaptations to environment through a process of natural selection and struggle for survival. Those strains, or "races," within a species that could get food best or run fastest survived, while the other strains died out. It was the same with whole species. But new species were not new "creations." They were rather the outgrowth of the "fittest" strains of older species.

In 1871, in his *Descent of Man*, Darwin extended his theory of the evolution of plants and animals to human beings. Man himself now became part of a unified history of evolution in which all life was interrelated and subject to the same laws. Darwin could not explain *how* individual variations were inherited, nor was he able to produce the "missing link" between the higher primates and man. The study of anthropolgy was still in its infancy, and Darwin knew virtually nothing of cytology, which might have helped him to understand the evolutionary modification of the cells of which an organizm is composed. Still, his general theory of evolution provided a tentative synthesis of all the biological sciences. It also had immediate reprecussions on the religious, political, and economic aspects of European civilization.

Referring to his evidence that man is related to all animal life, he wrote in his *Descent of Man:*

> "The great principle of evolution stands up clear and firm, when these groups of facts are considered in connection with others, such as the mutual affinities of the members of the same group, their geographical distribution in past and present times, and their geological succession. It is incredible that all these facts should speak falsely. He who is not content to look, like a savage, at the phenomena of nature as disconnected, cannot any longer believe that man is the work of a separate act of creation. . . ."

Darwinism not only dethroned man from his central place in the history of the earth, it also seemed to minimize the importance of individual behavior and moral values. The first reactions to it were mostly bigoted and hostile; the long-range reactions were very diverse. For Darwinism was an explosive compound of several ingredients, each of which could be interpreted differently. If the material environment itself were the determining factor in evolution, then Darwinism denied spiritual qualities and degraded men to the level of soulless animals in a blind struggle for survival. If adaptation to environment were more important, then the possibility of conscious adaptations restored scope for voluntary progress and free will. If one emphasized the struggle for survival as the main cause of successful adaptation, then one had to admit that the best adaptation was achieved by selfishness, greed, violence, competition, and conflict. But if the struggle were between species rather than between individuals, it could become an argument for closer cooperation among human beings and even for socialism.

The champions of many different ideologies could find support for their beliefs in Darwinism. Nationalists and imperialists could use it to justify the survival of the fittest in war and the rule of the weak by the strong. Racists could argue that natural selection had made white men more intelligent and more virtuous than non-white men and had even made northern Europeans superior to southern Europeans since the fall of Rome. Freethinkers and anticlericals of all kinds hailed Darwinism as an ally against the "superstitions" and bigotry expounded by the churches. On the one hand, socialists used Darwinism's emphasis on the importance of material conditions as a scientific endorsement for their belief that human progress must come from a better organization of social and economic activity. On the other hand, laissez-faire liberals could claim that natural selection and the struggle for survival supported their goals of free enterprise and cut-throat competition. Had not Darwin himself been strongly influenced by Malthus' idea that there were always more human mouths to feed than food and then simply extended it to the whole world of plants and animals?

Of course nobody really thought of society as a jungle "red in tooth and claw," as Tennyson called nature. All might be fair in love, or war, or business, but men, at least middle- and upper-class Europeans, were civilized; they had learned to be thrifty, self-controlled, morally responsible, and, above all, scientific. As a popularizer of Darwinism the English publicist Herbert Spencer (1820–1903) insisted that the education of the child must be in harmony with the natural stages of the human mind. As a popularizer of positivism he strongly emphasized the value of scientific knowledge, which alone could train human beings in the skills necessary for complete living.

### Positivism

Just as Darwinism stressed progress in biological evolution, positivism stressed progress in human knowledge. The founder of positivism, the French philosopher Auguste Comte (1798–1857), believed that all knowledge had evolved through three stages. The first stage had appeared in primitive times and was purely religious, or "theological"; the second stage had been initiated by the ancient Greek philosophers and was purely "metaphysical"; the third, or "positive," stage had been achieved in the physical sciences by the end of the seventeenth century. Comte set himself the task of bringing the study of social phenomena up to this positive stage. In this way he hoped to assemble all positive knowledge into a single synthesis in which the laws of the more complex sciences rested on the laws of the less—from the most general and abstract theorems of mathematics to biology and finally to the study of human society.

Comte's particular brand of positivism was restricted to a small group of admirers, including John Stuart Mill in England and influential intellectuals in Brazil, Chile, and Mexico, but his general faith in the scientific method as the key to progress dominated European thought during the last third of the nineteenth century. In this broader sense positivism was no longer a formal philosophy but a popular ideology. Science was the key to knowledge and power; anyone who cared to could see this in industry, in warfare, in medicine. All that needed to be done was discover the general laws governing any type of phenomenon or activity, and these phenomena and activities could be made to aid human progress.

As in the case of Darwinism, people of all sorts found their particular beliefs confirmed by positivism. Radicals, anticlericals, and atheists could now claim that their rejection of traditional institutions and values was scientific. Positivism also supported the idea that all citizens could be educated to play a responsible role in a democratic society. By the late nineteenth century the feminists could argue that, since there was no scientific basis for the age-old assumption that women were inferior to men, women should be given the same rights as men. Socialists stressed the scientific virtues of a planned economy; liberals, those of individualism.

The most far-reaching influence of Comte himself was in the new fields of social science. Sociologists, anthropologists, psychologists, political scientists, and even some economists began to operate under the assumption that all human behavior could be predicted and controlled. Men had base instincts, certainly, but they could be diverted into harmless and even constructive channels. Herbert Spencer, for example, thought that betting on horseraces and speculating on the stock exchange could take the place of war in satisfying men's craving for violence and excitement.

## The Resistance of Religion

In the latter part of the nineteenth century religion was on the defensive against science, the "isms," and most aspects of modern civilization. Industrialization and urbanization uprooted masses of people from their traditional religious beliefs and practices; strong national states took over the functions of the churches in education and social welfare. The liberal belief that each individual should think for himself and the democratic notion of the sovereignty of the people also challenged the authority of organized religion, as did the new ideology of Marxism. But religion was most directly threatened by Darwinism and positivism, which used science to challenge the fundamental beliefs of all sects.

### *Protestantism*

Darwinism acted as the greatest single challenge to traditional dogma, especially among Protestants. The obvious analogy between biological evolution and the material progress about which mid-nineteenth-century Europeans seemed so complacent was temporarily obscured by the implications of Darwin's theory for the dignity of man and the literal truth of the Bible as a revelation of Divine actions. The theory of evolution denied all the major events in the Old Testament, events that were "fundamental" to Protestant belief. Original sin and Divine creation had no meaning without Adam and Eve or Noah's ark. How could the "descendant of monkeys" have a soul? Darwin had never said that man was "descended from monkeys," but the Anglican clergy and Protestant ministers in Europe and North America fulminated against such supposed implications of evolution. On one famous occasion Bishop Wilberforce of Oxford taunted the prominent Darwinist Thomas Huxley by asking: "Is it through your grandfather or your grandmother that you are related to the monkey?" Much of this trivial reaction soon died down. But Fundamentalism, the belief that everything in the Bible is literally true and the only proper guide to human conduct, remained strong, especially in the United States, where the controversy over the teaching of evolution in the schools of Tennessee led to the famous Scopes trial in 1925.

Most European Protestants gradually became "modernists," that is, willing to be scientific and to interpret much of the Bible as allegory. Those who continued to go to church out of custom had their minds on more secular matters; many reasserted the value of Christianity, not because of the truth of its doctrines, but because it promoted morality. Even Spencer, in the ripeness of age, had to admit that "the control exercised over man's conduct by theological beliefs and priestly agency has been indispensable." Less socially conscious people than Spencer lauded Christian morality as a bulwark of social order against the "revolt of the masses." Yet their "modernism" did not often prompt them to face the social and economic problems of modern industrial society. The main new Protestant group to take an interest in the poor and the downtrodden, the Salvation Army, was Fundamentalist to the core.

PICTURE GROUP D

# *Nineteenth-Century Art and Architecture*

EUGENE DELACROIX: *Death of Sardanapalus*
Musée National du Louvre, Paris

LONDON, *Houses of Parliament*
British Overseas Airways Corp.

ADOLPH MENZEL, *Early German steel mill*
Staatliche Museum, Berlin

GUSTAVE COURBET: *The Ladies of the Village*
French Cultural Services

JOSEPH MALLORD WILLIAM TURNER: *The Harbor of Dieppe*
Copyright The Frick Collection, New York

LEFT:
JEAN-FRANÇOIS MILLET:

Musée Boymans; French Cultural Services

BELOW:
HONORE DAUMIER: *The Third-Class Carriage*

The Metropolitan Museum of Art, Bequest of Mrs. H. O. Havemeyer, 1929, The H. O. Havemeyer Collection

NEOBAROQUE ARCHITECTURE: *Opéra, Paris*

French Cultural Services

CLAUDE MONET: *Saint Lazare Railroad Station*
Art Institute of Chicago; French Cultural Services

EDGAR HILAIRE GERMAN DEGAS: *Rehearsal of the Ballet on the Stage*
The Metropolitan Museum of Art, Gift of Horace Havemeyer, 1929. The H. O. Havemeyer Collection

RIGHT
PAUL GAUGUIN: *Ia Orana Maria*
The Metropolitan Museum of Arts,

Bequest of Samuel A. Lewisohn, 1951

BELOW:
PIERRE AUGUSTE RENOIR: *In the Meadow*

The Metropolitan Museum of Art, Bequest of Mrs. H. O. Havemeyer, 1929, The H. O. Havemeyer Collection

PAUL CEZANNE: *The Gulf of Marseilles Seen from L'Estaque*

The Metropolitan Museum of Art, Bequest of Mrs. H. O. Havemeyer, 1929, The H. O. Havemeyer Collection

### *The Roman Catholic Church*

Positivism posed a greater threat than Darwinism to the Roman Catholic Church. Catholicism could ultimately accommodate itself to specific scientific theories like evolution; what it fought most was the positivist attempt to substitute faith in science for faith in the only true Savior. The positivist glorification of material progress denied spiritual values; the positivist demand for educational reform threatened the hold of the Church on the minds of the young. It was not so much science itself that the Church condemned as the kinds of things modern-minded people—which to the Church meant positivists—wanted to do in the name of science.

The first official treatment of positivism came in 1864, when Pope Pius IX (1846–1878) published his *Syllabus of Errors.* This document condemned faith in science and modern civilization as a whole and became the ideological manifesto of Integral Catholicism everywhere in Europe. It declared that the Church was a complete and perfect society, independent of and superior to all governments, with the exclusive right to educate and the power to use force if necessary. It denounced freedom of worship for non-Catholics, as well as freedom of the press, universal suffrage, and all theories of national or political sovereignty. The Church had the final authority in everything. It alone could tell Catholics what to believe and which governments to obey; its sacrament alone constituted a true marriage. The last article of the *Syllabus* concluded by warning that it was an error to believe that "the Roman pontiff can and ought to reconcile himself or compromise with progress, liberalism and modern civilization."

Not only did Pius IX reaffirm the "integral" character of Catholicism, he made the authority of the Holy See more absolute than ever. In 1869, 9 months before losing his temporal authority in Rome to the new Kingdom of Italy, he convened a Vatican Council which proclaimed the dogma of papal infallibility. This dogma holds that the pope, when speaking *ex cathedra,* possesses infallibility regarding faith or morals by virtue of his supreme apostolic power. The Holy See continued to have its preferences for the more reactionary political forces in Europe, but it gradually accepted the separation of spiritual and temporal power in the succeeding decades. The dogma of papal infallibility climaxed centuries of development toward a truly international Church in an age when nationalism, state sovereignty, and materialism divided Catholics into increasingly diverse cultural and social groups.

The next pope, Leo XIII (1878–1903), urged Catholic laymen to combat both capitalist and socialist materialism through organizations that would concern themselves directly with the human problems of industrial society. Since the Middle Ages the Church had accepted the economic and social order as God-given; but God had certainly not created industrial capitalism and the social injustice and class conflict it brought with it. These were new, man-made things, and the Church had to guide its followers in dealing with them. Hence, in 1891, Leo XIII issued his encyclical *Rerum Novarum* ("of new things"), which upheld private property but criticized capitalism for the poverty, insecurity, and degradation it imposed on many workers. This encyclical also acknowledged that much in socialism was Christian in principle but criticized its materialistic and anti-religious bias. Just as the Holy See was officially indifferent to forms of government, it now declared itself adaptable to either a capitalist or a socialist society, provided that such a society upheld the spiritual and moral values of Christianity. For this purpose, *Rerum Novarum* suggested that Catholic laymen form political parties, labor unions, and other mass organizations, especially where the anticlericals and socialists were winning large numbers of people away from the true Church.

*Rerum Novarum* was a turning point in the relations between the Roman Catholic Church and modern European society. In the early twentieth century Christian Socialist parties and labor unions appeared in Italy, France, Belgium, Germany, and Austria. And, in the second half of the century, the Church was even able to adapt itself to the Communist regime in Poland.*

On questions of dogma, however, the Holy See made no compromises. Leo XIII reasserted the theological position of Saint Thomas Aquinas in his counteroffensive against irreligion. In another encyclical, his successor, Pius X (1903–1914) condemned efforts of certain "modernist" theologians to make the teachings of the Church conform to new scientific theories of man and nature. In practice, Catholics were able to separate spiritual truth from most scientific theories, as well as from particular forms of government, capitalism, and non-Catholic socialism. On "fundamentals," however, there could be only one kind of Catholic.

### Judaism

Like Protestantism and unlike Catholicism, Judaism was unable to resist religious division. As long as the majority of the Jews lived in the ghettos of Eastern Europe, they managed to maintain their religious and cultural heritage intact. Since the late eighteenth century, however, a handful of Jews in Western and central Europe had chosen the alternative path of assimilation to the dominant culture of the country in which they found themselves. Then, beginning in the late nineteenth century, hundreds of thousands of Eastern European Jews migrated to Austria, Germany, France, Great Britain, and especially the United States. The immigrants generally clung to their Orthodox ways, but the second generation often chose the path of assimilation to the predominantly secular and scientific culture of the age. These Jews imitated the Protestant "modernists" in "reforming" the ritual and practices of their religion in keeping with the needs of modern civilization. The new, Reformed Judaism no longer insisted on the cessation of all activities on the Saturday Sabbath and on eating strictly "kosher" food. Orthodox Jews opposed the use of the organ in religious services because it is not mentioned in the Old Testament; Reformed Jews used organs. Orthodox Jews clung to the story of the Creation as told in the book of Genesis; Reformed Jews accepted Darwin's theory.

The split between Orthodox ("fundamentalist") and Reformed ("modernist") Judaism was complicated by the peculiar status of all Jews in European society. By the late nineteenth century they had been given the same rights as the dominant majority in all countries except Russia; legally, they could vote, own land, and enter any business or profession they chose. Modern-minded Europeans prided themselves on their toleration of the Jews and other minority groups. But there is a difference between toleration and assimilation (integration)—when all are completely assimilated, there are no more minority groups. Neither the majority of Christians nor many Jews were ready for such a situation in the late nineteenth century. Indeed, a minority of non-Jews began to give racial overtones to their nationalism and to advocate new forms of persecution.* Their antisemitism, in turn, gave some Jews a new sense of national identity. These Jews, mostly Orthodox, decided that the only solution to their plight was to have a national state of their own, in Zion, their biblical homeland. To this end they formed the Zionist movement and held their first congress at Basel in 1897.

The condition of the Jews typified the changes that had taken place in European society as a whole by the late nineteenth century. Liberalism and scientific thinking tended to free it from many traditional constraints, but old group differences persisted and new ones asserted themselves. The pride and wonder of the age was that all these different groups could live together in relative harmony.

The impact of science not only challenged traditional religious dogma, it drastically reduced the role of organized religion in modern society. By and large, the modernists in religion held liberal and even democratic attitudes toward government, social organization, and education. The fundamentalists tended to be reactionary on these matters, that is, to feel that their church should still have the final authority regarding them. Funda-

*See Chapter XXI.

*See p. 513 and p. 584.

mentalist Protestants wanted to enforce their strict moral code on everyone in the form of blue laws against gambling, drinking, or working on the Sabbath. Integral Catholics opposed democracy and public education. Orthodox Jews refused to modify their dietary laws or even to turn on a light on Saturdays. In most European countries, however, the state and private individuals and groups tended to go their own ways. Each church became just another private group, and each religion just another compartment of busy people's lives. By the end of the century the controversy between science and religion had died down, and Europeans of diverse faiths resigned themselves to living together in a pluralist society and culture.

## CULTURAL RESPONSES TO A CHANGING CIVILIZATION

In the late nineteenth century an unprecedented development took place: culture became divorced from civilization. Culture means those forms of behavior, thought, and art which express the distinctive way of life of a particular nation or social group; it includes the highest artistic and intellectual creations and those symbolic forms whose primary function is entertainment or embellishment. Civilization means the basic technology, institutions, and values shared by a number of nations or groups. Until a hundred years ago or so the various cultures of Europe had given meaning to the traditional civilization that most Europeans shared. Then as European civilization became more scientific, more industrial, more urban, and more democratic, both old and new cultural forms failed to help any nation or social group adjust its way of life to it adequately.

Of the major nations, England had adapted herself to the new civilization most successfully, Russia least successfully, by 1905. An obvious factor here was the length of time each nation had been industrialized. It seems equally obvious that the bourgeoisie should have found industrial civilization more compatible with its way of life than the nobles, the clergy, or the peasants. After all, its rational principles of organization in business, government, and technology had made industrialization possible in the first place. But, as we have seen, the bourgeoisie came to include more than just wealthy commercial and professional people in the nineteenth century. It was a large and heterogeneous class whose diverse sections coped with their rapidly changing civilization in different ways. In fact, a number of creative artists and intellectuals of bourgeois origin began to define themselves as a distinct social group by *rejecting* this civilization outright. Finally, the industrial workers themselves had to make the most extreme adustment with the least cultural capital.

### Popular Culture

The middle-brow culture of the urban bourgeoisie set the dominant tone for the late nineteenth century; and the first point to note about it is that it was not all waltzes and antimacassars. Real artists as well as hacks produced its various forms. Johann Strauss (1825–1899), the Viennese waltz king, was eminently talented, and his operetta *The Bat* (*Die Fledermaus*), though no *Marriage of Figaro*, was certainly not the work of a mere hack. Alfred, Lord Tennyson (1809–1892), the Victorian Poet Laureate, did not have very much to say, but he said it with a fine sense of language and lyrical precision. What made Strauss and Tennyson essentially middle-brow was the fact that they were content to give artistic decorum to an undecorous world.

The function of middle-brow culture is implicitly dual: veneer and entertainment. In a number of ways the nineteenth-century urban bourgeoisie showed its unwillingness to accept industrial civilization unadorned. These people filled their homes with useless, elaborate bric-à-brac, and their fashions in dress and grooming, especially those of women, were as cumbersome and nonfunctional as the designers could make them. At the height of the industrial boom of the 1850s every woman who could afford one wore a hoop skirt; ten years later the equally impractical bustle replaced it. As late as 1905 steamboats still had sails, railroad stations

*Parisians out for a stroll on a hot summer night in the 1890s*

looked like medieval fortresses, and electric streetcars sported cowcatchers. Even the first skyscrapers were camouflaged with gothic ornamentation.

Operetta, was the most typical middle-brow form of entertainment, and, like all the others, it sacrificed reality for complacency. It provided innocent diversion for the tired businessman and his bored wife in a make-believe, preindustrial world of gypsy barons, merry widows, and student princes. Unlike grand opera, which at least expressed deep emotions, operetta gave its audiences sentimentality and satire in small and often sparkling doses. Jacques Offerbach (1819–1880) was the first to perfect this form, which was then taken up by a long series of composers. Though essentially harmless, it could occasionally be misleading if taken too literally. For example, Parisian audiences gained a false conception of German political life from Offenbach's *The Grand Duchess of Gerolstein*, which confirmed their stereotyped image of Germany as a conglomeration of petty courts and incompetent rulers and generals, and thus made them unprepared for Prussian power in 1870.

Just as they preferred operetta to grand opera, the middle-brows preferred melodrama to tragedy. For in melodrama too, everything came out "all right" in the end. Unlike operetta, melodrama often dealt with the victims of urban industrial civilization: orphans, unwed mothers, working-class families with alcoholic fathers. The shame and injustice of it all brought many tears to many eyes until the last act or the final chapter. Then melodrama cheated the laws of true drama and real life. After leading up to an obviously inevitable disaster, it saved the poor hero or heroine with an unforeseen legacy or the sudden appearance of a brave or rich benefactor.

The over-all message of nineteenth-century middle-brow culture was: everything is understandable and everything can be domesticated. This basic optimism and complacency dominated operetta, melodrama, the science-fiction novels of Jules Verne, and the detective story, which also brought in the theme of science. These forms, like gothic skyscrapers, made what was distant or different seem near and familiar.

Most of the cultural responses that appealed to the uneducated urban masses were watered-down versions of bourgeois models. The low-brows found solace in melodrama long after the middle-brows abandoned it. In a world increasingly dominated by impersonal things and contractual relations, exaggerated sentimentality seemed to be the only alternative to despair. Even in the great cities the working classes produced few original cultural responses of their own.

### Literature and Art

The most original artists and writers protested against the mendacity of bourgeois culture, the evils of industrial civilization, and the failure of this culture and this civilization to offer meaningful solutions to the human predicament. Some sought to redeem humanity through art itself, others through anarchism or socialism.

#### *Realism and Naturalism*

In the novel, especially in France and Russia, romanticism gave way to realism. In his monumental series of novels, *The Human Comedy*, Honoré de Balzac (1799–1850) had launched the realist criticism of an essentially false way of life in which the quest for things, money, and power obscured the basic truths of human relationships. Gustave Flaubert (1821–1880), in his *Madame Bovary*, exposed the heart's corruption brought about by the discrepancy between illusory ideas about life and the reality of living. In the *The Brothers Karamazov* Fedor Dostoevsky (1821–1881) showed that every human situation, even the most trivial, may find itself at the crossroads between Heaven and Hell. Leo Tolstoy (1828–1910) challenged everything: the family, marriage, morals, state, church, education. He strove for nothing less than a renovation of Christianity and the establishment of his own brand of religion on earth. *War and Peace*, *Anna Karenina*, and *Resurrection* expressed his hostility to prevailing social and cultural norms with merciless realism.

Toward the end of the century realism was succeeded by an almost clinical naturalism. In *Hedda Gabler* and *A Doll's House* the Norwegian playwright Henrik Ibsen (1828–1906) depicted the human problems created by the divorce between culture and civilization with a poetic rather than a naturalistic kind of realism. But his younger contemporary, the Swede August Strindberg (1849–1912) exposed with excruciating frankness the personal corruption this divorce engendered in plays like *Miss Julie* and *Dance of Death*. In Russia Maxim Gorky (1868–1936) became the father of the style later known as "socialist realism," but in his early writings culminating in *The Lower Depths* (1902), the theme of man's inhumanity to man ran parallel to the equally powerful themes of humanity amid beastliness and man's yearning for liberation. For Gorky evil was not an "existential" problem, as it was for the author of *The Brothers Karamazov*, or the discrepancy between the truth of religion and the wrongs of civilization, as it was for Tolstoy. Evil was caused by the faulty organization of society, and according to Gorky, it could be remedied by socialism.

#### *Impressionism and Symbolism*

After 1870 a number of painters and poets in the West came to view high culture as a private domain of beauty and truth, which, like religion, was becoming increasingly separate from industrial civilization. French impressionist painters sought to make art "quicken" in a new kind of light. Manet, Renoir, Monet, and Degas were primarily concerned with showing the play of light on the changing surface aspects of nature and movements. They transmuted ugly details through soft hazes and startling colors and avoided any suggestion of deeper meaning in their paintings.* Monet once said that he wished that he could have begun to paint without knowing what the objects before him were. Like many other late-nineteenth-century painters, he wanted to detach himself and his works from everything material, everything literary, everything moral.

Symbolism expressed the doctrine of art for art's sake in poetry as impressionism did in painting. The pioneer of symbolism, which was to dominate European

*See pp. 492-493.

poetry until the 1930s, was the French poet Arthur Rimbaud (1854–1891). He announced the poet's isolation from and opposition to all forms of contemporary civilization: democracy, industry, sordid cities; and even the grammar, syntax, and accepted meanings of words that stood in the way of the poet's vision of the absolute. At the age of twenty Rimbaud felt that he had exhausted all the possibilities of the poetic imagination in three short books, one of which he called *A Season in Hell.* He then renounced literature and Europe altogether and spent the rest of his life as a drifter in Africa.

The French symbolists of the 'eighties and 'nineties tried to remove their poetry from all contamination by the vulgar, modern world. Stéphane Mallarmé (1842–1898) said that poems are made of words, not ideas. His ambition to write poetry that would live by itself and for itself was a form of exile comparable to the physical escape from European civilization sought by a number of creative artists—like Paul Gauguin's flight to Tahiti. One of Mallarmé's sonnets, perhaps the most famous, describes a swan whose wings are caught in a frozen lake. The obscurity of his language (which he self-consciously cultivated) presents difficulties, but Mallarmé seems to be using the swan to symbolize the sensitive man prevented from developing his personality fully in the crass, smug society of the late nineteenth century.

Some of the symbolists did not limit their protest to the nebulous villainy of bourgeois values and taste; they wanted to change both life and art. The Belgian poet Emile Verhaeren (1855–1916) anticipated twentieth-century efforts to find aesthetic meaning in modern life, the pulsation of machines, and the slow rise of the masses. What he indicted was the capitalist system itself. In France, Mallarmé and his companions flouted conventional manners as well as traditional artistic forms in order to "exasperate the bourgeoisie." Their nonconformist behavior paralleled the bombings and other outrages perpetrated by the political anarchists in the early 1890s. The radicalism of the poets had less impact on society than that of the anarchists and socialists,* but it indicated an intensification of social and cultural conflict that was later to lead to greater upheavals.

### Morris and Wagner

In Britain the effort to redeem civilization through a cultural renovation took a different form. Edward Carpenter, a thoughtful reformer, published a book entitled *Civilization: Its Cause and Cure* (1889); another reformer, William Morris, advocated "simplicity of life" as the only cure. As one means of restoring simple meaning to the lives of England's industrial workers Morris led a campaign for the revival of folk dancing; the special kind of dance he advocated was performed by people in costumes representing personages of the Robin Hood legend. Morris also decried the heavy, ornate, and gloomy architectural style of the mid-Victorian period and said that "the world should sweep away all art for a while . . . that it might yet have a chance to quicken in the dark."

In Germany Richard Wagner† went to the most elaborate lengths to make high culture a renovating force. He conceived of his opera as a synthesis of all the arts, combining the arts of vision—gesture, drama, color, painting, architecture—with the arts of sound—poetry, song, music, orchestration. Like William Morris and the symbolist poets, Wagner loathed the soulless materialism of his age, which was especially oppressive in the new German Empire. Since this age lacked any spontaneous feeling for the dramatic significance of life, Wagner turned to the age portrayed by German mythology for inspiration. The *Ring of the Niebelungen* provided him with "material" for a cycle of four long operas of the same name in which Siegfried and Brunhilde, among others, dramatically sought power and glory and challenged the gods themselves. In *Parsifal* Wagner gave his version of the medieval legend of the search for the Holy Grail. Never before or since has any form of high culture provided a challenge to

*See pp. 517-524.

†See p. 418.

contemporary civilization on as grandiose a scale as Wagnerian opera.

### Nietzsche

The German philosopher Friedrich Nietzsche (1844–1900) was the profoundest critic of bourgeois culture and modern civilization. His short-lived admiration for Wagner, added to later misinterpretations of his idea of the "will to power," gave rise to the legend that he saw his fellow Germans as a "master race" destined to conquer the world. Nothing could have been further from Nietzsche's mind. Although he loved Wagner's music, Nietzsche as well as Wagner himself was revolted by the way the German middle class, whose "cultural philistinism" he despised, "appreciated" this music at the Bayreuth festivals and tried to see in it an expression of their antisemitic nationalism. Nietzsche's response to modern civilization was not Wagner's alleged mixture of Christianity and "blonde beasts." It was a reasoned search for new values.

Like Socrates, his real hero, Nietzsche saw himself as the "gadfly" of his society and the "vivisectionist" of contemporary conceit and hypocristy. In his *Untimely Meditations* and *The Birth of Tragedy* he argued that culture—by which he meant the spontaneous creation of original norms and values—was the only goal that could give meaning to life. In *Thus Spake Zarathustra* and *Beyond Good and Evil* he exposed the inconsistencies involved in the attempt to harmonize the ancient moral code of Christianity with modern civilization and the compromises that were constantly being made between moral theory and social practice. Nietzsche also opposed liberalism, socialism, nationalism, and democracy as inimical to culture as he saw it. Concerning the belief that whatever is later in the evolutionary scale is necessarily more valuable, he said that "the goal of humanity cannot lie in the end [that is, the species in its present form] but only in its highest specimens." This assertion from the *Untimely Meditations* gives the clue to Nietzsche's theory of values and to his "aristocratic" ethics.

Nietzsche is justly famous for his concept of the "superman," but we must be careful to understand what he meant. He believed that it was up to "free spirits," creative artists and philosophers like himself, to show superior individuals how to surpass themselves and to make a better world for the future. But Nietzsche did not intend these "supermen" to take over political supremacy. They were antipolitical individuals seeking self-perfection—the only ultimate value—far from the modern world. Their "will to power" was directed more toward overcoming their own mediocre qualities than toward transforming society, and society was to be censured insofar as it insisted on conformity and impeded their development.

The shrill and provocative quality of Nietzsche's writings often obscured his basic intentions. He insisted that "war and courage have done more great things than brotherly-love" and left it to the context to show that "war" meant strife, "courage" exertion, and "brotherly-love" the ineffectual sentiment of sterile souls who fled their task of self-perfection. In an age when science and techology made bourgeois life complacent and when the state began to take the masses in tow, Nietzsche insisted (in *The Gay Science*):

> "that a human being *attain* his satisfaction within himself . . . only then is a human being at all tolerable to behold. Whoever is dissatisfied with himself is always ready to revenge himself therefor; we others will be his victims. . . ."

Many artists and writers sympathized with Nietzsche's views, but none could resolve the growing conflict between culture and civilization. All the cultural responses of the late nineteenth century were somehow contradictory and inadequate. For all its sugar coating, the outlook of the middle-brow bourgeoisie was secular and materialistic; for all its emphasis on competition and self-help, it showed some concern for the plight of the poor and the downtrodden. Just as some of the poor and the downtrodden turned to socialism, others tried to ape the ways of the lower middle class. The upper middle class tried to adopt the social

Karl Marx

graces and paternalistic outlook of the older ruling elite it was displacing. Meanwhile, a new outlook, Marxism, began to challenge all nineteenth-century cultural responses—from Wagner to melodrama—as mere window-dressing that camouflaged the obvious injustice of the whole economic, political, and social order.

## MARXISM

At this point we must consider the ideology of Marxism, for it gave a quite different view from that shared by the apparently dominant bourgeoisie. The Marxist view, which also drew on the prestige of science, had two main aspects: (1) a system of ideas showing that the existing order in all fields—government, society, religion, culture, the economy—was a mere superstructure by means of which the bourgeoisie exploited the worders; (2) a program of action—proletarian revolution—to overthrow the dominant bourgeoisie and establish a truly proletarian society and culture.

The need to understand Marxism is obvious. Today half the people of Europe and almost a third of the people of the world live in officially Marxist societies. Never before in history has any government succeeded in using a system of ideas to achieve, or even try to achieve, the kind of totalitarian rule that now exists in Russia, China, and every country from East Germany to North Vietnam. No one else has ever approached it—not Calvin in Geneva, not Louis XIV, not even Hitler. Although its first triumph was not to come until the Russian Revolution of 1917, the Marxist view of the world already began to challenge the prevailing view of Europe in the late nineteenth century. We shall see how this happened in the next chapter but first we must examine the ideology of Marxism itself.

Marxism made its first appearance in 1848 in *The Communist Manifesto*, an obscure pamphlet written by two Germans, Karl Marx (1818–1883) and Friedrich Engels (1820–1895). Marx, the son of a lawyer in the Prussian Rhineland, had studied law and philosophy and then begun a career as a publicist and political journalist, mainly in France and England. Engels, the son of a well-to-do German textile manufacturer, also spent much of his time in England, where he managed one of his father's factories. The two men originally met in Paris in the 1840s. There they joined the Communist League (also called the League of the Just), which in Engels' own words, was "not actually much more than the German branch of the French secret societies." Marx and Engels decided to make it much more. The closing words of their *Manifesto* foretold exactly what they had in mind: "Let the ruling classes tremble at a communist revolution. The proletarians have nothing to lose but their chains. They have a world to win. Workingmen of all countries, unite!"

Why should the ruling classes tremble? Why did the workers of the world have nothing to lose but their chains? Why should they unite?

In *The Communist Manifesto* and many later books Marx and Engels constructed a theory of man, society, and history to show why these developments were inevitable. They claimed that this theory superseded the theories of the utopian socialists* because it was *scientific*. According to Marx and Engles, it was scientific because it was based on the actual conditions of early industrial civilization as they observed them in England in the mid-nineteenth century. It was also scientific because it gave a more adequate explanation of man, society, and history than any other theory.

Whether or not Marxism is in fact more scientific than other socialist theories is, of course, open to question. But it is distinguishable from them in its three basic assumptions: (1) that the ways in which men produce goods and services to satisfy their needs determine the general character of social life; (2) that class warfare is the determining factor in history; (3) that every class-dominated society has a moral code peculiar to itself. These three assumptions may be summarized as materialism, class warfare, and class morality. They are a far cry from the utopian socialists' preoccupation with the progress of knowledge, with social harmony, and with universal moral values.

According to Marxism, the basis of civilization is mainly material. Man is primarily a practical animal; he must, if he is to keep alive and propagate his species, learn to control external nature. The ways in which he produces goods and services to satisfy his needs determine the general character of social life, including the ideas with which he explains both the world and his position in it. As he subdues nature to his purposes he transforms himself and his social environment; as his needs grow indefinitely greater, they require more complex techniques and more elaborate systems of thought. Yet no matter how sophisticated his civilization becomes—even when it seems to be beyond his control—the way is changes is still determined by how he produces goods and services to satisfy his needs.

The way men produce what satisfies their needs also divides society into classes. According to Marx, social relations either are, or correspond to, what he calls "the relations of property." He never explains just how they correspond; he merely assumes that the division of any society into classes depends on how the rights of property over external objects and human services (that is, "the means of production"—land, capital, and labor) are distributed. This distribution depends on what the rules of property are, and these, in turn, are determined by how men produce what satisfies their needs. In the agricultural economy of the Middle Ages the feudal lords established rules of property that gave them the exclusive right to own and to employ the labor of serfs. Thus, medieval society was divided into two classes: the exploiting landlords and the exploited peasants. In modern times, the bourgeois capitalists have property rights over the industrial means of production, rights that enable them to appropriate a large part of what the propertyless workers produce. Thus modern society is divided into two classes: the capitalists and the proletariat.

The state too is an instrument of class domination, according to Marx. The dominant class creates and uses the type of political system that will best preserve the system of property on which its superiority rests. Thus, in the Middle Ages, the feudal system concentrated all political and military power in the hands of the landowning nobility, with the king, the Church, the law courts, and the army under their control. In nineteenth-century Europe too, the dominant class used the state to maintain its economic interests. No matter what concessions were made in the way of constitutional rights and representative assemblies, the bourgeois capitalists used all branches of government to maintain a system of property that allowed them to exploit the proletariat. For example, they made laws against strikes and used the police and the army to enforce these laws.

Nevertheless, social relations and government are not static. If they were, then the evolution from feudalism to capitalism could never have occurred. The fact that it did occur was due to changes in productive methods—in the material basis of civilization. As this happened, the medieval businessmen, the precursors of the modern capitalists, grew in numbers and in

*See pp. 389-391.

strength until they finally destroyed the feudal system. They abolished or transformed the rights of property on which the superiority of the feudal nobles rested and replaced the political system of the Middle Ages with new methods of protecting property rights and keeping the peace.

This explanation illustrates the historical determinism of Marxism. Changes in productive methods create new classes whose material interests clash with those of the ruling classes. As the prevailing system of property "fetters" production, the class that stands to benefit the most from the new productive methods challenges it and eventually overthrows it. This had begun to happen at the end of the Middle Ages, and it was happening again in the nineteenth century, for as the productive methods of capitalism changed, they enlarged and strengthened the proletariat. Technological advances and expanding production increased its size, while the concentration of capital in a few giant monopolies reduced the formerly independent producers to the level of propertyless workers. (That is, it "proletarized" them.) As the rich prospered and the poor grew hungrier, the latter, with "nothing to lose but their chains," would inevitably unite and overthrow the former. History determined this outcome, and nothing could stop it.

Still, there are class wars and class wars. The bourgeois capitalists who triumphed over the feudal nobles misunderstood the nature of their revolution. They were unconscious innovators, and as often as not they put forward demands they believed to be rooted in tradition. Marx spoke quite differently of the proletariat. It was destined to become a revolutionary class of a kind that the bourgeoisie never had been. Unlike the bourgeoisie, it would aim deliberately at the destruction of one social order and the establishment of another. In fact, to the extent that the industrial workers accepted socialist ideologies, especially Marxism, they were already aiming at it. Although their goal was historically determined, their destiny was unique. They were to be the only self-consciously revolutionary class.

Not only would the proletariat understand the historical significance of its activities as the bourgeoisie never had understood its own, it would also have the Communists to enlighten it. In the *Communist Manifesto* Marx and Engles spoke of the Communists as "the most resolute and advanced section" of the working class, who understood "the line of march, the conditions, and the ultimate general results of the proletarian movement." One of the first things the Communists should show the workers was that they had to reject the whole superstructure of bourgeois society.

Marx and Engels recognized that there were more than two classes in a given society. For example, they showed their awareness that in the nineteenth century there were also petty bourgeois shopkeepers and white-collar employees, whose interests did not exactly coincide with those of the monopoly capitalists. They also recognized the existence of a *Lumpenproletariat*—a proletariat of vagrants, criminals, and other "ragged" types—which had no morality of its own and which spawned the strike-breakers and other saboteurs of the interests of the true proletariat of honest workers. Nevertheless, Marx and Engels usually singled out two classes as protagonists in the class war, and treated the others as subordinate allies or as neutrals. In the class war of the late nineteenth century, it was the rich bourgeoisie that was the main enemy of the proletariat, and it was the interests of this class that the superstructure was designed to preserve.

As we know, Marx believed that this superstructure included law, government, art, and religion—which served as "the opiate of the people" in making them accept the status quo. It also included the dominant morality.

The idea that each class tended to have its own class morality "corresponding to" its class interests is the third basic assumption of Marxism. When there is a ruling class, like the bourgeoisie, its class morality will be accepted more or less by all classes until its supremacy is challenged. This was so not only because the ruling class had a monopoly of power to enforce its ideas about justice and right conduct but also because all men's ideas about justice and right conduct tended everywhere to be influenced by the rules actually enforced. Thus, it was up to the workers to see, and the Communists to show them, that the dominant morality of the late nineteenth century was opposed to their interests and had therefore to be rejected, along with the rest of the bourgeois superstructure.

Marxism does more than show that the moral and other values of bourgeois society are the values of a class; it also argues that they are "objectively" bad. This argument is logically inconsistent with the doctrine that there are no "eternal" moral rules and that every system of morality serves to justify group interests. But Marx and Engels wanted to transform society as well as explain it, and in order to do this they had to condemn the society they wanted to destroy. They had to convince the proletariat that its morality was superior to bourgeois morality, even though their deterministic philosophy denied the superiority of one morality over another (somewhat as "bourgeois" thinkers like Mill and Spencer continued to accept Christian morality while denying it any theological basis). Unless they could change the workers' ideas about what was just, they could not hope to persuade the proletariat to assume its "true" revolutionary role.

So Marx and Engels gave a brilliant, if no longer convincing, appraisal of the "evils" of bourgeois society. They showed how bourgeois society drove both the workers *and* the capitalists into lives that did not bring happiness. The capitalists had to inhibit some of their natural affections and capacities in order to compete successfully with other capitalists for profits. The workers too, with nothing to sell but their labor, had to compete for jobs, and their work was monotonous and depressing. Both the capitalists and the workers were thus forced to lead lives that exhausted them without providing release for their creative energies. And there was no hope for anything better, given the capitalist system of economic organization, which increasingly threatened the less successful capitalists with ruin and disgrace and the workers with unemployment. (We must remember that Marx and Engels saw many examples of periodic unemployment and overproduction in the period in which they wrote, especially in the 1840s and 1870s.)

But how would the proletarian revolution be different from all previous revolutions? Would it not merely substitute the interests and morality of one class for those of another?

In answering these questions Marx and Engels seemed to abandon all pretense of being scientific and to become as utopian as the earlier socialists whom they condemned. They argued that the proletarian revolution would create a classless society in which there would be no need for an artificial superstructure to preserve the interests of one class against those of the rest of society. The state, which by the Marxist definition was an instrument of class rule, would serve no useful function in such a society and would "wither away." In the Communist utopia religion too would disappear as men come to understand the purely material and practical basis of civilization and morality. Art would survive as a means of helping the toiling masses to gain this kind of understanding, instead of perpetuating the false values of the ruling class as it always had in the past. The morality of the classless society would consist of rules which, given men's capacities and the resources at their disposal, would make for the greatest human happiness. Shades of Saint-Simon, Comte, and Fourier!

Marxism turned out to be wrong on many points. It did not foresee that the ownership of capital would become more widely diffused, and that industrial progress would alter the class structure without reducing the number of classes or aggravating conflicts between them. It did not anticipate that the working class might become so formidable through labor unions and political parties that it would be able to extort concessions making revolution unnecessary. In the twentieth century Marxist leaders were to despair at the stupidity of workers who, in flagrant contradiction to their class interest, gave their enthusiasm and their lives to causes like nationalism and fascism, which the decaying bourgeoisie allegedly promoted in order to forestall its ultimate collapse. Finally, Marxism failed to see that industrial civilization did not remove the need for hierarchy but merely changed its character—that the Communist "utopias" of today would produce their own "new [ruling] class."

Still, Marxism had an irresistible appeal for many alienated workers and intellectuals beginning in the late nineteenth century. It raised, more acutely than any other theory, important questions about how social phenomena should be classified and about causal relations between them. Also, its "scientific" approach and its materialism were in keeping with the temper of the age. Marx himself has been called the Machiavelli among socialist thinkers. He advocated a new kind of *Realpolitik*, not for princes or states but for a chosen class. His assessments of actual situations were incisive, and the advice that he gave to the workers or to the groups in which he took an interest was often well given. Marx helped to destory many illusions and, in an age when culture was at odds with civilization, he showed a way of bringing them together through a new system of distribution, socialism.

: : :

By 1905 scientific and technological advances had not only altered the material basis of European civilization, they had also affected all fields of human activity, from procreation to politics. The number of Europeans had increased at a prodigious rate, and these people were on the move, especially to the cities. This physical uprooting spelled doom for the traditional folk cultures of Europe's masses. At the same time, Darwinism and positivism fatally weakened the hold of traditional religion on the educated bourgeoisie. Many old attitudes survived, including Christian morality. Indeed, all levels of culture changed more slowly than science, technology, and the economic structure. The urban and rural masses remained culturally and socially isolated from the ruling elites, but these elites were not as united in their desire to preserve the status quo as Marx claimed they were. As we shall see in the next chapter, they did not hesitate to cater to the masses in their political conflicts with each other. For industrialization, urbanization, and population growth made mass movements possible, and the divorce between culture and civilization favored those movements that offered new values and programs of action for achieving them: democracy, socialism, and nationalism.

## SUGGESTED READINGS

Hayes, Carleton J. H., *A Generation of Materialism, 1871–1900*. New York: Harper and Row, 1963. Torchbook.*

An excellent volume in the Rise of Modern Europe series.

Eco, Umberto and G. B. Zorgoli, *A Picture History of Inventions*. New York: The Macmillan Co., 1963.

Good descriptions of nineteenth-century inventions.

*The Cambridge Economic History of Europe*, Vol. VI, *The Industrial Revolutions and After*.

See comments in readings for Chapter X.

Morton, Frederick, *The Rothschilds*. Greenwich, Conn.: Fawcett World Library, 1964. Crest.*

Entertaining history of Europe's most famous banking family.

Landes, David, *Bankers and Pashas*. Cambridge, Mass.: Harvard Univ. Press, 1958.

The early chapters give a very good summary of the development of European investment banking in the mid-nineteenth century.

For a more detailed, older treatment, see:

Edwards, George W., *The Evolution of Finance Capitalism*. New York: Longmans, Green and Co., 1938.

Feis, Herbert, *Europe, the World's Banker, 1870–1914*. New York: W. W. Norton, n.d.*
Rich in detail on European investments abroad.

Wilson, Charles H., *History of Unilever: A Study in Economic Growth and Social Change* . 2 vols. London: Cassel, 1954.
The first volume gives a good case study of the rise of big business in the late nineteenth century.

Bruck, W. F., *Social and Economic History of Germany from William II to Hitler, 1888–1938*. London: Oxford Univ. Press, 1938.
The early chapters describe the impact of rapid industrialization in the late nineteenth century.

Thistlethwaite, Frank, "Migration from Europe Overseas in the Nineteenth and Twentieth Centures." Chapter IX of *Population Movements in Modern European Society*, ed. Herbert Moller. New York: The Macmillan Co., 1964.*
Summarizes recent research on the subject.

Métraux, Guy S. and François Crouzet, eds., *The Nineteenth-Century World*. New York: New American Library of World Literature, 1963. Mentor.*
A selection of articles from UNESCO's *Journal of World History*. Though somewhat advanced, they are so up-to-date and authoritative that they can be read with profit by the student. See especially the articles on technology, biology, medicine and public health, religions, artistic expression, and philosophy.

Dampier, William C., *A History of Science and Its Relations with Philosophy and Religion*. 4th ed. Cambridge, Eng.: Cambridge Univ. Press, 1961.
A standard account, although it does not always deliver what the title promises.

Irvine, William, *Apes, Angels, and Victorians: The Study of Darwin, Huxley and Evolution*. Cleveland: World Publishing Co., n.d. Meridian.*
A popular account.

Himmelfarb, Gertrude, *Darwin and the Darwinian Revolution*. Garden City, N. Y.: Doubleday and Co., n.d. Anchor.*
A scholarly interpretative study.

Masur, Gerhard, *Prophets of Yesterday: Studies in European Culture 1890–1914*. New York: Harper-Row,1966.*
An excellent survey of the major thinkers and literary writers of the time.

Williams, Raymond, *Culture and Society*. New York: Harper-Row. 1966*
A thoughtful essay on the divorce between culture and civilization in England—especially good on the late nineteenth century.

Barzun, Jacques, *Darwin, Marx, Wagner: Critique of a Heritage*. New York: Doubleday and Co., 1958. Anchor.*
A provocative essay in intellectual and cultural history.

Kaufmann, Walter, *Nietzsche: Philosopher, Psychologist, Antichrist*. Cleveland: World Publishing Co., 1956. Meridian.*
A brilliant and on the whole successful attempt to rehabilitate this much misunderstood genius.

Berlin, Isiah, *Karl Marx, His Life and Environment*. New York: Oxford Univ. Press, 1959.* The best biography.

Wilson, Edmund, *To the Finland Station: A Study in the Writing and Acting of History*. Garden City, N. Y.: Doubleday and Co., 1953. Anchor.*
A classic essay on Marxism.

CHAPTER XIV

# DEMOCRACY, SOCIALISM, AND NATIONALISM 1871–1905

The *Communist Manifesto* had urged the workers of all nations to unite in a common cause and to reject any alliance with nationalism or bourgeois parliamentary democracy. Democracy, socialism, and nationalism were not mutually exclusive movements; they could be allied, as well as in conflict, in different countries. Though opposed to the existing economic structure, the British socialists supported British parliamentary democracy and British national interests. Socialists on the continent adopted an internationalist outlook, but even there the majority gradually came to believe that true democracy could be achieved without revolution. And some industrial workers began to see trade-unionism and state initiative as alternative means of improving their lot. Thus, despite the pronouncements of the socialist International, the masses of working people in Western and Central Europe identified themselves increasingly with the national interests and hardening political systems of their native lands.

Like the bourgeoisie, the modern state seems always to have been "rising," but only after 1870 did it seriously undertake the regulation of society. There had been earlier steps in this direction in Great Britain and France: Napoleon I's University of secondary and higher education (1806), Robert Peel's London Metropolitan Police (1829), the British Poor Law Commissioners (1834), and the "Haussmannization" of Paris (1850s and 1860s).* In the late nineteenth century, however, the powers and functions of the state increased at an unprecedented rate in the more advanced countries. The changes that were producing the urbanization and industrialization of society also gave governments the technical and organizational means of dealing with them. The increase in the activities of the state was both the cause and the effect of far closer reciprocal relations between government and society. Even in less advanced countries the growth in the state's power tended to buttress the existing form of government.

These developments led to the decline of the earlier type of liberalism almost everywhere. In the least authoritarian countries the democratization of government policies and the extension of the franchise hastened its decline. Elsewhere, the small minorities of liberals were either driven underground by the government,

*See pp. 342, 396, 382, and 442, respectively.

as in Russia, or weakened by the government's use of authoritarian methods, as in Germany and Austria-Hungary.

## THE PATTERNS OF PARLIAMENTARY DEMOCRACY

Two trends dominated the political life of Western and Central Europe: democratization and the extension of the power of the state. By 1871 industrialization and war had already strengthened the authority of the British and French governments and created strong national states in Germany and Italy. Thereafter the changed material and cultural conditions of industrialization made many governments begin to modify their laissez-faire attitude and aroused popular demands for more general participation in the shaping of national policies. As both the state and society changed, the need to bind them together more closely became increasingly important.

Parliamentary democracy filled this need, at least provisionally, in the advanced countries. In essence it was the old parliamentary system of the liberals with a wider suffrage and better-organized parties grafted onto it. By the end of the nineteenth century every advanced country had some kind of constitution limiting the powers of the different branches of government and guaranteeing the civil liberties of its citizens, as well as some kind of representative assembly: the British House of Commons, the French, Belgian, and Italian Chambers of Deputies, the German Reichstag and the Austrian Reichsrat. But the extent to which governments were truly democratic—of the people, for the people, by the people—varied widely, even when the forms were the same. The key test was not universal suffrage but ministerial responsibility: the degree to which the government ministries, or cabinets, were accountable to and controlled by the representatives of the people.

Neither democratization nor the extension of state power was achieved without conflict. Many conservatives and moderate liberals resisted universal suffrage as a "leap in the dark," while enthusiastic radicals endowed it with a magic power to

RIVAL STARS.
MR. BENDIZZY (HAMLET). "'TO BE, OR NOT TO BE, THAT IS THE QUESTION:'—AHEM!"
MR. GLADSTONE (out of an engagement). [Aside.] "'LEADING BUSINESS,' FORSOOTH! HIS LINE IS 'GENERAL UTILITY!' IS THE MANAGER MAD? BUT NO MATTERRR—A TIME WILL COME—"


*Cartoon on the alternation of Disraeli and Gladstone as Prime Minister (Punch, 1868)*

sweep away the last vestiges of privilege, squalor, and ignorance. The attempt of the state to limit the influence of the Roman Catholic Church brought especially bitter struggles in France and Germany. Like universal military training, free compulsory education forged new ties between the nation and the citizen. Nevertheless, in education, in the army, and in government the democratic principle of mass participation at the bottom did not apply at the top. The gap between the rulers and the ruled remained, and repression and revolution survived as possible alternatives to reform.

### Great Britain

Until the 1890s Disraeli and Gladstone kept Great Britain on the path of moderate reform. Benjamin Disraeli, the leader of the Conservatives, represented a new type of conservative nationalism. He was primarily concerned with British prestige and interests abroad but he recognized the need to mollify the working class by showing a paternalistic concern for it. William Gladstone, the Liberal leader, represented a quite different temperament and outlook—that of a liberal with a religious conscience. He combined the reforming zeal of the Methodists with the utilitarianism of the Philosophical Radicals* in a latter-day crusade for political justice for all. Hence, the alternating ministries of Disraeli and Gladstone were not mere shifts from "Tweedledee" to "Tweedledum." Yet neither statesman challenged the parliamentary system, the power of the traditional elites, or free enterprise.

The reforms of Disraeli and Gladstone made the British government more democratic and tied it more closely to British society without altering the basic structure of either the government or society. We have already noted Disraeli's extension of the franchise in 1867 and Gladstone's institution of the secret ballot and his reforms in education, the civil service, and the judiciary between 1870 and 1873. During Disraeli's second ministry (1874–1880) Parliament extended and codified existing acts regulating conditions in the mines and factories and setting minimum standards of sanitation. It also passed a Public Health Act and an Artisans' Dwelling Act that was the first serious attempt by any British government to deal with the problem of low-income housing. The main reforms of the second Gladstone ministry (1880–1885) were political rather than social. His Franchise Bill of 1884 provided nearly universal manhood suffrage; all male adults could now vote except domestic servants, bachelors living with their parents, and casual laborers with no fixed residence. A year later Gladstone's Redistribution Bill abolished the historic counties and boroughs as the basis for representation in the House of Commons; the individual now became the sole voting unit.

British parliamentary democracy thus came a long way toward government of the people and for the people, but it was not a government by the people. Parliament, the cabinet, and the high administrative posts were still virtually monopolized by men from the middle and upper classes. Although both the Liberals and the Conservatives developed mass followings at the polls and party discipline in the House of Commons, neither party represented the working class or that other mass minority, the Irish. In fact, it was Gladstone's insistence on Irish Home Rule that split the Liberal Party and prepared the way for a decade of coalition government by Conservatives and Liberal Unionists (advocates of the continuing union of Ireland and Great Britain) after 1895.

*See p. 407.

### *The Irish Question*

In the late nineteenth century most Britishers would have said that there was no "Irish Question, " that Ireland was a part of the United Kingdom, and that anyone who challenged this "fact" was a traitor and a fanatic. The most that the Conservatives and many Liberals were willing to offer by way of reform was to help the individual Irish tenant buy out his absentee landlord and become a peasant proprietor. Yet even these concessions indicated liberal Britain's bad conscience. Gladstone and his followers tended to think of the Irish as an underprivileged minority group that was entitled to freedom from the obligation to support an alien church (he "disestablished" the Church of Ireland in 1869) and to a degree of political autonomy. But his Home Rule Bills were defeated in Parliament in 1886 and in 1893, and the more ardent Irish patriots would settle for nothing less than national independence and complete separation from England. For them the Irish were a nation, not just a minority group.

In the 1880s Charles Stewart Parnell (1846–1891) tried to unite all Irish opponents of English rule. As a member of the British House of Commons he obstructed the business of that body with filibustering speeches. Parnell and other nationalist leaders also intimidated Irish tenants taking advantage of British efforts to give them more land, though Parnell himself repudiated out-and-out acts of terrorism, like the murder in broad daylight of two prominent British officials by members of the extremist Fenian Brotherhood. In 1890 Parnell's reputation was ruined by his role as "the other man" in a divorce suit. After that the Irish nationalists split into two groups, and Ireland was comparatively peaceful for the next two decades. Nevertheless, the Irish Question was to remain one of the great unsolved problems of British parliamentary democracy.

### France

The pattern of parliamentary democracy in France differed from that in Great Britain in some ways. First, the Third Republic was a new regime, and just how it would work out was a problem in itself. In addition, France already had universal manhood suffrage in 1871, and her voters had a wider choice of political parties than the British. Her liberal leaders were more systematic than Gladstone in curbing the influence of the Church, but there was no French Disraeli to lead a strong conservative nationalist party. Indeed, there were times when the most extreme conservatives and nationalists became the most implacable enemies of the existing regime. Despite these differences, the French pattern of parliamentary democracy produced similar results to the British: the triumph of moderate constitutional government, the strengthening of the authority of the state, and the failure to integrate the working class into the dominant political and social structure. In France, however, these results were achieved in a far more dramatic fashion.

The Third Republic came into being in the aftermath of a lost war and a bloody revolution. As we have seen, republican mobs in Paris had overthrown the Second Empire on September 4, 1870 and set up a provisional government that defended their city against the Germans until the end of January, 1871. In February Bismarck insisted that France elect a National Assembly that would sign a peace treaty with the new German Empire in the name of the French nation. Under the leadership of the Orleanist liberal Adolphe Thiers, this Assembly accepted Bismarck's peace terms in March and then moved from Bordeaux to Versailles. The radicals in Paris resented these developments bitterly. Already overwrought by the physical suffering and nervous tension of a four-month siege, they felt themselves further humiliated by the peace settlement and by the entry of German troops into the capital. Because they also feared that the National Assembly at Versailles would try to make France a monarchy again they repudiated its authority and set up the Paris Commune in its place.* This revolution and its ultimate suppression were far more violent than the overthrow of the Second Empire.

#### *The Commune*

Isolated from the National Assembly and the rest of the country, the government of the Commune controlled the capital for over two months (March 18-May 28). Its leaders included some socialists, but it was not primarily a movement for economic and social change; it did not touch the contents of the Bank of France, and its most "socialistic" decree prohibited night work in bakeries. Most of its supporters were moved by a combination of wounded patriotism, equalitarianism, anticlericalism, and hostility toward the provinces. But Thiers, the provisional President of the Republic, viewed the Commune as a proletarian insurrection against the legally elected national government—which it certainly was—and when he finally gathered enough troops at Versailles to attack the city, the working-class districts offered the most stubborn resistance.
attack the city, the workingclass districts offered the most stubborn resistance.

From May 21 to May 28 Paris experienced the bloodiest civil war in her history. In their last-ditch defense, the supporters of the Commune killed a whole group of hostages, including the Archbishop of Paris, and set fire to many public buildings. Thiers' forces, in turn, shot everyone caught with weapons and executed thousands of prisoners. In all, 20,000 persons died in the crushing of the Commune, and thousands of others were deported to penal colonies.

*Together, the 200 Legitimists and the 200 Orleanists in the National Assembly constituted an antirepublican majority. Many Frenchmen had voted for these deputies because of their pledge to make peace with Germany as soon as possible. Nevertheless, the February 1871 election had been hastily arranged in an emergency situation and consequently may not have expressed many people's true feelings on the question of a new regime.

The repression of the Commune had long-lasting effects on the political life of the Third Republic. On the one hand, it provided the partisans of order and laissez faire with a label, Communards—which they often identified with Communists—with which to oppose social reform. On the other hand, the workers blamed the bourgeoisie as a whole for the executions and mass deportations, and the socialists later organized yearly pilgrimages to the cemetery where the Commune's last defenders had fallen. For the first time, Marxism began to attract some French workers away from the patriotic radicalism that had dominated most Parisian uprisings since 1789. Socially conservative Frenchmen, especially in the provinces, came to view the Republic as a bulwark of order because it *had* successfully liquidated the Commune. The Third Republic still had to cope with its monarchist and clerical opponents on the extreme Right, but it was quickly to win the majority of the peasants and the urban middle classes to its defense of political democracy and social conservatism.

### The Victory of Republicanism

At first the new regime was in the hands of the monarchists—both Legitimists and Orleanists. The main thing that prevented them from reestablishing an out-and-out monarchy was the attitude of the Count of Chambord, the last Bourbon Pretender. He refused to ascend the throne except as a divine-right ruler, with the white flag of his dynasty instead of the revolutionary tricolor. Since only a minority of the monarchist deputies was willing to go this far, the majority framed a constitution that was nominally republican but that could be adopted to a more flexible monarch.* The republicans did not completely wrest the Republic from the monarchists until 1879

In the 1880s and 1890s a group of moderate liberals called Opportunists controlled the government most of the time, though they frequently faced strong opposition from the monarchist conservatives on the Right and the Radicals on the Left. When the conservatives seemed to threaten the very existence of the regime, the Opportunists and the Radicals temporarily joined forces to defend it. When the socialists elected fifty deputies in 1893, the Opportunists composed some of their differences with the less obstinate conservatives in order to preserve the nation's economic and social structure. Even the Radicals, who corresponded most closely to the Gladstone Liberals in Great Britain, showed no desire to alter this structure.

Still, the leaders of the Third Republic did strengthen the authority of the state in several ways. They instituted the Prussian system of universal military training for all Frenchmen and passed increasingly high tariffs to protect the farmers. In the 1890s, despite their hostility to basic social reforms, the Opportunists enacted several laws to ensure rules of hygiene in mines and factories, to shorten the working hours of women and children, and to prevent industrial accidents. The most controversial form of state intervention sponsored by both the Opportunists and the Radicals was in education.

The school issue brought the Republic into a heated conflict with the clericals in the 1880s. Imbued with the positivist ideology, the Opportunists made primary education compulsory for all children. They believed that a modern economy needed people who could read and write and that a modern democracy required civic-minded citizens. Furthermore, they were determined to "laicize" the public schools by eliminating religious teaching and clerical influence from them. The Integral Catholics fought this program in the press and in electoral campaigns, but the new laws survived. In addition to making the first six years of schooling compulsory and free, they substituted civics for religion in the curriculum and provided for the elimination of Catholic brothers and nuns from the faculty, though they left the Catholic school system itself untouched. Actually, the so-called laic laws were laxly enforced, and some brothers and nuns continued to

*Since the Count of Chambord was already fifty years old and childless, the moderate monarchists hoped that, upon his death, the Count of Paris would fill this role. The Count of Paris was the heir of Louis Philippe and hence represented the principle of constitutional monarchy. And he was young and already had several children.

teach in the public schools for several decades. Meanwhile, the bitter debate over the schools encouraged extremists on both sides to keep the clerical issue alive into the early twentieth century.

Toward the end of the nineteenth century a new kind of nationalism altered the nature of the opposition to the Third Republic. From the Revolution of 1789 through the Commune of 1871 militant nationalism had been associated with the Left. This situation began to change in the late 1880's when the monarchists tried to use the popular General Georges Boulanger in their effort to overthrow the regime. To many Frenchmen, especially Parisians, Boulanger symbolized the spirit of *revanche* (vindication) for the humiliating defeat in 1870 and the annexation of Alsace-Lorraine by Germany. Although he lost his nerve when the time for a *coup d'état* seemed favorable, henceforth the monarchists and other Rightist opponents of the regime understood that they could only hope to overthrow it by appealing to a mass following in the name of nationalism.

### *The Dreyfus Affair*

The next Rightist assault on the Third Republic came in the late 1890's in connection with the Dreyfus Affair. In 1894 Captain Alfred Dreyfus was court-martialed and sent to the penal colony of Devil's Island for allegedly having offered military secrets to Germany. For more than three years almost everyone considered the case closed. Then new information about the case prompted a group of prominent journalists and politicians to open a campaign for a revision of Dreyfus' conviction. The first dramatic gesture of this campaign was the novelist Emile Zola's inflammatory newspaper article accusing the army of gross injustice. Zola's trial for slander in February 1898 sparked the first serious riots in Paris and divided almost the entire educated elite in France into two opposing camps. Antisemitic newspapers and leagues used the excuse that Dreyfus was a Jew to attack all French Jews indiscriminately. Many former supporters of Boulanger tried once again to discredit the Republic for neglecting France's national interests, and they even sought to persuade another general to lead an attack on the presidential palace in December 1898.

*The degradation of Captain Dreyfus*

Thus the Affair became a political and ideological issue. Military circles were all against revision, so that the campaign for a new trial took on an anti-militarist character. One group of intellectuals—a term that first came into general use at this time—organized the League for the Rights of Man, which argued that individual justice must triumph over all else, even the honor of the army; a rival group, the League of the French Fatherland, argued that national interests came first. In addition, a number of Radical and Socialist politicians used the Dreyfus Affair to take political power away from the Opportunists.

Dreyfus was eventually exonerated, but more important than the fate of Dreyfus himself was the upsetting of political ideas and positions prompted by the Affair. First, the Radicals, helped until 1905 by the more moderate Socialists, replaced the Opportunists as the ruling party. Second, anticlericalism gained renewed vitality, since the most vocal clerical newspapers had supported the army against Dreyfus; the Radical government cracked down on many religious orders and, in 1905, ended the Concordat and state support for the Church. Third, the Right clung to its new nationalist ideology as the only means of attracting popular support in the future.

Yet the Third Republic itself remained unchanged. The governments of the early 1900s were not essentially different from those of the preceding decades, and they too failed to integrate the working class into the national community. They did, however, succeed in splitting it by drawing a large number of Socialists closer to the Republic, thus wiping out their sense of alienation from the aftermath of the Commune.

### Germany

In Bismarck's new German Empire the strengthening of the authority of the state was not accompanied by a comparable advance toward political democracy. Even more than in Great Britain, the ruling elite excluded the masses and much of the middle class from power. Since the German Empire, like the Third Republic, was a new regime, its rulers had to find a middle course between the still active forces of tradition and those of nationalism, democracy, and socialism, which pressed for further changes. Here the resemblance between France and Germany ended. Although the German people elected their representatives through universal suffrage, the emperor, not Parliament, was sovereign, and until his forced retirement in 1890 Bismarck, not the emperor, made the crucial decisions.

The constitution of the German Empire itself hindered the growth of parliamentary democracy. Bismarck had conceived it as a compromise between making the empire a mere extension of Prussia and giving it a truly federal structure. The lower house of the imperial Parliament, the Reichstag, was elected by universal manhood suffrage; the upper house, the Bundesrat, represented the individual member states. In order to humor these states, Bismarck intentionally avoided the creation of imperial ministries. Instead, he accepted the new post of imperial chancellor responsible only to the emperor, rather than the head of cabinet responsible to either house of Parliament. As imperial departments (not ministries) were created for the Postal Services, the Navy, Justice, and the Interior, each one was headed by a secretary of state without ministerial responsibility. The Reichstag voted on all legislation, including the budget, but it had practically no control over the executive branch of the government, praticularly in foreign and military matters. Furthermore, Prussia had a check on imperial legislation through the Bundesrat, where its predominance remained. Since the lower chamber of the Prussian Parliament was elected on the basis of a three-class suffrage system favoring the propertied classes, this meant a strong conservative influence off-stage, so to speak.

#### *Bismarck and the Political Parties*

In addition to trying to discredit representative institutions, Bismarck frustrated the growth of parliamentary democracy by weakening the party system. We have already seen how he forced the National Liberals to sacrifice liberty for unity during the period of unification. He also succeeded in dividing them into two factions, using them when he needed them after 1871 but playing them off against the two wings of the Conservatives and the newly formed Catholic Center Party. The Liberals lost out not only to a powerful government but also to the trend toward an increasingly democratic mass society, which they, like liberals elsewhere, vainly tried to resist.

The founding of the Catholic Center Party in 1871 prompted Bismarck to use authoritarian methods to reduce the influence of the Church in education and to strengthen state control over the clergy. He viewed the Catholic Church and the Center Party as mass organizations dangerous to the state because of their claims to autonomy and their international outlook. Diplomatic considerations were also at work, since Bismarck feared a hostile alliance of Catholic powers within and without his new empire. The Catholic clergy in Prussia resisted his repressive laws; in 1876 every Prussian bishop was either in prison or exile, and many parishes had no priests. Two years later, Bismarck changed his tactics and persuaded the new pope, Leo XIII, to withdraw his support from the Center Party. Thereafter the chancellor relaxed his attacks on the Catholic clergy, while retaining state inspection of schools and civil marriage. Yet even though the state increased its authority, the political Catholicism of the Center Party emerged from the struggle stronger than ever.

Bismarck's effort to curb the new socialist party—the Social Democrats—failed in a similar way. In 1878 he banned their meetings and publications and expelled some of their party officials, although he still allowed them to run candidates for public office. The growth of the German Social Democratic Party will be discussed presently; here all we need to note is that it grew despite Bismarck's restrictions on its activities. He viewed it as he viewed the Center Party, a dangerous mass organization with supranational loyalties, but he linked his struggle against the Social Democrats with a determined effort to outbid them for the allegiance of the working class.

In the 1880s Bismarck launched a state system of social insurance covering sickness, accidents, old age, and disability. The system established compulsory contributions from employers and employees with additional financial help from the state. In this way authoritarian Germany forged far ahead of the Western democracies in meeting some of the problems of an industrial mass society. Still, Bismarck made no effort to reduce the hours of work; on this point his experience as a landowner accustomed to rural conditions of work hindered him from understanding the realities of industrial exploitation, especially of women and children. In any case, his steps toward state socialism failed to exorcise the specter of Marxism.

Bismarck tried to manipulate the masses as he had manipulated the middle-class parties and the other states of Europe. He never seemed to have understood that no enduring political system can be the achievement of one man, whatever his strength and determination. In other hands the power that Bismarck had given to the state could easily be misused. This was to happen within a decade after the impetuous new emperor, William II (1888–1918), unceremoniously dismissed the "iron chancellor" in 1890.

*Prince Otto von Bismarck*

### *William II*

At first William II tried to win the workers over to the regime by removing the limitations on the Social Democrats and by granting further concessions to labor, but he refused to relinquish any of his authority to Parliament. He made his position clear in a speech in 1894 in which he said that he was "for religion, for morality and sound order, against the parties of destruction." By "parties of destruction" he meant not only the Social Democrats but the small states' rights parties and the remaining minority of liberals which wanted constitutional reform. During the course of his reign Emperor William II was to be even less successful than Bismarck in integrating the industrial workers and other dissident minorities into a truly national community.

The most significant sign of the disaffection of the urban masses with the imperial regime was the growing electoral strength of the Social Democratic Party. In 1871 only 52 per cent of the eligible voters took advantage of their franchise; by 1912 the figure was 84 per cent, and nearly all of these new voters cast their ballots for the Social Democrats. These were mostly young urban workers who acquired a growing political awareness. Their numbers increased as the total population grew—from 41 million in 1871 to 56 million in 1900 and 65 million in 1913—and as the proportion of this population employed in industry increased—from 35.5 per cent in 1882 to 42.8 per cent in 1907. Between 1871 and 1912, the Social Democratic vote grew from 2 to 29 per cent, while the percentage of the total electorate that voted for the other parties remained about the same.

Without ministerial responsibility, the pattern of parliamentary democracy in Germany could not reflect the new demands of the growing mass of urban workers. The emperor and his chancellor continued to discount the wishes of the Reichstag, and the big landowners and big industrialists helped to maintain the army and the bureaucracy as the real powers behind the throne.

### Italy

The majority of Italians were less involved in the national life of their country than the British, French, and Germans. This fact was due partly to Italy's lower level of industrialization, partly to the persistence of local and regional loyalties, and partly to the nature of Italian parliamentary democracy itself. Nevertheless, the state did assert its authority over the Church, and it increased taxes, promoted the building of railroads and a merchant marine, and made a half-hearted attempt to enforce compulsory education and a law making employers liable for accidents involving their workers.

Italian parliamentary democracy operated under a limited franchise and a political system in which strong leaders used Parliament for their own purposes. The franchise was extended from 600,000 to 2,000,000 (out of a total population of around 30 million) in 1881, but universal suffrage was not to be enacted until 1912. By "transforming" the old, incoherent party groupings into new government coalitions a few prime ministers obtained parliamentary majorities that would pass their legislative programs. Cavour had originated this practice in the name of national unity in the struggle against Austria. After 1871 both Right-wing and Left-wing prime ministers resorted to "transformism" as the main means of gaining working majorities in Parliament.

The trouble with "transformism" was that it prevented the growth of strong political parties. Center coalitions are all very well when they really respond to public needs, but when they do not, as was often the case in Italy, the lack of strong opposition parties makes peaceful political change almost impossible. In Italy party lines were so blurred, and the issues of politics so confused, that in constituencies where no candidate had an absolute majority the two extremes sometimes voted together on the second ballot. Both the moderate Right and moderate Left depended on the same class of people and had common interests against clericals and reactionaries on the one hand and radicals and socialists on the other. Hence party rivalries over policy gave way to "parliamentary incest." This phrase was uttered by the most energetic prime minister of the late nineteenth century, Francesco Crispi (1818–1901), before he became a practitioner of "transformism" himself.

During his two ministries (1887–1891, 1893–1896) Crispi tried to combine democracy with nationalism. This mercurial Sicilian, who had sailed with Garibaldi's famous Thousand in 1860, always remained a revolutionary patriot by temperament. But he matured, in part, into a political conservative once he had to defend the position his great energy and talents had won him. Like Bismarck, whom he admired, Crispi became a confirmed believer in paternalistic government and wanted to increase the power of the throne "lest Parliament should become a tyrant and the cabinet its slave." Yet the plebeian Crispi was far more responsive to the aspirations of the common people than the aristocratic Bismarck. He introduced a Public Health Act and a long-overdue prison reform; he set up special tribunals for redress against abuses by the bureaucracy; he allowed workers a limited right to strike. He also anticipated twentieth-century dictators by trying to divert attention from domestic unrest and corruption by constantly proclaiming that the nation was in danger. In particular he used colonial expansion in Africa to try to give the Italian people the feeling that their country, whose unification had depended so much on foreign help, was really a great power.

In 1896 Crispi's unsuccessful attempt to conquer Ethiopia ended in a disastrous defeat for Italian arms and in his own political eclipse. Social and economic unrest racked the country for the next four years. In the face of peasant uprisings in the south and bread riots in Milan the government temporarily ruled by military decree. When constitutional rule was restored at the turn of the century many workers in the increasingly industrialized north were turning more and more toward antiparliamentary movements of the extreme Left for the solution of their problems.

Great Britain, France, Germany, Italy, and the smaller countries of Western Europe all made notable advances toward democratization and closer ties between the state and society by the turn of the century. All the materials of the histories of these countries are the same; only their proportions and interactions are different. Every country except Italy, Portugal, Denmark, and the Netherlands had universal or nearly universal manhood suffrage; and these exceptions were to disappear by 1914. Every country except Germany, Spain, Portugal, and Denmark had ministerial responsibility. After Norway gained her independence from Sweden in 1905, the Irish were the only suppressed nationality in the West. The material and cultural effects of industrialization at home and the international anarchy abroad made the nation-state the dominant force in most people's lives, and with the advent of compulsory primary education it had a powerful instrument for instilling patriotism at an early age. Yet despite these advances the working class still tended to feel like a segregated minority group. To many workers national pride and the right to vote were inadequate substitutes for true social justice. Consequently a number of them turned to mass movements that promised to achieve this goal in one way or another. Trade-unionism and socialism experienced varying degrees of success from one country to another, but they were basic ingredients in the development of all.

## THE QUEST FOR SOCIAL JUSTICE

In the late 1880s new kinds of trade-unionism and new kinds of socialism took over the task of fighting for social justice. Previously both movements had been small in numbers, loosely organized, and restricted in their activities by law. Now the same forces that led to the growth of big business produced larger, more unified labor organizations, while the same forces that led to the increasing authority of the state and the participation of the masses in politics produced Marxist political parties organized on a national and even an international scale. These new working-class movements were most willing to seek reforms within the existing political structure in those countries where the traditions and institutions of parliamentary democracy had already become most fully established. They tended to be most revolutionary in those countries where parliamentary democracy was the weakest or—as in Russia—nonexistent. Whether reformist or revolutionary, the new trade-unionism and the new socialism fought for the "emancipation" of labor through a higher standard of living, better working conditions, and the removal of all the disabilities that kept the workers an underprivileged class.

These disabilities were still considerable in the late nineteenth century, for the democratization of European society proceeded more slowly than the democratization of government. It manifested itself in universal primary education, universal military training, and the beginnings of state regulation of public health and working conditions. But despite these gains and despite the extension of the right to vote, the aristocratic and bourgeois elites continued to dominate the social, economic, and political life of Europe. As late as the 1890s both the Liberal and Conservative Parties in Great Britain furnished a peer as prime minister, and the German chancellor was invariably an

*Belgian miners rioting*

important nobleman in the early 1900s. While most cabinet ministers were of upper middle-class rather than noble origin, the nobility were strong at the royal courts, in the highest ranks of the civil service, in the upper houses of Parliament, and especially in the diplomatic corps and army. The upper and middle ranks of the bourgeoisie virtually monopolized business and the professions. Urbanization, primary education, and the advent of the penny press did very little to help members of the working class to improve their social status. What they did do was to make the workers more conscious of the injustices they were forced to suffer at a time when their economic condition showed some signs of improvement.

### The Trade-Union Movement

The power and influence of trade-unions today—especially in the predominantly Anglo-Saxon countries—make it difficult to imagine the obstacles encountered by organized labor in earlier times. Unions did not gain the full right to strike in Great Britain until 1871, in France until 1884, and in Germany until the repeal of Bismarck's antisocialist laws in 1890; in Great Britain and the United States they were not made immune from ruinous civil suits by employers until the twentieth century. Furthermore, their membership was too small to achieve more than limited gains for particular trades on a local level. The organization of the mass of unskilled workers did not begin until the late 1880s, and the movement for unification and federation at the national level came to fruition only at the turn of the century.

Until the 1880s labor unions were predominantly craft unions consisting of the more skilled workmen in building, mining, textiles, printing, and the mechanical trades—called engineering in those days. These craft unions occupied themselves mainly with mutual insurance and self-help against the hazards of accident, sickness, and death, and only occasionally used strikes to reinforce their economic demands against the employers. Their members looked upon themselves as a kind of working-class elite and showed little interest in their less skilled comrades or in national politics.

The new unionism that made its first dramatic appearance after 1886 was, like so many other things of the period, a phenomenon of the masses and therefore different in character from all that had come before. It began with a series of long and bitter strikes by the hitherto unorganized or almost unorganized Belgian miners and glass workers in 1886, the London match girls in 1888 and the London dock workers in 1889, the Ruhr coal miners in 1889, and the French wood cutters in 1891 and 1892. The enlistment of these masses of less skilled workers into the ranks of trade-unionism quickly transformed the structure and significance of the labor movement. New types of labor organization came into existence on an industry-wide basis, as in coal and transportation, and these industrial unions often became linked with competing political and social creeds; there were now socialist unions, syndicalist* unions, and Catholic unions. The growing size and diversity of unions made the second major development of the period—national federation—both more desirable and more difficult.

"Solidarity forever!" became the battle cry of organized labor almost everywhere around the turn of the century. But solidarity for what? And solidarity with whom? These questions received different answers in different countries. The British Trades Union Congress (TUC), originally founded in 1868, had proved able to hold together the old craft and the new industrial unions, and by 1900 it represented some half-million workers. In France, the *Confédération Générale du Travail* (CGT), formed in 1895, combined in 1902 with the *bourses du travail*, peculiarly French institutions that were a mixture of labor exchange, trades council, and workers' club. Both the British and French national federations were wedded to a policy of improving the workers' lot through collective bargaining backed by strikes. But whereas the CGT deliberately tried to divorce itself from political movements and parliamentary politics, the TUC joined with several small socialist groups to set up a Labor Representation Committee to put up workers' candidates in parliamentary elections. Within a few years this Committee was to become a full-fledged, socialist-oriented Labour Party in the service of the TUC. In Germany a third pattern developed. There the majority of the trade-unions had been established as "feeders" to the Social Democrats and gradually loosened their political ties with that party. In 1908 the Italian socialist unions formed their own General Confederation of Labor, but, as in France and Germany, the Catholic, socialist, and syndicalist unions remained separate and often hostile to each other.

Although the trade-union movement enrolled many new members in the early 1900s, it did not achieve complete solidarity of organization or purpose anywhere. Between 1900 and 1913 trade-union membership rose from 2 million to 4 million in Great Britain, from 850,000 to 3 million in Germany, and from 250,000 to 1 million in France. The concentration of the German workers in only 400 unions and the diffusion of the French workers in over 5,000 reflected the different levels of industrialization in the two countries. In France the smallness of the movement reduced whatever advantage its declared political independence may have had; in Germany the growing split between the reformist unions and the nominally revolutionary Social Democratic Party offset the advantage of numbers. The British movement, though less concentrated than the German, had an older tradition and was more firmly attached to parliamentary democracy, but it had its troubles too.

In England, the Taff Vale case of 1902 helped to solidify the trade-union movement, turn it into political channels, and make it the dominant spokesman for the British working class. In this case the House of Lords declared unions legal entities capable of being sued by employers

*So called because they rejected both collective bargaining and parliamentary politics in favor of class warfare through strikes by the *syndicats*—the French word for trade-unions.

for business losses suffered during a strike. It was this threat to their very existence that prompted the unions to organize the Labour Party and use it to get the Taff Vale decision reversed in Parliament in 1906. From then on the British unions dedicated themselves to industrial action and parliamentary politics as the two main ways of seeking social justice for labor. Some union leaders were to toy with the notion of political strikes, but the British trade-union movement usually considered this syndicalist tactic, as well as the Marxist belief in class warfare, a foreign importation.

To trade-unionists, "bread-and-butter" considerations outweighed all others. Collective bargaining, backed by strikes, was the main tactic they prescribed for the achievement of higher wages, better working conditions, and the general emancipation of labor. They were also willing to put pressure on Parliament to achieve these goals, but they had no thought of overthrowing the existing political system. On the continent, however, the trade-unionists were not as successful as their British counterparts in preventing socialist politicians from giving the labor movement a revolutionary tone. In fact, the syndicalist unions in France and Spain pushed the socialist politicians in a more revolutionary direction.

## Marxism and the Socialist Parties

By the beginning of the twentieth century socialism meant Marxism almost everywhere in continental Europe; only the Scandinavian Labor parties followed the non-Marxist British model. But the Marxist parties on the continent were only superficially more successful than the trade-union movement in achieving national unity and international solidarity. On both levels reformists and revolutionaries differed openly on questions of strategy, and theoretical differences were only partially hidden by the common "socialist" or "social democratic" label. Great Britain, Germany, and France had all passed the stage of industrialization on which Marx had based his critique of capitalism. At the turn of the century Russia was the only major country still at this stage, and it was the Russian Social Democratic Party, under the leadership of Lenin, that was eventually to bring about the first successful revolution in the name of "orthodox" Marxism.

The elimination of non-Marxist elements from European socialism took over three decades. Marx himself had played a decisive part in founding the First International Workingmen's Association in London in 1864. The workers' organizations from the individual countries were to count as subdivisions and in no sense as independent parties. But this First International was weakened by the rise of the Paris Commune, which frightened many of its moderate members, and by an open rift between Marx and the anarchist leader Michael Bakunin.* Marx succeeded in getting Bakunin expelled from the First International in 1872, but anarchists continued to attract workers away from the socialists in Southern and Eastern Europe after the First International finally collapsed in 1876.

In addition to anarchist rivals, the French Marxist party (*Parti Ouvrier Français*), founded by Jules Guesde in 1879, faced competition from the syndicalists, from a group following the revolutionary-activist tradition of 1789–1871, and from a moderate reform group called the "possibilists." Ironically, it was the "independent socialist" Jean Jaurès who finally became the leader of the union of all these factions under the Marxist banner in 1905. Even the German Social Democratic Party did not succeed in eliminating its syndicalist and anarchist elements until the 1890s.

### *The German Social Democratic Party*

Since it was the largest and best organized of all the European socialist parties, the German Social Democratic Party requires special attention. In the late 1860s it had had a formidable rival in Ferdinand Lassalle's Universal German Workers' Union, which favored Bismarck's unification of Germany and a strictly national brand of socialism. The two groups united under the so-called Gotha Program of 1875, which still incorporated some Lasallian doctrines. Then Bismarck's antisocialist

*See p. 523.

laws more or less froze the movement's theoretical position for over fifteen years. Only in 1890, after the repeal of these laws, did the party bring out a new program, this time avowedly Marxist, at its Erfurt Congress. From then on the party's principal organizer, August Bebel, developed and centralized its organization and made it a mass party, not only in numbers but in the variety of activities it sponsored. For, in addition to running candidates for the Reichstag, the party established an educational organization teaching social science in the spirit of Marxism. Working-class party members schooled in this way were able to acquire responsible positions in the party's hierarchy and in their own localities. A number of economic and cultural organizations—trade unions, cooperatives, youth groups—also centered around the party and formed a whole proletarian world within the dominant "capitalist" society.

Yet despite its strictly Marxist orientation, the German Social Democratic Party experienced the same division over strategy and tactics as its counterparts in other countries. The leading exponent of reformism—or "revisionism"—was Eduard Bernstein. In his book *Evolutionary Socialism* (1899) Bernstein still accepted a socialist society as the final goal but rejected the assertion of the *Communist Manifesto* that it would come as a result of the inevitable concentration of capital in a few hands and the increasing misery of the toiling masses. He showed statistically that the number of people with large and middle-sized incomes was increasing absolutely and relatively, and that the position of the workers was improving rather than deteriorating. Consequently Bernstein advocated the gradual transformation of capitalism by political pressure, which the workers would be able to exert more effectively, just because they were a rising and not a sinking class. Bebel chastized Bernstein for his "revisionism," and the party reaffirmed its dedication to the inevitability of revolution at its party congresses in the early 1900s. Behind the façade of revolutionary speeches, though, the German party, like all others except the Russian, played an active role in Parliament, and made practical compromises within the existing political and economic structure.

### The Second International

The fragile unity of reformists and revolutionaries at the national level had its parallel in the Second International. This organization, founded in 1889, differed from its predecessor in having no directing council and in being merely a consultative body formed by national parties that reserved the right to determine their own policies. Still, the resolutions of its international congresses had a high moral authority, as when, in 1900, all the member parties accepted the resolution that no socialist should hold a cabinet post in a bourgeois government. Each party was free to adjust its parliamentary tactics to national needs, but the congresses of the Second International consistently proclaimed the solidarity of the workers of all countries. On this point the reformist Jaurès and the "orthodox" Bebel could agree, as could their counterparts in Italy, Belgium, Austria, and the Netherlands, right up to the outbreak of the First World War.

### The British Labour Party

Although the British and Scandinavian socialist parties sent delegates to the congresses of the Second International, they shunned Marxist doctrines. As we have seen, these parties were primarily appendages of the trade-union movement, with its emphasis on "bread-and-butter" issues. The closest counterpart to continental reformisim in Great Britain was the Fabian* Society, founded in 1883 and including George Bernard Shaw, H. G. Wells, and Sidney and Beatrice Webb among its early members. But the Fabians were very un-Marxist. Their inspiration came more from the tradition of English Radicalism and Chartism, which saw social democracy as an extension of political democracy rather than the result of class warfare and the dictatorship of the proletariat. The small Indpendent Labour Party, founded in 1893, was more avowedly Marxist, but it was submerged, along with the Fabians, in the parliamentary Labour

*Named after the Roman general Fabius Cunctator, the "delayer," and believer in gradual methods.

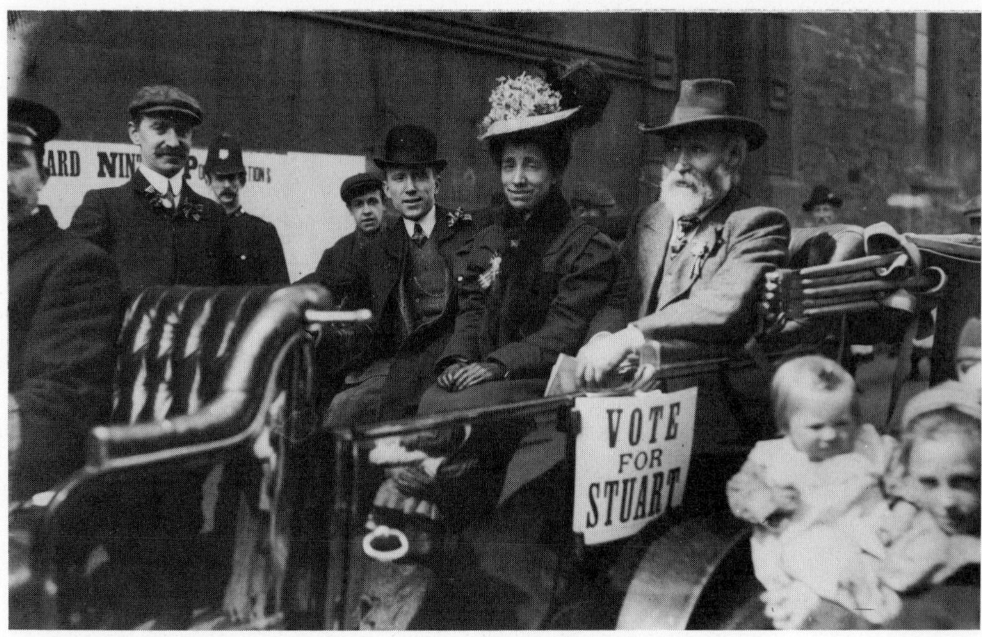

*A campaign of the British Labour Party*

Party of the early 1900s. Although this party continued to call itself socialist, both the bourgeois intellectuals and the trade-union leaders that directed its policies concerned themselves with economic realities rather than all-encompassing theories.

### *The Russian Social Democratic Workers' Party*

This party was as different from the British Labour Party as Russia was different from Great Britain. Its appearance at the end of the nineteenth century will be discussed later in this chapter as part of a peculiar series of developments in Russia. Nevertheless, we already know enough about that country to surmise that such a party was illegal and that its leaders could have little hope of achieving their goals by peaceful means. In the early 1900s some of them—called Mensheviks—resembled the reformist Marxists of the West in their desire to build a mass party and to postpone a full-scale revolution indefinitely. But the Bolshevik wing, led by Lenin, wanted a revolutionary action party with a general staff of professional revolutionaries. The Bolsheviks' ultimate strategy was to capture complete political power for themselves by the total overthrow of the existing regime.

Compared to the German and French Marxist parties, the Russian party seemed unimportant in the early 1900s. Its revolutionary wing was clearly a minority, and even that group rejected Lenin's novel conception of party leadership. The most notorious professional revolutionaries in the West were not socialists at all; they were anarchists or revolutionary syndicalists.

### *Revolutionary Syndicalism and Anarchism*

Whereas the trade unions and the reformist and orthodox Marxists all recognized the importance of the state in a highly industrialized society, the revolutionary syndicalists and anarchists sought to abolish it. In this respect these two movements resembled the utopian socialists of the first half of the nineteenth century, when industrialization was just beginning, but they rejected the ideal of social harmony as preached by Saint-Simon and Fourier. Both the revolutionary syndicalists and the anarchists agreed with their Marxist rivals that class warfare was inevitable, and the revolutionary syndicalists hoped to use strikes by the trade unions as the training ground for the proletarian revolution. With the notable exception of France, the goal of destroying the state had the most appeal in those countries of Southern and Eastern Europe—Italy, Spain, Russia—where industrialization was still a novelty in the late nineteenth century and where the mass of poor peasants felt as underprivileged and socially segregated as the town workers.

Significantly, Michael Bakunin (1815–1876), the prophet of anarchism, came from the country where the existing political system was most out of harmony with modern civilization. Bakunin rejected every aspect of the Old Regime in Russia, including his own noble status. He sought the salvation of society in the total destruction of all state institutions and the breaking down of nations into local groups, voluntary associations, and municipalities, and he believed that terroristic acts of violence and destruction were the only means of achieving this end. Forced to flee his native Russia in 1861, Bakunin spread his anarchist doctrine in Western Europe and, as we have seen, briefly took part in the activities of the First International. After his death the anarchists, though never a large movement, continued to frighten respectable society everywhere with their incitements to peasant and labor unrest and their spectacular political assassinations: President Sadi Carnot of France in 1894, Empress Elizabeth of Austria in 1898, King Humbert of Italy in 1900, and President McKinley of the United States in 1901.

Anarchists and revolutionary syndicalists developed a kind of working alliance in Spain and Italy, but they differed over doctrine and tactics. Syndicalism itself was simply the French, Spanish, and Italian name for trade-unionism; revolutionary syndicalism meant something more. Its spokesmen argued that the trade unions must remain independent of all political parties and train their members for class warfare through "direct action"—strikes whenever possible, sabotage and boycotts of employers when the workers were too weak to risk a strike. The workers' movement should also try to disrupt in advance the organization that enabled governments to coerce individuals: the army. The ultimate revolution would take the form of a general strike, which would paralyze the whole economy and bring about the total collapse of the state. After the revolution the state would be replaced by federal organizations of the unions, and society would thus consist of functional groups of wage earners, without class distinctions and without the need for parliaments, bureaucracies, law courts, and police, or the army. Unlike Marx, the revolutionary syndicalists did not want these instruments of class domination to be used by the proletariat.

Revolutionary syndicalism appeared in several countries,* but it was most important in France. There the CGT adopted it as its official philosophy, even though the union leaders did not always follow it in practice. Many French workers subscribed to the principles of the general strike and antimilitarism mainly as a symbolic gesture of class solidarity. Still, their suspicion of socialist politicians distinguished them from British and German workers and hampered the achievement of social justice by parliamentary means in France.

Thus the quest for social justice took a variety of forms. Both socialism and trade-unionism were theoretically split between those groups that were willing to come to terms with the institutions of parliamentary democracy and those that were not. The gradualists showed the greatest potential in Great Britain, where industrial capitalism had existed the longest and proved the most potent and flexible. Yet even the revolutionary syndicalists in France and the revolutionary Marxists in Germany became less militant in their actions by the turn of the century, and in the face of growing international tensions soon thereafter they tended to become more and more attached to their own nation-state. Anarcho-syndicalism was to remain popular in Italy and Spain, where industrial capitalism was still weak and on the defensive. But only in Russia, the most despotic and the least industrialized

*Even in the United States the International Workers of the World—called "Wobblies"—caused a certain amount of consternation until their brutal suppression in 1914.

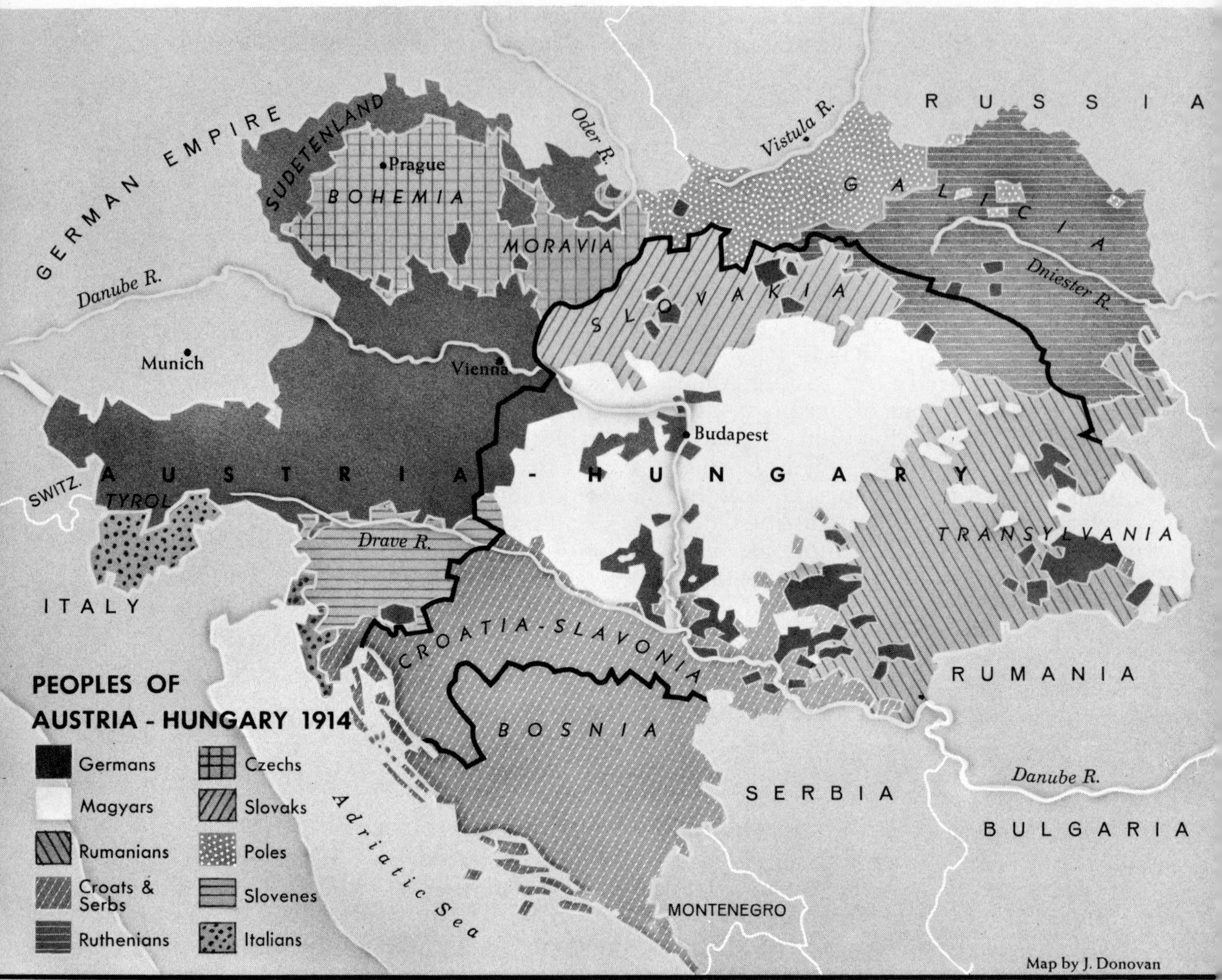


of the major powers, did a significant minority of professional revolutionaries continue to insist on a complete overthrow of the existing order as the only way to make social justice prevail.

### THREE IMPOSSIBLE EMPIRES

The political map of Eastern Europe in 1871 was deceptively simple. There was Austria-Hungary, the Russian Empire, and the Ottoman Empire, and that was about all. (Although Serbia and Rumania already enjoyed a large degree of autonomy within the Ottoman Empire, only Greece and tiny Montenegro were truly independent.) Yet each of these sprawling dynastic empires was on the verge of falling apart. The pressure of subject nationalities for self-rule threatened to bring about the complete disintegration of the Ottoman Empire and Austria-Hungary, and it aggravated the growing disunity within Russian society itself.

All three empires had reactionary monarchs dedicated to preserving as much of the old order as possible. The Russian tsars were the most consistent in their policies of forced assimilation of national minorities and repression of liberals and socialists within the dominant majority. The rulers of Austria-Hungary and the Ottoman Empire tried to bolster their shakier regimes by alternating reform and reaction. This approach merely raised false hopes and finally contempt. Even if all three empires could have isolated themselves from the outside world, it is doubtful that they could have survived unchanged for long. Actually, they were the instigators and the ultimate victims of the most chronic issue of European international relations—the Eastern Question.

### Austria-Hungary

The Dual Monarchy of Austria-Hungary had all the class and ideological cleavages of the other countries *plus* the nationality problems of Europe as a whole—in other words a "vertical" as well as a "horizontal" set of centrifugal forces. It survived because neither its own leaders nor those of the other European powers could think of anything to take its place. Its survival seemed the best way to maintain the new balance of power after 1870 and to avoid facing the nationalities question in Central and Eastern Europe. These reasons for preserving the Dual Monarchy were especially strong with Bismarck, and the suspended animation of Austrian politics in the late nineteenth century suited German needs. The Hapsburg emperor continued to play off one nationality against another. But his occasional political concessions merely intensified the mutual hostility of the disparate elements in his realm and made him reassert his own authority as the only unifying force therein.

Excluded from Germany and Italy in 1866, Austria concentrated more than ever on her "civilizing mission" among the Slavic peoples of Southeastern Europe. This policy reflected a continuing desire for prestige, a determination to preserve the balance of power in the Balkans against Russia, and an attempt to prevent Serbia (fully independent by 1878) from attracting the loyalty of the South Slavs within the Hapsburg lands. The catastrophic effects of this policy were not yet apparent at the end of the nineteenth century, but the opposition of many Magyars and Germans (for different reasons) to it was already isolating the dynasty from the two dominant elements in the Dual Monarchy. Thus Francis Joseph's expansionist aims in the Balkans* were to be as detrimental to the survival of the Dual Monarchy as his domestic policies.

*See pp. 588-589.

The Compromise of 1867 made a unified state under Emperor Francis Joseph impossible to maintain. A century earlier Maria Theresa had laid the foundation of a supranational empire to be held together by the aristocracy, the bureaucracy, the Roman Catholic Church, and the army. The Austrian Germans were to dominate this empire politically, and their language and culture were to integrate its non-German upper and middle classes. But with the Compromise of 1867 Hungary finally gained constitutional and practical equality with the larger and richer "other half," now called Austria, and destroyed the idea of a supranational empire. Moreover, Emperor Francis Joseph persisted in viewing this "other half" as a group of historic political units. Hence the Compromise of 1867 also challenged the predominance of the Germans in their own lands.

After 1867 the Germans were on the defensive in Austria. The first concession to non-German nationalist aspirations came in Galicia, where, in 1871, Polish was recognized as the language of administration and secondary education. Ten years later the Czechs received some of their demands when their language was given equality in the public affairs of Bohemia and Moravia, a national Czech university was founded in Prague, some Czech secondary schools were established, and some posts in the state administration were made available to Czechs. Germans of almost all shades of opinion opposed these concessions to the Czechs, and relations between the two nationalities became increasingly bitter toward the end of the nineteenth century.

After 1880 the Austrian Germans were united in their opposition to Czech demands for political and cultural autonomy, but they were divided on every other issue. The imperial government could thus make use of each German political party—Conservative Catholics, Liberals, Christian Socialists, Social Democrats—without allowing any of them to dominate it. This policy of "divide and rule" among the Germans themselves, as well as among the different nationalities, had an especially pathetic effect on Austrian liberalism.

Although weaker than the Prussian lib-

*Court Ball in Vienna, 1877; Emperor Francis Joseph is seated at the right*

erals, the Austrian liberals tasted real power before they too were dropped by their imperial rulers. We have seen how Bismarck had used the Prussian liberals in the 1860s and 1870s and then turned against them after they had served his purposes. In Austria, the defeats of the old order at the hands of foreign enemies forced Francis Joseph to establish a constitutional regime in 1867 and to accept a series of liberal ministries until 1879. Still, during their brief period of rule the Austrian liberals had to share power with the aristocracy and the imperial bureaucracy, and their social base was narrower than that of the Prussian liberals.

Francis Joseph appointed the conservative Count Eduard von Taaffe prime minister to strengthen imperial influence and authority. Taaffe broke the liberals' power by forming a coalition of conservative Catholics, Poles, and Czechs. The previously mentioned concessions to these nationalities made their representatives in the Austrian Parliament cooperate with Taaffe against the German liberals for a decade and a half. Under these conditions the "Austrian idea" could no longer command general political acceptance. It was nevertheless vindicated administratively by a competent and paternalistic bureaucracy, efficient state-controlled railroads, and a great extension of public services in health and education. Meanwhile, Taaffe managed to rule according to the constitution while serving as a loyal and accommodating servant of his emperor. He even proposed enfranchising the masses as a means of sweeping away the narrow issues that made up the political life of the existing parties. But the emperor balked at this "leap in the dark" and dismissed Taaffe in 1893.

Thereafter Austrian parliamentary politics became increasingly unreal. The unrepresentative governments of the next decade found no solution to renewed Czech demands and were unable to stop the growth of mass parties outside of Parliament. The antisemitic Christian Socialists gained control of the municipal government of Vienna in 1897, and the Social Democrats attracted many followers among the German and Czech industrial workers. All these developments completed the destruction of Austrian liberalism as a political force by the end of the century.

But even the combined political efforts of the bourgeois liberals and the conservative aristocrats could not have maintained the status quo in Austria. The emperor sabotaged constitutional rule and was no more willing to side with his German subjects than with any other nationality. Besides, not only the Czechs but the Magyars too were threatening the Dual Monarchy by the late 1890s.

The Magyar nationalists had always viewed the Compromise of 1867 with misgivings. Unlike the Germans in the "other half" of the Dual Monarchy, they remained firmly in power at all times. During the ministry of Kálmán Tisza, which lasted from 1875 to 1890, they accepted their "marriage of convenience" with Francis Joseph and strengthened their position in Hungary by various school and language regulations designed to "Magyarize" the new generation among the subject nationalities. The Croats offered more resistance than any of the others, but they were unable to play politics in the parliament at Budapest the way the Czechs did in the parliament at Vienna. Only Magyars had a voice in Budapest, and the only way for Tisza's Magyar opponents to unseat him was to stress the weakness of the Compromise and demand even fuller independence for Hungary. This they did by demanding the end of the common Hapsburg army, in which German was the language of command. By the early 1900s the only way Francis Joseph could check this demand was to threaten to introduce universal suffrage and thus break the political preponderance of the Magyars in Hungary.

Clearly, then, the Dual Monarchy was becoming an impossible empire by the turn of the century. Constitutional government collapsed in Austria, and Magyar nationalism became more and more unyielding, not only toward the Hapsburgs but toward the subject peoples of Hungary as well. Francis Joseph was having increasing difficulty in keeping the dominant and subject nationalities from tearing his empire apart. The fact that it survived until the First World War was due partly to the lack of an acceptable alternative and partly to the threat of Russia in the Balkans.

## Russia

On the surface the Romanov empire seemed to be in less danger of disintegrating than the Hapsburg empire in the late nineteenth century. The St. Petersburg government was no more successful than the Vienna and Budapest governments in "taming" its subject nationalities, but these were a smaller proportion of the total population in Russia than in Austria-Hungary. And whereas Austria-Hungary had some semblance of constitutional rule, Russia remained a pure autocracy, untroubled by parliaments, political parties, and mass movements. Industrialization, urbanization, and population growth were producing strains in the social order, to be sure, but the tsarist regime itself strengthened its authority and tolerated no open opposition to any of its policies. Yet beneath the surface large sections of Russian society became alienated from the regime and all it stood for.

### *The Reaction*

Alexander II had instituted reforms, but they had failed to accomplish their purpose of increasing the efficiency of the state and welding the nation together through the All-Class Principle.* Whatever efficiency the Russian state had was still due to the bureaucracy, the secret police, and the army. The All-Class Principle convinced no one and was contradicted both in practice and by the extremely reactionary tone of tsarist rule in the 1880s and 1890s. This reaction, which had already set in under Alexander II, grew worse after the terrorists who had been trying to assassinate him for years finally succeeded in 1881. From then until 1905 his

*See p. 459.

successors—Alexander III (1881–1895) and Nicholas II (1895–1917)—tried to reverse the democratization of society implicit in the All-Class Principle and to buttress the regime through the triple policy of Autocracy, Orthodoxy, and Russification.

But as in Austria-Hungary, the Old Regime in Russia had lost its basis with the emancipation of the serfs and the beginnings of industrialization. By the late nineteenth century it was becoming alien to the society it continued to rule, and the majority of people in this society felt increasingly alienated from it. And when large groups of people do not feel that they belong to the society in which they are born—when they feel alienated from it—then that society is not a real community.

### *The Revolutionary Intelligentsia*

The first social group in Russia to articulate its alienation was the intelligentsia. In the first half of the nineteenth century this group had been restricted mainly to sensitive young noblemen who felt "repentant" about serfdom, the police state, and their country's general backwardness as compared to Western Europe. Their consciousness of these evils prevented them from playing their expected roles as time-servers within the framework of the Old Regime, but under Nicholas I they could not organize movements of any kind, as the crushing of the Decembrist Revolt in 1825 had proved. They could not even study Western ideas at the universities, for the government prevented the teaching of philosophy in them. Their only recourse was to meet in study circles in private homes, where, over endless glasses of tea, they discussed the eternal question: What is Russia, and how must it develop by the laws of its own nature?

These study circles eventually came to include non-nobles—sons of priests, of minor officials, and of merchants. All these young men had obtained some education outside the universities, which were closed to them until the end of the 1850s. The government contemptuously referred to these self-educated—and often half-educated—commoners as "people of various ranks." Yet they, along with the "repentant noblemen," considered themselves a class apart because of their education and their concern for philosophical and social issues.

The intelligentsia, then, consisted of those educated Russians who could not accept the arbitrary and barbarous existing order but who felt helpless to do anything about it. The term "intellectual" does not describe them accurately, for not all Russian intellectuals shared their feeling of alienation. In Russia a member of the intelligentsia was called an *intelligent* (with a "hard" *g*.) To be an *intelligent* one had to have both an education *and* a guilty conscience; one had to want to change the existing order so that it would no longer give one a guilty conscience.

In the 'sixties and 'seventies, in the wake of Alexander II's partial reforms, a number of these *intelligents* made their first open attempt to destroy the Old Regime. This new type of revolutionary *intelligent* was portrayed in Nikolai Chernyshevsky's novel *What Is To Be Done?* in 1863. The hero, Rakhmetov, is a young nobleman who renounces material comforts and social status in order to devote himself completely to the cause of The Revolution. (Some observers have seen Rakhmetov as a fictional version of the famous anarchist, Michael Bakunin.) This fictional revolutionary socialist was an intransigent extremist ready for renunciation and sacrifice; he resembled a religious fanatic in his monastic austerity. Chernyshevsky himself was exiled to Siberia for his pernicious influence, but his message had already fired the imagination of Russia's educated young people and prompted some of them to lead a revolt of the peasant masses in the 1870s.

The cleavage between the intelligentsia and the masses, as well as the government, was dramatized by the attempt of this conscious minority of educated Russians to go directly "to the People." These self-styled Populists were agrarian socialists; they wanted the big estates broken up and the land distributed among all the peasants. After preparing themselves for the completely strange life that was ahead of them by learning humble trades such as carpentry or shoemaking, these youthful agitators from the city put on peasant

*Assassination of Tsar Alexander II, 1881*

costume and set out for the villages of Russia. But they rapidly discovered that they could not arouse what they thought was the people's "pent-up revolutionary energy." The lucky ones shared the experience of one of their comrades: the peasants listened to his speeches as they did to the priest who preached to them about the Kingdom of Heaven, calmly resuming their routine existence after the sermon was over, as if nothing had happened. The less lucky Populists were stoned out of the villages or turned over to the tsarist police by the peasants themselves, who distrusted even the most well-meaning outsiders.

Spurred on by the indifference of the peasant masses and by the determination of the government to suppress its spirit and its life, the revolutionary intelligentsia turned to the path of "direct action" through terrorism in the late 1870s. Both young men and young women threw bombs and fired pistols at the tsar for several years. Their assassination of Alexander II in 1881 led to the brutal suppression of all political movements, liberal and socialist alike, and to the sending of hundreds of young revolutionaries to Siberia. In the 1880s and 1890s the *intelligents* were again confronted with an alien and indifferent world, but this time they faced it with broken spirits and shattered dreams.

During those two decades almost every section of the Russian population had some grievance. The only groups that supported the regime whole-heartedly were the nobility and the clergy, and each of them was losing its power and influence. The small but growing class of industrialists and businessmen resented the interference of the bureaucracy in their affairs. A number of lawyers, doctors, and professors wanted to change the political system and give Russia a representative government and constitutional rights. Yet even the modest proposals of these liberals were branded as subversive by the government, and their advocates were forced underground or into exile abroad. Since trade-unions and strikes were illegal, the new industrial proletariat had little chance of achieving better working conditions and a higher standard of living. The peasants' perennial demand for more land was aggravated by continuing population pressure in the countryside, which migration to the cities and to new farmlands in Siberia hardly alleviated. Finally, there were millions of non-Russians in the empire's borderlands: Poles, Finns, Baltic peoples, Ukrainians, Jews, Georgians, and others. They wanted independence or at least freedom to follow their own way of life under Russian rule.

### Russian Marxism

Marxism was the first Western ideology to help the Russian *intelligents* reconcile their desire to assert themselves as a conscious, forward-looking minority with their emotional urge to retain their ties with the "unconscious" (spontaneous and unthinking) Russian masses. It suggested to many *intelligents* the realistic possibility of holding onto their distinctive Westernized identity while being at one with their Russian environment. In the proletariat, Marxist ideology gave the intelligentsia an image of a new and rising social force, born, as they had been, in the image of the West—whence industrialization came—and yet drawn from and nurtured by the very masses of the people. Marx had said that the industrial proletariat was bound to triumph eventually according to the laws of history. Thus, an *intelligent* who chose to identify himself with it would at last "belong" to a social group that would some day set the standards for society as a whole.

There were several competing Marxist theorists in Russia at the turn of the century, but the man who gave the movement its permanent direction and its final victory was Vladimir Ilyich Ulyanov, or to call him by his alias, V. I. Lenin. Like many underground revolutionaries of the time, he took his alias in order to confuse the authorities. Unlike them, he was a newer, more active, type of *intelligent.*

Vladimir Ilyich Ulyanov was born in 1870 at the provincial capital of Simbirsk, on the Volga. His father, who had been a teacher, became inspector of schools in the province in 1869. Reliable, respectable, and able, the elder Ulyanov climbed the bureaucratic ladder of state service to the rung of hereditary nobility. Thus, young Vladimir, born a commoner, became a nobleman at the age of four. His family's life was comfortable, cultured, quiet, and happy until the death of the father in 1886 and the execution in 1887 of the oldest son, Alexander, as a revolutionary.

Alexander Ulyanov had associated himself with a wholly idealistic but immature student group at St. Petersburg immediately after his father's death. This group of seven young men called itself "The Terrorist Section of the Populists"—though there were no other "sections," and the old organization was dead. Alexander was not its leader, nor did he organize the attempt which the group sought to make on the tsar's life. The plot was discovered, the conspirators tried, and five of them, including Alexander, were hanged.

This tragedy, which came when Vladimir was in his middle teens, had a profound effect on his life. It barred his path to respectability; it opened an unbridgeable gulf between him and the regime that had taken his brother's life; it inoculated him with a profound contempt for the respectable society that had abandoned the Ulyanov family in its time of trouble. Denied the right to study at the University of Kazan, young Lenin educated himself at home. Finally, in 1891, he was allowed to take examinations in law, given *in absentia* by the University of St. Petersburg. After passing these, with the highest honors, he became an "external graduate" of the university, and was admitted to the practice of law. He spent a dreary eighteen months at his profession as a junior lawyer in Samara, losing ten cases and winning one. Then, in 1893, he wrote his first Marxist work intended for publication and moved to St. Petersburg.

In the 1890s and early 1900s Lenin participated in the doctrinal disputes of the revolutionary intelligentsia and tried to organize a Marxist labor movement. He spent part of his time in Western Europe and three years in exile in Siberia. In the early 1900s he and other Marxist writers published a newspaper called *The Spark* in Germany and smuggled it into Russia.

The turning point in the development of the Russian Social Democratic Workers' Party came at a conference in London in 1903. There Lenin dramatically set forth a new conception of party organization. He said that "the organizations of revolutionists must be comprised first and foremost of people whose profession is that of revolutionists . . . not too extensive and as secret as possible." This tightly knit party of full-time agitators would not have to wait until Russia reached the degree of industrialization of Great Britain or Germany. It would hasten the inevitable course of history by acting as the vanguard of the small Russian proletariat as soon as the political and international situation was ripe for revolution. Lenin's opponents at the London meeting wanted the rank-and-file members of the party to guide its policies in a democratic way and they wanted Russia to go through its bourgeois-capitalist stage before launching the proletarian revolution. But Lenin's proposal won by two votes, and, for this reason, his wing of the party was henceforth called Bolsheviks (majority-men), while the rival wing was called Mensheviks (minority-men).

Despite their common allegiance to Marx, the Russian and Western Marxist parties developed along different lines. It could hardly have been otherwise in a country, unlike any in the West, where the bulk of the people were still miserable, illiterate peasants and where socialists of all varieties were hounded by the secret police and forced to live completely outside the respectable society into which most of them had been born. In the West avowedly revolutionary Marxists like Jules Guesde and August Bebel did not have to have their headquarters in foreign cities and smuggle their party newspapers into their homelands. Like them, the Russian Marxists rejected the anarchist-terrorist approach of Bakunin, and in the early 1900s they continued to oppose the Social Revolutionary Party, the direct heir of the bomb-throwing Populists of the late 1870s. Still, the Populist tradition had deeply affected many Russian *intelligents* who later became Marxists.

The fusion of Populism and Marxism in Russia was a crucial aspect of Bolshevism and helps explain its ultimate success in 1917. In 1902 Lenin acknowledged the link in a tract entitled *What Is To Be Done?*. By using the title of Chernyshevsky's novel Lenin tried to show that his brand of Marxism alone could bring social justice to Russia's urban *and* rural masses. Lenin had learned Marxism from George V. Plekhanov, a "repentant nobleman" who, having begun his career as a Populist agitator in the 1870s, became the main Russian theoretician of orthodox Marxism and who took the decisive step toward fusing the traditions of Marx and Chernyshevsky. In 1903 Lenin broke with his teacher over the Bolshevik-Menshevik dispute. But his conception of an elite of professional revolutionaries stemmed from the tradition of Chernyshevsky, through Plekhanov, just as his theories of history, society, and the state stemmed from Marx, again through Plekhanov. Lenin rejected the individual terrorism of the early Populists and adapted Marxism to the last country where Marx himself expected the proletarian revolution to occur.

Indeed, before the early 1900s no form of revolution seemed imminent in Russia. Neither the Bolsheviks nor the other revolutionary leaders could seriously challenge the overpowering authority of the tsarist regime. Beneath the surface order, however, Russians and non-Russians of almost all classes felt a growing sense of alienation from the Russian state. Even if this state could have isolated itself from "contamination" by Western ideas, it could not have remained the same. For it had never had the active allegiance of the majority of its subjects. Furthermore, increasing contacts with the rest of Europe pointed up the "impossibility" of an old-fashioned autocracy isolated from a whole population.

### The Ottoman Empire and the Emerging Nations of the Balkans

The government of Turkey was even more isolated from its own people than that of Russia, and even more unacceptable to its subject nationalities than that of Austria-Hungary. In all three empires wars prompted certain reforms, while prolonged periods of peace allowed their rulers to disregard many of these reforms. Like the Hapsburg emperor and the Romanov tsar, the Ottoman sultan managed to keep his autocratic power over the state through increasingly reactionary policies in the 1880s and 1890s. But the Turkish state lost considerable territory in the Balkans before attaining the precarious stability of this period, and it was to lose almost all the rest in the early 1900s. In addition to its own political decline and the awakening of its subject nationalities, the Ottoman Empire faced increasing intervention from the great powers in its internal affairs.

### Disintegration and the Reassertion of Authority

By the early nineteenth century the government in Istanbul had lost control over most of the Ottoman Empire, and it misgoverned the remainder. The janissaries, once the military backbone of the realm, had become a degenerate and insubordinate Praetorian Guard, feared only by the people they were supposed to defend. In the wars against Russia in 1809–1811 they had fled at the sight of the enemy, pausing only to plunder their own camp. The imperial bureaucracy bore little resemblance to the splendid organization of the sixteenth century, with its well-trained and loyal slave administrators. Like the officers of the janissaries, the administrators and tax collectors now bought their positions in order to make a profit at the expense of the central government as well as its subjects. Most of the provincial governors were semi-independent potentates, acknowledging only nominal allegiance to the sultan. Naturally all of these people opposed any reforms that threatened their vested interests.

The Greek Revolution in the 1820s convinced the sultans that their whole empire would disintegrate unless they reasserted the authority of the central government. In 1826 Sultan Mahmud II (1809–1839) finally took the first decisive step by destroying the janissaries. He did this by forming a new military corps of his own and then turning it loose against the main garrison of the janissaries in Istanbul. Within a few hours artillery fire reduced the barracks to a blazing ruins. Six thousand janissaries lost their lives in the holocaust, and another 18,000 were exiled to Asia Minor. Sultan Mahmud II also got rid of most of the semi-independent potentates in the provinces in the 1830s. In these and other ways the Ottoman government arrested the process of disintegration in its non-European territories, except for Egypt.* But by the middle of the century the peripheral Christian communities in Serbia, Montenegro, Greece, and the Danubian Principalities (Rumania) had gained virtual or complete independence. Hence, the mere reassertion of the authority of the central government was not enough to transform the Ottoman Empire into a workable modern state.

The Crimean War prompted the Ottoman government to launch a series of legal and administrative reforms. The most important of these was the *Hatt-I Humayun* of 1856, which promised the non-Muslim subjects equal rights in matters of justice, taxation, military service, public office, and social respect. This edict also proposed local reforms that would end the rapacity of their fellow Christian civil and ecclesiastical leaders. In the 1860s the Ottoman government tried to overhaul its own provincial administration and to implement a French-inspired law code. Finally, in 1876, a prominent minister, Midhat Pasha, framed Turkey's first constitution and planned to transform the empire into a truly national state in which Christians and Muslims would all have one nationality.

To the Western powers Ottoman reform meant the strengthening of the Turkish armed forces and the achievement of national solvency as well as legal and administrative changes designed to reconcile the sultan's provincial subjects to his government. Great Britain, France, and Austria had approved the *Hatt* in 1856 in order to forestall further Russian intervention on behalf of the oppressed Christians in the Balkans. The Turks also needed a strong army with which to defend themselves against such intervention,

*See p. 545.

and its creation was the most successful of the Ottoman reforms. Unfortunately, the empire's backward economy could not sustain the expense. To make matters worse, the sultans indulged their taste for new palace building, the harem, and personal favorites on a scale that seriously depleted the already inadequate state revenue. Beginning in the late 1850s Western European bankers lent large sums of money to the Turkish government to help cover the growing deficit, but the sultans showed no inclination to honor their debts, and their corrupt officials continued to mismanage the state's finances. In 1874 the government repudiated half the interest on its foreign debt.

Thus, by the mid-1870s the "Sick Man" of Europe seemed once again about to expire. The central government was bankrupt, and its reforms failed to neutralize the forces of Balkan nationalism. In 1875 the Christian Slavs of Bosnia and Bulgaria revolted against their Muslim overlords. The Turkish army supplemented by local Muslim irregulars put down the revolt in Bulgaria with savage brutality, slaughtering 15,000 helpless villagers. These "Bulgarian Horrors" made some Western European leaders conclude that the "Sick Man" was hopelessly unregenerate. Then, in 1876 and 1877, Serbia, Montenegro, and Russia sent their armies to the aid of the beleaguered rebels in Bosnia, and the Western powers prepared for war.

The international repercussions of the Russo-Turkish War of 1877–1878 will be discussed in the next chapter; here we note only its outcome for the Ottoman Empire in the Balkans. According to the peace terms imposed upon him by the powers, Sultan Abdul Hamid II (1876–1909) recognized the complete independence of Serbia and Rumania, the autonomy of Bulgariia, and the permanent occupation of Bosnia by Austrian troops. Although he was still nominally sovereign in Bulgaria and Bosnia, the only part of the Balkans he still governed directly was a strip of territory running westward from Istanbul through Thrace, northern Greece, southern Serbia, Macedonia, and Albania. Convinced of the pointlessness of further reforms, Abdul Hamid had already dismissed Midhat Pasha, closed down the first parliament in Turkish history, and allowed the constitution to lapse.

Henceforth this sultan earned himself the name Abdul the Damned for his merciless repression of all who challenged his authority. His secret police vigorously hunted down real and imaginary plotters against his person.* He trusted no one very far and tried to supervise all the affairs of state himself—from road building and minor diplomatic appointments to censorship and spying on his own ministers. The fact that the great powers were losing interest in the Eastern Question allowed Abdul Hamid to suppress the Armenian nationalist uprising in the 1890s with even greater savagery than in the "Bulgarian Horrors" of the 1870s. He also silenced those Turks who wished, by returning to the Constitution of 1876, to save what was left of the empire. Like many Russian liberals, these self-styled Young Turks carried on their campaign for reform in exile in the West. Yet even after they gained control of the government in 1908 they could not prevent the loss of the remaining Turkish territories in the Balkans.

### *The Balkan Independence Movements*

The emergence of the new nations of the Balkans occurred as a series of independent uprisings ranging from the early nineteenth century to the early twentieth; only the over-all pattern can be given here. Although hostile toward the Turks, the peoples of the Balkans were divided among and within themselves. Consequently, they could not offer a united front against Ottoman rule, and their struggles for independence involved continual rivalry and occasional open conflict.

No matter what categories are used, the peoples of the Balkan Peninsula were deeply divided. The most numerous of the four linguistic groups, the South Slavs, included the Roman Catholic Slovenes and Croats in Austria and Hungary

*It is said that he refused to allow an electric dynamo to be brought into Istanbul because he thought it had something to do with dynamite.

and the predominantly Orthodox Christian Serbs (including Montenegrins) and Bulgarians in the Ottoman Empire. There were also Orthodox Serbs in Hungary and Muslim Serbs (concentrated in Bosnia) and Bulgarians in the Ottoman Empire. The other three linguistic groups were the Rumanians to the north of the Slavs and the Greeks and Albanians to the south and southwest. Of these the Rumanians and Greeks were solidly Orthodox, the Albanians predominantly Muslim with Orthodox and Roman Catholic minorities.

The fact that all four linguistic groups suffered under the Turkish yoke did not prevent them from hating each other. Most persistent was the hostility between the Greeks on the one hand and the Slavs and Rumanians on the other. This hostility was due in part to the hold of the Greek language and Greek ecclesiastics on the Orthodox Christian churches and in part to the predominance of the Greeks in commerce, money lending, and tax collecting in the Balkans.

Even within each linguistic and religious group there were deep social cleavages. The higher clergy opposed revolutionary agitation for its rationalism and secularism and because it threatened their privileged position and their vested interests within the Ottoman structure. Another class that was lukewarm to change was that of the local leaders, who served as intermediaries between the Turkish overlord and the Christian subject. These "primates" were usually the biggest landowners. They also collected taxes, tried civil cases, and, in some places, attempted to raise the health and educational standards of the local population. Yet their very existence as a class required acceptance and, if necessary, support of Ottoman rule. For this reason their fellow Christians bitterly referred to them as "Christian Turks."

By 1878 the social and economic situation had changed little in Greece, Serbia, and Rumania, though the Serbs and Bulgarians now had their own, non-Greek Orthodox churches. In that year, when Bulgaria became autonomous, its peasants took over the land of the Muslim landowners who fled. After 1878 the local "primates" lost their power in Austrian-occupied Bosnia, but not in the provinces directly under Ottoman control. In 1908 Austria annexed Bosnia, and Bulgaria achieved full independence. Then, in 1912–1913, Greece, Serbia, and Bulgaria partitioned the remaining Ottoman territory in the Balkans among themselves—except for Albania, which became independent, and the area around Istanbul, which stayed Turkish. All the new Balkan nations adopted Western political forms, but these worked poorly in a context of chronic intrigue, general ignorance, fragmented parties, and recurring conflicts between foreign-born monarchs (except in Serbia) and elected assemblies.

In the late nineteenth and early twentieth centuries economic changes had an even more disruptive impact on the peoples of the Balkans than the winning of national independence. Western loans made possible the building of railroads, which led to the importation of machine-made goods, which in turn began to undermine many traditional handicraft industries. These foreign loans also created a rising national debt and heavier taxes. As a result, the peasant masses had to shift from their traditional subsistence farming to commercial forms of agriculture and animal husbandry in order to pay the taxes and to buy the new manufactured goods.

European nationalism reached its *reductio ad absurdum* in the Balkans. By the early twentieth century Ottoman rule there had been replaced by a half-dozen small, independent nations, too poor to support economic growth, too ignorant and corrupt to make democracy work, and too ridden with national hatreds to form a larger union. In 1913 Greece, Serbia, Rumania, and Bulgaria still claimed "unredeemed territories" from each other, from Austria-Hungary, and from Russia. Western Europeans and American knew only the comic-opera side of Balkan politics; otherwise, the whole area seemed as remote and worthless as it always had. When its peoples insisted on making headlines, the typical response in the West was the famous complaint of the American humorist Ogden Nash: "Rumanians and Serbs get on my nerbs."

Austria-Hungary, Russia, and Turkey were becoming "impossible" multinational empires in an age of the maturing nation-state. Each of them experienced a respite during the 1880s and 1890s, when temporary tranquility at home and on the international scene allowed their rulers to strengthen the authority of the central government to the detriment of liberalism, democracy, and nationalism. But in Austria, which was the most industrialized, the tide of mass unrest had already become strong by 1895. In Russia it was to come in 1905, and Turkey was to experience a series of liberal and nationalist revolts soon thereafter.

. . .

The developments described in this chapter and in Chapter XIII were directly related. Democracy made the most gains in countries where industrialism had been established the longest and was the most flexible, particularly Great Britain. Socialism had its greatest success in Germany, where industrialism was the youngest and the most inflexible. In France and Great Britain positivism and religious nonconformism prompted radical politicians to favor public education and social welfare; in Italy, where both democracy and industrialism were new and weak, politicians of similar temperament tended to ignore these issues. The Catholics in Germany were more liberal than those in France and Italy and were assaulted by the conservative Bismarck in the 1870s. By the turn of the century liberalism in most countries found itself on the defensive against socialist, conservative, and nationalist extremists.

Except in the Balkans, nationalism did not seriously threaten any established government between 1871 and 1905; and, except in Russia, socialism became less revolutionary than Marx had wanted it to be. The urban workers everywhere remained socially and culturally isolated, and they continued to support movements that tried to promote their solidarity as a class. But this very fact made them less isolated politically. The Socialists tended to follow the behavior pattern of other parliamentary parties. They refused to allow their leaders to accept cabinet posts, to be sure, but they competed for the mass vote and began making compromises with other parties in order to get laws favorable to labor passed. Despite their adherence to the Second International, the Marxist parties were really national parties, and despite their hostility to the bourgeoisie, most workers really wanted to be a part of their nation. Although nationalism and socialism were to remain bitter rivals until the First World War, the triumph of the nation-state over international class solidarity was already in prospect by 1905.

Almost everywhere in Europe the efforts of the state to regulate society were accompanied by some kind of democratization. Compulsory primary education, universal military training, and the beginnings of health and welfare legislation helped to make society, if no the state, more democratic. Universal or near universal male suffrage prevailed in Great Britain, France, and Germany and led to the growth of mass political parties. Here too, the effect on the democratization of the state depended on the political traditions of the country involved and the length of time it had been industrialized. Parliamentary democracy was a sham in Germany and Austria-Hungary, and it did not exist at all in Russia. Yet, in an age of international anarchy, the state, whatever its form of government, became the ultimate embodiment of power and security. Thus, the developments described so far were also directly related to the international situation.

## SUGGESTED READINGS

Anderson, Eugene N. and Pauline, *Political Institutions and Social Change in the 19th Century*. Berkeley: Univ. of California Press, 1967.
Excellent comparative history.

Hayes, Carlton J. H., *A Generation of Materialism, 1871–1900*.
See Readings for Chapter XIII.

Ruggiero, Guido de, *The History of European Liberalism*. Boston: Beacon Press, 1959.*
A classic study.

Thomson, David, *England in the Nineteenth Century.* Baltimore: Penguin Books, 1950.*
A good survey.
———, *Democracy in France: The Third and Fourth Republics.* 4th ed. New York: Oxford Univ. Press, 1964.*
A highly suggestive essay on the political problems of modern France.
Mansergh, Nicholas, *The Irish Question, 1840–1921.* New edition. Toronto: Univ. of Toronto Press, 1965.
Balanced and authoritative.
Mack-Smith, Denis, *Italy: A Modern History.* Ann Arbor, Mich.: Univ. of Michigan Press, 1959.
Excellent on the late nineteenth century.
Eyck, Erich, *Bismarck and the German Empire.* New York: W. W. Norton and Co., 1964.*
Detailed political history.
Medlicott, W. N., *Bismarck and Modern Germany.* (See Chapter XII) argues that Bismarck's diplomacy made for continuous tension in Europe and that, at home, he was conspicuously unsuccessful in developing a sense of political responsibility in the German people.
Landauer, Carl, *European Socialism: A History of Ideas and Movements.* 2 vols. Berkeley, Cal.: Univ. of California Press, 1959.
An advanced study. Particularly good on comparisons of socialist, anarchist, and syndicalist movements in the late nineteenth century.
Braunthal, Julius, *History of the International,* Vol. I, *1864–1914,* New York: Frederick Praeger, 1968.
Joll, James, *The Second International, 1889–1914.* New York: Frederick A. Praeger, 1964.
The best short history of the movement.
Lorwin, Val R., *The French Labor Movement.* Cambridge, Mass.: Harvard Univ. Press, 1954.
An excellent detailed history.
Pelling, Henry M., *The Origins of the Labour Party, 1880–1900.* New York: St. Martin's Press, 1954.
A solid study—sympathetic and authoritative.
Hobsbawm, Eric, *Labouring Men.* New York: Doubleday-Anchor, n.d.*
Outstanding social history.
Freemantle, Anne, *This Little Band of Prophets: The British Fabians.* New York: New American Library of World Literature, 1960. Mentor.*
Woodcock, George, *Anarchism.* Cleveland: World Publishing Co., 1962. Meridian.*
A sympathetic account.
Kann, Robert A., *The Multinational Empire: Nationalism and National Reform in the Hapsburg Monarchy, 1848–1918.* 2 vols. New York: Columbia Univ. Press, 1950.
Detailed, scholarly treatment of the nationalities problem and Austria's attempts to deal with it.
May, Arthur J., *The Hapsburg Monarchy,* 1867–*1914.* Cambridge, Mass.: Harvard Univ. Press, 1951.
Reliable general history.
Seton-Watson, Hugh, *The Decline of Imperial Russia, 1855–1914.* New York: Frederick A. Praeger, n.d.*
A very good survey.

Haimson, Leopold H., *The Russian Marxists and the Origins of Bolshevism.* Boston: Beacon Press, n.d.*

This and the following work are scholarly studies—difficult for beginners, but the best studies available on a very important subject.

Baron, Samuel H., *Plekhanov: The Father of Russian Marxism.* Stanford: Standford Univ. Press, 1963.

Stavrianos, Leften S., *The Balkans since 1453*. New York: Holt, Rinehart and Winston, 1958.

See the sections on Balkan nationalism in the late nineteenth century.

CHAPTER XV

# EUROPE AND THE WORLD TO *c.* 1905

By the early twentieth century Europe had reached the peak of her power and influence. She was the world's workshop, banker, and teacher, and she became the world's political master to a greater extent than she had ever been before or has ever been since. In addition to her economic and technological supremacy, she embarked on a spree of territorial conquest that brought almost all of Africa and a large part of Asia under her sway. In their competition for territory the Europeans put all sorts of economic and military pressure on the local rulers, but their own governments avoided open warfare with each other. Instead, they tried to divide the disputed areas into colonies, protectorates, and spheres of influence, with an almost complete disregard for the native inhabitants. Convinced of the superiority of their own civilization, many Europeans came to believe that they alone were fit to rule the world. As the Englishman Gilbert Murray put it:

"We are the pick and flower of nations; the only nation that is really generous and brave and just. We are above all things qualified for governing others; we know how to keep them exactly in their place without weakness and without cruelty. . . . The excellence of our rule abroad is proved in black and white by the books of our explorers, our missionaries, our administrators, and our soldiers, who all agree that our yoke is a pure blessing to those who bear it."

The diplomacy of the new imperialism reflected the uneasy stalemate within Europe itself. There were no major armed conflicts between the Franco-Prussian War (1870–1871) and the Russo-Japanese War (1904–1905). And as long as Bismarck was able to dominate European international relations he kept the antagonism between Austria-Hungary and Russia in check and prevented France from finding allies against Germany. Begining in the 1890s, however, the rulers of Germany had neither the wit nor the will to preserve the delicate balance of forces Bismarck had tried to create. Each power, including hitherto isolated Great Britain, then felt free to make new arrangements; for in their relations with each other the Europeans recognized no authority, principle, or system above the nation-state. This international anarchy not only marked the end of the Bismarckian system, it also intensified competition for empire overseas, where European power had to be maintained and expanded in the face of hardening rivalries and alliances at home.

In addition to the international anarchy within Europe, there were other underlying weaknesses behind the imposing façade of her world power. The rise of Japan and the United States posed a challenge to Europe's supremacy, though few Europeans understood the full implications of this challenge at the time. Furthermore, the first Asian and African nationalist movements, whose successors affect the present-day world so profoundly, appeared at the very zenith of the new imperialism. In view of these factors, the extent of European power by the early twentieth century is one of the most remarkable facts in the history of civilization.

## THE INTERNATIONAL ANARCHY

In the last three decades of the nineteenth century, European alliances and alignments took on a degree of complexity and commitment hitherto unknown in peacetime. Traditionally the states of Europe had cooperated in wars to keep one power from becoming too strong, and then had gone their separate ways. This traditional means of maintaining the balance of power had been abandoned in the wars of the 'fifties and 'sixties.* The emergence of Germany as the strongest power on the continent at the end of these wars created an unprecedented situation, for Bismarck not only announced that his dynamic new empire was "satiated," he accepted the international anarchy and used it to preserve peace, in the supreme interest of Germany, for almost twenty years. He involved Austria-Hungary, Italy, Russia, and, briefly, Great Britain, in an elaborate system of checks and balances against each other and against France. His master, Emperor William I, once said to him: "You seem to me at times to be like a rider who juggles on horseback with five balls, never letting one fall." But in the 1890s the consummation of the Franco-Russian Alliance brought an end to the Bismarckian system and divided Europe into two rival power blocs, each of whose members was committed to go to war if another member was attacked.

*See pp. 546-557.

### The Bismarckian System

After the Franco-Prussian War, Bismarck first devoted himself to stabilizing relations between victorious Germany and defeated France. He made certain that France remained diplomatically isolated by bringing Austria-Hungary, Germany, and Russia together in the League of the Three Emperors in 1873. Although ostensibly a conservative "Holy Alliance" against socialism, this League was really no more than an agreement among its members not to ally with France.

With relations between Germany and France stabilized, the powers turned their attention to the new crisis in the Balkans. As we have seen, this crisis had begun in 1875 with anti-Turkish revolts in Bosnia and Bulgaria, and it had brought Russia into a war against Turkey on the side of the Balkan Slavs in April 1877. The Turks, however, put up a surprisingly stubborn fight and wore the Russian armies down, so that by the time they reached the gates of Istanbul in January 1878 they could not give the final push. At this point the British government, forgetting the "Bulgarian horrors," decided to revert to its original policy of supporting Turkey. Anti-Russian feeling in England was expressed in the popular refrain, "We don't want to fight, but by jingo, if we do, we've got the men, we've got the ships, we've got the money too." (Thereafter, jingoism became a synonym for aggressive nationalism.) The rumor and then the reality of the British fleet at Istanbul brought the Russo-Turkish War to an end. In March 1878 the two countries signed the Treaty of San Stefano, which gave Russia a large indemnity and pockets of Turkish territory in the Caucasus, made Serbia and Rumania independent, and created an autonomous "Big Bulgaria" that was to extend from the Aegean to the Black Sea and to be occupied by Russian armies for two years. The British government refused to recognize the Treaty of San Stefano and stepped up its preparation for war until Russia finally agreed to submit the treaty to an international conference of the powers, with the understanding that "Big Bulgaria" would disappear.

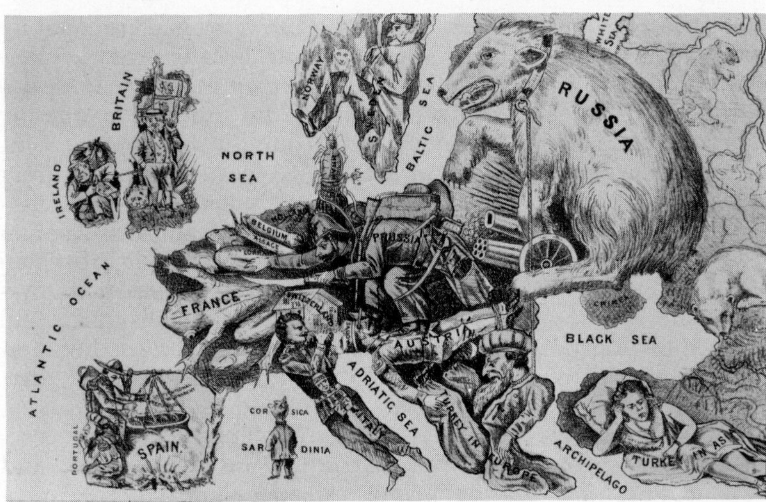


*The European Scene, 1871*

Most of the decisions confirmed at this conference, the Congress of Berlin (June–July 1878), had already been reached in secret agreements among the powers. Great Britain occupied Cyprus and undertook to support the Ottoman Empire against future Russian encroachments. Austria occupied Bosnia and some smaller territories on the northwestern border of Serbia. Macedonia was detached from "Big Bulgaria" and restored to the sultan, who promised the usual reforms. Bismarck himself had no territorial designs in the Balkans, which he said were "not worth the bones of a Pomeranian grenadier." He urged the other powers to turn their backs on the Eastern Question and suggested that France seek her compensation in Tunisia. But the basic conflict of interest between Great Britain and Russia continued in the months after the Congress, and Austria-Hungary and France supported Britain, which they took to be the winning side.

### The Austro-German Alliance

This apparent resurrection of the Crimean War coalition put Bismarck in a difficult position. For, if Austria-Hungary and France, the two powers whom Germany had defeated, succeeded in humiliating Russia, might they not then turn against Germany? On the other hand, Bismarck did not want to have to choose between Russia and Great Britain. He solved his dilemma in October 1879 by concluding a defensive alliance with Austria-Hungary against Russia. In this way he detached Austria-Hungary from the Western powers and saved Russia from the threat of a new Crimean coalition. Two years later Bismarck had no difficulty in persuading the now isolated Russian government to join a revived League of the Three Emperors, which guaranteed Russia's security in the Near East by promising to close the Straits between the Black Sea and the Aegean to British warships.

### The Triple Alliance

The Austro-German Alliance began an era in which every power except Great Britain formally committed itself to support some other power. Bismarck had not originally intended to lose his freedom of maneuver in this way. He had hoped to recover it by reconciling Austria-Hungary and Russia, but the Austrians refused to trust Russia's word and grumbled at the position into which Bismarck had forced them. In order to placate them he gave them a new ally, Italy. Thus, the Austro-German Alliance became the Triple Alliance in 1882. The Italians were delighted by the "great power" status this alliance conferred on them, especially after having come away from the Congress of Berlin empty-handed and then having "lost"

Tunisia to the French.* Austria-Hungary gained the assurance of Italian neutrality in any war between herself and Russia. Bismarck paid the price of committing Germany to defend Italy against France while at the same time cautioning Austria-Hungary that he would not support her expansionist aims in the Balkans.

Bismarck's elaborate system of checks and balances so tied up the European powers in the 1880s that none of them could make an independent move on the continent. The Triple Alliance eliminated any threat from France or Russia to its members. In 1887 Bismarck further satisfied Austrian fears of Russian expansion in the Balkans by encouraging a Mediterranean Agreement between Great Britain, Austria-Hungary, and Italy to check such expansion. Then, in that same year, he again rescued Russia from her diplomatic isolation by replacing the expired Alliance of the Three Emperors with a German-Russian Reinsurance Treaty. In this treaty Bismarck promised to recognize Russian interests in the Balkans, which he knew she could never satisfy because of British and Austrian opposition. At the same time he preserved his supreme achievement, which was the prevention of an alliance between the two powers he feared most: France and Russia.

Only Bismarck could make the Bismarckian "system" work, not only because of his diplomatic dexterity but also because he sincerely wanted peace. After the new emperor, William II, dismissed him in 1890, the makers of German foreign policy became impatient with his complicated checks and balances. They assumed that the main rivals in international affairs were Great Britain and Russia—in the Near East and in Central Asia—and they hoped to draw Great Britain into the Triple Alliance by abandoning Russia. But Great Britain remained aloof, and France and Russia entered negotiations that culminated in a formal alliance in 1894.

### The Franco-Russian Alliance

The Franco-Russian Alliance became an effective counterforce to the Triple Alliance. The two powers had reluctantly come together only because they wished to end their diplomatic isolation. The liberal republic and the despotic monarchy had nothing in common but a mutual interest in security from any German threat so that each could pursue its aims elsewhere. Yet, although the Franco-Russian Alliance seemed like a defeat for Bismarck's successors, it too helped to preserve the peace in Europe. Bismarck had always tried to prevent a war between Austria-Hungary and Russia. Now that France was committed to support Russia, she had the same objective. In any case, the Balkan conflict was dying away, and the Triple Alliance and the Franco-Russian Alliance alike became defensive combinations in which any member that was tempted toward adventure was restrained as much by its allies as by its opponents.

This restraint applied only in Europe, and their very security at home made it easier for the European powers to strengthen their positions overseas. The temporary stalemate in Europe and the new imperialism outside of Europe produced and reinforced each other.

## THE NATURE OF THE NEW IMPERIALISM

In the last two decades of the nineteenth century the Europeans expanded their overseas empires by over 10 million square miles and nearly 150 million people. Imperialism on this unprecedented scale was aided by new geographical explorations, improved communications, and a great military superiority than ever over non-Europeans. The fact that Europe itself was at peace also helped by allowing the employment of military and naval power elsewhere. But what made this late nineteenth-century imperialism *new* was the deliberate and noisily aggressive fashion in which it was carried out.

The new imperialism was not the first example of European expansion. In the twelfth and thirteenth centuries crusading Frenchmen and Englishmen had set up ephemeral empires in the Arab and Byzantine lands of the Near East. The second and more comprehensive wave of

*See p. 545.

*An American view of English imperialism characterizing Queen Victoria as the "old woman who lived in a shoe" (Puck 1883)*

European expansion included the Spanish and Portuguese penetration of Latin America in the sixteenth century, the British, French, and Dutch settlement of North America in the seventeenth century, and the British conquest of India in the eighteenth century. Between roughly the 1780s and 1880s the more advanced nations of Europe seemed to be too busy with their own industrial and political developments to bother very much about the rest of the world, but during that period a slower and usually quieter form of conquest was nevertheless taking place. The descendants of the Portuguese settlers on the coast of Brazil extended their control over that vast country; the descendants of the British settlers in Australia, Canada, and the United States pushed their frontiers across whole continents; the Russians conquered and occupied Siberia and much of Central Asia.

The British and the French were not entirely inactive during the period when the Americans and the Russians were pushing their frontiers to the opposite shores of the Pacific Ocean. Between 1830 and 1880 both nations extended their external sway over local rulers in Africa and Asia through loans, veiled protectorates, and on-the-spot "advisers." When local rulers resisted these kinds of pressure, the British and French governments were usually able to subdue them with a show of military or naval force. "Gunboat diplomacy" gave Algiers and Saigon to the French and Singapore and Hong Kong to the British. In two small wars with Afghanistan the British won control over that country's trade and foreign relations, and two other small wars led to the British annexation of Lower Burma. Although Napoleon III failed to maintain his puppet empire in Mexico, he established a firm grip on the most vital parts of South Vietnam and set up a protectorate over Cambodia.

The new imperialism of the 1880s and 1890s differed from both the American and Russian frontier movements and the earlier gunboat diplomacy of the British and the French. In addition to being more deliberate and more blatantly aggressive, it was more directly linked with the major forces of the age: economic competition, diplomatic rivalries, nationalism, and even Darwinism. Indeed, each of these has had its apologists as the sole cause of the new imperialism.

The economic explanation of imperialism was first set forth by J. A. Hobson in 1902, toward the end of the struggle between the British and Boer colonists for control of South Africa with its gold and diamonds. Hobson argued that the new imperialism was caused by the desire of European financial leaders to invest their surplus capital more profitably overseas. According to him, the declining rate of profit at home resulted primarily from underconsumption, which in turn reflected an unjust distribution of wealth. Hobson advocated social reform, including the nationalization of certain industries, as an alternative to imperialism, which enriched a few at the expense of the many. In 1915 Lenin carried Hobson's economic explanation much further. According to him, the new imperialism was a inevitable development in what he called "the highest stage of capitalism" — the stage in which the monopoly capitalists have eliminated their competitors at home and are hence forced to stake their claims on actual and potential raw materials, markets, and investment opportunities overseas in order to keep growing.

Other theorists produced evidence for non-economic causes of the new imperialism. Joseph Schumpeter, though an economist himself, blamed the new imperialism on the survival of feudal, warrior-class values among Europe's diplomats and army officers. Those theorists who stressed the role of popular nationalism could point to the British threat to declare war on Russia over the Straits in 1878 and the French humiliation by the British at Fashoda (in the Sudan) twenty years later. Strains in the European balance of power were certainly of major importance in the way tropical Africa was partitioned. Furthermore, the idea that colored peoples everywhere were the "white man's burden" could easily be associated with Darwinism.

A good deal of recent research and reconsideration has led to the conclusion that the new imperialism was as much the result as the cause of the actions it purports to explain. On the one hand the peoples and statesmen of Europe became increasingly conditioned to thinking in imperial terms — politically, strategically, economically, and above all psychologically. On the other hand, the local situations that arose in Africa and Asia seemed to invite imperial intervention. In many instances the European governments stumbled into actions that committed them to a more deliberate and aggressive policy of conquest than they had originally intended. We must therefore examine some of these major actions, as they happened, before coming to any conclusions about their over-all meaning.

## NORTH AFRICA

The situation in North Africa "invited" a new kind of imperialism. This was particularly true in Egypt, where the emergence of the military as the first native reformist force was fraught with meaning for the semi-colonial world, including Latin America, in more recent times. In the 1870s the whole area between Algeria and Persia was still under the nominal suzerainty of the Ottoman Empire. Although European penetration of the sultan's Asiatic territories was to increase, he was to retain them until the First World War. But, as we have seen, Abdul Hamid lost effective control over most of his European holdings and the island of Cyprus in 1878. In North Africa the rulers of Tunisia, Libya, and Egypt kept their formal ties with Istanbul while trying to behave as independent sovereigns in every other way. Unfortunately for themselves and their countries, the Bey of Tunis and the Khedive of Egypt became financially dependent on European investment bankers. In the eyes of their peoples these two potentates seemed to turn into mere debt collectors for the infidels. The more they squeezed money from the landlord and peasant, the nearer they came to internal revolt and political ruin, which overtook so many backward countries whose rulers had fallen under the external sway of Europe.

### Tunisia

In 1881 France sent a military expedition into Tunisia. The bey's government was bankrupt, and Italy was trying to gain the option over the economic and political future of the country. Such a move by Italy seemed to threaten both Franch prestige in the Mediterranean and the territorial security of Algeria.* At first the French government merely wished to reassert its external sway over Tunsia rather than acquire a new colony. Léon Gambetta, the President of the Chamber, defined the military expedition's aims as follows:

"We ought to extort a large reparation from the bey . . . take a large belt of territory as a precaution for the future, sign a treaty with effective guarantees, and then retire . . . after having made a show of force sufficient to assure forever a preponderant position there, in keeping with our power, our interests, and our investments in the Mediterranean."

The French show of force was sufficient to make the bey sign the Treaty of Bardo (May 12, 1881), which announced a French protectorate over his foreign relations. But the surrender of this discredited Muslim leader to France could not bind his subjects. The tribesmen of the interior rose in revolt, and the French were compelled to conquer and rule a people whom they could no longer dominate from the outside.

A similar pattern of economic, strategic, and diplomatic interests came into play in the British occupation of Egypt a year later. Since many historians consider the British action in Egypt to be the first major example of the new imperialism, the developments leading up to it will be described in greater detail.

*The French had begun their conquest of coastal Algeria in 1830 under Charles X and, with the assistance of the newly created Foreign Legion, had pacified the interior in the succeeding decades. By 1871 there were almost 300,000 European settlers in Algeria, and the Third Republic declared the territory a part of France itself.

### Egypt

The "opening" of Egypt to European influence began in the early nineteenth century under Muhammad Ali (1811–1848). Though illiterate, this pasha (viceroy) of the Turkish sultan set himself the task of introducing European—especially French—administrative, military, and economic techniques into his benighted Muslim land and of extending his territory. Most of Egypt is a desert, but the fertile valley of the Nile was capable of supporting far more than the 2 million peasants and their landlords who lived there in the 1820s. Indeed, this population more than tripled in the next half-century as a result of economic improvements intitiated bv Muhammad Ali and his successors. The mass of the peasants, however, remained poor and ignorant. All of them together owned only three-eighths of the land, whereas the same amount was owned by 11,000 rich families. When Muhammad Ali went to war against the sultan in 1839 over the Ottoman territories of Syria and Crete, the French encouraged him, but Great Britain and the other powers intervened and brought it to an end. Nevertheless, Muhammad Ali was able to establish a hereditary dynasty of khedives (kings) which was to rule Egypt for over a hundred years.

Muhammad Ali's grandson, Khedive Ismail (1863–1879), encouraged massive European penetration into his country, and even more than his grandfather, used the new wealth at his disposal for his personal ends. The Civil War in the United States had created a great demand for Egyptian cotton and resulted in widespread prosperity during the 1860s. The cotton boom encouraged European bankers to lend large sums of money to Ismail at usurious rates of interest. European merchants flocked to Cairo and Alexandria to dispose of third-rate goods at first-rate prices, and by 1870 there were 100,000 Europeans in these two cities. Under Ismail's rule French engineers built railroads, telegraph lines, and, above all, the Suez Canal. Some of Ismail's projects were economically sound; others were luxurious follies—like his new palace at Alexandria, whose entire parade ground he had covered with a platform of iron so that he would not be bothered by dust when reviewing his troops. Indeed, he brought the Egyptian government to bankruptcy. He issued all kinds of notes, bills, bonds, and similar instruments which fed the fires of Egyptian speculation and floated through the financial exchanges of Europe. He also borrowed cash outright from Parisian bankers.

By the late 1870s a running war had developed between the Egyptian treasury and European banking interests. Ismail's efforts to raise more money simply to serve his floating debt (at 25 per cent interest) caused him to sell the Egyptian government's ordinary shares in the Suez Canal Company to the British government in 1875 for £4 million and to mortgage almost half of the state's lands for a Rothschild loan of £8 1/2 million in 1878. In that year he was forced to suspend payment on his treasury bills and to establish an international Treasury of the Public Debt. An unedifying series of financial squabbles followed, many of which were settled by consular courts whose unannounced principle was to recognize only the claims of their own nationals. The British and French governments appointed a commission of inquiry, which quickly transformed itself into a responsible ministry of the Egyptian government. Ismail was now the prisoner of his creditors. When he tried to expel them in the spring of 1879, the European powers put pressure on the sultan to depose him, and the British and the French firmly subordinated his successor, Tewfik, to their "Dual Control."

This new arrangement prompted the first important nationalist movement against foreign subjugation. In 1881 Colonel Ahmed Arabi led a military revolt against Anglo-French control and Turkish influence and in favor of representative government and a larger army. The success of Arabi's revolt brought a sharp Anglo-French note (January 1882) designed to support the khedive against nationalistic pressures, but this note merely discredited Tewfik further, in Egyptian eyes, since it was not accompanied by any concrete action. A month later he appointed a nationalist government with Arabi as war minister.

Neither the British nor the French wanted to launch a military occupation of Egypt, yet something had to be done. Arabi threatened Britain's new "lifeline" to India, and the French feared the spread of his Muslim nationalist movement to their dissident subjects in Tunisia and Algeria. Anti-foreign riots in Alexandria killed fifty Europeans in June 1882. Whether or not it is true, as some historians claim, that Tewfik himself inspired these riots in order to force European intervention, this intervention came—in the form of a British naval bombardment of the city—in July. The French government declined to take part in any military action, so the British alone then sent an army into Egypt to protect the Suez Canal and to restore indirect European control over the Egyptian government. In mid-September Arabi and the Egyptian army surrendered, and the British occupied Cairo.

Having stumbled into Egypt in this way, the British soon found that they had to stay. At first they abolished the "Dual Control" and told the powers that they intended to leave. But they had overturned the only administrative system that Egypt possessed and they could not construct a new one without staying there to see that it worked. So in 1883 the British appointed the banker Sir Evelyn Baring —later Lord Cromer—as resident and consul-general to order the country's finances, develop its economy, and institute administrative reforms. Little was done, however, for popular education or for the development of self-government. British advisers supervised all native officials and exercised an ill-defined but effective control, backed up by a small but permanent army of occupation. For the next twenty-five years Cromer had to maintain British authority while at the same time posing as the custodian of the economic interests of the other Europeans in Egypt.

The French were particularly bitter. They announced that they "reserved their liberty of action" in Egypt, by which they meant that they would henceforth hamper British administration there and British foreign policy in general. For the French had considered themselves the dominant power in the Near East and North Africa since the early nineteenth century, and they refused to abandon this claim after 1882.

### International Consequences

The British occupation of Egypt had more important consequences for the European balance of power than any single event between the Battle of Sedan and the defeat of Russia in the Russo-Japanese War. By giving the British security for their route to India it made it unnecessary for them to stand in the front line against Russia at the Straits. This fact was crucial in shelving the whole Near Eastern Question as a major concern of the powers for over two decades. Britain's unilateral action in Egypt also encouraged France to unleash her colonial soldiers against British interests in unclaimed Africa and prepared the way for the Franco-Russian Alliance. Even Germany was able to use Egypt as a means of applying pressure on the British, in trying to draw them into her European affairs, and in allowing her to acquire colonies in tropical Africa and the South Pacific.

Along with the French occupation of Tunisia the British occupation of Egypt also opened the way for that intensive scramble in the rest of Africa which, more than anything else, justifies the label "new imperialism." In North Africa, the French began to assert their paramountcy in Morocco in 1905 and established their protectorate over that North African kingdom in 1912. Italy was thwarted in her attempt to conquer Ethiopia in 1896, but in 1912 she was to take over Libya, the last Turkish dependency in North Africa. Both strategic and economic interests had motivated the French in Tunisia and the British in Egypt, and economic interests were to be particularly important in the Congo, South Africa, and Morocco. But national prestige and diplomatic rivalries gave the major "push" to the new imperialism in almost all the rest of the African continent.

## THE PARTITION OF AFRICA

The partitition of tropical Africa is the classic example of the way in which the "push" of European imperalist interests coincided with the "pull" of local unrest. Until the 1880s the European powers had made no claims on the vast interior of the "Dark Continent," which was almost unknown except by a few explorers, missionaries, and soldiers. Once the British occupation of Egypt became an issue of European diplomacy, however, France and Germany entered an intensive competition with Great Britain for nominal control of the whole of Africa south of the Sahara. As in Tunisia and Egypt, the French and the British ran into strong Muslim resistance in the western and eastern Sudan and had to commit themselves to a more thorough policy of conquest and occupation than they had originally intended. Thousands of miles to the south, British efforts to bring Afrikaner (Dutch) nationalists under the control of the Cape Colony set off a second movement of expansion northward as far as Lake Tanganyika. Not wanting to be left out, the Germans and then the Italians began setting up paper protectorates on the east and west coasts of tropical Africa next to those of the British and the French. Acting as a private citizen, the King of the Belgians was able to carve out an empire for himself in the Congo. By the late 1890s the crescendo of European rivalries and local nationalist and religious resistance reached its peak. Consequently, the European powers had to colonize the whole of the territories they claimed, whether their original interests had been national prestige, strategy, diplomacy, or economic gain.

### Tropical Africa: The Period of Paper Partition

The only thing that the Africans south of the Sahara have in common is the color of their skin—and their color is only the same insofar as it is not "white." Until recent years only a mere handful of Europeans on the spot was aware of the bewildering variety of races, languages, religions, and societies that outsiders compressed into their stereotype of "Africa." Actually, there were at least five different "Africas" on the eve of partition. These five areas differed considerably in geography and in their contacts with outsiders.

The first of the five "Africas" was the broad belt of pastoral kingdoms of West Africa in the grasslands—called the Sudan—between the Sahara and the southern coastal regions from the Atlantic in the west of the Ethiopian border in the east. The Sahara was by no means an impenetrable barrier. Long before the Europeans began acquiring footholds on the African coast, Arab and Berber Muslims had been coming down to West Africa from the north in search of trade, slaves, and converts. Here dark-skinned Hamites* and true blacks had lived side by side and intermingled for centuries, tending their flocks, adopting each other's languages, and carrying out slave-raiding expeditions in the bush country to the south. Under the West African kingdoms—from Ghana in the eleventh century to the Fulani Empire in the eighteenth century—Islam was the religion and Arabic the language of the ruling classes only. Then, in the eighteenth and early nineteenth centuries, the Fulani people sharply accelerated the tempo of Islamicization throughout the Sudan, and the conversion of the masses continued during the period of European colonization.

In East Africa there were two distinct regions: the Arab-dominated coast and the Empire of Ethiopia. The population of Ethiopia itself was a mixture of dark-skinned Semites and blacks and was ruled by a Coptic Christian king who called himself the Lion of Judah. Along the east coast from the Equator to the Tropic of Capricorn the Arab sultan of the island of Zanzibar held a loose protectorate and extended his slave-raiding activities into the interiors of Kenya, Tanganyika (later German East Africa), Uganda, and Rhodesia. Indeed, the literal meaning of "Zanzibar" is "country of slaves." By the mid-nineteenth century the mixing of Arabs and Africans on the East African coast had produced an Arabized Bantu language known as Swahili. Thereafter Islam spread rapidly into the interior, and Swahili became the common language for much of the region.

The fourth "Africa" comprised the coastal areas of the West: Guinea, the Ivory Coast, the Gold Coast (Ghana), Nigeria, the Cameroons, Gabon. This was the area from which most of the slaves had been shipped to the Western Hemisphere, and which was best known to European traders for its frightful human sacrifices and its remarkable works of art: bronzes, clay statues, wooden and ivory masks. The fifth and most primitive "Africa" was the interior, from the Ubangi River in the north, through the jungles of the Congo, to the South African *Veldt*. Loose confederations of Bantu peoples controlled sections of this region, which also included such contrasting races as the stately blue-black Watusi and the shrunken, yellow-brown Hottentots, whom the Bantus considered subhuman.

During most of the nineteenth century European control in tropical Africa was largely restricted to coastal enclaves. In addition to the moribund Spanish and Portuguese colonies, the British and the French had established colonial outposts and trading stations between the mouths of the Senegal and Congo Rivers on the west coast and had tacitly agreed to leave the east coast alone. A number of British, French, and German explorers had made isolated expeditions into the interior in the 1860s and 1870s, but the traders and soldiers did not follow immediately. To them "Africa" was nothing but jungle and desert, and its inhabitants could never be trained to useful work by European standards. Only along the three great rivers—Senegal, Niger, and Congo—had the Europeans broken through the middleman chiefs who controlled all ways inland. Even here the British and French govern-

*It is believed that the original inhabitants of the northern third of Africa were "whites" who spoke Hamitic languages—from the Berbers of Morocco to the Egyptians in the Nile Valley. In addition, Semitic-speaking "whites" from southwestern Arabia presumably spilled over from Yemen into Ethiopia. Then, beginning in the seventh century, the Arabs—who are also Semites—conquered all of North Africa and periodically controlled the coastal regions of East Africa.

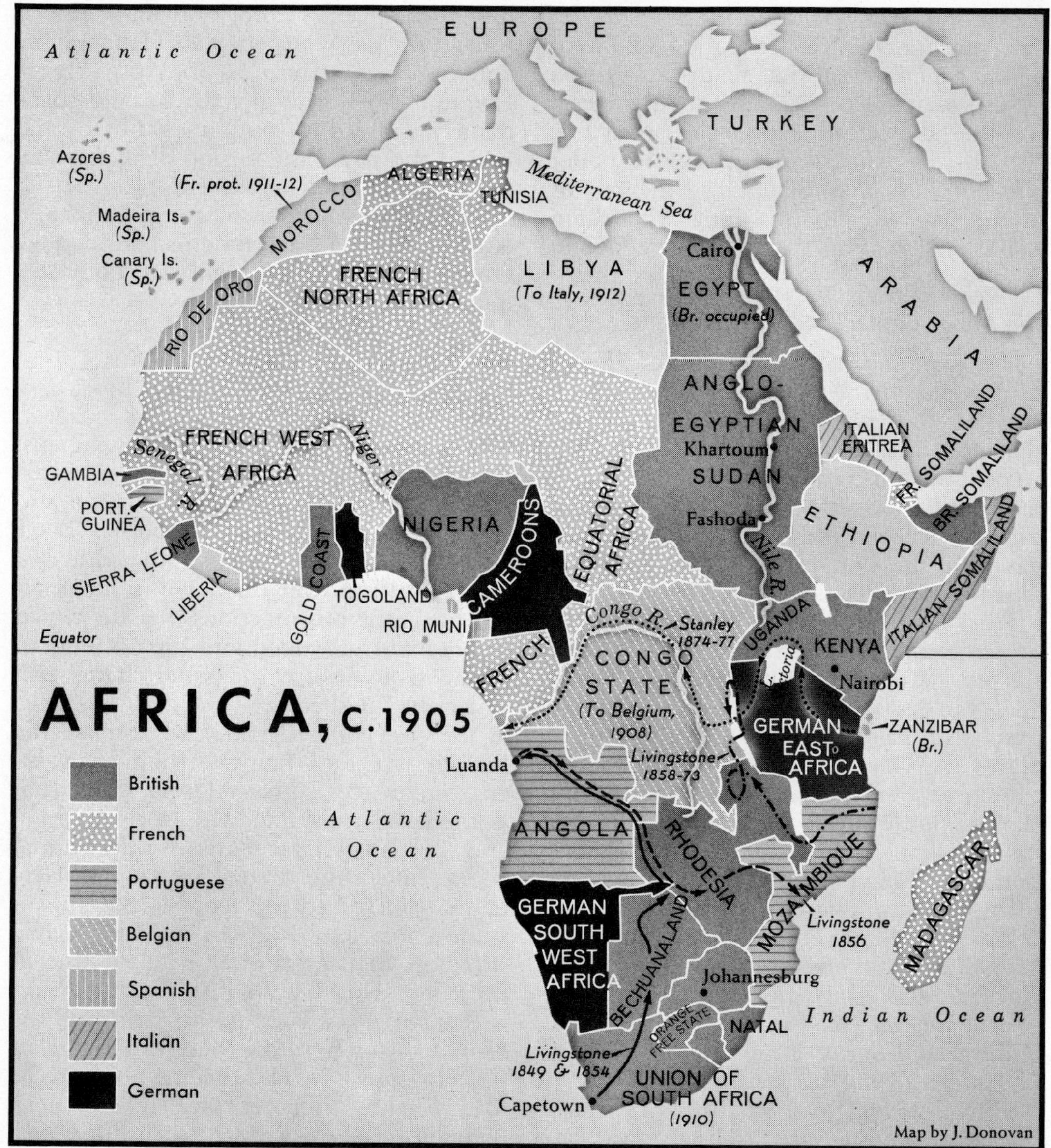


ments gave little support to the rival merchants and explorers who occasionally jostled each other. Leopold II, the King of the Belgians, plotted a private Congo empire (the Belgian government would have nothing to do with the scheme) under the guise of a free state, and in 1879 he sent in the British explorer Henry M. Stanley (who had "discovered" the dying missionary-explorer David Livingstone eight years earlier) to establish his claims.

Only in the mid-1880s did the rivalries among the European powers prompt them to begin the paper partition of Africa. In addition to Stanley, German and French explorers were moving into Central Africa from the east and west coasts respectively and persuading native chiefs to put their "X's" on blank treaty forms that placed their territories under European protection. British, French, and German traders were doing the same thing on the Ivory Coast, in Nigeria, and in the Cameroons. Their governments back home had let them off their leashes, now that the British occupation of Egypt had merged territorial claims in Africa with power-politics in Europe. Bismarck considered African colonies an absurdity, but he was willing enough to use paper partition as a momentary means of wooing the French by siding with them against British efforts to dig in deeper in Egypt.

### *The Berlin Conference*

For this dual purpose, Bismarck called a conference of the powers in Berlin (Nov. 1884–Feb. 1885). The delegates all agreed that the first "white man's burden" in Africa was the elimination of the slave trade. The second "burden" was the enforcement of freedom of trade and navigation in the Congo Basin, and the question was, who would enforce it?

In 1876, King Leopold had formed an International Association to repress slavery and to explore the Congo, and by 1879 the Association had begun to set up outposts in the area. In 1884, the United States and Germany recognized the Association as a territorial power. During the Berlin Conference, the British, French, and Russians followed, and the Association was renamed the Independent State of the Congo. Then, in April 1885, Leopold assumed sovereignty of the Congo Free State, thus making a mockery of its "independence." In these ways the King of the Belgians had acquired a personal empire almost as large as the United States east of the Mississippi.

Having given Leopold the lion's share, the lions contented themselves with scraps —a modest sphere on the north bank of the Congo around Brazzaville for France, Togoland in the Cameroons for Germany, and the division of the Niger basin between France and Great Britain.

The Berlin Conference declared that territorial claims on African coasts should depend on effective occupation, a magical phrase left purposely vague, so that the diplomats could wash their hands of their paper protectorates, once these had been saved from other European clutches. A year after the Berlin Conference Great Britain and Germany divided East Africa into a northern, British sphere of influence (Kenya and Somalia) and a southern, German sphere (Tanganyika and Zanzibar). Here, as in West Africa, London and Berlin gave these lands over to private trading companies, but by the end of the 1880s the period of paper partition was coming to a close. Most of the trading companies were going bankrupt, and their home governments had to make effective occupation a reality for both diplomatic and strategic reasons.

### Tropical Africa: the Period of Military Conquest

The longest and bloodiest fighting against European military penetration was carried out by the Muslims of the Sudan and the Coptic Christians of Ethiopia. Their opposition raised local crises that dragged the Europeans ever deeper into nationalistic and religious reactions that their own coming had provoked and forced them in the 1890s to occupy the paper claims with which they had colored the map of Africa in the preceding decade. In a sense the French extended their control in the western Sudan to protect Algeria, somewhat as the British occupied the eastern Sudan and the East African flank of the route to India (including Zanzibar, which Germany transferred to them in 1890 in her futile effort to woo them into the Triple Alliance) to protect their vital lifeline in the Nile Basin. The British did not object to Italian inroads into the lands of the Lion of Judah; these had the merit of blocking any French advance on the Nile Valley from their enclave in northern Somalia, at the entrance to the Red Sea. And in order to keep the Italians out of the Sudan the British recognized their claim to preponderance over Eritrea and eastern Somalia as far south as Kenya. Crispi's soldiers managed to subdue the black Muslim chieftains along the coast, but in 1896 20,000 Italians were slaughtered by 80,000 Ethiopians at the Battle of Adowa.

The Battle of Adowa was the first major defeat for European imperialism, but it was altogether exceptional in Africa. Everywhere else on that continent Europe's colonial armies broke native opposition to their presence. Having gone in

*Africa, 1894*

against its will in the 1880s, the French government gradually consolidated its haphazard conquests between Algeria, Senegal, and the Congo in the next decade. In the Sudan they defeated the Muslim slave-raiding princes one by one and took Timbuktu in 1893. They also added Dahomey, the Ivory Coast, and Guinea to French West Africa, which by the end of the century stretched from Senegal to Lake Chad. The French also subdued the more tractable natives from Lake Chad south to Brazzaville and organized the entire territory into French Equatorial Africa. Meanwhile, in Nigeria, the British defeated the warlike Ashantis and replaced the Royal Niger Company with a British protectorate.

### *The Sudan*

The struggle for control of the eastern Sudan offers the most dramatic and bloody example of native resistance and European rivalries. Mohammed Ali had conquered the entire area down to the middle reaches of the White Nile, and Khedive Ismail had laid heavy tribute on its people. At the same time, he had tried to suppress the slave trade—thus depriving the Sudanese of their chief means of paying this tribute—and employed British governors to impose Christian ethics on his Muslim subjects. The Sudanese detested the imperialism of Cairo, and they struck back at the Egyptians once the later had been disarmed by revolution and the British occupation.

As in other parts of Muslim Africa, the liberation movement took the form of a fanatical religious revolution against foreign overlords who had become too accommodating to the Europeans. The Mahdi (leader of the faithful) Mohammed Ahmed had begun his preaching in 1881, and in the next two years the revivalist Dervish orders forged the politically discontented sheiks, slave traders, and tribes into an army and a state. In late 1883 the Mahdists cut the Egyptian troops in the Sudan to pieces. Since Khedive Tewfik had no reinforcements at his disposal, the British authorities advised him to give up the Sudan and sent General "Chinese" Gordon (so called because he had helped suppress the T'ai P'ing Rebellion in China twenty years earlier, as we shall see presently) to Khartoum to negotiate evacuation terms with the Mahdi. The Mahdists and Dervishes refused to negotiate with the infidel; in January 1885 they occupied and ransacked Khartoum, killing Gordon and the 34,000 half-starved Egyptian troops under his command.

Not until the late 1890s were the Egyptians, under another British commander, finally able to subdue the "whirling Dervishes." In the Sudan, as in so many other places, the British went in to preserve a strategic area from incursions by rival European powers. For the French as well as the Italians were maneuvering around the upper Nile in 1896 from their Red Sea outposts, and two years later Major Jean-Baptiste Marchand was to establish himself at Fashoda (now Kodok) on the White Nile, after a long march northeastward all the way from Brazzaville. General Herbert Kitchener first reconquered the upper Sudan in a series of battles culminating in the massacre of 20,000 Dervishes near the spot where they had slaughtered Gordon and his Egyptians thirteen years earlier. Then he quickly marched southward to Fashoda.

In the fall of 1898 the Anglo-French struggle for the Nile approached its climax. The British were determined to keep the tricolor out of the eastern Sudan at almost any cost. Marchand had raised it at Fashoda in late August; Kitchener arrived there three weeks later; and both forces refused to give way. For the next two months the govenments in London and Paris seemed on the verge of declaring war, not simply for a lonely outpost in the heart of Africa but for all that it symbolized: British safety in Egypt and India and French security in the Mediterranean. In the end it was Paris that gave way, much to the indignation of the French nationalists, who were already anxious over the impending retrial of Captain Dreyfus. The exclusion of the French from the entire Nile Valley was ratified in the Anglo-French Declaration of March 1899.

Although the permanent "loss" of Egypt to Great Britain seemed like a humiliating defeat for France at the time, the settlement of the Nile issue actually prepared the way for a diplomatic understanding between the two countries in the face of a bellicose Germany five years later, when Anglo-German relations became strained over British imperialism at the other end of Africa.

### South Africa and the Boer War

In South Africa too the resistance of local nationalists sparked conflict. Only in South Africa, the nationalists happened to be white. The German emperor encouraged these Afrikaners in their struggle against the British, and the war that ensued—the Boer War—lasted from 1899 to 1902 and brought the military phase of European imperialism to a bloody end.

Beginning in the 1870s British policy in South Africa became far more imperialistic than it ever was in Egypt or tropical Africa. Until that time the government in London had been content to secure the southern route to India through colonial control of the Cape and Natal and to leave the inland Boer republics* of the Transvaal and the Orange Free State their ramshackle independence. Then the diamond discoveries at Kimberley and the beginnings of investment and railway building brought an influx of British colonists, and Disraeli decided to bring the coastal dependencies and the Boer republics together into a self-governing dominion on the model of Canada. In 1876 the British colonial office annexed the Transvaal, but three years later the Boer inhabitants took up arms and won back their independence from the Uitlanders

*Many of the descendants of the Dutch and French Huguenots who had settled the Cape and Natal in the seventeenth century had made their Great Trek inland in the 1830s, two decades after the British had taken over the Cape Colony from Holland at the end of the Napoleonic Wars. In the Transvaal and the Orange Free State they continued to speak seventeenth-century Dutch, which they preferred to call Afrikaans. Even after they formally abolished slavery, they imposed a rigid form of segregation on the black majority in their midst. The Afrikaners who remained in the Cape Colony became partly anglicized, but when the Boer War broke out, they sided with their distant compatriots to the North. Strictly speaking, the term Boer, which is the old Dutch word for farmer, applied only to the Afrikaners in the interior.

(foreigners). During the next two decades the Afrikaner nationalist movement spread to other parts of South Africa, and the British government waited for its collaborators in the Cape Colony, helped by the inflow of British capital and immigrants, to bring about an imperial union from within. But instead of becoming another Canada, South Africa turned into another Ireland.

The task of preserving the economic preponderance of the Cape and of extending British influence northward was undertaken by Cecil Rhodes, the greatest imperialist of them all. Compared to him even Leopold II himself took second place in his ability to put big business to work in politics and politics to work for big business, while at the same time pleading the cause of the "white man's burden." Rhodes carved out for himself a virtual monopoly of the South African diamond industry and got unlimited credit in the biggest banks in London. His swift mind thought big, and he then carried through schemes on an even more grandiose scale than his original intentions. Rhodes and the private army of his South Africa Company conquered Nyasaland and Rhodesia to the southern boundary of the Congo Free State in 1890. In that same year he became premier of the self-governing Cape Colony. Rhodes' ultimate dream was to place all of South Africa that was not already German under joint British-Afrikaner control and construct a railroad "from the Cape to Cairo."

But the diamonds of Rhodes were no match for the gold of President Kruger of the Transvaal. The British settlers who might have colonized Rhodesia began to join the Uitlanders of Johannesburg in the gold rush on the Rand instead. By the early 1890s these Uitlanders, mostly English, outnumbered the Afrikaners in the Transvaal, but the Kruger government put all sorts of obstacles in their way to naturalization and hence to equality of treatment. It also constructed, with German and Dutch capital, a railroad line connecting the Rand with Portuguese Delagoa Bay. There was also a line running to Capetown, but Kruger gave the Delagoa Bay line a monopoly over all exports from the Transvaal, which now became richer than the Cape Colony itself. Rhodes' dream of an imperial union based on the Cape's supremacy seemed increasingly remote by the mid-1890s. Kruger, not he, was now the arbiter over South Africa's commercial and political future, and Kruger seemed likely to opt for a Republic of South Africa under Afrikaner leadership.

In 1895 Rhodes and Joseph Chamberlain, the aggressive British colonial secretary, set out to topple Kruger. There is some doubt about how much Chamberlain knew of Rhodes' actual machinations; he was later reported to have said, "I did not want to know too much," But there is no doubt that Chamberlain was a rabid imperialist; in the 1880s he had been an outspoken opponent of Irish Home Rule, and in 1895 he urged Britain to tighten her hold on her white dominions by setting up an imperial tariff system. Rhodes gave Dr. Leander Starr Jameson 500 of his private mounted police to make a "raid" into the Transvaal which would coincide with a rising in Johannesburg. Jameson's Raid took place before the rising, however, thus exposing Rhodes' conspiracy and implicating the imperial authorities. On January 3, 1896, the day after Jameson's capture, the Kaiser sent a telegram of congratulation to President Kruger. The British never forgave the Kaiser for the Kruger telegram, and throughout South Africa, Afrikaner nationalists came together once more against British aggression. Those in Capetown ousted Rhodes from office, and those in the Orange Free State made a far-reaching alliance with the Transvaal.

In October 1899 the Boer War began after all British efforts to improve the status of the Uitlanders in the Transvaal and to bring the Rand into a South African commercial union had failed. Like Arabi in Egypt, it was Kruger who finally declared war, but unlike the Arabists, the Boers were able to put up a long hard fight. Even after British regulars captured Pretoria, the capital of the Transvaal, the Boers carried on a skillful guerrilla war. General Kitchener, fresh from his triumphs at Khartoum and Fashoda, reacted by setting up a system of block houses and concentration camps for Boer women and children, in which about 20,000 died. By 1902 the Boers finally capitulated. Their two republics were annexed by the British, who promised them self-government, granted their language official status, and compensated them for their war-devastated farms. Nevertheless, the war made Great Britain extremely unpopular in Europe, and the enmity of the Afrikaners prevented the Union of South Africa, established in 1910, from ever fitting comfortably into the British Empire or its successor, the Commonwealth.

Only in South Africa and the Congo was economic gain a major motive of the new imperialism on the Dark Continent. Everywhere else the powers' perpetual fumbling for safety in the world at large drove them to claim spheres, to proclaim protectorates, and to charter companies. In most cases they did these things with the largely negative purpose of keeping out others whose presence might threaten a national interest, no matter how remote. But European penetration provoked new African resistances, and these compelled further European exertions. As they sliced up and occupied more and more of the continent the politicians of Great Britain and France found it easier to justify their actions with talk about new markets and civilizing missions than with strategic concepts of lifelines to India and security in the Mediterranean. The Germans and the Italians were franker in their quest for national prestige, yet they too eventually took up the "white man's burden" as an excuse for maintaining their presence in the barren enclaves left over from the main struggle between the French and the British against each other and against the nascent forces of African nationalism.

## THE FAR EAST

In the period between 1885 and 1905 the imperialist powers advanced their control over an overwhelming list of new territories from Persia to the Hawaiian Islands. Even the list of imperialist powers involved is huge. The British, Dutch, Spaniards, and Portuguese were already well established in Southeast Asia, and Russia, Japan, the United States, and even Australia joined Great Britain, France, and Germany in the new competition for empire in the Far East and the Pacific. British policy in India will be discussed later; here we shall concentrate on the new imperialism in China and its nominal dependencies, with a brief description of the way in which Japan not only avoided China's fate but ultimately became one of the main aggressors against her.

### The "Opening" of China

At the beginning of the nineteenth century the Manchu dynasty held nominal sway over an immense empire that stretched from Central Asia to the Pacific and from Siberia to India. The Manchus had come down into China from Manchuria in the seventeenth century, overthrown the Ming dynasty, and set up their own dynasty, which the Chinese called Ch'ing. Although thoroughly assimilated culturally by the nineteenth century, the Manchus still excluded native Chinese from the top government posts and were still considered foreigners by their enemies. By then the population of China Proper (excluding Sinkiang, Mongolia, Tibet, Manchuria, and the tributary kingdoms of Korea, Indochina, and Burma) was 300 million, according to conservative estimates.

Like most Chinese dynasties in the past, the Manchus were isolated from the masses. The emperor lived in the Forbidden City of Peking, the prisoner of a majestic ceremonial. Units of the Manchu army protected the imperial palace, while other garrisons held the provinces in line. Like the Ottoman sultan, however, the Chinese emperor was also a religious and moral leader – all-knowing and the dispenser of justice according to the teachings of Confucius. Thus he was linked by an implicit pact of mutual affection with the people. His administrators, the mandarins, were also trapped by the rigid prescriptions of Confucianism, which, like those of Islam, served as an official political and religious cult, and which they had to learn by heart. Because they alone had mastered the difficult Confucian texts in classical Chinese, the mandarins considered themselves an intellectual as well as a social elite. But they were poorly paid, and in

1838 the emperor's government itself fixed the price of their bribes.

Despite the rigidity of its structure, Chinese society was not completely immobile. There was no hereditary nobility, but powerful warlords could sometimes gain control of whole provinces. The merchant class grew richer in the nineteenth century through growing trade with foreigners, through speculation on the fluctuating value of the silver currency, and through the sale of the products of village artisans. The overwhelming mass of Chinese were peasants who tilled the soil for their daily sustenance and who were organized in traditional family and village communities, protected by their ancestors. So slim was the margin of subsistence, however, that floods, drought, and local disorders periodically delivered whole communities into the hands of government administrators who practiced usury. As a result, the number of family holdings diminished. The rise of these wealthy administrators and merchants reinforced the regional particularisms that had always resisted a strong central authority.

Lacking any true national feeling, China's innumerable peasant communities still felt the common bond of a venerable and superior civilization—a civilization that had assimilated all its past conquerors—and they looked down on all foreigners with the same tranquility.

This pride in their civilization and this contempt for foreigners are extremely important in explaining the reactions of all classes of Chinese against foreign penetration in the nineteenth century. The prestige of the Manchus was especially weak in the south, where the British made their first inroads in the late 1830s. There numerous secret societies proclaimed the slogan: *fan Ch'ing, fou Ming* ("Let us overthrow the Ch'ing, let us restore the Ming"). As the British and other Europeans forced the "opening" of the country to traders and missonaries, anti-Manchu feeling became directly associated with antiforeign feeling. Throughout most of the century the foreigners supported the dynasty against its native enemies, thus aggravating both feelings. Indeed, the irony of China's relations with the West is that, in trying to maintain their own superiority, the Chinese at first refused to treat the Europeans as equals but in the end were forced to recognize *their* superiority.

Great Britain made the first breach during what came to be known as the "opium crisis." Since the late eighteenth century the East India Company had been smuggling opium into the port of Canton with the connivance of corrupt Chinese officials and greedy Chinese merchants. The government in Peking made feeble efforts to end this illegal trade, which had allowed opium-smoking to become a national vice. But since opium was the only product the Europeans could exchange for Chinese tea, silks, and porcelains without dipping into their own silver reserves, they refused to stop selling it. The situation became more acute when, in 1834, the British government broke the East India Company's monopoly and opened the China trade to all British merchants. Four years later the Manchu emperor declared: "This people, not having enough to live on at home, seeks to enslave other countries, whose inhabitants it first debilitates." Then the emperor ordered the seizure of all consignments of opium in Canton. The British government was more concerned with receiving equal treatment commercially and diplomatically from the Chinese than it was with the illicit opium trade itself, but British persistence on this point was hard for the Manchu government to understand. From its point of view the hostilities that followed were merely an "Opium War."

### The "Opium War"

This Anglo-Chinese War lasted from 1839 to 1842 and opened China to systematic foreign penetration. British gunboats bombarded several ports and captured Canton itself in 1841. Even the proud Chinese had to admit the superiority of British arms and equipment and the ineffectiveness of their own. They reluctantly accepted British terms in 1842 in the Treaty of Nanking. Specifically, this treaty ceded the island of Hong Kong to Great Britain, opened Canton and several other ports to British trade, and forced the Chinese to pay a war indemnity of £21 million. The treaty also forced the Chinese, for the first time, to conduct diplomatic relations on a basis of equality —first with the British, and, by 1844, with the Americans and the French.

Actually, these foreigners gained more than mere equality. For one thing, they compelled China to accept the humiliating principle of extraterritoriality, whereby she lost her sovereign jurisdiction over the persons and property of foreigners within her own boundaries to the consular officials of these foreigners. In addition, the principle of the "most favored nation" forced the Chinese to extend to the British, the French, and the Americans all trade privileges granted to any other power in the future. Although this principle was frequently to work to the disadvantage of China, it was also to protect her somewhat against the claim of exclusive monopoly by any single power. Yet the immediate effect of the "opening" of China in the early 1840s was the blow it gave to Chinese pride and to the prestige of the Manchu dynasty itself.

The dynasty faced mass discontent on several counts. Some traditionalists denounced the collusion of government officials with the barbarians who defiled their country with their opium and their Bibles and who exported "coolies" as cheap contract labor for the plantations of Latin America, the mines of Australia and South Africa, and the railroad gangs of the United States. The export of silver for European manufactured goods worsened the lot of peasants and taxpayers, who had to meet their obligations with money that became rarer and therefore dearer. In the ports the merchants prospered, but the village and urban artisans were hurt by the importation of machine-made products. The discontent of all these people finally erupted in the greatest and bloodiest civil war of all time.

### *The T'ai P'ing Rebellion*

The T'ai P'ing Rebellion was a full-scale revolution in every respect. It began in 1850 when the leader of one of the southern secret societies began calling himself the "Heavenly Prince," and proclaimed a new "Celestial Kingdom of the Great Peace." (T'ai P'ing means Great Peace.) The "Heavenly Prince" and his followers cut off their pigtails—which the Manchus had forced all Chinese to wear as a sign of submission—and launched military operations throughout the south and the central Yangtze Valley, where they occupied Hankow and made Nanking their capital. Some of them had read the Bible, and though not formally Christians they replaced Confucianism with monotheism and identified their "Celestial Kingdom" with the Kingdom of God. In the areas of China they controlled they raised the status of women, prohibited opium-smoking and gambling, preached a kind of agrarian communism, and even proposed the development of industry and commerce by the state. Much of their program anticipated that of the Chinese Communists a century later, yet it also borrowed elements from pre-Manchu China and from Western Christianity. The T'ai P'ing leaders' immediate goal was to overthrow the Manchus, and in order to do this, they created an army based on universal military service.

Throughout the 1850s and into the early 1860s China was on the verge of chaos. In addition to the T'ai P'ing Rebellion, the Muslim Chinese in the western provinces and in Sinkiang rose up in revolt in 1856. In that same year the British, now joined by the French, again declared war on the beleaguered Manchu government, accusing it of refusing to protect their nationals against attacks from hostile Chinese. Although the T'ai P'ing rebels had no love for the Western barbarians, their own attacks on Manchu authority actually helped the Europeans to gain new concessions.

### *Diplomatic and Territorial Gains*

Between 1858 and 1860 Great Britain, France, and Russia "opened" China to foreign penetration on a major scale. In the Treaties of Tientsin (1858–1859) the British and the French gained the right to have permanent legations at Peking; their traders as well as their missionaries were now to have freedom to travel and work in the interior of China; their merchant ships and gunboats received the right to navigate the Yangtze River; the opium trade was legalized; the terms of extraterritoriality were spelled out in greater detail; five more ports were opened. The most humiliating stipulation forced the Chinese to cease referring to foreigners as barbarians. Meanwhile, Russian emissaries engaging in separate negotiations persuaded the Chinese government to cede the territory north of the Amur River in 1858 and the territory between the Ussuri River and the sea in 1860.* In this way Russia transformed the former Chinese territories north of Manchuria into the Maritime Territory of Eastern Siberia and founded the town of Vladivostok at a great warm-water harbor on the Pacific. Also, Russia gained the right to send goods into Manchuria and the same extraterritorial and commercial privileges as Great Britain and France in China itself. But the Chinese government still hedged on its "treaty obligations" to these two countries, and in 1860 it refused to allow the British diplomatic corps to proceed to Peking. The British and the French decided to take drastic retaliatory action. They sent a military force to Peking and burned the emperor's summer palace. Then they forced the emperor to express his regret and to promise not to interfere further with the setting up of foreign legations in Peking.

Once they had gained all these concessions the Western powers decided to support the Manchu government against the T'ai P'ing rebels. Despite their Christian leanings and their hostility to Peking these rebels were, after all, opposed to Western penetration. In 1861 an American military adventurer, Frederick Townsend Ward, formed a small army of European freebooters to help the imperial government. After he was killed in action a year later the English Major Charles George Gordon took his place and gradually forced the T'ai P'ing rebels to retire southward. The Manchu army had proved its utter worthlessness in the wars of the late 1850s, but a new army, led by native Chinese, showed remarkable efficiency. Together with Gordon's forces, it recaptured the major cities held by the rebels and dispersed their forces by 1864. In the fourteen years it had lasted the T'ai P'ing Rebellion had taken 10 million lives and devastated large sections of the country. Besides, it had been bad for business, and this was the main reason the West had decided to "support" the legal government against it.

The establishment of the foreign legations in Peking and the crushing of the T'ai P'ing Rebellion ended the first phase in the "opening" of China—a phase which, as in the Mahdist uprising against the Egyptians, had involved a religion-inspired revolt against the indigenous, collaborating old regime. Between 1864 and 1894 the Western powers made no major inroads on China Proper, but the Manchu dynasty failed to use this breathing spell to modernize the country and to initiate desperately needed reforms. When foreign agression was resumed in 1894 it came not from Europe but from Japan. We must therefore turn to the situation in that country and see how differently its rulers behaved under the impact of the West.

### The "Opening" of Japan and the Meiji Restoration

Like China, Japan went through a period of internal revolt and foreign penetration in the 1850s and 1860s, but the outcome differed for several reasons. First of all, the Japanese rebels were members of the gentry, not plebeian fanatics. Second, their goal of "restoring" the "divinely descended emperor" (*Mikado*) was made easier by the fact that the real rulers of Japan, the *shōgun*, had preserved the imperial dynasty and had ruled in its name. What the rebels wanted was to eliminate the power of the *shōgun* in favor of the emperor. Third, though basically hostile to the "barbarians," some Japanese leaders were willing to learn Western technology and organizing principles. Fourth, Japan alone understood the quite different conceptions of international relations and obligations that governed East and West. Finally, the Meiji restoration took place before Western penetration had reached the stage of open warfare.

Until the middle of the nineteenth century the island empire of Japan had been almost completely isolated from the rest of the world. The vast majority of its 30 million people were poor peasants who

*See map p. 566.

*Commodore Perry meeting the Japanese Imperial Commissioners in March 1854.*

eked out a precarious living from their rice paddies and from the fruits of the sea. In Kyoto the emperor performed the sacred rituals of his office and remained aloof from practical matters. In Edo (present-day Tokyo) the office of *shōgun*, which the Tokugawa family had held since the early seventeenth century, combined the duties of generalissimo and prime minister. Chinese and Dutch merchants made periodic visits to Nagasaki and brought news as well as wares from the outside world, but the rest of the country was closed to outside influence.

Nevertheless, the Japan of the *shōgun* underwent a series of internal crises in the first half of the nineteenth century. In the west the great feudal lords—*daimyō*—ruled their provinces in virtual independence from Edo. The professional warrior gentry—*samurai*—was becoming impoverished and restive and turning back to the old national religion of Shintōism, which, in contrast to the Buddhist and Confucian rites patronized by the shōgunate, stressed the secular as well as the religious authority of the emperor. The merchant class, centered in Osaka, grew rich from internal commerce and from loans at usurious rates to the *samurai* and the peasants. In the 1830s widespread famine and local uprisings against the rich dramatized the need for reforms, but the *daimyō* of the west and the merchants of Osaka resisted all efforts of the *shōgun* to relieve the grinding poverty of the masses.

This was the situation in Japan when, in 1853, the American Commodore Matthew Calbraith Perry first sailed into Tokyo Bay with four warships. Unlike the British, French, and Russians in China, all that the Americans wanted in Japan (at first) was a coaling station on the long sea route from San Francisco to Shanghai, better treatment for the shipwrecked, and the opening of two ports to limited trade. Commodore Perry delivered these demands to the *shōgun* and warned that, if they were not met when he returned in a year, he "would not be accountable for the consequences." This was gunboat diplomacy of the most classic kind. A strong party favored defying the "barbarians," but the *shōgun* decided that it would be more prudent to sign a treaty with a relatively weak Western power and to play the stronger powers off against it. Thus, in March 1854, he consented to the Treaty of Kanagawa, which met the demands of the United States government.

Once this initial breach in Japan's isolation was made, other openings could not be prevented. Great Britain and Russia quickly forced the *shōgun* to sign "pacts of friendship" with them, and by 1858, the shogunate faced a crucial dilemma. If it did not grant further concessions, it risked the kind of military aggression that China was already undergoing. If it granted further concessions, it risked open opposition from all its enemies at home. In an effort to cover itself, the government at Edo sought the emperor's sanction for a new treaty negotiated in 1858 with the American envoy Townsend Harris. This treaty went far beyond the previous agreements with foreign powers: it provided for diplomatic representation at Edo, the opening of additional ports, rights of permanent residence and freedom of travel, and the now familiar system of extraterritoriality. At first the emperor in Kyoto refused to sanction the treaty, and the *daimyō* of Chōshū and Satsuma tried to stop the entry of foreign ships into Japan's western waters. In the end the barbarian gunboats prevailed, and the emperor had to ratify the Harris Treaty.

In the next decade Japan's internal political crisis merged with an unsuccessful effort to "drive out the barbarians." The enemies of the *shōgun* used his inability to accomplish this task as an excuse to end his power. In 1867, after surprisingly few military engagements, they finally succeeded in deposing him, restoring the secular authority of the emperor, and transferring the imperial court to Edo (renaming it Tokyo). But the leaders of the revolt, for the most part disgruntled retainers of Satsuma and Chōshū, had also come to realize that Japan could not oppose Western power without learning the secrets of its success. Thus, in 1868, they persuaded the new emperor to take the "charter oath," in which was inserted the clause that "knowledge shall be sought all over the world."

The new imperial reign was given the name Meiji—enlightenment—and the Meiji reformers launched Japan on the road to modernization and a carefully controlled program of political and social change. Between 1868 and 1894 Japan became superficially Europeanized. From Prussia she borrowed a constitution that gave a nominal voice to the legislature (diet) but that restricted effective authority to the emperor and his ministers. The feudal power of the *daimyō* was ended, and they were appointed governors of their provinces, directly responsible to the central administration in Tokyo. Japan's new civil code also showed the influence of Western, especially French, models. The nation instituted compulsory education and universal military training. Although its economy remained predominantly rural before 1894, Japan acquired the structural framework of an industrial society: railroads, a telegraph network, a modern banking and fiscal system, and —most important—a modern armaments industry.

Japan's government directly aided all these developments by bringing in foreign technicians, sending Japanese students abroad for training, and providing part of the capital. In 1884 it recouped part of its investment in the industries it had launched by selling them to rich men with government connections, including former *daimyō*, thus crating the close relationship between government and the great financial-industrial combines (*zaibatsu*) which characterized later economic development. It should be noted, however, that the modernization of Japan was superimposed on the nation's traditional way of life. Only in the twentieth century were the Japanese gradually to take on the culture as well as the civilization of the West.

The Japanese succeeded where the Chinese failed for a number of reasons. Unlike T'ai P'ing Christianity, which attacked and antagonized the main traditional forces of society, the Meiji reforms were carried out in the name of the nation's oldest institutions and gods. Also, Japan's new leaders, drawn from the military class, were fully persuaded of the need for change by the argument of military defeat, whereas the scholar-officials of China—the mandarins—refused to see the potency of barbarian gunfire as proof of the inadequacy of Confucian culture. The rulers of China did not use the period of relative peace between the late 1860s and the mid-1890s to put their own house in order. Instead, the Empress Dowager Tzu Hsi forced a completely reactionary policy on her hand-picked officials and puppet emperors. Distrusting all foreign innovations, they were unable to strengthen China militarily or to improve communications and develop industry, which might have prevented further rebellions by alleviating the misery of the peasant masses.

### Imperialism in China's Borderlands

China herself had a partial reprieve from aggression until 1894, but her weakness encouraged foreign penetration in the tributary states along her borders. The French annexed the bulk of Indochina (all of Vietnam plus Cambodia) in 1884; the British annexed Upper Burma a year later; and the long-term Japanese campaign to detach Korea from Chinese suzerainty culminated in a full-scale ware against China in 1894–1895. This Sino-Japanese War was to end China's reprieve from foreign aggression and to initiate the most active phase of the new imperialism against her own territory.

France's conquest of Indochina was precipitated as much by Frenchmen on the spot as by the government in Paris. French forces had conquered the southern portion, known as Cochin-China, in the 1860s, but the central part, Annam, and the northern part, Tonkin, had remained independent and tributary to China. In 1873 French merchants tried to force the Vietnamese officials in Tonkin to allow them to export salt from that area to the southern provinces of China. The government in Paris warned Admiral Dupré, the governor-general of Cochin-China, not to become involved, but Dupré said, "To establish ourselves in the rich country bordering on China is a question of life and death for the future of our rule in the Far East," and he himself was killed in the attempt to seize Tonkin. The Chinese government signed a treaty, in March 1874, which permitted the French to trade and maintain small garrisons in Hanoi and other Tonkinese ports. In 1882 another admiral, formerly stationed in Indochina and now minister of the navy and colonies, prodded the French government into sending 3,000 men to Tonkin. The Chinese government also sent troops to the border, and in 1883 and 1884 French and Chinese forces engaged in open warfare. Despite the effect of initial setbacks in this war in temporarily discrediting the current French government, by 1885 the Chinese withdrew from Tonkin, recognized the French protectorate over Annam, and gave France preferential trading privileges in Yünnan, China's southernmost province.

True to the pattern of the new imperialism, the British sought a counterweight to French expansion in Southeast Asia. They attacked Upper Burma in 1885 and annexed it to the British Crown a year later. Their excuse for this action was that the king of Upper Burma was trying to restrict British trade, but imperialist rivalry with France was the main cause for putting their colonial troops in Rangoon (capital of Lower Burma) "on the road to Mandalay" (capital of Upper Burma). Unlike the French, they did not have to cope with Chinese military retaliation. For the Chinese government did not advance its tenuous claims to suzerainty in Burma with the same vigor as it had in Indochina, partly because of its defeat by the French there and partly because of its involvement in Korea. But the end result was the same for both Great Britain and France, who were now saddled with the formidable task of pacifying the natives and setting up full-scale colonial administrations in their new Southeast Asian territories.

China's involvement in Korea was more complicated and more crucial than in Indochina and Burma. Her goal was to increase her own influence in Korea and keep that country free from foreign penetration without wars. In order to check Japanese and Russian designs, China urged the king in Seoul to "neutralize one poison with another" by signing treaties with the Western "barbarians"—a practice that had worked badly in her own case and that showed how little she understood the Western conception of international obligations. In 1876 Japan, a country that *did* understand this, had persuaded Korea to sign a treaty providing for trade and diplomatic relations with her, and now she resented the reassertion of Chinese influence, despite Korea's status as a nominal tributary of China. Furthermore, the Korean leaders themselves became divided between a conservative, pro-Chinese faction and a progressive, pro-Japanese faction. In the mid 1880s a clash between these two factions brought both Chinese and Japanese troops into the country, but the dispute was settled peacefully, and the pro-Chinese faction returned to power in Seoul. Ten years later a more serious rebellion broke out in Korea; this time it was both anti-Japanese and anti-Chinese. The Korean nationalist rebels defeated the king's troops and threatened to close their country to all outside influences. Again both China and Japan sent their own troops into Korea to restore order, but this time the Japanese decided not to withdraw and insisted that the two countries should join in carrying out extensive reforms in Korea. When the Chinese refused to share their traditional influence, the Japanese declared war on them in August 1894.

The Sino-Japanese War was the turning point of the new imperialism in the Far East. Japan's position was now quite different from China's as a result of twenty years of internal progress. Not only did the new Japanese army and navy drive the Chinese forces out of Korea, they also conquered southern Manchuria and captured its main harbor at Port Arthur (Lushun). In April 1895, in the Treaty of Shimonoseki, Japan forced China to recognize the complete independence of Korea and to cede Formosa (Taiwan), the Pescadores Islands, and the southern tip of Manchuria containing Port Arthur. The peace terms also included an indemnity, the opening of new Chinese ports, freedom of navigation on the Yangtze, and the right to set up factories in China. Great Britain did not challenge these terms; at least they had the merit of thwarting Russian ambitions in Manchuria and Korea. But Russia persuaded France and Germany to join her in forcing victorious Japan to give up all her conquests on the continent in exchange for a larger indemnity. Japan was to get her revenge for this humiliation by Russia ten years later. Meanwhile, she had made her own debut as an imperialist power and had inadvertently drawn the attention of all the other imperialist powers to the imminent collapse of the "Sick Man of Asia."

### China on the Brink of Partition, 1895–1901

In 1895 the European powers began their scramble for China Proper. They extended loans that enabled China to pay the Japanese indemnity and thus put her deep in their debt. Her weakness, now made clear by her defeat by Japan, "invited" new demands for Chinese wealth and territory, demands that were also stimulated by the effects of the recent Franco-Russian Alliance on international alignments. Like the new imperialism in Africa, the rivalry of Great Britain, Russia, France, and Germany in China was inspired by fears of the advantages that competitors might gain in the exploitation of the country. As in Africa, native nationalist resistance was to force the European powers into military actions that they had not originally intended. Unlike Africa, however, the whole of China had a central, "civilized," government with which all the European rivals had to deal directly. This situation was unique, and its outcome was unique.

The scramble for China took a form known as the "Battle for the Concessions." Between 1895 and 1898 the imperialist powers extracted from the Peking government concessions for the right to build railroads, mines, and telegraph networks, for the securing of favored positions for trade, and for the leasing of coastal and harbor areas for naval bases and commerce. The French demanded and received railroad construction rights in south China and took Kwangchow Bay for 99 years; the Germans obtained a 99-year lease on the port of Kiaochow in the Shantung Peninsula; the Russians secured a 25-year lease on Port Arthur and the

Boxer Rebellion: the fighting at Tientsin

right to build the Chinese Eastern Railroad across Manchuria to Vladivostok (with money borrowed from their new French ally); the British then asked for and got a 99-year lease on Kowloon and a 25-year lease on Weihaiwei, a port in Shantung opposite Port Arthur. There were no Fashodas in China, but each power demanded new concessions whenever another power seemed to be gaining more than its "share." And they all sent soldiers and gunboats as well as missionaries, merchants, and engineers into their newly acquired spheres of influence.

### The Boxer Rebellion

In 1898 the Chinese government and the Chinese people each responded to this new surge of foreign encroachment in its own fashion. At court the Kuang Hsü emperor, Te Tsung, inspired by a group called the Scholars of the New Learning, embarked on a last desperate effort to reform and modernize his country as the Meiji reformers had done in Japan. In his "Hundred Days" of reform (June-September 1898) he issued a number of decrees which, if carried out, would have overturned customs and institutions venerated for centuries. Unfortunately, the emperor's aunt, Tzu Hsi, reasserted her sway, imprisoned the reforming emperor, and rescinded most of his decrees. Meanwhile, the Society of the Harmonious Fist, a militantly antiforeign sect that the Westerners nicknamed "Boxers," spread rapidly among the peasants of Shantung, who were starving as a result of a flood on the Yellow River. Foreign pressure was also especially acute in the province at the time, and the Boxers promised their followers immunity in battle if they rejected every foreign influence, object, and practice.

The attitude of the government toward the Boxers was ambivalent, to say the least. On the one hand, these fanatics recalled the T'ai P'ing rebels—even though they loudly proclaimed their loyalty to the Manchus—and the provincial governors of Shantung and other provinces used their regular armies to repulse the Boxers. On the other hand, the empress dowager and a strong party at court favored support and approval of these antiforeign reactionaries. As a result of this ambivalence, many Chinese military and civil officials received contradictory instructions and took refuge in total inaction. But the pro-Boxer faction at court soon prevailed. The government removed its garrison from Peking and, on June 13, 1900, Boxer bands entered the capital in force and immediately began massacring Chinese Christians and molesting foreign residents.

The Boxer Rebellion quickly led to war between China and the principal imperialist powers. In Shanghai and the south the provincial Chinese officials undertook to protect foreign residents, suppress Boxer infiltration, and maintain normal trade if the powers refrained from landing troops or sending warships up the Yangtze. Northern China, however, suffered the full consequences of the Boxer Rebellion and its repression by the powers. In order to safeguard the lives and property of their nationals, these powers landed troops at Tientsin in mid-June. The empress dowager regarded this as an act of war and ordered the powers to evacuate their legations in Peking under guard of Chinese troops. The foreign diplomats refused, believing with every justification that to leave would be to invite a general massacre. In fact, on the day before China declared war on the Western powers (June 21), the German minister in Peking was murdered by a Manchu soldier acting under the direct orders of a pro-Boxer imperial prince.

Concern for the safety of their legations in Peking momentarily united all the imperialist powers, including Japan. For two months the foreign residents fortified themselves in these legations and waited for relief from Tientsin. During this time the situation in the capital was one of the utmost confusion. The court appeared unable either to control the armed bands that roamed the streets or to comprehend the disaster that was overtaking the dynasty and the nation. Finally, in mid-August, an international force of 20,000 men entered Peking almost without any resistance and relieved the besieged legations.

The failure of the Boxer Rebellion and the implication of the dynasty in its misdeeds brought China to the depths of degradation. In the panic and confusion that accompanied the allied entry into Peking, the empress dowager had been forced to disguise herself as a Chinese peasant woman and to flee the palace and the city with the emperor, the heir apparent, and a handful of attendants. When peace negotiations began in September the court was in a distant provincial capital in the west. The final peace terms, known as the Boxer Protocol (1901), forced the dynasty to make a number of humiliating concessions in order to prevent the partition of the helpless empire. It had to punish its pro-Boxer princes and ministers and liquidate all antiforeign organizations. In addition, it had to promise to enact Western-inspired administrative reforms, to make a formal and general apology, with special regrets to Germany and a special idemnity to Japan (one of whose diplomats had also been killed), and to accept military occupation of strategic points between the capital and the sea.

Half a century was to pass before once-

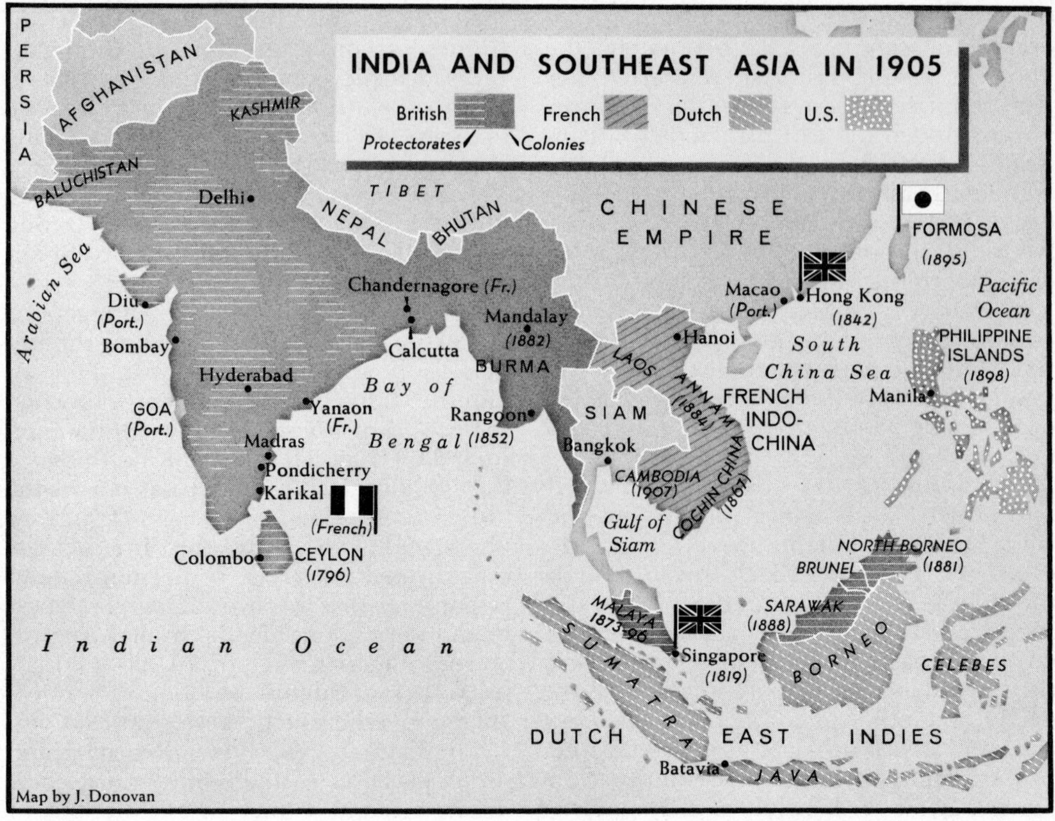


proud China recovered from the degradation to which the suppression of the Boxer Rebellion had brought her. The Manchus were to be overthrown in 1911 and a new nationalist organization, the Kuomintang, was to emerge. In its turn, it was to be ousted by the Communists in 1949. Like the T'ai P'ing rebels, and the Boxers, the Kuomintang leaders in their early years and the Communists after them were the indirect—some observers say the inevitable—consequence of the failure of the Manchus to protect their country from Western penetration. Even today, amidst industrialization and the forced breakup of her traditional civilization and culture, China remains the most anti-Western nation in the world.

Nevertheless, the very existence of the Manchu government saved China from the fate of Africa at the height of the new imperialism. Japan seemed willing to make Korea another Tunisia. Russia's projected Chinese Eastern Railroad across Manchuria was somewhat comparable in economic and strategic importance to the Suez Canal, and it showed signs of a Russian desire to make Manchuria another Egypt. But no power was yet prepared to annex and administer directly territories inhabited by millions of Chinese. Such an undertaking would have been far more troublesome than the partition of Africa, and it might also have brought about a war among the European powers themselves. So the powers decided to crush the nationalist Boxers, to preserve the nominal authority of Peking, and to accept the American-inspired policy of the "open door"—that is, equal commercial opportunities for all. Finally, by the end of 1901, Great Britain began negotiating an alliance with Japan which was to preclude any Japanese-Russian cooperation to partition China between themselves.

Although it left China nominally intact, the new imperialism transformed the map of the Far East and the Pacific almost as much as it had the map of Africa. Indochina was French, Burma became part of the British Empire in India, and, in 1896, the British set up a protectorate over the Federated Malay States. Meanwhile, Great Britain, France, Germany, and the United States annexed most of the islands in the Pacific, and Australia advanced into southern New Guinea. The Dutch retained their empire in the East Indies (Indonesia), but the United States took the Philippines from Spain in 1898.* By the early twentieth century Japan and Siam (Thailand) were the only truly independent countries in the whole of the Far East.

### The Anglo-Japanese Alliance and the Russo-Japanese War

In the ten years between her war with China and her war with Russia, Japan made her bid for recognition as a great power more and more effective. Once her civil code went into effect, the Western powers gave up their rights to extraterritoriality on Japanese soil. Her military victory over China marked her emergence as an active participant in the international affairs of the Far East, but she had had to give up her territorial gains in Manchuria at the "advice" of Russia, France, and Germany. These events prompted the Japanese to make expansion rather than mere equality their new goal. The realization of this goal would inevitably bring rivalry with Russia, perhaps an open clash. Hence, the Japanese government encouraged the acceleration of economic growth and military preparedness. It sponsored the creation of new investment banks, the building of a merchant marine, and the large-scale export of silk and cotton textiles. By 1904 population growth had finally overtaken agricultural production, and Japan had become a net importer of foodstuffs. Coal, steel, and armaments production had increased threefold in the period 1895–1904.

Still, Japan carefully avoided an open breach with Russia until she had secured an alliance with the greatest imperial power in the world. Russia's expansion in Northeast Asia alarmed everybody except the French. Her penetration of Manchuria had begun in 1860 and been accelerated by her acquisition of Port Arthur and her control of the Chinese Eastern Railroad in the late 1890s. During the Boxer Rebellion Russia had occupied all of Manchuria, and she kept her troops there after the other powers had removed theirs from Peking. In fact, she tried to force the Chinese to grant her a permanent protectorate over Manchuria, thus threatening Japan's interests in Korea. This Manchurian crisis was the main stimulus to negotiations for an Anglo-Japanese Alliance.

This alliance, which was signed in January 1902, had important long-range consequences. First of all, it changed the balance of power in Europe, for with Japan now a threat to Russia's "rear," the two continental alliances seemed to cancel each other out. Second, the Anglo-Japanese Alliance finally established Japan's formal status as a great power. Third, contrary to all expectations, the alliance was soon to turn international relations upside down. For it was to encourage Japan to force a showdown with Russia; and Russia's defeat was to upset the new balance of power in Europe and bring Great Britain out of her "splendid isolation" in an effort to redress the balance by coming to an understanding with France in 1904 and with Russia in 1907. The effects of these events on Germany and on the coming of the First World War will be discussed in the next chapter.

The immediate effect of the Anglo-Japanese alliance was to cause Russia to promise to withdraw her troops from Manchuria, but the expansionist faction in St. Petersburg soon decreed otherwise. These Russians wanted not only to exploit Russia's sphere of influence in Manchuria

*Like Japan, the United States became a world power at the end of the nineteenth century by engaging in its own version of the new imperialism. After defeating Spain in 1898, she not only seized the Philippines but also annexed Puerto Rico and established a military protectorate over Cuba. Except in Puerto Rico and the Panama Canal Zone (acquired in 1903), United States imperialism in the Caribbean was of the older type of external sway—promoting capital investments and periodically sending in the marines to "restore order." Nevertheless, *Yanqui* imperialism ultimately was to have as serious consequences in Havana and Santo Domingo as British and French imperialism in Cairo and Algiers.

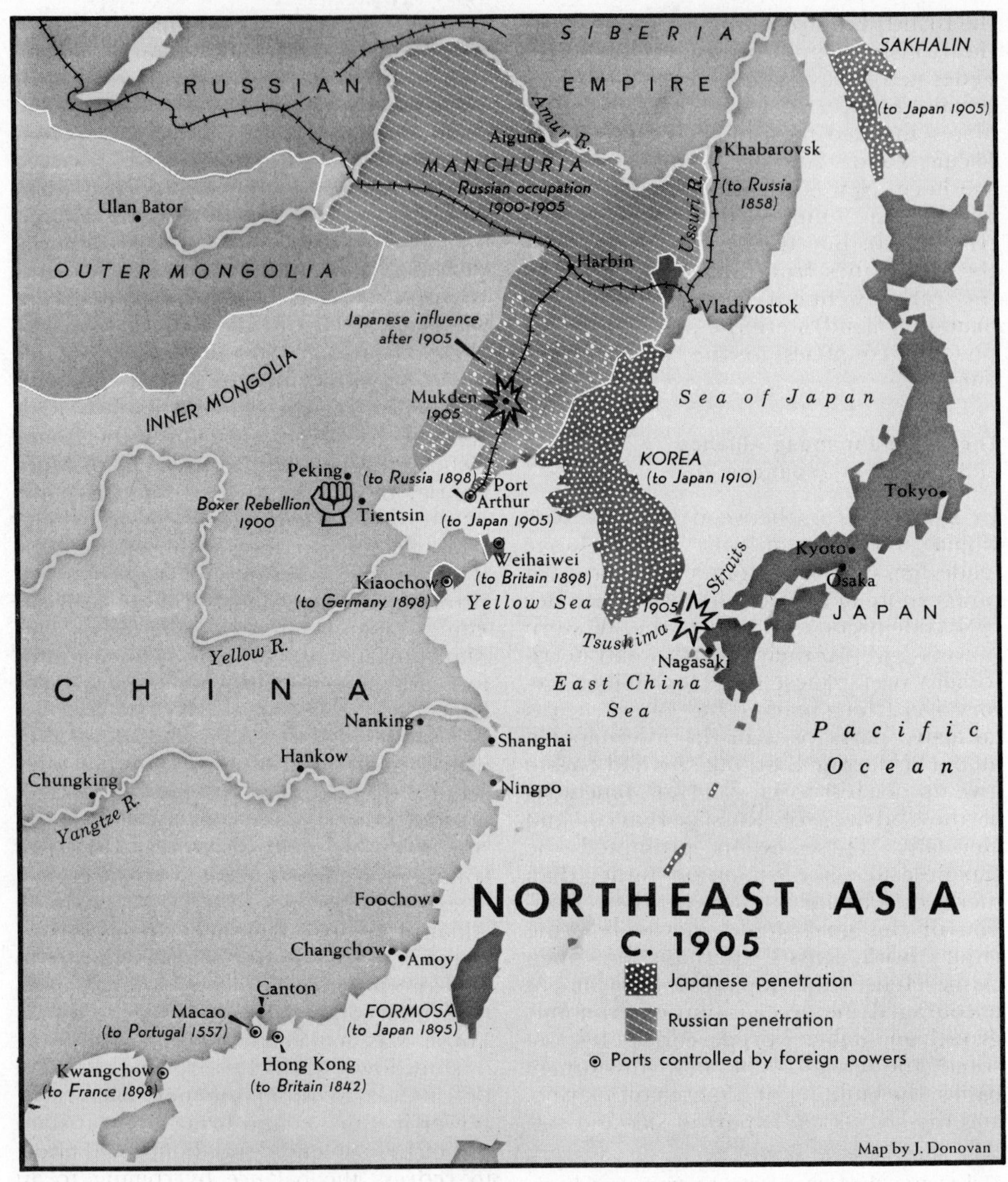


to the full but to move into Korea as well. Japan was willing to concede Manchuria but not Korea. After almost a year of negotiations Japan broke off diplomatic relations with Russia on February 3, 1904, and launched a sudden attack on Russian warships at Port Arthur six days later.

The Russo-Japanese War lasted for sixteen months and cost each side about a quarter of a million casualties. Russia had a larger army and navy than Japan, but Japan had larger forces on the spot and somewhat better equipment and leadership. Most important, Japan had the initiative from beginning to end. Her forces cut off Port Arthur from the main Russian army in Manchuria at Mukden, over 300 miles to the north. The British would not allow the Russian fleet to use the Suez Canal, so it had to take the longer route around the Cape of Africa.* Though be-

*In its passage through the North Sea the Baltic fleet opened fire on the British Dogger Bank fishing fleet (October 21, 1904), which it mistook for Japanese torpedo boats. War with Great Britain was narrowly averted by international arbitration.

sieged Port Arthur held out for almost a year, it finally surrendered on January 1, 1905, before the Russian Baltic fleet arrived. When this fleet finally entered the China Sea in late May, the Japanese navy annihilated it in the Straits of Tsushima. Meanwhile, the main Russian army had been defeated in a fifteen-day battle before Mukden. These Japanese victories were won at the price of financial exhaustion and heavy sacrifice of lives. Russia had more reserves than Japan, but these were still over 5,000 miles away on the single-track Trans-Siberian Railroad, and the unpopularity of the war had already sparked a major revolution in Moscow and St. Petersburg, as we shall see in the next chapter. Thus both sides accepted an American invitation to discuss peace terms at Portsmouth, New Hampshire.

The Treaty of Portsmouth (September 5, 1905) made Japan the most important power in Northeast Asia. Specifically, it gave her Russia's holdings in the Liaotung Peninsula, including Port Arthur, as well as the southern half of Sakhalin Island. It also strengthened her hold on Korea, which she was to annex formally five years later. Finally, it forced Russia to evacuate Manchuria and to pay Japan a substantial indemnity.

The outcome of the Russo-Japanese War was a major turning point in European and world history. It marked the climax of the crescendo of violence that characterized the new imperialism at the turn of the century. Equally important, Russia's defeat temporarily upset the balance between the Triple and Franco-Russian alliances. Japan's victory not only assured her status as a world power, it had great repercussions throughout Asia, for it showed vividly that a nonwhite people could take up arms against a major European power and win.

## THE IMPACT OF COLONIALISM ON NATIVES AND EUROPEANS

The difference between imperialism and colonialism is that the former does not take the natives into account, whereas the latter does. Colonialism consists of the policies and attitudes of a dominant foreign minority toward the subject native majority in whose midst it has chosen to live. It expresses itself in economic exploitation, in double standards of justice, in racial discrimination, in master-servant relationships, and in the suppression of native political aspirations. The colonialist outlook oscillates between a feeling of responsibility for civilizing the natives—by giving them Christianity, minimum health services, and even primary education—and a desire to keep them different. For when a handful of "us" is surrounded by masses of "them," it is difficult to think of letting down the barriers. As long as "they" are docile, "we" can treat them with paternalistic kindness and admire some of their quaint, though "childish," ways. After all, "they" do all the work, even if "they" are incorrigibly "lazy," and their presence, at a proper distance, reassures "us" of our own superiority.

At the turn of the century, Western supremacy in power seemed to leave only two alternatives to non-Europeans who wanted to retain their cultural identity. They could seek out and adopt those techniques and institutions from which the white man derived his power, or they could accept a subordination to which there was no foreseeable end and which might involve cultural disintegration as well. Actually the situation was rarely reduced to this cruel dilemma. The first reaction of most native leaders to the impact of the West was an antiforeign defense of the old order, but later generations of leaders began to accept the notion of the superiority of European civilization, which the white man so confidently used to humiliate them. These new leaders embraced not only the outward forms of the West—its gadgets, its languages, its style of dress—but also its scientific and rational outlook, even though this outlook undercut old ways of life and thought. A third phase of response among the leading and vocal elements of the population combined an assertion or reassertion of pride in the native community and its past with a continuing desire for westernization and modernization. The fourth phase was a drive for political independence.

The timetable of these four phases varied from place to place, depending upon local conditions and the policies of the colonial authorities. India had gone through the first three phases by the beginning of the twentieth century, and it achieved its political independence in 1947. At that time most of Black Africa was still only in the second phase, and, as this book goes to press, the blacks in Angola, Mozambique, and the Union of South Africa are still under the rule of white men who refuse to give up their claim to being a master race. The effects of the decolonization of the past two decades on both natives and Europeans will be described in Chapter XXI; here we are concerned with the impact of colonialism itself.

### Black Africa

European colonialism in Black Africa took the natives into account with a vengeance. Some of the early explorers and missionaries had warned incoming entrepreneurs and administrators against exploiting the natives too rigorously before they were taught what was expected of them. For their traditional village and tribal societies knew nothing of such European concepts as money, wages, property, or taxes. Furthermore, the kinds of dirty work the Europeans wanted the men to do was traditionally performed by women; African men prided themselves on being hunters or fighters. When the Europeans tried to make the Bantus dig for gold, serve as porters, or work on plantations, their first response was either to repeat the words *mbiambi* (I'm worn out) and *kokolo* (mercy) or to run away. The promise of wages meant little to them. What could they buy with money to restore their self-respect? Hence the whip often became the supreme persuader. One early plantation owner justified this instrument of forced labor by saying: "If you are good to the Negro, he will think you are afraid. If you mistreat him, he will believe in your superiority."

King Leopold's private empire in the Congo was especially notorious for its cruel exploitation. With no public authority to check them, European entrepreneurs ravaged the territory's resources and decimated the population. First they denuded the forests of their precious tropical woods and, beginning in 1895, they literally milked the rubber trees dry in ten years. The natives, already afflicted by the disease and enervation of an equatorial climate, died in droves as they were forced to work under conditions of inhuman severity and compulsion. The worst excesses of Leopold's regime were removed after the Congo came under the direct control of the Belgian government in 1908, and the copper mines of Katanga began to yield a more permanent form of wealth during the First World War. But forced labor was widely practiced in the Congo Basin well into the twentieth century. Across the river, in French Equatorial Africa, the noted author André Gide was to be horrified at the examples of it he saw there as late as 1926.

A native of Malawi (Nyasaland) recently said of Livingstone: "How could he have discovered us? We were always here!" This response to the "opening" of Africa by the Europeans is thoroughly understandable in newly independent nations, but it is important to note the conditions under which most Africans lived when the first Europeans arrived. Anthropologists have shown that primitive peoples do not necessarily lead happy, carefree lives—not even in the highly romanticized South Sea islands. In Africa especially they were constrained by taboos, debilitated by disease, and in frequent danger of enslavement and deportation by their own chiefs and by Arab slave traders. A good index of their unfortunate situation is the fact that between 1800 and 1900, while the population of Europe more than doubled, the population of Africa increased by a bare 40 per cent.

Livingstone was not alone in wanting to help the Africans out of the poverty, disease, and brutality that was their lot—or to stop the Arab slavers who were making it worse—by European control. He had no illusions about his missionary efforts as long as African conditions remained barbarous and he recommended the introduction of trade, industry, and better agriculture, as well as Christianity, as the only means of changing these conditions. It is easy to be cynical about traders and entrepreneurs who regarded philanthropy at 10 per cent as a natural, reasonable, and honorable way of bearing the "white man's burden." But except for Leopold's vile regime and a few other pockets of depravity, European colonial administration began to dispel the long night of terror in which most Africans lived.

The tragedy of Africa was not the arrival of the Europeans but the fact that they took so long in helping the Africans replace their traditional ways of life with something better. The uprooting of the African from his old tribal or village society was painful and often brutal. Hundreds of thousands of able-bodied men died in forced labor compounds, and millions more suffered silently the humiliation and submission imposed upon them even by the more enlightened colonial administrators. These administrators ended outright slavery, improved health standards, and supervised the building of roads, schools, and hospitals. By the 1920s the British and the French—though not the Belgians and the Portuguese—began to create a small minority of African priests, clerks, and petty government functionaries and even to send some young Africans to the universities of Oxford and Paris. Still, the European settlers from Dakar to Nairobi continued to view all Africans as children and to refuse to believe that they would ever be able to build bridges, cure the sick, or govern themselves. They laughed at the quaint way in which the partially westernized natives spoke English or French, and they would not think of inviting them to dinner or to their clubs. Not until the 1950s was the educated native minority able to move from the phase of imitating the ways of its white overlords in the hope of becoming more acceptable to them to the phases of national pride and political independence.

### India

British rule in India was also colored by imperial arrogance and assumed racial superiority, but it differed markedly from colonialism in Africa. India too had its taboos and its tradition-bound village societies, but it also had great cities, fabulously wealthy princes, and elaborate Hindu and Muslim cultures. Whatever the British thought of some of their customs, they treated the Indian aristocrats as equals at first. British rule had been established in India long before the age of the new imperialism, and it fostered a far greater degree of economic development and westernization than any colonial administration in Africa. Again, population figures offer a good index of the situation, for the population of India grew from 100 million to 300 million between 1800 and 1900.

In the early nineteenth century the British took three decisions that were to be the basis of their rule in India thereafter: political supremacy, economic colonialism, and westernization.

At the end of the Napleonic Wars the British decided that they had to have political supremacy in India as a necessary condition of continued trade. They achieved this supremacy by 1818 by extending their direct rule over half the area and two-thirds of the population of India and by forcing the remaining native rulers to accept British military and administrative advisers. By the 1850s the government of India, though still ruled by the cumbersome combination of the East India Company and a governor-general, had attained a high degree of centralization, with broad legislative powers and a civil service recruited by open competition. This government had also reduced princely India by a quarter in area and population through further annexations. It also whittled away the imperial status of the phantom Mughol empire in Delhi until in 1856 it induced the heir to vacate the palace and to renounce the imperial title on his father's death.

The second decision involved the economic subordination of India to Great Britain. Already in 1813 the Company's monopoly had been broken by allowing private traders (and missionaries) into the country. By the 1820s British cotton manufacturers began selling the finished article more cheaply in India than the native hand-weavers using their own raw materials. In this way India became a market for British industry in a way it had not been before. Henceforth her exports to the "mother country" were to be mainly raw materials.

In the 1820s the British also decided to introduce Western institutions, ideas, and education into India. They implemented

An Indian view of British justice

this decision by building schools, by introducing English procedure and legal assumptions in the Company's courts, and by launching public works involving western techniques and a western-trained class of natives for their maintenance. The medium of western influence was to be the English language, which Thomas Babington Macaulay, the eminent historian, helped to introduce in the schools in the early 1830s.

By the middle of the century westernization had advanced in both a material and a cultural sense. India acquired a telegraph network, canals, and her first railroad; these public works began to knit the vast subcontinent together in a way unknown before. Irrigation brought new lands under cultivation and made the first serious inroads against the tyranny of periodic famine among the peasant masses. Education in English had advanced far enough by the 1850s to allow its establishment as the language of all official business. Government servants, merchants, lawyers, and other professional men now needed English for their work, and in the process of learning it they tasted, however slightly, the flavor of its culture. This cultural revolution also had the unplanned effect of undermining the old dominant classes, which clung to the old ways of life and thought, and of promoting the rise of a new class whose interests were intertwined with the new regime.

These examples of decorous mid-Victorian improvement inspired confidence in the British, but they caused deep unrest among the Indians. Both the new measures and the new thought challenged traditional customs and their underlying assumptions. The caste taboos of the Hindu majority were threatened in various ways, such as the legal abolition of *suttee* (the burning of an Indian widow on her husband's funeral pyre), the accordance to Christians of the right to inherit family property, and the spread of new ideas of equality and moral obligation through the law as well as the colleges. Deeply disturbed by these and other threats to their religion and custom, Hindu Indians found a convenient scapegoat in the activities of some Christian missionaries, who were allegedly trying to convert the sepoys (native troops led by British commanders) in the army of Bengal. The Muslims too had a horror of innovation and change.

In 1857 all this unrest finally erupted in a major rebellion, called the Great Mutiny, led by the sepoys. The incident that sparked the rebellion was the issue of greased cartridges for new Enfield rifles. Due to administrative bungling and a whispering campaign, the Hindu sepoys believed that these cartridges were greased with beef fat (cows were sacred to all Hindus) and the Muslim sepoys believed that they were greased with pork fat (pork was considered unclean by all Muslims). The sepoys seized Delhi in May, and the British were unable to recapture the city for over a year. Meanwhile the rising spread through northern and central India, accompanied in some places by massacres of British missionaries and women.

Once British troops restored order in the country the first reaction of the authorities was "never again." Their precautions included a reorganization of the army which replaced the fanatical sepoys with more tractable northern tribesmen and increased the proportion of British troops. It was recognized that the aloofness of the officials from the people and of the officers from their men had been a major cause of the rebellion. Thus, the relationship between the British officers and the native enlisted men was also made much closer. In another permanent reaction to the rebellion the native princes —who had opposed the revolt—were treated with more respect and strengthened in their own states. The government kept strictly apart from the activities of the Christian missionaries and avoided interfering in social matters dictated by Hindu and Muslim religion. It also filled the provincial civil services almost entirely with Indians, and by the end of the century one-sixth of the all-India civil service was Indian. This policy, plus the creation of local advisory councils, was aimed at securing closer touch with Indian opinion.

Nevertheless, the general British attitude remained that of trustees of an estate that was likely to remain in their charge indefinitely. The British tended to ignore what they took to be Indian apathy, to avoid open clashes with tradition, and to press on with public works and education. They were wrong, however, in assuming that the Indians would look on apathetically at the modernization of their country so long as they religious feelings were not touched. Some Indians resented the economic exploitation of their country for the benefit of foreigners. Others resented the disruption of traditional ways—especially the breakdown of caste distinctions in the factories—by industrialization.

Even the partially westernized classes felt ill at ease in their ambiguous new status. These classes grew ever more rapidly in the late nineteenth century, for the teaching of English in the schools, the building of bridges, or the operation of coal mines could not be advanced without skilled Indian assistants. These people were torn between the traditional patterns that still prevailed in their private lives and the western notions to which they adhered in their public lives. The British official class amused itself over the awkwardness of these half-westernized Indians, with their sing-song English and their ill-fitting clothes. Although these new classes of Indians were forming themselves into a dynamic minority that was eventually to take over the country, their day was still far off in the last decades of the nineteenth century. In 1904 the current viceroy, Lord Curzon, declared that

> "British rule in India is the greatest achievement of the English people . . . a rule of justice, bringing peace, order, and good government to almost one fifth of the human race and . . . with such gentle fetters that the rulers are only a small handful among the governed, a minute spot of white foam on a dark and tumultuous ocean."

This declaration reveals the zeal and vigor of British officialdom, its latent anxiety with respect to the ruled oriental masses, and its insensitiveness to the aspirations of an Indian nationalism that it was helping to create.

The movement for a self-governing Indian nation began in the 1880s under the stimulus of renewed national pride. The rediscovery of India's glorious past by European scholars made thinking Europeans aware of India as the birthplace of Buddhism, of the fact that its ancient Sanskrit language was related to the languages of Europe, of the subtleties of Hindu philosophy, and of the great Indian empires of the pre-Christian and early Christian eras. The favor that Hindu India found in European learned circles encouraged westernized Indians who were looking for a past to be proud of.

Another stimulus to Indian nationalism was increasing irritation at British racial discrimination. This discrimination was practiced especially by the less-educated commercial classes, whose rudeness was more galling than the aloofness of the higher officials. The latter lived apart from the Indians in fashionable European enclaves. In 1885, when there was an official proposal to make Europeans subject to certain courts presided over by Indian judges, the rank-and-file Europeans protested loudly. They even plotted to kidnap the viceroy, and thus forced a

*The Imperial Assembly of India at Delhi—the Vice-Regal Procession passing the Clock-Tower and Delhi Institute*

compromise that satisfied neither side. The westernized Indians felt themselves especially challenged in the one field of law where they had made a considerable advance. These were the circumstances that, with liberal European support, brought the Indian National Congress into existence.

At first the leaders of the Congress, which met annually, took a moderate stance and supported the reforms of Lord Curzon (viceroy from 1898 to 1905). This greatest of British colonial administrators served India with integrity and unremitting toil, but he could not understand the working of the new Indian mind, appreciate its feelings, or sympathize with its aspirations. Otherwise he would not have decided to partition Bengal in the interest of administrative efficiency in 1905.

This fateful decision caused the Indian National Congress to change from a middle-class movement into a semi-popular party, for it rankled with all Bengalis and brought them into a passionate understanding with the westernized Indians. The nationalist movement therefore became popular in Bengal, through the public meetings and demonstrations, the boycott of foreign cloth, the *swadeshi* movement—which promoted the use of homemade and the exclusion of foreign goods—and the outer fringe of terrorist activity under religious sanction. A pan-Indian Muslim League soon appeared and reinforced Hindu opposition to British rule. Thus, in 1905, India entered an era of unrest. The Indian National Congress remained in the hands of a moderate majority, but extremists began to demand complete independence and to perpetrate acts of terrorism. And during the First World War Mohandas K. Ghandi (1869–1948), the leader of the Indians in South Africa, returned to his homeland and initiated his policy of nonviolent resistance.

The forms of native nationalism varied from place to place, but the effect of European colonialism in disrupting traditional ways of life and in humiliating the natives was its catalyst everywhere. It appeared first in those countries that had experienced the largest measure of westernizing change and where a westernized native minority began to oppose both the Europeans and their puppet native rulers. We saw the first example in the Arabist revolt in Egypt in 1881. By 1905 nationalism was most active in India, but a new nationalist movement had also appeared in China – or rather among Chinese exiles in Japan. There Dr. Sun Yat-sen organized the T'ung Meng Hui, a union of patriotic societies dedicated to overthrowing the Manchus. After it finally succeeded in doing so in 1911, this organization became the Kuo-mintang – the Chinese Nationalist Party.

Among the Europeans both at home and in "the colonies" colonialism inspired unprecedented feelings of superiority well into the twentieth century. Great Britain produced a whole breed of colonial administrators who ruled one-fourth of the people in the world with a true sense of dedication. Yet even they assumed that colonial status was degrading, and less enlightened Englishmen openly discriminated against colonial peoples wherever they came into contact with them. Until they actually lost their colonies, every European colonial power taught its schoolchildren geography with maps showing itself as the center of a great empire that somehow made its citizens superior to other peoples. Even in the 1960s tourists at the border of Portugal could see a map showing Angola and Mozambique as Portuguese "provinces" and a sign saying: "Portugal is not a small country."

But the new imperialism did not involve large-scale and permanent colonization of foreign lands by Europeans. Singapore and Saigon remained oriental cities, despite the banks, casinos, hotels, and beauty salons in their European quarters, and despite the union-jacks or tricolors atop their government buildings. In Europe's new colonies in Africa and Asia, as in older ones like British India and the Dutch East Indies, the European population was a small minority living almost completely apart from the mass of natives. These Europeans always felt a little like foreign campers in tropical and semitropical lands thousands of miles from their real home. They were colonialists, not colonists. Their purpose was to extract as much wealth as they could from this alien soil, use the natives to do all the work, and maintain their own status as a privileged elite. Well-meaning administrators, soldiers, and missionaries tried to make the presence of the Europeans palatable to the natives, but even they never forgot that they were white men whose first "burden" was to protect other white men from people who could never be quite like them.

## THE "CAUSES" OF THE NEW IMPERIALISM

The white men's second "burden" – civilizing the natives – was not a cause of the new imperialism but a rationalization after the fact. The most famous missionary of them all, David Livingstone, declared that the cure for the ills of Africa – especially the slave trade – was "Christianity and commerce." Livingstone was no imperialist; like Albert Schweitzer, he wanted to be a one-man "Peace Corps." The missionaries in China, whose occasional lynchings served as excuses for European armed intervention, were not imperialists either. They wanted to win souls for Christ, not subjects for Queen Victoria, the Kaiser, or President McKinley.

What, then, *were* the causes of the new imperialism?

First of all there was an evident "will to power" among certain influential government leaders, soldiers, and businessmen in the industrialized nations – which included Russia, Italy, the United States, and Japan as well as Great Britain, France, and Germany by the end of the nineteenth century. It has often been said that Great Britain, the first industralized nation and the one with the largest world empire to start with, did not want to undertake a new series of conquests in the late nineteenth century. But it was the British who took Cyprus in 1878, who occupied Egypt in 1882, who annexed Upper Burma in 1886, and who conquered all of South Africa up to Lake Tanganyika, not to mention the Gold

Coast (Ghana), Nigeria, the eastern Sudan, and Kenya, by 1902. Political power over foreign lands—which is what imperialism *means*—was the main goal of men like Joseph Chamberlain, General Kitchener, and Cecil Rhodes. Similar examples could be given for every other nation involved in the new imperialism.

Another cause was a heightened desire for national prestige in a period when nation-states were becoming the only foci of mass loyalty and when the rivalries among them were becoming increasingly acute. National prestige was the only conceivable explanation for Crispi's ill-starred effort to conquer Ethiopia for Italy. The French people may not have wanted Tunisia, Indochina, and West Africa, but their political leaders and soldiers wanted them as compensation for their defeat by Prussia and for the British occupation of Egypt—so much so that when Kitchener forced Marchand to evacuate Fashoda in 1898 the issue of French national prestige brought the two countries to the brink of war. National prestige was also the obvious inspiration of Kaiser William II's demand for "a place in the sun" and for Theodore Roosevelt's forcing the United States to "carry a big stick." In all countries the advocates of imperialism were a small but influential minority. Yet even in Great Britain many workers enjoyed discussing in the local pub the way imperial troops were crushing "our rebellious subjects" during the Boer War.

Imperialist nationalism as a strong alternative to socialism also deserves mention among the causes of the new imperialism. Beginning in the 1880s this ideology seemed especially attractive to the aristocracy and the middle classes as they drew together against the rising socialist threat. Some of the imperialist nationalists integrated it with a commitment to social reform. Those liberals who fought the losing battle against both imperialist expansion and social reform did so in the name of political and economic laissez faire. The socialists themselves faced a similar crisis as a result of the new imperialism. Increasingly those who wished to collaborate with the existing order for social reform gave their assent to overseas expansion, while those who stuck to the revolutionary creed became the staunchest opponents of both imperialism and war.

The desire for economic gain helped to encourage the expansion of some countries in some places, but it cannot be considered the major cause for the new imperialism in general. Great Britain, France, and Germany had surplus capital that they were eager to invest overseas; Russia, Italy, and Japan did not. The Russian capital that financed the building of the Chinese Eastern Railroad was mostly borrowed from the French, who invested very little of their surplus capital in Africa or Asia. South Africa was literally a gold mine for British investors, but such opportunities were exceptional. The Near East and China seemed to offer both investment opportunities and markets for manufactured goods, and the long depression from 1873 to 1895 certainly intensified the search for markets in these areas, especially by the British and the Germans. But the partition of tropical Africa, which was the outstanding example of the new imperialism, can hardly be said to have been caused by the desire for investment opportunities or markets for European manufactured goods.

We must also look to the areas conquered as well as to the conquerors for the causes of the new imperialism—for the "pull" as well as the "push." Loans and gunboats had been the instruments of European external sway from North Africa to the Far East during much of the nineteenth century, but these instruments proved absolutely useless against the Arabists of Egypt, the Mahdists of the Sudan, and the Boxers of China. The mass defiance expressed in these movements made it almost impossible for the Europeans to protect their interests in Africa and Asia through "moral influence" over the local pashas and mandarins. They had to move in themselves.

Finally, the new imperialism was intimately connected with the prevailing international anarchy and the new power alignments in Europe at the turn of the twentieth century. Italy joined the Triple Alliance largely out of hostility toward France for taking Tunisia. The Franco-

Russian Alliance was directed against Germany and Austria-Hungary, but it also allowed France and Russia to pursue their imperialist goals outside of Europe. The Anglo-Japanese Alliance made it possible for Japan to defeat Russia in a major war, thus upsetting the balance of power in Europe and bringing Great Britain directly into the continental alliance system in order to restore the balance.

## SUGGESTED READINGS

Taylor, A. J. P., *The Struggle for Mastery in Europe, 1848–1918.* New York: Oxford Univ. Press, 1954.
Provocative but informed analysis of the formation of rival alliance systems at the turn of the century.

Langer, William L., *European Alliances and Alignments 1871–1890.* New York: Vintage, n.d.*
The standard work, though not easy to read.

———*The Diplomacy of Imperialism, 1890–1902.*
2 vols. New York: Alfred A. Knopf, 1935.
A monumental study. Difficult reading, but useful as a reference for specific events.

Mansergh, Nicholas, *The Coming of the First World War.* London and New York: Longmans, Green and Co., 1949.
Stresses the relationship between imperialism and European power conflicts.

While Langer and Mansergh stress the political and diplomatic "causes" of imperialism, the following works by Hobson and Lenin stress the economic "causes." It should be noted that Lenin wrote his study during the First World War to discredit the major belligerents. Schumpeter, who also wrote his study during that war, stresses the incorrigible militarism of the aristocracy in explaining the imperialism of his native Austria.

Hobson, J. A., *Imperialism: A Study.* Ann Arbor: Univ. of Michigan Press, n.d.*

Lenin, Vladimir I., *Imperialism, the Highest Stage of Capitalism.* New York: International Publishers Co., 1939.*

Schumpeter, Joseph, *Imperialism and Social Classes.* Cleveland: World Publishing Co., 1955. Meridian.*

Robinson, Ronald and John Gallagher, *Africa and the Victorians.* New York: Doubleday-Anchor, 1967.* Stresses British reactions to political developments in Africa itself as the main motive behind British expansion. These two authors were the first to relate imperialism to native reactions against European penetration.

Landes, David S., *Bankers and Pashas.* Cambridge, Mass.: Harvard Univ. Press, 1958.
Excellent description of European economic penetration of Egypt in the 1860s and 1870s.

Holt, Edgar, *The Boer War.* London: Putnam, 1958.
Readable and up-to-date.

Thornton, Archibald Paton, *Doctrines of Imperialism.* New York: Wiley, 1965.*
An excellent survey of a controversial subject.

Kiernan, V. G., *The Lords of Human Kind. Black Man, Yellow Man and White Man in the Age of Empire.* Boston: Little Brown, 1969.
Brings alive the human aspects of the "new imperialism."

Pratt, Sir John Thomas, *The Expansion of Europe into the Far East.* London: Sylvan Press, 1947.
Stresses Britain's role.

Goodrich, Luther Carrington, *A Short History of the Chinese People.* 3rd ed. New York: Harper and Row, n.d.*
The best general introduction.

Clyde, Paul H., *The Far East: A History of the Western Impact on Asia.* 3rd ed. Englewood Cliffs, N.J.: Prentice-Hall, 1958.
An up-to-date general history of the nineteenth and twentieth centuries.

Nelson, M. Frederick, *Korea and the Old Orders in Eastern Asia.* Baton Rouge, La.: Louisiana State Univ. Press, 1945.
This scholarly study shows how Japan alone understood the quite different conceptions of international relations and obligations in the West and the traditional societies of the East.

Fleming, Peter, *The Seige at Peking.* New York: Harper and Row, 1959.
Exciting description of the Boxer Rebellion and foreign intervention in China.

CHAPTER XVI

# THE COLLAPSE OF THE EUROPEAN SYSTEM, 1905–1919

In the early 1900s neither the British nor anyone else could make the traditional European state system work satisfactorily. By then the territorial boundaries of Europe were already an unworkable compromise between the idea of the nation-state and inherited dynastic rights. This fact alone produced the incident—the assassination of the Hapsburg heir-apparent by Serbian nationalists in the summer of 1914—that was the immediate cause of the First World War. The more general causes of the war must be sought in the growing nationalist and imperialist rivalries and mounting domestic tensions, all within the framework of an increasingly uncontrollable international anarchy.

Although the First World War itself brought about a precarious new balance of power and momentarily rallied the citizens of each belligerent nation to "Sacred Unions" in the face of foreign aggression, the political and social tensions that had left their mark on prewar diplomacy remained unresolved. On the contrary, the hyperbolic mobilization of resources, manpower, and mass passions and the unprecedented scale of mass slaughter accentuated divisions at home and led, sooner or later, to revolutions throughout Central and Eastern Europe. By 1919 the Hohenzollerns, the Hapsburgs, and the Romanovs had been defeated in war and overthrown at home, and their former territories were being fought over by Bolsheviks and nationalists; by 1922 victorious Italy was to become the first fascist state in Europe. The hyperbolic character of the war encouraged the play of ideological forces in international relations as well as in domestic politics. Then the crucial role of the United States in the last year of the war and at the peace conference made it clear even to the victorious British and French that the traditional state system of Europe could never be fully restored.

In the postwar years many Europeans were to look back to the pre-1914 era as "the good old days." Except for two small-scale wars in the Balkans in 1912–1913, Europe itself had been at peace for as long as most people could remember. The stability of the pound, the franc, and the mark had seemed to make life itself predictable. The middle and upper classes had still dominated political, social, economic, and cultural life, and the lower classes had apparently known their "place." Perhaps most important of all,

Europe's world supremacy had never been more complete.

Nevertheless, this nostalgic image of the immediate prewar era was false in several respects. The war can certainly be blamed for weakening Europe's economic preponderance in the world and for inflation and unbalanced budgets at home in the 1920s. It also accelerated the demands of the masses for a greater voice in all fields of public life. But the international anarchy and political and social unrest that have plagued the twentieth century originated in the so-called "good old days" before the war.

## STRAINS IN THE POLITICAL AND SOCIAL SYSTEM, 1905–1914

In the early 1900s European society seemed calm and prosperous. Economic progress had raised the standard of living of the middle classes to new heights, and its effects were even filtering down to the urban masses. Europe was the world's workshop and the world's banker. Its science and technology were producing new marvels for all the world to see in the great 1900 Paris Exposition. High-principled statesmen were guiding the nations of Europe along the path of peaceful accommodation to change. Never had so many people had the vote; never had so many people gone to school. Except for a handful of fanatical anarchists, the working classes seemed to have been tamed. Even the discontented subject nationalities were quiet for the moment.

After 1905, however, the political and social consciousness of the underprivileged could no longer be kept in check. Their new social consciousness sprang from the changed material and cultural conditions of industrialization, and it sought to modify these new conditions further. Now that the urban workers were experiencing a slowly rising standard of living, they longed for more social justice and greater equality. Now that more and more people had been taught to read, they developed a heightened awareness of national political issues. This awareness also reflected the increasingly active role the state was playing in industrial society.

The more power the state exercised, the more the struggle for its control mounted. Now that a large proportion of the male adults had the vote, disenfranchised men—and even some women—demanded to have it too. New social groups reached out for political power, challenging the entrenched authorities with new demagogic slogans. Finally, as the great powers became more intensely nationalistic, so did many of their subject peoples.

Thus, democracy, nationalism, and socialism were breaking down the old order in many parts of Europe; the First World War simply accelerated the process. We must not be deceived by the fact that the existing power structure maintained itself almost everywhere until 1914. In some cases it did so by repression, in others by reform. But, as we shall see now, each major country had its internal strains, and, as we shall see later, the existing power structure was to collapse under these strains in Russia, Germany, Austria-Hungary, Italy, and Turkey between 1917 and 1923.

### Liberal Europe

#### *France*

In the early 1900s France seemed to be the most liberal and democratic country in Europe. Where else could individuals express themselves so freely and go about their business with so little interference from the authorities? Where else had anything like the Dreyfus Case aroused so many champions of justice for one individual—and a member of a minority group at that? Where else did a legislature elected by universal male suffrage have such complete control over the government? Between 1900 and 1905 Radical-dominated cabinets brought the army under strict civilian control and ended state support to the Church. By curbing these two remaining forces of reaction the Third Republic had gone about as far as it could in making France safe for democracy.

The fact that, until 1905, the leaders of the Third Republic had to spend so much time and energy defending the regime against its political enemies had tended to divert their attention from economic and social problems. After 1905, when labor unrest forced them to face these problems, they did so with repreesion rather than reform. The urban workers remained a despised, feared, and segregated class. In 1905 the various wings of the Socialist Party had united in the name of "proletarian unity," but the workers did not really accept their leadership. Instead, the more militant ones clung to the revolutionary syndicalist idea of "direct action" as the only means of achieving their goal of social justice. Between 1906 and 1911 they launched a wave of strikes and labor unrest. The former Communard Georges Clemenceau (premier, 1906–1909) and the ex-Socialist Aristide Briand (premier, 1909–1911) put down these strikes with severe measures. Clemenceau proudly labeled himself "France's Number One Cop," and Briand called out the troops. This kind of repression confirmed the belief of many workers that the state, the police, and the army were their enemies. Thus, the Third Republic failed to solve the problem of integrating its "proletariat" into the political and social community.

In addition to class divisions, Frenchmen became divided over the issues of nationalism and militarism in the immediate prewar years. The Socialists, the labor movement, and many middle-class Radicals opposed both on moral grounds, but growing international tension beginning in 1911 stimulated a nationalist and militarist revival. Nationalist and pacifist demonstrators clashed in the streets. The conflict mounted in 1913 over a government proposal to extend the period of compulsory military service from two to three years in order to raise the size of France's standing army to that of more populous Germany's. Jean Jaurès proposed a militia system as being more democratic, but the three-year law passed the Chamber of Deputies. Undaunted, he continued to preach pacifism and to threaten the government with a general strike if it went to war. (He was assassinated by a nationalist fanatic on July 31, 1914.)

### Great Britain

The British political system became more democratic in the pre-1914 decade. As we have seen, Gladstone's attempts to give Ireland Home Rule had shattered the Liberal Party toward the end of the nineteenth century. Between 1895 and 1906 a number of dissident Liberals who wanted to preserve the union of Great Britain and Ireland joined the Conservative cabinets of that period under the label of Unionists.* Meanwhile, the growth of the trade-union movement and the foundation of the Labour Party prompted the remaining Liberals to adopt a more radical program of political and social reform at home. It was this new, radical Liberal Party that regained power in 1906. Although the prime minister until 1915 was Herbert Asquith, a Liberal imperialist, the cabinet put through the reform program of the more radical David Lloyd George (1863–1944), chancellor of the exchequer and the son of a Welsh coal miner.

In 1911 the Liberals, supported by the Labour Party, instituted two major reforms which were Britain's principal advances toward political democracy in the pre-1914 decade. First, they greatly reduced the power of Britain's main stronghold of reaction, the House of Lords, by ending its absolute veto power and reducing the period for which it could delay legislation to only two years. Then the Liberal-Labour majority instituted its second reform, the payment of salaries to members of the House of Commons. This measure allowed men without independent incomes or without trade-union financial support to seek office on the Labour ticket. The Parliament Bill and the salaries bill at last gave Britain a government by the people as well as of and for the people.

Lloyd George also wanted the state to concern itself with the welfare of the working class. This New Liberalism went against the laissez-faire convictions of most traditional liberals, but it seemed necessary as a means of keeping the new Labour Party from getting the bulk of the working-class vote. Besides, Lloyd Geroge had a real sympathy for the plight of the workers—at least before 1914. As in

*The Unionists included imperialists who supported Britain's war against the Boer Republics in South Africa between 1899 and 1902.

An anti-suffragette cartoon (Punch, 1913). Militant Suffragette, after futile efforts to light a fire: "And to think that only Thursday I burnt two pavillions and a church!"

France, they had to fight for the right to strike, and they had practically no protection against the hazards of sickness and unemployment. In 1911 Lloyd George and the then Liberal Winston Churchill pushed the National Insurance Act through the House of Commons. It was primarily a contributory scheme to insure the working population against sickness, with a somewhat less comprehensive scheme for insurance against unemployment. In this way the champions of the New Liberalism hoped to integrate the working class into the national community.

This effort to mollify the working class did not completely succeed. As in France, where no such effort was made, some of the trade-unionists veered toward the syndicalist "direct action" policy of using strikes for political as much as for purely industrial purposes. There was a series of strikes of this kind in 1911, and in 1913 the railway men, transport workers, and miners began talking about a general strike, though they were not to call it until after the war.

Nor were the workers the only "disadvantaged minority" to use violence to gain their ends. The women's suffrage movement waged a sensational campaign to gain the vote in the immediate prewar years. These "Suffragettes" started fires, put bombs in mailboxes, and chained themselves to lampposts while haranguing the crowds; one "Suffragette" even sought martyrdom by throwing herself in front of the horses at the Derby racetrack. If caught and imprisoned, they went on hunger strikes, to which the jailers responded with forced feedings.

Finally, there were the Irish. In 1912 the Liberals introduced a Home Rule Bill that provided for an Irish Parliament in Dublin and a limited Irish representation in London. This bill made no provisions for the Protestant minority in Ulster, and the Ulstermen began organizing a military force of volunteers to resist it. While the Irish (Catholic) Nationalists were on the point of seeing their aims realized by parliamentary means, behind their backs a younger, more extreme Sinn Fein movement was recruiting its own force to counter the Ulstermen. In March 1914 the situation in Ireland threatened to get completely out of hand when 58 British officers stationed in Ulster resigned rather than use force against the Ulstermen.

The outbreak of the European war ended the violence of Great Britain's "disadvantaged minorities," but her internal strains showed how far she still had to go to achieve a political and social system adequate to the needs of the twentieth century.

### *Italy*

Like Great Britain, Italy seemed to be moving toward real democracy in the early 1900s. The man who dominated the government until 1914, Giovanni Giolitti (1842–1928), was a liberal. He tried to make reforms in tune with the times without changing the country's economic or social structure. He sponsored legislation to improve wages and working conditions in industry, partly out of humane conviction and partly to weaken the Socialist and Syndicalist movements. At the same time, he refused to suppress the general strike of 1904 by force. He feared that such a policy would drive the Socialists and the Syndicalists to greater extremes. As a true liberal Giolitti also tried to foster public education. Despite earlier compulsory education acts, millions of children did not attend school, and almost half of the population was still illiterate according to the 1911 census. But the new regulations of that year hardly went into effect before the First World War upset everything. In 1912 Giolitti made his most notable political reforms: the extension of suffrage to all male adults and the payment of salaries to parliamentary deputies.

After the extension of the franchise in 1912 the Italian masses gradually defected to the more extremist factions. The liberal ruling class included many men of integrity, but it winked at corruption and it seemed insensitive to the rest of the nation. The Socialists gained more votes, and in the spring of 1914 nationalists and antimilitarist workers clashed in the streets. The government had to use troops against an incipient general strike.

While an unhealthy political system can be partially blamed for the weakness of Italian democracy in the North, other factors were at fault in the South. There were really two Italies, with the dividing line just below Rome. South of this line most people lived in poverty. As in many other underdeveloped areas, the introduction of modern hygiene from the outside (in this case from the more advanced North) allowed more people to live longer and to become a glut on the limited labor market. Several million southern Italians emigrated in the period 1900–1914; the rest remained at home and lived on the sufferance of those who could give them a little land or part-time work. In some places the big landlords continued to behave like feudal seignors. Local gangs in Sicily (the *Mafia*) and Naples (the *Camorra*) protected pockets of graft from the law, organized smuggling and kidnapping, and administered their own brand of justice.

Centuries of exploitation by foreigners and by native landlords and bosses had given the Italian masses an ineradicable streak of anarchism which made them resent all legally constituted authority. The Sicilian *Mafia* was a perfect expression of this outlook, and southern Italy in general remained unassimilable into a liberal democratic society. But lawlessness and exaggerated individualism manifested themselves in other parts of the country. (When the government passed a law restricting the length of knives, manufacturers simply made hilts that would enter the wound along with the blade; for millions of honest Italians wanted to be able to protect themselves.) Anarchism also had a strong influence in the labor movement and inspired many purely political strikes. Italy needed more time than the impending world war allowed to eradicate the anarchic individualism of millions of her people and make them accept a liberal regime of law and order.

Thus, on the eve of the First World War Italy was an even more deeply divided nation than Great Britain or France. Great economic strides had been made in the North, but the urban workers still nursed deep grievances. In the South, neither the government nor private capitalists did anything to alleviate poverty and underemployment—and the *Mafia* and the landlords reigned supreme in Sicily. Noble-minded liberals like the philosopher Benedetto Croce denounced the nationalist rantings of the rabble-rousing poet Gabriele d'Annunzio, but the more down-to-earth liberalism of Giovanni Giolitti had been unable to provide a meaningful set of ideals for the Italian masses.

With the exception of Germany the more advanced countries of Europe had crossed the democratic watershed by

1914. Let it be repeated here that "advanced" had nothing to do with "racial" or national superiority. It simply meant such things as a high per capita income, a high literacy rate, a low mortality rate. By these standards all the smaller countries of Northwestern Europe – Switzerland, Belgium, the Netherlands, Norway, Sweden, and Denmark – were "advanced." They were also becoming more democratic. On the other hand, the countries of Southwestern and Southeastern Europe – Spain, Portugal, Serbia, Montenegro, Bulgaria, Rumania, Albania, Greece – were backward and had authoritarian governments. We shall now examine the internal strains in the major authoritarian states.

## Authoritarian Europe

### *Germany*

Compared to most European countries, pre-1914 Germany was a model of progress and stability. The overwhelming majority of the German people was proud of the tangible successes of the imperial system. The Empire had achieved national unity and, after centuries of weakness, made Germany the strongest power in Europe. It maintained law and order with the most efficient and least corrupt administration on the continent. Economic gains occurred at a dazzling pace; German scholarship was the envy of the world. The German people as a whole seemed as little inclined to revolution as any people could be. The country's rulers had little idea that their splendid Empire was about to face an international catastrophe that would find it handicapped by deep, unresolved domestic problems.

The major problem was the gulf between the government and the people. Despite Germany's immense prosperity and power, it became increasingly clear that the majority of the people could not be reconciled to the autocratic regime of Emperor (Kaiser) William II (1888 – 1918) and that he would never consent to a diminution of his power. By 1912 the imperial Reichstag included a liberal-democratic-socialist majority, elected on the basis of universal male suffrage; the Social Democrats alone held one-fourth of the seats. Nevertheless, the chancellor of the Kaiser's government was not responsible to it on many matters, and the Kaiser's known contempt for it gave its actions a note of impotent futility.

Furthermore, the Reichstag faced the overwhelming power of reactionary Prussia, with its three-class system of voting and its unreformed power structure. We have seen how the constitution of the German Empire clumsily intertwined Prussian and imperial affairs. This state aroused the resentment of millions of Germans, based as it was upon a divine-right monarch whose position as King of Prussia required close cooperation with the outmoded Junker class, the army, the bureaucracy, and an authoritarian, anti-Catholic Lutheran Church. Bismarck had made it work by adapting it to new needs as they arose, masterfully playing off one group against another, and always retaining the upper hand himself. But the system produced no other statesman of Bismarck's stature. Kaiser William II never understood the inadequacies of his regime; he mistook bravado for policy and had little understanding of modern society.

Because of its remoteness from the people the Kaiser's government could not mold them into a modern political community. They had not fought for their national unity and for what liberties they had – as the British and French had done. The nation had been imposed on them from above too recently to have given them a common set of values around which they could rally. Despite the unifying influence of compulsory education and universal military training the German people remained divided from each other by conflicting regional, social, economic, and religious interests. Since the government handled national problems without paying much attention to party leaders in the Reichstag, they did not have to find a common line through compromise – as in the parliamentary democracies of the West. Instead, they acted as spokesmen for narrower interests.

Lack of agreement on fundamental values did not prevent the conflicting groups in German society from working fairly well together before the First World

War. Only a handful of Left-wing liberals sought constitutional reform. The main opposition to the imperial system came from the Social Democrats, and even the majority of them hoped to change it by peaceful means, in spite of their talk about revolution. National pride and deeply ingrained habits of discipline and obedience to authority made even the underprivileged workers accept their lot with a minimum of protest. Yet the ordeal of the First World War was to show the shaky foundations on which Germany's apparent stability rested and to turn Germany into the most unstable country in Europe.

### Austria-Hungary

The internal strains in Austria-Hungary make one wonder how it managed to survive even until 1914. Magyars and Austrian Germans remained at odds with each other and with their own subject nationalities. In each half of the Dual Monarchy the government was legally responsible to its own legislature, yet in Austria after 1907 and in Hungary after 1912 these governments ruled without parliamentary majorities. In addition, Emperor Francis Joseph still fancied himself a divine-right monarch and tried to impose his will in both halves of his realm. Finally, new mass movements raised claims to political participation, especially in Austria.

Hungary resisted all these disruptive forces more successfully than Austria. The Magyar government used stronger measures to keep its subject nationalities in line and faced less opposition from its own peasants and urban artisans and workers. A strong party of Magyar nationalists demanded fuller independence from the Vienna government, but the Magyar liberals successfully insisted on strengthening the common Hapsburg army in the face of the mounting international tensions.

It was in Austria that the strains in the established order were most apparent. The Austrian upper middle class had given a liberal stamp to the country's legal, educational, and economic life beginning in the late 1860s. But it had had to share power with the aristocracy, which was staunchly reactionary, and the imperial bureaucracy, which was still committed to enlightened despotism in the style of Joseph II. Then, toward the end of the nineteenth century, the disenfranchised masses began supporting mass movements that attacked both the ruling classes and each other. The antisemitic Christian Socialists, who drew most of their early support from the German-speaking peasants, ruled the municipal government of Vienna. The Marxist Socialists gained many followers among the urban workers and craftsmen and clashed in the streets with the Christian Socialists and the police. These collectivist movements, along with the Czech nationalists, had destroyed the political influence of the German-speaking liberals and were threatening to paralyze the business of government altogether.

Austria's ruling classes found no effective way of coping with the unpleasant world of increasingly threatening political reality. The bourgeois liberals sought escape in the arts and in the life of the senses; the aristocrats at the Hapsburg court clung to their collective sense of caste and function. Neither they, nor the generals, nor the bureaucrats could infuse new life into the moribund political system. When universal suffrage was introduced in 1907, the Socialists and Christian Socialists gained so many seats in the legislature that the government took to ruling by decree. Some of the emperor's closest advisers were to welcome war as a possible means of staving off a revolution.

### Russia

The experience of Russia in 1905 should have warned the Hapsburgs that going to war was not the way to prevent a revolution. In 1904 Tsar Nicholas II had been told that "a little victorious war" against Japan would rally dissatisfied Russians to the regime. It might have if it had been both "little" and "victorious," but it was neither, and it led directly to the Revolution of 1905.

On the eve of this revolution the power of the reactionary tsarist regime rested mainly on the bureaucracy, the army, the police, Siberia, and centuries of tradition—and not on the confidence of its subjects. Almost every social group in the

*"Bloody Sunday," St. Petersburg, January 22, 1905*

Russian Empire had grievances that could be focused against the regime. The peasants wanted more land and the abolition of the redemption payments, which, according to the terms of their emancipation, they had to pay on the land they farmed. The subject nationalities violently resented some of the stupidities of the official policy of Russification. Even the nobles tended to sulk at home and leave the government to its own devices, for they had lost their former place in the economic life of the country, first with the abolition of serfdom and then with the rapid rise of large-scale industry which favored the capitalist entrepreneurs. This group in turn resented its total exclusion from the formation of government policy. Finally, the new urban proletariat was fighting against the extremes of exploitation that had accompanied the early stages of industrialization in Western Europe.

Until 1904 the government had managed to keep these discontented groups under control in one way or another. It suppressed strikes by force and even tried to organize pseudo-trade unions under police supervision; it also played off one national minority against another. For example, when the Ukrainians terrorized the Jews, the tsar's government not only failed to stop the pogroms but considered them a good way of side-tracking Ukrainian nationalism and of intimidating the Jews. Meanwhile, it continued to repress the organized opposition movements – Social Revolutionaries (Populists), Social Democrats, and Liberals – driving their leaders underground or into exile.

The Japanese war increased political discontent in Russia and weakened the government's ability to repress it. As in 1848 in Western and Central Europe, the Revolution of 1905 began with the massacre of working-class demonstrators by government troops in front of the sovereign's palace. This "Bloody Sunday" (Jan. 22, 1905) provoked a wave of strikes and demands by the Liberals for a constitutent assembly. In the spring disastrous military defeats in the Far East further weakened the government's prestige. All the underground protest movements emerged and began organizing political parties.

The climax of the revolution came in October. During that month the whole country went on a general strike—the only *successful* example of this technique in pre-1914 Europe. Initiated by factory and railroad workers, this strike became a kind of national passive resistance among all occupational groups. Teachers refused to teach, doctors refused to operate, businessmen shut down their plants. In desperation the tsar finally issued the Manifesto of October 30, which established civil liberties, a constitution, and a legislative assembly, called the Duma.

On paper the Revolution was accomplished; actually, the regime had given itself a respite during which to subdue its opponents separately. While the tsar's government kept the representatives of the professional and business classes arguing in the Duma about the form of the constitution, it repressed the national minorities and the working-class movement. Beginning on the very day after the issuance of the October Manifesto a new wave of pogroms was unleashed against the Jews in the Ukraine by a number of organizations popularly known as "Black Hundreds" and evidently supplied with funds by the secret police. The "success" of these pogorms steadied the nerves of the tsar's reactionary ministers and encouraged them to refrain from any hasty implementation of the promised constitution. Then, in December, Bolshevik-led Moscow workers turned from political to economic demands and rioted for an 8-hour day. These riots, which were crushed by government artillery and machine guns, played into the hands of the regime by turning the moderate businessmen away from any form of violent action. In 1906, Prime Minister Peter A. Stolypin finally mollified the peasants by abolishing their redemption dues and offering them the opportunity to become individual proprietors. This Stolypin Reform temporarily ended the peasant uprisings.

Having dealt successfully with the more extreme revolutionary forces, the government dissolved the duly elected Duma in June 1907 and packed the next Duma with its own supporters. From then on the tsarist regime maintained its power without really eliminating the major sources of domestic tension, and the next time it went to war these internal strains were to destroy it altogether.

By 1914 internal strains in each major country had weakened the illusory stability of the prewar era. The Russian Revolution of 1905 had a tremendous effect on Revolutionary Socialists and Syndicalists in Western Europe. For it made revolution still seem possible *if* the working class refused to identify itself with war or imperialism. Almost everywhere the liberals were fighting a losing battle against collectivist movements of the Left and extreme nationalist movements of the Right. In Austria-Hungary and Russia they were reduced to self-pitying impotence; elsewhere they were forced to make concessions to the more moderate nationalists and socialists. The Reformist Socialists avoided an open alliance with the New Liberals in order to preserve party solidarity with their more revolutionary brothers. But they failed to gain social justice by peaceful means, and their alleged betrayal of working-class goals by their decision to support the war effort in 1914 was to open the way for the revival of revolutionary socialism three years later.

## THE ROAD TO WAR

In the pre-1914 decade an explosion of tensions became as much of a threat in international as in domestic affairs. Here too 1905 was the turning point. The revolution of that year transformed Russia from being the Ajax of reaction into its Achilles' heel; the Japanese victory showed the danger of Asian conquest of "superior" Europe and the possible interaction of such a conquest with revolution at home. Meanwhile, Russia's defeat by Japan marked the end of the overseas safety valve to European rivalries and brought international friction closer to home, in Morocco and the Balkans. After 1905 each power took an ever more uncompromising stand. Militarism had spread to the masses, and the General Staffs were stepping up their preparations for war. Nationalism was rampant in the Balkans where, backed by Russia, Serbia could resist the most extreme pressures from Austria-Hungary. The existence of two major alliance systems made it almost inevitable that any conflict between two major powers would bring general war. Even Great Britain had come out of her "splendid isolation" in response to Germany's challenge to her naval supremacy. In July 1914, in the face of all these tensions, the diplomats could no longer save the peace.

### Diplomatic Crises and the Hardening of Alliances

The international tensions of the pre-1914 decade helped solidify the rival alliance systems in Europe. In the only major war of the period, Japan's defeat of Russia had great significance for the balance of power in Asia. Moreover, American mediation of the conflict at Portsmouth pointed toward a system of world politics involving Japan and the United States as well as the European powers. For the moment, however, the Europeans ignored this new situation and concentrated on their own affairs. The three main causes of tension among them were: (1) Austro-Russian rivalries in the Balkans, (2) the Franco-German conflict over Morocco, and (3) the arms race—on the sea between Great Britain and Germany and on land among all the powers.

Of all the tension-producing issues, the Anglo-German naval race was the most senseless. On rational grounds Germany did not need a big navy; she was basically a land power, guarded by the strongest army in the world. Yet in 1898 her government launched a major naval building program under the supervision of Admiral Alfred von Tirpitz with the avowed purpose of annoying the British and deterring them from risking a war. During the next sixteen years both the British and the Germans periodically stepped up their naval expenditures, and this race embittered relations between the two countries, without, ironically, altering the fundamental balance of military power between them. Its main effect was to make Great Britain seek to counteract German aggressiveness by coming to an understanding with France.

The Moroccan crises of the early 1900s helped to bring Britain and France together. They had recently been rivals for control of Egypt and the Sudan, but now that the British had taken over these two African territories, France began extending her influence in the independent but weak Kingdom of Morocco. The British were willing to give diplomatic support to French interests there in return for France's reconciliation to the British occupation of Egypt. An Entente (understanding) to this effect was finally signed in 1904. Then France began making the usual imperialist demands on the Sultan of Morocco, demands which, if met, would have given her a virtual protectorate over that country. At this point (March 1905) the Germans became belligerent when they saw France's major ally, Russia, completely bogged down in the Far East. The Germans too wanted to share in the partition of Morocco; they also wanted to test the strength of the Anglo-French Entente. The Kaiser himself was persuaded to visit the city of Tangiers as a symbolic gesture of Germany's interests in Morocco. His visit precipitated the First Moroccan Crisis, which lasted from March 1905 to April 1906. The British gave the French only partial backing, and the crisis was settled by a Franco-German compromise. Nevertheless, the Entente survived the German test, and Britain established the practice of joint military talks between her General Staff and that of France.

When the Second Moroccan Crisis broke out in 1911, the French had consolidated their hold on Morocco. In July of that year the German gunboat *Panther* arrived at the Moroccan port of Agadir, ostensibly to protect German interests. In reality, the purpose of the Agadir coup was to intimidate the French into ceding their colony in the Congo in return for the abandonment of German claims in Morocco. This time the British gave much stronger support. The British chancellor of the exchequer, Lloyd George, made a

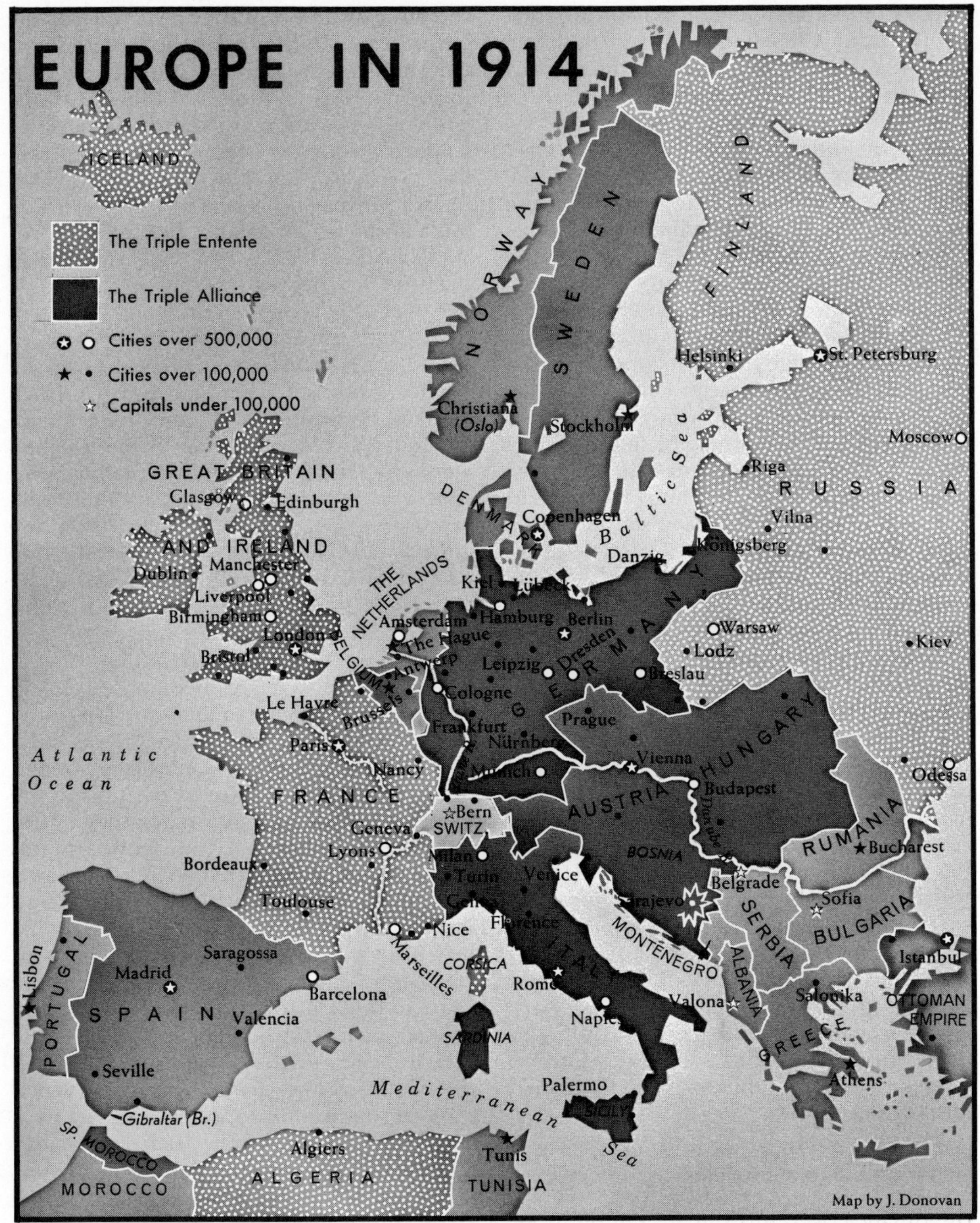


threatening speech against the Germans. As a result, the Germans backed down, accepting a token strip of the Congo and leaving France the right to set up a protectorate in Morocco, which she did in March 1912. In addition, Italy took advantage of the Second Moroccan Crisis to ensconce herself in Libya and the Dodecanese Islands—a feat she was able to accomplish without arousing the other powers.

Great Britain's mounting fear of German aggressiveness made her come to an understanding with Russia as well as with France. Here too, old imperialist rivalries had to be liquidated first. Russia's defeat by Japan in 1905 had removed the Russian threat to British interests in the Far East, and in 1907 the British and the Russians settled their antagonism in Persia by simply dividing that country into spheres of influence. The Entente between the two powers was less extensive than the one between Great Britain and France. Nonetheless, people began talking about a Triple Entente, and Germany began talking about how it was a plot to encircle her. The more she seemed to be losing out diplomatically, the more uncompromising she became, much to the gratification of her weaker partner, Austria-Hungary.

The most serious cause of international tension was the crises in the Balkans, where Austria-Hungary and Russia had old and irreconcilable interests. The first Balkan crisis occurred in October 1908, when Austria annexed the Turkish provinces of Bosnia and Herzegovina, which she had occupied since 1878. Russia protested against this unilateral action, which strengthened her rival's position in the Balkan Peninsula without giving Russia any "compensation."* Only Russia's momentary weakness from her recent defeat by Japan kept her from precipitating a war over the Bosnian Crisis of 1908. Both Austria and Russia kept out of the two Balkan Wars of 1912 and 1913, in which Serbia, Greece, Rumania, and Bulgaria divided what was left of Turkish territory in Europe (except for a small triangle west of Istanbul) and then fought each other over the spoils. But when Austria and Serbia came into direct conflict in the summer of 1914, Russia began to mobilize, and this Balkan crisis exploded into a full-scale war.

### Militarism and Nationalism

Diplomatic crises and the tightening of alliances were only partly responsible for the intensification of the "cold war" of the early 1900s. Within each country generals who had never seen a real war were urging military solutions to international problems. Nationalist and imperialist leagues sprang up everywhere. Industrialists, politicans, and the military establishment itself often backed the sabre-rattling journalists who brought the message of these leagues to the easily aroused urban masses.

Never before had militarism – the attitude that glorifies the military way of life – been so widespread. In Germany, in France, and in Italy a handful of civilian poets were so revolted by the "decadence" of bourgeois society that they glorified war as the noblest form of human expression. As international tensions mounted, armies became more popular with the general public. Even in the militantly pacifist working-class districts of Paris, the citizens began to enjoy watching military parades after the Agadir coup.

The most influential advocates of militarism were the professional soldiers themselves. German militarism was especially dangerous because there was little parliamentary control over the army and the Junkers held a favored position in the officer corps. Still, every major power except Great Britain and the United States had adopted the German system of short-service conscription. Although many conscripts never stopped being civilians at heart, each major power had millions of reservists who had spent two or three years in the army, where they had learned to obey orders without question, to salute their officers, to drill in unison, to polish their buttons and clean their rifles (which they were told were their "best friends"), and to take pride in their particular "outfit." When the mobilization orders were finally announced in the summer of 1914, the reservists responded almost to a man. They shook the moth balls out of their uniforms and rejoined their "outfits" to become soldiers again.

Mass armies had acquired a life of their own. By 1914 Germany and France each had about 800,000 men in uniform and millions of trained reserves. The General Staff of every power had its mobilization plans to regulate the movement of mil-

*A month earlier the Austrian foreign minister had promised the Russian foreign minister that Austria would not oppose Russia's efforts to force the opening of the Straits to Russian warships if Russia would not oppose Austria's annexation of Bosnia and Herzegovina. Since Austria took over these territories without first notifying Russia, she in effect cheated Russia out of her "compensation" in the Straits.

lions of men, hundreds of thousands of horses, and millions of tons of supplies. Even the railroad systems of certain countries, especially Germany, had been organized with "mobilization day" in mind. The influence of the General Staffs on civilian policy in the immediate prewar years is difficult to measure, although it was undoubtedly greatest in Germany and Austria-Hungary. While the diplomats were urging negotiation, the generals were assuring their governments that their strategy and mobilization plans would assure a quick victory. By the summer of 1914 the generals and diplomats were working at cross-purposes. The diplomats wanted partial mobilizations as a means of strengthening their bargaining position. (The Russian foreign minister did not even know that the Russian army had *no* plan for partial mobilization.) For the generals, mobilization was all or nothing. Once set into motion, it could not be stopped.

### Sarajevo

The event that finally set Europe's mass armies into motion was the assassination of the heir to the Hapsburg throne, Archduke Francis Ferdinand, at Sarajevo, the capital of Bosnia, on June 28, 1914. Austria blamed the Serbian government for this atrocity and issued the ultimatum that turned what seemed to be just another Balkan crisis into a world war. We must therefore try to understand the significance of what happened at Sarajevo.

Ever since Austria's annexation of Bosnia in 1908, Serbian nationalists had felt increasingly frustrated in their desire to bring all Serbs into an independent state. They were determined to free the Serbs of Bosnia from Austrian rule in one way or another. This determination became especially acute because of the Archduke Francis Ferdinand's known plan to give local autonomy to all the Slavs of the Hapsburg lands. If such a plan went through, "Greater Serbia" might lose its appeal to the Serbs in Bosnia and to other South Slavs in the neighboring provinces of Austria-Hungary. Emperor Francis Joseph was already in his eighties, and Francis Ferdinand might become emperor any day. His assassination was therefore not a mere act of terrorism; it was a deliberate attempt to eliminate the main exponent of Slav autonomy in Austria.

Although a young Bosnian revolutionary actually fired the shots, he was merely the agent of an ultra-nationalist secret society, the Black Hand, with headquarters in Belgrade. The Black Hand had supporters in the Serbian army, but the Serbian government opposed the assassination. In fact, Premier Pashich tried to warn the Austrian authorities of the danger to the Archduke. The Serbian ambassador in Vienna failed to deliver the message, and the Austrian government immediately blamed the Serbian government for the assassination. Two weeks later it sent an ultimatum to Belgrade, demanding that the Serbian government punish the culprits and that Austrian investigators supervise the proceedings. Since no sovereign state could accept such terms, war became inevitable. Thus, an extremist nationalist organization with support in the Serbian army perpetrated the act that started the First World War.

In July 1914 the holocaust began. Austria—though not Hungary at first—was determined to "teach a lesson" to the Serbs and to all other nationalities that were trying to break up her empire. She asked for German support, and, although not obliged by its alliance to aid Austria as an aggressor, the German government felt that it had to prop up its weaker ally. At the same time, Russia's imperialist aims in the Balkans led her to back Serbia. As diplomatic negotiations failed to ease the tension, Russia and Austria began to mobilize their armies. Germany viewed the Russian mobilization as a threat and ordered her own army to mobilize. France decided to stick by her ally Russia and mobilized too. Between July 28 and August 3, Austria, Serbia, Germany, France, and Russia went to war. Then Great Britain's desire to prevent Germany from dominating the continent made her enter the war on August 4, though her ostensible reason was Germany's violation of Belgian neutrality on that day.

There is no longer any point in trying to blame the First World War on any specific country or policy. Each government had added to the mounting tension by increasing its armed potential and extending its alliances. The crises of 1905–1913 had blown over because, in each case, someone had finally given way. By 1914 no one was willing to lose prestige by giving way again. Austria had to prove to herself and to her German ally that she could take a strong stand against the nationalist elements that threatened to break up her empire. Russia could not afford another diplomatic setback like the one of 1908. Germany could not afford a repetition of 1905 and 1911. France could not ask Russia to back down in the face of German threats, so she too had to be "firm." No one may have wanted war, but most people wanted to feel reassured of their own country's prestige—a feeling that in the end only war could give. The miscalculations of diplomats and generals did the rest.

One more factor in the outbreak of the war must be mentioned, namely national frenzy. To a large extent the mass social frustration of the preceding years found temporary release in war. With few exceptions the Socialists, who had consistently opposed "imperialism," also supported the war aims of their respective governments at the last minute. Even if the diplomats and generals had hesitated, they probably could not have "turned off" the hysteria their actions had generated. Too many Fatherlands had been declared in danger for their citizens to believe that it was all a mistake. The sight of millions of soldiers marching to join their regiments evoked emotions too strong to be quelled by official bulletins urging calmness and forbearance—even if such bulletins had been issued. Everywhere people cried for their departing loved ones, cursed "the enemy," and sang patriotic songs until they were hoarse—in the village taverns, in the railroad stations, in the vaudeville houses, in the cabarets, and in the great public squares of Europe's capitals. The newspapers whipped up this spontaneous hysteria to fever pitch. In the end, the responsible leaders of each power fell victim to it as helplessly as the cheering, singing, marching masses about them.

## THE FIRST WORLD WAR

The First World War was the bloodiest and most revolutionary upheaval that Europe had ever experienced. More people died in 4 years than the combined total of all the other wars in the preceding 400 years. Over 10 million soldiers were killed in battle, and millions of civilians died of hunger and disease, especially in Eastern Europe. The war destroyed three ancient empires—Russia, Austria-Hungary, and Turkey—and warped the German people for two generations. Tens of millions of formerly subject peoples suddenly found themselves living in new states, some with strange names and all with untried political leaders. Even the victor powers were never to be the same again: France suffered an irreparable loss in manpower, Great Britain lost her economic supremacy, Italy was soon to turn Fascist. The war gave birth to a "lost generation" in the West and to a Communist revolution in the East.

### The Failure of Military Strategy, 1914–1916

When the war began everyone expected his side to win before the first snow fell; even the General Staffs had based their strategic plans on this expectation. The French planned a mighty offensive through Alsace. By the time their crack troops had liberated that "lost province" and reached the Rhine, the Russian "steamroller" would begin pushing through East Prussia and approaching the Vistula. The German General Staff anticipated this attack on two fronts. In the early 1900s its chief, Count Alfred von Schlieffen, had devised a plan that would use the main force of the army to knock France out of the war in six weeks while a small defensive force held the Russians at bay in East Prussia. The Schlieffen Plan assumed that the Russian "steamroller" would not be ready to move before France was defeated. In the six weeks allotted for France's defeat 78 German divisions were to move through neutral Belgium, sweep down through northeastern France, and encircle the bulk of the French army.

Two major factors upset all military plans and changed the whole character of the war. First, people did not behave as the General Staffs had expected them to. In the West the German High Command was unable to coordinate—or even keep track of—the movements of all its forces as they advanced into France. Army commanders took the initiative at the wrong time, and their inexperienced peacetime soldiers were weary from forced marches, which had often taken them beyond their main supply lines. On the other hand, the French High Command successfully adjusted itself to the bad situation in which its own prewar plans had placed its armies. Instead of disintegrating, as the Germans thought they would, the French armies kept regrouping themselves for the next attack.

In the East the Russians attacked East Prussia before they were fully mobilized. Consequently, the Germans transferred 4 divisions from the Western Front in order to stop the Russians at the Battle of Tannenberg (August 26–30), around eighty miles south of the old Prussian capital of Königsberg. A week later the French stopped the German advance at the First Battle of the Marne (September 5–12), about fifteen miles east of Paris. In November, a small British expeditionary force stopped a German push toward the Channel ports at the First Battle of Ypres. Each of these battles brought victory to the *defensive* rather than the *offensive* forces. For the next four years neither side succeeded in destroying the enemy's defense in the West—on a virtually static front from the English Channel to Switzerland. In the East the front was to shift back and forth considerably, but it continued to tie down almost half of Germany's army until the end of 1917.

The second major factor that made the war different from what anybody had planned was the approximately equal strength of the opposing sides. The Central Powers—Germany and Austria-Hungary—were outnumbered by the principal Allies—France, Russia, and Great Britain, but the Allies' numerical superiority was more potential than real. The Russian "steamroller" of 16 million men required arms and equipment from more heavily industrialized Great Britain and France. When Turkey joined the Central Powers in October 1914, she closed the Straits to Allied shipping. Thereafter, Russia never had enough matériel to supply all her troops. In total power Russia and Austria-Hungary canceled each other out. Austria-Hungary had fewer troops, but she had the advantage of immediate military support from Germany whenever she needed it. In the West, Germany's forces approximately equaled the combined armies of France and Great Britain in size (Great Britain was unable to put more than six divisions on the Western Front before the end of 1915). The Germans were also technically superior for at least two years. British dominance of the seas was largely balanced by the continental communications system of the Central Powers.

After the collapse of the Schlieffen Plan, the war in the West went into an agonizing deadlock. The Allies had won the First Battle of the Marne by refusing to admit the possibility of defeat and by taking advantage of the momentarily exposed flank of the westernmost German army. But they were too exhausted to pursue the retreating Germans, who reformed their line near Noyon, about 50 miles northeast of Paris. In 1915 the Allied commanders persisted in believing that an offensive victory could be won along this line and pitted more and more men and guns against it. As a result, 1,430,000 French soldiers were killed, wounded, or missing, as opposed to 955,000 for five months in 1914 and 900,000 in 1916. The Germans again took the initiative in February 1916 by trying to break through the fortified area around Verdun. They kept up their attack for ten months, hoping that the loss of this supposedly impregnable position might cause a French collapse. The Allies in turn were trying equally hard to break the deadlock, this time on the Somme River. In the Battle of Verdun the Allies lost 315,000 men (mostly French), the Germans 281,000. In the Battle of the Somme (July-November 1916) the Germans lost 450,000 men, the Allies 614,000

Germans going "over the top"

(mostly British). All this carnage had failed to move the front more than a few miles in either direction.

How could ordinary men endure so much? For weeks, sometimes months, before each major offensive they could not move from their trenches, which were separated from those of the enemy by a desolate space called "No Man's Land." Unable to bathe or even to remove their boots, they were plagued by lice and running sores. They spent most of their time scratching themselves and cursing everyone and everything. Their prolonged idleness made them willing to do anything, even without purpose; sometimes they fired blindly, without knowing their exact target. Finally, when the offensive came, everything changed. For several days and nights their artillery batteries maintained a steady barrage of explosive shells—to "soften up" the enemy's position for an attack. The sound was deafening and nerve-racking and paralyzed many men with "shell shock." Then came the fateful command, "over the top."

What made hundreds of thousands of men go "over the top" in the face of almost certain death? The main answer is social pressure, which willed that men suffer and die in battle. Fear of society—of being exposed as a coward—drove former bank clerks, peasants, and professors forward in the face of enemy shells, mines, machine guns, grenades, and the screams of their fallen comrades. As they advanced, some said to themselves "I won't die today." Others became fatalistic; still others shut all thoughts out of their minds and succumbed to their bloodthirsty destructive drives. Those men who managed to reach the enemy's front-line trenches had to stab the individual soldiers there with their bayonets. Then they had to kill the retreating survivors to prevent them from reaching the next line of trenches and launching a counter-attack.

"We do not fight, we defend ourselves against annihilation." This attitude prevailed everywhere. Most front-line soldiers gave little thought to the abstract ideals and hatreds that propagandists used to organize the flagging enthusiasm of the civilians back home. French, German, and British fighting men were basically more patriotic than those of Austria-Hungary, Russia, and Italy. (Italy joined the Allies in 1915, but the war was never popular in that country.) Still, until late 1916 neither side was in danger of collapse because the men refused to go on fighting.

On the Eastern Front the Germans had achieved great military successes, but not a complete or a decisive victory. As we have seen, they had stopped the Russian advance into East Prussia in the summer of 1914. At that time Austria-Hungary had been unable to prevent the Russians from occupying the province of Galicia, but with German help they drove the Russians out in May 1915. Then the Germans conquered all of Russian Poland by mid-September. Half-armed, underfed Russian soldiers surrendered by the tens of thousands, but the Russian army as a whole continued to retreat into its own country. With winter approaching and their communications line overextended, the Germans had to call a halt to their offensive. By late 1915 the Central Powers had pushed the Eastern Front back two hundred miles. The following spring the Russians launched another major offensive into Galicia. Their initial success led Rumania to join the Allies in August and to be conquered by the Germans in the next four months. The Germans also stopped the Russian offensive and set up a new command structure making Field Marshal Paul von Hindenburg, the hero of Tannenberg, the supreme commander of all the Central Powers' armies.

It was in the Balkans that the Central Powers had the greatest edge over the Allies. Austria-Hungary had failed to conquer Serbia—her prime objective—at the beginning of the war; again it was Germany, now joined by Bulgaria, that took the initiative in the fall of 1915. The armies of these three countries overwhelmed the hard-fighting Serbs by mid-November. A few weeks later the British lost their foothold on the Gallipoli Peninsula on the European side of the Dardanelles, a position they had taken in April 1915 in the hope of attacking Istanbul and forcing Turkey out of the war. By October 1915 they had thrown in almost half a million troops without breaking Turkish resistance. In December the British finally withdrew their exhausted forces from Gallipoli.

### The Home Fronts

The failure of military strategy to end the war quickly placed unforeseen burdens on the civilian population in each belligerent country. For the first time in history there was a "home front" as well as a fighting front. In 1914 no government had considered questions of raw materials, food, and noncombatant manpower beyond the needs of a few months. Hence they had to improvise ways of "regimenting" all sorts of civilian resources and activities as the war dragged on. Little by little all the governments became "totalitarian" in their effort to wage total war. They even discovered that civilian morale had military repercussions and tried to organize it too, for the social frustrations of the prewar years reemerged as national glory turned to dross.

*The "Home Front"*

### *Economic Regimentation*

On the economic "front" almost every major government eventually had to deal with a munitions crisis, a food crisis, and a manpower crisis. In a war fought with unprecedented concentrations of firing power the munitions crisis came first. Within two months each side had almost exhausted its peacetime stockpiles and everyone was crying for "more guns, more shells!"

Germany was the first country to introduce economic regimentation in order to meet the munitions crisis. Under the overall direction of an industrial executive, Walter Rathenau, she quickly formed a War Raw Materials Department and a

Central Purchasing Company for the allocation and procurement needs of a well-organized munitions industry under mixed state and private control. (When nitrates essential for explosives became impossible to get from abroad, the German chemical industry developed a way of manufacturing them from the air.) Germany's economic regimentation was more thorough than that of any other country. The German government began food rationing in 1914, adding more and more items to the list each year, and also introduced synthetic substitutes for some things that were simply unattainable. In 1916 it tried to cope with a growing labor shortage by an Auxiliary Service Law, which required the compulsory employment of every noncombatant male between the ages of seventeen and sixty. But in the last two years of the war neither Rathenau's organizing genius nor the chemists' ability to invent synthetic products could solve the shortages of food and manpower. (Not even the Germans could manufacture full-grown men out of the air.)

In France and Great Britain too, new government agencies deprived "nonessential" enterprises of resources and labor, rationed consumer goods, and decided who would go to the front and who would stay in the factories and mines. The French government supervised the construction of a whole new industrial complex around Paris to replace the industries in the German-occupied provinces of the northeast. These new factories made France the leading producer of aircraft and artillery among the Allies by 1917, but this achievement occurred at the expense of other manufactured goods, especially textiles. The British government introduced compulsory military service in 1916 and tried to alleviate the manpower shortage in the civilian economy by encouraging the employment of women in jobs formerly held by men. By the end of 1916 well over 800,000 British women were working in munitions plants, plowing farm lands, and driving buses and ambulances. British women in military uniforms also provided auxiliary services for all branches of the armed forces.

Everywhere economic regimentation gave priority to military needs and tried to spread the resultant hardships on civilians as equally as possible. As a result, the daily lives of the rich and the poor alike took on a common drabness. French women made their families' old clothes last for the duration by turning them inside out and restitching them each year. In the "Turnip Winter" of 1916–1917 Germans of all classes grew thin on a diet of turnips and synthetics because an early frost had ruined the potato harvest. Germany did the most with the least; Russia did the least with the most. Despite the apparent advantages of a ready-made bureaucratic structure, a vast prairie agriculture, and over twice as many people as Germany, Russia was the least successful of all the belligerents in regimenting her resources and manpower. Although this failure was due in part to bungling at the highest levels of administration, it also involved another crucial factor on the home front—civilian morale.

### Civilian Morale

The situation in Russia was the extreme example of the reemergence of the prewar social cleavage in the form of outright revolution. Imperialism versus socialism before the war became international versus class war as the military conflict lost thrust. By 1917 France, Germany, and even Great Britain were to face serious unrest at home. Almost everywhere civilian morale was highest at the top of the social ladder and lowest at the bottom. But unlike the Western democracies and the Hohenzollern Monarchy, the tsarist regime could not persuade its citizens to make ever-increasing personal sacrifices. Its failure to do so was to lead to its overthrow in March 1917 and to Russia's withdrawal from the war ten months later.

Propaganda and ideology took the place of genuine feeling everywhere as the sterile process of slaughter numbed the initial enthusiasm for the war. Each government had to maintain the nation's unity and its will to go on fighting. Defeat had to be made to appear catastrophic; victory had to promise the realization of vague and sublime principles, such as "the war to end war" and the right of peoples to self-determination. Newspapermen, artists, advertisers, historians, and clergymen pooled their skills in the common propaganda effort. In Germany they made people fear devastation by the "hordes of Asia" (the Russians); in France they played up the atrocities* of the "barbaric Huns" (the Germans). Hatred of the enemy had to be publicized in every conceivable way. England, for example, found it essential for the war effort to delete German music from its concerts and to rename hamburger "Salisbury steak."

In August 1914 all sections of opinion had supported their respective governments nearly unanimously, and all political parties had agreed to bury their differences and join the "Sacred Union." As the war wore on, the desperate need for national unity still precluded dissent of any kind. Thus all governments accompanied their propaganda with censorship to silence criticism and to cover up their mistakes. Dissent was viewed as treason; doubt and lethargy were equated with defeatism.

By the end of 1916, propaganda and censorship for home use had been joined, on both sides, by deliberate attempts to stir up defeatism and revolution in the enemy camp. The Germans spread defeatist propaganda in France and promised to help the Poles, the Finns, and the Irish gain their national independence.† The Allies began making even more effective promises to the subject nationalities of the Hapsburg and Ottoman Empires,* which, along with the Romanov Empire, were close to military collapse and domestic upheaval. Great Britain, France, and Germany resisted both defeatism and revolution, but at the price of increased political regimentation.

*The Germans gave themselves a bad reputation from the start by invading neutral Belgium, by executing innocent civilians in order to terrorize the population into submission, and by destroying the precious library of the University of Louvain. But they did not, as one famous atrocity story said, hang the priests in Brussels by their feet to serve as living clappers for the bells that celebrated the end of Belgian resistance.

†A German attempt to land munitions in Ireland to support the Easter Rebellion against the British in April 1916 was intercepted, and the British suppressed the rebellion. But in doing so they turned Irish sentiment away from the more moderate nationalists and toward the Sinn Fein revolutionaries who were to lead a more successful revolt a few years later.

### *Wartime "Dictatorships"*

Great Britain, France, and Germany all became dictatorships in everything but name. In Great Britain the Liberal David Lloyd George finally replaced Herbert Asquith as prime minister of a coalition government in December 1916. His new war cabinet contained a majority of Conservative nationalists, and he ruled the country with a strong hand for the rest of the war.

In Germany Hindenburg's chief of staff, General Erich von Ludendorff, had set up a virtual dictatorship, civilian as well as military, by the end of 1916. Ludendorff's power became especially clear in July 1917, when the Reichstag broke its "Sacred Union" with the government and demanded democratic reforms and a compromise peace. Behind the scenes Ludendorff prevented the implementation of the Peace Resolution, ended the July Crisis, and continued to run the country and the war effort as he saw fit.

France too faced a serious crisis in 1917 and solved it with its own dictatorial ruler, Georges Clemenceau. In May her army was demoralized, and some of the soldiers pushed their "passive resistance" to their officers to the point of open mutiny. General Henri Philippe Pétain, the "hero of Verdun," managed to restore discipline by satisfying some of the soldiers' grievances and by tempering severity with mercy in dealing with the mutineers. Meanwhile, however, the coalition government had lost the support of the Socialists, and the "Sacred Union" threatened to collapse. By autumn war-weariness had spread dangerously, and some prominent politicians were talking about a negotiated peace. From the time he took

*The British encouraged the Arab revolt against Turkish rule in 1916. By July 1917 the controversial war hero, Colonel T. E. Lawrence, galvanized the movement in the Arabian desert and led open attacks against Turkish garrisons.

office in November Clemenceau changed the whole tone of government. He silenced its critics, jailed the defeatists, and restored the nation's morale sufficiently to prosecute the war to the end.

As the cost of winning mounted, the major governments expanded their original war aims. In 1914 no country had set out to annihilate its enemies, except possibly Austria regarding Serbia. By 1917, however, Germany's rulers were already planning vast acquisitions in Russian Poland and the Ukraine; Great Britain, France, and Russia had agreed to partition Turkey's Asian territories among themselves; all the powers began to contemplate huge indemnities from their defeated enemies. In the face of these expanded war aims Socialist proposals—as in the Reichstag Peace Resolution—for an end to the war "without annexations and indemnities" had little chance of success.

The developments on the home fronts had consequences that were to outlast the war. Clemenceau and Lloyd George were to put their characteristic stamp on the making of the peace as well as on the final year of the war effort. The organization of mass passions in order to sustain wartime sacrifices was to have a revolutionary effect on each country's demands at the peace conference and on the whole character of international diplomacy thereafter. For everything about the First World War had expanded beyond all preconceived limits—military casualties, civilian sufferings, mass passions, national war aims, and the number of belligerent states.

## From Deadlock to Armistice: The Prosecution of the War, 1917–1918

By 1917 the war had expanded to many parts of the world without breaking the deadlock in Europe. The Central Powers constituted an unbroken mass of territory from the North Sea to the Persian Gulf. Great Britain and France had persuaded Japan to join the Allied side in late August of 1914 by promising her Germany's possessions in the Far East. All the British Dominions had also declared war in 1914, and both Great Britain and France used troops from their overseas territories on the European fronts. In May 1915 Italy had come into the war on the side of the British and the French in return for promises of Austrian territories in the southern Alps and along the Adriatic coast and a share in the partition of Turkey. British and French intrigue forced the resignation of the pro-German Greek king and the entry of Greece into the war on the Allied side in June 1917. The most important extension of the war came with the entry of the United States in April 1917. China, Thailand, Liberia, and a number of Latin American republics also declared war against the Central Powers in 1917 and 1918. Before the First World War ended 1,400,000,000 of the then-estimated world population of 1,600,000,000 may be said to have been involved. Yet, despite this hyperbolic expansion of the war, Europe remained the center of conflict, and no break in the deadlock was in sight before the beginning of 1917. In that year, however, several crucial changes in the military situation made it seem possible that each side in turn would break the deadlock and win the war.

### *The War at Sea*

Germany's resumption of unrestricted submarine warfare on February 1, 1917, marked the climax of a long effort by the two most highly industrialized European powers to starve each other out. Since August 1914 Great Britain's control of the seas had allowed her to land troops in France and to import food and raw materials from her empire and the United States. It had also enabled her to blockade the entrance to the Baltic Sea and the German ports on the North Sea. This blockade antagonized the neutral nations, especially the United States, but it effectively strangled Germany's overseas trade. In retaliation, Germany had announced her own submarine blockade of the British Isles in February 1915. Thereafter German U-boats sank armed merchant ships and passenger liners indiscriminately and without warning. This was the only possible procedure for the small and undermanned U-boats, but it scandalized the other nations far more than the

*Submarine warfare, 1917*

British practice of confiscating the cargoes of neutral ships in the North Sea. The sinking of the British liner *Lusitania* in May 1915, which killed 1,000 civilians (including 100 Americans), aroused a wave of indignation in the United States. This reaction, plus lack of sufficient U-boats for an effective blockade, prompted Germany to abandon her first unrestricted submarine campaign in September 1915.

In 1916 the Germans again tried to challenge Great Britain's control of the seas. The German High Seas Fleet had not ventured out of its home ports since the beginning of the war. It finally made its one major effort to defeat the British Grand Fleet at the Battle of Jutland (May 31-June 1, 1916). In this battle, which took place at the entrance to the Baltic Sea, the British were outmaneuvered and lost almost twice as much tonnage as the Germans. Even so, the High Seas Fleet retired behind its minefields, never to emerge again. By the winter of 1916 Germany was suffering serious shortages of food and raw materials. Unable to break the stranglehold of the British blockade, the German High Command decided to resume unrestricted warfare in a new effort to win the war by starving the British out.

Hindenburg and Ludendorff concluded that they had enough submarines to accomplish this task in five months if they were allowed to attack all ships approaching British shores. Such a decision risked bringing the United States into the war, but since Germany's civilian leaders, including the Kaiser, had no alternative proposals for victory, Hindenburg and Ludendorff resumed unrestricted submarine warfare on February 1, 1917. By April they were sinking four times as much shipping as in January, and Great Britain was indeed only a few months from starvation.

Under Lloyd George's strong leadership the British soon alleviated their desperate situation. They set up a convoy system that cut their losses of merchant ships to a tolerable level. Then they instituted a comprehensive system of food rationing. By the spring of 1918 nearly 95 per cent of everything eaten and drunk in Great Britain was subject to government control. In the long run, then, Germany's unrestricted submarine warfare not only failed to drive Great Britain out of the war, it brought the United States in.

### America Declares War

America's entry in the First World War was the climax of a complex and sometimes contradictory situation. From the beginning of the war in Europe American public opinion had been divided. The majority had tended to favor the British and the French—though several million "German-Americans" and "Irish-Americans" felt otherwise—but few Americans wanted to enter the war directly before 1917. In fact, President Woodrow Wilson had been reelected in November 1916 largely on the basis of the slogan: "He kept us out of war." Wilson, who pictured himself as the great mediator, made his famous "peace without victory" speech in January, 1917. Two weeks later (February 3), however, he asked Congress to break off diplomatic relations with Germany after that country announced its intention to resume unrestricted submarine warfare. He then presented a Selective Service Act to Congress for passage. Thus, by early February Wilson was preparing for the worst but still not ready to believe that it was at hand. Hoping that the German announcement might prove to be only a diplomatic threat, he decided to wait for some "actual overt acts" before asking Congress to declare war.

These acts came quickly. German submarines did indeed sink several American ships in February and March, but that was not all. Germany was also intriguing with Mexico behind America's back. On January 19 the German foreign secretary, Arthur Zimmermann, had sent a coded telegram to Mexico City via Washington through the American State Department's cable line from Berlin. In it he said that, if the United States should declare war on Germany, the German government would help Mexico reconquer her "lost provinces" of Texas, New Mexico, and Arizona. British Naval Intelligence picked up the Zimmermann telegram, deciphered it, and handed it over to the American government. When it was finally released to the press on March 1, it aroused the whole nation. Less than two weeks later the first news of the Russian Revolution arrived. With the tsar overthrown and a liberal Provisional Government, Russia had become a democracy, like the other major Allies. The way was clear for Wilson's war message to Congress on April 2. He could now say that the United States was entering the war to make the world "safe for democracy." Four days later Congress declared war on Germany.

### The Russian and Italian Fronts

Whereas American intervention was to tip the military balance a year later, the rest of 1917 brought two major setbacks to the Allies. Russia's Provisional Government could not restore morale at home or on the battle front. By midsummer millions of Russian soldiers were deserting, and the Eastern Front was crumbling when the Bolsheviks overthrew the Provisional Government in November. By December the Bolsheviks asked the Germans for a cease-fire and began discussing peace terms at the town of Brest-Litovsk. When the Treaty of Brest-Litovsk* was finally signed in March 1918, Germany immediately began transferring troops to the Western Front, and the French and the British would now have to face them alone. Meanwhile, German and Austrian forces broke the deadlock on the Italian Front at Caporetto in late October. During the next two months the Italians fell back in disorder to within twenty miles of Venice. There the line held, and the French and the British quickly sent help to their hard-pressed ally. But the year 1917 had brought the Central Powers close to complete victory.

### The Western Front

In March 1918 Hindenburg and Ludendorff decided to launch a decisive offensive on the Western Front. With fresh reinforcements from Russia they were able to achieve the same slight numerical superiority over the French and the British that they had had in August 1914. Furthermore, they had more control over what happened; at the end of 1916 they had made themselves the supreme commanders of all the forces of

*See p. 605.

WORLD WAR I 1914-1918
NORWAY
SWEDEN
North Sea
UNITED KINGDOM
DENMARK
Petrograd
RUSSIA
NETHERLANDS
Berlin
GERMANY
Warsaw
BELGIUM
German U-Boats
1917
Paris
FRANCE
Vienna
AUSTRIA-HUNGARY
SWITZ.
Caporetto 1917
RUMANIA 1916
Black Sea
SERBIA
BULGARIA 1915
ITALY 1915
MONTENEGRO
ALBANIA
Istanbul
TURKEY
GREECE 1917
Gallipoli
PAIN
Allied Nations
Central Powers
Occupied area to the end of 1917
Occupied area after Treaty of Brest-Litovsk
Neutral Nations
Dates indicate entry into war.
THE WESTERN FRONT
London
ENGLAND
NETHERLANDS
Antwerp
Dunkirk
Calais
Ypres
Brussels
BELGIUM
Liège
Cologne
Bonn
Lille
GERMANY
Coblenz
Somme R.
Amiens
Sedan
LUXEMBOURG
Meuse R.
Le Havre
Saarbrücken
Seine R.
Château-Thierry
Reims
Metz
Verdun
Paris
St. Mihiel
Nancy
Strasbourg
Rhine R.
FRANCE
Limit of German advance, Sept. 1914
Trench warfare, 1914-1917
Armistice line, Nov. 11, 1918
0 25 50 mi.
Map by J. Donovan

the Central Powers. Now they managed to achieve strategic surprise and they used the new tactic of having special assault teams infiltrate soft spots in the enemy lines. By July 1918 they had again reached the Marne, only 37 miles from Paris. They had caused a million Allied casualties, although they had lost a million of their own men, including most of the soldiers of their assault teams.

Two factors helped the Allies turn the tide on the Western Front: unity of command and numerical superiority. In the spring of 1918 General Douglas Haig and General Henri Philippe Pétain were still directing the British and French armies with a minimum of cooperation. When the Germans launched their offensive, Haig insisted that the French appoint someone who could force Pétain to coordinate his efforts with those of the British. Haig's choice was Ferdinand Foch, the general who, at the First Battle of the Marne, had supposedly telegraphed: "My center is giving way; my right wing is bending back. Situation excellent. Tomorrow I attack." Since then Foch's military superiors had considered him too reckless, but on April 14, he was finally named Allied Supreme Commander. By the time he launched his counteroffensive in July his forces were being rapidly augmented by American divisions under General John J. Pershing. The American troops had limited training and combat experience, but they were soon attacking some of the strongest parts of the German lines. Arriving in France at the rate of 250,000 a month by August, American soldiers tipped the numerical balance in favor of the Allies and may have speeded up the German collapse by as much as a year.

### *Military Technology*

Since the First Battle of the Marne the Allies and the Germans had faced each other on the Western Front with their infantry and artillery virtually immobilized and with little information about what was going on behind the enemy's lines. Military aircraft and tanks altered this situation somewhat without changing it fundamentally. Primitive planes and dirigibles were used first to reconnoiter and photograph enemy installations and ultimately to attack troops, railroad centers, factories, and cities. But enemy fighter planes thwarted most reconnaissance missions, and the small carrying capacity and short range of planes on bombing missions limited the damage they could do. In the last year of the war the British and the French began using concentrations of slow-moving light tanks to clear a gap for their advancing infantry. With their heavy armored plate and caterpillar tracks these tanks were impervious to machine-gun bullets and could move over trenches. Even so, the artillery still had to knock out the enemy's heavy artillery batteries further back behind the lines, and the infantry had to survive in the gap and exploit it.

The First World War—like the Second—was won mainly by means of the same weapons with which it began. The increasing use of tanks and aircraft after 1917 showed what the Second World War would be like, just as the original atomic bomb that was used in 1945 showed what the next war might be like. In both cases, these new weapons merely hastened the defeat of an enemy that was already running out of men and matériel. By the summer of 1918 both the Germans and the Allies had developed infantry-artillery tactics that could create a gap in the enemy's lines. Germany, however, had no more reserves left for the battle front, and shortages of workers and raw materials prevented her factories from supplying sufficient guns and ammunition for current needs. Thus, after four years, Allied infantry and artillery were finally able to break the deadlock in a war fought primarily by men and guns.

Germany began to collapse at the end of September 1918. In the West the Allies had been rolling back the whole front since early August. Then, in mid-September, the Allied army in Greece broke out of its confines, forced Bulgaria to surrender (September 29), and began to liberate Serbia. This disaster in the Balkans was too much for Ludendorff; on the day of the Bulgarian surrender his officers found him on the floor, foaming at the mouth. That night he urged the Kaiser to request an immediate armistice in the West. Although Ludendorff and his associates soon recovered their nerve and the German army was still on French soil, news of the temporary "crack up" within the High Command had broken German morale, at home and at the front.

The final collapse of the Central Powers came more suddenly than anyone expected. Turkey accepted armistice terms on October 30. The Italian army won its only significant victory at Vittorio Veneto and broke up the last resistance of the disintegrating Austro-Hungarian army. Austria-Hungary signed an armistice on November 3. In Germany the Kaiser tried to create the impression that his country was to receive democratic reforms by appointing a well-known liberal, Prince Max of Baden, as chancellor on October 2, but neither Wilson nor the German people were deceived. Wilson insisted on unconditional surrender, and the German people revolted. A German commission—headed, significantly, by a civilian—accepted armistice terms from Generalissimo Foch on November 11. Ludendorff had resigned on October 26 and the Kaiser had abdicated on November 9, but Hindenburg and the High Command approved the signing.

The First World War may be said to have ended with the German Armistice on November 11, 1918. The people of the great Western democracies cheered and danced in the streets, just as the people of all the belligerent countries had done when they had gone to war four and a quarter years earlier. But no one cheered in the streets of Berlin, Vienna, or Petrograd. Even before the final armistice the great empires of Central and Eastern Europe had succumbed to revolutions at home, revolutions that had been in the making before the war temporarily sidetracked them and then intensified them as defeat seemed imminent. These revolutions transformed the old Europe to a greater extent than Western arms had done by November 11, or than Western statesmanship was to do at the peace table in the following months. We must therefore examine them before turning to the final peace settlement.

## THE REVOLUTIONS IN CENTRAL AND EASTERN EUROPE

At the end of the war Generalissimo Foch said: "Bolshevism is the disease of defeated nations." This disease was indeed ravaging the defeated nations of Central and Eastern Europe between the fall of 1917 and the summer of 1919. First Russia, then Germany, then Hungary experienced Bolshevik attempts to seize power. Only Russia succumbed to a permanent Bolshevik dictatorship, but all three of the great imperial dynasties—Romanovs, Hapsburgs, Hohenzollerns—were overthrown by democratic political forces and deserted by their subject nationalities. By the time the Western statesmen had formulated their peace settlement, the old order in Central and Eastern Europe was already gone. It was "succeeded" by a Bolshevik Russia and a democratic Germany, with ten completely new or radically transformed small states lying between them.

### The Russian Revolutions and the Beginnings of World Communism

Russia underwent a more profound transformation than any other European country. Beginning in March 1917 she went through a democratic political revolution, a Bolshevik revolution, and a devastating civil war. Not since the French Revolution had any nation experienced such a series of upheavals, and the events of 1917 in Russia were eventually to have as far-reaching effects on the rest of the world as the events of 1789 in France. These effects will be described, as they unfold, throughout the rest of this book. In this section we shall examine the story in Russia itself from the fall of the tsarist regime in March 1917 to the permanent triumph of the Bolsheviks by late 1920.

The tsarist regime collapsed in March 1917 mainly because it was unable to pursue the war effectively. As in other countries, the Russian people had united behind their rulers when the war had broken out, but Russia's rulers soon proved themselves incompetent in their conduct of military affairs and in their ability to sustain the patriotism of the ordinary soldiers and civilians. Tsar Nicholas II went to field headquarters near the front in August 1915, naïvely hoping to restore the situation there by his presence. From then on government affairs fell into the hands of his unstable wife, Alexandra, and her confidant, the unscrupulous mystic Gregory Rasputin. These two deranged persons disbanded the Duma and appointed their own inept and even corrupt favorites to the chief government ministries. As a result, supply, communication, and the army medical services were mismanaged, causing growing resentment among the fighting men. Since Russia's small industrial capacity was totally committed to the production of arms, people went hungry in the cities because they could produce practically no consumer goods to exchange with the peasants for food. By the beginning of 1917 even the middle-class members of the reassembled Duma, the generals, and Russia's allies wanted drastic political changes in the tsarist regime.

### The Democratic Political Revolution

On March 9 the Revolution "erupted" spontaneously. In Petrograd (as St. Petersburg had been rechristened in 1914 because it sounded too German) there were strikes by factory workers and bread riots. These had occurred before and had been put down. By March 12, however, the troops in the garrison, who were mostly conscripts, refused to fire on the crowds and joined them instead. There was a feeling of exuberance in the air which caught up both soldiers and civilians. Regular army officers and police officials disappeared from the scene, and the crowds were unopposed. Then soviets (popularly elected councils) of soldiers and factory workers sprang up and took over control of the capital.

Although the Duma was at first unwilling to depose the tsar, who was on his way back from field headquarters, the generals persuaded him to abdicate in favor of his brother, the Grand Duke Michael. Michael saw the hopelessness of the situation and refused to take the throne. Then on March 16, the Duma formed a Provisional Government composed of liberals and Right-wing Socialists. Russia had ceased to be a monarchy and it had two kinds of government: a national one emanating from the Duma and, in each major city, a soviet representing the workers and soldiers. By late spring soviets of peasants appeared in the rural towns as well.

The authority of the Provisional Government was weak because it did not represent the broad masses and because it *was* only provisional until a constituent assembly could be called to determine what kind of regime should replace the fallen monarchy. It tried to satisfy the demand for political democracy and civil liberties and immediately proclaimed an amnesty for all exiled political leaders. But, from the beginning, it was dependent on the Petrograd Soviet; for example, the soldiers would not obey its orders unless these were approved by that body. Since the Provisional Government, aided by immediate recognition and support from Russia's allies, was committed to continuing the war effort, it could not satisfy the demands of the workers for a higher standard of living (Bread), the peasants' demands for Land, and the general longing for Peace. These were the reasons for its ultimate downfall.

The failure of the Provisional Government and its supporters to make Russia a Western-style democracy was to be repeated in many countries that had just gotten rid of an authoritarian monarchy but where the masses of the people lived in poverty. A similar pattern of development from monarchy to a brief period of liberal democracy to a dictatorship had already occurred in many countries in Latin America, and was to occur in Spain and East Central Europe in the 1930s, and, more recently, in parts of Asia and Africa. In each case a small group of liberals wanted to graft the political system of the advanced countries of the West onto states where the cultural traditions of the West were lacking and where the masses of people were more interested in land and bread than in the right to vote and write letters to the editor. The liberals invariably looked to England, France, or the United States as cultural and political models to be copied—even to the point of wearing Western clothes and speaking English or French. They were well-meaning, humanitarian, reasonable men who felt that if only they could set up a constitution, schools, and birth control, they could lift their less fortunate countrymen out of squalor and superstition and drag them up to their own bourgeois standards. Unfortunately they had no real contact with the rural and urban masses and felt a good deal of contempt for them.

In Russia two outstanding examples of this type of liberal were Paul Miliukov and Alexander Kerensky. Miliukov was a university professor and author of many excellent books; he was also the leader of the Liberal Party in the Duma and the foreign minister in the Provisional Government until May 1917. Kerensky became the minister of justice in April and prime minister in July. As a nominal member of the Social Revolutionary Party (the successor of the Populists) he believed in agrarian reform as well as political democracy. He too, however, was oriented toward the West, essentially bourgeois, and out of touch with the ignorant masses. Furthermore, once he became the head of the Provisional Government Kerensky lost what little revolutionary spirit he had and behaved like any ruler trying to maintain order and stay in power. Both Miliukov and Kerensky and most of the other liberals and Right-wing Socialists wanted Russia to stay in the war, not only as a matter of keeping her pledged word to her allies, but also in the hope that by being on the winning side with the Western democracies, they would benefit by the prestige of these countries and thus assure the triumph of democracy in Russia.

By postponing any basic economic and social changes until this political triumph was assured, men like Miliukov and Kerensky damned themselves as selfish "bourgeois" in the eyes of the Russian masses. It should be remembered that the word "bourgeois" had a cultural rather than a purely economic connotation to almost everybody except the Marxists. A bourgeois was someone who valued comfort, respectability, and moderation. He washed regularly, respected the law, and disapproved of extreme behavior of any kind.

Not only was the Provisional Government weakened by the bourgeois "image" the masses had of it, it soon alienated the more conservative forces in the country as well. By the late summer of 1917 the army General Staff concluded that, like the tsar, the new regime could not carry on the war effectively. Discipline had almost completely broken down in the army, and several million soldiers deserted in order to share in the land seizures the peasants were carrying out in the countryside. Hoping to revive the army and strengthen the authority of the state, the Commander-in-Chief of Russia's armed forces, General Kornilov, tried to overthrow the Kerensky government in September. With the help of Bolshevik-inspired railroad workers—who stalled the trains carrying Kornilov's troops—Kerensky thwarted this attempted coup. But the division between the government and the generals further weakened the liberal cause and paved the way for a second revolution, led by the Bolsheviks, in November 1917.

### *The Bolshevik (November) Revolution*

The amnesty law of March 1917 made possible the return of Lenin and the other exiled Bolshevik leaders a month later, but in April 1917 there were only about 25,000 Bolsheviks in all Russia, an empire of over 150 million people. How could they hope to seize power? Since the masses of Russians looked to the soviets as their true representatives, Lenin's answer was "all power to the soviets!" By this he meant that the Bolsheviks would try to gain control of the soviets—which were dominated at first by Mensheviks and Social Revolutionaries—and then use them to overthrow the Provisional Government. This was the tactic that the Bolsheviks followed during the seven months leading up to the November Revolution.

During this time the Bolsheviks also increased their party membership to 200,000 and their popular following among the workers and soldiers. Lenin was accused of being a German agent because he urged the Russian soldiers to fraternize with the German soldiers. He and his party did indeed receive funds from Germany to spread defeatist propaganda among soldiers and civilians alike, but this propaganda would not have been

Storming of the Winter Palace

so effective had not the patriotism of many Russians already been displaced by their desire for peace and more radical reforms. By gaining popular support among the soldiers and workers the Bolsheviks were able to increase the proportion of their representatives in the soviets in the large cities, where elections were held frequently. By mid-September they had obtained narrow majorities in the Petrograd and Moscow soviets and acquired their main executive posts. As the disloyal opposition to the Provisional Government, the Bolsheviks were able to promise the masses the three things it could not give them: Land, Bread, and Peace.

On the eve of the November Revolution the Bolshevik, Menshevik, and Social Revolutionary leaders were still divided among themselves on what to do about the Kerensky regime, but Lenin's insistence on party discipline gave the Bolsheviks an advantage over their rivals. When the majority of the Bolshevik party leaders decided on an insurrection for early November, the minority that opposed this decision either submitted or temporarily resigned. Since the revolution was to be made in the name of the soviets, and not the Bolsheviks alone, the Bolsheviks were able to gain support from a number of Leftwing Mensheviks and Social Revolutionaries. This Bolshevik tactic of gaining power through temporary alliances with Leftwing movements worked so well in Russia in 1917 that Communists all over the world have used it periodically ever since.

Unlike the events in March, the November Revolution was carefully planned and carried through by a dynamic minority of professional revolutionaries. The Bolshevik president of the Petrograd Soviet, Leon Trotsky, organized a Military Revolutionary Committee. By his fiery oratory he swung the wavering garrison of the Peter-and-Paul Fortress from loyalty to the Provisional Government to the side of the insurrection on November 5. Since this fortress was stocked with thousands of rifles, its seizure was comparable to the fall of the Bastille in Paris in 1789. During the next two days Trotsky skillfully directed the capture of the capital's railroad and communications centers and the Winter Palace, the seat of the Provisional Government. Incapable of defending itself, this government collapsed almost as ignominiously as its predecessor, and Kerensky escaped in an automobile borrowed from the American embassy. On November 7 the Bolshevik Revolution had been completed, and with a minimum of bloodshed.

Within a few weeks the triumphant Bolsheviks set up a new government in the name of the All-Russian Congress of Soviets and passed a number of sweeping reforms. They preserved their momentary popularity by beginning negotiations for peace, confirming the peasants' land seizures, granting the workers a large share in the management of the factories, and discriminating against everything connected with the hated Old Regime, especially the Church and the former ruling classes, whom they called collectively the "bourgeoisie."

But the other parties in the soviets began deserting them and going into the opposition in the early months of 1918. The two events that prompted this desertion were the closing of the Constituent Assembly by the Bolsheviks in January and the Treaty of Brest-Litovsk in March.

The elections to the Constituent Assembly had shown that the Bolsheviks did not have the support of more than 25 per cent of the people in Russia as a whole, though they had greater strength in a few of the larger cities. Hence, when the delegates refused to accept the Bolshevik government's program, the Bolsheviks dissolved it.

Peace negotiations with the Germans had begun in December 1917 and culminated in March 1918 with the Treaty of Brest-Litovsk. From the point of view of Russian patriots this treaty was disastrous. It gave the Germans over 1 million square miles of the most highly developed Russian territory, with a population of 60 million people: the Ukraine, Belorussia, and the Polish and Baltic provinces. The Bolsheviks signed the treaty in order to get out of the war, so that they could consolidate their regime at home. They also believed that the treaty would have no permanent meaning once the Revolution spread to Germany and the rest of Europe. For unlike Kerensky, Lenin was not at first primarily concerned with remaining the ruler of Russia but with spreading the Revolution throughout the world. As a revolutionary Marxist he believed that once World Revolution was achieved, national states would cease to be rivals and would "wither away." Nevertheless, it was the Treaty of Brest-Litovsk, more than any other Bolshevik act, that sparked the outbreak of counterrevolution.

### *The Civil War*

For almost three years revolutionary and counterrevolutionary forces fought each other throughout the Russian Empire. The fury began in May 1918 with a revolt by 50,000 Czech prisoners from the Austro-Hungarian army. These Czechs, who had volunteered for service in France, were to be evacuated by way of Vladivostok, but when the Bolshevik leaders demanded that they disarm, they seized control of the Trans-Siberian railroad and thereby encouraged various opposition groups in western Siberia to similar defiance. In the next two months dissident Social Revolutionaries set up an anti-Bolshevik government in Samara and launched uprisings in the upper Volga and Moscow itself. By September the Bolsheviks had temporarily beaten off the Social Revolutionaries only to encounter a more formidable onslaught of tsarist officers. Thereafter the new Red Army fought the Whites (as the counterrevolutionaries were called) in the east, the south, and the far north. In addition, the civil war pitted Bolsheviks against Social Revolutionaries and Mensheviks, poor peasants against kulaks and Cossacks, city people against villagers, socialists against capitalists, Christians against Jews, and non-Russians against Russians.

This fratricidal orgy was even more devastating than the war against the Central Powers. People in the cities could not obtain enough to eat, despite forced requisitions by the government from the peasants. By the end of 1920 Petrograd and Moscow—both cities of over 1 million people—had been deserted by over one-half of their inhabitants, who became refugees in the rural areas where they hoped to find food. In the countryside itself the armies of both sides pillaged and spread terror, executing innocent civilians and killing prisoners-of-war.

The Russian Civil War also brought outside intervention. The Japanese occupied the Far Eastern provinces, and the British, French, and Americans sent aid to the Whites. But the separate counterrevolutionary armies were never able to join physically, and the Allies, though eager to see them win, limited their aid mainly to money and supplies. After the peace settlement in the West the peoples of the Allied nations were unwilling to get involved in another war, especially a civil war in another country. The new Polish government was less squeamish. It took advantage of the situation to push its frontier 150 miles eastward into Russian territory after a French military mission had saved it from a Bolshevik advance on Warsaw. Meanwhile, British and German aid helped Finland and the Baltic states retain their independence. Aside from these losses, however, the Bolsheviks cleared all Russian territory except the Far Eastern provinces (evacuated by Japan only in 1922) of counterrevolutionary forces. At the end of 1920 a million White Russians fled the country and the Bolshevik victory was assured.

The Russian Bolsheviks had not only eliminated their rivals for power at home, they had changed their name to Communists and tried to direct the spread of the Revolution throughout the world. To this end they founded the Third International in March 1919 to replace the Second International, which had collapsed in August 1914 when the majority of the Socialists had supported the war effort in all countries. By the beginning of 1919 Communists outside of Russia were trying to repeat the success of their Russian brethren. Lenin and Trotsky earnestly believed that the former Central Powers were bound to turn Communist in the wake of their military defeat, and that once this happened the working classes in the rest of Europe would soon rise up against their capitalist governments. These anticipated events did not occur, but Lenin and Trotsky consolidated their control of Russia and turned it into the first Communist state in history. At the same time their control of the Third International—also called the Communist International, or Comintern—caused an irreparable breach between the Western democracies and the new Soviet regime, home of the "Red menace."

### The Revolutions in Germany and Austria-Hungary

Germany might have succumbed to the "disease" of Bolshevism if the war had not ended when it did. In early November 1918 revolutionary defeatism was sweeping the country. On November 3 the German fleet mutinied and took over the country's main naval base at Kiel. Together with the enlisted men of the army garrison, the revolutionaries set up a soldier's council similar to the soviets that had sprouted in Russia in March 1917. On November 6 and 7 the garrisons of Hamburg, Bremen, and Cologne revolted and formed similar councils. On November 8 Bavaria, the second largest state in Germany, overthrew its king and set up a republic dominated by a coalition of the Right- and Left-wing Socialists. Finally, on November 9 the Socialist leaders in Berlin ordered the workers into the streets. Within a few hours the Kaiser abdicted, and the government passed into the hands of the Right-wing Socialists.

Two things saved this Socialist-dominated German Provisional Government from the fate of the Kerensky regime a year earlier: it no longer had a war on its hands, and the army remained loyal to it. In January 1919, it was threatened by an uncoordinated series of street demonstrations, seizures of newspaper offices, and skirmishes by several groups of revolutionary militants. One of these groups, the Spartacus League, had just joined the newly formed Communist Party of Germany, and it bore the brunt of the reprisals that accompanied the suppression of the revolt by special shock troops assembled by the Socialist minister of the interior, with help from the regular army. Unlike General Kornilov, the German General Staff had no need to oppose its Provisional Government for failing to carry on the war effort. The war was over, and the General Staff was concerned primarily with maintaining itself as an independent institution. In return for helping the Provisional Government put down the Communist (Spartacist) revolt, it forced the Socialist leaders of this government to promise not to meddle in its affairs.

After the suppression of the Spartacist revolt, Germany quickly built up an immunity to the Communist "disease." In the next few months a Constituent Assembly meeting at Weimar gave her a democratic constitution. Meanwhile, the army and the Free Corps (civilian volunteers under the leadership of former army officers) crushed the workers' and soldiers' councils in other parts of the coun-

*Arms inspection of the Spartacists*

try and in April 1919 overthrew the Communist regime that tried to rule Bavaria from Munich. The overthrow of the Bavarian Soviet Republic marked the end of the Communist danger in Germany. The large German middle class was staunchly anti-Communist, and the majority of the population was tired of war and revolutionary violence. Thus, Germany survived as a political unit and was soon to become an apparently orderly constitutional republic.

Austria-Hungary suffered a far more drastic fate than Germany at the end of the war. There, too, moderate Socialists forced the overthrow of the monarchy, and in Hungary, as in Bavaria, a Soviet Republic managed to establish itself for a short time in 1919. Unlike Germany, Austria-Hungary did not survive as a political unit. The former subject nationalities were already declaring their independence before the Armistice was signed. In the north the Czechs of Austria and the Slovaks of Hungary formed a new state in late October of 1918. The Serbs, Croats, and Slovenes in the south joined Serbia to form the new state of Yugoslavia; the Poles of Austrian Galicia deserted to the new state of Poland; Rumania, which had re-entered the war at the last minute, took over the Hungarian province of Transylvania. All that remained of the old Hapsburg Monarchy were German Austria and the Magyar districts of Hungary. Shorn of their subject nationalities and with the Hapsburg tie gone, the rump states of Austria and Hungary went their separate ways at the end of the war.

The upheavals at the end of the war and during its immediate aftermath brought revolutionary changes to Central and Eastern Europe. A dozen new states—the Russian Socialist Soviet Republic, the Ukraninian Socialist Soviet Republic, Finland, Estonia, Latvia, Lithuania, Poland, Czechoslovakia, Yugoslavia, the German Republic, Hungary,* the Austrian Republic—replaced the three great empires that had ruled most of that area

*In 1920 the new Republic of Hungary declared itself a monarchy again but left the throne vacant.

for so long. Hunger and disease ravaged the major cities; the Europe-wide epidemic of a particularly virulent form of influenza was especially severe in the former Hapsburg lands. Local fighting also continued in many places; aside from border disputes between the new states, most of this fighting involved the Bolsheviks and the conservative and nationalist forces opposing them. Though legally in the process of demobilization, units of the German army crushed Bolshevik uprisings at home and helped drive the Russian Bolsheviks out of the new states of Estonia, Latvia, and Lithuania. No one, however, could dislodge the Bolsheviks from control of Russia itself.

## THE PEACE SETTLEMENT AND THE REVOLUTION IN INTERNATIONAL RELATIONS

While most of these revolutionary changes were taking place, the statesmen of the victorious Allied powers were meeting in Paris. They tried to isolate the "Red menace" and to integrate the new national states of Central and Eastern Europe into a peaceful, democratic order. But, in addition to the new political situation in Central and Eastern Europe, the delegates to the Paris Peace Conference faced their own conflicting conceptions of what kind of peace to make. The hyperbolic character of the war had expanded the aims of all the belligerent governments and aroused exaggerated hopes among their citizens. Great Britain, France, Italy, and Japan all demanded "compensation" at the expense of the defeated countries. Among the major victor powers only the United States renounced all annexations and indemnities. The Allied statesmen argued over the major issues that divided them, and in the end they all had to make some compromises, but their diplomacy was unlike any other diplomacy in history. For the First World War had been a war of peoples, and the peacemakers had to reflect the will of the masses that had won it.

The Paris Peace Conference differed from all previous international meetings of comparable magnitude. First of all it was shorter; its first full session met in January 1919, and in less than four months its major work was finished. Second, the defeated powers were not represented at its deliberations; the final treaties were simply imposed on them. Third, the chief delegates of the victor powers were elected heads of government, responsible to their national assemblies and under great pressures from organized opinion. Fourth, ideology played a greater role than ever before.

### The "New Diplomacy"

In January 1918, President Wilson had issued a statement of Allied war aims known as the Fourteen Points. The points may be summarized:

1. Open covenants openly arrived at (no more secret diplomacy).
2. Absolute freedom of the seas.
3. The removal, as far as possible, of all economic barriers.
4. Adequate guarantees that armaments will be reduced to the minimum consistent with domestic safety.
5. Adjustment of colonial claims on the principle that the interests of the population should have equal weight with the claims of the government.
6. The evacuation of all Russian territory, the free determination by Russia of her own political and national policy, and an unselfish effort to help her regain her place among the free nations under institutions of her own choosing.
7. Evacuation and restoration of Belgium.
8. Evacuation and restoration of French territory and the return of Alsace-Lorraine.
9. Readjustment of Italian frontiers along clearly recognizable lines of nationality.
10. Autonomous development for the peoples of Austria-Hungary.
11. Evacuation and restoration of Rumanian, Serbian, and Montenegrin territory with access to the sea for Serbia.
12. The Turkish parts of the Ottoman Empire to be given a secure sover-

eignty, but the other nationalities to be given an opportunity for autonomous development, and the Dardanelles to be permanently opened to the ships of all nations.

13. An independent Poland to include territories indisputably Polish, with free and secure access to the sea.
14. A general association of nations to be formed for the purpose of guaranteeing the territorial integrity and political independence of great and small states alike.

At the time these points were issued, Russia was negotiating for its separate peace at Brest-Litovsk. This fact colored, and perhaps provided, the motive for issuance. It was felt to be vital to keep Russia in the War—hence Point 6, which guaranteed that the Bolshevik regime would be respected. moreover, the Bolsheviks were issuing pronouncements calculated to rouse the hopes of subject peoples everywhere. Hence Wilson tried, with Points 10, 11, 12, and 13, to show that the Allies would reward these people too once the war was won. Lenin called for a proletarian revolution, to be followed by a classless society in a warless world; Wilson too had to promise the elimination of the causes of war and the establishment of a peaceful world order (Points 1 through 5 and 14).

Wilson's statement was not simply a reaction to the Bolshevik activities, it was also a direct appeal to the world's masses—a propaganda weapon to aid the Allied victory. The British, French, and Italian governments had endorsed the Fourteen Points, and even the defeated Germans had welcomed them as the basis for a just and lasting peace. Thus they could not be ignored at the peace conference. Neither Lenin nor Wilson got the kind of world he wanted in 1919; the old-fashioned national interests of the victor powers won out over idealistic principles in the Peace of Paris. Nevertheless, the conduct of international relations had been revolutionized, and henceforth, all major international agreements would require popular support and ideological justification.

### The Big Three

Just as Clemenceau had believed that war was "too serious a business to be left to generals", all the Allied leaders felt that peacemaking was too important to be left to professional diplomats. Of the five principal powers all but Japan were represented by their heads of government. These four men—President Wilson, Prime Minister Lloyd George, Premier Clemenceau, and Premier Orlando of Italy—dominated the peace conference as the Council of Four. They were aided by 58 committees and commissions, but they, especially the first three, made all the important decisions. Wilson, Clemenceau, and Lloyd George were seasoned politicians; they knew exactly what they wanted and used all their political, rather than diplomatic, skills to get it.

Above all else Wilson wanted the League of Nations, Clemenceau wanted security from German invasion, and Lloyd George wanted to restore the balance of power in Europe so that Great Britain could once again concentrate on her imperial interests. When Clemenceau and Lloyd George demanded that Germany pay the cost of the war, Wilson had to give in to an indemnity disguised by the word "reparations." When Lloyd George and Wilson opposed French control of Germany's Rhineland provinces, Clemenceau had to accept an Anglo-American guarantee of military support instead. When all three statesmen agreed that Italy should not get the port of Fiume and the surrounding Adriatic lands inhabited by Croats and Slovenes, Orlando left the peace conference in a huff. Aside from the League of Nations itself, the Fiume question was one of the few issues on which the Big Three did agree. Their disagreements led to compromises that looked good on paper but that were not to work out as planned. When the peace treaty with Germany was completed, Wilson, Lloyd George, and Clemenceau each said it was a good treaty. But, as we shall see later, France did not get permanent security against a German invasion, the balance of power was never restored in Europe, and the League of Nations did not fulfill the task Wilson had set for it.

### The Treaty of Versailles

Before making a final judgment on the Peace of Paris let us briefly examine the treaties themselves. There were five of these, each named for the place in suburban Paris where it was signed: The Treaty of Versailles with Germany (signed in June 1919), the Treaty of Saint-Germain with Austria (signed in September 1919), the Treaty of Neuilly with Bulgaria (signed in November 1919), the Treaty of Trianon with Hungary (signed in June 1920), and the Treaty of Sèvres (signed with Turkey in August 1920 and replaced by another treaty in 1923). The first of these was by far the most important. All followed its general model, beginning with the Covenant of the League of Nations and followed by territorial, military, and reparations clauses.

The Treaty of Versailles deprived Germany of considerable territory, but it left most of the country intact. In the West, France got back Alsace-Lorraine and received the right to exploit for fifteen years the industrially rich Saar basin in compensation for the coal mines the Germans had flooded in northern France. Denmark and Belgium received small strips of territory too. In the East, Poland got the former provinces of Posen (Poznan) and West Prussia, the so-called Polish Corridor, which gave her access to the Baltic Sea and completely separated East Prussia from the rest of Germany. The German-speaking seaport of Danzig became a free city under the supervision of the League of Nations. In addition, the League was to supervise a plebiscite in Upper Silesia to determine which parts should go to Poland. Finally, Germany lost all her colonies in East Asia to Japan and in Africa to Great Britain, France, and the Union of South Africa. Here too the League of Nations was to have some supervisory powers, through its Mandates Commission.

More crippling were those clauses of the treaty that sought to prevent Germany from ever again becoming a major military power. They forbade her to build offensive weapons such as submarines, military aircraft, tanks, and heavy artillery; they limited her army to a small professional force of 100,000 men; they imposed equally drastic limits on her navy. The treaty demilitarized a zone thirty miles wide on the right bank of the Rhine and provided for a fifteen-year Allied occupation of the left bank.

Most severe were the reparations clauses. Article 231, the notorious "war guilt" clause, stated that "the Allied and associated Governments affirm and Germany accepts the responsibility of Germany and her allies for causing all the loss and damage to which the Allied and Associated Governments and their nationals have been subjected as a consequence of the war imposed upon them by the aggression of Germany and her allies." No total sum was mentioned. A Reparation Commission was to add up the total bill and see that Germany paid it "within a period of thirty years." Meanwhile, she was to turn over 5 billion dollars within the next two years, and to deliver coal and timber to France, livestock to Belgium, and merchant ships to Great Britain.

The other four treaties were mainly concerned with reshaping Central and Eastern Europe according to the principles of national self-determination and security. Austria and Hungary lost nearly three-quarters of their former area and over two-thirds of their inhabitants. Wherever possible, boundaries were drawn to coincide with ethnic communities, but the Succession States got the benefit of the doubt where the population was mixed or where a defensible frontier was needed. Thus, 3 million Austrian Germans were left in Czechoslovakia so that state could have the Sudeten Mountains as its frontier. Most of the 6 million people in Austria proper wanted to join the new German Republic, but the Allies refused to allow the union between their two main enemies. Several million Hungarians found themselves living in Rumania, Czechoslovakia, and Yugoslavia. A League of Nations commission was to see to it that national minorities in the new states got adequate protection of their rights.*

*During the Russian Civil War Poland advanced her frontier about 150 miles east of the boundary assigned to her at the Paris Peace Conference. After 1920, 10 million Belorussians, Lithuanians, Ukrainians, and Jews found themselves living under Polish rule.

## The Impact of the Peace Settlement

Such was the Peace of Paris. Whatever else one may say about it one must admit that it reflected the desires of the peoples who happened to be on the winning side. It was they who insisted that Germany pay for the cost of the war and for all her past sins. The French people, for example, took great satisfaction in the fact that the German delegates were forced to sign the treaty imposed on them in the Hall of Mirrors of the Palace of Versailles, where in 1871 Bismarck had first proclaimed the German Empire. The British people were satisfied that, on the question of reparations, their delegation had done its best to "squeeze the German orange till the pips squeak." The Italians were less satisfied, but the peoples of the Succession States were jubilant. Ironically, the American Congress refused to ratify Wilson's signature on the Treaty of Versailles. The United States made separate peaces with the former Central Powers, not because the Peace of Paris was too harsh, but because it embodied the League of Nations, the one institution that Wilson had thought would mitigate its harshness.

Another important consequence of the Peace of Paris was the way it temporarily oriented the small states of East Central Europe toward the West. During the war the British, French, and Italians had promised Austro-Hungarian territories to the Yugoslavs and the Rumanians to keep them fighting. By summer of 1918 Wilson had made special pledges to the Poles and the Czechs. The smaller nationalities of East Central Europe looked to the Western Allies to help them gain as much territory as possible, not only from the defeated Central Powers but from defeated Russia as well. Poland took the most Russian territory, Rumania got the province of Bessarabia (as well as Transylvania from Hungary), and Finland, Estonia, Latvia, and Lituania all detached themselves from the former Romanov empire. A glance at the map* will show how these six states effectively sealed off Bolshevik Russia from the rest of Europe. The French called this barrier a *cordon sanitaire*—a kind of sanitary screen to quarantine the source of the Communist "disease." Along with Czechoslovakia and Yugoslavia these small states also formed a barrier to German and Hungarian expansion to the East and a potential combination of allies to help keep Germany from threatening France in the West.

*See map, p. 684.

*"Open Covenants": a hostile American view of the Peace Conference*

Fear of Communism had begun to overshadow fear of Germany during the last months of the Peace Conference, and the policies of the Western Allies in East Central Europe had expressed their will to stop its spread. Indeed, some observers argue that this became their main purpose and that they succeeded in this purpose under the guise of supporting "national self-determination" in those small states that vaunted their anti-Communism the loudest. Fear of Bolshevism also softened the attitude of the Western Allies toward the new German government that had quelled the Spartacist revolt. But their attitude did not change sufficiently to reconcile the Germans to their defeat; it merely weakened the will of Western liberals to defend the settlement in East Central Europe when a revived Germany challenged this settlement in the 1930's.

The security and the very existence of the new small states of East Central Europe depended on the will of the strongest power on the continent. Lenin, Wilson, and Clemenceau had supported the principle of self-determination there, though for different reasons, but by 1920 Wilson and Lenin had nothing more to offer them. Hence, for the next fifteen years they became clients of France and enjoyed a greater degree of independence than they were ever to know again. After the mid-1930s, first a revived Germany and then a revived Russia were to take these small states out of the Western orbit. Thus, a major weakness of the Peace of Paris was its failure to give Europe as a whole a durable political structure.

Another major weakness of the Peace of Paris was its neglect of economic problems. The United States generously sent emergency aid to Europe's war-torn areas, including Russia. But none of the major delegations at Paris had given serious consideration to the long-range economic consequences of the war and the peace settlement. The war had disrupted normal production in Western Europe and stimulated the expansion of industry in the more advanced non-European countries—especially the United States and Japan. Nothing was done at the peace conference to help Western Europe revive her own production and recover her markets overseas. Austria-Hungary had disappeared as a large economic unit and been replaced by a number of mostly backward small states; their economic needs also received no consideration from the peacemakers. The Western European Allies had borrowed billions of dollars from the United States, transforming her into the world's largest creditor nation. How were they to repay these war debts in their weakened condition? Finally, the exclusion of any discussion of inter-Allied war debts from the peace conference hampered the efforts of the Reparations Commission to arrange a realistic financial settlement with Germany.

Even as a purely political settlement the Peace of Paris did not recognize how the world had changed. It failed to integrate the two largest states, Germany and Russia, into the new European structure it created. Furthermore, the delegates' Europe-centered frame of reference, plus American isolationism, masked the new actualities of the world power situation. British and French statesmen overestimated the strength of their own countries and the importance of the Succession States. They ignored the temporary nature of German and Russian weakness and the growing power of Japan in the Far East.

The French were soon left to enforce the terms of the peace treaties by themselves. The United States refused to join the League of Nations, and both the United States and Britain refused to ratify the treaty guaranteeing military assistance to France. The British followed the Americans into a policy of isolation. Consequently, the French sought allies in Eastern Europe to maintain their security against an embittered and by no means permanently crippled Germany. All three of the great Western democracies thus reverted to their respective prewar foreign policies. In this situation, the League of Nations could never play the role Wilson had planned for it. Even if it had had more arbitration and enforcement powers it was doomed from the start by the absence of the three most powerful states of the twentieth century: the United States, Germany, and Russia.

⁝ ⁝ ⁝

The First World War accelerated the collapse of the European system in almost every respect. It destroyed forever the traditional state system of Europe; it produced a new diplomacy based on appeals to mass passions; it brought a revolution in world power. The war had also gravely weakened Europe's economic supremacy over the rest of the world. Nationalism, socialism, and democracy scored notable gains at the expense of the defunct authoritarian empires of Central and Eastern Europe, and revolutionary Marxism, which had seemingly been tamed by 1914, took on a new life in Russia. Under Bolshevik guidance the Third International became a greater menace to the bourgeois capitalist countries of Europe than the old Second International had ever been.

Although the victor nations were to

survive the First World War with their governments intact, they were profoundly altered by its social effects. Mass suffering in the trenches and at home had made it the first great democratic war. While wartime governments had become more dictatorial, people of all classes had shared a common drabness in their day-to-day existence. The extremes of these developments did not outlast the war, but the brotherhood of the men in the trenches was to survive in politically oriented veterans' organizations; the economic emancipation of women was to accelerate their political and social emancipation; and the uprooting of millions of men from isolated rural areas was to broaden their social horizons. (As the song said, "How're you gonna keep' em down on the farm after they've seen Paree?") The urban workers also got a taste of belonging to a larger community and a desire to preserve their improved status after the war.

Europe's aristocracies went to their final ruin everywhere. The older aristocrats lost their control over diplomacy, and a high proportion of the younger ones died leading the early offensives of the war. After this peoples' war Europe's political elites were to become more middle class and—with the rise of Mussolini, Stalin, and Hitler—plebeian.

Finally, the war intensified the moral and cultural crisis that a few sensitive writers and artists had already begun to depict at the beginning of the century. It produced a "Lost Generation" that self-consciously rebelled against the remaining vestiges of prewar "bourgeois morality." Just as Maurice Ravel's symphonic poem *La Valse* (1920) expressed the ruin of the old aristocratic world, Igor Stravinsky's *L'Histoire du soldat* (1917) gave a musical forecast of the style that was to appeal to the "Lost Generation" of the 1920s.

## SUGGESTED READINGS

Dangerfield, George, *The Strange Death of Liberal England.* New York: G. P. Putnam's Sons, 1961.*

Especially suggestive on the domestic problems of the pre-1914 decade.

There is no general account in English of France in the early twentieth century. The following work, which covers the period 1870–1939, contains many details on the politics of the pre-1914 decade:

Brogan, Denis W., *France under the Republic.* New York: Harper and Row, 1940.

Salomone, A. William, *Italy in the Giolittian Era: Italian Democracy in the Making.* Philadelphia: Univ. of Pennsylvania Press, 1960.

An excellent scholarly study—sympathetic toward Giolitti.

Rosenberg, Arthur, *Imperial Germany: The Birth of the German Republic, 1871–1918.* Boston: Beacon Press, 1964.*

The best short analysis of the inner weaknesses of the German empire.

Balfour, Michael, *The Kaiser and His Times.* Boston: Houghton Mifflin Co., 1964.

A comprehensive, well-written, and balanced account.

Schorske, Carl E., *German Social Democracy 1905–1917: The Development of the Great Schism.* New York: Wiley, 1966.*

A scholarly study. Shows the split among the Socialists over the war.

May, Arthur J., *The Hapsburg Monarchy, 1867–1914.* Cambridge, Mass.: Harvard Univ. Press, 1951.

See the last chapters on the pre-1914 decade.

Seton-Watson, Hugh, *The Decline of Imperial Russia, 1855–1914.* New York: Frederick A. Praeger, n.d.*

A good survey.

Taylor, A. J. P., *The Struggle for Mastery in Europe, 1848–1918*. New York: Oxford Univ. Press, 1954.
Very good on the power politics of the pre-1914 period. Lively and informative.

Albertini, Luigi, *The Origins of the War of 1914*. 3 vols. New York: Oxford Univ. Press, 1952–1957.
Extremely detailed—more balanced than earlier works on the subject, though still more critical of Germany's role than some.

Vagts, Alfred, *A History of Militarism: Civilian and Military*. Rev. ed. Cleveland: World Publishing Co., 1959. Meridian.*
See especially on the rapid militarization of Europe in the pre-1914 decade.

Falls, Cyril, *The Great War, 1914–1918*. New York: G. P. Putnam Sons, 1967.*
A well-written, balanced account.

Taylor, A. J. P., *An Illustrated History of the First World War*. New York: G. P. Putnam's Sons, 1964.
Evocative illustrations accompanied by a provocative narrative chastising everyone except Lloyd George and Foch.

Fischer, Fritz, *Germany's Aims in the First World War*. New York: W. W. Norton, 1967.*
A brilliant and controversial book; its thesis is that German policy deliberately aimed at world domination in 1914–1918.

Tuchman, Barbara, *The Guns of August*. New York: Dell Publishing Co., n.d.*
A vivid description of the first month of fighting.

Ritter, Gerhard, *The Schlieffen Plan: Critique of a Myth*. London: O. Wolff, 1958.
A scholarly critique of Germany's plan to defeat France in six weeks.

King, Jere C., *Generals and Politicians: Conflict between France's High Command, Parliament, and Government, 1914–1918*. Berkeley, Cal.: Univ. of California Press, 1951.
On internal politics in wartime France.

Chambers Frank P., *The War behind the War, 1914–1918: A History of the Political and Civilian Fronts*. London: Faber and Faber, 1939.
A specialized study—well written and rich in details.

Carmichael, Joel, *A Short History of the Russian Revolution*. New York: Basic Books, 1964.
The most reliable and readable work on the Bolsheviks' rise to power.

Curtiss, John S., *The Russian Revolutions of 1917*. Princeton, N. J.: D. Van Nostrand, 1957.
An Anvil original.*
A good short account.

Wolfe, Bertram D., *Three Who Made a Revolution*. New York: Dial Press, 1964.*
This triple biography of Lenin, Trotsky, and Stalin has become something of a minor classic, though the final word has yet to be said about these three men.

Von Laue, Theodore H., *Why Lenin? Why Stalin?: A Reappraisal of the Russian Revolution, 1900–1930*. Philadelphia: J. B. Lippincott Co., 1964.*
Explains the Revolution in terms of the need for industrialization and the need for identification between rulers and ruled.

Mamatey, Victor S., *The United States and East Central Europe, 1914–1918: A Study in Wilsonian Diplomacy and Propaganda.* Princeton, N. J.: Princeton Univ. Press, 1957.

A scholarly study of the effect of Wilson's policies on the breakup of the Austro-Hungarian Empire.

Mayer, Arno J., *The Origins of the New Diplomacy.* New Haven: Yale Univ. Press, 1959.

An advanced analysis of the influence of Wilson and Lenin in creating a diplomacy appealing to mass passions.

——— *Politics and Diplomacy of Peacemaking: Containment and Counterrevolution at Versailles.* New York: A. Knopf, 1967.

The author shows how fear of the spread of Bolshevism affected the peace settlement; he also stresses the influence of domestic politics on the peacemakers.

Holborn, Hajo, *The Political Collapse of Europe.* New York: Alfred A. Knopf, 1951.

A perceptive analysis of Europe's changing position in international affairs owing to the First World War.

Marston, F. S., *The Peace Conference of 1919: Organization and Procedure.* New York: Oxford Univ. Press, 1944.

A good concise account.

Czernin, Ferdinand, *Versailles, 1919.* New York: G. P. Putnam's Sons, 1964.*

A good balanced account of the behavior of the "Big Three."

Birdsall, Paul, *Versailles Twenty Years after.* Hamden, Conn.: Shoe String Press, 1941.

Thoughtful and balanced reappraisal of the Treaty of Versailles.

Keynes, John Maynard, *The Economic Consequences of the Peace.* London: Macmillan, 1919.

A scathing condemnation of the peace makers for their economic treatment of Germany.

Mantoux, Etienne, *The Carthaginian Peace—Or the Economic Consequences of Mr. Keynes.* New York: Oxford Univ. Press, 1946.

With the benefit of hindsight, Mantoux disproves Keynes' charge that Germany was seriously crippled by the reparations imposed on her at Versailles.

CHAPTER XVII

# EUROPEAN CIVILIZATION, C. 1905–C. 1940

The First World War hastened the transformation of European civilization and culture. Before 1914 Henry Ford had introduced the assembly line and the nine-hour day in his automobile factory; by the end of the war these innovations began to take hold in Europe. In 1909 Louis Blériot had flown the first monoplane across the English Channel; in 1916 Igor Sikorsky developed the first twin-motored plane, essential for bombing operations and for the later development of commercial transports. Since the turn of the century the new departures of Freud, Einstein, and Picasso had been indicating what life in the twentieth century would be like. But it took the catastrophe of the war to make educated laymen see that it would be drastically different from the reasonable and ordered existence they had taken for granted.

The war and the dramatically obvious political and economic instability it engendered reinforced the cultural confusion that new artistic forms and new scientific and philosophical theories had previewed in the early 1900s. In the 1920s intellectuals and artists reflected in their works a troubled and unstable society which, confronted with the breakdown of traditional values and rules of conduct, rejected sentiment and lyricism, forced itself to ignore the war and its consequences, but also betrayed a general uneasiness of mind. After 1930 the intellectual and artistic climate began to change in response to the worldwide depression and the threat of fascism. Literature and art became more "committed" than they had been in the 1920s; systems of thought turned more toward the solution of current human problems. The theme of an absurd world appeared in many forms. It reflected the breakdown of earlier beliefs in determinism, the findings of psychoanalysis about human irrationality and, by extension, the idea of relativity in all areas of culture. While some artists, composers, writers, and philosophers tried to create new forms befitting a scientific age, others voiced their alarm at the mechanization and dehumanization of life.

## TECHNOLOGY AND ORGANIZATION

Having got under way in the late nineteenth century the "Second Industrial Revolution"* gained momentum in the twentieth. New discoveries brought forth new products and new techniques for

*See pp. 464-473.

manufacturing them on a mass scale. Mechanization and scientific management made possible greater output in fewer hours of work. The trend toward monopolies and cartels, stimulated by the depression of the late nineteenth century, was reinforced by the economic crises of the postwar years. Although the United States led the world in all these developments, and her workers experienced their economic and social consequences most fully, Europe also underwent significant technological and organizational changes, despite her structural, psychological, and economic handicaps between the two world wars.

The Hindenburg

### Advances in Industry and Transportation

In the early twentieth century the metallurgical and chemical industries made the greatest advances. Nonferrous alloys, stainless steel, and aluminum were produced at low cost in improved electric furnaces. Petroleum as well as coal began to be used as fuel and to yield a host of new by-products. Industrial chemists invented artificial textiles, like rayon, and plastics, like celluloid, both of which were being mass-produced by 1914. All these innovations helped to upset the hierarchy of the old raw materials. The war accelerated the pace of change; one has only to recall German successes in extracting nitrogen from the air and in manufacturing synthetic rubber. By 1919 it was no longer possible to return to the old ways.

During the postwar period whole new industries used petroleum or coal as their basic raw material. Oil refineries became as familiar a sight as steel mills and electric power stations. The production of gas from the coking of coal was concentrated in large installations that made it possible to distribute the gas economically and to recover its by-products. By 1930 the artificial gas industry of the Rhineland and the Ruhr distributed its product to 10 million consumers; three coking plants in Belgium served over half the country; two such plants in France filled the needs of over 6 million people in the Paris metropolitan area.

Plastics became the characteristic material of twentieth-century civilization. Between 1900 and 1940 hundreds of new ones appeared. The American firm Du Pont de Nemours produced nylon, the French firm Rhône-Poulenc acetates, the German firm I. G. Farben over a hundred varieties of buna (synthetic rubber), of which Buna S became the standard American synthetic rubber during the Second World War.

Another characteristic of modern technology has been growing speed in transportation. Streamlined design and more powerful motors made possible speeds unimaginable at the turn of the century. In 1929 Sir Malcolm Campbell's 1,000 horsepower, ice-cooled racing car "Golden Arrow" attained 231 mph. In the late 1930s sleek 80,000-ton ocean liners like the *Normandie* were crossing the Atlantic in a little over four days, and a Messerschmidt airplane had flown at 515 mph. A second form of air transport, the dirigible, showed great promise; in 1936 the *Hindenburg* flew from Lakehurst, New Jersey to Frankfurt, Germany in less than

42 hours.* Most Europeans still used the railroads (now with diesel and electric locomotives), but the automobile was beginning to alter social and cultural life, as it had already done profoundly in the United States. Commercial airlines were also becoming an integral part of European civilization. By the late 1930s they were providing regular service to the far corners of the world.

Electricity and, even more, the internal combustion engine also helped the spread of industrial technology to new areas. Electric power could be transported over long distances and used in mines, in ports, and on small farms. Factories no longer needed to be located near coal mines; electrically driven motors could run conveyor belts wherever electric power was available. Nor did factories and warehouses have to be near railroads or waterways any longer; diesel-powered trucks could transport raw materials and finished goods almost anywhere.

### Advances in Agriculture

In agriculture mechanization, artificial fertilizers, pesticides, and improvements in plant and animal breeding brought a revolution in productivity. Tractors, threshing machines, and combines eliminated most of the manual labor in sowing and harvesting. Motorized farm equipment also allowed the pasture land formerly used by draught animals to be converted to the production of marketable crops. New chemical compounds enriched the soil and destroyed insects, thus greatly increasing the yield of the seed. Hybridization produced hardier plants; artificial insemination multiplied the number of offspring of a single bull by ten.

Until the Second World War this agricultural revolution affected North America and Australasia far more than Europe. England and Denmark made greater gains in productivity than France, Germany, northern Italy, and the smaller countries of Northwestern Europe, while traditional farming methods prevented any significant advances in Southern and Eastern Europe—with the major exception of the Soviet Union. Even so, throughout the 1920s and 1930s, Europe as a whole and the main areas of European settlement overseas were producing more food than their markets could absorb.

The achievement of increased production and productivity with a reduced labor force had important social and economic consequences. Generally it was the day laborers who were eliminated, though in certain regions of large-scale farming they were found to be more economical than tenants or sharecroppers. The surviving day laborers tended increasingly to be machine operators. With less need than in the past for farming experience, they almost resembled factory workers. In parts of Western Europe, as in the United States, mechanization, rural electrification, the telephone, and the radio completely upset traditional rural life and narrowed the gap between it and life in the city. Unfortunately for most farmers, they could not revamp the economic structure to suit their needs the way the industrialists did.

### Transformations in the Economic Structure

In the twentieth century new techniques of management brought the change from empirical industry to scientific industry. Heretofore improvements in efficiency had been made through trial and error by the workers themselves or by imaginative inventor-producers like Henry Ford, and not even he understood all the possibilities for increased efficiency on an assembly line. The pioneer theorist of the scientific, or *rational*, organization of work was the American engineer Frederick Winslow Taylor (1856–1915), whose theories so impressed certain Europeans in the 1920s that they labeled all methods for rationalizing industry "Taylorism." The fact that Taylor was an American is significant; perhaps the most amazing feature of the interwar European economic structure was how much America was a part of it.

Rationalization brought increased efficiency in the use of plant, raw materi-

*Commercial dirigible flights were abandoned, however, after the *Hindenburg* exploded at its Lakehurst mooring in May 1937.

als, and labor. Outside experts showed factory managers how to save money by purchasing raw materials in larger quantities and by reducing their line to a few standard models that could be produced and distributed on a mass scale. In addition to the standardization of products, scientific management discovered ways to eliminate unnecessary effort on the assembly line through time-and-motion studies among the workers.

Progress varied in different countries and in different industries. In Germany, where rationalization was introduced on a large scale, many plants were liquidated or absorbed by larger ones, and improvements in labor efficiency allowed the Ruhr coal fields to increase their output with three-fifths of their former work force. In the 1920s Germany's total productive capacity increased by 40 per cent, despite the loss of heavily industrialized areas in the Saar and Upper Silesia. In France, Taylorism was applied mainly in the steel and automobile industries, though there was nothing comparable to the giant steel complexes in Germany and the United States.

Concentration transformed the European economic structure more than rationalization. Cartels and other monopolistic organizations that had appeared in the 1880s multiplied especially fast after 1925, when Europe's prewar productive capacity was restored and competition for limited national markets became keener. Industrialists in a number of countries formulated plans for fixing production quotas, distributing sales, and dividing up the export market. On the international level the Steel Cartel included producers in Germany, France, Belgium, Luxembourg, Austria, and Czechoslovakia. Three times a year its directing board fixed the steel tonnage that each national group was to produce. By 1930 there were two hundred cartels in Europe, of which forty-eight were in iron and steel and forty-seven in chemicals. American companies also made agreements with the European cartels to share markets, exchange trade secrets, and cooperate in repressing new inventions instead of competing in cheaper and better products.

*Man and Machinery (painting by Diego Rivera)*

### Social Consequences

Technological and organizational advances had important effects on the industrial worker. In Europe they reduced the average work-week from 60 hours in 1900 to 44 in 1937. They also raised wages in the long run, though this effect was partly offset by periods of unemployment. In general, shorter hours and higher wages improved the level of living of European workers, but the standardization of work provoked some disheartening human problems.

Work became uninteresting. Studies in the 'thirties and 'forties showed that the fatigue caused by a given task varied inversely with the interest felt in it by the same or different workers at different times. This correlation also held true for monotony. Thus, a skilled craftsman could work ten hours a day on a custom-built automobile and feel less tired and bored than a semiskilled assembly-line worker in eight hours. The craftsman's interest was held by the prospect of seeing the finished product he had created with his own skills. The assembly-line worker who spent the whole day turning one kind of bolt forty-five degrees could get no such feeling of satisfaction. More and more the extreme specialization of various phases of production separated the worker from his work.

Technological change made the semiskilled worker or employee an anonymous element in his firm. In Europe, with its strong craft traditions, this change had particularly demoralizing effects; it inhibited the worker's skill, his knowledge of the tricks of the trade, and his gift for technical invention. By the 1930s even office work was being transformed by adding machines, stamp-licking machines, and sorting machines, though these innovations were introduced more slowly in Europe than in the United States. In both factory and office the really skilled workers were now the expert mechanics and technicians who serviced the machines. The bureaucratic structure of a modern firm made people at all levels play roles in which they treated other people—and were themselves treated—as mere objects. This persistent role playing tended to encourage mental rigidity and lack of warmth and spontaneity as the only means of coping with what would otherwise have been serious conflicts between one's role and one's own personality and between the different roles one was forced to play.

Until the 1950s Europe lagged far behind the United States in institutionalizing adjustments to such conflicts and to the nervous tension and lack of motivation provoked by new conditions of work. There were no bowling leagues or "piped-in" music. The European worker sought his real "life" in outside distractions: gambling, sports, movies, and other forms of mass culture. By the 1930s mass culture was becoming as highly organized in Europe as in America, indeed more so in the totalitarian countries. On the job, however, the European worker, even in Communist Russia or Nazi Germany, felt a greater distance between himself and his immediate superiors than the American worker. In the United States traditionally democratic social relations were institutionalized in office parties, company picnics, and the habit of using first names. In Europe social relations had always been more formal, and little was done to change them to meet the needs of modern working conditions.

## ECONOMIC INSTABILITY

The gravest social problem of the postwar period was widespread unemployment. Already chronic in the 1920s in the most highly industrialized countries, it became catastrophic as prices fell during the world depression of the early 1930s. The immediate causes were the disruption of multilateral world trade and the collapse of the credit structure. Although provoked by the stock market crash in the United States, these calamities had deeper causes.

Europe's economy had never recovered completely from the disruptive effects of the war or adjusted adequately to the "Second Industrial Revolution." These weaknesses were partly due to the inability of the Europeans to reestablish the old channels of worldwide trade which had stimulated their economic expansion. In addition, specific errors of policy intensified the new weaknesses of the European economy. The first such error was the failure to develop a scheme like the Marshall Plan after the Second World War to provide the credit and raw materials essential for European reconstruction; this failure worsened the budgetary deficits and monetary inflation in France, Italy, Germany, the smaller countries of Central and Eastern Europe, and to some extent even in Great Britain. The second error was the superimposing of reparations payments and war debts on the already unbalanced international flow of money and credit. The third error was imprudent, large-scale, private American capital investment in Europe after 1925, 6 billion dollars of which went to Germany alone.

### Weaknesses of the European Economy in the 1920s

Europe's financial and monetary instability became apparent in the immediate postwar years. From the spring of 1919 until the fall of 1920 most countries experienced an economic boom. Wartime personal savings could at last be used to buy consumer goods not produced for four years, and manufacturers could hardly keep up with the backlog of orders. At first inflation helped this boom too, for governments had printed large quantities of paper money to meet their expenses during the war and continued to do so after it was over. But the boom gave way to a recession when Europe ran out of credits with which to import raw materials vital to her industries. These credits were lacking because Europe's income from overseas investments and from the export of goods and services had declined.

Inflation had especially serious psychological and social consequences in Germany and France. By the fall of 1923 the German mark was literally worthless; it took a trillion marks to buy a postage stamp. Loss of their cash savings lowered the level of living of salaried employees and much of the middle class. In contrast, the ability to negotiate loans that could be paid back in inflated currency favored the big industrialists, who concentrated and rationalized their production. Inflation brought similar, though less extensive, consequences in France, where by 1926 the franc had declined to one-fifth its prewar value. In all countries where it occurred, monetary instability prompted people to put their money in goods, foreign banks, and especially gold rather than invest it in productive enterprises at home.

The problem of gold remained insoluble throughout the 1920s. Every country wanted to put its currency back on the gold standard (which had been abandoned during the war), but the fixing of a suitable gold value caused difficulties. In 1925 the British government tried to restore London's position as the world's money market by overvaluing the pound. This action did attract money from people who wanted pounds for savings or business transactions, but it made British manufactured goods too expensive for foreigners who had to buy pounds to get them. Hence, British exports, on which the country's economic health depended, continued to decline. The French government, on the other hand, undervalued the

PASSING THE BUCK.

*The reparations problem (The Daily Express, London, 1923)*

franc in 1926, thus giving a temporary boost to French exports. Many countries that lacked sufficient gold used dollars, pounds, or francs to back their paper money and therefore became dependent on the stability of these three currencies.

Difficulties of international monetary exchange were aggravated by the problems of war debts and reparations. The payment of war debts to the United States by her former European allies increased their budgetary deficits and reduced their funds for importing raw materials. The payment of reparations by Germany worsened her inflation and delayed her recovery. In 1924 the German government established a new, stable mark, and an international loan under the auspices of the Dawes Plan (named after the American banker and statesman Charles Gates Dawes) temporarily alleviated the problems of reparations and war debts. Foreign loans to Germany allowed her to pay reparations to France, Belgium, Great Britain, and Italy; these reparations in turn helped these countries to pay their war debts to the United States. Nevertheless, the amount of capital available for further economic growth in Europe was sharply reduced.

Small markets also prevented Europe from resuming her prewar rate of economic growth—3.25 per cent annually before 1913 as opposed to 1 per cent after 1920. The domestic markets of all European countries (except the Soviet Union) were too small to sustain the same rate of growth as in the early stages of industrialization. Especially in Great Britain, older equipment and conservative financial and marketing practices limited the use of mass-production techniques. In France most consumer goods were still produced by small units at high costs, thus restricting the demand for them. In Germany, which made the most technological and organizational advances, the nation's total industrial capacity was too large for the domestic market alone. Like that of Great Britain, Germany's industry was geared to the world market, and after the war this market was being pre-empted by others.

In the 1920s the dislocation of world trade favored the newer industrial nations outside of Europe, especially the United States and Japan. The war had accelerated the industrialization of these countries by cutting off their imports of European manufactured goods, and by allowing them to take over European markets elsewhere. As a result, total industrial production in the postwar years was rising faster than the total world market, and the share of the European nations in this market was shifting. Compared to the prewar period Great Britain's share declined from 13.9 to 10.8 per cent, Germany's from 13.1 to 9 per cent, France's from 7.2 to 6.1 per cent; the United States' share rose from 13.3 to 15.8 per cent, and Japan's from 1.7 to 3 per cent.

The advanced European countries also lost much of their "invisible exports" and the economic and political influence that often went with them. Before the war they—especially the British—had earned income from distributing raw materials and farm goods from countries like Australia, South Africa, and Argentina. These countries began selling direct during the war and continued doing so afterward. Income from foreign loans was also lost: the 4 billion dollars the French had invested in Russia became a total loss when the Bolsheviks repudiated all debts contracted under the tsarist regime; other loans, especially in the United States, had been cashed in to pay the costs of the war. The United States, a former debtor nation, was now overtaking Europe as a source of foreign investment, while the loss of income from overseas loans reduced Europe's ability to import goods and to influence the political and economic life of underdeveloped countries overseas.

Economic nationalism further dislocated the world market by restricting imports in many countries. The United States had always maintained high tariffs, and in the 1920s these were increased at the very time when Europe needed to earn dollars to pay its war debts. After the war the Soviet Union itself was virtually lost as a market for the rest of Europe, and the new states in Central and Eastern Europe became extremely nationalistic economically as well as politically. In order to protect budding industries at home they put up high tariffs and established quotas limiting imports, but their domestic markets were far too small to support any significant expansion.

In these new states and in most of Eastern and Southern Europe population growth actually retarded economic development by aggravating the chronic problem of rural underemployment. This problem became more serious in 1920s when the United States cut off the prewar safety valve of emigration with restrictive quotas. France, whose stagnant population was especially weakened by wartime losses, temporarily welcomed almost 3 million foreign laborers, mainly from Poland and Italy. But emigration was not the answer for most underemployed men in Spain, southern Italy, Yugoslavia, Greece, Poland, or Lithuania. They did odd jobs whenever they could and spent most of their time idling in the village square. Underemployment wasted the manpower of growing populations, thus limiting the supply of goods and services. It also kept the demand for goods and services small, since the underemployed had almost no purchasing power.

Continuing poverty in the predominantly rural parts of Europe also reflected a worldwide slump in agriculture. This slump was caused by overproduction, especially in the prairies of North America, where new land had been brought under large-scale cultivation to meet wartime demand in Europe. As European agriculture returned to its own normal level of production, farm prices declined everywhere. For example, between 1919 and 1928, the price of wheat fell by two-thirds in Canada and by one-half in the United States. By 1929, 42 per cent of American, British, and German farms were mortgaged, as compared to 28 per cent in 1890. The farmers' declining purchasing power reduced the national and world markets for manufactured goods. This situation helped to cause the world depression in 1929 and to multiply its effects thereafter.

In addition to chronic *under*employment in the less developed areas, there was chronic *un*employment in some of the most highly industrialized countries. Throughout the 1920s the average rate of unemployment in Great Britain and Germany was 1 million; in the United States it was 2 million. These countries had known periodic unemployment in the past, but chronic unemployment was a new phenomenon, the product of the postwar slowdown in the rate of economic growth.

Thus, in the 1920s, important sections of the European economy suffered from a kind of chronic depression. The main reason was the contradiction between expanding production and limited markets, both at home and in the world at large. The brief prosperity in Europe between 1926 and 1929 and the somewhat longer prosperity in the United States from 1922 to 1929 masked this basic contradiction. When a "normal" depression—that is, falling prices due to temporary overproduction—occurred in 1929, it was intensified by the chronic depression, the dislocation of world trade, the problems of international payments, and the American investments in Europe which tied her economic fate to events in the United States.

## The World Depression and Its Consequences

By the fall of 1929 the American economy was well into a "normal" recession. Inventories were up, industrial production and wholesale volume were down; homebuilding had been falling for several years. Finally, down came the stock market. This crash reflected, in the main, the change already apparent in the industrial situation; yet its cause was loss of confidence in the market once the wave of selling began. Had the economy been fundamentally sound in 1929, the effect of the crash might have been small. Alternatively, the psychological shock and the loss of spending by those who were caught in the market might soon have worn off. Unfortunately, American business in 1929 was not sound; it was exceedingly vulnerable to the kind of blow it received from Wall Street. The crash therefore transformed what might have been an ordinary cyclic depression into a national and world disaster.

The mania for speculation which led to the crash was the most extreme example of the new American culture of the 1920s. On the one hand, President Calvin Coolidge (1923–1928) personified the older American virtues of abstinence—which had been institutionalized in the Eighteenth Amendment—hard work, and thrift. On the other hand, millions of American citizens were guzzling bootleg liquor in "speakeasies" and trying to make quick profits through speculative ventures. Easy credit allowed ordinary workers to purchase radios, refrigerators, and even automobiles; and second and third mortgages helped impoverished farmers to maintain a decent existence despite falling agricultural prices.

Easy credit also enabled almost anyone to speculate in the stock market. Although only about a million people were actively involved, speculation had become central to American culture. The broker's loan was an ingenious device for permitting the speculator to purchase securities on margin. The banks supplied the funds to the brokers, the brokers supplied the funds to the customers, and the collateral went back to the banks in a smooth and almost automatic flow.

Despite the seemingly endless supply of credit, however, there were limits to the amount of capital that existing enterprises could use or that new ones could be created to employ. As we have noted, the total demand for goods and services was already declining by 1929. Consequently, the real value of the securities of the companies that furnished these goods and services was also beginning to fall. When the stock market panic of 1929 exposed the widening gap between the real and market values of these securities, the credit, with the "prosperity" founded on it, disappeared.

The American stock market crash soon brought chaos to Europe's financial and monetary structure. Austrian and German investment banks were hit especially hard by the withdrawal of American capital to cover losses in Wall Street. The crisis began with the failure of the Austrian *Creditanstalt* in May 1931. Soon thereafter other Central European investment banks closed down, thus ruining their stockholders and removing the main sources of loans for Central Europe's manufacturers, who were also feeling the pinch of the depression. The financial collapse in Germany made it impossible for her to meet her reparations payments. Despite President Hoover's temporary moratorium on all intergovernmental debts (July 1931), and despite emergency credits from foreign banks, Germany was never again able to meet all her international obligations. Finally, in September 1931, the British government devalued the pound as a result of foreign withdrawals of the gold reserves that had heretofore backed it. This devaluation played havoc with all the currencies that had been tied to the pound, especially those of the Scandinavian countries.

In industry the Central European bank failures caused production to be reduced and workers laid off. The loss of American dollars in the form of loans plus the devaluation of the pound reduced the ability of many European countries to pay for imports of any kind. At the same time economic nationalism increased, and the decline in world trade intensified the crisis in Great Britain and in the agricultural exporting countries. By 1933 only the Soviet Union was unaffected by the depression that held all of Europe in its grip.

Meanwhile, farmers all over the world kept producing more food. Unlike the big manufacturers, the small farmers had no big production costs to limit output when market prices fell below these costs, and they had no savings to fall back on in a depression. Actually the real demand for agricultural products might have revealed underproduction and scarcity, but the industrial countries of Western Europe put up high tariffs on agricultural imports in order to protect their own farmers, thus artificially limiting demand. The agricultural countries of Eastern Europe and the rest of the world glutted the world market, causing prices to fall further. In Western Europe, as in the United States, the unemployed had no money to buy food, but here too the farmers produced more as prices fell.

For the world as a whole the main problem was restricted trade and broken markets. By 1932 world industrial production had fallen almost 40 per cent below the 1929 level as a result of both price movements and structural changes in the national economies and the world market. In their efforts to soften the blow at home many governments restricted imports of manufactured goods and manipulated their currencies. These policies failed to stimulate a real recovery. Only new investments could have put industry back on its feet, and these were simply not forthcoming in the depths of the depression.

Mass unemployment was the most dramatic consequence of the industrial depression. By 1932, 22 per cent of the labor force in the United States, Great Britain, and Sweden and 43 per cent in Germany was unemployed. Local and national governments set up soup kitchens and other kinds of emergency relief, and in some countries there were movements to reduce the work week in order to provide more jobs. The extension of short-time and irregular work became common; unemployed workers sold pencils in the street and did odd jobs whenever they could get them. As we shall see in the next two chapters, the anxiety and demoralization caused by unemployment was to attract people to all kinds of extremist political movements.

*Handing out bread and soup to the hungry in Detroit, 1930*

## SCIENCE

The major upheavals of the twentieth century altered the attitudes of the general public, of governments, and of the scientists themselves toward science. Until the end of the nineteenth century everyone had accepted the Newtonian view of a physical world governed by immutable natural laws. Darwin had shown that living things, including man himself, were also subject to such laws. Adam Smith and David Ricardo had extended the principle of natural law to the operation of a market economy; the English publicist Walter Bagehot had even applied it to society in his book *Physics and Politics* (1873). Even in the late nineteenth century, however, ordinary people were only faintly aware of the effects of science on their daily lives; governments gave only nominal financial support to research; and the typical scientist remained an isolated scholar independent of governments, foundations, industry, and society.

Around the turn of the century new scientific theories began to challenge the old certainties and the positivist, determinist, materialist creed they supported. Thereafter the scientists themselves came to regard scientific theory as a policy—a guide to action—rather than a creed. Governments intervened increasingly in financing and controlling research related to national defense, especially after 1940. Giant industrial firms like I.G. Farben and Du Pont set up their own research laboratories in which teams of scientists and technicians worked on prescribed projects. The general public eagerly accepted the practical applications of science through electricity, labor-saving devices, and the mass media of communication. Yet it continued to desire common-sense knowledge about nature, man, and society; instead, twentieth-century science gave it relativity, indeterminacy, and irrationality. None of these principles "made sense," but then neither did the depression nor the two world wars.

Some people remained optimistic about the ability of science to improve the conditions and even the length of human life, to eliminate poverty, and to allow each individual to develop his personality to the fullest. The majority, especially during times of crisis, felt uneasy and insecure about the impact of science on civilization. Whether optimistic or pessimistic, the general public became fascinated by science as a new kind of wizardry carried on by slightly mad men in white coats surrounded by test tubes and high-voltage conductors. This image was reinforced by the new genres of popular science and science-fiction in best-selling books, magazines, newspapers, and the movies.

### Theoretical Physics and Atomic Energy

Around 1900 new theories in physics brought into question the belief in a mechanistic universe governed by fixed laws, a belief that had gone practically unchallenged for two hundred years. These new theories were evolved to take care of newly discovered phenomena that mechanics alone could not explain. Scientists like Pierre and Marie Curie and Wilhelm Konrad Roentgen discovered that some forms of "matter" had radioactive properties whose powers could not be predicted by the old theory. In 1901 the German physicist Max Planck (1858–1947) launched the first revolution against it by saying that energy was a kind of "matter" emitted as particles, or quanta, of atoms and electrons. Planck's quantum theory of energy also replaced the old wave theory of light. The second revolution in physics followed from the theory of relativity put forth in 1915 by the German mathematical physicist Albert Einstein (1879–1955).

Einstein challenged the accepted notion of an absolute space and an absolute time in which physical events occur. According to him, both space and time are relative to the observer. (Einstein is said to have replied to a coed who asked him how time could be relative: "When you are sitting on a hot stove, a minute seems like an hour, when you are kissing your boy friend, a minute seems like a second.") The first fixed point of his new theoretical physics was the experimentally demonstrated fact that the velocity of light is always the same for any observer: 186,000 miles per second. To the ordinary layman this new "fixed point" was a poor substitute for the established image of matter-in-motion. Indeed, it was no image at all, it was a mathematical abstraction.

In his famous formula $E = mc^2$ Einstein used the constant $c$ to stand for the velocity of light, $E$ for energy, and $m$ for mass. With this formula he challenged the accepted distinction between matter and energy by saying that they are merely different forms of the same thing. Thus, if one page of this book could be converted into energy through some process of disintegration it would yield as much heat as 3,000 tons of burning coal. One gram of matter would yield 20 million million calories of heat energy or 22,000 kilowatt hours of electrical energy. The particles of the nucleus of an atom are "screwed together," so to speak, by a certain amount of energy; Einstein's formula predicted that, if these particles could be separated, the energy that held them together would be released, the total of their separate weights would be less than that of the nucleus when it was "whole," and the loss in mass would equal the amount of energy made available by their separation.

Planck and Einstein not only destroyed the old mechanistic theory of the natural world; their theories implied that the "laws" of nature could not be derived from direct observation and measurement. The common-sense assumptions of the observer would get in his way, as in the case of absolute time and space and the absolute distinction between matter and energy. The theoretical physicist would therefore have to rely on his ability to invent conceptual schemes that were uncontaminated by the senses, "common" or otherwise. He would have to derive these conceptual schemes from a "closed field" of pure thought and express them in the abstract language of mathematics. Then he could test them and see how much they explained about the natural world. But he would always have to be ready to modify them, or even replace them by others. The world "out there" and its "laws" could be grasped in no other way.

In the 1920s and 1930s new theories of bewildering complexity and diversity began competing for acceptance. In France,

PICTURE GROUP E

# *Twentieth-Century Art and Architecture*

MARCEL DUCHAMP: *Nude Descending a Staircase, Number 2*

Philadelphia Museum of Art, Louise and Walter Arensberg Collection

GEORGES BRAQUE: *The Table*

Collection, The Museum of Modern Art, New York, Acquired through the Lillie P. Bliss Bequest

LEFT:
ROBERT DELAUNAY: *Eiffel Tower*

The Solomon R. Guggenheim Museum

BELOW:
FERNAND LEGER: *The City*

Philadelphia Museum of Art, A. E. Gallatin Collection;
Photograph by A. J. Wyatt, Staff Photographer

PICASSO: *Guernica*

Musem of Modern Art New York

LEFT:
HENRI MATISSE: *Vase of Marguerites*

Paris Museum of Modern Art; French Cultural Services

BELOW:
MARC CHAGALL: *Birthday*

Collection, The Museum of Modern Art, New York, Acquired through the Lillie P. Bliss Bequest

**DESSAU, GERMANY,** *Bauhaus*

Museum of Modern Art, New York

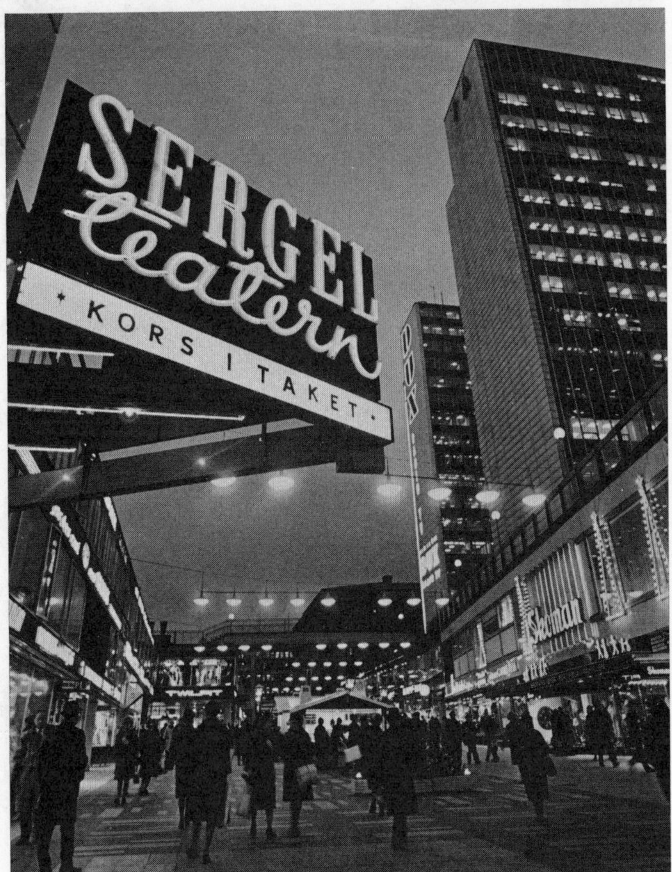


*Downtown Stockholm*

American Swedish News Exchange

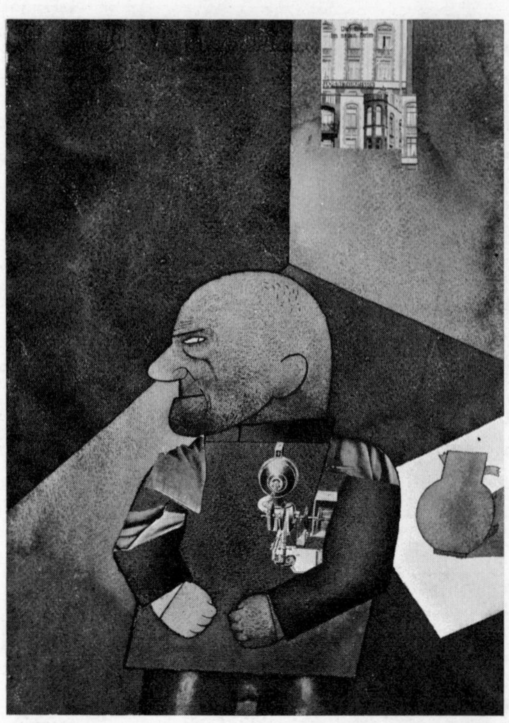

LEFT:
GEORGE GROSZ: *The Engineer Heartfield*

Collection, The Museum of Modern Art, New York, Gift of A. Conger Goodyear

BELOW:
VASILY KANDINSKY: *Painting Number 199 (Winter)*

The Solomon R. Guggenheim Museum

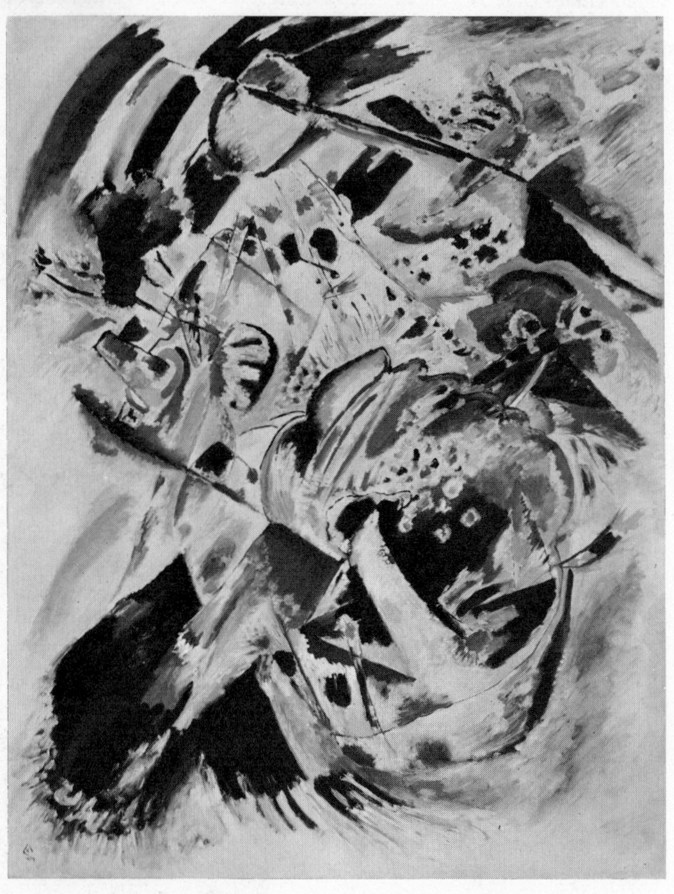

RIGHT:
WILLEM DE KOONING: *Untitled*

Collection, The Museum of Modern Art, New York, Gift of Mrs. Bliss Parkinson

BELOW:
JEAN DUBUFFET: *The Cow with the Subtile Nose*

Collection, The Museum of Modern Art, New York, Benjamin and David Scharps Fund

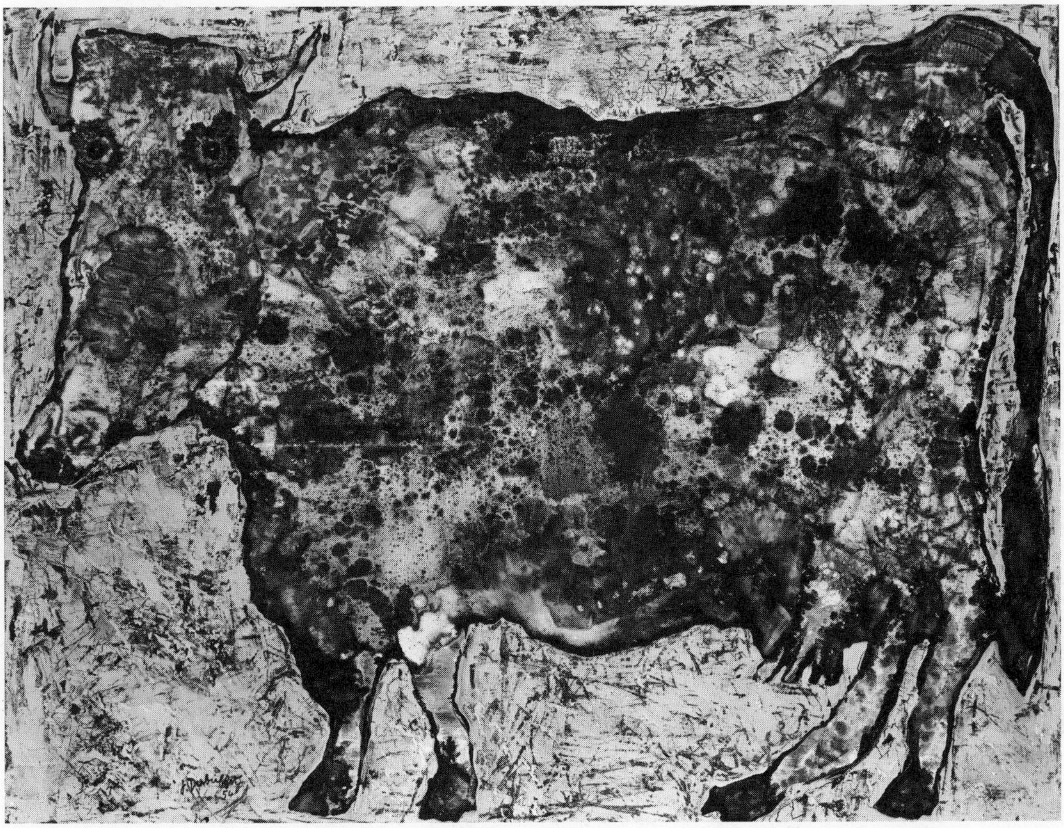

TWENTIETH-CENTURY ARCHITECTURE: *Nôtre Dame du Haut, Ronchamp,* by Le Corbusier

French Government Office

TWENTIETH-CENTURY ARCHITECTURE: *Trans World Airlines Terminal, New York,* by Eero Saarinen

TWA by Ezra Stoller Associates

Prince Louis de Broglie tried to reconcile the wave and quantum theories by asking: "Since light waves behave in certain situations like particles, why should not particles behave, from time to time, like waves?" In his famous equation the German Erwin Schrödinger used De Broglie's wave mechanics to demonstrate mathematically that a stream of electrons may be regarded as having certain properties of a wave as well as those of a series of particles. Schrödinger's compatriot Werner Heisenberg argued for a complete discarding of hypotheses based on physical analogies in favor of the more abstract language of differential equations. He said, in effect: "You make me laugh with your waves and your electrons. Have you ever *seen* them?" Heisenberg maintained that the nature of the movement of electrons around the nucleus of an atom was uncertain and indeterminate. According to him uncertainty and indeterminacy are the only "principles" we can know.

While these new theories dissolved all previous notions of "reality" into mathematical equations, atomic physics was translating new discoveries about the composition of the atom into practical applications. In 1919 the New Zealand-born Ernest Rutherford (later made a peer) made the crucial discovery that it was possible to break up a nucleus of hydrogen by a direct hit from an alpha particle. Further experiments with controlled atomic transformations revealed the fact that elements containing chemically identical atoms were capable of dividing into scores of different isotopes, some stable, some radioactive. In 1932 the Englishman Sir James Chadwick showed that the neutron (which may be regarded as a proton without its positive charge) was the central feature of nuclear structure. Soon thereafter the Frenchman Frédéric Joliot-Curie discovered that nearly all atoms bombarded with neutrons become radioactive. In 1936 the Italian Enrico Fermi bombarded heavy elements with neutrons and claimed to have produced a number of elements heavier than any found in nature. These discoveries opened the new fields of nuclear chemistry and atomic energy. By 1938 atomic physicists realized that if any nuclear process could be persuaded to yield more than one effective neutron per neutron originally supplied, the reaction would proceed faster and faster. If uncontrolled this chain reaction would be an explosion, if controlled it would be an energy-producing atomic reactor.

### Biochemistry and Medicine

As in the physical sciences new discoveries in the biological sciences were given practical application within an increasingly shorter time span. Unlike those in physics, however, these discoveries did not lead to a revolution in theory, nor were they related to the names of particular men. Nevertheless, the progress of biology and medicine has been closely linked with developments in physics, chemistry, and even psychology, as well as the major events of contemporary history. It was the world depression that stimulated research in nutrition and vitamins; it was the Second World War that provoked the mass production of penicillin and the spectacular advances in surgery.

In the twentieth century research in biology has taken two general directions, opposed yet related, which have been of prime importance for biological theory and for medical and surgical practice. On the one hand, as scientists penetrated increasingly the elementary composition and functioning of living things—with isotopic tagging, electron microscopes, and other aids—they were led to consider the total structure of an organism. On the other hand, this organism was seen to be inseparable from a larger structure in which diverse types of organic and inorganic substances were associated.

Born in the twentieth century, biochemistry is distinct from the organic chemistry of the nineteenth century, which studied the products of life. Biochemistry studies the chemical elements essential to the normal functioning of life itself. At the turn of the century research in fermentation showed that this process was due to chemical substances known as enzymes. Since then extremely complex and varied experiments have helped to build an understanding not only of the role of enzymes in other essential life processes like photosynthesis, but also of other chemical bodies indispensable to these processes. Traces of certain metals were also discovered to be necessary; for example, the absence of cobalt in pasture soil was found to produce sleeping sickness in cattle. Until 1929 the chemistry of all vitamins, except D, remained a mystery. Thereafter, beginning with the chemical breakdown of vitamin A, rapid progress was made in the analysis and synthetic production of these substances.

In addition to the substances that the living organism gets from its nourishment, it needs substances that it produces itself through the endocrine glands, namely hormones. In the 1920s this discovery inaugurated the new science of glands and internal secretions known as endocrinology. The importance given to hormones has been one of the main features of modern biology; they have been found to influence most physiological mechanisms, from the growth of animals and plants to the functioning of both the organs that secrete them and other organs. New discoveries relating to adrenalin, insulin, thyroid hormones, and sex hormones had obvious relevance for medicine, which, beginning in the mid-1920s, made more progress in a single generation than in all previous human history.

Another new science, cytology, concerned itself with the internal life of individual cells. This study in turn forced biologists to recognize the intimate connection between the cells themselves and the organism of which they were a part. It was found that tissue cultures separated from an organism continued to live at low temperatures and to adapt themselves to their isolation but that they did not form new organisms with a life of their own. The cell was thus seen as an integral part of an organism which, when full-grown, could not be altered at will. Embryologists demonstrated that artificial stimulation in the egg could alter the pattern of development, such as the growth of a third eye.

**AVERAGE EXPECTATION OF LIFE AT BIRTH FOR SELECTED COUNTRIES IN EUROPE, NORTH AMERICA, AND OCEANIA, BY SEX, DURING VARIOUS PERIODS, 1875–1945[a]**

| Country | Sex | 1875 | 1885 | 1895 | 1905 | 1915 | 1925 | 1935 | 1945 |
|---|---|---|---|---|---|---|---|---|---|
| Australia | M | – | 47 | 51 | 55 | – | 59 | 63 | 66 |
| | F | – | 51 | 55 | 59 | – | 63 | 67 | 71 |
| Austria | M | 31 | – | 37 | 39 | – | – | 55 | – |
| | F | 34 | – | 39 | 41 | – | – | 59 | – |
| Belgium | M | – | 44 | 45 | – | – | 56 | – | – |
| | F | – | 47 | 49 | – | – | 60 | – | – |
| Finland | M | – | – | 43 | 45 | 43 | 51 | 54 | 55 |
| | F | – | – | 46 | 48 | 49 | 55 | 60 | 61 |
| Germany | M | 36 | 37 | 41 | 45 | 47 | 56 | 60 | – |
| | F | 38 | 40 | 44 | 48 | 51 | 59 | 63 | – |
| Italy | M | – | 35 | – | 44 | 47 | 49 | 54 | – |
| | F | – | 36 | – | 45 | 47 | 51 | 56 | – |
| New Zealand | M | – | – | 55 | 58 | 61 | 64 | 65 | – |
| | F | – | – | 58 | 61 | 63 | 67 | 68 | – |
| Switzerland | M | 41 | 43 | 46 | 59 | 51 | 58 | 61 | 63 |
| | F | 43 | 46 | 49 | 52 | 54 | 61 | 65 | 67 |
| Union of Soviet Socialist Republics | M | – | – | 31 | – | – | 42 | – | – |
| | F | – | – | 33 | – | – | 47 | – | – |
| United States | M | – | – | – | 48 | 50 | 56 | 61 | 64 |
| | F | – | – | – | 51 | 54 | 59 | 65 | 70 |

[a]From United Nations, *The Determinants and Consequences of Population Trends* (1954), p. 54.

These demonstrations were of some help to medicine; they incidentally confirmed the popular image of the mad scientist busily creating new kinds of monster. Both cytology and embryology also showed that each living organism had a built-in regulatory power which, when disturbed in any way, could cause illnesses other than those induced by microorganisms or by lack of some essential chemical substance. Cancer, for example, came to be viewed as the abnormal growth of certain tissues.

The discovery of hitherto unknown microorganisms has made microbiology one of the most challenging of all the new sciences. Whereas microbiologists are still debating the question as to whether viruses are really organisms at all, the electron microscope has revealed the complex structure beneath the morphological simplicity of bacteria. The use of microorganisms as antibiotics began with Sir Alexander Fleming's almost accidental discovery of penicillin in 1928. Since then one new drug has followed another in a rapid succession of new experiments leading to commercial production: streptomycin, aureomycin, chloromycin, etc. Their side effects, however, (heavy doses of streptomycin, for example, impair some people's hearing) have yet to be understood. This problem is directly related to the complex regulatory mechanisms that maintain all parts of a living creature in a delicate functional balance and that can be disoriented when the organism lacks some chemical product it needs or when its functioning is upset by some extraneous chemical product.

This conception of the interrelations within the total organism has revolutionized both medicine and surgery. More attention has been paid to the disrupting effects of surgical operations; anesthesia and tranquilizers have come to be administered by specialists. The study of different blood types, especially the discovery of the RH factor in 1941, has shown that unsuccessful transfusions and certain diseases of newborn infants are due to the ill effects of the proteins in one blood type on another. Experiments in the late 1930s revealed the basic role of the sympathetic nervous system as an agent in all tissue diseases. Finally, the realization that certain diseases and organic malfunctions can be initiated by psychological disturbances opened up the new field of psychosomatic medicine.

### Psychology

While the new biochemistry stressed the delicate equilibrium necessary to the

*Pavlov and his staff with one of the dogs used in his conditioned reflex experiments*

healthy functioning of the human body, and the new physics made the world "out there" increasingly remote and abstract, the new psychology of Sigmund Freud (1856–1939) brought the world "inside" —the *unconscious*—into painfully clear focus. In the early twentieth century other schools of psychology tried to explain human behavior without resorting to the unconscious. In Russia, Ivan Pavlov stressed the importance of *conditioned reflexes* through the nervous system. In the United States John B. Watson maintained that internal feelings were directly observable in outward behavior, a position that gave his theories the label *behaviorism*. In Germany the Gestalt psychologists held that the way to understand an individual mind was through the painstaking study of all the subtle connections of its whole form, for which the German word is *Gestalt*. Though oriented more toward philosophy than clinical practice, the Gestalt movement made outstanding experimental contributions to the psychology of perception and thought.

Among all these developments, it was the *psychoanalytic* theories of Freud that had the greatest influence in the first third of the twentieth century. Not only did Freud talk about things that everyone could recognize in his own experience, he said them in language that educated laymen could understand. He tried to give a coherent explanation of the workings of the unconscious, to define the strange rules by which its illogical logic operated. Freud's mighty effort directly challenged the nineteenth-century liberal conception of man as essentially rational and moral and replaced it with a conception of man largely dominated by unconscious drives, most of which were in direct conflict with the standards of conventional morality.

Primarily concerned with helping the mentally ill, Freud devised the method of psychoanalysis to probe the hidden causes of his patients' illnesses. He found that most of their neuroses and psychoses were the result of painful experiences in childhood, and that when these were brought out into the open the patient's symptoms disappeared. Freud used various techniques—from hypnosis to "free association"—to penetrate the unconscious, but the basic one was the interpretation of his patients' dreams. From his clinical practice Freud became convinced that "the interpretation of dreams is the royal road to a knowledge of the unconscious activities of the mind."

Freud's ideas about the role of the unconscious in human behavior have now become so commonplace that only a brief summary is necessary here. Each child brings into the world an unorganized chaotic bundle of urges called the *id*, whose sole aim is the gratification of basic instincts. As the child grows older he acquires an *ego*, which is aware of the cultural environment and self-consciously seeks a place in it. But through his parents and parental substitutes (schoolteachers, clergymen, etc.) the cultural environment teaches him that certain kinds of behavior are forbidden. The child incorporates these rules of conduct into a *superego*, or conscience. Henceforth, his *ego* tries to develop a personality of its own by expressing the drives of his *id*—especially the energy of his sexual instinct of *libido* —in ways acceptable to his *superego*, that is, to society.

The *ego* is frequently torn between the demands of the *id* and those of the *superego*. Neuroses and psychoses develop when these conflicts get out of control, though ordinarily the forbidden urges are suppressed below the conscious level. Even in dreams, these urges express themselves only in indirect, symbolic ways whose "rules" Freud sought to interpret. Freud also believed that certain primitive myths—like the story of the Greek king Oedipus who killed his father and married his mother—expressed forbidden urges experienced by all male children in modern society. In all instances these urges strive for some form of expression. Some of these forms are socially unacceptable and cause trouble with the *superego*; others are inadequate substitutes for real gratification and cause trouble with the *id*. The most satisfactory adjustment to these conflicts is *sublimation*, the process of deflecting *libido* drives from human objects to new objects of a nonsexual, socially valuable nature. This unconscious process allows the *ego* to maintain its self-respect and develop a healthy personality.

A few months after the outbreak of the First World War Freud wrote the following to a Dutch colleague:

"Psychoanalysis has concluded from a study of the dreams and mental slips of normal people, as well as from the symptoms of neurotics, that the primitive, savage and evil impulses of mankind have not vanished in any individual, but continue their existence although in a repressed state . . . and that they wait for opportunities to display their activity.

It has furthermore taught us that our intellect is a feeble and dependent thing, a plaything and tool of our impulses and emotions."

Yet Freud had faith in the liberating quality of reason. Toward the end of his life, in his *Future of an Illusion*, he said: "The voice of the intellect is a soft one, but it does not rest until it has gained a "hearing." Thus Freud provided an image of man that made him understandable without making his utterly contemptible.

Since the mid-1930s a basic controversy has developed between the psychoanalytic school and the newer schools that stress the importance of the social context to the individual. The psychoanalytic school maintains that human personality is shaped in the first six years of life and that early characteristics are extremely resistant to change. According to the post-Freudians, the *ego* is a more important instrument of adjustment than it had been for Freud himself, but psychoanalytic theory still focuses its study of personality on what goes on *inside** the individual. Thus, it differs markedly from theories like that of the late Harry Stack Sullivan, who contended that personality is shaped in large part by the *social interactions* within the situation in which it develops. Some psychologists now feel that mentally ill individuals can be treated most effectively in a situation in which they "interact" with other people besides the psychiatrist.

*Since, strictly speaking, a theory is scientific only if it is—at least in principle—refutable by experiment, psychoanalytic theory is dogmatic rather than scientific.

Freud himself thought it probable that every culture had to be built upon coercion and the suppression of instincts. The best he hoped for was a lessening of some of the sexual sacrifices imposed by the moral code and some sort of compensation for the sacrifices "that must necessarily remain." Indeed, his own labors as ethical liberator and educator were to change the sexual outlook of the society (middle-class, pre-1914 Vienna) whose dictates he treated as essentially unalterable in most of his work. More than any other individual Freud has colored our whole contemporary view of the human mind and human values, but it was another new science of man, cultural anthropology, that emphasized the relativity of all human values.

### Anthropology and Sociology

Educated Europeans had long been aware of the diversity of the world's cultures, but, as we have seen, in the nineteenth century most of them had become more convinced than ever of the superiority of their own. They viewed other peoples' customs and beliefs as not only different but wrong. Anthropology as it was practiced during most of the nineteenth century also seemed to confirm their belief in their own superiority as a "race," for it concerned itself almost exclusively with the physical differences among men.

When some anthropologists finally began studying cultural differences they showed that every culture is essentially an adaptation to the physical and social environment in which it develops. Thus, what is "good" for one environment may be "bad" for another. Who was "right": the Frenchman who believed that "a meal without wine is like a day without sunshine," or the Muslim who abstained from all alcoholic beverages because they were forbidden by the Koran?

By the beginning of the twentieth century investigators of the world's cultures were telling Europeans some startling things. In *The Golden Bough* Sir James Frazer (1845–1941) concluded that primitive religion originated in magic and that some of the most sacred practices, rites, and beliefs of modern Christianity were only thinly disguised versions of primitive forms. Frazer also showed that all peoples invent myths to explain everything from the weather to the origins of their society. Could it not be that many of the explanations currently accepted by Europeans were also merely myths?

In *The Elementary Forms of the Religious Life*, the Frenchman Emile Durkheim (1858–1917) argued that the basic beliefs in any society are "collective representations." These express the combined ideas and sentiments of the society as a whole about reality, and they are reinforced for each member of the group through a program of ritual acts. Durkheim maintained that it was not important to inquire whether one or another set of beliefs was "true" or "false." All are true in their own fachion; all answer, though in different ways, to the given conditions of human existence. Durkheim was mainly interested in cultural anthropology for the insights it provided into European society of his own time. Aside from his study of primitive religion, his main works dealt with two specific problems of modern urban society: the division of labor and suicide. Here Durkheim tried to make sociology more empirical and less dogmatic than its original founder, Comte, had envisioned it.

It was not Durkheim, however, but the German sociologist Max Weber (1864–1920) who gave sociology and all the social sciences a new methodological base. Weber reconciled the empirical, idealist, and intuitionist* theories of knowledge with his definition of the "ideal type." According to Weber, ideas like "the economic man," "feudalism," "the state," "capitalism," are abstract constructions with which real situations or actions are compared in order to explain certain of their significant components. In other words, the social scientist should observe phenomena (empiricism), see certain basic similarities in the phenomena, and construct an "ideal type" that accentuates these similarities. Because the "ideal type" ignores individual variations, it is abstract. In this respect it resembles the pure idea of the idealist theories of knowledge; but, unlike the idealists and intuitionists, Weber maintained that the "ideal type" was purely fictional. Its only "truth" lay in the rational understanding it gave of the human world. With the intuitionists, however, Weber recognized the importance of imagination and insight as sources of the "hunches" that help us to see the crucial similarities in phenomena.

Weber stressed the relative character of knowledge and insisted that it be judged by its results. If the "ideal type" "capitalism" helps us to understand economic behavior in modern Europe, it is a valid concept in this context; if it does not help us to understand economic behavior in ancient Egypt, it is not a valid concept in that context. Validity, rather than "truth," is the ultimate test. Like Freud, Weber abandoned to the realm of the unconscious a vast field that could never be more than partially understood by our rational intellects. According to Weber, the social scientist should limit himself to those fields in which he can operate rationally. Within these fields he can add to our fund of knowledge, if he follows rigorous scientific procedures. But he can never know the whole truth about human behavior, as men like Comte and Spencer had thought he could. Finally, Weber said that all "ideal types" are subject to revision and refinement "through the expansion and shift of the scientific horizon." In other words, they are relative to some function.

Sociologists have tried to show how the group or class to which a person belongs provides him with status and gives meaning to the role he plays in it and in other groups. For each role-player has a number of "reference groups" whose expectations he would like to fulfill and whose beliefs (Durkheim's "collective representations") he shares. In fact, scholars concerned with the sociology of knowledge maintain that the beliefs of social groups and of whole societies are mainly determined by the functional context whose needs they serve.

*See p. 642.

Since the mid-1930s all the social sciences have adopted something of this functionalist approach, which interprets the world in terms of interconnection of operation rather than in terms of separate units like individuals and institutions. This trend parallels relativity theory as the basis for explaining physical phenomena and the new biological theory, which sees every organism as inseparable from a larger structure in which diverse types of organic and inorganic elements contribute to its proper functioning. Political science has analyzed the hidden factors that determine public policy and the informal ways in which official policy may be modified, subverted, or even destroyed in actual practice. History has been slower in adopting the functionalist approach, though few historians any longer view the past as a mere series of unique events. The experiences of the twentieth century have made many historians see that change does occur in patterns and that these patterns are heavily influenced by forces beyond the decisions of rulers and statesmen.

### Economics

In economics the theories of John Maynard Keynes have been particularly influential on public policy. By the 1920s the Scandinavian countries were already beginning to engage in government planning along lines parallel to those suggested by Keynes. In the 1930s the American New Deal used his theories to justify the measures it took to cope with the problems of the depression. Since the Second World War Great Britain, France, and many other countries have adopted the Keynesian approach in order to stimulate economic growth.

Keynes blamed the classical economic dogmas of "sound" financing, deflation in time of crisis, and free enterprise at all costs for the economic stagnation and chronic unemployment in his native Britain during the 1920s. From then on he undertook to prove that governments could manipulate the economy without resorting to socialism. He argued that the normal levels of capital inventment and consumption were insufficient to create full employment. His solution was government encouragement of more private investment (called "pump-priming" in the United States) through a lower interest rate, monetary expansion, long-term credits, and public works. Keynes contended that even "wasteful" public works were justified if they created jobs and thus stimulated consumption.

Keynes based his theories on the new functionalist approach. The classical economists, whom he scorned even more than he did the socialists, had analyzed the factors of supply and demand in the context of the individual business firm. In place of this "microeconomics" Keynes stressed "macroeconomics," the analysis of interconnections within the economy as a whole. He also said that psychological factors had to be taken into account in economic behavior and charged that the economic man of the classical economists was a myth. Real human beings were not that rational: consumers often bought things they did not need; labor leaders stubbornly denied the logic of taking a wage cut in a time of depression and falling prices. Like so many theorists in other fields, Keynes judged economic policy by how well it worked, by the total output of goods and the volume of employment it succeeded in creating. He also emphasized short-run considerations. The classical economists argued that, in the long run, the natural laws of economics would set things right. "In the long run," Keynes retorted, "we are all dead."

Thus, since the turn of the century the social sciences have drastically altered the eighteenth- and nineteenth-century image of man as a rational being making choices among properly weighted alternatives. Freud, Durkheim, and Keynes stressed man's irrational behavior; Weber raised once again the age-old riddle of how the human mind can arrive at knowledge of man and society at all. More recently, the three social sciences that deal most directly with human behavior—anthropology, psychology, sociology—have presented still another image of man. These sciences, which have taken the name behavioral sciences, have replaced earlier images of philosophical man, political man, economic man, and even psychoanalytic man with a new one, social man—man the social product, social producer, social seeker. In the words of David Riesman, behavioral science man is "other-directed." The traditional images of man emphasized reason or faith or impulse or self-interest as prime motives; the behavioral science image stresses the social definition of all of these. It is based on studies of Western man in a context of industrial civilization and mass culture, and no validity is claimed for it outside of this context. For behavioral scientists, like natural scientists, assure us that their findings are relative to both the setting they study and the conceptual framework within which they operate.

## PHILOSOPHY

The tendency of science to treat men as objects widened the gap between civilization and culture, between those things that merely support life and those that give it meaning. Although the attack on science as "inhuman" had already been voiced in the eighteenth century by Diderot, most nineteenth-century philosophers had reconciled their systems of thought to the emerging scientific-technological civilization of their time. The main cultural opposition to it had come from creative artists like Rimbaud, Gauguin, Wagner, and Dostoevsky, and reformers like William Morris. Before the 1890s Nietzsche had been the only major philosopher to launch a full-blown attack on modern civilization as totally stifling to culture. Thereafter, the divorce between the two was to become the overriding concern of philosophers. Yet even they become split between those who still tried to see life as part of some meaningful process and those who declared this effort bankrupt.

In the early 1900s Nietzsche's idea that superior men could surpass themselves had widespread appeal. It attracted a humanitarian socialist like the Irish playwright George Bernard Shaw and action-for-action's-sake poets like the Italian Gabriele D'Annunzio and the German Stefan George. In different ways each of them was reacting against the smugness with which his bourgeois contemporaries accepted the purely material progress of the age. According to these writers, nineteenth-century culture had come to a dead end, and they wanted to replace it with something that would give life new meaning. The Frenchman Henri Bergson (1859–1941) voiced this desire for a cultural regeneration in a way that made him the most popular and most widely translated philosopher of the early twentieth century.

In his *Creative Evolution* (1907), Bergson urged his contemporaries to shake off their complacency and sterile theorizing and to seek direct contact with life instead. He emphasized the primacy of intuition and instinct over intellect: "You must take things by storm; you must thrust intelligence outside itself by an act of will." Only in this way, according to him, could men achieve a higher stage of evolution, for living is a far more basic process than knowing. The knowledge revealed by science and mathematics is abstract; it facilitates action, but it does not penetrate to the instinctual stream of consciousness that surges beneath it. Bergson argued that only at this level of experience do we become aware of the life force (*élan vital*) which is the true reality. Men raise themselves to a higher plane through an increasingly precise, complex, and supple adaption of their consciousness to the conditions under which they live.

Bergson rejected the mechanistic-materialistic-deterministic views of life with which nineteenth-century thinkers had strait jacketed human freedom. According to him, there was room for real change and real freedom once men threw off this strait jacket "by an act of will." The life force, rather than mind or matter, is the fundamental reality. Intuition alone brings us into immediate contact with real life. The intellect misses what is unique and original, unforeseeable and irreversible—and it is from these sources that true human progress stems.

Bergson remained in the continental philosophical tradition, which sought verbal solutions to general problems on a theoretical level. In contrast, the American pragmatists William James (1842–1910) and John Dewey (1859–1952) sought contact with science, life, and culture while maintaining certain logical and analytical standards. Pragmatism was therefore a kind of intellectual half-way house between the speculative continental tradition and the noncommittal reportage of the British analytic philosophers, whom we shall discuss presently.

The essence of pragmatism is that the truth of any statement lies in its practical operation. If you want to know whether a theory of any kind is true, try believing it and see whether satisfactory results follow from it. James set forth this relativistic conception of knowledge in his *Pragmatism* (1907). It caused some Europeans to hail him as a savior, some to condemn him as an enemy of abstract speculation, and others to attack him for his denial of absolute moral standards. In his *Varieties of Religious Experience* (1902) he had shown how different types of belief were possible among individuals—just as anthropologists were showing how beliefs varied among individual cultures. But James earnestly felt that everybody should base his moral conduct on some belief. Put rather baldly, his argument went something like this: the truth is that which we ought to believe; that which we ought to believe is what is best (that is, which helps us function most effectively) for us to believe; therefore, the truth is that which is best for us to believe.

James remained ambiguous about the meaning of "we" and "us" in these propositions; Dewey said forthrightly: "What is utility if it is confined to a single person? Truth is public." More than any other philosopher Dewey tried to reconcile empirical science with the "normative" disciplines of logic, ethics, and aesthetics. In logical theory he held that the laws of deduction arise in the context of scientific inquiry. In politics he contended that intelligence was man's chief weapon in his fight for a free society and that both Communist and fascist totalitarianism were man's chief enemies. By the time his *Art as Experience* appeared in 1934 Dewey had given pragmatic treatment to the Beautiful as well as the True and the Good. In all cases, the test was empirical: "If operation $O$ is performed on this, then $E$ is experienced."

Dewey's "operational" criterion was close to that of the analytic philosophers, who maintained that concepts and assertions are meaningless if no operations can be specified that define the former and test the latter. Unlike the pragmatists, however, they have attached small importance to philosophy as a social force or as an instrument of cultural criticism. These philosophers stemmed from the tradition of British empiricism, especially David Hume; they were also part of an international movement that sprang from important logical, mathematical, and scientific developments in the nineteenth and twentieth centuries. This movement, called first logical positivism and later logical empiricism, had its roots in Cambridge University, particularly in the prewar writings of Bertrand Russell (1870–1968), and in postwar Vienna, particularly in the writings of Rudolf Carnap (b. 1891) and Ludwig Wittgenstein (1889–1951).

Russell and Carnap argued that only by using the unambiguous language of symbolic logic could philosophy speak with clarity and precision; Wittgenstein hoped to achieve this goal through the careful use of ordinary language. But all three men tried to clear away the "verbal magic" from philosophy and thus show how most of its traditional issues were meaningless. Hegel had tried to synthesize these issues through the added dimension of the Absolute; Marx had tried to do so by reducing everything to material conditions. The analytic philosophers rejected both Hegel's "something more" and Marx's "nothing but" and concerned themselves exclusively with "what is what."

This revolution in philosophy reflected the other revolutionary developments in twentieth-century civilization and culture. We have already noted the new "languages" that physical and social scientists invented in their efforts to explain phenomena beyond the ken of traditional "common-sense" language; we shall discuss similar efforts in literature and the arts later. Problems in semantics also arose in political life, where familiar words like democracy came to mean different things to an American liberal, a British socialist, and a Russian Communist. Analytic philosophers have tried to analyze all these new problems of language.

The approach to Wittgenstein has had the most influence. In his *Tractatus Logico-Philosophicus*, published in Vienna in 1921, he used a set of terse and intentionally provocative propositions of his own to show how the propositions of traditional philosophy were devoid of meaning—how they did not really say anything that could be verified by any objective standard. The last proposition of the *Tractatus* reads: "Whereof one cannot speak, thereof one must be silent." Having thus given the death sentence to traditional philosophy, Wittgenstein gradually modified his extreme position. In 1929 he settled in Cambridge, England, where he devoted his efforts to clarifying the meanings of words by examining their use.

In his *Philosophical Investigations* (published posthumously by his former students in 1953) Wittgenstein said that the rules by which we use words are like the rules of a game. Since we use several sets of rules for different purposes (naming, describing, commanding, evoking, etc.) we play several language games. We learn each game by seeing how examples are used in a particular way, rather than by learning abstract definitions. "*The meaning is the use.*"

This analytic conception of language has had a widespread impact. In the academic world it spread from the philosophy department at Cambridge to Oxford and to a number of American universities. It has helped science rid itself of such unverifiable entities as "ether" and "essences"; it also shows signs of spreading to the language of law, history, politics, literature, and aesthetics. Present-day diplomatic and military strategists play language games in trying to decipher the pronouncements of the Kremlin and in anticipating the number of bombs enemy *x* may use in his first strike. Even computers can play.

Long before the explosion of the first atomic bomb made everybody anxious about the future of civilization, a number of continental philosophers became preoccupied with the anxiety, boredom, and dread of human existence in an alien and hostile world. These men, the existentialists, rejected logical empiricism and pragmatism without, however, reverting to neo-idealism or intuitionism. Their concerns had first been expressed by the Dane Sören Kierkegaard in the first half of the nineteenth century. Dostoevsky and Nietzsche have also been seen as forerunners of existentialism because of their interest in dark emotions and uncommon men. After the First World War the writings of Martin Heidegger and Karl Jaspers had a certain vogue among Germans haunted by despair, anguish, and forlornness; the Second World War was to provoke a similar interest in existentialism in France.

The basic thesis of existentialism is that human existence has no rhyme or reason; a man simply *is*. When existentialists speak of the "absurdity" of this situation they mean that it cannot be explained by anything more fundamental. Christian existentialists like Jaspers save themselves from complete despair by an act of blind faith in a God whose mode of existence they cannot understand. Atheistic existentialists like the Frenchman Jean-Paul Sartre (b. 1905) accept the absurdity of existence as the basis of a "dreadful freedom" from any external guidance or restraint.

Like analytic philosophy, existentialism rejects all traditional certainties and all determinisms, but instead of ignoring moral issues it maintains that these are the *only* issues. Dostoevsky once wrote "If God did not exist, everything would be permitted." Sartre agrees. Yet he contends that even though man does not know how or why he was created he is nevertheless responsible for everything he does, not only to himself but to all mankind. Sartre bases this contention on the following agrument (in his *Existentialism and Humanism*):

> "The man who lies in self-excuse, by saying "everyone will not do it," must be ill at ease in his conscience, for the act of lying implies the universal value which it denies."

One does not have to be a Wittgenstein to see flaws in Sarte's argument. The important point is that it expressed the anguish of many sensitive Europeans faced with difficult choices in a world dehumanized by science, machines, bureaucracies, world world wars, fascism, Communism—in other words, by a civilization of their own making.

## CRISIS IN THE ARTS

Europe's artists and poets made the earliest and most creative cultural responses to their changing civilization. As in the past, the degree to which they broke with traditional forms reflected the degree of change they saw. In the fifteenth and sixteenth centuries they had forecast the transition from medieval to modern civilization with radically new aesthetic forms. Since then new styles had highlighted new cultural concerns without completely abandoning the aesthetic framework of the Renaissance. For all its revolutionary pronouncements, even romanticism had remained representational in painting and had preserved traditional tonalities in music and conventional language and syntax in literature. By the 1880s post-impressionist painters like Van Gogh and symbolist poets like Mallarmé were heralding certain twentieth-century trends, but the real revolution in the arts began around 1905. It was unique in both its extremes and its duration. Indeed, if we were to judge twentieth-century culture from the arts alone, we would see it as reflecting a permanent state of crisis.

The political and economic upheavals of the period 1905–1940 changed the way in which many artists and writers viewed their scientific-technological civilization without deterring them from their basic search for new kinds of truth and beauty. This search took two basic forms—Expressionism and abstractionism—both of which destroyed the façade of conventional realism in nineteenth-century art and literature. Expressionism and the related movements of Neoprimitivism, Futurism, and Surrealism all asserted the primacy of emotion. The trend toward abstraction, beginning with Cubism and continuing in Constructionism and Purism, sought to impose some kind of new order on the world through the intellect. This abstractionist tendency paralleled new developments in theoretical physics, while Expressionism and its sister movements paralleled new developments in psychology and anthropology, especially the new stress on the unconscious and the "discovery" of primitive art. It should be noted, however, that many creative artists moved from one new "language" to another and that some combined both in a single work.

### New Forms For a New Civilization

The Expressionist revolt had its roots in Van Gogh and Rimbaud. Like Rimbaud, Expressionist writers longed for reality in terms of an inner vision; like Van Gogh, Expressionist artists wanted to penetrate beneath the world as we see it, in order to bring out those basic urges they believed to lie behind visual reality. Expressionism dominated German avant-garde literature and drama from 1910 to 1925. Among the most prominent Expressionist painters were the German Emil Nolde (1867–1956) and, before 1914, the Frenchman Henri Matisse (1869–1954) in his *fauve* (literally, "wild beast") period. The Italian poet Filippo Tommaso Marinetti (1876–1944) wrote a *Manifesto of Futurism* (1909) demanding the creation of a dynamic personal experience as an end in itself. In its revolt against nineteenth-century bourgeois culture Expressionism resorted to caricature, ugliness, the sounds and images of primitive tribes, and anything else that would expose the raw emotions underneath the polite façade.

The revolution in the arts around 1905 manifested itself in many parts of Europe, but Paris was its center. There the Polish-French poet Guillaume Apollinaire (1880–1918) tried to cope with the modern world on its own terms, and to describe it energetically and precisely; he was not afraid to write about automobiles, airplanes, the Eiffel Tower, or gas lamps spurting their flames in the moonlight. There the Spanish painter Pablo Ruiz Picasso (b. 1881) and the Russian composer Igor Stravinsky (b. 1882) rejected the egocentric cult of personal sensitivity and harked back to the most elemental, that is primitive, expressive forms they could recapture. Picasso drew his inspiration from African masks. Stravinsky combined Russian folk legend with strident tones

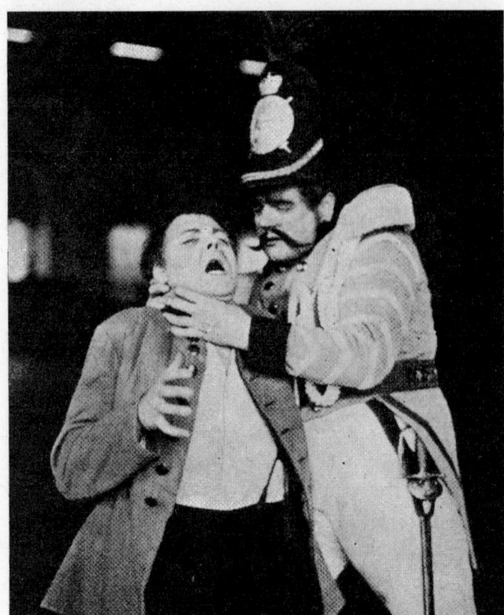

A scene from Alban Berg's opera, Wozzeck

and barbaric rhythms in his music for the ballet "The Rite of Spring," which caused a riot at its first performance in 1913. For in Paris, more than anywhere else, the creators of new artistic forms pitted themselves against growing social conformity and passionately asserted their belief that there *can* be something new under the sun. They sought to blend art and life as a means of preserving spiritual meaning in a godless universe.

Cubism was the second new aesthetic form, or "language," of the pre-1914 decade. Originally applied to painting, the term came to include the other arts; Apollinaire, for example, called himself a Cubist poet. Cubist painters tried to show the public what is actually seen in the kaleidoscope of modern life. Instead of portraying whole individuals discreetly draped and at the center of interest they painted tangles of limbs and heads caught in motion, anonymous, and with no order among themselves except for that given by the observer. In Marcel Duchamp's "Nude Descending a Staircase" (1912)* the subject and the occasion no longer matter. What matters is the interest of seeing a new vision of the human form, conditioned by the abstract idea of motion and by the added dimension of time. the art of Cubism tried to make the peculiar complexities and abstractions of the industrial age tangible.

The most important new "language" in twentieth-century music was also invented before 1914. This was the twelve-tone serial system of Arnold Schoenberg (1874–1951), who lived in the Vienna of Freud and Wittgenstein. Schoenberg abandoned all traditional chordal combinations and melodic contours and based his compositions on an arbitrary arrangement of the twelve chromatic tones, called a tone-row or series. The inversions and transpositions of these series follow strictly arithmetical rules. The resultant sound is grating, tense, and often frenetic, suggesting the feeling of an Expressionist painting or play. In 1922 Schoenberg's pupil Alban Berg (1885–1935) combined a modified form of the twelve-tone system with a half-spoken, half-sung kind of dialogue which heightened the eerie effect of his opera *Wozzeck,* whose macabre story prefigured the Czech novelist Franz Kafka.

In the 1920s the educated public became more tolerant of new aesthetic forms than it had been before the war. This change was due partly to the shock the war had given to bourgeois complacency, partly to the growing influence of science and technology, and partly to the tendency of some creative artists to use "tamer" though still unconventional forms. Matisse, for example, abandoned his prewar "wildness" for a polished semi-representational style; Stravinsky turned to neoclassicism; German Expressionist writers adopted a "New Realism" after 1925. The popularity of Freudian psychology made the public more receptive to Surrealism, which tried to give pictorial and literary form to the "language" of dreams. The Purist works of the painter Piet Mondrian and the sculptor Constantin Brancusi, the Constructionist paintings of Fernand Léger, and even the Abstract Expressionist paintings of Vasily Kandinsky, were easier to accept, if not understand, than Cubism.*

The new architecture tried most con-

*See p. 627.

*See pp. 627-628.

sistently to blend art and life, though at first the buildings of the German Walter Gropius, the Belgian-born Auguste Perret, and the American Frank Lloyd Wright seemed as bare, abstract, and indifferent to individual sensitivity as Cubist and Purist paintings. They looked raw with their concrete façades, their vast expanses of glass, and their undisguised metal beams and trim. By the 1930s skyscrapers had shed their Gothic and baroque ornaments for hard edges and bleak surfaces. their height was out of scale with humanity, but they were light and airy, and they visibly suggested the austere beauty of machinery. They were also eminently *functional* in serving social needs in a mass age. As Nikolaus Pevsner suggested over three decades ago: "Nearly every building that is designed nowadays serves masses, not individuals. Must not therefore our style be one adapted to mass production, in the sense of production not only in masses but also for masses?" In the 1930s strikingly successful examples of such adaptation included the London subway stations designed by Charles Holden, the 1937 Paris Exposition, and Rockefeller Center in New York.

### Literature and Drama in the Interwar Years

Whereas the new architecture accepted contemporary civilization on its own terms, avant-garde literature and drama were preoccupied with cultural and social criticism and the quest for personal identity in a disoriented world.

In the 1920s a number of important novels portrayed the young men and women who considered themselves a "lost generation" because they had grown up during the First World War. Having lost faith in the old certainties, they wanted to reject bourgeois moral standards, savor new experiences, and assert their personal independence. In England D. H. Lawrence's glorification of natural sexual desire, expecially in his *Lady Chatterley's Lover* (1928), reflected the postwar liberation of manners among that country's "lost generation." Hermann Hesse's *Demian* (1919) and *Steppenwolf* (1930) profoundly stirred the youth of Germany with their assaults on bourgeois hypocrisy and their pleas for the free expression of personal values. In France André Gide's *The Counterfeiters* (1925) depicted a bewilered and confused generation reacting against a rigid society whose traditional values were losing their meaning. While Gide's fictional heroes asserted their individuality through wanton misdeeds, real bohemians and flappers in Paris, London, Berlin, and New York were also trying to forget ethics, science, and history in their pursuit of fleeting pleasures in sex and sport.

The heroes of Marcel Proust and James Joyce were more introspective, and in their efforts to probe the basic mystery and anguish of life in the twentieth century these authors created new dimensions of time and experience. Proust's multivolume *Remembrance of Things Past* (1914–1922) is a semi-autobiographical work in which time is the world's fourth dimension and the ultimate realities are unique events. In this novel the protagonist tries to recapture all the events in his life in a gigantic dense mesh of complicated relations, with innumerable cross-references between different groups of characters. Proust felt that it was hopeless to seek his true identity in his ever changing consciousness and in the continual transformation of the world. Hence he sought to preserve his unconscious memories in a work of art, which alone might endure. In Joyce's *Ulysses* (1922) the hero is also searching for his lost self. The author transposes the myth of the Greek wanderer Ulysses to twentieth-century Dublin, where through an apparently hopeless confusion of word plays, parodies, and scraps of recollection, he has his hero carry out his lifelong quest for identity in a single day.

According to the symbolist poet T. S. Eliot, Joyce's use of mythical parallel in *Ulysses* was "simply a way of controlling, of ordering, of giving a shape and a significance to the immense panorama of futility and anarchy which is contemporary history. . . . It is a step toward making the modern world possible in art." Eliot's poem *The Waste Land* (1922) is itself the best known poetic criticism of the modern epoch, of the dreariness and desolation of a world of discarded ideals, frayed nerves, and meaningless pleasures. It too relies on "difficult" language and obscure allusions to primitive myth and ritual to "expose" the real inner world. The Austrian poet Rainer Maria Rilke used a similar symbolist approach in his *Sonnets to Orpheus* (1922) and, like Eliot, turned to religion in order to assuage his feelings of despair.

In Italy the playwright Luigi Pirandello took a different approach; he wanted to portray a reality that was valid psychologically rather than aesthetically. Thus in *Six Characters in Search of an Author* (1922) he brought two sets of players simultaneously on the stage: the members of a family desolated by domestic tragedy and the professional actors whom they implore to act out their personal drama. Each character offers his own version of the truth, and the audience is left to draw its own conclusions. Like most creative artists Pirandello was expressing his own personal convictions rather than reflecting the cultural climate. But the emotional desperation of his characters can be related to the growing concern over the meaninglessness and absurdity of conventional norms for behavior, which did not help individuals learn the truth about themselves, others, or life in general. Pirandello's outlook also had its parallels in Freud's stress on the irrational and the unconscious, Einstein's relativity, and Heisenberg's indeterminacy.

Poles apart from Pirandello's plays in both form and content were those of the German Berthold Brecht. They blamed the existing social structure for man's degradation and offered a kind of Marxist humanism as the means for ending this degradation. According to Brecht, man could acquire true individual dignity only under socialism. Like George Bernard Shaw, he was always lecturing his audience, but unlike Shaw he heightened the emotional impact of his message with all sorts of stage tricks and popular songs. His style, which he called "epic realism," was most effective in his plays of the 1920s, such as *A Man's a Man* and the *Threepenny Opera,* both of which used Expressionist symbols and jazz in lambasting the social evils with which they dealt.

In the 1930s many other writers became preoccupied with the evils of capitalist society. Some blamed these evils for the depression and the rise of fascism and turned to Marxism; The Frenchman Jacques Prévert began his poem *Late Rising* as follows:

*Terrible*
*is the soft sound of a hardboiled egg*
*cracking on a zinc counter*
*and terrible is that sound*
*when it moves in the memory of a man*
*who*
*is hungry.*

Other Western writers, including the American expatriate poet Ezra Pound, turned to fascist authoritarianism in their rejection of capitalism and its materialistic civilization. In many ways, however, the so-called literature of commitment was a new expression of the cultural alienation of Europe's artists and intellectuals, an alienation that the avant-garde of the prewar decade and the 1920s had tried to overcome through new aesthetic forms.

Despite their increasing tolerance for new forms, most educated Europeans preferred the "classics" to the avantgarde. They wanted to be reassured, not tormented; thus they chose Renoir over Picasso, Dickens over Joyce, *Lohengrin* over *Wozzeck.* But since the "rise of the masses," the consumption of artistic and intellectual culture increased faster than its production. Most creative artists and intellectuals did not "betray" their true calling by selling out to politics and business—as the French critic Julien Benda charged in *The Betrayal of the Intellectuals* (1927). Rather, their best works, along with those of the past, simply reached a growing audience through paperback books, radio, and state-sponsored musical and theatrical performances. Adult-education programs in the 1930s also increased the appreciation of the products of high culture. Still, the masses, including the bulk of the middle class, went on consuming *re*productions and watered-down versions of both the "classics" and the avantgarde: from Michelangelo to Mondrian, from Descartes to Dewey, from Italian provincial to Swedish modern.

## Mass Culture and Its Critics

Culture in the broadest sense makes life worthwhile by giving it meaning. Before the advent of industrial civilization each homogeneous society had its own culture, often with regional or class variants. This culture, and its variants, consisted of traditional patterns of behavior which in turn were based on certain shared values. The slow pace of change allowed ample time for new patterns of behavior and even new values to be integrated into the traditional way of life. In the history of European civilization we have seen many examples of the manner in which innovations were integrated into the cultural outlook of the upper and middle classes. The artistic innovations of the Renaissance, the religious innovations of the Reformation, the growth of capitalism, the development of representative government, the theories of Copernicus, Newton, and even Darwin—all were reconciled with the basic imporance accorded to the *individual* and his happiness.

In the twentieth century all traditional cultures have succumbed to mass culture. This has happened for two reasons: the rapid pace of industrialization and the "rise of the masses." The urban masses have asserted themselves more and more in politics, in economic life, and in the realm of taste. Once they got the vote, all political parties and movements catered to them; once they gained the right to strike, they were able to influence wages and prices (since their employers usually passed wage increases on to the consumer in the form of price increases): once they became large-scale consumers of cultural products, their level of taste began to determine the nature of these products.

Since there have not been enough products of high culture to give meaning to the lives of the masses, what about the cultural products created specifically for them? Before 1940, to what extent did mass culture give new meaning to life in a scientific-technological civilization? In the first quarter of the twentieth century American mass culture led the world in taking modern technology into account. Millions of American boys read *Tom Swift and His Motorcycle* and *Tom Swift and His Flying Machine;* millions of people of all ages saw the automobile chases in the silent films. By the 1930s radio, films, newspapers, and picture magazines in Europe also began to convey up-to-date, though superficial, images of scientific-technological civilization—and the media themselves were obviously technological marvels. But the deeper implications of this civilization rarely came through in the mass media, which lacked the power of the true art to bring out such implications. There were occasional exceptions in motion pictures such as the German-made *Metropolis* (1925) and the American-made *Modern Times* (1936), starring Charlie Chaplin. Otherwise mass culture before the 1940s gave as meaningless an interpretation of modern civilization as Jules Verne and the Ferris Wheel.

Even when dealing with basic human emotions mass culture failed to provide meaningful norms and models for behavior. It can be argued that that was not its function, and that it misappropriated this function when it took it in order to sell soap or a party line. Nevertheless, the masses had nowhere else to turn for such norms and models. Hence they got wrong ideas about basic human emotions from "soap operas," true-confession magazines, and the propaganda films of Nazi Germany and Soviet Russia. By the 1930s mass culture was creating a completely artificial and self-contained world of its own. A Dutch factory worker could listen to a football game on the radio, read a commentary on it in the next day's newspaper, and then go outside and see a billboard advertisement for razor blades or bottled drinks with an endorsement by one of the stars in the game. A French shopgirl could see Douglas Fairbanks or Rita Hayworth on the screen and then read an equally fictitious account of their private lives in a movie magazine while sitting under the hair-dryer.

During the interwar years a number of European intellectuals attacked both mass culture and the civilization that spawned it. In his book *The Revolt of the Masses* (first

*Douglas Fairbanks in a scene from The Three Musketeers*

published in Spanish in 1928) the philosopher José Ortega y Gasset blamed democracy, socialism, fascism, and sheer population growth for the overwhelming of traditional standards of good taste and self-discipline by the uncritical outlook of the ubiquitous masses. In France the novelist Georges Duhamel blamed the mechanization and dehumanization of modern life on "Americanization" in his *Scènes de la Vie Future* (1930), which was translated under the more telling title of *America the Menace*. Perhaps the most widely read indictment of modern technology and mass culture was the English novelist Aldous Huxley's *Brave New World* (1932). Here everyone and everything was completely controlled by a new brand of scientists and engineers, called "technocrats." They produced babies from test tubes, they "brainwashed" them as they grew up, and they supplied them with completely synthetic emotional sustenance through "feelies"* and a euphoria-producing drug called *soma*.

In Europe, as in the United States, the current media of mass communication have preserved the products of the mass culture of earlier decades for all to see. These old movies, old songs, old novels, old vaudeville routines, and even old billboards are already museum pieces, so fast has popular taste evolved. But for all its current sophistication, most mass culture remains what it has always been: pseudo-art and pseudo-thought. This is a fact, not a condemnation, and this fact is important because it helps us to understand the cultural crisis as it has affected the masses

*In the early 1930s movies were just becoming "talkies." Huxley added another dimension by imagining theater seats that would allow the spectators to share, vicariously, the sense of touch of the actors on the screen.

since the beginning of the twentieth century.

: : :

Huxley gave *his* "brave new world" the motto: "Ford's in his heaven; all's right with the world." It would have been just as ironical to replace Ford with Freud, Picasso, Einstein, or Wittgenstein, each of whom had anticipated some aspect of twentieth-century civilization and the culture it would produce. Huxley was writing for a depression audience that longed for the supposed security of preindustrial times, but there were other solutions and other gods. In the Soviet Union Marx was in *his* heaven and all was right with the world—at least according to the government-controlled mass media. Many writers in the West agreed, and without irony, but the majority did not. For them *anything* was better than the "brave new world" of Communism. Democracy muddled through without new gods or demigods in those countries of Northwestern Europe where it was most firmly entrenched. It failed to survive the First World War in Italy and the depression in Germany. Hence, along with Stalin, Mussolini and Hitler created the principal "brave new worlds" of the interwar years.

## SUGGESTED READINGS

Ellul, Jacques, *The Technological Society.* New York: Alfred A. Knopf, Inc., 1964

An eminent sociologist-historian's analysis of the triumph of technique and its inhuman consequences. Difficult reading, but provocative.

Friedmann, Georges, *Industrial Society.* New York: The Free Press of Glencoe, 1964.

An analysis of workers' attitudes and problems by a sociologist.

There is no satisfactory book on the world depression and its origins. Much information and analysis may be found on pp. 16–58 of the following technical study—the only one of its kind in any language:

Svennilson, Ingvar, *Growth and Stagnation in the European Economy.* New York: United Nations, 1954.

For a general interpretation, stressing the United States, see:

Berle, Adolf A., *The Twentieth-Century Capitalist Revolution.* New York: Harcourt, Brace, and World, 1955.

Heilbroner, Robert L., *The Worldly Philosophers.* Rev. ed. New York: Simon and Schuster, 1961.*

General history of the development of economic theories—see especially the section on Keynes.

Jones, Alan Pryce, ed., *The New Outline of Modern Knowledge.* New York: Simon and Schuster, 1956.

Excellent articles on the sciences and the arts.

Conant, James M., *Modern Science and Modern Man.* New York: Doubleday and Co., n.d. Anchor.*

Excellent description of what twentieth-century scientists do and how they have modified their earlier assumptions.

Barnett, Lincoln, *The Universe and Dr. Einstein.* Rev. ed. New York: New American Library of World Literature, n.d. Mentor.*

A first-rate explanation of Einstein's theories.

Heisenberg, Werner, *Physics and Philosophy: The Revolution in Modern Science.* New York: Harper and Row, n.d. Torchbook.*

By one of the leading participants in the twentieth-century revolution in physics.

Hall, Calvin S., *A Primer of Freudian Psychology.* New York: New American Library of World Literature, 1954. Mentor.*
A simplified account.

Hughes, H. Stuart, *Consciousness and Society: The Reorientation of European Social Thought, 1890–1930.* New York: Random House, 1963. Vintage.*
See especially the thoughtful analyses of Freud, Weber, and Durkheim.

White, Morton, *The Age of Analysis: 20th Century Philosophers.* New York: New American Library of World Literature, 1956. Mentor.*
Selections from all the major philosophers, with commentaries by a major authority.

Kaufmann, Walter, ed., *Existentialism from Dostoevsky to Sartre.* Cleveland: World Publishing Co., 1956. Meridian.*
Selections accompanied by an astute commentary.

Read, Herbert E., *Art and Society.* New York: Schocker, n.d.*
A thoughtful work by an outstanding critic.

Finney, Theodore M., *A History of Music.* Rev. ed. New York: Harcourt, Brace and World, 1947.
A good survey.

Pevsner, Nikolaus, *An Outline of European Architecture.* Baltimore: Penguin Books, 1960. Pelican.*
Especially interesting on the twentieth century.

Shattuck, Roger, *The Banquet Years: The Origins of the Avant-Garde in France, 1885–1918.* Garden City, N. Y.: Doubleday and Co., 1961. Anchor.*
Brilliant cultural history.

Samuel, Richard and R. Hinton Thomas, *Expressionism in German Life, Literature, and the Theatre.* Cambridge, Eng.: W. Heffer and Sons, 1939.
Detailed cultural history.

Cassou, Jean and others. *Gateway to the Twentieth Century: Art and Culture in a Changing World.* New York: McGraw-Hill Book Co., 1962.
A magnificently illustrated volume on the artistic revolution of early 1900s.

Barr, Alfred H., *Masters of Modern Art.* Rev. ed. Garden City, N. Y.: Doubleday and Co., 1959.
A fine survey—richly illustrated.

Golding, John, *Cubism, a History and Analysis, 1907–1914.* New York: George Wittenborn, 1959.
A good technical study.

Wilson, Edmund, *Axel's Castle: A Study of the Imaginative Literature of 1870–1930.* New York: Charles Scribner's Sons, n.d.*
Written over three decades ago, this is still the best general study of the literature of the early decades of the twentieth century.

Tindall, William York, *Forces in Modern British Literature 1885–1946.* New York: Vintage, n.d.*
Suggestive studies by an eminent literary critic.

Peyre, Henri, *French Novelists of Today.* New York: Oxford Univ. Press, n.d.*
See especially the sections on Proust and Gide.

Crossman, R. H. ed., *The God That Failed.* New York: Harper and Row., n.d. Colophon.*
Revealing "confessions" of six major writers who were attracted to Communism during the interwar years.

CHAPTER XVIII

# TOTALITARIAN EUROPE, 1919-1939

In 1919 Russia was already Communist, but Spain and Portugal, Germany and Italy, and almost every small state in Eastern Europe had at least the formal trappings of parliamentary democracy. By 1939 all had succumbed to some form of dictatorship. Only Italy and Germany became truly fascist, but all these dictatorships were part of a general trend toward the replacement of liberal societies with totalitarian rule.

Totalitarianism, which means state control over all aspects of national life, has taken hold wherever the existing regime has failed to fulfill the aspirations of large sections of the community. Today it is most familiar in its Communist variety, but from the end of the First World War to the end of the Second, Communism held sway only in the Soviet Union. Except where it has been imposed by an outside power, Communist totalitarianism has arisen in societies that were economically backward and lacking in a liberal tradition. Fascism, on the other hand, the main form of totalitarianism during the interwar period, developed most fully in economically advanced nations whose citizens felt cheated by the outcome of the First World War and whose liberal governments could not hold them together morally in the face of economic hardship, rabble-rousing nationalists, and fear of a Communist revolution.

The two kinds of totalitarianism also differ widely in their goals. The main goals of fascism were to replace the "decadent" liberal society that had spawned it with a militaristic state and to end the "dreadful freedom" of individual existence by fostering feelings of national or racial pride. The main goal of Communism has been to end poverty and social injustice through material progress.

Totalitarianism was more than just a one-party political system; it was a technique for creating a new way of life—the "perfect final society of mankind. Once in power a totalitarian party, whether Communist or fascist, did more than eliminate all political rivals. It also tried to take over all organizations that might promote competing values: churches, labor unions, schools, youth groups, and fraternal societies, as well as the mass media of communication. The party directed its system of terroristic police control not only against demonstrable opponents of the regime but against arbitrarily selected sections of the population as well: the "bourgeoisie" in Russia, the Jews in Germany. Minority groups and cultural pluralism had no place in the "brave new worlds of Communism and fascism.

## COMMUNIST RUSSIA

For all its pretensions toward being the wave of the future, the Communist regime of the Soviet Union was the product of a series of historical accidents and of the determined efforts of two powerful leaders: V. I. Lenin and Josef Stalin. In Chapter XVI we saw how the unpopularity of the First World War and the weakness of Kerensky's Provisional Government created the opportunity for the Communists to seize power in November 1917. The ability of the Communists to take advantage of this opportunity rested on the absolute party discipline that Lenin had been fostering since 1902, the lack of coordination among the counterrevolutionary forces, and the lack of large-scale Allied intervention in the Russian Civil War. Here the organizing genius of Leon Trotsky was crucial. In the 1920s, however, Trotsky was downgraded and finally eliminated by Stalin, who gave Communist totalitarianism the stamp of his own personality until his death in 1953.

Yet it was Lenin himself who laid the foundations of a monolithic state and who temporarily abandoned the Marxist goal of world revolution, thus paving the way for Stalin's un-Marxist one of "socialism in one country." All rival parties were eliminated at the end of the Civil War, and periodic purges thereafter rid the ruling party of nonconformists. The party shifted its economic, social, cultural, religious, and nationalities policies without ever abandoning its goals of material progress and the total regimentation of Soviet life. Through an accident of history the state and the party were separate, but by 1939 all high-and medium-ranking government officials were members of the Communist Party. So were most army officers, school teachers, factory managers, and heads of collective farms. The party dictated the standards of personal morality, aesthetic taste, and scientific truth. In its combined role of entrepreneur, Big Brother, cheer leader, and policeman, it tried to create a new, socialist civilization.

### Lenin's Consolidation of Power, 1921–1922

At the end of the Civil War the Communist Party faced the severest crisis in its history. This small band of men had grappled with enemies on all sides and had won in the face of incredible hardships. Their victory enhanced their conviction that they alone were on the side of history, but the country was devastated, and even Lenin conceded that the "overwhelming majority" of the people had turned against Communist rule. By 1921 production on the land had fallen to half the total for 1913, industrial production to between a quarter and a third. Peasants in bands of tens of thousands rebelled against the government's forced food requisitions and shouted "Down with the Communists!" Hundreds of thousands of homeless children roamed the countryside in wolf packs and terrorized the authorities in the largest display of juvenile delinquency on record. The Mensheviks and the Social Revolutionaries were gaining new followers, and there was growing dissension within the top rank of the Communist Party itself. In late February 1921 a wave of strikes in Petrograd was suppressed only through wholesale arrests. Finally, on March 2, six days before the opening of the Tenth Party Congress, the party was shaken to its very foundations by the news that the garrison of the naval base at Kronstadt and the sailors of the Baltic Fleet had revolted and had set up a Provisional Revolutionary Committee.

The Kronstadt revolt was something neither Marx nor Lenin had foreseen: a proletarian uprising against the dictatorship of the proletariat. Long renowned for their savage revolutionary ardor, the sailors voted a resolution demanding new elections for the workers' and peasants' soviets, freedom of speech for all workers' and peasants' political parties (Mensheviks and Social Revolutionaries), the abolition of the privileged position of the Communist Party, and equal rations for all. Lenin, however, had decided that Communist Party rule and socialism were identical. Despite the obviously spontaneous and popular character of the Kronstadt uprising, the Tenth Party Congress called it

*Lenin Addressing an outdoor meeting in Moscow*

"counterrevolution." The Red Army was dispatched from Moscow, and the soldiers' reluctance to fire on sailors and workers was overcome by skillful propaganda, threats, and lies. The revolt ended on March 18 with the fall of the Kronstadt fortress. Then Lenin quickly applied himself to consolidating party rule on a new and more secure basis.

### *NEP and New Party Machinery*

By 1920 Lenin had defined the role of the party as "unlimited power based on violence, and bound by no laws." The party should use terror not only in repressing those elements regarded as by nature opposed to the revolution—the bourgeoisie, and the "petty bourgeoisie" among the peasants—but also against those sections of the proletariat that resisted Communist rule. In 1921 Lenin declared that the dictatorship of the proletariat, which meant the dictatorship of its vanguard, the party, was in itself "the continuation of the class struggle by other means." It would have to go on indefinitely, but it would also have to increase its support from the toiling masses.

As a means of placating the dissident workers and peasants. Lenin persuaded the Tenth Party Congress, against considerable opposition, to adopt the New Economic Policy (NEP). Its first two steps were the replacement of forced requisitions of produce from the peasants with a graduated tax in kind and the sanctioning of a limited form of local trade. These moves favored the rich peasants, known as kulaks, and the petty traders, who were soon nicknamed Nepmen, though NEP's main purpose was to stimulate the production and distribution of food for Russia's starving millions. The news of the concessions to the peasants encouraged the peasant soldiers who were putting down the Kronstadt rebellion, but it caused a deep division within the ranks of the party itself. Trotsky and other "orthodox" Marxists condemned NEP as a "surrender" to capitalism. They argued that since the political superstructure of every society is determined by its economic base, the revival of private enterprise, even on a limited scale, would inevitably bring a revival of the bourgeois state, thus negating the gains of the Revolution. Lenin condemned this line of thinking as "The Children's Disease of 'Leftism' in Communism." He contended that the only way of saving the Revolution was with the support of the peasants and that, as long as the state retained control over the "commanding heights" of heavy industry and foreign trade, the socialist Revolution could eventually be completed.

Lenin considered NEP subsidiary to his main purpose of consolidating the power of the party. In the face of continuing hostility from the great mass of the population he insisted that the only way the party could maintain its supremacy was through absolute unity within its own ranks. At the Tenth Party Congress he inaugurated stiffer standards for recruitment and membership. By the beginning of 1922, through purges and defections, the number of members and candidate members fell from 730,000 to 515,000. Most of the defectors were revolutionary romantics who became disillusioned with the growing bureaucratization of the party; most of those expelled were "careerists" who had joined at the end of the Civil War, when membership in the party no longer called for self-sacrifice. Henceforth, all members of the party had to submit unquestioningly to "proletarian" orthodoxy and discipline as defined by the Politburo (Political Bureau).

The Politburo was the high command of the party. Originally composed of five men, its membership was increased to seven in 1922 and fifteen in the 1930s. These men made all the major policy decisions in both the party and the government, where they held the most important cabinet posts.

After 1919 no one outside the Politburo could successfully challenge its authority. At the time of the Revolution the nineteen-member Central Committee had been the party's only coordinating agency at the national level. Theoretically, the local cells elected members to regional organizations which in turn chose the delegates to the national Party Congress, which met only once a year. The rest of the time the Central Committee made all the major decisions, but within its ranks the members of the Politburo gained supreme power during the Civil War.

Two other organizations created during the Civil War to strengthen the party apparatus were the Orgburo (Organizational Bureau) and the Secretariat. In contrast to the Politburo, which dealt with public policy, the Orgburo concerned itself with internal party matters, especially discipline. The third subcommittee, as it were, of the Central Committee was the Secretariat, a kind of permanent administrative board for dealing with routine party affairs not requiring the attention of the Orgburo. Controlling as they did virtually all aspects of the country's life, these party agencies offered great opportunities to the man who could manipulate them in pursuit of his own ends. Stalin, who from 1922 onwards was the only man to be a member of all of them, was to make the most of his opportunities.

### The Structure of the State

Parallel to the structure of the party was the structure of the Soviet state. The relations between the two had grown out of the conditions and circumstances of the Revolution, without being willed or planned by anyone. As we saw, the local and regional soviets had their own Congress and their own Central Executive Committee, which, renamed the Union Soviet of the Supreme Soviet in 1936, became a rubber-stamp legislature for the decisions of the Politburo. In the executive branch of the government the party used the internal security police to eliminate its enemies. Founded during the Civil War as the Cheka, this agency was transformed in 1922 into the GPU (State Political Directorate) of the People's Commissariat of the Interior (the NKVD), and in 1923 into the OGPU, or Unified State Political Administration. The Soviet state had its own legal and judicial system, but the party infiltrated it through its "procurators" and was itself above the law. Discretionary repressive powers were not confined to the OGPU but were made an integral part of normal criminal law and procedure.

Meanwhile, when NEP was introduced, the Communists used all the police and judicial powers at their disposal to persecute their old rivals the Mensheviks and the Social Revolutionaries. These two socialist parties could no longer be tolerated now that their more gradualist policies had been adopted as a matter of expediency. Otherwise, people might have asked why they should not be allowed to share power with the Communists. Thus in the spring of 1921 a legal ban on both parties was adopted. It effectively eliminated the last organized political opposition to Communist rule. The show trial for the Social Revolutionary leaders took place in 1922; the main one for the Mensheviks, not until 1931. The next few years after 1922 emphasized peaceful consolidation rather than terror.

### Picking Up the Pieces, 1921–1927

Freed from the threats of political opposition at home and military intervention from abroad, the Communist Party of the Soviet Union lost some of its revolutionary ardor. Though only a temporary expedient, NEP seemed to be a real return to a limited kind of free enterprise. Both peasants and craftsmen were encouraged to sell their products on the open market with the help of a new class of commercial traders, the Nepmen. Even the state-controlled sector of the economy was somewhat decentralized, and trade agreements were sought with the "capitalist" countries, especially Great Britain and France. By 1924 the peasants were paying their taxes in a new, stable currency issued by a new state bank. There was no limit on private incomes, and property in land could be passed on to one's offspring. In Moscow rich Nepmen patronized reopened night clubs and gambling houses, where the doormen greeted them with the prewar title of *barine*. Dedicated party members deplored all this "bourgeois decadence." They wanted to institute a new Communist morality based on self-sacrifice, free love, and proletarian comradeship. The party leadership temporarily tolerated their experiments in both morality and the arts, but its main concern lay in more "practical" matters.

Still suspicious of the outside world, the Politburo nevertheless sought to establish normal diplomatic relations with other countries. In 1921 the Soviet government signed treaties with all of Russia's neighbors except Poland, and ambassadors were exchanged with Great Britain and France three years later. The failure of the world revolution in the immediate postwar period prompted the Politburo to abandon the policy of "revolutionary adventurism," that is, aid to foreign Communist uprisings, in Europe by 1923 and in China by 1927.*

Neither Lenin nor his successors renounced the *idea* of world revolution, but they began to use the new Communist International, or Comintern, more as an instrument of Soviet foreign policy than as a means of overthrowing foreign governments. Technically, the Comintern was simply an organization of world Communist leaders meeting "temporarily" in Moscow but not directly associated with the Soviet government. Thus, even when these foreign Communists were instructed to foment trouble in their respective countries, the Soviet government could disavow any responsibility for their actions. It wanted to be free to put its own house in order without the danger of foreign reprisals; it also needed foreign trade and foreign specialists, especially for the initial stage of its program of rapid industrialization, which began in 1928.

#### *The Nationalities Problem*

Since the revolution was apparently not going to spread in the foreseeable future, the Russian Communists had to give their own country a new constitution. A major problem here was what to do about the non-Russian nationalities within its borders. During the Revolution and the early stages of the Civil War the Communists, wishing to end all vestiges of tsarist imperialism, had offered these nationalities the right to a separate, independent existence. By 1920 the party's obsession with centralized control won out, and within the next two years all the territories of the former tsarist empire except Estonia, Latvia, Lithuania, Bessarabia, and Poland were forcibly reintegrated. In the Constitution of 1924 the Ukrainian, Belorussian, and Transcaucasian Soviet Republics were joined with the Russian Socialist Federated Soviet Republic in the Union of Soviet Socialist Republics (USSR). Excluding the Ukrainians and Belorussians, the Great Russians were a bare majority in this multinational union, but the Constitution, though federal in structure, left to the member republics sole competence only in matters of economics, justice, education, and welfare. Even in these areas their competence was limited by the party machine, controlled in Moscow, of which the Constitution made no mention. And everyone know that the right of secession, "guaranteed" by the Constitution, was no more than a mockery. The backward areas of the Caucasus and Central Asia were soon to benefit from the economic and technological advances promoted by the Five Year Plans. But their nationalist aspirations, even when voiced by native Communists, were never allowed to get out of hand.

### *The Emergence of Stalin*

Stalin, the main proponent of this nationalities policy, was himself a Georgian, born in 1879 of peasant stock in a small town near Tiflis. His real name was Josef Vissarionovich Dzhugashvily, but like all revolutionaries under the tsarist regime he adopted several aliases, finally settling on Stalin (from the Russian word for "steel"). It was a most suitable name for such a hard, tenacious, and apparently feelingless man. Since 1912 he had been a member of the Bolshevik Central Committee, a member of the Politburo since 1919, and Party Secretary beginning in 1922. Although Lenin found him too "rude," and Trotsky described him as "the outstanding mediocrity of the Party," Stalin had made himself indespensable as a party organizer behind the scenes. He became the chief contender for party leadership after Lenin's death in January 1924.

The story of how Stalin eliminated Trotsky and all other opponents to his control of the party is too complex to tell in a short space; only his basic methods can be mentioned. One method was to build up an anti-Trotskyite coalition within the seven-man Politburo itself. This group's hostility to Trotsky, based more on political rivalry than on ideology, illustrates the kind of ruthless in-group fighting typical of most totalitarian, one-party states. Stalin's allies in this coalition were discarded later. His second method was to use his powers as Party Secretary to gain support within the rank-and-file of the party. Trotsky was better known and more popular with the urban masses than Stalin, but he was too proud and vain to engage in the kind of back-room intrigue at which Stalin was so adept.

In spite of Trotsky's public popularity and his ability as a theoretician, the majority of party members found him tiresome in his demands that the party think in terms of an imminent world revolution. They wanted to concentrate on ruling Russia, and Stalin won their backing with his new slogan of "socialism in one country." As for the proletariat, it remained an apathetic spectator while the two factions, each claiming to speak in its name, fought out their battles. These were strictly a party matter and Stalin had made himself master of the party. Within three years he stripped Trotsky of his posts in the government and the party and finally had him expelled from the party altogether. In 1928 Trotsky began a period of exile that was to end twelve years later in Mexico City with assassination by an agent of Stalin's police. Meanwhile, Stalin inherited Lenin's mantle and inaugurated an economic program that was to transform the daily lives of the Russian people far more than the political revolutions of March and November, 1917.

## Stalin's Third Revolution, 1928–1940

Under Stalin Russian Communism deviated increasingly from orthodox Marxism. Soon after the November Revolution Lenin had heralded this deviation with the slogan; "Electrification plus Soviet power equals communism." During the Civil War Trotsky as well as Lenin had sanctioned police-state methods that would have horrified Marx. Then, beginning in the late 1920s, Stalin carried through an un-Marxist Third Revolution with his "socialism in one country" and his personal dictatorship. But Stalin was not simply a ruthless politician; he was determined to catapult Soviet soceity into the industrial age both economically and culturally by "catching up with and overtaking" the capitalist countries. This was an extraordinary goal, given the backwardness of the country in 1928 yet it was already being partially realized by 1940. In this respect at least, the great Soviet experiment won the admiration of Marxists and non-Marxists alike in the West.

### *The Five Year Plans*

The First Five Year Plan and its successors, with their dual goal of industrialization and the collectivization of agriculture, revolutionized every aspect of Soviet life. Between 1928 and 1940 the gross national product doubled. In addition to furnishing capital for further industrial expansion this increase provided unprecedented revenues for other purposes. For example, in 1940 the government could spend twenty-six times as much on defense as in 1928, and thus make the Soviet Union a first-class military power. Expenditures on communal services quadrupled, raising the standard of living in terms of education, health, and welfare far more than the mere 10 per cent increase in consumers' goods would indicate. Furthermore, by monopolizing these vastly expanded services, the government partially offset the public dissatisfaction it provoked through its administrative and police regimentation (now getting 3 1/2 times as much money as in 1928). The most dissatisfied group, the peasants, was also the largest—82 per cent of the total population in 1928, 60 per cent in 1940. Of those who remained on the land, 95 per cent were forced to work on collective farms. The 18 per cent who left the land went to the cities and the mines, where they helped to increase the industrial labor force from 10 to 30 per cent of the economically active population.

How were these remarkable advances achieved? By 1928, Russian industry had barely regained its prewar level, with no further rapid advance in sight. Industrial expansion requires capital, and there were no hopeful prospects of attracting foreign capital or of increasing foreign trade. It was therefore obvious that the peasants would have to provide the capital. The state forced the new collective farms to sell it their produce at one-eighth of the market price, the remaining seven-eighths constituting in effect a tax. That tax, plus the sales tax charged the consumer, and the ability of the government to keep real wages down while productivity went up, provided the main source of investment capital for the industrialization of the Soviet Union.

Although the collectivization of agriculture served this economic function, its original purpose has been different. All Communists agreed in principle that it represented the all-important step away from an individual, bourgeois system of ownership and production to a collective, socialist, economy; this was its ideological purpose. All Communists also resented the strengthening of "petty bourgeois" elements like the kulaks and the Nepmen and wanted to see them eliminated; this was the social purpose of collectivization. Stalin himself had a political purpose in mind, namely, to end the relative independence from all party control which the peasants enjoyed under NEP. He may also have calculated that to unleash a new class war in the countryside was the most certain way of assuring his own survival as dictator.

Planned originally as a gradual advance, the subjugation of the peasants was carried through at breakneck speed. In 1929, 25,000 party zealots were sent from the cities into the villages to organize collective farms and establish socialism. As peasant resistance mounted, their methods became more ruthless, not only against the so-called kulaks, but against the poorer peasants who refused to cooperate. Soon the brunt of the operation fell on the OGPU, whose officials participated in every one of its grim phases. Over half of the total peasant households were collectivized in five months.

This spectacular feat brought chaos to the countryside. The poorer peasants, convinced that all their needs would be met in a collective farm, slaughtered and ate their cattle and horses. During the process of "dekulakization" some 5 million people either died from hunger or

*Propaganda poster urging collective Farm workers to keep physically fit*

were sent to "re-education centers" (forced labor camps) in far-off Siberia and Central Asia. In March 1930 Stalin himself, in his famous article "Dizzy with Success," chastized the collectivizers for their excessive enthusiasm and their indiscriminate use of force. During the temporary respite that followed almost two-thirds of the 14 million peasant households that had been collectivized left the collective farms. Before long, however, their number began to increase again as the government resorted to less direct pressures. By 1931 almost 53 per cent of the farms were once again collectivized, by 1934 nearly three-quarters. But contrary to the lavish promises of the Plan, agricultural production was lower in 1933 than in 1928, and the number of cattle had declined by almost half. The peasants learned that resistance to collectivization did not pay; but they did not learn to like being forcibly deprived of their produce at compulsorily low state prices, and most of them failed to meet their production quotas through the 1930s.

Organization and regimentation of labor were much more successful in industry than in agriculture. Lack of knowledge and experience had led to many mistakes at first. Supply and demand were often not coordinated; goods were almost uniformly shoddy. Industrial workers fresh from the farm jammed the machinery and dropped their tools on one another's heads. Party zealots turned factory-managers did not know how to make their workers meet production quotas. Gradually, however, the Soviet authorities got more work out of the industrial labor force. They raised individual incentive by means of piece work, increasingly wide wage differentials, and "socialist competition." They made an example of a particularly energetic coal miner named Alexei Stakhanov, who reportedly overfulfilled his daily quota of hewing coal by 1400 per cent. "Shock brigades" of "Stakhanovites" were sent into all sorts of industrial enterprises to show the other workers how to speed up production and thus raise productivity. In the capitalist West the labor unions resisted these methods, but in the USSR the unions served as tools of the universal employer, the state, rather than as representatives of labor interests.

### *Stalin's Personal Dictatorship: The Great Purge*

From the Communist point of view the toiling masses could have no other interests than those of the state; after all, it *was* the dictatorship of the proletariat. Following the elimination of the regime's bourgeois and petty bourgeois enemies the main function of the party membership — over 2 million in the 1930s — was to promote the economic, social, and cultural policies of the Politburo. But the nature of Soviet politics changed under Stalin, who often ruled *over* the party — including the Politburo — rather than *through* it.

In the 1930s Stalin purged the party and the state of all opponents and suspected opponents of his absolute personal dictatorship. The great purge began in December 1934 with the assassination of Sergei Kirov, the party boss of Leningrad. His assassin, proclaimed to be a member of the Left (Trotskyite) Opposition, was shot, along with about a hundred alleged accomplices. Actually, Stalin himself had Kirov murdered in order to have an excuse to get rid not only of Trotskyites, "wreckers," and traitors, but also of the "Old Bolshevik" leaders who had participated in the 1917 Revolution and who had ideas of their own. After three public trials in 1936, 1937, and 1938, almost no leaders of any prominence were left. All but four had received the death penalty after having confessed — some under torture, others out of heroic loyalty to Soviet Communism — to the most fantastic charges.

The purge was not limited to party leaders; it spread to the rank-and-file membership of the party, virtually all branches of the government, the armed forces, and finally the political police itself. The total number of people arrested has been estimated at 8 million, and the survivors unanimously testify to teeming forced labor camps and crowded prison cells. The extraction of real confessions to imaginary crimes became a major industry among NKVD examiners. Fear of arrest, exhortations to vigilance, and perverted ambition generated new waves of denunciations, interrogations, and detentions. Most of the accused were utterly bewildered by the fate that had befallen them — from the obscure Communist Youth leader accused of talking to the wrong people, to Marshal Tukhachevsky, hero of the Civil War and suppressor of the Kronstadt revolt, accused of conspiring with Nazi Germany. In the end, two successive heads of the NKVD themselves fell victims to the purge.

Although the major purpose of the great purge was the violent transformation of Lenin's revolutionary party into a privileged and imperialistic caste, its magnitude reflected Stalin's psychotic fear of wholesale conspiracy and of constant threats to his power and his very life. Stalin understood that he could maintain the new order only if the purged Communist elite served his dictatorship in the name of "building socialism," and if it reasserted Russia's imperialist ambitions in the name of "the leading role" of Russian Communism in world Communism. Yet there was madness in his method. Undoubtedly there were real conspiracies and real threats to Stalin's personal dictatorship. But the man was also obsessed with phantom enemies.

Stalin went further than any other dictator in imposing his will and his ideas on his followers. This fact was all the more remarkable in view of his compulsive aloofness from the public and his almost total lack of human warmth. While Hitler and Mussolini ranted and strutted before huge crowds, Stalin always seemed like a remote demigod to the Soviet people and even to most party members. It was easy enough to manufacture an "image" of him as everybody's Big Brother — smiling benignly at admiring children, prize-winning writers, or dedicated coal miners, in posters and newsreels — to erect statues of him and to name streets and cities after him. Yet Stalin exerted his main leadership behind the scenes as the Party Secretary who, beginning in 1930, intervened personally in every branch of art and learning and in the rewriting of history. It was Stalin who defined "socialist realism" as a doctrine which, "being the basic method of Soviet artistic literature and literary criticism, demands of the artist a truthful, historically specific depiction of reality in its revolutionary development." It was Stalin who, in 1938, wrote the famous *Short Course on the History of the All-Union Communist Party* which for years thereafter was to remain the primary subject of study for young Communists, replacing not only other histories but the sources of Marxism as well. Finally, in

Stalin with two women collective farmers of Tadzhikistan at a conference of champion workers in cotton farming

1939, it was Stalin who "revised" Marxism and Leninism by announcing that the state would never "wither away" in the USSR as long as it was encircled by capitalist countries.

One of the supreme ironies of Stalin's dictatorship was the introduction of a new Constitution just before the height of the great purge. This 1936 Constitution was far more democratic than its 1924 predecessor, and it contained a long list of civil rights as well as obligations. It reemphasized the federal character of the USSR, whose component units were increased to eleven. The Soviet of Nationalities represented each of these eleven units and their national subdivisions; the Union Soviet represented the entire Soviet people on the basis of one deputy for every 300,000 inhabitants. Stalin claimed that the new Constitution was "the only thoroughly democratic constitution in the world" and that its international significance "could hardly be exaggerated" at a time when the "turbid wave of fascism . . . is besmirching the democratic strivings of the best people in the civilized world." But the niceties of this Constitution, which Stalin initiated for its propaganda effect at home and abroad, mattered little under his personal dictatorship. The great purge showed *that.*

**Soviet Society and Culture**

There was more to Soviet civilization than dictatorship, state socialism, and collectivized agriculture. From the beginning the party had tried to promote new, "proletarian" values to go along with the new political and economic structure: a classless society, "to each according to his needs," progressive education, free love, and the like. Slogans like these did not survive the First Five Year Plan. Instead, there was a return to values and institutions previously defined as typically bourgeois and now called socialist: "socialist competition," "socialist intellectuals," the socialist family," "socialist discipline," and—during the Second World War—"Soviet nationalism." The shift in usage from "proletarian" to "socialist" to "Soviet" by the early 1940s is significant, for it reflected the amalgamation of old and new, Western and Russian, elements in the society and culture of the Soviet Union.

The creation of a new, classless society on the ruins of the old seemed a relatively easy task at first. In 1917 and 1918 the landowning gentry disappeared rapidly as the peasants seized their land; the upper bourgeoisie was similarly eliminated when the Bolsheviks nationalized industry, finance, and trade. Most people in these two classes emigrated, along with many intellectuals. The clergy also suffered harsh persecution—low rations, lack of civil and political rights until 1936, loss of their property—though they were never completely annihilated. After having staged a brief comeback during the years of NEP, the petty bourgeois traders and kulaks were destroyed during the First Five Year Plan. Theoretically, then, all that was left were the "toiling masses" and their "vanguard," the Communist Party, whose leaders carefully nurtured their proletarian "image" by their simple style of living and dress.

### *Stratification and Regimentation*

This "idyllic" state of affairs gave way to a new system of stratification in the 1930s. Industrialization differentiates people according to their role—even under socialism. So do government bureaucracies—even under socialism. One observer found ten levels of occupation and status, from party chiefs, generals, and scientists at the top, through middle-range managerial and technical personnel, through lesser party and government functionaries, through teachers and bookkeepers, through the most productive ("Stakhanovite") workers, through the less productive workers and the more productive peasants, through the less productive peasants, to the bottom, where in 1939 there were some 10 million people in forced labor camps. Altogether, the "new class" of managers, intellectuals, and engineers came to compose about 15 per cent of the total population. It was distinguished by special privileges and high income as well as by occupation. Even the distribution of medals, prizes, and other material and psychological rewards for achievement was graded according to the recipient's status. The 1936 Constitution itself recognized the principle "to each according to his ability" and the existence of three classes: intellectuals, workers, peasants.

Although these arrangements seem terribly capitalistic and Western, Soviet society developed certain distinctive features of its own. First of all, of course, Soviet citizens could not accumulate fortunes based on profits, rent, or interest. Second, the emancipation of women, carried through in the early 1920s, was never rescinded: divorces and abortions became harder to get, but Soviet women worked in all occupations—from street cleaners to atomic scientists—as the equals of men in every respect. By the middle 'thirties, for example, almost half the doctors in the USSR were women. The third distinctive feature of Soviet society was its extensive welfare services, such as day nurseries for the children of working mothers, free medical and health care for all, prepaid resort vacations for the more productive workers, and a wide variety of organized leisure-time activities.

To Westerners, at least, the most notorious feature of Soviet society has been its high degree of organization and regimentation, which reached its peak in the 1930s. The labor unions were the main force for disciplining the workers. In trying to regiment and indoctrinate the peasants the party used not only its own local cells but the Machine Tractor Stations. Until they were finally abolished in 1958, these agencies provided indispensable mechanized aid to the collective farms, especially at harvest time; they also inculcated Communist propaganda and rooted out slackers and "wreckers." The party has been especially active in influencing the young through its youth organizations: Little Octobrists for children under nine, Pioneers for those aged nine to fifteen, and the Union of Communist Youth, or Komsomol, with members up to age twenty-six. The party has also worked with or directed innumerable organizations of all types: social, professional, cultural, athletic. Regimented leisure was first introduced in the Soviet

Union and soon became a hallmark of all totalitarian societies.

Regimentation and the Communist ideology developed an unmistakably Soviet style of culture: materialistic, optimistic, serious, over-organized, favoring quantity over quality, and always subject to the latest party "line." First of all, everyone had to be taught to read and write. In 1922 the government began to implement a large-scale educational program to establish schools for all children and to eliminate illiteracy among adults. Through a liberal expenditure of funds and a spirit of determination on the part of the teachers this program raised the literacy rate for all Soviet citizens over the age of ten from 51 per cent in 1926 to 83 per cent in 1940. Secondly, these citizens had to be provided with something to read. By the 1930s the State Publishing House was printing hundreds of thousands of books a year: technical books, self-improvement books, literary classics, and third-rate novels in the "socialist realism" vein. These novels praised Machine Tractor Stations, heroes in the battle to increase steel production, reforestation, or whatever the party decided had to be praised, or condemned, that year. Newspapers, magazines, radio, films, the theater, and even the circus acquired a distinctly Soviet flavor.

One of the main functions of Soviet education and culture was to instill the party "line" into the entire population. From kindergarten to university there were required courses in Marxism-Leninism. (Indeed, there were no "electives" in the Soviet curriculum.) In 1932 the party replaced the short-lived Russian Association of Proletarian Writers with the Union of Soviet Writers; again the changes in language are significant. The members of this new Union were required to act as "engineers of human souls" in the "building of socialism." Soviet science and scholarship continued to be directed by the prerevolutionary Academy of Sciences, though with a new attention to ideological considerations, even in such unlikely fields as physics and genetics.

Yet "building socialism" was more than a mere propaganda slogan imposed on an indifferent population. In the cities at least, millions of young Russians took pride in the regime's industrial achievements and in their own role in making these possible. Those workers who earned government-subsidized vacations at the once fashionable Black Sea resorts looked awkward in their sleeping pajamas, which were all they had in the way of "leisure apparel"; but the fact that they were there at all was a great advance over tsarist times. Hackneyed artistic and literary works in the "socialist realism" style had almost as much appeal to the Soviet masses as the works of Norman Rockwell and Edgar Guest (which they resembled) had to the American masses in the 1930s. In that period the main difference between "Andy Hardy" movies and Soviet films about ideal family life was "ideological"; in style they were equally banal. Three decades later both the Soviet and American masses were to acquire more sophisticated tastes. Meanwhile, for all its political excesses, Stalin's regime was molding the Russian people into a national community to an extent unmatched by the tsars. This fact was to become clear during the Second World War, when, contrary to their behavior in 1917, the Russians – if not the other peoples of the USSR – were to remain loyal to their leaders and to national – if not strictly Marxist – cultural values.

### *Relics from the Past*

Already in the 1930s Soviet education and culture began to borrow heavily from the prerevolutionary legacy. The high standards and serious academic character of Soviet schools dated from tsarist days; what the Communists did has been to disseminate education at all levels and on a vast scale. In general, the quality of Soviet creative work was highest – as in science and music – where prerevolutionary achievements were developed with the least interference from Marxist doctrine. On the level of popular culture the Communists finally discovered that traditional folk dances and folk songs had more appeal than synthetic "proletarian" models. By the late 1930s some of the "new class" of managers, engineers, and professional people even began to bow, kiss hands, and don impressive uniforms, as in tsarist times.

The one relic from the past which the

Communists were unable either to destroy or absorb has been religion. Outright persecution of the Russian Orthodox Church lasted well into the 1930s. Yet despite all the confiscations, executions, and exiles, and despite the efforts of the Militant Atheists' League, over half the Soviet citizens, mostly peasants, remained religious. This stubborn fact, along with the general social stabilization of the 1930s, persuaded Stalin and the Politburo to assume a more tolerant attitude toward religion. During the Second World War the Church gained added acceptance and standing through its patriotic behavior. Since then it has maintained complete loyalty to the regime in return for a constricted and precarious existence. But as the purveyor of an alternative set of values and beliefs, organized religion—Christian, Muslim, or Jewish—has no future in a system in which the only acceptable view is the Communist view.

Soviet civilization, then, is a unique blend of Western and Russian elements. Like Peter the Great, Stalin wanted Russia to "catch up" with the West in industrial and military power without abandoning state socialism and social regimentation. He also tried to make his new elite more "cultured," partly by reviving tsarist social niceties and partly by imitating outdated Western aesthetic models, reclassified "socialist realism." Still, because the Russian Communists believed that they were true Marxists, they continued to *talk* about world revolution and the victory of socialism over capitalism. By doing so they maintained their hold over the Comintern throughout the interwar years and continued to frighten the West. In Italy in 1922 and in Germany in 1933 the party "line" was "obstructionist" rather than revolutionary. Yet *fear* of a Marxist revolution helped the rise of fascism in these two countries.

## FASCIST ITALY

Fascist rule, a kind of totalitarianism peculiar to the interwar years, resembled Communist rule in maintaining a one-party dictatorship through police terror, thought control, and social regimentation; but the resemblance ended there. Despite Stalin, glorification of a magnetic leader has not been fundamental to Russian Communism. Ideologically, fascism dedicated itself to nationalist and militarist values, whereas Communism, at least until 1939, remained internationalist and pacifist. Most important of all, fascism did not alter the basic economic and social structure. In fact, its underlying purpose seemed to be to shore up this structure against real or imagined threats to it in the wake of the First World War, the Russian Revolution, and the world depression.

### The Nature of Fascism

Fascism has been said to be a radicalism of the Right. This definition brings out the basic inconsistency of the movement. While seeking power the fascists used methods usually associated with the revolutionary Left—brutality, mass meetings, civil disobedience—in order to reinvigorate conservative values like loyalty, honor, family, and nation. Once in power they continued to speak the language of socialism but adopted an economic policy favoring the forces of large capital. Fascism was blatantly anti-Marxist, yet it used a similarly radical ideology and almost identical methods to destroy Marxism within a strictly national framework. Most fascists hated the traditional privileged orders, who in turn looked down on them as gangsters and rabble-rousers. But when power came within their grasp the fascist leaders made their peace with these orders, and the bulk of the prelates, magistrates, and generals accepted these new champions of the radical Right, if not with joy at least with the hope that they would save the values and institutions of the traditional Right from a *real* revolution.

Contrary to Marshal Foch's famous remark, fascism, not Communism, was the "disease of the defeated nations." The disease metaphor is apt because it implies both the susceptibility of its victims and the actual disruption of their "organisms" over a significant period of time. There were Communist *scares* in many European countries during the interwar years, but Communism did not actually take hold anywhere outside of Russia before the Second World War. Yet in Germany in 1933, as in Italy in 1922, fear of a native

Communist revolution brought crucial financial aid to the fascists from Big Business as well as moral support from the older elites.

Above all, the backing of the masses explains the rise of fascism; without it the gold of the industrialists and the good will of the Right-wing elites would never have brought Mussolini and Hitler to power. Both men were demogogues; they knew what the masses wanted and they knew how to appeal to their longing for something to believe in, something bigger than themselves and untainted by association with the regime that had let them down. We are talking here about the disoriented "little men"—mainly lower-middle class—not the organized industrial workers for many of whom Marxism was still the answer. These "little men" knew that their country had lost—or, in the case of Italy, almost lost—the war and that it might eventually have to bow to "Americanization" or "Bolshevization." These were unpalatable facts to people who wanted desperately to belong to a great, independent, national community of which they could be proud. Nationalism, then, was what was wanted, and that was what the fascists gave them, consistently and with an intensity only possible in a modern industrial society.

### The Origins of Italian Fascism

In the immediate postwar years Italy resembled the defeated nations of Central Europe more than Great Britain and France. Being on the winning side had not given the Italians the kind of moral unity that had rallied the British and French peoples to their governments. There was considerable labor unrest in the great Western democracies, as we shall see, but middle-class values and the middle-class way of life held firm. In Italy, as in Germany, Austria, and Hungary, these values and this way of life were less deeply entrenched and hence less capable of resisting severe political, economic, and ideological shocks. The glory of the liberal tradition had been its faith in self-criticism and in the ability of the bourgeois elite to carry out its self-imposed duty of bringing about the technological and economic unity of the world, emancipating all peoples as part of this effort, and doing this through peaceful compromises with the earlier aristocratic elite. This kind of liberal synthesis had been in the making before 1914 in Italy and Central Europe as these areas became increasingly industrialized. But it had begun much later than in Great Britain and France, and at the end of the war an old-fashioned rural and paternalistic society continued to live alongside and entangled with a modern industrial society in Italy and Central Europe.

In Italy, then, the bourgeois-liberal tradition was too weak to prevent its critics from destroying it. These critics represented a wide range of interests. On the extreme Right were the reactionary landowners, generals, and bureaucrats; on the extreme Left were the Marxist-oriented industrial workers. In addition to the traditional hostility of these groups, the war and postwar inflation and unemployment caused growing resentment toward the existing regime among large numbers of people who now found themselves on the margins of respectable society: discontented war veterans, small shopkeepers, petty office employees, and assorted drifters. These people were too proud to turn to Marxism; most of them considered themselves superior to the working class, which that ideology was dedicated to liberating. They had already been emancipated, or so they thought, by bourgeois-liberal society. And now this society, for all its intellectual, economic, and technical rationality, no longer seemed able to give them the kinds of security and well being they had come to expect from it. Consequently, many of them turned to fascism, the new radicalism of the Right.

### Mussolini and the Rise of Italian Fascism

The history of Fascism* is largely the his-

*Fascism with a capital "F" refers to the regime of the Fascist Party in Italy. Fascism with a small "f" refers to similar regimes and movements in other countries, whatever the name of the party involved may have been. Hitler's Nazi—or National Socialist—regime emphasized ideology somewhat more than Mussolini's Fascist regime, but the similarities outweighted the differences, as we shall see.

tory of the dealings of Benito Mussolini (1883–1945) with the Italian people. More than Stalin, though less than Hitler, Mussolini was a truly popular dictator. There was opposition to him from the start, and the persistence of the monarchy made it possible for the same Victor Emmanuel III (1900–1946) who appointed him premier in October 1922 to dismiss him in July 1943. Nevertheless, during his twenty-year rule, Mussolini's regime satisfied at least some of the aspirations of many of the people most of the time. The propertied and educated classes were not taken in by Fascist propaganda, but they supported Mussolini as long as he safeguarded their private interests. The rural masses, especially in the south, were cowed, as always, by superior power; to them Mussolini was a kind of super-*Mafia* strong man whom they respected and feared. The urban masses, both working-class and petty bourgeois, were also impressed with the power of the regime, and many of them were taken in by the myth of national glory. The most enthusiastic supporters of the regime were the more than one million members of the Fascist Party and the hangers-on to whom it gave jobs, uniforms, and status. Mussolini failed to solve Italy's chronic economic problems, but he did maintain domestic order and bolster national pride. These were the main reasons for his success.

### Mussolini's Beginnings

What was the background of this flat-faced, square-jawed, solidly packed little man whose strutting and posturing symbolized "the dictator" to millions of people throughout the world during the interwar years? The son of a village blacksmith, he grew up in a section of north central Italy famous for its petty despots in Renaissance times. Despite his father's socialist and anticlerical leanings young Benito attended a Catholic seminary until he was finally expelled for having stabbed a fellow pupil. In 1901 he began teaching in a public elementary school, but a year later, to avoid being drafted into the army, he fled to Switzerland. There he led a bohemian existence, doing odd jobs, begging, reading revolutionary books, and dreaming of revolutionary deeds. In 1904 he returned to Italy and modified his "principles" sufficiently to undergo military service. Thereafter he combined his primary interest, which was always journalism, with working his way up in the Italian Socialist Party. Considering his later pose as a superpatriot it is interesting to note that in 1910 he had called the Fatherland "a fiction, a mystification, a conventional lie." By 1912 Mussolini was one of the outstanding personalities in Italian Socialism and the editor of the official party newspaper *Avanti!*.

Despite his prewar effort to parade as an orthodox Marxist, Mussolini gradually abandoned his belief in class solidarity for a growing attachment to revolution for revolution's sake, power for the sake of power. A few weeks after the outbreak of war in 1914 Mussolini again changed his "principles" from ardent neutralism to ardent interventionism. He was moved by an instinctive feeling that war would pave the way for revolution. With money from Italian interventionists he set up his own newspaper, the *Popolo d'Italia*, to which he devoted most of the war years. He was in uniform for a while, however, and like Hitler attained the rank of corporal. In March 1919, at a meeting in Milan, he helped to found the Fascist Party, along with several score discontented zealots. They were still socialists of a sort, and Mussolini, fancying himself as the Lenin of Italy, still talked of expropriating exploiters and seizing factories as a first step in social revolution. But Mussolini already stressed his "elasticity" by declaring: "We allow ourselves the luxury of being aristocrats and democrats, conservatives and progressives, reactionaries and revolutionaries, legalists and antilegalists. . . ." The elections of November 1919, in which not a single Fascist was successful, convinced Mussolini that he could never compete with the Marxist socialists for working-class support. He then revealed his true colors as those of pure opportunism by changing to the conservative side.

### Italy's Postwar Crises

Although the nationalist frustration and economic hardship of 1919 and 1920 helped give the Fascists the beginnings of a mass following, other parties benefited more than they from the growing dissatisfaction with the existing political system. This dissatisfaction had already appeared in 1912 when universal male suffrage had first been instituted. The Socialists, who had gained 50 seats in the Chamber of Deputies at that time, raised their representation to 156 in the 1919 election. Easily the largest party in Italy, they were also better organized and disciplined than any other, though that was no great achievement. Many people took fright, and fear of socialism was to be the most important single factor in Mussolini's favor by 1921. Before then, however, another new mass party, the *Popolari*, or Christian Democrats, had come into existence and gained 100 seats in Parliament. Whereas the Socialists got their main backing from the urban workers in the industrial North, the *Popolari* appealed strongly to the discontented agricultural workers. Both turned against the old-fashioned liberals like Giolitti who continued to rule through minority coalitions and who refused to inaugurate urgently needed economic and social reforms.

More than government reforms were needed to solve Italy's economic and social problems. The basic problem was that the country's economy was not expanding fast enough to meet the needs of a rapidly growing population (which had passed 37 million by 1919). Despite prewar advances in the industrial north, the nation as a whole lacked the natural resources and the investment capital necessary for the kind of economic development that would have benefited all regions. The southern third of the country was especially poor, and its chronic problem of underemployment became worse as the war and postwar American immigration restrictions reduced the possibility of emigration abroad. *Popolari* demands for dividing up the big estates among the peasants and Socialist demands for steep income taxes on the rich and higher wages for the workers did not go to the root of the problem. But neither did the government, and that was why the rural and urban masses voted for "antigovernment" parties. Unfortunately, neither the *Popolari* nor the Socialists were willing to join coalitions with other parties, and in 1921 the Socialists, already divided, were badly weakened when their extreme Left wing broke away and formed the Italian Communist Party.

Impatient with both the government and the "antigovernment" parties, large numbers of peasants and urban workers took matters into their own hands in 1920. There were sporadic peasant revolts against the local authorities, and in some areas the peasants began redistributing the land themselves. As in other Western countries, there were also industrial strikes for higher wages to combat the rising cost of living. Finally, in September 1920, the industrial workers in the North copied the peasants' land seizures by occupying a number of factories. There is evidence that some of the factory owners provoked the spread of these "sit-in" strikes by threatening to lock the workers out. They hoped that the Prime Minister Giolitti would use force against the workers, but Giolitti fell back on the same technique he had used against socialist strikers in 1904; he waited for the workers themselves to see the futility of their purely negative action. In the end, he brought about a compromise between the employers and the strikers. Nevertheless, the so-called occupation of the factories helped the Fascists more than anybody else, for it dispersed the energies of the Left and made many wealthy people willing to turn toward anyone who would save them from a socialist revolution.

### The Rise to Power

In 1921–1922, while a number of industrialists gave financial aid to the Fascist Party, the Liberals and Conservatives allowed Mussolini to rise to power rather than take any action of their own. His party had gained only 35 seats in the 1921 elections, and he continued to flirt with all factions, including the Socialists, as a means of augmenting his strength. But he soon decided that saving Italy from socialism was the best way to gain backing from the forces that really counted: the monarchy, the army, the magistrates, and even some members of the Church hierarchy. His blackshirted *Squadristi* had become notorious for being able to tame agrarian and industrial disorder with clubs and heavy doses of castor oil. In August 1922, in response to a Socialist call for a general strike, he sent these thugs on a rampage of looting and burning Socialist offices and meeting halls. Neither the government, the army, nor the police interfered with these acts of criminal rowdyism. Finally, in October, a new premier asked the king to sign a decree for martial law. The king refused to sign it, and many politicians hesitated to take a stand against Mussolini and thus antagonize a possible premier.

For Mussolini wanted above all else to become premier. Since his party had only 35 seats in Parliament, he had no legal claim to this post. Hence, he engineered the so-called March on Rome beginning on October 26, 1922. While his Fascist gangs congregated on the outskirts of the city, Mussolini remained in his newspaper office in Milan until October 29, when the king sent him a telegram asking him to form a government. The Fascist *Duce* then arrived in the capital in a Pullman car and asked that his forces camped outside the city be allowed to parade with him in front of the king's palace. Fascist propaganda later glorified the "March on Rome" as a great revolutionary event. Actually this parade was a sorry aftermath to a set of circumstances in which the forces of the Left refused to unite against Mussolini and in which those of the Right backed him against a phantom threat of socialist revolution and against a kind of lawlessness that their own selfishness had helped to create.

*IL Duce*

### Fascist Totalitarianism

From October 30, 1922 to January 3, 1925 Mussolini consolidated his power while maintaining a pretense of legality. Still unsure of his tenure he left a margin of liberty to the parties in Parliament, the trade unions, and the press. He reduced the strength of the opposition parties in rigged elections, but Nationalists, Liberals, and even a few Right-wing *Popolari* continued to support his government, cherishing the illusion that they could influence it toward a milder course. The Socialists suffered most from *Squadristi* beatings, doses of castor oil, and outright assassinations. In the summer of 1924 their outspoken leader, Giacomo Matteotti, was murdered, apparently on official orders. Public revulsion against this brutal act was so strong that, at first, Mussolini feared dismissal by the king. Nothing happened, however, and on January 3, 1925 he announced that Italy would henceforth be a totalitarian state in which all opposition parties would be disbanded and all dissenting elements crushed.

In 1926 the Fascist government became openly totalitarian. It made Parliament, the courts, and the monarchy rubber stamps of the one-party state, and the armed forces became its obedient servants. Mussolini ruled by decree, with the advice of the Fascist Grand Council, the highest party organ. Like Stalin and Hitler, Mussolini purged his party of many of the revolutionary enthusiasts who had brought him to power and tamed the others. In Fascist Italy, unlike the Soviet Union, the state bureaucracy, rather than the party, was supreme. Its secret police silenced all dissenters; its ministry of education indoctrinated the young. The state also passed laws prohibiting strikes and organizing Italian workers into Fascist unions.

By 1929, the only part of the Italian "establishment" with which Mussolini had not yet come to terms was the Church; in that year he did this through the Lateran Treaty with the Vatican. An atheist himself, Mussolini fully appreciated the influence of Catholicism in Italian life; he also saw that preceding parliamentary governments had lost the support of millions of Italians by their anticlericalism. Since Cavour the liberals had held this attitude, and since 1870, when the new Kingdom of Italy had deprived the pope of his sovereignty over Rome, the Vatican had been hostile to all Italian governments. The Lateran Treaty ended this hostility by giving the Vatican territorial sovereignty over a few acres around St. Peter's and by giving the Church a privileged position in Italian public education. This reconciliation with the Church, plus Mussolini's milder manner in foreign and domestic policy, made Fascism seem respectable to the democratic leaders of other Western countries.

But beginning in 1931 the Fascist regime made it clear that it would stop at nothing less than the totalitarian absorption and control of all areas of national life. Despite the Lateran Treaty, it launched a campaign against the lay organizations of the Church, especially the youth groups run by an agency called Catholic Action. The regime's foreign policy became more belligerent as its ideology increasingly emphasized the restoration of the grandeur of Imperial Rome. This ideology called for conquest abroad and the regimentation of the whole Italian people in order to achieve this conquest.

The most extreme phase of Fascist totalitarianism began with the invasion of Ethiopia in October 1935.* Regimentation was extended to a "reform of custom" campaign with the purpose of eradicating the more civilized and gracious manners of the Italian people and replacing them with hard, efficient, ruthless, and militaristic habits of talking, acting, and thinking: the polite and slightly subservient *Lei* was replaced by *voi* for addressing strangers; instead of shaking hands, Italians now had to greet each other with an outstretched arm, like the ancient Romans. Finally, in 1938 antisemitism became the official policy of the Italian state.

*See p. 717.

### *Ideology and Propaganda*

Long before this final phase Mussolini was almost deified as *Il Duce*, The Leader. This inveterate opportunist had no scruples and no faith in anything or anyone but himself, yet he must have had something more to keep a modern, individualistic nation like Italy under his control for twenty years. What he had was the ability to make himself appear to be a strong leader. He used the party apparatus, the mass media, and public posturing to nourish this "image": Mussolini the athlete jumping through fiery hoops; Mussolini the soldier who had refused to take chloroform when his wounds were being treated during the First World War; Mussolini the lover with a string of beautiful and brilliant mistresses. Far more than Stalin—and even Hitler—Mussolini personified the male stereotype of his countrymen: vain, loquacious, and a ladykiller. Still, he was more than a synthetic demigod embodying the hopes and dreams of unsuccessful young Italians (the way a hero like Errol Flynn enacted the fantasies of American gas-station attendants and office clerks). He also gave them something bigger than themselves in which to believe, namely national glory.

A skilled journalist, Mussolini used propaganda slogans to glorify himself and his regime. The key slogan, stenciled on walls and buildings throughout the nation, was "Mussolini is always right." Other refrains given nationwide display were:

*Believe! Obey! Fight!*
*He who has steel has bread!*
*Better to live one day like a lion than a hundred years like a sheep!*
*War is to the male what child-bearing is to the female!*

*High Fascist Party Officials "keeping fit" in the required annual exercises prescribed by Mussolini*

### *Regimentation and Economic Troubles*

Fascist regimentation was in certain respects almost as effective as that of Communist Russia and Nazi Germany. At first it controlled the mass media through strict censorship, but in 1937 these were placed under the direct control of the new Ministry of Popular Culture. Leisure time activities for adults were supervised by an organization called Dopolavoro. The Opera Nazionale Balilla, with subdivisions for boys and girls, began as an agency for training future Fascists, but in 1937 all young people from six through seventeen were required to participate in the various subgroups of the Fascist youth movement, which stressed propaganda, sport, and discipline for all, and premilitary training for boys. By the late 1930s the work of these youth organizations was showing real results, and the younger generation was becoming one of the bulwarks of the regime. But in the use of terror Italian Fascism was milder than German Nazism and Russian Communism; there were a smaller number of political prisoners and no concentration camps.

One respect in which Fascism differed markedly from Communism was its failure to regiment the nation's economy. Fascists in general were not much interested in economic matters, and Mussolini never tackled the basic needs for Italian economic development. He built a few showy public buildings and drained a few marshes, but he made no effort to stimulate capital investment, especially in the South, and he failed to solve the problem of unemployment. In fact, he tried to stimulate more births for military purposes without providing new jobs. In the early 1930s he pretended to set up a corporatist state by combining the trade-unions and the employers' associations into "corporations" that were supposed to eliminate class conflicts through cooperation among people at all levels of the productive process. But these "corporations" were merely a ruse for subordinating labor to the interests of Big Business, which had been so helpful during Mussolini's rise to power and which in 1925 had agreed to cooperate with the regime in the Palazzo Vidoni pact. Even after the regime set up its Ministry of Corporations and began to disregard the advice of the business community in fiscal matters it left the profits of industry and commerce largely in private hands.

For all its regimentation, Italian Fascism developed more slowly and was milder in tone than Nazism or Russian Communism. Mussolini himself thought that the Italian people were inferior material for his dictatorial work of art; they were too individualistic, too skeptical, and too easygoing. The "reform of custom" campaign was supposed to change them, but it came too late to have any real effect. Italy's relatively small size and population were also hindrances to Mussolini's grandiose ambitions. Nevertheless, by 1939 the Fascist youth groups had created real enthusiasm for the regime, and if Mussolini had had the wit to stay out of the Second World War he might have become irremovable. But the will to power and empire was to be the cause of Mussolini's undoing as well as Hitler's.

## NAZI GERMANY

On January 30, 1933 Adolf Hitler became chancellor of the German Reich; on March 23 the Reichstag and the Reichsrat passed the Enabling Act establishing the Nazi dictatorship, which was to last for the next twelve years. This regime resembled Mussolini's sufficiently to rate the label "fascist," but its methods were more brutal, its control over national life more thorough. Instead of castor oil the Nazis used concentration camps to terrorize the "enemies" of the nation. The churches, the army, and the business community were more completely subdued than in Fascist Italy. Most important, the Nazis were extremely popular—so popular that their rise to power constituted a real revolution.

### The Nazi Revolution

Like the French Revolution of 1789, the Bolshevik Revolution of 1917, and the Chinese Communist Revolution of the late 1940s, the Nazi Revolution took place in a situation in which the old order had come to be viewed as no longer capable of fulfilling the aspirations of large sections of the nation. Indeed, the absence of agreement on fundamental values was one of the two necessary conditions for the success of these revolutions, the other condition being the political impotence of the existing regime. In each instance, national political unity had become a strong enough habit to overcome "feudal" and separatist tendencies without providing new symbols of loyalty sufficiently strong to hold the whole community together morally. The main difference between the Nazi Revolution and the others was that it made no basic changes in the economic and social structure—partly because the Nazis had no wish to do this, but primarily because they took over an industrial society in which the major job of technical and economic rationalization had already been accomplished.

In spite of this difference, the Nazi Revolution fits the pattern of the others. Two of its three main ingredients were the weaknesses of the Weimar Republic and Germany's social disorganization. The third was the personality and political gifts of Adolf Hitler.

#### *Weaknesses of the Weimar Republic*

Like the parliamentary regime in Italy, the Weimar Republic collapsed for lack of a deeply entrenched democratic tradition. Germany's military defeat, the Revolution of November 1918, and the adoption of the Weimar Constitution in July 1919 had paved the way for a parliamentary democracy modeled after French and American patterns. But during the 1920s this new regime was unable either to reconcile or to eliminate the prewar ruling elites. These army generals, high civil servants, and declining aristocrats never really thought of the Weimar Republic as "theirs." Their antidemocratic influence might have declined in time, but there was not enough time. For German democracy was weakened when it was just getting established: by the danger of a Communist revolution in early 1919, by attempted Rightist *putsches* in early 1920, and by a renewal of threats from both extremes during the crises caused by inflation and the French occupation of the Ruhr in 1923. The conflicting interests that had been held in check under the imperial regime came out into the open in the freer atmosphere of the Weimar Republic and were sharpened through the activities of powerful political parties, trade-unions, and Big Business organizations.

Germany lacked the moral cohesiveness of France, Great Britain, and the United States. Unlike these nations, the Germans had not fought to achieve their democracy, and they did not value it as highly. It is unlikely, however, that the Germans rejected democracy merely because it was "imposed" on them by the victorious Allies. The Treaty of Versailles was extremely unpopular, to be sure, and it was always referred to as the *Diktat.* Nevertheless, Germany's territorial losses were not crippling, and after 1924, the reparations' burden was considerably lightened by the Dawes Plan.

Through the efforts of the conservative statesman Gustav Stresemann (1878–1929) Germany resolved many of her differences with France in December 1925 through the Locarno Pact,* and in 1926 she was admitted to the League of Nations and given a permanent seat on its Council. Stresemann's diplomatic achievements restored Germany's status as a great power in every respect except equality in arms. Hence, the effects of the Versailles Treaty were no longer serious by the late 1920s, and most Germans thought little about them. The inflation of the early 1920s had dislocated German society to some extent, but it was the depression of the early 1930s that provided the degree of social and economic disorganization favorable to the rise of the Nazis. Only under these extreme conditions was it possible for them to equate the *Diktat* with the democratic regime itself and to demand the repudiation of both.

*See pp. 694-695.

### *Hitler's Early Career*

Before examining the conditions under which almost half of the German people rejected democracy for a Nazi dictatorship, let us turn briefly to the early history of the party and its leader. Adolf Hitler (1889–1945) was born at Braunau, across from Bavaria, on the Austrian side of the river Inn. Though the son of a minor customs official, young Adolf rejected the prospect of a respectable lower-middle-class life in a small provincial town. At the age of twenty he went to Vienna to seek his fortune. His experience there was one of uniform failure: he was refused admission in the state school of architecture and led a drab and aimless existence—coloring picture post cards, steeping himself in Wagnerian opera, talking politics, and absorbing extremist ideologies. It was not surprising that this bewildered and humiliated young man from the provinces should learn to hate the cosmopolitan, sophisticated, and "decadent" atmosphere of prewar Vienna, with its prominent Jewish minority and its class-conscious socialist movement.

On the eve of the First World War Hitler moved to Munich, where he was soon to begin his active political career. During the war he served as a volunteer in the Bavarian infantry and was decorated for bravery. In army life he seemed at last to have found the comradeship and discipline he had longed for. The war also intensified his German nationalism, and during the five years following the Armistice Hitler led a turbulent existence as a political agitator in the Bavarian capital, specializing in rabble-rousing speeches with a strongly nationalist and antisemitic flavor. He attached himself to a group of jobless veterans, artistic bohemians, and political drifters who in 1920 began calling themselves the National Socialist German Workers' Party (*National-Sozialistische Deutsche Arbeiterpartei*—the first two syllables of *National* are pronounced *natzi*, which became the popular name for the party) and quickly became its *Führer*, or Leader.

The Nazi Party quickly acquired its fascist trappings. Like the *Popolo d'Italia*, the *Völkischer Beobachter* claimed to be the newspaper of the real "people," or "folk." The party had its own version of Mussolini's *Squadristi*—the *Sturmabteilung* (SA), or Storm Troopers—and it adopted the Fascist salute with the outstretched right arm. The "*Heil Hitler!*", the swastika, and the technique of the public meeting with its flags, marching, and songs all came into use in the early 1920s. Hitler greatly admired Mussolini, and though some of the early Nazis were socialists of a sort, he stressed nationalism, antisemitism, and anti-Communism rather than justice for the workers.

At the height of the 1923 crisis the Nazis made their first bid for power. It began with a tumultuous meeting in one of Munich's vast beer halls and ended in a street demonstration in which old General Ludendorff also participated and which was intended to turn into a general revolution. This so-called "Beer-Hall *Putsch*" was a fiasco; the police quelled it with little difficulty, and Hitler was imprisoned for over a year.

### Social Disorganization

During the last half of the 1920s the Nazi Party languished; it was the coming of the depression that gave this clique of malcontents a new and better chance to gain power. As we saw in Chapter XVII, the depression of the early 'thirties hit Germany harder than any major European country. Out of a total population of 68 million, 6 million were fully unemployed, and many others eked out a precarious existence from part-time work and dwindling savings. The last governments of the Weimar Republic were more energetic than those in Italy which had preceded Mussolini's rise to power, but their efforts to curb political extremism were hampered by the worsening of the economic crisis in 1931 and 1932. Big industrialists, factory workers, and millions of lower-middle-class people uprooted and disinherited by the depression all sought extreme solutions to an extreme situation. In the 1930 elections the Communists won 77 seats in the Reichstag, the Nazis 107; in July 1932 the Communists raised their representation to 89, the Nazis to 230.

The threat of economic and social ruin turned millions of middle- and lower-middle-class Germans toward the Nazis, but the fears and prejudices the Nazis played on had deep roots in German life. Belief in the uniqueness of Germany stemmed from the writings of Herder and Fichte. Aggressive nationalism dated back to the early reign of Emperor William II; it had reached its first climax during the First World War, and it had shown signs of returning in 1925, when the German people had elected Field Marshal Paul von Hindenburg President of the Republic. "Ordinary" antisemitism was not unique to Germany; as a heritage of medieval prejudice supplemented by modern petty bourgeois resentments, it thrived in dozens of countries. But in the late nineteenth century a new kind of *political* antisemitism had appeared in Germany (and Austria) and was closely associated with the belief in the uniqueness of Germany and with aggressive nationalism. The Nazis made this kind of antisemitism a means of intensifying German feelings of national self-awareness, which previous regimes had been unable to provide.

The Nazis were extremely successful in appealing to the mass of disoriented "little men" against the powers-that-be and their "henchmen." The disruption of the German sense of community, which had never been strong, prompted millions of people to reject the authority of the Weimar Republic and its institutions. As in other major revolutions, the "have-nots" also vented their rage on the "haves." The Nazis managed to direct most of this hatred against the Jews, and huge crowds of respectable burghers held their children on their shoulders to watch Nazi Storm Troopers beat up helpless Jews in the streets. This sadistic response reflected a possibly sincere, but wholly misguided, belief that the Jews were alien subversives whose strangelehold on business, the professions, and, who knows, even the government, had to be broken before honest Germans could call their homeland their own again.

While antisemitism won many adherents to Nazism from the lower middle classes, anti-Communism was more important in gaining support from many members of the older elites and the more prosperous sections of the middle class. The declining landed and military aristocracy had never become reconciled to the Weimar Republic. Though they hated it privately because it was *democratic*, publicly they attacked it for being "soft on Communism." Thus, in the turmoil of 1932 and early 1933, they were ready to make deals with the Nazis. The rising middle class had been denied political power by Bismarck and William II, and under the Weimar Republic it had been divided between conservatives and democrats. Lacking in self-confidence to rule directly, it was large enough and strong enough to assure the success of an anti-Communist party, the Nazis, which promised to save it from a proletarian revolution.

### *The Seizure of Power: The Legal Phase*

Like the Russian Communists and the Italian Fascists, the German Nazis were an "antigovernment" party, but, unlike them, they sought power by *legal* means. To succeed in this endeavor they had to have a large enough representation in Parliament to merit consideration as a governing party. They also required behind-the-scenes allies to persuade that aged Junker President Hindenburg to appoint Hitler to the chancellorship. Once they controlled the cabinet, they also needed enough parliamentary votes from other parties to sanction the revolution they intended to carry out from above.

At the end of 1932 the Nazis seemed to be losing some of their appeal, and they needed funds to maintain themselves as the most powerful party in the country. The November election had bankrupted the party treasury and reduced the Nazis' parliamentary representation from 230 to 196, while increasing that of the other parties of the extreme Right to 70 and that of the Communists to 100. Hundreds of thousands of frustrated young men continued to swell the ranks of the Storm Troopers, but they had to be paid to keep them active in the streets: shouting "*Heil Hitler!*", smashing Jewish shop windows, beating up Communists, and the like. Money was also needed to step up the party's campaign propaganda for the next election.

On January 4, 1933 a group of German industrialists came to the rescue. Like the Italian businessmen who had helped Mussolini, these industrialists feared both a proletarian revolution and the inability of the existing regime to suppress it. At a meeting in the home of a Cologne banker they promised to pay the Nazis' election expenses and the wages of the Storm Troopers. In return Hitler let it be understood that when he became chancellor he would not interfere with the activities of the business community. He was to keep this part of the bargain, but he had no intention of becoming a mere hireling of the industrialists or of the other elites who facilitated his rise to power.

Hitler's aristocratic and military backers were represented by Baron Franz von Papen and General Kurt von Schleicher respectively. Papen had headed a "Baron's cabinet" from June to December 1932, after which Schleicher had replaced him as chancellor. Unable to maintain their majorities in Parliament, both men schemed to create a reactionary government which, with a few Nazis holding key posts, would benefit from that party's strength in Parliament and in the country while keeping the reins of power in their own hands. But Hitler would settle for nothing less than the chancellorship for himself, and President Hindenburg balked at appointing a "Bohemian corporal" to this post. In the end it was Papen who convinced Hindenburg and other key Junkers that a reactionary-nationalist coalition cabinet headed by the Nazi chief was the only alternative to chaos. Only a minority of the aristocrats and generals were involved in the "deal" that made Hitler chancellor in January 30, just as only a minority of the industrialists had agreed to the pact of January 4. Nevertheless, their backing was crucial in bringing him to power in a perfectly legal way.

Once in office Hitler took only a year and a half to consolidate his dictatorship, and he carried out the first phase of this process within the letter—if not the spirit—of the law. The first step was the elimination of the 100 Communist deputies in the Reichstag. Conveniently, a demented Dutch Communist set fire to the Reichstag building on February 27. Although this spectacular act was never convincingly linked to the responsible leadership of the German Communist Party, the Nazis were able to use it as an excuse to outlaw the party and to arrest its parliamentary deputies. They also used the "Red peril" as a campaign slogan in the new election they called for March 5. With the Storm Troopers spreading violence and terror in the streets and with Nazi officials in control of the state radio network, the Nazi Party gained 44 per cent of the total vote. Still, all the other parties ran candidates, and the polling itself was done without interference. If one adds the votes for the Right-wing nationalists who were part of the Nazi coalition government, it seems fair to say that almost half the German people and an even larger proportion of those under twenty-five wanted Hitler to stay in power in the last relatively free election of the 1930s.

By passing the Enabling Act on March 23 the German Parliament gave Hitler's government dictatorial powers for four years, thus allowing him to make further legal changes. In effect, the Reichstag surrendered its own power in this way. With his dictatorial mandate Hitler was also able to destroy the federal character of the German Republic by stripping the individual states of their powers, abolishing the Reichsrat, and concentrating all political power in the hands of the central government in Berlin. The final legal act of the Nazis was the Civil Service Law of April 7, 1933, which eliminated Jews and anti-Nazis from all national and local branches of government, including public school teachers. Within a short time Nazi Party members filled all the high administrative offices, and they eventually took over all the lower ones as well.

### *The Illegal Phase*

The *illegal* phase of the Nazi Revolution began with the creation of a one-party state. By July 1933 the government had forced all the opposition parties to dissolve themselves. Why did these parties not put up a fight? The Social Democrats still had 120 seats in the Reichstag, the Center Party with its Bavarian Catholic allies had 92, yet these two parties showed less willingness to save parliamentary institutions than their Italian counterparts in the early 1920s. Unlike the Italian Socialists, the German Social Democrats had been a government party for over thirteen years, but since their harsh treatment under Bismarck they had never lost the habit of thinking of themselves as the "victims" of whoever was in power. Also, like the Center Party, they had feared the extreme Left more than the extreme Right since the first Communist uprising in January 1919. The fact that the Center Party itself had voted for the Enabling Act did not save it from dissolution. Even the Nationalists, who had participated in Hitler's coalition cabinet, disappeared in the summer of 1933.

After that Germany became a police state. The Nazis perverted the legal and judicial systems to suit their own purposes, thus ending the proud German tradition of rule by law. In May 1934 they set up a "People's Court" for treason trials; its proceedings were secret, and there was no appeal. Political offenders, with or without a trial, were sent to concentration camps. The Gestapo (State Security Police) enforced its own laws and its own diabolical brand of terror.

The final phase in the Nazi seizure of power came in the summer of 1934; as in Russia and Italy, once the revolutionary party had become the ruling party, it purged itself of dissidents within its own ranks. The main victims of the purge were the "Left-wingers" in the party, who still took the "socialist" part of its name seriously, and the leaders of the 2,500,000 Storm Troopers, whose continuing unruliness was no longer necessary to Hitler and whose desire to be incorporated into the regular army was anathema to the generals. During "the night of the long knives" (June 30, 1934) Hitler's personal elite guard, the SS, slaughtered almost 1,000 "undesirables," including former chancellor Kurt von Schleicher, who had consorted with the Nazis and the generals and who was now repudiated by both.

In Germany, unlike Russia, the party purge was part of a "deal" with a nonrevolutionary organization, the professional army. Hitler agreed to eliminate the Storm Troopers as rivals of the regular army; the generals agreed that Hitler would succeed the moribund Hindenburg as head of the state and that all army officers would take an oath of personal loyalty to him as their *Führer*. By late August all the terms of this "deal" had been carried out by all parties concerned.

The execution of this "deal" had crucial consequences for the future of the Nazi regime. By combining the offices of president and chancellor in his own person Hitler rid himself of a competing head of the state, like the Italian king who was ultimately able to dismiss Mussolini. Once they had taken their personal oath of loyalty to their *Führer*, even those army officers who disliked him felt that any open opposition would be dishonorable. The gradual replacement of the SA by the SS gave the party a select, highly disciplined, paramilitary arm that was to play an ever more important role in the Nazi state.*

## The Nazi Regime

### The Führer

"In a world of normalcy a Nothing, in chaos a Titan." This was what Konrad Heiden said of Hitler in his biography. Physically the man was unimpressive, with his little mustache, his dark forelock, his rasping voice. Yet the mightiest and most blasé men, both Germans and foreigners, came away from his presence curiously shaken. Part of this response was due to a knowledge of his unlimited power, but Hitler also had the uncanny ability to make people see him as a Titan in the chaotic world in which he achieved this power and which he made more chaotic.

Today the things that Hitler was able to make the German people believe and do seem demented, but at the time they *did* believe and do these things. Why? In *Mein Kampf* (*My Struggle*), a book written long before he gained power, Hitler said the following about the persuasiveness of the Big Lie:

". . . In the size of the lie there is always contained a certain factor of credibility; since the great masses of a people may be more corrupt in the bottom of their hearts than they will be consciously and intentionally bad, therefore with the primitive simplicity of their minds they will more easily fall victims to a great lie than to a small one, since they themselves perhaps also lie sometimes in little things, but would certainly still be too much ashamed of too great lies."

Irrational? Cynical? Yes. But there are many irrational and cynical aspects to politics, and Hitler was master of them all. He knew well how to bring out the worst in the German political tradition since unification. Alan Bullock, another biographer of Hitler, calls him the *reductio ad absurdum* of *Realpolitik*, nationalism, militarism, authoritarianism, the exaltation of the state, and the worship of success and force for their own sake. In the prosperous late 'twenties the "good Germans," led by Stresemann, had made a more liberal and humane tradition prevail; in the critical 'thirties, haranguing rapt and responding multitudes at innumerable party rallies, Hitler was the symbol of the Germany that worshipped him and which he led into the greatest political and moral excesses since those of Attila the Hun.

For all his ability to "utter the thoughts of millions," Hitler was a unique person, combining outstanding qualities of leadership with an utterly contemptible meanness of spirit. As Bullock says, no one can deny his ability to simplify—to exploit the irrational longings of his followers and the weaknesses of his opponents, to take risks with an uncanny sense of timing. Completely unprincipled, he showed a remarkable degree of consistency and perseverance in the pursuit of whatever course of action he finally decided on. Although he was both calculating and cynical in manipulating the masses, he never lost his belief that destiny had called on him to change the course of history. Yet the slightest shift of fortune could make him vacillate between mystical elation and suicidal dejection. Above all moved by ignoble hatred and resentment, he had an insatiable lust for power and for the destruction of everyone and everything that he could not dominate.

### Ideology and Racism

The Nazi ideology, like that of Fascist Italy, was imperialistic and militaristic. It too

*See pp. 738-739.

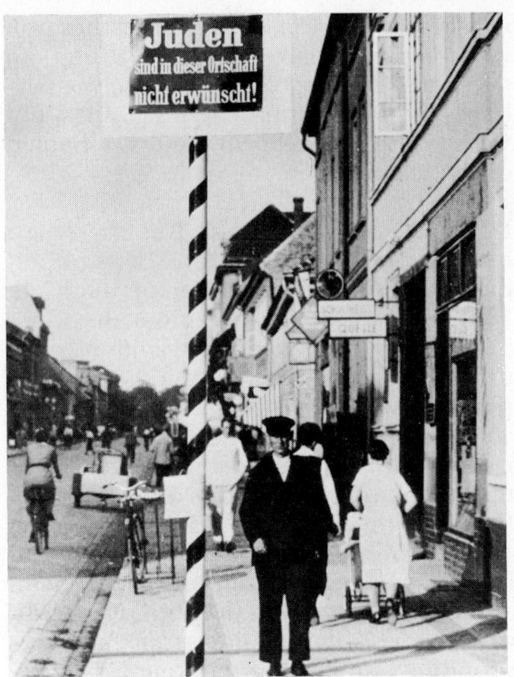


*"Jews not wanted in this place"—hundreds of signs like this were placed all over Germany*

wanted to restore an ancient empire, or Reich. The First Reich, the Holy Roman Empire of the German Nation, had lasted for nine hundred years; the Second Reich, the Wilhelmine Empire, a mere fifty years; the Third Reich was to last for a thousand years. Geared for war, it would find its "natural" area for expansion in Eastern Europe against the "naturally" inferior Slavic peoples there. But first it must "purify" itself of alien and inferior racial elements within its own midst.

Racism was the basic "principle" from which the rest of the Nazi ideology followed. The goal of all Nazi racial policies was to restore the "health" of the German race (*Volk*) by isolating and weeding out all undesirable elements. In the end this included the congenitally ill, the feebleminded, and even old people, but the first and most important "cancer" to be attacked was the Jews.

At first the Nazis restricted their attacks on Jews to sporadic boycotts and street campaigns, but in April 1933 they instigated their first legal act of discrimination. This was the Civil Service Law, which barred all Jews from government service. The bar was soon extended to the armed forces, the schools, and the professions. In 1934 the Nazis, as we have seen, were busy consolidating their political power, but in 1935 they initiated new antisemitic legislation, the Nürnberg Laws. These were a completely new phenomenon in history, a *rescinding* of the civil and political rights of a whole group of people, without exception. They differed from the "Jim Crow" laws in the United States, whose victims had never enjoyed these rights in practice. The Nürnberg Laws also differed from the early discriminatory laws against the "bourgeoisie" and the kulaks in the Soviet Union, which were based on social, not racial, criteria and whose victims could be "reeducated" and reintegrated into the community. The Nürnberg Laws decreed that no Jew or Jewess—that is, anyone with one Jewish grandparent—could have sexual relations with an "Aryan." In order to forestall temptation they even forbade Jews to employ an "Aryan" maid under forty-five years of age.

Outright persecution began in 1938. Until then, Jews were allowed to stay in business in order to help the country's recovery, though they were often harassed. Thereafter Jews were excluded from business and their property was "Aryanized"—that is, bought by non-Jews at a fraction of its worth; Jews were ordered to have fewer children; Jews had to adopt easily identifiable first names, like Sarah or Israel, and to wear a yellow Star of David at all times. The assassination of the German embassy secretary in Paris by an enraged Jew was made the excuse for a wholesale pogrom in Germany. By 1939 the German Jews were reduced to the status of pariahs, as in the Middle Ages—without even the benefit of the money they had had then.

The beginning of the Second World War cut off all possibility of emigration. In 1933 there had been a little more than half a million Jews in Germany, less than 1 per cent of the population. By 1939 about half of them, including the wealthiest, the most talented, and, ironically, the most assimilated, had left the country. Many of those who remained still could

*A party rally in Nürnberg*

not believe in the inhuman treatment in store for them at the hands of the "civilized" and law-abiding Germans. Yet during the Nazi occupation of Europe they were to be almost totally annihilated along with several million other European Jews.

### *"Togetherness" Nazi Style*

At the annual Party Rally in Nürnberg in September 1937 Hitler had already said that the new "thousand-year Reich" required complete "racial purification." This Party Rally also dramatized the new kind of "togetherness" (*Gemeinschaft*) that the Nazis were bringing to the "purified" German people. First, Hitler arrived by airplane (a gift from heaven?) and was cheered by hundreds of thousands of citizens as he drove through the streets of the city to its gigantic stadium. Then, in a sea of devoted party members and swastika flags, precision marching, fanfares, and floodlights, the *Führer*, followed by his chief lieutenants, mounted the steps of the rostrum. More fanfares, solemn introductions, and the *Führer* finally saying: "The fact that you have found me and believe in me has given your life a new meaning and a new purpose." In other words, he, Hitler, had acted like a magnet in attracting the racially pure elite of the reborn German race—namely, the Nazi Party.

The party in turn would give the mass of the German people a new culture and society worthy of a "master race." The new Germany was to be free of decadent Western influences in culture, just as it had freed itself from the shackles of Versailles.* Modern art, for example was condemned as decadent, liberal, Jewish, and Bolshevik; Nazi art would be an art for the masses (shades of "socialist realism"), with a touch of Wagner and a heavy handful of pseudo-Roman, "classical," architecture. (Even Mussolini supported a more modern, though still "accessible," style of architecture.) Under the Nazis, Germany would also rid herself of class conflicts. "No more employers or workers; only soldiers of work." And these "soldiers of work" would find fulfillment in their leisure time in the Labor Front's "Strength through Joy" movement.

The reduction of leisure to a mere auxiliary of work was the official Nazi philosophy. It was all the more brutal because it coalesced with the policy of social regimentation. In "Strength through Joy" and other organizations the workers submerged their individuality in the group. They marched, sang, and hiked together; they went on inexpensive vacation tours together.

Like the Soviet Union and Fascist Italy, Nazi Germany paid special attention to the regimentation and indoctrination of the country's youth. In the schools pupils learned the Nazi ideology and "racial science" from textbooks purged of Jewish, Bolshevik, democratic, and other subversive elements. The teachers who refused to teach these subjects fled; those who were considered unfit to teach them were fired. Outside of school the boys were required to participate in the activities of the Hitler Jugend, the girls in the Bund Deutscher Mädel. Amid the marching, singing, and games these young people, always *together*, made the perfect captive audience for Nazi propaganda.

As in all totalitarian societies, propaganda was the staple fare of the mass media of communication in Nazi Germany. Under the brilliant though sinister direction of Dr. Joseph Goebbels, Nazi propaganda showed no concern for truth or logic. It could be for and against the same thing, like capitalism; it could condemn the Jews for being both capitalists *and* Bolsheviks; in 1939, it could suddenly reverse its habitual antibolshevism with the signing of the Moscow Pact.* Yet, because the Nazi regime was more truly popular than Russian Communism or Italian Fascism, its propaganda was probably closer than theirs to what the majority of people wanted to believe.

### Economic Policies

A major reason for the popularity of the Nazi regime was its speedy solution of the problems of the depression. Unemployment, which had stood at 6 million in early 1933, declined to 1 million by 1937 and disappeared soon thereafter. Several distinct policies were responsible for this remarkable achievement. First, the Nazi finance minister, Dr. Hjalmar Schacht, substituted an inflationary policy for the deflationary one of the Weimar Republic. By extending short-term credit to banks and businesses, the Reichsbank improved the liquidity of the former and reduced the debts and inventories of the latter. As national income grew, so could the public debt. Second, the government launched an extensive public works program, which provided jobs and stimulated business; the most notable example was the network of superhighways (*Autobahnen*), which, not incidentally, had military significance as well. Third, the government's rearmanment program began in 1935. It became the main stimulus to recovery.

The price of this recovery was economic regimentation. Labor was regimented the

*In 1935, Hitler had repudiated the demilitarization clauses of this treaty.

*See p. 722.

most. Limitations were placed on the workers' physical movements, and their wages were frozen. The Labor Front, which replaced the free trade-unions, was a tool of the state, as in the Soviet Union. Its main job was to keep the workers docile; it also administered social security taxes and benefits and provided shop stewards. The government also set up extensive controls over agriculture. It set production quotas for the farmers, and those who did not meet them were threatened with the loss of their land. Between 1933 and 1936 these controls, plus the general economic recovery, helped Germany to increase the amount of foodstuffs produced from 75 to 81 per cent of total consumption.

Big Business underwent the least amount of regimentation. Hitler kept his promise not to interfere too much in its activities; indeed, he favored it over those of the smaller enterprises, through tax relief and big government contracts. The cartels, which had been growing since the mid-twenties,* ran large sections of the German economy far more efficiently than Mussolini's government-sponsored "corporations," while giving Hitler a larger source of income.

By the outbreak of the Second World War the Nazis had given most Germans good cause to be content. The workers were underpaid, but at least jobs were plentiful. Industrialists were prospering; the army was being revitalized; and good party members could make their fortunes in "Aryanized" businesses, in the government bureaucracy, and in the party itself. The Jews and the churches had the most cause for complaint.

### The Churches

The hostility between Hitler and the Protestant and Catholic churches was mutual. Hitler despised Christianity because of its Jewish origins and its gospel of brotherly love. Also, like Mussolini, he wanted to dissolve the Catholic schools and youth organizations, which threatened the monopoly of the Hitler Jugend. The churches in turn condemned racism, the glorification of the *Führer,* and all attempts to subordinate Christianity to the state.

In general Hitler acted most harshly toward dissident Protestants, who for their part were the most courageous in their defiance. At first he had tried to unify and to "Nazify" the Protestant churches by forcing them into a single Reich church with an "Aryan ethic." The majority of the bishops and pastors resisted this effort and managed to keep their organizations out of the political struggle. A strong minority, however, formed a "confessional" Church, preaching open opposition to Nazi doctrines. This group fought a long, hard battle against Nazi persecution until 1937, when its leader, Pastor Martin Niemöller, and eight hundred of his fellows were sent to concentration camps.

The Catholic Church suffered less and offered less resistance. In July 1933 Hitler had signed a concordat with Pope Pius XI granting freedom of faith and worship, recognizing the secrecy of the confessional, and guaranteeing the maintenance of Catholic organizations, orders, charities, and schools. Hitler soon broke his promises. Concentrating his persecution on the teaching orders, whose members were unjustly accused of smuggling and of sexual offenses, he effectively destroyed the Catholic schools and youth groups. In 1937, Pope Pius XI denounced Nazism in his encyclical *Mit brennender Sorge* ("With burning sorrow"). This encyclical was read from all Catholic pulpits in Germany, and its charges were repeated thereafter by a number of German prelates. The government did nothing to redress their grievances, but it left them personally unharmed.

### Limits of Nazi Totalitarianism

Despite its efforts to regiment all aspects of German life, the Nazi regime was not completely totalitarian. Hitler's successes rested on his transformation of the old Prussian-German "barracks state" into a "state barracks" with the aid of modern technology. In Nazi Germany the bureaucracy, the party, and the army executed Hitler's orders with machine precision and without question, but these institutions, along with the churches and the business community, were never com-

*See p. 619.

*Book burning by Nazi storm troopers May 10, 1933*

pletely integrated into a monolithic whole. The Nazis' much vaunted regimentation of the economy for war proved to be no more effective than that of the British and the Americans once they embarked on a similar program. The only truly totalitarian structure within the Nazi regime, the SS, did not make its bid for power until the Second World War; it will be described in Chapter XX.

Within its limits, however, Nazi totalitarianism profoundly affected the German people. On the one hand, they were numbed by the unprecedented scale of militarization to which they were subjected. On the other hand, the regime fulfilled their longing, in an impersonal industrial society, for a moral and spiritual union – a longing that neither the Kaiser nor Weimar had been able to satisfy. For many Germans Nazi totalitarianism meant not terror or fear but unity – against the enemy within, against the pure materialism of the United States, and against the Bolshevism of the Soviet Union.

## EAST CENTRAL EUROPE

Beginning in 1938 Hitler was to impose Nazi rule on all twelve of the smaller states of Central and Eastern Europe, but the way had been paved before his arrival. Reacting against an unsuccessful Communist coup, Hungary had already reverted to authoritarian rule in 1919. Poland and Lithuania had succumbed to dictatorship in 1926, Yugoslavia in 1931, Austria in 1933, Estonia and Latvia in 1934, Bulgaria and Greece in 1935, Rumania in 1938. Albania had been virtually an Italian protectorate since the late 1920s; Austria was incorporated into the Third Reich in March 1938; Czechoslovakia was dismembered in October 1938 and occupied in March 1939. The manner in which parliamentary democracy was overthrown in these countries varied considerably, and most of them lacked the economic and technological base for a fullfledged fascist regime. Nevertheless, some of the conditions that had helped to bring fascist totalitarianism to Italy and Germany also existed among the smaller countries to the east.

Just before sacrificing Czechoslovakia to Hitler in 1938 Prime Minister Neville Chamberlain spoke of "a quarrel in a faraway country between people of whom we know nothing." It was both ironical and sad that the British leader should have felt this way: ironical because Czechoslovakia was socially and culturally a "Western" country; sad because she had remained democratic while so many others, including more familiar ones like Germany and Italy, had not. Yet even Czechoslovakia was handicapped by two of the conditions that fatally weakened her less fortunate neighbors. She had a severe nationalities problem, as the quarrel between the Sudeten German minority and the Czech majority showed; she was also a pawn in the struggle among the great powers, as the way they "resolved" this quarrel at Munich showed.*

The other countries of Central and Eastern Europe had other weaknesses as well. Torn by class conflicts, they all lacked the liberal tradition that had at least partially reconciled these conflicts in the West. Parliamentary democracy was new to all of them, including Czechoslovakia, but the Czechs were better able to maintain it because they had a healthy balance of social classes – prosperous peasants, skilled workers, a numerous and well-educated bourgeoisie – an honest and efficient administration dating from Hapsburg times, and a strong religious and moral tradition stemming from Hus. None of these conditions prevailed in the greater part of any of the other countries. Furthermore, most of them were dissatisfied with their 1919 territorial boundaries. Hungary, Austria, and Bulgaria, the countries that had lost the most in the peace settlement, were the most "revisionist." Even those that had benefited sought to gain more: Poland from Russia, Poland and Lithuania from each other, Rumania from Hungary, Greece from Turkey, Yugoslavia from Italy. Finally, almost all of Eastern Europe was poor.

### Economic Problems

Aside from Austria, the Czech lands, parts of Hungary, and the western fringe of Poland, all the small countries of Central and Eastern Europe were economically underdeveloped. Predominantly agricultural, they all suffered from low productivity and underemployment. Little was done to modernize agriculture during the interwar years. Land redistribution had a political rather than an economic purpose wherever it was tried: Rumania, Czechoslovakia, Estonia, Latvia, Lithuania, and parts of Yugoslavia. In most of these places it merely reinforced the pattern of small, inefficient farms, which already prevailed in Bulgaria, Greece, and the Serbian part of Yugoslavia. The fact that land reform was not introduced in Poland and Hungary perpetuated the hostility of the peasants toward their landlords without improving agricultural productivity. The backwardness of Eastern European agriculture also prevented the creation of mass markets for industry and services and, as we saw in Chapter XVII, it aggravated the effects of the chronic depression of the 'twenties and the world depression of the early 'thirties.

The development of industry was limited not only by lack of a mass market but also by lack of capital. When foreign capital did come in it was used to produce armaments for the state or luxury goods for a small urban market. These enterprises did not necessarily help build a native industrial base. What was needed were industries to transform the agricultural products of these countries into jam, butter, cheese, canned meat, and timber products for the home and international market, as well as cheap textiles for the peasant masses. But both the capital and the entrepreneurs were lacking. What little new industry was developed did not provide enough unskilled jobs for peasants coming to the cities from the overpopulated countryside.

Trade was limited by both small domestic markets and economic nationalism. We have noted how most European countries tried to build tariff walls around themselves during the interwar years. This policy was especially ill-advised in the nations of Eastern Europe because of their small populations. If France, with 40 million people, constituted too small a market to stimulate economic growth, the situation was disastrous in Bulgaria, with 6 million people. In each East European country there was a more or less glamorous capital city, where a few thousand middle-class people traded goods and services with each other, and a hinterland, where several million debt-ridden peasants sold little and bought nothing. Business was certainly better in Budapest or Warsaw than in Athens or Sofia, but the basic pattern was the same.

*See p. 721.

## Social Cleavages

Town and countryside were two different worlds socially as well as economically. In Poland and Hungary and even in Rumania and Croatia an important section of the urban middle class had an aristocratic rather than a bourgeois outlook, especially those in the bureaucracy, the army, and the liberal professions. These people were the children and grandchildren of former landowning gentry who had moved to the cities in the second half of the nineteenth century, when the abolition of serfdom and competition from American grain had forced them to sell their estates. The fact that they still identified themselves socially and politically with the big landowners made them indifferent and even hostile to the kinds of reforms the Western European bourgeoisie had sponsored in an effort to reduce class conflicts. To them anyone who worked with his hands was still a peasant and anyone in trade was a Jew or some other kind of "foreigner." Although most middle-class people in Warsaw, Budapest, and Bucharest were of humbler origin, they often adopted similar attitudes out of snobbery. In the Balkans the urban bourgeoisie was more capitalistic than in Poland or the Danubian states, but it too felt an unbridgeable cleavage between itself and the rural masses.

In the 1920s parliamentary democracy, free public education, and even land reform where it was tried, could not mitigate the severe class antagonisms in most of Eastern Europe. Like Miliukov and Kerensky in Russia in 1917,* a handful of well-meaning liberal politicians was unable to force the social and cultural values of the West European bourgeoisie on societies where most people thought of themselves as either the rulers or the ruled. The ruling class consisted of four elements in varying mixtures: landowners, wealthy businessmen, bureaucrats, and "intellectuals"—particularly professors and lawyers; the ruled included the peasant masses and a minority of urban workers, shopkeepers, and clerks. Land reform merely reinforced the poverty and inefficiency of the small peasant proprietors rather than transforming them into the kind of prosperous, independent farmers found in Northwestern Europe. As in so many underdeveloped countries, village boys who managed to obtain a higher education too often studied law, the key to a government job, settled down in the cities, and cut themselves off from peasant life. Meanwhile, the spread of literacy among the masses exposed the younger generation to extremist political ideologies that aggravated existing social tensions. In most places these ideologies found expression in antigovernment parties, thus preventing the minority of bourgois liberals from creating the kind of agreement on fundamental values that made parliamentary democracy work in the West.

*See p. 603.

### Nationalism

The most disruptive ideology in Eastern Europe was nationalism; even when the bourgeois liberals were in power they often used it to divert discontent from domestic problems. In the new schools that they themselves had helped to found, children were taught to regard neighboring nations as culturally and morally inferior to their own. This kind of indoctrination had especially unfortunate consequences in a "revisionist" state like Hungary, many of whose former nationals now found themselves under the rule of "inferior" Rumanians and Czechs. Neither the Rumanians nor the Czechs were responsible for the fact that most of Hungary's peasants still did not own even a small plot of land. But hatred of these "wicked" neighbors was used by Hungary's rulers as a means of avoiding the question of land reform.

Nationalism created other kinds of tension in the newer multinational states. In addition to its Sudeten German and Hungarian minorities Czechoslovakia was a union of two separate nationalities, Czechs and Slovaks; the fact that they both spoke the same language did not prevent the Slovak nationalists from wanting autonomy or outright independence. A similar situation prevailed in Yugoslavia, or the Kingdom of the Serbs, Croats, and Slovenes, as it was called when it was founded in 1918; the Croats prided themselves on their "thousand years of history" under the Hapsburgs and resented their political subordination to the "oriental" Serbs. Poland and Rumania had large ethnic minorities in the provinces they had taken from the former Russian Empire. These Belorussians, Ukrainians, and Jews were more "assimilable" than the Slovaks and

Croats, but the Polish and Rumanian governments found it more convenient to use them as scapegoats for their own ethnic majorities.

The most vicious kind of nationalism was directed against the Jews, especially in Rumania, Hungary, and Poland, where they constituted 5 to 10 per cent of the population. This antisemitism was motivated in part by competition in business and the professions between the "natives" and the more assimilated Jews, but it was also encouraged by the government itself. University students in these three countries behaved like Nazi Storm Troopers in their attacks on Jews, and they formed the hard core of the fascist parties that arose in the early 1930s: the National Radical Camp in Poland, the Arrow Cross in Hungary, the Iron Guard in Rumania.

### The Road to Dictatorship

The greater the hostility between social and ethnic groups, especially in poor countries, the more likely it is that violence and strong-man rule will ultimately prevail. Some of the military dictatorships that replaced parliamentary democracy in Eastern Europe were more fascist than others. Marshal Pilsudski, the war hero who ruled Poland from 1926 until his death in 1935, merely superimposed the trappings of fascism on his reactionary regime with no intention of transforming it into a totalitarian state. In Hungary General Gömbös, who was premier from 1932 to 1936, represented the same tendency. On the other hand, in 1938 King Carol II of Rumania tried to make himself a miniature Mussolini, introducing a one-party state, a party uniform, Roman salutes, and a bombastic fascist rhetoric. King Boris of Bulgaria modestly avoided such extravagances. The dictatorship that General Metaxas set up in Greece in 1936 came nearest to true fascism, with its extremely efficient repressive machinery, its youth movement modeled on the Hitler Jugend, and its glorification of Metaxas as the founder of a new Hellenic civilization.

Whether ruled by generals or kings the dictatorships of Eastern Europe did not try to approach the degree of totalitarian control that existed in Germany and Italy.

They lacked both the mass support and the economic and technological base for that. There were few attempts at social regimentation; there was no conflict with the Catholic and Orthodox churches, both of which shared the essentially reactionary goals of these dictatorships. Even some of the bourgeois liberals came to admit that strong-man rule was the only way to preserve order and to quell revolutionary threats to an economic and social structure that they themselves did not really want to change. Both they and the other members of the ruling elite deplored the brutality of the police and the corruption of the bureaucracy. In the end, however, they felt that even this was better than the darkness and chaos that a revolt of the masses would bring to them and to the veneer of "civilization" they tried to maintain.

## PORTUGAL AND SPAIN

As in the smaller countries of Central and Eastern Europe, the fundamental reason for the collapse of parliamentary democracy in Spain and Portugal was the conflict between the interests of the ruling elite and the majority of the population. Portugal's democratic republic led a stormy and precarious existence from 1910 to 1932, Spain's from 1931 to 1939. Both had come into being through anticlerical, antimonarchical revolutions; both were destroyed by dictators who, if they could not restore the monarchy, at least restored the dominant position of the Catholic Church, the wealthy employers and landowners, and the army.

Portugal's dictator until his stroke in 1968 was Antonio de Oliveira Salazar (1889-1970). This pious, retiring professor began his rise to power as the advocate of a national renaissance under a "new state." Before he became dictator in 1932 he had already founded the fascist-inspired National Union Party as the instrument of this renaissance. Once in power he declared all other parties illegal and promulgated an authoritarian constitution. In the "new state" the Catholic

*Portugal: a typical small-country dicatorship. The figurehead chief-of-state, General Carmona, center; Prime Minister Salazar, left.*

Church regained its monopoly over education and its pervasive influence over all aspects of Portuguese life. Salazar also set up a corporative chamber on the Italian model, though with only advisory power. Within the limits of an extremely backward economy and a politically indifferent population Portugal became a totalitatian state that was clerical-reactionary rather than fascist.

Salazar's regime resembled the one set up across the border by General Francisco Franco (b. 1892) in the late 1930s. But unlike Portugal, Spain suffered through a bloody civil war between the overthrow of its monarchy in 1931 and Franco's final victory in 1939.

The background of the war in Spain lay in that country's lack of political community and social cohesion. At the beginning of the nineteenth century the Spanish masses had momentarily united in resisting the Napoleonic occupation, but thereafter the traditional ruling classes retained their power over the government and public life in general. When these classes disapproved of a particular government, the army overthrew it and "pronounced" the installation of a new one, this method of political change being called a *pronunciamento.*

Between 1875 and 1931 Kings Alfonso XII and XIII did the bidding of the ruling classes—thus eliminating the need for further *pronunciamentos*—but the chasm between the elites and the masses remained. A sizable middle-class minority opposed the established order and tried to foster the goals of nineteenth-century liberalism. Because of the reactionary character of the Spanish Church these middle-class liberals also tended to be strongly anticlerical. The mass of the country's peasants were poor agricultural workers, resentful of their absentee landlords and far less docile toward the

Church than their Portuguese cousins. Even more than the exploited peasants, Spain's industrial workers and miners wanted to destroy the existing society, and all three groups were attracted to anarcho-syndicalism.* Finally, Catalan and Basque separatist sentiment became increasingly vocal in the face of corrupt rule in Madrid and declining national prestige.†

By 1931 the army could no longer resist the accumulated demands for change. Alfonso XIII left the country, Spain became a republic, and the middle-class liberals set up a democratic political regime. But these liberals soon antagonized the ruling classes by attacking the position of the Church, especially in education. The urban workers in turn found the liberals too "bourgeois," and the mass of poor peasants resented their unwillingness to redistribute the country's farm land. Although almost all Spaniards wanted the Republic to change *something,* they remained as divided as ever.

The chaotic life of the Spanish Republic soon led to civil war. Churches were pillaged; political leaders of both the Left and the Right were murdered; laws became increasingly difficult to enforce; there were frequent armed uprisings. In late 1933 the electoral victory of the more moderate republicans gave the reactionary forces enough influence on the government to satisfy them. This situation ended with the election of February 1936, which was won by a Popular Front coalition of liberal republicans, Socialists, and Communists. Now the traditional ruling classes decided that the Republic itself had to be destroyed; they planned a new *pronunciamento.* At the same time, the anarcho-syndicalists and the handful of Communists wanted the new Popular Front government to initiate a real social and economic revolution. Thus, both the extreme Right and the extreme Left were sabotaging the regime when the civil war broke out on July 17, 1936.

*See pp. 522-524.

†Spain's military defeats by the United States in 1898 and by Moroccan tribesmen in 1921 accelerated this decline.

Actually, the army generals who tried to "pronounce" the republican regime out of existence had no intention of starting a civil war. But, in flagrant violation of all the rules, the legal government began arming the people; the "rabble" was to be permitted to "pronounce." Since the navy, the air force, and some of the generals remained loyal to the regime, the few rebellious garrisons in Spain itself could not hold out for long without outside reinforcements. Under the leadership of General Franco these reinforcements came from Spanish Morocco in transport planes furnished by Adolph Hitler. From the beginning foreign intervention influenced the course of the Spanish Civil War.

The war dragged on for almost three years. Within the first few months, the rebels, or Nationalists, established themselves in the western part of the country, with Franco as their "head of state." For over two years the Republicans, or Loyalists, held much of the eastern part, including the three biggest cities: Madrid, Barcelona, Valencia. It was a bloody war, with innumerable atrocities committed on both sides, though the Nationalists were especially cruel. Before it was over, 600,000 Spaniards died, and the country, already poor, became destitute. The Nationalists' ultimate victory in March 1939 dashed all hopes for a liberal society and brought wholesale reprisals against the defeated Loyalists. Over half a million of them fled into exile, and almost half a million were imprisoned.

Why did this war last so long? The regular armed forces of each side were fairly evenly matched, but foreign intervention was crucial, not only for the war in Spain but also for the European balance of power. As we shall see in the next chapter, Germany and Italy aided the Nationalists while the Soviet Union aided the Loyalists. Both Hitler and Stalin deliberately limited their aid in order to keep either side from winning. They did this so that the major powers that favored the losing side would not come into the war directly.

In the end, however, Franco imposed his quasi-fascist dictatorship on the whole of Spain. Taking the title *El Caudillo*, he seemed like another *Duce* or *Führer.* The *Falange,* an avowedly fascist party founded in the early 'thirties, became the only legal party, though, as in Italy and Germany, its storm troopers soon lost out to the politicians and generals. Franco's regime suppressed the labor movement, instituted strict censorship, and enforced obedience to the state through terroristic police control. Yet his regime was *not* truly fascist. Unlike Hitler and Mussolini, Franco remained the tool of those conservative elites that had helped him gain power: the landowning nobility, the Church hierarchy, the directors of large corporations, the professional officers of the armed forces. They had no interest in fostering a new ideology or in creating a "brave new world." Consequently, Franco was obliged to restore the economic and social status quo as it had been before 1931. Despite its fascist trappings, the most accurate label for his regime is authoritarian-reactionary.

: : :

European Communists had to win in the first round, as they did only in Russia; if a second round had to be fought, the ruling elites, including some self-styled liberals, would be ready to go to whatever extremes they felt were necessary to stop any kind of social or economic revolution. In all Germany and Italy they went all the way to fascism; in Hungary and Spain they reverted to an older type of authoritarian rule. By 1939 only Great Britain, France, and the smaller countries of Northwestern Europe had escaped the trend toward anti-Communist totalitarianism. Such was the final outcome of the war that had supposedly been fought to "make the world safe for democracy."

Anti-Communism and dissatisfaction with the results of the First World War were not the only reasons for the rise of fascism. The inability of the Italian and German bourgeois liberals to do their job properly was also to blame. Their job, as we know, was to find ways of reconciling the older elites and the masses to the economically and technologically rational civilization they had created. They had good excuses for having failed to provide the necessary degree of social synthesis and moral cohesiveness: lack of time, lack of power, lack of cooperation. The point is that they *did* fail, and the fascists forcefully rejected the whole liberal tradition as decadent and contemptible.

Like the Communists, the Fascists and the Nazis used totalitarian methods to create their "brave new worlds" on the ruins of the liberal regimes they had overthrown. All parties except The Party were eliminated, and the struggle for power henceforth took the form of ruthless in-group fighting within its top ranks. The Party placed itself above the law and maintained its dictatorship over the rest of the population through police terror, thought control, and social regimentation. In order to promote a more positive feeling of "togetherness" within the cowed majority, The Party also tried to direct its hatred against arbitrarily selected minority groups.

Despite these similarities in method, Communism and fascism had different goals. The long-range goals of the Russian Communists were *revolutionary-aggressive* ones: to end poverty and social injustice through material progress and to spread their revolution throughout the world. During the interwar years, however, they concentrated on overthrowing the existing economic and social structure in Russia and on giving socialism an industrial base there.

In Germany and Italy the task of technical and economic rationalization had been largely accomplished, and neither the fascists nor their supporters wanted to overthrow the existing economic and social structure. Their main goals were to shore up this structure and to strengthen the nation in the face of real or imagined threats to its power and glory. In the long run these were *reactionary-defensive* goals, given the growing might of the United States and the Soviet Union, but during the 1930s they made Hitler and Mussolini more aggressive than Stalin.

## SUGGESTED READINGS

Nettl, J. P., *The Soviet Achievement.* New York: Harcourt Brace and World, 1967.*

An excellent survey.

Von Laue, Theodore, *Why Lenin, Why Stalin?* Philadelphia: Lippincott, 1964.*

Argues that only dictatorial means could have modernized Russia in so short a time.

Fainsod, Merle, *How Russia is Ruled.* Rev. ed. Cambridge, Mass.: Harvard Univ. Press, 1969.

An advanced analysis by a leading expert.

Deutscher, Isaac, *Stalin: A Political Biography.* 2nd ed., New York: Oxford Univ. Press, 1967.*

A first-rate study—lively, detailed, and provocative.

Warth, Robert D., *Stalin.* New York: Twayne, 1969.

Brief and up-to-date.

Simmons, Ernest J., ed., *Through the Glass of Soviet Literature.* New York: Columbia Univ. Press, 1953.

Attempts—through selections from literary works—to show changes in Soviet society during the interwar years.

Borkenau, Franz, *World Communism.* Ann Arbor, Mich.: Univ. of Michigan Press, 1962.*

Though rather opinionated, this remains the most thorough account of the international Communist movement during the interwar years.

Weber, Eugen, *Varieties of Fascism.* Princeton, N.J.: D. Van Nostrand, 1964. An Anvil original.*

An excellent analytical survey. Covers all European countries that had fascist movements.

Nolte, Ernst, *The Three Faces of Fascism.* New York: Holt, Rinehart and Winston, 1967.*

Good on fascist theory.

Woolf, Stuart J., ed., *European Fascism.* London: Weidenfeld & Nicolson, 1968.*

Brief essays on fascism in a dozen countries.

Halperin, S. William, *Mussolini and Italian Fascism.* Princeton, N.J.: D. Van Nostrand, 1964. An Anvil original.*

The best short history in English—accurate and up-to-date.

Tasca, Angelo, *The Rise of Italian Fascism, 1918–1922.* New York: H. Fertig,1966.

A comprehensive account—puts heavy blame on the industrialists for helping Mussolini gain power.

Kirkpatrick, Sir Ivone, *Mussolini: A Study in Power.* New York: Hawthorn Books, 1965.

The best biography in English so far.

Bullock, Alan, *Hitler: A Study in Tyranny.* Rev. ed. New York: Harper and Row, 1964.*

Probably the best political biography of any twentieth-century dictator.

Meinecke, Friedrich, *The German Catastrophe, Reflections and Recollections.* Boston: Beacon Press, 1963.*

A great German historian who had held aloof from Hitlerism analyzes the modern history of his country.

Bracher, Karl Dietrich, *The German Dictatorship.* New York: Praeger, 1970.
The most recent and most authoritative work on the subject in any language.

Schoenbaum, David, *Hitler's Social Revolution.* New York: Doubleday-Anchor, 1967.*
Excellent analysis of the effects of the Nazi regime on different sections of German society.

Allen, William Sheridan, *The Nazi Seizure of Power: The Experience of a Single German Town.* Chicago: Quadrangle Books, 1967.*
A remarkable study of the rise of the Nazis at the grass roots.

Klein, Burton H., *Germany's Economic Preparations for War.* Cambridge, Mass.: Harvard Univ. Press, 1959.
The pioneering study that first challenged the legend that Hitler put the Germany economy on a war footing in the 1930's.

O'Neill, Robert J. *The German Army and the Nazi Party, 1933–1939.* New York: Heineman, 1967.
Shows how Hitler manipulated the generals.

Seton-Watson, H., *Eastern Europe between the Wars,* 1918–1941. New York: Harper and Row, 1965, Torchbook.*
A comprehensive survey—written over two decades ago and still the most balanced presentation of the interwar period.

Wiskemann, Elizabeth, *Europe of the Dictators 1919–1945.* New York: Harper and Row, 1967.*
Especially good on Central European developments.

Thomas, Hugh, *The Spanish Civil War,* New York: Harper and Row, 1963. Colophon.*
A very satisfactory history of this tragic series of events.

Jackson, Gabriel, *The Spanish Republic and the Civil War, 1931–1939.* Princeton, N.J.: Princeton Univ. Press, 1965.*
The best analysis of Spain's troubled history in the 1930's.

CHAPTER XIX

# THE WESTERN DEMOCRACIES AND THE WORLD, 1919–1939

To most people in the Western democracies the Communist and fascist regimes of the interwar years were inexcusable deviations from the European tradition. Like the victors of 1815, the victors of 1919 wanted to resume their "normal" pattern of existence. Although the United States clung to its old attitudes the most tenaciously, President Warren G. Harding's 1920 campaign slogan "back to normalcy" also expressed the outlook of the British and the French during the 'twenties and early 'thirties. "Back to normalcy" meant political democracy, laissez faire, bourgeois ascendancy at home, and white supremacy in the colonies. All these "normal" conditions had begun to be challenged before 1914, but the war had seemingly eliminated "internal" unrest in the face of the "external" enemy. Once victory had been won, the British, French, and American governments continued to expect conformity and obedience from their citizens and colonial subjects. Communist Russia, of course, was beyond redemption, but, hopefully, she could be isolated. Italian Fascism was not the kind of regime one would ever want for one's own country, but perhaps a little discipline would be good for "those over-emotional Italians." The brutality of the German Nazis, however, turned one's stomach; Hitler really *was* no better than Stalin. And the worst thing about all those dreadful dictators was their threats to the peace.

The last thing the Western democracies wanted was another war—any kind of war. They convinced themselves of their innocence in provoking the holocaust they had just been through and of their righteousness in ending it on their own terms. In the 1920s they made concessions to their former enemy Germany and their former ally Japan in the interest of preserving international peace. Their "colonial" dependencies remained docile for the most part, though the French had to suppress rebellions in Morocco and Syria, and the British gave up Ireland rather than continue fighting to keep it. The real challenge to the territorial and military status quo came in the 1930s, when Japan, Italy and Germany, declaring that the legal framework of the peace settlement deprived them of their equal rights as nations, proceeded to flout it with wanton acts of aggression. Few Britishers, Frenchmen, or Americans really believed that the three aggressor nations were morally justified in asserting their rights by destroying those of other nations—even "faraway" ones like China, Ethiopia, and Czechoslovakia. Yet so averse were they to war that not until 1940 did the British and the French take any major military action; the majority of Americans remained doggedly isolationist until the Japanese attack on Pearl Harbor in December 1941.

During the interwar years the Western democracies were on the defensive against domestic as well as foreign threats to the status quo. Small countries like Sweden and New Zealand might experiment with the welfare state, but the Big Three clung to laissez faire and "business as usual" as long as they could. In 1919 women got the vote in Great Britian and the United States, and in the 1930s French and American labor gained some long overdue reforms. In general, however, new policies were adopted only to meet emergencies. Even the American New Deal and the French Popular Front were viewed by their supporters as temporary, while their opponents saw these innovations as the end of everything they held dear. Neither the "lost generation" of the 'twenties nor the "committed generation" of the 'thirties spoke for the majority. The majority thought of themselves as unlettered and apolitical "little men." They believed that, given the chance, they could run their lives in the good old ways without assistance from Big Government, Big Business, Big Labor, or Big Brother. Just as peace turned out to be an illusion, so did this belief.

## FRANCE

The French had had a Pyrrhic victory, and both the victory and its Pyrrhic quality profoundly influenced their postwar development. They felt that the First World War—"The Great War"—had been the final reckoning in their struggle to preserve their nation and their way of life against German aggression. Like the British and the Americans, the French wanted to believe that the war had made the world safe for democracy and a return to "normalcy." The French, however, had a stronger sense of having exhausted their moral and physical reserves, and their manpower losses were particularly crippling in view of the country's declining birth rate. At first they tried to preserve their temporary preponderance in Europe by insisting on strict enforcement of the Treaty of Versailles, by maintaining a large military establishment, and by building up a new alliance system against Germany. After 1925, however, pacifist sentiment and sheer exhaustion led to a laxer foreign policy, and when the Germans became aggressive again in the mid-1930s, fear of another bloodletting won out over fear of Germany.

By the mid-1930s the new challenge to France's international position helped to break down the prewar liberal synthesis at home, but as long as France's rank among the world powers remained undisputed this synthesis survived almost intact. It was a stalemate between old and new elements in the political, economic, and social systems of the Third Republic; and it accepted social mobility and industrialization as long as they did not disrupt the country's traditional way of life too sharply. This "stalemate society," dominated by the upper and middle bourgeoisie, had the moral approval of the majority of the population—small farmers, shopkeepers, craftsmen, and white-collar employees—but it could not reconcile the extreme reactionaries or the militant workers. Nevertheless, the political system of the Third Republic worked fairly effectively as long as the economic and social balance was maintained. Until the 1930s it provided temporarily strong and stable cabinets during real crises. Otherwise the state let most citizens alone, providing a Parliament and a highly centralized bureaucracy that ran the country between election days. By 1932, however, the depression was already challenging the economic and social balance and by 1934 it was challenging the political balance.

### The Quest for Security

In the 1920s "international relations" seemed to be largely restricted to Europe, like the League of Nations itself. Specifically, they seemed to be centered on the continuing conflict between France and Germany. France tried to preserve her version of "normalcy" as embodied in the artificial securities of 1919; Germany tried to restore her "natural" status as the strongest power on the continent. This conflict was bound to go on as long as the belief persisted that Europe was still the center of the world, and neither the United States nor the Soviet Union did anything to destroy this illusion.

### *The League of Nations*

The League of Nations was the most elaborate and most nearly worldwide international organization ever before devised. Its Assembly consisted of fifty-odd sovereign states each having an equal vote; its Council included Great Britain, France, Italy, and Japan as permanent members anf four (later increased to six) temporary members. Both the Assembly and the Council met in Geneva, where the permanent Secretariat, heavily staffed with Frenchmen, did much useful work of a nonpolitical nature during the interwar years.

From the start, however, France sensed the inadequacy of the League as an instrument for fostering her security or anyone else's. The League was fatally weakened by the permanent absence of the United States and by the fact that at no time were all the great European powers simultaneously members of it. (Germany was admitted in 1926 and withdrew in 1933, the year before the Soviet Union was admitted.) This situation gave France and her East European satellites an unwarranted influence in both the Assembly and the Council, but it did not make up for the fact that the League lacked effective machinery for preventing armed aggression against any of its members.

The weaknesses of the League were especially disconcerting to France in view of the "desertion" of her wartime Allies. We have seen how both the American Congress and the British Parliament rejected the Treaty of Guarantee, in which Wilson and Lloyd George had pledged their nations to defend France against further German aggression. France's only alternative therefore was to safeguard her security through her own military and diplomatic efforts.

### *Alliances to the East. The Locarno Pact*

The French alliance system comprised those small countries that had the most to fear from the powers that wanted to "revise" the peace settlement. First there was Belgium, obviously exposed to a repetition of the Schlieffen Plan without a clear military understanding with France; such an understanding was reached in 1920. Then there was Poland, a client state of France from the day of her foundation, saved by her from the Bolshevik invasion of 1920, and fearful of German designs on her Corridor to the sea: in 1921 a Franco-Polish treaty bound the two countries to a common defense against unprovoked aggression. Finally, three other Succession States in Eastern Europe—Czechoslovakia, Yugoslavia, and Rumania—had formed the Little Entente mainly against Hungarian revisionism. France signed her alliance with Czechoslovakia in 1924, with Rumania in 1926, and with Yugoslavia in 1927. She reinforced the several agreements from time to time with loans.

France's commitments in Eastern Europe overstrained her resources without giving her real security against a German decision to upset the Versailles settlement. Hence the French tried to enforce the terms of this settlement to the fullest. When the Germans defaulted on their reparations payments in 1923, France placed the Ruhr district under military occupation in order to force them to pay. The occupation ended with a surrender by Germany, but it antagonized world opinion and taught the French the folly of unilateral coercion.

By late 1924, then, the French were again trying to strengthen the League and to negotiate a military agreement with Great Britain. Germany's new foreign minister, Gustav Stresemann, initiated a countermove by offering to respect the western frontiers established at Versailles in return for a general attempt to relax international tensions. The outcome of Stresemann's proposal was the Locarno Pact, signed in December 1925. The circumstances leading to the signing of this pact epitomized the new diplomacy of the 1920's. With the British foreign secretary, Austen Chamberlain, playing the role of mediator, Stresemann and his French counterpart, Aristide Briand, held a highly publicized "summit meeting" at the Swiss lakeside resort of Locarno. As a means of showing the world that the two habitual enemy nations had now resolved their differences, the two aging foreign ministers had themselves photographed relaxing in their shirt-sleeves and rowing around in a small boat.

The pact that emerged from all this was a limited and rather vague achievement. It included a main treaty in which Germany, France, and Belgium agreed to respect one another's existing frontiers and in which Great Britain and Italy promised to see that they did so. Germany also agreed to settle her disputes with Poland and Czechoslovakia by arbitration, but she did *not* agree to accept her existing frontiers with these two countries. In return for these commitments, Germany was to be accepted back into the family of "respectable" nations, and her "great power" status was to be recognized by a permanent seat on the Council of the League.

Once the pact was signed, statesmen and journalists in every European country—with the important exception of the Soviet Union, which we shall discuss presently—magnified the significance of Locarno out of all proportion. They spoke of the "Locarno spirit" and the "Locarno era" as if all the old problems had been settled. This was, of course, illusory. The "Locarno spirit" was based on a fundamental misunderstanding: Briand assumed that by abandoning their insistence on armed security the French had already conceded enough to Germany to expect her to become reconciled to her new token status as a great power; Stresemann intended to use this "foot in the door" as a means of making further demands for revision until Germany should at last achieve her rightful place as the number one power in Europe. Meanwhile, Stresemann secretly condoned the German General Staff's illegal rearmament program.

Later observers have argued that France's real purpose at Locarno was to bring Germany clearly into the Western camp against the Soviet Union. There is little evidence that the French were thinking in these terms in 1925, although the Soviet Union itself charged that they and the British were. As early as 1922 Germany and Russia had broken the diplomatic isolation imposed on them by France by coming to a mutual understanding with each other at the Italian resort town of Rapallo. Ostensibly a trade agreement, the Rapallo understanding secretly provided Soviet factories and training areas for Germany's illegal rearmament in return for German technical assistance. Locarno weakened this arrangement without destroying it. The main point is that Briand, though he knew about the Rapallo agreement, chose to ignore it in the futile hope that Germany would eventually come around to the French point of view.

### Disarmament

One thing the "Locarno spirit" did was stimulate the movement for disarmament. At the Washington Conference in early 1922 the French had strongly objected to the formula that put their navy on a par with that of Italy and at a much lower total tonnage than that of the British, American, and Japanese navies.* During the Locarno era the French were more willing at least to listen to proposals for disarmament of all kinds. Indeed, in 1928, Briand and the American secretary of state, Frank B. Kellogg, initiated a worldwide agreement to renounce war altogether. If the Kellogg-Briand Pact was merely a pious hope, the Disarmament Conference that finally met in Geneva in 1932–1933 brought the French and everyone else back to their senses; for it was there that Germany made clear her demand for "equality of rights" in armaments as well as in diplomatic status. Her withdrawal from the Disarmament Conference and from the League in October 1933 initiated a new period of international tensions.

*The Washington Conference was also noteworthy for establishing a status quo in the Far East comparable to that of the Versailles settlement in Europe. In the Nine-Power Treaties signed at Washington the five signatories of the Naval Armaments Treaty, along with China, Belgium, the Netherlands, and Portugal, guaranteed the territorial integrity and administrative independence of China.

The failure of the Disarmament Conference signaled the breakdown of the Versailles settlement. This settlement had not removed the disequilibrium that had precipitated the First World War; it had merely created a new and quite artificial status quo. The Locarno Pact, the French alliance system, and even the League of Nations had become the custodians of this status quo. Hence, any changes in it could only be made in defiance of the Versailles settlement itself, and any such changes were bound to threaten France's security.

### Social Conservatism

In the 1920s French society resisted change more successfully than most other European societies, but their very conservatism hampered the French in adapting themselves to the economic and political crises of the 1930s. The persistence of strong family ties fostered emotional and social stability; it also retarded economic growth by preserving many small family firms that were reluctant to expand at the price of losing their control to outside investors. The class structure gave the majority of Frenchmen an acceptable status in good times, but it was ill suited to the needs of an industrial economy and an egalitarian ideal. In addition, France's educational system divided people socially and failed to provide enough technicians for an industrial economy.

Although social distinctions based on education prevailed almost everywhere in Europe, the French educational system seemed especially designed to perpetuate the dominance of the bourgeoisie. Elementary education was free to age fourteen, but most pupils going on into secondary education—which was not free and which was virtually restricted to middle- and upper-class children—were separated from the others at age twelve. The classical education and baccalaureate degrees they received from these secondary schools set them apart from the majority of young people and gave them a monopoly of the best jobs.

During the interwar years the entrenched bourgeoisie tried to resist every kind of change. The dearth of young men caused by heavy wartime casualties allowed the older generation to maintain its hold on business, government administration, and the army, as well as education. The French bourgeoisie feared everything from the Bolsheviks and the "lost generation" to "Americanization," by which it meant technological and organizational innovations. The leading bourgeois politicians opposed female suffrage on the ground that most women would vote for the clerical-minded Rightist parties but also because they continued to believe that woman's place was in the home and not in public life. As for the workers, the big businessmen believed that any concessions to them would make them lazy and more demanding then ever.

#### *French Labor*

Mutual hostility between the working class and the bourgeoisie was an ingrained habit in France. With the exception of the brief Popular Front episode in 1936, nothing was done during the interwar years to break it. The workers continued to view all bourgeois as selfish capitalists; the employers continued to view all union leaders as dangerous revolutionaries—a view shared by large sections of the rest of the population in times of labor unrest. During the war French labor had abstained from strikes and demonstrations, but in the spring of 1919 the trade-unions launched a series of strikes culminating in an abortive general strike a year later. Although only a minority of the CGT leaders—partly Communist and partly revolutionary syndicalist—had approved this general strike, it turned the government and the public against the labor movement as a whole.

From the 1919–1920 strikes onward, international Communism served as a bogeyman with which to frighten the general public, and it divided the labor movement itself. In January 1921, the defeated and discredited CGT was temporarily disbanded by the government. Hope for a solution to the labor problem waned rapidly thereafter. In 1921 normal trade-union activities were further curtailed by a demoralizing internal struggle that led to an open split when the revolutionary wing, inspired by the Communists, broke away from the CGT. Always a small minority, the Communist-controlled CGTU nevertheless confirmed the conservative belief that all union leaders were committed to class warfare and violent revolution and that any labor legislation would be a mistake. The only such legislation passed before 1936 was the very modest National Workmen's Insurance Law of 1930. Otherwise, the conservative forces blocked all measures to improve the workers' lot until the "dreadful year," 1936, when the Popular Front government came to power and the whole liberal synthesis seemed threatened by nationwide sit-in strikes.

The sit-in strikes of May and June, sparked by the Popular Front's victory in May, resembled those in Italy in September 1920, though they were more effective and more widespread. Their main purpose was to achieve recognition of the right of the labor unions to conclude collective trade agreements, plus a forty-hour week and paid vacations. These demands seem modest enough today, but in 1936 they fed Rightist fears of an economic and social revolution. After all, the workers' "occupation" of the factories seemed to threaten the very principle of private property.

Instead of declaring martial law and forcibly evacuating the plants, the new Popular Front government forced the employers to sign an agreement at the Hôtel Matignon, the official residence of the prime minister, Léon Blum. The Matignon Agreement and the supplementary legislation that followed it met all the demands of the strikers, and also provided small wage increases, the appointment of shop stewards, and a government arbitration system for labor-management disputes. Blum did not stop there. He fixed prices and established government control of wheat, he reorganized the Bank of France by placing it under government control, and he took steps to nationalize the armaments and aviation industries. Not only the employers but other sections of the bourgeoisie felt their dominant position in French society threatened by a government that gave in to the "revolt of the masses" in this way, especially when its prime minister was both a Socialist and a Jew. Most of the bourgeois elite merely grumbled and sent its gold out of the country. A significant minority, however, began to abandon the liberal synthesis for quasifascist movements.

### Political Weaknesses

The Third Republic survived the First World War and all the crises of the interwar years. In 1873 Adolphe Thiers had called it the regime that divided Frenchmen least, and it had little more to recommend it thereafter—except its survival. The politicians were as divided as the French people themselves, but their lines of division did not concide on different issues. Furthermore, the political leaders of the Third Republic had to make so many compromises in order to hold shaky coalitions together that they were unable to carry through positive solutions to the nation's most pressing problems. Most parties rarely won a majority of the votes on the first ballot. Consequently, on the run-off ballot, the leaders of one party would make agreements to support the candidate of a "like-minded" party with a larger plurality in one constituency in return for that party's support in a constituency where its own candidate had the larger plurality. In the elections of 1920 and 1928 the Radicals formed such alliances with the Right-Center parties, while in 1924, 1932, and 1936 they worked with the Socialists. These electoral alliances dissolved once the Chamber was in session: then Right-Center coalitions were threatened by the possibility that the Radicals might leave them, and Left-Center coalitions were weakened by the same danger plus the fact that the Communists usually did not suport them.

The shifts of the Radicals back and forth from the Left Center to the Right Center reflected in part the ambivalence of the mass of lower-middle-class voters that supported them. These people opposed the conservatives on ideological grounds, but they also feared the kinds of economic and social change demanded by the Socialists and especially the Communists. The Radical deputies also shifted as they played politics in voting against a particular government in order to get more cabinet posts in the next government. Because of their prominence in

*One of the many demonstrations immediately preceding the February 6 riot*

nearly all governments, the Radicals had more opportunities than any other party to institute policies in keeping with the new needs of postwar France. Their failure to do so was attributable not only to the ambivalent desires of their constituents and to their own desire to stay in office by not "rocking the boat," it was also due to ineffectual leadership.

Between the fall of Georges Clemenceau in 1920 and the emergence of Charles de Gaulle in 1944, the French democractic process failed to turn up a really creative and dynamic leader. From 1922 to 1924 and from 1926 to 1929 Premier Raymond Poincaré guided the country through the crises created by the occupation of the Ruhr and by the fall of the franc, but he lacked both popularity and imagination. He was essentially a conservative nationalist holding the line against threats to France's military and financial security. Of the dozen or so other men who served as premier during the interwar years, only Léon Blum offered anything resembling a consistent program of reform; yet he too lacked the strong personality and will of a true leader.

### An Uneasy Democracy

While the majority of Frenchmen continued to support the parliamentary regime despite its weaknesses, a growing minority turned away from it during the depression years. The first overt "attack" against it was the riot of February 6, 1934, by

Right-wing nationalist leagues intent on storming the Chamber of Deputies. Over a hundred thousand Parisians gathered in the Place de la Concorde to watch the members of these leagues—mostly war veterans and college boys—battle the police who were defending the bridge leading to the Chamber. Most of the rioters wanted to force the legally constituted government out of office because of its alleged involvement in a financial scandal; a small minority wanted to overthrow the regime itself. There was considerable bloodshed, but the police held the mob in check, and the rioters did not get the chance to throw the deputies into the Seine. Law and order were restored within a few days, and a new conservative government temporarily placated many Rightists. Nevertheless, the specter of fascism had appeared in the riot, and the French Communists, remembering what had happened to the German Communists a year earlier, abandoned their antiparliamentary tactics and began trying to form a Popular Front of all the Leftist parties.

Politically the Popular Front was an electoral alliance and a parliamentary coalition of Radicals, Socialists, and Communists, which supported the Blum government from June 1936 to June 1937. Socially it was a temporary coming together of workers and middle-class liberals in the face of a threat to democratic liberties and institutions. It also stood for a program of economic reform. Finally, it was a tactical and propaganda device which the Russian-controlled Comintern used to forestall possible German and Japanese aggression against the Soviet Union. In this respect the Popular Front was not restricted to France; the Communists promoted it in many other countries, with special success in Spain and China.

For all its good intentions, the Popular Front government of Léon Blum failed to meet the challenges of the depression and German aggression. Its foreign policy was no more effective than that of the governments that preceded and followed it. At home its leaders had proclaimed the advent of a New Deal and a moral regeneration, but unlike the American New Deal, the French Popular Front tried to foster economic recovery without the extreme measures of government loans and public works. Its efforts to stimulate spending through modest wage increases were soon threatened by inflation and by the massive hosility of the French business community, which preferred to invest its capital abroad. In June 1937, when Blum finally tried to restrict the outflow of capital, the Radical-dominated Senate overthrew his government.

Despite its other failures, the Popular Front saved French democracy. It was the menacing activities of the Rightist leagues and the impulse toward republican defense that had prompted the Radicals to rally to it in the first place. Without the threat of fascism—both at home and from the outside—the Communists would probably have continued to sabotage the democratic system, and millions of impoverished lower-middle-class Frenchmen might also have turned against it. Anti-Communism might have become an irresistible slogan for them as the depression continued. It is true that the various reactionary and fascist movements in France were weak and divided and lacking a Mussolini or Hitler to lead them. Still, one of them might have succeeded in setting up an authoritarian government had there been an alliance among the Leftists.

Since the Communists ceased to denounce the parliamentary regime (though they often opposed the current government), the main threats to it continued to come from the extreme Right in the late 1930s. Some people in this camp may have thought in irritation "better Hitler than Blum," but none of their demonstrations or conspiracies toppled the hated "system." Only the military defeat of 1940 was able to do that.

## GREAT BRITAIN

In may ways postwar Great Britain resembled France. Like the French, the British wanted to preserve as much of the prewar order as possible, both at home and in the world. As in France, the labor movement in Great Britain showed considerable militancy in the early postwar years only to see its hopes frustrated. Britain's wartime casualties had been smaller than France's, but many of her most talented and energetic young men had volunteered and been killed in the first two years of the war. Thus she too suffered a dearth of dynamic leadership in both business and politics. Finally, as in France and all advanced countries, her state administration grew in size and power and played an ever larger role in national life.

In some respects Great Britain made a better adjustment than France to the new problems of the interwar years. Her less rigid social structure and the strength of her labor movement reduced class conflict and reinforced the liberal synthesis. Her more advanced economy, despite chronic weak spots, recovered more quickly from the depression of the 1930s. After a good deal of splintering and individual desertions her major political parties came to represent more distinct points of view than those in France. But British foreign policy was as unimaginative and defensive as that of the French, especially in the face of the new aggressors of the 1930s.

### Society

In the 1920s British society was less tradition-bound and more democratic, at least in outward appearance, than it had been before the war. The fact that 90 per cent of the population was urban (the largest percentage of any major country) helped to break down traditional values of all kinds. Respectable women wore short skirts and smoked in public; young people asserted their freedom from sexual restraints that their elders had taken for granted. In Britain, as in the rest of Northern Europe and the United States, women finally won the right to vote. Social democratization was accelerated by economic growth and technological changes, which increased the number of people who thought of themselves as middle-class. The greatest increase occured within the ranks of the white-collar employees, who were bourgeois rather than proletarian in dress, in manners, and in thought. In addition to this upward leveling, there was some downward leveling of those people whose fixed incomes had been reduced by high taxes and inflation. Even the rich wore simpler clothes, had fewer servants, and entertained less lavishly than in prewar days.

Despite increased social mobility and the democratization of manners, economic and social differences remained. There were still great disparities of income between the rich and the poor, and, as in France, the educational system separated the middle and upper classes from the rest of the population. Only one child in eight went to secondary school, and, of these, most went to state schools rather than exclusive private schools like Eton and Harrow (the state secondary schools were called "grammar schools"; the private ones were called "public schools"); only four in a thousand went on to a university. Different speech patterns and other subtle distinctions also separated one class from another. Possession of a degree from a secondary school or even a university was not enough to get a man into an exclusive London club; the degree had to be from the right school, and he had to have the right social connections. Ramsay MacDonald could become the prime minister of Great Britain; as a Labourite of humble origin he could not have hoped to become the director of a big insurance company.

The ruling "establishment" remained virtually closed to outsiders. Education, birth, and wealth still determined its membership, which included the key people in the high civil service, the armed forces, the universities, the Church of England, industry, and finance. The "establishment" was not a class in itself, but it drew its members exclusively from the upper and upper-middle classes. Titled or untitled, they all called each other "old boy," moved in the same social circles, and shared the same gentlemanly code of behavior. No peer had been prime minister since the turn of the century; still, members of the "establishment" dominated British political life throughout most of the interwar years. In the end they even took mavericks like Lloyd George and MacDonald into their outer ranks, if not into their inner sanctums.

### *British Labor*

British labor was less hostile to the ruling elite than French labor; it too had profound social grievances, but its main de-

*London's East End dock district during the General Strike*

mands for reform were economic. The war had postponed, and in postponing had aggravated, prewar demands for a better life. Higher wages and the right to engage in collective bargaining put the trade-union movement in a recalcitrant mood. As in France, there was a wave of strikes in 1919, including the threat of a general strike in Scotland. Unlike its French counterpart, the Trades Union Congress survived this episode unscathed and became increasingly militant in its demands. It objected particularly to the inadequacy of the government's relief program for the million or so chronically unemployed workers, and to the efforts of mine owners to reduce wages in what had become a declining industry. Finally, in May 1926, the coal miners tried to force the Conservative government – which sided with the mine owners – out of office through the continental technique of "direct action."

The General Strike initiated by the miners brought the nation's industries to a standstill. Railroad men, transport workers, iron and steel workers, builders, and printers quit work out of sympathy for the miners. For nine days 2,500,00 laboring men stayed away from their jobs, an unprecedented situation. Equally unprecedented were the enthusiasm and efficiency with which the government mobilized upper-middle- and upper-class volunteers to run the essential services. Oxford and Cambridge students drove the buses and unloaded the food ships in the docks; there were even a few peers at the throttles of the railroad trains. The strikers had prepared no revolutionary organs for seizing control of the government, and there was only sporadic local violence. Nevertheless, the country as a whole, while sympathizing with the miners, condemned the "class rebellion" of the trade-unions.

The mutual antagonism of the propertied classes and the workers also showed up in the way the General Strike was ended. Having been forced to support it against their will, the leaders of the TUC called off the strike as soon as they saw that it had no chance of success. On the other hand, the miners, "betrayed" by their follow workers, continued their own strike for another six months. This desperate and hopeless struggle finally ended with a complete surrender on their demands. The Conservative government then added to the bitterness of labor's failure by passing the Trade Disputes Act of 1927, which banned all sympathy strikes and weakened the Labour Party's ility to get financial aid from the trade unions.

During the remainder of the interwar period unemployment replaced trade-union militancy as the main social issue. All through the 'twenties over a million British workers had been without jobs. In 1921 Parliament had passed an Emergency Unemployment Act—familiarly called the "dole"—to provide continuing relief for those industrial workers whose three months of unemployment insurance had run out. In the early 'thirties the worldwide depression more than doubled the number of chronically unemployed; in the depressed areas of the midlands and around Glasgow, many grown men had never worked in their lives. In 1933 middle-class Britons were shocked to learn from Walter Greenwood's best-selling novel *Love On The Dole* that some of these men got married and raised families. But the men themselves were demoralized by their inability to find work and humiliated by the "means test" they had to pass periodically in order to continue receiving their welfare checks.

Except for the resentment of the "forgotten men" in the depressed areas, class antagonisms abated somewhat during the 1930s. Vast differences in income persisted, and the upper classes retained their dominant position, but the British workers, both white-collar and blue-collar, were more integrated into the national society than these classes were on the continent. Paid vacations and cheap transportation allowed them to flock to the less fashionable seaside resorts; the movies, the radio, and the illustrated Sunday supplements gave them at least the illusion of participating in the national mass culture.

### Politics

British politics reflected a changing society more than French politics did. Like the French, the British soon rejected their strong wartime chief; unlike the French, they also changed their voting habits. The Liberals, who had furnished every prime minister since 1905, ceased to be a ruling party after Lloyd George was forced to resign in 1922. The subsequent decline of the Liberal Party showed that the changing society of the postwar years preferred a clear-cut choice between the Conservative and Labour parties—both now national rather than class parties—to the Conservative-dominated coalitions headed by the maverick Liberal Lloyd George during the past few years. The British public did not always get this choice after 1922, but the political process was moving in this direction.

The British Liberals resembled the French Radicals in many ways. In the late nineteenth century both had stood for democratic political and educational reforms, anticlericalism, and laissez faire. At the turn of the twentieth century both parties were divided over imperialism. By the First World War both had acquired the habit of participating in Right-Center coalitions. In fact, by the early 1920s the old issues between them and the parties immediately to the Right of them had been swept away.

Yet the two parties had quite different histories thereafter. As we have seen, the Radicals remained the leading party in France throughout the interwar years. This situation was partly due to the lack of a strong conservative party in that country. It also reflected the slower rate of economic and social change, which allowed millions of small independent proprietors to cling to a middle-of-the-road party that no longer stood for any vital issue. In Great Britain there were fewer small proprietors, especially in agriculture, and the new issues were more pressing. Even if Lloyd George had not split the Liberal Party over the question of cooperating with the Conservatives, it would have been less able than the Conservatives and Labourites to represent a distinct position on the new issues of the day. The Conservatives had taken over its older idea of laissez faire at home, while the Labourites had taken over its later reforming zeal as expressed by Gladstone and the prewar Lloyd George.

Aside from these party realignments, however, the British political system was only slightly more adaptable to new needs than the French. The Conservative and Labour governments that succeeded each other between 1922 and 1931 were willing to compromise their principles—tariffs for the Conservatives, the welfare state for the Labourites—but they were unable to solve the chronic problems of declining exports and unemployment. In the election of October 1931, held in the midst of a financial crisis, the Conservatives revived the wartime idea of a National Government to meet an emergency situation. Promising protective tariffs and the preservation of the overvalued pound, their coalition won 80 per cent of the seats in the House of Commons. Although the Conservatives alone had an overwhelming majority, they tried to preserve the fiction of coalition rule by maintaining Ramsay MacDonald, the former Labourite prime minister, as head of the National Government until 1935. Thereafter, they ruled alone.

The governments of the 'thirties had no consistent plan for dealing with the problems of the depression. They used the dole, rather than public works, to handle unemployment. Their most "revolutionary" achievement was the Import Duties Bill of 1932, Britain's first tariff in eighty years. Contrary to their 1931 campaign promise, the Conservatives reduced the value of the pound from $4.96 to $3.40, in the interest of making British goods cheaper than imports. They also tried to stimulate business by lowering the interest and discount rates, and housing construction by lowering the mortgage rate. None of the government's policies was the main source of economic recovery, though all contributed to it. The most important stimulus was increased consumption, which, as in France, took place at the expense of capital investments needed for economic growth.

As in France, there was a dearth of dynamic and creative leadership. Stanley Baldwin, the Conservative prime minister during the second half of the 'twenties and again in 1935–1937, characterized himself best in his 1929 campaign slogan, "safety first." His outstanding achievement was his delicate handling of the abdication of King Edward VIII in 1936.* Ramsay MacDonald was handsome and eloquent, and his whole manner suggested a born leader, but he turned out to be merely vain, hesitant and lacking in a creative program; his own party repudiated him when he became head of the National Government in 1931. Neville Chamberlain, prime minister from 1937 to 1940, was the most forceful of Britains's interwar leaders, but he lacked warmth and popular appeal. Still in the international crises of the late 'thirties his policy of appeasement represented the British mood as accurately as the policy of "squeeze the German orange till the pips squeak" had in 1918. Thus, the British people got the leaders they deserved.

### Isolation and Appeasement

In the early 1920s the exhausted British wanted to isolate themselves from the continent and concentrate on home and imperial affairs. They persisted in referring to "Europe' as if it were another part of the world, like the Middle East or North America. At the Peace Conference, Lloyd George had tried to reassert Britain's traditional role as mediator and peacemaker in the new Europe created by the last war, but as in the past, Britain had taken her share of the spoils before assuming this role. Now that they had helped to render Germany militarily powerless, the British wanted her as a market for their goods and they wanted the French to stop provoking her. In their effort to restrain the French they alternately used the sugar of promised military assistance and the whip of restraining

*Edward VIII succeeded his father George V in January 1936. He was forced to abdicate eleven months later owing to his insistence on marrying a divorcee.

pressure. Most of all, they wished that the two continental rivals would settle their differences and not force the British to keep intervening in their disputes. The Locarno Pact seemed to bring Britain out of her isolation; actually it merely satisfied this wish.

The Labourites were more internationalist than the Conservatives. They tried to combine their traditional pacifism with the idea of collective security through the League of Nations. But these two ideas were potentially incompatible, since collective security against overt aggression might well necessitate the use of military force. Although the issue remained an academic one in the 'twenties, it became menacingly real in the late 'thirties. By then not only the Labourites but the majority of the British people were in the same quandary, as the National Peace Ballot of 1934 had already shown.

In this ballot, in which 40 per cent of the British electorate participated, the voter was invited to answer "Yes" or "No" to the following questions:

> "Should Great Britain remain a member of the League of Nations? Are you in favor of an all-round reduction in armaments by international agreement? . . . Do you consider that, if one nation insists on attacking another, the other nations should combine to compel it to stop by (*a*) economic sanctions, (*b*) if necessary, military measures?"

The overwhelming majority answered "Yes" to all these questions. Yet, when the first acts of aggression began, the British people, like their leaders, preferred to give in rather than to commit themselves to collective security. Unfortunately, the day of disillusionment for appeasement was near at hand.

## TOWARD THE WELFARE STATE

Developments in a number of Western democracies merely paralleled those in Great Britain or France. Like Britain, Switzerland and the Netherlands remained politically stable and economically conservative, despite the fact that, like France, they operated under the multiparty system. This system also prevailed in the four Scandinavian countries—Denmark, Norway, Sweden, and Finland—but only in Finland did fascism make serious inroads against democratic rule. In Belgium, however, coalitions of Catholics, Liberals, and Socialists did not work well, and, as in France, extremist groups on both the Right and the Left gained many followers in the mid-thirties.

Only the United States, Scandinavia, and one British Dominion—New Zealand—succeeded in combining political democracy with economic and social selfare. Belgium was handicapped by conflicts between her French- and Flemish-speaking inhabitants. Canada and white-controlled South Africa were also divided along ethnic lines; Anglo-Saxon and French in the former, Anglo-Saxon and Afrikaner in the latter. Australia, though ethnically homogeneous, was seriously split along regional and party lines. Consequently, these three Dominions, and Belgium, struggled through the 'thirties with less unity of purpose than the United States or Scandinavia.

### The United States: Isolationism and the New Deal

The position of the United States in world affairs during the interwar years was paradoxical. On the one hand, the American government wanted as little diplomatic contact as possible with foreign governments; it never joined the League of Nations and, until 1933, it refused even to "recognize" the Soviet Union. On the other hand, the United States had an unprecedented economic influence overseas, especially in Europe. As late as the summer of 1933, in the very depths of the depression, President Franklin D. Roosevelt's refusal to let the American observer discuss currency exchange rates was enough to wreck the World Economic Conference meeting in London.

The depression reinforced American isolationism in foreign affairs, but it brought great changes in American opinion on domestic policy. A sizable and influential minority continued to believe that the "betrayal" of freedom began in 1933, the year in which the United States went off the gold standard, "recognized" the Soviet Union, and launched the New Deal. To the majority of Americans, however, the depression was a shattering experience. In January 1933, 15 million people were out of work, billions of dollars in savings had been lost, and the closing of the banks threatened the loss of billions more. Hence the majority accepted the New Deal as a series of practical measures designed to meet an extraordinary situation.

The most striking feature of all these New Deal measures was the augmented role of the government: in stimulating business recovery through loans and public works, especially through the Works Progress Administration; in controlling private financial operations and the relations between capital and labor, especially through the short-lived National Recovery Administration; in subsidizing the nation's farmers, through the equally short-lived Agricultural Adjustment Administration; and even in planning future economic development, through the Tennessee Valley Authority. Such policies were a far cry from the laissez-faire "normalcy" of Presidents Harding and Coolidge.

In addition to emergency measures, with their temporary government controls, the New Deal permanently improved the status of American labor in the summer of 1935. The National Labor Relations Act (Wagner Act) restored collective bargaining and defined unfair labor practices on the part of employers. As a result, the CIO was able for the first time to organize the workers in the automobile, steel, and other mass production industries on the basis of industrial unionism. The Social Security Act provided for old-age and unemployment insurance, financed in part by compulsory contributions from employer and employee. Taken for granted by everyone today, the principle of government-sponsored social security was truly revolutionary in 1935 in the United States.

The flexibility of the American political process allowed the United States to avoid both the totalitarianism of Nazi Germany and the muddling-through tactics of Great Britain and France. Like most Britishers and Frenchmen, most Americans considered themselves capable of providing for their own needs. Still, the severity of the depression convinced them that the government would have to step in where their own efforts failed, at least for the duration of the emergency. Furthermore, the Democratic Party furnished a strong leader to foster this kind of intervention. Only in the United States and Canada* could a major nonsocialist party have gone so far in the direction of the welfare state. The last example of this kind in Europe had been the Liberal Party under David Lloyd George around 1910. And we saw how the Labour Party, avowedly socialist, took away most of the Liberals' votes in the 1920s.

### Scandinavian Social Democracy

The Scandinavian countries moved further toward the welfare state than the United States, but they did so under socialist leadership. Though nominally moderate Marxists, the Scandinavian socialists rejected class struggle and the nationalization of private business as necessary merely to satisfy a principle. Like the British Labour Party, with its slogan "fair shares for all," they derived their outlook more from the socialists of the 1830s, especially Robert Owen, than from Marx. Their brand of socialism opposed extremes of wealth and poverty and sought to raise the level of the poor by taxing the rich. It was the socialism of a skilled working-class elite that had achieved a decent standard of living for itself and that wanted to spread the benefits of its way of life to the whole society. It was also the socialism of a handful of middle- and upper-middle-class people with a bad conscience.

After the First World War many continental socialists were also moving away from the idea of class conflict toward this kind of democratic socialism. One notable example was Léon Blum in France; there were others in Germany, Austria, and Ita-

*In 1935 the Conservative Party got the federal Parliament of Canada to pass a sweeping program of social legislation similar to the New Deal in the United States. The supreme courts of both countries nullified most of these measures. Thereafter the individual Canadian provinces varied considerably in their acceptance of the welfare state.

ly. In these three countries the Social Democrats were stifled by fascist totalitarianism, and in France they were unable to revamp the economic and social structure under the brief Popular Front coalition. The British Labour Party was also unable to institute basic reforms before the end of the Second World War. During the interwar years it was in Scandinavia that democratic socialism made the greatest strides.

Sweden, Norway, and Denmark had many advantages in their effort to solve the problems of twentieth-century civilization. First, they had all escaped the First World War and its after-effects. Second, they were small countries whose citizens had a high degree of ethnic and religious homogeneity and a strong respect for the law. Third, these features, along with a severe climate, had given them a talent for working in common without destroying their robust sense of personal freedom. In the late nineteenth century the advent of industrialization had disrupted traditional cultural and social values, and the early emancipation of middle- and upper-class women led to the kinds of intrafamily conflict depicted in the plays of Henrik Ibsen and August Strindberg. But class conflict was not as severe as in the larger continental countries. When the depression struck, the Scandinavian labor unions were the strongest in Europe and the most willing to settle their differences with employers through peaceful bargaining and government-sponsored arbitration.

Another distinctive feature of the Scandinavian scene was its sizable cooperative movement. Although even today the consumer cooperatives handle less than 15 per cent of the total retail trade, since the beginning of the century both consumer and producer cooperatives have been stronger than anywhere else in the world. In agriculture the cooperatives helped to eliminate middle men in the marketing process and to improve productivity through the spread of technical knowledge. The main function of cooperative factories was not to supplant private enterprise but to force it to keep its prices competitive. This was an especially important problem in dealing with the monopolistically organized manufacturers of light bulbs, overshoes, bread, and rubber tires. The cooperatives also served as a means of strengthening economic democracy through the effective participation of their members in actual decision-making.

Working from their tradition of common action, the Scandinavians met the depression with the idea that society should determine what is to happen, not merely adjust to what does happen. The chief agent of society was the state. It tried to avoid coercion, but it frankly assumed leadership in stabilizing employment and setting standards of efficiency. It controlled and limited the profits of the entrepreneur and raised the standards of living of the wage earner. Through its tax policies it sought to reduce inequalities in income and to obtain revenue for extensive social services. The state also planned for basic facilities and the use of natural resources, though usually leaving the execution of these plans to private business.

Scandinavia's mixed economy has been called a "middle way" between capitalism and socialism. Private enterprise still accounts for a far greater proportion of total production than the nationalized industries. Yet social controls—from the state, the cooperatives, and the labor unions—have limited its freedom of action as well as its profits. Capitalist in form, the Scandinavian economy has been directed by coalition governments imbued with socialist philosophy since the 1930s. At that time it was a "middle way" between the economy of France and that of the Soviet Union, but the main purpose of its planners was to combine political democracy with economic and social security.

The Scandinavian countries were the first full-fledged welfare states in the West. During the depression they provided comprehensive protection against the hazards of unemployment, sickness, and old age. They also established minimum wages and shorter working hours. In order to encourage people to use their new leisure "constructively," they fostered adult education and the performing arts on a large scale. Businessmen in all three countries complained about government paternalism and high taxes. Nevertheless the majority of Scandinavians managed to adapt their traditional individualism to the requirements of the welfare state.

## THE LATE SUMMER OF IMPERIALISM

The governments of Great Britain and France did not show as much concern for the welfare of their citizens as the governments of Scandinavia did, although by the late 1930s they had begun to redress some of the grievances of their laboring classes. This was more than they were willing to do for their subjects overseas. The problem was not that the colonial powers were uninterested in the welfare of these "natives"; it was that the French refused to admit that the natives might prefer self-government to good government and that the British, though they understood this preference, refused to grant it.

The year 1919 marked both the apogee of European imperialism and the beginning of the reaction against it. With the collapse of the Ottoman Empire and the assignment of most of its Arab-speaking areas to Britain and France as mandates, the Europeans controlled an unprecedented extent of territory. The mandate system itself, however, was a late-summer variety of imperialism, and at the same time the Turkish war hero Mustapha Kemal (1880–1938) began his campaign to drive the Allies out of Anatolia, to end the capitulations, and to bring about a national revival along modern lines. While the Big Three at Paris disregarded China's territorial sovereignty by transferring Germany's former holdings to Japan, a group of Chinese nationalist students launched the "May Fourth Movement" for the independence, unity, and modernization of their country. At Amristar, India, following the murder of four Europeans by a mob, an unarmed crowd assembled in an enclosed garden. When it failed to disperse the British commander ordered his troops to fire, killing 379 persons and wounding 1208. This "error of judgment," as his fellow officers called it precipitated a campaign of passive resistance and noncooperation led by Mohandas K. Gandhi. And at the beginning of 1919 the British already faced the most serious threat ot their sovereignty in their oldest "colony" of all – Ireland.

### From Empire to Commonwealth

The decline of a great imperial power is difficult to measure. During the interwar years Britain's national lassitude and weak foreign policy certainly indicated a retreat from greatness. Yet one-quarter of the earth's land surface and almost one-quarter of the human race remained under some form of British rule. Only Ireland and Egypt broke loose completely, and Egypt still had to tolerate British armed forces on her soil. All the same, the ideology of self-determination, which had already made self-governing Dominions of Canada, Newfoundland, Australia, New Zealand, and South Africa, was being taken up in other parts of the old Victorian empire. Along with a combination of indifference and bad conscience at home, this ideology brought concessions that appeared to have been extorted from a sort of moral impotence rather than to have been granted by a power in the full consciousness of its rightness and strength.

#### *Ireland*

The Sinn Fein ("We Ourselves") nationalists in Ireland were living proof that the need to belong to a community of their own kind can make men demand independence from alien rule at all costs. In January 1919 they set up their own Parliament in Dublin, and soon thereafter their self-styled Irish Republican Army initiated a campaign of assassinating members of the Royal Irish Constabulary. If it had had the will, the government in London undoubtedly could have crushed the Sinn Fein movement with a massive military invasion. Instead, it reinforced the local police with a force of volunteers, the "Black and Tans," authorizing them to take reprisals against the inhabitants of every area where IRA terrorism occurred. For more than a year the two irregular armies fought a brutal undeclared war involving ambushes, bomb explosions, torture, arson, and the seizure of hostages. The fact that they were tearing their country apart did not deter the more extreme Sinn Feiners from demanding not only complete independence from England but also the forcible incorporation of the six Protestant counties of

*Dublin during the Irish Rebellion, 1920*

the northeast (Ulster) into their new Catholic republic.

In December 1921 the British government and the more moderate Sinn Feiners finally agreed on a compromise. They signed a treaty making the southern two-thirds of Ireland, under the name of the Irish Free State, a self-governing Dominion. The members of its Parliament had to take an oath of allegiance to the Crown; they also had to concede several naval bases to the British Admiralty—to allay the strategic fears that always colored England's attitude toward Ireland. Ulster was granted a special status as an autonomous region of the United Kingdom under the name Northern Ireland.

These arrangements did not solve the Irish Question; they merely allowed England to wash her hands of it. Eamon de Valera, the leader of the Sinn Fein extremists, refused to accept the 1921 treaty, and it took the new Irish government over another year to subdue his forces. There were also border disputes between Northern and Southern Ireland and anti-Catholic riots in Belfast. In the late 1920s the country as a whole was more peaceful than it had been in years, but De Valera returned to the political arena and became president in 1932. One by one he repudiated the clauses of the 1921 treaty; in 1937 he introduced a new constitution which completely ignored both Crown and Commonwealth.

### The Statute of Westminister

The other Dominions did not share Ireland's hatred for the "mother country," but they too wanted complete independence. They had entered the First World War of their own free will; they had separately signed the Treaty of Versailles; they had become separate member states of the League of Nations. Still, they wanted to retain their ties with the Crown and the Commonwealth. In an attempt to give legal meaning to a unique and basically illogical relationship the Imperial Conference of 1926 defined Great Britain and the Dominions as:

". . . autonomous communities within the British Empire, equal in status, in no way subordinate one to another in any aspect of their domestic or external affairs, though united by a common allegiance to the Crown, and freely associated as members of the British Commonwealth of Nations."

In 1931 this definition was incorporated into the Statute of Westminster, which completed the transfer of sovereign power to the already self-governing Dominions under their several constitutions. This was a great step forward for the Dominions, but it still did nothing for those parts of the Empire—India, the crown colonies, protectorates, and mandates—which were decidedly not self-governing.

### *India*

Each concession from London merely provoked increasing pressure from the native nationalists in India, the largest and most populous (over 350 million in 1939) colony within the British Empire. Like the Dominions, India had made a massive contribution to the British war effort; between 1914 and 1918, 620,000 Indian soldiers had served overseas and 62,000 had been killed. In recognition of these services the Secretary of State for India, Edwin S. Montagu, and the viceroy, Lord Chelmsford, issued a report recommending "the increasing association of Indians in every branch of the administration and the gradual development of self-governing institutions with a view to the progressive realization of responsible government in India as an integral part of the British Empire." The more extreme nationalists demanded "Home Rule." In 1920, when the India Act gave effect to the Montagu-Chelmsford Report by setting up new institutions, the Indian National Congress Party, now under the leadership of Gandhi, boycotted them. By the early 'thirties the British government began talking about "Dominion Status." The National Congress, now moving toward the "extremist" position of Jawaharlal Nehru (1889–1964), began demanding "Independence"; so did the Muslim League as it came under the control of Mohammed Ali Jinnah. In 1935 the British Parliament passed a new India Act inaugurating a federal constitution under a viceroy, governing with the assistance of a bicameral legislature to be elected through a complicated adjustment between general and communal electorates. When hostilities broke out in Europe in 1939 this new constitution was still not in full operation, and India was once again dragged into war by the "mother country."

The pattern of Anglo-Indian relations illustrated the basic and irreconcilable conflict between the colonial powers and the anticolonial nationalists. The British argued that they could not abandon their responsibility to the mass of the Indian people until they were sure that the small number of educated Indian politicians could rule just as well. Meanwhile, they would gradually give these educated Indians administrative experience, at the same time throwing them in jail if they challenged the existing political order. The Indian leaders argued that the British were stalling, that they did not want to lose India, and that they only made concessions under pressure. The fact that the arguments of both sides were partly true only made matters worse. In essence the British were saying that good government was better than self-government; in essence the Indians were saying the opposite.

In India, as elsewhere, the conflict was complicated by divisions among the natives themselves. The Indian princes, technically "sovereign" over almost half the land, were generally loyal to their British "advisers." As the novelist E. M. Forster said when he was serving at the court of one of these princes in 1921: "There is no anti-English feeling. It is Gandhi whom they dread and hate." They dreaded and hated Gandhi not only for his nationalism but also because he wished to emancipate the lower classes from social ostracism, thus threatening the traditional caste system of the Hindus. Gandhi, however, was a traditionalist in

*Nehru and others welcoming Gandhi Back after his prolonged fast undertaken to bring about improvement in the administration of Rajkot State, 1939*

his own way. Unlike the other leaders of the National Congress, he rejected economic modernization and preached a return to handicraft production. When he was not dramatizing his hostility to the British by hunger strikes, he was demonstrating his economic ideal by operating a spinning wheel. More than anyone else it was the saintly Gandhi who unleashed the nationalist feelings of the Indian masses. But by the late 1930s Nehru emerged as the most dynamic leader of the National Congress. And Nehru, like the majority of anticolonial nationalists, accepted the superiority of European civilization and sought to use it as a model for a truly independent India.

### The Near East Astir

The First World War had not begun as an imperialist war, but once under way it had stimulated imperialist ambitions. The Treaty of Brest-Litovsk had shown Germany's imperialist ambitions in Eastern Europe, ambitions that were revived by Hitler; and Japan's Twenty-One Demands on China in 1915 anticiptated full-scale aggression two decades later.

Great Britain and France, however, were able to realize their imperialist ambitions in the Near East at the end of the war. In a secret agreement in 1916 these two powers had already allotted themselves the lion's share of the Ottoman Empire in Asia. The British had then complicated matters by encouraging the Arabs to revolt against their Turkish overlords and promising them "national governments and administrations that shall derive their authority from the free exercise of the initiative and choice of the indigenous populations." This complication was not resolved by the mandate system.

The Arab national awakening had begun before 1914 with a literary revival. As in Eastern Europe in the preceding century, cultural nationalism had soon developed into political nationalism and a desire for self-determination. In Egypt the British occupation had already turned Arab nationalism against the Europeans; in the Arab lands to the east the main enemy had still been the Turks. During the war these Arabs had participated in their own liberation with British and French help. Instead of giving them their promised Arab National State, France set up mandates in Syria and Lebanon, while Great Britain carved out mandates in Palestine, Transjordan, and Iraq. (Only the desert kingdom of Saudi Arabia gained full independence.) Technically, the Mandatory Powers held these lands in trust on behalf of the League of Nations until their eventual independence. Actually, neither the British nor the French anticipated giving them their independence in the foreseeable future. The Arab leaders naturally felt cheated.

Throughout the interwar years anti-European feeling mounted among the Arab nationalists. As in the Sudan and China, the earliest resistance against European rule tended to come from religious and tribal leaders who wanted to preserve their traditional way of life from foreign contamination. A good example was the revolt of the Druses mountain chieftains of Syria against the French; it lasted from 1925 to 1927 and had to be put down by a massive military campaign. As in India, the second wave of resistance was led by more modern-minded nationalists. For example, in 1936 Syria's new Nationalist Party declared a general strike and thus obliged the French to let it form a cabinet and to promise to end their mandate in three years. This promise was not kept. Before the Second World War only Egypt and Iraq gained their nominal independence, and in each country the British reserved certain military and economic rights.

Whereas the frustration of their nationalist goals made the Arabs increasingly anti-European, the Turks went through an entirely different experience. In 1919 victorious British, French, and Italian forces occupied parts of Anatolia, and the Greeks landed at Izmir (Smyrna). In Istanbul (Constantinople) the sultan's government helplessly resigned itself to the partition of the country. But the presence of these foreigners (especially the Greeks, who seemed bent on restoring the old Byzantine Empire) aroused a resistance movement, under the leadership of Mustapha Kemal. In Ankara (Angora), Mustapha drafted a program for a new and independent National Turkey. Then he led a brilliant military campaign against the Greek invaders, recaptured Smyrna, and forced its centuries-old Greek population to flee; by 1923 a million refugees had been forced to move to Greece. In that year Mustapha also negotiated a new peace treaty with the Allies giving Turkey all of Anatolia and Eastern Thrace. Thereafter he led the Turkish people in a general reform of their political and cultural life along Western lines.

Mustapha Kemal was the Western-oriented nationalist lead *par excellence.* Born in Salonika of European Turkish parents, he had taken part in the Young Turk revolt of 1908, which had ended the despotism of Sultan Abdul Hamid II and restored the Constitution of 1876. He had also distinguished himself in the fighting at Gallipoli, though he disapproved of Turkey's entry into the war on the side of Germany. In the 1920s, once he had cleared his country of foreign troops, he decided to break with all the forces of the past. He abolished the sultanate and made Turkey a republic with the usual democratic forms. He made primary education free and obligatory for both sexes. His most radical reform was to sever all connections between the state and the Muslim religion. Religious tribunals were abolished; Sunday replaced Friday as the weekly day of rest. Men were forbidden to wear fezzes; women were discouraged from wearing veils. Polygamy was prohibited, divorce permitted, and civil marriage made compulsory. The old Koranic law was replaced by new civil, criminal, and commercial codes, based respectively on Swiss, Italian, and German models. Mustapha even introduced the Latin alphabet in place of the intricate Turkish script.

The new Turkey became a model for other westernizing nationalists who wanted to free their countries from foreign domination. In addition to its political and cultural reforms, it adopted a nationalist economic policy, discouraging foreign investments and encouraging government-sponsored industrial enterprises. It was also a dictatorship. Only strong authoritarian powers on the part of the government could have forced so many reforms upon an ignorant and occasionally hostile population. But Kemal was a benevolent dictator. There was no significant opposition to his leadership, and in 1934 the Grand National Assembly gave him the family name of Atatürk, "the Father of the Turks." He had not been able to raise the economic and educational level of his countrymen as high as he would have liked. Still, his regime and his reforms outlasted him. There was no return to the past and no move toward Communism.

## China

China was ultimately to pose a quite different type of model for nationalists trying to free themselves from Western imperialism. In the nineteenth century her internal history and her relations with the European powers had resembled those of Turkey in many ways,* and these resemblances continued into the early twentieth century. Both countries had undergone revolutions in the immediate prewar years; both had lost out in the peace settlement; both came under the leadership of Western-oriented nationalist leaders in the 1920s. Thereafter, however, China's development was determined by two factors absent in Turkey: a strong Communist Party and a full-scale war against a militarily superior aggressor.

Japan's defeat of Russia in 1905 had marked the beginning of the twentieth-century retreat of the West from the East, but China, the principal victim of Western imperialism in East Asia, had gained nothing from Russia's defeat. On the contrary, political disintegration at home soon made her an easy prey for a much more determined imperialist power, the Land of the Rising Sun.

The Chinese Revolution that began in 1911 was the earliest and most important upheaval in the non-Western world. Most of the other non-Western countries were eventually to follow a similar pattern: (1) resistance of the traditional monarchy to reform; (2) overthrow of the traditional monarchy by revolutionary nationalists; (3) subsequent struggle for power among military dictators, civilian "liberals," and Communists; (4) foreign intervention, invited or uninvited.

After the Manchu dynasty was overthrown in 1911–1912, there were two chief rivals for power. When the old order collapsed amid general rioting in 1911, General Yüan Shi-k'ai headed an army of 80,000 men, and he was elected premier of the new national assembly at Peking. Yüan's main opponent was Sun Yat-sen (1866–1925), who had been organizing revolutionary activities in China from abroad for years. He returned home from Europe in 1911 and momentarily became the head of a rival government at Nanking. To unite the country, he soon recognized Yüan as the President of the new Chinese Republic. Then, however, he assumed a new role as leader of the Kuomintang—or National People's Party—which championed parliamentary government. Yüan wanted neither opposition nor a Parliament, and in 1913 he suppressed both. When the European war broke out in 1914 Yüan was firmly established in power at Peking and had the support of the Western Allies. Sun again went into exile.

During the First World War the new Chinese Republic fell apart, as Japan took advantage of her Allies' preoccupation with their war in Europe. In 1915 she handed President Yüan the notorious Twenty-One Demands, an ultimatum that would have reduced China to the status of a Japanese protectorate. The publicaction of these demands and Yüan's partial acceptance of them were very damaging to Yüan and to the unity of his government. When he died in 1916, the country lapsed into a confused civil conflict of provincial "war lords." A "legitimate" government persisted at Peking under Yüan's successors, and it declared war on Germany on behalf of all of China in 1917. Meanwhile, Sun returned to China and set up a rival government in Canton. American pressure limited Japan's implementation of her Twenty-One Demands, but at Versailles Japan was allowed to take over Germany's concessions on the Shantung Peninsula. Both the Peking and the Canton governments protested this action and both refused to sign the Treaty of Versailles. As in Turkey, the movement for national revival and modernization in China began as a reaction against mistreatment by the Western Allies at the end of the First World War.

Unitl the mid-1920s civil war among local military dictators prevented the unification of China under any native government; it also provided an opportunity for Soviet "aid" in a new form that

*See pp. 531-533.

anticipated the foreign "advisers" in Asia and Africa in the 1960s. In 1923, the Soviet Union helped Sun Yatsen reestablish his authority at Canton, whence he had been expelled by local war lords. For the next four years Russian "advisers" and native Chinese Communists tried to help the new Kuomintang regime in Canton gain control of the rest of the country and to eliminate the remaining Western concessions. Under Sun Yat-sen's leadership the Kuomintang proclaimed the "Three Principles of Nationalism, Democracy and Social Progress" as the goals of the Chinese Revolution, but the war lords were not impressed, and the revolution could not be achieved until they were subdued by military force.

After Sun Yat-sen's death in early 1925 the leadership of the Kuomintang passed to General Chiang K'ai-shek (b. 1887). In 1924 Chiang had become the head of a new military academy near Canton. This academy, staffed by Soviet officers, created and trained the army that Chiang then used to conquer northern China beginning in 1926. By mid-1927 he had conquered Shanghai and made Nanking Nationalist China's new capital. With over half of all Chinese territory now in his hands Chiang repudiated Soviet support, purged the Kuomintang of native Communists and allied himself with the wealthy Chinese businessmen. He sought Western recognition for his new regime by softpedaling nationalist demands for the elimination of foreign rights in China. In December he married Soong Meiling (Wellesley, Class of 1917), a member of the richest banking family in the country, thus strengthening his ties with the business community. German officers replaced the now banned Russians, and with their help Chiang resumed his conquest of the rest of China in 1928. When the war lord of Manchuria recognized the Nanking government in November, the nominal unification of China was complete.

During the next ten years Chiang's government launched a vigorous program of modernization—very much like Atatürk's. It introduced administrative efficiency, a new criminal and civil law code, and monetary and banking reforms; it sponsored the development of transportation and industry; it fostered higher education. Unfortunately, Chiang was never able to create the kind of China proclaimed in Sun Yat-sen's "Three Principles." He promised to do so, but his preoccupation with the Chinese Communists and with Japanese aggression prevented him from following through.

The Chinese Communists were a new force. Founded in 1919, their party adhered to strict Leninist principles until Stalin abandoned it to Chiang's vengeance in 1927. This "betrayal" was never to be forgotten. The party acquired new leaders and a new character as the remnants fled to the hills in the southeastern part of the country. There Mao Tse-tung (b. 1893), a former librarian, teacher, newspaper editor, and union organizer, began to emerge as the new Communist leader. Associated with him was General Chu Te, who had traveled and studied in Europe and who had held a high rank in the Kuomintang army. These men organized the Chinese Red Army, which specialized in guerrilla tactics. They also set up a network of peasant soviets and combined them into a Chinese Soviet Republic in 1931. Their special appeal to the peasants, rather than to the urban workers, marked them off from the Russian Communists. It also gave them a permanent advantage over Chiang, who could never offer the mass of Chinese peasants the basic land reforms they wanted above all else. Even when he finally dislodged the Chinese Communists from their southeastern stronghold in 1934, he could not destroy them. In a virtual mass migration they made their "Long March"—almost 5,000 miles—to Yenan, on the borderlands of Mongolia. Although Japanese aggression brought the Nationalists and Communists into an uneasy "Popular Front" alliance in 1937, they were ultimately to prove to be irreconcilable enemies.

Chiang abandoned his liberal Western orientation after the Japanese invasion. He was forced to move his capital from Nanking to the remote provincial city of Chungking, and there he lost contact with the modern-minded business communities in Shanghai and Nanking and came under the influence of conservative landowners. By the early 1940s Chiang had turned back toward Confucianism. He repudiated both the Communists and the liberals in the Kuomintang, and his resurgent traditionalism paved the way for a new and tougher modernization under Mao Tse-tung.

### The Three Kinds of Anticolonial Nationalism

In the late summer of imperialism native nationalists felt all forms of foreign influence and control to be humiliating. Although China was not a colony in the same sense that India or the Congo was, Christian missionaries, extraterritoriality, and even foreign businesses came to be viewed as forms of colonialism: the concessions that Atatürk finally persuaded the Western powers to renounce in 1923 had been viewed in a similar way.

The native leaders who opposed colonialism were divided into three groups: (1) traditionalists, (2) westernizing nationalists, (3) national Communists. The traditionalists were usually most active during the early stages of European control or influence. Their response was a defensive reaction rather than true nationalism —from the Sepoy Mutiny in India in 1857 through the Boxer Rebellion in China in 1900 to the Druse Revolt in Syria in 1925. The leaders of these movements had little contact with European civilization and wanted to keep it from contaminating their own. With the exception of Gandhi, who *was* Western-educated, no traditionalist took over command of a major nationalist movement once imperial controls began to give way.

When this happened, the westernizing nationalists usually took command. Sun Yat-sen and Nehru were outstanding examples; like almost all the others, they had achieved substantial acquaintance with the West and its ideologies of national self-determination, democracy, and socialism. The West also gave them the model for material advancement so necessary, in their minds, for the survival of their nations after the achievement of full independence. On the other hand, this small elite of westernizing nationalists lacked contact with the masses everywhere. This separation, traditional in most underdeveloped countries, was to become a handicap once war, continued poverty, and Communist propaganda aroused the masses themselves.

Before the Second World War the national Communists offered no serious competition to the westernizing nationalists, except in China. Thereafter, however, they were to gain increasing strength wherever vestiges of Western imperialism and colonialism remained. They too had learned their lessons from Europe: nationalism, industrialization, *and* Marxism. As we have seen, the stated goal of Communism is to end poverty and social injustice through material progress. When combined with nationalism, as it was by leaders like Mao Tse-tung, this ideology was to have widespread appeal in emerging nations. But in the 1930s the West was more concerned with a new wave of imperialist aggression by advanced nations than with anticolonial nationalism in backward ones.

## AGGRESSION AND APPEASEMENT TO 1939

It is difficult today to imagine any major state deliberately embarking upon a program of military conquest; the risk of immediate and devastating retaliation is too great. In the 1930s the situation was different. On the one hand, Germany, Italy, and Japan were willing to risk war to satisfy their "will to power"; on the other hand, Great Britain, France, and the United States were unwilling to stop them by risking war themselves. The position of the Soviet Union, the remaining great power of the period, was less clear-cut, though, publicly, that country was the most consistent advocate of collective military measures against aggression between 1934 and 1938.

Aggression fed on appeasement. Each time Germany, Italy, or Japan committed an aggressive act with impunity, its leaders' appetite for empire increased. Hitler wanted *Lebensraum* (living space) in Eastern Europe and victory over the Soviet Union; Mussolini wanted to make the Mediterranean an "Italian Lake"; Japan's military leaders wanted dominaton over all of East Asia. At first the Western democracies thought that Italy was bluffing and that Germany and Japan would not dare to extend their power at the expense of others. Then, after the first bluffs and dares had worked, the British and the French refused to believe that the aggressor states would try such tactics again. They abhorred the prospect of war, and their pacifism was a major motive for their own acts of appeasement—even when these meant going back on their pledged word to the victims of aggression. The United States had no foreign commitments and refused to become involved.

Hitler was especially adept at using propaganda to befuddle the democracies. His argument that it was only right for all Germans to belong to one Reich worked until 1939. His raucous antibolshevism led some people in the West to hope that as long as he directed his aggression eastward, they were safe; he might even go to war against the Soviet Union, a war in which Nazism and Communism would destroy each other. Most people in Western Europe did not succumb to this kind of wishful thinking, but even the staunchest advocates of a Soviet alliance against Hitler were suspicious of Russia. When Hitler finally began adding non-Germans to the Reich and wooing the Russians himself, the war that the British and French had hoped to avoid began under circumstances far less favorable to them than those of the preceding years.

## The First Acts of Aggression, 1931–1936

In the 1930s each of the future Axis powers began to challenge the international political framework established by the Versailles Settlement (1919) for Europe and by the Washington Conference (1922) for the Far East. These treaties and agreements had created a territorial and military status quo, which had been reconfirmed for the Rhineland in the Locarno Pact of December 1925. They set up the legal framework and norms for the peaceful negotiation of differences as well as the League of Nations to enforce them. But Germany, Italy, and Japan argued that these arrangements deprived them of their equal rights as nations. Hence, Japan invaded Manchuria in 1931 and China itself in 1937, Italy invaded Ethiopia in 1935, and Germany took over the demilitarized zone of the Rhineland in 1936. Each of these three powers justified its first aggressive acts in the name of its national rights: Japan's right to be the number one power in the Far East, Italy's right to an African empire, Germany's right to military equality with France, which had the Maginot Line* while the German frontier was defenseless.

### *Manchuria and China*

Japan did not want a strong, united China of the kind Chiang K'ai-shek began to create in the late 1920s. Such a state would threaten her own claim to be the number one power in the Far East; it might also try to produce its own manufactured goods instead of buying them from her. This second consideration became particularly serious as the depression caused Japanese foreign trade to fall by one-third between 1929 and 1930. To make matters worse, the Chinese had already begun to boycott Japanese wares in resentment against Japan's interference with their occupation of Peking in 1928. During most of the 1920s civilian, liberal, Western-oriented leaders had kept control of the Japanese government. Like the big industrialists, they had wanted to attain new markets and an expanding empire without open warfare.

But Japan also had its own brand of nationalism, and the more aggressive elements in her army and navy gave this nationalism a strongly militaristic tone. They regarded the West as decadent and their own liberal politicians as flabby. Most of all, they wanted to weaken their country's new rival on the Asian mainland, and in 1931 they became determined to conquer Manchuria—in the name of Japan's national interests. As in the case of German and Italian aggression

*Named after the French minister of war who began its construction in the late 1920s, the Maginot Line was an ultra-modern system of border fortifications, with heavy guns enclosed in concrete pillboxes, and with a complete system of underground barracks and railroads. The Line ran from the Swiss to the Belgian border.

a few years later, suitable incidents were easy to find, or arrange. First there was the murder of a Japanese army captain in civilian dress at Mukden, which received highly colored accounts in the Japanese press on September 17. The next night some Chinese soldiers were reported to have blown up a short stretch of track on the Japanese-operated South Manchuria Railway (31 inches according to later estimates) and to have resisted Japanese patrols. Japan's national honor and her economic interests were obviously at stake! Within five months her army eliminated all organized resistance in Manchuria. The local war lord fled, and the victors replaced him with a puppet "emperor" in the renamed independent state of Manchukuo.

The Japanese had timed their act of aggression well. Preoccupied with the depression at home, the United States at no time contemplated the use of force to aid China; she simply refused to recognize Japan's conquest of Manchuria. Great Britain, whose naval strength in the South Pacific was less than that of the United States, tried, along with France, to get the League Council to apply sanctions. There Japan, also a member, used delaying tactics until her conquest of Manchuria was completed. Finally, in December 1931, the Council sent an investigating commission headed by Lord Lytton to the Far East. Ten months later the Lytton Commission reported that the Manchurian campaign could not be justified as a legitimate defense of Japan's national interests, described Manchukuo as a puppet creation, and recommended its replacement by an autonomous regime under nominal Chinese sovereignty. The League finally adopted this report in February 1933; a month later Japan gave notice of her own withdrawal from the League. She had acquired a large satellite state on the Chinese mainland with impunity. Only direct military intervention by the major Western democracies could have stopped this flagrant challenge to the international order they themselves had set up. Their failure to intervene is understandable in view of their domestic difficulties and Japan's sense of timing. It was nonetheless regrettable, for it weakened the League and encouraged other states to commit acts of aggression under the pretense of protecting their own national interests.

During the next few years Japan made several forays into Chinese territory during the undeclared war that she chose to call the "China Incident." Meanwhile, the militarists assassinated or otherwise eliminated all Japanese politicians who opposed their plan to dominate East Asia. In June 1937 they launched their full-scale invasion of China, capturing most of her major cities in a little over a year. The "China Incident" was now a life-and-death struggle between the two most populous independent nations in Asia. As in 1931, the Western democracies took no action to stop the aggressor. Only now they faced other aggressors much closer to home.

### *The Beginnings of Appeasement. Ethiopia*

By 1935 Germany and Italy were showing their separate intentions of upsetting the international status quo, and France and Great Britain were beginning to appease them. In July 1934 Hitler had tried to take over Austria with the help of local Nazis, but Mussolini had prevented the coup by sending 200,000 troops to the Austro-Italian frontier. Mussolini's gesture prompted the new French premier, Pierre Laval, to try to gain Italy as an ally against future German aggression. In January 1935 Laval visited Rome and gave Mussolini the impression that France would allow Italy to conquer Ethiopia as the price for Italian friendship. Then, in March, Hitler declared his intention of ignoring the Treaty of Versailles by reintroducing mass conscription for a new German army. Two months later Laval visited Moscow and persuaded Stalin to join France in guaranteeing the territorial integrity of Czechoslovakia, against whom German aggression might soon be directed. But while Laval was building paper alliances against a resurgent Germany, the British decided to accept Hitler's demands for "equality of rights" in armaments. In June 1935 they signed an agreement with him legalizing his new naval building program—again, in violation of the Treaty of Versailles. Thus, while Italy was preparing to conquer Ethiopia and Germany was rearming, the

French and the British launched their separate policies of appeasement.

The "incident" that gave Mussolini his excuse for attacking Ethiopia had occurred in December 1934 at Walwal, on the ill-defined border separating that country from Italian Somaliland. It was simply a local clash between the troops of the two countries—and may well have been deliberately provoked by Italy—but Mussolini made it an issue of national honor. He argued that Ethiopia was a backward and barbarous kingdom, and that Italy could not tolerate its threats to "her own security, rights, and dignity." Besides, it was the only major African territory not under European control, and Italy had a right to take it over, just as the British and the French had taken over most of the rest of Africa. He made this intention very clear in his response to attempts by the League of Nations to settle the border dispute through exchanges of territory:

"Italy's need for expansion in East Africa is not to be satisfied by the cession of a couple of deserts, one of salt and one of stone. The League Council seems to think I am a collector of deserts."

On October 3, 1935, Mussolini launched his attack.

Italy conquered all of Ethiopia in seven months. Mussolini took no chances. He poured a quarter of a million troops into this "colonial" war, supported by a formidable array of tanks, motorized units, and aircraft. The poorly equipped Ethiopians were no match for such a force. They fought bravely but they had no defense against the weapons of modern warfare, including poison gas. On May 9, 1936, Mussolini proclaimed the annexation of Ethiopia to Italy and the King of Italy's assumption of the title of Emperor of Ethiopia.

No major power did anything to stop this act of aggression. The British government weighed the potential danger to its control of the Red Sea plus Italy's obvious guilt against the cost of a war to defeat Italy. It decided that the cost would be too high. The French government still hoped to retain Mussolini's friendship and opposed any effective sanctions against Italy. Sections of public opinion in both Great Britain and France wanted their governments to help Ethiopia. So did many of the smaller states. In November 1935 the League of Nations voted to deprive Italy of arms, loans, and certain raw materials, but not the one raw material she really could not do without: oil. Mussolini had declared that oil sanctions would lead to war, and he appeared to mean what he said. Nobody called his bluff. Finally, in July 1936, the League removed its sanctions, and the powers accepted Mussolini's conquest.

### Remilitarization of the Rhineland

To Mussolini's aggressive technique of the bluff, Hitler added that of the dare. On March 7, 1936, while the Ethiopian War was still in progress, he marched his troops into the demilitarized zone of the Rhineland and dared the French to expel them. A glance at the map will show that, if Hitler fortified the Rhine, France would no longer be able to send troops across Germany to Czechoslovakia. Not only was the French alliance system thus compromised, but Hitler's act was clearly a violation of the Treaty of Versailles and the Locarno Pact. Why, then, did the French not meet Hitler's dare?

The answer is relatively simple, though not very edifying. In addition to dreading another war, Frenchmen were now divided by ideological and political conflicts. Under these conditions no political or military leader was willing to take the responsibility for using force to dislodge Hitler's troops from their new positions on France's border. The cabinet sought British backing before taking any action, but Great Britain, despite her pledge at Locarno to guarantee the status quo in the Rhineland, convinced herself that Hitler was within his "national rights" in reoccupying "his own backyard." The French government then used Britain's counsel of caution as one excuse for its own inaction. Another excuse was that the army leaders had no plan for moving a large task force into German territory; their strategy was a defensive one based on the supposedly impregnable Maginot Line. The government also argued that France's Eastern European allies—the Soviet Union,

*Hitler and Mussolini dancing beside Franco while he tells Chamberlain and Daladier: "Honest, Mister, there's nobody here but us Spaniards."*

Czechoslovakia, and Yugoslavia—could furnish no effective military help, despite their offers to do so. Like the army, it began to succumb to the "Maginot mentality."

By sheer daring, Hitler gained a decisive advantage over a more powerful adversary. France virtually abandoned her dominant position even though she was still militarily stronger than Germany. Hitler had gambled from a position of weakness and won, thus making the year 1936 the turning point in the European balance of power.

### The Spanish Civil War

Four months after Hitler reoccupied the Rhineland and two months after Mussolini completed his conquest of Ethiopia, civil war broke out in Spain. This war, which lasted from July 1936 until March 1939, was the most devastating experience of the Spanish people in modern times.* It also became an international moral issue, creating a tragic test case for the advocates of appeasement against aggression.

In order to prevent the Spanish Civil War from becoming a major European war the interested powers set up a Nonintervention Committee in London in September 1936. Great Britain, France, Germany, Italy, and the Soviet Union were its principal members, but only the Western democracies—including the United States, which passed its own Neutrality Act in 1937—really honored the principle of nonintervention.

Each of the three totalitarian powers intervened to further its own ends. The Soviet Union, whose intervention began several months after that of Germany and Italy, sold the Republicans arms, aircraft, transport, fuel oil, and machinery and lent them Russian technicians. Stalin's goal was to turn a Republican victory into a revolution led by Spanish Communists. But, as we have seen, Stalin was having his own difficulties at home, and he abandoned the Spanish Communists in 1938, just as he had abandoned the Chinese Communists eleven years earlier. Unlike the Soviet Union, Germany and Italy had strategic as well as ideological stakes in the Spanish Civil War. At the time, Franco not only seemed close to being a fascist but also seemed willing to grant considerable concessions to Hitler and Mussolini. During the course of the war, 20,000 German and 50,000 Italian troops participated directly in the fighting. In return, Mussolini and Hitler hoped to receive Spanish naval bases; Mussolini even hoped for Britain's base at Gibraltar. The two fascist dictators also hoped to gain a military ally on the southwestern border

*See p. 688 for more on this war.

of France, and Hitler wanted to divert the attention of Great Britain and France from his designs on Austria and Czechoslovakia.

Great Britain and France, though threatened by German and Italian aggression in Spain, chose to buy peace at the price of their vital interests. The British government hoped to detach Italy from the Rome-Berlin Axis, which had been formed in October 1936. At first Léon Blum's Popular Front government wanted to help its Spanish namesake. Within a few months, however, Blum decided that it was more important to cultivate France's only sure ally, Great Britain, and he closed the French border. Thereafter only a trickle of supplies reached the Spanish Loyalists from the great power to which they had looked for the most aid.

The governments of Great Britain and France enforced the policy of nonintervention, but public opinion in the major Western democracies was divided along ideological lines. In general the political conservatives and most Catholics favored the Nationalists, while the political liberals and the Extreme Left supported the Loyalists. For the former, the Spanish Civil War was a Christian crusade against Communism; for the latter, it was a democratic defense against fascism.* Both were right, in part, but the ideological issue in Spain was not the main point.

The main point was that German and Italian armed forces were killing Spanish soldiers, blockading Spanish ports, and bombing Spanish cities. Not only were these atrocities and aggressive acts illegal, they gave the Axis powers valuable military experience. For example, German planes dropped bombs on the defenseless town of Guernica "to see what would happen." As in the case of Ethiopia and the Rhineland, the British and French preferred to appease the aggressors rather than risk a general war. They were soon to learn to their sorrow that their appeasement had only strengthened the Axis and weakened them when the war they had tried to avoid finally came.

*13,000 individual volunteers from many countries fought for the Loyalists in the International Brigades. They included talented writers like the Frenchman André Malraux, the Englishman George Orwell, and the American Ernest Hemingway. Though the majority of the volunteers were not Communists, those who were tried to indoctrinate the others. Before the end of the Spanish Civil War many sensitive intellectuals became disillusioned by Communist efforts to use their heroic sacrifices for undemocratic ends.

### Austria and Czechoslovakia: The Munich Agreement

In 1938 Hitler emerged as the greatest danger to the peace of Europe. He boasted that he was building the mightiest military machine the world had ever known, and in February he rid the German army of the generals who opposed his plans for territorial expansion Then, in early March, he decided to seize Austria. As in July 1934, he used local Austrian Nazis to harass the existing government there, but he now sent German troops across the frontier as well. On March 12, swastikas adorned the main buildings of Vienna, Austria was annexed to the German Reich, and Hitler sent Mussolini a telegram thanking him for not interfering this time. Henceforth, Mussolini became a loyal junior partner in the Rome-Berlin Axis. Hitler was the main aggressor now.

"Horrible, horrible! I never thought they would do it!" This was the British foreign secretary's first reaction to the Nazis' seizure of Austria. But neither the British nor the French government *did* anything. Wildly cheering crowds in the streets of Vienna convinced the outside world that the Austrian people were glad to be "reunited" with their German kinsmen. The tens of thousands of Austrians who opposed the Nazis suffered greatly. The ex-chancellor was bullied by the Gestapo and then put in a concentration camp. Leaders of the Fatherland Front (a Right-wing organization), Social Democrats, and Jews bore the main brunt of Nazi violence. The Catholic Church in Austria also had its organizations dissolved and its properties confiscated. Still, Austria was a German-speaking land, and the usual 99 per cent voted "*ja*" in the Nazi-engineered plebiscite in early April. The other powers accepted the situation, and Austria did not become an international issue.

*Hitler entering the city limits of Vienna*

Czechoslovakia, Hitler's next target, did become an international issue. There too he was aided by local Nazis, who claimed to represent the 3 million Sudeten Germans in that multinational state of 15 million people. The Sudeten Nazis demanded autonomy from the Prague government, and Hitler posed as the champion of these "oppressed" Germans outside the Reich, ready to intervene and "free" them. Unlike the Austrian government in March, the government of Czechoslovakia was not helpless in May 1938. It had a well-armed military establishment and an alliance with France and the Soviet Union. When Hitler seemed about to strike, the Czechs moblized half a million men, and the French and Russian governments and even the British warned him that such a move might lead to war. These momentary demonstrations of firmness ended the May Crisis and saved the Czech state from immediate partition.

Far from ending his designs on the Sudetenland, the May Crisis irritated Hitler so much that he told his generals: "Czechoslovakia must be wiped off the map." During the summer of 1938 he publicly demanded only the Sudetenland, although he had no intention of tolerating a rump Czech state standing between Germany and her new province of Austria. He hoped that the British and French governments would convince themselves that the Sudeten Germans, like the Austrians, wanted to "rejoin" the Reich.

The British and French governments overfulfilled Hitler's hopes. Neville Chamberlain took the lead. In the early summer of 1938 he sent Lord Runciman, a wealthy businessman, to Czechoslovakia to "mediate" between the Sudeten Germans and the Czech government. His purpose was to extricate France from her treaty obligations to Czechoslovakia by forcing the Prague government to give Hitler the Sudetenland without starting a war; for if France went to war with Germany over the Sudetenland, Great Britain could not remain aloof for long. Edouard Daladier, the French premier, frowned on

Chamberlain's willingness to sacrifice France's most loyal ally in Central Europe, but his foreign minister, Georges Bonnet, was a firm advocate of appeasement, and most of his countrymen were in no mood for war. So Daladier let Chamberlain do the appeasing and became his accomplice.

By mid-September Hitler was talking so belligerently that Chamberlain flew to Germany to negotiate with him personally. At Hitler's Bavarian retreat at Berchtesgaden Chamberlain agreed to persuade his own government, the French, and Czechs to accept a plan of "self-determination" for the Sudetenland. He performed his part of the bargain. Then, on September 22, Chamberlain flew to his second meeting with Hitler, at Godesberg, to settle the technical details, but Hitler now declared that "self-determination" was not enough. He wanted Czechoslovakia to surrender the Sudetenland immediately. Chamberlain was truly shocked. He viewed himself as an "honest broker," trying to make the best "deal" for all parties concerned. Now he had to fly back to London with Hitler's ultimatum.

During the last week in September, Europe seemed to be on the brink of war. The Czech government ordered general mobilization; France began calling up 600,000 army reservists; and Chamberlain reluctantly agreed to put the British navy on a war footing. Nobody in Europe wanted a full-scale war, however, and Hitler, Chamberlain, and Daladier agreed to the suggestion of Mussolini that the four of them meet in Munich and settle the Czech crisis peacefully.

The tragic story of aggression and appeasement reached its climax at Munich on September 30, 1938. There Chamberlain agreed to deliver the Sudetenland to Germany. Daladier signed the Munich Agreement for France, and, along with Chamberlain, pledged his country to guarantee the new Czechoslovak frontiers. Hitler and Mussolini agreed to guarantee the frontiers of the reduced Czech state as soon as the territorial claims of Hungary and Poland in the eastern part of the country were settled (which happened a few weeks later). The victim of this partition was not represented at all at Munich; nor was the Soviet Union, which was certainly an interested party. It looked to her as if the British and the French were deliberately trying to divert Hitler's expansionist energies toward the East. This was not really true of Chamberlain and Daladier; like their countrymen, all they wanted was "peace in our time." As the London *Times* said on October 1, "No conqueror returning from a victory on the battlefield has come home adorned with nobler laurels than Mr. Chamberlain from Munich yesterday." The price the British and the French soon paid for Chamberlain's "laurels" has made the Munich Agreement the symbol of the folly of appeasement. Not only had Chamberlain and Daladier abandoned an innocent ally, they had subverted the whole Versailles system, strengthened the power and prestige of the Third Reich, and lost most of their remaining friends and influence in Eastern Europe.

All this became clear six months later. On March 15, 1939, Hitler declared that Czechoslovakia had fallen apart. He recognized the newly "independent" clerico-fascist regime in Slovakia, marched his own troops into Prague, and turned the Czech provinces into a German protectorate. Chamberlain was again shocked, but he accepted the "fact" that Czechoslovakia had disintegrated without external aggression, so that legally neither Great Britain nor France had to go to war to save it. They had already paid the price for peace at Munich.

### Poland: The Moscow Pact

By the summer of 1939 Hitler seemed to be able to get anything he wanted without a general war. His demand for Danzig, in the Polish Corridor, prompted Great Britain and France to guarantee the territorial integrity of Poland. Mussolini's annexation of Albania prompted them to guarantee the territorial integrity of Greece, Rumania, and Turkey. Hitler was convinced that the Western democracies would not honor these guarantees, even to Poland. Still, he had one more step to take to give him a serious chance of winning a general war: to neutralize the principal enemy in the East (the Soviet Union) while he liquidated the secondary enemy in the East (Poland) and then the main continental enemy in the West (France).

The Soviet Union was the key power in European diplomacy on the eve of the Second World War. Without her military support the British and the French could do little to save Poland from annihilation by the Germans, although the Poles themselves feared the Russians as much as the Germans and refused to allow Russian troops on their soil. The British and French governments dragged out their feeble negotiations for a Russian alliance in July and August of 1939. They had a low opinion of the Russian army and an unrealistically high one of the Polish army. They haggled over Stalin's demand for the right to intervene in Estonia, Latvia, and Lithuania in order to prevent an internal pro-German coup in these small Baltic states. Most important of all, they thought that they could keep the Soviet Union dangling indefinitely and that no one else would seek an understanding with this unsavory outcast nation.

Behind the scenes, however, Stalin was playing off the French and the British against the Germans. Hitler's timetable for the invasion of Poland could not be postponed beyond the end of August, and he was ready to promise Stalin anything in order to gain his benevolent neutrality. On August 23, the German and Soviet foreign ministers signed the Moscow Pact. In return for her neutrality, the Soviet Union was promised a free hand in the three Baltic states, a large slice of eastern Poland, and a sphere of influence in part of the Balkans.

The significance of the Moscow Pact cannot be overstressed. It assured Hitler of an easy victory over Poland without the danger of a two-front war. It ended the diplomatic isolation of the Soviet Union and gave her a breathing space in which to improve her military defenses against a future German attack. It also showed that power considerations outweighed ideological ones; Germany's antibolshevism and Russia's antifacism were no longer mentioned once the Pact was signed. Finally, the Moscow Pact ended any hope for an independent Eastern Europe. Hitler and Stalin simply divided the whole area into spheres of German and Russian influence.

Hitler won his greatest diplomatic victory with the Moscow Pact, and the British and the French knew it. They had already begun to abandon their policy of appeasement by giving guarantees to Poland, Greece, and Rumania and by stepping up their own military preparedness. Now they clearly saw that appeasement had been a total failure. The British and French ranted at the Soviet Union for its "betrayal." Having been beaten at their own game by the Bolsheviks, they were now angry enough to stop Hitler at any cost. The cost was a general war in which they had no effective allies. Nevertheless, two days after Hitler's troops and planes crossed the Polish border on September 1, 1939, Great Britain and France declared war on Germany. The war that nobody had wanted had begun on the best possible terms for the aggressor.

⁝ ⁝ ⁝

The record of the Western democracies during the interwar years was a mixed one. Their greatest failure was in foreign affairs, where they did not preserve the international order that they themselves had created. They managed to retain their hold on their overseas empires, but they were even less responsive to the aspirations of their colonial subjects than to those of their underprivileged citizens at home. Like many continental countries, France failed to intergrate her working class into her national society. Great Britain was more successful than France in this respect, but she was surpassed by New Zealand, the United States, and especially Scandinavia.

Whether one counts the shift from laissez-faire "normalcy" to what a spiritual descendant of President Harding called "welfarism" as a gain or a loss depends on one's point of view. The fact remains that the depression of the 1930s forced a number of Western democracies to make this shift. Like the social integration of labor, with which it was closely linked, the welfare state was accepted most eagerly in Scandinavia and resisted most vociferously in France. Yet, whatever people thought about them, unemployment insurance, minimum wages, paid vacations, and the forty-hour week had come to stay. Not only did the state itself enforce these measures, it also played an increasingly active role in the national economy, regulating it and sometimes even planning it in the interest of the common welfare.

The greatest achievement of the Western democracies was in preserving their traditional liberties while the rest of Europe was succumbing to totalitarianism. For all her internal divisions and weaknesses, France remained the citadel of European freedom in the eyes of the refugees who flocked there from Italy, Germany, and Spain, just as their ancestors had done a century earlier. But the days of this freedom were numbered, and the Fall of France in June 1940 was to dramatize in an extreme way the failure of the statesmen who had met in her capital twenty-one years earlier to make the world safe for democracy.

## SUGGESTED READINGS


Werth, Alexander, *The Twilight of France, 1933–1940.* New York: Harper and Row, 1942.
A high-level journalistic account by an on-the-spot observer.

Tannenbaum, Edward R., *The New France.* Chicago: Univ. of Chicago Press, 1961.
Examines the social, cultural, and economic factors in French life.

Joll, James, ed., *The Decline of the Third Republic.* New York: Frederick A. Praeger, 1959.
Suggestive essays on France's tribulations in the 1930s.

Mowat, Charles, *Britain between the Wars.* Chicago: Univ. of Chicago Press, 1955.
A comprehensive, detailed study.

Taylor, A. J. P. *English History, 1914–1945.* New York: Oxford Univ. Press, 1965.*
Lively and informative.

McElwee, William L., *Britain's Locust Years, 1918–1940.* London: Faber and Faber, 1962.
A brief, readable account.

Graves, Robert and Allan Hodge, *The Long Weekend: A Social History of Great Britain, 1918–1939.* New York: W. W. Norton, 1963.*
Amusing and penetrating social history.

Knaplund, Paul, *Britain: Commonwealth and Empire, 1901–1955.* New York: Harper and Row, 1957.
See the section on the interwar years.

Holt, Edgar, *Protest in Arms; the Irish Troubles, 1916–1923.* New York: Coward-McCann, 1961.
A very satisfactory account of Ireland's struggle for independence.

Wolfers, Arnold, *Britain and France between Two Wars: Conflicting Strategies of Peace since Versailles.* Hamden, Conn.: Shoe String Press, 1940.
Balanced diplomatic history based on materials then available.

Jordan, W. M., *Great Britain, France and the German Problem, 1918–1939: A Study of Anglo-French Relations in the Making and Maintenance of the Versailles Settlement.* New York: Oxford Univ. Press, 1943.
A scholarly study.

Sturmhal, Adolph, *Tragedy of European Labor, 1918–1939.* New York: Columbia Univ. Press, 1944.
Shows how the failure to integrate the labor movement into the national societies of Europe weakened their ability to remain democratic.

Scott, Franklin, *The United States and Scandinavia.* Cambridge, Mass.: Harvard Univ. Press, 1950.
An excellent, readable survey.

Childs, Marquis, *Sweden: The Middle Way.* New Haven: Yale Univ. Press, 1961.*
A reprint of a sympathetic report that alerted the Western world to the nature of the welfare state in Scandinavia in the 1930s.

Kinross, Lord, *Atatürk: A Biography of Mustapha Kemal, Father of Modern Turkey.* New York: Morrow, 1965.
A balanced and comprehensive account.

Schwartz, Benjamin I., *Chinese Communism and the Rise of Mao.* New York: Harper and Row, n.d., Torchbook.*
Excellent scholarly study.

Walters, Francis P., *A History of the League of Nations.* New York: Oxford Univ. Press, 1952.
A comprehensive history by a British member of the League Secretariat.

Carr, E. H., *The Twenty Years' Crisis, 1919–1939: An Introduction to the Study of International Relations.* New York: Harper and Row, n.d. Torchbook.*
A critical study of the character of international relations during the interwar period—particularly severe toward the Wilsonian tradition.

Thomas, Hugh, *The Spanish Civil War.* New York: Harper and Row, 1963. Colophon.*
Especially good on the international aspects of this war.

Wheeler-Bennett, John W., *Munich: Prologue to Tragedy.* New York: Viking Press, 1964. Compass.*
Well-written and comprehensive.

Eubank, Keith, *Munich.* Norman, Okla.: Univ. of Oklahoma Press, 1963.
A scholarly study bringing in information from captured German documents.

Craig, Gordon A. and Felix Gilbert, eds., *The Diplomats, 1919–1939.* Princeton, N.J.: Princeton Univ. Press, 1953.
A useful collection of studies of leading diplomats.

Taylor, A. J. P., *The Origins of the Second World War.* Greenwich, Conn.: Fawcett Publications, 1963.*
A provocative and sometimes perverse attempt to absolve Hitler from blame for "starting" the war. Especially severe toward British policy.

Bullock, Alan, *Hitler: A Study in Tyranny.* Rev. ed. New York: Harper and Row, 1964.*
The sections on Hitler's diplomacy are excellent.

Weinberg, Gerhard, *Germany and the Soviet Union, 1939–1941.* Leyden: E. J. Brill, 1954.
A detailed, scholarly study of the first of the "strange alliances" of the mid-twentieth century. See particularly the concluding chapter, which summarizes the author's main arguments.

Wiskemann, Elizabeth, *Europe of the Dictators.* See comments in readings for Chapter XVIII.

CHAPTER XX

# THE SECOND WORLD WAR

The Second World War came as much less of a surprise than the First. Mounting tensions in the pre-1914 decade had not prepared Europeans for war nearly as effectively as the international events leading up to 1939. These events reinforced the wish of many people to avoid another bloodletting while at the same time making them understand how precarious world peace was.

Actually, the Second World War consisted of four different wars. The war between the Western Allies and the Germans – the Second German War – began in September 1939, when Great Britain and France declared war on Germany following her attack on Poland. In June 1940 Italy joined Germany, and France signed an armistice. The British then fought the two Axis powers alone until June 1941, when Hitler launched the Russo-German War. In December 1941 the United States became involved in the Second German War and two other major wars: the Great Pacific War and the War for East Asia. Now the three Axis powers – Germany, Italy, and Japan – were fighting the three principal Allies – the United States, Great Britain, and the Soviet Union – in theaters of war thousands of miles apart. The two wars in Europe ended in May 1945, and the Great Pacific War ended in September 1945. But the War for East Asia, which had begun in 1931 when Japan conquered Manchuria, did not really end until 1949, when the Chinese Communists drove the Chinese Nationalists off the Asian mainland.

The Second World War affected the lives of even more people – especially civilians – than the First. The total armed forces of the European belligerents were no larger than they had been in 1914–1918, but those of the United States, Japan, and China added millions more soldiers, sailors, and airmen. Hundreds of thousands of guerrillas also took part in the fighting in both Europe and Asia. During the course of the war millions of civilians became displaced persons, and millions more were killed in cold blood. In fact, new weapons and new methods of mass destruction did much more harm to the civilian population than to the fighting men. Finally, new forms of political coercion were applied to large sections of Europe and Asia during and immediately after the war.

## THE COURSE OF THE WAR, 1939–1943

During the first three years of the war in Europe Hitler strengthened Germany considerably. Of the six other great powers, three—Italy, Japan, and the Soviet Union—were on his side at the start, and the United States remained isolated. He conquered Poland in the first three weeks of September 1939 and overran Norway, Denmark, Belgium, Luxembourg, the Netherlands, and France in the spring of 1940. The following winter he had made satellites of Hungary, Rumania, and Bulgaria and occupied Yugoslavia and Greece. Hitler therefore controlled almost the whole European continent when he invaded the Soviet Union in mid-1941. In December of that year his armies were 40 miles from Moscow and less than 100 miles from the Suez Canal. At the same time, his Japanese ally took over Southeast Asia and forced the United States into the war. Hitler's military successes made him overconfident and indifferent to the kind of diplomatic strategy that had made them possible. In the long run, the involvement of the Soviet Union and the United States was to prove fatal to Germany and her Axis partners, but throughout most of 1942 they still held the upper hand.

### Blitzkrieg in Poland and the West, 1939–1940

Hitler's speedy conquest of Poland introduced a new kind of warfare to the world: the Blitzkrieg. This "lightning war" was organized around large Panzer (armored tank) units in conjunction with the Luftwaffe, which maintained mastery of the air. The Luftwaffe carried out the first phase. In forty-eight hours it destroyed Poland's 500 first-line planes by the concentrated bombing of her airfields. Simultaneously, dive bombers, or Stukas, took over the former function of the long-range artillery in demolishing rearward communications and also spread terror among civilian refugees fleeing the advancing ground forces. The second phase was effected by the heavy tanks, followed by lighter motorized divisions. The self-sufficient Panzer units often raced several days' marching distance ahead of the main body of infantry, maintaining contact with each other by radio. Their function was to penetrate deep behind the weak points in the enemy's lines and to capture road and railroad junctions, bridges, airfields, and military headquarters. The infantry "mopped up" afterward with air and artillery support.

Only an armored counterattack of equal strength could restore the defense, once a deep armored penetration had been made and fully exploited, and the Poles had no means of launching such a counterattack. They met the German invasion of 1,000,000 men—including nine armored divisions and 1,500 planes—with about 500,000 fully mobilized infantrymen, a single armored brigade, and, incredibly, twelve fully horsed, booted, and spurred cavalry brigades. Their organized resistance collapsed in three weeks, and Warsaw fell on September 27.

Poland was to suffer a worse fate than any other nation during the Second World War. Germany occupied the western two-thirds of the country, where the bulk of the Poles themselves lived. Russia occupied the eastern third, which was inhabited mainly by Belorussians, Ukrainians, and Jews. Both the Germans and the Russians ruthlessly crushed all lingering manifestations of Polish patriotism, and the Nazis eliminated all the leading Polish intellectuals and Jews they could find.

None of the major powers was prepared for Hitler's new kind of warfare. They all had some light and medium tanks; in fact, France had almost as many as Germany by May 1940. But they all simply parceled them out to the infantry, rather than organizing them into self-sustaining combat units with heavy tanks for the initial breakthrough. Only the British had built up sufficient air power to cope with the Luftwaffe when their turn came to face it; indeed, Italy was the only other country with a separate air force. Neither the Soviet Union nor the United States could build up their armored and air forces sufficiently to overwhelm the Germans anywhere before 1944.

France, which was obviously to be Hitler's next major victim, did not change her basic military strategy in the light of the Blitzkrieg in Poland. She continued to put her main trust in fixed land defenses, even to the neglect of her air defense system (which relied on observers using civilian telephones and was deficient in antiaircraft guns and fighters). The Maginot Line was indeed a formidable obstacle to any frontal attack. Although it tapered off at the Belgian border, the Forest of the Ardennes and the Meuse River would supposedly serve from there on as natural barriers to German tanks. France's "Plan D" assumed that the Germans would come through Belgium, as they had during the First World War. When they did, the French and British armies would advance across the Belgian frontier and take up positions between Antwerp and Namur. This plan was to be no match for the Blitzkrieg in the West in May 1940, with its dive bombers, armored tanks, paratroopers, the terror bombing of towns, the deliberately induced exodus of the civilian population, the chaos of communications and services, and organized treachery in the rear.

The long delay preceding this German attack in the West tended to reassure the French and their British allies that their land defenses were secure. Having "neutralized" Russia and conquered Poland, Hitler was ready to turn his country's full might against France as early as November 1939, but bad weather stopped him then and again in January. For six months there was no important military action. After the Blitzkrieg in Poland, this *Sitzkrieg* (sitting war) seemed strangely "phony" to the British and the French.

### *The West and the Russo-Finnish Campaign*

While the two Western powers sat out the "phony war" in the winter of 1939–1940, the Soviet Union tried to strengthen her own strategic position in the Baltic area, particularly in Finland. The Finnish border was almost within artillery range of Leningrad, and Stalin feared an eventual German attack through Finland, just as the French feared one through Belgium. Unlike the Belgians, however, the Finns had fortified their own frontier against their powerful neighbor. Stalin offered to trade Soviet territory further north for the Carelian Isthmus. When the Finns refused, he attacked them, determined to push the frontier back by force, just as he had pushed his frontier in Poland back in September. Less than a month after her occupation of Eastern Poland the Soviet Union had signed treaties with Estonia, Latvia, and Lithuania entitling her to establish military, naval, and air bases there.* Finland alone remained uncooperative.

In the early months of 1940 the four major powers centered their attention on the Baltic and the Scandinavian countries. The whole Western world was indignant over Russia's invasion of Finland; the British, who wanted to safeguard the Gallivare mines, and the French, for less practical motives, prepared to send an expeditionary force through Norway and Sweden to help the beleaguered Finns. If the Norwegian and Swedish governments had not refused to permit the passage of this force through their territories, Great Britain and France might well have gone to war against the USSR, even though they were already at war with Germany. The German government, in turn, planned to invade Norway and Denmark in anticipation of an Allied occupation of Norway. It also wanted an Atlantic base for its submarines and an ice-free sea route for Swedish ore, which would be shipped through the Norwegian port of Narvik. The Allied expedition to Finland never got started, for the Finns made peace with the Russians in March, ceding the Carelian Isthmus to the USSR. But on April 8 the British, following repeated German violations of Norway's neutrality in coastal inlets, began mining Norwegian waters. On the next day, Hitler's land, sea, and air forces launched a lightning invasion of Denmark and Norway. The Danes could offer no serious resistance; the Norwegian forces fought as best they could, but the Germans occupied all the key points in a few days, even though British and French forces retook (and lost) Narvik in May and June.

### *Invasion of the Low Countries*

Having secured his northern flank, Hitler began his Blitzkrieg against the West on May 10. Within a week his tanks and

*She was to take these three countries over completely after the Fall of France in the summer of 1940.

planes overran Holland, Luxembourg, and most of Belgium. Further south a German armored spearhead broke through the supposedly impenetrable Ardennes and raced to the French Channel coast, thus trapping twenty French divisions and the whole of the British and Belgian forces in Flanders. On paper the total manpower of each side had been about equal at the beginning of the campaign: 136 German divisions against 135 Allied divisions, of which 94 were French, 22 Belgian, 10 Dutch, and 9 British; but the Dutch army capitulated on May 15 and the Belgian on May 28. By then the British and French forces in Flanders held only a beachhead at Dunkirk. Instead of destroying them, Hitler began regrouping his Panzers for the main battle against France. Consequently, British and French naval units and hundreds of private vessels were able to evacuate 366,000 men, about two-thirds of them British, from Dunkirk by June 4. On the next day the Battle of France began.

### *The Fall of France*

Never in modern times has a great power been defeated so quickly; it was all over on June 25. In less than three weeks the Germans overran the northern two-thirds of France. The Maginot Line, in which the French had placed so much hope, had been outflanked, and it stood like a stranded battleship, with its guns still pointing eastward. The French fought as well as they could, but, like the Poles, they were unable to launch a major armored counterattack against the German Panzer thrusts. Division after division found itself isolated and forced to surrender. Meanwhile, German dive-bombers disrupted their rearward communications, and machine-gunned the civilian refugees fleeing southward. Over a million Parisians alone left their homes just before the capital fell, on June 13. In Bordeaux Paul Reynaud, who had replaced Daladier in March, resigned as premier on June 16 in the face of pressure for an armistice within his own cabinet. He was succeeded by the eighty-four-year-old "Victor of Verdun," Marshal Pétain, whose delegates accepted Nazi Germany's armistice terms on June 22. The armistice went into effect three days later.

France did not suffer the fate of Poland. Only the northern two-thirds of the country was to be occupied, and it was to remain under the legal jurisdiction of Pétain's government, which soon established its capital at Vichy, in the unoccupied zone. Still, the French armed forces were to be demobilized, almost 2 million French prisoners of war were to remain in German hands until the conclusion of peace, and the French navy was to be kept in ports and under no circumstances to be allowed to fall into British hands.

At the height of the Battle of France, Mussolini finally entered the war. (It is humiliating," he once said, "to sit with one's arms folded while others make history.") Like almost everybody else, he thought that Great Britain too would soon fall, and he wanted his share of the spoils. He got only a strip of French Alpine territory in Europe, and, as we shall see, he was to become more of a liability than an asset to Hitler in the Eastern Mediterranean. Nevertheless, Italy's entry into the war compounded the terrors that the Nazi Blitzkrieg held in store for Great Britain, which now had to face the enemy alone.

## Britain Fights Alone, 1940–1941

In June 1940 Great Britain's position seemed almost hopeless. The British Chiefs of Staff admitted that "should the Germans succeed in establishing a force with its vehicles in this country, our army forces have not got the offensive power to drive it out." The expeditionary force evacuated at Dunkirk had lost all its tanks and artillery; the Royal Navy had lost a third of its already inadequate destroyer force in this and other operations. Only the Royal Air Force remained essentially intact at the end of the Battle of France, but it was still only half the size of the Luftwaffe.

In these circumstances, it was fortunate indeed for Britain—and the rest of the world—that Hitler delayed his invasion of England. Some historians explain this delay by Hitler's alleged belief that the British would see the hopelessness of their

*London during an air raid: Henry Moore's "Tilbury Shelter Scene"*

situation and make a compromise peace. Certainly his main ambition was to control the continent and defeat the Soviet Union; in fact, he was already planning his invasion of Russia on July 31, two weeks before he launched his air attack on England. It is more likely, however, that the delay was needed for the preparation of an amphibious attack for which the German High Command lacked both equipment and experience. Even after Hitler issued his first directive for "Operation Sea Lion" for mid-August, the German service chiefs spent much precious time in acrimonious discussions over the technical problems of a Channel crossing. Admiral Raeder gave no assurance of success, and all of Hitler's advisers agreed that the Luftwaffe would first have to gain complete mastery of the air.

To Britain the delay was invaluable. It allowed her factories to reequip her land forces and to turn out hundreds of new fighter planes; it strengthened the determination of her people to resist; it gave the new prime minister, Winston Churchill (1874–1965), time to reorganize the war effort and to bolster the nation's morale with his rhetoric. The disastrous Norwegian campaign shook the British people and government out of their complacency and forced Chamberlain out of office. When Churchill became prime minister on May 10,1940, his first speech struck an entirely different note:

"I have nothing to offer but blood, toil, tears and sweat. . . . You ask, what is our policy? I will say: It is to wage war, by sea, by land, and air, with all our might and with all the strength that God can give us. . . ."

During the next five years Churchill's audacity and impatience sometimes caused difficulties with his generals. Still, with his drive, vigilance, joy of battle, love of responsibility, and above all, courage and faith, he was unsurpassed as a national leader in wartime.

The Battle of Britain, which began on August 12, 1940, was primarily a contest for mastery of the air. For a month the Luftwaffe bombed RAF airfields, factories, and radar stations as well as England's southeastern harbors and her Channel shipping. Although the British lost fewer planes than the Germans, their reserves of both fighter planes and pilots were seriously weakened. A few hundred young British and Commonwealth fighter pilots, and a few score French, Poles, Czechs, and Belgians, repulsed Germany's armada of bombers by flying in shifts around the clock. Then on September 7, the Luftwaffe turned on London. Its leaders believed that the enemy's reserves were already gone, and Hitler wished to retaliate for British raids on Berlin. In reality, the Luftwaffe was already admitting that it had failed to destroy RAF fighter strength. German bombers continued to bomb London and Midland manufacturing towns into the fall and winter, but in October Hitler postponed "Operation Sea Lion" indefinitely.

For the next three years the main struggle between Great Britain and Germany took place in the Atlantic and the Eastern Mediterranean. As in the First World War, Germany's grand strategy was to cut the island kingdom's sea communications and starve its people into submission. German submarines attacked their Atlantic convoys in "wolf packs" of eight to twenty. By November 1942 they were sinking 200,000 tons of British shipping a month, and an equal amount of other Allied shipping. In the Eastern Mediterranean, Italy launched the first major attacks against the British, but her navy never captured Malta, and her army's effort to penetrate Egypt and seize the Suez Canal ended in failure. By December 1940, British forces were driving the Italians back into Libya. Then in April 1941, the Germans took over the initiative. They captured Crete and, under the leadership of the shrewd and colorful General Erwin Rommel, they forced the British out of Libya. The campaigns in Libya and Egypt continued throughout 1941 and 1942, but Hitler was now devoting the main body of his army and air force to his new war in Russia, and he never gave Rommel enough forces to permit him to gain a decisive victory over the British.

The fact that the British kept fighting had crucial significance for the eventual outcome of the Second World War. Without this British effort, especially in 1941, American power might never have been brought to bear on Germany, and the Russians might have been completely defeated. In the end, Germany and her Axis partners were to be overwhelmed by the unprecedented might of the United States and the Soviet Union. In 1941 and most of 1942, however, these two superpowers needed time to transform their industrial and manpower potential into a fighting reality. They were given this time by the sacrifices of bombed-out Londoners, British seamen in the Atlantic, and British and Commonwealth desert fighters in North Africa.

### The Russo-German War to December 1941

By any reasonable estimate, the Germans had sufficient superiority over the first-line strength of the Red Army to defeat it in a few months. Moreover, the Tripartite Pact, signed by Germany and Italy with Japan in September 1940, had given Hitler an ally in the Far East in case the United States should enter the war on the side of Great Britain. And, as in the cases of Poland and France, Hitler secured his flanks before pushing forward. In the winter of 1940–1941 he forced Hungary, Rumania, and Bulgaria to sign the Tripartite Pact. Then, in April 1941, German forces defeated and occupied Yugoslavia and Greece—including the island of Crete. With the Balkans secured and the British pinned down in Egypt, Hitler felt ready to begin his conquest of the Soviet Union.

But Hitler made two grave mistakes. Politically, he underestimated the loyalty of the Russian people to the Stalin regime in the face of a German invasion. Diplomatically, he failed to gain a Japanese commitment to join him in attacking the Soviet Union, while he committed Germany to joining Japan in an eventual war against the United States. Actually, in April 1941 Japan and the Soviet Union had signed a Neutrality Pact. Coming after a decade of clashes between these two powers along the borders of China and Manchukuo, this agreement was as much a diplomatic surprise as the Moscow Pact of August 1939 had been. In each case two hostile nations had come to terms in order to concentrate their military forces elsewhere. (Unlike the Germans, however, the Japanese were to keep their part of the bargain throughout the war, and the Russians were to keep theirs until after the United States dropped atomic bombs on Hiroshima and Nagasaki in August 1945.)

Hitler's goal in the Soviet Union differed from what it had been in the West. It was not just to possess territory, capture cities, win battles, or break the fighting will of the enemy. It was to destroy Russia. The Moscow Pact had been a mere expedient for both sides; Hitler never gave up his ultimate goal in the East. Relations between Germany and the Soviet Union had deteriorated steadily since the autumn of 1940, and, as we have seen, Hitler had already begun his invasion plans by then. Stalin may have been surprised—he later told Churchill, "I thought I might gain another six months or so." Or he may have overestimated the efficiency of his own massive forces. Regardless of Stalin's response, the Germans were committed to a war of annihilation, and the Russians were soon to retaliate in the same spirit. As Hitler told his commanders just before the invasion:

"The war against Russia will not be of a kind that can be conducted in knightly fashion. It will be a struggle of ideologies and racial differences and will have to be waged with unprecedented, unmerciful, and unrelenting harshness. All officers must rid themselves of old-fashioned and obsolete doctrines [of mercy and basic human decency]."

When Hitler declared war on the Soviet Union on June 22, 1941, he unleashed the most gigantic military struggle in the history of mankind. Nine million fighting men were eventually to join battle along a thousand-mile front from the Baltic to the Black Sea. The invaders seem to have been slightly superior in numbers and greatly superior in air power and armored techniques, though not in number of tanks. From the beginning, there were small contingents of Finns, Rumanians, and Hugarians on the German side.*

Within a few weeks the invaders had breached the Soviet frontier throughout its length and were pushing deep into Russian territory. Military "experts" throughout the world predicted the country's imminent collapse. Then, instead of concentrating his main attack on Moscow—as Napoleon had done and as a number of his own generals wanted to do—Hitler diverted some of his forces into the Ukraine. There General Gerd von Rundstedt captured a whole group of Russian armies, thus giving Hitler his greatest single victory. It was probably also his greatest blunder though, for it meant that he could not regroup his forces for his drive on Moscow until October 2, 1941, over two weeks after Napoleon entered that city a century earlier.

Hitler's other blunders stemmed from his political underestimation of the

*The Finns joined the Axis in June 1941 for revenge against Russia's war on them in the winter of 1939–1940; the Rumanians and Hungarians, already members of the Axis, also gave their anti-Russian prejudices free rein. They had no love for each other, though, especially since Hitler had allowed Hungary to annex about half of Transylvania in August 1940. But the Soviet Union had already taken over Bessarabia six weeks earlier. Both these seizures of Rumanian territory had discredited the existing government and left the pro-Nazi General Ion Antonescu as the real ruler of the country. Although the Hungarian and Rumanian units on the Russian front were carefully separated from one another, they fought there in ever increasing numbers. As the war dragged on, small pro-Nazi contingents from other European countries were also to fight on the Russian front.

strength of Stalin's dictatorship and from his racist prejudice, which blinded him to the ability of Russian junior officers to make up for the inexperience of their commanders by improvising their own tactics. Over 2 million Russian troops had surrendered in the Ukraine, long a center of anti-Bolshevik feeling and a major German political target; but Nazi ruthlessness against the "racially inferior" Ukrainians soon turned them against the invaders. The rest of the country was becoming enraged at the sufferings and deaths of Russian soldiers in German prison camps.

By mid-November, German advanced units were within forty miles of Moscow, but once again Hitler overruled his generals. Bad weather was already upon them, and they advised settling down into winter quarters; Hitler insisted on pressing forward toward final victory. By the first week in December, even he had to admit that winter weather prevented any further operations. Indeed, the Red Army had already begun its counteroffensive, and Russian guerrilla fighters harried German rearward communication lines and garrisons. Just before Christmas, 1941, Hitler took over the supreme army command himself and relieved the commanders who had failed in the great offensive.

The Russian front was to remain the main theater of war until the Allied landing in Normandy two and a half years later. There were to be German offensives and Russian counteroffensives on a scale that staggers the imagination. Hitler had not destroyed the Soviet Union by December 1941, as he had planned, and his troops, short of winter clothing and equipment, suffered appalling hardships. The Russians themselves were barely able to regroup and re-equip their beleaguered fighting forces. Meanwhile, the United States was dragged into the war, under most unfavorable circumstances, when Japan began its full-scale offensive in Southeast Asia. Throughout 1942 and 1943 the British and the Americans were to increase their economic and military aid to the Soviet Union and to prepare for their own ultimate counteroffensive against the Axis. Until they finally launched it, however, the Russians bore the full brunt of the war.

### The United States Enters the War

As in the First World War, American opinion was divided over what to do about the conflict in Europe. Like President Wilson, President Roosevelt had promised to keep the United States out, though he saw the danger of German world conquest sooner than Wilson had. Pacifists, isolationists, and "America Firsters" had much public support, especially in the Middle West and the South. Hence, aside from allowing the British and the French to buy American arms and ammunition on a cash-and-carry basis, the American government maintained strict neutrality until the summer of 1940. Then the Fall of France and the possible defeat of Great Britain startled most Americans into a realization of how defenseless they were. After weeks of debate, Congress passed the Selective Service Act in September. In that same month the United States government gave the British government fifty over-age destroyers in exchange for a string of British naval bases in the Western Atlantic. After being reelected for an unprecedented third term in November, President Roosevelt declared that the United States must be "the great arsenal of democracy," and he set up plans for a two-ocean navy, production of 50,000 planes a year, and a modernized army of 1 million men.

During 1941 America's policy shifted decisively from neutrality to "all aid to Britain short of war." By March, Congress passed the Lend-Lease Bill to provide economic and military aid to any country "whose defense the President deems vital to the defense of the United States." Its initial appropriation was for $7 billion. (The Canadian Government made its first billion-dollar gift to Britain soon thereafter.) The United States also became increasingly involved in the Battle of the Atlantic, for Lend-Lease goods were of no value unless they could get past Hitler's submarine "wolf packs." America gave naval protection to British shipping as far as Iceland. Within a few months, however, the field of American operations had widened, and her destroyers were convoying British troops as far as Capetown. On September 4, the American destroyer *Greer* exchanged shots with a German U-boat.

Meanwhile, in August, Roosevelt, Churchhill, and their Chiefs of Staff held a full-scale "summit meeting" on a battleship in the Atlantic and issued the Atlantic Charter. In this expression of their war aims the two powers, one belligerent and one technically neutral, explicitly referred to "the final destruction of Nazi tyranny."

Still, it was Japan, not Germany, that forced the United States into the Second World War. Japanese-American relations had been slowly deteriorating since 1937. The United States government refused to recognize any of Japan's conquests in China and had curtailed all trade with the Asian aggressor by July 1941. A year earlier the fall of the Netherlands and France had left their respective possessions in Southeast Asia open to Japanese invasion, and by September 1940 the Governor-General of French Indochina was forced to permit the Japanese to build air bases there. In 1941 Japan's relations with the United States became increasingly bitter as her preparations for taking over all of Southeast Asia became known. "Magic" —the Cryptanalytic Division of the United States Army and Navy—had broken the Japanese radio code and was informing the State Department of all major decisions of the Japanese government. In November two Japanese emissaries arrived in Washington to negotiate the differences between the two powers, but Tokyo had already resolved to go to war.

On December 7, 1941 the Japanese attacked Pearl Harbor. "Magic" had informed the Army Chief of Staff, General George C. Marshall, of the impending attack, but static difficulties prevented the relaying of his alert to Honolulu by Army radio. He finally had to send his message by Western Union! By the time the Honolulu messenger boy was carrying it to military headquarters on his bicycle, the first bombs fell. Never had a single attack —surprise or not—caused so much initial damage to an enemy. Almost half of the American Pacific Fleet was destroyed or put out of commission.

The Second World War now became a truly global conflict. The United States, Great Britain, the British Commonwealth nations, and the Dutch government-in-exile in London declared war on Japan on December 8. Three days later, in accordance with the Tripartite Pact, Germany and Italy declared war on the United States.

On the same day as Pearl Harbor, Japanese planes destroyed most of the United States Army's planes in the Philippines. Three days later they sank the only two British capital ships in the Pacific off the Malay coast. Within three months, Japanese forces overran Malaya, Burma, the Philippines, and the Dutch East Indies, and they were threatening Australia, New Zealand, India, and all United States outposts in the Pacific. American picture magazines printed lurid drawings of Japanese marines sacking San Francisco.

But Japan never intended to invade the continental United States. Her aims were (1) to conquer Southeast Asia—especially for its oil and rubber; (2) to destroy American and British seapower in the Pacific; (3) to make counterattacks on her Far Eastern empire so expensive that the American and British people would force their governments to make a compromise peace. This extreme example of the "dare" in international relations seems insane in retrospect. It counted on a German victory or a stalemate in Europe; it underestimated the damage that American submarines could do to Japanese shipping and that American aerial bombing could do to Japanese cities; it did not foresee the Allied strategy of bypassing the Japanese strongholds in the South Pacific and concentrating on cutting the sea routes from Southeast Asia to Japan.

Nonetheless, during most of 1942 the Axis powers were still winning on all fronts. It was the "year of agony" for the Allies. In August American marines seized beachheads on Guadalcanal in the Solomon Islands, and the Japanese in northern New Guinea began to give ground under American and Australian counteroffensives. Still, Japan remained in control and was to retain almost all of her Far Eastern empire until 1945. For the United States and Great Britain decided to concentrate their main effort on the European Theater. Only there could they cooperate effectively against the common enemy.

## The Turning of the Tide, 1942–1943

In late 1942 the Allies gained their first victories over Germany and Italy. November saw the greatest tonnage losses in the Battle of the Atlantic, but it was the last month in which losses exceeded new construction. In that same month the British and the Americans also began to drive the Axis powers out of North Africa and the western Mediterranean. Their growing sea power enabled them to assemble and equip widely separated forces for these operations. It also enabled them to send substantial aid to the Soviet Union.* In that country, at the besieged city of Stalingrad (now Volgograd), occurred the third and most important turning point of the war.

### *North Africa*

The events in North Africa involved German, Italian, British, American, and hitherto quiescent French forces. In August 1942, the new commander of the British Eighth Army, General Sir Bernard Montgomery, stopped Rommel's last big drive into Egypt at El Alamein, only fifty-five miles from Alexandria. During the next three months the Allies were able to re-equip the Eighth Army in Egypt via the Cape and the Red Sea and to assemble eight hundred and fifty ships—warships, transports, and landing craft—for a seaborne invasion of Morocco and Algeria. Meanwhile, Italy's Mediterranean Fleet was almost immobilized by lack of oil, and two-fifths of the oil sent to Rommel from the Balkans was lost in transit. In late October, Montgomery finally launched his counteroffensive, which we know as the Battle of Alamein. Outnumbered and short of matériel, Rommel could not prevent the German and Italian armies from being totally routed in 12 days. Churchill later called the battle "the turning of the Hinge of Fate . . . Before Alamein we never had a victory. After Alamein we never had a defeat." On November 7, three days after it was over, the Anglo-American invasion of Morocco and Algeria began.

This invasion led to the complete expulsion of the Axis from North Africa. Since June 1940 Morocco, Algeria, and Tunisia had been under the control of Pétain's government, and the Americans and the British were uncertain about the reaction of the local authorities to their landing. In order to achieve it with as little bloodshed as possible they accepted the collaboration of Admiral Darlan, a former Vichy premier and foe of the British, who was conveniently on the spot. Darlan officially ordered the cessation of French resistance in North Africa within forty-eight hours after the first landings.* At the same time, Montgomery's army was chasing the Germans and Italians across Libya. By the end of January, 1943, it was approaching the southern borders of Tunisia, having covered 1,400 miles since the Battle of Alamein in October. The Germans and Italians made a gigantic delaying action in Tunisia against the Eighth Army and the Anglo-American forces in Algeria, but by May 1943 they were all forced to surrender.

The Allied victory in North Africa provided a base for an attack on southern Europe and the elimination of Italy as an active belligerent in the war. In July, a few days after the Allied invasion of Sicily, King Victor Emmanuel III dismissed and arrested Mussolini after the majority of his own Fascist Grand Council had desert-

*Churchill and Roosevelt's "strange alliance" with the Soviet Union did not seem so strange at the time. Arch-conservative society matrons in London and Washington held fund-raising drives for the relief of the heroic Russian people in their resistance to the Nazis; Hollywood produced a number of films on the theme of Soviet-American friendship. Roosevelt even more than Churchill insisted on preserving the alliance—no matter what the cost—until the complete collapse of the Third Reich.

*The Germans retaliated by occupying the southern third of France itself, thus ending the dwindling degree of independence Pétain had managed to maintain there. Just before their arrival at Toulon, the French naval commanders scuttled their ships, rather than allow them to fall in German hands. Seven weeks later a young French patriot assassinated Darlan in Algiers. During the next six months two anti-Vichy generals, Giraud and De Gaulle, vied for political leadership in liberated French North Africa.

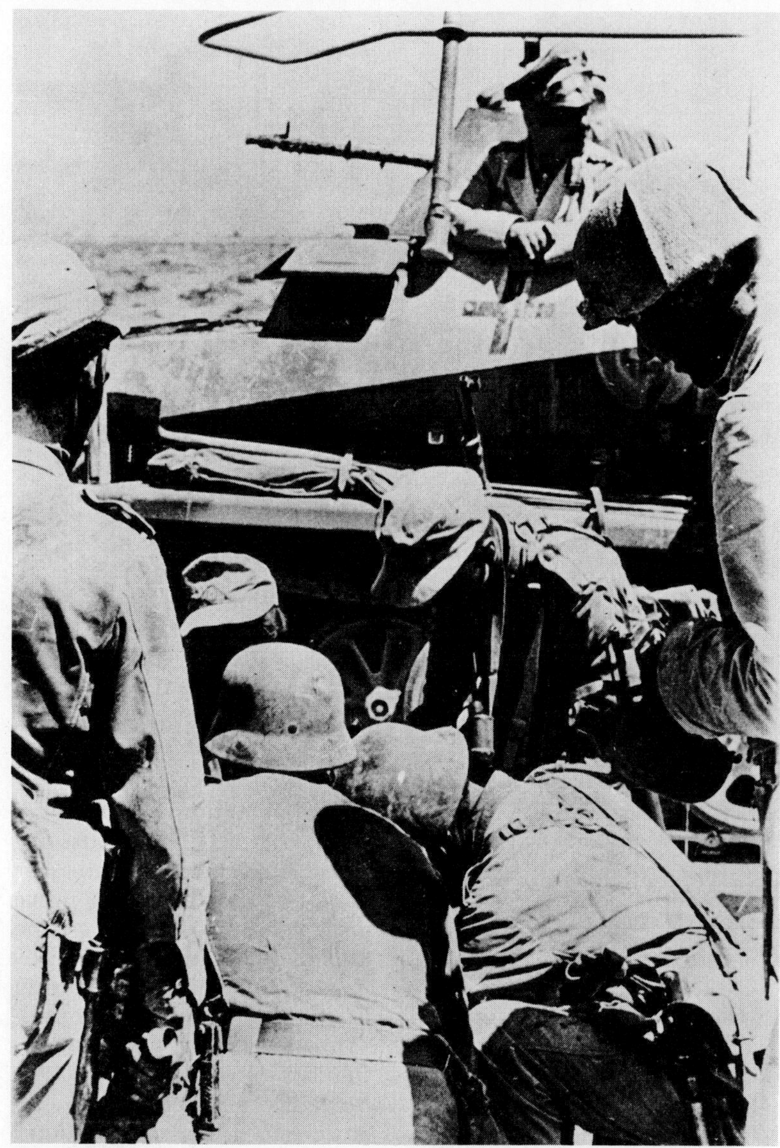

General Rommel during a lull in his North African campaign

ed him. The new government, under Marshal Pietro Badoglio, tried to stall both the Germans and the Allies; not until September 3 did it sign an armistice (made public only on the eighth) with the latter, and it did not use this respite to prepare itself against the inevitable reprisals from the former. As a result, Hitler's armies occupied the northern two-thirds of the country, which became a new battleground between the Allies and the Germans. Mussolini himself was rescued by German glider-borne troops and set up a puppet "Fascist Republic" in the north, thus preparing the way for a bloody civil war with the anti-Fascist resistance movement.

### The Russian Front

Heartening as all these events were to the Allied cause, they were not as crucial to it as those in the Soviet Union. It was there, not in North Africa or Italy, that Hitler irretrievably engaged the bulk of his ar-

*The Battle of Stalingrad*

mies and his own prestige. His goal was to capture Stalingrad, move northward up the Volga, and effect the final envelopment of the Red Army. In this way he would have brought the war in Russia to an end, and the Western Allies alone might never have defeated him.

The Battle of Stalingrad almost defies description. It lasted from early November, 1942, until the end of January, 1943. Two anonymous masses of men fought relentlessly in sub-zero weather in the ruined streets and shattered buildings of the city, with a vast snow-covered steppe on the one side and a frozen river two miles wide on the other. Russian civilians as well as soldiers took part in the fighting. They held out while two Russian armies advanced from the north and the south to encircle the German forces. Once again Hitler overruled his generals and insisted that his 250,000 soldiers at Stalingrad should die rather than retreat. By the new year, hunger, frost, and typhus had reduced the German army to a tattered rabble of broken men. Only 80,000 remained alive when the final surrender came on February 2.

The failure of simultaneous operations in the Caucasus brought Germany's losses to one-fifth of her total strength on the Eastern front since September 1942. By the spring of 1943, further Russian counteroffensives pushed the Germans back to where they had been a year earlier.

Hitler began his last offensive on July 5, 1943, but within two weeks the Russians had irreversibly turned the tide of the war in their favor. By November, they were across the Dnieper and had cut the escape routes from the Crimea. Henceforth they were superior in both numbers of fighting men and armaments to their Axis opponents. Even though Hitler had the resources and manpower of almost all of the rest of Europe at his disposal, he still had to station a large part of his own military forces in the occupied countries: 1,370,000 men in France and the Low Countries, 612,000 in the Balkans, 486,000 in Norway and Denmark, and 412,000 in Italy. He had to do this to prevent an Allied landing and to maintain his own "New Order" in Europe.

## HITLER'S EUROPE

Hitler's New Order shows us what all of continental Europe might be like today, if Germany had won the war. It now seems like a monstrous nightmare. But it was agonizingly real for the over 200 million non-Germans who managed to survive it and for the over 7 million who were slaughtered in the Nazi concentration camps. For almost four years the Germans tried to regiment the entire continent according to Nazi "principles" and to exploit its human and physical resources for the needs of their total war. In every occupied country the New Order also created a moral crisis over the issues of collaboration and resistance – issues that were to have crucial military and political consequences during the Liberation period.

### The New Order

Despite its name, Hitler's New Order was not a unified and consistent plan for the reorganization of Europe according to a clearly defined set of principles. The only "principles" involved were the superiority of the "Master Race" and territorial aggrandizement. Otherwise, the New Order varied from place to place and with the course of the war. At the outset of his conquests, Hitler was mainly interested in victory, not the organization of a New Order. Nevertheless, his long-term aims are well-known, from the Nürnberg trial after the war and from *Mein Kampf* itself.

In *Mein Kampf* Hitler had visualized a Greater Germany including all of Central Europe, surrounded by a certain number of associated and satellite nations. This whole community would be integrated economically. Its industrial production would be concentrated in Greater Germany, and the states to the east and the west would furnish mainly agricultural products and livestock. Hitler viewed territorial conquests in the Soviet Union as the means of permanently safeguarding his European empire. Even more than the struggle against Bolshevism, the mission of his New Order in occupied Russia was to incorporate her territories into his empire and to create in them a "wall of peasants," fortified by German colonists. After the defeat at Stalingrad, Hitler's plans changed. The New Order was less a matter of German overlordship in Europe and the reorganization of the territories in the East, than of defending "Fortress Europe" against Bolshevism and its appetite for conquest. Now the associated and satellite states were to be treated as free partners in the common endeavor.

While Hitler's ideological pronouncements changed in these ways, occupied Europe remained enslaved to its German masters until the Allies drove them out. Each satellite and puppet government passed laws embodying Nazi "principles" of antisemitism, regimentation of labor, suppression of civil rights, and persecution of Marxists, democrats, and other political opponents of the New Order. Everywhere German military personnel demanded and received preferential treatment over the natives. Everywhere the local police and courts had to carry out Nazi orders.

The peoples in the West received less harsh treatment than those in the East. This was due partly to the circumstances under which they were conquered and partly to the status assigned to them in Hitler's racial hierarchy. The Danes, Norwegians, Dutch, and Flemings were considered "almost as good" as Germans and were allowed a certain amount of local autonomy at first. Hitler viewed the French as inferior racially, but he found it more convenient to tolerate the Pétain regime than to try to administer directly the whole occupied zone and the rest of the country, after his troops occupied it in November 1942. Still, as we have seen, he stationed large numbers of troops in all of Western Europe. The Gestapo eliminated political undesirables, Jews, and all who tried to oppose the puppet governments there.

In the German-occupied territories in the East there were no local puppet regimes, and the Nazis treated the Slavic peoples as subhuman beings, fit only for slavery or extermination. They incorporated much of western and northeastern Poland into Greater Germany and partially repopulated these territories with Germans. (The Protectorate of Bohemia-Moravia was also designated for incorporation into the Reich, but it received somewhat better treatment than Poland.) They transformed the southeastern half of Poland into the Government-General of Poland. This colonial dependency was exploited exclusively for the benefit of Germany, and its national intellectual and cultural life was systematically stifled. The Russian territories under German control consisted of two Governments-General: Ostland (Estonia, Latvia, Lithuania, and Belorussia) and the Ukraine. In addition, the Germans and Italians carved up Yugoslavia and Greece into military occupation zones. There was little pretense of a New Order there.

The satellite countries had the status of privileged subordinates in the New Order. Slovakia, Hungary, Croatia, Rumania, Bulgaria, and Finland retained a good deal of local autonomy, and Italy remained independent until the summer of 1943, when she suffered German military occupation and Gestapo terror.

Whereas the Nazi government itself had no over-all plan for the New Order, the SS did. After 1939 this organization, originally Hitler's elite guard, had quickly expanded its size and functions until it became a kind of state within the state. Hitler made it independent of the German government and the Nazi Party itself. It absorbed the secret police into its own "security services"; it built up its own administrative hierarchy; it acquired its own economic resources. By 1943 it also had its own army, the Waffen-SS, of 600,000 shock troops. All members of the SS were carefully trained to be utterly fearless in combat and totally ruthless in dealing with political undesirables and subject peoples. By the end of the war, they had come closer than the military and Party authorities to making the New Order a truly totalitarian regime in the image of their own special world—the world of concentration camps.

Originally the function of the Nazi concentration camps was to imprison the enemies of the Reich. Until the outbreak of the war the inmates were primarily German political undesirables, although the SS authorities mixed them with common criminals in order to break their morale. They devised all sorts of techniques to turn them into groveling animals. The prisoners were also tortured physically and made to do forced labor. Half-starved, subjected to a brutal discipline, and condemned to live and work under conditions of howling filth and misery, many died of exhaustion or from the blows of the guards. The sick and the incapacitated were put to death in gas chambers and crematoriums.

The camps acquired new functions as they became filled with non-Germans from conquered countries. One was the brutalization of the SS troops, who got their "basic training" in inhumanity by torturing the prisoners. A recruit who winced or showed any sign of pity was "washed out" of the service. Another function of the camps during the war was to provide human guinea pigs for "scientific" experiments. SS doctors inoculated healthy male and female prisoners with typhus and malaria germs in order to observe the development of these diseases. They inflicted abscesses and cancerous tissues on others; they killed twin infants in order to perform autopsies on them. Those subjects who did not die when their bodies were cut open were killed by injections of pure phenol directly into the heart.

After 1941 the camps acquired an economic function too. Hundreds of thousands of prisoners were used as slave labor in fifteen large camps (among them Dachau, Buchenwald, and Mauthausen) and 900 secondary ones in underground armament and chemical factories. They worked without rest until they collapsed.

The ultimate function of the camps was the mass extermination of whole peoples. Hitler said:

> "If I can send the flower of the German people into the hell of war without the least pity for the spilling of precious German blood, then I certainly have the right to destroy millions of beings of an inferior race that proliferates like vermin."

Hitler's "final solution" for peoples of "inferior race"—Gypsies, Slavs, and especially Jews—was mass murder. This operation was carried out with a bureaucratic efficiency that was a horrifying version of the rationalization of industry in the prewar years. Special extermination camps were equipped with mammoth crematoriums and gas chambers. As each shipment of victims arrived, it was "processed" and then "disposed of" on an assembly-line basis. The bodies from the gas chambers were rendered into fat for use in

Captured guards from women's concentration camp

soap; the gold from their teeth was collected and melted into bars. At Auschwitz the SS authorities were especially proud of the fact that they could gas 2,000 persons at a time in half an hour and repeat the operation four times a day. By the end of the war over 5,000,000 Jews alone had been slaughtered in this way.

Thus, the SS empire was a super-efficient hell where the unfit and the racial undesirables were systematically annihilated, and where the physically able were brutalized and worked to death in the interest of the Nazi war effort. Above the whole structure of the camps—and even the German army and the Nazi Party—stood the elite of the "Master Race," its leaders responsible only to Hitler himself. Alongside this SS New Order the other forms of German exploitation in Europe seem almost humane. And they were severe enough.

### The Occupied Countries

The expolitation of the physical and human resources of occupied Europe greatly aided the Nazi war economy. In every country that fell into their hands the Germans took the same preliminary measures: representatives of the Office of Economic Warfare immediately seized existing stocks of raw materials, semifinished goods, and manufactured products and tried to put the local economy back into operation. Thereafter they applied different measures according to the nature of the country and its future place in the New Order. In those territories incorporated, or to be incorporated, into the Reich, the industries were directly and completely integrated into the German economy. Some of these, like the Skoda armaments works in the Protectorate of Bohemia-Moravia, were expanded because their location gave them a relative immunity from aerial bombing. On the contrary, in the "colonial" areas of Eastern Europe, industry was limited to production for the armed forces and for a bare minimum of the needs of the local population.

In Eastern Europe the Germans took over many factories, banks, mines, and oil wells directly; in the West they followed a different policy. There they left the operation of the economy in native hands, while supervising it closely. They could exert irresistible pressure in several ways. The German authorities controlled the allocation of raw materials, bank credits, and, eventually, the licensing of imports and exports. They also forced the local manufacturers to give priority to their war orders. In France, for example, they bought 75 per cent of the aluminum and copper, 65 per cent of the leather, 70 per cent of the automobiles, and 45 per cent of the electrical appliances and radios. The Germans also acquired controlling interests in a number of Western European enterprises at prices fixed by themselves.

German control of Europe's food production and distribution had adverse effects almost everywhere outside the Reich itself. Farmers had to plant what the occupation authorities told them to, and all basic foods were rationed everywhere. Only the Danes ate as well as the Germans. Frenchmen were limited to half their usual supply of bread, and the bread itself was dark and had a disagreeable taste. In most of Europe, malnutrition took a smaller toll in life and health than it had during the First World War, but agricultural production declined almost as much in the Second. City dwellers not engaged in war work, old people, and children suffered most, especially if they did not have the means to supplement their meager rations with purchases in the black market.

Germany's financial exploitation provoked the growth of a black market in all the occupied countries. On the one hand, the occupation authorities bought a large percentage of local production. On the other, they accumulated massive means of payment: by seizing existing gold supplies, by issuing paper money that could not be exchanged against German currency, by holding payment for goods in the form of "blocked marks" in Germany, and by resorting to all sorts of confiscations and fines. For example, they made the French pay the costs of the German occupation at an annual rate that equalled France's 1940 war budget. Inflation plagued all the occupied countries as a result of declining supplies of goods and increasing German orders purchased with paper money. The black market was a natural outgrowth of this situation, and the Germans did nothing to curb it. Indeed, their own military and construction agencies, with their unlimited means of payment, outbid the natives for goods available only in the black market.

The Nazis relieved their labor shortage at home by importing several million workers from the occupied countries. They introduced their levies of forced labor in Poland as early as 1939. In the West, they tried to use persuasion at first, promising workers who came to Germany high wages and good working conditions, but the number of volunteers was disappointingly small. By 1942, every able-bodied German male was serving in the armed forces—and the Russians alone still outnumbered them. Since the only manpower available for German industry and agriculture lay in the occupied countries, the Nazis resorted to mass deportations everywhere. The treatment of forced labor in Germany was regulated by the following policy statement of Fritz Sauckel, Pleinpotentiary for Labor Allocation: "All men [and women] will be fed, housed, and treated in a way that will allow them to furnish the highest production at the lowest price."

More than any other form of exploitation, Germany's massive deportations of workers aggravated the issues of collaboration versus resistance in the occupied countries. For this mass procurement of human beings required the active help of many native administrators.

### Collaboration and Resistance

The unprecedented severity of the German occupation forced its victims to take some kind of stand. At one extreme, the puppet and satellite governments had to collaborate with the Germans—that is, to help make their war machine and their oppressive regime function effectively. At the other, organized resistance groups and each country's exiled political and military leaders opposed the Germans in every way possible. The majority of people in the occupied countries did not have to go to either of these extremes, but few could remain entirely aloof from the demands of those who did.

There were many kinds and degrees of active collaborators. First there were those who, because of fascist sympathies or personal ambition, had aided the Axis powers during the conquest of their homelands and who served them until the end. The Norwegian Nazi Vidkun Quisling is the most notorious example of this type, and his name became a symbol for it everywhere. Second, many members of national minorities in Eastern Europe supported the Axis in the hope of becoming independent from their former overlords: Slovaks in Czechoslovakia, certain Croats in Yugoslavia, Magyars and Germans in Rumania. Third, there were those political and military leaders who had remained loyal to their own governments until these had gone down in defeat, and who then tried to conciliate the conqueror in order to protect their own countrymen. Marshal Pétain was the best-known example of this type,* but even he could not avoid giving increasingly active help to the enemy in the struggle against the French resistance forces and in furnishing forced labor to the German war machine. Finally, there were self-styled patriots who remained hostile to the invader but who informed on the resistance forces. They feared the resistance as a threat to the conservative social order, and they also feared that the complete annihilation of the German army would open the way to Communism.

In addition to all these active collaborators, a much larger number of ordinary citizens was forced to aid the enemy in one way or another. Most of them were frightened, bewildered individuals swept into situations beyond their control. There were the Czech munitions manufacturers who produced weapons for the Nazis; there were the Belgian construction workers who helped build Hitler's Atlantic Wall against an Allied invasion from England; there were the French civil servants who administered the Vichy government's antisemitic laws. And there were millions of other people whose occupations required them either to serve the enemy or starve: railroad conductors, printers, clothing workers, bank clerks, entertainers, shopkeepers.

*Meeting for the last time at Vichy on July 10, 1940, the Parliament of the Third Republic had given Pétain a free hand in reshaping the country's institutions. He set up an authoritarian nationalist regime and purged the government and the civil service of its democratically minded personnel. At first the Vichy regime maintained some degree of independence, both from the Germans and from the French fascists in occupied Paris. But its hostility to democracy and pressure from the Nazis combined to make it increasingly collaborationist and fascist after 1942.

The line between passive collaboration and passive resistance is hard to draw, for many people engaged in a little of both: the Greek ship's captain who carried German supplies to North Africa but who arrived behind schedule, the Dutch policeman who arrested Jews in their homes but neglected to look in the attic, the Norwegian singer who entertained German troops in public but listened to radio broadcasts from London in secret.

As hope for an Allied victory grew and as the Germans became more oppressive, more and more people in the occupied countries felt guilty about having served the enemy. Although only a minority joined the active resistance, the majority of collaborators gradually began to practice some form of passive resistance. Some simply refused to speak to the German soldiers in their midst, or else gave them false information. Others sheltered Jews and Allied airmen and prisoners of war trying to escape. Workers producing weapons for the Germans engaged in slowdowns and made defective equipment.

Active resistance meant sabotage and guerrilla warfare. It often involved liaison with exiled political leaders, and it sometimes included the preparation of programs and shadow governments for the Liberation period. Every country in Hitler's Europe had some kind of resistance movement. In Poland, Norway, and Yugoslavia they appeared immediately after the German invasion and had widespread public support. In Rumania, and Hungary a mere handful of patriots began to resist the Germans only at the very end of the war. The French resistance lay somewhere between these two extremes. It swelled as Nazi occupation policy grew more oppressive and disappointment with the Vichy regime spread. In Italy the war itself disillusioned most people, and an Italian resistance movement sprang up almost overnight when the country changed sides in 1943. Even in Germany a small group of army officers and civilian leaders tried to overthrow Hitler. Their most famous act was their attempt to assassinate him on July 20, 1944, with a time-bomb in a brief case.

Like collaboration, resistance had many

varieties as well as certain common features. Large-scale guerrilla activities were confined to wooded and mountainous areas that offered sufficient cover. Some men and women joined the resistance out of patriotism or hatred of fascism, others to avoid the labor draft. Whatever their motives or activities, most members of the resistance led a life apart from the community as a whole. The Polish resistance maintained a regular underground government, with law courts, bond issues, and even a rudimentary education system to preserve the nation's cultural heritage in the face of Nazi efforts to destroy it. In Norway, the Netherlands, and Belgium the clergy openly protested Nazi exploitation, and some of them resigned their posts. The resistance movements in all these countries kept close ties with their governments-in-exile in London; those in occupied Russia received material and moral support from Moscow. In France, Italy, Yugoslavia, and Greece the resistance movements played a significant military role in the liberation of their homelands. Meanwhile, native Communists cut off from Moscow tried to transform the resistance movements in these countries into truly revolutionary forces.

In addition to their struggle against the Nazis and their collaborators, the more important resistance movements became involved in internal conflicts between Communists and non-Communists. The examples of Yugoslavia and France suggest how this conflict developed in two widely different stettings.

### Yugoslavia

Yugoslavia produced two rival resistance movements. In 1941 Colonel Draja Mihailovich led a number of Serbian army officers into the mountains and organized bands of guerrilla fighters called Chetniks. The Yugoslav government-in-exile appointed him minister of war, and the British and Americans were soon sending him considerable material aid. But Mihailovich did not appeal to the Croats and other minority peoples of Yugoslavia in his struggle against the Germans. Indeed, he made no secret of his intention of restoring the reactionary Serbian monarchy on the country's liberation. Mihailovich's behavior prompted the rise of a second resistance movement under the Croatian Communist Josip Broz, better known as Tito.

This most successful of all resistance leaders organized his Partisans over a year after the Chetniks had formed, but he soon outdistanced them. Though his bands of Partisans included many non-Communists, they were carefully indoctrinated by Communist commisars. Tito adopted the Popular Front slogan and preached reconciliation between Serbs and Croats. He also fought the Germans much more resolutely than Mihailovich, who held his forces in reserve for an eventual day of reckoning with the Croats and the Communists.

The Yugoslav government in London continued to support Mihailovich, but Churchill and Roosevelt abandoned him in 1943 and gave their help to Tito instead. In late 1944 Tito's Partisans drove the Germans out of Yugoslavia while the Russians were still advancing into Hungary. His success as a leader of the resistance made him a national hero, and as soon as the war was over, he was able to set up the first Communist regime outside the Soviet Union.

### France

France found a military and nationalist leader who was far more effective than Mihailovich in counteracting Communist influence in her resistance movement. This influence was considerable. Not only did the Communists maintain their own Partisans, they also tried to gain control over the union of all other resistance groups—the National Council of the Resistance—which came into being in late 1943. In France too, the Communists used Popular Front and antifascist slogans to mask their real purpose, and their undeniable bravery and sacrifices won widespread admiration among non-Communists. But, unlike Yugoslavia, France had a fighting force overseas. Composed of defectors from the regular army and navy, this force gained the allegiance of a sizable part of the French Empire and took part in Allied operations in North Africa, the Middle East, and Italy. Its leader was Charles de Gaulle (b.

1890), a brigadier general who had refused to accept Pétain's armistice and who had established a Free French National Committee in London in the summer of 1940.

By early 1942 the majority of the still small resistance forces in France began to recognize De Gaulle as its nominal chief. The British government, which had no relations with Vichy, gave him some support from the start; the Americans maintained an ambassador there until April 1942 and refused to recognize De Gaulle's National Committee until more than a year later. De Gaulle himself was haughty and uncompromising, and his relations with both the Allies and the resistance leaders in France itself were often strained. Nevertheless, his voice became familiar to millions of Frenchmen from his frequent radio broadcasts on the BBC, and the exploits of his Fighting French Forces stimulated their patriotism.

By the end of 1943, after having moved his headquarters from London to Algiers, De Gaulle had eliminated all rivals for the leadership of the French resistance movement both underground and overseas. Still the Allies held back their formal recognition of his Provisional Government in Algiers, and prepared their own military government for liberated France. De Gaulle himself, however, was determined to obtain administrative control of the country. He was aided in this endeavor in April 1944, when the underground military forces in France, which had banded together as the FFI (French Forces of the Interior), accepted him as their supreme commander.

Once the invasion of France began, the French resistance forces as well as the Allied armies turned the liberated areas over to De Gaulle's representatives. Even the Communists did so with no more than a mild protest. Many resistance leaders besides the Communists had hoped that their country's physical liberation would be accompanied by a moral renovation and a more just social order. They had drawn up a program embodying these ideals and spread their message in their widely circulated clandestine newspapers. Unlike Yugoslavia, France was not to have a real revolution; De Gaulle saw to that. But he paid at least some heed to the ideals of the wartime resistance movements, including the Communists, and he helped to reunite his countrymen, almost all of whom had turned against the puppet Vichy regime by 1944.

In Italy and Greece, as well as in France and Yugoslavia, tens of thousands of resistance fighters took part in the military defeat of the Germans. They held dozens of enemy divisions at bay and liberated a number of major cities. (They also captured Mussolini in April 1945, shot him, and hung his corpse upside down in a public square in Milan for the angry crowd to vilify.) But the important role of these resistance movements during the Liberation period should not deceive us into thinking that the victims of totalitarian rule can ever overthrow it by themselves. It took the combined military power of the United States, Great Britain, the Soviet Union and the other Allies to defeat Nazi Germany. The impending Allied victory encouraged the resistance forces to come out into the open and weakened the ability of the Germans to repress them, but Hitler's New Order prevailed until the eve of Liberation almost everywhere. Without the Allied military victory it might still prevail today.

## THE ALLIED VICTORY, 1944–1945

The Western Allies won the Second German War and the Great Pacific War in 1945 and tipped the balance in the Russo-German War. In addition, their contributions of air power, military equipment, and advice seemed to be giving Chiang K'ai-shek the upper hand in the continuing War for East Asia. Most military critics agree that the Western powers deployed their forces correctly in these four wars. There is less agreement about the diplomatic and political decisions of their civilian leaders, and there is still considerable controversy over strategic decisions affecting the outcome of the two wars in Europe.

In early 1944 "Fortress Europe" still stood. The landing at Anzio, south of Rome, on January 22 had been costly and indecisive, and the Allies were to remain bogged down in southern Italy for several months. In the East the Germans were retreating from the Ukraine, but their satellite empire was in no immediate danger. In the West Hitler's "Atlantic Wall" seemed almost impregnable, and until the opening of the Second Front in June the British and American people saw no end to the war.

### Organization and Cooperation for Victory

The United States, Great Britain, and the Soviet Union mobilized all their economic and labor power earlier than Germany, and by 1942 each of them alone surpassed German arms production. Only then did Hitler finally allow his new minister of armaments, Albert Speer, to set up an economic dictatorship. Speer regimented foreign as well as German labor, but German women were never used to the same extent as in the major Allied countries. German arms output more than doubled by May 1943 and was more than three times as great in July 1944 as in February 1942. Yet, even with all the resources of the continent at her disposal, Germany fell further and further behind the Allies in total production.

It must be remembered that the Allies had to produce things that the Germans did not need after 1942. The United States, Great Britain, and Canada built over 40 million tons of merchant shipping. Almost a third were "Liberty" ships, built in the United States from an old-fashioned British design adapted for quick construction by the extensive use of welding. Canada specialized in destroyers and corvettes for escorting convoys. Finally, the Allied needed landing craft. They produced many new types: the smaller ones could bring infantry troops straight to the beaches; even the larger ones could come practically up to the shore, open their big doors, and pour forth tanks, self-propelled guns, and trucks.

As in the First World War, each major belligerent used all sorts of controls and administrations in its mobilization of industry and labor, but the degree of economic cooperation *among* the Allies was unprecedented. Lend-Lease took the place of outright sales and piling up of inter-Allied debts. About three-fourths of American Lend-Lease materials went to Great Britain and the Commonwealth countries. In turn they supplied the American forces on their soil with many items. The total of their reverse Lend-Lease was smaller than the American contribution, but it was about as large a portion of their total production. The Western Allies also sent considerable aid to the Soviet Union, via the North Cape and Persia. This supplement to Russian munitions production was never more than one-tenth of the Russian total, but the 400,000 trucks, 22,000 planes, and 12,000 tanks sent by the Americans and the British enabled the Russian counteroffensive to keep moving past the Soviet frontier. With them the Russians could bypass river crossings, cities, and road and rail junctions—the key points in Eastern Europe's plains, marshes, and forests—which the Germans stubbornly defended.

The Western Allies did not allow the problem of a unified command (which had caused so much resentment in the First World War) to arise in Europe. They all willingly accepted General Dwight D. Eisenhower as the Supreme Commander at Supreme Headquarters, Allied Expeditionary Force (SHAEF). Eisenhower had already directed the Allied landings in North Africa, and although he had had no previous experience in the field, his earlier staff appointments, especially in Washington and Manila, had taught him the political aspects of his service well. He now proved to be the ideal coalition leader—a statesman as well as a soldier. General (later Field Marshal) Montgomery was his deputy commander for the ground assault against Germany. The fiery Montgomery found Eisenhower over-cautious, but Eisenhower was a decisive commander, even though he did not always decide in favor of Montgomery.

Allied miliary cooperation was much more difficult to achieve in the other three wars of the Second World War. In the Russo-German War the Russians carried out their counteroffensives independently. The United States was primarily responsible for the Pacific War, which was commanded by Admiral Chester W. Nimitz and General Douglas MacArthur. In the Far East, however, overlapping mili-

*An American landing in New Guinea*

tary commands led to confusion and mutual recriminations among the Americans, the British, and the Chinese.

The Allied conquests of Germany and Japan posed unprecedented problems in logistics and amphibious campaigns. Massive operations over vast distances required complex organizations using hundreds of thousands of men who were exclusively occupied with preparing these operations down to the last detail months in advance. In the Pacific, the Americans had to send whole Fleet Trains, complete with floating dockyards and warehouses, thousands of miles to the area of operations. They had to bring everything with them to each Japanese-held island they captured. In addition to food, fuel, ammunition, and medical supplies, the Pentagon sent 14,000-ton "logistic packages" for the outfitting of improvised airdromes with 66 officers and 1600 enlisted men. "Operation Overlord"—the code name for the Allied landing in Normandy—involved the most massive preparations of all. General Eisenhower later (in his book, *Crusade in Europe*) enumerated the prerequisites for a successful cross-Channel invasion:

> (1) that our Air Force would be, at the chosen moment, overwhelming in strength; (2) that the German air forces would be virtually swept from the skies and that our air bombers could practically isolate the attack area from rapid reinforcement; (3) that the U-boat could be so effectively countered that our convoys could count on . . . a safe Atlantic crossing; (4) that our supporting naval vessels would . . . batter down local defenses and (5) that specialized landing craft could be available in such numbers as to make possible the pouring ashore of a great army through an initial breach.

Logistics was to remain a problem long after the first landings. Rather than try to capture the well-defended Channel harbors, the Allied towed five floating ports from southern England to the Normandy beaches. Even after they broke out of their beachheads they had to rely on trucks and even air transport to supply their advancing troops, for their bombers had disrupted the French railroads. The Russians, who fought the Germans almost exclusively on land, were also to have their problems of supply once they crossed their own borders.

### Decision in the West

The delay in opening a Second Front irritated both the Russians and some Americans. When the victory in North Africa opened the way to further Mediterranean campaigns, many people thought that Churchill wanted to divert forces from a cross-Channel assault to the "soft underbelly" of Europe in an effort to gain a foothold in the Balkans before the Russians got there. Geographically, however, the "underbelly" of Europe is not "soft." Churchill's undertaking would have been slow and costly, as the Italian campaign showed; the Allies had landed at Salerno, just south of Naples, on September 9, 1943, and they did not reach Rome until June 5, 1944, one day before the invasion of Normandy. More important, a major Anglo-American landing in the Balkans might have prompted the Russians to make a separate peace with the Germans. The Americans felt that the only way the Western Allies could defeat Hitler was to keep the Soviet Union in the war until the end and to launch their own land offensive as close to the heart of Germany as possible: namely, the Channel coast of France.

Not until May of 1944 were all of General Eisenhower's conditions met. Victory in the Battle of the Atlantic helped to meet the third and fourth conditions. The shortage of landing craft—the fifth condition—was the last to be met, but it was more a matter of sheer production, than of strategy. The first and second conditions—those involving air power—presented the most difficult strategical problems.

The strategic use of air power was (and still is) experimental. Beginning in June 1943, the American and British air forces waged a long battle of attrition over Germany with the ultimate purpose of destroying the Luftwaffe. At first the Americans depended on unescorted precision bombings of German factories to disrupt the enemy's aircraft production and to destroy his fighters in the air; but German aircraft production kept increasing, and the unescorted American bombing crews suffered heavy losses. Only by the beginning of 1944 were the Allies able to provide sufficient long-range escort to cut these losses. In the "Big Week" of February 20–25 the RAF, still sticking to its strategy of "area" bombing at night, dropped over 9,000 tons of bombs on five industrial cities, with the loss of only 157 bombers in 2,351 sorties. The USAAF, having modified its faith in unescorted attacks but not in precision attacks by daylight, dropped almost 10,000 tons of bombs on German airdraft plants and lost only 226 planes in 3,800 sorties.

The Air Battle over Germany was won by the end of March 1944. The enemy was forced ro disperse his entire aircraft industry, and his fighter losses had been so heavy that he no longer opposed every attack. In the words of General Carl Spaatz, the United States air commander in Europe:

> When our ground forces stormed the beaches [of Normandy], . . . our fighters were not needed to form a protective umbrella . . . and could be used almost exclusively as fighter-bombers against enemy troops. Our armies were thus assured of freedom of movement by day or night, whereas the German troops were constantly harried. . . . These advantages . . . were gained through the strategic use of air power to destroy the German air force.

On June 6, 1944, with all of General Eisenhower's preconditions thus met, "Operation Overlord" began. Initial surprise was complete, mainly owing to disagreements between Hitler, Rommel, and Rundstedt as to where the attack would come. Despite heavy losses, 130,000 men and 20,000 vehicles were landed in western Normandy on the first day. By July 2 there were 13 American and 11 British divisions, and 1 Canadian division—a million men in all—on French soil. During

*The Liberation of Paris*

most of July the Germans held the British off at Caen and confined the Americans to the Cotentin Peninsula, with its great port at Cherbourg. By the end of the month, however, the Americans broke out and the German rout began. Thereafter, the Allied armored divisions swept relentlessly eastward toward the Seine and the Rhine.

Most of France was liberated in the month of August. On August 15, 3 American and 7 French divisions invaded the Riviera beaches and began their triumphal march up the Rhône Valley. As they advanced northward to meet General Patton's forces southeast of Paris, the French resistance fighters liberated sizable areas of central and southwestern France and prevented many German divisions from escaping the gigantic trap that was closing on them. In Paris itself the Germans were frantically burning their files and loading cases of champagne into their trucks. At the same time they had to fight bitter street battles with the resistance forces, which had risen on August 19. Six days later De Gaulle's prize armored division under General Leclerc de Hauteclocque arrived in the city and settled the issue; De Gaulle himself walked in triumph down the Champs Elysées and took over authority. Within a week after the liberation of Paris the Allied armies coming from the west and the south were converging on France's eastern frontier.

But the war in the West was not yet won. Montgomery and some American generals criticized Eisenhower for not pushing forward immediately. Unlike him, they underestimated the logistical problem involved. The Allies had outrun their supply lines. By late September they had liberated most of Belgium, but the Germans still held Antwerp and the

Dutch ports, thus impeding the arrival of Allied reinforcements by sea. In a heroic gamble to gain a foothold across the Rhine, Montgomery launched an airborne attack at Arnhem, in southern Holland. It failed, and his defeat meant more months of hard fighting. In November and early December the Germans made a major stand in Lorraine, and the campaign there cost the Americans more casualties than Normandy. Meanwhile, since June, Hitler had been bombarding London with new terror weapons. His V-1's were pilotless jet planes with warheads of about a ton of high explosive; his V-2's were single-stage supersonic rockets against which no defense was then possible. In the late 1944 the Germans produced and launched thousands of these V-1's and V-2's. Then, in mid-December, Hitler began his last big counteroffensive in the West. His armies pushed back through the Ardennes and threatened to destroy the Allied position in Belgium. It took the Allies over a month to win this "Battle of the Bulge" and force the Germans back to their original positions.

### The Russian Advance

Although the Red Army pushed the retreating Germans out of Soviet territory within a month after the Normandy invasion, the wars in the East and West remained separate. During July Soviet forces advanced on an 800-mile front: those in the north invaded the Baltic states and reached the border of East Prussia; those in the center were well into Poland; those in the south crossed the Rumanian frontier. In Warsaw, as in Paris, the resistance forces rose against their German oppressors as liberation from the outside seemed imminent. Unfortunately for them, the army of Marshal Rokossovsky failed to maintain its advance, and the Germans began to cut them down in the streets of the city. The Americans and the British pleaded with the Soviet High Command to allow them to use airfields behind the Soviet lines for a shuttle service to drop arms and supplies to the beleaguered Poles. Stalin remained adamant. He argued, with some justification, that the Polish uprising had been premature and irresponsible in view of his own overextended supply lines. The more likely reason for his inaction was his desire to see the non-Communist Polish resistance (whose loyalty was to the Polish government-in-exile in London) eliminated so that his own puppet regime in Lublin could take over the country.

Much as the Western Allies regretted this ghastly episode they had no desire to stop the Russian advance against the common enemy. By September this advance was engulfing Hitler's entire satellite empire in Eastern Europe. Finland escaped a Soviet occupation by signing a separate peace. After the Russians occupied Bucharest the Rumanians opened the way into the Balkans by signing an armistice and reentering the war on the side of the Soviet Union. Bulgaria, which was also occupied, soon followed Rumania's example. The Red Army crossed the borders of Hungary and Slovakia by October, and their regular armed forces went over to the Russians. The Germans managed to hold out in Warsaw until mid-January 1945 and in Budapest until mid-February. But with the bulk of Eastern Europe* under Soviet domination Stalin had achieved the essentials of his purpose. With final victory in Europe in sight, he, Roosevelt, and Churchill could no longer postpone the fateful political decisions that would affect the whole world.

### From Yalta to Potsdam: The Final Collapse of Germany

The Second World War did not alter the nature of international politics. Each of the major Allies wanted to help destroy the common enemy and to further its own interest. The United States and Great Britain had differed on questions of military strategy, but they agreed on the political goal of a free Europe in which each nation would determine its own destiny. The Soviet Union had other plans, at least for Eastern Europe. This conflict of interests over the political future of Europe

*Tito's Partisans liberated Yugoslavia by themselves. The British landed in Greece, the only East European country to escape Soviet influence.

WORLD WAR II
EUROPE AND NORTH AFRICA: THE ALLIED VICTORY
ICELAND
Atlantic Ocean
NORWAY
SWEDEN
FINLAND
Archangel
USSR
Leningrad
ESTONIA
LATVIA
Jan. 1945
LITHUANIA
Moscow
UNITED KINGDOM
IRELAND
DENMARK
NETHERLANDS
London
BELGIUM
Berlin
Danzig
June 1944
D-Day June 6, 1944
V-E Day May 8, 1945
POLAND
Stalingrad
(Nov. 1942 - Jan. 1943)
German U-Boat operations
Paris
GERMANY
FRANCE
HUNGARY
RUMANIA
SWITZ.
Vichy
Free French and U.S.
ITALY
YUGOSLAVIA
Yalta
Black Sea
SPAIN
(Aug. 1944)
Aug. 1944
BULGARIA
ALBANIA
Rome
GREECE
TURKEY
Nov. 8, 1942
Algiers
Invasion of Italy Sept. 3, 1943
Tunis
Sicily
MOROCCO
Oran
ALGERIA
Conquest of Tunisia May 1943
Malta
Crete
SYRIA
(Vichy France to July 1941)
IRAQ (Br.)
TUNISIA
Mediterranean Sea
Axis powers in 1939
Joined Axis in 1941
Limit of Axis occupation, 1942
Vichy France
Neutral nations
PALESTINE (Br.)
TRANS-JORDAN (Br.)
LIBYA
El Alamein (Oct. 1942)
Cairo
EGYPT
EUROPE
0
200
400 mi.
Map by J. Donovan
Suez Canal
Teheran
ALGERIA
LIBYA
EGYPT
Free French
FRENCH WEST AFRICA
FR. SOMALILAND
BR. SOMALILAND
ETHIOPIA
FRENCH EQUATORIAL AFRICA
ITALIAN EAST AFRICA
Atlantic Ocean
KENYA

came out into the open in 1945 at Yalta (February 4–11) and at Potsdam (July 17–August 2).

Roosevelt, Churchill, and Stalin kept up an appearance of unity and cordiality when they met at Yalta, a Russian resort on the Black Sea. They agreed on general principles and postponed discussion of the controversial details. Their first item of agreement was the transformation of the wartime alliance against the Axis into a permanent world organization, the United Nations.* The second item was a Declaration on Liberated Europe, in which the "Big Three" promised to help the conquered and satellite states to solve their pressing political and economic problems by democratic means. The "Big Three" also agreed to divide Germany—which was still fighting—into four military occupation zones (one for each of them and one for France), to disarm and demilitarize her, to make her pay reparations, and to try her major war criminals.

The most troublesome issue at Yalta was Poland. As the Red Army liberated that country, the Soviet-sponsored Lublin government set itself up there. Roosevelt and Churchill persuaded Stalin to allow Polish leaders in London to join it and to make it hold free elections. They, in turn, agreed that Russia's western frontier should include those parts of prewar Poland inhabited by Belorussians and Ukrainians.

In view of Soviet imperialism in Eastern Europe since Yalta, President Roosevelt has often been blamed for making too many concessions to Stalin at that conference. His kinder critics attribute his "mistakes" to his failing health (he died two months after the Yalta Meeting); others say that he allowed himself to be hoodwinked. But Roosevelt did not decide all these matters himself. He listened to his military advisers, who told him that it was essential to preserve the anti-Axis alliance until Germany's final defeat and to get the Soviet Union into the war against Japan. At Yalta, Roosevelt did gain a commitment from Stalin to declare war on Japan three months after the end of hostilities in Europe. This commitment seemed like a major Russian concession at the time. Yet, it is also true that, unlike Churchill and Stalin, Roosevelt and his military advisers never fully grasped the relationship between war and politics.

After Yalta both the Western Allies and the Russians moved into the heart of Central Europe. The Red Army took over Warsaw and Budapest and advanced into East Prussia and Silesia. In early March the Americans crossed the Rhine on a bridge that had for some strange reason not been destroyed; soon thereafter British paratroopers also established a foothold on the opposite side of the river. By the end of the month the two forces had occupied the whole west bank and were rapidly expanding their bridgeheads on the east bank. Rumors of a last-ditch stand by the Nazis in the mountains of southern Bavaria prompted Eisenhower to divert some of his troops in that direction. These rumors—plus his overextended supply lines and his wish to cooperate with the Russians—made him stop at the Elbe. Meanwhile, Vienna fell on April 13, and at that very moment Marshal Zhukov was bombarding the eastern suburbs of Berlin.

The end of Hitler and the Third Reich now came quickly. On July 20, 1944, a small group of anti-Nazis from all walks of life had already made an attempt to get rid of Hitler. This group, which even included a few generals, had planted a brief case containing a time-bomb in a temporary shelter where the *Führer* was holding a staff conference. Surprisingly he suffered what seemed to be only minor injuries, even though several others standing near him were killed. The failure of the bomb plot meant that the Germans would be unable to escape from total defeat, as the Italians had a year earlier with the overthrow of Mussolini. By April 1945 there was no hope left: Allied bombers were destroying German cities at will; on the Western Front German soldiers were being taken prisoner at the rate of 50,000 a day; on April 25 the Russians and the Western Allies met at the Elbe, thus cutting the country in two.

With Zhukov's troops fighting in the

*The fifty "original" United Nations were those that had declared war on Germany and then attended the United Nations Conference at San Francisco in April, 1945.

*Berlin, May 1, 1945*

streets of Berlin, Hitler moved his government into an air-raid bunker in the Chancellery garden. In that "subterranean madhouse" he still gave the orders, but some of his oldest and most trusted lieutenants were either turning away from him or competing for the positions of those who had just deserted. The *Führer* appointed Admiral Doenitz as the new military commander in the northern half of Germany and sent him off to field headquarters. Then he married Eva Braun, his faithful mistress, in a macabre ceremony, wrote his will, and expelled Hermann Goering and Heinrich Himmler from the Nazi Party because of their alleged efforts to end the war behind his back. Finally, on April 30, Hitler and Eva Braun committed suicide, and—in accordance with his will—their bodies were destroyed by flames. It was a fitting end for the man who had destroyed so much of Europe and then brought even worse destruction on his own country.

The Third Reich died seven days after its *Führer*. Doenitz offered to capitulate in the West but he wanted to continue fighting in the East. The Western Allies rejected this offer and demanded unconditional surrender on all fronts. Hostilities in Italy ceased on May 2, and beginning on May 4, units in Germany surrendered to the Allied commanders on the spot. On May 7 the general instrument of surrender was signed at Eisenhower's headquarters at Reims; May 8 was proclaimed V-E Day, the day of victory in Europe. Zhukov then ratified the Reims surrender in Berlin, and in the next few days isolated German units in Norway, Bohemia, and the Aegean laid down their arms.

Two months after the wars in Western and Eastern Europe had been won, the Allied leaders met at Potsdam to deal with the former aggressor. President Harry S Truman now represented the United States; Clement Attlee, the head of a new Labour government, replaced Churchill in the middle of the conference; Stalin still represented the Soviet Union.

Germany was the main order of business at Potsdam. The "Big Three" spelled out the Yalta principles of disarmament, demilitarization, reparations, the elimination of Germany's industrial war potential, and the punishment of war criminals. They also agreed to "denazify" the country and to establish democratic procedures in its courts and civil life. All political authority was to be in the hands of the military governments of the four occupying powers. As for Germany's frontiers, they were to be reduced to their pre-1938 status. (Austria was detached and also occupied by the United States, Great Britain, the Soviet Union, and France.) This provision was purely formal, however, for Poland was allowed to occupy German territory up to the Oder and Neisse Rivers, in "compensation" for Polish territories ceded to Russia in the East—which were actually much further west than the line agreed on at Yalta. Poland soon annexed the area east of the Oder-Neisse line and forced the German inhabitants to leave. Thus, Prussia and Silesia ceased to be German. This was the most crushing punishment of all.

### The Atomic Revolution and the Defeat of Japan

A day before the beginning of the Potsdam Conference, the first nuclear explosion was achieved at Alamogordo, in the New Mexico desert. Four days after the Conference ended, the first atomic bomb was dropped on Hiroshima. The world immediately recognized its revolutionary consequences. Although the United States carried the technological and financial burden, the perfection of the atomic bomb was a European achievement as well. Scientists in Italy, France, Germany, and Great Britain had begun experimenting with isotopes of uranium in the late 1930s. Albert Einstein had already come to the United States, and Enrico Fermi, another refugee from fascism, came in 1938. From 1941 on, the British, Canadian, and American governments agreed that all research on nuclear fission should be conducted in the United States. This research, under the code name Manhattan Project, was distributed among plants and laboratories in different parts of the country. On December 2, 1942, the first atomic chain reaction was achieved under the grandstand of the University of Chicago stadium. Thereafter, European and American scientific workers quickly found the way to incorporate this new source of energy into a devastatingly explosive force.

By the time the first bomb fell on Hiroshima, Japan was already suffering crippling losses. She had suffered her "Trafalgar" at Leyte Gulf in the Philippines in late October 1944. By the beginning of 1945, MacArthur was gaining control of the Philippines and cutting Japan's lifeline to the resources of Southeast Asia. In early March, American planes began their intensive fire bombings of Tokyo. A month later American marines landed on Okinawa, only 350 miles from Japan. Henceforth, the Japanese industrial economy deteriorated rapidly as a result of declining imports and intensive air attacks. The German surrender compounded Japan's troubles.

In the end, the Japanese *army* was to become little more than a spectator in a war for which its leaders had been primarily responsible. As MacArthur was to explain later on:

"At least 3,000,000 of as fine ground troops I have ever known . . . laid down their arms because they didn't have the materials to fight with . . . and the potential to gather them . . . where we would attack. . . . When we disrupted their entire economic system, . . . they surrendered."

The war against Japan could have been won without the atomic bomb. Nevertheless it was this bomb that made the Japanese surrender come as quickly as it did. In late July 1945 the extreme militarists in Tokyo wanted to go on fighting indefinitely, even though the Americans and the British were beginning to transfer large numbers of troops from Europe to the Far East. Russia declared war on Japan two days after Hiroshima and occupied Manchuria and North Korea, but the official American history of the war against Japan does not think that even this action was as significant in forcing the Japanese surrender as the bomb. The bombing of Hiroshima killed 78,000 persons immediately and injured almost as many; a second bomb caused comparable losses in Nagasaki four days later. Such destructive power so terrorized the Japanese that Emperor Hirohito was able to override the objectors and sue for peace. The instrument of unconditional surrender was signed in Tokyo Bay aboard the battleship *Missouri* on September 2, 1945.

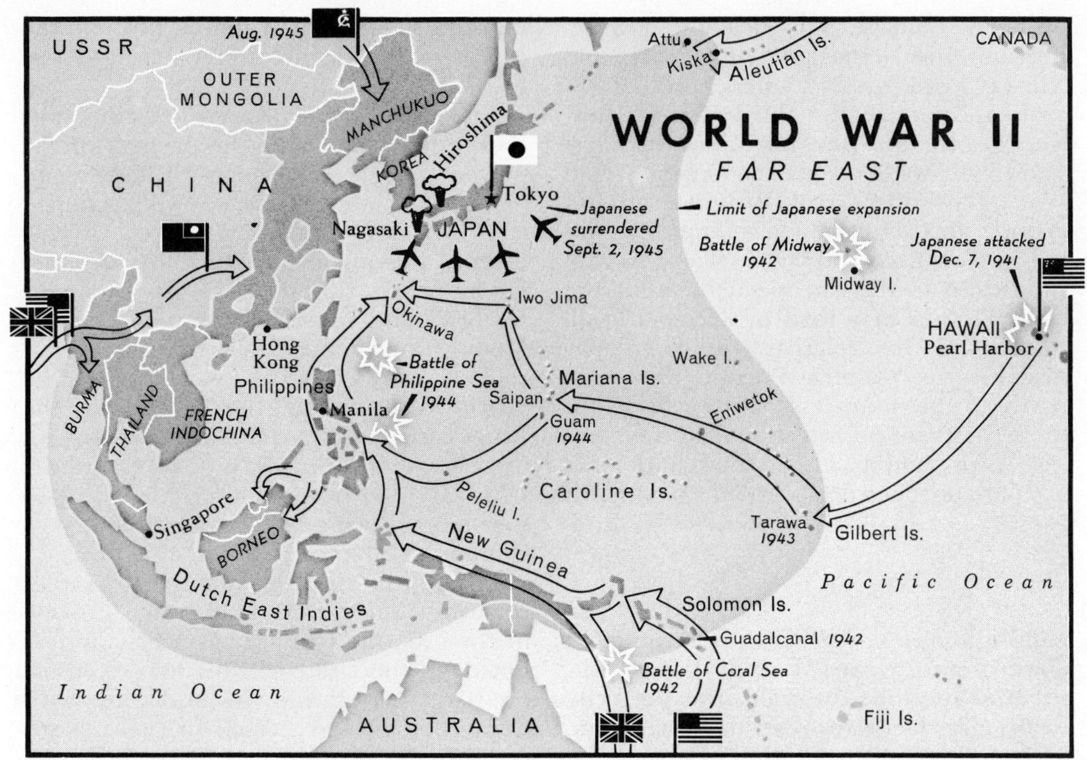


## The Balance Sheet

Despite the effect of the bombing of Hiroshima in hastening Japan's surrender, the Second World War, like the First, was won with essentially the same weapons with which it had begun. Air power was crucial in strategic bombing, in tactical support of ground forces, and in landing combat troops behind enemy lines. Amphibious and naval operations were carried out on an unprecedented scale. At the end of the war armored tanks continued to function effectively—though no longer independently—in mechanized infantry and artillery units. Jet planes, guided missiles, and atomic bombs showed how future wars would be fought. So did the guerrilla tactics developed by the resistance forces—especially the Communists—in Europe and the Far East. Yet these innovations did not change the basic character of the Second World War, any more than the tank and the airplane had changed that of the First. The Allies won the Second World War for the same reasons they had won the First: superior industrial production and manpower and control of the seas.

More Europeans died during the Second World War than in any war in history. In the Russo-German War alone military casualties were as large as those of the First World War; civilian casualties were larger. The Soviet Union lost approximately 20 million military and civilian dead, a tenth of her population. Germany lost about 3,500,000 military dead on all fronts and about 525,000 civilians, not including 280,000 Jews. In addition, almost 3 million German-speaking inhabitants of Hitler's defunct East European empire died in the forced migrations that followed the Russian advance. The other peoples living in areas of combat had also suffered terribly since 1939. Poland, Czechoslovakia, Rumania, Hungary, Yugoslavia, Greece, and Bulgaria lost 1,070,000 military dead and 7,700,000 civilians; half of these were Jews. Western Europe's human losses were much smaller than during the First World War, though property damage was heavier. France, Belgium, the Netherlands, Denmark, and Norway lost 284,000 soldiers and 610,000 civilians, more than a third of them Jewish. (France the Belgium alone had lost 1,371,000 soldiers in the First World War.) Italy and Great Britain each lost about a third of a million military personnel and less than 100,000 civilians. American deaths in the European theater were 260,000—out of a total of 389,000 in all theaters. These relatively light military casualties in Western Europe were due partly to the shortness of the campaigns there, partly to improvements in the medical corps, and partly to new antibiotics—sulfa and penicillin—which saved many lives.

: : :

Hindsight has partially obscured the main point of the Second World War in Europe. At the time the point was perfectly clear: Nazi Germany was destroying the independent states in the East *and* the West, subjecting their people to a sickening reign of terror, and fighting the Allies to the bitter end. Although Hitler had expressed his partiality toward the Americans and the British as against the Russians, he had shown none. He began sending his V-1 and V-2 "retaliation" bombs against England in June 1944, and he unleashed the Ardennes Offensive against the Americans in December. The people in almost all the occupied countries welcomed their liberators from whatever direction they came, and the Allies had no alternative except the complete defeat of Nazi Germany.

The Second World War began as a struggle between the liberal states of the West and the nationalist states of Central Europe. Between 1941 and 1945 the Communist East joined the West, and together they eliminated the nationalism of Central Europe. After the cessation of hostilities all the states on the continent were completely dependent on the American and Soviet giants for their very survival. In Europe nationalism of the fascist variety was completely eliminated, and the liberal West and Communist East stood face to face on a line running through the center of the main country that had fostered it.

The ideological aspects of the war should not blind us to the primacy of the power struggle. Hitler may not have *wanted* a general war, but he was willing to risk it in his drive for control over all of East Central Europe and western Russia. Once he launched this drive, Mussolini made his brief and inept bid for power in the Mediterranean, and Stalin began his long-range push westward. As in the First World War, neither the British nor the Americans had any territorial designs on the continent, but they now set out to destroy German power forever. In doing so they helped bring Soviet power, as well as Communism, into the heart of Europe.

Despite the drafting of high principles regarding the future of liberated Europe in the Atlantic Charter, at Yalta, and at Potsdam, the United States never considered associating the Soviet Union with Great Britain and herself in the military government of Italy or with herself alone in Japan. Churchill wanted to bargain with Stalin for Western and Soviet spheres of influence in the Balkans, but, aside from Greece, the United States and Great Britain had little hope of participating in the military government of the liberated countries of Eastern Europe. The Soviet Union believed—and was encouraged to believe—that the Western Allies would tolerate an orbit of states friendly to her on her western borders, but she did not maintain even minimum respect for democratic processes in the states she liberated.

Furthermore, Stalin was to resume his policy of "revolutionary adventurism" in 1946 and to try to take advantage of the economic and social disintegration in Western Europe to extend Russian influence there through the local Communist Parties. Some observers say that only the American monopoly over atomic weapons prevented him from marching to the Atlantic in the late 1940s. At any rate, the beginning of the "Cold War" was to halt progress toward a general European peace settlement. The 1945 status quo was to be altered somewhat by peace treaties with Italy and the smaller countries of

Eastern Europe and by the defection of Yugoslavia from the Soviet bloc, but the problems of Berlin and a divided Germany were left unresolved.

## SUGGESTED READINGS

The literature on the Second World War is overwhelming. In addition to the multivolume official histories of the major powers, there are hundreds of memoirs, specialized military and diplomatic studies, and superfical surveys.

Wright, Gordon, *The Ordeal of Total War, 1939–1945.* New York: Harper and Row, 1968, Torchbook.*

This last volume in the "Langer series" is also the best analysis of all aspects of the war to date.

Collier, Basil, *The Second World War.* New York: Morrow, 1967.

A good, up.to-date survey.

Young, Peter, *A Short History of World War II, 1939–45.* New York: Crowell-Apollo, 1968.*

A readable brief military history; it describes operations on all fronts, paying appropriate attention to technological developments.

Taylor, Telford, *The March of Conquest.* New York: Simon and Schuster, 1958.

A good account of Hitler's Blitzkrieg tactics—argues that the gains thus achieved were offset by shortcomings of strategy.

Churchill, Winston S., *The Second World War.* 6 vols. New York: Bantam Books, 1962.*

Already a classic, these colorful memoirs give a grandiose picture of the war as Churchill saw it and participated in it.

Toynbee, Arnold J. and Veronica Toynbee, eds., *Hitler's Europe*, Vol. IV of *Survey of International Affairs, 1939–1946.* New York: Oxford Univ. Press, 1954.

The best reference for occupied Europe—especially good on Vichy France.

Milward, Alan S., *The German Economy at War.* New York: Oxford Univ. Press, 1964.

A scholarly study that shows the lack of full-scale economic mobilization before 1943.

Hilberg, Raul, *The Destruction of the European Jews.* Chicago: Quadrangle Books, 1964.*

The most authoritative study to date.

Kogon, Eugen, *The Theory and Practice of Hell: The German Concentration Camps and the System behind Them.* New York: Berkley Publishing Corp., n.d.*

A clinical analysis of a phenomenon whose horrors almost defy description.

Maclean, Fitzroy, *Disputed Barricade: The Life and Times of Josip Broz-Tito, Marshal of Jugoslavia.* London: Cape, 1957.

The author, Churchill's personal representative to Tito, writes with a combination of understanding and detachment of the Yugoslav resistance and its political problems.

Deakin, Frederick W., *The Brutal Friendship: Mussolini, Hitler and the Fall of Italian Fascism.* New York: Doubleday-Anchor, 1964.*

Very detailed; particularly useful on Mussolini's Italian Social Republic.

Delzell, Charles F., *Mussolini's Enemies: The Anti-Fascist Resistance.* Princeton, N. J.: Princeton Univ. Press, 1961.

A brilliant work; most of it deals with the Italian resistance movement toward the end of the war.

Gaulle, Charles de, *Complete War Memoirs of Charles de Gaulle.* New York: Simon and Schuster, 1964.

Rivals Churchill's work in style, though far less comprehensive. Unfortunately, there is no book in English on the French resistance movement.

Eisenhower, Dwight D., *Crusade in Europe.* Garden City, N. Y.: Doubleday and Co., n.d. Dolphin.*

Still the best general account of the Allied victory.

Werth, Alexander, *Russia at War, 1941–1945.* New York: Avon, 1966.*

A lively, first-hand account by a noted British journalist.

Ryan, Cornelius, *The Longest Day.* Greenwich, Conn.: Fawcett World Library, 1960. Crest.*

An exciting description of the Normandy invasion.

Trevor-Roper, Hugh R., *The Last Days of Hitler.* New York: Berkley Publishing Corp., n.d.*

A colorful account of the end of Hitler in the Berlin bunker.

There are numerous studies of the diplomacy of the war. For a good bibliography and a general survey see:

Snell, John L., *Illusion and Necessity: The Diplomacy of Global War 1939–1945.* Boston: Houghton Miflin; 1963.*

Chapter XXI

# EUROPE AND THE WORLD SINCE THE SECOND WORLD WAR

In 1945 much of Europe was in ruins. Industry, commerce, transportation, and agriculture were thoroughly disrupted. The great capitals of East Central Europe—Berlin, Vienna, Warsaw, Budapest—had been pounded to rubble by every form of modern combat. In the West, Coventry, Rotterdam, and Le Havre had been gutted by aerial bombing. Whole sections of Germany and Russia had been laid waste. Most distressing of all, millions of displaced persons were living in improvised camps, with no hope of finding a permanent home anywhere.

Yet in hardly more than a decade Europe achieved a greater degree of prosperity and stability than it had ever known. In the West, unprecedented economic aid and military protection from the United States were crucial, but even more remarkable was the determination of the Europeans to build a better life for themselves. In the East, they did this entirely with their own resources, though, of course, under the heavy-handed control of their Communist governments. Not all the peoples of Eastern Europe accepted their new Communist masters without protest, as the 1956 revolts in Poland, Hungary, and East Germany showed. Democracy was far more widely accepted in the West than Communism in the East, though for a few years it was threatened in France by disgruntled army officers.

The temporary threat to French democracy was a by-product of the process of decolonization. This process was second only to the overwhelming power of the United States and the Soviet Union in depriving Great Britain and France of their former influence in the world. It was most painful in Algeria, but it created serious troubles for both the "depossessors" and the "depossessed" in many parts of Africa and Asia.

In addition to having rid themselves of almost all their former colonial masters, the non-Europeans have outstripped the Europeans in numbers. In 1970 the proportion of Europeans (including the Soviet Union) in the total world population was 19 per cent, compared to 24 per cent in 1950 and 26.5 per cent—the peak figure—in 1930. This relative decline is all the more dramatic in view of the fact that the population explosion has hit Europeans and peoples of European extraction too. France, whose population was static in 1930, has had an annual growth rate of 1.2 per cent since the Second

World War. In the 1960s the rate for Europe without the USSR was 0.9 per cent; for the United States and Canada, 1.6 per cent; for the Soviet Union, 1.7 per cent. But in Asia the rate was 2.3 per cent; in Africa, 2.4 per cent; in Latin America, 2.8 per cent. Thus, Europe's position in world population as well as world power has changed at a faster pace in the last generation than at any time in history.

## THE LIBERATIONS AND THEIR AFTERMATH, 1945–1948

The liberation of Europe heralded sweeping changes of all kinds. Hitler and his henchmen had overthrown the national institutions of over a dozen countries and had imposed the hated New Order. In both Eastern and Western Europe the governments of the Liberation period immediately tried to purge the remaining fascists and collaborators. These governments also faced popular pressure for industrialization and land reform in the East and for the welfare state and the nationalization of Big Business in the West, but these spontaneous demands for economic and social changes were soon to give way to other, more powerful, forces. In the East a major revolution was to be imposed by local Communist parties, sometimes backed by the Red Army. In the West, native conservative leaders, sometimes bolstered by the presence of American and British armed forces, were to help bring a substantial return to the prewar of prefascist situation.

### Western Europe

Until 1948 Western Europe lived in a state of chronic emergency. First the resistance movements and then the Communists alone tried to bring about a real revolution. Those who wanted to return to the old ways, though more numerous, remained for the most part inarticulate and absorbed in their private concerns. Actually, the main problem—both public and private—was economic. Communications, essential services, and foreign trade had to be restored; factories and houses had to be rebuilt; the cost of living had to be regulated in the face of a dearth of consumers' goods. In Great Britain, Norway, and Belgium strong government action prevented inflation and the growth of a black market; in France, Italy, and Germany, these evils completely escaped control. Not until the American government launched the Marshall Plan did Western Europe at last emerge from its postwar economic crises, and it was in the context of these crises that the struggle for political and social change took place.

#### *Postwar Political Changes and the Failure of the Resistance Ideology*

Although the Second World War, like the First, had been a war of peoples, this fact had a greater effect on domestic politics in 1945 and 1946 than in 1919. In the first postwar elections the voters in the major countries seemed to favor the parties that promised the most sweeping changes. Even the British voted Churchill and the Conservative Party out of power in mid-July, 1945. During the war they had expressed their solidarity in the first experiment in economic equality ever made by a major Western nation, and now a majority of them viewed the Labour Party as better suited than the Conservatives to continue a policy of "fair shares for all." The French and Italian people also voted overwhelmingly for the parties that promised "social justice"—in France in October 1945, in Italy in June 1946.

Ironically, those countries that changed their political systems least achieved the greatest measure of social justice. At one extreme, Great Britain experienced no break in the continuity of its government. The newly elected Labour Party simply put into effect the program it had been advocating since the turn of the century: nationalization of basic industries and utilities, social security, and a steeply graduated income tax. The smaller countries of Northwestern Europe also moved in the direction of the welfare state without changing their constitutions: in Norway, the Netherlands, and Belgium the legitimate governments-in-exile simply returned from London; in Denmark the government had managed to survive the German occupation unsullied. At the other extreme were Germany and Austria, where the Nazi regime was complete-

*Nürnberg Trial of Nazi War Criminals*

ly replaced by an Allied military government. As we shall see later, West Germany was to acquire a democratic constitution in 1949 and to stick more closely to a policy of laissez faire than any country in Europe. The situation in France and Italy was the most complex. There new governments had joined the Allied war effort before the Liberation, and local resistance forces had played an active military role.

Before examining the relationship between political change and social and economic reform we must note the failure of both the Western Allies and the resistance movements to fulfill a great moral task they had set for themselves during the war. This task was to punish all fascists, collaborators, and war criminals. In France, Italy, the Low Countries, and Scandinavia, the new, resistance-inspired governments tried to establish degrees of guilt and mete out just punishments, but the results of their efforts were disappointing to almost everyone. Preoccupied with getting food and keeping warm, most people soon lost interest in the moral issue of collaboration. Besides, they viewed the "purge" increasingly as a mere exercise in revenge by the victors against the vanquished. The German public was especially apathetic toward efforts of the Allied military authorities to "denazify" the country. Even more than in France and Italy, the purge in Germany bogged down in a backlog of untried cases, for almost all Germans had been associated with the Nazi Party in one way or another. Millions of them filled out elaborate questionnaires and then joined a conspiracy of silence. They, too, viewed the punishment of their defeated wartime leaders as only an act of revenge by the victors.*

During the Liberation period the main spokesmen of the French and Italian resistance movements wanted to create a new society. They were mostly Communists, Socialists, and Catholics of advanced social views who called themselves Christian Democrats. Although their ideology resembled that of the prewar Popular Front in its emphasis on political democracy and social justice, it went much further. It sought to bridge the gap between Catholics and anti-clericals by creating a new and nonsectarian socialism; it hoped to reconcile conflicting social classes; it wanted to provide new leaders who were

*The Nürnberg trial lasted from November 1945 to September 1946. Great Britain, the United States, France, and the Soviet Union provided the judges and prosecutors of the top twenty-two Nazi leaders who were still alive. The case against them was meticulously prepared, and they all described their respective roles in waging aggressive war and their "crimes against humanity" in minute and gruesome detail. Three were acquitted, seven imprisoned, and twelve sentenced to be hanged. Only ten of these twelve were in fact hanged; Goering took poison in his cell; Bormann, who had been sentenced *in absentia*, is presumably still at large.

more concerned with the public welfare than the traditional parliamentary politicians.

Several factors frustrated the realization of this resistance ideology. First the resistance movements lost their illusory unity once the common enemy was gone. The Communists and Socialists split with the Christian Democrats on economic policy—the issue being state action versus free enterprise; the Socialists and the Christian Democrats championed personal liberty against the authoritarian Communists. Second, the resistance leaders lost control of these three parties to the more seasoned politicians and were unable to form a party of their own. As we have seen, these three parties gained three-fourths of the votes in the first postwar elections in France and Italy, and they were to work together in tripartite coalitions in both countries until May 1947. From the beginning their main concerns were framing new republican constitutions and staying in office.

A third factor working against the resistance ideology in Italy and France was the overriding power of two strong conservative leaders. From the time of Liberation until the end of 1945 Charles de Gaulle ruled France as a benevolent dictator, while Italy foundered under a weak coalition government. Then the situation in the two countries was reversed. In Italy, Alcide de Gasperi, the head of the Christian Democratic Party, became prime minister in November 1945; in France, De Gaulle retired from office in January 1946. But both men managed to block the more extreme reforms advocated by the resistance ideology.

Under De Gasperi and even after De Gaulle, Italy and France became gradually more conservative. Both countries extended the franchise to women and nationalized the utilities and a few banks and key industries. Although France also expanded her social security program and initiated a long-range plan for economic development—eventually named after its organizer, Jean Monnet—these modest economic and social reforms fell considerably short of the resistance ideology. In 1946 the tripartite governments in France and Italy framed new democratic constitutions that were also more conservative than the resistance movements had wanted. Actually, the constitution of the Fourth French Republic soon began to operate very much like that of the Third, while the constitution of the Italian Republic resembled the prefascist constitution, except for the abolition of the monarchy.

### *The Beginning of the Cold War and the Marshall Plan*

The trend toward conservatism in France and Italy was reinforced by the growing rift between the Soviet Union and the Western Allies. This rift had already become apparent in the spring of 1946 at the Paris meeting of the foreign ministers of the United States, Great Britain, the Soviet Union, and France. It hampered the drafting of peace treaties with the Axis satellites and postponed indefinitely the peace settlement with Germany. The Soviet Union accused the Western powers of trying to form an "Anglo-Saxon bloc" to "contain" her; the Americans and the British in turn accused her of threatening the independence of Greece and Turkey. In March 1946 former Prime Minister Churchill coined the phrase "Iron Curtain" to describe the division between "Free Europe" and Russian-controlled Europe.

A year later the "Cold War" was "on," and Stalin began to use the Communist parties in France and Italy as his agents in waging it. Under these circumstances, the heads of the tripartite governments dropped their Communist ministers (in May 1947), with strong encouragement and promises of economic aid from the United States. The dismissal of the Communist ministers settled the two issues that had split the French and Italian governments since the Liberation by insuring the triumph of free enterprise and traditional Western freedoms. Thwarted in their efforts to bring about their revolution legally in France and Italy, the Communists launched political strikes and tried to obstruct their countries' economic recovery under the Marshall Plan.

At first, General Marshall, the man for whom this plan was named, wanted to help *all* European countries toward economic recovery. His goal was to extend substantial dollar credits to them for two main purposes: to purchase equipment and raw materials abroad, especially in the United States, where their dollar credits were exhausted; and to increase their own industrial and agricultural production. By the spring of 1948 all the countries of East Central Europe had Communist regimes, and Stalin forbade them to accept such credits. Thus, only sixteen nations joined the Marshall Plan. According to its terms, they had to decide their needs among themselves, submit their report to the American government, and then create an Organization for European Economic Cooperation to channel the forthcoming funds among themselves. For the Marshall Plan, or European Recovery Program, was designed not only to aid recovery in individual countries, but to stimulate permanent economic cooperation among these countries.

Through launched after the beginning of the "Cold War" the Marshall Plan was not just another "Cold War" measure. It was a generous and far-sighted policy for creating an economically and politically stable Western Europe. It did help to eliminate Communist influence in the governments of France and Italy, but this was not its main purpose. Moscow thought it was and ordered the French and Italian Communists to obstruct it in every way possible. By doing so they isolated themselves politically, since almost everybody else was willing to accept American economic aid at its face value. Hence it was the Marshall Plan plus Communist obstruction that strengthened the more conservative forces in France and Italy and finally brought these countries out of the political and economic crises of the Liberation period.

## Eastern Europe

Eastern Europe's experience was dramatically different from that of the West. The Red Army had liberated most of the territory east of the Elbe and stationed its troops in Poland, Hungary, Rumania, Bulgaria, East Germany, and, temporarily, Czechoslovakia. Under the protection of Marshal Tito of Yugoslavia, whose movement it resembled, the Communist-led Albanian resistance drove out the Italians. Yugoslavia and Albania, though free of Soviet occupation troops, maintained close ties with their Big Brother in Moscow, and by 1948 the five countries directly liberated by the Russians were all to have native Communist regimes under Soviet control. This crucial development took place somewhat differently in each country, but it was marked everywhere by a continually frustrated effort on the part of non-Communist native leaders to bring about a spontaneous and democratic revolution of their own.

Under Communist leadership the countries of Eastern Europe underwent a more profound and complete revolution—albeit "from above"—than any other part of the world except China. As in Russia, in 1917, thrones were toppled, the old nobility was dispersed, the big estates were broken up, and the old political leaders disappeared in exile or in death. The non-Communist political parties disintegrated or were transformed, and they too finally disappeared. Whereas the former ruling classes had looked to London, Paris, Washington, and Rome for intellectual and economic guidance, after 1945 the new rulers looked to Moscow.

### *"Satellization"*

Subordination to the Soviet Union, one of the two major trends in postwar Eastern Europe, was completed by 1948; "Communization" continued into the 1950s. "Satellization" was Stalin's foremost postwar aim. He was determined to transform the belt of small countries east of Germany into Russian satellites. After the First World War, France had sought to organize these states into a *cordon sanitaire* against the westward spread of Bolshevism, and in the 1930s French influence had been replaced by German influence, which was equally hostile to the Soviet Union. Hitler's East European satellites were forced to contribute considerably to his war against Russia. Stalin wanted to make certain that this situation would never arise again; under Communist control the new *cordon sanitaire* would be turned against the West.

Although the Red Army was on the

scene, Russia preferred to give the processes of "satellization" and "Communization" the outward appearance of orderly, legal, and spontaneous changes, at least until the conclusion of the peace treaties with the former Axis satellites. These were drafted by the Allies in Paris, between July and October 1946, for Italy, Rumania, Hungary, Bulgaria, and Finland. In contrast to the Paris Peace Conference of 1919, the one in 1946 allowed the defeated nations to plead their case. The "victorious" nations of Eastern Europe – Poland, Czechoslovakia, and Yugoslavia – also had their say. Great Britain and the United States kept their wartime promise to let Russia retain the territories she had gained from Finland, Poland, and Rumania as well as the three Baltic states. In addition, "victorious" Czechoslovakia ceded her easternmost province, Ruthenia, to the USSR, and the Russians also took over the northern half of East Prussia, changing the name of its ancient capital from Königsberg to Kaliningrad. In all, the Soviet Union acquired about 200,000 square miles of territory and 22 million people and pushed her pre-1939 border almost 300 miles westward. The Conference also sanctioned minor territorial changes between Yugoslavia and Italy and between Rumania and Bulgaria, but Poland's large acquisitions from Germany did not come within its purview.

Forced transfers of population in 1945 and 1946 made the political map of Eastern Europe correspond more closely with the ethnic map than at any time in modern history. Aside from hundreds of thousands of voluntary refugees from Russia's western borderlands, millions more were forced to leave other East European countries. The Soviet Union expelled the Finnish and German populations from the territories it annexed from Finland and East Prussia; it "exchanged" the Poles left in territories it annexed from Poland for some Russians still left in Poland; it helped Rumania rid itself of the sizable German minority in Transylvania. Poland, Czechoslovakia, and Hungary also expelled their large German minorities – over 6,500,000 persons in all.

The peace treaties, which were signed in February 1947, also gave Russia the lion's share of reparations from Finland, Rumania, and Hungary. Even though the "victorious" East European states got something too, they had to pay equally heavy, albeit disguised, economic tribute to the Soviet Union.

Meanwhile, the Russians had cautiously consolidated their hold on Eastern Europe. As the Red Army advanced in 1944–1945, Soviet security police arrested all known anti-Communists and other "fascists" who had not already fled with the retreating Germans. The Soviet occupation authorities then forced the inclusion of Communists in the first coalition governments of the Liberation period. Thereafter they left most domestic matters in the hands of native Communists, but they exerted strong pressure on the new governments in several ways. The mere presence of Soviet troops prevented any real independent action. Besides, the Russians could blackmail these governments with the reparations they collected and with the German economic assets in Eastern Europe, which they now controlled. Finally, they strengthened their control over the Eastern European countries by exploiting their old nationalist rivalries and their fear and hatred of Germany.

After the signing of the peace treaties the Soviet Union quickly transformed the bulk of Eastern Europe into satellite states. The formal distinction between victors and vanquished disappeared; now, all signed treaties of alliance with the Soviet Union. In September 1947 their Communist Parties also joined the newly founded Cominform (Communist Information Bureau), which coordinated their activities and those of the French and Italian Parties with the needs of Soviet foreign policy. The "Cold War" had begun, and Stalin effectively prevented any of his satellites from being lured into the Western camp, either ideologically or economically – especially under the Marshall Plan.

### *"Communization"*

While outside pressure from the Soviet Union made satellites of most Eastern European countries, their native Commu-

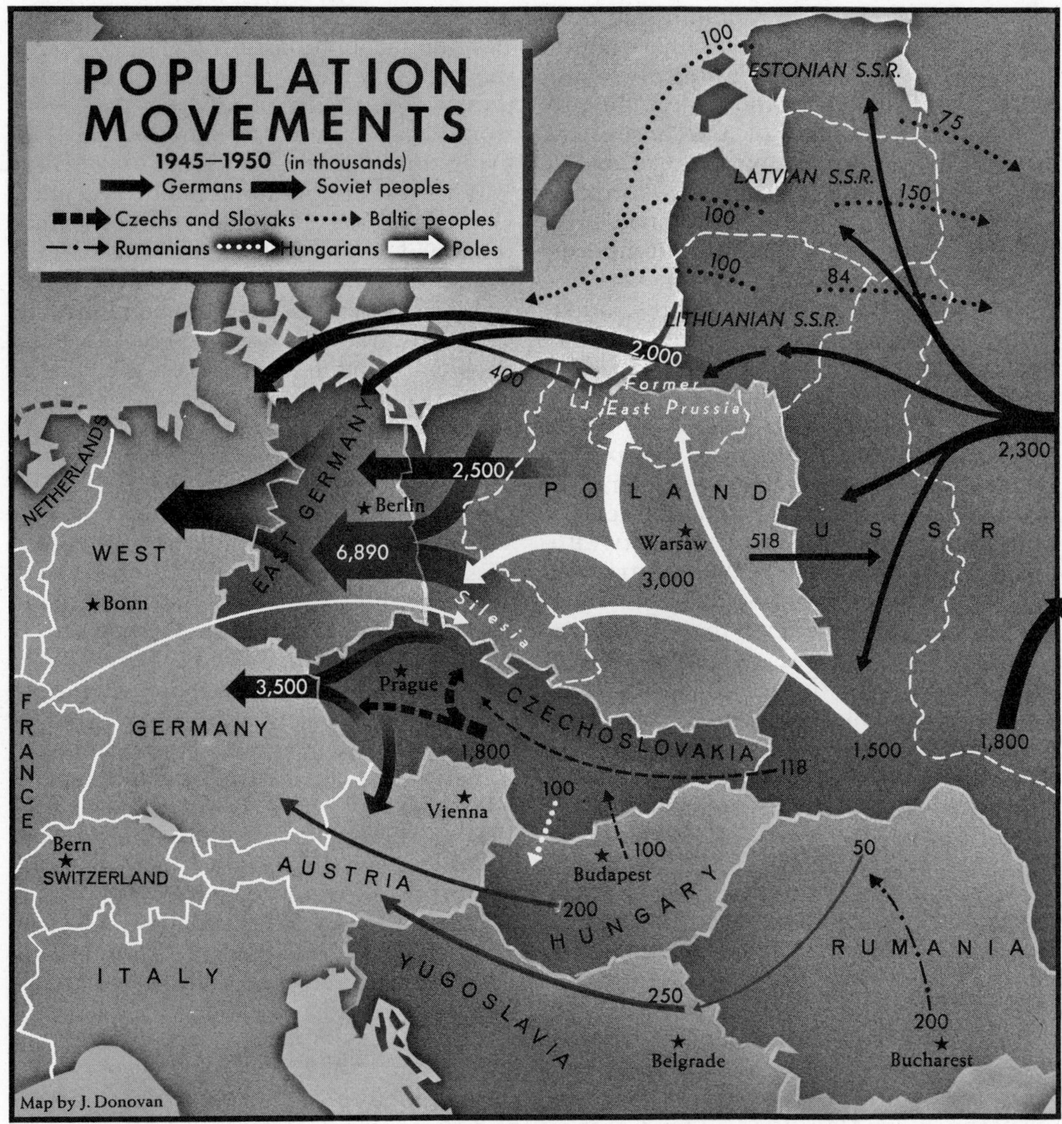


nist parties made them adopt Communist goals as well. The suppression of organized opposition proceeded in stages: first the democratic political leaders were attacked, then prominent churchmen; after 1948 the Communists began to purge their own ranks of "national deviationists."

In the first phase of the Liberation period, the majority of the states under Soviet occupation had coalition governments called Peoples' Democracies. The political parties involved—Communists, Socialists, Agrarians, and sundry democrats—all agreed on three policies to be carried out immediately in the wake of Nazi tyranny: the purge of fascists, land reform, and other acts of social equalization. Agrarian reforms and the nationalizations destroyed the former ruling classes: petty noblemen, big landowners, industrialists, and bankers. They also revolutionized the lives of the peasants. The rural underemployed of prewar days began to move to the new urban factories, while the peasants who remained were all given land. There was real popular support for this democratic revolution, and the Communists' view of Peoples' Democracy as a mere prelude to true Communism was not universally shared. A number of unimpeachably democratic leaders believed in Peoples' Democracy and were willing to try it: Eduard Beneš of Czechoslovakia and Ferenc Nagy of Hungary were able to exert significant influence for two or three years in their respective countries. In Bulgaria and Rumania the Communists gained the upper hand more quickly.

Poland and Yugoslavia, on the other hand, did not experience a true Peoples' Democracy phase. Under Tito's leadership the Communists in Yugoslavia were so strong that they did not have to share authority with other political groups. In Poland they were so weak that they relied openly on the Red Army to keep them in power and refused to share authority with the most popular party in the country, the Peasant Party of Stanislaw Mikolajczyk.

The timing varied, but the pattern of "Communization" was the same almost everywhere. From the beginning the local Communists controlled three vital levers of power: the ministry of propaganda, the ministry of the interior (in charge of the police and local administration), and the army. They used these levers to eliminate the other political parties and overthrow the monarchy, which was destroyed in Bulgaria by September 1946 and in Rumania by the end of 1947. By then the Polish United Workers' Party—Communist in all but name—was the sole party in that country, and Mikolajczyk had fled back to London. The Hungarian Communists forced Ferenc Nagy to resign as premier in May 1947. The Czechoslovak Communists eliminated all non-Communists from their government in February 1948; President Beneš resigned in April and died in September. All these countries, as well as Yugoslavia, adopted similar constitutions and called themselves Peoples' Republics. All began to collectivize the farmland that had been redistributed to individual peasants, but most of the peasants resisted, and forced collectivization proceeded slowly. All adopted Two-, Three-, or Five-Year Plans for industrialization and for the completion of the nationalization of all existing industries and banks. Industrialization increased the size of the urban working class, and Communist propaganda exalted the formerly despised workers. Even so, they were strictly supervised and overworked and saw no rise in their level of living until the late 1950's.

With the opposition political leaders eliminated, the Christian churches alone remained as possible opponents of the Communists. The Orthodox clergy in Bulgaria, Rumania, and the Serbian parts of Yugoslavia did not present a serious problem. Some merely bowed their heads and did what was expected of them; others actively supported the new Communist regimes. The Catholic clergy reacted differently. They had more support from their own parishioners, from the Vatican, and from millions of Catholics in Western Europe and the United States. Consequently, the Communists did not proceed directly against religion itself in the Catholic lands. Instead, they limited the Church's role in education and in Croatia, Czechoslovakia, and Hungary frightened the clergy into submission by bringing the chief figure, or primate, to trial. The trial of the Hungarian Cardinal Joseph Mindszenty recalled earlier Soviet purges in the defendant's public confession to the most unlikely charges. Only in Poland, the most solidly Catholic country in Eastern Europe, did the Communists allow the Church some measure of independence.

### *How Eastern Europe Was "Lost"*

One main difference between free peoples and those in totalitarian countries is that the former tend to feel guilty about what they consider to be their past mistakes. During the interwar years many Britishers and even some Frenchmen had shown his tendency regarding the Treaty of Versailles. Since the late 1940s many Western Europeans and Americans have come to believe that they were responsible for the "enslavement" of Eastern Europe by Communist Russia; some Americans also feel guilty about having "lost" China to the Communists. But it is hard to see how the comparatively small mechanized forces of the Americans and the British could have advanced much farther than

Berlin and Prague by the summer of 1945; it is even harder to see what the United States, which was rapidly demobilizing in 1946, could have done militarily to prevent China from falling into the hands of native Communists.

Perhaps the Western Allies could have done more politically and diplomatically, but the Axis powers were largely responsible for opening the gates of Europe and Asia to Communism. In China, Japan's occupation largely discredited Chiang K'ai-shek's regime and thus gave the Chinese Communists the chance to take over the Nationalists' former appeals of social justice and of freeing the country from all foreign domination. Native Communists in Southeast Asia also gained followers during the Japanese occupation. By signing the Munich Pact in 1938 Great Britain and France may have forced the Soviet Union to appease Hitler in her own way, but by signing the Moscow Pact a year later it was Hitler who first opened the gates of Europe to the Russians by giving them eastern Poland and spheres of influence in the Baltic and Balkan states. His attack on the USSR in 1941 then brought about the "strange alliance" between that country and the West. During the next four years the Western Allies urged the Soviet Union to make its way into Nazi-occupied Eastern Europe and sanctioned its presence there at Yalta and Potsdam. Still, it was Hitler's reign of terror that made many Eastern Europeans welcome the Russians as liberators in 1945.

## INTERNATIONAL RELATIONS

The Second World War and its aftermath drastically altered the relations of the European states among themselves and their relative power in the world as a whole. Perhaps the most striking change was the polarization of power in the United States and the Soviet Union, apparently placing the countries west of the so-called Iron Curtain under the protection of the former and leaving those countries east of it at the mercy of the latter. By the 1950s the reintegration of Italy and most of Germany into Western Europe was a second major change; the "Communization" of East Germany and the smaller countries of Central and Eastern Europe was a third. The emergence of dozens of new nations in the former colonial territories of Africa and Asia has complicated but not basically altered the new pattern of international relations. Even with their colonies Great Britain and France would no longer be able to compete with the two giants in the struggle for world power. In Asia, China is bidding for the role of the former colonial powers, and she is challenging the ideological predominance of the Soviet Union everywhere, but in Europe itself the Soviet Union has no rival for her role as the number one power.

However unpleasant these changes may seem, they are closer to the "natural" order of things than was the pattern that had emerged at the end of the First World War. Today no serious-minded German dreams of restoring his country's "natural" role as the predominant power in Europe, as many did during the interwar period. That dream rested on the assumption that Central Europe, which had been dominated by Germans for so long, was the key position to hold in any struggle for European and world supremacy. After the end of the Second World War there was no longer a Central Europe for Germany to dominate and to use as a base for expansion. Hence, she was no longer the "natural" number one power. West Germany is now fairly well integrated with France, Italy, and the Low Countries economically and closely tied to the Atlantic alliance militarily and diplomatically. She still has opportunities to assert herself within this alliance, especially by playing off France against the United States, and she may once again, as in 1922 and 1939, try to negotiate pacts with the Russians. But there is only one way for West Germany—or the rest of Western Europe—to compete with the United States or the Soviet Union as a superpower: to transform the six-member European Economic Community (the Common Market) into a military and political power bloc. So far, this has not happened, despite De Gaulle's efforts to promote such a bloc under French leadership during the early 1960s.

# EUROPE, 1970

ICELAND
NATO (North Atlantic Treaty Organization)
Common Market (European Economic Community)
Warsaw Pact and
COMECON (Council for Mutual Economic Aid)
0
200
400 mi.
Map by J. Donovan
NORWAY
SWEDEN
Oslo
Stockholm
SCOTLAND
Glasgow
Edinburgh
N. IRELAND
Belfast
IRELAND
Dublin
North Sea
Göteborg
Newcastle
UNITED KINGDOM
DENMARK
Liverpool
Manchester
Copenhagen
Baltic
Kaliningrad
Birmingham
Cardiff
ENGLAND
London
NETHERLANDS
Hamburg
Gdansk
(Danzig)
The Hague
Amsterdam
Bremen
Atlantic
Ocean
Rotterdam
Hanover
EAST GERMANY
Berlin
POLAND
Vistula R.
English Channel
Antwerp
Brussels
Düsseldorf
Elbe R.
Oder R.
BELGIUM
Cologne
Le Havre
Bonn
Leipzig
LUXEMBOURG
Frankfurt
Wroclaw
Paris
Seine R.
WEST GERMANY
Prague
CZECHOSLOVAKIA
Krakow
Rhine R.
Stuttgart
FRANCE
Bay of
Biscay
Munich
Zürich
Vienna
Bern
LIECHTENSTEIN
SWITZERLAND
AUSTRIA
Bordeaux
Lyons
Geneva
Budapest
HUNGARY
Bilbao
Rhône R.
Milan
Venice
Trieste
Toulouse
Turin
Po R.
PORTUGAL
Lisbon
Madrid
SPAIN
ANDORRA
Marseilles
MONACO
Genoa
Bologna
SAN MARINO
Florence
YUGOSLAVIA
(Nonaligned)
Belgrade
Adriatic
Barcelona
Corsica
ITALY
Valencia
Rome
VATICAN CITY
Seville
ALBANIA
Tirana
(Aligned with China)
Balearic Islands
Sardinia
Naples
Gibraltar (Br.)
Mediterranean Sea
Palermo
Sicily
MOROCCO
ALGERIA
TUNISIA
GREECE

Barents Sea
Murmansk
Archangel
FINLAND
Lake Ladoga
Helsinki
Leningrad
ESTONIAN S.S.R.
Riga
LATVIAN S.S.R.
LITHUANIAN S.S.R.
Vilna
Minsk
BELORUSSIAN S.S.R.
Moscow
Gorki
Volga R.
Kazan
RUSSIAN SOVIET FEDERATED SOCIALIST REPUBLICS
Kuibyshev
UNION OF SOVIET SOCIALIST REPUBLICS
Saratov
KAZAKH S. S. R.
Ural R.
Dnieper R.
Kiev
Kharkov
Volgograd (Stalingrad)
UKRAINIAN S. S. R.
Don R.
Astrakhan
Donetsk (Stalino)
Rostov
MOLDAVIAN S.S.R.
Kishinev
RUMANIA
Odessa
Sea of Azov
Caspian Sea
Yalta
Bucharest
Danube R.
Black Sea
GEORGIAN S.S.R.
AZERBAIJAN S.S.R.
ARMENIAN S.S.R.
Baku
BULGARIA
Istanbul
Ankara
TURKEY
Aegean Sea
Teheran
IRAN
IRAQ
SYRIA
CYPRUS
NORTH AMERICA
North Pole
Arctic Ocean
Atlantic Ocean
ASIA
AFRICA
Indian Ocean

## Europe and the "Cold War"

The Cold War began in 1947 with Soviet pressure on Greece and Turkey and with American retaliation against this pressure. In Turkey the Russians wanted military bases at the Dardanelles; in Greece they allegedly encouraged the Communist guerrillas against the Right-wing regime—the only monarchy left in Eastern Europe—which remained in power mainly with British military support. By early 1947, however, Great Britain informed the United States that she could no longer provide this support. In March President Truman took up the challenge by announcing that henceforth the United States would "support free peoples who are resisting attempted subjugation by armed minorities or by outside pressure."

The Truman Doctrine launched a new phase of American intervention in European affairs. Soon after its announcement the United States sent military missions to Turkey and Greece and gave $400 million to the governments of the two countries. The Marshall Plan, though originally conceived as a program of economic aid for *all* of Europe, also became transformed into an instrument of the "Cold War" once the Soviet satellites were prevented from participating. In 1948 efforts to link the American, British, and French occupation zones in Germany to the Marshall Plan, to give these zones a stable currency, and to organize them into a West German government, elicited counter-pressure from the Russians in the form of the Berlin Blockade. They cut off all ground transportation between the occupation zones of the three Western powers in that city and the outside world. In retaliation, the American government sent sixty superfortresses to Europe and strengthened the "airlift" of food, fuel, and other necessities to the citizens of West Berlin. Like the aid to Greece and Turkey, the Berlin "airlift" made the Russians back down, but by intensifying the "Cold War," these events prompted the American government, for the first time in its history, to enter into a peacetime alliance for collective defense.

The North Atlantic Treaty Organization, or NATO, was launched in April 1949 with the signing of the North Atlantic Pact by the United States, Canada, Great Britain, France, Belgium, the Netherlands, Luxembourg, Italy, Norway, Denmark, Iceland, and Portugal. These twelve states agreed that an armed attack against one or more of them should be considered an attack against them all and committed themselves to resist it with armed force. They then set up a Council and a Defense Committee, which were to determine joint policy and to organize the ground, air, and naval contingents contributed by each member under a unified command. The keystone of NATO military policy was to be the defense of West Germany, with an army that was eventually to consist of fifty divisions. Such a force could obviously only delay a major Soviet advance, but its very existence, plus the American arsenal of atomic bombs, would presumably deter Stalin from risking the consequences of overt aggression in Western Europe.

In 1950 the Korean War led to a strengthening of NATO. Although this conflict began with an attack by North Korea on South Korea, everyone in the West assumed that it was inspired by the Soviet Union and that it might soon be followed by a Soviet push into Western Europe. It induced the NATO members to reinforce their military alliance. In January 1951 General Eisenhower went to Paris to take command at the Supreme Headquarters Allied Powers Europe (SHAPE), the military arm of NATO. A few months later Greece and Turkey joined NATO. Since the defense of West Germany was its main task, and since the bulk of British and French armed forces were fighting Communist guerrillas in Southeast Asia,* the United States put strong pressure on the NATO Council to establish an integrated European Defense Force containing a sizable German contingent. Faced with the fearful prospect of a German military resurgence, France made an alternative proposal for the creation of a European Army in which German battalions could not act independently. In

*See p. 776.

May 1952 the foreign ministers of France, Italy, Belgium, the Netherlands, Luxembourg, and West Germany signed the European Defense Community (EDC) Treaty with the purpose of creating such an army.

But the EDC was stillborn. The parliaments of the six signatory states delayed their ratification of the treaty for two years. Meanwhile, in 1953, the Korean stalemate and the death of Stalin led many people to hope for a relaxation of tensions. In August 1954 most of the signatory states had finally ratified the treaty when it came to the floor of the French Assembly. Hostility toward the EDC in France was not merely the result of opposition to German rearmament; it was based on a fear of losing her national independence. A few months earlier she had suffered a disastrous defeat in Indochina;* now she was being asked to incorporate a large part of her armed forces into an international community. Her Assembly said "no."

France's rejection of the EDC did not prevent the rearmament of Germany. In the fall of 1954 the French accepted a British proposal for the inclusion of a fully sovereign West Germany in the Western European Union (WEU), consisting of Great Britain, France, Belgium, the Netherlands, Luxembourg, and Italy. They also agreed to accept West Germany into NATO and to the use of German troops "in accordance with NATO strategy." Beginning in 1955 these agreements went into effect, and the Allied occupation came to an end. West Germany was not to manufacture atomic weapons or missiles, but a new German Army came into being. By 1957 it numbered 125,000 men; by 1965, 500,000.

In response to the rearmament of West Germany the Soviet Union brought East Germany and her other satellites into a new alliance called the Warsaw Pact. Signed in May 1955, this treaty of mutual assistance was to be a counterforce to NATO. As was to be expected, the armed forces of Poland, Czechoslovakia, East Germany, Hungary, Rumania, Bulgaria, and Albania were more thoroughly subordinated to Red Army Command than were those of the NATO allies to the American commander at SHAPE.

Even so, the year 1955 marked the beginning of a new phase in the continuing "Cold War." With NATO balanced by the Warsaw Pact on May 14, with the Austrian Treaty (which ended the four-power occupation and guaranteed Austria's independence and neutrality) signed a day later, and with East and West in a "nuclear stalemate," the time seemed opportune for a "summit conference." In July 1955, exactly ten years after the last such meeting at Potsdam, the leaders of the United States, the Soviet Union, Great Britain, and France met at Geneva. Although they came to no formal agreements, they maintained an outwardly cordial spirit which, in the jargon of the new diplomacy, was dubbed the "Geneva Spirit." This spirit did not prevail at the 1960 "summit conference" in Paris, which Khrushchev broke up following the capture of an American U-2 pilot flying over Soviet territory. A year later a new crisis arose when the East German government built a wall separating West Berlin from the eastern sector of the city. But except for this new Berlin crisis, which soon died down, Europe ceased to be the main center of conflict in the "Cold War."

By the mid-1960's the lessening of international tensions made it increasingly difficult for the United States to hold NATO together. Greece and Turkey came close to war in their efforts to keep the Greek and Turkish populations of Cyprus from massacring each other. America's deepening involvement in the Vietnam War caused growing consternation among her Western European allies. President de Gaulle was particulary critical of American policy everywhere and, in September 1965, he announced that France would end "the subordination known as integration . . . which puts our destiny in the hands of foreigners." Soon thereafter, he said that France would withdraw from NATO's 15-nation defense force and demanded that American bases and NATO headquarters be removed from French soil. This process was completed by 1968 when NATO

*See p. 777.

*President Charles DeGaulle visits the Soviet Union, June 1966*

moved its headquarters to Brussels. De Gaulle still claimed to support NATO as a system of defense pacts between individual states. But his efforts to strengthen France's ties with the Soviet Union, Poland, and Rumania clearly showed that he no longer believed in the "Cold War."

### Western European Integration

Since the late 1940s the nations of Western Europe have moved toward closer cooperation on nonmilitary matters. The sixteen members of the OEEC, the European agency of the Marshall Plan, worked together in allocating American economic aid, and they also reduced their own import quotas, thus reversing a twenty-year trend in European commercial policy. In January 1948, Belgium, the Netherlands, and Luxembourg became a nucleus of Western European integration when they formed an economic union called Benelux, within which practically all customs duties were abolished. Then came the establishment, in May 1949, of the Council of Europe, with permanent headquarters at Strasbourg. The Council's original members included the Benelux countries, Great Britain, France, Ireland, Italy, Norway, Denmark, and Sweden; and West Germany was soon admitted as an "associate member." Its sponsors hoped that it would gain real political power in certain limited spheres, but it failed to fulfill their hopes. Nevertheless, it held the germ of development away from the traditional pattern of intergovernmental relations on the political level.

The first step toward true integration came on the economic level with the European Coal and Steel Community (ECSC). The original plan, though inspired by Jean Monnet, was named after French Foreign Minister Robert Schuman, who announced in May 1950 that: "The French government proposes to place the whole of Franco-German coal and steel output under a common High Authority in an organization open to the participation of the other countries of Europe." This High Authority, independent of national supervision, was unprecedented, yet the response was immediate. Within a few weeks, West Germany, Italy, Belgium, the Netherlands, and Luxembourg agreed to consider the Schuman Plan, and two years later the parliaments of the six countries ratified the ECSC Treaty. In effect the ECSC created a common market for coal and steel. The High Authority, with headquarters in Luxembourg, became an independent executive and legislative directory. Not only did it eliminate all import and export duties, it also equalized prices in the six member countries for coal, steel, coke, iron ore, and scrap.

The successful operation of the ECSC suggested that "the European Community" of "the Six" might become the framework for other kinds of integration. France's rejection of the EDC in 1954 precluded military integration, but in the next two years the ministers of the same six countries met periodically to propose further economic steps toward the goal of unity. The Suez Crisis of 1956,* which threatened Europe's oil supply, gave special import to their deliberations. Finally, in March 1957, "the Six" signed the Treaty of Rome establishing the European Community for Atomic Energy, or Euratom, and the European Economic Community (EEC), or Common Market.

By far the most important move toward Western European integration, the EEC bound its members to a wide range of goals. First, they agreed to a progressive elimination of all tariffs and other trade barriers between themselves within fifteen years. Second, they agreed to cooperate in their agricultural, transport, investment, and labor policies. Third, they agreed to present a common tariff to the outside world. The EEC would function through a Council of Ministers, a Parliamentary Assembly (superseding the Coal and Steel Assembly), a Court of Justice, and an independent executive European Commission with headquarters in Brussels. In practice, this last institution and its planners, nicknamed "Eurocrats," have come to dominate the EEC on all but the highest policy matters, which are still decided by representatives of the national governments.

The most remarkable thing about the EEC has been the determination of the member states to make it work. They have disagreed on specific policies, especially the equalization of agricultural prices, yet, despite these disagreements, the Rome Treaty has been applied more rapidly than had originally been planned. Within six years after its signing the customs duties between the member states had been cut across the board by 40 per cent; the second of three moves had been made toward the establishment of the EEC's single external customs tariff; unconditional freedom of movement was granted to broad categories of investment capital; few restrictions remained on the free movement of labor from one country to another. Yet, in July, 1968, when the full customs union was achieved, the EEC Commission said:

"Europe is not only a matter of customs tariffs. It does not belong just to the manufacturers, the farmers or the technocrats. It is not only the Europe of 180 million Europeans living in the Community. It is not just the Europe of governments, parliaments and administrations. It must also be the Europe of the peoples, of the workers, of youth. All—or nearly all—still remains to be done."

The main controversies over the EEC have concerned its relations with nonmembers, particularly Great Britain. In November 1959 the British launched a counter-organization, the European Free Trade Association (EFTA) to include "the Seven"—Britain, Austria, Denmark, Norway, Portugal, Sweden, and Switzerland. These states agreed to reduce and eventually abolish trade restrictions among themselves without adopting any common policy toward the outside world. By the end of 1962, however, the EFTA had not alleviated Britain's chronic trade problem, and the British, after much soul-searching and some prodding from the United States, applied for membership in the EEC. In January 1963, to their dismay, and to the irritation of the other five members, France vetoed the acceptance of their application. President de Gaulle justified this action on the ground that Britain was not prepared to accept all the terms of the Rome Treaty, but this real motive was political. He had his own con-

*See pp. 785-786.

ception of European integration: he wanted to make "the Six" into a "third force" between the United States and the Soviet Union. Britain's membership would not only have weakened the political cohesiveness of such a force, it would, in De Gaulle's view, have entailed the indirect influence of the United States, with whom he believed Britain had closer ties than with any continental country.

In the late 1960's France's continued opposition Britain's entry into the Common Market indicated the limits to be anticipated regarding the integration of Western Europe. Aside from a common external tariff—which was not likely to be raised to a point that would seriously block trade—"the Six" did not agree on what their relations with the outside world should be. France was not alone in having her own policy. West Germany wanted to keep the benefit of American protection while continuing the work of European integration. The other members of "the Six" were divided between the vague desire to be less dependent on the transatlantic Big Brother and the fear of compromising their security by accepting the leadership of France, which had neither the immense resources nor the nuclear power of the United States. Political integration was held in check less by the survival of old-style nationalism than by the fact that the mixture of cooperation and integration in Europe and within NATO was sufficient to assure prosperity and security. Only a hardening of Soviet policy toward the United States and the Eastern European satellites could give the Western European nations a common goal. And, despite the Soviet occupation of Czechoslovakia in 1968, the recent trend of Soviet policy seems to be in the opposite direction.

### Europe and the World

The reduced influence of the nations of Western Europe in the world has become apparent in several ways. In the United Nations Organization, for example, they constitute a bare 13 per cent of the 121 members of the Assembly. Great Britain and France hold permanent seats on the Security Council; the other three seats belong to the United States, the Soviet Union, and, so far, the Republic of China (Taiwan). Unlike the old League of Nations, whose headquarters and Secretariat were in Geneva, the central organs of the United Nations are located in New York City. Some of France's former territories in Africa supported the French position in the Assembly, but the growing Chinese Communist influence in Africa was beginning to change this pattern. The French, British, Dutch, Belgians, and Portuguese have been frequently censured by the non-European majority of the Assembly for alleged colonialism and neocolonialism.

Along with the appearance of dozens of new nations in Asia and Africa and the continuing preponderance of the United States and the Soviet Union, the emergence of mainland China as an independent power further altered the framework of international relations and the place of both Western and Eastern Europe within it. The new China has already shown her territorial designs on India, Southeast Asia, and even Soviet Siberia. Coupled with her effort to outbid the Soviet Union for the leadership of world Communism, these designs seemed to turn the Russians' wrath more against her than against the West. At the same time, China's bid for ideological leadership* gave some of the

*In the early 1960s the controversy between the Chinese and Russian Communists was over the *means*, or strategy, of bringing about the triumph of world Communism. Khrushchev argued that Communist influence—and ultimately Communism itself—could expand most successfully under conditions of "peaceful coexistence." Mao Tse-tung, on the other hand, argued that the capitalist world's retreat had to be hastened by means of revolutionary wars. In September 1965 Marshal Lin Piao, China's defense minister and Deputy Premier, outlined the global strategy for a "people's war" in Asia, Africa, and Latin America. This strategy was to be the same one that Mao had used in winning the Chinese civil war: establishing bases in rural areas to encircle and conquer cities. Lin Piao likened the United States and Western Europe to cities and the rest of the world to rural areas. He also charged the Soviet "revisionists" with being afraid of war and or revolution. Revolutionaries, he concluded, "never take a gloomy view of war."

Communist countries of Eastern Europe more leeway in pursuing their own paths toward socialism and in following their own foreign policies. By 1960 Albania had already opted for China and was being vilified by Khrushchev. Yugoslavia became more independent than before. In 1964 Rumania was trying to play the role of mediator between the Soviet Union and China and seeking economic and cultural contacts with Western Europe, especially France. President de Gaulle was not alone in foreseeing the day when the Iron Curtain might lift and all the nations of Europe, including the Soviet Union, might be forced to cooperate against the new "yellow peril."

Nevertheless, in the late 1960s, the assumptions of the "Cold War" still dominated the foreign policies of the major powers. The mutual suspicion between the United States and the Soviet Union remained, and the leaders of both countries continued to view international rivalries in ideological terms. This habit went back to the new diplomacy inaugurated by Wilson and Lenin in early 1918 and especially to the beginning of the "Cold War" in the late 1940s. But the Sino-Soviet split and France's independent course away from American domination were clear indications that Communism versus Democracy was not the main issue in international relations. As usual, national self-interest, rather than ideology, was the determining factor. Otherwise, the main division in the world seems to be between the rich and the poor nations, which corresponds largely to the division between the "white" and "colored" peoples, with the notable exception of Japan. It is unlikely that Russia and the Communist countries of Eastern Europe will align themselves with the other "white" nations against China—the habit of ideological thinking is still too strong. But change is as much a part of history as habit.

Meanwhile, aside from their participation in the now defunct Southeast Asian (SEATO) and Middle Eastern (Bagdad Pact) counterparts of NATO, the main diplomatic and military activities of Great Britain and France have concerned their role as colonial powers.

## THE END OF EMPIRE

In 1912, when European imperialism was at its peak, Lord Crewe, Secretary of State for India, proclaimed that Dominion status under the control of "a race which is not our own" would never work in that country.

> "There is nothing whatever in the teachings of history . . . or in the present condition of the world which makes such a dream even remotely probable. . . .Is it conceivable that at any time an Indian Empire could exist, on the lines, say, of Australia and New Zealand, with no British officials, and no tie of creed and blood, which takes the place of these material bonds? . . . To me that is a world as imaginary as any Atlantis."

Four decades later, after the inconceivable had happened, and India, partitioned to provide for an independent Pakistan and Ceylon, was fully sovereign, another British colonial official, Lord Milverton, said the following, not of the ancient civilizations of Asia but of semi-primitive Africa:

> "Whether Africans are ready or not for self-government, whether independence is reasonable or not, has become irrevelant. Africa is in a hurry and in no mood to wait. . . . The nascent nations of Africa do not accept Western timetables of the proper or prudent timing of independence, and when we talk of the premature grant of self-government the adjective presupposes a point of view which is not admitted by Africans."

The contrast between these two statements highlights the degree to which the world has been transformed within the lifetime of many of the leading participants. Native nationalists who on the eve of the First World War barely merited the attention of European statesmen became the heirs of empire in the aftermath of the Second. Nations whose very existence was denied and whose colonial status seemed permanent enforced their claim to be their own masters. In 1955, the leaders of twenty-nine Asian and African countries gathered at Bandung, Indonesia, to declare that "colonialism in all its manifestations is an evil which should speedily be brought to an end." In this way they gave formal notice to the world that European sponsorship or protection had been replaced by a new order of legitimacy.

Paradoxically, the imperialist powers themselves provided most of the ideas and techniques that hastened the end of empire. In trying to reshape the territories under their control in their own image they ruthlessly upset ancient societies and tried to drag them into the modern world. In doing so they unleashed the very forces—industrialization, nationalism, socialism, democracy—that had engineered their own transformation in the nineteenth century. As had happened in Europe, these forces were promoted first by the middle-class elite and ultimately by the broader masses. Just as the bad conscience of European liberals had made them grant concessions to their underprivileged minorities at home, so it weakened their resistance to the demands of the revolutionary nationalists in their colonies.

Yet the process of "decolonization" was painful and often violent. For all their sympathy with native aspirations, the colonial authorities felt morally bound to maintain their own conception of law and order not only as a matter of principle but also to protect European investments and strategic positions* and—as in Algeria and Kenya—the interests of the white settlers. Clashes occurred because the revolutionary nationalists rejected this conception of law and order for a "higher" law that denied the right of foreigners to "possess" them and that asserted their own right to a sense of dignity and cultural individuality. Whereas the existing authorities treated them as lawbreakers or treaty violators, men like Nehru in India, Nkrumah in the Gold Coast (Ghana), and Ben Bella in Algeria saw themselves as patriots. Indeed, they prided themselves on having been imprisoned by the British or French for their revolutionary activities, which ranged from passive resistance in India to terrorism and war in Algeria.

*The traditional anticolonialism of the United States has been tempered by the need to maintain good relations with her allies and by embarrassment over her strategic interest in the Far East, where she has tended to take over the imperialist role of the British, French, and Japanese in the face of the new menace of the Chinese Communists.

## Paths to Independence: Asia

After the defeats suffered by the Western powers in the war against Japan, colonial authority could never be the same again. This was especially true in the Dutch East Indies, French Indochina, and the British crown colony of Burma, where the Japanese were still in possession at the end of hostilities. Although India had escaped a Japanese occupation, the British had brought her into the war without consulting the leaders of the Congress Party, Gandhi and Nehru (whom they soon jailed), and it was clear that these men would accept nothing less than complete independence as soon as possible. Only the United States ended its colonial rule without regrets when, in July 1946, it recognized the independence of the Republic of the Philippines. The paths to independence in the rest of Southeast Asia and in India were marked by wars against the "returning" Europeans and strife among the natives themselves.

### *India*

By 1947 the British were willing to grant complete independence to India, but the transfer was complicated by the Muslim League, which insisted on the establishment of a separate state for the country's large Muslim minority. In 1946 differences between the Congress Party and the Muslim League had already developed into an open struggle for political power, and large-scale civil strife between Hindus and Muslims was causing thousands of deaths. By early 1947 the British authorities in India were finding it increasingly difficult to maintain law and order, and in June the government in London bluntly announced a one-year deadline for the transfer of power to Indian hands, whatever India's constitution might be. It also reluctantly accepted partition as the only solution to the irreconcilable conflict between the Hindus and the Muslims. In August, India and Pakistan became two separate Dominions with full sovereignty within the British Common-

Arctic Ocean
ASIA, 1970
UNION OF SOVIET SOCIALIST REPUBLICS
L. Baikal
Irkutsk
Ulan Bator
MONGOLIAN PEOPLE'S REPUBLIC
L. Balkash
Aral Sea
Alma Ata
SINKIANG
Lop Nor
(Atomic test site)
INNER MONGOLIA
Harbin
Vladivostok
Kamchatka
Sakhalin
Hokkaido
Sea of Japan
NORTH KOREA
Peking
Tientsin
Pyongyang
Seoul
SOUTH KOREA
Honshu
Kyoto
Tokyo
Osaka
JAPAN
AFGHANISTAN
WEST PAKISTAN
KASHMIR
Sian
Yellow Sea
PEOPLE'S REPUBLIC OF CHINA
Nanking
Shanghai
TIBET
Lhasa
SIKKIM
NEPAL
BHUTAN
Delhi
Hankow
Chungking
Okinawa
(U.S.)
Taipei
REP. OF CHINA
(Taiwan)
INDIA
Calcutta
EAST PAKISTAN
Canton
Hong Kong
(Br.)
Pacific Ocean
Bombay
BURMA
Hanoi
LAOS
Vientiane
NORTH VIETNAM
Rangoon
Luzon
THAILAND
Bangkok
Quezon City
Manila
PHILIPPINES
Bay of Bengal
Madras
CAMBODIA
SOUTH VIETNAM
South China Sea
Andaman Is.
Pnompenh
Saigon
CEYLON
Colombo
Mindanao
MALAYSIA
BRUNEI
SABAH
Celebes Sea
Kuala Lumpur
MALAYA
SARAWAK
Singapore
Indian Ocean
Equator
Sumatra
Borneo
Celebes
New Guinea
INDONESIA
Djakarta
Bandung
Java
Bali
Ocussi
(Port.)
Port. Timor
AUSTRALIA
Map by J. Donovan

wealth. In February 1948, Ceylon likewise achieved Dominion status,* and a few years later all three countries transformed themselves into republics. Thus, Great Britain stretched the definition of the Commonwealth one degree further by allowing them to participate in an institution that necessarily honored a monarch as its symbolic head.

Although the British withdrew quickly and with good grace, the partition of their former Indian empire perpetuated the ethnic and religious antagonisms among the natives. The frontiers of India and Pakistan left millions of Hindus and Muslims in the wrong country; by the end of 1948, 5 million persons had moved from one Dominion to the other in order to find security among their coreligionists. There was no war between India and Pakistan—as there was in 1948 following the partition of Palestine between Israel and Jordan—but two major Indian states caused considerable trouble. Hyderabad, with its Hindu majority and Muslim Nizam, had to be forcibly occupied by Indian troops; Kashmir, with its Muslim majority and Hindu Maharajah, was the scene of intermittent fighting throughout 1948, and its status has still not been settled.

In general, however, India and Pakistan became more viable new states than many others whose frontiers remained the accidental ones of imperial rule and which included mutually hostile ethnic and religious communities. The independence of Malaya, Indonesia, and Indochina involved not only native uprisings against the British, Dutch, and French, respectively, but also prolonged conflicts among the natives themselves. In each case these conflicts were complicated by guerrilla bands of national Communists, who fought both the Europeans and the new native governments. In Indonesia the Dutch withdrew by the end of 1949, leaving the "pacification" of this far-flung and heterogeneous republic to President Achmed Sukarno; in Malaya, British troops fought the Communist guerrillas (who were largely Chinese rather than Malayans) until 1957 before granting complete independence.

*Burma, which had been occupied by the Japanese in the last year of the war, did not join the Commonwealth on gaining her independence.

### *Indochina*

The conflict over former French Indochina was the longest and bloodiest in the annals of "decolonization" in Asia. It began in the summer of 1945, when the national Communist leader, Ho Chi-minh, proclaimed Vietnam an independent democratic republic and declared all former treaties with France null and void (the Kingdoms of Cambodia and Laos remained outside the struggle). For over a year Ho had been waging guerrilla war against Japan and her puppet Vietnamese "emperor," Bao Dai, with whom she had finally replaced the Vichy authorities. When Gaullist forces began "returning" in the fall of 1945, Ho, now styling himself the leader of the Vietminh ("Revolutionary League of Vietnam"), soon withdrew to Hanoi, in the north, in an embittered, belligerent mood. In March 1946 a provisional cease-fire was negotiated in Saigon, in the south, and in November Ho went to Paris to discuss the future of Veitnam in a peaceful way. While he was there, however, the French commander in northern Vietnam bombarded Haiphong, the port of Hanoi, and captured both cities. Ho quickly returned to lead the Vietminh rebellion against the French.

For seven years the French fought an expensive and demoralizing war against the Vietminh rebels. In 1949 they "restored" Bao Dai to his throne in the hope that he would continue to serve their interests after Vietnam was given its token independence. But the Communist triumph in China in that same year gave the Vietminh diplomatic support from both Peking and Moscow, and the Korean armistice in 1953 released a considerable amount of Chinese arms for its use. Meanwhile, the struggle was costing the French over a billion dollars annually and killing her best army officers. The war became increasingly unpopular at home, although no conscripts were sent to Vietnam. Yet the government in Paris was unwilling to abandon its Vietnamese protegés to the Communists and often unable to control its own military commanders,

*A student demonstration in Saigon, South Vietnam*

even when it doubted their assurances that they would ultimately "pacify" the country. Finally, in April 1954, the local French commanders made a desperate effort to defend the northern fortress of Dienbienphu, but after a heroic defense lasting over a month they were finally forced to surrender. The fall of Dienbienphu shattered all remaining hopes of the French in Indochina.

Unfortunately for all concerned, the cease-fire of July 1954 did not achieve permanent peace in Indochina. This cease-fire, arranged at Geneva by the foreign ministers of fourteen countries, temporarily divided Vietnam itself at the seventeenth parallel, giving the Vietminh control of the north and creating the new independent state of South Vietnam until the day when national elections would reunite the two Vietnams. Cambodia and Laos were also made independent, and their neutrality was guaranteed by the fourteen states at the Geneva Conference. These arrangements brought peace for several years. In 1961, however, local Communists resumed guerrilla warfare in Laos and in South Vietnam. The United States then took over the "pacification" of these territories and the effort to prevent them from falling into the hands of the Communists.

### *The American Involvement in Vietnam*

Although Cambodia managed to maintain its independence from outside interference, and a precarious truce was forced on the opposing factions in Laos in 1962, the war in South Vietnam continued to "escalate" throughout the 1960's. At first the American armed forces there were called military "advisers" whose task was to help the government in Saigon maintain its military control of the country. Yet this government itself was being harassed not only by the Vietcong (the guerrilla army of the Communist-led National Liberation Front) but also by civil strife between Buddhists and Catholics and by the constant threat of military coups from within its own ranks. By the mid-1960's, the Saigon regime had lost control of half of the countryside to the rebels. As the United States stepped up its military and material aid to the rulers in Saigon, the government of North Vietnam increased its aid to the Vietcong and began sending its own troops into South Vietnam.

Under the Johnson Administration the United States government made a major military commitment to the Saigon regime in order to "contain" Communism in Southeast Asia. It told the American people and its allies that this commitment was essential in order to prevent the Chinese Communists from taking over the area, although the foreign Communist soldiers in South Vietnam were North Vietnamese and most of the military equipment used by the Vietcong was either imported from the Soviet Union or captured from the Americans. By 1967 Hanoi, instead of Peking, was defined as the main enemy, and American bombers made a concerted effort to cripple the economic and military capacity of North Vietnam. Despite this effort, North Vietnamese soldiers continued to move into the battle areas of the south, and American military units suffered increasing casualties on the ground. The much vaunted "beefing up" of the South Vietnamese army did not occur, and the American "presence" took on the form of an outright occupation: by early 1969 there were 600,000 American troops in South Vietnam (whose total population was 17 million) and 200,000 foreign civilians, mostly American.

The peace negotiations in Paris, which were still going on at the time of this writing, had begun in the spring of 1968 after President Johnson called a halt to the bombing of North Vietnamese cities. The United States and North Vietnam, later joined by the Saigon regime and the National Liberation Front, used these peace talks for propaganda purposes while striving for a better military bargaining position. As the fighting in South Vietnam continued without breaking the military stalemate the war became increasingly unpopular in the United States, where a minority of militant opponents of the war had already been active for several years. In early 1970 President Nixon reasserted the policy of "Vietnamization" and began bringing some American troops home. But this process was slowed down in May and June by American incursions into Cambodia. Agonizing as the issue of the war was for many Americans, especially in view of the cost in lives and in money that could have been used better in solving the nation's urban crisis, it was also the last chapter in the struggle of the peoples of Asia for national independence. From the point of view of many South Vietnamese, the Americans were simply the heirs of the French.

### Paths to Independence: Africa

In Africa independence came later, more quickly, and often more dramatically than in Asia. The independence of the former Italian colony of Libya in 1951 and the withdrawal of the British from the Suez Canal Zone in 1954 were relatively peaceful affairs. But France's "disengagement" from Tunisia and Morocco in 1956 was preceded by considerable violence on all sides, and in Algeria it entailed an even more demoralizing and costly war than in Indochina. On the other hand, in 1958, the French allowed all their colonies south of the Sahara to determine their future status in a plebiscite. The twelve new states that emerged out of former French West Africa and French Equatorial Africa experienced far less internal strife and maintained far more cordial relations with their former colonial masters than the Congo, where anarchy and terrorism followed the precipitous Belgian withdrawal in 1960. Great Britain presided over the peaceful independence of Ghana (former Gold Coast), Nigeria, and Tanganyika between 1957 and 1961, but in Kenya and

AFRICA
1970
Independent states
Colonial territories, Rhodesia and Republic of South Africa
EUROPE
ASIA
Mediterranean Sea
Red Sea
Atlantic Ocean
Equator
Algiers
Tunis
TUNISIA
Rabat
MOROCCO
Madeira (Port.)
Canary Is (Sp.)
Villa Cisneros
SP. SAHARA
ALGERIA
Tripoli
Benghazi
LIBYA
Cairo
EGYPT
MAURITANIA
Nouakchott
Cape Verde Is. (Port.)
Dakar
SENEGAL
GAMBIA
PORT. GUINEA
Conakry
GUINEA
Freetown
SIERRA LEONE
Monrovia
LIBERIA
MALI
Bamako
UPPER VOLTA
Ouagadougou
IVORY COAST
Abidjan
GHANA
Accra
TOGO
Lomé
DAHOMEY
Porto-Novo
NIGER
Niamey
NIGERIA
Lagos
CHAD
L. Chad
Ft. Lamy
Khartoum
SUDAN
AFAR-ISSA TERR. (Fr.)
Djibouti
Addis Ababa
ETHIOPIA
SOMALIA
Mogadishu
CENTRAL AFRICAN REP.
Bangui
CAMEROON
Yaoundé
FERNANDO PO
Bata
EQUATORIAL GUINEA
RIO MUNI
Libreville
GABON
São Tomé (Port.)
CONGO REP.
Brazzaville
Kinshasa
REP. OF THE CONGO
UGANDA
Kampala
L. Victoria
KENYA
Nairobi
RWANDA
BURUNDI
TANZANIA
ZANZIBAR
Dar es Salaam
CABINDA (Angola)
Luanda
ANGOLA (Port.)
ZAMBIA
Lusaka
MALAWI
Zomba
Salisbury
RHODESIA
MOZAMBIQUE (Port.)
MALAGASY REP.
Tananarive
SOUTH WEST AFRICA
Windhoek
(Rep. of S.A. Mandate)
BOTSWANA
Gaberones
Pretoria
Lourenco Marques
SWAZILAND
REP. OF SOUTH AFRICA
LESOTHO
Map by J. Donovan

Rhodesia, like France in Algeria, she was caught between the demands of the African nationalists and the European settlers.

### French North Africa. The Agony of Algeria

The half a million French settlers in the protectorates of Morocco and Tunisia could not prevent the government in Paris from ending the repressive measures of the local military authorities—especially the famed Foreign Legion—and from acceding to native nationalist demands for independence. Algeria, however, was legally as much a part of France as Normandy or Provence. One million Europeans, a tenth of the total population, considered it their homeland; indeed, in the major cities they constituted a slight numerical majority and had virtually no contact with the Muslims. Even a small minority of the Muslims seemed content to remain second-class citizens of France. Still, Muslim demands for complete independence had been brewing since 1945, and in 1954 the nationalists began a guerrilla campaign that eventually became a full-scale war. This war tied down almost half a million French troops, now including conscripts.

The Algerian War was the agony of France as well as Algeria. By 1957 rebel terrorism was being met with counterterrorism by French police and soldiers. Army officers who had fought in Indochina prided themselves on having learned the latest techniques of revolutionary warfare—guerrilla tactics, enlisting civilian loyalty, "brainwashing" and pitiless torture of prisoners—from the Vietminh (who in turn had learned them from Mao Tse-tung's lectures on the subject, first published in 1941). "Intoxicated" by their mission of outdoing the FLN (Front of National Liberation), they regrouped whole villages into compounds and perpetrated atrocities of which no other Europeans except the Nazis had been thought capable. Stories of these atrocities brought forth a number of protests both in France and in the outside world; Jean-Paul Sartre and over a hundred other prominent Frenchmen signed a manifesto supporting the native "resistance movement" and urging Frenchmen of good faith to help it actively. On May 13, 1958, sections of the army and the European population in Algiers rose up against the government in Paris for fear that it would "abandon" them to the Muslims. General de Gaulle, who returned to power in June, faced similar pressures, for the complete abandonment of Algeria was as agonizing a prospect to millions of Frenchmen as the continuation of the war.

Finally in the spring of 1962, the French government recognized the independence of Algeria. On "freedom day" downtown Algiers, formerly the bastion of the European settlers, witnessed the triumphal scene of Muslims dancing in the streets to celebrate their "dispossession" by the "colonialists"—an echo of similar celebrations all over the world. Despite the continued presence of the French army and the new Algerian government's assurances regarding their safety and their property, the European settlers flocked to the docks and the airport. *Their* Algeria was dead. The new Algeria would have to get along without them; by the beginning of 1965 over 800,000 of them had left. As in Morocco, Tunisia, and most of her other former territories in Africa, France has continued to supply teachers, technicians, and economic aid. But memories of colonialism die hard, and the leaders of independent Algeria began looking elsewhere, including Moscow and Peking, for the kind of help so urgently needed.

### Black Africa.† Ghana and Kenya

Black Africa has become "decolonized" at a dizzying pace. At the beginning of 1957 the only independent native states were still Ethiopia and Liberia; at the beginning of 1965 the only important colonial ones were Rhodesia, Portuguese Angola and Mozambique, and the dependencies of the Union of South Africa. Between these two dates almost two dozen new nations had emerged. Aside from the Congo (formerly Belgian) and Somalia (formerly

†The designation Black Africa is used here to highlight the natives' basis for awareness of themselves as peoples. In Chapter XV Tropical Africa was used to emphasize the Europeans' view of the same general area as territories to be partitioned among *themselves*.

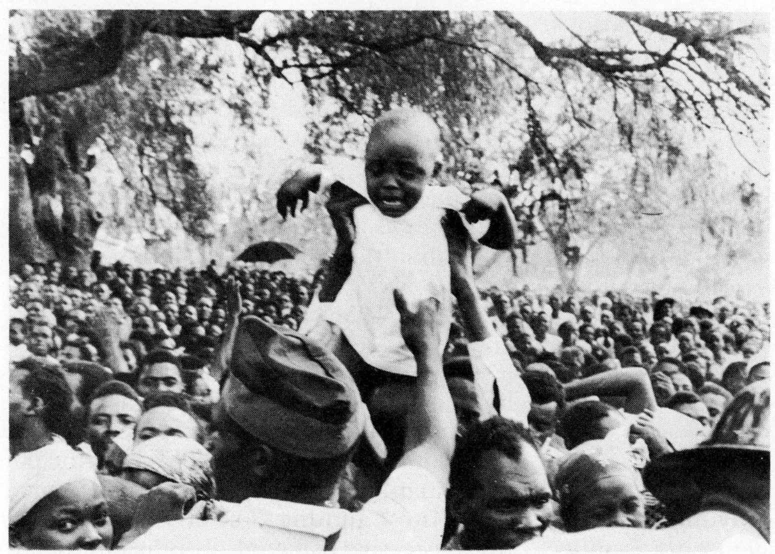

*A crowd in Nairobi celebrating Prime Minister Jomo Kenyatta's return*

Italian), all were former colonies of Great Britain and France.

The British and French colonies followed three main paths to independence. In 1958 all the French ones except Guinea accepted President de Gaulle's offer of independence within what was then called the French Community, but which was dissolved in 1961; so far many of their leaders have remained friendly to France. The second and third paths, the most instructive from the European point of view, are best exemplified by Ghana and Kenya.

In 1948 the British had set up in Ghana, then called the Gold Coast, the first Legislative Council in Africa to have an African majority; a year later the first clearly defined African nationalist revolt took place. It was led by Kwame Nkrumah and his United Gold Coast Convention Party. Some thirty Africans were killed in the rioting, and Nkrumah was put in jail. But in 1951 the British governor abandoned his policy of repression; instead, he courageously released Nkrumah from jail and made him virtually prime minister of the territory. For the next six years this English- and American-educated nationalist, curbing his flamboyant personality and his Marxist sympathies, cooperated with the British authorities in preparing native administrators and legislators to take over the country. In 1957, against a background of complete apathy in London and amid friendly ceremonies in Accra, Ghana became the first African territory to gain its independence.

The British found it much harder to turn Kenya over to native rule. Whereas Ghana had no significant community of white settlers, over 50,000 Europeans occupied the cities of Kenya and its "White Highlands," whose temperate climate and fertile soil they had monopolized for several generations. Here was Nairobi, made famous in novels and films as the coastal base for white hunters and their native safaris. And here was the Mau Mau, the secret society of the Kikuyu tribe, which, in 1952, launched the most savage wave of atrocities on record against the Europeans and their alleged native lackeys. During the mid-1950s, when the Gold Coast was moving tanquilly toward independence, Kenya was in the grip of Mau Mau terrorism, a terrorism inspired by primitive witchcraft rather than any modern ideology. Army units were flown in from Britain, and the local leader, Jomo Kenyatta, was imprisoned for seven years for his alleged part in the rebellion. After relative peace was restored, the

British authorities proposed various forms of multiracial rule, but, as in Algeria, the white settlers saw no future for themselves in an African-dominated state. In the late 1950s and early 1960s such an eventuality still seemed a long way off; but finally, in 1964, the British government relinquished power to an all-African regime headed by Kenyatta. In Nairobi, as in Algiers, the native Africans danced in the streets, while the Europeans bid farewell to their adopted homeland. As in all the emerging nations, the struggle for survival began.

### Politics of the Emerging Nations

The survival of the newly independent nations has been contingent on a number of questions. After the withdrawal of European troops, who was to protect the current rulers from domestic coups and foreign aggressors? How were these underdeveloped countries to industrialize and to feed and educate their rapidly growing populations? Should they accept aid from the advanced nations of the West and the East, and if so, how could they remain "nonaligned" in the Cold War?

#### *Nationalism and Nonalignment*

With few exceptions—most notably India—the emerging nations quickly abandoned democracy for dictatorship. This was not surprising. It had happened in Latin America in the nineteenth century and in Turkey in the 1920s. In most places only a strong man could break the hold of the traditionalist princes, priests, and tribal chiefs on the benighted masses. Only a dictator, it seemed, could mold them into a nation and force them to go to school and to meet the occupational and psychological demands of industrialization. Not only the traditionalists but also the westernizing liberals were soon forced out of power almost everywhere. It took Achmed Sukarno almost ten years to secure his control over the islands of the Indonesian republic from his base in Java. In Egypt, on the other hand, Colonel Gamal Abdel Nasser was able to eliminate all his rivals in a little over two years after the overthrow of King Farouk in July 1952. In Ghana, Kwame Nkrumah also outlawed all opposition to him in two years. Yet despite their political strength these dictators were unable to provide the material progress that their peoples are beginning to expect. Like so many dictators in the past, they promoted aggressive nationalism as a substitute.

At first the emerging nations tried to achieve a certain solidarity among themselves. In 1955, at the Bandung Conference, they condemned colonialism where it still prevailed and declared their "nonalignment" in the "Cold War." The neutralist ideology was made acceptable by the conviction and prestige of its principal spokeman, Indian Prime Minister Nehru. After the Bandung Conference, however, the aggressive behavior of some of its leaders—especially Nasser's designs on the South Arabian Federation and Sukarno's attacks on Malaysia—weakened the solidarity of the nonaligned "bloc" and partially discredited the neutralist ideology itself.

By October 1964, Nehru was dead, and at the meeting of this "bloc" in Cairo many of the delegations showed more concern with furthering their own nationalist interests than with international solidarity. Ghana, Algeria, Guinea, and Kenya were too eager to acquire economic and military aid from Russia and China to attach much importance to nonalignment. Indonesia urged military aid for rebel "freedom fighters" against "neocolonialism" all the way from Malaysia—where the British were helping the government fight off Sukarno's guerrillas—to Portugal's African territories. Most of the delegations approved a resolution that peaceful coexistence was impossible without the "abolition of imperialism, colonialism, and neocolonialism," but India's Prime Minister Shastri, Yugoslavia's President Tito, and Egypt's President Nasser opposed overt military support.*

Ironically, the explosion of China's first atomic bomb occurred less than a week after the Cairo Conference had passed a resolution urging Peking to renounce the

*During the late 1960s the Left-wing nationalist dictators of Algeria, Ghana, and Indonesia had all been ousted by more moderate military leaders.

development of such weapons. It is too early to gauge the implications of this event for the emerging nations. Clearly, however, China now looms as a greater military threat than ever to her neighbors. And she will undoubtedly use her achievement as the first nonwhite nation to join the hitherto all-white "nuclear club" in trying to persuade others that her brand of Communism is the answer to their military as well as economic and social problems.

#### *Marx, Malthus, and Mao Tse-Tung*

The manner in which Mao Tse-tung took over China has become the model for Communist leaders in many underdeveloped countries. In 1945, while defeated Japan came under the firm grip of the American occupation,* China reverted to the rule of Chiang K'ai-shek. He moved the capital from Chungking back to Nanking and, at first, controlled the whole country except the Communist stronghold in the distant northern province of Yunan. But the Communists, following Mao's guidelines of revolutionary warfare, had been widening their popular appeal during the long struggle against Japan. After 1945 the weakness of Chiang's government, its corruption, and its inability to cope with an inflation that further ravaged the country's war-torn economy, played into the Communists' hands by alienating not only the peasants but also many disillusioned intellectuals. American efforts to reconcile the Communists to Chiang failed, and in early 1947 civil war broke out. During 1948 and 1949 the Communists brought the whole of the Chinese mainland under their control and forced Chinag's government to flee to the island of Taiwan (Formosa). Their astounding success was abetted partly by the low morale of Chiang's army but mainly by their combination of guerrilla tactics and subversion of the already demoralized civilian population.

*By 1952, when the occupation ended with the signing of the Japanese peace treaty, the country had a democratic government and was entering an economic boom comparable to that of Western Europe. Though Japan has a militant Communist Party, it has had less popular support than the Communist parties of France and Italy.

In their new capital at Peking the Communists immediately launched their drive to make China a great military and industrial power. The Russian Communists had given them only limited aid—mainly captured Japanese weapons from Manchuria—in their battle against Chiang, and now they rationed money and technicians to them until 1959. The Chinese Five-Year Plans of the 1950s and early 1960s brought notable gains in the production of steel, in railroad construction, and in the electronic and optical industries, but China's over-all capital equipment is still incomplete and she has been unable to use what industrial plant she already has to full capacity. In 1959–1961, as in the Soviet Union thirty years earlier, the forced collectivization of agriculture was accompanied by a severe famine. Since then the regime has concentrated on trying to increase agricultural production to feed a population that was over 800 million by 1970 and growing at the rate of 12 to 14 million a year. The regime has modified the organization of the peasant communes (which were even more severely regimented than Soviet collective farms) and allowed the peasants to grow their own vegetables, poultry, and livestock on adjoining plots. China still had to import some grain in 1962 and 1963 and to pay for it with money that might otherwise have gone into industrial expansion, but the food problem was practically solved by 1964. From 1965 to 1967 the Chinese economy suffered new setbacks during "the great proletarian cultural revolution," in which Mao pitted youthful Red Guards against the party bureaucracy. Now that the party's "bourgeois revisionists" have been eliminated, the young revolutionaries have—reluctantly, it seems—given up the joys of political warfare for the more prosaic task of becoming productive members of the economy.

Communist successes in solving the food problem and in exploding nuclear devices have strengthened domestic support for the regime and given it increased prestige in the non-Western world. As in the Soviet Union, there was considerable resistance to totalitarian rule at first, but even more than the Russians, the Chinese Communists have sought popular backing

*Anti-American demonstration in Peking*

at home by mixing Marxist goals with nationalist slogans. Recently they also stepped up their attacks on the Soviet Union. Ever since 1931, Mao has made no secret of his belief that the Revolution in Russia could be the model only for "imperialist" countries, while the Revolution in China must be the model for "colonial and semicolonial" countries.

Mao's "revision" of Marxism has taken a leaf from Malthus. According to Mao, the white world, including the Soviet Union, will grow richer and better educated, while the nonwhite world will grow poorer and more illiterate. The population explosion, not capitalism, will make this development inevitable. In fact, says Mao, the white world, again including the Soviet Union, will accelerate it by "misplaced" aid in the form of better hygiene and improved technology, which will widen the gap between agricultural production and population growth. Mao estimates that by the end of the twentieth century 5 billion out of 6 billion people in the world will be poor nonwhites, half of whom will be under fourteen (hence nonproducers) and illiterate. He believes that these people will be easily persuaded to follow native Communists, just as hundreds of millions of poor and illiterate Chinese did in the late 1940s. According to him, the Soviet Union, which is already becoming a "land of plenty," cannot hope to compete successfully for leadership of the miserable masses in the nonwhite world.

Mao has also "revised" the Leninist doctrine that the capitalist nations will destroy one another in imperialist wars. He has said that if the Soviet Union, the United States, and China should come to a nuclear war, China could lose as many people as the total population of either of the other countries and still have 500 million left. In the end, when civilization advanced once again, China would be the leading country in an all-Communist world. It is unlikely, however, that the Chinese Communists in their less boastful moments desire a nuclear war or are confident that their regime could survive one.

The impact of Communist China on the European world is twofold. On the one hand, China has set herself up as the rival of Russia for the leadership of world Communism; she has even tried to lure some of Russia's East European satellites out of the Russian camp. On the other hand, China wants to be the heir to European colonial rule in Southeast Asia. This desire and its implementation have been clearest in Indochina, first against the French and more recently against the Americans. On a less obvious level China has tried to subvert the new regimes in Burma, Malaya, and Indonesia.

Just as the spread of European Communism did not come the way Marx had foreseen, the advance of Chinese Communism in the non-European world may not follow Mao's blueprint. China may *impose* her brand of Communism on Southeast Asia, just as Russia imposed hers on Eastern Europe. This is unlikely to happen in the near future for several reasons. First, the party apparatus was permanently weakened by the "cultural revolution" of the mid 1960's. Second, China is still predominantly an agrarian country; despite its nuclear weapons, it lacks the industrial base for large-scale expansion beyond its immediate neighbors. Finally, after Mao's death, the military and the state bureaucracy probably will become the decisive political forces as provincial and other traditional Chinese inclinations assert themselves in the face of doctrinaire Maoism. The ideological crisis of Communism, which already plagues the Soviet Union,* is not likely to bypass China in the long run.

Nevertheless, Mao's revolutionary ideology could have at least as broad an appeal—especially as preached by politically ambitious native Communists—to the world's nonwhite masses as Marx's revolutionary ideology had among Europe's industrial masses at the beginning of this century. The population explosion is real, and Mao may not be as far wrong in calculating its effects as Marx was in predicting the effects of capitalism. For in Western Europe capitalism has not only survived the end of empire, it has accommodated itself to the welfare state and brought unprecedented prosperity, as Mao himself admits.

*See pp. 807-811, 815.

### Effects in Europe: The Suez Crisis

Despite the end of empire the former colonial powers are trading more than ever, and on more favorable terms, with the nonwhite agricultural nations. Does this mean that Mao is right, that in the 6 billion people's world of the 1990s Europe plus the Soviet Union and the United States will become ghettos of affluence defending themselves with nuclear weapons against the starving nonwhite masses? Whatever the answer may be then, the last two decades have shown conclusively that colonies are irrelevant to the European economy. Even the total loss of investments in former colonial territories has been no greater than, say, the cost of the Algerian War or a first-class depression.

The most important effects of the end of empire in Europe have been noneconomic. At strategic bases from Dakar to Singapore the tricolor and the union jack have been lowered forever; each instance was a blow to the national pride of the French and the British as well as to their military and naval power. Although the British suffered no humiliation comparable to Dienbienphu, the cumulative psychological effect of the end of empire has touched them more deeply than any other nation. Just as the former colonial peoples continued to bear the scars of inferiority and subjection thrust upon them by the colonizers, many Europeans remained unpersuaded in their hearts that they were not in fact superior to peoples of darker skins and were ready to call a halt to further attacks on what remained of their overseas holdings.

These tensions came out in the open in the Suez Crisis of 1956. In July of that year President Nasser had announced the nationalization of the Suez Canal.* Nasser said he needed the revenues to build a dam on the upper Nile, but he also want-

*The Canal itself was only one asset of the 200-million-dollar Suez Canal Company, whose largest stockholders were in London and whose headquarters was in Paris. Its loss was so far from being disastrous that in the late 1960's Suez stock was selling at almost $100 a share on the Paris Bourse, and the total assets of the company—now called the Suez Finance Company—had increased to 235 million dollars.

ed to demonstrate the strength of his regime to the Egyptian people and their Arab neighbors; perhaps he also wished to distract attention from his own economic failures. The British and French governments condemned the nationalization as illegal and determined on a show of power. On October 31, British and French aircraft began bombing Egyptian airfields preparatory to landing operations in the Canal Zone. The British were primarily concerned with the maintenance of unimpeded passage through the Canal and made it plain that they regarded the Egyptians as incompetent to assure this. The French also wanted to eliminate the dictator who was aiding the Algerian rebels; in fact, the French paratroop commander promised to "bring Nasser back to Paris in a cage."

The Anglo-French task force was obviously capable of routing the Egyptians, but at the United Nations the Soviet Union and even the United States (as well as the Bandung anticolonialists) condemned the invasion. The task force then withdrew. In contrast, the Soviet Union continued to crush a national uprising in Hungary* with no apparent concern for United Nations condemnation. It took the French over five years more to give up Algeria, but to the British, the bitter setback at Suez marked the true end of the imperial era. Meanwhile, Egypt, by blocking passage through the Canal with sunken ships, threatened Western Europe's oil supply from the Middle East.

Egypt naturally broke all relations with Great Britain and France, but in the post-imperial era many emerging nations retained some of their cultural and economic ties with them. The profusion of native languages in India, Southeast Asia, and Africa practically forced the new governments to use English or French in administration and education. They have also retained many of the legal and judicial practices of their ex-masters and they still accept economic and technical assistance from them. France has continued to admit workers from Africa, and Great Britain to admit workers from Pakistan, India, and the West Indies. This policy had the unfortunate effect of transplanting racism from the lost colonies to Marseilles and Birmingham.

Although the Suez Crisis marked the end of British and French imperialism in the Middle East, the questions of the Canal and of Israel's relations with her Arab neighbors brought a new crisis to that area beginning in 1967. From the Arab point of view the Israelis represented a European occupation of their territory, even though more than one-third of the Jews in Israel were refugees from other Arab countries, which had expelled them because of Israel's participation in the Anglo-French invasion of Egypt in 1956. Indeed, these Jewish refugees from North Africa, Yemen, and Iraq almost equaled in numbers the one million Arab refugees who had fled from that part of Palestine out of which the United Nations had sanctioned the creation of the state of Israel in 1948. Israel's neighbors, particularly Egypt, Jordan, and Syria, took up the cause of these Palestinian Arab refugees and refused to accept the very existence of Israel. Then, in the mid-1960's, the Soviet Union tried to foster its own imperialistic aims in the Middle East by siding with the Arabs against Israel and by arming the Egyptians. In the spring of 1967 Egypt, which had closed the Suez Canal to Israeli shipping in 1956, threatened to close off the Gulf of Aqaba, which the Israelis had been using as an alternative route. With war obviously imminent, Israel took the initiative and launched an offensive against her Arab neighbors.

The "Six Day War," in early June 1967, was a humiliating defeat for Israel's Arab enemies. Israel's armed forces destroyed their Soviet planes and tanks on the ground and occupied the right bank of the Suez Canal, Jordanian territory up to the Jordan River, and the Syrian highlands within thirty miles of Damascus. This military tour de force was carried out with "European" precision and dispatch; indeed, Moshe Dayan, Israel's commander in chief, reminded everybody—ironically—of a Prussian general. More Palestinian Arabs were now refugees or forced to live under Israeli rule, and by 1969 some of them formed a Liberation Front and began to use terrorist

*See pp. 812-813

tactics against Israeli installations. At the time of this writing the situation in the Middle East remained explosive, with neither side showing any willingness to compromise and with the Big Four (United States, Soviet Union, Great Britain, and France) engaging in apparently fruitless efforts to settle the dispute.

: : :

Just as the Second World War made the liberal states of Western Europe dependent on the United States for their economic recovery and military survival, it also hastened the end of their colonial empires. They had apparently eliminated one variety of nationalism from their own midst and then been forced to retreat before other forms of it overseas. By the 1960's, the masses of Asia and Africa had achieved their formal independence, and, one by one, Western-built strategic installations had also been seized or threatened by the aggressively nationalist governments on these continents. Even long-entrenched European settlements in South Africa were no longer safe from domination by the non-European natives. Ironically, the United States, the first overseas country in history to achieve its independence from Europe, found itself accused of colonialism by native nationalists in Asia and Africa as well as in Latin America and became bogged down in a demoralizing war in South Vietnam.

As long as the "Cold War" seemed limited to the Soviet and NATO blocs, each side tried to gain the political and military cooperation of the new revolutionary-nationalist regimes overseas. Sometimes these two blocs used the promise of economic aid, sometimes direct intervention. Although each side had its failures, the Communist nations seemed to have the advantage over the West in extending their influence over the newly independent nations, but this situation is neither permanent nor hopeless for the West. Wherever the leaders of the new nations are true nationalists—and not mere tools of some outside power—there is a strong movement for developing their own native traditions. By the late 1960's, the Soviet Union clearly was losing whatever influence it had ever had in the "Third World", and the United States, although it maintained a watchful eye over its traditional preserve in Latin America, seemed increasingly resolved to avoid "more Vietnams." Furthermore, as in Europe in the past, nationalist and imperialist aspirations are already leading to power struggles within the so-called nonaligned bloc. The student of European history has learned that nations will fight, negotiate, or unite when it suits the interests they ascribe to themselves, Ideology is not all.

The decline of "Cold War" tensions made the nightmare of a nuclear holocaust somewhat less compelling. This nightmare haunted the popular imagination during the 1950's and reached its climax in 1962, at the time of the Cuban missile crisis, when the Soviet Union and the United States seemed on the brink of warfare over the installation of Russian missiles on Cuban soil. The effects of this crisis on Soviet domestic politics will be mentioned in the next chapter. Here, all we need to note is that the withdrawal of the Russian missiles was followed in 1963 by the signing of a treaty banning nuclear weapons tests in the atmosphere. In 1968, the Soviet Union and the United States sponsored a treaty banning the spread of nuclear weapons to countries that did not already possess them. Although both powers continued to build up their nuclear weapons systems, they virtually ceased to threaten one another with actually using them. The emergence of an anti-Soviet China as a major power with a nuclear capacity altered the assumptions of the "Cold War" by showing the world Communism was obviously not a monolithic force. In fact, in 1969, the Chinese began to demand that the Russians return some of the far eastern territories taken from them in tsarist times, and a series of border clashes ensued. No one seriously believed that the Russians or the Chinese would use nuclear weapons over this matter and certainly not over their rivalry for leadership of world Communism. Meanwhile, the easing of "Cold War" tensions in Europe prompted the European allies of the United States and the Soviet Union to continue reasserting their own independence of action. They, too, wanted to establish their relations with each other and with the rest of the world on a new, more peaceful, basis.

In past centuries Western Europeans had brought a good part of the rest of the world under their political control and cultural influence; today the forces that made this possible have spread all over the globe. Men of all races now control governments, armies, and business corporations; hold press conferences; compose symphonies; cure diseases; and operate nuclear reactors. As they come to deal with their former masters as equals, and as both Europeans and Americans extend their growing affluence to all members of their own societies, we may begin to take a new pride in the role of the West in the progress of all mankind.

## SUGGESTED READINGS


Einaudi, Mario, and Jean-Marie Domenach and Aldo Garosci, *Communism in Western Europe.* Ithaca, N.Y.: Cornell Univ. Press, 1951.

A good survey of Communist activities in France and Italy in the immediate postwar period.

Seton-Watson, Hugh, *The East European Revolution.* 3rd ed. New York: Frederick A. Praeger, 1956*

Especially good on the "Communization" and "satellization" of Eastern Europe.

There is no adequate survey of international relations during the Cold War period, and most of the specialized studies go out of date very fast. The following are useful:

Beloff, Max, *The United States and the Unity of Europe.* New York: Vintage, 1966.*

Kissinger, Henry A., *Troubled Partnership: A Re-Appraisal of the Atlantic Alliance.* New York: Doubleday-Anchor, 1967.*

McLellan, David S., Cold War in Transition. New York: Macmillan, n.d.,*

Emerson, Rupert, *From Empire to Nation: The Rise to Self-Assertion of Asian and African Peoples.* Cambridge, Mass.: Harvard Univ. Press, 1962.

A thoughtful, topical approach.

Latourette, K. S., *A History of Modern China.* Baltimore: Penguin Books, 1954. Pelican,* A fine short history by a major authority.

Barnett, A. D., *Communist China and Asia.* New York: Vintage, n.d.*

Stresses international relations.

Moraes, Frank, *Jawaharlal Nehru, a Biography.* New York: The Macmillan Co. 1956. The best study to date of India's foremost political leader.

Cameron, James, *The African Revolution.* New York: Random House, 1961.

Popular and authoritative.

Hatch, John, *A History of Postwar Africa.* New York: F. Praeger, n.d.*

A good summary.

Du Bois, W. E. B., *The World and Africa: An Inquiry into the Part Which Africa Has Played in World History.* Rev. ed. New York: International Publishers Co., 1965.*

Presents ideas and historical materials not readily accessible elsewhere, but is somewhat slanted in its interpretation.

Schmitt, Hans, *The Path to European Union: From the Marshall Plan to the Common Market.* Baton Rouge, La.: Louisiana State Univ. Press, 1962.

This and the following work are two fine examples of the many books on European economic cooperation.

Mayne, Richard, *The Community of Europe.* New York: W. W. Norton, 1962.*

CHAPTER XXII

# EUROPEAN CIVILIZATION IN A TECHNOLOGICAL AGE

The overwhelming fact of modern civilization is the extension of ever more efficient techniques to all domains of life. Techniques are not restricted to machine technology. Any standardized means of attaining a predetermined end is a technique. There are economic techniques, political techniques, military techniques, and techniques for manipulating human beings in education, work, counselling, propaganda, public relations, sport, entertainment, and medicine. As techniques become more elaborate, pervasive, and self-perpetuating, they tend to suppress the human ends they were devised to achieve and to become ends in themselves. Anxiety concerning the dehumanizing effects of our technological age has been felt most strongly in those parts of the world that became modern the earliest and the most gradually: Western Europe and, to a lesser extent, the United States. Yet, even in these areas, most people are fascinated by successful techniques in everything from football and heart transplants to group therapy and public opinion polls. In more recently modernized countries, like the Soviet Union, technology tends to be viewed as almost sacred.

It is difficult to imagine how a mass society could be organized on a nontechnical basis. No one willed that growing masses of human beings be integrated into ever larger communities; this development was the result of improved techniques in food production, medicine, communication, warfare, and government. Nor did anyone will that techniques be extended to all domains of life; once begun, the process became self-generating. The only way to limit the undesirable consequences of one technique is with still another technique: air pollution control for incinerators, government arbitration for prolonged strikes, improved police methods for organized crime. Even if all the political leaders, generals, bureaucrats, and technical experts in the world could be overthrown, they would have to be replaced by new ones capable of using similar techniques. Otherwise, the richest nations would immediately plunge into chaos and the poorest ones would quickly starve to death.

Not only does technique know no ideology but modern economic systems are no longer dependent solely on their heritage of physical resources. The rapid recovery of those countries most devastated by the Second World War—Germany, the USSR, and Japan—was inevitable because their economic systems carried within themselves the seeds of their own resurgence. Their capacity for producing material things was based on their knowledge of the techniques for sustained growth. This knowledge, plus the survival of some machine tools under the rubble, allowed them to surpass prewar production figures within less than ten years and to move forward steadily ever since. Already in the late 1940's, France adopted the "socialist" technique of planning; in the mid-1960's, the USSR introduced the "capitalist" technique of a free market for some consumer goods.

## WESTERN EUROPE

The most striking feature of Western Europe in recent years has been the almost universal desire for economic advancement, both collective and individual. Stimulated by the problems of postwar recovery, this desire soon became self-sustaining, creating an unprecedented openness to new ideas like managerial efficiency, state planning, and mass consumption. In the 1950s the application of some or all of these ideas brought a wave of growth and affluence to most of the already industrialized societies of Western Europe; by the 1960s it was spreading to Austria, Spain, Portugal, and Greece. Contrasts between advanced and backward areas remain, but the inhabitants of the latter are less resigned to their lot than in the past.

One of the most dramatic consequences of Europe's rapid economic growth since the Second World War has been a widespread desertion of the countryside. In 1945, French farmers still constituted a third of the working population; by the early 1960's this figure had declined to 20 per cent and by 1970 to less than 15 per cent. Between the early 1960's and 1970, the percentage of farmers declined from 14 per cent to less than 10 per cent in West Germany, from 29 per cent to 21 per cent in Italy, from 12 per cent to 8 per cent in Switzerland, and from 42 per cent to 30 per cent in Spain. By the end of the 1960's, French farmers were leaving their small, inefficient holdings at the rate of 280,000 a year; Italians were moving to the cities at the rate of 360,000 a year. Spanish agricultural workers were abandoning agricultural labor for new jobs in Madrid and Barcelona or even Bordeaux and Düsseldorf.

Economic growth has been accompanied by social and political changes. Although ruling groups still exist, they are recruited increasingly from the upper middle class of outstanding professional people, higher civil servants, independent businessmen with large enterprises, and better-paid executives. Furthermore, there have been more opportunities for talented and ambitious individuals to rise into these middle ranks of the power structure. Higher wages and an abundance of mass-produced consumer goods have permitted many skilled workers and employees to attain a bourgeois level of material comfort, if not social status. This development, along with the growth of the welfare state, has lessened traditional class antagonisms.

Political ideologies based on class interest began to decline by the beginning of the 1950s as the general desire for economic growth and government efficiency spread. This decline was then reinforced by economic improvement and increased social mobility. On the other hand, the ascendancy of bureaucrats and other kinds of "organization men" in all areas of modern life has reinforced a trend toward moderate conservatism and, in certain nations, authoritarianism in politics.

Bigness breeds bureaucrats. The more people and things there are to be "handled" in a given situation, the more elaborate the bureaucratic structure doing the "handling" becomes. This "law" applies to big business, big unions, big education, and, most of all, big government. Bureaucracies that carry out the decisions of governments are not new; what is new is the growing tendency of high-level bureaucrats to take over the decision-making process itself. They do this partly because they feel that they alone understand the organizational means by which particular decisions can be executed and partly because the technical aspects of such matters as public finance, defense, and economic planning are too complex for the ordinary legislator to understand. He will haggle over the cost of a parking lot for government employees, but he will allow fantastically expensive military proposals by technically trained bureaucrats to pass with a minimum of discussion.

The intensity of all these developments has varied from country to country. At the end of the war, the more complete the breakdown in social continuity, the greater the challenge it posed to the nation involved. Thus, in the 1950's, economic growth was most extensive in West Germany, followed by Italy, France, and Great Britain.* West Germany made the fewest advances toward the welfare state, Great Britain the most. Since 1958 France has gone the furthest in downgrading the power and prestige of parliament. The relative eclipse of parliamentary democracy has been due not only to bureaucratization and to the "domestication" of the Leftist parties but also the tendency of individual Europeans to give increasing attention to private over public affairs. Yet they can still be aroused when the occasion demands, and democracy in its broadest sense is stronger than ever.

### Great Britain

The Second World War and its aftermath brought profound changes in British life. Having played as great a role during the war as the United States and the Soviet Union, Great Britain soon had to accept both the loss of her overseas empire and the reduction of her international status to that of a second-rate power. These were hard blows for patriots of all classes, and the delayed reaction against them may partially explain the renewed popularity of the Conservatives, the party of power and empire, in the 1950s; even the "angry young men" who riduculed the old-fashioned patriotism fostered by the "establishment" were not entirely unmoved by feelings of hurt national pride. For most Britishers, however, economic and social considerations came first. As we have seen, in July 1945 they had shown their determination to preserve the wartime principle of "fair shares for all" by voting the Labour Party into power. In its effort to fulfill this mandate the government of Clement Attlee, which remained in office until 1951, made Great Britain a welfare state with socialist overtones.

Labour's goal – to insure the security and welfare of all citizens "from the cradle to the grave" – was embodied in a legislative program that was pushed through Parliament in two years. The National Insurance Bill consolidated existing schemes of social insurance and extended them to a larger section of the population: the National Health Service Bill made free medical services available to everyone. Henceforth the state paid for everything from maternity benefits to old age pensions, from eyeglasses to false teeth. Educational facilities were expanded, and the government made university scholarships available to thousands of talented young people from all social classes. There was also an integrated program for new housing and for the rehabilitation of depressed areas.

But Labour instituted no overall plan for a socialist economy. Its frankly socialist reforms were limited to a steeply graduated income tax and the nationalization of certain key industries. The new tax scale was partly designed to redistribute the nation's wealth but also to provide additional revenue for increased social services and subsidies to enterprises facing foreign competition, especially in air and sea transport, or, like the BBC, unable to pay their way at home. The nationalizations were restricted to the railroads, road transport, and inland waterways, the gas and electricity supply industries, the

*Between 1948 and 1958 the gross national product increased in Great Britain by 26 per cent, in France by 73 per cent, in West Germany by 197 per cent, in Italy by 73 per cent. Between 1958 and 1963 the increase in Great Britain was 14 per cent, France 29 per cent, West Germany 35 per cent, Italy 59 per cent. During this same period the poor showing (15 per cent) of Belgium and Luxembourg lowered the average for the EEC to 26.5 per cent, which was still above the 22.5 per cent of the United States; in industrial production alone the figures were EEC 47.7 per cent, Great Britain 16 per cent, the United States 33.5 per cent.

coal mines, and the Bank of England.* After compensating the former stockholders, the government reorganized these industries into autonomous public corporations, often under the same managers as before. Technically under public ownership, these corporations (like the Transit Authorities in many American cities) had their own budgets and their own powers to deal with labor, the consumers, and even the government itself. Although 80 per cent of the total British capital has remained in private hands, the nationalized industries together have provided almost half of the new investment capital. Still, unlike the Soviet Union or even France (which made no pretense of establishing socialism), Great Britain under Labour rule shied away from any kind of systematic planning for economic growth.

On several occasions both the Labour and Conservative governments have had to restrict economic expansion because of difficulties in the nation's balance of payments. These difficulties—summed up in the slogan "Export or Die"—have been caused by a combination of factors. The British trade-unions, which are among the most powerful in the world, have succeeded in raising wages and preventing technological changes that might threaten full employment. In doing so, however, they have made some British manufactured goods, especially ships and automobiles, too expensive to compete abroad. The need to maintain the pound's stability, basically precarious because the pound performs an international function disproportionate to the present dimensions of the British economy, has forced the government to institute periods of "austerity" in order to prevent the outflow of its gold reserves. Some of Britain's balance of payments difficulties may also be due to the inefficiency of the Treasury, which unlike that of France, Italy, or the United States, was run until recently by educated amateurs rather than experts.

The relative smallness of Great Britain's postwar economic gains can also be partly explained by the fact that she had more to start with. In 1945 her level of production was considerably higher than that of any continental country, and her industrial and transportation facilities had suffered far less wartime damage than those of France, Italy, and especially Germany. Throughout the 1950s she somehow managed to import the raw materials essential to her industry and the food and consumer goods essential to her rising standard of living, though in the early 1960s it was obvious that her shortage of gold and foreign currency would not allow this situation to last indefinitely.

Class distinctions have also remained more persistent in Great Britain than in most highly industrialized countries, despite growing affluence and the reforms of the first postwar Labour government. The general rise in the real income of the blue-collar and white-collar workers has narrowed the gap between the middle and lower classes; the extension of opportunities for higher education has raised the level of aspiration of the masses. But, as in the past, the "proper" social background has been vital for entry into prestige professions like the higher civil service, banking, and the military, ecclesiastical, judicial, and educational hierarchies. Beginning in the early 1950s a number of talented young writers openly criticized the "establishment" for this social injustice: Kingsley Amis did this in his novel *Lucky Jim*, John Braine in his novel *Room at the Top*, and John Osborne in his play *Look Back in Anger*. By the early 1960s, however, it was becoming clear that the "establishment" lacked the cohesiveness these men attributed to it—that it was a chain of autonomous overlapping circles rather than one ruling circle. Moreover, a ruthless new group of "American-style" entrepreneurs was increasing its power in commerce and industry, while the authority of the older ruling circles was being diffused as a result of bureaucratization and a growing sense of lack of purpose. Traditional social and cultural values persist among men in high official places, but

*In 1949, when the government tried to nationalize the iron and steel industries, the Conservatives in the House of Lords raised so many objections that Attlee and his colleagues modified the Parliament Act of 1911 by reducing the remaining powers of the upper house to a one-year suspensive veto. Although the nationalization itself went into effect in 1951, the Conservative government that took office in that year quickly nullified it.

*English pop music festival*

the Labour Party, which returned to office in October 1964 after thirteen years, promised to weaken further the power of these men.

The performance of the Labour government during the rest of the 1960's belied the hopes of its early supporters on several counts. Although the traditional social and cultural values declined and the spread of higher education had a democratizing effect, the government of Harold Wilson had to face unrest from new quarters. Many lower- and lower-middle class whites became increasingly racist in their resentment toward the three quarters of a million "colored" workers in their midst from the West Indies, India, and Pakistan. On the other hand, middle-class liberals and radicals condemned the government for publicly condoning the Vietnam War. British workers disregarded Wilson's pleas for holding down demands for wage increases in the interest of keeping the prices of British' industrial goods competitive at home and abroad. The devaluation of the pound in 1967 was partly a legacy of an earlier government, but the subsequent rise in prices brought new wage demands. Economic reasons pushed the leaders of the Labour Party reluctantly toward joining the Common Market, only to be rebuffed by De Gaulle. Wilson's government had little room for maneuver, and its lack of decisiveness brought a continuing decline in its popularity even within the ranks of the trade-union movement, whose interests it had to balance with those of the country as a whole. In June 1970 the Conservatives were voted back into power with Edward Heath as the new prime minister.

Despite her economic and social limitations, Great Britain has made a remarkably satisfactory adjustment to changing conditions in the last twenty-five years. Her former colonial officials and the upper class from which most of them came have "retreated in good order." She has taken diplomatic rebuffs like the United Nations condemnation of her invasion of Egypt and De Gaulle's veto of her entry into the Common Market with her traditional "stiff upper lip." A continual wave of building is beginning to change the face of her cities, and her people are better fed and better clothed than ever before. Finally, democracy has been extended from politics to economic and social welfare.

## France

As in earlier times, France has pushed to extremes tendencies that have been general but less pronounced in other European countries. She has moved from a kind of Peoples' Democracy at the end of the war through the parliamentary coalitions of 1948–1958—coalitions attacked by mass movements on the extremes of both Left and Right—to the quasi-monarchical rule of President de Gaulle and, since 1969, the less authoritarian presidency of Georges Pompidou. She has achieved one of the highest rates of economic growth in Europe in the face of the most massive resistance to change. She has abandoned class hatred for a wholly unprecedented "live-and-let-live" attitude. And, as we have already seen, her colonial and foreign policies have been the most dramatic expressions of national pride reacting against declining power.

As the Fourth Republic came to resemble the Third, more and more Frenchmen turned against it. Beginning in the late 1940s they voted for both antigovernment parties of the Right and Communists. With almost half the deputies refusing to participate in parliamentary coalitions, the ministerial instability that had plagued the Third Republic returned with a vengeance. Since the government parties—Independents, Radicals, Socialists, and Christian Democrats (MRP)—were divided among themselves, they had even greater difficulty than their predecessors in maintaining their shaky coalitions. In fact, *any* positive policy risked the withdrawal of one or more of the parties. Hence, in the early 1950s, the "immobilism" of the government became increasingly intolerable.

Much as Frenchmen wanted the state to let them alone as individuals, as members of pressure groups they wanted it to support their interests. The labor unions preferred strikes to lobbying, and by 1953 they had forced the government to institute a sliding wage scale geared to the cost-of-living index. Other groups, however, lobbied diligently. Together the sugar beet and alcohol lobbies forced the government to continue subsidizing their market prices by buying up excess sugar and storing it after it had been distilled. (In 1954 the government had such a large stock of alcohol that it even considered mixing some of it with automobile fuel, an idea that was immediately opposed by the gasoline lobby.) The state's subsidies to agriculture and certain industries were a constant drain on its already inadequate revenue; but an extremely vocal antitax lobby delayed any reform in the tax structure. Meanwhile, the National Committee of French Employers, representing Big Business, concentrated its pressure on the higher bureaucrats, whose power grew as that of the government declined.

Between June 1954 and February 1955 Prime Minister Pierre Mendès-France tried to break the deadlock between the government and the pressure groups. He succeeded in forcing the collection of taxes from delinquent shopkeepers and farmers, but he did not remain in office long enough to carry through his other proposals for reform. One of these, a campaign to persuade Frenchmen to drink milk instead of wine, was designed to combat widespread alcoholism; it merely antagonized the wine producers without having any visible effect on the consumers. Mendès-France also wanted to reduce the nation's overseas commitments, especially by granting independence to Morocco and Tunisia. During the parliamentary debate on Tunisian independence the colonial lobby combined with the alcohol lobby to force him out of office.

After the fall of Mendès-France the hostility of the colonists and the army in North Africa toward the Fourth Republic reached its climax. Mendès-France himself had got France out of Indochina in July 1954, and in 1956 his successors recognized the independence of Morocco and Tunisia. The million settlers in Algeria feared that they might be abandoned next, and the military leaders in charge of the "pacification" of that war-torn country were determined to prevent another "betrayal" by the "decadent" politicians. Finally, on May 13, 1958, a European mob captured the government buildings in Algiers and, backed by some leading generals, set up a "committee of public safety" that demanded the overthrow of the government in Paris.

General de Gaulle himself had not participated in any of the plots that helped bring him back to power. For over a decade he had preached the need for a strong presidential form of government, but he had insisted that the change should be made legally. Now, in the last weeks of May 1958, the rebellious generals in Algiers were planning to invade France and install a military dictatorship of their own. On June 1, De Gaulle temporarily thwarted this plan by accepting the premiership from Parliament, with the proviso that he would also be allowed to frame a new constitution. A few days later he went to Algiers and, raising his arms to the mob that had invoked his name, he said: "I have understood you!"

De Gaulle had understood *them*, but they had not understood *him*. At first he too hoped to keep Algeria French, but more important to him was his desire for France herself to be strong. In September 1958 he submitted the Constitution of the Fifth Republic, designed according to his specifications, to a plebiscite. With the situation in Algiers still tense, the French people accepted the new constitution —that is, the continued rule of De Gaulle —by a majority of 80 per cent. De Gaulle now had his strong presidency, and he soon recognized the need to "disengage" France from Algeria. In January 1960 the European settlers rose up against him; in April 1961 the generals did the same. De Gaulle repressed these last-ditch rebellions against the inevitable with his usual firmness and in April 1962 signed the agreement that turned Algeria over to the FLN nationalists.

The army's part in these rebellions was not unique. Powerful military supporters of "victory no matter what the cost" have spoken out, in other Western countries, including the United States. The section of the French army that rebelled wanted to "purify" the political and social system in France in the same way it had tried to remold Algerian society: through a benevolent military dictatorship. De Gaulle saved France from this fate, and though people still called him "General," he reshaped the army to prevent it from ever threatening the civilian regime again.

But the price of De Gaulle's achievement has been high. The Fifth Republic has reduced the functions of Parliament and the traditional parties in political life. Until his retirement in April 1969 De Gaulle's radio and television speeches took over Parliament's function as a transmission-belt of political information from the state bureaucracy to the people; the press, the public opinion polls, and the plebicite have taken over its function of informing the government of the national mood. As in other Western democracies, the bureaucrats, through the cabinet, have increasingly initiated legislation, which the legislators themselves may amend but rarely reject outright. In France, however, even under De Gaulle's successors, Parliament and the political parties have had less control over executive action than elsewhere.

The Fifth Republic is more stable than the Fourth, but in many ways it has merely consolidated the gains made under its predecessor. The Fourth Republic helped to stimulate France's extraordinary growth; between 1947 and 1953 the Monnet Plan had channeled nearly 40 billion dollars into the modernization and requipment of the nation's industrial plant. This was done by technical experts rather than politicians, but Parliament had approved the Plan in principle. Mendès-France initiated a stronger fiscal policy and the reduction of government subsidies, thus helping to weed out marginal enterprises and restore competition. The Common Market, atomic research, and "decolonization" all date back to the Fourth Republic. It was also under that regime that French women got the vote and lost their traditional inferiority in property rights, professional opportunities, and wages. Neither the Fourth nor Fifth Republic has eliminated the housing shortage, class distinctions, or many of the inadequacies of the educational system. But the "revolt of the masses" is an accomplished fact; every Frenchman now wants a modern standard of living and is less and less satisfied with the old ways of doing things. This dissatisfaction became dramatically evident in the spring of 1968, when 150,000 students and 10 million workers brought the life of the country to a standstill for more than three weeks (see p. 800.)

### West Germany

Of all the peoples of Europe the Germans had the most to forget and the furthest to rise. It was easier for them to forget their own follies under the Nazi regime than the final disaster to which Hitler had led them: the physical ruins, the military occupation, and the likelihood of permanent national partition were constant reminders. Yet under the occupation and the stable regime of Konrad Adenauer, West Germany rebuilt her economy to the strongest point in its history. This "economic miracle" owed most to the efforts of the German people themselves, but it was also stimulated by the "Cold War," which brought an equally extraordinary change in West Germany's status from foe to friend.

The "German miracle" began when the Western Allies changed their policy of holding their occupation zones down to building them up. In 1948 Marshall Plan aid was instituted; a year later the three Western powers accelerated the transfer of political authority from their military government to the new Federal Republic, with its capital at Bonn. The new constitution followed that of the Weimar Republic with three major exceptions: it gave the individual states (*Länder*) a greater voice; it deprived the President of the Republic of emergency powers; it assured the chancellor a more stable tenure of office through an ingenious device that permitted a vote of "no confidence" only when the opposition had already agreed on a candidate for the succession. Actually, Konrad Adenauer (1876–1967), a former mayor of Cologne, who had stayed aloof from the Nazis, remained chancellor until 1963. Under the laissez-faire policy of his economic minister, Ludwig Erhard, the government did not try to stimulate production by public investments. Instead, it channeled private capital into productive enterprises and housing through tax exemptions and by maintaining a strong currency. The Korean War boom also stimulated the revival of the West German economy by raising the demand for its exports of machinery and other capital equipment. Another stimulus was the fact that, unlike Great Britain and France, West Germany did not have to maintain an expensive military establishment.

From the start the West Germans had other advantages too. The amount of war damage turned out to be less than originally estimated; beneath the rubble many machine tools were still intact or capable of repair. With the help of its well-trained managers, engineers, and technicians the country quickly restored its prewar industrial structure. The workers accepted low wages and long hours and, unlike those in Great Britain and France, they launched no crippling strikes; overtime earnings were tax exempt and consumer goods were more abundant than at any time since 1939. The government also encouraged large profits for private businessmen if these were reinvested. All people had the built-in incentives of overcoming the consequences of a lost war, of recovering their material possessions, and of reestablishing their personal status.

Social progress has lagged behind economic progress. The Federal Republic has not yet integrated the mass of wage earners into the national society, despite having improved their material lot. Organized labor has remained weak and has had no real representation in the government, even though the Socialists increased their representation in Parliament and, between late 1966 and late 1969, became part of a Grand Coalition government with the Christian Democrats. The social structure has retained more of its traditional rigidity than in other Western countries, and conservative values are reinforced by the education system and the churches.

In West Germany the ruling groups are quite different from the traditional British "establishment." In Britain a member of the established elite could follow a career leading him successively from a professorial chair to the directorship of an investment trust, a brigadier general's commission, or a cabinet position, and finally to the post of ambassador or

*West Germany Today*

director-general of the BBC. Such a career would be unthinkable in West Germany, where each of these "estates" remains exclusive and defends its own standards and interests against competing and often hostile groups. Even though the traditional Junker aristocracy has lost its power and influence, the members of Germany's segmented ruling groups remain separated from each other, as well as from the mass of the ruled, by great social distance.

But man does not live by bread—or status—alone. The British and the French have seen their traditional cultures modified by industrialization, the "revolt of the masses," and declining world power, without abandoning their basic values completely; in other words, there has been some continuity in their recent history. In contrast, since 1918 the Germans have twice been reduced from mastery of Europe to abject defeat, as well as having experienced a paralyzing depression, the Nazi Revolution, and the still unresolved burden of guilt for the massacre of the Jews.

Since the Second World War the West Germans have exhibited a high degree of moral and cultural apathy. Perhaps their capacity for enthusiasm had been drained to the limits by Nazism. In any case, the Nazi period has been ignored as far as possible. Only in 1960s were schoolchildren first taught some of the evils of Hitler's regime. Rolf Hochhuth's play *The Deputy* (1962) attacked the silence of Pope Pius XII and the German Catholic hierarchy toward Nazi persecution, but it did not condemn the German people. Günter Grass, on the other hand, in novels like *The Tin Drum* and *The Dog Years*, openly ridiculed the actions of his countrymen over the past three decades. In *Local Anaesthetic* (New York: Harcourt, Brace & World, 1970, p. 186) Grass has a seventeen-year-old student watching overdressed women eating rich cakes in a café say: "Freedom of choice and second helpings. That's what they mean by democracy." Most West Germans seemed to be trying to substitute exaggerated materialism for cultural continuity and moral purpose. Those who did seek a meaningful moral and cultural orientation looked to the values of the pre-1914 era—when defeat and genocide were still in the future.

During most of the 1960's the West Germans, like most Europeans, seemed apathetic politically. Reunification was a *national* issue; it remained outside the realm of politics and did not generate much spontaneous enthusiasm. A major stir occurred over the arbitrary arrest in 1962 of an editor of the *Spiegel* (West Germany's counterpart to *Time* magazine) for allegedly publishing military secrets. Public indignation over the *Spiegel* affair forced Adenauer to dismiss its instigator, Defense Minister Franz Joseph Strauss, from his cabinet and seriously damaged his own public image. Although Adenauer himself remained in power for another year, German opinion had expressed its opposition to any overt threat to the democratic liberties guaranteed by the 1949 constitution. From 1963 to 1966 Christian Democratic rule limped along under Chancellor Ludwig Erhard until it was succeeded by the Grand Coalition, with the ex-Nazi Kurt-Georg Kiesinger as its Christian Democratic chancellor and the anti-Nazi Willy Brandt as its Socialist foreign secretary. With the Socialists arguing that "the classic division between Left and Right is no longer valid in the country," the government had virtually no legal opposition, except for a small group of Free Democrats (liberals) and the budding National Democratic Party (see p. 799) on the extreme Right. Under these circumstances, the radical Left-wing student group, the SDS (*Sozialistische Deutsche Studentenbund*), violently denounced the Socialist Party and began the now familiar campaign of revolutionary gestures aimed at "das Establishment." These students did not relent even after the Socialists became the ruling party in October 1969, with Willy Brandt as chancellor.

### Italy

In the twentieth century Italy's principal dilemma has been to find a regime that would bridge the differences between rich and poor, Catholics and anticlericals, and north and south, and at the same time provide the dynamic leadership necessary to bring the economy and society up to the level of France, Germany, or Britain. It has yet to find one. In 1922 it was the failure of the liberal regime and leaders like Giolitti which had prompted many Italians to turn to Mussolini. Although Mussolini brought Church and state into harmony with the Lateran Treaty of 1929, Italy's other problems remained unsolved. After the nation's defeat and disgrace of 1943 the resistance movement tried to reform society and create a broadly based regime, but, as in France, the experiment in Peoples' Democracy ended in 1947.

Alcide de Gasperi emerged from the Peoples' Democracy period at the head of the Christian Democratic Party; he remained prime minister until his death in 1953, and his party has controlled the government without interruption ever since. Because of its growing conservatism it was unable to integrate the lower classes into the national society, despite a rising standard of living. Moreover, the Christian Democrats themselves came to resemble the splintered parties of the Fourth Republic in France, and Italian politics in general has followed the pattern of that unfortunate regime. In the mid-1950s the Christian Democrats tried to rule through coalitions with parties further to the Right; by the early 1960s the Left wing within the party sought an alliance with the Socialists. In the election of 1963, however, the "opening to the Left" did not prevent the Communists from gaining 25 per cent of the vote, an increase of 3 per cent over the result of the preceding election.

This Communist showing at the polls is the result of several factors: the increase in urbanization, which has turned "immigrants" from the rural south into Communist voters in Milan and Turin; the achievements of the Communists in local administration, where they have been strong since resistance days; and the astuteness of their national leader, Palmiro Togliatti, who died in 1964. Togliatti was able to appeal to a wide variety of people—including many who voted Communist out of protest or even to preserve the status quo. He quickly understood that a large number of these voters did not really want to see the regime overthrown, and his party has long abandoned its efforts to sabotage economic growth. Thus, as in France, the Communist leaders seem to be transforming their party into a kind of legal pressure group on the extreme Left.

The idea of voting Communist to maintain the status quo may seem very odd to North Americans; what is perhaps even odder is the idea that the Italian status quo of the last twenty years has seemed worth preserving. Yet, in the absence of decisive national government or a sense of national purpose, Italy's economy has undergone phenomenal expansion. Since 1953 her growth rate has been the highest in Europe. The fact that she started from a lower base, and hence would naturally rise more dramatically, does not nullify her achievement; she has been able to hold her own in the Common Market and to develop a thriving export trade in calculating machines, automobiles, and other products. Italy has no formal economic planning comparable to that of France. Until recently the bureaucrats, especially those in the Bank of Italy, have made most of the economic decisions in the absence of effective governments. Nevertheless, as in Great Britain, widespread governmental ownership of industry, banking, and transportation involves the state in piecemeal planning of the nation's economy. In the underdeveloped south extraordinary efforts at growth have been aided by the discovery of natural gas and oil, and despite numerous handicaps the southern third of the country shows signs of moving toward a greater degree of industrialization.

Since the "opening to the Left" in 1963, Italy, like West Germany after 1966, has been ruled by a coalition of Christian Democrats and Socialists, with the former as the senior partners. But, unlike West Germany, the Left in Italy includes a large Communist Party, which opposes the coalition. As a result of this opposition and of the divisions within the ruling parties, the Italian coalition government has had far less support among the people, especially the workers, than its West German counterpart. Italy has been by far the most strike-ridden country in Europe, and many of her strikes have been against government-controlled enterprises. This and other kinds of direct action have been common in a country where most people have been traditionally suspicious of overcentralized government and cynical toward their national leaders. They argue, somewhat unjustly, that the material gains of recent years have occurred in spite of the government rather than because of any initiative it has taken.

Italy, like most of Western Europe, has acquired the trappings of a modern, technological society. Faith in continued economic growth is almost universal, and as the actual rate of growth remains almost double that of the United States, the gap between per capita income in the most advanced countries in Europe and the United States continues to narrow. The following figures are for 1967: United Kingdom, $1910; West Germany, $2010; France, $2060; Switzerland, $2480; United States, $3159. Although there are proportionately more Americans than Europeans with a high average income, there is proportionately less poverty in the more advanced European countries; national income is most evenly distributed in the Scandinavian countries, where hard-core poverty has virtually disappeared. In many Western European countries technical and economic values now constitute effective standards of selection at all but the top managerial levels in the state and in private enterprise, thus creating greater social mobility for people who can meet these standards. Even so, few working-class children seek high-school and university education, which are among the most unevenly distributed "commodities" in Western Europe. Furthermore, the mechanism of progress and renewal is not entirely dependent upon internal conditions or even the Common Market. The future of Western Europe is still linked with that of the rest of the world by a network of cultural, political, and economic relationships that are more intricate than ever.

### The End of Ideology?

In the early 1960's many observers interpreted the growing apathy of most Europeans (and Americans) toward national politics as a sign of the "end of Ideology." This trend seemed to be reinforced by De Gaulle's downgrading of political activities in France, by the governing coalition of Christian Democrats and Socialists in Italy after 1963 and in West Germany after 1966, and by the declining appeal of the British Labour Party and the Scandinavian Socialist parties in the late 1960's. Even the large Communist parties in Italy and France seemed bent on playing down their revolutionary slogans and becoming respectable. Meanwhile, with economic prosperity and law and order well established, the parties of the extreme Right lost supporters almost everywhere. The most important of these parties, the *Nationaldemokratische Partei Deutschlands* (NPD) won a bare 10 per cent of the West German vote in the late 1960's. The prevailing materialism seemed to bring a growing indifference toward public affairs among all people except a minority of disenchanted youths.

The student protests of the late 1960's will be duscussed in the next section; here we are concerned with the question of whether or not the 1960's did indeed witness an "end of ideology." The answer must be yes, if by ideology one means a belief in the possibility of setting down blueprints and, through "social engineering," bringing about a new utopia of social harmony. Both the British and the continental Socialists were forced to abandon this belief by the responsibilities of power; most Communist leaders have clung to this belief as an article of faith, but their appeal to the masses is more against existing injustices than for any specific utopia. On the extreme Right, nationalism and even racism ("Keep Britain white.") are also defensive reactions rather than programs for a new order. Finally, as we shall see, the "New Left" among the students rejects all existing ideologies and leaves its utopia undefined. But the "end of ideology" in the traditional sense does not mean a lack of concern for the quality of life in a technological mass society.

## RECENT UPHEAVALS: THE CHALLENGE TO TECHNOCRACY AND BUREAUCRATIZATION

The upheaval of May-June 1968 in France made that country once again the barometer of new developments in European civilization. Beginning as a student revolt, it culminated in the biggest general strike in history. For three weeks, 10 million workers (out of a total population of 50 million) brought the nation's economic life to a standstill. Neither the trade-union leaders nor the Communist Party could control the strikers. The government of President De Gaulle itself seemed on the verge of collapse. Yet even this was not the ultimate goal of "the movement." A large percentage of young Frenchmen was saying "no" to the technocratic, bureaucratic society of the modern world. More specifically, the rebels were protesting against the efforts of the new managerial elite to condition them, manipulate them, and integrate them into this society. Although no other country experienced a general strike, students in Italy, Germany, Czechoslovakia, Yugoslavia, Japan, Mexico, and United States engaged in similar protests.

Many explanations have been given for the protest of the younger generation, especially students, against the existing society. One explanation views it as a craving for action and drama by youths no longer content to be mere consumers and spectators. This explanation blames the mass media for glorifying violent demonstrations and parents for permissiveness toward their children. According to another view, we are witnessing a political struggle of young people against the "power structure," which rules their lives without consulting them. This explanation has the merit of including the demands of oppressed and "colonized" minority groups for freedom and equality in many countries. One observer considers confrontation tactics on the domestic scene to be a reflection of the diplomatic "brinkmanship" of the "Cold War" a few years earlier. According to this explanation, domestic confrontations will increase as the danger of a major war recedes. All of these explanations assume the breakdown of the "moral consensus" in many countries and the failure of existing societies to integrate young people and minority groups into a meaningful new social and cultural order.

Although this assumption may be correct, we still need to know why the old consensus has broken down and why no new one has yet emerged.

Perhaps the old consensus was mainly a function of the national crises of the 1930's and 1940's—a willingness to work together against a common peril. Since the end of the Second World War, young men who had experienced it and the depression that preceded it brought these experiences with them as they became mature leaders in a world no longer plagued by depression or a major war. Hence, there is a generation gap between these leaders and young people who have never had a compelling reason to unite with the rest of their nation. Indeed, in

*Paris, May 1968*

1968, some extremist American students openly supported their nation's enemy in Vietnam, and extremist French students shouted "We are all German Jews" when President De Gaulle hounded one of their leaders who was. None of the earlier religious or national models appeals to these extremists any more, not even the Soviet Union, which they consider as bureaucratic and imperialistic as their own country.

Until some new national or world crisis forces a new moral consensus into being many young radicals in the West will probably continue to seek models for their ideal society in the less modern parts of the world. Many of the French students who rose up in 1968 had a vague vision of some kind of Communist utopia. Needless to say, neither Mao's China nor Castro's Cuba provided the kind of unstructured society, participatory democracy, and cultural freedom that these students desired. They simply idealized these real models to fulfill their own wishes, just as their Communist elders used the Soviet Union as their ideal model. To a radical some other country's revolution always looks better than the status quo at home. If the revolution is still going on, so much the better, as in the case of certain Latin American countries.* But the "New Left" among today's students in France and elsewhere is less concerned with importing foreign models than with destroying existing institutions at home. Thus far these students have rejected the very means by which Mao and Castro made their revolutions—namely, a strong, strictly disciplined organization.

Neither in France nor anywhere else did the students or workers develop an effective political organization for achieving their goals; in fact, their goals were not really the same. The young French workers who occupied their factories in May 1968 refused to have anything to do with the student rebels. They were not trying to "change society" but to gain a voice in managing their plants. The workers came from a lower social class than the students and viewed them as pampered bourgeois. Similar class differences divided most black militants from the white student radicals as much as race in the United States. Clearly, the new ruling elite in the modern countries of the western world is now technocratic rather than bourgeois. But class, race, and even language (as in Belgium and Canada) determine people's goals as much as hostitlity toward any "establishment."

Whatever their causes and whatever their goals, mass protests and confrontation politics ushered in a new era of instability and tension in the late 1960's. In Western Europe and North America

*The movement has already found a glamorous martyr in Ernesto Che Guevara, who was killed in 1967 in his effort to liberate Bolivia's peasants through guerrilla warfare.

growing affluence seemed to foster new forms of discontent and alienation. The historian cannot predict the future. Nevertheless, it is clear that the technocratic bureaucracies that rule modern societies have more power to quell revolutions than any despotic government in the past. They also know how to fragment the opposition and to adopt its propaganda slogans—such as "participatory democracy" and "community control"—for their own purposes better than earlier liberal regimes. Thus, it is unlikely that mass protests and confrontation politics will overthrow any ruling establishment in the foreseeable future. Instead, the mass media, which are always committed to the status quo, are likely to institutionalize them as familiar news items, like electoral politics, strikes, and football games.* Every society finds its own techniques for relieving tensions and keeping instability within controllable bounds.

In 1969 student unrest in Italy prompted the government of that country, along with that of France, to sponsor sweeping university reforms. In both countries the main emphasis of these reforms was on increasing participation by students and nontenured faculty members in decision making. Not only were the full professors to lose their "feudal" powers in their own bailiwicks and in formulating university policy but also they were to spend more time attending to their teaching duties. In addition, France's and Italy's large universities were to be broken up into autonomous units with a minimum of control by the ministry of education. The radical extremists who wanted to use the universities as a base to "change society" opposed these reforms from above, which were obviously designed to cut the ground out from under them. But it is difficult to understand how the majority of students and young faculty members could reject the opportunities for participation and control which these reforms offered them. By adapting themselves to the new demands for mass education the reformed French and Italian universities also hope to meet the new needs of a technological mass society for highly trained people capable of running such a society.

*Already in 1968 some American television networks were "staging" campus riots with artificial lighting and faked injuries.

Much of the recent student protest has been directed against two alleged evils of modern society: (1) the authoritarian ( or "bureaucratic") control, which decides what happens to people without consulting them or allowing them to participate in the decision-making process, and (2) the manipulative techniques that make individuals serve the needs of impersonal systems, especially, the economic system, or, more specifically, the "consumer society." The rebellious students believe that they are being conditioned—both in school and by the mass media—to become "organization men" and consumers—that modern society rewards conformity and penalizes individual self-expression.

The fact that traditional societies rewarded conformity and penalized individual self-expression to a far greater extent than modern society may be a small comfort; so may be the fact that totalitarian political regimes are worse in this respect than liberal regimes. History, after all, is not supposed to comfort us but to enlarge our understanding. The crucial question today is: Are things getting better or worse than they are now?

Many intelligent observers are extremely pessimistic; they feel that the manipulators of techniques are even able to integrate the very movements that challenge them into the dominant technical society. During the 1960's those movements included the Theater of the Absurd, a pornographic literature of revolt (à la William Burroughs), hippies, yippies, crazies, and other kinds of long-haired, unwashed romantic rebels. These movements were based on authentic impulses and valid feelings, and they did allow a few individuals to express themselves in uninhibited ways. But independently of the will or desire of these individuals, their movements vicariously satisfied the revolutionary and ecstatic impulses of millions of other people and, thus, integrated these impulses into the technical society. Television, popular magazines, and the world of fashion, constantly searching for new models and life styles, took over the outward forms of these movements and literally domesticated them for mass consumption—sometimes as objects of curiosity and sometimes as watered down imitations emptied of even symbolic meaning.

Rock music is a good example. Like earlier jazz, it originated among American blacks as a means of soothing their bitter longing for freedom by giving them the illusion of freedom through rhythm and sound. Then it was taken up by American whites and quickly spread to all the industrialized societies of the world—from France to Japan, from Czechoslovakia to Australia. By the late 1960's Rock music had become so completely domesticated that it was used in commercials to sell soap and automobiles. Some youthful militants recognized the hoax and took their revolt into the streets and onto university campuses. Then that form of revolt was domesticated through ritual battles with the police staged for the benefit of the "prime time" television audience.

Jacques Ellul, a brilliant French commentator on the allegedly inexorable effects of the manipulation of all human feelings, including the most intimate ones, says:

"With the final integration of the instinctive and the spiritual by means of these human techniques, the edifice of the technical society will be completed. It will not be a universal concentration camp, for it will be guilty of no atrocity. It will not seem insane, for everything will be ordered, and the stains of human passion will be lost amid the chromium gleam. We shall have nothing more to lose, and nothing to win. Our deepest instincts and our most secret passions will be analyzed, published, and exploited. We shall be rewarded with everything our hearts ever desired. And the supreme luxury of the society of technical necessity will be to grant the bonus of useless revolt and of an acquiescent smile." (*The Technological Society,* N.Y.: A. Knopf, 1964, pp. 426–7.)

This gloomy forecast is based on the assumption that, because the complexities of our technological age require an increasing level of rationalization at all levels, technical experts and managers—often called technocrats—are coming to hold more and more power in society as a whole. But another French observer, the sociologist Michel Crozier, is more optimistic. According to Crozier's careful analysis of modern decision-making:*

". . . the expert's success is constantly self-defeating. The rationalization process gives him power, but the end results of rationalization curtail this power. As soon as a field is well covered, as soon as the first intuitions and innovations can be translated into rules and programs, the expert's power disappears. . . . It can be less and less consolidated in modern times, inasmuch as more and more rationalized processes can be operated by nonexperts."

Crozier's analysis of "the bureaucratic phenomenon" is most illuminating with regard to the second alleged evil of modern society against which so many young people have been rebelling. Instead of viewing bureaucratic organizations as self-sustaining "monsters" Crozier shows how they are affected by the social and cultural environment in which they function. Seen in this light, the bad features—or dysfunctions—of bureaucracy are not inherent in their utilitarian, rational goals; they spring instead from the incompatibility of these goals with the means of social control, through rewards and sanctions, of the society it serves and from which it recruits its personnel. These means of social control, in turn, are determined by the basic values and norms for behavior of that society's cultural system.

Thus, the "pathology" of bureaucratic organizations differs in countries like France, the Soviet Union, and the United States. All bureaucratic organizations are unable to correct their behavior in view of their errors and are too rigid to meet without crisis the need for change required by the accelerated evolution of industrial society. These problems are especially acute in the Soviet Union, where—despite certain provisions for self-criticism and informal networks of complicity among people who know and trust each other—autocratic means of social control make for more rigidity than in Western countries. In the Russian cultural

*_The Bureaucratic Phenomenon_, Chicago, The University of Chicago Press, 1967, p. 165.

setting, people accept favor and arbitrariness as normal and protect themselves either by remaining apathetic or by building informal groups based on traditionally warm human relationships. In the French cultural setting, people find face-to-face dependence relationships difficult to bear; they reconcile this attitude with their recognition of the need for absolute authority by stressing impersonal rules and centralization. In this way they can always obey the rules but need not submit to the whims of their immediate superiors. But as a result, French bureaucratic organizations suffer from preoccupations with status, difficulties of communication between isolated hierarchical strata, and limitations on initiative. In the American cultural setting, people do not try to avoid face-to-face relationships, and it is easier for them to cooperate. Their individual rights in both public and private bureaucratic organizations are not so universal as the ones of their French counterparts, but they are better protected by due process of law. The main handicaps of American bureaucratic organizations concern the strictness and the arbitrariness of jurisdictional delimitation of competence. (One has only to think of the problems of dealing with different labor unions or government agencies.)

Despite their dysfunctions, modern bureaucratic organizations are becoming more liberal, at least in Western Europe and North America. The traditional debate on the standardization and the threatening enslavement of modern man misses the point that these organizations use much more liberal sets of pressures than their predecessors.

"They deal with people who, through their education, have already internalized a number of basic conformities and a general ability to conform easily to an organization's way. Then, too, there has been a great deal of progress in the field of training, and no one feels obliged any longer to make people spend months trying to master the exact observance of petty details. Most important of all, human behavior is now better understood and therefore more predictable. Because of this, a modern organization does not need the same amount of conformity to get as good results as did earlier organizations." (Crozier, *op. cit.*, p. 184.)

Today's revolutionary activists recognize these trends when they speak of the "repressive tolerance" of liberal institutions, but it is difficult to comprehend how riots or even revolutions can stop the irresistible development of rational techniques. Liberalization is logical because it makes it easier for individuals to participate in the controlled and standardized activities of large-scale organizations. The successes of liberalization allow modern man to push the logic of standardization, that is, the goals of efficiency, much further than was possible under the older authoritarian methods. The men who run large-scale organizations are becoming increasingly aware of the need for more flexibility and for the elimination of bureaucratic waste. Big business leaders see partial decentralization as a necessary condition for further growth. The decentralization of the French and Italian university systems is designed to achieve more effectively the goals of these systems in a mass society. In the big cities of the United States there is also a growing demand for breaking up bureaucratic public school systems in favor of greater community control. All of these changes give people both the advantages and the burdens of more complex entaglements and greater sophistication. Participation entails responsibility; cooperation requires tolerance of other people's views. These are the facts of life in any age and, most especially, in an advanced technological civilization in which the needs of billions of people must be met.

## EASTERN EUROPE

Like Western Europe, Eastern Europe has changed considerably since the late 1940s. The fact that in 1956 the Hungarian Revolution had to be crushed by the Red Army showed how little the wishes of the people still counted in the East in contrast to the West. But they count more now than they did when the Communist regimes were first set up in the satellite countries. Even in the Soviet Union, which the Communist Party has controlled for over half a century, industrialization and the consequent growth of a new middle class have made the country's leaders seek popularity by raising the standard of living and by reducing the needless severity of the Stalin era—without, however, altering the basic pattern of totalitarianism. For the one thing that has *not* changed in Communist Eastern Europe is the determination of those in power to stay there at all costs.

## The Soviet Union

Despite Russia's remarkable successes in foreign expansion, economic recovery, and scientific and technological development, the Communist regime has suffered a profound crisis involving the ideological basis of the state and society. Lenin and Stalin, for all their departures from orthodox Marxism, could channel the almost religious enthusiasm of their devotees into building socialism through industrialization. But once the Soviet Union was essentially industrialized, the historic mission of Communism became less and less clear. Where would Marxism lead that country next? To the "withering away of the state," to perfect equality? These slogans have come to sound unreal and distant to those considerable parts of the population that have imbibed the spirit of industrialism and become middle class in their values and views.

Neither Stalin nor any of his successors have been able to reverse the trend toward ideological apathy under the impact of industrialization. The leaders of the Soviet Union know that the achievement of a higher standard of living gives people further economic, and eventually political, aspirations, and they know that any increase in the people's political power will be a decrease of their own power. Consequently, they try to "prove" that the Communist ideology has a continuing mission abroad in order to solidify and justify popular support for the regime at home. In this way, Soviet successes against the retreating Western powers and other Communist states have been directly linked with domestic politics.

### *The Last Years of Stalin*

No relaxation and no reward to the Soviet people followed the appalling sacrifices of the Second World War. In 1946, new political repression took the form of a purge of local party leaders, whose numbers had grown in the wartime effort to reestablish contact with the masses. Unlike the purge of the late 'thirties, however, demotion or transfer took the place of execution or exile. The Fourth Five Year Plan, also launched in 1946, was designed not only to rebuild the economy—at least one-fourth of the total capital of which had been destroyed in the war—but also to "catch up with and overcome the West" in technological development. It heaped renewed sacrifices on the Soviet people, sacrifices both of consumer goods and housing, and of leisure time; the 48-hour week and drives for greater productivity were restored. Thus victorious Russia reverted to her prewar routine.

Nowhere was this reversion clearer than in Stalin's personal dictatorship. The party as a policy-making organization practically ceased to exist. No Party Congress met between 1939 and 1952; only one meeting of the Central Committee took place between 1945 and 1952; even the Politburo met irregularly. The party and the state bureaucracy confined themselves to the day-to-day functioning of the government machinery. As a result, the average party member—like the average army officer, state bureaucrat, or trade-union leader—came to think of himself in professional rather than ideological terms. Indeed, there was a real danger that, following Stalin's death, a clash between leaders of the army, the secret police, and other professional and bureaucratic interests would result in one of them gaining power, leaving the party to rule only in name.

Government-sponsored Russian nationalism also contributed to the dilemmas of the Soviet regime in the late 1940s. National pride among the non-Russian peoples of the USSR was condemned; "cosmopolitanism" was labeled a sin next to treason; antisemitism became almost an official policy. All these attitudes were repudiations of Marxism. One motive for them was to spur on the new industrial effort and its accompanying sacrifices. Another reason was to counteract the postwar "seduction" of Russian soldiers, to whom battered cities like Berlin, Vienna, and Budapest—and especially their women—seemed glamorous compared to the austerity and backwardness of life in the Soviet Union.

The identification of Russian nationalism with Communitst orthodoxy was extended to all fields of culture. In 1946 the poet Anna Akhmatova was expelled from the Union of Soviet Writers for having displayed an "unsocialist loneliness," and other "decadent Western" vices. Not until the early 1960s did Soviet biology recover from the theories of Trofim Lysenko, who with Stalin's blessing substituted the scientifically doubtful, but attractively Marxist, notion that acquired characteristics could be inherited for the "bourgeois capitalist" theory that denied this possibility. Finally, Stalin's cultural nationalism brought forth claims that Russians had invented practically all the marvels of modern science and technology.

This kind of cultural nationalism was inherently contradictory and dangerous. It antagonized the Communist intelligentsias both in the satellite countries and among the Ukrainian, Uzbek, Tartar, and other non-Russian national cultures in the Soviet Union. Antisemitism, though it had deep roots in Russia, was so incompatible with Marxism that its spread threatened the declining morale of the party itself.

Like party-state relations and nationalism, the peasants posed basic problems in the postwar years. More than two decades of collectivized farming had not succeeded in integrating them into the new industrial society as workers, and by the early 1950s Soviet agricultural output barely surpassed the precollectivization figures. The contradictory policies tried and then abandoned by the regime failed to bring the desired results. Sometimes it sought to eliminate the peasants' private plots by severely limiting their size and taxing their products more heavily. At other times the regime tried to win over the peasants by lowering their taxes and giving them more latitude in running the collective farms. Meanwhile the breach between the peasants and the regime continued.

Still another problem was that the prodigious growth in industrial production created new class attitudes among the growing number of professional people and technicians. Proletarian romanticism gave way to Communist-style Horatio Alger stories about poor boys becoming, through hard work, engineers, factory managers, doctors, and deputies to the Supreme Soviet. Citizens who had improved their status and income did not dream of seeing Soviet totalitarianism transformed into a democracy under the rule of law, but their modest desire for a modicum of personal security and legality and for some minimal contact with the outside world was an inevitable offspring of their success. Hence the resumption of prewar repressive policies threatened to undermine the morale, and eventually the economic and scientific efficiency, of all of Soviet society.

In 1952 Stalin made his last efforts to resolve the mounting problems of his dictatorship. At the Nineteenth Party Congress the ailing despot tried to launch a new purge and a new industrial advance; he also laid the framework for an orderly succession by creating a Presidium of the Central Committee—with twenty-five members and eleven alternates—to replace the old Politburo and Orgburo. All these efforts were interrupted by Stalin's death on March 5, 1953. The next day a new Presidium was announced, consisting of only ten members and four alternates. Though the new name persisted, the old Politburo was in effect restored, with some changes in personnel. Stalin's successors inherited the problems created by both the successes and the failures of his policies, but none of them inherited his power and prestige, which had allowed him to solve some of these problems merely by compulsion.

### The Struggle for Stalin's Mantle

Since Stalin's death, competing leaders have attempted to gain credit for liberalizing policies while trying to brand their opponents as diehard defenders of the old, bad, order. Personal intrigue, deception, and occasional violence have remained part of the atmosphere of Soviet politics. Nevertheless, the main contenders for power have had to take a much greater account of public sentiment than at the time when one man stood so far above everybody and everything.

During the "thaw" following Stalin's death, his successors granted a number of concessions. They softened the edge of immediate economic grievances by improving living standards; they abolished secret trials by the political police and largely disbanded the forced-labor camps; they permitted a limited degree of intellectual freedom and contact with foreigners. Their "sane" totalitarianism reflected not only a response to social pressures but also a confidence in the ability of the regime to withstand an occasional outspoken novel or news about the number of washing machines in the United States. But the concessions of the "thaw" period did not constitute even a first step toward the rule of law, not to mention democracy. They were mainly the by-products of the struggle for Stalin's mantle.

By late 1954 Nikita Khrushchev (b. 1896) was sharing public honors with Georgi Malenkov, Stalin's immediate successor as prime minister. A prewar favorite of Stalin, Khrushchev had held a number of important posts in the party since the mid-1930s, and in September 1954 he acquired Stalin's old post of First Secretary. Like his predecessor, he prepared his bid for power by putting his own men in key positions in the party. When in February 1955 Malenkov stepped down in favor of Nikolai Bulganin, the power struggle was far from settled, although to obscure the situation increased emphasis was placed on the principle of "collective leadership."

It took Khrushchev almost four years to establish his supremacy. His first open move was a spectacular speech to the Twentieth Party Congress (February 1956), in which he denounced certain excesses of the Stalin regime and specifically condemned the "cult of personality." Implicitly, this speech called into question the credentials of three members of the Presidium who had been closely associated with Stalin toward the end of his life. Then in June 1957, these three men, joined by four other members of the Presidium, including the war hero Marshal Zhukov and Bulganin himself, tried to oust Khrushchev by dismissing him from his party post as First Secretary. Khrushchev retaliated by calling a meeting of the Central Committee, which, packed with his supporters, reversed the decision of the Presidium. The three leaders of the "antiparty group" were stripped of their posts; in November Zhukov was also dismissed; Bulganin was removed as prime minister in March 1958 and expelled from the Presidium soon thereafter. Once Khrushchev had replaced all his rivals in the Presidium with his own men his triumph seemed complete. In December 1958 he himself assumed the office of prime minister.

#### *Continuing Dilemmas*

Khrushchev's rule, though it restored the role of the party, was less stable than Stalin's (except during the height of the terror in the late 1930s). The basic dilemmas—agriculture, the aspirations of the middle class, and the use of ideology to justify totalitarianism in a highly industrialized society—remained. The growing conflict with Communist China posed an additional danger to the ideological structure by showing at least some of the younger party members that the interests of the Soviet Union and those of world Communism had begun to diverge.

Stalin's successors cannot admit even to themselves that their monopoly of power, the interests of the nation, and the cause of world Communism might not coincide. They have used the repressive instruments of totalitarianism more sparingly than Stalin while basing their policies of the moment on their ability to prove to Soviet citizens that Communism is a superior way of life: How illusory are obsolete democratic and liberal ideas compared with Russian achievements in the harnessing of nuclear energy and space exploration! Was not the fact that the Russians were the first to put a satellite into orbit (1958), to launch a rocket to the moon (1959), and to send a man around the world in a space ship (1961) necessarily connected with the totalitarian rule exercised by the Communist Party?

In the late 'fifties and early 'sixties the limited liberalization of Soviet life, sometimes called "de-Stalinization," gave Khrushchev's government a greater measure of popularity and acceptance than any of its predecessors. The West should not take the rebellion of a poet or restlessness among a group of intellectuals or students as evidence of a widespread desire for democracy as we understand it. The hopes of most Soviet citizens probably do not go beyond an improvement in their standard of living and a final obliteration of Stalinism—that is, a regime that will grow more humane and tolerant, while remaining totalitarian.

Still, the desire for a freer life has not been entirely stifled in the Soviet Union, nor is there universal contentment with a regime that can arbitrarily order a thaw or a period of renewed vigilance. The policy of "de-Stalinization" was itself a clever attempt to persuade the Soviet people that the cause of their past sufferings was the criminal personality of one man rather than the system under which they still live. Furthermore, current acceptance of that system may give way to future aspirations for a freer society as material improvement continues.

More important than future discontent is the perennial problem of political infighting in a one-party dictatorship. The continuation of this problem was evident in 1961 at the Twenty-Second Party Congress, where new revelations about the crimes of Stalin and the "antiparty group" of 1957 were made public. The official explanations for rehashing these sordid matters are not very convincing. One guess is that the main impetus for the further downgrading of Stalin* came in part from a group of party functionaries too young to have been intimately involved in the terroristic policies of the Stalin era. Their emotional revulsion is understandable, but they were also moved by political calculation: What better way of replacing the older party officials than by harping on their associations with Stalin?

*Such as the removal of his embalmed body from the Mausoleum in Red Square, its subsequent cremation, and the renaming of Stalingrad Volgograd.

Another possible reason for the renewal of the anti-Stalin campaign in 1961 was that Khrushchev and his supporters needed a counteroffensive against the powerful Stalinists in the Presidium to whom they were losing ground in the face of defeats in foreign policy. The first such defeat came in May 1960, when an American U-2 spy plane was brought down by a Soviet rocket over the Urals. This incident created a serious setback to Khrushchev's efforts to ease tensions with the United States and forced him to wreck the Four-Power Summit Conference in Paris later in May. It also resulted in a reshuffle of top party officials to his disadvantage. The Cuban missile crisis of October 1962 further weakened Khrushchev's authority, especially among the Soviet "hawks." In this crisis President Kennedy overruled the American "hawks" and offered Moscow a relatively dignified way of removing its missiles from Cuban soil, but this was a defeat nonetheless. Finally, during the early 1960's Khrushchev was unable to prevent the Chinese Communists from going their own way and from tempting other foreign Communists to follow their example.

It is conceivable that Khrushchev really did rise above his grimy Stalinist past and was genuinely fired by the will to reform the Soviet system. He seemed to think so when he told a group of writers in 1962: "Some people are waiting for me to croak in order to resuscitate Stalin and his methods. That is why, before I die, I want to destroy Stalin and to destroy those people, so as to make it impossible to put the clock back" (quoted in Michel Tatu, *Power in the Kremlin: From Khrushchev to Kosygin*, N.Y.: Viking, 1969). In October 1964, however, "those people" had the satisfaction of seeing him overthrown. Leonid Brezhnev took over his post as First Secretary of the party, Alexei Kosygin his post as Prime Minister.

The men who replaced Khrushchev did not put the clock all the way back to Stalin's time, but they did pursue a more reactionary line. Liberal writers were imprisoned at home, and the Soviet government became embroiled in Stalin-like foreign adventures in Vietnam and the Middle East. In August 1968 Soviet armies invaded and

*Brezhnev and other Soviet leaders reviewing May Day parade*

occupied Czechoslovakia. Soviet determination to suppress Czech Communism's program of liberalization was also an international act of re-Stalinization as well as the final stage in the transformation of Soviet Russia from a world ideological power into a world imperialist power.

The reaction of one-party dictatorships to their internal difficulties is often a lessening of outward expansiveness and aggressiveness. Thus, during the years of political uncertainty following Stalin's death the Russian Communists softened their attacks on the West and stressed "peaceful coexistence." In a dictatorship, however, as in an individual, a major crisis can lead to a violent and irrational hostility toward the outside world. Thus, an outright threat to the basis of Soviet totalitarianism—such as a movement of national separatism within the USSR—could make Russia's rulers adopt aggressive policies with catastrophic implications.

So far the Russians have accepted a certain weakening of their control over the European satellites, but the greater flexibility of the Communist regimes in some of these countries, their wider range of intellectual and professional freedoms, may make the younger Soviet generations question the ideological basis for totalitarianism in their own country. It may also eventually become evident to them that the spread of Communism to foreign countries does not reinforce the logic of Marxism or of totalitarianism in Russia. Hence the nature of both "isms" at home is likely to be increasingly affected by the future development of other Communist states.

Meanwhile since the late 1960's, the party elite has tried to preserve its own power and privileges by balancing among various forces within the Soviet Union and world Communism. Aside from the demoralization of younger party members over the regime's ideological weaknesses, the technical elite has begun to realize that, under the rule of the party apparatus, the Soviet Union has lagged behind the United States and even Western Europe in technological advances. In addition, the generals were becoming increasingly dissatisfied with setbacks in Soviet foreign policy—in the Middle East, in Czechoslovakia, and in China. Lacking in strong leaders and unwilling to accommodate itself to new democratic ideas the party elite may well be paving the way for militaristic saviors of the state and of socialism. Barring a major confrontation with China, the ascendancy of the army is most likely to come from internal, not external, causes. As Milovan Djilas says: "The Soviet Union is no longer capable of bringing forth a Napoleon."

## East Central Europe and the Balkans

Communist regimes crave power and industry. Just as Lenin and Stalin subordinated their internationalist ideological goals to these cravings once they gained control of the government, so did Communist leaders in other countries. Former humble servants of the Comintern began to plot fantastic schemes of industrialization and expansion, sometimes territorial, of their national states. Beginning with the defection of Tito in 1948 Moscow and its new international extension, the Cominform, incited purges of "national deviationists" in the satellite countries and forced them to follow strictly Russian models in social and economic policy. By the mid-1950s, however, the satellites were again demanding greater autonomy from Moscow, and by the mid-1960s some of them were seeking to exploit the Sino-Soviet rift to further their own independence.

### *Yugoslav-Russian Relations to 1958*

From the beginning, Tito had kept his country free from significant Soviet aid and the Red Army. In September 1947, in a bid to gain his loyalty, Stalin made Belgrade, rather than Moscow, the headquarters of the new Cominform (Communist Information Bureau). But Stalin could not make Tito his puppet; and in June 1948 Stalin expelled the Yugoslav Communist Party from the Cominform. Tito was able to maintain his regime because he had the party, the police, and the army completely under his control—and because he had no common frontier with the Soviet Union. In addition, Tito entered into moderately friendly relations with the West, and by the early 1950s he was receiving substantial economic and military aid from the United States.

Tito's quarrel with the Kremlin has never been completely resolved. In 1955 it was patched up temporarily by Khrushchev; the disbanding of the Cominform a year later also helped to create more cordial relations between Yugoslavia and the Soviet Union. Nevertheless, Tito remained determined to follow "his own path to Socialism," and his conflict with Russia flared up again as a result of the revolts in Poland and Hungary in October 1956. Not only did these revolts seem to have been inspired by Titoist "national deviationism," but Tito welcomed thousands of Hungarian refugees to his country. In 1958 Khrushchev placed a perpetual quarantine on the Yugoslav Communist Party.

Yugoslav society had changed so much that it has become virtually immune from Soviet influences, short of a military invasion. For two decades, Yugoslavia has followed a zigzag but inexorable course toward nondogmatic forms. It is a much more truly federal state than the Soviet Union. The Serbs, Croats, and Slovenes are disparate by cultural and historical development, and the Communist parties of the six Yugoslav republics have become increasingly nationalistic as their dogmatism has declined. Although, outside of agriculture, nonsocialist forms of ownership have been suppressed, they have not been destroyed, and they are growing in strength. Even the socialist sector of the economy is developing in opposite ways from that of the Soviet Union: in the Soviet Union the emphasis is on increasing centralization, whereas in Yugoslavia the initiative of local plant managers is being extended. Furthermore, the Yugoslav economy has long been tied more to the West than to the East.

### *The Satellites*

In 1948 Tito's original expulsion from the Cominform accelerated a new phase in Soviet policy toward the satellite countries. Until then political persecution had been directed only against the anti-Communist opposition. Thereafter "Titoists" or "national deviationists" within the Communist Parties themselves also began to be purged, a trend that culminated in 1951 in the arrest of many of the top Communist leaders. In its "Sovietization" of the satellite regimes the Kremlin insisted on slavish imitation of the Russian example in everything. The Russian language was made compulsory in the schools, and Western cultural influences were eliminated.

The Soviet Union forced the satellite countries to concentrate their production on heavy industry, coal, and oil—products that would serve its own military and economic needs. Impressive results were achieved by 1954, when, together, Poland, Czechoslovakia, Hungary, Rumania, and Bulgaria produced 10 million tons of steel. This was one-fourth the production of the USSR and equal to it on a per capita basis. Still, the standard of living in the satellites showed no improvement comparable to that of Western Europe in the early 'fifties or of the Soviet Union and Yugoslavia in the mid-fifties. Not until the early 1960s was it to rise appreciably.

Meanwhile the death of Stalin had important repercussions in the satellite countries. In June 1953 antigovernment demonstrations spread to many Czech industrial towns, while in East Germany the workers launched an open revolt. The Czech riots were quickly put down by reliable militia forces from Prague, but the Red Army had to intervene directly to crush the East German revolt. The new Soviet leaders, sensing the broader implications of these episodes, did not punish the rebel leaders with the customary brutality. As in Russia itself, they adopted a "gentler course."

This "gentler course" lasted less than two years. It was carried furthest in Hungary, where, in July 1953, the Stalinist Mátyás Rákosi was replaced by Imre Nagy as prime minister. Nagy criticized the "grave mistakes" of the political persecution under his predecessor and promised that legal procedure would replace police despotism. He also halted the forced collectivization of the land and pronounced himself in favor of the production of more consumer goods. No other satellite leader went as far as Nagy, and in February 1955 Khrushchev forced him to step down. Rákosi was then restored.

Beginning in 1955 the Kremlin reasserted its determination to dominate the satellites. By forcing them to sign the Warsaw Treaty of Mutual Assistance as a counterforce to NATO the Soviet Union confirmed its long-established military control over Eastern Europe and afforded legal justification for maintaining Russian troops in Hungary and Rumania. Khrushchev also tried to increase economic "cooperation" between the satellites and Russia, but his plans were spoiled by the 1956 uprisings in Poland and Hungary. These uprisings were partly inspired by Khrushchev's anti-Stalin speech in February, which the satellite leaders learned about through broadcasts from the West in June.

### The Polish Revolt

On June 28, 1956, a strike among the workers of Poznan developed into a general anti-Russian uprising in that city. Though crushed with despatch, it was a symptom of widespread unrest. Sensing the popular character of the revolt the Polish government quickly raised wages and promised to improve living conditions. Yet its efforts to retain power by real concessions failed to appease the Polish people. Only a change in leadership and some sense of independence could do that.

In October the Polish Communist Party was ready to install Wladyslaw Gomulka as the new head of the party. Gomulka had been arrested in 1951 as a "national deviationist," and Khrushchev and other top Soviet leaders descended on Warsaw in order to prevent this action. They gave way, however, in the face of the open defiance of the Polish Communist leaders, and Gomulka took power. He retained good relations with the Soviet Union and told the Polish people that Russian troops had to remain in their country to protect her frontier with East Germany. This was a convincing argument in view of West German hostility to the Oder-Neisse Line. Moreover, the brutal crushing of the Hungarian revolution had shown the

*A Russian tank in Budapest during the Hungarian Revolution*

Poles the danger of open opposition to Russia.

### *The Hungarian Revolution*

The Hungarian Revolution was the most serious postwar threat to Soviet domination in Eastern Europe. It began as opposition by intellectuals and students to the Rákosi regime and the demand that he be replaced again by Imre Nagy; it soon became something more. On October 23, 1956, street demonstrations in Budapest turned into riots; government buildings were attacked, statues of Stalin and his followers toppled. The next day, there were two announcements: Nagy was now premier, and Russian troops would be used to restore order. But the people were led to believe that Nagy had called in the Russians and they lost confidence in him.

A mass upheaval followed. Workers, students, and even units of the Hungarian army and police fought against Soviet tanks. Hungarian "soviets"—including both Communists and non-Communists—arose spontaneously and demanded political and civil liberty, free and secret elections, free competition among political parties, parliamentary democracy, independent trade-unions, the right of workers to run the factories, the abolition of compulsory membership in collective farms, and the abolition of the secret police. Although many of the Hungarian rebels wanted to return to the old capitalist order, they publicly supported the idea that their country remain a socialist democracy. The protest against Rákosi had turned into an anti-Russian revolution.

By October 30, Nagy persuaded the Red Army to withdraw, and the Hungarian people learned that a close friend of Rákosi, not Nagy, had called it in. Nagy also announced the end of one-party rule, and the appearance of a liberal coalition government filled everyone with hope. On November 3, however, the Soviet Union decided on massive intervention when Nagy withdrew from the Warsaw Pact. The next day fifteen Russian divisions, with six thousand tanks, began an all-out attack on Budapest and other towns. Tens of thousands were killed in the fighting, which continued into December. Thereafter, 200,000 Hungarians (2 per cent of the population) fled across the border to Austria and Yugoslavia, whence many later emigrated overseas, especially to the United States and Canada. The Russians dissolved Nagy's coalition and replaced it with a puppet government under János Kádár, but the repression was not completed until the spring of 1957, when the number of political prisoners had climbed to fifteen thousand.

### East Germany (German Democractic Republic)

The Polish and Hungarian uprisings prompted the immediate recognition by Moscow of East Germany as "an equal and especially cherished member of the Communist bloc alliance." In this way the Soviet leaders put a tighter ring around Poland and strengthened the Czechoslovak Communists, who feared that a rising in East Germany would spread to their country, particularly if it elicited Western help. The East German Communist regime was more unpopular than any other, as the growing stream of refugees in the late 1950s showed. In August 1961, the East German government built a wall between East and West Berlin to cut off the main path of the refugees, but by then the country had lost a large share of its professional and technical people. A year later it had to "import" replacements, including five hundred Bulgarian doctors. For all its agricultural resources and heavy industry East Germany was becoming an actual burden to the the rest of the Communist bloc. Prague and Warsaw had a higher standard of living than East Berlin or Leipzig. By 1965, however, economic conditions were improving, and, though still a satellite with little national feeling, the German Democratic Republic was beginning to make a life of its own.

### Trends in the 1960's

By 1960 a new, uneasy balance was established in Soviet relations with the other Communist states. Both the unreasonable terror of the old Stalinism and the permissiveness of the mid-fifties were dead. The Russians have continued to try to forge unifying links through common ideological and economic interests, and by late 1964 even Yugoslavia was increasing its economic ties with the Comecon, an East European version of the Common Market. At the same time, the Sino-Soviet rift induced Khrushchev to end the "perpetual" quarantine he had imposed on Yugoslavia in 1958 and to make frequent trips to the satellite countries to seek their support in his quarrel with the Chinese Communists.

Soviet hopes as to the future of the satellites are bound to be disappointed. They are developing into troublesome dependents—demanding, ungrateful, always in need of being watched. The results of industrialization and forced collectivization in Bulgaria or Rumania are even less likely to conform to the Communist dream than in Russia. For the Communist parties have been in power for a much shorter time in the satellite countries, and their hold on the people is much less secure than in the Soviet Union. Gomulka will undoubtedly continue to repress Polish intellectuals whose criticism of the regime becomes too blatant, but the ideological justification for totalitarianism in all the satellites is so unconvincing to most educated people that the party leaders are virtually forced to allow more intellectual and professional freedom than in Russia. It was after all a Yugoslav writer, Milovan Djilas, who first publicized the growth of the "new class." In Yugoslavia, as in the satellites, this "new class" is likely to become increasingly resentful of both Soviet interference and of what it considers unwarranted rigidity on the part of its own leaders. The day of real freedom, however, is probably as far off for the satellites as it is for the Soviet Union.

*Prague, August 1968*

### *Czechoslovakia*

The Czech crisis of 1968 dramatically illustrated the difficulties in bringing about political reforms in the satellite countries. In January of that year a new group of Communist leaders wrested control of the party from the Stalinists and launched a sweeping program of liberalization: they abolished censorship, permitted the public expression of non-Communist political views, and began to make Czech life a little more democratic at all levels. Except for the Stalinists themselves the whole nation backed these reforms, which the younger generation of Communists had been advocating for several years. Led by Alexander Dubcek the new Czech government continued to profess its friendship for the Soviet Union, but Moscow could not tolerate a further weakening of its hold over its remaining satellites. Albania had switched its allegiance to Peking by 1960, and Rumania had already begun to pursue an independent foreign policy by 1964. If Czechoslovakia should also choose to do so, only Hungary, Poland, Bulgaria, and East Germany would remain in the Warsaw Pact.. Hence, the press in these four countries and in the Soviet Union stepped up its criticism of the Czech experiment in the spring and summer of 1968. Then, in August, half a million troops from the Warsaw Pact countries invaded and occupied Czechoslovakia. The bloodbath of 1956 in Hungary was not repeated, but the blow was no less shattering to the Czech people.

Throughout the rest of 1968 and into 1969 the Soviet government continued its efforts to make Czechoslovakia submit to its will. The leaders of the Czech government were whisked off to Moscow and forced to make a number of concessions. They fired several of their vociferous liberal colleagues and limited freedom of speech. Like the Nazis twenty years earlier, the Russian Communists pitted the more conservative Slovaks against the liberal Czech leaders; they also forced the Czech party hierarchy to restore some of the ousted Stalinists to positions of power. Czech students, intellectuals, and workers led many protest demonstrations against the Soviet occupation, and one student burned himself to death in downtown Prague. Finally in September 1969, Dubcek and his liberal colleagues were stripped of all influence in party affairs. At the time of this writing the outcome of the Czech crisis is still in doubt. But it is unlikely that the Soviet Union will be able to repeat its earlier victory in Hungary. The Czech dissidents have not obliged the Russians by leaving the country, and the majority of the Czech people is too sophisticated to be taken in by trumped up charges of counterrevolution against its own Communist leaders. On the other hand, Moscow and its Czech stooges have the power to suppress new demands for reforms indefinitely.

### The Unfinished Revolution

Utopias, by definition, are not of this world. The Soviet Union was the classic example of a society revolutionized in the name of Marxist principles. The Five-Year Plans of the 1930s generated mass enthusiasm of a kind unknown in tsarist days. For the first time in their history the Russian people felt that they were building a better future for themselves, but the first signs of the betrayal of Marxism had already appeared in the form of terror and dictatorship. Then came the rise of the new middle class, to which efficiency, status, and comfort meant more than ideology. According to Marx, Communism was a classless, stateless utopia based on the principle "to each according to his needs." In this sense, the revolution in the Soviet Union is unfinished and will undoubtedly remain so.

Marxism has had special appeal to both the grievances and aspirations of societies in the process of transition. It has told the "victims" of the old order that this order was doomed and that its downfall could, and should, be hastened by revolution; it has also inspired utopian visions of social justice and material well being in an industrial future. The greater the degree of poverty and injustice, the greater the appeal of Marxism has been. Today its appeal is the greatest among the alienated intellectuals of the emerging nations. In the West it has lost its appeal as continuing industrialization has fostered the inelegant values of materialism and industrialism and the growing integration of the working class into Western European society. As the Soviet Union and the other Communist countries of Eastern Europe try to catch up with the West in material culture, may they not eventually discover that they too have left Marxism behind?

For all their growing similarities in technology, bureaucratization, and materialist values, Western Europe is still democratic and Eastern Europe is still totalitarian. On October 15, 1964, this basic difference was made dramatically evident to the whole world. The British people decided what the change would be in a completely free and open election; the Soviet people were told what the change had been by the men who had engineered it in complete secrecy. Even more important than the replacement of Sir Alec Douglas-Home by Harold Wilson and of Nikita Krhushchev by Leonid Brezhnev and Alexei Kosygin (or whoever may replace *them*) was the fact that the opposition party was given power in Great Britain whereas in the Soviet Union the Communist Party's monopoly of power remained unaffected by the change in personal leadership. The probability that Khrushchev was removed partly for having failed to maintain Russian control over the other Communist parties of the world indicated once again the importance of the revolutionary ideology in foreign policy as a justification for totalitarian rule at home.

## CIVILIZATION AND CULTURE IN A MASS AGE

Contemporary civilization and culture are changing literally from day to day as a result of the "revolt of the masses," the population explosion, and the "cybernetic revolution." The third of these revolutions, in which programmed commands and controls are carried out by electronic computers, is still restricted to the most advanced industrial societies, but, like everything else, it will undoubtedly spread to the rest of the world very soon. Meanwhile, the feedback from the new technology has already stimulated new discoveries in the sciences. How have all these changes affected the way contemporary man thinks, feels, and behaves? Only the briefest survey of a few outstanding examples is possible here.

### The Cybernetic Revolution

Cybernetics is the theory of communications and of command in machines and living things. Its goal is to assure the most efficacious action through programming, learning, and method. In human beings it operates entirely within the context of nerves, muscles, and sense perceptions, which transmit information in the form of symbols back and forth from the brain to the agents of action: limbs, vocal cords,

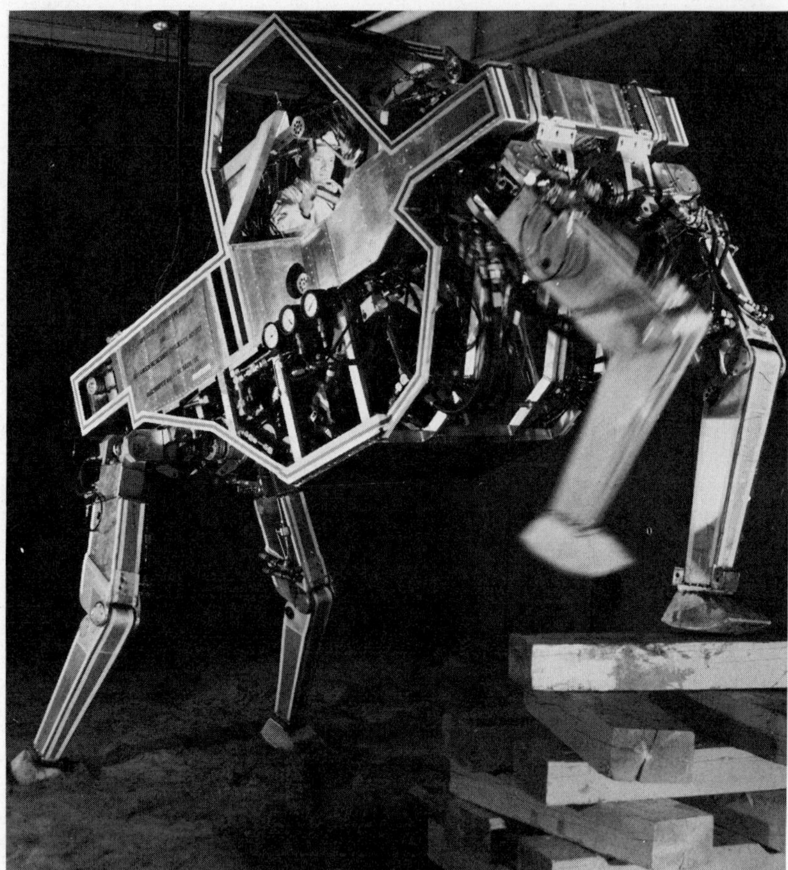

*General Electric's "Walking machine"*

etc. In machines it operates entirely within the context of electronic circuits. Regarding the crucial factor of feedback, Norbert Wiener (d. 1964), the inventor of the term cybernetics, said:

"Again, feedback is the control of a system by reinserting into the system the results of its performance. If these results are merely used as numerical data for the criticism of the system and its regulation, we have the simple feedback of control engineers. If, however, the information which proceeds backward from the performance is able to change the general method and pattern of performance, we have a process which may well be called learning."

The consequences of the cybernetic revolution are manifold. For one thing, it has altered the general research model of the scientific theorist, who has traditionally tried to isolate the variable he is studying from all the others. To "think cybernetically" is to examine an actual situation with all the changes actually going on in it and to devise a program of action that will alter this situation in accordance with some preconceived goal. This new method, known also as operations research, is a kind of creative engineering.

Automation, the replacement of men by "thinking machines," is already having important economic and social effects in the most advanced countries. There is a potential danger of overproduction from machines operated by computers, for they can produce almost limitless goods and services (vending machines, shoe-shining machines, and even "programmed" works of art). While the population explosion expands the labor force, automation whittles down the number of jobs. Many people who have jobs find no meaning in their work; indeed, it may become increasingly difficult to maintain the idea that people should work at all—in the sense of producing goods and services for the market. The cyberneticists tell us that the most advanced societies will soon reach the point where people will have to be *given* the purchasing power they formerly earned by working. Then even their leisure may have to be "automated." Thus, the cybernetic revolution confronts contemporary society with the desperate necessity of adapting its values and rules for behavior to the dynamics of an automated civilization.

Shortly before his death Norbert Wiener said that we may soon reach the point where we will have to adopt a strategy to counter the autonomous "will" of complex computer systems. Already human beings have been "phased out" of such systems in industry and government at all but the final decision-making level, and those who remain may also become "obsolete" shortly. Computers are becoming self-programming through their own feedback and through coupling with other computer systems. In Saudi Arabia, for example, there is a completely automated oil refinery which, if coupled with an automated distribution system, could continue to produce and distribute oil without regard to market demands or human decisions. The need for counter strategies against the computers seems most pressing in the military field. In the United States the relaying of a "beep" on a radar screen—be it caused by a Canadian goose or a Russian missile—to the President sitting next to "the button" is already completely "computerized."

### Science

The recent explosion of scientific knowledge has been the result of a chain reaction begun at the turn of the century through a combination of new theories, measurements, instruments, and experiments. First came the new physics and the new chemistry. With knowledge based on these solid foundations engineers were able to build the most elaborate technology in history, a technology that in turn has fed instruments back into science to provide the means of even more sophisticated measurement, such as computers and the electron microscope. Since 1945 biology and medicine have been among the main beneficiaries of this science-technology feedback. They now stand where physics did in the 1920s and 1930s during the ferment of new atomic discoveries.

Since the first spectacular "fruit" of atomic research was dropped on Hiroshima in August 1945, further advances have been made. Fusion has replaced fission, and its larger "fruits" have proliferated, but the energy created in nuclear chain reactions has been adapted to peaceful purposes as well, and dozens of countries now have nuclear reactors. New breakthroughs have also been made in probing the nature of subatomic particles. In the early 1930s physicists assumed that there were only three: electrons, protons, and neutrons. Thereafter they added antielectrons (positrons), antiprotons, and antineutrons and introduced the neutrino as a hypothetical particle, which they first captured in 1955. Recent additions include muons, pions, kaons, nucleons, and hyperons. The question remains: Are these elementary particles *really* elementary, or do they possess their own internal structures? As in the past, the search continues for a new all-embracing theory to bring order to these subatomic particles.

Meanwhile, the life sciences have come within reach of fulfilling the promise made over a century ago by a rash German biologist, Emil Du Bois-Reymond, who declared that eventually they would "dissolve completely into organic physics and chemistry." Today molecular biology tries to deduce the biological function of a molecule from its structure and structural changes. It aims at using atomic and molecular science to clarify all the basic phenomena of life. Other branches of the new biology are on the threshold of understanding the chemical basis of such life processes as the use of energy, the control of infectious disease, the production of new living substance, the removal of disabilities, and, the best known example, heredity.

In the early 1960's biochemists and geneticists made remarkable progress in

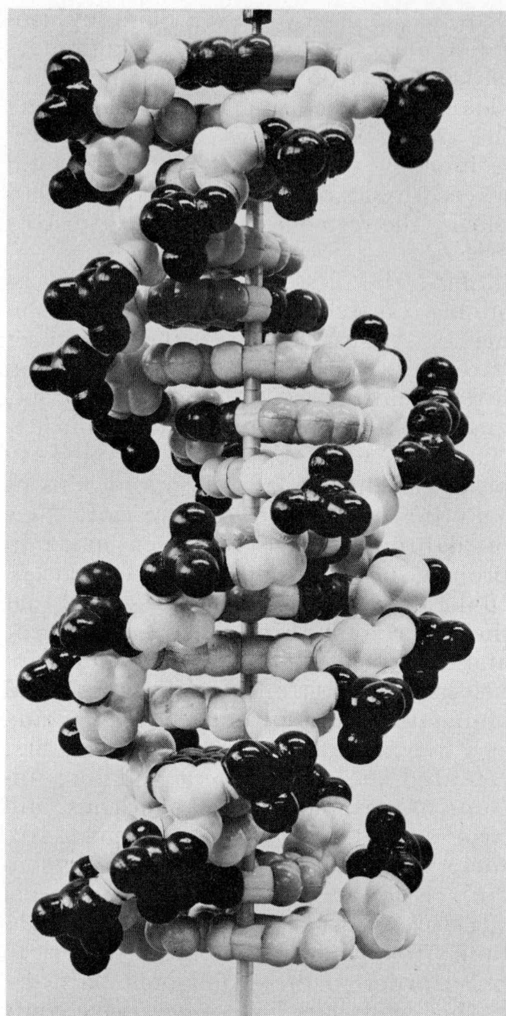

*Model of a DNA molecule*

"breaking the code of life" through discoveries regarding the functions of deoxyibonucleic acid, or DNA. DNA operates like the memory of a giant computer, substituting chemicals for mechanical and electrical links. It stores the instructions for controlling the various forms of protein synthesis which give all living things their specific characteristics. Each molecule of DNA has the form of a double-coiled helix in which sugar molecules held together by phosphorus form the backbone. Sticking out from the coils, like leaves from a vine, are sequences of four nitrogen-containing clusters of atoms, called organic bases. The sequences (arrangements) of the four bases—known by the initials of the chemicals involved, A,G,U,C—determine the genetic information stored by the DNA. In 1961 it was discovered that another chemical, ribonucleic acid, or RNA, actually "carries" this information to the ribosomes that manufacture protein. Also in that year some of the sequences were deciphered.

Apparently all attributes of living things are determined by the sequences of the "code." Thus, the sequence

AAUACUUCGCUA

may mean a human female with dark hair, blue eyes, blood type O, tendency toward diabetes, etc., while the sequence

UAUGCUGGAGGU

may code an orchid with petals of a certain shape, colored violet with yellow spots, etc. All higher forms of life are more like each other than, say, a streptococcus is like a tuberculosis bacillus. A brave man and a timorous mouse—or a brave mouse and a timorous man—share about 25 per cent of all their inherited characteristics: red blood cells, two eyes, one nose, one mouth, etc. Monkey DNA resembles human DNA more than it does that of a mouse, though there are still variations for different types of "moral character."

In science, as in technology, anything now seems possible. A giant pulse laser (light amplification by the stimulated emission of radiation) can deliver millions of watts for 10 to 25 billionths of a second—enough to disintegrate the largest diamond. With lasers and "computerized" robots yesterday's science fiction becomes today's reality. Just as the cyberneticists are divising new strategies for (and against) computers, the scientists are conceiving new theories of the structure of the physical universe and the nature of life itself. In the late 1960's, for example, astronomers were discovering new thresholds by means of radio signals from pulsars (apparently neutron stars), exploding galaxies, and quasars (possibly, quasi-stellar gas clouds from exploding galaxies) These discoveries have made nuclear physicists question accepted notions of the forces of nature, which cannot explain the violence of quasars.

### The Arts and Literature

These new scientific theories are also altering the common guiding ideas of a generation ago in many fields of art and experience. Our civilization is moving away from formalism and abstraction—from nonrepresentational painting, atonal music, and symbolic logic—into a period in which computers stimulate the activities of men, and buildings imitate the operations of living organisms. The new biology, for example, has its counterpart in the new architecture. Eero Saarinen's TWA terminal at New York's International Airport* has softened the Euclidean severity of glass-box skyscrapers with the more flexible outlines of an amoeba, complete with "tentacles" to stretch out to the aircraft and exchange the passengers who "nourish" them.

The change that is taking place in painting can be seen by comparing the works and opinions of Willem De Kooning and his younger contemporary Jean Dubuffet. De Kooning has written:

> "The space of science—the space of the physicist—I am truly bored with now . . . . The stars I think about, if I could fly I could reach in a few old-fashioned days. But physicists stars are used as buttons, buttoning up curtains of emptiness. If I could stretch my arms next to the rest of myself and wonder where my fingers are—that is all the space I need as a painter."

Here hope is denied for a common world that unites the motivating heart, the thinking mind, and the active body. In contrast, Dubuffet says: "This much is sure, a picture interests me to the degree I succeed in kindling in it a kind of flame—the flame of *life*, or presence, or *existence*, or *reality*." He adds that this reality "has nothing to do with the objects represented, rather it is distinct from them, pre-existent, surging up like an electric flow, without your ever knowing where it comes from."

In music, as in art and architecture, today's avant-garde is abandoning yesterday's ultramodern styles. Even those who still compose in the twelve-tone serial system use it in a more melodic, luminous, and restrained way than Schoenberg and his school. Except for Stravinsky, the major composers of the first half of the century are all dead; the works of Bartok, Honegger, Prokofiev, and Hindemith have already become classics. Whereas Bartok's *Music for Strings, Percussion, and Celeste* evoked the fast-moving tempo of machines in the 1930s, two decades later the chamber pieces of Pierre Boulez and Karl-Heinz Stockhausen expressed a more personal outlook by combining atonality with a haunting lyricism. These two composers, both in their early fifties, were also pioneers in electronic music, which some observers hail as the wave of the future. By dispensing with performers and traditional instruments electronic music gives the composer direct contact, so to speak, with his audience.

While the educated public balks at experimental music, it accepts avant-garde novels and plays fairly readily. There are two possible reasons for this. First, their language is still comprehensible (James Joyce's *Finnegan's Wake*, written in 1939, seems to have been a dead-end to prewar literary experimentation). Second, their themes of isolation, breakdown, failure to communicate, and relationships seen as illusion are coming, under crisis, to dominate society as a whole. Indeed, much popular fiction and drama expresses the themes of the avant-garde in a more commonplace way. In the late 1940s the moral nihilism and gratuitous violence of Meursault, the protagonist of Albert Camus' novel *The Stranger* (1942), had a direct parallel in Mike Hammer, the "private eye" hero of Mickey Spillane's detective stories. In the late 1950s the conventions of the Theater of the Absurd appeared in many second-rate movies and television scripts. Samuel Beckett, an Irishman writing in French, remains the outstanding exponent of existential anguish in his plays and novels, which tell us that, for all our civilized distractions, we can do little more than invent stories out of nothing, fill up the day with nonsense, or attempt the hopeless task of find-

*See Picture Group E.

*Scene from Peter Weiss's* Marat/Sade

ing out just who, why, and where we are.

But in recent years soul-searching existentialism, like passionate commitment to disappointing causes à *la* Brecht and Sartre, has given way to a more detached view of the world. The outstanding literary experiments of the 1950s—the "new novels" of Alain Robbe-Grillet and Nathalie Sarraute in France—rejected story-telling for meticulous description of bits of physical and emotional reality. Using more conventional—one might almost say Balzacian—techniques, the Italian novelist Alberto Moravia continues his criticism of the emptiness of bourgeois society. Like those of the German Günter Grass, the novels of the Englishman Joyce Cary use hilarious satire to expose current idiocies. By the late 1960's, more brutal expressions of violence and sexual frankness were being used in film and drama for this same purpose, as in Jean-Luc Godard's *Weekend* and Peter Weiss's *Marat/Sade*. Although most literature in Eastern Europe has remained strait-jacketed in official canons of socialist realism, a number of highly imaginative films have been produced in the Soviet Union, Poland, and Czechoslovakia. And from Sweden to Japan, talented film-makers are creating a new art of poetry and fantasy—less optimistic than that of the early twentieth century but just as determined to give meaning to life in a rapidly changing civilization.

## Religion

Mass civilization and mass culture have gravely weakened the influence of religion in European life. By the 1890s the "dechristianization" of Europe's masses had already provoked countermeasures ranging from the encyclicals of Pope Leo XIII to the activities of the Salvation Army. As one French priest poignantly exclaimed at the turn of the century: "It's the bicycle that has dechristianized my parish!" Since then the number of practicing Christians (and Jews) has declined steadily everywhere. Continuing industrialization and urbanization, the automobile and the movies, and all the other forms of mass transportation and communication have multiplied the effects of the bicycle. Among Roman Catholics the number of communicants in Italy has declined almost 50 per cent since 1938; in West Germany and Belgium about 25 per cent attend Mass regularly. Among Protestants the numbers are even smaller; according to a recent estimate, only 5 per cent of the population in England and 20 per cent in Scotland are active members of any church.

Religious practice seems to be directly related to the degree to which different kinds of people are affected by mass civilization and mass culture. City-dwellers are less religious than country-dwellers, young people less than old people, the lower classes less so than the middle and

*Ecumenism: Pope Paul VI and Patriarch Athenagoras of Jerusalem*

upper classes. In Paris, for example, the most active Catholics are upper-middle-class matrons and their elderly, country-bred maids; the least active are working-class men and teen-agers of all social levels.

Since the Second World War the churches have tried to revivify Christianity in several ways. In an effort to combat the prewar tendency to view religion more as a matter of good intentions than dogma, Protestant theologians like Karl Barth, Reinhold Niebuhr, and Paul Tillich have forcefully reasserted the original Reformation view of salvation solely through the divine grace of "Christ the Lord and only Savior." The Roman Catholic Church has sent missionaries into "dechristianized" areas of the French countryside and even into the factories. As a means of regrouping their forces the Protestant churches have tried to resolve some of their differences through international conferences. The Roman Catholic Church has also taken important steps toward making itself more ecumenical. Initiated by Pope John XXIII (1958–1963) and continued under Pope Paul VI, the Vatican Ecumenical Council of the early 1960s resolved a number of its differences with the Greek Orthodox and Anglican churches and proclaimed the goal of reuniting all the Christian churches. Finally, this Council went a long way toward renovating Catholicism itself; it "democratized" the Church hierarchy by making the bishops collaborators with the pope on matters of high policy; it sanctioned the use of the vernacular for parts of the Mass. But in 1968 Pope Paul VI reaffirmed the Church's ban on artificial methods of birth control—despite the dangers of the population explosion—and he lamented the demands for more radical changes that the liberlization of the early sixties had sparked.

### Mass Culture and Mass Society

The population explosion and the "revolt of the masses" have made both society and culture more democratic. Already directed toward materialistic values by its bourgeois creators, mass culture now reflects the desire of most Europeans to become bourgeois in their whole style of life. Growing affluence has permitted wage earners to spend less of their income on food and at the same time have as nutritious a diet as most middle-class people. As a result, class differences in physical appearance are becoming less and less obvious, and those that remain can be partially offset by cosmetics and well designed ready-made clothing. Even the universities—those last strongholds of Europe's bourgeois elites—are being expanded to accommodate increasing numbers of students from more modest backgrounds. This expansion still lags behind that in the United States and the Soviet Union. Nevertheless, the majority of English, French, and German youths now attends some kind of secondary school and views education as the key to a higher level of living.

Contemporary mass society is unique in the history of Europe and the world. It has been condemned on many counts: atomization, belieflessness, alienation, egotism, conformity, facelessness, moral emptiness, evaporation of loyalty, rootless homogeneity. Actually, many of these indictments apply to earlier societies. Facelessness and conformity characterized the masses of ancient Egypt for thousands of years; beliefIessness, egotism, moral emptiness, and the evaporation of loyalty were widespread in the Roman Empire during its long decline; the alienation of large sections of the population precipitated the French Revolution, and the critics of this now venerable event have never tired of condemning the atomization of society it produced. Only rootless homogeneity is really new, and it has its positive as well as its negative side. Long-haired waifs from London trying to "sing" and gyrate like commercialized hillbillies from West Virgina are indeed blatant examples of the rootless homogeneity fostered by contemporary mass culture. Yet the society that tolerates them has also achieved a closer *integration* of the mass of the population into its institutions and value systems than any other society in history.

Indeed, mass culture has provided mass society with commercialized versions of symbolic protest against itself. By the late 1960's, rock and pseudo-folk music, miniskirts and long hair (or at least long sideburns and heavy mustaches) became the rage, first among the "in" members of the upper-middle classes and then among the fashion-conscious lower-middle classes. This happened not only in New York and Montreal, London and Stockholm, Paris and Rome but also in Prague and Belgrade. Two centuries ago, Queen Marie-Antoinette played at being a milkmaid in her custom-built village amid the splendor of Versailles. Today, college-educated office clerks and shop assistants play at being peasants or gypsies in their mass-produced high-rise apartment buildings. Mass culture has the techniques for making everything available to everyone—from the most exotic forms of dress and grooming to the most outrageous forms of political and artistic expression. But the mass media of communication and merchandising, by emptying forms of symbolic protest of their original meaning, in effect, integrate them into prevailing life styles.

Social and cultural integration are the unique features of the mass society that became visible between the two world wars and that has been pushed ever forward since then in Europe, North America, Australasia, and Japan. As China and other non-European countries become industrialized they too will undoubtedly move in the same direction. Mass society is vertically integrated in a hierarchy of power and status; it is horizontally integrated through the unity of its political, economic, social, and cultural elites and through the "agreement on fundamentals" of the whole. There was little vertical integration in preindustrial societies, where the people at each level lived in a world of their own; there was little horizontal integration at the lower levels. The nation was the first important integrating idea in modern society, and it has lost little of its appeal in Europe, let alone the rest of the world. Parliaments, pressure groups, and collective bargaining have also helped to settle differences among conflicting sections of society. Mass society is not the most orderly ever, but it gives the largest proportion of its members a common ground. The main problems in the 1970's are to make the power structure in this society more truly democratic and to find a new basis for integration in the face of conflicting demands for individual freedom and social justice.

## SUGGESTED READINGS

Graubard, Stephen R., ed., *A New Europe?* Boston: Beacon Press, 1965.*
A collection of astute and readable essays on all aspects of the streamlined and affluent Western European society that had arisen by the early 1960's.

Lichtheim, George, *The New Europe: Today and Tomorrow.* New York: F. Praeger, 1963.*
Another fine work on the same subject.

Sampson, Anthony, *Anatomy of Europe.* New York: Harper and Row, 1969.
A more recent survey of all aspects of contemporary life in Western Europe, including the student revolts of 1968.

________, *Anatomy of Britain Today.* New York: Harper and Row, 1965.*
An amusing and often penetrating description of contemporary British institutions and leaders—argues that there is no one central establishment but many overlapping circles of leadership, not always working together.

Young, Michael, *The Rise of Meritocracy.* Baltimore: Penguin Books, n.d. Pelican.*
A stimulating satire by a British sociologist on the rise of a functional society and the educational system it is producing.

Tannenbaum, Edward R., *The New France.* Chicago: Univ. of Chicago Press, 1961. Explains the sweeping changes in French life since the early 1950's.

Ardagh, John, *The New French Revolution.* New York: Harper and Row, 1969.
Carries the changes through the 1960's.

Hoffman, Stanley, and others, *In Search of France.* New York: Harper and Row, 1964. Torchbook.*
Six revealing studies on various aspects of contemporary France.

Lacouture, Jean, *De Gaulle.* New York: Avon-Discus, 1968.*
The best short analysis of this controversial leader.

The following three books are very good on West Germany:

Grosser, Alfred, *The Federal Republic of Germany.* New York: F. Praeger, 1964.

Merkl, Peter H., *Germany: Yesterday and Tomorrow.* New York: Oxford University Press, 1965.

Dahrendorf, Ralf, *Society and Democracy in Germany.* New York: Doubleday, 1967.

Hughes, H. Stuart. *The United States and Italy.* Cambridge, Mass.: Harvard Univ. Pres., 1965.
The revised edition of this excellent survey is most useful.

Carlyle, Margaret, *Modern Italy.* New York: F. Praeger, 1968.
A good summary of recent developments.

Almond, Gabriel and Verba, Sidney, *The Civic Culture: Political Attitudes and Democracy in Five Nations.* Boston: Little, Brown & Co., 1967.*
The three European nations analyzed are Great Britain, West Germany, and Italy.

Fainsod, Merle, *How Russia Is Ruled.* Rev. ed. Cambridge, Mass.: Harvard Univ. Press, 1963.
This revised edition adds some of the changes of the Khrushchev era.

Tatu, Michel, *Power in the Kremlin: From Khrushchev to Kosygin.* New York: Viking, 1969.
A penetrating account by an outstanding French journalist.

Ulam, Adam B., *The Unfinished Revolution: An Essay on the Sources of Influence of Marxism and Communism.* New York: Vintage, n.d.*
A sober reappraisal of Soviet Communism.

Djilas, Milovan, *The New Class: An Analysis of the Communist System.* New York: F. Praeger, n.d.,*
The pioneering analysis of the new social structure of Communist societies in Eastern Europe.

Warth, Robert D. *Soviet Russia in World Politics.* New York: Twayne Publisher, 1963.
See particularly the section on the period since 1945.

Ripka, Hubert, *Eastern Europe in the Postwar World.* New York: F. Praeger, 1961.
Especially good on the 1950's.

Hoffman, George W. and Neal, Fred W., *Yugoslavia and the New Communism.* New York: Twentieth Century Fund, 1962.
Detailed and scholarly.

Mehnert, Klaus, *Peking and Moscow.* New York: New American Library of World Literature, 1964. Mentor.*
A perceptive analysis of Russian and Chinese Communism and their relations.

White, William H., Jr., *The Organization Man.* New York: Simon and Schuster, 1961.*
Compare White's pessimistic view with Crozier's newer, more optimistic view below.

Crozier, Michel, *The Bureaucratic Phenomenon.* Chicago: Univ. of Chicago Press, 1964.*

Ellul, Jacques, *The Technological Society.* New York: A. Knopf, 1964.
Pushes the logic of the triumph of technique to its extreme.

*London Times Literary Supplement.* "Critical Moment." New York: McGraw-Hill, n.d.*
Excellent essays on the literature of contemporary Europe.

# ILLUSTRATION CREDITS

CHAPTER ONE. 15: New York Public Library. 17: Historical Pictures Service. 20: Historical Pictures Service. 23: New York Public Library. 29: Walter Steinkopf/Staaliche Museen, Berlin. 33: New York Public Library. 36: New York Public Library. 41: Historical Pictures Service. 45: Bettmann Archive. 52: Historical Pictures Service.

CHAPTER TWO. 61: Anderson/Art Reference Bureau. 75: Historical Pictures Service. 81: Bettmann Archive. 85: National Portrait Gallery, London. 89: Bettmann Archive. 92: Bettmann Archive.

CHAPTER THREE. 102: Historical Pictures Service. 107: Historical Pictures Service. 110: H. Roger Viollet. 116: New York Public Library. 117: New York Public Library. 119: Historical Pictures Service. 127: Bettmann Archive.

CHAPTER FOUR. 135: Bulloz/Art Reference Bureau. 137: Bibliothèque Nationale, Paris. 140: Historical Pictures Service. 142: New York Public Library. 149: Historical Pictures Service. 157: Historical Pictures Service. 164: New York Public Library.

CHAPTER FIVE. 173: New York Public Library. 176: New York Public Library. 180: The Granger Collection. 185: Culver Pictures. 189: American Museum of Natural History. 197: Historical Pictures Service.

CHAPTER SIX. 216: New York Public Library. 222: The Granger Collection. 226: Bettmann Archive. 229: Historical Pictures Service. 236: Historical Pictures Service. 239: Bibliothèque Nationale, Paris.

CHAPTER SEVEN. 255: Historical Pictures Service. 258: Historial Pictures Sėrvice. 263: Historical Pictures Service. 267: H. Roger Viollet. 270: Historical Pictures Service.

CHAPTER EIGHT. 283: Bettmann Archive. 287: Historical Pictures Service. 289: New York Public Library. 294: Culver Pictures, Inc. 298: Historical Pictures Service. 300: Historical Pictures Service. 311: Bettmann Archive. 315: Colonial Williamsburg. 320: The Wallace Collection.

CHAPTER NINE. 326: Historical Pictures Service. 329: Bulloz/Art Reference Bureau. 331: Historical Pictures Service. 334: Historical Pictures Service. 337: Musée Carnavalet; Historical Pictures Service. 338: Historical Pictures Service. 339: Historical Pictures Service. 349: Historical Pictures Service. 357: Museo del Prado, Madrid. 359: Bettmann Archive.

CHAPTER TEN. 365: Historical Pictures Service. 367: Historical Pictures Service. 373: Historical Pictures Service. 377: Culver Pictures, Inc. 379: Historical Pictures Service. 383: Deutsches Museum, Munich. 386: Bibliothèque Nationale, Paris. 390: Historical Pictures Service.

CHAPTER ELEVEN. 397: Austrian Information Service. 398: National Archive, Berlin. 404: Bettmann Archive. 411: Historical Pictures Service. 414: Bettmann Archive. 419: Historical Pictures Service.

CHAPTER TWELVE. 433: Historical Pictures Service. 435: Bettmann Archive. 442: George Eastman House Collection. 449: Bettmann Archive. 456: Bettmann Archive. 458: Bettmann Archive.

CHAPTER THIRTEEN. 466: Archives of Casa Editrice, Valentino Bompiani and Company, Milan. 468: Marius Fontane (Voyage pittoresque a travers l'isthme de Suez,) (Paris, 1870). 478: The Museum of Modern Art, New York. 484: Historical Pictures Service. 498: Bibliothèque Nationale, Paris. 502: Bettmann Archive.

CHAPTER FOURTEEN. 509: Historical Pictures Service. 513: Bettmann Archive. 515: Culver Pictures, Inc. 518: Bettmann Archive. 522: Radio Times Hulton Picture Library. 526: Bettmann Archive. 529: Bettmann Archive.

CHAPTER FIFTEEN. 541: Bettmann Archive. 543: Historical Pictures Service. 551: The Mansell Collection. 558: Bettmann Archive. 562: Historical Pictures Service. 570: Historical Pictures Service. 572: Historical Pictures Service.

CHAPTER SIXTEEN. 580: Historical Pictures Service. 584: Historical Pictures Service. 592: Bettmann Archive. 593: Bettmann Archive. 597: Imperial War Museum, London. 604: Historical Pictures Service. 607: Historical Pictures Service. 611: Historical Pictures Service.

CHAPTER SEVENTEEN. 617: Bettmann Archive. 619: Historical Pictures Service. 621: Historical Pictures Service. 625: Bettmann Archive. 637: Bettmann Archive. 646: Bettman Archive. 650: Bettmann Archive. Bettmann Archive.

CHAPTER EIGHTEEN. 655: Bettmann Archive. 660: Historical Pictures Service. 662: Sovfoto. 669: Historical Pictures Service. 671: Wide World Photos. 678: Wide World Photos. 679: Wide World Photos. 682: Historical Pictures Service. 687: Wide World Photos.

CHAPTER NINETEEN. 698: United Press International. 701: Wide World Photos. 708: United Press International. 710: United Press International. 718: David Low cartoon, Low All Countries; Copyright Curtis Brown, Ltd. 720: Wide World Photos.

CHAPTER TWENTY. 729: The Tate Gallery, London. 735: Wide World Photos. 736: Wide World Photos. 739: Imperial War Museum, London. 745: Wide World Photos. 747: AP Newsfeatures Photo. 751: Pictorial Parade.

CHAPTER TWENTY-ONE. 759: United Press International. 770: Sovfoto. 777: AP Newsfeatures Photo. 781: Wide World Photos. 784: Eastfoto. 793: Camera Press, PIX. 797: Pictorial Parade. 801: Black Star. 809: Sovfoto. 812: Wide World Photos. 814: Pictorial Parade.

CHAPTER TWENTY-TWO. 816: General Electric. 818: John Oldenkamp. 820: Friedman-Abeles. 821: United Press International.

# INDEX